International Directory of
COMPANY
HISTORIES

International Directory of

COMPANY HISTORIES

VOLUME 73

Editor

Jay P. Pederson

ST. JAMES PRESS

An imprint of Thomson Gale, a part of The Thomson Corporation

Detroit • New York • San Francisco • San Diego • New Haven, Conn. • Waterville, Maine • London • Munich

International Directory of Company Histories, Volume 73

Jay P. Pederson, Editor

Project Editor
Miranda H. Ferrara

Editorial
Virgil Burton, Donna Craft, Louise Gagné,
Peggy Geeseman, Julie Gough, Linda Hall,
Sonya Hill, Keith Jones, Lynn Pearce,
Maureen Puhl, Holly Selden,
Justine Ventimiglia

Imaging and Multimedia
Lezlie Light, Michael Logusz

Manufacturing
Rhonda Dover

Product Manager
Gerald L. Sawchuk

LIBRARY OF CONGRESS CATALOG NUMBER 89-190943
ISBN: 1-55862-548-8

BRITISH LIBRARY CATALOGUING IN PUBLICATION DATA
International directory of company histories. Vol. 73
I. Jay P. Pederson
33.87409

Printed in the United States of America
10 9 8 7 6 5 4 3 2 1

CONTENTS _____

PREFACE

The St. James Press series *The International Directory of Company Histories (IDCH)* is intended for reference use by students, business people, librarians, historians, economists, investors, job candidates, and others who seek to learn more about the historical development of the world's most important companies. To date, *IDCH* has covered over 7,550 companies in 73 volumes.

Inclusion Criteria

Most companies chosen for inclusion in *IDCH* have achieved a minimum of US$25 million in annual sales and are leading influences in their industries or geographical locations. Companies may be publicly held, private, or nonprofit. State-owned companies that are important in their industries and that may operate much like public or private companies also are included. Wholly owned subsidiaries and divisions are profiled if they meet the requirements for inclusion. Entries on companies that have had major changes since they were last profiled may be selected for updating.

The *IDCH* series highlights 10% private and nonprofit companies, and features updated entries on approximately 50 companies per volume.

Entry Format

Each entry begins with the company's legal name, the address of its headquarters, its telephone, toll-free, and fax numbers, and its web site. A statement of public, private, state, or parent ownership follows. A company with a legal name in both English and the language of its headquarters country is listed by the English name, with the native-language name in parentheses.

The company's founding or earliest incorporation date, the number of employees, and the most recent available sales figures follow. Sales figures are given in local currencies with equivalents in U.S. dollars. For some private companies, sales figures are estimates and indicated by the abbreviation *est.* The entry lists the exchanges on which a company's stock is traded and its ticker symbol, as well as the company's NAIC codes.

Entries generally contain a *Company Perspectives* box which provides a short summary of the company's mission, goals, and ideals, a *Key Dates* box highlighting milestones in the company's history, lists of *Principal Subsidiaries, Principal Divisions, Principal Operating Units, Principal Competitors,* and articles for *Further Reading.*

American spelling is used throughout *IDCH*, and the word "billion" is used in its U.S. sense of one thousand million.

Sources

Entries have been compiled from publicly accessible sources both in print and on the Internet such as general and academic periodicals, books, annual reports, and material supplied by the companies themselves.

Cumulative Indexes

IDCH contains three indexes: the **Index to Companies**, which provides an alphabetical index to companies discussed in the text as well as to companies profiled, the **Index to Industries**, which allows researchers to locate companies by their principal industry, and the **Geographic Index**, which lists companies alphabetically by the country of their headquarters. The indexes are cumulative and specific instructions for using them are found immediately preceding each index.

Suggestions Welcome

Comments and suggestions from users of *IDCH* on any aspect of the product as well as suggestions for companies to be included or updated are cordially invited. Please write:

The Editor
International Directory of Company Histories
St. James Press
27500 Drake Rd.
Farmington Hills, Michigan 48331-3535

AB	Aktiebolag (Finland, Sweden)
AB Oy	Aktiebolag Osakeyhtiot (Finland)
A.E.	Anonimos Eteria (Greece)
AG	Aktiengesellschaft (Austria, Germany, Switzerland, Liechtenstein)
A.O.	Anonim Ortaklari/Ortakligi (Turkey)
ApS	Amparteselskab (Denmark)
A.Š.	Anonim Širketi (Turkey)
A/S	Aksjeselskap (Norway); Aktieselskab (Denmark, Sweden)
Ay	Avoinyhtio (Finland)
B.A.	Buttengewone Aansprakeiijkheid (The Netherlands)
Bhd.	Berhad (Malaysia, Brunei)
B.V.	Besloten Vennootschap (Belgium, The Netherlands)
C.A.	Compania Anonima (Ecuador, Venezuela)
C. de R.L.	Compania de Responsabilidad Limitada (Spain)
Co.	Company
Corp.	Corporation
CRL	Companhia a Responsabilidao Limitida (Portugal, Spain)
C.V.	Commanditaire Vennootschap (The Netherlands, Belgium)
G.I.E.	Groupement d'Interet Economique (France)
GmbH	Gesellschaft mit beschraenkter Haftung (Austria, Germany, Switzerland)
Inc.	Incorporated (United States, Canada)
I/S	Interessentselskab (Denmark); Interesentselskap (Norway)
KG/KGaA	Kommanditgesellschaft/Kommanditgesellschaft auf Aktien (Austria, Germany, Switzerland)
KK	Kabushiki Kaisha (Japan)
K/S	Kommanditselskab (Denmark); Kommandittselskap (Norway)
Lda.	Limitada (Spain)
L.L.C.	Limited Liability Company (United States)
Ltd.	Limited (Various)
Ltda.	Limitada (Brazil, Portugal)
Ltee.	Limitee (Canada, France)
mbH	mit beschraenkter Haftung (Austria, Germany)
N.V.	Naamloze Vennootschap (Belgium, The Netherlands)
OAO	Otkrytoe Aktsionernoe Obshchestve (Russia)
OOO	Obschestvo s Ogranichennoi Otvetstvennostiu (Russia)
Oy	Osakeyhtiö (Finland)
PLC	Public Limited Co. (United Kingdom, Ireland)
Pty.	Proprietary (Australia, South Africa, United Kingdom)
S.A.	Société Anonyme (Belgium, France, Greece, Luxembourg, Switzerland, Arab speaking countries); Sociedad Anónima (Latin America [except Brazil], Spain, Mexico); Sociedades Anônimas (Brazil, Portugal)
SAA	Societe Anonyme Arabienne
S.A.R.L.	Sociedade Anonima de Responsabilidade Limitada (Brazil, Portugal); Société à Responsabilité Limitée (France, Belgium, Luxembourg)
S.A.S.	Societá in Accomandita Semplice (Italy); Societe Anonyme Syrienne (Arab speaking countries)
Sdn. Bhd.	Sendirian Berhad (Malaysia)
S.p.A.	Società per Azioni (Italy)
Sp. z.o.o.	Spólka z ograniczona odpowiedzialnoscia (Poland)
S.R.L.	Società a Responsabilità Limitata (Italy); Sociedad de Responsabilidad Limitada (Spain, Mexico, Latin America [except Brazil])
S.R.O.	Spolecnost s Rucenim Omezenym (Czechoslovakia)
Ste.	Societe (France, Belgium, Luxembourg, Switzerland)
VAG	Verein der Arbeitgeber (Austria, Germany)
YK	Yugen Kaisha (Japan)
ZAO	Zakrytoe Aktsionernoe Obshchestve (Russia)

$	United States dollar	ISK	Icelandic krona
£	United Kingdom pound	ITL	Italian lira
¥	Japanese yen	JMD	Jamaican dollar
AED	Emirati dirham	KPW	North Korean won
ARS	Argentine peso	KRW	South Korean won
ATS	Austrian shilling	KWD	Kuwaiti dinar
AUD	Australian dollar	LUF	Luxembourg franc
BEF	Belgian franc	MUR	Mauritian rupee
BHD	Bahraini dinar	MXN	Mexican peso
BRL	Brazilian real	MYR	Malaysian ringgit
CAD	Canadian dollar	NGN	Nigerian naira
CHF	Swiss franc	NLG	Netherlands guilder
CLP	Chilean peso	NOK	Norwegian krone
CNY	Chinese yuan	NZD	New Zealand dollar
COP	Colombian peso	OMR	Omani rial
CZK	Czech koruna	PHP	Philippine peso
DEM	German deutsche mark	PKR	Pakistani rupee
DKK	Danish krone	PLN	Polish zloty
DZD	Algerian dinar	PTE	Portuguese escudo
EEK	Estonian Kroon	RMB	Chinese renminbi
EGP	Egyptian pound	RUB	Russian ruble
ESP	Spanish peseta	SAR	Saudi riyal
EUR	euro	SEK	Swedish krona
FIM	Finnish markka	SGD	Singapore dollar
FRF	French franc	THB	Thai baht
GRD	Greek drachma	TND	Tunisian dinar
HKD	Hong Kong dollar	TRL	Turkish lira
HUF	Hungarian forint	TWD	new Taiwan dollar
IDR	Indonesian rupiah	VEB	Venezuelan bolivar
IEP	Irish pound	VND	Vietnamese dong
ILS	new Israeli shekel	ZAR	South African rand
INR	Indian rupee	ZMK	Zambian kwacha

International Directory of
COMPANY
HISTORIES

Abengoa S.A.

Avda de la Buhaira 2
Seville
E-41018
Spain
Telephone: +34 95 493 71 11
Fax: +34 95 493 70 02
Web site: http://www.abengoa.es

Public Company
Incorporated: 1941
Employees: 9,318
Sales: EUR 1.69 billion ($2.01 billion) (2004)
Stock Exchanges: Bolsa de Madrid
Ticker Symbol: ABG
NAIC: 238210 Electrical Contractors; 221122 Electric
  Power Distribution; 221310 Water Supply and Irriga-
  tion Systems; 221320 Sewage Treatment Facilities;
  236115 New Single-Family Housing Construction
  (Except Operative Builders); 236116 New Multi-
  Family Housing Construction (Except Operative
  Builders); 236117 New Housing Operative Builders;
  237990 Other Heavy and Civil Engineering Construc-
  tion; 334511 Search, Detection, Navigation, Guidance,
  Aeronautical, and Nautical System and Instrument
  Manufacturing; 334512 Automatic Environmental
  Control Manufacturing for Regulating Residential,
  Commercial, and Appliance Use; 334513 Instruments
  and Related Product Manufacturing for Measuring,
  Displaying, and Controlling Industrial Process Variables; 334515 Instrument Manufacturing for Measuring and Testing Electricity and Electrical Signals;
  334519 Other Measuring and Controlling Device
  Manufacturing; 335311 Power, Distribution, and Specialty Transformer Manufacturing; 335931 Current-
  Carrying Wiring Device Manufacturing; 336510 Railroad Rolling Stock Manufacturing; 541710 Research
  and Development in the Physical Sciences and Engineering Sciences; 541910 Marketing Research and
  Public Opinion Polling; 562111 Solid Waste
  Collection

In slightly more than a decade, Abengoa S.A. has transformed itself from a company focused almost exclusively on the
engineering and industrial construction market into a diversified, international corporation. Abengoa's operations are conducted through four primary divisions: Bioenergy; Environmental Services; Industrial Engineering and Construction; and
Information Technologies. The company's Bioenergy division
is centered on Abengoa Bioenergía, the largest European, fifth
largest American, and second largest global producer of
bioethanol, with an installed capacity of more than 700 million
liters. Bioenergy accounted for nearly 20 percent of Abengoa's
EUR 1.69 billion ($2.01 billion) in 2004 sales. Environmental
Services operates through Abengoa's majority control of publicly listed Befesa, acquired in 2003, and focuses especially on
recycling and industrial waste management, as well as engineering and construction for water treatment and waste management. This division added 21.3 percent to company revenues.
Information Technologies focuses on providing network systems and integration for the energy, traffic control, transportation, and environmental markets, accounting for 16 percent of
group revenues in 2004. Finally, Industrial Engineering and
Construction represents Abengoa's historical core, with a particular focus on the electrical and telecommunications markets,
as well as the construction of industrial facilities and power
plants, including fossil fuel and renewable energy (bioethanol,
wind, solar, geothermal, and biomass) plants. This division accounted for nearly 43 percent of the group's sales in 2004. Spain
remains Abengoa's major market, accounting for nearly 60
percent of group revenues. The company is listed on the Bolsa
de Madrid; the founding Benjumea family maintains a 55 percent stake in the company. Felipe Benjumea Llorente and Javier
Benjumea Llorente, son and grandson of Abengoa's founder,
serve as company co-chairmen.

Construction Business in the 1940s

Abengoa was founded in Seville, Spain, in 1941 by Javier
Benjumea Puigcerver to provide installation services as Spain
built out its electricity grid. After conquering the Seville region,
Abengoa launched a national expansion drive. The company also
broadened its capabilities, beginning installation services for the
country's telephone network as well. By the end of the 1950s, the

company had grown into one of Spain's leading providers of engineering and construction services to both industries.

Having consolidated its hold on the Spanish market, Abengoa turned to international growth in the 1960s. The South American market was the logical choice for the next phase in the company's development. Before long, Abengoa had added operations in Chile, Brazil, Argentina, Peru, and elsewhere in South America, becoming a leader in that market. The company also extended its operations as far north as Mexico. Abengoa developed operations in other European markets, primarily in France, Belgium, and Switzerland, over the following decades. Its main focus outside of Spain, however, remained the Latin American market.

Abengoa not only expanded geographically, it expanded into new areas of business, adding new expertise in areas such as instrumentation, automation, supervision, and surveillance systems. A major milestone in this effort came with the take-over of Sociedad Anonima de Instalaciones de Control (Sainco) in 1969. Sainco, founded in 1963, focused on developing, manufacturing, and maintaining control systems and related industrial process supervisory systems, while entering the road traffic control market in 1968. As part of Abengoa, Sainco took over the company's existing operations in the electronics field.

The company proved especially strong in developing its own proprietary systems and technology, helping to consolidate its position as a market leader both in Spain and abroad. The company's technology capacity also enabled it to expand its capacity for control systems, such as traffic control systems, with the launch of turnkey systems in 1974. This activity in turn allowed the company to develop a level of expertise in information systems, digital electronics, and real-time computing. In 1989, Abengoa created a new Communications Division, which combined the company's interests in control systems and telecommunications systems integration, with Sainco as its core.

Nonetheless, the large majority of the group's revenues came from its construction and engineering operations. Into the 1990s, the focused nature of Abengoa's operations had become something of a liability. The downturn in the construction market at the beginning of the 1990s especially exposed the group's vulnerability to cycles in the market. At the same time, the market for installations had become relatively mature, promising slower growth in the near future. Abengoa was all the more vulnerable because of its reliance on the public sector—in

particular, the Spanish telephone monopoly Telefonica—which represented 80 percent of its sales in the early 1990s.

Restructuring in the 1990s

Under its new chairman and son of the company's founder, Felipe Benjumea Llorente, Abengoa launched a restructuring of its operations in 1992. As part of this effort, which required four years to complete, the company cut back its workforce by 14 percent; it also boosted its use of temporary workers by some 50 percent during this period.

The group's restructuring effort, however, went further than a mere streamlining. The company adopted a policy of seeking out partnerships, especially in its Latin American market, which enabled it to achieve strong international growth during the 1990s. Back at home, Abengoa made an effort to expand its customer base beyond its reliance on the public sector, successfully reducing the part of public works projects to just 12 percent of its sales.

In 1992, the company adopted an entirely new strategy, one focused on diversifying the company's operations beyond its reliance on the construction and engineering markets. The company developed four key areas of interest, creating four new divisions: Energy; Environmental and Urban Systems; Control Systems and Telecoms, led by Sainco; and Installation. The underlying strategy to develop fully integrated operations, including not only the engineering, manufacturing, and installation, but also sales, financing, maintenance, and even plant management services.

In 1995, Abengoa launched its entry into the Environmental and Urban Systems sector with the acquisition of a stake in Befesa, via one of its subsidiaries. Befesa had been established just two years earlier when a number of Spanish companies, led by BUS and including Metall Capital, Duro Felguera, and Indumetal, merged their environmental systems businesses, including industrial waste management and recycling operations, into a single entity, which was then listed on the Bolsa de Madrid. In 1999, Abengoa acquired its first direct shareholding in Befesa, buying up 7.44 percent of the company. By 2000, Abengoa had bought out BUS's 50.01 percent holding in Befesa, and by the end of that year, Abengoa had increased its position to nearly 83 percent, at a total investment of EUR 300 million ($250 million). The following year, Abengoa transferred its existing environmental businesses into Befesa.

Diversified Success in the 2000s

In the meantime, Abengoa also had launched its entry into the energy market, choosing to build a presence in the market for renewable fuels. The company's first effort in the renewable energy market was in the operation of a wind farm, based on the company's own proprietary technology. The company then launched construction of a bioethanol plant. Completed in 2000, at an investment of EUR 94 million ($80 million), the plant initially produced 100 million liters per year, before rising to 150 million liters by 2005. The success of this plant led Abengoa to sell off its wind farm operations in 2001, to The Netherlands' Nuon, raising nearly EUR 110 million. Abengoa then used the proceeds of the sale to boost its ethanol opera-

Key Dates:

1941: Javier Benjumea Puigcerver founds Abengoa as a provider of electricity installation services.

1950s: The company launches national expansion.

1960: International expansion begins, with entry into the South American market.

1969: The company acquires Sainco and enters Control Systems.

1992: A restructuring and diversification strategy is initiated.

1995: The company acquires a stake in Befesa as an entry into environmental services.

1999: The company launches Telvent, which takes over Sainco operations.

2000: Abengoa acquires control of Befesa; construction is completed on the first bioethanol plant in Spain.

2001: The company sells its wind farm operations to Nuon in The Netherlands.

2002: High Plains Corporation, a bioethanol producer, is acquired.

2003: Metso Corporation's U.S. and Canadian Network Management Solutions division is acquired.

2004: Telvent is listed on the NASDAQ.

tions, buying up High Plains Corporation, in the United States, for EUR 100 million in 2002. High Plains was then renamed as Abengoa Bioenergy Inc. In that year, as well, Abengoa added a second Spanish ethanol plant, in Galicia, with a production capacity of 126 million liters per year.

In 1999, Abengoa had launched Telecom Ventures, or Telvent, which took over from Sainco as Abengoa targeted an expansion into the wider telecommunications arena. Telvent also became responsible for Abengoa's systems and networks operations, which were relaunched under the new brand names Abentel, Carrierhouse, and Internet Datahouse. The company added a number of new brands, including Telvent Interactiva in 2000 and Telvent Outsourcing in 2002. In 2003, Telvent acquired Mesto Corporation's Network Management Solutions divisions, based in the United States and Canada. Soon after, Telvent rebranded its operations, placing all of its business under the single Telvent banner. This led to Telvent's public offering, in 2004, with a listing on the NASDAQ.

By the end of that year, Abengoa had become a much different company from what it had been just ten years earlier. The company's sales had nearly quadrupled, nearing EUR 1.7 billion ($2.1 billion). The company also had succeeded in reducing reliance on its original construction and engineering business. While this unit remained the company's largest, at nearly 43 percent of sales, Abengoa had gained a strong presence in its new Energy and Environmental Services, while expanding its Information Technologies operations as well. Abengoa appeared to have engineered strong growth for the new century.

Principal Subsidiaries

Abecnor Subestaciones, S.A. de C.V. (Mexico); Abecom, S.A.; Abeinsa, Ingeniería y Construcción Industrial, S.L.; Abelec, S.A. (Chile); Abema Limitada (Chile); Abenasa Transmissao de Energia, Ltda. (Brazil); Abener Energía, S.A.; Abengoa Bioenergía, S.L.; Abengoa Bioenergy Inc. (U.S.A.); Abengoa Brasil, S.A. (Brazil); Abengoa Chile, S.A.; Abengoa Limited (U.K.); Abengoa México, S.A. de C.V.; Abengoa Perú, S.A.; Abengoa Puerto Rico, S.E.; Abenor, S.A. (Chile); Alianza Befesa Egmasa, S.L.; Asa Bioenergy Holding, AG (Switzerland); Befesa Aluminio Bilbao, S.L.; Befesa Argentina, S.A.; Befesa Brasil, S.A.; Befesa Chile, S.A. Santiago (CL) 160 100.00 A. Chile/AMA a-b (2).

Principal Competitors

Telefonica de Espana SAU; Energie Baden-Wurttemberg AG; ACS Actividades de Construccion y Servicios S.A.; Roggio E Hijos Benito S.A.; Fomento de Construcciones y Contratas S.A; Gas Natural SDG S.A.; Groupe Fabricom S.A.; Ferrovial Agroman S.A.; Sociedad General de Aguas de Barcelona S.A.

Further Reading

"Abengoa Buys High Plains," *Chemical Market Reporter,* November 5, 2001, p. 3.

"Abengoa Expands U.S. Bioethanol Capacity," *Chemical Market Reporter,* May 19, 2003, p. 3.

"Abengoa Wins Concession," *Latin American Power Watch,* November 23, 2004, p. 4.

—M.L. Cohen

ACCU WEATHER®

AccuWeather, Inc.

385 Science Park Road
State College, Pennsylvania 16803
U.S.A.
Telephone: (814) 235-8650
Fax: (814) 235-8609
Web site: http://www.accuweather.com

Private Company
Incorporated: 1975 as Accu-Weather, Inc.
Employees: 335
Sales: $100 million (2003 est.)
NAIC: 513220 Cable and Other Program Distribution;
   514110 News Syndicates; 514191 On-Line
   Information Services

AccuWeather, Inc. is the leading commercial weather service in the world. It provides forecasting, graphics, and other information to more than 235,000 print and broadcast media clients, as well as users in business, government, and institutions. More than 850 newspapers around the world print weather pages created by AccuWeather, which also supplies the Associated Press. Its content appears on 1,200 Internet sites as well, including its own AccuWeather.com. The company also has pioneered graphical weather content for wireless devices. The company gathers meteorological information from more than 200 countries through an array of 35 satellite receivers. It keeps about 100 meteorologists on staff, the largest assemblage of forecasters under one roof. It claims greater accuracy than either the National Weather Service or its archrival, The Weather Channel.

Origins

AccuWeather, Inc.'s origins can be traced back to November 15, 1962, when Dr. Joel N. Myers, then a graduate student at Penn State, began forecasting winter weather for Columbia Gas, a Pennsylvania gas utility. According to the *Encyclopedia of Entrepreneurs,* Myers had begun logging weather conditions at the tender age of seven and within a few years was dreaming of starting his own forecasting business. Myers obtained raw data from government institutions such as the National Weather Service. He performed his own analysis to create more accurate forecasts.

Myers soon began helping ski resorts determine the best times to make artificial snow. Other early clients included government agencies. Myers continued to teach and study at Penn State's leading meteorology program, earning a Ph.D. in 1971. He retired from the university ten years later. (Myers's younger brother Barry joined the business in 1964, eventually becoming executive vice-president and general counsel.)

In the Media in the 1970s

Myers started reading the weather on Penn State's public TV station (WPSX) in 1968. In 1971, he landed AccuWeather's first radio account, with WARM of Wilkes-Barre/Scranton, Pennsylvania. In late 1971 Philadelphia's WPVI became the first television station to subscribe.

The AccuWeather name was unveiled in 1971. A product for newspapers was introduced in 1974. The business was incorporated in November 1975 as Accu-Weather, Inc. The same year, the company came out with customized seven-day forecasts for local markets.

1980s Enhancements

AccuWeather developed the weather page for the national daily *USA Today,* launched by Gannett Co. in 1982. In 1986, AccuWeather began producing weather maps for the Associated Press. Business blossomed in the early 1980s. According to *Forbes,* revenues were about $2 million in 1983, when AccuWeather had 500 clients.

The company's AccuData real-time weather database was introduced in 1984. It originally incorporated 12,000 different weather products; this number would nearly triple over the next several years. Subscribers included home, business, and educational users. In pre-Internet days, users could access AccuWeather's database via modems and the Accu-Weather Forecaster program. The software displayed the raw data with a number of graphics. Users were charged sign-up and connection fees.

Key Dates:

1962: As a Penn State grad student, Dr. Joel N. Myers begins forecasting for a local gas company.
1968: Myers begins forecasting weather for a local public TV station.
1971: Myers lands his first radio account; the AccuWeather name is introduced.
1974: The newspaper product is introduced.
1979: The AccuData database is introduced.
1986: AccuWeather begins producing weather maps for the Associated Press.
1997: The Exclusive AccuWeather RealFeel Temperature index is introduced as an improvement to the heat index.
2001: Galileo Weather System is offered to TV stations.
2003: AccuWeather launches the first high-definition TV weather system.

AccuWeather streamlined its data delivery for various media. It introduced broadcast-ready color graphics for television in 1983 (it began supplying weather graphics computers systems to TV stations three years later). It also began transmitting weather data directly to newspapers' typesetting systems.

The company expanded into the aviation and education markets in the mid-1980s. AccuWeather's main challenge over the next 20 years would be to successfully meet the demands of new broadcast technologies. One of these, cable television, provided a platform for the emergence of a powerful new rival, The Weather Channel.

At the end of the 1980s, AccuWeather had about 2,000 clients. It limited its franchise to one television and one radio station per market. It was also supplying Reuters Ltd., the U.K.-based wire service, as well as scores of private businesses and government agencies. AccuWeather acquired Oklahoma City's WeatherScan International Corporation in 1989.

New Media in the 1990s

New methods of delivery were developed in the early 1990s, including an automated service and broadcasts via CompuServe. By 1991, AccuWeather had begun transmitting print-ready pages directly to newspaper printing systems.

There also were new sources of weather information, such as NEXRAD Doppler radar data acquired from Unisys, made available through the Accu-Data database. New sources of weather imagery continued to emerge in the mid-1990s. AccuWeather was a leader in providing images from weather satellites. VirtualWeather offered computer-generated 3-D representations of storm systems.

AccuWeather.com was launched in 1996, the same year the company introduced local weather for cable TV systems. An aviation-related weather site debuted in 1998.

The detail of AccuWeather's local forecasting was extended with 10-Day Hour-by-Hour forecasts introduced for 55,000 cities in 1997. Widespread Weather Services was acquired during the year.

A new interpretive tool introduced in 1997 was The Exclusive AccuWeather RealFeel Temperature, which described what the temperature really felt like to someone appropriately dressed for the weather. It was a unique composite of everything that affects how warm or cold a person feels, and measured the effects of temperature, wind, humidity, sunshine intensity, cloudiness, precipitation, and elevation on the human body.

The late 1990s was a time of celebration and success at AccuWeather. In 1997, company founder Dr. Joel N. Myers was recognized as a major American entrepreneur by *Entrepreneur Magazine*. The next year, the company moved to a new $5 million, 52,000-square-foot headquarters. In the late 1990s, AccuWeather had 345 employees and 15,000 customers, including 280 radio stations, 250 TV stations, and 400 newspapers.

As a side venture, AccuWeather also was distributing other types of information and content such as crossword puzzles and lottery results. According to the *Pittsburgh Post-Gazette*, though, most of its revenues came from analyses provided to businesses, not the media. The company had to be vigilant, however, to fend off advances from The Weather Channel on its traditional media and corporate weather businesses.

In early 1999, AccuWeather rolled out Forecast Center, a turnkey, automated service that allowed local television stations to transmit graphics and live, two-way footage of AccuWeather's own meteorologists.

New Standards for the New Millennium

AccuWeather brought out a new PC-based Galileo Weather System in 2001. It soon became a leader in the TV broadcast industry, which had been dominated by the SGI platform for several years.

The company helped Allentown, Pennsylvania's WFMZ-TV develop an all-local, 24-hour weather channel for digital TV. Another new offering, Weather-Triggered Marketing, matched online ads to weather conditions based on users' zip codes.

In 2002, AccuWeather acquired the United Kingdom's OnlineWeather, as well as the newspaper businesses of Weather-Data, Inc. and Meteorlogix, LLC. AccuWeather was providing graphical weather data for a variety of wireless devices. It was also at the forefront of an industry trend to provide increasingly more precise local weather data. In 2003, AccuWeather launched the world's first high-definition TV weather system via Cablevision's VOOM service.

Also in 2003, AccuWeather launched its Wireless Weather application that provides 24-hour weather forecasts, radar images, and severe weather watches and warnings to cell phones. In 2005, AccuWeather launched its Local AccuWeather Channel, an automated around-the-clock loop of customized local weather and news information for cable stations.

Principal Competitors

AWS; Baron Services, Inc.; DTN; National Weather Service; Universal Weather and Aviation, Inc.; The Weather Channel.

Further Reading

AccuWeather, Inc., "AccuWeather Highlights: A Compendium of AccuWeather Firsts, Innovations, Awards and Interesting Tidbits," State College, Penn.: AccuWeather, Inc., 2005.

"AccuWeather Leads the Nation and Serves the World," State College, Penn.: AccuWeather, Inc., 2005.

"The AccuWeather Story: Excellence in Weather Forecasting Since 1962," State College, Penn.: AccuWeather, Inc., c. 2003.

"AccuWeather Uploads Advanced Doppler Radar Images," *Link-Up,* May/June 1993, pp. 1 +.

Adler, Roger, "Eye of the Storm; In-House Counsel: Barry Myers, AccuWeather Inc.," *National Law Journal,* April 5, 2004.

Altman, Burt, "Accu-Weather Brings Graphic Forecasts Online," *Link-Up,* May/June 1991, pp. 1 +.

Anderson, Karen, "AccuWeather Debuts Forecast Center," *Broadcasting & Cable,* January 4, 1999, p. 70.

Astor, Dave, "Four Decades for Forecasting Firm: Newspaper List Growing As AccuWeather Marks Anniversary," *Editor & Publisher,* June 23, 2003, p. 21.

Balas, Janet, "Accu-Weather: Getting Your Data and Using It, Too," *Computers in Libraries,* April 1990, pp. 37 +.

Beebe, Paul, "AccuWeather Builds Media Base," *Centre Daily Times* (State College, Penn.), November 7, 2002.

Carmichael, Mary, "Hot and Bothered," *Newsweek,* June 24, 2002, pp. 90 +.

"Clear and Increasingly Accurate: Advanced Weather Radar Technology," *Document Delivery World,* April 1, 1993, p. 44.

Cooper, Jim, "The Business of Weather," *Broadcasting & Cable,* May 31, 1993, p. 46.

Cotlier, Moira, "Climate-Controlled Banner Ads," *Catalog Age,* March 15, 2001, p. 7.

Dixon, Glen, "Weather Right or Wrong," *Broadcasting & Cable,* December 15, 1997, p. 129.

Fish, Larry, "Forecast for Accu-Weather: Great," *Houston Chronicle,* March 13, 1988, p. 3.

Gannon, Joyce, "Joel Said It Would; AccuWeather's Myers Has Built a Big Business on a Tricky Subject," *Pittsburgh Post-Gazette,* January 4, 1998, p. F5.

Grotticelli, Michael, "Talk About the Weather; With Help from Accu-Weather, Allentown, Pa., Station Airs 24-Hour Local Service Via DTV," *Broadcasting & Cable,* May 28, 2001, p. 40.

Guterl, Fred, "The Nerds of Weather: Where Does Your 'Local' AccuWeather Forecast Come From? A Little Building in Rural Pennsylvania," *Newsweek,* September 30, 2002, p. 48.

Hallett, Anthony, and Diane Hallett, "Joel N. Myers (AccuWeather, Inc.)," *Entrepreneur Magazine Encyclopedia of Entrepreneurs,* Hoboken, N.J.: John Wiley & Sons, 1997.

Herrera, Stephan, "Weather Wise," *Forbes,* June 14, 1999, p. 90.

Keegan, Paul, "Stormy Weather," *Business 2.0,* June 2005, pp. 130B136.

Kerschbaumer, Ken, "Storm Warning: AccuWeather Introducing a PC-Based System for Graphics, a New Challenge for SGI," *Broadcasting & Cable,* September 10, 2001, p. 50.

Mackinnon, Jim, "Pennsylvania-Based AccuWeather to Build New Headquarters," *Knight Ridder/Tribune Business News,* March 27, 1997.

Mari, Christopher, "Myers, Joel N.," *Current Biography Index,* April 2005, pp. 44 +.

Moss, Linda, "Forecast: Weather Rivalry to Heat Up," *Multichannel News,* March 24, 1997, p. 54.

St. Goar, Jinny, "First Degree," *Forbes,* December 19, 1983, p. 206 +.

Smeltz, Adam, "AccuWeather Trims Workforce, Tightens Belt as Economy Struggles," *Knight Ridder/Tribune Business News,* September 30, 2002.

Wind, Gregory, "A Climate Control; Forecast: Weather Data That Is More Local and Precise," *Broadcasting & Cable,* March 22, 2004, p. 43.

—Frederick C. Ingram

Acer Incorporated

9F, 88 Hsin Tai Wu Rd., Sec 1
Hsichih, Taipei 221
Taiwan
Telephone: 886-2-696-1234
Fax: 888-2-696-3535
Web site: http://www.acer.com

Public Company
Incorporated: 1976 as Multitech International
Employees: 6,560
Sales: $7.03 billion (2004)
Stock Exchanges: Taiwan
Ticker Symbol: ACER
NAIC: 334111 Electronic Computer Manufacturing;
    334613 Magnetic and Optical Recording Media
    Manufacturing; 334290 Other Communications
    Equipment Manufacturing; 334119 Other Computer
    Peripheral Equipment Manufacturing; 334310 Audio
    and Video Equipment Manufacturing; 511210
    Software Publishers

Acer Incorporated is Taiwan's leading exporter and the world's fifth largest computer manufacturer. The company designs, manufactures, and sells computer hardware and software products; it ranks among the world's largest manufacturers of individual components such as keyboards, motherboards, set-up boxes, storage drives, monitors, CD-ROM drives, keyboards, printers, scanners, and software. Acer's nearly 30 years of growth results primarily from its business of manufacturing and assembling branded and contract PCs in several locations throughout the world. The company sells its products through dealers and distributors in more than 100 countries.

Taiwan's high-tech industry pioneer Stan Shih cofounded Acer. Over the years Shih guided his company through several corporate restructuring processes as well as financial ups and downs of the 1980s and 90s. In a significant restructuring in 2000 Acer spun off its lucrative contract manufacturing business and renamed it Wistron Corporation. This helped position Acer on a growth curve in several markets. When Stan Shih retired in early 2005 Acer's branded products had strong sales figures worldwide, and the company was poised to make a larger impact in the U.S. market through its desktop and notebook PCs.

Business Origins

Acer's founder was born Shih Chen Jung in 1945. A shy youth, Shih blossomed at National Chiao Tung University, where his natural math aptitude helped him graduate at the top of his class. Shih, who later westernized his given name to Stan, earned a master's degree in 1972 and went to work as a design engineer at Qualitron Industrial Corp.

It was not long, however, before the entrepreneurial bug bit Shih; in 1976, he and several friends founded Multitech International with a $25,000 initial investment. The new firm started by designing hand-held electronic games, then expanded into the distribution of imported semiconductors. Shih renamed his company Acer Incorporated in 1981. The name was derived from the Latin word for acute or sharp.

The company enjoyed its first international success that year with the launch of MicroProfessor, a teaching tool. The company began manufacturing PC clones—computers and components that were sold to larger companies with strong brand names—in 1983. Acer diversified vertically in the late 1980s, soon becoming "one of the most vertically integrated microcomputer manufacturers in the world," according to *Los Angeles Business Journal*.

In 1995, *Fortune*'s Louis Kraar called Stan Shih "a fascinating combination of engineering nerd, traditional Chinese businessman, avant-garde manager, and international entrepreneur, with an outsize ambition and vision to match." The young CEO applied all of these talents to his young enterprise. In stark contrast to the micromanagement, nepotism, and profit-taking typical of Taiwanese companies, Shih established a modern, progressive corporate culture. Although Shih's wife, Carolyn Yeh, served as the company's first bookkeeper, the founder vowed that his three children would have to look for jobs elsewhere. Time clocks were anathema, even in production

Company Perspectives:

Acer ranks among the world's top five branded PC vendors, designing and marketing easy, dependable IT solutions that empower people to reach their goals and enhance their lives.

plants. In 1984 he established Taiwan's first stock incentive program. Within four years, 3,000 of Acer's employees were also stockholders.

In 1981, Acer hinted at a sweeping change in strategy with the establishment of Third Wave Publishing Corp. The term "third wave" referred to the most recent phase of the history of Taiwan's computer industry: the first was characterized by trademark and patent piracy, the second by clonemaking, and the third by technological innovation. Instead of simply churning out other companies' designs, Acer began to set itself apart from most of its Taiwanese competitors by doing its own research and development. For example, the company developed one of the world's first Chinese language computer systems. In 1986, Acer was second only to Compaq to introduce a 32-bit PC with an Intel 386 microprocessor.

Acer went public in 1988, having chalked up average annual growth of 100 percent from 1976 to 1988. In 1988, net profits totaled more than $25 million.

Early 1990s Setbacks

The late 1980s brought internal and external changes that had a devastating effect on Acer. The internal problems were completely unexpected. In 1989, Shih hired Leonard Liu away from a 20-year career with International Business Machines Corp. (IBM), making him president of the Acer group and chairman and chief executive officer of Acer America Corp. Described in an October 1995 *Fortune* article as "a cerebral Ph.D. in computer science from Princeton," Liu had previously been the "highest-ranking Chinese American executive" at IBM. Liu's managerial style reflected his experience at "Big Blue": in contrast with Shih's traditionally progressive corporate culture, Liu tried to centralize control of Acer. His off-putting approach has been blamed for a management exodus in the early 1990s.

At the same time, the computer industry quickly matured, shifting from a high profit margin business to a low margin commodity practically overnight. Price wars pushed component prices down so rapidly, and a strong New Taiwan dollar made the country's goods so expensive, that it became difficult to make a profit on the finished product.

Acer's sales rose from $530.9 million in 1988 to $977 million by 1990, but its profits dropped from $26.5 million to $3.6 million during the same period. In 1991, Acer posted its first ever annual loss, $22.7 million. More than $20 million of that shortfall came from Acer America, which had struggled since its inception. Acer's stock dropped to 50 percent of its initial public offering price. Shih had to sell Acer's headquarters to make a profit in 1992.

These difficulties, however, did not deter Shih from making several expensive, and oft-criticized, expenditures during the late 1980s and early 1990s. In 1989, Acer invested $240 million in a joint venture with Texas Instruments and China Development Corporation, a Taiwanese development bank. The cooperative enterprise built Taiwan's first DRAM (dynamic random access memory) factory. Half of its output was sold to Acer, and the other half was sold on the world market. Some industry observers ballyhooed the project, noting a glut in the global DRAM market. Acer also expanded production capacity at its main plant, spent $36 million on a global marketing campaign, and made questionable acquisitions in the United States and Germany. *Financial World*'s Jagannath Dubashi was skeptical that the company's investments would pay off, noting in her July 1991 coverage of the company that "this new aggressiveness seems both poorly timed and unrealistic." She even characterized the company's bold moves as "a desperate gamble."

At the time, Shih would have been the first to agree with such an assessment. In January 1992, he offered to resign from the company he had founded. Acer's board of directors turned down Shih's resignation, but accepted Leonard Liu's withdrawal three months later. By mid-year, Shih had resumed day-to-day administration of Acer and its American subsidiary.

Instead of being cowed by the setback, Shih was determined to cement Acer's future in the PC industry by transforming it from just another OEM into one of the world's leading computer brands. He would achieve this goal via several revolutionary strategies.

New Methods Pace Mid-1990s Turnaround

In a 1995 *Financial World* article, Shih compared Taiwanese computer manufacturing to Chinese restaurants, saying that "Chinese food is good, and it is everywhere, but it has no uniform global image or consistent quality." The same was true of personal computers; although most were made in Taiwan, they were sold under several (primarily American and Japanese) brands, with varying levels of quality. Shih wanted Acer to be more like McDonald's, the quintessential fast food restaurant that boasted a strong brand image and strict quality standards.

This unique paradigm shift required a complete overhaul of Acer's production and distribution scheme. Instead of assembling computers in Taiwan, as it had done for more than a decade, the company began to ship components to 32 locations around the world for assembly. Shih compared computer components including casings, keyboards, and mice to such staples as ketchup and mustard that could be shipped slowly and stored indefinitely. He likened the motherboard, which had to have the "freshest" technology possible, to the meat in a sandwich. It was shipped by air from Taiwan to each assembly operation. Finally, Shih compared the CPU and hard drive to "very expensive cheese: we try to source them locally." Shih's adoption of this unique strategy earned him the nickname "the Ray Kroc of the PC business."

This production scheme saved on shipping costs and enabled Acer to include the most up-to-date (Shih liked to call it the "freshest") technology available. In Acer-speak, "fresh" meant innovative. Not content to rely on low-end knockoffs of other

Key Dates:
1976: Multitech International is founded by Stan Shih and four others.
1981: Multitech is renamed Acer, Inc.
1983: Acer begins manufacturing PC clones.
1988: Acer Incorporated goes public.
1991: Acer posts its first loss.
1994: Acer Computer International (Asia-Pacific distributor) completes its initial public offering (IPO).
1995: Acer is top selling PC brand in Mexico, Bolivia, Chile, Panama, Uruguay, Thailand, Philippines, and Taiwan.
1996: Acer expands into consumer electronics.
1998: Company reorganizes into five units.
2000: Acer restructures, breaking off several operating units; contract manufacturing spins off to become Wistron Corporation.
2003: Acer becomes the world's fifth largest PC maker.
2005: Stan Shih retires; J.T. Wang is named CEO and Gianfranco Lanci becomes president.

companies' technology, Acer stayed abreast of the industry's latest developments. In 1992, it launched a multi-user UNIX system as well as 386- and 486-based PCs. That year also saw the introduction of an international service and support network, a vital element of any successful PC business in the 1990s. In 1993, Acer unveiled a new PC that came equipped with a RISC (reduced instruction-set computing) chip and Microsoft's most recent version of the Windows operating system.

Shih hoped to bring the "fast food" concept all the way to the retail level, so that customers could custom-order computers with peripherals and memory capacity specifically suited to their needs. Acer tested this concept at a company-owned retail store in Taipei. It seemed to be as close as Acer could come to McDonald's-style service: only two hours passed from the time a system was ordered to the time it was booted.

Shih's "global brand, local touch" strategy was closely related to the "fast food" distribution concept. Instead of creating a series of centrally controlled foreign subsidiaries, Acer established a network of virtually autonomous affiliates, much like a fast food franchise system. Each of these affiliates was managed by a group of locals who determined product configurations, pricing strategies, and promotional programs based on national or regional preferences. The affiliate would usually have just one Taiwanese person on staff to facilitate interorganizational communications. *Sales & Marketing Management* characterized the system as a "revolutionary departure from the traditional hierarchical model of worldwide branches and subsidiaries reporting to a head office." Instead, it was "a commonwealth of independent companies, united only in their commitment to a common brand name and logo."

This strategy gave each Acer affiliate the semblance of a local company, an image that carried with it several benefits. Perhaps most important, it helped to downplay Acer's Taiwanese roots. Despite the country's large strides in the area of quality, "made in Taiwan" continued to carry negative connotations in the minds of many consumers. While Shih was proud of his company's heritage, individual affiliates often found it efficacious to de-emphasize that aspect of the business.

Globalization at Acer employed a third strategy adapted from an Asian chess-like game called "Go." Instead of jumping directly into the world's largest and most important computer markets, Acer conquered the surrounding markets before entering the United States. For example, Acer established itself as the leader in less hotly contested markets in Latin America, Southeast Asia, and the Middle East. By 1995, it was the top-selling computer brand in Mexico, Bolivia, Chile, Panama, Uruguay, Thailand, and the Philippines, not to mention Taiwan.

This combination of tactics worked quickly and well, vindicating many of Acer's previously criticized moves. In 1993, Acer posted record profits of $75 million; 43 percent of that year's net was generated by the DRAM joint venture, considered "the most efficient in the DRAM industry" by some observers. From 1994 to 1995, Acer advanced from 14th to ninth among the world's largest computer manufacturers, surpassing Hewlett-Packard, Dell, and Toshiba. Total sales grew to $3.2 billion in 1994, and net income increased to $205 million, as Acer America turned its first annual profit in the 1990s.

Strategies for the Mid-1990s and Beyond

In the mid-1990s, Acer began to globalize production as well as assembly, building a keyboard and monitor plant in Malaysia in 1994. The company planned a motherboard and CD-ROM factory for the Philippines and hoped to set up production in Argentina, Chile, Thailand, Dubai, South Africa, Brazil, India, the People's Republic of China, and the former Soviet Union.

In 1994, Shih unveiled a plan to "deconstruct" Acer into 21 publicly traded business units by the end of the 20th century. Acer Inc. would continue to own anywhere from 19 percent to 40 percent of the firms' stock, but Shih hoped that their independent status would enable the individual units to compete more effectively by facilitating entrepreneurship, inspiring research and development, and allowing for corporate fundraising through stock and bond offerings. Michael Zimmerman of *PC Week* speculated on another possible motivation behind the plan, known internally as "21-in-21." His June 1994 piece on Acer noted that "Separating the divisions will also clear a path for Shih to retire and, as one observer said, 'to leave his legacy intact' by not risking the future of his brainchild to a successor." In fact, Shih told *PC Week* that he "expects to withdraw from Acer and the workforce" by 1999.

Acer Computer International, the company's Asia-Pacific distributor, had its initial public offering in September 1994. The approximately $55 million flotation was oversubscribed by about 20 times. Spinoffs of Acer Peripherals, the corporation's manufacturer of keyboards and monitors, and Acer Sertek, the Taiwanese distribution operation, were planned for 1996. Stock in Acer America and certain Latin American operations was slated to go on the auction block by 1997.

The *Economist* reported that Acer's revenues had increased by 75 percent from $3.2 billion in 1994 to $5.7 billion and that

Shih hoped to increase that figure to $15 billion by 1999 via expansion into consumer electronics including televisions and fax machines. Global sales did strengthen, but Acer's performance lagged in the U.S. market due to intense competition from rivals with stronger brand presence.

Acer America was reorganized in both 1996 and 1997 in an attempt to stem the tide of loss. In 1997 Acer America lost $141 million. This had a significant impact on the company's bottom line because at the time, one third of Acer Inc.'s business was in North America. Its branded PCs were ranked ninth in sales in the U.S. PC market. That same year Acer America purchased Texas Instruments' notebook sector.

On a global scale, Acer was seeing a turnaround; its net profits in 1997 were $115 million, up 22 percent from the previous year. That year Acer negotiated significant partnerships with IBM and Apple to manufacture PCs. At the time it had 37 assembly sites worldwide, but no manufacturing outside of Asia. Later that year the company opened its first manufacturing plants outside of Asia, in Mexico, in order to reduce shipping time to the Latin and North American markets. By late 1998 Acer was the top brand in South Africa, Mexico, and several other emerging markets.

While Acer had successfully concentrated its efforts on emerging markets, corporate leaders were still dissatisfied with its weak showing in the United States and Europe. In the United States, Acer's share of the PC market slipped from 5.4 percent of PC sales in 1995 to 3.2 percent in late 1998. In an effort to recoup some of that market share, Acer America planned to streamline efforts toward less complicated systems targeted toward schools, governments, and businesses.

In 1998 Acer reorganized into five groups—Acer International Service Group, Acer Sertek Service Group, Acer Semiconductor Group, Acer Information Products Group, and Acer Peripherals Group. Two years later that corporate restructuring did not appear to have made a significant impact on the company overall, and stock prices were sliding. Shih restructured again. To dispel complaints from clients that Acer competed with its own products and to alleviate the competitive nature of the branded sales vs. contract manufacturing businesses, Shih spun off the contract business, renaming it Wistron Corporation. The restructuring resulted in two primary units—brand name sales and contract manufacturing. The restructuring also resulted in Acer breaking off several of its smaller operations, including semiconductor design, consumer electronics, and liquid-crystal displays.

Early signs indicated that the spinoff strategy had worked well, especially in Europe, where Acer became a popular PC brand. In 2003, company sales increased 48 percent to $4.6 billion, and helped Acer surpass Japan's Toshiba and NEC, making it the world's fifth largest manufacturer of PCs.

Acer had also adopted a more focused ''channel'' approach to distribution. Instead of a multi-tiered strategy, the company simplified the sales/distribution process by eliminating direct sales, and fostering closer working relationships with dealers and distributors. Acer also focused on selling to corporations through distributors rather than trying to win the sales from individual consumers.

The restructuring, combined with the 100 percent focused channel strategy, increased Acer's success in the European markets. Acer applied the same channel strategy in the United States, where sales figures eventually began to turn around—so much so that Acer America was on track to break even by the end of 2004. Acer America had also worked hard to reinforce product support services since early 2000.

By late 2004, the industry rankings were in Acer's favor. In Europe Acer was number two in PC brand sales in the second quarter of 2004. In the third quarter, Acer was the top PC notebook brand in Italy and Germany, the region's biggest PC markets. Acer had also climbed to number three in PC shipment volume to the entire pan-European market which included the Middle East and Africa.

Gianfranco Lanci, who had overseen and orchestrated Acer's success in Italy and then throughout Europe, began managing the U.S. market operations. Lanci became Acer president, and president J.T. Wang was promoted to CEO, while Stan Shih planned to retire. After putting it off for several years, Shih finally announced his upcoming retirement, sensing his company was in good hands and positioned for continued growth.

Forecasting into 2005, the company anticipated its global revenue would increase by 30 to 40 percent. Acer leaders hoped to become the world's third largest PC maker by surpassing Fujitsu Siemens Computers and IBM. To reach that goal, Acer planned to further expand desktop market penetration. At the time notebook PC sales represented 58 percent of Acer's earnings. Comfortable with its leading presence in Asia and Europe, the company was ready to position itself to increase sales in China and North America, turning up the competitive heat on rivals Dell and Hewlett Packard.

Principal Subsidiaries

Acer Computer International; Acer Information Products Group; Acer Internet Services; Acer NeWeb Corp.; Acer Peripherals, Inc.; Acer Property Development, Inc.; Acer Semiconductor Manufacturing; Addonics Technologies Corp. Aegis Semiconductor Technology; Aopen, Inc.; Acer Technology, Inc.; Darfon Electronics Corporation; Hitrust Incorporated; Vision Tech Information Technology; Weblink International, Inc.; Wistron Nexus Inc.; Acer America Corporation (U.S.A.); Acer Latin America, Inc.; Acer Peripherals America, Inc.; Acer Africa Pty. Ltd.; Acer America Corp. (Canada); Acer CIS, Inc. (Russia); Acer Computec Latino America S.A. (Mexico); Acer Computer Australia Pty. Ltd.; Acer Computer Benelux (Netherlands); Acer Computer Co., Ltd. (Thailand); Acer Computer Czech and Slovak Republics; Acer Computer (Far East) Limited (Hong Kong); Acer Computer Finland Oy; Acer Computer France S.A.R.L.; Acer Computer GmbH (Germany and Poland); Acer Computer Handels gmbH (Austria); Acer Computer Iberica S.A.U. (Spain); Acer Computer (Singapore) Pte. Ltd.; Acer Computer Magyarorsz-g (Hungary); Acer Computer (M.E.) Ltd. (United Arab Emirates); Acer Computer New Zealand Ltd.; Acer Computer Norway A/S; Acer Computer Sweden AB; Acer Computer (Switzerland) AG; Acer Computer Turkey; Acer do Brasil Limitada; Acer India (Pvt.) Ltd.; Acer Information Services International (Costa Rica); Acer Italy S.r.l.; Acer Japan Corporation; Acer Marketing Services (China); BenQ (formerly Acer Peripherals Holland) (Netherlands); Acer Peripherals Japan; Acer Peru S.A.; Acer Philippines, Inc.; Acer Sales and Service Sdn.Bhd. (Malaysia); Acer Scandinavia A/S (Denmark); Acer UK Limited; Acer Vietnam Co. Ltd.; ONC Technologies Inc. (South Korea); PT Acer Indonesia; Servex Singapore Pte. Ltd.

Principal Competitors

Dell Inc.; Fujitsu Siemens Computers (Holding); Hewlett-Packard Company; NEC Corporation.

Further Reading

"Acer Chairman to Retire," *Asia Pacific Telecom*, October 2004, p. 19.

"The Acer Group," *Los Angeles Business Journal,* September 2, 1991, p. S10.

"Acer Ranked No. 3 in Pan-Europe Computer Market in 3Q," *Asia Africa Intelligence Wire*, October 26, 2004.

"Acer Reorganizes into Five Units," *Computer Dealer News*, August 17, 1998, p. 8.

"Bits and Bytes," *Economist,* March 9, 1996, p. S20.

Brennan, Laura, "High-Tech Union Shatters Merger Myth: Acer, Altos Upbeat on Profits, Channels," *PC Week,* March 4, 1991, p. 123.

Burke, Steven, "Acer on the Move," *Computer Reseller News*, November 8, 2004, p. 31.

"Business Briefs: Acer Slims Down," *Infoworld*, December 18, 2000, p. 16.

Carlton, Jim, "Compaq and Acer Are Slashing Prices on Entry-Level PCs to Expand Market," *Wall Street Journal,* November 17, 1995, p. A3.

Chong, Lim, "Ace of Acer," *New Straits Times (Malaysia)*, December 18, 2003.

"Computer Giant Acer Forecasts Bright 2005," *Newsday.com,* November 10, 2004.

DiCarlo, Lisa, "Acer to Expand Beyond PCs," *PC Week,* April 22, 1996, p. 125.

Dubashi, Jagannath, "The Dragon's Curse: Why Taiwan's $1 Billion Acer Group Is Betting the Store on PCs," *Financial World,* July 23, 1991, p. 46.

Einhorn, Bruce, "Acer: How Far Can It Ride This Hot Streak?" *Business Week,* May 17, 2004, p. 52.

——, "For Acer, a Bad Year Turns Brutal," *Businessweek Online,* January 15, 2001.

Engardio, Pete, "For Acer, Breaking Up Is Smart to Do," *Business Week,* July 4, 1994, p. 82.

Engardio, Pete, and Neil Gross, "Acer: Up from Clones—and Then Some," *Business Week,* June 28, 1993, p. 54.

Hamm, Steve, "Ace in the Hole," *PC Week,* June 13, 1994, p. A1.

"High-Tech Union Shatters Merger Myth: Acer, Altos Upbeat on Profits, Channels," *PC Week,* March 4, 1991, p. 123.

Huang, Charlene, "Acer Group Plans Major Leap in PC Market," *Electronics,* January 23, 1995, p. 13.

"Inferiority Complex," *Economist,* February 1, 1992, p. 78.

Kovar, Joseph F., "Acer's Channel Strategy Pays Off," *Computer Reseller News*, November 8, 2004, p. 6.

Kraar, Louis, "Acer's Edge: PCs to Go," *Fortune*, October 30, 1995, p. 186.

Kunert, Paul, "Can Acer Play Another Ace?" *Microscope*, August 23, 2004, p. 1.

Lazlo, J.J., "Electronics Industry 1995 Far East Review," *PaineWebber Inc.,* January 2, 1996.

Mantel, Kimberly, and Carol Wei, "The Datamation 100: Acer Inc.," *Datamation,* September 1, 1992, p. 89.

Moore, Jonathan, "Stan Shih's Moment of Truth at Acer," *Business Week*, October 12, 1998.

Moore, Jonathan, Peter Burrows, and Joan Oleck, "Acer Scales Back Its Aspirations," *Business Week*, October 26, 1998, p. 8.

Morris, Kathleen, "The Disintegration Model," *Financial World,* June 20, 1995, p. 32.

Shapiro, Don, "Ronald McDonald, Meet Stan Shih," *Sales & Marketing Management,* November 1995, p. 85.

"Stan Shih, Acer," *Computer Reseller News*, June 7, 2004, p. 62.

"Stan Shih: Setting the Standard; Chairman, Acer, Inc., Taiwan," *Business Week*, July 12, 2004, p. 62.

Tanzer, Andrew, "The Great Leap Forward," *Forbes*, April 15, 1991, p. 108.

——, "Made in Taiwan," *Forbes*, February 26, 1996, p. 134.

"TI Enters Taiwan Venture to Make DRAMs," *Electronic News*, May 15, 1989, p. 1.

Whelan, Carolyn, "Why Acer Lags in the U.S.," *Electronic News (North America)*, June 29, 1998, p. 1.

Whiting, Rick, "Getting Acer Back on Track," *Electronic Business,* February 1993, p. 76.

Zimmerman, Michael R., "Acer to Divest into 21 Public Businesses: Growth Plan to Be Complete by Year 2000," *PC Week,* June 20, 1994, p. 109.

—April Dougal Gasbarre
—update: Susan B. Culligan

Advanced Neuromodulation Systems, Inc.

6901 Preston Road
Plano, Texas 75024
U.S.A.
Telephone: (972) 309-8000
Toll Free: (800) 727-7846
Fax: (972) 309-8150
Web site: http://www.ans-medical.com

Public Company
Incorporated: 1979 as Medicor, Inc.
Employees: 529
Sales: $120.7 million (2004)
Stock Exchanges: NASDAQ
Ticker Symbol: ANSI
NAIC: 339112 Surgical and Medical Instrument
   Manufacturing

Advanced Neuromodulation Systems, Inc. (ANS) is a medical device company that makes implantable spinal cord stimulators and drug pumps to help alleviate chronic pain. Neurostimulation products include Renew, an externally powered radio-frequency system that uses an implanted receiver to send electrical energy to relieve pain caused by damaged nerves; Genesis, an internally implanted, adjustable device that sends energy to the spine through a pulse generator; GenesisXP, offering a larger battery than the Genesis system; GenesisRC, and the Eon Neurostimulation System, rechargeable implantable pulse generator (IPG) systems; and Rapid Programmer, a handheld, easy-to-navigate programmer for clinicians, allowing them to test and program ANS devices. The company's implantable drug pump therapy line consists of the AccuRx, which delivers a measured amount of intraspinal drugs to key points on the spine. The device's precision allows doctors to cut back on the amount of drugs a patient is required to take, thus limiting side effects. ANS is a public company based in Plano, Texas, listed on the NASDAQ.

Beginnings in Late 1970s

ANS was incorporated in May 1979 as Medicor, Inc. by veterans of the medical device field, including its president, Thomas C. Thompson, who had earlier founded a company that made intravenous catheters. After the intravenous catheter company was sold to Baxter Travenol, Thompson joined forces with seasoned executives who had worked at Johnson & Johnson, Eli Lilly's IVAC unit, and IMDE, a Warner-Lambert subsidiary. The partners got into business in October 1979 through acquisition, picking up a four-year-old Dallas company called Med-Pro Ltd., which made its money selling surgical tape but harbored a great deal of potential in the intravenous (IV) tubes and electronic IV devices it had under development. A few months later, in January 1980, Medicor changed its name to Quest Medical, Inc. The company went public in April 1981 selling shares at $2. The timing of the offering proved to be propitious. The company's Intelligent Infusor IV device was unveiled to investors in 1982 at an ideal time, as the fast-growing intravenous market was receiving a great deal of attention on Wall Street, due in no small measure to Warner-Lambert's $468 million buyout of IMED. As a result, Quest's stock price approached $9 by the end of 1982.

Quest began selling the infusor in 1983 and appeared poised to enjoy a prosperous future, but changes in the marketplace derailed the company's plans. First, Medicare and Medicaid reimbursements became more stringent, causing hospitals, Quest's main customers, to become more cost-conscious and to turn to less expensive technologies. By making intravenous tubes and accessories, and blood pressure and electronic pulse rate measuring devices, the company was able to scrape by until hospitals became more comfortable with the government's tighter reimbursement policies and infusor sales picked up. Quest's revenues grew from $4.8 million in 1983 to $10.7 million in 1985, when the company turned a profit of nearly $200,000. Arguably, Quest offered the best infusion device in the industry, but the competition was larger and better funded. Both Abbott Laboratories and Baxter Travenol Laboratories Inc. brought out their own IV pumps, and what they may have lacked in quality they compensated for in pricing, bundling the devices with IV solutions and offering them at a discount. Quest continued to grow sales in 1986 to $13.7 million but posted a loss of $323,000.

Unable to compete against its much larger rivals, Quest decided in September 1987 to sell its IV infusion device business to Colgate Palmolive Co.'s subsidiary Kendall McGaw for $9 million. Additional payments were contingent upon the favorable outcome of a patent infringement suit brought by Minnesota Mining & Manufacturing Co. (3M). After a federal district court judge ruled in its favor in April 1989, Quest received another $2.8 million from Kendall McGaw. While Quest continued to manufacture surgical tapes and IV tubing sets, Thompson and his management team scouted for a good use for their reserve of cash—and executive experience—primarily targeting for acquisition medical companies that manufactured disposable products sold directly to hospitals. Ideally the manufacturing could be relocated and consolidated with Quest's Dallas operation.

Although it was keen on finding a new business as soon as possible, management was also determined to make sure an acquisition was a good fit. As a result, Quest's search lasted several years. Along the way, the company tried in 1988 and 1989 to acquire HemoTec Inc., a Colorado maker of blood coagulation products used during heart surgery. HemoTec rejected an initial offer, and after Quest improved the bid and acquired 23 percent of its stock, HemoTec merged with another company rather than be acquired by Quest. Still, the episode proved profitable to Quest, which pocketed $1.1 million after selling HemoTec stock. Ironically, in August 1990 Quest found itself the object of an unsolicited merger offer from Titan Holdings Inc., a San Antonio-based private insurance holding company that considered Quest, as currently configured, more of an investment company than a medical products company. Hence, Titan's management team believed it was more suited to optimizing shareholder value. From the point of view of Quest's management, however, Titan was simply looking for a chance to go public while picking up an attractive investment pool. The bulk of Quest's shareholders agreed, putting an end to the bid.

Early 1990s Acquisitions

Part of Quest's difficulties in finding suitable acquisitions were the high prices medical companies were seeking, but in the early 1990s Quest was finally able to buy appropriate assets at a desirable price level. In the fall of 1990 Quest bought certain assets of Clini-Therm Corp. out of bankruptcy. Also based in Dallas, Clini-Therm developed and manufactured hypothermia systems used to treat cancer and other diseases with heat. Quest was especially interested in Clini-Therm's Prostek 3000 sys-

tem, a prostate treatment that relied on disposable catheters, an item that Quest was well suited to mass produce. Three more acquisitions followed in 1991 and 1992: the $2.3 million purchase of American Omni Medical and the $2 million purchase of Delta Medical Industries, both makers of heart surgery devices; and the addition of assets related to McGaw, Inc.'s activated clotting time instrument.

It was in 1995 that Quest became involved in the spinal cord stimulation (SCS) field with the acquisition of Neuromed, Inc. for $15.2 million in cash plus stock. It fit in well with Quest's competencies in medical device manufacturing, and was an attractive acquisition because of the key patents it held in a fast growing niche. Moreover, it would be difficult for other companies to enter the market, providing Quest with some assurance that it would not be easily nudged aside by larger players as had been the case with infusors a decade earlier.

Integrating Neuromed into Quest proved problematic, however. Neuromed's devices were not easily manufactured, forcing Quest to make a major investment in reengineering the products. The sales infrastructure also had to be beefed up in order to properly market the line. Quest experienced problems with some of its other units as well. The introduction of the company's Myocardial Protection System of hardware, software, and disposable products designed to offer protection to the heart during open-heart surgery was met with ongoing delays. By the time the $11 million project was ready for launch, the market had changed, with hospitals no longer interested in buying such systems, preferring instead to rent them. But such an arrangement offered little payoff to Quest. The company posted sizable losses in 1995 and 1996, leading to a drop in the price of the company's stock and pressure from some investors for Quest to seek a merger or sale.

In March 1997 Quest retained Smith Barney and Rauscher Pierce Refsnes to help it sort out strategic alternatives, whether it be a sale, merger, or joint venture. While management weighed the options, Quest rebounded somewhat in 1997, recording revenues of more than $14.7 million and returning to profitability, netting nearly $725,000. The main reason for the improvement was the performance of its Advanced Neuromodulation System business. It was no surprise that after a year of deliberation management decided to divest its cardiovascular and intravenous fluid delivery products division, selling the business to Atrion Corporation for about $23 million in January 1998. Quest kept the Advanced Neuromodulation Systems product and also changed its corporate name to Advanced Neuromodulation Systems, Inc. in June 1998.

New Leadership in Late 1990s

While Quest was completing its transformation, Thompson retired in December 1997, replaced as president and CEO on an interim basis by Chief Financial Officer F. Robert Merrill III. A permanent replacement, Christopher G. Chavez, was hired in April 1998. A Harvard Business School graduate, Chavez had more than 20 years of experience in the medical device industry, 16 of which were at Johnson & Johnson Medical Inc., where he served stints as general manager of the Infection Prevention business unit, director of international marketing, and director

---

Key Dates:

1979: Company is founded as Medicor, Inc.
1980: Name changes to Quest Medical, Inc.
1987: IV infusion device business is sold.
1995: Neuromed, Inc. is acquired.
1998: Cardiovascular and IV product lines are divested; name changes to Advanced Neuromodulation Systems, Inc.
1999: Renew is launched in U.S. market.
2002: Genesis is launched in U.S. market.

---

of new business development. He was attracted to ANS because of its promise, telling *Dallas Business Journal* in 2004, "The company had a beautiful idea that was poorly executed." Moreover, he took over a company that was essentially debt-free, holding $19 million in cash.

Shortly after Chavez took over, ANS took steps to transfer its expertise in electrical stimulation technology to other markets. It forged an alliance with Sofamor Danek Group Inc. to develop a deep brain stimulation system to treat Parkinson's disease, epilepsy, and other conditions. A few months later, however, Medtronic, Inc. acquired Sofamor Danek and ANS completed a buyout of its contract with Sofamor Danek. ANS also became involved in the programmable intrathecal drug pump business through an alliance with a German company, Tricumed Medizintechnik Gmbh.

After three years of research and development, ANS launched the Renew RF stimulation system in the U.S. market in June 1999. Sales were so strong that by the end of the year ANS controlled a 50 percent share of the radio-frequency SCS market. Product sales grew by 21 percent to $20.6 million. Overall, revenues grew to $35.8 million and net income totaled $5.8 million. Also during the year, ANS opened a new, state-of-the-art facility to position the company to handle even greater levels of demand for its products.

ANS completed development of AccuRx, its implantable drug pump, in 2000. Much of the technology used in the device was licensed from Implantable Devices Limited Partnership (IDP). In January 2001, ANS acquired IDP, along with another company, ESOX Technology Holdings, LLC, to solidify the company's leading position in implantable drug pump technology. AccuRx began clinical trials in the United States in the first quarter of 2001, and during the second quarter of the year the company began selling the device in foreign markets.

While AccuRx was being launched internationally, ANS was also developing its Genesis IPG SCS system, working closely with a New Jersey company, Hi-tronics Designs, Inc. (HDI), which ANS also acquired in January 2001. Not only did HDI bring with it technology used in Genesis but also expertise in the design of energy-efficient electronic circuits that could be used in the design of products to help in the pain management of numerous conditions. Moreover, HDI was a contract developer and OEM supplier of electromechanical medical devices, thus adding an additional revenue stream. ANS began selling Genesis in Europe in 2001 and in the United States in 2002. After

receiving FDA approval, GenesisXP was launched in the U.S. market in the fourth quarter of 2002.

Revenues increased to $37.9 million in 2001, $57.4 million in 2002, and topped $91 million in 2003. Net income during this period improved from $1.5 million in 2001 to more than $13.2 million in 2003. The company was expanding on a number of fronts. It was especially aggressive in building up its sales force, in an effort to switch from a distributor network to a direct sales force. In 2003 the company acquired the pain management system of three of its top distributors in the United States: Seattle-based Comedical, Inc.; Clifton, New Jersey-based State of the Art Medical Products; and Arlington, Texas-based Sun Medical, Inc. Combined they had done about one-third of ANS's business. As a result of these acquisitions, in just a matter of five years, ANS had gone from being a company that was 100 percent dependent on distributors to one that did just 10 percent of its business through independent distributors. To accommodate its growing business, ANS also moved into a new facility in Plano, Texas, in 2004. ANS looked to expand its product lines as well as markets. In November 2002 it acquired MicroNet Medical, Inc., adding spinal cord stimulation leads that might prove useful in the treatment of Parkinson's disease and migraines. ANS also teamed up with Boston Scientific to enter the Japanese market and established subsidiaries in Germany and Australia.

ANS received some unwanted publicity in 2005 when it announced that it was the subject of a federal investigation of certain of its sales and marketing practices. According to the *Wall Street Journal* in February 2005, "U.S. regulators are looking into past promotional practices at Advanced Neuromodulation Systems Inc., which several years ago offered doctors $1,000 if they implanted a pain-management device in certain patients for a five-day trial. . . . A question that investigators have studied in prior cases has been whether payments to individual doctors constituted compensation for clinical trials, or inducement to use a medical device or drug." In fairness to ANS, it appeared that the federal government was targeting the industry as a whole. Within weeks, investigations were launched concerning the sales and marketing practices of numerous orthopedic spine companies and other medical device manufacturers.

Sales improved to $120.7 million in 2004 and net income grew to $18.2 million. Despite the cloud of investigation, ANS seemed well positioned for the future. Baby Boom patients, unlike their stoic parents, were not shy about demanding pain management products, an attitude that translated into continuing sales growth for ANS products. In addition, neuromodulation held great promise in a wide variety of applications, such as depression, obesity, Alzheimer's, Lou Gehrig's disease, stroke, and obsessive-compulsive disorder. Should ANS successfully apply its technologies to the treatment of some of these areas, its future was indeed promising.

Principal Subsidiaries

Advanced Neuromodulation Systems Australia Pty Limited; ANS Germany GmbH; Hi-Tronics Designs, Inc.; MicroNet Medical, Inc; SPAC Acquisition Corp.

Principal Competitors

Medtronic, Inc., Boston Scientific Corp. (Advanced Bionics).

Further Reading

Abboud, Leila, ''Medical–Device Industry Faces More Scrutiny by U.S. Officials; ANS Is Under Investigation As Federal Regulators Probe Use of Marketing Incentives,'' *Wall Street Journal,* February 25, 2005, p. A2.

Belli, Anne, ''Quest Targets Acquisition to Restore Growth,'' *Dallas-Fort Worth Business Journal,* January 18, 1988, p. 2.

Brady, Lorraine, ''Pile of Cash Keeps Quest in Market for Health Care Firm,'' *Dallas Business Journal,* October 5, 1990, p. 2.

Fine, Jennifer, ''A Local Medical Concern's Quest for Profitability,'' *Dallas Business Courier,* January 13, 1986, p. 1.

Lau, Gloria, ''Pain Relief Equals Big Bucks for These Guys,'' *Investor's Business Daily,* August 13, 2002, p. A07.

Reeves, Amy, ''Beefed-Up Sales Team Lifts Results Here,'' *Investor's Business Daily,* April 9, 2003, p. A08.

Rosenberg, Daniel, ''Pain Control Gets Rechargeable with Latest Neurostimulators,'' *Wall Street Journal,* April 19, 2005, p. D4.

Tanner, Lisa, ''Former Quest Medical Changes Name, Focus,'' *Dallas Business Journal,* November 13, 1998, p. 14.

Yu, Roger, ''Plano, Texas, Medical-Device Maker Experiences Growing Pains,'' *Dallas Morning News,* June 23, 2004.

—Ed Dinger

Aga Foodservice Group PLC

4 Arleston Way, Shirley
Solihull B90 4LH
United Kingdom
Telephone: +44 121 711 6000
Fax: +44 121 711 6001
Web site: http://www.agafoodservice.com

Public Company
Incorporated: 2001
Employees: 4,745
Sales: £435 million ($833.2 million) (2004)
Stock Exchanges: London
Ticker Symbol: AGA
NAIC: 335221 Household Cooking Appliance Manufacturing; 335211 Electric Houseware and Fan Manufactur- ing; 339999 All Other Miscellaneous Manufacturing; 551112 Offices of Other Holding Companies

Aga Foodservice Group PLC manufactures and distributes high-end kitchen equipment and interiors for the residential market, as well as a line of kitchen equipment for the commercial and industrial foodservice and bakery markets. Aga's core product category is its line-up of cast-iron stoves, ranging from the entry-level Falcon (stoves priced up to approximately $4,000), to the mid-priced Rangemaster and (starting at approximately $10,000 per stove) Aga brands, and up to the ultra-high-end La Cornue brand, which costs as much as $40,000 each. Aga Foodservice has been engaged in an acquisition drive during the first half of the 2000s to develop a full-service home furnishings product offering. As such, the company has acquired a number of high-end interiors brands, such as the United States' Domain and its line of kitchen, bedroom, and bathroom furnishings; terracotta tile specialist Fired Earth; and a 40 percent stake in French furniture maker Grange. In 2003, the company developed a new catalog, the *Address Book,* gathering its brand family into a single, coherent product offering. Concurrently, Aga has developed its institution division, Aga Foodservice Equipment, which includes Adamatic, Belshaw, Bongard, Falcon Foodservice Equipment, Miller's Vanguard,

Victory Refrigeration, and Williams Refrigeration. The company's acquisitions in this category have enabled it to present a full range of kitchen equipment, including stoves, ovens, refrigeration, fryers, and doughnut makers and the like for the commercial foodservice and bakery markets. Aga Foodservice was formed from the breakup of former conglomerate Glynwed in 2001. The company is listed on the London Stock Exchange and is led by CEO William McGrath.

Starting Out at 150 Years Old in 2001

Glynwed International PLC was a highly diversified and ultimately unfocused collection of mostly industrial companies at the beginning of the 2000s. Founded in 1939, Glynwed began its march toward conglomerate status—a popular trend among companies in the United Kingdom in the late 1960s—when in 1969 it acquired Allied Iron Founders. Glynwed not only boosted its revenues by more than 100 percent in the deal, it also acquired a business that served as the basis for its later transformation into a focused kitchen equipment company. That business was Aga, a manufacturer of cast-iron stoves.

In the meantime, Glynwed continued to expand its industrial holdings. In 1981, for example, the company acquired Durapipe, which, together with another company holding, Vulcathene, launched Glynwed's industrial pipes division. The company continued adding acquisitions through the 1980s, both in the United Kingdom and in the United States, Australia, Italy, Monaco, and elsewhere. By the mid-1990s, Glynwed's operations spanned the construction, steel and engineering, metal distribution, tubes and pipe systems, and real estate industries, as well as a small consumer products division developed around the Aga stove and other brands. That division was known as Leisure Consumer Products.

Large overly diversified conglomerates such as Glynwed fell out of favor with the global investment community in the 1990s, however. More and more companies began to streamline their structures, focusing on a narrower core of operations, and an increasing number of corporations presented themselves as "pure play" stocks as the dawn of the 21st century neared.

An important result of this trend was that Glynwed and other highly diversified companies saw their stock prices slip, in part

---
Company Perspectives:

Strategy: A strategy for growth. Aga Foodservice Group starts with a strong balance sheet, a young and energetic management team, a strategy for growth and the determination to push it through. We continue to invest in the existing businesses and indeed, our new product developments and upgrades are testament to this.

---

because of the difficulty of comparing their operations with the more easily quantified pure play stocks. The pressure to steamline began to build at Glynwed as well, and by the late 1990s, Glynwed announced that it was refocusing on just two core operations, its Pipe Systems division and its Consumer and Foodservice Operations, the latter grouped around Aga. In 2001, however, Glynwed was approached by a Belgian company, Etex, with an offer to buy out its Pipe Systems division. Glynwed agreed, and then announced that it would reform itself around its remaining business, which was then renamed as Aga Foodservice Group.

By then, the Aga name had been a British mainstay for more than 70 years. Yet the technology it represented had its roots in the late 1770s when John Flavel established a foundry specialized in producing "vapour baths" modeled after those at nearby Leamington Spa. By 1803, however, Flavel had moved the foundry to Leamington Spa, where the company began to specialize in the production of cast-iron stoves. Flavel was later joined by son William, and by 1833, the company had established the Eagle Foundry, described as one of the world's largest at the time. The new site provided the testing grounds for William Flavel's invention—a cast-iron stove that offered boiling, roasting, baking, and warming functions in a single unit, and that also used solid fuel. Flavel named his stove "The Kitchener range cooker."

The Kitchener quickly became a British institution, and Flavel's company earned a number of accolades, including a coveted gold medal at the 1851 Exhibition. The invention became known the world over. Rangemaster continued improving its cooker, adding colors to the exterior, and dual fuel cookers, as well as a fold-away grill. The Kitchener, and the later Flavel brand Rangemaster, also inspired a number of imitators, notably the Falcon and Rayburn brands in Scotland, and the Stanley brand in Ireland, both founded in the 1920s and linked together into the 1950s.

In the meantime, the Kitchener had attracted interest outside of England. Sweden's Nils Gustaf Dalen, who had been awarded the Nobel Prize for Physics in 1912, had been blinded in an accident that same year. While convalescing, Dalen became interested in cooking, and specifically, in resolving a number of problems associated with cast-iron cookers at the time. Dalen began searching for a means for developing a fuel-efficient stove capable of remaining warm 24 hours per day. Basing his design on the Kitchener type of cooker, Dalen developed a highly insulated cast-iron stove capable of operating on small amounts of fuel. Cooking was done using the radiant heat of the stove, while different types of cooking were performed in one of several oven compartments, as well as on the stove top.

Dalen patented his invention in 1922, and launched a new company, called the Svenska Aktiebolaget Gas Accumulator. The stove itself became known as the Aga.

The Aga's real success came in England, however. Sales in the United Kingdom began in 1929, and by 1931 the stove had been introduced in Ireland. At first, the Aga (which weighed some 1,300 pounds) was imported by a licensee, Bell's Asbestos & Engineering based in Slough. Before long, however, the Aga's success led Bell's to begin manufacturing the stove in England. That plant was later acquired by Allied Ironfounders Ltd., which also acquired the Flavel company. By the time of Allied's acquisition by Glynwed, the company's line of stoves had been expanded to include the Scottish Falcon and Rayburn brands as well.

The Aga's true success came when David Ogilvy, then an Aga salesman in Scotland, published *The Theory and Practice of Selling an Aga Cooker* in 1935. Ogilvy went on to found the famed advertising agency Ogilvy & Mather. In the meantime, the Aga came to represent a British tradition, particularly among the British country gentry. The company launched the New Standard Aga in 1936. In 1941, however, the company replaced all of its existing Aga models with a new series of models using standardized parts, called the Aga Standard. The Aga Standard remained the company's mainstay into the 1970s. Color was introduced in 1956, and in 1964, the first Aga model using oil was launched. By the end of the century, solid fuel was replaced by gas or electricity.

Behind the Aga Banner in the New Century

The development of a new strategy of Aga Foodservice Group was turned over to William McGrath, who had joined Glynwed in the late 1990s, and who became CEO of the now smaller company. McGrath and his executive decided to recreate the company around the Aga cooker line as its core. As McGrath told the *Times*: "Aga has been merrily sitting in the group since 1969 and wasn't quite getting the time, love, attention and resources that it could. The group was a good, solid business, but not really brand-oriented. The idea was to bring Aga to the centre and build the business around that."

As part of that effort, the company launched a new marketing effort designed to reposition the Aga brand. Long synonymous with a country gentry lifestyle (and even inspiring its own category of fiction, called the "Aga Saga"), Aga faced only limited growth in that market. One of the major limiting factors of the group's growth was the high degree of durability of its cookers. Indeed, an Aga cooker often lasted for decades, a fact that also had given rise to a thriving secondhand market.

Instead, Aga decided to target a younger, more urban market, introducing a new and more compact model and launching a successful advertising campaign. By the middle of the 2000s, Aga had succeeded in repositioning the brand as an urban up-and-comer's status symbol. Until 2004, the Aga brand represented the high point of the company's line of cooker brands, with the price of its cookers ranging from $10,000 to $20,000. The "entry level" Falcon brand featured cookers starting at just $4,000, and the Rangemaster represented the group's mid-point brand. In 2004, Aga was dethroned as the company's top-of-the-line brand, with the acquisition that year of France's La Cornue. With hand-

Key Dates:

1777: John Flavel opens a foundry in Leamington, which later specializes in cast iron cookers, launching the "Kitchener" in 1835.

1922: Nobel Prize winner Nils Gustav Dalen develops the Aga cooker.

1929: Aga sales are launched in the United Kingdom.

1939: The industrial manufacturing group Glynwed is founded.

1969: Glynwed acquires Allied Iron Founders, including Aga, Flavel, and other brands, which are later grouped as the Leisure Consumer Products division.

1998: Glynwed launches a restructuring around the core of pipe systems and Leisure Consumer Products.

2001: Glynwed sells the pipe operations to Etex, and renames Leisure Consumer Products as Aga Foodservice; the company acquires Fired Earth and Elgin & Hall.

2002: The company acquires Domain Home Fashions and Belshaw in the United States and Bongard in France.

2003: Northland Corporation, including Marvel Industries, is acquired.

2004: The company acquires La Cornue in France.

2005: The company acquires Waterford Stanley in Ireland.

built, made-to-order ranges priced as high as $40,000, the Cornue brand boasted an impressive clientele, including French President Jacque Chirac, Italy's Silvio Berlusconi, and international stars such as Brad Pitt and Celine Dion.

Aga Foodservice now set out to expand beyond being a manufacturer of stoves to develop itself as a high-end kitchen equipment and interior furnishings provider. The company used the proceeds from the sale of Glynwed's pipe division to finance an aggressive acquisition drive into the mid-2000s. In 2001, for example, the company purchased U.K.-based interiors retailer Fired Earth, adding that company's 55-store retail network. Also that year, the company purchased Elgin & Hall, a manufacturer of high-end fireplace surrounds.

Aga also launched an entry into the institutional and commercial kitchen equipment market at the end of 2001. The company first purchased Bury-based Millers Bakery Machinery in the United Kingdom, then turned to the United States, buying up New Jersey-based Adamatic, a maker of equipment for producing specialty breads and pizzas. That purchase boosted the group's U.S. presence, begun with Glynwed's acquisition of Victory Refrigeration, also in New Jersey.

The United States played host to two more Aga purchases in 2002. In April of that year, the company bought Belshaw, the world's top manufacturer of doughnut machines, based in Seattle. Belshaw controlled a 50 percent share of the global market for doughnut machines and included major clients such as Dunkin' Donuts, Krispy Kreme, and Wal-Mart. At the same time, Aga expanded its U.S. consumer presence, with the acquisition of Boston-based retailer Domain Home Fashions, pro-

viding the company with its first showroom presence in the United States. Back in Europe, the company became a leading bakery equipment supplier on the continent with the acquisition of France's Bongard.

Aga's acquisition drive continued into the mid-2000s. The company acquired a stake in exclusive French furniture maker Grange, then expanded its commercial equipment business by acquiring Northland Corporation, including its Marvel Industries unit, specialized in refrigeration equipment, in 2003. The La Cornue purchase followed in 2004; by 2005 the company had extended its cooker line again, acquiring Ireland's Waterford Stanley. In the meantime, Aga raised its European presence with the acquisition of three bakery equipment factories in France in September 2004. Aga Foodservice promised to play a leading role in the international kitchen equipment market into the new century.

Principal Subsidiaries

Adamatic; AFE Online; AFE Serviceline; Aga Ranges (U.S.A.); Belshaw; Bongard (France); Domain Home Fashions (U.S.A.); Falcon Foodservice Equipment; Fired Earth; Grange (France; 40%); La Cornue (France); Miller's Vanguard Ltd.; Mono Equipment; Northland/Marvel; Pavailler; Rangemaster; Victory Refrigeration; Williams Refrigeration (U.S.A.).

Principal Competitors

Siemens AG; Samsung Electronics Company Ltd.; Sanyo Electric Company Ltd.; Electrolux AB; Sibtyazhmash Joint Stock Company; Whirlpool Corporation; Aisin Seiki Company Ltd.; LG Electronics Inc.; BSH Bosch und Siemens Hausgerate GmbH; GE Appliances; Liebherr-International AG; Maytag Corporation; De' Longhi S.p.A. Treviso; Fagor Electrodomesticos Soc Cooperative Ltda.; Elco Brandt S.A.

Further Reading

"Aga Adds to Brand Portfolio," *Appliance,* November 2004, p. S2.

"Aga Buys: Group Acquires French Factories," *Birmingham Post,* September 10, 2004, p. 21.

Ashworth, Jon, "Cooker Manufacturer Turns Up the Heat in Campaign to Extend Reach," *Times,* February 21, 2005, p. 44.

Gibson, Helen, "Aga Keeps on Cookin'," *Time International,* August 20, 2001, p. 54.

Griffin, Jon, "Aga's Saga of Success in 2004," *Birmingham Evening Mail,* January 12, 2005, p. 38.

Howard, Philip, "An Aga Saga: How Emblem of Gentry Won Urban Chic," *Times,* March 20, 2004, p. 3.

"Rival Stove Manufacturers Cook Up a Reunion," *Birmingham Post,* June 7, 2005, p. 18.

Rozhon, Tracie, "Get Ready for Britons Bearing 1,290-Pound Stoves," *New York Times,* May 10, 2003, p. C3.

Waller, Martin, "Aga Develops a Cast-Iron Strategy to Boost Its Sales," *Times,* June 11, 2002, p. 26.

"Welcome to the Iron Age," *Foundry Trade Journal,* March 2002, p. 12.

Williams, Penny, "Aga Expands into Cooling Market," *ERT Weekly,* July 25, 2002, p. 4.

—M.L. Cohen

Agrium

Agrium Inc.

13131 Lake Fraser Drive Southeast
Calgary, Alberta T2J 7E8
Canada
Telephone: (403) 225-7000
Toll Free: (877) 247-4861
Fax: (403) 225-7609
Web site: http://www.agrium.com

Public Company
Incorporated: 1992 as Cominco Fertilizers Inc.
Employees: 4,667
Sales: $2.83 billion (2004)
Stock Exchanges: Toronto New York
Ticker Symbol: AGU
NAIC: 325320 Pesticide and Other Agricultural Chemical
    Manufacturing; 325312 Phosphatic Fertilizer
    Manufacturing

Agrium Inc. is a producer and retailer of nitrogen, phosphate, potash, and sulfate fertilizers. Agrium produces its fertilizer at a dozen plants in Canada and the United States. The company also owns a 50 percent stake in a production facility in Argentina. Agrium sells its fertilizer through 206 retail centers in the United States, marketing fertilizer as well as crop protection products, seeds, and services to growers in 22 states. In South America, Agrium operates 33 farm centers in Argentina, four stores in Chile, and two stores in Bolivia.

Origins

Although much of what constituted Agrium in the 21st century was built during the 1990s, the company's roots stretched back to the beginning of the 20th century. Agrium was formed as a business unit within the corporate structure of another company, The Consolidated Mining and Smelting Company, which was formed in 1906 when several businesses controlled by the Canadian Pacific Railway were consolidated into a single entity. Consolidated Mining, which changed its name to Cominco Ltd. in 1966, operated a number of mining operations throughout its history, but relied on its core Sullivan Mine for much of its business during the 20th century. The Sullivan Mine began producing in 1909, yielding $20 billion worth of lead, zinc, and silver by the time it was shuttered in 2001. From the success of the Sullivan Mine and the other mines owned and operated by the company, Cominco gained the size and the financial resources to fashion itself into an integrated metals concern. As part of its development into a more well-rounded company, Cominco formed a division to market fertilizer byproducts from its British Columbia metals plants, a division that became known as Cominco Fertilizer Ltd., the predecessor to Agrium.

Cominco's involvement in the fertilizer business began in 1931 when the company began producing ammonia—the basic building block of nitrogen fertilizer—and phosphate fertilizer in British Columbia. During the ensuing decades, Cominco Fertilizer emerged as an innovator in its field, developing the first nitrate prilling (pellet-forming) process in the 1940s and the first granulation process for urea and ammonium nitrate during the 1960s. The division's first decades also included an increase in the number of fertilizer facilities under its control, constituting the assets that would be inherited by Agrium. In 1965, the division's Homestead nitrogen operations in Nebraska began operating, followed by the addition of nitrogen operations in Borger, Texas, three years later. In 1969, a potash facility was established in Saskatchewan. In 1977, nitrogen operations in Carseland, Alberta, began production, followed a decade later by the establishment of nitrogen facilities in Joffre, Alberta. Despite the division's pioneering work and its lengthy involvement in the fertilizer business, Cominco gave relatively little management attention to Cominco Fertilizer. Fertilizer sales represented only a small portion of the mining company's total revenue volume, relegating Cominco Fertilizer to a minor role within Cominco Ltd.'s operations. Consequently, the division received limited financial support from its corporate parent, never realizing its full potential while governed by Cominco Ltd.

1993 Spinoff

Cominco Fertilizer's fortunes improved dramatically when the company gained its independence, an event that ended decades of passive management and replaced it with dynamic leadership intent on pursuing growth aggressively. During the early 1990s, Cominco Ltd. decided to spin off its fertilizer division to the public, a decision that led to the incorporation of Alberta-based Cominco Fertilizer in December 1992 in preparation for the division's initial public offering of stock. Several months later, in mid-1993, Cominco Ltd. spun off its fertilizer business, retaining an 18 percent stake in the business and selling the remainder to the investing public. Cominco Fertilizer's debut as an independent company gave investors an opportunity to invest in one of only a few public companies in North America exclusively involved in the fertilizer business, referred to as a "pure play" in investing circles. Investors were presented with a company involved in producing nitrogen and potash (a compound containing potassium), two of the four major nutrients essential to the growth of all plants. (Nitrogen, phosphorous, potassium, and sulfate are the four major nutrients. They are depleted when crops are grown and replaced by the application of fertilizer.)

Cominco Fertilizer, as it set out on its own, was heavily reliant on nitrogen fertilizer, deriving 72 percent of its production value from nitrogen production facilities in Alberta, Nebraska, and Texas. The company derived the remaining 28 percent of its production value from potash, which it produced from a single mine in Saskatchewan. Aside from the production, or wholesale, part of its business, Cominco Fertilizer was supported by retail operations consisting of farm centers that sold fertilizer directly to growers. The cornerstone of the company's retail operations was its investment in Crop Production Services, a major U.S. retailer of fertilizer. Cominco Fertilizer had purchased a 33 percent stake in Crop Production Services in 1989, which was increased to 86 percent in 1993, giving the company control over approximately 120 farm outlets in the United States. Cominco Fertilizer also operated storage facilities placed strategically to support its fertilizer activities, the third dimension of the company's business.

Once set free from the control of Cominco Ltd., Cominco Fertilizer flourished, developing into one of the largest fertilizer concerns in the Western Hemisphere. Under the leadership of President and CEO John Van Brunt, who would guide the company during its first decade of independence, Cominco Fertilizer recorded impressive growth, expanding its production, retail, and distribution holdings, broadening its geographic scope of operations, and increasing its market exposure by adding phosphorous and sulphur to its product mix, making the

company a producer of all four major nutrients. Cominco Fertilizer's maturation as a fertilizer producer and retailer was highlighted by acquisitions, Van Brunt's primary means of increasing the company's revenue volume from CAD 290 million in 1993 to more than CAD 2 billion by the time he departed.

Van Brunt's expansion program began in earnest in 1995, the year the company changed its name to Agrium Inc. The year began with the acquisition of Western Farm Services, a deal that added 100 retail outlets in California and the Pacific Northwest. The acquisition, coupled with the company's purchase of the 14 percent of Crop Production Services it did not already own in 1995, doubled its retail base, giving it more than 200 farm centers that sold fertilizer and chemicals to growers. The company's revenue from the retail side of its business shot upward as a result, jumping from CAD 365 million in 1994 to CAD 753 million in 1995. On the production side, a major addition to the company arrived in October 1995 when Van Brunt completed the CAD 290 million acquisition of Nu-West Industries, a phosphate fertilizer producer that had filed for bankruptcy in 1990 after expanding imprudently during the late 1980s and reemerged recapitalized in 1993. Nu-West's core product was superphosphoric acid, a liquid fertilizer used for corn, wheat, alfalfa, and soybean crops. Once Agrium absorbed Nu-West's operations, it had the capability to produce three of the four major fertilizer compounds.

While Agrium strengthened its business in North America, Van Brunt announced his ambitions for the company's growth abroad. In 1995, when Agrium conducted all of its business in North America, Van Brunt revealed his intention to have one-sixth of the company's assets located outside North America by 2000. To achieve this goal, he set his sights on Argentina, a country whose economy relied heavily on agricultural activity. Van Brunt planned to build the first major nitrogen fertilizer plant in Argentina, ordering the construction of a facility in the Neuquen province, where production was slated to begin by the end of the decade. Van Brunt also pushed forward with plans to develop a retail presence in Argentina, forming Agroservicios Pampeanos S.A., which became an Agrium retail subsidiary. Construction of 18 retail centers in Argentina began in 1996, adding the first overseas dimension to the rapidly growing Agrium.

While construction was underway in Argentina, Van Brunt plotted what would be his boldest move on the acquisition front. In 1996, he targeted a company named Viridian Inc. as his next acquisition candidate. Viridian's background was similar to Agrium's origins: a fertilizer business that grew out of a metals business. Viridian began its business life as Sherritt Gordon Mines Limited, which owned a nickel-copper mine in Lynn Lake, Manitoba. As part of its mining business, the company developed a hydro-metallurgical process that used ammonia, which eventually led the company to establish a fertilizer plant, becoming, like Cominco Ltd., a vertically integrated company. Instead of spinning off its fertilizer business, Viridian's management chose to spin off all of the company's other assets. After acquiring a fertilizer plant from Imperial Oil in Redwater, Alberta, in 1994, Viridian quickly divested its other assets, spinning off its metals, oil and gas, and technology businesses in 1995 and 1996. By the time Viridian was acquired by Agrium in December 1996, the company operated solely as a fertilizer business, generating $527 million from fertilizer sales in 1995. When Viridian's operations were absorbed by Agrium, the combined company boasted annual revenue of $1.67 billion. The acquisition primarily strengthened Agrium's nitrogen and phosphate business, but Viridian's Redwater plant also produced sulphur, giving Agrium the capability of producing all four major fertilizer compounds.

Agrium in the Late 1990s

Agrium's progress between 1993 and 1996 did much to increase the company's stature. Entering 1997, the company ranked as the Western Hemisphere's second largest nitrogen producer, its third largest potash producer, and its fourth largest phosphate producer. In the wake of this substantial surge in growth, the company expanded at a slower pace, focusing instead on improving its balance sheet and the efficiency of its operations. The company did add to its operations on several occasions, however, ensuring its prominence within the fertilizer business. In 1998, the company acquired a phosphate mine in Idaho. The following year production at its phosphate mine in the province of Ontario commenced. The end of the 1990s also saw the company come closer to realizing its objective of establishing a production facility in Argentina. In early 1999, the company increased its interest in a joint venture project from 33 percent to 50 percent, giving it an equal stake with its partner Repsol-YPF S.A. in the construction of ammonia and urea plants in Bahia Blanca, Argentina. Production at the facility, managed by the joint venture company Profertil S.A., commenced in 2000.

As preparations were being made to begin production in Bahia Blanca, Van Brunt prepared to make another large acqui-

sition, the last purchase he would make at Agrium. In September 2000, he acquired the agricultural products division operated by Union Oil Company of California, a CAD 321 million deal that gave Agrium ammonia and urea production facilities in Alaska and nitrogen production and distribution assets in Washington, Oregon, and California.

During the first years of the 21st century, depressed conditions in the fertilizer industry forced Agrium to reduce capital spending and to shelve plans for expansion. Van Brunt, after a decade of leading the company, retired in 2003, leading to the promotion of Agrium's chief operating officer, Michael Wilson, to the chief executive officer post. By the time Van Brunt retired, conditions in the fertilizer industry had improved, but Agrium did not make any meaningful move toward expansion until 2005. In February, the company began expanding throughout South America, acquiring 12 retail farm centers in Argentina, four retail locations in Chile, and two outlets in Bolivia. By this point in the company's development, annual sales eclipsed $2.8 billion, having grown nearly tenfold since Van Brunt began orchestrating Agrium's fast-paced expansion. The company's pace of growth during its first decade of independence made Agrium a global leader in the fertilizer industry, a standing that Wilson was charged with maintaining in the years ahead.

Principal Subsidiaries

Agrium U.S. Inc.; Agrium Nitrogen Company; Crop Production Services, Inc.; Western Farm Service, Inc.; Agroservicios Pameanos S.A. (Argentina); Nu-West Industries, Inc.; Viridian Inc.; Viridian Fertilizers Limited; Profertil S.A. (Argentina; 50%); Canpotex Limited (33.33%).

Principal Competitors

Potash Corporation of Saskatchewan Inc.; Terra Industries Inc.; CF Industries Holdings, Inc.

Further Reading

"Agrium Acquires 18 Retail Outlets in Argentina, Chile, and Bolivia," *Canadian Corporate News,* February 2, 2005, p. 43.
"Agrium and Viridian Merge," *European Chemical News,* October 28, 1996, p. 4.
"Agrium Buys Unocal Ag Products Business for Roughly $325 MM," *Chemical Market Reporter,* January 24, 2000, p. 3.
Wareing, Andrew, "Phosphate Producer Plans Expansion," *Northern Ontario Business,* December 2003, p. 6C.
Westervelt, Robert, "Agrium Acquires Unocal's Nitrogen Operations," *Chemical Week,* January 26, 2000, p. 12.

—Jeffrey L. Covell

The Anschutz Company

---

555 17th Street, Suite 2400
Denver, Colorado 80202-3941
U.S.A.
Telephone: (303) 298-1000
Fax: (303) 298-8881

Private Company
Incorporated: 1992
Employees: 100
NAIC: 551112 Offices of Other Holding Companies

The Anschutz Company and its affiliates, including the Anschutz Corporation and Anschutz Investment Company, are the investment vehicles for the diversified interests of Philip F. Anschutz. Originally funded by the oil and gas holdings of his father, the publicity-shy Anschutz quietly became a billionaire in the early 1980s as a result of his oil and gas exploration ventures. Consistently ranked as one of the richest persons in Denver, Anschutz became better known nationally in the late 1980s and early 1990s for acquiring railroad lines, including the small Rio Grande Railroad and a railroad giant, Southern Pacific Rail Corporation. In 1996 he engineered the sale of Southern Pacific to rival Union Pacific Corporation, pocketing $1.4 billion in profits from an initial $90 million investment. By that time he had invested about $55 million into a sleepy offshoot of Southern Pacific to develop what would eventually become Qwest Communications International Inc., a major telecommunications firm based in the western United States that acquired U S West Inc., one of the Baby Bells, in 2000. In the early 2000s Anschutz moved aggressively into entertainment and media. AEG (formerly Anschutz Entertainment Group) is the nation's second largest producer of concerts and other events; owns stakes in the Los Angeles Kings hockey franchise, the Los Angeles Lakers basketball team, and the state-of-the-art Staples Center; and owns five Major League Soccer teams. Anschutz also controls Regal Entertainment Group, the largest movie theater chain in the United States. His evangelical Christian beliefs have also led him to form Anschutz Film Group, which through two film production companies, Walden Media and Botany Bay Productions, aims to produce ''family-friendly'' films. His newspaper holdings include the *San Francisco Examiner* and the *Washington Examiner*. In addition to being the largest shareholder in both Union Pacific (6 percent stake) and Qwest (16.5 percent), Anschutz continues his involvement in the energy sector through a 16 percent stake in Forest Oil Corporation, a Denver-based oil and gas exploration and production company, and a 59 percent interest in Long Beach, California-based Pacific Energy Partners, L.P., which is involved in gathering, blending, transporting, storing, and distributing crude oil in the western United States and Canada. He also has extensive real estate holdings. His estimated net worth of $5.8 billion is well down from the $18 billion of the late 1990s when Qwest was riding the tech stock bubble. A marathon runner in his younger years, Anschutz has built this fortune through tenacity, savvy dealmaking, strategic timing, and a knack for spotting trends.

From Struggling Wildcatter to Billionaire Dealmaker: 1960s to Early 1980s

Philip F. Anschutz was born in Russell, Kansas, in 1939 (some sources say it was Grand Bend). His father, Fred Anschutz, was a renowned oilfield wildcatter who made and lost several fortunes. It was Fred Anschutz who founded the Anschutz Corporation, which was called Anschutz Dunwoody Drilling Co. Inc. when it was formed in 1960. At that time, Philip Anschutz was in college at the University of Kansas, where he earned a bachelor's degree in finance, with honors, in 1961. The following year, the younger Anschutz was days away from starting classes at the prestigious University of Virginia law school, when his father became ill; he returned home to take over the family businesses, including Anschutz Corporation and the oil wildcatting company, Circle A Drilling. He also relocated to Denver that same year.

Success did not come immediately for the young wildcatter. It was not until 1968 that he made his first major strike—and his first million—while contract drilling for Chevron near Gillette, Wyoming. When the huge oilfield caught fire soon after its discovery, Anschutz averted disaster by persuading the famed oil-fire fighter Red Adair to take on the blaze despite Anschutz's shaky finances, and by securing $100,000—enough to tide him over until he could get financing from his bankers—from Uni-

Key Dates:

1960: The Anschutz Corporation, originally called Anschutz Dunwoody Drilling Co. Inc., is founded by Fred Anschutz, an oil wildcatter.

1962: Philip Anschutz takes over Anschutz Corporation from his father, setting up shop in Denver.

1968: The younger Anschutz makes his big strike as a wildcatter.

1982: Anschutz sells a half-interest in the mineral rights on his ranchlands to Mobil Corporation for $500 million.

1984: Anschutz acquires the Denver & Rio Grande Railroad.

1988: Anschutz purchases Southern Pacific, merging it with the Rio Grande.

1991: Anschutz separates SP Telecom from Southern Pacific, retaining the right to lay fiber-optic cable along the railroad's rights-of-way.

1992: The Anschutz Company is formed and made parent company of Anschutz Corp.

1995: With Edward Roski, Jr., Anschutz purchases the Los Angeles Kings hockey team; Anschutz acquires Qwest Communications and merges SP Telecom into it.

1996: Union Pacific acquires Southern Pacific; Anschutz pockets about $1.4 billion from the sale; Qwest announces that it will build a nationwide, state-of-the-art, fiber-optic network.

1997: Anschutz hires AT&T executive Joseph Nacchio to head Qwest, which is taken public later in the year; Anschutz retains an 84 percent stake in Qwest, which is worth $4.9 billion by year-end.

1998: Anschutz gains part-ownership of the Los Angeles Lakers basketball team.

1999: The Staples Center, part-owned by Anschutz, opens in Los Angeles.

2000: Qwest acquires U S West in a $43.5 billion stock swap, which reduces Anschutz's stake in Qwest to 38 percent, or about $12 billion.

2001: In partnership with Cary Granat, Anschutz forms the film production company Walden Media.

2002: Qwest collapses amid a scandal involving accounting and other financial improprieties; its stock plummets to 90 percent below its all-time high, cutting the value of Anschutz's stake to as low as $322 million; three Anschutz-controlled movie theater chains are combined into Regal Entertainment Group, which is taken public.

2004: Anschutz buys the *San Francisco Examiner* newspaper.

---

versal Studios. Universal just happened to be filming *Hellfighters,* which had John Wayne playing Adair, and were pleased to be able to shoot footage of a real fire and the real Adair in action.

Over the next several years, Anschutz's fortunes waxed and waned, and it was during this period that he began to expand outside of the oil industry while continuing to own oilfields in Montana, Texas, Colorado, and Wyoming. Anschutz purchased cattle ranches, uranium and coal mines, and wheat and vegetable farms, and launched a New York-based commodity trading company specializing in oil and metals. He was nearly ruined by a disastrous coal mining investment before managing to sell the money-losing mines to an electric utility.

Among the real estate Anschutz purchased in the early 1970s was a property on the Wyoming-Utah border, known as Anschutz Ranch East. In 1978 Amoco Corporation discovered a huge reservoir of oil and natural gas adjacent to this ranch—what turned out to be one of the largest discoveries since Alaska's Prudhoe Bay. Amoco attempted to buy Anschutz's mineral rights but he refused. Instead, he expanded his holdings of what became known as the Overthrust Belt, acquiring leases on ten million acres. Then in a prime example of his exquisite timing, Anschutz sold a half-interest in the mineral rights on his ranchlands to Mobil Corporation for $500 million in 1982, not long before the 1980s oil crash. Were it not for this shrewd maneuver, which made him a billionaire, ranking 13th on *Forbes* magazine's list of the richest Americans, Anschutz could have been one of the crash's casualties.

Anschutz parlayed his oil and gas wealth into the stock market, downtown real estate (primarily in Denver) and, ultimately, the railroad industry. Anschutz contemplated and then abandoned takeovers of two publicly traded companies in the 1980s, ITT and Pennwalt; in the process of buying and selling shares in the companies, he pocketed more than $100 million. In the early 1980s, Anschutz spent $61.5 million for a nearly 25 percent stake in troubled Ideal Basic Industries, one of the largest companies in Colorado and one of the country's leading producers of cement and potash. Anschutz ended up clearing a $30 million profit on what had looked like an extremely risky investment.

Anschutz's first major venture into real estate began in 1974 when he secured a 30 percent interest in all projects developed by the Oxford-AnsCo Development Co.—a subsidiary of a leading Canadian development company, Oxford Properties Inc.—for $1 million and downtown property owned by Anschutz in Denver and Colorado Springs. By the early 1980s, Oxford-AnsCo had developed several major skyscrapers in Denver, including the 56-story Republic Tower and the 39-story Anaconda Tower, worth an estimated $250 million. The relationship with Oxford-AnsCo soured when Anschutz gained the vast real estate holdings of the Denver & Rio Grande Railroad in 1984 and wanted to begin to develop real estate on his own rather than through the Oxford partnership. Late in 1984, the partnership was dissolved and the holdings divided between Anschutz and Oxford, with Anschutz keeping the Anaconda Tower (where the company's offices were still located in the early 21st century), Denver's Fairmont Hotel, and a half-block of undeveloped land in Denver.

Mid- to Late-1980s: Modern-Day Rail Baron

Soon after becoming president in 1981, Ronald Reagan deregulated the U.S. railroad industry. Anschutz spotted a huge opportunity here, anticipating that the deregulation would inevitably lead to consolidation and the possibility of profiting from dealmaking. He started modestly, with the 1984 purchase of the Denver & Rio Grande Railroad, commonly known as the Rio Grande, a small railroad that then consisted of more than 3,400 miles of track from Missouri to Utah. Anschutz Corp. purchased the Rio Grande's parent, Rio Grande Industries, Inc., for $500 million, $90 million of which was in cash and the remainder in loans. This heavy debt load, coupled with competition from the Union Pacific line and several lost coal-hauling accounts, led to an approximate revenue loss of 20 percent over the first four years under Anschutz and a net loss of $1.8 million over an 11-month period in 1987 and 1988.

The Rio Grande's small size and its position as a bridge carrier (providing connections between other rail lines) led Anschutz to pursue the acquisition of the railroad giant Southern Pacific (SP) in an attempt to save the much smaller Rio Grande. With 20,000 miles of track thoroughly covering the West Coast and a line through the southern United States to the Mississippi River, SP was even more attractive to Anschutz for its connections to the Rio Grande lines in Kansas City and Ogden, Utah, making for a synergistic coupling.

Anschutz had to overcome a major hurdle to achieve his objective of solidifying his railroad holdings. Santa Fe Industries Inc. had purchased Southern Pacific in 1983 with the intention of merging SP with the Atchison, Topeka & Santa Fe Railway (known as the Santa Fe), one of SP's main competitors. The proposed merger elicited immediate opposition from government officials and Santa Fe's competition, and with the added impetus of pressure from Anschutz, whom *Forbes* called "politically influential," the Interstate Commerce Commission (ICC) in 1987 blocked the Santa Fe–SP merger as anticompetitive. Robert Krebs, the chairman of Santa Fe Industries, was forced to sell one of his lines and chose SP, which he felt was the weaker of the two.

Anschutz closed the deal for Southern Pacific in the fall of 1988. Similar to many other takeovers of the 1980s, Anschutz engineered a highly leveraged purchase in which Rio Grande Industries paid Santa Fe Industries just over $1 billion in cash, most of it borrowed, for SP, assuming more than $700 million in SP debt. After the deal, Anschutz held 71 percent of the Rio Grande, which now controlled SP, while Morgan Stanley as a minority partner controlled the remaining 29 percent through its purchase of $111 million in Rio Grande common stock. As William P. Barrett noted in *Forbes,* "Beyond the original cash stake in the Rio Grande, Anschutz put not a penny more into the deal," thereby making him the first individual to own a major railroad in decades.

Early 1990s: Turning SP Around

In the initial years after the purchase, Rio Grande Industries struggled to overcome its huge debt load, which had led to $100 million-plus interest payments each year, as well as the decline in SP's traditional accounts in auto parts, lumber, and food; increased competition from Union Pacific and Santa Fe; and more rigorous safety inspections in California, where SP trains were involved in two chemical spills in July 1991. Amid speculation that he would be better off breaking up SP and

selling it piecemeal (Krebs of the Santa Fe still coveted much of the SP line and approached Anschutz about a deal several times without success), Anschutz told *Forbes:* "I said in my original ICC filing that we would turn this railroad around; I'm in it for the long haul." Anschutz also foresaw that Southern Pacific would be far more valuable intact than in parts, especially after industry consolidation proceeded to its endgame when one of the western railroads, in order to remain competitive, would pay dearly for SP.

To reduce the debt load, Anschutz sold large portions of Southern Pacific's vast real estate holdings, more than $1 billion worth by the end of 1991 and nearly $400 million in 1992 alone. Anschutz also began to improve the quality of its service through heavy expenditures to maintain its track and hiring a quality expert, Kent Sterett, from its competitor Union Pacific. As trade between the United States and Mexico increased in the early 1990s, SP seemed best positioned to profit from it with its six Mexican gateways in California, Texas, and Arizona. Anschutz's strategy appeared to be working as an operating loss of $347.7 million in 1991 had been reduced to $24.6 million in 1992. But in 1993, SP slid back to a loss of $149 million.

In the summer of 1993, Anschutz turned to a railroad company veteran, Edward Moyers, to assist in turning SP around. Moyers had retired after a very successful four-year stint at Illinois Central, where he cut its operating ratio (operating expenses as a percentage of revenues) from 98 percent to 71 percent. Anschutz hired Moyers as chief executive, and Moyers immediately focused on Southern Pacific's operating ratio, which stood at 96.5 percent in 1993. The hiring enabled Anschutz to embark on a new and surprising strategy for a man who preferred to keep his dealings private: taking SP public.

In another effort to reduce the debt load, 30 million shares were offered in August 1993. Although the initial offering price was estimated at $20 per share, the actual price of the shares as issued was $13.50. Still, that the offering was successful at all was attributed by many to the hiring of Moyers. Investor interest in Southern Pacific increased in the several months that followed, so that by February 1994, when a second stock offering of 25 million shares was initiated, the stock sold for $19.75 per share. Following these sales, Anschutz owned 41 percent of the shares outstanding. Henry Dubroff of the *Denver Post* estimated that Anschutz had pocketed pretax profits of as much as $500 million from the stock offerings.

Meanwhile, Moyers started a multipronged strategy for revitalizing Southern Pacific. First, he planned to cut costs by reducing the employee ranks through a buyout program and a reorganization. In his first year, he reduced the labor force by more than 3,000 to about 19,000 jobs. Second, Moyers focused on service to SP's customers, putting pressure on his subordinates to improve the operations. This initiative saved a lucrative Georgia-Pacific account by increasing on-time Georgia-Pacific deliveries from zero to 80 percent in three months. Overall, on-time deliveries were up by more than 50 percent in his first year. Moyers also sought to bolster Southern Pacific's equipment through the purchase of new locomotives, the rebuilding of existing locomotives, and better maintenance of both trains and track. Although SP was still in weak financial condition, Moyers had managed to make a number of improvements, and in February 1995 he once again retired. Moyers was succeeded as president and CEO by veteran railroader Jerry R. Davis.

Anschutz was also attempting to leverage the real estate holdings of Southern Pacific by developing some of the land rather than selling it to other developers. Starting around 1994, Anschutz was involved in the planning of a downtown development in his base city of Denver on land along the South Platte River that he had purchased from SP. Anschutz and Comsat (later Ascent Entertainment), then owners of the National Basketball Association's Denver Nuggets and later the owners of the National Hockey League's Colorado Avalanche, developed a proposal for a $130 million sports and entertainment center that would include a new basketball and hockey arena and film and television studios. But the plan fell through when Anschutz insisted that Ascent sell him 50 percent of the Avalanche and Ascent refused. In the end, Anschutz sold the land underneath what would eventually become the Pepsi Center to Ascent for top dollar; he would also turn away from Denver and seek his entrée into the sports world to the west, in Los Angeles.

Mid- to Late 1990s: Exit Railroads, Enter Qwest and Sports, Reenter Oil

By 1995 railroad industry consolidation was reaching a crescendo, with the number of major railroads having been reduced from 40 in 1980 to ten, and with the completion of the merger of Burlington Northern and the Sante Fe. There were now just three major rail companies in the western United States: Southern Pacific, Union Pacific, and the newly named Burlington Northern Sante Fe, which was about the size of the other two combined. Not surprisingly, then, the Southern Pacific and Union Pacific entered into what turned out to be lengthy discussions about a merger. Finally, in November 1995 Union Pacific filed an application with the ICC to acquire Southern Pacific.

Completion of the merger was by no means certain. The rail systems of Burlington Northern and the Sante Fe scarcely had any overlap, while the merger of SP and UP would eliminate competition on certain runs, most notably in Texas and between Colorado and California. Meanwhile, the U.S. Congress, under full Republican control for the first time in decades, was considering the abolition of the ICC and its replacement by a more industry friendly Surface Transportation Board (STB). With Anschutz once again wielding political pressure, the Congress passed the legislation that replaced the ICC with the STB in December 1995. In July 1996—despite opposition from the U.S. departments of Justice, Transportation, and Agriculture; from such rival railroads as Kansas City Southern and Consolidated Rail; and from the governor of Texas, George W. Bush— the STB approved the merger in July 1996, with the only major stipulation being that UP grant trackage rights for about 4,000 miles of track to Burlington Northern Sante Fe.

Union Pacific paid $5.4 billion for Southern Pacific, with Anschutz pocketing about $1.4 billion from the sale. Part of this came in the form of stakes of more than 5 percent each he gained in Union Pacific (a stake initially worth about $700 million) and in Union Pacific Resources Group Inc., a leading independent oil and gas exploration and production company that was spun off from Union Pacific in 1995 and 1996 (the

stake in the latter was worth about $300 million). The $1.4 billion figure was an astounding gain on what had essentially been Anschutz's initial cash investment (in the Denver & Rio Grande Railroad) of $90 million.

Anschutz continued to hold his 5 percent stake in Union Pacific into the 21st century. UP suffered from highly publicized difficulties integrating SP, resulting in massive gridlock in the summer of 1997 and extending into 1998; it was estimated that by March 1998 delays in UP shipments had cost rail customers about $1 billion in curtailed production, reduced sales, and higher shipping costs. The *New York Times* called the takeover "the most spectacular merger fiasco of modern times."

While Anschutz's railroading venture garnered him the most publicity in the early to mid-1990s, other activities stepped into the spotlight in the late 1990s. Emerging seemingly out of nowhere to replace Southern Pacific as Anschutz's key venture was Qwest, a company whose lineage came straight out of Southern Pacific. Beginning in 1987, the railroad operated a sleepy subsidiary called SP Telecommunications Company, which installed fiber-optic cable along its tracks for the use of the railroad and for telephone companies. In 1991 Anschutz carved SP Telecom out of Southern Pacific, taking full control of it for an investment of $55 million. SP Telecom continued digging trenches along the tracks and laying fiber-optic cable, then leasing the lines to such telecommunications firms as AT&T and MCI. The company began offering its own long-distance service to business customers in the Southwest in 1993. Two years later, Anschutz acquired Qwest Communications Inc., a Dallas-based digital microwave company, and merged SP Telecom into it, setting up headquarters in Denver. He also began securing the rights to lay cable along the tracks of other railroads, eventually gaining agreements to lay cable along 40,000 miles of railway.

In the fall of 1996, perhaps not coincidentally soon after Union Pacific's takeover of Southern Pacific was consummated, Qwest announced that it planned to develop a nationwide fiber-optic network, using the most advanced technology and offering the highest capacity of any U.S. telecommunications network. With the Internet beginning its explosive late 1990s growth, telecommunications companies were clamoring for additional capacity. To fund the cost of constructing the massive network—initially estimated at $1.4 billion—Qwest in 1996 reached an agreement with Frontier Corporation, whereby Frontier, at the time the number five U.S. long-distance company, would invest $500 million in Qwest in exchange for the right to 25 percent of the capacity of the Qwest network for the following 50 years. Anschutz next pulled off a coup by hiring Joseph Nacchio, a top AT&T executive, to run Qwest as CEO (Anschutz remained chairman). Following Nacchio's hiring in January 1997, Qwest inked two additional deals with WorldCom and GTE, similar to the one with Frontier, for another $600 million. To pare down the company's $311 million in debt, Anschutz took Qwest public in June 1997 through an IPO that raised $321 million. Anschutz retained an 84 percent stake in Qwest, whose stock soared from $22 per share at offering to more than $50 by the end of 1997. At that point, Anschutz had managed to turn his initial $55 million investment in SP Telecom into $4.9 billion. He had now made billion-dollar fortunes in three separate industries: oil, railroads, and telecommunications.

Over the next few years, Qwest grew rapidly through acquisitions. In 1998 the company became the number four long-distance company in the United States through a $4.4 billion stock-swap purchase of LCI International. The following year Qwest battled for control of local telephone provider U S West Inc., one of the original Baby Bells, with another upstart telecommunications company, Global Crossing Ltd. Qwest eventually won the battle, acquiring U S West for about $43.5 billion in stock in 2000. These and other deals diluted Anschutz's stake in Qwest by mid-2000 to about 38 percent, which still translated into about $12 billion.

Meanwhile, Anschutz began his move into the sports world in 1995 when he teamed with Los Angeles developer Edward Roski, Jr., to buy the Los Angeles Kings hockey team for $114 million. Anschutz also bought three professional soccer teams, the Los Angeles Galaxy, the Colorado Rapids, and the Chicago Fire, all part of Major League Soccer, which Anschutz owned a part of as well. In 1997 Anschutz and Roski inked a deal to build a state-of-the-art sports arena in Los Angeles that would become the home ice for the Kings. The following year the partners purchased a 25 percent stake in the Los Angeles Lakers, one of the premier teams of the National Basketball Association. The Lakers, the Kings, and another NBA team, the Los Angeles Clippers, began playing in what became the $400 million, 20,000-seat Staples Center in the fall of 1999. Anschutz also owned 30 acres of land around the arena that he planned to develop into a vast entertainment complex with hotels, restaurants, theaters, and offices. Filling the Staples Center on off nights became the inspiration for Anschutz's entrance into concert promotion. Anschutz Entertainment Group eventually became the second largest promoter of concerts and other events in the United States.

While his ventures into telecommunications and sports grabbed most of the headlines in the second half of the 1990s, behind the scenes, Anschutz became increasingly active in the industry in which he made his first fortune, petroleum. In 1995 Anschutz purchased a 40 percent stake in Forest Oil Corporation, a Denver-based oil and gas exploration and production company founded in 1916, for $45 million. Anschutz attempted to build Forest Oil into a major independent oil company through mergers and acquisitions. In 1996 and 1997 Forest Oil acquired two Canadian exploration and production companies, Saxon Petroleum Inc. and ATCOR Resources Ltd. Forest Oil then purchased some of Anschutz's oil and gas properties in 1998 for about $80 million in stock. In 2000 the company agreed to acquire a Miami, Florida-based exploration and production firm called Forcenergy Inc., which Anschutz had gained control of after it went into bankruptcy.

Early 2000s: Qwest Implosion, Expanding into Entertainment and Media

Anschutz's reputation as a modern-day Midas took a serious hit in the early 2000s with the collapse of Qwest, a central event in the wave of accounting scandals that rocked corporate America in the wake of the bursting of the late 1990s tech/telecom stock bubble. Not only was Qwest accused of various accounting improprieties, the company and its competitors overbuilt their fiber-optic networks, essentially squandering billions of dollars creating unneeded capacity. Qwest was eventually forced to lower its reported profits for 2000 and 2001 by $2.5 billion because of the improper accounting practices. By August 2002 Qwest's stock had plummeted more than 90 percent, wiping out the paper profits of the company's shareholders. The largest of these was of course Anschutz, who saw the worth of his shares fall from $17 billion to $322 million; according to *Forbes,* his overall net worth plunged from the high of $18 billion in early 2000 to $4.9 billion in early 2003. Anschutz nevertheless had managed to sell about 20 percent of his Qwest holdings between 1997 and 2001—before the collapse—thereby logging profits of $1.85 billion. This led *Fortune* magazine in September 2002 to name him the nation's ''greediest executive,'' prompting his company to release a rare public statement calling the article ''inaccurate and unfair.''

Although a number of Qwest executives were the subject of a variety of criminal and civil indictments and lawsuits in connection with the financial scandal, and the company itself settled a Securities and Exchange Commission fraud suit in October 2004 by paying a $250 million fine, Anschutz was never directly implicated. As nonexecutive chairman until June 2002, when he resigned that position while staying on the board, Anschutz claimed that he was not involved in the day-to-day operations, a contention that Nacchio disputed. The closest that Anschutz came to prosecution was a case involving IPO ''spinning,'' that is, receiving IPO shares from a Wall Street firm in exchange for directing investment-banking business to the firm. New York State Attorney General Eliot Spitzer accused Anschutz, Nacchio, and several other top executives of telecommunications firms of spinning, and in May 2003 Anschutz agreed to a settlement whereby he donated $4.4 million to New York law schools and charities, without admitting or denying wrongdoing.

In the meantime, Anschutz used part of the proceeds from his sales of Qwest stock to make major moves into the entertainment industry, specifically film production and movie theaters. In the case of the former, Anschutz was apparently at least partly motivated to act based on his conservative Christian beliefs. This seemed to be a departure for the billionaire dealmaker, whose previous forays had been strictly business (though his Anschutz Foundation was well-known for funding right-wing, conservative Christian causes). Anschutz's goal in setting up Anschutz Film Group was to create family-friendly films. In a February 2004 speech, he played down the money angle, saying, ''My friends think I'm a candidate for a lobotomy, and my competitors think I'm naive or stupid or both. But you know what? I don't care. If we can make some movies that have a positive effect on people's lives and on our culture, that's enough for me.'' Crusader Entertainment was created in 2000 to produce films free of violence, sex, drugs, tobacco, and profanity. Anschutz established Walden Media the following year in partnership with veteran film producer Cary Granat, formerly of Miramax, to make G and PG movies that could tie into schools' reading lists. None of Crusader's movies made much money, however, and it was shut down in 2004. Crusader was replaced by Botany Bay Productions, which found success with *Ray* (2004), a biopic about the life of singer Ray Charles that was awarded two Oscars and grossed $125 million at the box office. Walden, meantime, scored a minor hit in 2003 with a film adaptation of the award-winning teen novel *Holes,* but then suffered a major flop the next year when a remake of *Around the World in 80 Days,* which cost $110 million to make, grossed only $75 million at the box office. The film group's biggest bet, however, came when Walden teamed with Walt Disney Company to develop C.S. Lewis's *Chronicles of Narnia,* a series of religious allegorical fantasies set in the mythical kingdom of Narnia, into a series of movies—hoping for a *Lord of the Rings* type of blockbuster payoff. The first of these was a $150 million version of *The Lion, the Witch, and the Wardrobe,* slated for release in late 2005. More than one observer noted the parallels between filmmaking and oil wildcatting—box office flops/dry holes, smash hits/gushers—which seemed to suggest that Anschutz possessed the temperament needed to succeed in Hollywood. It also did not hurt that the nascent movie mogul's focus on P and PG movies also made business sense: films with those ratings made more money than the ubiquitous R-rated fare.

The move into movie theaters seemed more typical for the Denver billionaire: building an empire by buying low. In the mid- to late 1990s the major U.S. theater chains participated in a debt-fueled building spree, eventually creating too many screens and seats in relation to patron demand and saddling themselves with unsustainable amounts of debt. Four major exhibition companies filed for bankruptcy in 2000 alone. Anschutz's approach was to buy a large portion of the distressed bank debt of a particular chain (at fire sale prices); take the company into bankruptcy where unprofitable leases could be jettisoned, underperforming locations shut down, and the debt restructured; and then turn his share of the debt into majority equity control of the company when it emerged from bankruptcy. Anschutz in this way took over, from 2000 to 2001, United Artists Theatre Company, Edwards Theatres Circuit Inc., and Regal Cinemas Inc., the latter being the largest movie theater operator in the United States. In 2002 the three companies were then combined into Centennial, Colorado-based Regal Entertainment Group, which started out with 561 theaters and 5,885 screens located in 36 states—nearly twice as large as its nearest competitor, AMC Entertainment Inc. The new Regal had debt of just $700 million, compared to the combined $3 billion of its three predecessor firms. In May 2002 Anschutz took Regal public, through an IPO that raised $342 million from the sale of 18 million shares at $19 apiece. Regal posted profits of $334 million on revenues of $2.5 billion in 2004. Future plans for Regal included making its thousands of screens the centerpiece of a digitally wired network that could display an unprecedented amount of advertising as well as stage corporate meetings and other events during the many hours during the day when few people go to the movies.

Anschutz's expansion into newspapers seemed on the surface to be another case of bargain hunting, though there was much speculation about possible hidden agendas. In early 2004 Anschutz bought the money-losing *San Francisco Examiner* for $20 million. Once the flagship of William Randolph Hearst's newspaper empire, the 145-year-old *Examiner* had long been in decline as San Francisco's second major paper, straining to survive as a free daily in the shadow of the *San Francisco Chronicle.* Anschutz next bought three struggling dailies in suburban Washington, D.C., and then relaunched them in February 2005 as the *Washington Examiner.* These two papers formed the basis for a new Denver-based company, Clarity

Media Group, which signaled its ambitions for expansion by trademarking the *Examiner* name in 67 additional cities. Clarity's strategy was to distribute its tabloid-style newspapers free of charge to the most affluent zip codes in an area, focusing on young, college-educated homeowners—the demographic most desired by advertisers. By the spring of 2005 the print runs of both papers had been doubled, but when—if ever—they might turn a profit was an open question.

At this same time, the twists and turns at Qwest continued. The company, whose largest shareholder remained Anschutz with a 16.5 percent stake, was saddled with $17.3 billion in debt, and it seemed to need either a major recapitalization of its balance sheet or a bankruptcy filing to survive. Its financial health was further imperiled by fierce competition and a steady erosion in landline customers, and it also lacked a wireless division. New CEO Richard Notebaert attempted to move the company forward by buying MCI Inc., but by mid-2005 he appeared to have failed after a lengthy battle with Verizon Communications Inc. Meanwhile, Anschutz Company's newly renamed AEG unit (the former Anschutz Entertainment Group) was moving ahead with two high-profile projects. In London, AEG was investing $1.8 billion to develop the failed Millennium Dome into The O2 (named after the British wireless firm O2 in a naming-rights deal). The O2 was slated to include a 23,000-seat indoor arena, ten restaurants, eight bars, a British music hall of fame, a theater and a music hall, and possibly a major casino. In Los Angeles, groundbreaking was scheduled for September 2005 on a $1 billion project on property around the Staples Center. This endeavor, dubbed ''Times Square West,'' was slated to include a 55-story Hilton hotel, a music museum for showcasing and hosting the Grammy Awards, theaters for movie premieres, shops, restaurants, offices, and residential units.

As always, Anschutz was keeping numerous irons in the fire. Although his golden touch had certainly been tarnished by the Qwest debacle, and a number of observers questioned his moves into media and entertainment, it still seemed unwise to bet against him. He had already cashed in on the Regal Entertainment venture to the tune of a few hundred million dollars, and there was the potential for other gushers from his media/entertainment ''wildcatting.''

Principal Subsidiaries

Anschutz Corporation; Anschutz Investment Company; The Anschutz Overseas Corp.; Pacific Energy Partners, L.P. (59%); Regal Entertainment Group (78%).

Principal Operating Units

AEG; Anschutz Film Group; Clarity Media Group.

Principal Competitors

Hicks, Muse, Tate & Furst Incorporated; Kohlberg Kravis Roberts & Co.; Thomas H. Lee Partners L.P.

Further Reading

Anders, George, ''New Role: Financier Bets Big on Risky Venture—Family Values,'' *Wall Street Journal,* April 22, 2004, p. A1.

Barrett, William P., "Working over the Railroad," *Forbes,* October 31, 1988, pp. 51–54.

Berman, Phyllis, and Roula Khalaf, "I Might Be a Seller, I Might Be a Buyer," *Forbes,* February 3, 1992, pp. 86–87.

Bing, Jonathan, "Who Is Philip Anschutz?," *Variety,* October 14, 2004, pp. S62–S65.

Blackhurst, Chris, "Mr. Dome," *Evening Standard* (London), May 27, 2005.

Bryer, Amy, "Anschutz Expands Empire: Qwest Founder Buys Calif. Newspapers," *Denver Business Journal,* February 20, 2004.

Burke, Jack, "With Alameda Corridor Deal in Hand, Southern Pacific Prepares to Sell 25 Million More Shares," *Traffic World,* December 20, 1993, pp. 26–27.

Caulk, Steve, "SP Deal Forges Biggest Railroad," *Rocky Mountain News,* August 4, 1995, p. 62A.

Couch, Mark P., "Publicity Casts Greedy Glare on Anschutz's Image," *Denver Post,* August 18, 2002, p. K1.

"A Cowboy's Dream," *Financial Executive,* March/April 1993, pp. 32–33.

Curtis, Carol E., "Take a Ride on the Rio Grande," *Forbes,* May 20, 1985, pp. 106–07.

DiOrio, Carl, "Mystery Mogul Flexes Plexes," *Variety,* September 17, 2001, pp. 5, 12.

Douthat, Ross, "The Apocalypse, Rated PG: Can a Socially Conservative Christian Republican Succeed in Hollywood?," *Atlantic Monthly,* May 2005, pp. 36+.

Dubroff, Henry, "Anschutz's Ride on Southern Pacific Has Been a Profitable One," *Denver Post,* November 13, 1994, p. 1H.

Everitt, Lisa Greim, "Anschutz Works Behind Scenes to Secure Deals," *Denver Rocky Mountain News,* July 19, 1999, p. 9B.

Fridson, Martin S., "How Phil Anschutz Made His Fortune," *Denver Rocky Mountain News,* January 16, 2000, p. 2G.

Grover, Ronald, "Now That's Entertainment: Phil Anschutz Is Making a Big Bet on Everything from Sports to Cinema," *Business Week,* April 22, 2002, pp. 62, 64.

Hudson, Kris, "Pay Attention to the Man Behind the Curtain: Philip Anschutz Is Focused on Changing the Movie Business, from the Files We Watch to How Theaters Make Their Money," *Denver Post,* December 7, 2003, p. K1.

MacAdams, Lewis, "The Invisible Man," *Los Angeles Magazine,* October 1998, pp. 70–78+.

Machan, Dan, "The Man Who Won't Let Go," *Forbes,* August 1, 1994, pp. 64–65.

Mack, Toni, "The Next Quest," *Forbes,* July 26, 1999, p. 53.

——, "Remember the Name: Anschutz," *Forbes,* June 8, 1981, pp. 36+.

——, "Stark Raving Rich," *Forbes,* February 26, 1996, p. 44.

Mahoney, Michelle, "Southern Pacific Going Public," *Denver Post,* May 14, 1993, p. 1C.

McCool, John H., "The Man Who 'Sees Around Corners,'" http://www.kuhistory.com/proto/story.asp?id=77.

McGhee, Tom, "Anschutz Looks for Gold Under the Dome: The Denver Financier Is Taking His Talents Global," *Denver Post,* May 27, 2005, p. C1.

——, "A Paper Chase for Anschutz: San Francisco Purchase a Typical Bargain Deal," *Denver Post,* May 30, 2004, p. K1.

Milstead, David, "Regal Unveils King-Sized Dividend," *Rocky Mountain News,* June 12, 2003, p. 3B.

Moore, Paula, "Anschutz Tackles Sports," *Denver Business Journal,* September 13, 1999.

Morris, Kathleen, and Steven V. Brull, "Phil Anschutz: Qwest's $7 Billion Man," *Business Week,* December 8, 1997, pp. 70, 72, 74.

O'Reilly, Brian, "Billionaire Next Door," *Fortune,* September 6, 1999, pp. 139–40+.

Ortega, Bob, "Southern Pacific's Chairman Turns Attention to Oil and Gas and New Areas," *Wall Street Journal,* August 4, 1995, p. B8.

Palmeri, Christopher, "Media Wildcatter: Anschutz Is Bringing His Contrarian Style to Newspapers and Films," *Business Week,* April 25, 2005, pp. 100–01.

Palmeri, Christopher, Ronald Grover, and Amy Borrus, "What Did Phil Know?," *Business Week,* November 4, 2004, pp. 114–16.

Pomerantz, Dorothy, "Morality Play," *Forbes,* October 16, 2000, pp. 58, 60.

Raine, George, and Jenny Strasburg, "New Owner Is Reclusive, a Conservative Christian," *San Francisco Chronicle,* February 20, 2004, p. A1.

Rebchook, John, "King of the Silver Screen: Anschutz Set to Own United Artists," *Denver Rocky Mountain News,* January 21, 2001, p. 1G.

Sandberg, Jared, "Qwest Is Building the Basics of Better Communications," *Wall Street Journal,* December 24, 1996, p. B3.

Shafer, Jack, "The Billionaire Newsboy: Making Sense of Philip Anschutz's *Examiners*," *Slate,* March 24, 2005, http://slate.msn.com/id/2115253/.

Sherer, Paul M., "Anschutz Group Scores Big by Moving Against the Grain," *Wall Street Journal,* May 24, 2001, p. C1.

——, "Anschutz May Be Making Play for United Artists," *Wall Street Journal,* June 1, 2000, pp. C1, C23.

Shin, Annys, "A Low Profile and a Large Footprint: Anschutz Makes Mark on Area with Soccer, Newspapers," *Washington Post,* November 21, 2004, p. A1.

"Shrewd Deals Helped Propel Anschutz," *Denver Post,* August 18, 2002, p. K1.

Smith, Jeff, "Is Troubled Qwest Missing Anschutz's Golden Touch?," *Rocky Mountain News,* April 27, 2002, p. 1C.

Smith, Jeff, et al., "Split Decisions: Phil Anschutz Rarely Seeks the Spotlight, but the Collapse of the Market Has Illuminated Founder's Overlapping Business Deals," *Rocky Mountain News,* February 8, 2003, p. 1C.

Smith, Jerd, "The Man with the Cash: Phil Anschutz Pours Success into Almost Any Deal," *Rocky Mountain News,* December 21, 1997, p. 5W.

Smith, Randall, and Dennis K. Berman, "Anschutz Settles IPO 'Spinning' Case with Donation Pact," *Wall Street Journal,* May 14, 2003, p. C1.

Weaver, Nancy, "Denver's Billionaires: Low-Key Anschutz Built His Empire Quietly," *Denver Post,* October 9, 1983, pp. 1A-17A.

—David E. Salamie

ArthroCare Corporation

680 Vaqueros Avenue
Sunnyvale, California 94085-3523
U.S.A.
Telephone: (408) 736-0224
Toll Free: (800) 348-8929
Fax: (408) 736-0226
Web site: http://www.arthrocare.com

Public Company
Incorporated: 1993
Employees: 643
Sales: $147.8 million (2004)
Stock Exchanges: NASDAQ
Ticker Symbol: ARTC
NAIC: 334510 Navigational, Measuring, Electromedical,
    and Control Instruments Manufacturing

Based in Sunnyvale, California, ArthroCare Corporation is a medical device company, relying mostly on its patented Coblation technology. Coblation-based products use radiofrequency energy to dissolve soft tissue without burning, unlike other radiofrequency-based products, like lasers, that are heat-driven. ArthroCare organizes its business around four medical specialties. The ArthroCare Sports Medicine unit is devoted to products used in arthroscopic joint surgery, the company's first application for Coblation. It has found a ready market among surgeons using single-use ArthroWands repairing the knees and shoulders of athletes. The division also treats chronic tendon pain through the TOPAZ procedure. The ArthroCare Spine unit uses the company's minimally invasive DISC Nucleoplasty procedure to treat back conditions such as herniated discs. In addition, vertebral compression fractures and spinal tumors can be treated with the CAVITY SpineWand. The ArthroCare ENT business unit leverages Coblation technology to perform tonsillectomies as well as procedures to address disorders such as chronic stuffy noses and problem snoring. The unit also represents the company's cosmetic surgery product line, which offers a wrinkle-reducing procedure that rivals laser techniques. Finally, the Coblation business unit looks to develop new devices for laparoscopic and general surgical procedures. In addition to Sunnyvale, the company also maintains a campus in Austin, Texas, a manufacturing plant in Costa Rica, and an international office in Stockholm, Sweden. ArthroCare is a public company listed on the NASDAQ.

Company Founding in the Early 1990s

ArthroCare was founded in 1993 by Hira V. Thapliyal and Philip E. Eggers. Born in India, Thapliyal received his higher education in the United States, earning a B.S. in electrical engineering from Washington State University, followed by an M.S. in electrical engineering from the University of Idaho and a Ph.D. in materials science and engineering from Cornell University. Before teaming up with Eggers, Thapliyal gained experience in the medical device field while working for Vascular Interventions, maker of atherectomy systems. In 1986 he cofounded Cardiovascular Imaging Systems, Inc., a company that developed catheters for the ultrasonic intraluminal imaging of human arteries. Three years later he became CEO of Micro-Bionics, Inc. Eggers came to the medical devices industry from a different direction, earning an M.S. in physics and an M.B.A. from Ohio State University. He then went to work at Battelle Columbus Laboratories, where he spent a dozen years involved in both the nuclear and medical fields.

When Thapliyal and Eggers began working together their goal was to find a way to use electrosurgical energy to unblock coronary arteries. Hence, the original name of their company was Angiocare. But an accidental discovery changed the direction their start-up company would take. Typical electrosurgical tools drove energy through tissue, which was then burned away, but Thapliyal and Eggers, working with conductive fluid, became puzzled by the results they were getting. Although tissue was clearly being removed, they could find no evidence of burned edges. After some investigation they realized that the radiofrequency energy they were using had ionized the electrolytes in the conductive fluid, and these ions in turn possessed enough energy to break down the molecules of the soft tissue, essentially dissolving the tissue without generating enough heat to burn surrounding areas. It was apparent that this phenomenon held great promise, since it offered surgeons greater precision than could be found with traditional electrosurgical instruments, lasers, or even scalpels.

Although the partners were excited by the Coblation technology they had stumbled upon (it could be used to clear a clogged artery without causing harm to surrounding tissue) they began having second thoughts about trying to enter the highly competitive cardiac product field, requiring a great deal of seed money and years to gain FDA approval. Instead they decided to look for surgical applications in which precision was a major selling point and settled on arthroscopic joint surgery. Arthroscopy's $600 million market may have been dwarfed by cardiology's $10 billion market, but it was a field that had not seen a new development in quite a few years and regulatory approval could be gained in a few months. Thus when Thapliyal and Eggers incorporated their new company in April 1993 they called it ArthroCare Corporation, originally based in Sunnyvale, California. Thapliyal served as the company's initial president and chief executive officer.

In 1995 ArthroCare had completed the development of a commercial product using Coblation technology. The company hired a number of doctors as consultants and they began spreading the word throughout the arthroscopy field that an exciting new product was on the horizon. As a result, when ArthroCare unveiled its first Coblation wands at an arthroscopy trade show in 1996 a crowd of surgeons circled the company's booth. In short order the company had the foundation of a sales and distribution network in place and began selling its product. The initial marketing approach was simple yet effective: Surgeons were given a chance to use the product for free on surgeries they already had scheduled. Once they tried the wands, they were convinced of the product's efficacy and asked their hospitals to buy the controlling devices and supply the single-use wands. Sports medicine was one of the early users of the product, since athletes undergoing arthroscopic surgery could reduce their recovery times and be back in action much quicker and with less pain.

Going Public in the Mid-1990s

In the fall of 1995 the company began the process of going public, reincorporating in Delaware, and then in December filing with the Securities and Exchange Commission (SEC). The initial public offering of stock, managed by San Francisco investment banks Robertson, Stephens & Co. LLC and Volpe, Welty & Co., was conducted in early February 1996, selling more than 2.5 million shares of common stock at $14 per share and netting nearly $32 million. After sales of just $200,000 in 1995, ArthroCare began making significant inroads into the arthroscopic market during its first full year in operation. By the end of 1996 it had a 2 percent market share, resulting in sales of $6 million. Close to 600 controllers were installed and more than 40,000 disposable wands were shipped. Already the Coblation device was being used in more than 10 percent of all arthroscopic rotator cuff procedures done on shoulders in the United States.

ArthroCare received a patent on its Coblation technology in 1997. Sales continued to mount and new markets were beginning to open up, but to achieve the kind of growth its founders envisioned it was time to bring in a more seasoned executive to take the business to the next stage in its development. In July 1997 Michael A. Baker replaced Thapliyal as president and CEO. A graduate of West Point with an M.B.A. from the University of Chicago, Baker had managed the coronary angioplasty unit at giant Medtronic, Inc., where he spent eight years and played a key role in the development and commercialization of a number of medical products. After Baker joined ArthroCare, Thapliyal stayed on as chief technology officer (CTO) and Eggers remained involved on a consulting basis. Fourteen months later Thapliyal retired as CTO, turning his attention to other projects.

Baker continued the strategy of identifying new medical applications for the Coblation technology, focusing on areas in which precision was at a premium and the elimination of collateral damage important. The company decided to revisit cardiology. About six months after Baker took over, ArthroCare forged a partnership with Boston Scientific to develop a Coblation system suitable for cardiac surgery. Several months later the two partners began to look for ways to apply the technology to ear, nose, and throat surgery. ArthroCare then formed an alliance with medical device company Inamed Corp. to become involved in cosmetic surgery. In early 2000 ArthroCare received FDA approval for its method of facial resurfacing, that is, wrinkle reducing. Also in 2000, the company introduced DISC Nucleoplasty to treat herniated back discs by inserting a Coblation needle into the center of a bulging disc and removing some of the tissue, with the goal of returning the disc to its normal size and reducing the pressure on nerves that often caused patients severe leg pain. The procedure required local anesthesia only and could be done in less than an hour.

Although ArthroCare enjoyed rapid growth during the late 1990s and into the 2000s, it also faced challenges on a myriad of fronts. It had to turn to the court system to protect the patent on its technology. In 1998 it sued Ethicon Inc., a Johnson & Johnson medical device maker involved in fields such as sports medicine. The two sides settled in July 1999 with Ethicon agreeing to license some of ArthroCare's technology. In addition to Johnson & Johnson, ArthroCare had to contend with other well-funded companies such as the United Kingdom's Smith & Nephew and Oratec Interventions. In the cosmetic surgery field the company faced a market saturated with alternative procedures, leaving little revenue potential despite the effectiveness of ArthroCare's method.

Accounting Concerns in the Late 1990s

Although the company had branched into a variety of fields, arthroscopic surgery continued to supply the bulk of sales. Revenues essentially doubled each year, improving to $12.8 million in 1997, $24.6 million in 1998, and $44.2 million in 1999, before tapering off in 2000 when the company posted sales of $64 million. But questions were being raised about ArthroCare possibly inflating its numbers, due to the company's policy of booking all licensing and royalty fees from multiyear contracts at the time of signing. As a result, ArthroCare in 1999 showed a profit for the first time. According to an October 2000

Forbes article, the company's "stock, which had been dragging along at around $6 per share, took off. After it hit its high of $62 in late February, Chief Executive Michael Baker began unloading shares, reaping $10.6 million." ArthroCare was not the only company that accounted for licensing in the way it did, prompting the SEC to crack down on the practice, implementing a new accounting rule that called for licensing fees, and royalties (if applicable), to be recognized over the life of the contract. The company announced that it would begin to spread out revenues starting with the first quarter of 2000, but what *Forbes* called the "day of reckoning" kept getting pushed back later into the year. The SEC mandated that the accounting change begin no later than the fourth quarter.

In 2001 ArthroCare received approval to use Coblation technology to remove tonsils, opening up yet another source of revenues. But the company had now reached a crossroads in its history; management had to determine the best way to take the company to the next level, whether to sell the business to a giant rival or commit the necessary funds to augment the company's infrastructure to support continued growth. In the end, the decision was to remain independent. With almost $100 million in cash at its disposal, the company began making a number of long-term investments that resulted in a short-term drag on profits, which management hoped would hit $13 million in 2002 after reaching $10 million the prior year. Instead, net income totaled just $1.1 million on sales of $85 million. Primary reasons for the shortfall was the hiring of a sales force to free the company from its dependence on U.S. and European distributors to become more involved in direct sales, and the cost of building a new manufacturing plant in Costa Rica. Previously, ArthroCare relied on suppliers who did subassembly in Mexico. In addition, the company vacated its headquarters-manufacturing facility for a new Sunnyvale campus offering twice as much space. Unfortunately, the transition was costly and took longer than expected. The balance sheet also was adversely impacted by the unexpected write-off of inventory. Once the company worked through this transitional phase, profits improved, approaching $7.5 million in 2003 on revenues of nearly $115 million.

ArthroCare continued to build research partnerships with other companies. It worked with Johnson & Johnson to develop gynecology products and teamed up with Lawrence Berkeley Laboratories and a pair of Russian institutes, the High Current Electronics Institute and the Russian States Research Center Troitsk Institute for Innovation and Fusion Research, to find more applications for Coblation. ArthroCare also became active on the acquisitions front in the early 2000s. To build on its direct sales efforts in the sports medicine field, it acquired Atlantech Medical Devices, Ltd. and its sister companies in Germany and Australia, which had distributed Arthrocare's products in the United Kingdom, Germany, and Austria. In 2004 ArthroCare completed a pair of significant acquisitions. First it bought Medical Device Alliance along with subsidiary Parallax Medical, Inc., which brought with it the back treatment method of percutaneous injections of bone cement and bone augmentation. In addition, ArthroCare gained the distribution rights to a line of medical screws used in arthroscopy, thus helping the company to round out its product line in the United States. Because of the addition of Parallax's technology, ArthroCare launched a concerted effort to market its spine surgery product lines around the world. In November 2004 ArthroCare acquired Opus Medical in a $130 million cash and stock deal, adding an anchoring system, AutoCuff, to help surgeons more easily use ArthroCare wands while performing arthroscopic rotator cuff surgery.

Sales approached $150 million in 2004, but it was very likely that ArthroCare was just beginning to realize its potential as its Coblation technology continued to find new applications.

Principal Subsidiaries

AngioCare Corporation; ArthroCare Costa Rica S.R.L.; Atlantech Medical Devices Ltd.; Medical Device Alliance Inc.; Parallax Medical, Inc.

Principal Competitors

Smith & Nephew PLC; Tyco Healthcare Group; United States Surgical Corporation.

Further Reading

Austin, Deborah, "New Medical Technology Builds ArthroCare's Revenues," *Industry Week Midmarket,* March 3, 2000.

Chandler, Michele, "Sunnyvale, Calif., Scalpel Seller Maps High-Stakes Strategy of Independence," *San Jose Mercury News,* November 12, 2003.

Keeney, Jennifer, and Andrew Rafalaf, "Ready to Run," *Fortune Small Business,* May 2002, p. 32.

MacDonald, Elizabeth, "Jam Today or Jam Tomorrow," *Forbes,* October 30, 2000, p. 64.

Moore, Brenda L., "ArthroCare's Wrinkle Treatment Draws Fans to Its Sagging Shares," *Wall Street Journal,* April 19, 2000, p. CA2.

Reeves, Amy, "ArthroCare Corp. Sunnyvale, California; Medical Tech Firm Is Focused on Staying a Step Ahead," *Investor's Business Daily,* October 9, 2003, p. A08.

—Ed Dinger

Arthur J. Gallagher & Co.

2 Pierce Place
Itasca, Illinois 60143-3141
U.S.A.
Telephone: (630) 773-3800
Fax: (630) 285-4000
Web site: http://www.ajg.com

Public Company
Incorporated:
Employees: 8,200
Sales: $1.48 billion (2004)
Stock Exchanges: New York
Ticker Symbol: AJG
NAIC: 524210 Insurance Agencies and Brokerages

Arthur J. Gallagher & Co., ranked among the largest insurance brokerages in the world, offers property and casualty, reinsurance, and surplus lines. The company also provides risk management services and manages employee benefits programs, including claims management, loss control consulting, and workers' compensation investigations. The brokerage grew steadily by way of acquisitions beginning in the mid-1980s.

Innovation Driving Growth: 1920s to Mid-1980s

Arthur J. Gallagher & Co. (AJG) was founded in 1927 by a native Chicago insurance agent ready to strike out on his own. In addition to offering commercial insurance, Gallagher helped his customers identify and reduce risks. The stock market crash of 1929 and subsequent economic depression elevated interest in the concept and Gallagher's business grew. In 1938, Gallagher helped The Hartford Group develop a system to reward customers minimizing losses. Late in the decade, Gallagher wrote a large-deductible fire policy written for a Chicago dairy. Both moves were innovative for the times.

The end of World War II brought Gallagher's three sons, John, Jim, and Bob, into the business. The company incorporated in 1950 when the revenues were $175,000. In 1957, Arthur J. Gallagher & Co. reached a high point of its history

thus far, winning Beatrice Foods Company as a client and usurping the nation's largest brokerage.

The 1960s marked Gallagher's entry into the life and benefits business, planting the seeds for the company's employee benefits and human resources consultant division, Gallagher Benefit Services. Meanwhile, Beatrice Foods proposed a novel idea: a self-insurance program on multiple lines of coverage. The insurance broker brought in a top claims adjuster, Sterling Bassett, to direct the claims management aspects of the new program. In November 1962, Gallagher Bassett Services, Inc. was formed. In March 1963 Beatrice became self-insured. Bob Gallagher took over as president and CEO that year.

In 1965, Gallagher implemented the Bishop's Plan for Self-Insurance, a Lloyd's of London program. A deadly fire in a Chicago Catholic school in 1958 led to the development of the plan, one that took hold nationally and raised Gallagher's profile. Revenues exceeded $1 million in 1968.

Gallagher's expertise in the self-insurance market led to international expansion. In 1974 the company cofounded Lloyd's broker Gallagher, Hinton & Vereker Ltd. Gallagher later purchased the remaining interest in the entity. The American-owned subsidiary then broke ground when it was independently accepted as a Lloyd's broker in 1981.

During the mid-1970s, the company established a Bermuda office to engage in offshore alternative markets; laid the groundwork for the later development of Gallagher Captive Services; and wrote its first self-funded employee benefits plan.

The innovations drove growth. During the decade, average annual revenue grew 36 percent, earnings 56 percent, and employees 27 percent, Revenues climbed from $10 million to $25 million between 1976 and 1978.

Gallagher continued to evolve in the 1980s. By 1982, *Business Insurance* magazine had ranked Gallagher as the tenth largest broker in the United States. The company introduced an online risk management information system in 1983 to allow its ever-growing list of clients to instantly access claims and loss information.

Gallagher made its initial public offering in 1984 and a few years later joined the ranks of the New York Stock Exchange.

Acquisitions Driving Force: Late 1980s to 1999

Gallagher was ready for a shopping spree. An acquisition and merger plan set in place in 1985 would drive the company's growth for the next decade and a half.

As the company grew, it made structural changes. Late in the 1980s Gallagher Bassett services were unbundled and offered individually for the first time and then made available through other brokers and agents. Business skyrocketed.

Leadership shifted in 1990. CEO Bob Gallagher was named chair and his brother John, vice-chair. John's son J. Patrick Gallagher took over as president and would succeed his uncle as CEO.

The properties and casualty business was organized under the Brokerage Services Division about this time, replicating the structure under which Gallagher Bassett and Gallagher Benefits Services had been formed. A fourth division was established in 1997. AJG Financial Services managed the company's own investment portfolio and engaged in alternative investment strategies.

By 1998, Gallagher had climbed into the number four spot in the *Business Insurance* rankings of the world's brokerages and risk management services providers.

During the mid-to-late 1990s the Brokerage Services Division concentrated on growing its Specialty Marketing and International segment. The division engaged in new ventures in the United Kingdom, Canada, Australia, and elsewhere.

Meanwhile, stiff competition in a crowded domestic market had put steady downward pressure on property and casualty premiums during the 1990s and dating back to the late 1980s. But Gallagher was still able to secure double-digit growth in all but three years from 1990 through 2000, according to *Investor's Business Daily*.

Highs and Lows: 2000–05

Gallagher's size gave it an advantage and helped it gain larger, more profitable clients and outpace the thousands of small brokerages vying for a piece of the market. Those smaller firms also had been buyout targets for Gallagher. The firm scooped up 16 more during 2000. Gallagher had grown its presence to include about 50 U.S. cities.

A downswing in the economy in 2000 served to push rates higher and widen the profit margins for the property and casualty industry. ''Higher prices help Gallagher because its broker-age commissions are tied to the amount of insurance it sells and brokerage commissions make up two-thirds of its revenue,'' wrote Steve Watkins for *Investor's Business Daily*.

Gallagher's 2000 revenue climbed 13 percent to $740.6 million. Earnings climbed 25 percent to $87.8 million, the biggest gain since 1993. Premiums rose 6 to 10 percent on most policies during the year.

The risk management segment of the business continued to bring in earnings as more companies self-insured and hired third parties to pay claims. The consulting end of Gallagher's business helped companies determine whether or not to take on the risk of self-insurance.

Since 1986, Gallagher had acquired 92 companies, primarily brokerages with sales of $5 million to $10 million. The company had been making six to 12 purchases per year, according to a 2001 *Crain's Chicago Business* article.

During 2001, Gallagher made its biggest acquisition to date, purchasing The Galtney Group Inc., a Houston-based property and casualty broker for healthcare providers. The company's largest division brought in $30.4 million in brokerage revenue during 1999.

The vast majority of purchases had been in the property/casualty area, but not all. During 2000, for example, Gallagher bought New Jersey-based John P. Woods Co., Inc., the world's ninth largest reinsurance broker, according to *Business Insurance* rankings. The deal put Gallagher in position to compete with Marsh and Aon in the treaty reinsurance sector, Dave Lenckus reported.

Gallagher Bassett Services Inc., meanwhile, offering claims and information management services, risk control, security consulting and surveillance, had been ranked by *Business Insurance* as the nation's third largest claims administrator based on claims paid for self-insured clients during 2000.

The years 2000 and 2001 saw stock prices of brokerages rise in response to the positive pricing trend. Gallagher's more than doubled over the period. But its acquisition strategy was threatened by the rising sale price of small firms. Regional bankers had entered into the bidding.

Continued favorable pricing could ease the pressure on Gallagher to drive growth through acquisitions. Claims processing and other services to the self-insured, which brought in about one-quarter of the company's income, was less affected by the insurance business cycles. Another 10 percent was generated by tax-advantaged investments, primarily alternative fuel plants and low-income housing, according to *Crain's Chicago Business*.

Gallagher's stock price sank as the company hit choppy waters. Late 2002 into early 2003 Gallagher's Financial Services segment wrote off $59 million in bad investments, primarily venture capital business, which it subsequently dropped. Then profit margins suffered when an unusually large number of new brokers came aboard. The company was criticized for the slow start-up of earnings generation by the new hires and questioned about its choice to hire large account brokers from companies such as Marsh and Aon, according to *Crain's*.

Key Dates:

1927: Arthur Gallagher founds an insurance agency in Chicago.
1950: Gallagher's three sons come on board following World War II.
1962: Gallagher Bassett Services, Inc. is formed.
1963: Bob Gallagher steps in as head of the firm.
1968: Revenues top $1 million.
1974: International expansion begins.
1976: Revenues top $10 million.
1984: The company makes its initial public offering.
1995: The grandson of the founder becomes the third leader in company history.
2002: Revenues top $1 billion.
2004: The company completes a record 19 acquisitions.

Gallagher's recruitment expenditures began paying off in 2003: revenue per employee and total brokerage commissions and fees climbed. Concurrently, risk management services, benefits consulting, and wholesale operations experienced growth.

The brokerage business increased its revenue via expansion in niche businesses. New business areas such as higher education and agribusiness risks joined more established niches of church and real estate risks. J. Patrick Gallagher told *Business Insurance* he expected niche areas to bring in more than 90 percent of business, up from 67 percent, over the next five years. Although brokerage growth in 2003 lagged behind its peer group leaders, profits were up by more than 12.5 percent versus 3.7 percent in 2002.

During 2004, Gallagher completed a record 19 acquisitions, bringing the total since 1986 up to 144.

Gallagher began 2005 mired in uncertainty on two fronts. Insurance companies, including Gallagher, were under the scrutiny of investigators looking into contingency commissions and the likelihood of conflict of interest. Gallagher stopped making the agreements in January 2005.

In addition, Gallagher found itself in a Utah court, being sued for failure to pay license fees and royalties promised in an alternative fuel licensing agreement with Headwaters Inc. Synthetic coal tax credits related to the plants built reduced Gallagher's corporate tax rate to 20 percent in 2004. In February 2005, Gallagher was ordered to pay $175 million in damages to Headwaters.

In May, the investigation by the Illinois Attorney General Lisa Madigan ended when Gallagher agreed to pay $27 million in restitution to policyholders nationwide and reform its business practices. Sally Roberts reported for *Business Insurance:* "While no lawsuit was filed against Gallagher, the Illinois investigation revealed that Gallagher accepted millions of contingent commissions from insurers in return for steering business their way, according to a statement from Ms. Madigan's office."

Marsh & McLennan Co. Inc., Aon Corp., and Willis Group Holdings Ltd., the top three brokerages in the world, had already made similar agreements. The company hoped the agreement could be used as leverage to bring the more than dozen other investigations to an end. The loss of contingent commissions would reduce Gallagher revenues and hamper the company's ability to buy smaller brokers still able to accept the highly profitable but controversial payments, according to *Crain's.*

Principal Subsidiaries

Gallagher Bassett; Gallagher Benefit Services.

Principal Competitors

Aon Corporation; Marsh & McLennan Co. Inc.; Willis Group Holding Ltd.

Further Reading

Daniels, Steve, "Gallagher Buys Its Way to Big Leagues," *Crain's Chicago Business,* February 11, 2002, p. 3.
——, "Gallagher's Deal Flow Clipped," *Crain's Chicago Business,* May 23, 2005, p. 4.
——, "Street Snubs Gallagher," *Crain's Chicago Business,* July 14, 2003, p. 4.
"Gallagher Buys Its Way to Big Leagues," *Crain's Chicago Business,* February 11, 2002, p. 3.
Lenckus, Dave, "Arthur J. Gallagher & Co.," *Business Insurance,* July 16, 2001, p. 40.
——, "Arthur J. Gallagher & Co.," *Business Insurance,* July 19, 2004, p. 44.
Murphy, H. Lee, "Rate Increase Launching Upward Trend at Gallagher," *Crain's Chicago Business,* June 4, 2001, p. 17.
Roberts, Sally, "Gallagher Settles with Illinois for $27 Million," *Business Insurance,* May 23, 2005, p.1.
Sachdev, Ameet, "Fuel Venture May Backfire for Major Insurance Broker," *Chicago Tribune,* February 6, 2005.
Watkins, Steve, "Art of the Sale Is Key to This Insurance Firm," *Investor's Business Daily,* April 25, 2001, p. A10.

—Kathleen Peippo

The Associated Press

450 West 33rd Street
New York, New York 10001
U.S.A.
Telephone: (212) 621-1500
Fax: (212) 621-5447
Web site: http://www.ap.org

Private Cooperative
Incorporated: 1848 as Associated Press of New York
Employees: 3,700
Sales: $630.1 million (2004)
NAIC: 519110 News Syndicates; 519190 All Other
Information Services

The Associated Press (AP) describes itself as the largest newsgathering organization in the world. Organized as a non-profit cooperative, AP provides news and graphics to over 1,700 member newspapers in 121 countries around the world. To collect the news and photographs it supplies to its members, AP maintains 242 worldwide news bureaus. AP also provides a broad range of other services including up-to-the-minute financial and sports news; entertainment segments; Freedom of Information issues and updates; and a historic archive of hundreds of thousands of photos and images.

Early Years: the 1800s

The Associated Press was first established in 1848, when six of the most prominent daily newspapers in New York City decided to pool their resources to cut costs. Representatives of the six papers—the *Journal of Commerce,* the *New York Sun,* the *Herald,* the *Courier* and *Enquirer,* the *Express,* and the *New York Tribune*—were able to put aside their competitive differences and the Associated Press of New York was created. David Hale, publisher of the *Journal of Commerce,* was its first president. In the beginning the purpose of the organization was strictly financial; by sharing all the news that arrived by telegraph wire and dividing the expenses evenly, each member was spared the dangers of losing wire-borne information to a higher bidder.

By 1850 the group had its first paying customers, the *Philadelphia Public Ledger* and the *Baltimore Sun,* which were given access to AP dispatches for a fee, without becoming actual members of the collective. A seventh full member (another New York paper) was admitted in 1851. Over the next several years, the number of client newspapers outside of New York grew and AP was able to recover about half of its expenses. AP kept its transmission costs in check by sending out news to each geographical area only one time. The newspapers in each area were left to distribute the news among themselves. This led to the formation of several regional associations modeled on the original AP. The Western Associated Press (WAP) was created by a group of Midwestern daily newspapers in 1862. Other groups sprang up over the next few years: the Northwestern Associated Press, the New England Associated Press, the Philadelphia Associated Press, and the New York State Associated Press.

As the regional associations, especially the WAP, gained strength, friction developed between them and their New York parent. The Western papers felt they were being overcharged for European news, which by the 1860s was flowing steadily to the United States by underwater telegraph cable. Concessions were made, and peace reigned for several years. Several competitors to AP arose during the 1870s, but none were able to break the virtual monopoly AP held on the transmission of domestic and international news by wire. The first serious rival emerged in 1882 when the United Press (UP), led by William M. Laffan of the *New York Sun,* was formed.

In 1891 Victor Lawson of the *Chicago Daily News* produced evidence that top executives of AP and UP had engaged in a secret agreement that gave UP free access to AP News. Outraged by this revelation, AP's Western members broke from the association and established the Associated Press of Illinois under the leadership of general manager Melville Stone in 1892. The New York AP quickly folded and its original members defected to UP. Stone then pulled off a major coup for the new AP by obtaining exclusive arrangements with three major European news agencies: Reuters in England, Havas in France, and Wolff in Germany. These contracts put UP in an untenable position, and by 1897 UP had thrown in the towel. All of the New York dailies except the *Sun* and William Randolph Hearst's *Journal* were given memberships in the new AP.

Dissolution and Rebirth: 1900 to Early 1920s

Controversy erupted near the close of the century and again Laffan of the *Sun* was involved. Laffan had set up his own agency, the Laffan News Bureau, following the collapse of UP. When AP discovered one of its client papers, the *Chicago Inter Ocean,* had used Laffan copy it sought to punish the *Inter Ocean* by cutting off its AP service. The *Inter Ocean* sued to block AP from severing its service. The Illinois Supreme Court ruled in 1900 that AP's bylaws were broad enough to make the organization akin to a public utility, which meant AP must provide service to anyone who wanted it. Rather than comply with the Illinois Court's conclusion, the Associated Press of Illinois was dissolved and the organization set up shop once again in New York. The new AP was organized under New York State law as a nonprofit membership association, with Stone continuing in his role as general manager.

By reorganizing, rather than by complying with the Illinois Supreme Court's decision, AP was able to maintain control over who was allowed to become a member. The new AP of 1900 was a cooperative, whose members shared news as well as the costs of maintaining staff to control the flow of news among members. By 1914 AP had about 100 member newspapers. Until 1915, AP members were prohibited from buying news from other services. There were, by this time, two viable competitors from whom AP members could get additional news: the United Press Association, formed in 1907, and the International News Service, founded by Hearst in 1909. Laffan's agency, after thriving for a few years, was out of the picture by 1916.

In 1910 a young Indiana journalist named Kent Cooper approached Stone with the idea of using telephone rather than telegraph to feed news to out-of-the-way newspapers. Although this method was only put to use for a few years—due mainly to the emergence of the teletype machine in 1913—Stone was impressed and hired Cooper as AP's traffic chief. Cooper worked his way up to assistant general manager by 1920. A year later, Stone retired, and was succeeded by Frederick Roy Martin. Cooper replaced Martin as general manager in 1925 and remained with AP for a total of 41 years.

Growth Under Kent Cooper: 1925–45

Under Cooper AP grew into a gigantic international news machine. From the beginning, Cooper saw countless ways to improve the organization's methods of collecting and distributing information. One of his most important moves was to free AP from its obligations to import European news by way of news agencies there—ironically, these were the same arrangements that had given AP its decisive edge over UP years earlier. Cooper believed news from European agencies was often slanted in favor of their home governments and figured the only way for AP to receive accurate accounts of events abroad was to use its own reporters. AP opened bureaus in Great Britain, France, and Germany in 1929 but it took until 1934 to break free of the European agencies completely.

One of Cooper's most important domestic improvements was the development of state bureaus as AP's primary operating units. Cooper also widened coverage to better reflect the public's changing interests, adding an afternoon sports service, financial information, and features. AP's new acceptance of human interest stories, which it had historically disdained, led to the organization's first Pulitzer Prize awarded to Kirke L. Simpson in 1922 for a series on the Unknown Soldier buried in Washington, D.C.'s Arlington Cemetery. In 1927 AP started a news photo service and the improved AP Wirephoto system gained approval eight years later.

In 1931 member editors formed the Associated Press Managing Editors Association to review the organization's work. By 1940 there were more than 1,400 member papers in AP, the year the organization began selling its news reports to radio stations. Six years later radio stations were allowed to become associate AP members, without voting rights. Meanwhile, another legal skirmish forced AP to change its bylaws concerning membership. Since 1900 AP had generally been regarded as a private association with the right to refuse membership to any outfit it did not want to admit. When the *Chicago Sun*—a paper launched by Marshall Field in 1941 to compete with the *Tribune*—sought entry into the AP collective, it was denied membership by the publishers of AP's member newspapers. At the *Sun*'s urging, the matter was investigated by the Justice Department, which found AP's exclusionary rules to be in violation of federal antitrust regulations. The Associated Press changed its rules at its next meeting and the *Sun* was granted membership. As a result, any publisher who wanted access to AP news reports could become an AP member.

Expansion and World War II: Late 1940s to 1970

With the onset of World War II came further breakthroughs in international news coverage, including the additions of transatlantic cable and radio-teletype circuits, leased land circuits in Europe, and an overseas radiophoto network. In 1946 AP launched its World Service and two years later, in 1948, Cooper retired. He was succeeded as general manager by Frank J. Starzel, who had joined AP in 1929. The organization continued to grow steadily through the 1950s under Starzel. Broadcast media began playing an increasing role in news coverage in the United States and in 1954 the Associated Press Radio-Television Association was formed. By 1960 this subgroup represented over 2,000 domestic stations, while AP's newspaper count had risen to nearly 1,800 members. In addition, about 3,500 news outlets outside of the United States were receiving AP reports.

Starzel retired in 1962 and the general manager position was assumed by Wes Gallagher, who had led AP's World War II coverage as a reporter. By 1962 the organization had total

Key Dates:

1848: Associated Press of New York (AP) is formed to share the news gathering costs of six newspapers.
1892: AP of Illinois is founded by Melville Stone.
1900: AP reorganizes with its headquarters reestablished in New York.
1922: AP receives its first Pulitzer Prize.
1927: News Photo service begins.
1929: AP opens bureaus in France, England, and Germany.
1945: Open membership in AP is offered for all who wish to join.
1954: Associated Press Radio-Television Association is formed.
1967: Partnership with Dow Jones offers business news service.
1982: AP begins transmitting news by satellite.
1994: APTV, an international video newsgathering service, is launched.
1996: The WIRE Internet news service begins operation.
1998: AP buys Worldwide Television News and combines it with APTV.
2000: A new Internet division, AP Digital, is launched.
2004: AP moves its headquarters from Rockefeller Center to West 33rd Street.
2005: AP unveils a Freedom of Information Act web site.

revenues of $44 million. Although the number of domestic newspapers subscribing to AP reports had begun to decline, broadcast members were joining at a brisk pace. Advancing technology made it easier to collect and spread news faster than ever before; the use of computers was expanded to include typesetting. Wire systems were overhauled and modernized, and a direct Teletype line connecting Moscow, London, and New York was installed. AP also established a book division during 1963.

AP teamed with Dow Jones & Company, Inc. in 1967 to launch a new, ambitious business reporting service. AP-Dow Jones Economic Report was an in-depth business newswire service transmitted to governments, corporations, trading firms, and other interested entities in nine European, Asian, and African countries. The following year, the same team launched AP-Dow Jones Financial Wire, a teleprinter news service aimed primarily at stockbrokers in all of Europe's financial centers. By 1970 these services were being offered in 17 countries. Broadcast stations continued to join AP in droves, with a total net increase of 1,224 member stations by the end of the 1960s.

Improved Newsgathering Technology: 1970s to Early 1990s

Technological progress continued to improve AP services during the 1970s. One of its breakthroughs during this period was the Laserphoto news picture system, developed jointly with researchers at the Massachusetts Institute of Technology (MIT). The Laserphoto system allowed AP to transmit photographs of a much higher quality than previously possible to both print and broadcast members. Another new general manager, Keith Ful-

ler, was named upon Gallagher's retirement in 1976. The following year three new seats, bringing the total to 21, were added to the AP board of directors to give AP broadcast members board representation. In 1977 the same MIT team who had developed Laserphoto introduced the Electronic Darkroom, a system capable of transmitting, receiving, and storing pictures in digital form.

By the early 1980s newspapers were generating about half of AP's revenues, as new media, particularly cable television, emerged to dilute print's role in delivering news to Americans. In 1982 the organization amended its bylaws to allow the use of its news reports by member newspapers on cable systems. AP also began developing ways of transmitting news reports via satellite. By 1984 AP's global network included over 300 news and photo bureaus throughout the world, delivering reports to 1,300 daily newspapers and 5,700 broadcast stations in the United States alone. In addition, there were 8,500 subscribers in foreign countries. Fuller retired as both president and general manager that year, and was replaced by Louis D. Boccardi, a 17-year veteran of AP.

Under Boccardi AP continued to enhance its services through the rest of the 1980s. A new graphics department was added in 1985, and a year later, a transition began to make all photos offered to member newspapers available in color. By this time AP's network of satellite receiving dishes had grown to 3,000. Further improvements were made on transmission speed, business coverage, and graphics over the next few years. In 1989 the organization developed a fully designed sports page that could be delivered over its GraphicsNet system. Other new services included state weather maps and a biweekly package of stories and columns aimed at senior citizens.

AP collected revenue of $329 million in 1991. As the 1990s progressed, the organization focused on ways to make more money from nontraditional sources, such as the sale of photo technology and through its AP-Dow Jones financial services outside the United States. By early in the decade, all of AP's photo members had the Leaf Picture Desk (a digital photo compression and transmission system) and PhotoStream (its high-speed digital photo service) in place. Domestic newspapers began to take on a more colorful look and the combination of the Leaf and PhotoStream systems was a big part of this trend.

As the 1990s continued, AP focused on adding video news coverage to its arsenal. In 1994 the organization launched APTV, an international video newsgathering service based in London. Other developments included a 24-hour broadcasting operation, All News Radio, and the commercial sales of AP's television newsroom software, called NewsCenter. In order to remain a leader in the international newsgathering community, AP expressed its intention to devote vast resources to research and development for the rest of the century, in recognition of how technology had become an essential element to maintain the attention of news consumers.

Further Growth and Change: 1995–99

In 1995 came the introduction of AP AdSEND, a digital advertising delivery service. For a small per-use fee, advertisers could upload copy and images into an AP database, which could then be downloaded by newspapers and other users. The system saved both time and money for advertisers, and enabled wider and easier distribution of advertising messages. A competitor, AD/SAT, sued AP for allegedly monopolizing the market, but the suit was dismissed and AD/SAT folded soon thereafter.

The next year the company formed a new multimedia unit which created The WIRE, AP's public news web site. The WIRE, which was also featured on many member web sites, contained text, sound, and image information, and was updated continuously. Digital technology had become a key part of every aspect of AP's business, particularly photography. Advances in digital photo quality allowed AP to discard film and shoot the 1996 Super Bowl entirely by digital cameras, developed in conjunction with Eastman Kodak. The digital process also enabled reporters in far-flung locations to instantly send out images using only a laptop computer and modem. AP's immense photo archive was also being digitized, allowing anyone to download a high-resolution copy from a collection of hundreds of thousands of images for a small fee.

In 1998 AP celebrated its 150th anniversary. The company's video service was expanded during the year with the purchase of the Worldwide Television News agency from ABC. APTV was subsequently renamed APTN, or Associated Press Television News. In the last year of the decade AP reached two interesting milestones: its Havana news agency, closed by Cuban dictator Fidel Castro 30 years earlier, was allowed to reopen; and its news bureau in Bonn, Germany, was closed and employees were transferred to Berlin to serve the unified German market. With the addition of two more Pulitzer Prizes for 1999, AP's total awards climbed to an impressive 45 as the 20th century came to a close.

The 21st Century: 2000–05

AP had come a long way by the dawn of the new millennium, from using the telegraph to transmit news to the advances of the electronic and digital age. By the year 2000 AP was owned by 1,500 member newspapers and over one billion people saw, heard, or read its news reports on any given day. Yet with such advances came problems, like when a simple keystroke in August halted satellite transmissions to AP radio and television stations nationwide for several days. While the glitch caused quite a commotion, most of AP's affiliates were able to receive news updates via the Internet until the satellite connections were fixed. The incident, however, made both AP and its rivals realize how important it was to have backup systems in place.

After its satellite snafu, AP stepped up research and development to remain at the cutting edge of digital technology. The organization established an Internet unit, AP Digital, to provide news and photos to the burgeoning online market and the service was expanded to Spanish language markets in 2001. An online entertainment news service was launched in 2001 as well.

In 2002 AP updated its partnership with Dow Jones & Company by revamping its financial wire services. On the political front, AP acquired the Washington, D.C.-based Capitolwire (later sold) and initially planned to retool its Voter News Service, the election service it shared with ABC, NBC, CBS, Fox, and CNN. Instead the Voters News Service was disbanded and the National Election Pool was formed with its affiliates to conduct exit polls during elections.

The year 2003 heralded major change for AP with the retirement of Louis Boccardi after 18 years as chief executive of worldwide operations and a total of 36 years at the organization. Boccardi was succeeded by Tom Curley, who had served as a senior vice-president at Gannett Company, Inc. from 1998, and had run *USA Today* as publisher since 1991 and its president since 1986. Another watershed moment was the announcement that AP would move its headquarters from Rockefeller Center—after 65 years—to West 33rd Street near Madison Square Garden and Penn Station.

In April 2004 President George W. Bush spoke at AP's annual luncheon on the opening day of the Newspaper Association of America's convention. Three months later, AP had completed its move to Manhattan's West Side, consolidating its operations from four city locations to one. During the year AP also redesigned its web site (www.ap.org), launched the online AP Financial News service, and unveiled its first political ''blog'' to provide continual reporting from the national Democratic and Republican conventions. As the presidential election approached, AP was selected to count votes on election night, while the National Election Pool conducted exit polls.

In early 2005 AP had launched a new web site dedicated to the Freedom of Information Act, making consumers aware of their rights toward governmental disclosure, hoping to prompt more openness after the terrorist attacks of 2001. AP joined a group of journalists and newspaper organizations to form the Sunshine in Government Initiative, to fight increased secrecy in the government. By this time, AP had brought its total of Pulitzer Prizes to 48; news writing had garnered 19 prizes, while the remaining 29 were shared by AP photographers.

As the Associated Press approached its second century in operation, the organization could look back on an impressive list of accomplishments in the field of newsgathering. It had come a long way—bringing news to the masses through increasingly sophisticated technology—in an organization with over 240 bureaus worldwide, 1,700 newspaper members, 5,000 radio and television outlets, and 8,500 international broadcasters in 121 countries who received their news in five languages (Dutch, English, French, German, and Spanish).

Principal Operating Units

AP Ad Services; AP Broadcast; AP Digital; AP ENPS; AP International; AP Photo Services; APTN (Associated Press Television News).

Principal Competitors

Agence France-Presse; Bell & Howell Company; Bloomberg L.P.; Dow Jones & Company, Inc.; Gannett Company, Inc.; Knight Ridder-Tribune News Service; New York Times Company; Reuters Group PLC; United Press International, Inc.

Further Reading

Alabiso, Vincent, ''Digital Era Dawns,'' *Editor & Publisher*, March 2, 1996, p. 8P.

Alabiso, Vincent, Kelly Smith Tunney, and Chuck Zoeller, *Flash! The Associated Press Covers the World*, New York: Associated Press in association with Harry N. Abrams, 1998.

"AP in 'Healthiest Condition,' 1963—$44 Million News Year," *Editor & Publisher*, April 25, 1964, p. 20.

"AP Offers New Member Services," *Editor & Publisher*, April 29, 1989, p. 20.

"AP's Digital Darkroom Breaks New Ground," *Editor & Publisher*, June 11, 1977, p. 15.

"AP's Sweep of the Century," *Editor & Publisher*, October 9, 1999, p. 36.

"AP Upgrades," *Editor & Publisher*, April 30, 1994, p. 14.

"Associated Press Taps Boccardi As President and General Manager," *Wall Street Journal*, September 14, 1984, p. 24.

Bedway, Barbara, "U.S. Military Won't Do It: AP Counts the Civilian Toll," *Editor & Publisher*, June 23, 2003, p. 6.

Brown, Robert U., "Transition at AP," *Editor & Publisher*, April 21, 1979, p. 130.

Consoli, John, "AP's Online Wire Making Strides," *Editor & Publisher*, May 3, 1997, p. 12.

——, "Improvements at AP," *Editor & Publisher*, April 26, 1986, p. 20.

"Dow Jones, AP Plan International Service to Report Business News, Starting April 1," *Wall Street Journal*, January 23, 1967, p. 26.

Emery, Edwin, and Michael Emery, *The Press and America*, Englewood Cliffs, N.J.: Prentice-Hall, 1977.

"Gallagher: AP Geared for 'News Explosion,' " *Editor & Publisher*, March 21, 1970, p. 11.

Garneau, George, "AP Archive Set to Fly," *Editor & Publisher*, June 22, 1996, pp. 38–39.

——, "AP Leads Pack in Moving Ads," *Editor & Publisher*, May 11, 1996, pp. 22–23.

Gersh, Debra, "State of the AP," *Editor & Publisher*, May 1, 1993, p. 15.

Giobbe, Dorothy, "AP Chief Upbeat About Newspapers," *Editor & Publisher*, April 29, 1995, p. 12.

"Keith Fuller Chosen As A.P.'s President at Annual Meeting," *New York Times*, May 4, 1976, p. 14.

Kobre, Sidney, *Development of American Journalism*, Dubuque, Iowa: Wm. C. Brown Co., 1969.

Lafayette, John, "Stations Turn to Internet After AP Snafu," *Electronic Media*, September 4, 2000, p. 3.

McClellan, Steve, "Getting the Count Right," *Broadcasting & Cable*, October 28, 2002, p. 28.

Moses, Lucia, "The Business of Newspapers," *Editor & Publisher*, June 5, 1999, p. 14.

Nelson, Kristie, "AP's ENPS Breaks Language Barrier," *Electronic Media*, April 8, 2002, p. 14.

Nicolas, Alex, "Broadcast Rights and Wrongs," *Broadcasting & Cable*, March 24, 2003, p. 2.

Rathbun, Elizabeth, "Associated Press Tackles International Video," *Broadcasting & Cable*, July 18, 1994, p. 44.

Robins, Wayne, "Wire Provides Line on Net," *Editor & Publisher*, December 10, 2001, p. C8.

Rosenberg, Jim, "AP Expands Photo Archive, Rolls Out Server," *Editor & Publisher*, August 1, 1998, p. 22.

Scully, Sean, "AP Determined to Stay on Cutting Edge," *Broadcasting & Cable*, September 27, 1993, p. 44.

Shmanske, Stephen, "News As a Public Good: Cooperative Ownership, Price Commitments, and the Success of the Associated Press," *Business History Review*, Spring 1986, p. 55.

Stein, M.L., "AP Reports to Its Member Editors," *Editor & Publisher*, November 10, 1990, p. 18.

"A Strong Year for Associated Press," *Editor & Publisher*, May 9, 1992, p. 16.

"What's New? That's a $42 Million Question," *Editor & Publisher*, April 6, 1963, p. 12.

Whitney, Daisy, "AP Rolls Out Broadcast News Services," *Electronic Media*, November 18, 2002, p. 12.

——, "Expanding News Coverage Beyond TV," *TelevisionWeek*, April 18, 2005, p. 59.

Williams, Jason, "AP Introduces Streaming News," *Editor & Publisher*, February 10, 2000, p. 10.

—Robert R. Jacobson
—updates: Frank Uhle, Nelson Rhodes

Aviall, Inc.

2750 Regent Boulevard
DFW Airport, Texas 75261-9048
U.S.A.
Telephone: (972) 586-1000
Toll Free: (800) AVIALL-1
Fax: (972) 586-1361
Web site: http://www.aviall.com

Public Company
Incorporated: 1981
Employees: 939
Sales: $1.16 billion (2004)
Stock Exchanges: New York
Ticker Symbol: AVL
NAIC: 421840 Industrial Supplies Wholesalers; 421860
    Transportation Equipment and Supplies (Except Motor
    Vehicle); 514191 On-Line Information Services;
    541614 Process, Physical Distribution, and Logistics
    Consulting Services

Aviall, Inc. is the world's leading supplier of new aftermarket aerospace parts. It provides supply-chain services for the aerospace, defense, and marine industries through two operating units. Both are U.S. companies with long histories and global reach. Aviall Services, Inc., based in Dallas, is a leading distributor of aftermarket aerospace parts. It buys them from about 220 original equipment manufacturers (OEMs) for resale to more than 18,500 customers in government, commercial, and general aviation. This unit also performs repair work and handles supply chain management and other services. Inventory Locator Service LLC (ILS), based in Memphis, specializes in e-commerce services for the aviation, defense and marine industries. Its more than 15,000 users buy and sell 55 million line items through ILS's electronic marketplaces.

Origins

Aviall, Inc. was formed by the 1981 merger of Burbank, California-based Aviation Power Supply Inc. (APS) and Cooper Airmotive, formerly a division of Cooper Industries Inc. These two companies each had numerous precursors.

Cooper Airmotive's history dates back to the formation of Edward F. Booth Inc. in 1932. This was launched as an aircraft dealership at Dallas's Love Field by former Army flyer "Doc" Booth. The company became Booth-Henning Inc. in 1934 when Texaco avgas salesman Hall Henning joined the business. It was renamed Southwest Airmotive Co. in 1940 after an investment bank acquired control.

Two important industry developments occurred after the war. Southwest began supplying parts to the airlines, which had previously dealt only with manufacturers. In 1950, the company also won a novel contract to overhaul piston engines for the U.S. Air Force.

There were several other early predecessors. One was Standard Aircraft Equipment, which mechanic Louis Bollo formed in 1933 from Bendix's old operations at Roosevelt Field in Long Island. Another future component, Van Dusen Aircraft Supplies, was formed during World War II by G.B. Van Dusen, who delivered parts himself by plane. It acquired several competitors in the 1960s. Aviation Power Supply was established in 1952 by three aircraft mechanics. Focusing on the commercial market at first, it eventually expanded to include engines for business jets and helicopters.

Cooper Industries acquired Southwest Airmotive in 1973, and the next year merged it with Dallas Airmotive, which had been acquired in 1970. Standard Aircraft Equipment was added in 1975.

At the time of its creation in 1981, Aviall, Inc. was probably best known as a fixed base operator (FBO) at three Dallas airports, fueling and servicing general aviation planes. However, it was also the world's largest independent jet engine maintenance company. Overhauling engines for several southern airlines and industrial users accounted for about two-thirds of revenues.

Heavy Acquisition Activity in the 1980s

The relatively small Aviation Power Supply (APS) had to borrow heavily to finance the $150 million acquisition of Cooper Airmotive that formed Aviall in 1981. Company President Robert G. Lambert later lamented to the *Dallas Morning News* that the

Company Perspectives:

Aviall delivers—on our commitments to customers, suppliers, employees and shareholders. Aviall delivers—across worldwide markets, with unmatched product breadth and value, and through leading-edge technologies. Aviall delivers—corporate ability, strength and growth, sustained business momentum and evolutionary industry transformation and vision.

highly leveraged company had been created right before a recession that was particularly harsh to the general aviation business. "It was a rough start," he said. Compounding the challenge was the bankruptcy of Braniff, a $25 million a year customer.

Revenues rose 33 percent to $400.5 million in the fiscal year ended August 1984, with profits of $8.1 million after a loss the previous year. The company had 2,600 employees, about two-thirds of them in Dallas. There were a half-dozen turbine maintenance shops in the United States, and 50 distribution offices around the world.

Aviall had a successful initial public offering on the New York Stock Exchange in the fall of 1984. Within a year, though, Ryder System Inc. announced it was buying the company for $125 million.

Aviall then acquired the assets of Minneapolis aviation parts distributor Van Dusen Air Inc. in late 1986. Van Dusen had about 60 branch offices through the world and had a handful of shops to overhaul engines and other components. Its sales were about $190 million a year. Aviall also acquired Ellis-Horn Company in 1986.

Aviall's Love Field general aviation facility underwent a $1.5 million upgrade in 1988. In the same year, ILS headquarters moved to a new location in Memphis. ILS began serving the marine industry the same year, while introducing new DOS software for PC users. Its first Windows software followed in 1994.

Aviall greatly expanded its European operations with the £50 million purchase of Caledonian Airmotive in 1987. The Scottish firm, an offshoot of British Caledonian Airways, specialized in overhauling jet engines for airliners. It had revenues of more than $100 million a year. Aviall bought USAir's Pacific Southwest Airmotive subsidiary in 1991.

Focusing on Distribution in the 1990s

Aviall and Aviall Services became Delaware corporations in 1993 and Ryder System, Inc. spun off the companies to its shareholders in December of that year. Company President Marshall B. Taylor explained to *Air Transport World* that Ryder was unwilling to continue to invest the levels of capital needed in a demanding industry that had suffered greatly in the early 1990s recession. Many airlines declared bankruptcy, forcing Ryder into unwelcome decisions about their creditworthiness. Aviall itself, however, remained profitable until it lost $146 million in 1993 as revenues slipped 25 percent to $895 million.

In 1993, Aviall acquired Memphis-based Inventory Locator Service (ILS), which had started operations in May 1979.

Formed by John Williams, founder of The Memphis Group, ILS provided a business-to-business marketplace for its subscribers to search among millions of parts and negotiate orders. Users could connect via cheap, "dumb" terminals rather than expensive mainframes. Much business was done by phone and fax before the development of the Internet.

Aviation Sales, Aviall's used parts distribution subsidiary, was sold off in December 1994. Aviall also divested its engine repair and overhaul businesses between 1994 and 1996. Together, these had about 1,900, or two-thirds of Aviall's total.

As the airlines staggered to recovery following a global recession, a predicted trend toward more outsourcing in the industry failed to materialize to the degree expected. Both airlines and jet engine manufacturers were performing more maintenance work.

The company's Aviall Dallas Engine Services unit was hammered by penalties and losses under a fixed-rate contract. This put Aviall at risk of defaulting on its debt covenants. Aviall's small engine subsidiaries were sold off in the spring of 1995. Privately owned Dallas Airmotive bought several of these.

Greenwich Air Services Inc. (GASI) of Miami bought Aviall's Commercial Engine Services Division for around $270 million in early 1996, making GASI one of the largest independent MRO (maintenance, repair, and overhaul) companies in the world.

Robert G. Lambert, president and CEO of Aviall and its predecessors from 1973 to 1992, returned to these roles in December 1995 as Marshall B. Taylor left the company. Lambert was already chairman. Eric E. Anderson was named president and CEO in 1996, and succeeded Robert Lambert as chairman as well in December 1997. Anderson had joined Aviall in 1988 and became head of its ILS unit in 1993.

Aviall was quick to embrace the web, becoming, according to Anderson, "the first independent aviation services company to offer electronic services over the Internet." By 1998, the ILS e-commerce unit had revenues of $28 million, with income of $16 million. It had about 85 employees, most in Memphis.

The Asian financial crisis was preventing Aviall from seeing much of a return on its efforts in the Far East. The company also had to deal with significant IT problems in 1999. It was a difficult year; the company's lagging share price put the company into play.

Nolan Acquisition Partners, then Aviall's largest shareholder with 9 percent of shares, offered to buy the company for $280 million in April 1999. This led to a fruitless, several-month search for a strategic buyer, as opposed to a financial one. The company's market capitalization was reported between $200 million and $300 million at the time. Aviall's board ultimately opted to keep the company independent.

Tech Investments for 2000 and Beyond

Paul E. Fulchino replaced Eric E. Anderson as Aviall's chairman and CEO in January 2000. Fulchino had formerly been president and COO of BE Aerospace, Inc. Aviall soon began overhauling its e-business processes in 2000 in order to

Key Dates:

1932: Edward F. Booth Inc., predecessor to Cooper Airmotive, is formed at Dallas's Love Field.

1933: Standard Aircraft Equipment is formed in Long Island.

1940: Former Edwin F. Booth Inc. is renamed Southwest Airmotive Co.

1955: Southwest Airmotive is formed.

1973: Cooper Industries merges Southwest Airmotive with Dallas Airmotive.

1979: ILS is formed in Memphis.

1981: Aviation Power Supply Inc. and Cooper Airmotive merge to form Aviall, Inc.

1984: Aviall goes public on the New York Stock Exchange.

1985: Ryder System, Inc. acquires Aviall for $125 million.

1986: Aviall buys Van Dusen Air Inc.

1987: Caledonian Airmotive signals major European expansion.

1991: Aviall buys USAir's Pacific Southwest Airmotive subsidiary.

1993: Aviall is spun off to Ryder shareholders; Aviall acquires ILS.

1994: Aviall begins major divestment of engine maintenance operations.

1999: Board keeps Aviall independent after evaluating takeover offers.

2000: ILS's IT systems undergo major overhaul.

2003: Growth prompts facilities upgrade and expansion.

streamline parts buying and supply chain management for its customers. New state-of-the-art technology was installed to support this. According to *Computerworld,* this investment helped push Aviall to the top of its field.

ILS introduced web access to its database in 1999/2000. In 2001, ILS was changed from a Tennessee corporation to a Delaware limited liability company. It was seeing record usage while other dot-coms folded in the collapse of the Internet bubble. It had about 6,000 subscribers at the time and was succeeding in the face of new competition from start-ups, airlines, and OEMs.

Aviall's overall revenues were growing by leaps and bounds. In fiscal 2002, sales rose 59 percent to $803 million. The company was representing 180 manufacturers and had more than 10,000 customers in general aviation, plus 300 airlines.

Sales exceeded $1 billion in 2003. The growth prompted the expansion of Aviall's Dallas central distribution facility and headquarters over the next couple of years. The Houston customer service center was also relocated to larger accommodations. The company continued to take advantage of acquisition opportunities. It bought the hose assembly business of McAVIAN Aircraft Supply in 2004.

In December 2004, the U.S. Supreme Court ruled against Aviall Services in an environmental case. Aviall had discovered contamination at some former Cooper Industries sites, and took a proactive approach to cleaning them up before they were sold off to another party. However, the Supreme Court decided Aviall could not recoup costs from Cooper since it had not been ordered to clean up the sites by the government.

Principal Subsidiaries

Aviall Services, Inc.; Inventory Locator Service–UK, Inc. (USA).

Principal Operating Units

Aviall Services, Inc.; Inventory Locator Service LLC.

Principal Competitors

AAR Corp.; The Fairchild Corporation; First Aviation Services Inc.; The Memphis Group, Inc.

Further Reading

"Aviall Closes on Deal to Sell Engine Unit to Dallas Airmotive," *Weekly of Business Aviation,* March 20, 1995, p. 121.

"Aviall Sells Re-Distribution Business, Concentrates on Big Engine Work," *Airline Financial News,* December 12, 1994.

"Aviall Spares Venture Could Save Airlines Billions," *Airline Financial News,* December 25, 1995.

"Aviall to Buy Van Dusen Assets," *Dallas Morning News,* October 29, 1986, p. 2D.

"Aviall to Sell Remaining Engine Units, Focus on Distribution," *Weekly of Business Aviation,* February 5, 1996, p. 54.

Cantu, Tony, "Ryder Ponders Sale of Texas Aviation Unit: American Airlines Parent Named As Potential Buyer," *South Florida Business Journal,* June 18, 1993, pp. 1+.

"CEO Interview: Paul Fulchino - Aviall Inc. (AVL)," *Wall Street Transcript,* July 17, 2000.

"CEO Interview: Paul Fulchino - Aviall Inc. (AVL)," *Wall Street Transcript,* June 18, 2001.

"CEO Interview: Paul Fulchino - Aviall Inc. (AVL)," *Wall Street Transcript,* June 24, 2002.

"CEO Interview: Paul Fulchino - Aviall Inc. (AVL)," *Wall Street Transcript,* May 5, 2003.

Civins, Jeff, and John Eldridge, "Cleanup Help Not Available," *Texas Lawyer,* January 10, 2005.

Donoghue, J.A., "Aviall, Alone and Assured," *Air Transport World,* February 1, 1994, p. 97.

"Facing Default, Aviall Strikes Potential Deal with Greenwich Air; If It Goes Through, Once-Tiny GASI Could Become Biggest Independent," *Aerospace Propulsion,* February 15, 1996, p. 5.

Feuerstein, Nora, and Lynn Cornwell, "ILSmart Review: Accelerating Buying and Selling Time," *Contract Management,* April 2005, pp. 58+.

Field, Alan M., "No Respect," *Forbes,* July 1, 1985, p. 46.

Fulton, Dennis, "Low Profile Belies High-Flying Aviall; Jet Support Firm on Fast Growth Track," *Dallas Morning News,* February 3, 1985, p. 1H.

"Greenwich to Buy Aviall's Engine Service Business," *Aviation Daily,* February 6, 1996, p. 193.

Harrington, Lisa H., "Bulking Up; Independent Sites Fight for Mass As Major Vendors and Buyers Throw Their Weight Around," *Air Transport World,* November 2000, p. 16.

"Lambert Takes Over Top Jobs at Aviall Following Taylor's Departure," *Weekly of Business Aviation,* January 1, 1996, p. 2.

Leland, Richard G., "Court Decision Shows No Good Deed Goes Unpunished," *Real Estate Weekly,* February 2, 2005.

Mathews, Jim, "Girding for Aviall Proxy War, Nolan Brings Ex-GE Chief Aboard," *Aero Safety & Maintenance,* April 2, 1999, p. 1.

Maxon, Terry, "Aviall Chairman Lambert Returns As President, CEO," *Dallas Morning News,* December 21, 1995, p. 11D.

——, "Aviall Plans to Sell Jet Repair Unit; Company Cites Decline in Profits for Action," *Dallas Morning News,* February 1, 1996, p. 1D.

Melymuka, Kathleen, "Going for Broke: When the Chips Were Down, Aviall Invested $40 Million in IT: The Payoff Is a $431 Million Boost in Sales," *Computerworld,* May 26, 2003, pp. 41+.

Paulk, Michael, "Commercial Aviation Companies Take Their Battle Online," *Memphis Business Journal,* August 4, 2000, p. 6.

——, "ILS Bucks Dot Com Slowdown, Reports Record Business Levels," *Memphis Business Journal,* April 20, 2001, p. 7.

Pratt, Ben, "Aviall, at Last, Hovers Closer to a Sale: After More Than Six-Month Exploration, Aviation Co. Should Land a Buyer," *M&A Reporter,* October 18, 1999.

Reed, Arthur, "Caledonian Airmotive Expanding with Ryder," *Air Transport World,* April 1, 1989, pp. 62+.

Ridgway, Nicole, "Aviall Buyout Talk Gains Momentum As Deadlines Near," *Dow Jones News Service,* August 12, 1999.

Robertshaw, Nicky, "ILS Creates a Global Market for Aviation, Marine Parts," *Memphis Business Journal,* March 26, 1999, p. 32.

Robinson, Teri, "Get Buy-In from Sales Force to Ensure E-Biz Success," *InternetWeek,* September 27, 1999, p. 22.

Stuart, Scott, "Aviall Faces Potential Proxy Pounding: Frustrated Shareholders Bemoan Aerospace Supplier's Grounded Stock," *M&A Reporter,* February 15, 1999.

——, "Deal Engines Hum for Aviall: Would-Be Buyer May Lack Financial Lift to Raise Its Bid," *M&A Reporter,* April 19, 1999.

"Stung by Fixed-Rate Engine Contracts, Aviall to Exit Engine Arena," *Aerospace Daily,* February 2, 1996, p. 168.

"Superior Terminates Deal for Acquisition by Aviall," *Weekly of Business Aviation,* November 27, 2000, p. 245.

Tan, Kopin, "Analysts Expect Aviall to See Much Interest from Aerospace Buyers," *Dow Jones Business News,* February 24, 1999.

Tan, Kopin, and Steven M. Sears, "Aviall Said to Be Mulling at Least Two Purchase Offers," *Dow Jones News Service,* June 16, 1999.

"USAir to Sell Pacific Southwest Airmotive to Aviall," *Aviation Daily,* April 19, 1991, p. 140.

Velocci, Anthony L., Jr., "Market Focus," *Aviation Week & Space Technology,* March 8, 1999, p. 15.

Weinberger, Joshua, "Secret of My Success: Aviall Services Uses CRM to Improve Collaboration—and Revenue," *CRM Magazine,* January 1, 2005, p. 50.

Weiss, Michael, "Ryder System to Buy Dallas-Based Aviall for $125 Million," *Dallas Morning News,* August 23, 1985, p. 3D.

Zimmerman, Martin, "New Aviall Facility to Open Thursday," *Dallas Morning News,* July 28, 1988, p. 2D.

—Frederick C. Ingram

BAE Systems Ship Repair

750 West Berkley Avenue
Norfolk, Virginia 23523
U.S.A.
Telephone: (757) 494-4000
Fax: (757) 494-4184
Web site: http://www.usmarinerepair.com

Wholly Owned Subsidiary of BAE Systems
Incorporated: 1997 as SWM Holdings, Inc.
Employees: 2,200
Sales: $545.3 million (2003)
NAIC: 336611 Ship Building and Repairing; 811310
    Commercial and Industrial Machinery and Equipment
    (Except Automotive and Electronic) Repair and
    Maintenance

BAE Systems Ship Repair, formerly United States Marine Repair, Inc., is the nation's largest nonnuclear ship repair, overhaul, and conversion company. It has sites near the huge Navy bases at Norfolk, Virginia; San Diego, California; and Pearl Harbor, Hawaii, as well as smaller facilities in California and Texas. The company's prime customers are the U.S. Navy and other government entities, as well as owners of large commercial ships.

Origins

The history of BAE Systems Ship Repair's predecessor, United States Marine Repair, Inc., can be traced back to Southwest Marine, Inc., which according to the *San Diego Business Journal* was formed in 1977 when Art and Herb Engel won a contract to repair landing craft for the U.S. Navy. The brothers had grown up in the ship repair business around San Diego, which was the headquarters of the Pacific Fleet. Art Engel, who would be CEO, was just 30 years old at the time Southwest Marine was founded.

The company started out with just a half-dozen employees, according to *Lloyd's List International.* By the mid-1980s, it employed 1,500 people. Art Engel invested millions of dollars in productivity training, he told *Lloyd's List.*

U.S. shipyards emerged from the lean 1980s better able to compete with their subsidized European and Asian rivals for price-sensitive cruise ship business. In August 1990, Southwest landed a colossal $75 million contract to convert Royal Caribbean Cruise Line's *Viking Serenade* from a car ferry to a passenger liner. (Unfortunately, this project was stopped when Southwest claimed that it required an extra $38 million in work.)

Consolidation in the 1990s

The nation's shipyards would be hard pressed to find work in the military downsizing following the end of the Cold War. During the 1990s, the size of the Navy's fleet would be nearly halved to around 300 ships.

By 1990, Southwest was taking in revenues of $350 million a year and had 4,000 employees. It had recently acquired Portland, Oregon's Northwest Marine but would close it within two years after failing to see an expected boost to the commercial repair business that it was trying to build. In fact, Southwest remained 70 to 85 percent dependent upon government contracts. Southwest attributed the Northwest closure to a lack of protection against foreign subsidies.

In 1993, Southwest Marine refurbished its operations at two drydocks leased from the Port of San Francisco. The business was renamed San Francisco Drydock Inc.

In spite of renewed demand from the cruise ship industry, Southwest's business would be nearly cut in half due to the military downsizing that followed the end of the Cold War. Revenues were approximately $200 million in 1996. The contracting market led to a period of consolidation in the industry.

Acquired by Carlyle in 1997

B. Edward Ewing, a former executive at International Harvester, Lockheed Martin, and General Dynamics, was hired as president and chief operating officer in 1996 to help reverse Southwest Marine's fortunes. According to the *San Diego Business Journal,* he followed a philosophy akin to that of the similarly named (but unrelated) Southwest Airlines: putting the employees first in order to motivate them to deliver great customer service. Ewing became CEO in the fall of 1997 as

Company Perspectives:

We are the leading provider of non-nuclear ship repair services in each of our strategic markets, and we maintain operations in major Navy megaports, including Hawaii.

Key Dates:

1915: Northfolk Shipbuilding (Norshipco) is founded as F.O. Smith Shipbuilding & Drydock.
1976: Southwest Marine is formed.
1997: The Carlyle Group buys a controlling interest in Southwest Marine through SWM Holdings, Inc.
1998: Norshipco is acquired; SWM Holdings is renamed United States Marine Repair, Inc. (USMR).
2002: USMR is acquired by fellow Carlyle company United Defense Industries.
2005: BAE Systems acquires United Defense and renames the shipyards.

Engel stepped down in advance of the company's acquisition by The Carlyle Group (through the holding company SWM Holdings, Inc.). The Carlyle Group was a Washington, D.C. investment bank that had considerable defense-related holdings. It paid $25 million for controlling interest in the shipyard.

At this time, Southwest Marine had shipyards in San Pedro and San Francisco, California, and Ingelside, Texas. Southwest acquired Virginia's Norfolk Shipbuilding & Drydock Corporation (Norshipco), another large naval contractor, in 1998. This gave Southwest a base on the Atlantic, and created the country's largest nonnuclear ship repair company, with annual revenues of $400 million.

Norfolk Shipbuilding's history dated back to 1915, when it was established as F.O. Smith Shipbuilding & Drydock. It had been run by the Roper family for several decades. Norshipco employed more than 5,000 people at its peak in World War II.

Norshipco maintained a reputation as one of the country's most modern naval repair sites. It found a thriving business repairing oil tankers in the 1970s (revenues were about $50 million in 1979) and the Reagan years greatly expanded the naval business. Revenues reached $200 million in 1990, when an executive told *Lloyd's List* that Norshipco was "probably the most successful repair yard in the U.S." The company had three shipyards and two drydocks; it then employed around 3,000 workers.

While demand from the cruise ship business rebounded in the 1990s, Norshipco, like other private shipyards, was hit hard by the Navy's policy of doing more of its repair work, particularly at the Norfolk Naval Shipyard. Norshipco had scaled back to about 1,500 employees at the time of the merger. The new owner further cut the headcount to just 700 workers; a majority of those laid off, however, were recalled within a year.

Southwest's parent company, SWM Holdings, Inc., was renamed United States Marine Repair, Inc. (USMR) in November 1998 to reflect its new geographic scope. At the time, USMR had revenues of about $400 million a year.

The headquarters was relocated from San Diego to the 110-acre Norshipco site in Virginia, which underwent a $12 million renovation, with $3 million spent on repairs and improvements such as landscaping and painting (including a $1 million, 60,000-square-yard paving project).

Purchased by United Defense in 2002

USMR filed for an initial public offering in March 2002, but that deal would not go through. Instead, in the spring of 2002, another Carlyle-controlled company, United Defense Industries Inc., bought USMR from The Carlyle Group for $316 million (most of it borrowed). United Defense, which was publicly traded, gained a business complementary to its military vehicle maintenance unit, Barnes & Reinecke.

According to the *Daily Deal,* Carlyle reaped cash proceeds of $150 million on its original $25 million investment. Carlyle had spent a total of $100 million in acquisitions (including the original 1997 buy of Southwest Marine and San Francisco Drydock) in building up USMR, noted the *Washington Post.*

USMR had 2,500 employees at six shipyards (USMR had entered the Honolulu market through a September 2001 agreement with Pacific Shipyards International). It was expected to benefit from the U.S. military's operations in the Middle East and the aging of the Navy fleet.

USMR bought Corrosion Engineering Services, Inc. (CES) in April 2005. CES was based in San Diego and employed 370 people at several facilities in the mainland United States and Hawaii. It specialized in providing corrosion control on both military and commercial vessels, including submarines.

Acquisition of United Defense by BAE Systems: 2005

BAE Systems, Inc., a unit of British defense giant BAE Systems PLC, acquired USMR's parent company, United Defense Industries, in June 2005. USMR subsidiary Southwest Marine was subsequently renamed BAE Systems San Diego Ship Repair. The other shipyards in San Francisco, Hawaii, and Norfolk also were prefixed with the BAE Systems name.

Principal Subsidiaries

Corrosion Engineering Services, Inc.; BAE Systems San Diego Ship Repair; San Francisco Drydock, Inc.; Norfolk Shipbuilding & Drydock Corporation; Capital Air Services, Inc.; Marepcon Financial Corporation.

Principal Divisions

BAE Systems Hawaii Shipyards; BAE Systems Norfolk Ship Repair; BAE Systems San Francisco Ship Repair; BAE Systems San Diego Ship Repair.

Principal Competitors

General Dynamics Corporation; Norfolk Naval Shipyard (U.S. Navy); Northrop Grumman Corporation.

Further Reading

Abrahamson, Eric, "Ship Shade: A New Awareness at City Hall Spurs a Ship Repair Renaissance," *San Francisco Business Magazine,* October 1, 1992, p. 16.

Calbreath, Dean, "Southwest Marine Sheds Its Time-Tested Name," *Knight Ridder/Tribune Business News,* June 29, 2005.

Carey, David, and Lou Whiteman, "Carlyle Does $174M In-House Deal," *Daily Deal,* May 29, 2002.

Dinsmore, Christopher, "Norfolk Yard in Ship Shape; Norshipco's New Owners Unveil Face Lift; Employment Is Back Up After Layoffs," *Virginian-Pilot* (Norfolk), July 20, 1991, p. D1.

——, "Norshipco Cuts Work Force in Half: Company Blames Navy for Taking Work from the Private Sector," *Virginian-Pilot* (Norfolk), October 10, 1998, p. A1.

——, "Norshipco's Owner Moves in with New Name; U.S. Marine Repair Shifts Headquarters to Norfolk," *Virginian-Pilot* (Norfolk), November 13, 1998, p. D1.

——, "An Old Yard Stays Afloat; The Purchase of Hampton Roads' 2nd Largest Yard by an Outside Firm Marks a Dramatic Shift for the Region," *Virginian-Pilot* (Norfolk), October 4, 1998, p. D1.

Glass, Joel, "Fresh Start for Southwest Yard," *Lloyd's List International,* January 27, 1993.

——, "Northwest Marine Yard to Be Mothballed by Southwest Marine," *Lloyd's List International,* September 11, 1992, p. 1.

——, "Shipbuilding Industry Boosted by Southwest Marine Winning Ship Conversion Contract from Royal Caribbean," *Lloyd's List International,* August 9, 1990, p. 7.

Merle, Renae, "United Defense to Buy Ship-Repair Firm," *Washington Post,* May 29, 2002, p. E1.

Mott, David, "Two-Year 'Viking Serenade' Row Ends," *Lloyd's List International,* July 9, 1993.

O'Brien, Dennis, "Newport News, Va., Shipyard Closes Part of Facility, Spruces Up the Rest," *Daily Press* (Newport News), March 7, 1999.

Pelline, Jeff, "S.F. Drydock's Bind Mirrors Shipyard Industry's Woes," *San Francisco Chronicle,* November 6, 1993, p. D1.

Peterson, Gordon I., "Spotlight on Industry: United States Marine Repair," *Sea Power,* August 1, 2001, p. 64.

Siedsma, Andrea, "Carlyle Buys Southwest Marine," *San Diego Business Journal,* October 20, 1997, p. 1.

——, "The Master of the Turnaround," *San Diego Business Journal,* April 6, 1998, p. 8.

——, "Shipyard Acquires East Coast Counterpart," *San Diego Business Journal,* August 3, 1998, p. 1.

——, "Southwest Marine Parent Firm Gains New Name," *San Diego Business Journal,* November 23, 1998, p. 3.

——, "U.S. Marine Buys Second Local Shipyard," *San Diego Business Journal,* December 21, 1998, p. 1.

"Special Report on Virginia Ports—Business Booming at Norfolk Shipbuilding and Drydock Corp.," *Lloyd's List International,* June 19, 1990.

Taylor, Marisa, "Shipyard Defends Hiring in Immigrants Case," *San Diego Union-Tribune,* September 25, 2003.

Thorpe, Kris, "Norshipco Extends Norfolk Facilities," *Lloyd's List International,* August 21, 1996.

—Frederick C. Ingram

Ballard Power Systems Inc.

4343 North Fraser
Burnaby, British Columbia V5J 5J9
Canada
Telephone: (604) 545-0900
Fax: (604) 412-4700
Web site: http://www.ballard.com

Public Company
Incorporated: 1979 as Ballard Research Inc.
Employees: 1,099
Sales: $81.37 million (2004)
Stock Exchanges: NASDAQ
Ticker Symbol: BLDP
NAIC: 335999 All Other Miscellaneous Electrical
   Equipment and Component Manufacturing

Ballard Power Systems Inc. is the world leader in developing and manufacturing fuel cells based on proton-exchange-membrane technology. Ballard Power's product line includes vehicular fuel-cell power trains, fuel-cell engines, fuel-cell power generators, power-conversion systems, electric drive trains, fuel-cell stacks, and carbon materials. The company's power products provide environmentally clean energy, combining hydrogen fuel and oxygen to produce electricity, releasing steam as the only waste byproduct. DaimlerChrysler AG and Ford Motor Co. own 18 percent and 20 percent of Ballard Power, respectively.

Origins

Ballard Power's role as a technological pioneer began in 1979, when Geoffrey Ballard, a dual U.S.-Canadian citizen, formed Ballard Research Inc. Ballard, whose father had worked on the Manhattan Project, which produced the atomic bomb during World War II, started the company as a research and development firm to conduct work on high-energy lithium batteries. Before starting his company, the Harvard-educated Ballard spent a decade conducting military and energy research for the U.S. government, including a brief term as research

director of the Office of Energy Conservation—a fitting post for the founder of Ballard Power. Within several years of its founding, the small start-up's research on rechargeable lithium batteries turned to broader exploratory inquiries into environmentally clean systems with commercial potential. With funding from the Canadian government, the company began focusing on fuel cells during the early 1980s, endeavoring to make technology nearly 150 years old practicable in the commercial sector.

Developed by a Welsh physicist and patent attorney named Sir William Grove in 1839, fuel cells are electrochemical devices that produce electricity without combustion, extracting exponentially more electricity from a fuel- rather than combustion-based technology. Internal combustion engines operate by converting fuel into heat, heat into mechanical energy, and mechanical energy into electric power, with each step in the conversion process leading to decreased efficiency because of heat and friction losses. Fuel cells, in contrast, are elegantly simple and efficienct. Fuel cells use hydrogen fuel (obtained from methanol or natural gas) and oxygen from the air to produce electricity, a highly efficient, one-step conversion process that converts fuel directly into electricity and leaves only heat and water as its waste.

The fundamental design aspects of fuel cells were simple, but turning the technology into a practicable energy system for widespread use proved exceptionally difficult. The size and cost of fuel-cell energy systems rendered them virtually useless in nearly all applications. The National Aeronautics and Space Administration (NASA) used fuel cells to generate electricity aboard space missions during the 1960s, but Sir William Grove's invention found little use in any other setting. Ballard's small group of scientists sought to bring Grove's pioneering work to the masses, beginning, in 1983, with the development of proton-exchange-membrane (PEM) fuel cells. PEM fuel cells were regarded as the most suitable form of fuel cells for vehicles, promising the arrival of zero-emission, highly efficient vehicles with the capability to eliminate vehicular pollution and dramatically reduce the world's dependence on oil. It was Ballard Power's job to turn the promise of a hydrogen-based economy powered by fuel cells into reality, a task that fell to

Company Perspectives:

At Ballard Power Systems, our vision is Power to Change the World. Our mission is to develop fuel cell power as a practical alternative to internal combustion automotive engines through technology leadership.

several dozen scientists gathered on the outskirts of Vancouver, British Columbia, in a small town named Burnaby.

Relying solely on government funding, Ballard and his research team worked on perfecting the fuel cell, beginning a laborious process that would distinguish Ballard Power as the worldwide leader in advancing fuel-cell technology. By taking the lead in developing fuel-cell technology, Ballard Power had to become both innovator and promoter, responsible for reaching performance targets and convincing the rest of the world that fuel cells were commercially viable. Specific goals were set to judge the viability of fuel cells, including size and weight, power density (the ratio of power output to weight), manufacturing cost, durability, and the ability to start up in extremely cold conditions. Geoffrey Ballard and his team of 30 scientists experimented with new materials and techniques to improve the performance of PEM fuel cells according to such criteria, registering their first major success in 1987 when they recorded a dramatic fourfold increase in power density. The increase was significant, but Ballard soon began to worry about his firm's future, realizing that its own viability in the business world demanded an experienced management team to help it become more than just a laboratory. To become a profit-making, commercial enterprise, capital needed to be raised, partnerships needed to be formed, and managerial expertise was required to bring the firm's technology to market. Ballard needed help to complete Ballard Power's transition from laboratory to company, hiring Firoz Rasul in 1989.

Rasul at the Helm Beginning in 1989

Born in India, raised in Uganda, and educated in Europe and Canada, Rasul spearheaded the company's efforts to become a commercially active manufacturer of fuel cells. Rasul's goal was to wean Ballard Power from its reliance on government contracts and to develop and then dominate the global market for fuel cells. ''If you guys are looking for a Nobel Prize, you are in the wrong place,'' Rasul informed Ballard Power's research team upon his appointment as president and chief executive officer, according to an account quoted in the March 1998 issue of *Ward's Auto World*. ''If you are here looking to make a lot of money, you are in the right place,'' Rasul added.

Committed to delivering its technology to market, Ballard Power pressed forward with perfecting PEM fuel cells under Rasul's command. The company developed sub-scale and full-scale prototype systems between 1992 and 1994, a period that included two significant events, one on the technological front and the other on the corporate front. In 1993, Ballard Power demonstrated the world's first zero-emission, fuel-cell bus, the same year Rasul completed the company's initial public offering of stock. Ballard Power's conversion to public ownership

made its share price a barometer of the investing public's belief in the viability of fuel cells, with gains and losses indicating the prevailing faith in the technology. Ballard Power's stock debuted at $6 per share. By 1997, it had soared to $82 per share, reflecting optimism roused by several important events that augured well for the future of Ballard Power.

After dedicating itself to perfecting fuel cells for roughly 15 years and devoting $200 million to the cause, Ballard Power had much to celebrate in 1997. In the fall, it became the only company in the world to put a fuel-cell vehicle on the road when it delivered three fuel-cell powered buses to the Chicago Transit Authority (public transportation became the first market for the company's fuel cells). The year also brought much needed capital to the company, conferring, as well, legitimacy to its campaign of promoting the use of fuel cells in the automotive industry. By 1997, 11 of the leading car manufacturers were developing emission-free, fuel-cell drive trains, and eight of those manufacturers were working with Ballard Power, led by Daimler-Benz AG, the parent company of Mercedes-Benz. During the year, Daimler-Benz invested $325 million for a 20 percent stake in Ballard Power, becoming the company's partner in reaching the goal of mass-producing fuel-cell vehicles by 2004. Before the end of the year, Ford Motor Co. followed suit, investing $420 million for a 15 percent stake in the company. Together, the three partners were investing nearly $1 billion in the belief that fuel cells would power the cars of the future, a belief grounded in the significant advances in fuel-cell technology made by Ballard Power.

By the late 1990s, Ballard Power was the undisputed expert in fuel cells, maintaining an estimated three- to five-year lead over the technological accomplishments of all of its rivals. ''Ballard has the best road map to solve technology, packaging, and cost problems,'' a Ford Motor Co. executive said in a March 1998 interview with *Ward's Auto World*. The company's biggest challenge was lowering the cost of a fuel-cell engine, which was $35,000 in 1998, or more than 15 times that of a conventional internal combustion engine. Although the high cost of the engines in 1998 kept the emergence of a fuel-cell car on the drawing board—the hand-built fuel cells in a prototype Mercedes-Benz unveiled in Washington, D.C., in 1999 cost a staggering $350,000—Daimler-Benz AG, Ford Motor Co., and the investing public were encouraged by the advances in technology. By 1998, Ballard Power had lowered fuel-cell costs by 80 percent since 1990, achieving the reduction by advances in materials technology. The company, for instance, had reduced the use of expensive platinum by 90 percent (platinum is the catalytic material that coats the two electrodes found at the fuel cell's core). The results were promising, fueling optimism in the advent of a hydrogen-powered world, but much remained to be done. Further improvements in size and cost needed to be completed, as well as the enormous task of building either a regional or national re-fueling infrastructure, a project that would require billions of dollars of investment.

Moving into the 21st Century

As Ballard Power entered the late 1990s, it chased its objective with purpose. Geoffrey Ballard resigned from the company because of health problems in the late 1990s, leaving Rasul in sole command over the company's progress. In the fall of 1998,

Key Dates:

1979: Ballard Power is formed to conduct research on rechargeable lithium batteries.
1983: The company focuses its research and development efforts on proton-exchange-membrane fuel cells.
1989: Firoz Rasul is appointed president and chief executive officer.
1993: Ballard Power completes its initial public offering of stock.
1997: Daimler-Benz AG and Ford Motor Co. take substantial equity stakes in Ballard Power.
1999: Ballard Power completes construction of the world's first high-volume, fuel-cell manufacturing plant.
2003: Dennis Campbell is named chief executive officer.

Vancouver followed Chicago as the second city in the world to make zero-emission, pure-hydrogen buses part of its public fleet. The city purchased three buses, each priced at $600,000 and powered by stacks of fuel cells that converted hydrogen, which was stored in tanks on the roof, and oxygen drawn from the air, into water to produce electricity. In October 1999, Ballard Power completed construction of the world's first high-volume, fuel-cell manufacturing plant, a facility situated adjacent to the company's headquarters in Burnaby. The plant was officially opened the following October by Canadian Prime Minister Jean Chretien, and the manufacturing infrastructure was put in place by the end of the year, completing the final stages of preparation for manufacturing to commence in 2001.

The first years of the 21st century included promising advances toward Ballard Power's vision of the future, but the period failed to usher in the age when large fleets of hydrogen-powered cars filled the highways. Ballard Power, as it had been for more than 20 years, was a company built on expectations. The company also, as it had done for more than 20 years, continued to make progress toward its goal. In 2001, Rasul completed two acquisitions that made the company a more comprehensive player in the industry it dominated. In mid-2001, Ballard Power acquired the carbon products business unit of Wilmington, Massachusetts-based Textron Systems. The unit, which became a Ballard Power subsidiary named Ballard Material Products, developed and manufactured several carbon materials for automotive and fuel-cell applications, including a gas diffusion layer for use in PEM fuel cells (gas diffusion layers allowed the even diffusion of gases against the membrane at the heart of PEM fuel cells). In October 2001, Ballard Power completed an all-stock deal valued at $348 million to acquire the interests held by DaimlerChrysler (formerly Daimler-Benz) and Ford Motor Co. in XCELLSIS GmbH and Ecostar Electric Drive Systems, two companies formed in 1998 through the partnership of DaimlerChrysler, Ford, and Ballard Power. XCELLSIS developed and manufactured PEM fuel-cell engines and integrated fuel-cell engines and electric drive trains to form fuel-cell power trains. Ecostar developed and manufactured electric drive trains for use in electrically powered vehicles and power conversion systems for microturbines, internal combustion engines, and fuel-cell products. In 2003, Daimler-Chrysler delivered to public transportation authorities in Madrid the first zero-emission Mercedes-Benz Citaro Bus, powered with a Ballard fuel-cell engine The bus was the first of 30 buses to be delivered by 2004 to nine other European cities: Amsterdam, Barcelona, Hamburg, London, Luxembourg, Porto, Reykjavik, Stockholm, and Stuttgart.

As the company prepared for the future, one that it desperately hoped would herald the dawn of a hydrogen economy powered by fuel cells, a new leader took the helm. Rasul, whose masterstroke had been forming an alliance with Daimler-Chrysler and Ford Motor Co., handed the responsibilities of chief executive officer to Dennis Campbell in March 2003. Campbell had joined Ballard Power the previous year after serving as president and chief executive officer of Home Care Industries, a filter manufacturer. Rasul stayed on as chairman until May 2004, when he was named chairman emeritus and replaced by John Sheridan, former president and chief operating officer of Bell Canada, who was named chairman in a non-executive capacity. The challenge of making Ballard Power's vision of the future a reality fell in large part to Campbell, whose thoughts on the company's immediate future were captured in his letter to the company's shareholders written in March 2005. "I sit down to write this letter at a time when the hydrogen fuel cell future seems increasingly clouded in uncertainty," Campbell wrote. "Competing automotive technologies such as hybrid electrics and advanced diesels are making headlines while the pundits are dismissing fuel cells as too costly, too frail or too fraught with challenges. Early optimism around fuel cell commercialization has been replaced in many cases with discouragement and pessimism. While I won't deny the considerable challenges we continue to face, if I might borrow the words of Mark Twain, 'the reports of our death have been greatly exaggerated.' It's worth noting that in 1901, two years before that historic day at Kitty Hawk, Wilbur Wright told his brother, Orville, that it would take at least 50 years before man could learn to fly."

Principal Subsidiaries

Ballard Power Systems AG; Ballard Power Systems Corporation; Ballard Material Products Inc.; Ballard Generation Systems Inc.

Principal Competitors

FuelCell Energy, Inc.; Plug Power Inc.; United Technologies Corporation.

Further Reading

"Ballard Awaits Hydrogen Economy," *Ward's Auto World,* June 1, 2005, p. 21.
"Ballard Completes Acquisition of Carbon Products Division of Textron Systems," *Advanced Materials & Composites News,* June 18, 2001, p. 32.
"Ballard Power Systems Commissions Initial Manufacturing Facility," *Canadian Corporate News,* June 8, 2001.
"Ballard Powered Fuel Cell Bus Begins Field Trials in Europe," *Canadian Corporate News,* May 5, 2003.
"Ballard Signs Agreement to Sell German Subsidiary to DaimlerChrysler and Ford," *Canadian Corporate News,* June 23, 2005, p. 32.

Cook, William J., "A Mercedes with a Future," *U.S. News & World Report,* March 29, 1999, p. 62.

Ghazi, Polly, "Love Story with a Cleaned-Up End," *New Statesman,* September 25, 1998, p. 28.

Hauke, Keenan, "Fuel-Cell Maker Warrants a Look in Light of Blackout," *Indianapolis Business Journal,* August 25, 2003, p. 37A.

Lewin, Tony, "Daimler Zooms Ahead in Fuel Cells," *Automotive News,* October 27, 1997, p. 28Z.

Mertl, Steve, "Primed for Competition," *Automotive News,* March 4, 2002, p. 8i.

Nauss, Donald W., "Ballard Battling to Break Through," *Ward's Auto World,* March 1998, p. 75.

Truett, Richard, "Ballard Chief Says Wall Street's Wrong About Fuel Cells," *Automotive News,* May 16, 2005, p. 16.

—Jeffrey L. Covell

Bank of Hawaii Corporation

130 Merchant Street
Honolulu, Hawaii 96813
U.S.A.
Telephone: (808) 537-8430
Toll Free: (888) 643-3888
Fax: (808) 537-8440
Web site: http://www.boh.com

Public Company
Incorporated: 1971 as Hawaii Bancorporation, Inc.
Employees: 2,600
Total Assets: $9.76 billion (2004)
Stock Exchanges: New York
Ticker Symbol: BOH
NAIC: 522110 Commercial Banking; 551111 Office of
    Bank Holding Companies

Bank of Hawaii Corporation is a holding company for Bank of Hawaii. Through its bank, Bank of Hawaii Corporation provides financial services in Hawaii and the Pacific Islands. Subsidiaries of the Bank of Hawaii are involved in equipment leasing, securities brokerage and investment services, and insurance and insurance agency services. Bank of Hawaii Corporation serves business, consumer, and government customers.

Origins

The Bank of Hawaii, often referred to as Bankoh, was established more than 60 years before Hawaii gained statehood. Bankoh was organized in December 1897, its mission to provide banking services to its community, a community heavily reliant on the pineapple trade for its subsistence. Like any bank, Bankoh could not grow unless the community it served grew, a dependence that was directly related to the growth of Hawaii's pineapple industry. During the first years of the 20th century, at roughly the same time the territory's political leaders first pushed for statehood, advances in the efficiency of canning methods fueled the expansion of pineapple production. Sugar production increased as well, providing the seeds for Bankoh's

growth: waves of new immigrants and new businesses, both attracted by the flourishing pineapple and sugar industries. Efforts to attract American settlers largely failed, but Hawaii's population swelled with the arrival of Japanese immigrants, followed by waves of Filipino, Korean, Puerto Rican, Spanish, and Portuguese workers. Between 1900 and 1940, the territory's population increased substantially, nearly tripling from 154,001 to 422,770. The growth in population represented the growth of Bankoh's potential customer base, providing a fertile economic climate that enabled Bankoh to establish itself as the territory's largest bank, a standing it would hold throughout the 20th century and into the 21st century.

Bankoh's development was aided greatly by Hawaii's population growth, but the structure of the territory's society was not as conducive to the bank's growth as it could have been. Power was concentrated in the hands of the owners of five major sugar companies—Hawaii's "Big Five"—resulting in a plantation society with virtually no middle class. Without the lending needs, deposits, and small businesses that a middle class would have generated, Bankoh was deprived of a considerable amount of business, holding its development in check. The bank's business prospects increased when Hawaiian society began to lose its feudal trappings and adopt a more democratic profile, a gradual evolution aided by an organized labor movement that began developing in the 1930s, a more diverse manufacturing sector, the rising influence of the Democratic Party in the 1940s and 1950s, and the rapid growth of tourism. The number of visitors to Hawaii increased exponentially during the 1950s, spawning an industry that became Hawaii's most important source of revenue and no longer left it dependent on a one-industry economy.

Post-World War II Expansion

By the time Hawaii gained statehood in 1959, there were nearly 600,000 residents on the eight major islands, outranking Alaska, Nevada, Wyoming, Vermont, and Delaware. The state's population provided an ample customer base with a sizeable middle class for Bankoh to serve. Bankoh's development by this point, after more than 60 years of existence, had been shaped by the two great movements of the era: the growth of Hawaii's

---

Company Perspectives:

Bank of Hawaii remains steadfastly focused on building value for our customers. We're committed to doing all we can to deliver exceptional service and enhance customer satisfaction. Our approach centers on developing long-term banking relationships, based on offering quality products and services that meet our customers' full range of financial needs. Our business units work closely with one another to ensure we not only meet clients' current needs but also help them plan for their future needs.

---

population and the emergence of a diversified economy supported by a middle class. In the second half of the 20th century, the bank used its standing as Hawaii's largest bank to expand its scope beyond Hawaii, ushering in an era that would see Bankoh spread its presence in the Pacific Islands, Asia, and eventually onto the U.S. mainland. One of the first major indications of the bank's more expansive geographic strategy was the formation of Bank of Hawaii International, Inc. in 1968. Through its international subsidiary, the bank began taking equity interests in foreign financial institutions, using its wealth to invest in banking activities in places such as Tonga, New Caledonia, Tahiti, and Samoa. Bankoh's journeys abroad, however, did not begin in earnest until several years after the formation of Bank of Hawaii International, when the company adopted the corporate structure to facilitate its maturation into a diversified, internationally oriented financial services institution.

A milestone in Bankoh's development from a community bank to an international financial services firm occurred in 1971, the year Hawaii Bancorporation, Inc. was formed. Hawaii Bancorporation became the first bank holding company in Hawaii, the corporate umbrella under which Bankoh and other subsidiaries such as Bank of Hawaii International would operate. Bankoh continued to represent the principal operating entity of the holding company—four decades later Bankoh held 90 percent of the holding company's assets—but the creation of a holding company enabled the bank to reach farther geographically and to broaden its services both in Hawaii and abroad.

The formation of Hawaii Bancorporation in 1971 marked the beginning of a 30-year period that would see the company spread its influence far and wide, a period punctuated by the formation of subsidiaries that operated alongside or underneath Bankoh. In 1973, Bancorp Leasing of Hawaii, Inc. was formed to provide, as its name suggested, leasing and leasing services primarily to commercial customers. After the name of the holding company was changed to Bancorp Hawaii, Inc. in 1979, the company threw itself into expanding its operations during the 1980s. In 1985, the company acquired Hawaiian Trust Company, a company founded in 1898, one year after the formation of Bankoh. Hawaiian Trust provided trust services primarily in Hawaii and Guam, operating as a subsidiary of Bankoh. In 1986, FirstFed America, Inc. (later renamed Bancorp Pacific, Inc.) was formed to acquire First Federal Savings and Loan Association, a savings and loan association founded in 1904 that operated in Guam and on the island of Saipan in the Commonwealth of the Northern Mariana Islands. The following

year, Bancorp Hawaii's management directed their expansion efforts in the opposite direction, turning to the U.S. mainland for the first time. In October, the company acquired First National Bank of Arizona, which offered commercial banking services through branch offices in Arizona. The company ended the decade by establishing an insurance company to serve the holding company and its subsidiaries. Bancorp Hawaii Insurance Service, Ltd., formed in 1989, provided bankers professional liability insurance and, after 1992, workers compensation for Bancorp Hawaii and its subsidiaries.

Bancorp Hawaii continued to expand during the 1990s, a decade that marked the 100th anniversary of Bankoh and the arrival of unsettling times at the venerable financial institution. Lawrence M. Johnson, who held senior management positions throughout Bancorp Hawaii's development from a community bank into an international financial services firm, completed his rise up the company's managerial ranks during the 1990s, taking the helm during one of the most significant decades in the bank's long history. Johnson, who joined Bankoh in 1958 as a teller, was named president of Bankoh and the holding company in 1989, adding the titles of chairman and chief executive officer five years later when Howard Stephenson retired. When Johnson took over, Bankoh held $11.3 billion in assets, more than 90 percent of the holding company's total assets.

Johnson followed the course set by Stephenson, looking for growth opportunities beyond Hawaii's shores. The need to expand overseas became increasingly important in Johnson's mind as the decade progressed. The Hawaiian economy stagnated during his tenure in command, experiencing a nearly decade-long period of anemic growth that fueled his desire to look elsewhere for building the company's business. Toward this end, the bank's centennial marked a turning point in its history that hinted at the beginning of a new era. In July 1997, Bancorp Hawaii acquired California United Bank, an Encino, California-based bank with 21 branches in Southern California. The company also offered syndicated lending services in Asia, extending credit to customers in countries such as South Korea, Malaysia, Thailand, and Indonesia. To reflect its increasingly international focus, which had been developing for decades, the holding company changed its name in 1997, adopting Pacific Century Financial Corporation as its new corporate title.

With a new name, the holding company appeared to be embarking on a new era of existence, but the adoption of the Pacific Century name marked the beginning of arguably the most troubled period in Bankoh's history. The onset of the Asian economic crisis in 1997 delivered a serious blow to the company's fortunes, leaving it exposed to the financial turmoil experienced by troubled Asian countries. The Asian crises exacerbated the problems stemming from Hawaii's lackluster economy, the source of roughly two-thirds of Pacific Century's assets and earnings. The first signs of the holding company's troubles were made public in early 1998, acknowledged by Johnson in a February 19, 1998 interview with *American Banker*. "Hawaii's stagnant economy," he said, "coupled with economic turbulence in Asia has thwarted our attempts to significantly improve our performance." Johnson shuttered 25 of the company's 100 branches, trimmed payroll by 11 percent, and consolidated the company's California and Arizona banking operations in Encino (renamed Pacific Century Bank).

As the late 1990s progressed, Johnson continued to look for salvation from overseas, pressing ahead with the international orientation of Pacific Century. In 1998, the company invested in Brisbane, Australia-based Bank of Queensland, a $1.8 billion asset bank. In mid-1999 the company more than doubled its original investment in the Bank of Queensland, increasing its ownership stake to 17 percent. "This is a continuance of Pacific Century's Pacific Rim strategy," an analyst remarked in a June 30, 1999 interview with *American Banker*. Investments in foreign financial institutions, made through Bank of Hawaii International, also increased, giving the company a 96 percent stake in Bank of Hawaii-Nouvelle Caledonie, 95 percent of the Banque de Tahiti, 100 percent of Banque d'Hawaii (Vanuatu). Ltd., and 51 percent of the National Bank of Solomon Islands.

Johnson staked his future at Pacific Century on the success of the company's numerous forays abroad. He promised to retire if the company's stock value failed to recover. As Pacific Century entered a new century, Johnson offered a self-assessment of his efforts to revive the company in an August 23, 2000 interview with *American Banker*. "After several years of not creating shareholder value, I acknowledged that this was one of my primary responsibilities. In fact," he said, "it's my entire report card with investors." Johnson announced his departure, effective as soon as a replacement was found. Before leaving he offered an explanation of the reasoning behind his decision to enter syndicating lending abroad, stressing that he had few other options. "We were faced with virtually no revenue growth from our primary market, Hawaii," he said in his interview with *American Banker*. Forced to look beyond Hawaii, the company pursued opportunities that, in Johnson's words, possessed "a degree of risk that was unacceptable." Looking back, however, Johnson believed his moves might have saved the company. "If we hadn't done that, we probably would have been acquired," he said.

Pacific Century was in need of a savior as the 21st century began, and it found one in November 2000. Michael E. O'Neil, formerly the vice-chairman of Bank of America, replaced Johnson and immediately began unraveling the sprawl that had been created during the previous three decades. When he joined Pacific Century, O'Neil announced he would accept no salary other than stock options and he invested $10 million of his own

money in Pacific stock. His divestiture program began the month after his arrival, starting with the announcement that Pacific had agreed to sell its banking operations in Arizona. The deal was completed in April 2001, followed by the sale of the company's California banking operations in September 2001. In November 2001, O'Neill announced he had entered negotiations to sell Banque de Tahiti and Bank of Hawaii-Nouvelle. As the divestiture program swept away business units abroad, O'Neill jettisoned a number of bad loans, clearing up the company's troubled loan portfolio. He recruited new executives and substantially increased the bank's efficiency and return on capital, reinvigorating Pacific Century and Bankoh and narrowing the focus for the future on markets in Hawaii, American Samoa, and the Western Pacific. As progress was being realized, O'Neill gave the company the symbolic stamp of his influence, formally bringing an end to a period that had seen the holding company stray from its course and stumble. In April 2002, the Pacific Century name was dropped, replaced by a corporate title reflective of the narrowed focus of its operations: Bank of Hawaii Corporation.

By 2003, O'Neill's turnaround efforts were nearly complete. His $10 million investment was made when Pacific Century's stock was trading for $15 per share. By the spring of 2003, Bank of Hawaii Corp.'s stock was trading in the $30 range. In mid-2004, when Bank of Hawaii Corp.'s stock was trading for more than $45 per share, O'Neill announced his three-year restructuring program was complete, having trimmed the holding company's assets from $14 billion in 2000 to $9 billion by 2003. "My work at the bank is done," he said, as quoted by the July 31, 2004 issue of *Asia Africa Intelligence Wire*. Allan R. Landon, Bank of Hawaii Corp.'s president and chief operating officer, was selected as O'Neill's replacement, inheriting a healthy company that had been comprehensively restructured by his predecessor. As Landon plotted the company's future course, he concentrated on controlling costs, increasing revenue, and reducing credit risk, employing a strategy that had been put in place by O'Neill.

Principal Subsidiaries

Bank of Hawaii; Bancorp Hawaii Capital Trust I; Bank of Hawaii International, Inc.; Bankoh Investment Services, Inc.; Bankoh Investment Partners, LLC; Pacific Century Insurance Services, Inc.; RGA Corp.; Pacific Century Advisory Services, Inc.; Bank of Hawaii Leasing, Inc.; Pacific Century Life Insurance Corporation; Triad Insurance Agency, Inc.; Bank of Hawaii Insurance Services, Inc.

Principal Competitors

American Savings Bank, FSB; Central Pacific Financial Corp.; First Hawaiian Bank.

Further Reading

"Bank of Hawaii Names New Chairman and CEO," *Asia Africa Intelligence Wire*, July 31, 2004, p. 43.
Cole, Jim, "Bank of Hawaii Keeps on Riding Cost Saving Wave," *American Banker*, April 26, 2005, p. 18.
——, "Cost Control, Consumers Bolster Bank of Hawaii," *American Banker*, October 26, 2004, p. 27.

Domis, Olaf De Senerpont, "Bank of Hawaii's Parent to Double Stake in Northern Australian Bank," *American Banker,* June 30, 1999, p. 1.

——, "Hawaii's Top Bank to Bid Aloha to 550 Workers, 25 Branches," *American Banker,* February 19, 1998, p. 1.

Julavits, Robert, "From CFO to Heir Apparent," *American Banker,* April 27, 2004, p. 1.

Mandaro, Laura, "Bank of Hawaii Chairman to Quit, True to His Word," *American Banker,* August 23, 2000, p. 2.

Reiker, Matthias, "Bank of Hawaii Turnaround CEO Steps Aside," *American Banker,* July 27, 2004, p. 1.

Salkever, Alex, "Online Extra: Bank of Hawaii," *Business Week Online,* April 9, 2003, p. 32.

Sundaramoorthy, Geeta, "Bank of Hawaii Seen Still Needing Some Fine-Tuning," *American Banker,* August 18, 2004, p. 20.

Trifonovitch, Kelli Abe, "Ready, Set, Charge!," *Hawaii Business,* February 2004, p. 52.

"Whatever Happened to . . .?," *Pacific Business News,* November 2, 2001, p. 3.

Wood, Christopher, "Executive Changes," *American Banker,* June 6, 2005, p. 2.

—Jeffrey L. Covell

BE&K, Inc.

2000 International Park Drive
Birmingham, Alabama 35243
U.S.A.
Telephone: (205) 972-6000
Fax: (205) 972-6651
Web site: http://www.bek.com

Private Company
Incorporated: 1972
Employees: 7,700
Sales: $1 billion (2004 est.)
NAIC: 233320 Commercial Building Construction

BE&K, Inc. is a major U.S. engineering and construction contractor serving the pulp and paper, cement, chemical, petrochemical, power generating, environmental, and telecommunications industries. The Birmingham, Alabama-based private company does business through a group of subsidiaries, including Allstates Technical Services, Inc., providing engineering and information technology outsourcing solutions; As-Built Services, which offers such high-tech services as 3D-CAD modeling, digitized photography, and computer analysis; BE&K Building Group, provider of construction services for commercial, healthcare, industrial, and institutional projects in the Southeast and Mid-Atlantic region; Enprima, serving power companies, municipal utilities, and other clients with consulting, design, engineering, and project management services; MEI Consultants, Inc., dedicated to the hydrocarbon sector, providing a variety of engineering services related to oil and gas production, pipelines, terminals, and storage; NorthStar Communications Group, Inc., providers of wireline and wireless telecommunications services, including engineering, network installation, construction management, maintenance, and staffing; QBEK, which tests equipment and offers other quality assurance and quality improvement services; Rintekno Group, primarily an engineering and contracting company in the Life Science and Chemical Process industries; BE&K's Saginaw Warehouse, which offers a full line of construction equipment for rent; SW&B Construction Corporation, offering general contracting services primarily to the pulp and paper industry; and Terranext, LLC, an environmental consulting and engineering service company.

Formation in Early 1970s

BE&K was incorporated in April 1972, its name drawn from the first letters of the last name of the company's three founders: C. Peter Bolvig, William F. Edmonds, and Ted C. Kennedy. Of the three, Kennedy, longtime chief executive and chairman, was the driving force behind the company's growth. The son of an ironworker, Kennedy worked for his father at Birmingham's Rust International as a water boy when he was a teenager. He studied at Duke University, where he graduated Phi Beta Kappa with a civil engineering degree, then returned home to work for Rust. He stayed for 20 years before growing frustrated with Rust's bureaucracy and elected to strike out on his own with Rust colleagues Edmonds and Bolvig. They also took on a fourth, silent, partner in Henry Goodrich, a Rust senior vice-president. Goodrich's son, T. Michael (Mike) Goodrich, also joined BE&K in 1972, serving as assistant secretary and general counsel, destined to one day succeed Kennedy as CEO and chairman.

Although BE&K has grown into a large organization, the founders' intent was to remain small, but the firm's ability to attract and retain talented employees all but forced the company to continue growing. Kennedy also took charge of the new firm, convinced from his experience at Rust that union wages and restrictive rules were making it increasingly difficult for builders to remain competitive. According to some, BE&K was founded intentionally as an open (nonunion) shop, although Kennedy, who insisted he was not actually antiunion, disagreed with that assessment, telling *Engineering News-Record* in 1999, "That was the growth part of the market." Regardless, he did not hesitate to cross a picket line to take a job, a fact that down the road would lead to controversy and make him a marked man for union organizers.

In the beginning BE&K concentrated on providing engineering and construction services to the pulp and paper industry. The first major contracts, won during its first year of operation, included a job for South Carolina Industries to expand a linerboard mill. It also landed a big job with Southern Energy as well as 19 smaller contracts, enough business to establish BE&K as number 285 on *Engineering-News Record*'s top 400 construction firms. Two years later BE&K ranked number 64. It was in 1975 that the company firmly established itself as a leader in the pulp and paper industry after it succeeded in installing a newsprint

Company Perspectives:

BE&K's three founders began business with a simple philosophy: support our clients, our employees, and our community. Over 30 successful years, providing engineering, construction, and maintenance services for clients in a variety of markets, attests to these core values.

machine for Southland Paper in Lufkin, Texas, 33 days ahead of schedule. Other major pulp and paper projects in the 1970s included serving as construction manager of a corrugating medium mill built for Inland Container Corporation and the expansion of a bleachboard mill for Continental Forest Industries, both in 1975; the design and construction of an expansion for Weyerhaeuser's paper mill in Pine Bluff, Arkansas; the building of the first recycled newsprint mill in the South, built for Southeast Paper Manufacturing Company; and the introduction of the tube conveyor, first installed in the Jackson, Alabama bleached paper mill owned by SCM Allied Paper.

Diversification Picking up in 1980s

Although BE&K was now very much identified with the pulp and paper industry, it made inroads in the energy sector as well. In 1977 it won the design and construction contract for a Louisiana oil and gas processing facility for Sonat Corporation. A year later BE&K formed an Industrial Power Division to handle this new line of work. It was not until the 1980s, however, that BE&K began to actively pursue diversification, evolving from a pulp and paper business into an industrial design and construction firm. In 1981 the company formed Poyry-BEK, a joint venture with the Finland-based company of Jaakko Poyry Group to serve as a high-technology consulting firm to the pulp and paper industry. The following year BE&K acquired Brazos Construction Company, forming a major part of subsidiary BE&K Construction Company. BE&K also won a major communications job in 1982, selected by Media General to serve as the construction manager for one of the country's largest cable television installations. In 1983 the company launched BE&K Communications in Atlanta to pursue cable television, fiber optics, and other communications projects. That same year the company started an industrial maintenance division and completed another significant acquisition, picking up Danco Construction Company to form BEK-Danco in Lynn Haven, Florida, which quickly became a leader in plant shutdown work. BE&K also solidified its relationship with Jaakko Poyry, which bought a 15 percent stake in the company as part of a technology exchange agreement. Two years later, in 1985, BE&K teamed up with another Finnish company, Polar Construction Company of Helsinki, to form a real estate development joint venture, Polar-BEK. In that same year, Poyry-BEK formed PBI Maintenance, a joint venture with Sweden's Idhammar Konsult involved in industrial maintenance consulting. Also of note, the first of the BE&K founders, Peter Bolvig, retired.

In the second half of the 1980s BE&K continued to enjoy strong growth. Sales reached $650 million in 1986, $870 million in 1987, and then leaped to $1.3 billion in 1988. Highlights during this period included the construction of the $423 million Project Gamecock mill in Cattawba, South Carolina, for Bowater Carolina Company in 1986, BE&K's largest project to that point;

a 1987 steel mill modernization project in Pittsburg, California, for USS-POSCO Industries; a major expansion of a Dublin, Georgia mill for Southeast Paper Manufacturing Company in 1987; and in 1988 the company established its first Canadian operation. In 1989 BE&K completed a major acquisition, picking up the 1,300-employee engineering firm of Allstates Design & Development Co., heavily involved in the chemical industry.

The year 1989 brought the retirement of William F. Edmonds, who had been the firm's chairman, a post turned over to Kennedy, who remained CEO while Mike Goodrich was promoted to president. BE&K also garnered unwanted publicity in 1989, the result of its contentious relationship with labor unions. *Engineering News-Record* offered a picture of BE&K's reputation in a 1990 article: ''BE&K arguably is the country's most aggressive open shop contractor. Some building trade unions claim that the firm markets itself to owners as a 'union buster.' '' In 1987 during the Pittsburg steel upgrade project, for example, BE&K brought in out-of-state non-union workers, leading to a confrontation with unions, which held up the project and caused cost overruns by filing a host of environmental, permit, and health and safety petitions. BE&K sued the labor organizations, claiming unfair labor tactics, resulting in a series of back-and-forth filings in a legal squabble that would not be resolved for another decade. Also in 1987, BE&K became involved in a strike against an International Paper Co. mill in Jay, Maine. BE&K maintained the paper machines that the supervisors manned while replacement workers were hired. The strike ended in failure after 16 months, leaving many union members without jobs and harboring animosity toward BE&K. In addition, Kennedy had become president of the Associated Builders & Contractors, representing 23,000 open-shop companies. According to the *Wall Street Journal,* ''Kennedy became a lightning rod. His speeches drew pickets. Protesters threw beer on him and once clubbed him with a picket sign.''

Kennedy's relationship with labor became even more strained when Boise Cascade named BE&K the general contractor for a $535 million paper mill expansion at International Falls, Minnesota, close to the Canadian border. Not only was it the largest project in the history of BE&K, it was the largest industrial investment in the history of Minnesota, a strong union state, and with BE&K involved it was guaranteed to receive a great deal of attention. The project was hit with wildcat strikes by union workers of some subcontractors upset that BE&K was bringing in out-of-state non-union workers, who lived in what was called the ''man camp.'' One night the camp was set on fire in a riot between union and non-union workers, causing an estimated $1.3 million in damages. Smaller acts of violence continued in the weeks that followed. In the end, 58 men pled guilty to charges connected to the riot, although few served jail time. BE&K was also pitted against elected officials, whom the company claimed were currying favor with union workers by making life difficult for the firm and by strictly imposing a number of work rules.

It was around this time that Kennedy, according to the *Wall Street Journal,* began to have private misgivings: ''He feared the warfare was weakening the industry, that cost cuts had gone too far. 'We'd reached the point where we weren't paying a fair wage to our employees, or providing them with adequate benefits.' he said. He soon ''turned his artillery on his own side. In a 1992 convention speech, he attacked fellow contractors. . . . "We could all raise craft wages a reasonable amount, provide benefits we're not ashamed of, create a career for young people instead of a revolving door,' he told a stunned audience. He also extended an olive branch to unions, offering $500,000 for a joint training venture. He got no takers.'' According to the *Wall Street Journal* he embraced ''other policies that belied his hard-line image. When workers told him child-care problems forced them to quit, he started work-site facilities. The company also began offering some workers a guaranteed annual wage to ease on-again, off-again construction schedules.'' As a result, BE&K would gain recognition as one of the best places to work. In the words of the *Journal,* ''Kennedy brushes aside questions about his transformation. He says simply that over the years, he's learned that you have to have faith that investing in people yields better work.''

Further Diversification in 1990s

BE&K continued to grow and diversify its business in the 1990s. The company launched a new Construction Management Department in 1992, as well as Fibertech, a full-service recycle fiber facility, and As Built Data Inc., which provided photogrammatic data on process plants. BE&K also established SBE Environmental Co., serving pulp and paper, semiconductor, consumer products, and general manufacturing companies in need of high-tech solutions for the treatment of pollutants. Another 1992 startup was QBEK, a quality-control inspection service. A year later QBEK expanded with the incorporation of SBE into its operations. BE&K also looked to international markets during the first half of the 1990s. In 1993 BE&K forged an alliance with a major French engineering firm, Technip S.A., and in 1994 the company became involved in the Polish market through its long-term relationship with International Paper, which bought a pulp and paper mill in Poland and needed an experienced hand in optimizing and then maintaining the facility. Out of this project emerged BE&K Europe in 1995, established to provide engineering, repair, and construction services to International Paper and other customers in Poland and elsewhere in Europe. To serve International Paper's expanding business in Russia, BE&K Europe and BE&K International formed BE&K East in 2000, dedicated to providing construction and maintenance services to customers in that market.

Mike Goodrich was named CEO in 1995, replacing Kennedy, who stayed on as chairman. The change did nothing to slow the company's growth, however. BE&K acquired SW&B

Construction Corporation, a Maine-based company that focused on mid-size projects and paper machine rebuilds. It was subsequently merged with Danco, creating the paper industry's premier small project firm. BE&K added to its environmental business with the acquisition of Terranext in 1997, the same year that BE&K Maintenance became BE&K Industrial Services and BE&K Telecommunications was established. The telecommunications business was further strengthened by the acquisition of North Star Communications Group Inc., a Bellevue, Washington-based company with five West Coast offices. In 1999 BE&K Telecommunications adopted the North Star name and continued to grow through acquisitions, picking up California-based Trans Tec Concepts, Inc. and Oregon-based Pacific Inter Tel, Inc. a year later in 2000. Also in 2000, BE&K expanded its hydrocarbons business with the purchase of Houston-based M-E-I. Other significant acquisitions in that year were Industra Engineers and Consultants, Inc.

Despite a sputtering economy in the early 2000s, BE&K continued to grow, winning important contracts in a variety of markets. In 2004 the company established a pair of new business groups—BE&K Building Group, providing construction services to the healthcare field, and BE&K Government Group, geared toward work for the federal government—in an effort to make up for declining business in the industrial markets. In the meantime, Kennedy turned over the chairmanship to Goodrich in 2003, but continued to remain involved with the company. During his more than 30 years with BE&K Kennedy saw the company grow from start-up to one of the top engineering and construction firms in the country, generating more than $1 billion in sales each year.

Principal Subsidiaries

Allstates Technical Services, Inc.; As-Built Services; BE&K Building Group; Enprima; MEI Consultants, Inc.; NorthStar Communications Group, Inc.; QBEK; Rintekno Group; BE&K's Saginaw Warehouse; SW&B Construction Corporation; Terranext, LLC.

Principal Competitors

CH2M Hill Companies, Ltd.; Parsons Corporation; URS Corporation.

Further Reading

Baker, Sharon M., ''Telecom Engineering Firm Acquired for $6M,'' *Puget Sound Business Journal,* December 18, 1998, p. 4.

Korman, Richard, ''The Town Where Unions Tangle with BE&K,'' *Engineering News-Record,* September 6, 1990, p. 31.

Krizan, William G., ''News Unions, BE&K Square Off,'' *Engineering News-Record,* April 13, 1989, p. 11.

''Labor's Love Lost,'' *Dallas Morning News,* September 5, 1989, p. 1D.

Park, Jennifer, ''Diversification Key to BE&K's Growth,'' *Birmingham Business Journal,* October 25, 1999, p. S15.

Powers, Mary Buckner, '' 'We Take Care of Our Own,' '' *Engineering News-Record,* November 22, 1993, p. 28.

Shellenbarger, Sue, ''A Long Career Gives Business Leader Lesson in How to Value Labor,'' *Wall Street Journal,* December 26, 2001, p. B1.

—Ed Dinger

Biosite Incorporated

11030 Roselle Street
San Diego, California 92121
U.S.A.
Telephone: (858) 455-4808
Fax: (858) 455-4815
Web site: http://www.biosite.com

Public Company
Incorporated: 1988 as Biosite Diagnostics Incorporated
Employees: 905
Sales: $240.6 million (2004)
Stock Exchanges: NASDAQ
Ticker Symbol: BSTE
NAIC: 325413 In-Vitro Diagnostic Substance
    Manufacturing; 339112 Surgical and Medical
    Instrument Manufacturing; 334516 Analytical
    Laboratory Instrument Manufacturing

Biosite Incorporated develops diagnostic products that use human biomarkers of disease to determine what is afflicting a patient. Biosite's devices provide rapid diagnoses at the point of care, eliminating the use of laboratory-based analyzers, which take longer and cost more to provide test results. The company offers diagnostic products for drug screening, heart attack, congestive heart failure, acute coronary syndromes, and for the evaluation of shortness of breath and certain bacterial and parasitic infections. Biosite's products are developed through an internal research program named Biosite Discovery. The company's products are sold in the United States and in Europe.

Origins

Biosite sprang from discontent, created by a trio of executives and scientists as a way of improving their professional lives. During the early 1980s, Kim Blickenstaff, Kenneth Buechler, and Gunars Valkirs enjoyed the success of developing an innovative product that became the financial backbone for their employer, Hybritech Incorporated, one of the first biotechnology companies based in San Diego. Of the three, Blickenstaff was the business executive, a certified public accountant with a master's degree in

business from Loyola University who was versed in finance, marketing management, sales, and strategic planning. Buechler and Valkirs were scientists, holding doctorate degrees in biochemistry and physics, respectively.

At Hybritech, within the company's diagnostics research and development group, the trio's pioneering work took shape. In a project headed by Blickenstaff, experimental work began on the development of a color-change-membrane pregnancy test, a test capable of determining pregnancy in the doctor's office, which eliminated the need to wait for results from a lab. Valkirs, who was credited as the inventor, developed the ICON hcG test, the first rapid, visual pregnancy test that was the precursor to over-the-counter pregnancy kits used by women in their homes. The test proved to be a market winner, becoming the primary source of revenue for Hybritech, generating $30 million in sales within three years. For Blickenstaff, Buechler, and Valkirs, the joy of bringing a revolutionary product to market and watching its success did not last long. In a way, their success became their own undoing, sowing the seeds of discontent that gave birth to Biosite.

The point-of-care, visual pregnancy test drew national attention to the small, biotechnology company based in San Diego. Eli Lilly and Company, the giant pharmaceutical company based in Indianapolis, took more than a casual interest in Hybritech, paying $300 million in 1986 to gain control of ICON hcG and the rest of Hybritech. The pleasure of being part of a successful start-up soon faded, as Blickenstaff later explained in an August 27, 2001 interview with the *San Diego Business Journal*. "After the company was acquired by Eli Lilly," he said, "we were really disenchanted with the change in culture from a stand-alone start-up environment to something that was much more structured and drug-company oriented." Blickenstaff, Buechler, and Valkirs were not the only Hybritech employees to chaff at the change in ownership: an exodus of talent began, including the trio's superiors, Timothy Wollaeger and Howard Greene, Jr., who left to start their own venture capital firm, Biovest Partners.

Biosite's founders decided to start their own company and return to the happier days of working for a start-up. In 1988, Blickenstaff wrote a business plan based on what he referred to

Company Perspectives:

"Novel" is a term we apply to the proprietary protein markers that form the basis of our unique diagnostic products. It's a description that can also be applied to the breadth and depth of scientific expertise that resides within Biosite Discovery, one of Biosite's research and development arms. Our team of multi-talented scientists provides us with the knowledge base to accelerate advancements in these varied disciplines. The overarching goal is to create a productive pipeline of cost-effective, easy-to-use diagnostic technologies that deliver accurate, reliable results with unusual speed.

as his "cute little product" in his interview with the *San Diego Business Journal*. The initial idea was to develop another color-change diagnostic kit, one that could test for illicit drug use and aid doctors in emergency rooms trying to identify which drug a patient had overdosed. For the money to start the company, Blickenstaff approached his former bosses, Wollaeger and Greene, who agreed to give Blickenstaff $600,000 to start his company, which was incorporated as Biosite Diagnostics Incorporated in March 1988. The seed money gave Blickenstaff, joined by Buechler and Valkirs, enough money to begin development work on the company's first diagnostic kit, work that was performed in Biosite's first headquarters, a 400-square-foot office. Each of the founders applied their particular skills to Biosite's first project, enjoying the freedom of working within a small company. "Gunars believed what I told him about marketing," Blickenstaff said of Valkirs in an October 23, 2003 interview with *Forbes*, "and I believed what he told me about the technology."

The freedom of running their own company soon gave way to a less attractive aspect of operating a start-up: finding the capital to keep the company alive. Within a year of starting out, the Blickenstaff-led company was in desperate need of cash, having quickly exhausted the $600,000 obtained from Biovest Partners. Blickenstaff, in his realm as the business executive among scientists, devoted his efforts to finding the financial support to keep the company's research and development efforts moving forward. He arranged meetings with more than 40 venture capitalists, pitching the prospects of a point-of-care drug-abuse diagnostic device, but his efforts were undermined when one of the venture capitalists he met with began spreading the word that there was no market need for a faster, cheaper test for illicit drug use. Blickenstaff was running out of time and options, prompting him to make a last-ditch appeal to Frederick Dotzler, a partner at Medicus Venture Partners. Dotzler was not convinced by the skeptical venture capitalist, but neither was he convinced by Blickenstaff's enthusiasm. With nowhere else to turn, Blickenstaff paid for a market research study, using the company's last $35,000 and borrowing another $35,000 to pay for evidence that could refute the assessment of the company's vocal critic and build confidence in Biosite's cause. "If we were wrong," Blickenstaff said in an October 23, 2003 interview with *Forbes*, referring to the market research, "the company was dead."

According to *Forbes*, the venture capitalist who had derided Biosite had based his marketability assessment on conversations with toxicologists, rather than emergency-room (ER) doctors—the people who would use Biosite's proposed device. When ER doctors and pathologists were asked in the market-research study if they would probably or definitely purchase the test, 75 percent responded in the affirmative, providing enough evidence for Dotzler to throw himself behind Biosite's cause. He raised $3.5 million from a group of investors to fund research and development work on the drug abuse device, enabling Biosite, which used the research data to aid in pricing and marketing the device, to introduce the Triage Drugs of Abuse Panel into the U.S. market in February 1992. The credit-card-sized device, using a urine sample, was able to determine which of seven drugs a patient had misused within ten minutes for $25 a test. Technology at the time relied on large analyzers the size of a mainframe computer that were kept in the central laboratories of hospitals and designed to conduct hundreds of blood tests at a time, requiring considerable time for hospital personnel to log and to load the blood samples. Biosite's device delivered the same results for a fraction of the cost in a fraction of the time. Within 18 months of the release of its testing device, Biosite celebrated its first profit, encouraging Blickenstaff, Buechler, and Valkirs to develop additional point-of-care products.

A Focus on Heart Disease in the Mid-1990s

Biosite altered its strategic focus in the wake of its initial success, but the basis of the company's technology already was established with the Triage console. In the future, the company's products would use the same basic Triage device, which sold for between $3,000 and $4,500, but they would use different, disposable cartridges to identify human biomarkers of disease, identifying certain concentrations of what were called analytes—proteins, peptides, enzymes, hormones, and other blood-borne molecules found in normal and diseased physiology. The change in strategy, begun as the company entered the mid-1990s, was the focus on diagnosing heart disease, a choice made because of the changing dynamics in the healthcare industry. "Rapid diagnosis wasn't important 20 years ago," Blickenstaff said in his August 27, 2001 interview with the *San Diego Business Journal*, "but with insurers and providers draining costs out of the systems, everybody is interested in diagnosing quicker."

The focus on a new market put Biosite in the red again. Research and development investments were made in designing a blood test for diagnosing a heart attack, chewing through the profits generated by the company's drug-abuse test. As work was underway on a product to detect a heart attack from a blocked coronary, the company turned to Wall Street for aid in funding its research and development efforts. Biosite completed its initial public offering of stock in February 1997, when the company's stock debuted at $12 per share on the NASDAQ National Market, raising $30 million. Roughly eight months after its conversion to public ownership, Biosite received U.S. Food and Drug Administration (FDA) approval to market its Triage Cardiac System for diagnosing heart attack, but Blickenstaff and his team barely had the opportunity to celebrate the achievement. Biosite was beset by manufacturing problems with its newest device: Half of all the disposable test devices were rejected on the assembly line, severely delaying the introduction of the Triage Cardiac System into the market. While Blickenstaff revamped the company's manufacturing operations, Biosite received FDA approval in 1998 to market two diagnostic kits, the Triage C. difficile Panel and the Triage Parasite Panel, developed to identify bacteria and intestinal parasitic disease, respectively. The new devices did little to offset the damage caused by problems with manufacturing the Triage Cardiac System, however. Biosite fell short of its earnings and revenues projections twice, a failure that whittled its share price down to $4.50 by October 1998.

The waiting was over in February 1999, when the Triage Cardiac System was released in the United States. The $3,000 system, which consisted of a main console and a one-time $25 cartridge, enabled doctors to monitor three heart proteins that were released into the bloodstream at higher levels during a heart attack. The system, introduced in Europe in November 1999, was the first of several products developed to diagnose heart disease, followed by the Triage BNP Test, which received FDA clearance in November 2000. Development of the device, which measured levels of B-type natriuretic peptide (BNP), was begun five years earlier at a time when there was no clear association between heart failure and BNP, and its novelty proved to be a hindrance to its market success. Biosite was unable to convince the medical community that Triage BNP worked, leading to a period of frustration that did not end until the March 2002 meeting of the American College of Cardiology. At the meeting, results of a clinical study were released, revealing that measuring levels of BNP represented the single most accurate indicator of congestive heart failure. Soon afterward, the company's 15-minute, $20 blood test was adopted for use in 1,000 hospitals. By the end of 2002, Biosite had sold $38 million worth of the kits.

By the time the Triage BNP began to stir excitement within the medical community, Biosite had a decade of new product introductions under its belt. The revenue growth between 1992 and 2002 described a company fast on the rise, with each of its innovative, cost-effective devices delivering surges of financial growth. Biosite was a $2.2 million company in 1992, a $28.2 million company in 1995, and a $51.6 million company in 2000

before eclipsing the $100 million mark in 2002. During the ensuing two years, the company's annual revenue total would more than double as sales of its existing devices matured and new devices were introduced. Biosite, which had struggled for years after its founding, entered the mid-2000s as a company planning to be a $1 billion-in-sales diagnostics company. Such confidence was drawn from its rapid growth, the pace of which surprised even Biosite's most ardent supporters. "Our growth is shocking to us," Blickenstaff said in a May 18, 2005 interview with *Investor's Business Daily.* During the previous five years, Biosite had recorded annual revenue growth of 46 percent, far outpacing the 6 percent annual revenue growth of the diagnostics industry.

As Biosite planned for its future, there was every expectation that the years ahead would witness the continued rise of the company. The establishment of overseas operations promised to boost foreign sales, deepening Biosite's presence in large medical markets. In mid-2003, the company organized Biosite France SAS to manage direct sales and distribution in France, tasks that also were assigned to a new German subsidiary, Biosite GmbH, formed in November 2003. Further European expansion followed in January 2004, when offices were opened in the United Kingdom and Belgium. On the new product front, high expectations were pinned on the company's kit for diagnosing stroke. Development of the Triage Stroke Panel began in 2001 when the company's stroke marker discovery program yielded an initial panel of markers capable of detecting stroke. In early 2005, the pre-market approval application for the Triage Stroke Panel was under review by the FDA.

Principal Subsidiaries

Biosite GmbH (Germany); Biosite France S.A.S.; Biosite Ltd. (U.K.); Biosite BVBA (Belgium); Biosite S.r.l. (Italy).

Principal Competitors

Avitar, Inc.; Dade Behring Holdings Inc.; Roche Holding Ltd.

Further Reading

"Biosite Announces FDA Clearance to Market Triage TOX Drug Screens," *Asia Africa Intelligence Wire,* March 2, 2005, p. 32.
"Biosite Inc.," *San Diego Business Journal,* April 4, 2005, p. 39.
Dolan, Kerry A., "Good Genes," *Forbes,* May 16, 2005, p. 106.
Kroll, Luisa, "Vital Signs," *Forbes,* October 27, 2003, p. 150.
Lau, Gloria, "From One Idea, Years of Success," *Investor's Business Daily,* August 30, 2004, p. A12.
Reeves, Amy, "Biosite Inc. San Diego, California; Shift in Thinking Gives Test Maker a Boost," *Investor's Business Daily,* September 30, 2002, p. A10.
Somers, Terri, "Biosite Heart Attack Meter Puts Lifesaving Speed in ER," *San Diego Union-Tribune,* February 11, 2005, p. B2.

—Jeffrey L. Covell

The BISYS Group, Inc.

90 Park Avenue, 10th Floor
New York, New York 10016
U.S.A.
Telephone: (212) 907-6000
Fax: (212) 907-6014
Web site: http://www.bisys.com

Public Company
Incorporated: 1989
Employees: 5,200
Sales: $1.03 billion (2004)
Stock Exchanges: New York
Ticker Symbol: BSG
NAIC: 541990 All Other Professional, Scientific and
Technical Services

The BISYS Group, Inc. provides outsourcing, back-office, and third-party services to the financial services industry. The company's business is divided between three units: Investment Services, addressing the needs of investment firms of all sizes; Insurance Services, providing life insurance and commercial insurance services; and Information Services, providing banking solutions to midsized and community banks, corporations, and healthcare companies. BISYS is a public company based in New York City and listed on the New York Stock Exchange.

Separating from ADP in the Late 1980s

BISYS grew out of Automatic Data Processing, Inc. (ADP), a pioneer in the field of outsourced payroll accounting. ADP was founded in the late 1940s by young accountant Henry Taub as Automatic Payrolls, Inc. At the time, small businesses were finding it increasingly difficult to comply with mounting government regulations brought on by the creation of Social Security in the 1930s and the system of income tax withholding introduced during World War II. Taub found a ready market for his innovative service and soon was joined by his younger brother Joe and a World War II veteran and Columbia graduate in economics named Frank R. Lautenberg, who would become better known as a U.S. Senator from New Jersey. The three men worked well together and expanded the company's offerings, primarily through acquisitions, transforming Automatic Payroll into Automatic Data Processing, Inc., a multibillion-dollar information services company. One of the acquisitions was United Data Processing, Inc., established in 1966 to provide processing services to banks and thrifts. In the 1980s ADP suffered some setbacks, prompting management to either sell off or downsize some of its product lines to focus on major revenue centers. In the wake of the Savings and Loan debacle of the 1980s, which resulted in a number of institutions closing their doors and a smaller client base for data processors dedicated to this sector, ADP's banking and thrift data processing operations were deemed expendable. In August 1989 a group of ADP executives incorporated BISYS Group, Inc. and with the financial backing of Welsh Carson Anderson & Stowe paid $78 million to acquire the banking and thrift data processing business.

Heading BISYS as chief executive officer and chairman of the board was Lynn J. Magnum, a 22-year ADP veteran who had served as division president for the Employer Services National Accounts Division prior to the formation of BISYS. Not one of the larger players in the field, BISYS in the beginning eschewed large banks as clients in favor of smaller institutions: community banks with less than $2 billion in assets and thrifts with less than $10 billion in assets. The company also adopted a "single product, single source" strategy, an outgrowth of management's experience at ADP, which in the early 1980s had attempted to run several different accounting systems for clients, only to find that such a broad approach proved difficult and expensive to run.

Learning from their mistakes at ADP, management now looked for an integrated set of software applications that would not only provide the flexibility to allow clients to grow but to support BISYS's own expansion plans. The result was a product called TotalPlus, a complete end-to-end solution that could be tailored to meet the needs of banks and thrifts of all sizes. Accessible on desktop computers, the system could produce all customer documents; handle all loan functions through Total Loan Manager; process checks; do research, create reports, and handle customer service requests through Total Report Manager; and help make marketing and financial decisions through the information compiled from Total Marketing Manager and Total Financial Manager. In addition, BISYS helped clients to design their computer networks to optimize connectivity internally or between the client and BISYS's hosted functions. The package of data processing services BISYS had to offer came at a lower cost per transaction than a bank or a thrift could hope to achieve through an in-house system.

Going Public in the Early 1990s

BISYS wasted little time in building on its base of operations through complementary acquisitions. In October 1989 it added Data Systems Corp., picking up a company that provided data processing services to the southeast Atlantic Coast area. A pair of acquisitions followed in 1991: Litton Mortgaging Servicing Center, which acted as a sub-servicer for mortgage and commercial real estate loans, and certain assets of JRS Inc., an item processing and vault servicing company. Early in 1992 BISYS acquired Tridatatron Software Services, Inc., a company that specialized in data processing for mortgage loans. Later in 1992 BISYS went public, netting approximately $50 million in an initial offering of stock, with the money earmarked to pay off the debt taken on in the 1989 buyout as well as to fund further acquisitions. At this stage, the company's stock traded on the NASDAQ. A secondary offering in February 1993 raised an additional $40 million.

At the time it went public BISYS serviced 214 thrifts, 39 commercial banks, and a handful of mortgage banks in 31 states. The company lost a few thrifts as clients in the early part of the decade when some of the institutions failed and were taken over by regulators. BISYS began to focus on increasing its slate of banking system clients and in 1993 looked to broaden its product offerings even further through acquisitions. In February of that year it spent $10 million in cash to acquire The Barclay Group, Inc., a Pennsylvania company that specialized in providing record-keeping and other support services for 401(k) plans, a service that BISYS could now offer to its small bank customers. As a result of the acquisition, BISYS became the country's largest third-party administrator of corporate-sponsored small to medium-sized 401(k) plans. Later in 1993 BISYS added another attractive service for banks, paying $60 million for Columbus, Ohio-based Winsbury Companies, a creator, marketer, and administrator of proprietary mutual funds for banks. Also of note in 1993, BISYS acquired Data Management Systems, Inc., a deal that added 30 banking customers in New England, and Meyer Interest Rate Survey of Calabasas, California, a company that tracked deposits and loan information for more than 3,000 banks, thrifts, and credit unions.

BISYS achieved some internal growth in 1994, as it beefed up its home banking services by creating a new position, vice-

president of electronic banking. Before the year was out the company introduced automatic teller machines and card management platforms, and in 1995 added point-of-sale services, home banking, and bill paying services. The thrust of the initiative was to provide the company's bread-and-butter small bank customers with the electronic capabilities they would need to compete against larger banks in a time of rapidly changing technologies and consumer demands. BISYS also continued to add banking customers through external means as well during 1994. The acquisition of Sun Trust Data Systems, Inc. brought with it 100 community bank customers in Alabama, Florida, Georgia, and Tennessee, significantly adding to the company's customer base in the Southeast.

BISYS added to its bank fund business in 1995 and complemented its Winsbury operation with the acquisition of Concord Holding Corporation in a stock swap valued at $120 million. Concord expanded BISYS's reach to include money center banks, as well as increased its overall stake in the fund services industry and established an offshore platform for fund services in Ireland. Also in 1995 BISYS used $38 million in stock to acquire Birmingham, Alabama-based Document Solutions, Inc., a check and document imaging software firm that was ideally suited for BISYS's core of community and mid-sized banks. As a result of expansion in the first half of the 1990s, the company's balance sheet grew at a similar pace. Revenues increased from $88.3 million in 1992 to more than $200 million in 1995.

Expansion on Many Fronts in the Late 1990s

In the second half of the 1990s BISYS evolved further into a multifaceted outsourcer, no longer limited to a single product and catering to a narrow market. The company raised its sights to include large banks as well as investment management and mutual fund companies, insurance companies, and consumer finance companies. The company also continued to grow through acquisitions. In 1996 BISYS added Strategic Solutions Group Inc., which provided automated telephone marketing systems to financial institutions. The purchase of The Underwriters' Group (TUG) in June 1996 allowed BISYS to sell insurance through banks. Harrisburg, Pennsylvania-based TUG was a major wholesaler of insurance products for agents, banks, and financial services companies and also provided back-office administration for insurance selling operations. The September 1997 acquisition of Benefits Services, Inc. enhanced BISYS's position as a single source outsourcer of insurance products and services, not only to insurance companies, but also to producer groups, securities firms, and financial institutions. Benefit Services was one of the country's leading providers of long-term care insurance products, a fast-growing segment of the insurance marketplace.

Starting in 1998 BISYS picked up the acquisition pace, bringing four significant companies into the fold: Underwriters Service Agency, bolstering the company's life insurance services; CoreLink Resources, improving BISYS's share of the fund service industry while adding sophisticated trade execution, settlement, and custody services; Potomac Group, supplementing the company's marketing sales support services for life insurance and estate planning; and Greenway Corporation, reinforcing the company's leading position in the check imaging field. BISYS closed out the decade with a bevy of acquisitions in 1999, including EXAMCO, Inc., which offered certification

Key Dates:

1989: The company is formed by acquiring assets from Automated Data Processing, Inc.
1992: The company is taken public.
1995: Concord Holding Corporation is acquired.
1999: The company's insurance business is established.
2002: The company is listed on the New York Stock Exchange.
2005: The Education Services unit is sold to Kaplan Professional.

training and continuing education programs to the securities and insurance industries; Poage Insurance Services, a life insurance wholesaler that greatly expanded BISYS's presence on the West Coast; Bachmann Asset Management's mutual fund administration business; Dover International, which added regulator education services for the investment industry; and State Street Bank and Trust Company's Retained Asset Account Processing business, which laid the foundation for BISYS's Asset Retention Solutions unit. When BISYS closed the decade, revenues totaled $473 million and the company was enjoying net profits in the $40 million range.

BISYS was well positioned for the new century, as the ongoing convergence of the financial services industry, globalization, the increasing use of the Internet, and the growing reliance on outsourcing all played into the company's strengths. BISYS continued to seek out strategic acquisitions, in particular to build on its Insurance and Education Services unit, the fastest-growing part of its business. In 2000 BISYS acquired Pictorial, a leading provider of pre-licensing and continuing education training programs in all 50 states for insurance carriers, agencies, and agents. BISYS also acquired Salt Lake City-based Ascensus Insurance Services, a broker of life and health insurance products that BISYS had been pursuing for four years. Ascensus, which provided insurance products to more than 50,000 agents representing some 100 life insurance companies from 13 offices across the country, added a great deal of business while also expanding BISYS's geographic reach. For fiscal 2000 revenues soared to more than $570 million and net income almost doubled to $70 million. The company also initiated a two-for-one stock split.

BISYS continued to fill out its business in 2001, completing seven complementary acquisitions to take advantage of convergence in the financial services industry and increased reliance on outsourcing. The company continued to devote a great deal of attention to growing the insurance and education business, with a particular emphasis on filling in geographic gaps. The acquisition of Insurance Exchange of America, Inc. increased BISYS's presence in the tri-state region of New York, New Jersey, and Connecticut; Toner Organization added customers in the mid-Atlantic region; and Life Brokerage Corporation bolstered the company's presence in the Florida market. Despite a softening economy, which was dealt a further blow by the September 11 terrorist attacks, BISYS continued to experience a rapid climb in revenues, which topped $700 million for the fiscal year, yielding profits of more than $85 million.

In 2002 BISYS gained a coveted listing on the New York Stock Exchange. The company continued to prosper, completing another half-dozen acquisitions, and despite sluggish sales in the insurance and education services unit the balance sheet remained strong. In 2002 revenues increased to $865.7 million and net income improved to $115.9 million, and for the second time in just 16 months management engineered a two-for-one stock split.

Fiscal 2003 proved to be more of a challenging year for BISYS due to some declining markets, yet the company continued to expand on a number of fronts, adding customers in all divisions and expanding geographically through acquisitions. Revenues grew to $958.4 million and a year later topped the $1 billion mark, although net income tailed off to $111.8 million in 2003 and $63.6 million in 2004. The company had to cope with a number of challenges in 2004 when earnings fell short in several key business segments. In February the company's CEO, Dennis R. Sheehan, was forced to step down due to medical problems caused by an accident. His successor, Russell P. Fradin, had to contend with a struggling insurance and education services unit. Not only were sales off, the company soon announced that it would have to restate its earnings for the previous three years. Fradin maintained that the problem was limited to the life insurance operations and the way commissions receivable were accounted.

BISYS adjusted its business mix somewhat in 2005, selling off its Education Services unit to Kaplan Professional. Nevertheless, BISYS remained well positioned to continue its steady growth for the foreseeable future.

Principal Subsidiaries

Ascensus Insurance Services, Inc.; BISYS Commercial Insurance Services, Inc.; BISYS Document Solutions LLC; BISYS Financial Services Ltd.; BISYS Fund Services, L.P.; BISYS Information Solutions L.P.; BISYS Insurance Services, Inc.; BISYS Retirement Services, Inc.

Principal Competitors

Electronic Data Systems Corporation; SEI Investments Company; State Street Corporation.

Further Reading

Bills, Steve, "Bisys CEO: Problem Under Control," *American Banker,* June 17, 2004, p. 11.
"BISYS Joins the Initial Public Stock Offering Derby," *Bank Network News,* February 26, 1992.
Blumenthal, Robin Goldwyn, "Bisys Believes It Was Profitable in Its 1st Quarter," *Wall Street Journal,* November 2, 1992, p. 6.
Crockett, Barton, "Concord Discussed Buyout with Bisys Before It Brought Its Stock to Market Last Year," *American Banker,* February 3, 1995, p. 10.
Markowitz, Michael, "Banks Do Business with BISYS," *The Record* (Bergen County, N.J.), November 13, 1996, p. B1.
Much, Marilyn, "Wide Reach Lifts Results at Outsourcing Firm," *Investor's Business Daily,* November 9, 2001, p. A08.
Tracey, Brian, "Bisys Group Thrives amid Shake-Up in Outsourcing Business," *American Banker,* September 27, 1993, p. 16.

—Ed Dinger

BÖHLER-UDDEHOLM AG

Modecenterstrasse 14/A3
A-1030 Vienna
Austria
Telephone: +43 1 798 69 01
Fax: +43 1 798 69 01
Web site: http://www.bohler-uddeholm.com

Public Company
Incorporated: 1991
Employees: 11,800
Sales: EUR 1.93 billion ($2.2 billion) (2004)
Stock Exchanges: Vienna
Ticker Symbol: BUD
NAIC: 333992 Welding and Soldering Equipment
    Manufacturing; 331111 Iron and Steel Mills; 331221
    Cold-Rolled Steel Shape Manufacturing; 331491
    Nonferrous Metal (Except Copper and Aluminum)
    Rolling, Drawing, and Extruding; 332111 Iron and
    Steel Forging; 332116 Metal Stamping

BÖHLER-UDDEHOLM AG (Böhler-Uddeholm) is a world-leading specialty steels and materials manufacturer focused on four core niche markets: High-Performance Metals; Welding Consumables; Precision Strip; and Special Forgings. The company's largest division is its High-Performance Metals division, which is the world's leading producer of tool steel—used in the creation of tooling dies and molds—and the world's number two producer of speed steel, used for drill bits and other related applications. The company's Precision Strip division holds top global positions for the production of bimetallic strips, cutting and creasing rules and rule die steel, which the group's Welding Consumables division ranks third worldwide. Formed through the merger of Böhler in Austria and Uddeholm in Sweden at the beginning of the 1990s, Böhler-Uddeholm operates additional production facilities in the United States, Mexico, Brazil, Italy, Germany, and Belgium. The company distributes its products to more than 100 countries, generating revenues of EUR 1.93 billion ($2.2 billion) in 2004. Böhler-Uddeholm, formerly controlled by the Austrian government's industrial holding company Osterreichische Industrieholding AG (OIAG), has been listed on the Vienna Stock Exchange since 1995 and completed its privatization in 2003.

Merging Steel Histories in the 1990s

The merger of Austria's Böhler and Sweden's Uddeholm in 1991 brought together more than six centuries of experience in metals production. Uddeholm grew from the first iron forge in Sweden's Värmland region, built in Stjärnfors in 1668. That forge was already known as Uddeholms Bruk and led to the later formation of Uddeholm AB.

Two years after the launch of the Stjärnfors forge, another forge appeared in Munkfors, built by Johan Bjesson. The Munkfors site grew into one of the country's major iron and steel producers. Uddeholm acquired the Munkfors mill in 1829.

Uddeholm added to its growing steel empire with the creation of a new steel mill at Hagfors in 1873. The Hagfors mill added a rolling mill in 1882, and Uddeholm expanded into the tool steel market, producing steel products for tool and die machinery. Under subsidiary Uddeholm Tooling, the company grew into a major global tool steel producer. By 1886, Uddeholm began experimenting with newly developed methods for producing cold-rolled steel at Munkfors. That facility then became specialized in the production of steel strips, and grew into one of the world's largest producers of thin and ultra-thin steel strips. In 1905, the Munkfors site constructed a dedicated cold-rolling mill. The boost in production enabled Uddeholm to begin targeting the foreign market, especially the booming U.S. market. Among the company's most prominent customers was the fast-growing Gillette company, which specialized in razor blades.

Uddeholm grew into one of the world's leading names in its specialty steel niches through the 20th century. The company also expanded internationally, acquiring steelworks in a number of foreign markets, such as Belgium's Stora in 1978. Closer to home, Uddeholm added AGA AB to its operations in 1985.

In 1988, Uddeholm itself was purchased by privately held Trustor Industrier AB. Soon after, however, Trustor put Uddeholm back up for sale. In 1991, Uddeholm was acquired

Company Perspectives:

Shared Values: We are the leaders in quality. BÖHLER-UDDEHOLM regards profitability and financial stability as a sound basis for growth and business development, and as a means of establishing long-term partnerships with our customers. BÖHLER-UDDEHOLM anticipates and identifies the needs of its customers and provides materials, products and services that demand consistent leadership in quality. This goal requires superior knowledge of processes, products and applications based on state-of-the-art technology. Quality leadership means continuous improvement across the entire value chain.

by Böhler of Austria. Böhler's operations proved complementary to Uddeholm's, as both companies had developed a strong presence in specialty steel niche markets. The combined company, known as Böhler-Uddeholm, took its place among the world's leading specialty steel groups.

Böhler's own history reached back even further than that of Uddeholm. The earliest part of the Böhler group stemmed from the opening of a hammer forge in Kapfenberg, part of the early Austrian empire, by Arnold Taubenprunner in 1446. The Kapfenberg site played host to an important center of the Austrian empire's steel industry, developing into a modern steel mill by the mid-19th century. That era also saw the arrival of a new range of competitors, one of which appeared in 1854, with the founding of a hot-rolling mill in Bruckbach on the river Ybbs by Josef Liebl. The Bruckbach site launched production in 1855.

In 1870, Albert and Emile Böhler purchased the Bruckbach mill, laying the foundation for one of Austria's major steel producers. The company's original name was Gebrüder Böhler & Co. Over the next decades, Böhler expanded strongly, in part through acquisition—in 1894, for example, the company acquired the Kapfenberg mill. In 1940, Böhler acquired the Gerstlmill, which specialized in the production of cold-rolled strip steel and galvanized steel.

Böhler played a significant role as an Austrian steel industry innovation leader. In 1900, the company introduced Böhler Rapid, one of the first high-performance, high-speed steels. Then, in 1908, Böhler became the first in Austria to build an electric arc furnace. Whereas that furnace was rated at just three tons, in 1910 the company opened a new hammer forge with a hammer weight of 30 tons.

The need to boost production during World War I led Böhler to build a new facility boasting six 30-ton furnaces in 1916. In that year, the company expanded its rolling mill as well. Following the war, Böhler began developing new products, such as blank welding wire, introduced in 1926. Welding consumables then became an important part of Böhler's operations, particularly after the company developed a new type of welding wire, called core wire, in 1927.

The buildup to World War II led Böhler to open a new facility, a steelworks at Deuchendorf, in 1938. By 1944, the company had expanded its capacity again, installing a press

with a force of 1,200 tons. Yet World War II, and especially its aftermath, were to have far-reaching consequences for Böhler.

Following the war, the Soviet Union launched a policy of confiscating the "German-owned" businesses within its zone of control. Because of Austria's active participation in the Nazi alliance, a large number of Austrian companies, including Böhler and other members of the country's steel industry, now fell under the Soviet Union's definition of a German-owned company. This definition included all businesses founded in Austria following the Anschluss of 1938, as well as companies that had been taken over during the war years by the German-Austrian government. Altogether, the businesses threatened by the Soviet Union's confiscation program—which involved the stripping bare of these businesses, transporting their machinery and equipment for use inside the Soviet empire—accounted for some 20 percent of Austria's total economy. In addition to the steel industry, the "German" definition targeted the country's banking industry, including its three largest banks, as well as its coal and metals mining industry, its oil refining and extraction businesses, as well as the country's leading industrial companies.

The Austrian government reacted quickly, passing new legislation in 1946 nationalizing all of its "German" companies. Yet the first Nationalization act, while protecting the businesses in the zones controlled by the British, French, and Americans—which respected Austria's claim—remained ineffectual in the Soviet zone. The nationalization of the remaining industries and businesses nonetheless gave the Austrian government oversight of the distribution of reconstruction aid provided by the United States in particular. In this way, the government was able to subsidize its nationalized businesses and aid in the reconstruction. Over the next decades, government control proved less than efficient; after a number of crises, the government instituted a series of reforms in the 1960s, leading to the creation of a new public limited company, Osterreichische Industrieverwaltungs AG (later Osterreichische Industrieholding AG, or OIAG), in 1970.

In the early 1970s, the OIAG began restructuring its vast holdings, which included the creation of industrial giant VOEST. The specialty steel sector's turn came in 1975, when Böhler and two other specialty steel producers, Schoeller-Bleckmann and Steirische Gusstahlwerke, were combined into a single company, known as Vereinigte Edelstahlwerke AG (VEW). Schoeller-Bleckmann, which traced its own history back to the founding of a forgery guild in 1496, had developed a specialty as a stainless steel producer. In 1988, the OIAG decided to split VEW's operations into two, creating Böhler on the one hand, and Schoeller Bleckmann on the other. By then, the OIAG, which faced losses in many of the businesses under its control, was under pressure to begin restructuring its holdings, including the privatization of many of its companies. The passage of new legislation in 1993 established a strict timeline for carrying out OIAG's privatization effort.

Global Niche Leader in the 21st Century

The acquisition of Uddeholm by Böhler in 1991 set the stage for the combined company's privatization in the mid-1990s. Before that event took place, however, Böhler-Uddeholm launched a thorough restructuring in an effort to cut its losses.

Key Dates:

1446: A hammer forge is founded in Kapfenberg, in Austria, by Arnold Taubenprunner.

1668: The first iron forge, known as Uddeholm, is built in Sweden's Värmland region, in Stjärnfors.

1670: An iron forge is built at Munkfors, in Sweden.

1829: Uddeholm acquires the Munkfors mill.

1854: A hot rolling mill is founded in Bruckbach, Austria.

1870: The Böhler brothers acquire the Bruckbach mill.

1900: Böhler introduces Böhler Rapide, the first high-speed steel.

1905: Uddeholm constructs a cold rolling mill at the Munkfors site and launches thin and ultra-thin steel production.

1926: Böhler develops welding wire, launching the Welding Consumables operation.

1946: Böhler is nationalized by the Austrian government.

1975: Böhler is combined with two other Austrian steel producers to form VEW.

1988: VEW is broken up, with Böhler taking over the specialty steel component.

1991: Böhler and Uddeholm merge, forming BÖHLER-UDDEHOLM (Böhler-Uddeholm).

1995: The Austrian government lists 25 percent of Böhler-Uddeholm's stock on the Vienna exchange in the first step of privatization.

1996: Böhler-Uddeholm's free float now tops 75 percent.

1997: The company acquires Martin Miller GmbH of Austria.

1998: The company acquires Allegheny Teledyne of the United States.

2000: The company forms a welding consumable joint venture with Thyssen Group.

2003: Böhler-Uddeholm's free float reaches 100 percent; the company acquires full control of the Thyssen joint venture.

2004: The company acquires Villares Metals of Brazil.

2005: The company acquires Edelstahlwerke Buderus in Germany.

By 1994, the company's reorganization had succeeded in transforming Böhler-Uddeholm into a streamlined and profitable company.

The first step in Böhler-Uddeholm's privatization came the following year, when the OIAG listed more than 25 percent of the company's shares on the Vienna Stock Exchange. In the meantime, Böhler-Uddeholm's restructuring continued, until, by the end of 1996, the company had sold off its noncore holdings and regrouped around four core businesses: High-Performance Metals; Precision Strip; Special Forgings; and Welding Consumables. The company then capped its restructuring with a secondary offering, which reduced the OIAG's stake in the company to just 25 percent, in 1996.

Böhler-Uddeholm then began a new growth phase, launching a number of major acquisitions. In 1997, the company purchased fellow Austrian firm Martin Miller GmbH, a pro-

ducer of strip steel. Founded in 1782 in Vienna, Martin Miller had been behind the invention of steel piano wire in 1840, before adding cold-rolling mill capacity at the beginning of the 20th century.

Böhler-Udderholm became the world's second largest high-speed steel producer in 1998, when it acquired Allegheny Teledyne. The Virginia-based company had been created in the early 1970s, and had risen to become the U.S. leader in the high-speed steel segment.

Into the beginning of the 21st century, Böhler-Uddeholm launched an expansion of its international sales network, setting up or consolidating subsidiaries in markets including Germany, the United Kingdom, Switzerland, The Netherlands, and elsewhere. The company also invested in expanding its own production capacity, opening electro-slag re-melting plants in Austria and Sweden, as well as a powder metallurgy steels facility in Kapfenberg in 1999. The company then built a new vacuum re-melting plant at the Kapfenberg site in 2000.

Despite the global slowdown following the September 11, 2001 terrorist attacks in the United States, Böhler-Uddeholm continued its expansion. In 2002 the company formed a number of joint ventures, including one with Fileur S.A. of Italy, and another with Dan Spray A/S, a Denmark-based spray forming specialist. In 2000, in addition, Böhler-Uddeholm had formed a joint venture with the Thyssen Group to form the 50–50 joint venture Thyssen Schweisstechnik GmbH. By 2003, however, Böhler-Uddeholm had acquired full control of the joint venture, making it the world leader in welding consumables.

The year 2003 also marked Böhler-Uddeholm's full privatization, as OIAG placed the last of its holdings on the Vienna Stock Exchange. Soon after, the company turned to a new part of the world, South America, buying up Brazil's Villares Metals S.A. That acquisition, completed in 2004, gave Böhler-Uddeholm the leading share of the South American tool steel and speed steel markets.

Böhler-Uddeholm showed no sign of slowing down into the middle of the 1990s. In 2005, the company returned to the acquisition trail, buying up Germany's Edelstahlwerke Buderus. That purchase gave the company production facilities in Germany, while boosting its specialty steels capacity. With operations dating back to the 15th century, Böhler-Uddeholm had forged a solid foundation for the future.

Principal Subsidiaries

ASSAB Pacific Pte. Ltd.; BÖHLER Bleche GmbH; BÖHLER Edelstahl GmbH; BÖHLER International GmbH; BÖHLER Schmiedetechnik GmbH & Co. KG; BÖHLER Schweisstechnik Austria GmbH; BÖHLER THYSSEN Schweisstechnik Deutschland GmbH; BÖHLER THYSSEN Schweisstechnik GmbH; BÖHLER-UDDEHOLM (UK) Ltd.; BÖHLER-UDDEHOLM Deutschland GmbH; BÖHLER-UDDEHOLM France S.A.S.; BÖHLER-UDDEHOLM Iberica S.A.; BÖHLER-UDDEHOLM Italia S.p.A.; BÖHLER-UDDEHOLM North America; BÖHLER-UDDEHOLM Precision Strip AB; BÖHLER-UDDEHOLM Precision Strip GmbH & Co. KG; BÖHLER-UDDEHOLM Specialty Metals, Inc.; BÖHLER-UDDEHOLM Strip Steel LLC; BÖHLER-

YBBSTAL Profil GmbH; BÖHLER-YBBSTALWERKE GmbH; ESCHMANNSTAHL GmbH & Co. KG; FONTARGEN GmbH; MARTIN MILLER GmbH; SOUDOKAY S.A.; UDDEHOLM Machining AB; UDDEHOLM Tooling AB; UTP Schweissmaterial GmbH; VILLARES Metals S.A.

Principal Competitors

Corus Nederland B.V.; Chongqing Special Steel Group Company Ltd.; Cargill Inc.; Aceros Chile S.A.; Arcelor S.A.; United States Steel Corporation; BHP Billiton Ltd.; ACINOX S.A.; JFE Steel Corporation.

Further Reading

"Acquisition of Villares Metals SA Completed," *Steel Times International,* May-June 2004, p. 9.

"Austria Readies Divestiture Plan for 25% Bohler-Uddeholm Stake," *American Metal Market,* April 9, 2003, p. 2.

"Böhler-Uddeholm," *Euroweek,* May 20, 2005, p. 28.

Burgert, Philip, "Böhler/Thyssen Accord Creates Tool Steel Giant," *American Metal Market,* April 20, 2000, p. 1.

"Fourteen Suitors Eye Böhler-Uddeholm," *American Metal Market,* September 5, 2001, p. 3.

Penson, Stuart, "Uddeholm's Privatization Moves Up," *American Metal Market,* March 15, 1995, p. 3.

"Steel Maker Turns 50," *Canadian Machinery and Metalworking,* August-September 2003, p. 11.

Wood, Peter, "Böhler Targets Further Acquisitions to Strengthen Forging Business," *Steel Times,* December 1999, p. 432.

——, "Böhler-Uddeholm's Profits Attract Investors," *Steel Times,* July-August 2001, p. 214.

—M.L. Cohen

Boiron S.A.

20 rue de la Libération
Sainte-Foy-les-Lyon 69110
France
Telephone: +33-4-72-16-40-00
Fax: +33-4-78-59-69-16
Web site: http://www.boiron.com

Public Company
Incorporated: 1967 as Laboratoire Boiron
Employees: 2,600
Sales: $427.1 million (2004)
Stock Exchanges: Euronext Paris
Ticker Symbol: BOI
NAIC: 325410 Pharmaceutical and Medicine Manufacturing; 325411 Medicinal and Botanical Manufacturing; 325412 Pharmaceutical Preparation Manufacturing

Boiron S.A. is a world leader in the production and distribution of homeopathic medicines. One of the oldest homeopathic manufacturers in Europe, the company has operations in more than 60 countries in Europe, North America, South America, Africa, the Middle East, and Australia. Boiron, which produces more than 1,500 homeopathic remedies, alone or in combinations, also funds scientific research, provides training to medical professionals, and distributes healthcare information to the general public.

Beginnings

In June 1932, René Baudry hired twin brothers Jean and Henri Boiron to found a homeopathic laboratory, the Laboratoire Central Homéopathique de France in Paris. Born in Paris in 1906, the Boiron brothers had each earned a degree in science in 1928 and a diploma in pharmacy in 1929.

Baudry was himself a pharmacist, who had long specialized in producing homeopathic medicines, or remedies. In 1911, he had founded a homeopathic pharmacy called the Pharmacie Générale Homéopathique Française, which he sold in 1922 when he left Paris. Eight years later, in 1930, Baudry joined a group of homeopathic physicians in Lyon to found the Lab-

oratoire Central Homéopathique Rhodanien. Shortly thereafter, when the Parisian physicians of the Ecole Moderne d'Homéopathique asked Baudry to found a national laboratory for the production of homeopathic medicines, he agreed, basing the company in Lyon, France, and hiring the Boiron brothers to head up a branch of the company in Paris.

Homeopathy is a branch of medicine that follows the maxim: "Like treats like." Each homeopathic remedy contains a minute dilution of a substance that, in a healthy person, will create symptoms similar to those the patient currently manifests. The remedy is the result of a series of successive deconcentrations of the substance, which may be plant-, animal-, or mineral-based, which is "potentized" homeopathically by a standardized shaking process called "dynamization." The homeopathic dilution, or "strain," may be added to a liquid base and used as a tincture or impregnated onto an inert pharmaceutical vehicle which may be granule, pill, or pellet. There are currently about 3,300 strains that serve as the starting point for homeopathic remedies.

Homeopathy was first developed in the late 1700s by Samuel Hahnemann, a German physician, who began to study the effects of various natural substances on his body. To avoid problems of toxicity, he used substances at smaller and smaller concentrations. Hahnemann became convinced that "the same things which cause the disease cure it," a principle espoused by Hippocrates. By the mid-1800s, there were several homeopathic medical colleges in Europe and the United States, and one in five doctors used homeopathy, but the move toward a more mechanistic view of the body and the growing use of pharmaceuticals pushed homeopathy into relative obscurity by the 1940s.

The Boiron brothers' Laboratoire Central Homéopathique de France was located on the premises of Baudry's original Pharmacie Générale Homéopathique Française. A year after its opening, in 1933, René Baudry joined Henri Boiron at the Paris laboratory, which became the Laboratoires Homéopathiques Modernes (LHM). Boiron and Baudry focused on developing a range of homeopathic combination formulas, which eventually became the foundation of the Boiron company's line of specialties. Specialties contain several homeopathic active ingredients traditionally used to treat an ailment.

Company Perspectives:

For more than 70 years, Boiron has been committed to funding scientific research and educating the public and healthcare professionals on homeopathic medicines. Boiron maintains the highest standards in manufacturing, complying with U.S. Food and Drug Administration regulations, the Homeopathic Pharmacopoeia of the U.S., and the Drug Good Manufacturing Practices.

At the same time, Jean Boiron took over development of the Laboratoire Central Homéopathique Rhodanien in Lyon, which became the Pharmacie Homéopathique Rhodanienne (PHR). His focus became and remained the production of classical homeopathic remedies, those that were developed in the 19th century by Hahnemann.

After 1941, while still maintaining a close connection to LHM, the Boiron brothers began an independent business under the trademark PHR. During the next two decades, homeopathy gained acceptance in France, and both LHM and PHR grew steadily. In 1967, PHR and LHM merged to form the Laboratoires Boiron. The company opened its first regional production and distribution facility in Toulouse in 1968.

Other distribution facilities followed throughout France starting in the 1970s, and the Laboratoire Boiron set up regional establishments in Lille, Belfort, Nantes, Avignon, and Grenoble. In 1974, it moved its head offices and production plant to Ste. Foy-lès-Lyon, near Lyon. The Laboratoires Boiron also undertook its first international development in 1979 with the establishment of a foreign branch in Milan, Italy. Additional branches followed soon afterward: in Spain in 1984, in Belgium in 1989. By the late 1980s, the company also had subsidiaries in the United States, Canada, and the Caribbean.

As the company grew, the Boiron brothers developed their commitment to promote homeopathy throughout the French and international medical communities. They founded the Centre d'Etude et de Documentation Homéopathiques and the Organisation Médicale Homéopathique Internationale. Jean Boiron also maintained his interest in producing classical homeopathy remedies and undertook extensive research to develop production processes such as triple impregnation. This is a process that guarantees impregnation of the homeopathic solution right to the heart of the inert substance. Meanwhile, Henri Boiron was elected president of the Syndicat National des Pharmaciens Homéopathes in 1953, and, in 1955, he founded the Comité International des Pharmaciens Homéopathes. One of the peak moments of his career was the inclusion of homeopathy into the Pharmacopée Française in 1965.

The next generation of the family took the reins of the Laboratoires Boiron in 1983 when Christian Boiron succeeded Jean Boiron as president. At the time, the company had 29 production facilities around the world. Boiron acquired Philadelphia-based John Borneman & Sons in 1983, further consolidating its presence in the United States.

Two years later, in 1985, the Institut Boiron opened, sealing the company's commitment to expand homeopathy throughout the international medical and scientific communities. This research institute drew on the clinical experience of homeopathic physicians with the goal of better understanding the active mechanism of homeopathic drugs. Institut Boiron began holding a symposium every other year for academics and doctors, the goal of which was to develop research in homeopathy; to reinforce medical training in homeopathy; and to foster communication about homeopathy among doctors of all backgrounds. The institute also aimed to educate the general public about homeopathy with its Club Boiron Santé.

The 1980s saw the expansion and establishment of Boiron as France's largest homeopathic laboratory and production facility and as the world's leader in producing homeopathic medicines. Boiron undertook to consolidate its presence in France where the social security system reimbursed the costs of homeopathic medicines and where 5,000 to 6,000 doctors were trained homeopathically. In 1987, the company went public, offering its stock on the Lyon Stock Exchange. The following year, it merged with the Laboratoires Homéopathiques de France, and its domestic market share reached 60 percent. Boiron's worldwide market share at the time was around 16 percent, well ahead of its French rival Dolisos and of the two leading West German homeopathic laboratories, Schwabe and Heel. Its total sales were almost $130 million in 1988, 90 percent of which occurred within France.

The company experienced continued growth at home and abroad through the first half of the 1990s as an increasingly liberalized European drug market created opportunities for niche companies in the healthcare sector. Two EEC directives in 1992 provided a legal framework for homeopathic remedies at the European Union level, which led to recognition of the status of homeopathic medicine in all member states and a procedure for registering homeopathic remedies. In 1990, Sibourg laboratories of Marseille, France, another producer of homeopathic medicines, merged with Boiron, and in the years following, competition intensified between Boiron and Dolisos. Also in the early 1990s, Boiron took advantage of the times to launch a line of food supplements called Bioptimum through pharmacies in France.

Boiron's French business slowed in 1994, but all foreign subsidiaries showed a profit for the first time that year, accounting for more than 36 percent of its profits. Sales continued to remain level in France in 1995, while international sales increased 5 percent. The situation at home notwithstanding, in 1995 Boiron built a new production facility in Messimy near Lyon. In the late 1990s, France still accounted for close to three quarters of all sales; however, when the French government capped homeopathic drug prices, the domestic market further stagnated. By 1996, when sales for the company reached $217 million, only about 73 percent of revenues occurred within France. Foreign sales grew by almost 20 percent in 1996.

Boiron also continued to develop its pharmacy market in the second half of the 1990s. Moving into the phytotherapy market, it launched a range of 16 plant-based skin, face, and hair care products, called Soins Quotidiens (Daily Care), for distribution through pharmacies only in 1996. In 1997, after two years

Key Dates:

1932: Henri and Jean Boiron establish the Laboratoire Central Homéopathique de France in Paris.

1933: René Baudry and Henri Boiron take over the development of the Laboratoires Homéopathiques Modernes (LHM) in Paris; Jean Boiron oversees development of the Pharmacie Homéopathique Rhodanienne (PHR) in Lyon.

1941: The Boiron brothers begin their independent business under the trademark PHR.

1967: The Laboratoires Homeopathiques Jean Boiron (PHR), the Laboratoires Homéopathiques Henri Boiron (LHM), and the Laboratoires Homéopathiques Modernes merge to form Laboratoire Boiron.

1968: The company opens its distribution facility in Toulouse.

1974: Laboratoire Boiron moves its head offices and production plant to Ste. Foy-lès-Lyon.

1983: Christian Boiron succeeds Jean Boiron as chairman; the company acquires John Borneman & Sons.

1985: The Institut Boiron opens.

1987: Boiron stock is offered on the Lyon Stock Exchange.

1988: Laboratoires Boiron merges with Laboratoires Homéopathiques de France.

1989: Boiron acquires a 35 percent interest in Unda of Belgium.

1990: Boiron purchases Les Laboratoires Sibourg.

2003: The company opens its HERBAXT industrial site in the Paris region.

2005: Boiron purchases UNDA.

of research and development, the company introduced classical herbal remedies in gel form. This introduction put Boiron in direct competition for the phytotherapy market in France with Arkopharma, which had entered the homeopathy market there in 1991.

During the second half of the 1990s, with the homeopathic world market worth about $21 billion, Boiron embarked on a trail of international expansion, moving into Eastern Europe and the United States and starting to penetrate the South American and Asian markets. Growth in the United States was initially slow despite 1,000 doctors and 4,000 healthcare professionals prescribing homeopathic remedies; however, by 1998, Boiron's U.S. market was increasing by about 5 to 10 percent annually to reach about $12 million in 1997. In 1999, Boiron acquired a 35 percent interest in Unda, Belgium's main homeopathic specialty company. To accommodate its international expansion, in the late 1990s Boiron instituted a new management structure, beginning in distribution and extending next to production and administration.

By 2000, Boiron had around 3,000 strains for developing homeopathic remedies. Homeopathic medicines were used in more than 75 countries, mainly in Europe. Despite the leveling off of the French market, France still remained the biggest market for homeopathic medicine in the world, with 40 percent of the population using remedies at least occasionally, and in 2003, the company opened its HERBAXT industrial site in the Paris region to specialize in the production of trace elements. Also in 2003, Boiron launched Camilia, the first homeopathic medicine in bottle packs for teething and Verrulia, a medicine in tablet form for treating warts. Camilia became the second most recommended over-the-counter product of the year at the Quotipharm trade fair. In addition, Boiron's Oscillococcinum flu remedy, became one of the most widely used homeopathic medicines in the world around that time.

The French government dealt a blow to homeopathy in January 2004, when it suddenly reduced coverage of homeopathic medicines from 65 to 35 percent. Then in September, the National Academy of Medicine launched an attack on homeopathic medicines, saying that they should not be covered by health insurance because they had not been proven in clinical trials. Both pronouncements met with opposition from the French public, and 650,000 physicians, pharmacists, and citizens signed a petition objecting to the reduction in reimbursement for prescribed homeopathic remedies.

Despite the official opposition to homeopathy, Boiron, which had been experiencing double-digit growth for the past several years, purchased Dolisos, one of its major competitors, from the French pharmaceuticals group Pierre Fabre in 2005. The merger meant that Boiron commanded 90 percent of the French homeopathy market. The company also increased its stake in Unda to 95 percent in 2005. Although homeopathic remedies still represented less than half a percent of the more than $450 billion world pharmaceutical market, Boiron was in a position to capitalize on a much larger share of that market.

Principal Subsidiaries

Unda; Boiron Srl; Boiron Inc.; Boiron Sociedad Iberica de Homeopatica; Boiron Canada Inc.; Boiron GmbH; Boiron Caraibes SARL; HERBAXT; Boiron CZ s.r.o.; Boiron SK s.r.o.; Boiron SP zoo; Boiron TN s.a.r.l.; Boiron RO s.r.l.; Boiron MA s.a.r.l.

Principal Competitors

A. Nelson & Co. Ltd.; Arkopharma; NBTY.

Further Reading

"Boiron in USA Pushes Alternative Medicines," *Nutraceuticals International*, December 1998.

"French Homeopathic Drugs Competition," *Pharma Marketletter*, May 4, 1992.

Graham, George, "Spreading Homeopathic Message," *Financial Times*, January 4, 1989, p. 21.

Ollivier, Debra, "Homeopathy," *Health & Body*, March 16, 2000.

—Carrie Rothburd

Busch Entertainment Corporation

231 South Bemiston, Suite 600
St. Louis, Missouri 63105
U.S.A.
Telephone: (314) 577-2000
Fax: (314) 613-6049
Web sites: http://www.4adventure.com
           http://www.anheuser-busch.com

Wholly Owned Subsidiary of Anheuser-Busch Companies, Inc.
Incorporated: 1959
Employees: 15,000
Sales: $923.9 million (2003)
NAIC: 713110 Amusement and Theme Parks; 722110
   Full-Service Restaurants

Busch Entertainment Corporation is the entertainment subsidiary of Anheuser Busch Companies, Inc., operating nine theme parks in the United States and maintaining an equity position in an amusement facility located overseas. Busch Entertainment ranks as the third largest theme park operator in the United States. The company owns Busch Gardens in Tampa, Florida, an African-theme park, and Busch Gardens in Williamsburg, Virginia, which replicates 17th-century European villages. The company owns SeaWorld parks in San Diego, California; Orlando, Florida; and San Antonio, Texas. Other properties include water park attractions in Tampa, Williamsburg, and Langhorne, Pennsylvania, where Adventure Island, Water Country USA, and Sesame Place are located, respectively. Busch Entertainment also operates Discovery Cove, a reservations-only attraction in Orlando that offers guests the opportunity to interact with marine animals. Through a Spanish affiliate, Busch Entertainment owns 13.3 percent of Port Aventura, S.A., which operates a theme park near Barcelona, Spain.

Origins

When Eberhard Anheuser, with the help of his son-in-law, Adolphus Busch, began brewing beer in 1852, the sole focus of the company was beer. A century later, after holding sway as the "King of Beers" for decades, the company could entertain other business interests. Busch Entertainment became one of those extracurricular interests, a subsidiary devoted to managing the brewer's diversification into the amusement park business. The move into what became the entertainment facet of Anheuser Busch Companies, Inc. was made by August "Gussie" Busch, Jr., and from the start one of the primary objectives of running an amusement park was to use it to promote the brewer's brands of beer.

Eberhard Anheuser passed day-to-day control of the company to Adolphus Busch in the 1870s, marking the start of a Busch family dynasty that continued into the 21st century. Adolphus Busch died in 1913, leading to the appointment of his son, August A. Busch, as the leader of the nation's largest brewing concern. Adolphus Busch III was next in line, guiding the company until shortly after the end of World War II, when August A. Busch's son, August A. "Gussie" Busch, Jr., was named president, inheriting a company renowned for its aggressive and effective advertising. August Busch, Jr., embraced the legacy handed to him and threw himself into promoting the company's brands, restoring the preeminence of Anheuser-Busch, Inc., as it was then known, after the company briefly relinquished its lead in the industry following World War II. One of the ways August Busch, Jr., sought to promote the company's beer labels was by opening an entertainment park. In 1959, 20 years before Busch Entertainment was formed, August Busch, Jr., opened a complex in Tampa named Busch Gardens. It was "Gussie Busch's idea of combining a bird garden and beer garden," August Busch, Jr.'s great-granddaughter said in an April 25, 1994 interview with *Amusement Business.*

The original vision of August Busch, Jr.'s entertainment attraction changed markedly over the years. The theme-park arm of Anheuser Busch would be neither a bird garden nor a beer garden, but the tie-in of operating amusement parks with the promotion of the company's beer brands did exist from 1959 forward. The Tampa Busch Gardens was expanded in 1962, one year before the company broke ground on a second Busch Gardens in Los Angeles. More pertinent to Busch Entertainment's future was the opening of a Busch Gardens in Williamsburg in 1975. The Los Angeles Busch Gardens did not last, but it was historically significant because it reflected the company's commitment to developing further its theme-park branch. The Williamsburg Busch Gardens, as the concept of the company's theme-park business evolved, offered a different attraction than the Tampa Busch Gardens. In Tampa, guests were treated to an African-themed park that contained one of the largest collections of wildlife under private ownership. Williamsburg offered an interpretation of 17th-century Europe, featuring representations of village-life in Germany, France, England, and Scotland.

As Anheuser Busch's theme-park business matured, it grew through internal development and through external means, blossoming into a chain of facilities that were either established by the company or acquired from other operators. Before further development of the theme-park business continued, the existing assets were organized into a distinct entity. In 1979, 20 years after "Gussie" Busch opened Anheuser Busch's first park, Busch Entertainment Corporation was formed as a subsidiary, giving the former division the corporate structure to accommodate its growth. Expansion resumed the following year, adding considerably to the managerial duties of the new subsidiary. In 1980, the same year Italy was added to the roster of cultures on display in Williamsburg, two new parks were added to Anheuser Busch's entertainment subsidiary, both developed by the company. In June, Adventure Island Water Park was opened, a 36-acre attraction featuring water-play areas that was situated next to the 335-acre Tampa Busch Gardens. The following month, the company unveiled Sesame Place in Langhorne, Pennsylvania, a family-oriented park jointly developed with The Children's Television Workshop, the creator of the seminal television show *Sesame Street.*

SeaWorld Acquisition: 1989

Busch Entertainment entered the 1980s organized as a distinct entity under the Anheuser Busch corporate umbrella. The company had four parks under its control when the decade began, a total that would more than double by the end of the 1980s when Busch Entertainment's management set its sights on a company created by four graduates of the University of California Los Angeles (UCLA). During the early 1960s, the group of graduates discussed building an underwater restaurant, an idea that was not technically feasible, but one that led to the founding of Mission Bay Research Foundation in 1963 and the development of a concept capable of becoming a reality. Backed by an initial investment of $1.5 million, the UCLA graduates built a marine zoological park on 22 acres along the shore of San Diego's Mission Bay. In 1964, the park, staffed with 45 employees and featuring a Japanese village, a Lagoon Stadium, and a number of dolphins, seal lions, and two seawater aquariums, opened to the public, marking the debut of SeaWorld.

SeaWorld was a success from the start. During its first year, the park, operating as a private partnership, drew more than

400,000 visitors. In 1965, the first killer whale was brought before audiences, the first of numerous attractions added to the popular marine zoological park. In 1968, SeaWorld offered its stock to the public in a bid to raise capital for expansion, leading to the establishment of the second SeaWorld in Aurora, Ohio, in 1970. A third SeaWorld, located in Orlando, Florida, followed, debuting in 1973. SeaWorld proved to be a replicable concept, capable of thriving in markets as dissimilar as San Diego and suburban Cleveland. Harcourt Brace Jovanovich, Inc., a publishing and insurance firm, seized the opportunity to acquire SeaWorld in 1976. Under Harcourt Brace's ownership, SeaWorld in 1988 opened the world's largest marine theme park, a SeaWorld located in San Antonio. The 250-acre, $170 million park took three years to plan and build, and it would be the last SeaWorld project overseen by Harcourt Brace. Saddled with debt, the company was forced to sell its four SeaWorld parks and another park, Cypress Gardens in Winter Haven, Florida.

A bidding war for Harcourt Brace's park assets began in 1989. Among the interested suitors were MCA, Inc. and Walt Disney Co., but Busch Entertainment came away with the prize, paying $1.1 billion for the four SeaWorld parks, Cypress Gardens, and Orlando-based Boardwalk and Baseball, a combined amusement park and baseball stadium that later was closed. The acquisition added more than $500 million in revenue to Busch Entertainment's annual total and gave the company a powerful new vehicle to promote its other parks and its parent company's beer. A little more than a year after the acquisition was completed, the company announced plans to invest tens of millions of dollars in a new master plan for the San Diego SeaWorld that included horse stables for Anheuser Busch's iconic Clydesdale horses and a new Anheuser Busch Hospitality Center, complete with a beer garden and an exhibit area about the history of Anheuser Busch, patterned after similar centers in the company's other parks.

Busch Entertainment entered the 1990s facing increased competition from its rivals. Six Flags, Inc., Universal Parks & Resorts, and Walt Disney Parks & Resorts, the largest players in the industry, represented formidable foes, forcing Busch Entertainment to expand and to consistently revamp its attractions, shows, and rides. The company also faced competition from family entertainment centers and Las Vegas attractions, among others. "The industry is changing," a Busch Entertainment executive observed in an April 25, 1994 interview with *Amusement Business.* "There are more smaller entities in the picture." The company kept pace by continuing to expand, acquiring Water Country USA, its 10th park, in 1992. A 450-acre complex located near the Williamsburg Busch Gardens, Water Country USA featured more than 30 water attractions. The addition of Water Country USA and record attendance at the Tampa Busch Gardens enabled the company to draw more than 19 million people to all its parks in 1993, an all-time high.

Busch Entertainment in the 2000s

Busch Entertainment was able to register record growth during the recessive early 1990s, but when the next economic downturn loomed the company did not rest on its laurels. The beginning of the 21st century brought economic conditions that did not encourage leisure travel, prompting Busch Entertainment to implement marketing strategies to promote visits to its parks. The company began its new marketing program in 2000 with the introduction of Florida Fun Cards as a way to boost its rolls of season pass holders. Florida residents, who constituted the bulk of the company's season pass holders, were offered the opportunity to obtain a seven-month pass for the price of a single admission. The promotion proved to be highly successful, flooding the parks in Florida with visitors and leading the company to introduce a marketing program for all its parks. Busch Entertainment began issuing Passport cards in 2001, a program with Bronze, Silver, Gold, and, in some areas, Platinum tiers that offered an ascending level of rewards, such as early entry or line-jumping privileges. The company's tiered loyalty program dramatically increased the number of season pass holders and gave the company a vast database of names, addresses, and telephone numbers to aid in its marketing efforts. "That Passport card gets in people's pockets and some will come back and some won't," the editor of a trade publication explained in a September 2, 2002 interview with *Amusement Business*. "Busch looks to see who uses it and hits them up next year by saying for $20 more you can get free parking and discounts on food and beverages. The next year they'll work their way up and pitch Platinum."

The introduction of Busch Entertainment's tiered loyalty program and its success occurred at a welcomed time. The influence of the economic downturn was exacerbated by reverberations from the terrorist attacks of September 11, 2001, which dealt another debilitating blow to amusement park owners because of anxieties about flying. By relying on Passport to boost season pass rolls and by targeting marketing in areas within a 500- to 600-mile radius from its parks, Busch Entertainment prospered during difficult times. Aside from adopting a new, more focused marketing stance, the company also made several other important moves during the first years of the decade. The Aurora SeaWorld was sold to Six Flags in early 2001, replaced by another property, Discovery Cove. Located in Orlando, Discovery Cove was unique in that it was a reservations-only park. Situated adjacent to the Orlando SeaWorld, the park offered its guests the opportunity to interact with marine life, featuring swims with dolphins, explorations of an aviary, and snorkeling along a coral reef.

As Busch Entertainment prepared for its future, the company was supported by nine, well-established theme parks. The properties generated record earnings in 2004, the 45th anniversary of Anheuser Busch's entry into the amusement park industry. The profits generated by Busch Entertainment provided its parent company with $173 million in operating profits, not a major reward for a company that netted $2.2 billion in 2004, but the value of the amusement parks as a promotional tool added an intangible worth to the contributions of Busch Entertainment. Its relationship with its parent company aside, the company ranked as the third largest theme park operator in the United States, an impressive industry standing that the company likely would not easily surrender in the years ahead.

Principal Subsidiaries

Busch Entertainment Company International, Inc.; SeaWorld, Inc.; SeaWorld of Florida, Inc.; SeaWorld of Texas, Inc.; Port Aventura, S.A. (13.3%).

Principal Competitors

Six Flags, Inc.; Universal Parks & Resorts; Walt Disney Parks & Resorts.

Further Reading

Aronson, Emily, "Post 9/11 Strategy: Theme Parks Find Success Targeting Regional Audiences," *Advertising Age,* July 29, 2002, p. 12.
Beirne, Mike, "After Unexpected Attendance Surge, Busch Tends to Gardens, Seaworld," *Brandweek,* February 18, 2002, p. 9.
——, "Getting to Know You," *Brandweek,* September 2, 2002, p. 14.
Brydolf, Libby, "Busch Puts Its Stamp on Sea World," *San Diego Business Journal,* September 16, 1991, p. 1.
Diamond, Randy, "Busch Gardens Keeps Tampa, Fla., Park Open into the Night to Attract Crowds," *Tampa Tribune,* July 26, 2004, p. B2.
Emmons, Natasha, "*Shrek, Haunted Lighthouse* Make 4-D Debuts with Busch, Universal," *Amusement Business,* January 27, 2003, p. 7.
Hardin, Angela Y., "SeaWorld's Latest Goes Under the Sea," *Crain's Cleveland Business,* September 27, 1999, p. 3.
"Kasen New Busch President," *Amusement Business,* March 10, 2003, p. 5.
Lewis, Connie, "Executive Profile: Dennis Burks," *San Diego Business Journal,* August 16, 2004, p. 39.
Magenheim, Henry, "Busch Parks Ready for Competition," *Travel Weekly,* May 28, 1990, p. 46.
O'Brien, Tim, "Busch Gardens Williamsburg," *Amusement Business,* October 28, 2002, p. 3.
Panczyk, Tania D., "Busch Gardens to Try Branding: DDB Ads Push Message of Togetherness," *ADWEEK Midwest Edition,* February 18, 2002, p. 3.
——, "Seaworld Seeks Ideas," *ADWEEK Southwest,* February 18, 2002, p. 6.
Powell, Tom, "Busch Parks Looking Forward to Another Banner Season," *Amusement Business,* April 25, 1994, p. 1.
Rodrigues, Tanya, "A Full Plate," *San Diego Business Journal,* March 19, 2001, p. 50.

—Jeffrey L. Covell

CALGON CARBON CORPORATION

Calgon Carbon Corporation

400 Calgon Carbon Drive
Pittsburgh, Pennsylvania 15205
U.S.A.
Telephone: (412) 787-6700
Toll Free: (800) 422-7266
Fax: (412) 787-4511
Web site: http://www.calgoncarbon.com

Public Company
Incorporated: 1985
Employees: 1,150
Sales: $336.6 million (2004)
Stock Exchanges: New York
Ticker Symbol: CCC
NAIC: 325998 All Other Miscellaneous Chemical
    Product and Preparation Manufacturing

Calgon Carbon Corporation is a Pittsburgh, Pennsylvania-based public company dedicated to granular activated carbon, a material that has the ability to absorb odors and chemical pollutants. Calgon Carbon divides its business into four units. The Activated Carbon unit is dedicated to the manufacture of 100 types of granular, powdered, and pelletized activated carbon products at four facilities located in the United States and China. The unit also sells custom-designed carbon adsorption, or particle collection, systems. The company's Engineered Systems division helps customers to design and build water purification and disinfection systems, odor control systems, and solvent recovery and distillation systems that rely on carbon adsorption as well as ultraviolet light and ion exchange separation technologies. The Services Options unit maintains air and water purification systems for customers on a fee basis, as well as picking up spent carbon for reactivation. Finally, the company's Consumer Products unit uses activated carbon to make carbon cloth, charcoal briquettes, and consumer products that include Purrfectly Fresh, a pet and household odor remover; PreZerve, tarnish-preventing jewelry storage products; and BreatheSafe, a washable respirator mask capable of filtering odors, gases, mists, fumes, and dust. Calgon Carbon also

maintains a European operation, Chemviron Carbon, based in Brussels.

Company Roots Dating to World War II

Calgon Carbon grew out of the Pittsburgh Coke & Chemical Company, Inc., which in 1942 as part of its military effort during World War II developed a way to use coal-based activated carbon in gas masks. As described by *Forbes* in a 1988 article, "Coal is 'activated' by heating it to temperatures as high as 1,800 degrees Fahrenheit, which opens up the coal's minute pore structure. When liquids or gases pass through the activated carbon, organic chemicals are attracted and cling to the coal grains' vast network of surfaces. Vast? One pound of activated carbon, which looks a lot like a pound of ground coffee, has a total surface area of 125 acres." After World War II the company's Activated Carbon Division continued its pioneering efforts, in the mid-1950s developing a sugar decolorization process using activated carbon and in 1960 finding a way to use granulated activated carbon to purify water. Two years later the division supplied 40,000 pounds of granular activated carbon for the groundbreaking water treatment system installed by the Virginia-American Carbon Company. Now called the Pittsburgh Activated Carbon Company, the business was acquired by Calgon Corporation in 1965, where it retained its autonomy, responsible for its own manufacturing and marketing. The unit changed corporate parents in 1968 when Calgon Corporation was acquired by pharmaceutical company Merck & Co., Inc. At the time, the activated carbon division, renamed Calgon Carbon, was generating about $11 million in annual revenues.

As the United States began setting more stringent clear air and water standards, Merck believed that there was major growth potential for activated carbon. Those expectations were heightened by the passage of the Safe Water Drinking Act and the Clean Water Act in the early 1970s. To make its products even more attractive, the company began offering its water treatment equipment on a lease basis, with trained company personnel providing maintenance. Calgon Carbon believed that not only was there business to be done in the United States but in Europe as well. In 1970 the company formed Chemviron Carbon, S.A. in Brussels in order to market its products, engineering services, and water pollution systems in Europe. Later in the decade Calgon Carbon looked to the Far East, in 1978 creating a joint venture with Mitsui Chemicals, Inc. and Mitsui & Co., Ltd. to serve markets in Japan, Korea, Taiwan, and later on in China.

Failed Investments in the 1970s and Management Buyout in the 1980s

During the 1970s Merck invested heavily to increase Calgon Carbon's production capacity, spending $75 million to open new activated carbon production and reactivation facilities in the United States, Belgium, and the United Kingdom. Merck was not alone in its belief that the market for activated carbon was about to explode because of environmental legislation. Competitors Westvaco and Carborundum also built new plants. By the end of July 1977 the water industry was supposed to be in compliance with the Clean Water Act. As the company manager at the time, Thomas McConomy, recalled in a 1991 *Executive Report* interview, ''Newspapers were full of all this being required, who was in compliance, who wasn't. The date came and went and nothing happened. No increased demand. Then a competitor started up a new production plant and they were hell-bent to sell it out so they cut prices, and margins were hurt.'' To make matters worse the United States implemented a payment in kind (PIK) program with farmers, providing them with certain materials in storage in lieu of growing crops. ''One of the big markets we were serving at that time was water treatment for the agricultural chemical industry,'' McConomy explained. ''Well, PIK drove them completely out of the game. And Merck said, this is not our business.'' Calgon Carbon's sales hovered around the $100 million mark, and in 1982 net income totaled $6.6 million, a far cry from the 15 percent on gross assets that Merck's management desired.

Merck put Calgon Carbon up for sale, attracting three offers, but the deal Merck chose fell through. Frustrated by the situation, McConomy began thinking about a leveraged buyout to take the company private and allow it to control its own future. McConomy had grown up in the Pittsburgh area, earned a chemical engineering degree from Carnegie Mellon University in 1955, gone to work for Calgon Carbon's predecessor, and begun making his way up the ranks of management. Once he became interested in buying the business McConomy sought advice from his brother, a partner at the Pittsburgh law firm of Reed Smith Shaw & McClay, who put him in contact with one of the firm's attorneys, Harry Weil. One afternoon over lunch, the two men sketched out some numbers on the back of a menu, according to McConomy (and on the back of a napkin according to Weil). McConomy then approached an investment banker, a former Calgon Carbon salesman who had intimate knowledge of the business. After he also received positive feedback about the idea of a management buyout from a local bank, Mc-

Conomy in January 1984 met with Merck President John Huck and broached the subject. ''John looked at me, then swung around in his chair and stared out the window for about five minutes,'' according to McConomy's recollection. ''He finally swung back around and said, all right, if you can make us a fair offer and you have an idea of where the money is coming from, we will give full consideration to it.''

McConomy recruited four other managers to join him in the buyout. Together they were only able to scrape together $817,000, of which $325,000 came from McConomy, who mortgaged his house, borrowed against insurance policies, and cashed in stock options early. Despite the lack of cash, McConomy was able to meet with the president of Merck's specialty chemicals division and make his pitch about Calgon Carbon's potential, maintaining that prices would soon stabilize and competitors were likely to drop out. At the very least McConomy kept his group in the game and was told to come back with an offer when they had secured their financing.

A year would pass before the management group was able to cobble together a $90 million package to buy Calgon Carbon, composed of $77.5 million in cash, a $5 million note, and $7.5 million in preferred stock. In addition, Merck held a $10 million note that became payable if Calgon Carbon went public within 20 years or other specified events occurred. The deal was almost scuttled at the 11th hour when the principal lender, Citibank, continued to try to extract better terms. Despite the risk, McConomy decided to ditch Citibank. He now turned to Bankers Trust, where he found more than a receptive lender. The bank, to his surprise, pitched him on why he should do business with them. In the end, Bankers Trust lent $51 million, Travelers Insurance contributed $25 million, and Teachers Insurance & Annuity Association bought one million shares for $500,000 and lent another $9.5 million. Teachers also received warrants to purchase 3.5 million shares. On April 1, 1985 the buyout was completed and Calgon Carbon Corporation was born.

McConomy and his managers were assuming a great deal of risk in what was one of the most highly leveraged management buyouts (LBOs) of an era filled with LBOs. Interest payments alone totaled almost $9 million a year, at a time when the company's cash flow was $11.3 million. But McConomy's rosy scenario of what awaited Calgon Carbon turned out to be understated. Competitors dropped out, sales surged, interest rates dropped, and the company's new production processes lowered costs. As a result, sales reached $138 million and net income totaled $11.4 million, well above management's projections. Business was so strong that the company was actually in danger of being victimized by its success. The deal struck with Teachers now became an issue. As McConomy explained to *Executive Report,* Teachers ''had warrants that could have taken their total holdings to 45 percent. Under our agreement, beginning [1991], they could have forced the company to buy those warrants and that stock from them. And it was to be at a certain multiple of earnings. . . . We would have actually had to releverage the company even more than it was originally leveraged, to pay Teachers.''

Because Teachers had never intended to become a long-term investor, Calgon Carbon offered the insurer a chance to cash out after just two years, offering to buy back half of its holdings at a premium, and then take the company public. Teachers agreed, the other lenders acquiesced, and in 1987 Calgon Carbon made an initial public offering (IPO) of stock. As a result, Teachers' $500,000 investment turned into a $77 million windfall. In addition, Merck was in line for another $13.4 million, the $10 million note plus interest that was triggered by the IPO. Calgon Carbon also benefited from the offering, which raised $30 million used to pay down the company's sizable debt.

Calgon Carbon prospered for the rest of the 1980s. After more than doubling in price the stock was split, as sales and earnings continued to build. About $40 million in sales came from the 1988 purchase of Degussa AG, a West German charcoal producer. At the start of the 1990s the company earned $38 million on sales of $285 million, but conditions would soon begin to deteriorate. Activated carbon was such an important material that most people considered it recession-proof, but the recession of the early 1990s dispelled that notion. Sales to municipalities, which accounted for 17 percent of sales, dried up. Revenues reached $308 million in 1991 and then began to slip. Two years later sales dropped to $269 million.

Introducing New Products in the Mid-1990s

Colin Bailey, a member of the management team that bought Calgon Carbon from Merck, was named CEO in 1994, while McConomy stayed on as chairman. Under Bailey the company launched a new line of purification products in an effort to improve the company's fortunes. After ten years of research and development the company introduced the Centaur family of activated carbon products with enhanced adsorptive ability and catalytic capabilities, making the material suitable for a wide range of commercial and home uses. Bailey also tried to grow the company through acquisitions, completing three deals in 1996. The company supplemented its activated carbon business by adding the perox-pure operations of Vulcan Peroxidations Systems, Inc. and Canada's Solarchem Enterprises, to become the world leader in advanced oxidation. Also in 1996 Calgon Carbon bought Advanced Separation Technologies Incorporated, a chromatographic separation equipment manufacturer, a transaction that proved less than satisfactory and led to Calgon Carbon suing the company's previous owners for misrepresentations and breaches of warranties in the acquisition agreement. A better fit was another 1996 acquisition, Charcoal Cloth (International) Ltd., a U.K. manufacturer of cloth-infused activated carbon.

Although Calgon Carbon added significantly to its sales, the acquisitions failed to live up to expectations, resulting in a sagging stock price. Bailey resigned suddenly in late February 1998, citing philosophical differences with the board, and McConomy stepped in as CEO on an interim basis. The company also hired Morgan Stanley & Co. to consider how best to maximize shareholder value. Calgon Carbon was soon put up for sale, but the bids were so low, reportedly half of the desired $13 to $15 range, that the company did not even bother to negotiate with any of the lukewarm suitors. Instead, the company elected to remain independent and made an effort to live within its means. A restructuring plan was implemented that included a 10 percent cut in payroll.

A new CEO, Jim Cederna, was hired in July 1999; he also would replace McConomy as chairman. He boasted more than 20 years of experience with Dow Chemical Company, where he gained a wide range of experience in research, commercial development, and sales as well as management. He did a great deal to restore morale at the company, which had seen the price of its stock sag to the $5 level and sales tail off. During Cederna's tenure, Calgon Carbon began offering consumer products in 2000, some of which were sold on QVC Inc.'s Home Shopping Network. They included Purrfectly Fresh, PreZerve, and WaveZorb, a product that protected cellular telephone uses from microwave radiation. Under Cederna, the company also established a manufacturing plant in China and created a joint venture with Mitsubishi Chemical Corporation of Tokyo to manufacture and sell activated carbon products and provide related services in Japan. But in the end Cederna's plan to broaden Calgon Carbon's customer base beyond municipalities and industrial clients to general consumers failed to gain enough traction to offset the loss of traditional sales to cheaper foreign competition. Sales fell from $270.6 million in 2001 to $258.1 million in 2002, both years in which the company reported sizable losses and the price of the company's stock fell as low as $4.

Cederna resigned in February 2003, replaced as acting chairman by McConomy and acting CEO by John Stanik, a 12-year veteran of the company. A few weeks later the board made both appointments permanent. The company's business rebounded somewhat in 2003, as the company returned to profitability on sales of $278.3 million. Calgon Carbon also developed a three-year plan to grow the business and acquired a company, Waterlink Specialty Products, in a deal that was completed in 2004. Waterlink supplied carbon-based air and water purification equipment to both the United States (through Barnebey Sutcliff Corp.) and the United Kingdom. Seven new products were introduced in 2003, which flowed out of the new Business Development Organization. The company had to contend with rising costs and competitive price pressure, yet enjoyed another year of improved performance in 2004, when sales reached $336.6 million and income totaled $5.9 million. On balance, management believed that the company was once again headed in the right direction.

Principal Subsidiaries

Chemviron Carbon GmbH; Calgon Carbon Canada, Inc.; Chemviron Carbon Ltd.; Solarchem Environmental Systems, Inc.; Charcoal Cloth Limited; Advanced Separation Technologies Incorporated.

Principal Competitors

MeadWestvaco Corporation; WEDECO AG Water Technology; USFilter Corporation.

Further Reading

Baughmanand, Hank, and David Hasley, "Pittsburgh's Newest $100 Million Man," *Executive Report,* May 1, 1991, p. 18.

Davis, Christopher, "Calgon Carbon Looks to Purchase to Expand Geographic Reach, Product Line," *Pittsburgh Business Times,* February 13, 2004, p. 6.

Gannon, Joyce, "Pittsburgh-Area Calgon Carbon CEO Makes Quick, Quiet Exit," *Pittsburgh Post-Gazette,* February 26, 2003.

Meeks, Fleming, "Perfect Timing," *Forbes,* June 13, 1988, p. 58.

Teaff, Rick, "McConomy Activating Public Calgon Carbon," *Pittsburgh Business Times,* February 20, 1989, p. 1.

——, "Officers Retaining Control in Calgon IPO," *Pittsburgh Business Times,* May 11, 1987, p. 1.

—Ed Dinger

China Netcom Group Corporation (Hong Kong) Limited

Bldg. C, No. 156 Fuxingmennei Avenue, Xicheng
   District
Beijing 100031
China
46 Floor, Cheung Kong Centre
2 Queen's Road Central
Hong Kong
Telephone: +852 2626 8888
Fax: +852 2626 8862
Fax: +8610 6642 9253
Web site: http://www.china-netcom.com

Public Company
Incorporated: 1999
Employees: 150,000
Sales: CNY 64.9 billion ($7.84 billion) (2004)
Stock Exchanges: Hong Kong
Ticker Symbol: CNC
NAIC: 517110 Wired Telecommunications Carriers;
   334210 Telephone Apparatus Manufacturing; 334220
   Radio and Television Broadcasting and Wireless
   Communications Equipment Manufacturing; 334290
   Other Communication Equipment Manufacturing;
   517212 Cellular and Other Wireless Telecommuni-
   cations; 517910 Other Telecommunications

China Netcom Group Corporation (Hong Kong) Limited is
the Hong Kong Stock Exchange-listed arm of state-controlled
China Network Communications Group (China Netcom), formed
from the breakup of the China Telecom monopoly. China Netcom represents the merger of the northern China operations of the
former China Telecom, including the cities of Beijing and Tianjin, and eight provinces, including Hebei, Henan, Shandong, and
Liaoning, in northern China, with broadband pioneer China Netcom and data communications group Jitong Communications.
China Netcom provides telecommunications and broadband and
Internet services, including IP-based telephony and television
services, as well as mobile telecommunications services through

Xiao Ling Tong. China Netcom controls about 30 percent of the
total national fixed-line network, including 35 percent of the
country's fixed-line customers and 30 percent of broadband
users. China Netcom's total subscriber base includes more than
80 million fixed-line subscribers, more than 15 million Xiao Ling
Tong subscribers, and 6.9 million broadband subscribers. The
company also has access to southern China's Shanghai Municipality and Guangdong Province, although the southern region
remains dominated by market leader China Telecom Corporation
Ltd.. China Netcom is ranked third in the market, behind China
Mobile Communications Corporation. China Netcom itself remains a state-owned company; the successful listing of its Hong
Kong subsidiary in 2004 has provided the company with funding
to pursue further expansion, both in China and into the greater
Asia-Pacific Region. China Netcom is led by CEO Edward Tian.
In 2004, the company posted revenues of nearly CNY 65 billion
($7.8 billion).

Building China's Internet Infrastructure in the 1990s

Telecommunications played only a marginal role in China,
despite the introduction of the first telephone services there in
1882. Yet no effort was made to create an integrated telegraph
and telephone network in the country through the first half of
the 20th century. Telephone use remained the perquisite of
Chinese royalty, high-ranking government officials, and the
wealthy. By the late 1940s, only about 10 percent of the country's provinces had any kind of telephone service and the total
subscriber base barely reached 0.05 percent of the population.

Telecommunications took on a greater role following the
Communist revolution of 1949 and the creation of the People's
Republic of China. The new government launched an effort to
wire the country's largest cities during the first of its many Five-
Year Plans, forming a network centered on Beijing. Over the
next several decades, Beijing remained the hub of the country's
telecommunications network, as it extended to the country's
other major cities. Nonetheless, large portions of the country
continued to be left out of the telecommunications loop.

The desire of the hardline Communist government, especially during the Mao-led Cultural Revolution, to control the

flow of information in the country limited investment in the development of a full-scale telecommunications network. As such, into the late 1970s, as the country's population topped one billion people, only about two million telephone lines had been installed.

The launch of economic reforms at the end of the 1970s and the reform-minded government's greater openness to the international community led to increased investment in the telecommunications system. The network began to grow strongly, under the government-controlled monopoly China Telecom. By the early 1990s, China's total telephone lines had passed the ten million mark. By 1998, the country's telephone system had grown into one of the world's largest, in terms of subscriber lines, with more than 100 million. China Telecom itself had grown into a corporate behemoth, with some 500,000 employees.

China Telecom's unwieldy size, and its position as an arm of the Chinese government, meant that, despite its strong growth in the 1990s, the country's telecommunications network remained more or less closed to the new revolution in telecommunications—that of the Internet. Indeed, the Chinese government remained wary, as always, of allowing the free flow of information, and recognized that the nature of the Internet made the control of information difficult, if not impossible. The Chinese government, therefore, dragged its heels on the introduction of a public Internet in China, which was finally launched only in 1995, and then, only reluctantly.

Yet that year marked the arrival of a new player in the Chinese telecommunications market: Edward Tian. Born in 1963 to Soviet-trained parents, Tian was raised in a family which suffered greatly during the Cultural Revolution. Both of his parents were sent to the country's reeducation camps. The Tian family's house was taken over by the Red Guard, and Tian and his grandmother were forced to live in a single room.

Inspired by the new era promised by Deng Xiaoping after Mao's death in 1976, Tian excelled as a student, attending the elite Chinese Academy of Science. In the late 1980s, Tian and his wife went to study at Texas Tech, in Lubbock, Texas, where Tian earned a doctorate degree in biology. The Tians remained in Texas, raising their daughter. Yet Tian sought a means of contributing to China, particularly to the growing momentum of the country's economic and social reforms.

Tian's introduction to the Internet pointed the way to his return to China. In 1993, Tian and friend James Ding founded a new company, AsiaInfo, which began providing Chinese news services for the American market. By 1994, however, the company had set up a second company with offices in Beijing, and began producing software for the newly developing information

technology (IT) market. The company's breakthrough came in 1995, when Tian and Ding launched AsiaInfo in China in order to secure a contract for building the backbone for China Telecom's new commercial Internet service, ChinaNet.

AsiaInfo quickly emerged as one of the major players in China's new Internet market. By the late 1990s, the company had gone public, listing its shares on the NASDAQ. AsiaInfo then became the first nongovernment-controlled Chinese company to see its market value top $1 billion. Yet, by then, Tian was no longer overseeing AsiaInfo's growth.

Broadband Start-up in the 2000s

The development of the Internet became a source of contention among members of the Chinese government in the late 1990s. Whereas many government officials remained wary of the new technology, and reluctant to roll out high-speed technologies, others recognized that the sustained development of the country's economy depended on its ability to build a national broadband infrastructure. This appeared particularly true as the date approached for China's entry into the World Trade Organization, at which point the entry of foreign IT players threatened to steamroll over China's own slowly developing technological infrastructure.

Few of the proponents of faster broadband development believed in China Telecom's ability to adapt and expand broadband capacity, given the slow pace of its dial-up Internet growth. In 1999, therefore, four state-owned entities—the Academy of Sciences; Information and Network Center of State Administration of Radio, Film and Television (INC-SARFT); China Railways Telecommunications Center (CRTC); and Shanghai Alliance Investment Limited (Shanghai Alliance)—decided to found a new start-up company, called China Netcom.

For this the partners turned to Tian, and finally persuaded him to take the new company's CEO spot by offering him an unprecedented degree of autonomy. Each of the four founding shareholders also agreed to put up some $75 million in start-up costs.

China Netcom quickly began building its own fiber-optic-based network. For this, the company was aided by founding member CRTC, which agreed to allow the company to lay cable along its extensive railway network. China Netcom's early efforts were impressive: Just two months after launching construction of the network, China Netcom had extended the network to reach more than 8,500 kilometers. By the end of the first year, the company also had completed construction of ten of its proposed 50 data centers. China Netcom's fiber-optic network not only rivaled the scale of those built by Sprint and Qwest in the United States, it also boasted far higher broadband capacity, enough to offer virtually unlimited bandwidth for the entire Chinese market. In 2000, China Netcom boosted its network again when it launched construction of the 500,000-square-foot Super Internet Center in Beijing, with room for 100,000 servers, and its own power plant.

China Netcom's original business model was to serve as a wholesale bandwidth provider, selling bandwidth to China's mobile telephone network, cable television, and others. The company also began extending its network into the more ne-

Key Dates:

1882: The first telephone network is installed in China.
1992: Telephone lines top ten million for the first time.
1993: Edward Tian sets up his first business, AsiaInfo.
1994: Tian establishes his first company in China.
1995: The first commercial Internet network in China is launched; Tian establishes a new AsiaInfo, which begins building an Internet infrastructure.
1999: Tian is asked to become head of China Netcom, founded by a group of government agencies to develop a broadband Internet structure.
2002: The government breaks up the China Telecom monopoly and merges northern operations as well as Jitong Communications into China Netcom.
2003: China Netcom absorbs Jitong as part of its integration effort.
2004: China Netcom forms a Hong Kong subsidiary, which launches a public offering on the Hong Kong and New York Stock Exchanges.
2005: China Netcom begins negotiations to acquire fixed-line operations in four more northern provinces.

glected regions of China, connecting up schools, libraries, hospitals, and other facilities in towns and even cities that until then had not even been served by the country's telephone network. China Network then began offering IP-based telephony and other services as a means to ensure its cash flow and fuel its continued expansion. The company's fiber-optic network, meanwhile, soon boasted the lowest wholesale rates in the world. In this way, the company helped providers slash online access fees—which remained at more than CNY 1,000 a month at China Telecom—by a factor of ten.

Joining China's Telecom Leaders for the New Century

Despite its successes, China Netcom struggled against continued losses. By 2002, the company was said to be heading toward collapse. The company received a temporary lifeline when the government allowed it to sell a 12 percent stake to a group of foreign investors, including News Corp. and Goldman Sachs, for $325 million—a rare event, considering that foreign ownership in the Chinese telecommunications industry remained prohibited.

Near the end of 2001, however, China Netcom appeared to be in line for a more permanent solution to its financial woes. By then the Chinese government was preparing to break up China Telecom. The government's plan called for the telephone monopoly to be divided roughly in half, into its northern and southern operations. Tian, who represented not only Western-style management techniques, but who also had established himself as China's leading Internet personality, was tipped to take over as the northern telecom business's new head.

The "new" China Netcom was established with the breakup of the China Telecom monopoly in 2002. At that time, the Chinese government decided to merge northern operations of

China Telecom into the existing China Netcom. The merger brought control of the fixed-line telecommunications market in the major urban centers of Beijing and Tianjin, as well as in eight other northern provinces, giving China Netcom control of roughly 30 percent of the Chinese fixed-line market, a subscriber base of more than 80 million (placing it among the world's largest) and an employee payroll of more than 150,000 (compared with the original China Netcom's less than 3,000). Also joining the merger was another Chinese IT pioneer, Jitong Communications, which had been established in 1993. Tian remained at the head of the new telecommunications leader, which took third place in the Chinese market, trailing only China Telecom and the cellular phone group China Mobile Communications.

Merging the three companies, which had very different corporate cultures, proved difficult at the start. The three entities continued operating more or less independently—even competing against each other—in the first year. In 2003, however, Tian began the process of integrating the businesses, announcing China Netcom's intention to buy out the government's share in Jitong Communications, then absorb that company's operations into its own. China Netcom then began the slower process of extending its full control over the former China Telecom business.

In the meantime, China Netcom continued to eye growth, not only within the northern region, but into southern China and, ultimately, throughout the Asia-Pacific region. By 2004, the company had succeeded in gaining access to six more provinces in southern China. The company also sought new resources to fund its expansion. At the end of 2004, China Netcom created a new subsidiary in Hong Kong specifically as a vehicle for a public offering. That offering came in November 2004, with a dual listing on the Hong Kong and New York Stock Exchanges, which raised more than $1.1 billion for the company.

By the beginning of 2004, China Netcom boasted revenues of more than CNY 64 billion ($7.8 billion). The listed vehicle had taken over most of its parent's northern China operations. In 2005, the two companies began negotiations that would transfer four more provinces, including Heilongjiang, Jilin, Shanxi, and Inner Mongolia, to direct control by China Netcom Hong Kong. Meanwhile, China Netcom enjoyed steady growth in its core markets, boosting its subscriber base by more than 145 percent in 2004. China Netcom appeared poised to become a major world player in the Chinese—and international—telecommunications markets.

Principal Subsidiaries

China Network Communications Group Corporation (parent company); China Netcom (Group) Company Ltd.; China Netcom BVI Ltd.; Asia Netcom Corporation Ltd.

Principal Competitors

China Railway Communication Corporation; China Mobile Communications Corporation; China Telecom Corporation Ltd.; China Unicom Ltd.; UTStarcom China Ltd.; China United Telecommunications Corporation; Wuhan Hongxin Telecommunication Technologies Company Ltd.; Fiberhome Telecommunication Technologies Group; Changfeng Communication Group Company Ltd.

Further Reading

Chen Zhiming, ''Netcom IPO to Increase Expansion,'' *China Daily,* November 18, 2004.
''China Netcom Consolidates Position,'' *China Daily,* May 12, 2005.
''China Netcom in Talks to Buy from Parent,'' *China Daily,* April 28, 2005.

''China Netcom to Fund Expansion with IPO Proceeds,'' *People's Daily,* November 8, 2004.
''Chinese Telephone Users Ranking World's Second,'' *People's Daily,* December 13, 2000.
Kuo, Kaiser, ''China Netcom's Merger Pains,'' *Telecom Asia,* July 2003.
''Merger to Consolidate China Netcom,'' *China Daily,* June 12, 2003.
''Netcom Expects Major Gains from Telecom Restructuring,'' *China Daily,* September 4, 2001.
Sheff, David, ''Betting on Bandwidth,'' *Wired,* February 9, 2001.
Tuinstra, Fons, ''China's Net Plumber,'' *Asiaweek,* August 18, 2000.

—M.L. Cohen

City Brewing Company LLC

925 South Third Street
La Crosse, Wisconsin 54601
U.S.A.
Telephone: (608) 785-4200
Fax: (608) 785-4300
Web site: http://www.citybrewery.com

Private Company
Incorporated: 1858
Employees: 220
NAIC: 312120 Breweries

City Brewing Company LLC is one of the leading small regional beer breweries in the United States. The company was formerly the G. Heileman Brewing Company, which was a powerful midwestern beer manufacturer for much of its long history. Heileman rose to become one of the nation's largest beer companies by the 1980s, but then suffered through two bankruptcies and several changes of ownership, until its brands were sold off in 1999. City Brewery was then resurrected out of the remaining Heileman physical plant in La Crosse, Wisconsin. City Brewery produces several of its own beer brands, including City Lager and La Crosse Lager, and the company also brews and bottles for other beverage makers through its Midwest Beverage Packers division. Contract brewing and beverage packaging is actually by far the greater part of City Brewery's business, with only 2 to 3 percent of the company's capacity going to its own brands. City Brewery's own brands are sold principally in Wisconsin, Minnesota, Iowa, and northern Illinois.

From the 1850s Through Prohibition

Two German immigrants founded City Brewery in 1858 in La Crosse, Wisconsin. John Gund bought a small brewery in La Crosse in 1854 after leaving a brewery business in Galena, Illinois. Then in 1858 he formed a partnership with Gottlieb Heileman to build a new brewery in La Crosse, on the corner of Third and Mississippi Streets. This business was called City Brewery until 1872, when Gund sold Heileman his share and founded another La Crosse brewery, Empire Brewery. City

Brewery then continued under the name G. Heileman Brewing Co. Gottlieb Heileman died in 1878, and his widow Johanna carried on the business. By 1880 G. Heileman was the third largest brewery in La Crosse, producing some 2,500 barrels of beer a year. In 1902 the company copyrighted its Old Style lager, which went on to become one of its most popular products. The company was run by R.A. Albrecht from 1911 until 1933. Johanna Heileman died in 1917.

The United States enacted Prohibition in 1919, and from January 1920 until the Prohibition amendment was repealed in 1933, the manufacture and sale of beer and other alcoholic beverages was banned nationwide. Many breweries went under during this time, but Heileman survived by manufacturing a nonalcoholic drink called ''near beer.'' Heileman was able to continue to brew throughout Prohibition and to keep its physical plant in fine shape by switching to near beer, and as a result, when Prohibition was repealed, the company had no difficulty going back to regular beer. The company was reorganized as a public company on the New York Stock Exchange in 1933, and Harry Dahl became president. By 1934, G. Heileman had doubled the output of its best years before Prohibition. The company extended its business outside the Upper Midwest, shipping as far west as Montana. The company began selling some beer in cans in 1935, instead of only in oak barrels or glass bottles.

Becoming a National Player: 1950s–80s

G. Heileman named a new president in 1936, Albert J. Bates. Bates led the company through World War II. Bates moved the brewery into producing beers with broader consumer appeal and lower price. This apparently did not go well with G. Heileman's longtime customers, and sales fell. A new president, Ralph Johansen, took over from Bates in 1951. He was replaced by Roy F. Kumm in 1956. Kumm and his son-in-law Russell Cleary were credited with moving G. Heileman from a regional brewer to a big national company with a large stable of brands and subsidiaries in all corners of the country.

In 1960, G. Heileman relied on only two beer brands, Special Export and Old Style. Heileman's sales were concentrated in Wisconsin, Iowa, Minnesota, and Illinois. At that time, the beer industry was highly fragmented, with many small regional breweries selling in their local markets, while five big companies among them controlled a third of the total beer market nationwide. Faced with this market picture, Heileman decided that its best strategy was to grow big enough to compete nationally. The company bought a Kentucky brewer, Wiedemann, in 1967 and then bought a large but ailing Milwaukee brewer, Blatz, in 1969. In 1971, Roy Kumm died, and he was succeeded by Cleary in the presidency. By that year, the company was selling ten different beer brands, and it had extended its market through the Midwest into Indiana, Ohio, and Michigan, and was selling in the South, too, at least as far as Kentucky, Tennessee, and West Virginia.

Cleary had been trained as a lawyer and served as Heileman's general counsel while his father-in-law was president. Apparently, many in the beer industry regarded him as an outsider who had only made it to the top of the company through his family connections. Yet Cleary seemed to have a better grasp of beer industry dynamics than many ostensibly more qualified executives, and G. Heileman did extraordinarily well throughout the 1970s. Its sales volume increased on average 11 percent a year through the decade, and the company made more acquisitions and achieved more market share, while some of the country's leading brewers were beginning to have trouble. The company made a total of 13 acquisitions between 1960 and 1980, and the company was the sixth largest brewer in the United States by 1979. As Heileman acquired other brewers, it was able to bring its raw materials costs down by buying on a larger scale. The company spent relatively little on advertising, concentrating its money on only a few brands in a few major markets. Its Old Style beer moved up from controlling 10 percent of the Chicago market in 1973 to more than 30 percent by 1979. This venerable brand accounted for 40 percent of Heileman's sales volume by the late 1970s. Heileman had 34 total beer brands by the end of the 1970s, including Colt 45 malt liquor, Black Label, Schmidt, Rainier, Blatz, and Sterling. A few of these brands, including Old Style, Special Export, Rainier, and Schmidt, were regarded as premium beers, and they sold in large quantities. Some of the remaining Heileman brands were small regional or seasonal sellers, yet these brands were often nicely profitable. By the late 1970s, Heileman seemed poised to overtake Coors and become the fifth largest U.S. brewer. It was still gaining in sales at a time when three of the top five largest brewing companies lost sales and saw declines in profits. G. Heileman's sales had risen from about $100 million in 1970 to $330 million in 1978.

Between the late 1970s and the early 1980s the company did even better. Earnings grew on average 35 percent annually between 1976 and 1983 as the company continued to make acquisitions. By 1985, G. Heileman had sales of $1.2 billion, and it had become the nation's fourth largest brewery. Yet by the mid-1980s, the beer market had started to slump, with beer

drinking on the decline and the top five brewers locked in an apparent stalemate over the 85 percent of the market they jointly controlled. Heileman remained a powerhouse in the Midwest, where half the nation's beer was consumed, but it had difficulties pressing into the growing Sunbelt states. The company's plants ran at only 75 percent capacity in 1985, as it could not sell all the beer it could make. The company diversified, moving into snack food manufacturing and then into the production of precision metal parts for vehicle engines. Heileman's nonbrewing division accounted for about 15 percent of sales. The company continued to have strong cash flow and relatively little debt, but there was no doubt that the beer market had become stagnant by the late 1980s.

A Takeover and Two Bankruptcies in the Late 1980s and 1990s

Despite clear competitive difficulties, G. Heileman continued to grow in 1986, with an earnings gain of more than 11 percent over the year previous, even as other big brewers sold their beer below production cost to sustain market share. The company had a strong cash flow, and Heileman responded to the dwindling beer market with new products such as mineral water and nonalcoholic beers. Then in 1987 G. Heileman was taken private in a leveraged buyout by Bond Corporation Holdings, an Australian company run by entrepreneur Alan Bond. Bond paid $1.3 billion for Heileman, and was successful in its bid even after the Wisconsin legislature took action to prevent the brewery falling into foreign hands. Bond owned a string of Australian breweries, and G. Heileman became the crown of the company's U.S. holdings. But in a saga that was repeated often in the 1980s, the leveraged buyout, in which the acquired company's cash flow is used to service the debt incurred by the acquisition, almost instantly put Heileman under an overwhelming burden. The amount of debt Heileman took on when it was acquired by Bond was first said to be $850 million, but by 1990 that figure had been revised upward, to more than $1 billion. In 1988, Heileman lost $5 million, and in 1990, with sales of slightly less than $800 million, the company was in the red by $126.7 million. Bond Corp. Holdings had its own difficulties, as Alan Bond was forced to resign in mid-1990 and the company sold its Australian brewing assets. Bond Corp. lost a spectacular $740.7 million that year, the largest loss in Australian history. In January 1991 G. Heileman filed for bankruptcy, listing debts of $1.4 billion and assets of $1.24 billion.

Heileman continued operating while bankrupt, though its market share sank and its president resigned. Its creditors owned 67 percent of the company after the bankruptcy reorganization. Then in 1993 a Texas firm known for its leveraged buyouts bought the company for $390 million. Hicks, Muse & Co. paid what amounted to a fire sale price for the company that had gone for $1.3 billion six years earlier. Hicks, Muse intended to bring Heileman back into viability, and it placed at the top a man who had turned around other ailing Hicks, Muse purchases. When Bill Turner became CEO, he instituted a number of strategies aiming to bring back market share. Turner launched a slew of brand extensions, such as ''Ice,'' ''Light,'' and ''Genuine Draft'' versions of existing Heileman labels. Heileman also came up with many new brands, in a bid to compete with the growing presence of small microbreweries.

Key Dates:

1858: Gund and Heileman found City Brewery in La Crosse.

1872: Heileman buys out Gund; the company is renamed G. Heileman.

1902: The Old Style brand is copyrighted.

1933: The company goes public under new ownership as Prohibition ends.

1956: Heileman begins national expansion under President Roy Kumm.

1971: Kumm's son-in-law Cleary becomes president, continues expansion.

1987: Heileman is taken private by Australian company Bond Corp. Holdings.

1991: Overloaded with debt, Heileman declares bankruptcy.

1993: Heileman is bought by Texas investment company Hicks, Muse.

1996: Heileman declares bankruptcy for the second time and is bought by Stroh.

1999: Stroh sells the Heileman brands; Platinum Holdings buys the La Crosse plant and changes the name back to City Brewery.

2000: Struggling City Brewery is bought from Platinum by La Crosse investors.

2004: Company is a leading "third tier" brewer in the United States.

Between 1993 and 1995 when he resigned, Turner had proposed as many as 150 product and packaging changes. Some of these new products were disastrous, such as a menthol-flavored Colt 45 malt liquor, which was allegedly so nasty that "... alcoholics on the sidewalk are turning it down," according to a beer wholesaler quoted in a *Brandweek* (February 6, 1995) profile of Heileman. Aside from the slew of new products, Turner also brought in several new top executives, including former president Russ Cleary, who had retired. None of these men lasted long, and in 1995 Heileman was led by Lou Lowenkron, who had formerly run the soft drink manufacturer A&W.

Despite creative attempts to revive the company, Heileman was still beset by dwindling market share and high debt. In late 1995, Heileman announced that it would not be able to meet next quarter's interest payments, and it planned to either sell assets or merge with another company. In 1996 the company filed bankruptcy for the second time, and it was then acquired by the nation's fourth largest beer maker, The Stroh Brewery Company.

Stroh obviously knew how to manage a beer company, having prevailed when rivals such as Pabst and Heileman struggled. Stroh used Heileman's huge La Crosse plant to brew several non-Heileman brands under contract, while it closed some unprofitable Heileman facilities in the West and South. The national beer market remained stagnant in the mid-1990s, and even small specialty brewers such as Boston Beer Co., maker of the Samuel Adams brand, began to report slower growth. Small brewers including Boston Beer and Pete's Brewing Co. had

seen lively growth while the biggest makers held steady or contracted, but even the specialty beer segment slowed somewhat in the middle to late 1990s. In 1999, Stroh Brewery Company announced that it would stop making beer, and sell its brands and some of its plants to competitors. Miller Brewing Co. and Pabst Brewing Co. between them split up the Heileman brands, and it seemed like Heileman's flagship La Crosse brewery would close.

New Life As City Brewery in the 2000s

Heileman's La Crosse plant had operated at Third and Mississippi streets since 1858. On August 8, 1999, the brewery closed, leaving some 500 employees without jobs. But the brewery reopened a few months later, now as City Brewery. A New York-based investment firm, Platinum Holdings, had raised $10.5 million to acquire the facilities. Platinum was fronted by James Strupp and a native of the La Crosse area, John Mazzuto. The new company started small, hiring back 52 former Heileman employees, and hoped to have several hundred La Crosse residents back at work within six months. The company launched four new beer brands, two so-called premium brands, City Lager and City Light, and two so-called super-premium brands, La Crosse Lager and La Crosse Lager Light. The initial market area was to be the city of La Crosse itself, followed by western Wisconsin, and then the Upper Midwest. This was a business on a far smaller scale than the old Heileman.

Unfortunately, the new owners quickly ran into trouble. The investors had borrowed about $900,000 from the city of La Crosse, which naturally was very interested in keeping a large local employer afloat. Platinum also had borrowed $4.5 million from a Chicago bank. Already in March 2000, City Brewery fell into default on the loans from La Crosse, and a few months later, the Chicago bank foreclosed. By July, the plant was unable to pay its bills, buy supplies, or give its workers their paychecks. Mazzuto and Strupp hoped to raise more cash to put into the business, but meanwhile, production at the plant stopped.

In November 2000, City Brewery President Randy Smith and 11 other investors put together $9 million to buy out Platinum Holdings. With the help of loans from the city and county, the new investment group got the company back on its feet. The former Heileman plant was producing six brands of beer by mid-2001, employing 185 people. The company also had eight contracts with other beverage makers to manufacture and bottle their products on contract. A year later, City Brewery had close to 300 employees and was producing at least 1.2 million barrels of beverage annually. Only 2 to 3 percent of the brewery's production was its own brands, meaning it did the bulk of its business contracting its plant to other makers. Its contract work included making Arizona Iced Tea for the New York company Ferolito, Vultaggio & Sons, and making some beer brands for Pabst. One of the brands City Brewery made for Pabst was the former major Heileman brand Special Export. By 2003, the company seemed to be doing well. It was by that time the second biggest brewer in Wisconsin, and it had paid off all its loans from the city of La Crosse and from the county and state governments. City Brewery was very interested in pursuing contracts for nonalcoholic products such as energy drinks and tea, since that niche was seeing growth within the beverage sector. By 2004 the company had become one of the leading brewers in what brewery analysts called the "third tier" of U.S. breweries. Competitors included the maker of the Samuel Adams brand, Boston Beer Co., and the owner of Pete's Wicked Ale and other brands, the Gambrinus Co. By the mid-2000s, the company was closer in aspect to what it had been in the 1850s than to Heileman in its heyday in the early 1980s. It was essentially a craft brewer, making a small number of brands that were sold in Wisconsin and surrounding states. But it was also a prominent contract brewer, able to produce a wide variety of beverages for companies across North America. The many changes in ownership after 1987 had marked hard times for the company, yet it seemed to have a solid formula for success in its new guise as City Brewery in the 2000s.

Principal Divisions

City Brewery; Midwest Beverage Packers.

Principal Competitors

Boston Beer Co., Inc.; D.G. Yuengling & Son, Inc.; The Gambrinus Co.

Further Reading

"Can Heileman's Ales Be Cured?," *Brandweek,* February 6, 1995, p. 21.

"Cash-Short G. Heileman Brewing Co. Says It Would 'Prefer' Not to Seek Chapter 11," *Modern Brewery Age,* September 11, 1995, p. 1.

"City Brewing Operation in Debt," *Wisconsin State Journal* (Madison, Wis.), March 24, 2000, p. 1E.

Daykin, Tom, "Brewing Problems in La Crosse," *Milwaukee Journal Sentinel,* May 28, 2000, pp. 1, 8.

——, "God's Country Diversifies," *Milwaukee Journal Sentinel,* July 21, 2002.

Delvers, Diane, "Competitors Eyeing Heileman Assets As Company Reorganizes," *Business Journal-Portland,* March 25, 1991, p. 1.

Frank, John N., "Heileman's New Brew," *Beverage Industry,* January 1994, p. 30.

"Future of La Crosse Brewery Is Dubious," *Modern Brewery Age,* February 22, 1999, p. 1.

"G. Heileman Purchased by Hicks, Muse & Co., TX-Based Leveraged Buyout Firm," *Modern Brewery Age,* November 8, 1993, p. 1.

"Heileman Bankruptcy Plan Looks Favorable for Banks," *American Banker,* August 12, 1991, p. 2.

"Heileman Debts Topped $1 Billion," *Modern Brewery Age,* February 19, 1990, p. 1.

"Heileman Files for Reorganization As Part of Merger," *Modern Brewery Age,* April 15, 1996, p. 1.

Imrie, Robert, "Big Trouble Brewing," *Capital Times* (Madison, Wis.), July 26, 2000, pp. 1E, 8E.

Ivey, Mike, "City Brewing Banks on Future," *Capital Times,* April 11, 2003.

——, "New Brew in God's Country," *Capital Times,* February 24, 2000, p. 1E.

Kinkead, Gwen, "Heileman Toasts the Future with 34 Beers," *Fortune,* June 18, 1979, pp. 124–30.

Kirchen, Rich, "House of Heileman Hopes Reorganization Allows It to Rebuild," *Business Journal-Milwaukee,* January 28, 1991, p. 30.

Kroll, Wayne L., *Badger Breweries Past and Present,* self-published, 1976.

"La Crosse Hopes to Retain Its Brewing Heritage," *Modern Brewery Age,* August 7, 2000, p. 1.

Mullins, Robert, "Life Is Not Good for State's Breweries," *Business Journal-Milwaukee,* December 28, 1996, p. 5.

"New Brewery Unveils Four Brands," *Wisconsin State Journal,* December 2, 1999.

"The Perils of G. Heileman: More Details," *Modern Brewery Age,* September 18, 1995, p. 1.

"Restructuring of Bond Corp. Won't Help G. Heileman, Analysts Believe," *Modern Brewery Age,* July 30, 1990, p. 3.

"Revived City Brewing to Offer Tours," *Modern Brewery Age,* July 23, 2001, p. 1.

Stavro, Barry, "I Wouldn't Rule It Out," *Forbes,* July 29, 1985, p. 123.

—A. Woodward

Clean Harbors, Inc.

1501 Washington Street
P.O. Box 859048
Braintree, Massachusetts 02185
U.S.A.
Telephone: (781) 849-1800
Toll Free: (800) 282-0058
Fax: (781) 356-1363
Web site: http://www.cleanharbors.com

Public Company
Incorporated: 1980
Employees: 3,800
Sales: $643.2 million (2004)
Stock Exchanges: NASDAQ
Ticker Symbol: CLHB
NAIC: 562211 Hazardous Waste Treatment and Disposal

Clean Harbors, Inc. is the largest hazardous waste clean-up firm in the United States. The company manages the treatment, storage, and disposal of chemicals, fuels, explosives, and industrial and household hazardous materials. Clean Harbors runs nine landfills, five incinerators, seven wastewater treatment plants, and a variety of other waste management facilities across North America. The company's services include materials recycling, lab chemical disposal, PCB disposal, site management, and laboratory packing and moving. Clean Harbors' customers include large and small oil, pharmaceutical, and chemical companies, technology and biotechnology firms, governments and government agencies, and schools and universities. The company does emergency work, such as responding to fuel spills, as well as ongoing site clean-up and hazardous materials management. The company began doing clean-up work in the Boston area and grew rapidly to cover the North American market. Clean Harbors made a significant acquisition in 2002, buying the chemical services division of the bankrupt Safety-Kleen Corporation, and thus transformed itself from a medium-sized company to a major player in the waste disposal industry.

Quick Growth in the 1980s

Clean Harbors, Inc. began in 1980 in suburban Boston, near the shores of the famously polluted Boston Harbor. Alan S. McKim, then only 24 years old, started the company with three friends and $13,000. The company's office was a trailer, and its facilities included little more than a truck that McKim and his fellows drove around the area, transporting, treating, and disposing of hazardous wastes. The company was no bigger than many local plumbing or yard care firms, yet within its first year it had landed one of the country's leading oil companies, Texaco, as a customer. At the end of its second year, Clean Harbors had revenue of $1.5 million and 18 employees. A year later, revenue had increased to $4.2 million, and the number of employees had grown to 34. Clean Harbors offered both emergency hazardous waste cleaning and ongoing management of hazardous material sites. In 1984, the company averted a potential oil spill by pumping more than 100,000 gallons of oil off the crippled tanker Eldia, which came to grief off Cape Cod in a snowstorm.

Clean Harbors also served many clients in the Boston corridor known as "Silicon Valley East" for its high concentration of high-tech and biotechnology companies. Handling of hazardous waste was a growing industry, as these many new high-tech companies contracted out their waste handling needs. Much hazardous waste produced on the East Coast had to be shipped down South to states that had disposal sites, and the collecting, packing, and tracking of such waste was a demanding job requiring specialized equipment and the ability to comply with complex federal and state regulations. Clean Harbors handled industrial waste that might contain any combination of thousands of chemicals. Waste such as mercury and PCBs had to be handled differently from industrial solvents or leaked gasoline, for example, as not every storage or disposal site accepted them. As more and more companies set up in the Boston area, Clean Harbors had a booming market. In 1985 it bought a solvent recovery plant and a transfer station in Braintree, Massachusetts, giving it more capacity to handle materials in its own facilities. By the mid-1980s, Clean Harbors was the largest so-called environmental services company on the East Coast. Sales rocketed from less than $5 million in 1983 to close to $50 million in 1986.

Becoming a Public Company in 1987

Clean Harbors grew very quickly through the 1980s, and it had taken out loans to finance its expansion. In 1986, founder McKim began receiving queries from parties interested in funding Clean Harbors. A venture capitalist asked if he would consider selling part of the company to raise money, while an investment banker asked if he would think about taking the company public. McKim considered both private placement and going public. By that time, Clean Harbors had more than $11 million in debt. McKim himself was personally liable for much of this. McKim was also interested in sharing profits with his employees by letting them own stock. McKim eventually decided to take both routes, first selling 18 percent of the company to Boston-area venture capitalists, and then taking Clean Harbors public. But the road to going public turned out to be bumpier than McKim expected.

McKim laid plans in the spring of 1987 to take Clean Harbors public in the early fall. This was a period of enormous growth on Wall Street, as measured by the Dow Jones Industrial Average, which went from 1,896 in December 1986 to 2,722 at the end of August 1987. The felicitous bull market seemed to promise good things for Clean Harbors' initial public offering (IPO). The company hoped to sell 1.5 million shares for $15 each, to bring in as much as $22.5 million. But the process of auditing the company before the IPO dragged on for longer than expected. One problem was that Clean Harbors had made some acquisitions within the last three years, but spun them off immediately. Although Clean Harbors no longer owned these companies, it still had to provide thorough paperwork for them. As adequate records had not been kept, the auditors had to painstakingly reconstruct the needed documents. The price Clean Harbors paid to its auditor, Arthur Anderson & Co., became vexingly steep. McKim considered changing his strategy and bringing the company public in London instead of on the NASDAQ because suddenly much of Clean Harbors' financial information was out in the open for competitors to read.

Finally all of the paperwork was ready, and Clean Harbors filed with the Securities and Exchange Commission (SEC) on September 30, to bring off the IPO within the next 45 days. McKim began touring the country to interest investors in the stock. But Clean Harbors' timing was poor. On October 19, 1987, the stock market slid, an enormous ''correction'' to the bull market memorialized as Meltdown Monday. From an August high of close to 3,000, the Dow Jones Industrial Average fell to 1,739. Clean Harbors' underwriters were nervous about the IPO, and discussed postponing the offering or canceling it. Ultimately, Clean Harbors and its underwriters decided to go ahead with the IPO, but to offer one million shares instead of 1.5 million, and at $9 instead of $15. This would bring in only $9 million instead of the hoped-for $22 million. The company went public on the NASDAQ on November 24. Clearly, the company

would have made much more money if it had debuted before the fateful Monday. Yet six months later, Clean Harbors' stock had risen from $9 to more than $15. The company then made a secondary offering later in 1987, and that year paid off some $12 million in debt. Founder Alan McKim retained about 60 percent ownership of Clean Harbors.

Diversification in the 1990s

Clean Harbors was somewhat stymied in its attempts to expand within its home state of Massachusetts, but it made key acquisitions in other parts of the country. It had attempted to add an incinerator to its waste disposal site in Braintree, and spent $15 million over four years in the late 1980s and early 1990s in its bid to get the local government to approve the addition. Massachusetts was supposed to follow federal regulations ordering it to deal with its own hazardous waste instead of shipping it out of state, but because of a lack of facilities, Massachusetts was unable to comply. Yet siting a new incinerator in such a densely populated area as Braintree was contentious if not impossible. Clean Harbors' incinerator permit was denied in 1991, and it later purchased incinerators in Texas, Utah, Nebraska, and in Ontario and Quebec. It bought the Nebraska incinerator in 1995, a new and state-of-the-art facility formerly owned by the Ecova Corp. The Kimball, Nebraska incinerator was the only hazardous waste incinerator in the United States that was allowed to ''de-list'' its ash. That meant that it was so efficient at destroying hazardous materials that the ash remaining from the incineration was not considered hazardous in itself.

Clean Harbors was well known for its emergency response work. It was considered one of the leading companies in this field. It cleaned up large oil spills in Narragansett Bay in Rhode Island and in the Delaware River in 1990. Taking care of leaking tankers or wrecked trains could be lucrative business, though it could also cause the company problems if it took workers away from ongoing projects. Although such jobs could provide a windfall for Clean Harbors and put it in the public eye, for long-term growth, the company needed to focus on day-to-day waste management and environmental services work. The company set up several new divisions in the 1980s and 1990s to focus on specific service areas. In 1986 Clean Harbors formed Clean Pack, which focused on collecting, packing, and disposing of chemicals, mainly from laboratories. Clean Pack's customers included schools and universities, industrial laboratories, and local communities with household hazardous wastes. Clean Pack at first focused on the Boston area and the East Coast, but later expanded into the South and West. In 1998, Clean Harbors initiated another division, Clean Harbors Industrial Services. This division offered a variety of cleaning and maintenance services, including chemical cleaning, vacuuming, steam cleaning, and hydroblasting. The company also created an information management services subsidiary, marketing Clean Harbors' considerable expertise in the complex data collection, tracking, and archiving that its industry required.

A Major Acquisition in the 2000s

Clean Harbors was actively involved in cleaning up the destroyed World Trade Towers in New York City after the terrorist attacks of September 11, 2001. The company also was hired to manage hazardous or potentially hazardous waste at the offices of NBC in New York after a letter containing anthrax was received there. By that time, the company had evolved a highly sophisticated information and data management capacity to go with its physical waste handling ability. Clean Harbors used a satellite tracking system to record the movements of its waste hauling fleet and high-speed Internet connections at its mobile command centers. Its fleet of vehicles had grown to 650 trucks, and its customer web site offered online quotes for transportation costs and online Department of Transportation regulatory forms. While leading the hazardous waste disposal industry in its region, Clean Harbors had become one of the top 50 waste hauling and disposal companies nationwide.

Whereas Clean Harbors made its mark by dealing with hazardous materials, many much larger companies dominated the general (hazardous and nonhazardous) waste hauling industry. The top player in the United States was Waste Management, Inc., with more than $11 billion in revenue in 2002, while 28 other companies had revenue of $50 million or more. The fifth-ranked company in the waste hauling and disposal industry was Safety-Kleen Corporation, with 2002 revenue of more than $870 million. Safety-Kleen, however, had declared bankruptcy in June 2000 and was operating under Chapter 11 while it resolved financial discrepancies in its 1997, 1998, and 1999 financial statements. Safety-Kleen decided to sell its chemical services division in 2002, a division that included four hazardous waste incinerators, six wastewater treatment plants, nine landfills, and some 90 individual parcels of real estate, spread across the United States, Canada, and Mexico. Clean Harbors put in a bid for the division.

The merger with Safety-Kleen's unit would triple Clean Harbors' size and make it the largest company in the U.S. hazardous waste niche. The company bid $46.3 million for the division. The deal was enormously complicated. Safety-Kleen's problems included allegations of fraud and ongoing litigation involving so-called Superfund hazardous waste sites. Clean Harbors was offering to swallow up a company more than twice its size, and it needed to procure financing from various sources. The other bidder (through its Onyx subsidiary) for Safety-Kleen's assets was a company 50 times the size of Clean Harbors, the international water company Vivendi. Clean Harbors put together the transaction using the small Boston legal firm that had first incorporated the company back in 1980, while

Safety-Kleen relied on one of the nation's largest and most prestigious law firms. The other bidder, Onyx, also had high-powered legal representation. But Clean Harbors and its lawyers persevered, wading through contracts, sorting out what exactly Safety-Kleen owned, and talking to workers in the field who could accurately assess the state of some of the Safety-Kleen division's assets. A bankruptcy judge finally approved Clean Harbors' offer in late 2002. The newly enlarged Clean Harbors expected to have annual revenue in the area of $750 million, and to call almost half of the *Fortune* 500 list of top companies its customers. Clean Harbors became the single largest hazardous waste disposal company in the United States, and moved up to the 15th largest company in the waste industry overall.

But revenue for 2003 was less than expected, at around $600 million. The company suffered a net loss of $17.6 million. Clean Harbors explained that it failed to meet the higher expected revenue figure quoted when it acquired the Safety-Kleen division simply because much of the math was based on estimates, and the estimates were off. Nevertheless, investor disappointment sent Clean Harbors' stock price way down. It dropped by almost 40 percent over 2003, and in mid-2004 groups of shareholders filed suit against the company. The suits alleged Clean Harbors had not been fully forthcoming about some of the problems with the Safety-Kleen acquisition. The lawsuits were dismissed in 2004. By that time, Clean Harbors appeared to be recovering from the shock of digesting such a large acquisition. It claimed its fourth quarter of 2004 was its best ever, and the company finished the year with a 5 percent increase in revenue over the year previous, to $643.2 million, and net income of $2.6 million. The company also did well into 2005. Its first quarter revenue grew twice as much as anticipated, and the company expected sales and earnings to do well for the year.

Principal Divisions

Technical Services; Clean Pack; Site Services; Industrial Services; Apollo Onsite Services; Clean Harbors Training Services; Service Chemical.

Principal Competitors

Onyx North America Corporation; OHM Corporation; Waste Management, Inc.

Further Reading

Brewin, Bob, "IT Helps Waste Hauler Handle Anthrax Safely," *Computerworld*, November 12, 2001, p. 8.
"Clean Harbors Completes Acquisition," *American Metal Market*, May 23, 1995, p. 6.
Cunningham, John O., "How a Small Firm Pulled Off One of the Year's Biggest Deals," *Lawyers Weekly*, January 27, 2003.
Glass, John, "Simplifying the Siting Process," *Boston Business Journal*, October 15, 1990, p. 5.
Johnson, Jim, "Clean Harbors Ascends 30 Rungs in Annual List," *Waste News*, July 21, 2003, p. 13.
——, "Clean Harbors Merger Spawns Class Action," *Waste News*, November 24, 2003, p. 23.
——, "Lighter and Faster," *Waste News*, June 24, 2002, p. 3.

Lanza, Julie, ''Legislature Limits Local Control of Waste Facilities,'' *Boston Business Journal,* April 20, 1992, p. 5.

Mamis, Robert A., ''Going Public,'' *Inc.,* October 1988, pp. 55–62.

Mandell, Patricia, ''Clean Harbors Relies on PC Database for System to Track Toxic Material,'' *PC Week,* August 18, 1987, p. 49.

Rowland, Christopher, ''Some Massachusetts-Area Firms Suffer As Spooked Investors Caused Stock Slides,'' *Boston Globe,* May 18, 2004.

Wald, Matthew L., ''Cleaning Spills: Is It Profitable?,'' *New York Times,* July 10, 1990, p. D8.

—A. Woodward

Compass Bancshares, Inc.

15 S. 20th Street
Birmingham, Alabama 35233
U.S.A.
Telephone: (205) 297-3000
Toll Free: (800) 266-7277
Fax: (205) 297-7363
Web site: http://www.compassweb.com

Public Company
Incorporated: 1964 as Central Bank and Trust Company
Employees: 7,832
Total Assets: $28.18 billion (2004)
Stock Exchanges: NASDAQ
Ticker Symbol: CBSS
NAIC: 522110 Commercial Banking; 551111 Offices of
   Bank Holding Companies

Compass Bancshares, Inc. is the holding company for Compass Bank, which operates primarily in Alabama, Arizona, Colorado, Florida, New Mexico, and Texas. The company expanded outside of Alabama by way of acquisitions, beginning in the late 1980s. With few desirable banks available for purchase at the onset of the 21st century, Compass turned towards internal growth and product diversification.

Alabama Bound: 1960s–80s

Compass Bancshares, Inc.'s roots lie in Birmingham, Alabama, where Central Bank and Trust Company was founded in 1964. Central Bank was the first new bank to open in the city for nearly two decades. As the 1970s began Central Bancshares of the South was formed as a holding company. In the 1980s, Central merged ten affiliate banks, creating the first statewide as well as the largest bank in the state.

Compass Bank, a spinoff of Central Bank of the South, was created in 1987 with the acquisition of First National Bank of Crosby, located in a rural Houston, Texas suburb. The purchase of the $8 million asset bank came during a troubled period in Texas banking. The Texas economy had been flattened by the collapse of oil prices and real estate, Kenneth Cline wrote for *American Banker*.

Between 1985 and 1991, the state's banking assets fell from $220 billion to $170 billion and the number of banks dropped to 1,200 from 2,000. A trend toward out-of-state ownership took hold during the period. Compass, according to the *Dallas Business Journal*, was positioning itself between the larger banks and single-location independents with a mix of healthy, failed, and newly established banks.

Going against common practice, Compass worked to retain the management of the banks it acquired. Employees benefited with a greater sense of security during the transition period. The practice was appealing to those bankers interested in a healthy future of the business they had established.

The bank concentrated on four loan areas: individuals, small-to-medium corporations, home mortgage lending, and income-producing real estate. Demographically, Compass had set its sites on banks serving wealthier individuals. The bank also emphasized its desire to build personal relationships with those customers.

Some on the local banking scene took a wait and see attitude regarding Compass's plan, questioning whether the drive for growth would override the more benevolent aspirations of the company.

Westward Ho: 1990s

From mid-1990 to mid-1992 Compass acquired 14 banks in Texas with combined assets of $1.5 billion. Its network of 18 banks in the state now totaled nearly $1.8 billion. Charles McMahen, chairman and CEO of Compass Bancshares, Inc. and a veteran Texas banker, directed the growth.

The largest single acquisition, $427 million asset River Oaks Bancshares, Inc., came in March 1991. The independent bank was located in Houston's ritziest neighborhood, according to the *Houston Business Journal*.

McMahen was pleased with the purchase, telling Jim Grier, ''It was such a well known and respected and coveted property.'' The bank's trust business was especially desirable to Compass.

Prior to the River Oaks acquisition, Compass's largest purchase was an $82 million asset bank in upscale Plano. Compass was set to buy a $239 million asset bank in a wealthy area of Dallas and interested in expanding into other prime locations in Texas.

Central Bancshares, with about $6 billion in total assets, had seen its stock price rise to $34.38, or some 145 percent from December 1990 to June 1992. Compass used Central Bancshares stock to pay for all its acquisitions in the first half of 1992, an enticement to the sellers.

D. Paul Jones, Jr., successor to Harry B. Brock, Jr., as chairman and CEO of Central Bancshares of the South, faced a challenging environment in 1993. Net interest margins were shrinking and loan demand was weak.

But *American Banker* reported the $7.1 billion asset bank had some strengths from which to draw: a quarter of its assets were going toward expansion in the fast growing Texas and Florida markets; its overhead was below most in its peer group, allowing for competitive pricing; and its $700 million indirect auto loan portfolio was expected to help out income during slow economic times.

Central Bancshares of the South changed its name in November 1993 to Compass Bancshares Inc. The company, for the time being, planned to limit its acquisitions to Florida, primarily the panhandle area; and Houston and Dallas, likely the source of greatest future earnings growth.

Just about 40 percent of Compass was internally held in the early 1990s, and one of the insiders thought a new direction was necessary. Brock, a founder as well as ex-leader of Compass, tried to take control again in 1994. Brock wanted the bank holding company to accept a $30.71 per share offer by First Union Corp. Jones, who had been handpicked by Brock, opposed the sale. Brock failed to earn enough votes in the proxy election and Jones stayed at the helm.

Earnings were driven down the first half of 1995 by proxy related expenses. But the company's shares climbed in the wake of other bank deals being played out. Compass headed further west in the late 1990s, buying $805 million asset Arizona Bank toward the end of 1998. Competition in the Southeast had heated up while the region's economic growth cooled off.

Backtracking: 2000–05

In January 2000, Compass acquired Western Bancshares Inc. of Albuquerque, New Mexico. Now at $19 billion in assets, Compass moved into Colorado in April. Denver's MegaBank

Financial Corp. held $300 million in assets and had nine branch offices. In September, Compass announced a deal to buy privately held Denver-based Firstier Corp. for $127 million in stock.

Jones told *American Banker*, "The deal 'is consistent with our strategy of acquiring well-managed, profitable banks in high-growth, high opportunity markets.' " Firstier had $880 million in assets, with 17 of its 19 branches in or around Denver.

In the summer of 2000 Compass added to its Arizona holdings with the acquisition of the Founders Bank in Phoenix. Competition in the West was similar to that of Texas and included much larger competitors Bank of America Corp., Wells Fargo & Co., and Bank One Corp.

Western Bancshares experienced a slump in business its first six months under Compass ownership. Market share and deposits dropped off further in 2001. The trend was reversed in 2002, and Compass brought in a local banker to head the New Mexico operation in January 2003.

The parent company posted record earnings and earnings per share for the 15th consecutive year in 2002, according to the *Albuquerque Journal*. Net income was up 16 percent to $314.4 million and earnings per share of $2.42 marked a 15 percent increase over the previous year. Compass's assets had climbed to $23.9 billion.

Acquisitions outside its home state helped Compass climb to the position as the 31st largest bank in the country. In 1990, just 10 percent of its investments were outside of Alabama, by 2003 that percentage had risen to 70. But a dearth of banks on the selling block forced Compass to shift its growth strategy, turning instead to bricks and mortar.

David Boraks wrote for *American Banker* in December 2003, "Since announcing the branch-building plan early last year, Compass has built 37 branches, including 11 in the Dallas/ Fort Worth area, nine in Phoenix, and four in Houston. Among the 23 remaining to be built, six will be in Phoenix and seven in Denver." Compass's last acquisition was in 2000.

Despite the prospects of a strengthening economy, Compass faced a period of depressed growth relative to its peer group. Todd Davenport explained in a March 2004 *American Banker*, "Several years ago Compass presciently added interest rate sways to guard against rate declines. But the historic period of low rates has outlasted the swaps, which now are rolling off the books."

Moreover, other business lines such as insurance and brokerage were not yet supplying any significant source of earnings. Compass had moved to increase product diversification during 2002, buying insurance agencies in Dallas, Denver, and Phoenix and a wealth management firm in Jacksonville.

As merger mania resurfaced, Compass once again became grist for the buyout rumor mill. Its Texas market of $6.4 billion of deposits in 129 branches was Compass's largest and sparked the interest of other companies wishing to enter the state.

Wachovia Corp. reportedly was one of them. Wachovia had tried to buy Compass in 1994 when it was operating under the name First Union Corp. Wachovia did buy a Birmingham-based

```
┌─────────────────────────────────────────────────┐
│                  Key Dates:                     │
│                                                 │
│ 1964:  Central Bank and Trust Company opens in Bir-│
│        mingham, Alabama.                        │
│ 1970:  Parent company is organized as Central Bancshares│
│        of the South, Inc.                       │
│ 1971:  State National Bank is acquired.         │
│ 1987:  Company implements repositioning strategy, enters│
│        Texas market.                            │
│ 1995:  Total assets top $10 billion.            │
│ 1998:  Company establishes presence in Southwest with│
│        purchase of an Arizona bank.             │
│ 2000:  Company enters Colorado and New Mexico mar-│
│        kets.                                     │
│ 2004:  Company is added to S&P 500 index and the Dow│
│        Jones Select Dividend Index.             │
└─────────────────────────────────────────────────┘
```

bank, in June 2004, not Compass but SouthTrust Corp. Regions Financial Corp. was also in a merger deal, and AmSouth Bancorp, another large Birmingham bank, was considered a prime buyout target.

In the spring of 2005, analysts were predicting a slowdown in growth for some midsize banks, including Compass. The company continued to see stiff competition in its six-state market, driving further speculation as to its future.

Principal Subsidiaries

Compass Bank.

Principal Competitors

AmSouth Bancorporation; Regions Financial Corporation.

Further Reading

Boraks, David, "Compass, AmSouth, SunTrust Seen Takeover Targets," *American Banker*, September 30, 2004, p. 20.

——, "Compass' New Direction in Southwestern Market," *American Banker*, December 2, 2003, p. 1.

——, "Without Potential Suitor, Compass' Stock May Slip," *American Banker*, June 29, 2004, p. 18.

Cline, Kenneth, "Alabama's Compass Holds Course in Rough Sea," *American Banker*, October 25, 1993, pp. 4+.

"Compass Proxy Rivals Keep Slugging After the Bell," *American Banker*, August 25, 1995, p. 4.

Davenport, Todd, "Heat's On, But Compass Is Still Playing It Cool," *American Banker*, March 2, 2004, p. 1.

Frames, Robin, "Newcomer Compass Is Settling In," *Albuquerque Journal*, August 25, 2003, p. 3.

Greer, Jim, "Compass Launches Bank Buying Blitz: Explosive Growth in Houston, Dallas Turns Small Bank into State Powerhouse," *Houston Business Journal*, June 8, 1992, pp. 1+.

Kulikowski, Laurie, "Sovereign, TCF, Compass Seen Hitting Profit Wall," *American Banker*, May 11, 2005, p. 18.

Lallier, Rob, "A Different Direction: Compass Bancshares Charts a New Course in Metroplex by Acquiring Solvent Banks," *Dallas Business Journal*, April 12, 1991, pp. 15+.

Moyer, Liz, "Compass' Denver Push Continues with Firstier: Fast-Growth Market Drive, Through Acquisition," *American Banker*, September 6, 2000, p. 1.

—Kathleen Peippo

Real Estate Information

CoStar Group, Inc.

2 Bethesda Metro Center, 10th Floor
Bethesda, Maryland 20814-5388
U.S.A.
Telephone: (301) 215-8300
Toll Free: (800) 204-5960
Fax: (301) 718-2444
Web site: http://www.costar.com

Public Company
Incorporated: 1998 as Realty Information Group, Inc.
Employees: 1,038
Sales: $112.1 million (2004)
Stock Exchanges: NASDAQ
Ticker Symbol: CSGP
NAIC: 518210 Data Processing, Hosting, and Related
    Services

Maintaining its headquarters in Bethesda, Maryland, CoStar Group, Inc. is a national provider of commercial real estate information services, relying on a massive proprietary database delivered through the Internet. Coverage includes 1.14 million properties in the top 50 markets in the United States, as well as London and portions of the United Kingdom. All told, some 30 billion square feet of real estate is covered, supplemented by 2.2 million high-resolution digital images of buildings, floor plans, and maps. Information is updated on a daily basis by a staff of more than 700 researchers, analysts, and photographers. Customers—which include brokers, owners, investors, and appraisers—are able to list properties and to manipulate the data in order to find properties that meet certain criteria or to conduct market analysis and other research. Through an acquisition in 2005, CoStar also offers a database of U.S. shopping centers. After fending off the challenges of numerous rivals, CoStar is the undisputed leader in its field. It is a public company, listed on the NASDAQ.

Launching the Company in the Late 1980s

CoStar was founded by its chief executive officer, Andrew C. Florance, who grew up in the real estate industry. His father was a top Washington, D.C. architect and other relatives were brokers. While earning an economics degree at Princeton University in the mid-1980s, he got his real estate license. He also made money writing software, experience that he would soon put to use while casting about for a business to start during his final months at Princeton. Florance considered launching a video delivery service, but abandoned the idea, afraid that any success he might achieve would only attract the notice of a larger competitor. He then decided to return home to Washington, after graduating from Princeton in 1987, to use the money he made writing software to buy and renovate abandoned buildings. ''I was going to become a real estate tycoon,'' he told the *Washington Post* in a 1994 profile. He quickly grew frustrated with the quality of real estate information that was available, and realized that he could use his knowledge of computers to develop a commercial multiple-listing database service. At the time, real estate brokers compiled their own information, at great cost, essentially calling one another to share information. Florance's concept was to centralize the process, to call all of the brokers, then make the information available to subscribers, putting economies of scale to work so that brokers could eliminate their research staffs and obtain more accurate and comprehensive information at less expense. To start out, Florance, who set up shop in his parents' basement laundry room, inputted information that could be gleaned from sources such as Dunn & Bradstreet and government economic development publications. According to the *Washington Post,* ''He proceeded to write software programs that could handle and sort the reams of data he collected. . . . 'I did it for a year, and I was broke,' he said.''

Florance worked nights as a freelance computer consultant to support his daytime work of compressing the real estate assessment data from a mainframe computer into a personal computer. His first company was called Real Estate Infonet, geared toward publishing real estate public records. He printed ten copies of the 1,200 pages of information he had compiled, using a rented laser printer, and then sold them for $800 a piece. The algorithms he had devised to compress the information proved attractive to a number of companies and he was on the verge of selling his software to Planning Research Corp. when he found a backer in Washington lawyer Michael Klein, who assembled an investment group, allowing Florance to start a new company, Realty Information Group (RIG).

Late 1980s Real Estate Crash a Boon to CoStar

While Florance developed software to make use of the data, his researchers began to contact brokers for current information about what local properties were available. A number of brokers were suspicious of Florance's intentions, and some even tried to drive him out of the field. Attitudes changed during the real estate market crash of the late 1980s, however. Brokers were less guarded about their listings, since the information had always been an open secret. Under pressure to cut costs, it now made sense for brokers to eliminate their research staffs and essentially outsource the work at much less expense to RIG and its main competitor at the time, Cor/Net, which published Black's Office Leasing guide. RIG's competing print product was called Cornerstone, a quarterly leasing guide first published in 1989. For the next few years, RIG offered both the guide and its evolving electronic product, sold under the CoStar name. Revenues were meager at this stage, totaling just $30,000 in 1989, while expenses ran $1 million. But sales began to accelerate in 1990, reaching well more than $500,000.

Early on, after it became apparent that RIG had great potential, Florance recruited a seasoned executive to serve as president. Florance concentrated on developing the company's technology platform, but he eventually grew disillusioned with the president, despite the man's competence, because of his lack of vision for the company. Realizing that he was the only one possessing such a vision, he reassumed the post and led RIG through a period of tremendous growth during the 1990s. By 1992 RIG was entrenched in Washington, D.C., and now entered the nearby Baltimore market it had been eyeing for some time, again in stiff competition with Cor/Net. The company learned a valuable lesson in the process: The product had to be tailored to individual markets. Because Baltimore had more industrial properties the inclusion of ceiling heights was important. Moreover, terminology varied between markets. Washington's "core factor" (the location of elevators and other mechanical functions) was Baltimore's "public factor." It was a lesson that would soon be applied in other new markets.

After establishing itself in Baltimore, Florance realized the company had reached a turning point in 1992. If he was content just to do business in the Washington-Baltimore region, his success would breed his own destruction, as one day a larger company would come in and use its economies of scale to crush RIG—the very reason he abandoned the idea of a video delivery service. Thus he concluded that he had no choice but to keep expanding into new markets. It was also at this stage, in 1993, that Florance elected to cast his fate with the CoStar product and

the electronic delivery of real estate information. He sold the Cornerstone print business to Black's and did not look back.

In an effort to ward off competition from better funded national companies, Florance eschewed secondary markets, electing instead to enter the largest markets, where cost of entry would become cost-prohibitive later on. Hence, his next strike was the largest real estate market of all, the New York City metropolitan area. In 1994 RIG gained a toehold in the market by acquiring Space Data Graphics. RIG did not enter New York unopposed, however. Two years earlier Realty Information Tracking Group began selling an electronic program, the RE/Locate system, which had won the lion's share of the market, and whose partners Michael Sapers and Bruce Weissberg were ready for a fight. Weissberg told the *Washington Post* at the time, "They'll [RIG] find out it's not quite the opportunity they thought it was." Weissberg was proved wrong, as RIG not only entrenched itself in New York City, it began spreading out across the country, initially entering a market by acquiring a local company and building on its base, but more often than not by starting an operation from scratch. RIG entered the Los Angeles market in 1995, California's Orange County and Chicago in 1996, followed by San Francisco, Philadelphia, and Wilmington, Delaware, by mid-1997. Boston, Atlanta, and Elmhurst, Illinois, were soon to follow.

With so many investors having a piece of RIG, there was talk in the industry that the company would be forced to make an offering of stock. In February Realty Information Group, Inc. was incorporated in Delaware. A month later the company filed for an initial public offering, revealing that its revenues from 1997 totaled $7.9 million, an 82 percent jump over the previous year, and that its accumulated deficit stood at $11.4 million. With the $23 million the July 1998 stock offering raised, plus a secondary offering of $100 million two years later, RIG was well positioned to continue its expansion. The acquisition of Atlanta-based Jamison Research in early 1999 moved the company into the Atlanta and Dallas markets, and later in the year RIG opened offices in south Florida. It was also in 1999 that RIG became more dedicated to the Internet, investing heavily in new online products and services and the development of a new browser-base interface to shift away from the delivery of information by CDs. Already about two-thirds of the company's corporate clients were receiving daily updates over the Internet. Although RIG predated the emergence of the Internet, it benefited from investor enthusiasm over online ventures in the late 1990s. Less than a year after going public, the company's stock grew nearly 400 percent, from its initial $9 price to $44.50 in mid-April 1999. RIG's main competition was now Internet-based, in particular Comps.com, a San Diego company that went public in May 1999, raising $100 million. Comps was devouring local research firms and appeared poised to go head-to-head with RIG, but in a matter of months it was swallowed by RIG in a cash and stock deal that closed in early 2000 and made CoStar the undisputed leader in its field. By this time RIG had taken on a new name, CoStar Group, Inc., which better aligned the company with its brand.

Completely Web-Based in 2000

In 2000 CoStar finished moving all of its information to the Internet, phased out CDs, and became completely web-based.

Although the leader in its field, it was not without challengers. Investment banking giant Goldman Sachs launched a web-based service, Zethus Inc., that had the potential to cut out the broker, directly connecting buyers and renters of property, a move that CoStar had assiduously avoided, instead building its business around the broker. CoStar also faced a renewed challenge from an old foe, New York's RE/Locate, which in 2000 bought the in-house database of information in 47 markets from New York brokerage Cushman & Wakefield Inc. With backing from venture capitalist FrontLine Capital Group, Re/Locate transformed itself into RealtyIQ.com. Ceding the high end of the market to CoStar, RealtyIQ.com hoped to price its service to attract small and medium-sized firms. Other online rivals included start-ups LoopNet, PropertyFirst, Commercial Realty Online, and Commercial Real Estate Exchange. Within a short period of time many of these players were struggling and looking to sell out. In January 2001 RealtyIQ.com agreed to sell itself to Zethus, which in turn tried to sell itself to CoStar and others. It eventually filed for Chapter 7 bankruptcy protection and closed its doors, while RealtyIQ.com was sold for less than $4 million after burning through 70 million in seed money. PropertyFirst and LoopNet also merged, bringing together two money-losing ventures.

While the national competition fell by the wayside, CoStar, after more than a decade of establishing itself, neared profitability. Sales grew from $58.5 million in 2000 to more than $95.1 million in 2002. The company's net losses quickly declined, from $49.7 million in 2000 to $20.2 million in 2001 and $4.8 million in 2002. Finally in 2003 the balance sheet produced black numbers, as CoStar earned $100,000. During the year the company also completed another offering of stock, netting $53.5 million. At the end of 2003 the company possessed no long-term debt and had in hand $97.4 million in cash, cash equivalents, and short-term investments. During the course of the year CoStar rolled out its new web-based technology platform, replacing all earlier versions of the company's software, the retirement of which not only saved money but allowed the company to focus its resources on its suite of web-based services. The new platform was appreciated by customers, who used the high-end product, CoStar Property Professional, at a

much greater rate than earlier services. The company's renewal rate approached 90 percent and one of the fastest-growing client segments was that of national customers, such as investment and commercial banks, life insurance companies, and institutional investment managers. A "light" version of the product called CoStar Property Express also was unveiled in 2003, targeting smaller real estate brokers and property owners who could either subscribe or use the service on an on-demand basis with a credit card. The year 2004 also marked CoStar's first foray overseas, when in January of that year it acquired London-based Property Intelligence PLC and its FOCUS brand. Because many of CoStar's largest U.S. clients also had operations in the United Kingdom, the company had a ready base of clients to draw upon.

CoStar followed an outstanding 2003 with an even better 2004. Sales increased to $112.1 million and net income soared to almost $25 million, due in large measure to a more mature sales force, which enjoyed the fruits of better retention of personnel. The company was even more flush with cash than in 2004, holding $117.1 million at year's end. The company continued to break into new markets, such as Nashville and Memphis with the acquisition of PeerMark. Also in 2004 it launched field research in the United Kingdom and began upgrading the FOCUS service in London and Manchester. The acquisition of Scottish Property Network in June 2004 allowed the operation to extend its coverage into Scotland as well.

CoStar was expanding on any number of fronts in 2005, entering new U.S. markets but also moving beyond commercial real estate. In early 2005 the company acquired National Research Bureau, the leading provider of shopping center information, opening the way for CoStar to become involved in the retail real estate sector. By the end of the year it planned to add 200,000 properties to its database. With other real estate sectors to tackle in the United States and the vast potential of applying its proven technology platform to the world stage, the future prospects for CoStar appeared bright.

Principal Subsidiaries

CoStar Realty Information, Inc.; CoStar Limited (U.K.); Property Intelligence Limited (U.K.).

Principal Competitors

The First American Corporation; Grubb & Ellis Company.

Further Reading

Abrahams, Doug, "Young Entrepreneur Cats About, Lands a Winner," *Washington Business Journal,* September 3, 1990, p. 24.
Fruehling, Douglas, "The Sky's the Limit: Realty Statistics Titan Hunts for New Conquest," *Baltimore Business Journal,* July 11, 1997, p. 19.
Grant, Peter, and Rich Motoko, "Looks Like Showdown Time in Broker Land—Goldman's Move to Develop Online Real Estate Site Threatens Brokers' Role," *Wall Street Journal,* April 12, 2000, p. B16.
Haggerty, Maryann, "Interest in Computers, Real Estate Leads to Thriving Business," *Washington Post,* August 15, 1994, p. F10.

Holusha, John, ''Web Services Take Measure of Markets,'' *New York Times,* June 17, 2001, p. 11.

Kleiner, Kurt, ''Listing Levels the Playing Field,'' *Baltimore Business Journal,* July 30, 1993, p. 15.

Lemke, Tim, ''Bethesda-Based Office, Industrial Specialist CoStar Group Gets into Retail,'' *Daily Record* (Baltimore), January 24, 2005, p. 1.

Misonzhnik, Elaine, ''CoStar on the Horizon,'' *Real Estate Weekly,* February 4, 2004, p. 8.

Rich, Motoko, ''Online-Data Shops Enter Click-for-Tat War—Frontrunner CoStar, Beset by New Challengers, Goes After RealtyIQ,'' *Wall Street Journal,* March 22, 2000, p. B14.

Tyman, Douglas, ''In the Real-Estate Data Market, CoStar Is the Rising Star,'' *Business News New Jersey,* February 7, 1996, p. 30.

Webb, Bailey, ''Connecting with CoStar's Andrew Florance,'' *National Real Estate Investor,* June 2001, p. 96.

—Ed Dinger

Dairyland Healthcare Solutions

625 South Lakeshore Drive
Glenwood, Minnesota 56334
U.S.A.
Telephone: (320) 634-5331
Toll Free: (800) 323-6987
Fax: (320) 634 -5316
Web site: http://www.dhsnet.com

Private Company
Incorporated: 1980 as Dairyland Computer and
    Consulting Company
Employees: 250
Sales: $30 million (2004 est.)
NAIC: 511210 Software publishers

Dairyland Healthcare Solutions (DHS) is a leading national provider of comprehensive computer information systems for community healthcare facilities. Located in the heart of "Dairyland" in the central Minnesota town of Glenwood (approximately 100 miles from the Minneapolis-St. Paul metropolitan area), Dairyland develops computer software systems for small and mid-sized hospitals as well as their affiliated clinics, long-term care facilities, and home healthcare services. The company's client base extends to 38 states across the country. With a product line that integrates financial and clinical applications, Dairyland helps customers more effectively and efficiently manage their information, operations, and patient care. The company has satellite offices in Louisville, Kentucky, and Lafayette, Louisiana, as well as staff members working in several other states to ensure expedient delivery of its products and software support. That commitment to customer service is a big part of what earned the company national industry recognition when it was given a "Best in KLAS" rating in the category of community hospital information systems by KLAS Enterprises. KLAS Enterprises is a nationally recognized and respected independent organization that evaluates healthcare information technology.

1980: Bringing Technology to Rural America

Steve Klick founded Dairyland Computer and Consulting Company in Sauk Centre, Minnesota, in 1980. At the time, personal computers (PCs) were just entering the market, and the computer industry was in its infancy in the small business sector. Then working as a computer audit specialist, Klick saw the potential for technology in the small business market. His initial vision was to bring technology to small business, providing "turnkey computer systems and consulting services to the rural marketplace."

Klick started out in Sauk Centre as a consultant, helping small business owners determine the best hardware and software packages. Eventually he realized that he could develop better software systems himself and could tailor programs specifically to each customers' needs. Within two years, Klick's company created 12 software prototypes. He had initially focused on the agricultural market. But working closely with Glacial Ridge Hospital in nearby Glenwood, Klick developed systems to manage the financial/billing side of the healthcare business.

As the PC market began to take hold, Dairyland Computer and Consulting Company found customers throughout rural America. By 1985 Dairyland had 52 customers in four midwestern states. The company's software and hardware packages focused on the financial needs of small business operations.

Late 1980s: Steady Growth Throughout the Midwest

In need of a larger space to accommodate the company's growing staff of nearly 30 employees, Dairyland Computer and Consulting moved to nearby Glenwood, Minnesota, in 1987. The new company headquarters was a brand new 12,000-square-foot facility overlooking Lake Minnewaska. By this time Klick's company had developed hardware-software packages to distribute nationally for hospitals, nursing homes, medical clinics, and implement dealers. The company also developed systems for implement dealers and distributors and construction firms by working closely with various local companies.

At the time, Dairyland had installed systems for businesses in 13 states with additional sales pending in another seven

---

Company Perspectives:

Dairyland is committed to providing highly functional, cost effective information systems, as well as the highest level of service possible to our customers. Further, we are committed to the continual improvement of our products and services to help ensure our customers can deliver on their vision of providing care to their respective communities.

---

states. It also set up small offices in Sydney, Nebraska; Spokane, Washington; and outside Tucson, Arizona. The firm's presence in Nebraska was the result of Dairyland acquiring a company there named Business Computers Assistance.

Dairyland had always placed customer service as a top priority. In the new Glenwood facility it was able to offer 24-hour service. The larger facility also gave Dairyland staff ample space to test systems on hardware there, prior to installing systems at the customer site. Dairyland technicians would not only install systems at a customer's facility, they would also conduct onsite training for new clients.

During the early 1990s, Dairyland continued to grow, finding most of its success in the healthcare market. By 1994 the company employed 75 people, most at the Glenwood headquarters. The existing garage space had been converted into needed office space. Growth required a new 48- by 90-foot addition to the facility, which would facilitate storage and shipping.

Early 1990s: Enhancing Systems and Training to Meet Changing Industry Needs

Each summer since the mid-1980s, Dairyland hosted a three-day conference for its system users from all over the country, providing training and retraining to customers. The company was committed to helping users get the most from their systems, but also encouraged customers to look forward in the rapidly changing healthcare field. Conference literature noted that "Industry trends are also examined in an effort to make rural healthcare a strong and viable part of our nation's economy."

By 1995, Dairyland had 291 customers in 24 states. By this time the company had developed clinical applications to complement and integrate with the financial systems. Annual sales figures for the company reached $15 million, and projections for the following year were $20 million. Dairyland was featured in *Minnesota Technology* magazine in 1996, where the company was described as the "nation's largest installer of software and computer services in hospitals with 100 beds or fewer. Dairyland's hospital management system tracks finances, materials, management patient care systems, medical records, nursing systems, practice management home health systems. Perhaps more important, it is designed and serviced with the limited resources of rural hospitals in mind."

Late 1990s: Strengthening National Presence Through Acquisitions and Partnerships

During the mid- to late 1990s, Dairyland expanded its national presence through a number of acquisitions, but the com-

pany maintained its focus on its core products. Purchasing smaller firms in Louisville, Kentucky, and Abbeville, Louisiana, helped the company increase its scope in both the medical and agricultural markets. Dairyland also entered into collaborative agreements with other firms to develop software and offer customer support. The medical division surpassed $15 million in sales by 1997. The company also enhanced its customer service focus by becoming an IBM business partner, and better serving the hardware and software needs of clients. The partnership gave Dairyland the ability to help customers leverage hardware support from IBM as well as system support.

In 1998 Dairyland acquired Integrated Health Systems, Inc. of La Jolla, California, resulting in the company changing its name temporarily to Integrated Health Systems-Dairyland. The California company had served a slightly larger hospital market with from 100 to 500 beds. Dairyland continued to succeed and grow by evolving and adapting to the changing market needs.

In 1998 Klick stepped back from day to day management of the company so he could instead focus on future growth and keep up with the rapidly changing industry. The company focused on harnessing the potential of the Internet in its systems as well as helping customers prepare for any Y2K glitches. According to a 1999 article in the *Pope County Tribune*, Klick's vision was to help create a healthcare system in which "all providers of health care services shared a common data base of information about patients."

1999–2000: Focusing on the Healthcare Market and Its Future

Dairyland's total sales reached $27 million by 1999. The company's primary products were the Vision 6000 system, created to meet the needs of hospitals with fewer than 150 beds. The company also offered and supported the Vision 400 for hospitals up to 500 beds, as well as the clinical package named Vision 2000, which integrated easily with both software systems. Dairyland put increasing emphasis and resources on developing clinical products to augment financial systems.

In 2001, Dairyland's leaders decided it was time to officially change the company's name in order to communicate more clearly its focus on the healthcare market. The new name was Dairyland Healthcare Solutions (DHS); previously, "healthcare" had never been part of the name. The company decided to keep "Dairyland" as part of the name because it was widely recognized and highly respected in the healthcare industry because of its excellent reputation.

2003: Recognized Nationally As an Industry Leader

Dairyland's highly regarded position in the industry was validated in 2003 when the company won a first place, "Best in KLAS" rating in the category of community hospital information systems by KLAS Enterprises. The recognition was based on feedback from healthcare executives about corporate and product performance details. KLAS Enterprises was established to provide the healthcare information technology industry with objective evaluation and facts about vendors via surveys of CEOs and IT officers in the healthcare field.

The company repeated the "Best in KLAS" distinction again in 2004, garnering first or second place ratings in 33 out

Key Dates:

1980: Dairyland Computer and Consulting founded in Sauk Centre, Minnesota.

1987: Company moves to Glenwood, Minnesota.

1994: Dairyland adds on to Glenwood facility to accommodate growth.

1996: Company is featured in *Minnesota Technology Magazine*.

1998: Dairyland is acquired by Integrated Health Systems, La Jolla, California.

2001: Name is officially changed to Dairyland Healthcare Solutions (DHS).

2003: DHS wins the highest industry honor, "Best in KLAS."

2004: DHS repeats first place "Best in KLAS" award.

of 40 measures of performance. Some of the performance indicators where DHS rated high were "executive's interest in you, lived up to expectations, telephone support, costs as expected, quality of releases and updates, commitment to technology, quality of training, documentation, and fair contract." J.P. Wenslick, publisher of *HIT Strategies Newsletter*, wrote "Dairyland offers an extraordinary range of applications to smaller . . . healthcare providers at prices they can afford. . . . KLAS ranked them number one in this space over QuadraMed, Meditech, HMS and CPSI."

DHS had developed nine clinical products and 23 financial products, all integrated to enhance flow of information, reduce errors, and save time in delivery of high quality medical care. The products also easily linked records from affiliated health clinics, hospitals, long-term care facilities and even home healthcare.

By 2005 DHS had approximately 400 customers in 38 states. The company was an industry leader in allowing community and specialty hospitals to meet their information systems needs. Dairyland clearly dominated the market throughout the Midwest, especially in its home state of Minnesota where 55 healthcare facilities were DHS customers. The company also led the markets in Kansas, Nebraska, Wisconsin, and Iowa.

2005: Continuing a Strong Tradition of Customer Service

Much of Dairyland's growth came from referrals from satisfied customers. Working closely with longtime customers allowed Dairyland to refine existing products and develop new systems. The company's commitment to remaining on the cutting edge was evident in that DHS released software upgrades regularly, integrating industry changes as well as recommendations and suggestions from customers.

The company's biggest challenges were managing growth and attracting and retaining high caliber employees. Company leaders expected continued growth in the Midwest, Southwest, and West. Dairyland was committed to the small and mid-sized community healthcare market, its focus for more than 20 years. Customers appreciated that the company was not trying to serve multiple market segments.

The company hoped to delve deeper into developing more information system solutions for doctors, nurses, and technicians. DHS was also working on developing a system for web-based personal health records, which could be accessed by individuals and would include more complete information than a clinic would maintain on an individual patient. Dairyland saw the benefits of this system in automating clinical data, reducing medical errors, tracking drug interactions, and more.

Dairyland executives believed they were well positioned to meet the future demands of the healthcare industry. They were especially committed to helping customers meet the requirements that might be forthcoming relating to the federal government's Electronic Health Records Initiative. DHS continued to monitor the status of the federal initiative, keep its customers informed, and remain prepared to address requirements through any existing or newly developed applications.

Principal Competitors

Medical Information Technology, Inc.; Computer Programs and Systems, Inc.; Health Management Solutions, Inc.; QuadraMed Corporation.

Further Reading

"Dairyland Computer Featured in Minnesota Technology," *Starbuck Times*, July 17, 1996.

"Dairyland Expansion Approved," *Pope County Tribune*, May 2, 1994.

"Dairyland Healthcare Solutions Names New President," *Starbuck Times*, October 31, 2001.

"Dairyland Open House Sunday Afternoon," *Pope County Tribune*, January 4, 1988.

"Dairyland Wins Prestigious National Rating, Recognition," *Pope County Tribune*, March 29, 2004.

"DCC to Host 10th Annual Summer Conference," *Starbuck Times*, July 10, 1996.

"Ground Broken for Computer Firm," *Pope County Tribune*, June 15, 1987.

Stone, John, R., "Dairyland on Track for Rapid Future Growth," *Pope County Tribune*, November 1, 1989.

——, "Integrated Health Systems-Dairyland Continues to Evolve and Change with the Times," *Pope County Tribune*, October 18, 1999.

"Welcome to Glenwood, Dairyland," *Pope County Tribune*, June 22, 1987.

—Mary Heer-Forsberg

DaVita Inc.

601 Hawaii Street
El Segundo, California 90245
U.S.A.
Telephone: (310) 536-2400
Toll Free: (800) 310-4872
Fax: (310) 536-2675
Web site: http://www.davita.com

Public Company
Incorporated: 1979 as Medical Ambulatory Care, Inc.
Employees: 15,300
Sales: $2.29 billion (2004)
Stock Exchanges: New York
Ticker Symbol: DVA
NAIC: 621492 Kidney Dialysis Centers

DaVita Inc. is the second largest dialysis services provider in the United States. The company operates approximately 660 outpatient dialysis centers in 37 states and the District of Columbia, serving roughly 54,000 patients. DaVita also provides acute inpatient dialysis services through contracts with 370 hospitals. The company's largest concentration of outpatient clinics is located in California, where it operates 95 facilities.

Origins

DaVita operated under three different names during its first quarter-century of existence, but under each identity the company pursued the same corporate objective: providing service to patients with chronic kidney failure. Chronic kidney failure, technically known as end-stage renal disease (ESRD), was treatable in three ways. A kidney transplant offered the only cure for ESRD; without a successful transplant, the disease was irreversible and ultimately fatal. A shortage of kidney donors severely limited the number of transplants, however. Only 5 percent of ESRD patients in the United States could hope for a transplant, leaving dialysis—the removal of waste and toxins from the blood—as the only treatment option for a vast majority of ESRD patients. With dialysis, there were two treatment options: peritoneal dialysis and hemodialysis. Peritoneal dialysis usually was performed in the patient's home, while hemodialysis, the most common form of ESRD treatment, typically was performed in a hospital or an outpatient facility. Of those on dialysis in the United States, an estimated 92 percent received hemodialysis, a treatment that used a dialyzer to remove toxins, fluid, and chemicals from the patient's blood and another device that controlled external blood flow and monitored the patient's vital signs. Hemodialysis typically was administered three times a week to an individual patient. DaVita and its two predecessor variants, Medical Ambulatory Care, Inc. and Total Renal Care, Inc., concentrated on providing hemodialysis at company-operated facilities, targeting the vast majority of all ESRD patients.

In macabre terms, providing service to ESRD patients represented a growth industry. Specifically, the number of patients requiring chronic dialysis services in the United States increased at a 9 percent compounded annual rate during DaVita's first decades in business, jumping from 66,000 in 1982 to 200,000 in 1995. By 2002, there were 309,000 individuals in the nation who required DaVita's services. Aside from the escalating need for dialysis treatment, DaVita, from a business standpoint, was aided by another trend. Historically, outpatient dialysis facilities composed a loosely-knit, fragmented industry, with ownership of the centers held by groups of nephrologists or by hospitals. During the 1980s and 1990s, however, a new breed of operators began to emerge: multi-center dialysis companies with national, if not global, aspirations of market domination. During the 1990s in particular, the industry began to consolidate, as companies of DaVita's ilk became more prominent within the dialysis services industry. For example, seven major multi-facility dialysis providers owned 45 percent of the 3,000 facilities in operation in 1996, a sharp increase from the 30 percent they operated four years earlier. During this same four-year period, the number of facilities owned by independent physicians declined from 37 percent to 27 percent as physicians—nephrologists, generally—sought relief from adhering to changing government regulations and administrative burdens. Hospitals, too, were bowing out of providing dialysis services, choosing, like much of corporate America, to outsource the management of their facilities. In 1992, 33 percent of dialysis facilities were based in hospitals. In 1996, 28 percent of the country's facilities fell under the purview of hospitals.

The two trends of the dialysis industry—growth in the number of ESRD patients in the United States and the consolidation of facility ownership—worked in DaVita's favor, serving as the impetus for its creation and, ironically, nearly causing its ruin. The company began in 1979 as part of another company, National Medical Enterprises, Inc. Santa Monica-based National Medical, perhaps foreseeing the changes to come in the dialysis services industry, formed Medical Ambulatory Care, Inc. to own and to operate its hospital-based dialysis services business as freestanding facilities. National Medical also directed Medical Ambulatory to acquire and to internally develop additional dialysis facilities in its markets. Medical Ambulatory was an early entrant into the national race for market share, expanding at a modest pace throughout the 1980s.

1994 Spinoff

DaVita, as Medical Ambulatory, spent its first 15 years operating under the control of a parent company. It did not begin to record strong growth until it gained its independence. Against the backdrop of an industry in the midst of consolidating, Medical Ambulatory was spun off from National Medical in a leveraged buyout led by the subsidiary's management and DLJ Merchant Banking Partners, L.P. in August 1994. The transaction created Total Renal Care Holdings, Inc. and its subsidiary, Total Renal Care, Inc., the new identity for Medical Ambulatory. When Total Renal Care entered the dialysis services industry on its own, the company operated 37 outpatient facilities and maintained 28 inpatient contracts with hospitals, the extent of its expansion under the aegis of National Medical (following a federal investigation, National Medical moved its headquarters to Dallas and changed its name to Tenet Healthcare Corp.).

Total Renal Care attacked expansion with ferocity once it was on its own, taking its cue from its new leader, Victor M.G. Chaltiel. Chaltiel was a veteran of the healthcare industry, having compiled an impressive résumé that included top executive positions at several well-known companies. Before joining Total Renal Care in 1994, Chaltiel served as chief operating officer of Salick Health Care Inc. between 1985 and 1988. Next, he served a four-year term as chairman and chief executive officer of Total Pharmaceutical Care Inc., leaving in 1993 to assume the office of chief executive officer of Abbey Healthcare Group Inc. Under Chaltiel's charge, Total Renal Care began adding substantially to its portfolio of dialysis facilities and hospital contracts. The company nearly doubled in size in little more than a year, adding 31 outpatient facilities and 20 inpatient contracts with hospitals by the end of 1995. For Chaltiel, the

progress by this point was merely a prelude to far more ambitious plans, for which he prepared by completing an initial public offering (IPO) of stock in October 1995. The IPO raised $107 million, giving Chaltiel a portion of the money to fund his ambitious plans.

In the two years following its IPO, Total Renal Care became one of the largest contenders for market dominance in the United States. By the end of 1996, the company controlled a network of 134 outpatient facilities, having added 66 new facilities during the year. It strengthened its business with hospitals as well, signing 39 inpatient contracts during the year for a total of 59 management agreements. The expansion achieved during 1996 was unprecedented in scale, but Chaltiel soon established a new benchmark to measure the company's expansion, by completing a deal that positioned Total Renal Care near the top of its industry. In November 1997, the company announced that it had agreed to acquire its closest competitor, Renal Treatment Centers. The $1.3 billion all-stock transaction nearly doubled Total Renal Care's size. The two companies also had expanded internationally, adding a piece of the overseas market to the combined entity. Total Renal Care had expanded first in Guam before either establishing or acquiring facilities in Puerto Rico and Europe in the months leading up to its acquisition of Renal Treatment Centers. Renal Treatment Centers, based in Berwyn, Pennsylvania, had established facilities in Argentina, operating, in total, 164 centers in 23 states, the District of Columbia, and Argentina. Total Renal Care, at the time the acquisition was announced, operated 194 freestanding dialysis centers in 18 states, the District of Columbia, and abroad.

Chaltiel's acquisition tightened up the national race for market share considerably. As Total Renal Care absorbed the operations of Renal Treatment Centers, it drew close to the second largest competitor in the United States, Lakewood, Colorado-based Gambro Healthcare, the U.S. subsidiary of a Swedish renal care company, Gambro AB. Total Renal Care and Gambro Healthcare each controlled approximately 15 percent of the U.S. market. The market's leading competitor was a German company, Fresenius Medical Care AG, which controlled 25 percent of the U.S. market. Chaltiel, intent on overtaking his competitors, commented on the acquisition in a November 27, 1997 interview with *Modern Healthcare*. ''We will now have the critical mass necessary to ensure our position as the leading independent provider of dialysis services in the United States and the resources to rapidly expand.'' His confidence soon faded, however. The acquisition that vaulted Total Renal Care into the industry elite nearly led to the company's collapse, bringing the Chaltiel era to a disastrous conclusion.

Total Renal Care's aggressive expansion caught up with it after the Renal Treatment Centers purchase. The acquisition doubled the company's patient and staff base overnight, putting an enormous strain on its infrastructure. Often, accounts were uncollected and patients were billed incorrectly, as the company's 600-person billing and bookkeeping office in Tacoma, Washington, struggled in vain to support the vastly larger network of dialysis facilities. Further, debt escalated, reaching $1.5 billion in 1999—the consequence of the numerous acquisitions that fueled Total Renal Care's expansion from fewer than 40 facilities to nearly 500 facilities during the previous five years. In 1999, the company's situation quickly deteriorated. In the

---

Key Dates:

1979: DaVita's earliest predecessor, Medical Ambulatory Care, is formed as a subsidiary of National Medical Enterprises, Inc.

1994: Medical Ambulatory Care is spun off as Total Renal Care Holdings, Inc.

1995: Total Renal Care Holdings completes its initial public offering of stock.

1997: Total Renal Care Holdings announces its acquisition of Renal Treatment Centers.

1999: After struggling to absorb Renal Treatment Centers, the company appoints Kent Thiry as its new chief executive officer.

2000: Total Renal Care Holdings changes its name to DaVita Inc.

2004: DaVita announces the acquisition of Gambro Healthcare.

---

spring, it announced that its earnings would fall short of expectations, causing its stock to plummet in value and triggering shareholder unrest. Exacerbating matters, the company defaulted on its loans to creditors, leaving it teetering on the brink of insolvency. Before the year ended, Chaltiel and the company's chief financial officer resigned.

Turnaround Beginning in 1999

Total Renal Care's bid to become the largest dialysis services company failed spectacularly at the end of the 1990s. One analyst, who referred to the Chaltiel-led organization as "a disaster of a company" in an October 23, 2000 interview with the *Los Angeles Business Journal,* also commented: "All they did was buy things instead of focus on running the company." Chaltiel's replacement arrived in October 1999, inheriting a company with profound problems that required wholesale changes. Kent J. Thiry, who had spent the previous decade leading a healthcare services company named Vivra Incorporated, assumed the responsibility of saving the company, realizing that it needed to be thoroughly revamped to have any chance to compete in the years ahead. Thiry divested nearly all of the company's international operations and he ploughed money, technological resources, and new management into the company's beleaguered Tacoma office. He began negotiating with Total Renal Care's lenders, hoping to win their trust. After making a $35 million payment, Thiry was able to obtain a new line of credit, giving the company the financial fuel to continue its rise in the dialysis services market. Once all the fundamental changes were made, Thiry let 600 members of the company's mid- and upper-management decide on one final change at a meeting in June 2000. The managers voted on a new name, selecting DaVita Inc. as the new name for the old Total Renal Care. "We are very much a new company," Thiry explained in an October 23, 2000 interview with the *Los Angeles Business Journal.* "The previous company was almost exclusively focused on shareholders, and our new mission is to be the provider, partner, and employer of choice. We realize that we have to satisfy our shareholders with a reasonable return, but that is not our primary mission."

DaVita continued to expand under Thiry's rule, but unlike earlier years, the company focused on building its infrastructure as well. The company's stock value responded well to Thiry's commitment "to be the provider, partner, and employer of choice," recovering from the precipitous drop recorded during the final months of Chaltiel's leadership. In mid-1998, the company's stock was trading for more than $30 per share before beginning its rapid decline, plummeting to $2.06 per share by the spring of 2000. When it emerged under the DaVita name, the company's stock debuted at $10.25 per share and began climbing toward $50 per share during Thiry's first five years of leadership, a period highlighted by relatively small acquisitions and a disciplined approach to growth. When Thiry acquired the 24 clinics operated by Physicians Dialysis, Inc. in September 2004, it was the largest acquisition completed during his tenure. Within months, however, he would complete the largest acquisition in the company's history, orchestrating a deal that outstripped by far the size of Chaltiel's Renal Treatment Centers purchase.

By 2004, DaVita ranked as the second largest provider of dialysis services in the United States. The company served more than 45,000 patients through nearly 600 clinics and through contracts with 300 hospitals, trailing only Fresenius Medical Care in the race for market share. Gambro Healthcare ranked just behind DaVita, followed by another competitor playing a prominent role as a consolidator, Renal Care Group, which controlled 9 percent of the U.S. market. Thiry, who had acquired 120 centers during the previous five years, greatly changed the dynamics of the race among the four contenders when he brokered a deal that would give DaVita 565 new clinics overnight. In December 2004, he announced that he had reached an agreement to acquire Gambro Healthcare in a $3 billion deal that would enable DaVita to overtake Fresenius Medical Care. The merger, combining DaVita's 664 clinics with Gambro Healthcare's 565 clinics, promised to create a new towering giant in the U.S. dialysis services market, presenting a threat to Fresenius Medical Care that did not go unanswered. In May 2005, Fresenius Medical Care announced that it had agreed to acquire Renal Care Group, a transaction that promised to return the German company to the leadership position. Once the two proposed mergers were completed, the race for dominance would be a contest between DaVita and Fresenius Medical Care, setting the stage for the ultimate battle in an industry shaped by consolidation.

Principal Subsidiaries

DaVita Nephrology Medical Associates of California, Inc.; DaVita Nephrology Medical Associates of Illinois, P.C.; DaVita Nephrology Medical Associates of Washington, P.C.; DaVita Nephrology Associates of Utah, L.L.C.; DaVita - Riverside, LLC; DaVita - West, LLC; Physicians Choice Dialysis of Alabama, LLC; Physicians Choice Dialysis, LLC; Physicians Dialysis Acquisitions, Inc.; Physicians Dialysis of Lancaster, LLC; Physicians Dialysis of Newark, LLC; Physicians Dialysis Ventures, Inc.; Physicians Dialysis, Inc.; Physicians Management, LLC; Renal Treatment Centers - California, Inc.; Renal Treatment Centers - Hawaii, Inc.; Renal Treatment Centers - Illinois, Inc.; Renal Treatment Centers, Inc.; Renal Treatment Centers - Mid-Atlantic, Inc.; Renal Treatment Centers - Northeast, Inc.; Renal Treatment Centers - Southeast, LP; Renal Treatment Centers - West, Inc.; Total Renal Care, Inc.; Total Renal Care of Colorado, Inc.; Total Renal Care North Carolina, LLC; Total Renal Care of Utah, L.L.C.; Total Renal Laboratories, Inc.; Total Renal Research, Inc.

Principal Competitors

Fresenius Medical Care Aktiengesellchaft; Gambro AB; Renal Care Group, Inc.

Further Reading

Alva, Marilyn, "DaVita Inc. El Segundo, California; Dialysis Clinic Owner Makes Full Recovery," *Investor's Business Daily,* January 21, 2005, p. A6.

Bowe, Christopher, "DaVita Pays $3 Billion for Gambro's U.S. Clinics," *Financial Times,* December 8, 2004, p. 21.

Brinsley, John, "Management Change Gives New Vigor to Health Firm," *Los Angeles Business Journal,* October 23, 2000, p. 38.

Cole, Benjamin Mark, "Total Renal Care Slates Secondary Offering," *Los Angeles Business Journal,* April 22, 1996, p. 12.

"DaVita Completes Acquisition of Physicians Dialysis, Inc.," *Blood Weekly,* September 30, 2004, p. 77.

"DaVita to Acquire Physicians Dialysis, Inc.," *Blood Weekly,* August 19, 2004, p. 83.

Eckart, Kim, "California-Based Kidney Dialysis Provider Resurfaces with New Name," *News Tribune,* October 8, 2000, p. B3.

Marcial, Gene G., "There's New Life at DaVita," *Business Week,* July 21, 2003, p. 90.

Snow, Charlotte, "Renal-Care Biggies Plan Merger," *Modern Healthcare,* November 24, 1997, p. 20.

—Jeffrey L. Covell

Dean Foods Company

2515 McKinney Avenue, Suite 1200
Dallas, Texas 75201-1978
U.S.A.
Telephone: (214) 303-3400
Fax: (214) 303-3499
Web site: http://www.deanfoods.com

Public Company
Incorporated: 1988 as Kaminski/Engles Capital Corp.
Employees: 26,000
Sales: $10.82 billion (2004)
Stock Exchanges: New York
Ticker Symbol: DF
NAIC: 311511 Fluid Milk Manufacturing; 311520 Ice
    Cream and Frozen Dessert Manufacturing; 311999 All
    Other Miscellaneous Food Manufacturing; 311421
    Fruit and Vegetable Canning

Dean Foods Company, the largest processor and distributor of milk and other dairy products in the United States, is the product of Suiza Foods Corporation's December 2001 acquisition of the "old" Dean Foods Company, after which Suiza adopted the acquiree's name. Prior to the takeover, Suiza and the old Dean had been leading consolidators of the highly fragmented U.S. dairy industry, buying up dozens of mainly family-owned operations that were ripe for acquisition. By the time of the merger the two firms had grown into the two largest U.S. dairy companies. The "new" Dean Foods was a dairy giant, its Dairy Group generating nearly $9 billion in sales by 2004. Of this total, 55 percent was generated by more than 30 well-established local and regional dairy brands—including Broughton, Dairy Fresh, Dean's, Melody Farms, Nature's Pride, and Shenandoah's Pride—with the remainder coming from a variety of private label brands. National in scope if not in brands, Dean Foods' Dairy Group operates more than 110 plants from coast to coast, producing milk, whipping cream, coffee creamers, ice cream, yogurt, cottage cheese, sour cream, and other dairy products, as well as fruit juice, fruit-flavored drinks, and water. Dean's WhiteWave Foods Company subsid-

iary, meanwhile, produces and sells a range of soy, dairy, and dairy-related products under national brand names, including Silk soymilk and cultured soy products; Horizon Organic dairy products, juices, and other products; International Delight coffee creamers; Marie's refrigerated dips and dressings; Land O'Lakes fluid dairy and cultured products; and Hershey's milks and milkshakes (the latter two under license from Land O'Lakes, Inc. and Hershey Foods Corporation, respectively). Outside the United States, Dean's Leche Celta division is the fourth largest dairy processor in Spain and operates in Portugal as well. Dean Foods also owns a 27 percent stake in Atlanta-based Consolidated Container Company L.L.C., a leading producer of rigid plastic containers. In June 2005 Dean Foods spun off its former Specialty Foods Group, maker of pickles, nondairy creamer, sauces, and salad dressings, into an independent, publicly traded firm called TreeHouse Foods, Inc.

Early-20th-Century Beginnings of "Old" Dean Foods

Samuel E. Dean, Sr., was working with a brokerage firm in Chicago when he decided to start his own company. As he had been brokering evaporated milk, it seemed logical to enter that business. In 1925 he bought the Pecatonica Marketing Company, which ran an evaporated milk processing facility in Pecatonica, located in northwestern Illinois. Dean changed the company name to Dean Evaporated Milk Company in 1927 and soon added two more Illinois dairy plants. The firm was renamed Dean Milk Company in 1929. Dean entered the fresh milk industry in the mid-1930s, and until 1947 Dean's market was mostly fluid milk in northern Illinois. In 1947 Dean also entered the ice cream business.

The company's strategy of growth through careful acquisition began with its founder. In order to expand geographically, Dean began acquiring solid performers in other regions. Until World War II, Dean had been strictly a Midwestern dairy. After the war, it spread further, going as far as Kentucky. A research and development lab was established as early as 1943. One of the lab's first innovations was a powdered nondairy coffee creamer. This marked the origin of another company strength: more than half of Dean's later growth came from expanded markets and new

Company Perspectives:

At Dean Foods, we are proud to be in the business of enhancing and enriching the lives of consumers. Our brands are known for freshness, purity, delicious taste and impeccable quality. We sell fresh, nutritious dairy products under an array of local brands that have been staples in their communities for generations. Meadow Gold, Alta Dena, Dean's, Country Fresh, Oak Farms, Mayfield, and Garelick Farms are just a few. Which one is on your table? We also are proud to be the nation's leading organic foods company. Through our Silk and Horizon Organic brands, we are bringing healthy, delicious alternatives to tables across the country. From nutritious foods and beverages for people on the go—like single-serve milks, soymilks, juices and yogurts—to the creamy goodness of International Delight coffee creamers, we make the products consumers rely on to enhance and enrich their lives.

products. In 1951 the company established new headquarters in Franklin Park, Illinois, in suburban Chicago.

A number of milestones occurred in the 1960s. Dean Milk Company completed its first public offering of stock in 1961. The following year Dean acquired Green Bay Food Company, a maker of pickles, marking Dean's entry into the specialty food business. Reflecting this expansion, the company changed its name to Dean Foods Company in 1963. Two years later, Howard M. Dean, grandson of the founder and at the time a supply officer for the U.S. Navy, was tapped by his uncle, who was then chairman, to join the company. Howard Dean became company president in 1970, along with some other changes in management that signaled a new era for Dean Foods. Included in that new era was an acquisition strategy—perfected by Kenneth J. Douglas—that set the stage for the company's next decade. Most often, Dean absorbed well-known regional brands and companies that were small and healthy. Dean provided them with infusions of capital—especially to upgrade facilities—and access to marketing and management expertise.

Dean was remarkable for its decentralized management structure, allowing acquired companies relative autonomy. In nearly all cases, acquired companies saw increased earnings within a year or two of joining the Dean family. With one exception, all acquisitions through 1992 were privately held companies, often family owned. While other industry giants relied on brand-name, premium-priced products, Dean made its reputation through low-margin markets, providing regionally labeled goods to leading grocery chains and restaurants. For this reason, the Dean name was often not as recognized as some of its regional product lines. The company built its success on local favorites.

Expansion in the 1960s Through 1980s

Dean acquired a few more Midwestern dairy concerns in the 1960s, including Wisconsin's Fieldcrest Sales, purchased in 1966. Changes in the dairy industry, where competition necessitated economies of scale, caused many smaller companies to look to Dean for survival. Seven out of the 12 companies Dean acquired up to 1991 had approached Dean. Gandy's Dairies, Inc., of Texas was acquired in 1976, followed by Bell Dairy Products and Price's Creameries in 1978. Creamland Dairy of Albuquerque, New Mexico, also joined the family that year. In 1980 Florida companies McArthur Dairy Inc. and T.G. Lee Foods, Inc. were purchased, granting Dean a solid entry into that region. Later, Hart's Dairy of Florida was added to that state's holdings. Moving out of the largely Midwestern markets proved profitable for Dean as early as 1985, when its Southern and Southwestern regions became the company's strongest performers.

Dean began serving Pennsylvania and eastern Ohio with its 1984 purchase of a Sharpsville, Pennsylvania, dairy. A Kentucky-based dairy specialty company brought Dean into that area through a 1985 acquisition. Dean's sales hit the $1 billion mark in 1985, after 13 consecutive years of record earnings. Early that year, Jewel Food Stores was forced to close its own dairy operations after an outbreak of salmonella. The Chicago-area Jewel stores at that time accounted for nearly one-third of retail grocery business there. Dean stepped in to assist Jewel, providing the stores' fluid milk supply within 48 hours of the onset of the crisis. That single market accounted for nearly 90 percent of Dean's sales growth that year; the growth, however, was not immediately reflected in profits because of the costs of expansion and start-up services.

Meanwhile, Dean's dairy division was also benefiting from increased public awareness of the health benefits of calcium. Fluid milk consumption, after 20 years of stagnation, increased in 1984 and 1985. Research linking osteoporosis, or bone deterioration, to calcium-deficient diets not only gave a boost to milk sales, it also generated a new product line, as Dean Foods quickly introduced Nature's Calcium Plus and other calcium-added items.

Dairy products accounted for nearly 70 percent of Dean's total sales in 1984. Fluid milk was the largest dairy category at that time, but Dean's ice cream business was also thriving. Dean was area franchiser and exclusive supplier to more than 400 Baskin-Robbins stores in the West and Midwest. Ice cream sales nearly doubled when Dean began supplying Jewel in 1986. Several more healthy dairy companies were added to the fold about this time, including Reiter Dairy, Inc., of Akron, Ohio, in 1986. Representing $100 million in annual sales in that state, with excellent brand identity and growth records, Reiter's product line included fluid milk, cottage cheese, and ice cream. Ryan Milk Company of Kentucky, also acquired in 1986, brought with it a line of aseptic products and a distribution network that reached 40 states. Ryan brought Dean solidly into the ultra-high-temperature (UHT) processed products market. UHT products have longer shelf lives and include such things as flavored milks, half-and-half, whipping creams, and nondairy coffee creamers, of which Dean eventually became the nation's largest producer. With the purchase of Elgin Blenders, Inc., in 1986, Dean began supplying stabilizers and other products to McDonald's Corporation.

While best known for its dairy products, Dean's fastest-growing area was its specialty segment. Specialty foods included such things as pickles, dips, sauces, and relishes. In 1986 Dean merged with Larsen Company to enter the vegetable

Key Dates:

1925: Samuel E. Dean, Sr., enters the dairy industry through the purchase of Pecatonica Marketing Company in northwestern Illinois.

1927: Company changes its name to Dean Evaporated Milk Company.

1929: The company's name is changed to Dean Milk Company.

Mid-1930s: Dean enters the fresh milk industry.

1961: Dean Milk goes public.

1962: Dean expands into specialty foods with the purchase of pickle maker Green Bay Food Company.

1963: Reflecting expansion, company is renamed Dean Foods Company.

1985: Following numerous acquisitions, Dean's revenues surpass $1 billion.

1988: Gregg L. Engles and Robert Kaminski form Kaminski/Engles Capital Corp. to purchase the Reddy Ice packaged ice business from The Southland Corporation.

1993: Engles and partners enter the dairy sector, purchasing Suiza-Puerto Rico, owner of the largest dairy company on that island.

1994: Engles incorporates Suiza Foods Corporation as a Dallas-based holding company for his dairy and ice operations.

1996: Suiza Foods goes public through an initial public offering.

1997: Dean's plastic, single-serving milk bottles called "Milk Chugs" become a consumer hit; Suiza enters the branded dairy and nondairy food sector through merger with Morningstar Group, Inc.

1998: Suiza sells off its packaged ice business and acquires a 12 percent interest in Horizon Organic Dairy, Inc.

1999: In this year and the next, Dean acquires a 36 percent stake in soymilk maker WhiteWave, Inc.

2000: Suiza and Southern Foods Group, L.P. combine their milk operations, enabling Suiza to overtake Dean as the leading U.S. milk processor.

2001: Suiza acquires Dean in a $1.7 billion deal and adopts the Dean Foods Company name, but remains based in Dallas.

2002: Dean purchases full control of WhiteWave.

2004: Dean increases interest in Horizon Organic to 100 percent; most of the company's branded businesses, including WhiteWave, Horizon Organic, and Dean Branded Products Group, are consolidated within a unit called WhiteWave Foods Company.

2005: The Dean Specialty Foods Group is spun off as TreeHouse Foods, Inc.

---

business. Considered the creator of canned mixed vegetables, Larsen was a cornerstone in the canned and frozen vegetables industry as the processor of such successful retail brands as Veg-All and Freshlike. Larsen's annual sales were $170 million. This acquisition was one of Dean's largest and represented a notable diversification. It also reflected a revised corporate strategy regarding acquisitions—one that targeted companies with larger sales and different markets. At the time, more than three-quarters of Dean's volume was in dairy operations. The expense of this merger, combined with a bountiful crop at that time which lowered prices, hurt Dean initially, but the company recovered. With increased public attention to diet and health concerns, sales of frozen vegetables especially soared in the 1980s. By 1987 Dean ranked third in frozen and canned vegetable sales, after Pillsbury's Green Giant and Nabisco's Del Monte. Dean also began to service international vegetable markets. However, the vegetable glut combined with higher raw-milk prices in 1987 to slow Dean's net income that year. Profits for the company were flat. Whereas the government stabilized prices in the milk industry by buying surpluses, a surplus of vegetables meant only waste and depressed margins.

Dean purchased Verifine Dairy Products Corp. at the end of 1987. The $25 million Wisconsin dairy was quickly computerized and its automated systems updated. Fairmont Products, Inc., of Belleville, Pennsylvania, came onboard that year as well. In large part because of these two purchases, Dean's fluid milk sales grew 14 percent in 1988. That same year, Dean spent $9 million to settle a price-fixing case brought by Florida school boards. The charge was that two of Dean's subsidiaries were among ten dairies and distributors that conspired to rig bids for school milk supply contracts in Florida between 1965 and 1987.

Dean greatly strengthened its position in the frozen vegetable market by purchasing Richard A. Shaw, Inc., in 1988. Shaw's annual sales in 1989 were $55 million. The California-based company supplied major grocery chains and foodservice accounts and was Dean's entry into the West Coast vegetable market. Shaw also helped round out Dean's Midwestern produce line with crops grown mostly in the West. Dean then expanded its canned vegetable business in 1989 with the acquisition of Big Stone Inc. This Minnesota-based vegetable processor had sales of $24 million and two processing plants located near thriving sources of corn, peas, and green beans. Still more prime growing areas were accessed with the 1990 purchase of Bellingham Frozen Foods, Inc., whose plants in Washington and Michigan garnered annual sales of $30 million. A 1988 drought brought prices back up after they had been depressed by the earlier crop surplus, though this same drought depressed milk production.

Dean also made some internal changes in 1989: Howard Dean became chairman; William Fischer became president; and Kenneth Douglas became vice-chairman. The cost of acquisitions and the antitrust settlement, combined with a drought-related fall-off in milk production, caused a dip in earnings going into 1989. Another drain was the company's unprofitable transportation unit, which operated in a highly competitive market, providing a wide range of transportation and distribution services. Only 20 percent of the division's business was transporting Dean's products.

Dean sold its retail Baskin-Robbins ice cream business in 1989, but continued to be the stores' sole supplier for two of their major distribution areas. Shortly after that sale, Dean acquired Charles F. Cates & Sons, Inc., a pickle processor based in North Carolina with annual sales of $84 million. This boosted Dean's presence in the East and Southeast. Meanwhile, the company was the target of takeover talk and updated its poison-pill strategy late in 1989. Dean also continued its product innovations, introducing a very successful nonfat yogurt with artificial sweetener and Extra Light sour creams and dips. A frozen yogurt, which Dean had introduced 14 years earlier with little success, suddenly began performing well with the trend toward nutritional and health awareness.

Continuing Acquisition Spree in the Early to Mid-1990s

Dean launched 1990 with the purchase of Mayfield Dairy Farms, Inc. As one of the largest remaining family-owned dairy farms, Mayfield was a force in the Southeast—primarily Tennessee and Georgia—with annual sales near $110 million. Another new product was introduced in 1990: a low-fat milk with reduced lactose, a sugar that causes digestion problems for some milk drinkers. Dean also acquired Ready Food Products, Inc., of Philadelphia, a specialty dairy processor representing sales of $28 million. Expanding its specialty food segment helped Dean to balance the shortfall in dairy profits caused by further increases in raw-milk prices in 1989 and 1990. The operating earnings in specialty foods exceeded Dean's dairy products segment for the first time in 1990.

Three more dairies acquired in early 1991 brought with them $150 million in annual revenues. At the same time, Dean sold its McCadam Cheese Company unit, a private-label, New York supplier of natural cheeses. As raw-milk prices returned to pre-drought levels by the summer of 1991, the company refocused on its acquisition program. Dean purchased Cream o'Weber Dairy, Inc., of Utah in April 1991. It also acquired Frio Foods, Inc., a Texas-based vegetable processor, and Meadow Brook Dairy Company of Pennsylvania. The Cream o'Weber purchase typified Dean's strategy: even before the acquisition was completed, Cream o'Weber's plants were being consolidated and updated. Another advantage of being part of the Dean team was the sharing between divisions. An example of this came during the frozen yogurt boom in 1990, when Dean's T.G. Lee and McArthur affiliates wanted to enter this market. Starting a new product from scratch might have taken more than six months. Instead, these dairies were able to take advantage of the expertise of a fellow Dean division, Mayfield Dairy Farms, which produced one of Dean's best frozen yogurts. In just about five weeks, these companies had a new product on the market under their own names. Sharing between companies and a decentralized management style were part of what made Dean so successful.

Dean passed the $2 billion mark for the first time in 1991. An excess of crops in 1992, however, put a squeeze on Dean's profits in the vegetable segment. While revenues increased to $2.3 billion, net income dropped to $62 million, down from $72.5 million the previous year. At this time, Dean's vegetable line was 55 percent frozen and 45 percent canned, with roughly two-thirds of its output for private labels. Dairy remained Dean's primary business, with more than 21 milk processing plants and nearly 6 percent of the total market, making Dean a very close second to Borden, the industry leader.

In early 1993 Dean acquired W.B. Roddenbery Co. Inc., a processor of pickles, peanut butter, and syrup that generated

approximately $57 million in annual sales. Based in Georgia, the company's brands had widespread regional name recognition and were expected to help strengthen Dean's existing Specialty Foods segment. Relentless rain in the summer of 1993 seemed to promise relief from the oversupply and resulting low prices that had plagued the vegetable business in recent years; Dean found, however, that the weather raised its processing costs without providing immediate price increases, as the company was locked into low-priced contracts with its retail customers.

In January 1994 Dean Foods completed negotiations with Yarnell Ice Cream Co. to manufacture and distribute a line of low-fat and nonfat dairy products under Yarnell's Guilt Free brand, and two months later Dean purchased Birds Eye frozen foods from Kraft General Foods for $140 million. Noting the strength of the Birds Eye brand name, Howard Dean called the purchase "a strategic acquisition" that "positions Dean for volume and profit growth." Dean also announced plans to purchase Curtice-Burns Foods for approximately $173 million; the companies, however, were unable to resolve obstacles to the acquisition, and the deal fell through. In early 1995 Dean's CFO, Tim Bondy, resigned abruptly, and Dean's stock dropped 8 percent on this news: according to observers, Bondy was the mastermind behind Dean's growth-by-acquisition strategy, and his departure raised eyebrows on Wall Street. Within a week, the company announced that earnings for its third quarter (ending in February) would be substantially lower than previously estimated, and its stock dropped an additional 6 percent. According to the company, interest costs and tax rates contributed to the earnings decline.

Throughout 1995 Dean continued its shopping spree, purchasing Rio Grande Foods, a $40 million frozen vegetable processor based in Texas; Noral Crosetti Foods, a $45 million frozen vegetable processor based in California; and the salad dressing and dairy operations of Merico Inc., worth about $70 million annually. Whenever possible Dean worked to consolidate operations of its new acquisitions, seeking to effect efficiencies and move production closer to retail markets to reduce transportation costs.

The following year, Dean invested heavily to update the brand image of its dairy line, redesigning its packaging in bright colors with eye-catching graphics. Seeking to strengthen the Dean brand identity in a commodity market, the company began advertising milk's rich calcium content on its cartons and to approach marketing in general with the mind-set of a large beverage producer. In this vein, Mayfield Dairy Farms, a Dean division based in Tennessee, developed a highly successful plastic, single-serving, resealable milk bottle with a twist-off cap. A hit with consumers following its introduction in 1997, the plastic bottles—called "Milk Chugs"—were convenient, portable, and saleable in vending machines. Industry consultant Jerry Dryer noted the potential of such packaging for expanding the portability and popularity of milk, observing: "A square carton doesn't fit in the cup holder of your minivan." Dean subsequently introduced the Milk Chug at other dairies it owned, always sold under the local or regional brand of the specific dairy.

Late 1990s: Divestment of Vegetable Operations, Battling to Become Number One in Dairy

By 1996 Dean's rapid expansion into the vegetable business was taking a severe toll on earnings, as excess production, stagnant prices, and weak demand hurt vegetable processors throughout the country. Dean announced that it would undergo a wholesale restructuring, closing 13 plants—including seven vegetable plants—eliminating 840 jobs, and hiring a consultant to examine every other aspect of its business. Its recent acquisitions had made Dean the third largest vegetable processor in the United States, with vegetables accounting for 20 percent of its revenues. Dean expected the restructuring to eliminate $50 million in costs annually. The restructuring also entailed a shift in focus, with Dean reemphasizing dairy and pickles at the expense of vegetables, particularly canned vegetables.

In January 1997 the company announced the selection of Phil Marineau, the former head of Quaker Oats' Gatorade unit, as president and COO. Marineau replaced Thomas L. Rose, who retired from those positions but maintained a position as vice-chairman of the board. Analysts applauded the selection of Marineau for his extensive experience in packaged foods marketing, an area in which Dean was not traditionally strong. Said analyst John McMillin of Prudential Securities, "As a Dean Foods stockholder, I am thrilled that Dean could find such a qualified person."

Dean soon announced the purchase of Meadows Distributing Company (a $70 million distributor of ice cream in the Chicago metropolitan area) and the $35 million Marie's line of salad dressings, dips, salsas, and fruit glazes. In addition, Dean entered into a joint venture with River Ranch, of Salinas, California, to produce a line of branded fresh vegetables under the Birds Eye name. Fresh produce in U.S. supermarkets was an $18 billion a year business; with the increasing popularity of branded fresh vegetable lines, Marineau speculated that the new venture could soon generate $100 million annually. At the same time, Dean announced that it was investing $10 million to promote its new line of Birds Eye frozen baby gourmet vegetables.

Dean Foods completed several more dairy acquisitions in 1998, pushing its share of the U.S. milk market past the 10 percent mark and solidifying its position as the leading U.S. milk processor. Among the largest of these purchases was that of Nashville, Tennessee-based Purity Dairies, completed in May. The family-owned Purity, with annual sales of $100 million, produced and sold milk, ice cream, and other dairy products in central Tennessee, southwestern Kentucky, and northern Alabama. Other 1998 acquisitions included the California dairy operations of Lucky Stores, Inc., a subsidiary of Salt Lake City-based food and drug retailer American Stores Company, which added a business with $250 million in annual sales. The Alabama-based Barber Dairies Inc. was also acquired, although Dean was forced to divest Barber's Huntsville plant to gain regulatory approval. Revenues for the acquired operations of Barber totaled $200 million in 1997. To fund these and future acquisitions, Dean elected to sell off its underperforming vegetable business. It was sold in 1998 to Agrilink Foods Inc., a unit of Pro-Fac Cooperative, Inc., for $400 million in cash.

During the second half of the fiscal year ending in May 1999, Dean bolstered its California dairy operations, buying the San Francisco Bay area firm Berkeley Farms, Inc. in November 1998 and Alta-Dena Certified Dairy, Inc., operating in Southern California, in May 1999. For the fiscal year, sales in Dean's dairy business jumped 45 percent, reaching $2.9 billion. Such

apparently strong growth, however, was not enough to keep Dean number one. In early 2000 the company was surpassed by the even-more-rapidly expanding Suiza Foods, which had completed more than 40 dairy acquisitions since 1996, coming seemingly out of nowhere to grab 20 percent of the milk market, while Dean's operations now claimed 14 percent. In the meantime, to improve its profit margins, Dean spent more than $15 million in fiscal 1999 to consolidate its burgeoning operations, closing ten dairy plants and centralizing engineering processes for the remaining 56 plants.

Dipping its toe into the burgeoning market for soy-based food products, Dean spent $15 million in 1999 and 2000 for a 36 percent stake in Boulder, Colorado-based WhiteWave, Inc. Founded by Steve Demos in 1977 to sell tofu in the Boulder area, WhiteWave was the U.S. pioneer in refrigerated soymilk, launching the top-selling Silk soymilk brand in 1996. At the time of Dean's investment, WhiteWave was generating annual sales of approximately $21 million. Also in 2000, Dean purchased the Upper Midwest fluid milk operations of Land O'Lakes, Inc., a business with $310 million in 1999 sales. Concurrently, Dean and Land O'Lakes entered into a 50–50 joint venture through which Dean would begin marketing sour cream, half and half, and cream nationwide under the Land O'Lakes brand. For the 2000 fiscal year, Dean Foods reported net income of $106.1 million on $4.07 billion in revenues. In April 2001 Dean Foods, after more than three-quarters of a century in the milk business, agreed to be acquired by the industry's upstart but now clear number one player, Suiza Foods.

Suiza Foods' Packaged Ice Beginnings

Suiza Foods Corporation had its start in 1988 when an investment firm, Kaminski/Engles Capital Corp., formed by Gregg L. Engles and Robert Kaminski, purchased the Reddy Ice packaged ice business from The Southland Corporation, owner of the 7-Eleven convenience store chain, for $26 million. It was ironic that Reddy Ice would be the company that Suiza Foods was founded upon, since Southland also traced its beginnings to Reddy Ice, which was launched in 1927 by 7-Eleven founder Joe C. Thompson. By the late 1980s, Southland had fallen on hard times, and the selling of its ice business was part of a divestiture program. Later in 1988 Kaminski/Engles bought Sparkle Ice from The Circle K Company, another convenience store chain, and combined it into Reddy Ice. Over the next several years, more than a dozen additional ice making and distribution operations were purchased and melded into Reddy Ice, creating abundant opportunities for consolidating facilities and achieving economies of scale. This pattern would be followed to an even larger extent by Engles in the dairy sector.

Engles's background was in investment banking, but he specialized in mergers and acquisitions, which was quickly apparent. In late 1993 Engles and a group of partners in Suiza Holdings L.P. acquired Suiza-Puerto Rico for $99.4 million, including $85 million in cash. Suiza-Puerto Rico's operations included Suiza Dairy Corp., the largest dairy company in Puerto Rico. Suiza Dairy ("Suiza" is Spanish for "Swiss") had been founded in 1942 by Héctor Nevares, Sr., and was owned by the Nevares family until the purchase by the Engles-led partnership. The company held 58 percent of the milk market on the island, had 850 employees, and generated annual revenues of $185 million. Suiza-Puerto Rico was also involved in the manufacture of fruit drinks and the distribution of third-party brand-name ice cream and other dairy products.

The dairy sector quickly became Engles's industry of choice. He had been searching for an area ripe for consolidation. In 1998, in explaining to *Dairy Foods* why he chose dairy, he said: "In large measure, because that's the opportunity that presented itself. I don't know of a bigger industry consolidation going on today. But I like dairy. Its dynamics are good. This industry is one in which there are real economic benefits in size and scale, but no one really has it, no one has capitalized on that." The U.S. dairy industry of the 1990s was highly fragmented, with numerous family-owned operations that were ideal acquisition candidates.

Engles's formula for growth was evident right from his first foray into dairy (and actually was earlier applied to ice packaging). His plan was to purchase the leading dairy in a region, then fill in with additional acquisitions in that region. By consolidating operations, closing plants, and cutting jobs, the first dairy acquired would gain market share, increase its efficiency, and become more profitable. In Puerto Rico, Engles followed his purchase of Suiza Dairy with the June 1994 $7 million acquisition of Mayaguez Dairy, Inc., the island's number three dairy. Mayaguez was subsequently consolidated into Suiza Dairy, whose market share increased to 66 percent, and the plan was put into practice.

In April 1994 Engles, through his Dallas-based investment banking firm Engles Management Corp., spent $48 million to acquire Lakeland, Florida-based Velda Farms, Inc., providing a regional base for the state of Florida. Velda Farms, which was founded in 1955, manufactured and distributed fresh milk, ice cream, and related products under its own brand names to about 9,500 foodservice accounts, convenience stores, club stores, and schools.

October 1994 Formation of Suiza Foods

Engles incorporated Suiza Foods Corporation in October 1994 as a holding company for Suiza-Puerto Rico, Velda Farms, and Reddy Ice. Engles was named chairman and CEO, while Cletes O. "Tex" Beshears—Engles's right-hand man—was named president and chief operating officer as well as a director. Beshears had been a vice-president at Southland and COO of its dairy group from 1980 to 1988. From 1965 to 1980 Beshears was division manager for a number of Southland's regional dairy operations, including Velda Farms. The headquarters for Suiza Foods was established in Dallas.

Suiza Foods was set up as a holding company, with a thoroughly decentralized management style. As with its previous acquisitions, the Suiza plan was to seek out companies with strong management teams that could be left in place for a smooth transition and the retention of local market experience, relationships, and knowledge. By and large, the company had no plans for creating national brands, concluding that the continuation of longstanding local and regional brands was critical for success in the dairy industry.

The newly formed corporation immediately set out on the acquisition trail. In November 1994 Velda Farms added to its dairy operations the Florida division of Flav-O-Rich Inc., which was purchased from Mid-America Dairymen, Inc. for $3.6 million. Similarly, Velda bought Skinner's Dairy Inc. of Jacksonville, Florida, in January 1996.

To help fund additional acquisitions and pay down debt, Suiza Foods went public in April 1996 through an initial public offering—priced at $14 per share—that raised about $48.6 million. Company stock was traded on the NASDAQ under the symbol SWZA. An additional $10 million was secured in August 1996 through a private placement of common stock to the T. Rowe Price Small Cap Value Fund. Then in January of the following year Suiza raised another $89 million through a secondary public offering, priced at $22 per share. Proceeds were again used to reduce debt. In March 1997 Suiza Foods began trading on the New York Stock Exchange under the symbol SZA. Company stock ended 1997 trading at $59.56 per share, after reaching a high of $62.50.

Meanwhile, in July 1996 Suiza acquired Garrido y Compania, Inc., the second largest coffee processor in Puerto Rico and operator of the island's largest office and hotel coffee service. The company paid $35.8 million for Garrido, which became part of Suiza-Puerto Rico. In September 1996 Suiza gained a regional milk producer in southern California through the $55.1 million acquisition of Swiss Dairy Corp., based in Riverside. The family owned and operated dairy was founded in the 1940s and had sales of about $126 million in 1995. Suiza Foods added another western dairy to its growing stable in December 1996 when it paid $27 million for Model Dairy, also family owned and operated since opening in 1906. Reno, Nevada-based Model Dairy was the largest milk distributor in northern Nevada. These acquisitions helped increase Suiza Foods' revenues from $431 million in 1995 to $521 million in 1996.

An Accelerating Acquisition Pace Starting in 1997

In July 1997 Beshears was named vice-chairman of Suiza and William P. "Bill" Brick added the post of president to his title as COO (which he had assumed from Beshears in October 1996). Brick, like Beshears, had experience in the dairy industry prior to joining Suiza in July 1996 as an executive vice-president.

During the later months of 1997 and all of 1998 Suiza Foods grabbed headlines with its ever-more acquisitive methods. In the second half of 1997 alone, the company acquired Dairy Fresh L.P. (renamed Dairy Fresh, Inc.) for $106.3 million (in July); Garelick Farms, Inc. for $299.6 million (also in July); the Nashville, Tennessee, dairy division of Fleming Companies, Inc. (in August); Country Fresh, Inc. for $135 million in stock and debt (in October); and The Morningstar Group, Inc. for $960 million in stock and debt (in November). Winston-Salem, North Carolina-based Dairy Fresh generated about $125 million in annual revenues through the processing of milk and ice cream products. The Fleming dairy division, which Suiza renamed Country Delite Farms, Inc., had revenues of $76 million. In February 1998 Suiza paid $248 million for Land-O-Sun Dairies, L.L.C., a Johnson City, Tennessee, processor of fluid milk and ice cream with revenues of $464 million. Dairy Fresh, Country Delite, and Land-O-Sun together formed the largest dairy manufacturing and distribution network in the Southeast.

Garelick Farms included three dairy companies in the Northeast—Franklin, Massachusetts-based Garelick, Fairdale Farms, Inc. in Bennington, Vermont, and Grant's Dairy, Inc. of Bangor, Maine—in addition to Mendon, Massachusetts-based bottled water firm Miscoe Springs, Inc. Garelick's operations also included 17 plastic bottle manufacturing operations located from Maine to Texas, which Suiza consolidated within a new subsidiary, Franklin Plastics, Inc. Collectively, the Garelick operations generated more than $370 million in revenues and provided Suiza a solid base for growth in the Northeast.

The acquisition of Country Fresh provided Suiza its first penetration of the Midwestern market. Based in Grand Rapids, Michigan, Country Fresh was a processor of milk, juice, and ice cream products, which it distributed in Michigan, Ohio, and Indiana. The company had annual revenues of $353 million. In early 1998 Suiza expanded its presence in the Midwest through the February acquisition of Oberlin Farms Dairy, Inc. of Cleveland, Ohio, and the March purchase of Louis Trauth Dairy, Inc., of Newport, Kentucky. Oberlin had revenues of $76 million, while Louis Trauth had sales of $67 million.

The merger—through a stock swap—with Morningstar was different in that it diversified Suiza's operations. Morningstar's history paralleled that of Suiza Foods. It, too, was born in 1988 through a Southland divestment. Since being sold that year to private investors, Morningstar had grown through acquisitions and become a publicly traded company (just as Suiza had). It had revenues of about $528 million through its manufacturing and distribution of branded and long-shelf-life dairy and nondairy specialty foods. Morningstar's array of brands included International Delight gourmet coffee creamers, Second Nature no-cholesterol egg substitute, Naturally Yours sour cream, Mocha Mix nondairy creamer, and Jon Donaire cheesecakes and desserts. The company also licensed the Lactaid brand for a line of lactose-free and lactose-reduced dairy products, as well as supplied its customers with private-label creamers, cottage cheese, prewhipped toppings, sour cream, and yogurt.

As a result of its aggressive acquisition strategy, Suiza Foods more than tripled its revenues for 1997, posting net sales of $1.8 billion. The company reported net income of $28.8 million. It now laid claim to the top position in the U.S. milk industry, although Dean Foods also boasted that it was number one.

Following the merger with Morningstar, Suiza shuffled its top management. Brick shifted over to become executive vice-president and president of the dairy group, making room for L. Hollis Jones to become president and COO, the position he had held at Morningstar. Jones, however, left Suiza in February 1998, becoming an exclusive consultant for Suiza, with a focus on acquisitions and strategic developments. Taking over as president and COO was G. Irwin Gordon, who had been a Suiza executive vice-president.

1998–2000: Shuffling of Plastic Assets, Divesting Ice, Acquiring More Dairies

Suiza Foods' acquisition of Garelick Farms—more specifically Franklin Plastics—had presented the company with another opportunity. Up until that purchase, Suiza was involved in the plastic packaging industry only through those dairies it had

acquired that made their own containers (such as Neva Plastics, which was acquired along with Suiza-Puerto Rico). Franklin Plastics, however, served outside customers as well. Suiza decided to build upon the expertise of Franklin by applying its consolidation strategy to plastic packaging. In an acquisition announced in January 1998 and consummated in June of that year, Suiza acquired Continental Can Company, Inc. for about $345 million. Norwalk, Connecticut-based Continental Can had revenues of $546 million and 15 plastic packaging plants in the United States, which when added to those of Franklin provided Suiza with a nationwide packaging network. Continental Can also had nine European plants that manufactured food cans and plastic packaging; these operations were almost immediately identified as likely candidates for divestment, and they were in fact sold off in 2000.

In March 1998 the company's board of directors adopted a shareholders' rights plan aimed at making a hostile takeover of Suiza more difficult. Two months later Suiza completed the sale of Reddy Ice—the business upon which the company was founded—to privately held Packaged Ice, Inc. of Houston, Texas, for $172 million. The move was intended to allow the company to focus on its core dairy and plastic packaging operations, with the proceeds slated for additional acquisitions in those sectors. In a somewhat similar move, Suiza in July 1998 exchanged its Jon Donaire desserts business for the retail refrigerated and frozen creamer business of Rich Products Corporation of Buffalo, New York. While desserts were outside Suiza's core food areas, the Coffee Rich, Farm Rich, Poly Rich, and Rich Whip brands acquired fit in perfectly with the other brands Suiza had acquired through Morningstar.

Suiza Foods added two more dairies to its northeastern region in 1998 by way of the June purchase of West Lynn Creamery, Inc., which had revenues of $215 million; and the August acquisition of the fluid dairy division of Cumberland Farms, Inc. of Canton, Massachusetts, which generated sales of about $200 million. In July 1998 Suiza spent about $12 million for a 12 percent stake in Boulder, Colorado-based Horizon Organic Dairy Inc., holder of 65 percent of the U.S. organic dairy product market. The transaction was made in concurrence with Horizon's initial public offering. Horizon also entered into dairy processing and distribution agreements with Suiza subsidiaries Model Dairy and Garelick Farms. Suiza Foods topped off 1998 with two more deals. In December Suiza agreed to purchase Broughton Foods Corporation for $123 million. Based in Marietta, Ohio, Broughton was a leading manufacturer and distributor of milk, ice cream, and other dairy products in Michigan, Ohio, West Virginia, Kentucky, Tennessee, and sections of the eastern United States. The company had revenues of about $200 million in 1997. Suiza planned to integrate Broughton facilities into its regional operations in the Midwest and Southeast. Also in December, Suiza and Dairy Farmers of America, Inc. (DFA), the nation's largest dairy cooperative, agreed to combine their northeastern dairy operations into a joint venture 75 percent owned by Suiza and 25 percent by DFA. With its various 1998 acquisitions, Suiza posted 1998 revenues of $3.32 billion, nearly double that of the preceding year. It now held more than 10 percent of the $25 billion fluid milk market in the United States, and Engles set a goal of increasing that figure to 30 percent by 2003.

The Broughton deal ran into a snag when the U.S. Department of Justice filed an antitrust suit to block the purchase because of concerns about how the combination would affect the pricing of milk contracts in certain Kentucky school districts. Suiza settled the suit by agreeing to sell one of Broughton's Kentucky dairies, and the deal closed in June 1999 at a reduced price of $86 million plus the assumption of $20 million in debt. In July 1999 Suiza exchanged its domestic plastic packaging operations for a 43 percent stake in the newly formed Consolidated Container Company L.L.C. (CCC), plus $502 million in cash and assumed debt. CCC was created by Vestar Capital Partners, a private equity firm, which contributed its Reid Plastics operations to the venture. The sale helped Suiza pay down some of its $900 million debt load and provided funding for further dairy acquisitions.

Of the dozen or so deals completed in 1999 and 2000, the most significant involved Southern Foods Group, L.P., the third largest dairy processor in the nation. In January 2000 Suiza merged its milk processing and distribution assets with those of Southern Foods in a deal valued at $435.6 million. Southern, whose annual sales totaled about $1.25 billion, operated in Texas, the Midwest, and the Rocky Mountains, marketing its milk under such names as Oak Farms, Schepps, Foremost, Borden, Elsie, and Meadow Gold. Southern had been half owned by DFA, so upon completion of the deal the newly created Suiza Dairy Group operated as a joint venture between Suiza and DFA, with Suiza owning 66.2 percent and DFA 33.8 percent. DFA would act as one of Suiza Dairy Group's prime milk suppliers. The addition of the Southern Foods' dairies to the fold made Suiza the clear leader of the U.S. fluid milk sector, with a market share of about 20 percent compared to Dean Foods' 14 percent. Following completion of the merger, Gordon resigned and his position as president and COO was not filled. Instead, Suiza began operating with two presidents of its two main units. Pete Schenkel, who had been CEO of Southern Foods, was named president of Suiza Dairy Group and vice-chairman of Suiza Foods. Bing Graffunder continued to serve as president of the Morningstar branded dairy product subsidiary. Also in 2000, Suiza entered the international dairy market by acquiring a 75 percent stake in Leche Celta, one of the largest dairy processors in Spain. Suiza was mainly interested in gaining access to Leche's pasteurization technology that prolonged the shelf life of dairy products. In August 2001 Suiza acquired the remaining 25 percent interest. Suiza revenues for 2000, meanwhile, totaled $5.76 billion, more than triple the total of just three years earlier.

2001 and Beyond: The New Dean Foods, a Creation of Suiza's Takeover of the Old Dean

In a move that some in the industry called unthinkable and some inevitable, Suiza Foods in April 2001 reached an agreement to acquire Dean Foods. When completed in December of that year, the deal was valued at $1.7 billion in cash and stock, with Suiza also assuming about $1 billion in Dean debt, pushing its total debt load to more than $3 billion. The company kept its headquarters in Dallas but elected to adopt the better-known Dean Foods Company name. Engles remained CEO and also served as vice-chairman, while Howard Dean assumed the chairmanship; in April of the following year, however, Dean

retired and Engles became chairman once again. Concurrent with completion of the takeover, the newly enlarged company purchased DFA's 33.8 percent stake in the Dairy Group unit, gaining full control of its milk operations once again. Dean conveyed to DFA $145.4 million in cash plus the operations of 11 milk plants (seven of Suiza's and four of old Dean's) located in nine states where the two predecessor firms had overlapping operations. The plant divestments were necessary to gain Justice Department approval of the transaction. Schenkel remained president of the Dairy Group, which now claimed 30 percent of the U.S. fluid milk market, achieving Engles's goal two years early. Dean Foods also ranked as the third largest maker of ice cream in the country. With operations in 39 states, and a total of 129 plants, the company was better positioned to serve the increasingly national operations of the major supermarket chains. Engles expected to achieve $120 million in cost savings through merger synergies by 2003. In 2002, its first full year of operation, the new Dean posted revenues just shy of $9 billion.

Integration activities were the main priority in 2002, and a few plants were shut down and three noncore businesses in the old Dean's Specialty Foods division were divested. Dean in December of that year sold its Puerto Rico operations to Grupo Gloria, a Peruvian conglomerate, for $119.4 million. The divested properties included the first dairy operation that Suiza had purchased. In May 2002 Dean spent $192.8 million for the 64 percent of WhiteWave it did not already own. Demos remained in charge of WhiteWave, whose annual sales had reached $125 million. Also acquired that year was the Marie's line of refrigerated dips and dressings, which were sold in the western United States and became part of the Morningstar Foods portfolio. In addition, Dean entered into an expanded alliance with Land O'Lakes giving Dean the right to use the Land O'Lakes name nationally on a range of value-added fluid milk and cultured dairy products.

Restructuring continued in 2003 as several more milk plants were closed and Morningstar Foods was transformed into the Dean Branded Products Group. Responsibility for private-label dairy products was shifted from Morningstar to the Dean Dairy Group, and the newly named Dean Branded Products Group refocused exclusively on national brand-name products, such as International Delight coffee creamers, Hershey's milks and milkshakes, Land O'Lakes value-added dairy products, and Marie's dips and dressings. In a move important more for its marketing potential than for the potential sales, WhiteWave entered into an agreement with Starbucks Corporation for Silk to become the exclusive soymilk used at the numerous Starbucks outlets located throughout North America, starting in the summer of 2003. On the acquisition front, Dean spent $158.6 million for Kohler Mix Specialties, Inc., maker of private-label, ultra-pasteurized ice cream mixes, creamers, and creams, mainly for the foodservice channel. The deal greatly expanded the Dairy Group's ultra-high-temperature manufacturing capacity. In June 2003 the Dairy Group bolstered its Michigan operations by acquiring Melody Farms, LLC, a producer of fluid dairy and ice cream products from two facilities with annual revenues of $116 million. Continuing to seek this type of fill-in acquisition, the Dairy Group in January 2004 acquired Ross Swiss Dairies, a Los Angeles dairy distributor with 2003 net sales of $120 million. Late in 2003 Dean's Specialty Foods

Group bought the Cremora brand of nondairy powdered creamer from Eagle Family Foods, Inc.

Dean further bolstered its brand-name operations through the January 2004 purchase of the 87 percent of Horizon Organic it did not already own. The purchase price was approximately $287 million. Horizon had achieved $187 million in sales by 2002, and its flagship brand dominated the U.S. organic milk market, with a 67 percent share. In addition to milk, Horizon's product line included butter, yogurt, cheese, juices, puddings, fruit jells, and eggs. Horizon also had an operation in the United Kingdom, marketing and selling organic milk, yogurt, and butter under the Rachel's Organic brand. The Rachel's Organic business was shifted into Dean's International division at the beginning of 2005. In August 2004, meanwhile, Dean launched a plan to consolidate by the end of 2005 its Branded Products Group, WhiteWave, and Horizon into a single, standalone operating unit called WhiteWave Foods Company, to be based in Broomfield, Colorado. These operations, boasting an impressive array of brands—Horizon Organic, Silk, Sun Soy, WhiteWave, Hershey's, Land O'Lakes, Dean, Marie's, and International Delight—produced $1.19 billion in revenues in 2004 and were growing at a clip in excess of 20 percent per year. Demos was initially placed in charge of WhiteWave, but he resigned in March 2005, apparently after Dean concluded that it needed someone at WhiteWave with more consumer packaged goods experience. Engles assumed leadership over the unit on an interim basis, while a search for a new leader commenced.

Revenues at Dean Foods surpassed $10 billion for the first time in 2004, but net income fell thanks to highly volatile raw milk prices, pressures stemming from a difficult environment in the retail grocery sector, and record costs for fuel, resin, and other commodities. Only $676.8 million of the $10.82 billion in revenues was attributable to the underperforming Specialty Foods Group, so Dean in January 2005 announced a plan to spin the operation off to shareholders in order to further focus on its core Dairy Group and WhiteWave units. Dean shifted its Second Nature egg substitute, Mocha Mix nondairy creamer, and foodservice salad businesses into the Specialty group before completing the spinoff in June 2005, which created the new, publicly traded TreeHouse Foods, Inc. In the wake of this important divestiture, Dean Foods was faced with the immediate tasks of successfully consolidating the WhiteWave Foods operations and finding a new leader for it, and taking further steps to cut costs and improve profitability at the Dairy Group.

Principal Subsidiaries

Alta-Dena Certified Dairy, Inc.; Barber Ice Cream, LLC; Barber Milk, Inc.; Berkeley Farms, Inc.; Broughton Foods, LLC; Country Delite Farms, LLC; Country Fresh, LLC; Dairy Fresh, LLC; Dean Dairy Products Company; Dean Foods Company of California, Inc.; Dean Foods Foundation; Dean Foods North Central, Inc.; Dean Milk Company, Inc.; Dean Puerto Rico Holdings, LLC; Dean Transportation, Inc.; Fairmont Dairy, LLC; Franklin Plastics, Inc. (88%); Gandy's Dairies, Inc.; International Milk Sales, Inc.; Land-O-Sun Dairies, LLC; Liberty Dairy Company; Louis Trauth Dairy, LLC; Maplehurst Farms, LLC; Mayfield Dairy Farms, Inc.; McArthur Dairy, Inc.; Meadow Brook Dairy Company; The Meadows Distributing

Company; Midwest Ice Cream Company; Model Dairy, LLC; Morningstar Foods Inc.; New England Dairies, LLC; Old G & Co., Inc.; Pet O'Fallon, LLC; Purity Dairies, Incorporated; Reiter Akron, Inc.; Reiter Springfield, LLC; Robinson Dairy, LLC; Schenkel's All-Star Dairy, LLC; Schenkel's All-Star Delivery, LLC; Shenandoah's Pride, LLC; Southern Foods Group, L.P.; Suiza Dairy Group, Inc.; Sulphur Springs Cultured Specialties, LLC; T.G. Lee Foods, Inc.; Tuscan/Lehigh Dairies, L.P.; Verifine Dairy Products Corporation of Sheboygan, Inc.; Wengert's Dairy, Inc.; WhiteWave, Inc.; Tenedora Dean Foods Internacional, S.A. de C.V. (Mexico); Dean Netherlands, B.V.; Carnival Ice Cream, N.V. (Netherlands Antilles); Leche Celta, S.L. (Spain).

Principal Divisions

Dairy Group; WhiteWave Foods Company; International.

Principal Competitors

The Kroger Co.; National Dairy Holdings L.P.; Prairie Farms Dairy, Inc.; Dreyer's Grand Ice Cream Holdings, Inc.; Parmalat Canada Limited; Dairy Farmers of America, Inc.

Further Reading

Adamy, Janet, "Behind a Food Giant's Success: An Unlikely Soy-Milk Alliance," *Wall Street Journal,* February 1, 2005, p. A1.

Alm, Richard, "Dallas-Based Dean Foods to Acquire Organic Dairy," *Dallas Morning News,* July 1, 2003.

Augstums, Ieva M., "Dallas-Based Dairy Distributor to Sell Puerto Rico Units to Peruvian Concern," *Dallas Morning News,* November 12, 2002.

Bailey, Ken, "Dean, Suiza Going Head-to-Head in Fluid Milk Business," *Feedstuffs,* September 13, 1999, pp. 22 + .

Balu, Rekha, "Dean Agrees to Sell Vegetable Division to Pro-Fac Unit," *Wall Street Journal,* July 28, 1998, p. A6.

——, "Dean Foods Attempting to Reintroduce Milk to Consumers," *Wall Street Journal,* March 26, 1998, p. B4.

Barnett, Tracy L., "Dean Pursues Consolidation Strategy," *Santa Cruz Sentinel,* February 4, 1996.

Byrne, Harlan S., "Dairy King," *Barron's,* February 23, 1998, p. 20.

——, "Dean Foods Co.: Diversification Paying Off for Big Seller of Dairy Products," *Barron's,* May 7, 1990.

——, "Dean Foods Co.: SeeSaw Markets Don't Slow Its Trek to Another Record Year," *Barron's,* June 3, 1991.

——, "Southern Exposure: Suiza's Joint Venture Gives Company More Clout," *Barron's,* October 18, 1999, p. 14.

Cahill, William R., "Galloping Gourmet," *Barron's,* December 8, 1986.

Clark, Gerry, "Think Nationally, Act Locally," *Dairy Foods,* December 1999, pp. 36–38 + .

Clark, Gerry, and Dave Fusaro, "$1.2 Billion Power Play," *Dairy Foods,* February 1999, pp. 20 + .

Clucas, David, "WhiteWave Founder Resigns from Dean Foods," *Boulder County (Colo.) Business Report,* March 18, 2005, p. 9A.

Cohen, Deborah L., "Dean Chugs with National Rollout," *Crain's Chicago Business,* March 20, 2000, p. 4.

Conlin, Michelle, "The Pastures Weren't Greener," *Forbes,* September 7, 1998, pp. 175 + .

Cook, Lynn J., "Got Growth?," *Forbes,* May 12, 2003, p. 102.

Crown, Judith, "Dean Foods Catches a Chill," *Crain's Chicago Business,* September 18, 1989.

Curriden, Mark, "Dallas-Based Dairy Processor to Pay $189 Million for Rest of Soy Milk Firm," *Dallas Morning News,* May 9, 2002.

"Dean Foods Co.: A Big Processor Survives a Dry Spell," *Barron's,* April 10, 1989.

"Dean Foods Gets License for 'Guilt Free' Products," *Frozen Food Age,* March 1994.

"Dean Foods to Cut 840 Jobs and Close 13 Plants," *New York Times,* May 29, 1996.

"Dean's List," *Forbes,* June 15, 1987.

Deogun, Nikhil, and Kevin Helliker, "Suiza Nears $1.5 Billion Deal for Dean Foods," *Wall Street Journal,* April 5, 2001, p. A3.

Dexheimer, Ellen, "Dean Dynasty," *Dairy Foods,* November 1991.

Donovan, William J., "Texas' Suiza Foods to Acquire Rhode Island's Garelick Farms," *Providence Journal-Bulletin,* June 24, 1997.

Dwyer, Steve, "Dean Got Milk Money," *Prepared Foods,* September 1998, p. 10.

Fink, James, "Coffee Rich Blends with Dallas Company," *Business First of Buffalo,* July 20, 1998, pp. 1+.

Fusaro, Dave, "Enigmatic Acquisition Machine," *Dairy Foods,* March 1998, pp. 18+.

——, "Suiza Foods," *Dairy Foods,* April 1998, pp. 69+.

Guy, Sandra, "Dean to Chug Along in Slow-Growth Area," *Chicago Sun-Times,* January 14, 2002.

"Horizon Organic Inc. Completes Its IPO and a Sale to Suiza," *Wall Street Journal,* July 6, 1998, p. C22.

Horwich, Andrea, "Boosting Sales by Boning Up on Calcium," *Dairy Foods,* October 1986.

Kuhn, Mary Ellen, "Dairy's Slam Dunk!: Dean and Suiza Capitalize on Consolidation with Aggressive Expansion Agendas," *Food Processing,* June 1998, pp. 22+.

Lee, Steven H., "Dallas-Based Dairy Processor Grows Through Steady Stream of Acquisitions," *Dallas Morning News,* August 15, 1999.

——, "Dallas-Based Foods Firm's Deal Will Create Dairy Giant," *Dallas Morning News,* April 6, 2001.

——, "Dallas-Based Suiza Foods to Buy Virginia Dairy Group," *Dallas Morning News,* July 24, 1999.

——, "With Acquisition, Dallas-Based Firm Becomes Nation's Largest Dairy Processor," *Dallas Morning News,* September 21, 1999.

Leibowitz, David, "Of Gum, Tools and Milk," *Financial World,* February 24, 1987.

Lingle, Rick, "A Tale of Two Lines," *Dairy Foods,* August 1991.

Lipin, Steven, "Suiza Foods to Buy Morningstar Group for $777 Million in Stock, Plus Debt," *Wall Street Journal,* September 29, 1997, p. A4.

"Lucky 13th," *Barron's,* July 5, 1985.

"The New Dean Foods a $10 Billion Business," *Dairy Foods,* February 2002, p. 8.

Otto, Alison, "The Year-End Juggling Act," *Dairy Foods,* December 1986.

Mans, Jack, "Hey, Big Spender!" *Dairy Foods,* November 1991.

Markgraf, Sue, "Chugging Along," *Dairy Foods,* May 1998, pp. 15–16, 18.

——, "Purely Strategic," *Dairy Foods,* June 1998, p. 16.

Montano, Agnes J., "Suiza Foods' Subsidiary Buys Flav-O-Rich Division," *San Juan Star,* November 29, 1994.

Nethery, Ross, "Food Company Raising $200M," *Dallas Business Journal,* October 21, 1994.

"New Faces in New Places," *Dairy Foods,* July 1998, pp. 10+.

Oloroso, Arsenio, "Dean Foods' Dry Spell Ends," *Crain's Chicago Business,* July 29, 1991.

Osterland, Andrew, "Dean Foods: Indigestion," *Financial World,* April 25, 1995.

Otto, Alison, "A Prognosis of Progress," *Dairy Foods,* April 1986.

Palmer, Jay, "Growing Again," *Barron's,* July 6, 1992.

Pico, Maria Bird, "Suiza Plans $80 Million Stock Offering," *San Juan Star,* November 4, 1994.

Reiter, Jeff, "All Together Now," *Dairy Foods,* November 1991.

——, "Small Niche, Big Potential," *Dairy Foods,* May 1991.

Rewick, C.J., "Dean Foods to Can Veggie Venture," *Crain's Chicago Business,* July 27, 1998.

——, "Hefty Merger Costs Halt Dean's Milk Run," *Crain's Chicago Business,* April 5, 1999, p. 3.

"Riverside, Calif., Dairy Has Gone Through 48 Years of Changes," *Riverside (Calif.) Press-Enterprise,* October 14, 1996.

Robinson-Jacobs, Karen, "Dean Foods Capitalizes on Rapid Growth in Soymilk Sales," *Dallas Morning News,* September 25, 2004.

——, "Dean to Spin Off Business," *Dallas Morning News,* January 28, 2005.

Schexnayder, Karla, " 'Whey' Ahead of the Game," *Dairy Foods,* March 1991.

Siler, Charles, "Ripe for the Picking," *Forbes,* April 3, 1989.

Smith, Pamela Accetta, "Dairy Dynamics," *Dairy Field,* October 2002, pp. 1+.

Smith, Rod, "Dean Foods Building Position As National, 'On-the-Go' Dairy," *Feedstuffs,* September 27, 1999, pp. 6+.

——, "Dean, Suiza Continue Strategy to Acquire Dairy Market Share," *Feedstuffs,* June 15, 1998, p. 7.

——, "Suiza Building Platforms to Shape Dairy Industry," *Feedstuffs,* May 11, 1998, pp. 6+.

"Suiza Foods Restructures Top Mgmt., Names Gordon President," *Nation's Restaurant News,* March 16, 1998, p. 116.

"Suiza Foods to Buy Plastics Manufacturers and Dairy Companies," *Wall Street Journal,* June 24, 1997, p. A12.

Tejada, Carlos, "Suiza to Combine Milk Operations with Company," *Wall Street Journal,* September 22, 1999, p. B11.

Therrien, Lois, "Dean Goes Looking for a Diet Supplement," *Business Week,* March 14, 1988.

——, "Making the Undrinkable Thinkable," *Business Week,* May 14, 1990.

Wren, Worth, Jr., "Two Southland Spinoffs Expected to Merge: Suiza Will Acquire Morningstar in a $960 Million Deal," *Fort Worth Star-Telegram,* September 30, 1997.

Zehr, Douglas, "Delaware Group to Buy Suiza Dairy," *San Juan Star,* September 30, 1993.

—Carol I. Keeley and David E. Salamie
—updates: Paula Kepos, David E. Salamie

DELUXE

Deluxe Corporation

3680 Victoria Street North
Shoreview, Minnesota 55126-2966
U.S.A.
Telephone: (651) 483-7111
Fax: (651) 481-4163
Web site: http://www.deluxe.com

Public Company
Incorporated: 1920 as DeLuxe Check Printers,
    Incorporated
Employees: 9,955
Sales: $1.57 billion (2004)
Stock Exchanges: New York
Ticker Symbol: DLX
NAIC: 323116 Manifold Business Forms Printing;
    323119 Other Commercial Printing; 454111
    Electronic Shopping; 454113 Mail-Order Houses;
    522320 Financial Transactions Processing, Reserve,
    and Clearinghouse Activities; 541214 Payroll Services

Best known as a check printer, Deluxe Corporation continues to be the largest supplier of checks and check-related products and services in the United States. It has diversified its operations, however, and the company's largest unit, and the one on which it intends to base its future, is its Small Business Services unit, which was built mainly through the June 2004, $639.8 million acquisition of New England Business Services, Inc. This unit serves six million small business customers, selling business checks, business forms, stationery, and related products; offering packaging, shipping, and warehouse supplies through an office supply catalog service; and providing payroll services. The Deluxe Financial Services unit supplies checks and related products and services to financial institutions. Direct Checks is the leading direct-to-consumer supplier of checks in the United States. Operating under the Checks Unlimited and Designer Checks brand names, this unit sells personal and business checks and related products via direct response marketing and the Internet. Although the demise of the check has been consistently—and wrongly—predicted

for years, its use is slowly declining, providing impetus to Deluxe's diversification efforts.

Early History

The foundation for Deluxe was laid in 1905 when William Roy Hotchkiss purchased a small Wisconsin newspaper named the *Barron County Shield Well.* Acquainted with the printing business since boyhood, Hotchkiss thought he had found his niche, particularly after he became publisher and co-owner of the more prestigious *Dunn County News* of Menomonie in 1908. For the next five years Hotchkiss oversaw the development of this paper into the largest and most respected weekly in the state. A protracted illness, however, forced his early retirement from the newspaper business and his relocation to the more congenial climate of southern California. His entrepreneurial drive still intact, Hotchkiss decided to raise chickens but failed, despite conceiving the idea of selling precut chickens to grocery stores.

In 1915 Hotchkiss returned to the Midwest and settled in St. Paul, vowing, according to company annals, "to do one thing and one thing only, but do it better, faster and more economically than anyone else." Recalling his printing days and a special assignment of printing bank checks for a friend, Hotchkiss decided to claim the creation and marketing of personalized checks as his business. The distinctive feature of his checks would be quality imprinting of information unique to each customer. Hotchkiss borrowed $300 to secure the necessary equipment and a small office in the People's Bank Building in downtown St. Paul. In the two months of operations for 1915 the eager salesman attracted $23 in orders against $293 in expenses. Despite such unpromising numbers, the company would soon find success. As Terry Blake wrote in *A History of the Deluxe Corporation, 1915–1990,* several factors favored Hotchkiss's enterprise, particularly the printer's choice of location. The Minneapolis/St. Paul area, already densely populated with financial institutions, was destined to become a major national banking center—and therefore a major check clearinghouse—through Minneapolis's selection as the site of the Federal Reserve Bank of the Ninth District. Equally important was Hotchkiss's timing. In 1915 approximately five billion checks were issued by American businesses each year. This immense market was being served by various printing houses, none of which was more than regionally dominant, particularly noteworthy for its service, or even remotely prepared to foster new business in a virtually untapped domain: individual consumers.

Hotchkiss's early marketing of his company's services consisted of mail-order brochures sent to all regions of Minnesota. His first customers were healthy outstate banks, with less deposits than the Twin Cities banks but also far fewer check-printing competitors. In 1916 Hotchkiss succeeded in tapping the metropolitan market with contracts from both the People's Bank and the Western State Bank of St. Paul. Sales for his first full year of business reached $4,173. This same year Hotchkiss welcomed printer Einer Swanson as a business partner. Swanson replaced Hotchkiss as chief salesman and may also have been responsible for determining the company's name. The new arrangement allowed Hotchkiss, an instinctive inventor, the freedom to design and develop new machinery to enhance printing quality, speed delivery time, and save money. By 1918 the company's sales had soared to $18,961 and Hotchkiss issued his first catalog. The following year, as sales more than doubled, the company relocated to its first, full-sized plant. In 1920 Swanson and Hotchkiss incorporated as DeLuxe Check Printers, Incorporated and became equal partners.

Growth during the 1920s was phenomenal because of both timing and the special imprint of Hotchkiss's vision. From the beginning he had decided that his business would emphasize quality and service. Service, for him, became synonymous with speed; he instituted the still standing company goal of 48-hour turnaround on any order, or "in one day, out the next." As the Federal Reserve established new banking districts, Deluxe, as soon as it was able, moved in to claim its share of the check business. First came Chicago, then Kansas City, then Cleveland, then New York. By the end of the decade, sales and net income had risen to $579,000 and $42,000, respectively.

Perhaps more indicative of the company's long-term prospects were Hotchkiss's unique advancements in check products and printing technology during the 1920s. In 1922 he developed one of the first small pocket checks—nicknamed the LH, or "Little Handy"—to complement the larger, end-register-style business check. The initial market for this new check was to be the wise and discerning consumer. As catalog copy from this era declared, "The Individualized Check today is considered almost as necessary in leading social and business circles as the calling or business card. It marks the user as a man of distinction and discrimination." Yet, as Blake pointed out, "Hotchkiss had no definite strategy for marketing the personalized Handy checks. Bankers, too, were skeptical of the horizontal register and deemed Hotchkiss's invention a fad. As a result, the LH, destined to become the most successful product in Deluxe's history, remained an obscure novelty for a number of years."

Hotchkiss realized more immediate profits from a series of important, speed-enhancing inventions, which included the Hotchkiss Imprinting Press (HIP), patented in 1925; a two-way perforator, perfected the same year; and the Hotchkiss Lithograph Press (HLP), patented in 1928.

Revolutionary Sales Program During Great Depression

An end to a free-spending era came with the stock market crash in 1929. From 1920 to 1929, Deluxe saw sales increase by an average of 32.3 percent annually. By comparison, from 1930 to 1939, sales increased only 55 percent for the entire ten-year span. After suffering its only full-year loss in 1932, the company began to rebound as newly elected President Franklin D. Roosevelt's sweeping reforms for the banking industry took hold. A potentially devastating period was transformed and, like F.D.R., Deluxe hastened the transformation with a revolutionary new sales program. The program was guided not by Hotchkiss but by George McSweeney, a former Deluxe paper supplier hired by the company in 1932 expressly for the task of building a sales force and boosting revenue. McSweeney emphasized personalized attention over catalog promotions and worked closely with bankers in developing personalized check programs. Viewing Deluxe as a service- (rather than product-) oriented business, he sought ways to aid financial institutions in boosting their own incomes. Promoting small checking accounts for individual customers, all of whom represented potential loan clients, became a mutual goal, and the LH, the mutually agreed upon tool to attract these customers. McSweeney also directed his sales force to refocus attention on serving rural banks; by 1939, this segment had grown to represent 58 percent of Deluxe's annual revenue. Finally, McSweeney instilled in his sales force a "guidance and counsel" approach. With the passing of the Social Security Act in 1935 came an opportunity for McSweeney and his representatives to thoroughly research the law and then educate their banking customers. "To McSweeney," writes Blake, "it was important for Deluxe to establish itself as a leader, and Deluxe's impressive anticipation of an industry-altering event like Social Security set a precedent the company has always followed."

In 1940 Deluxe saw sales surpass $1 million. A year later, McSweeney became company president at his own request. LH orders had multiplied from 1,000 in 1938 to 100,000 and would continue to grow exponentially. With World War II and the ration banking program that necessitated new ration checks, sales also jumped dramatically. A new service-monitoring system was instituted by Production Superintendent Joe Rose in 1948. Within a year, two-day delivery fulfillment advanced from 75 percent to nearly 90 percent. The advent of the teletypesetter and new plant construction in Chicago, Kansas City, and St. Paul capped the decade.

Steady Growth Continuing: 1950s–80s

During the 1950s, overall sales rose by 275 percent. Much of the company's growth could be attributed to the widespread popularity of the LH. Equally important was Deluxe's national coverage of the commercial banking industry. By 1960 it had contracted for a portion of sales with 99 percent of the country's commercial banks. Meanwhile, Deluxe's largest competitor,

Key Dates:

1915:   William Roy Hotchkiss begins printing and selling checks in St. Paul, Minnesota.

1920:   Hotchkiss and partner Einer Swanson incorporate their business as DeLuxe Check Printers, Incorporated.

1922:   Hotchkiss creates the LH (Little Handy) pocket check.

1964:   New Products Research Division is created, eventually developing loan coupon books, process control documents, and deposit/withdrawal slips.

1965:   Company goes public.

1988:   Company is renamed Deluxe Corporation.

1993:   A restructuring involves the closure of one-fourth of the company's check-printing plants and the first layoffs in Deluxe history.

1996:   John A. ''Gus'' Blanchard III, the first outsider to be named CEO, initiates a major reorganization.

2000:   Deluxe's electronic payment and information technology businesses are spun off into the separate firm eFunds Corporation.

2004:   New England Business Services, Inc. is acquired through an $800 million deal.

New York-based Todd Company, was struggling to hold market share after a corporate takeover. With ten plants strategically spread across the United States to better serve its customers, Deluxe could boast sales of $24 million and anticipate a bright future, with steadily rising numbers for total domestic checks written, which numbered nearly 13 billion. Furthermore, many bankers now accorded Deluxe special status as an industry leader. This was particularly true after Deluxe's fundamental involvement with the development of magnetic ink character recognition (MICR), which after years of back-and-forth negotiations between the American Bankers Association, leading high-tech companies, and check printers, was becoming the industry norm.

With McSweeney's death in 1962 and the continuing maturation of MICR technology came numerous changes for the company. McSweeney's successor, Joe Rose, was faced with dire predictions that a checkless society would be a reality by 1970. Deluxe's recourse was to embrace MICR for all types of document processing and to launch a New Products Research Division. By 1967, sales for the three-year-old division from loan coupon books, process control documents, and deposit/withdrawal slips topped $1 million. Deluxe underwent another difficult, though ultimately beneficial, change in 1965 when it went public after pressure from various estates who complained of the artificially low trading prices for their stock. This same year, Rose satisfactorily settled another potential setback when the U.S. Post Office announced new coding and presorting regulations. A major user of the public mails, Deluxe could ill afford increased expenses or undue delays caused by the new regulations. Consequently, Rose met directly with the deputy postmaster general and obtained permission to establish his own in-plant post offices where mail could be easily sorted and sent to save the company and the local post offices both time and money. Rose closed the 1960s with more than $85 million in sales.

Despite serious inflation during the 1970s, which caused production costs to rise, Deluxe performed well. By 1979 sales had risen to $366 million and net income to $39 million. This was especially impressive after considering the large capital expenditures involved in new plant openings, which arose at the pace of three per year. A considerable amount of new equipment, including minicomputers and the Deluxe Encoder Printer (DEP), also made their debut during this decade. Under Gene Olson, who became president in 1976 and CEO in 1978 (and stayed in these positions until 1986), Deluxe acceded to critics on Wall Street—long wary of the company's dependency on essentially one product—and cautiously diversified into pre-inked endorsement stamps.

Growth continued unabated during the 1980s; by 1988 sales had surpassed $1 billion. Among the new products that kept Deluxe firmly in place as a financial products market leader were three-on-a-page, computer-form business checks, pegboard checks, and money market related documents. Although the financial industry suffered repeatedly by failures of large-sized banks, such developments actually increased Deluxe's competitiveness, for as the institutions failed, numerous small check printers ceased business as well. By 1989, less than 10 full-service printers remained. In one sense, however, such events were singularly frightening, for few could anticipate the future of banking. Harold Haverty, a 32-year company veteran elected president in 1983 and CEO (the company's fifth) in 1986, wrestled anew with the problem of diversification (analysts for *Forbes* had twice predicted the company's downfall, because of its traditionally cautious acquisition policy). In part to satisfy the analysts, but also to increase its presence as a provider of wide business services, Deluxe purchased ChexSystems in April 1984, John A. Pratt and Associates in June 1985, and Colwell Systems in October 1985, consequently entering such new fields as account verification, marketing services, and direct-mail supply to the dental and medical industry. In December 1986 Deluxe purchased A.O. Smith Data Systems and instantly became a leader in the burgeoning electronic funds transfer (EFT) industry. In 1987 the company purchased Current, which soon became touted as ''the nation's largest direct mail marketer of greeting cards and consumer specialty products.'' The following year, in a move symbolic of the company's diversification, Deluxe Check Printers, Inc. became simply Deluxe Corporation.

First Serious Difficulties, in Early 1990s

Under Haverty's direction, Deluxe stayed on the same course through the early 1990s, continuing to cautiously diversify. In 1990 ACH Systems was acquired to bolster the company's electronic funds transfer operation. Deluxe, the following year, acquired the Seattle-based Electronic Transaction Corp., which provided electronic check authorization services for retailers. The acquired firm managed the Shared Check Authorization Network (or SCAN), an association of retailers nationwide who exchange information on bad checks and closed customer accounts. In 1993 Deluxe bought PaperDirect, a mail-order supplier of specialty papers and other products, while 1994 brought National Revenue Corporation, a leading U.S. collections agency, into the company fold.

By 1993 it was becoming evident that not all was well at Deluxe. Although revenues continued their yearly rise, return on equity dropped below 25 percent for the first time in years to 17.4 percent. Net income fell substantially as well, from $202.8 million in 1992 to $141.9 million in 1993, due in part to a restructuring charge incurred as a result of the closure of about one-fourth of the company's check-printing plants, which were made redundant by other, higher tech plants. For the first time in company history, workers were laid off.

The company would continue to struggle for the next several years, buffeted by a variety of factors. The bank merger mania of the mid-1990s resulted in larger institutions that could demand lower check prices. Its check-printing business was also being pressured by new competition from more than two dozen marketers using direct mail to sell checks to consumers. At the same time, its efforts at diversification were not paying off; although the new businesses were generating more than 35 percent of overall company revenues, they were contributing less than 10 percent of the profits.

Restructuring Under Blanchard: 1995–2000

It was thus in this troubled environment that for the first time ever Deluxe looked outside for new leadership. In May 1995 John A. ''Gus'' Blanchard III was named the company's sixth CEO (and then became chairman as well the following year). Blanchard had gained plenty of experience helping companies deal with technology change through stints at AT&T and General Instruments Corp. Once onboard at Deluxe, he moved quickly and decisively to restructure and streamline operations; to identify noncore, underperforming business that should be divested; and to reestablish growth through new products, alliances, and acquisitions.

In early 1996 Deluxe announced plans to trim operating costs by $150 million over a two-year period. Included herein was the planned closure of 26 of the company's 41 check-printing plants, a 30 percent reduction in capital spending, the implementation of a centralized purchasing function, and layoffs for 30 percent of the company's officers. Divested in 1996 were T/Maker Company (a maker of clipart and children's multimedia software, just acquired in 1994), Health Care Forms, Financial Alliance Processing Services, Inc. (a processor of credit and debit card transactions, just acquired in early 1995), Deluxe U.K. forms, and the internal bank forms business. Deluxe also placed PaperDirect and Current Social Expressions (i.e., the greeting cards, gift wrap, and related products—the Current Checks direct-mail operation was to remain with Deluxe) on the block, although it ran into initial trouble trying to find a buyer.

A restructuring of the remaining operations left Deluxe with four main business segments in 1997. Deluxe Paper Payment Systems consisted of the check printing services that remained the company's core, including Current Checks and Deluxe Canada Inc., which had been formed in 1994 to provide Canadian financial institutions with checks and financial forms. Deluxe Payment Protection Systems included account verification (ChexSystems), check authorization (SCAN), and collection agency (National Revenue) services, as well as the TheftNet employee screening service run by Deluxe Employment Screening Partners, Inc., a new subsidiary established in 1996. Deluxe Direct Response specialized in the development of

targeted direct-mail marketing campaigns for financial institutions, with four of its five units having been acquired or established in 1996 and 1997. Finally, Deluxe Electronic Payment Systems, Inc. grew out of the 1986-acquired A.O. Smith Data Systems and concentrated on electronic funds transfer services.

Blanchard's dramatic moves had quickly transformed Deluxe Corporation into a much more focused and strategically structured organization at a time when checks—though hardly dinosaurs—were beginning to show signs of decline. Checks had been growing at a rate of 6 percent a year in the early 1990s, but grew less than 1 percent in 1996—EFTs, telephone banking, and online banking were finally having a real impact.

In 1997 Deluxe began offering check ordering over the Internet. The following year brought several divestments. PaperDirect and Current Social Expressions were finally offloaded, as were the Deluxe Direct Response unit and the renamed ESP Employment Screening Partners subsidiary. Continuing to trim noncore operations, Deluxe sold NRC, its collection agency business, in December 1999. On the acquisition side, the company in February 2000 spent $97 million for Designer Checks, Inc., a producer of specialty design checks and related products for direct sale to consumers.

In the meantime, the company had acquired eFunds Corporation, a provider of electronic check conversion and electronic funds transfer services, for $13 million in February 1999. Then in January of the following year, Deluxe announced plans to combine all of its electronic payment and information technology businesses, including eFunds, Deluxe Payment Protection Systems, ChexSystems, and SCAN into a single entity, and then spin it off into an independent publicly traded firm called eFunds Corporation. These moves were designed to create two separate, ''pure-play'' companies, thereby unlocking value for shareholders. In June 2000 eFunds was taken public through an IPO of 12 percent of its stock, raising $71 million. In December of that year the remaining 88 percent stake was distributed tax free to Deluxe shareholders as a stock dividend. Blanchard left Deluxe to become chairman and CEO of eFunds. Taking over as chairman and the seventh CEO of Deluxe was Lawrence J. Mosner, who had been vice chairman and who had joined the company in November 1995 as president of Deluxe Direct.

Early 2000s: Newly Focused, Diversifying Through NEBS Acquisition

Deluxe, now focused exclusively on paper payment services, divided its operations into three segments in 2001: Financial Services, supplier of checks and related products and services to financial institutions; Direct Checks, direct-to-consumer supplier of checks; and Business Services, seller of checks, forms, and related products to small business/home office customers. According to the company's estimates, the total number of checks written by individuals and small businesses began to decline that year. The 2001 net sales of $1.28 billion represented only a small increase over the previous year, while net income jumped 15 percent, to $185.9 million.

In 2002 the Financial Services unit rolled out a new program called DeluxeSelect aimed at bolstering revenues when customers reorder checks from their bank or credit union. Under the program, Deluxe would take over the handling of such orders either over the telephone, via the company's voice response system, or through the Internet. Pilot programs showed that revenue increased by as much as 50 percent when the more marketing savvy Deluxe salespeople handled the reorders compared to when the financial institution fulfilled them.

In 2003 the use of checks continued to fall because of increasing use of credit cards, debit cards, and electronic payments. Deluxe responded with plans to close three more printing plants, which shaved 635 jobs from the payroll and entailed restructuring charges of $11.8 million. The following year the company began targeting the wider small business printing market as an area of potential growth. A big step in this direction was taken in June 2004 when New England Business Services, Inc. (NEBS) was acquired for $639.8 million in cash, plus the assumption of $160 million in debt. Based in Groton, Massachusetts, NEBS had a customer base of 3.1 million small businesses in the United States, Canada, the United Kingdom, and France, selling them checks, computer forms, stationery, and packaging supplies via direct marketing, direct mail, and an in-person sales force. The deal was viewed positively by many observers, who saw Deluxe diversifying itself through the addition of a highly complementary business. NEBS was merged with the Business Services unit to create the Small Business Services unit, which was the largest of Deluxe's three units. NEBS's European operations were sold off in late 2004. The impact of the acquisition was felt immediately as revenues that year jumped to $1.57 billion.

Late in 2004, however, Deluxe lost one of its largest bank clients, Wells Fargo & Company. This was a key factor in a 19 percent drop in net profits in the first quarter of 2005. Revenue for the same period surged 41 percent, a jump wholly attributable to the NEBS acquisition. It was an open question whether this one deal would be enough to offset the steady decline in Deluxe's core check-printing business. Check use was now declining at a rate of about 4.5 percent per year. It appeared that this challenge was to be faced by a new Deluxe CEO as Mosner announced that he planned to retire in 2005.

Principal Subsidiaries

Chiswick, Inc.; Designer Checks, Inc.; Direct Checks Unlimited, LLC; Deluxe Financial Services, Inc.; Deluxe Financial Services Texas, L.P.; Deluxe Mexicana S.A. de C.V. (Mexico; 50%); DGBS (UK) Forms Limited; DGBS (UK) Holdings Limited; DLX Check Printers, Inc.; DLX Check Texas, Inc.; McBee Systems, Inc.; NEBS Business Products Limited (Canada); NEBS Business Stationery Limited (U.K.); NEBS Capital (Canada); NEBS Payroll Service Limited (Canada); New England Business Services, Inc.; Paper Payment Services, LLC; PPS Holding Company, Inc.; Rapidforms, Inc.; Russell & Miller, Inc.; Safeguard Business Systems, Inc.; Safeguard Business Systems Limited (Canada); Shirlite Limited (U.K.); Sigma Afterprint Services Limited (U.K.); Stephen Fossler Company; VeriPack, Inc.

Principal Operating Units

Small Business Services; Financial Services; Direct Checks.

Principal Competitors

John H. Harland Company; Clarke American Checks, Inc.; American Banknote Corporation.

Further Reading

Abelson, Reed, ''The Check Is in the (Electronic) Mail,'' *Forbes,* January 6, 1992, p. 99.

Barthel, Matt, ''To Bolster Checks, Deluxe Buys Authorization Service,'' *American Banker,* January 4, 1991, p. 3.

Bills, Steve, ''Core Business Shrinking? Try Another One,'' *American Banker,* January 31, 2005, p. 1.

——, ''Printers' Divergent Responses to Check Drop,'' *American Banker,* May 14, 2004, p. 13.

Blake, Terry, *A History of Deluxe Corporation, 1915–1990,* St. Paul: Deluxe Corporation, 1990, 48 p.

Blumenthal, Robin, ''Deluxe's Divide,'' *Barron's,* February 15, 1999, p. 20.

Byrne, Harlan S., ''Deluxe Corp.: Diversifying Against Check-Free Banking,'' *Barron's,* April 26, 1993, pp. 39–40.

Chithelen, Ignatius, ''Printing Money,'' *Forbes,* March 18, 1991, p. 116.

Deogun, Nikhil, ''Deluxe Intends to Splits Its Operations, Take Two Technology Businesses Public,'' *Wall Street Journal,* January 31, 2000, p. C11.

DePass, Dee, ''Cashing Out,'' *Minneapolis Star Tribune,* January 17, 2002, p. 1D.

——, ''Deluxe Corp. Sells Two Units, Reports Earnings Increase,'' *Minneapolis Star Tribune,* October 23, 1998, p. 1D.

——, ''Deluxe's Mosner to Retire As CEO, Chairman,'' *Minneapolis Star Tribune,* December 14, 2004, p. 1D.

——, ''Deluxe Targets E-Commerce,'' *Minneapolis Star Tribune,* April 23, 1999, p. 1D.

——, ''Deluxe to Split into Two Separate Public Companies,'' *Minneapolis Star Tribune,* February 1, 2000, p. 1D.

——, ''Deluxe, Two Others Plan 'Debit Bureau,' '' *Minneapolis Star Tribune,* January 29, 1998, p. 1D.

——, ''Deluxe Will Buy eFunds,'' *Minneapolis Star Tribune,* February 4, 1999, p. 3D.

Krol, Carol, ''Deluxe Agrees to Acquire NEBS,'' *B to B,* June 7, 2004, p. 15.

Kutler, Jeffrey, ''Three ACH Operators Band Together,'' *American Banker,* April 20, 1992, p. 3.

Levy, Melissa, ''Checkmaker Deluxe Acquires Financial Direct Marketing Firm,'' *Minneapolis Star Tribune,* July 8, 1997, p. 1D.

Marjanovic, Steven, ''Deluxe Reorganization Targets Revenue Growth,'' *Minneapolis Star Tribune,* April 26, 1999, p. 14.

——, ''Though Hedging, Deluxe Isn't Writing Off Checks,'' *American Banker,* March 26, 1997, p. 4.

Melcher, Richard A., ''Deluxe Isn't Checking Out Yet,'' *Business Week,* February 26, 1996, pp. 94, 96.

Sawaya, Zina, ''The Underpaid: Relative Pain (Harold Haverty),'' *Forbes,* May 27, 1991, p. 222.

Serres, Chris, ''Deluxe Diversifies with Deal: $747 Million for Maker of Business Forms,'' *Minneapolis Star Tribune,* May 18, 2004, p. 1D.

Zemke, Ron, and Dick Schaaf, ''Deluxe Corporation,'' *The Service Edge: 101 Companies That Profit from Customer Care,* New York: New American Library, 1989.

—Jay P. Pederson
—update: David E. Salamie

Diagnostic Products Corporation

5210 Pacific Concourse Drive
Los Angeles, California 90045
U.S.A.
Telephone: (310) 645-8200
Toll Free: (800) 372-1782
Fax: (310) 645-9999
Web site: http://www.dpcweb.com

Public Company
Incorporated: 1971
Employees: 2,406
Sales: $443.1 million (2004)
Stock Exchanges: New York
Ticker Symbol: DP
NAIC: 325131 Inorganic Dye and Pigment Manufacturing;
    325413 In-Vitro Diagnostic Substance Manufacturing

Diagnostic Products Corporation (DPC) sells immunodiagnostic systems that provide information concerning diseases and medical conditions. The company's test kits diagnose thyroid, reproductive, and cardiac disorders, allergies, infectious diseases, anemia, and certain types of cancer by using samples of blood, urine, and other bodily fluids and tissues. DPC's tests are sold throughout the world to hospitals, physicians' office laboratories, and to veterinary, forensic, and research facilities. The company's test kits are manufactured in the United States, the United Kingdom, and China, marketed through a global distribution network covering more than 100 countries. DPC derives 70 percent of its annual revenue from foreign customers.

From Kassel to Los Angeles: Sigi Ziering's Epic Journey

For nearly all of its history, DPC was under the firm control of the Ziering family, whose patriarch, Sigi Ziering, took control of the company not long after its founding. In the years before Ziering took an interest in DPC, he achieved something far more remarkable than transforming a homespun business into a more than $200 million-in-sales company. Ziering's achievement was survival. Perseverance and luck, each exhibited to extraordinary degrees, enabled Ziering to endure the Holocaust and make a better life for himself after his harrowing teenage years. DPC, though trivial to the horrors of World War II, was a reflection of Ziering's determination, and, as such, the company drew its essence from its longtime leader, indelibly marked by the atrocities in Nazi Germany.

Ziering was born in 1928 in Kassel, Germany, one year after his brother Herman. The Ziering boys were the sons of a Polish citizen who made his living as a clothing merchant. In 1939, the father fled to England, leaving with the belief that his wife and two sons would join him as soon as they obtained their visas. Sigi, or Siegfried as he was then known, was 11 years old when his father left. The emigration restrictions for Jews tightened and then closed not long after Ziering's father left, leaving the family of three trapped in Germany to face the greatest crucible of their lives.

The Zierings managed to escape the attention of Hitler's SS for a while, but the family eventually became ensnared in Nazi Germany's pogrom against the Jews. In late 1941, the Zierings were among 1,000 Jews transported to Riga, Latvia, where a Jewish ghetto had been established. Once in the ghetto, the Ziering boys stopped attending school and began working, a decision made by their mother who believed her children's usefulness as workers might spare their lives. Of the original 1,000 Jews transported to Riga, Ziering later found 16 survivors, a group that included his brother and his mother.

The Zierings remained in the Riga ghetto until the approach of Russian troops near the war's end forced the Nazis to move the surviving Jews elsewhere. The Zierings were moved to a German prison, Fuhlsbuttel, on the outskirts of Hamburg that had been converted a decade earlier to a concentration camp. The struggle to survive became markedly more difficult at Fuhlsbuttel, as the Nazis stepped up their efforts to fulfill the mandate of Hitler's Total Solution pogrom ''with German precision,'' as Ziering noted in an April 13, 1998 interview with *Fortune*. Every week, eight or ten Jews were transported to Bergen-Belsen for elimination, a systematic weeding out of the Fuhlsbuttel population that was conducted alphabetically. As the Nazis began with the beginning of the alphabet and worked their way toward "Z," the Ziering family was spared execution. British troops closed off the roads to Bergen-Belsen before the Nazis reached the end of the alphabet, leading to another relocation of the Zierings north to a concentration camp in Kiel.

The survival odds in Kiel did not improve. Between 40 and 50 of the camp's population died daily, either because of the grisly conditions or from execution. One day all the males in the camp were forced to run a kilometer while carrying a heavy piece of wood. The Ziering boys passed the test, but 35 of the camp's prisoners failed to reach the finish line and were shot. As the Nazi's cause grew more desperate and the chances for survival diminished, the Ziering family again found themselves separated into a group of 1,000 Jews. According to unconfirmed reports, a member of Sweden's royal family, Count Folke Bernadotte, offered Henrich Himmler $5 million for 1,000 Jews, a deal that ultimately led to the Zierings' freedom. On May 1, 1945, Red Cross workers arrived in Kiel to transport the 1,000 Jews to Sweden. While on his way to Sweden, Ziering learned of Hitler's death, ending his extraordinary fight for survival and the horror of his teenage years.

The Zierings, who remarkably had remained together throughout the Holocaust, were reunited in London. Ziering was 17 years old when he was reunited with his father, who had spent the war years building a successful career as a diamond merchant. Ziering, who had only five years of elementary education, made up for lost time by pursuing his education with zeal. After entering a tutorial school, he enrolled at the University of London. He wanted to become a doctor, but his hopes were dashed when he learned nearly all medical school spots were reserved for war veterans. Ziering resumed his academic career after his family moved to the United States in 1949 and settled in Brooklyn, where he worked part-time while attending Brooklyn College. In 1953, the same year he married Marilyn Brisman, Ziering received his undergraduate degree in physics. In 1955, ten years after leaving the Kiel concentration camp, he earned his master's degree from Syracuse University, where his academic career culminated two years later with the completion of his doctoral studies.

Ziering's professional career began in Boston, where he would remain for a decade before moving to the West Coast. He joined Raytheon Co. the year he left Syracuse University, using his doctorate degree to land a job as a senior scientist. He spent two years working on research related to nuclear reactors, leaving in 1959 to become department head of space projects at another Boston company, Allied Research. After another two-year stint, Ziering struck out on his own, forming his own company, Space Sciences, located in the Boston suburb of Waltham, to perform work for the federal government. Space Sciences proved to be enough of a success to attract the attention of a larger conglomerate, Whittaker Corp., which purchased Ziering's company in 1968 for $1.8 million. The deal gave Ziering considerable financial security, but it led to a change in his working environment that he found unappealing. After the acquisition of his company, Ziering moved to Los Angeles to serve as a research executive for Whittaker, placing him in a corporate culture he disliked. He left Whittaker in 1970, but remained in Los Angeles, joining a company named Dynascis, where he spent a year serving as the vice-president of the company's medical group. Next, Ziering became an entrepreneur again, starting a company that made fishmeal. The business failed, but his next venture became the focus of his professional career for the rest of his life.

Taking Control of Diagnostic Products: 1970s

Ziering was 45 years old when he first heard of Diagnostic Products Corporation. Either through a friend or through an advertisement in a trade publication, Ziering learned of a chemist who had developed radioimmunoassay (RIA) diagnostic kits. The chemist, Robert Ban, had developed tests, or assays, that permitted the measurement of infinitesimally low concentrations of substances, such as drugs and hormones, in bodily fluids. He had formed DPC in 1971, but two years later, when Ziering first heard of his work, Ban was operating DPC out of his kitchen. He had advertised in a professional journal, claiming he had 30 different RIA kits, which produced a steady stream of orders. Ziering discovered Ban had far fewer than 30 RIA kits, but he was interested in DPC nevertheless, investing $50,000 in the business.

Once production was focused primarily on one kit of commercial value, the business began to record meaningful growth. DPC fared well, but the relationship between Ziering and Ban became strained, prompting Ziering to buy out Ban for $25,000 and hire his wife as a replacement. The company recorded robust growth during its first decade, establishing early on a presence overseas, where eventually DPC would generate nearly three-quarters of its annual sales. During the 1970s, the company's European expansion began in Switzerland, Italy, Germany, and the Netherlands. Domestically, the company moved its headquarters from a storefront on Venice Boulevard to a 5,000-square-foot facility in West Los Angeles. In 1978, demand from its domestic and European customers—hospitals and clinical laboratories—made the company the global leader in the fertility immunoassays market. Its growing business required its West Los Angeles facility to be expanded to 9,600 square feet before ever increasing growth demanded a move to a new location. In 1981, DPC established its headquarters near Los Angeles International Airport, occupying a 20,000-square-foot building. The following year Ziering took his company public, presenting to Wall Street the company he had developed into a more than $10 million-in-sales diagnostic concern. At the time, the company offered 52 different tests capable of detecting thyroid disorders, anemia, and other conditions.

During the 1980s, the company's expansion continued, producing impressive growth, particularly late in the decade. The company established a presence in Asia in 1986, organizing a joint-venture company named Nippon DPC Corporation. That same year, the company opened a combined research and manufacturing facility in the United Kingdom. The year also marked the arrival of Ziering's son Michael, who left his job as a public defender in Orange County, California, to become DPC's legal counsel. DPC's market value grew more than sevenfold during the late 1980s, swelling from $35 million to $429 million. Ziering presided over a company whose financial performance was impressive but otherwise attracted little attention. DPC, according to the September 16, 1991 issue of the *Los Angeles Business Journal*, was "both sexy and boring," a company "full of unsurprising moves." The "sexy" quality of the company was its financial success: DPC earned 22 cents profit for each $1 of sales. The "boring" aspect of the company was its unwillingness to initiate dramatic changes; the stuff of excitement for industry onlookers. Ziering chose not to diversify, deciding instead to chip away at the more than $10 billion diagnostics market by introducing assays to identify thyroid disease, fertility, illicit drug use, anemia, and prostate cancer, among a number of other conditions.

During the 1990s, DPC continued to sparkle unspectacularly, but for those pundits who clamored for more excitement, the decade included at least one event of significance. In 1992, DPC acquired Cirrus Diagnostics Inc., a purchase that included Cirrus's IMMULITE technology. IMMULITE became the central component of DPC's product portfolio in the years ahead, beginning in 1993 with the introduction of the first IMMULITE system, a computer-driven diagnostic device capable of measurements at exceptionally low concentrations that could process up to 120 samples per hour. By the following year, DPC, through its IMMULITE system, could claim to offer the most complete panel of thyroid, fertility, cancer, and allergy screening panels for any automated immunoassay system.

DPC in the New Millennium

As DPC prepared for its 30th anniversary and the beginning of a new century, the company offered more than 400 diagnostic tests to its customers. Ziering witnessed the company eclipse the $200 million-in-sales mark for the first time in 1999 during his last days in charge of the company he had transformed from kitchen-run operation. Ziering was diagnosed with brain cancer in December 1999, forcing him to hand the reins of command to his son Michael, who was promoted from the posts of chief

operating officer and president to become the company's chief executive officer. In November 2000, Ziering passed away, losing his last battle for survival.

Under Michael Ziering's control, DPC demonstrated vigorous financial growth and incurred one of the most threatening blows to its vitality since its formation. Sales shot upward during the early years of the century, spurred by advances in IMMULITE technology that spawned the IMMULITE 1000, the IMMULITE 2000, and in 2004 the IMMULITE 2500. By 2004, sales reached nearly $450 million, virtually doubling during the first years of the decade. In early 2004, however, a serious threat to its future financial growth arrived in the form of a letter from the U.S. Food and Drug Administration (FDA). The FDA placed DPC on its Application Integrity Policy (AIP) violations list—among the most serious offenses issued by the FDA—meaning the FDA could suspend the review of all pending products submitted by DPC. The problems stemmed from inspectional findings related to the company's diagnostic test application for Chaga's disease. Specifically, the problems included failure to report false negative and false positive study results, failure to report adverse precision studies from four clinical sites, misrepresenting data, and failing to monitor clinical studies. The FDA's findings did not affect the company's business overseas, where it derived 71 percent of its revenue in 2004. Although the FDA's actions represented a potentially significant impediment to DPC's progress in the future, Michael Ziering was confident that DPC would deal with the problems and move forward successfully. "We have initiated a process to identify and correct the causes of these issues," he explained in a March 2004 interview with *Bioresearch Monitoring Alert*. "Our understanding is that a reasonable time for the resolutions of these types of issues is approximately 12 months. . . . Our new instrument, the IMMULITE 2500, and 74 assays which run on it, have already been cleared by the FDA."

Principal Subsidiaries

DPC Cirrus, Inc.; EURO/DPC Limited (U.K.); Diagnostic Products International Inc. (Barbados); DPC Analytic (Slovenia); DPC Holding GmbH (Germany); DPC Biermann GmbH (Germany); DPC Czech s.r.o. (Czech Republic); DPC d.o.o. Zagreb (Croatia; 50%); DPC Polska sp.z.o.o. (Poland); DPC Slovensko (Slovakia); DPC Benelux B.V. (Netherlands); DPC Nederland B.V. (Netherlands); DPC Belgium b.v.b.A./s.p.r.l.; DPC Finland OY; Bio-Mediq DPC Pty. Ltd. (Australia); DPC Dipesa S.A. (Spain); DPC France SAS; Tianjin De Pu (DPC) Biotechnological and Medical Products Inc. (China); Diagnostic Products DPC Norway A/S; DPC Medlab (Bolivia; 28%); DPC Medlab Productos Medico Hospitalares Ltda. (Brazil; 56%); DPC MEDLAB BRAZIL (56%); DPC Medlab Productos Medico Hospitalares Ltda. (Dominican Republic; 56%); DPC Venezuela C.A. (Venezuela; 56%); DPC Medlab de Uruguay S.A. (56%); DPC Medlab Panama, S.A. (29%); DPC Medlab Guatemala (29%); DPC Medlab Centroamerica S.A. (Costa Rica; 29%); Nippon DPC Corporation (50%); DPC Skafte AB (Sweden); DPC Scandinavia AB (Sweden); DPC Baltic Estonia OU (Sweden); DPC Baltic Latvia SIA (Sweden); DPC Baltic UAB Lithuania (Sweden); D.P.C.-N. Tsakiris S.A. (Greece) (50%); Medical Systems S.p.A. (Italy; 45%); DPC Amerlab Lda. (Portugal; 47.5%); Lumigen, Inc. (10%).

Principal Competitors

Abbott Laboratories; Chiron Corporation; Dade Behring Holdings Inc.

Further Reading

Darmiento, Laurence, "Problems at Testing Firm Exceed Disclosures," *Los Angeles Business Journal,* April 5, 2004, p. 1.

——, "Firm Hit with One-Year Ban by FDA After Testing Probe," *Los Angeles Business Journal,* March 29, 2004, p. 1.

——, "Maker of Medical Test Kits Registering Healthy Results," *Los Angeles Business Journal,* October 15, 2001, p. 32.

——, "Public Company, Private Perks," *Los Angeles Business Journal*, August 9, 2004, p. 1.

"Diagnostic Products Corporation Announces Fourth Quarter and Full Year 2004 Results," *Business Wire,* February 10, 2005, p. 43.

Galperin, Ron, "Diagnostic Products Corp.," *Los Angeles Business Journal,* April 10, 1989, p. 6E.

Loomis, Carol J., "Everything in History Was Against Them," *Fortune,* April 13, 1998, p. 64.

Sami, Tamra, "Diagnostic Products Corp., Says It Is Placed on FDA's AIP List," *Bioresearch Monitoring Alert,* March 2004, p. 5.

"Sigi Ziering, Chairman of Diagnostic Products Corporation, Succumbs to Cancer," *Business Wire,* November 13, 2000, p. 0864.

Taub, Daniel, "Mystery Behind Stock Price Rise for Diagnostic Products," *Los Angeles Business Journal,* June 28, 1999, p. 45.

White, Todd, "Diagnostic Test Kit Maker Tools Down Wall Street," *Los Angeles Business Journal,* September 16, 1991, p. 47A.

—Jeffrey L. Covell

DSW Inc.

4150 East 5th Avenue
Columbus, Ohio 43219
U.S.A.
Telephone: (614) 237-7100
Fax: (614) 238-4200
Web site: http://www.dswshoes.com

Public Subsidiary of Retail Ventures, Inc.
Incorporated: 1969 as Shonac Corporation
Employees: 4,800
Sales: $961.1 million (2004)
Stock Exchanges: New York
Ticker Symbol: DSW
NAIC: 448210 Shoe Stores

DSW Inc. is a discount retailer of shoes, operating a chain of approximately 180 stores in 32 states. The chain's stores feature self-service fixtures displaying more than 30,000 pairs of shoes in more than 2,000 styles. The stores, operating under the name DSW Shoe Warehouse, typically measure 25,000 square feet with nearly 90 percent of the square footage used as selling space. The company completed its initial public offering (IPO) of stock in July 2005. DSW anticipates developing into a 500-store retail chain.

Origins

DSW was created within the corporate folds of the retail operations owned by the Schottenstein family. As such, the company's roots stretched to the beginning of the Schottenstein family business empire, back to the first store opened by the patriarch of the family, Ephraim L. Schottenstein. Ephraim Schottenstein opened his first store, the E.L. Schottenstein Department Store, in Columbus, Ohio, in 1917. His son, Jerome M. Schottenstein, began working for the family business as a teenager, taking on his first executive responsibilities in 1946 when he was 20 years old. Jerome Schottenstein spent nearly a half-century building his father's business into a modern corporation, becoming chief executive officer and chairman of the family's business interests, organized as a privately held enter-

prise named Schottenstein Stores Corporation, in 1972. Jerome Schottenstein invested in a number of retail concerns, creating the corporate folds that constituted the Schottenstein empire, but the core of the family's empire sprang from the Schottenstein department stores in Columbus. The stores operated under the Schottenstein banner in Columbus; but outside Columbus, where a retail chain developed, customers knew the Schottenstein retailing business as Value City Department Stores. Value City operated as a discount retailer, offering a broad selection of merchandise with an emphasis on apparel items.

DSW was created within the Schottenstein Stores Corp. corporate structure, its initial mission to serve the family's core retail business. The business began in January 1969 as Shonac Corporation, a venture formed by the Schottensteins and another family, the Nachts. Shonac was created to manage the leased shoe departments of Value City and other retailers, the sole function of the company for more than 20 years. Although the company continued to manage the shoe departments of other retailers in the 21st century, its prominence in the retail sector was associated with another aspect of its business, one that did not come into being until the beginning of the 1990s.

The 1990s marked an eventful time for the Schottenstein-controlled businesses. Years of expansion and acquisitions had created an impressive retail empire, one created almost entirely by Jerome Schottenstein. Under Schottenstein's orders, the company had acquired equity stakes in a host of retail businesses, including Hoffman's Ready to Wear, American Eagle Outfitters, Gee Bee Stores, Dollar Bargain, and Sciffran Willens jewelry stores. Together, the company's numerous affiliates, subsidiaries, and divisions represented a $1.5 billion retail empire, the legacy Schottenstein left to his family after he passed away in March 1992. In the months before the transfer of power between Jerome Schottenstein and his son Jay Schottenstein, there were two significant events that had a bearing on the future of DSW. In June 1991, Schottenstein Stores Corp., which was a privately held company, decided to spin off Value City to the public, selling approximately half of the company to investors and keeping the remainder of the company under its control. At the time of the public offering, Value City Department Stores, Inc. operated approximately 60 stores. The following

Company Perspectives:

Since its founding in 1991, DSW has grown into a major force in retail footwear. Conceived originally as a warehouse-format "category killer" for shoes, DSW has evolved into a unique, upscale, consumer-friendly shopping environment. It is distinguished by the vast merchandise selection, the efficiency and convenience of the shopping experience and the exceptional values offered—current styles of quality designer and famous name-brand shoes, sold every day at up to 50% off department store regular prices.

month, Schottenstein Stores Corp. formed DSW Shoe Warehouse, Inc. as a subsidiary of Shonac. The move marked Shonac's beginning as a stand-alone retailer. In the years ahead, DSW developed into a chain of stores, eventually eclipsing the importance of its most immediate parent company, Shonac.

DSW opened its first store in July 1991 in Dublin, Ohio. Like Value City, the retailer it had long served, DSW started in Ohio before making any significant geographic leap, first building a base in the Schottensteins' home state before expanding throughout the Midwest and Northeast. Also like Value City, the company positioned itself as a discount retailer, inheriting the signature trait of the Schottenstein empire. As DSW gradually developed into a chain, its format found a receptive audience, attracting consumers who helped make the 1990s the decade that warehouse, or "big-box," discount retailers flourished. DSW's white-and-black striped color theme, most visible on the awnings in front of the company's stores, became a familiar sight in certain markets, but it was the stores' layout and their merchandising mix that won over consumers and earned their loyalty. A typical DSW store measured 25,000 square feet, with 90 percent of the square footage used as selling space. On display were more than 30,000 pairs of shoes that customers could browse through and try on themselves, a vast selection available for between 20 percent and 50 percent below usual retail prices. Unlike most other discount shoe chains, DSW offered a sizable collection of current-season, designer-label shoes rather than focusing exclusively on mass-market shoe brands.

Blossoming in the 1990s

DSW developed into a regional chain during the 1990s, becoming a small but burgeoning aspect of Schottenstein Stores Corp.'s business. During the first years of the company's existence, an average of seven new outlets were opened every year, as DSW fanned out from its base in Ohio and established itself throughout the Midwest and into the Northeast. Later in its development, the company pursued expansion more aggressively, but before it did so, control over the concept changed hands several times—albeit within the confines of the Schottensteins' business interests. In 1998, Value City acquired Shonac from Schottenstein Stores Corp. and Nacht Management, Inc., paying $100 million for full control over the business that operated as the shoe department licensee in all of its stores—Shonac—and for ownership of the DSW chain of stores. In the seven years since Schottenstein Stores Corp. had spun off Value City, the chain had expanded from 60 stores to 95 stores. During

this same period, DSW had developed from a single store in Dublin into a 47-store chain, demonstrating a level of commercial success that eluded its new corporate parent as the 1990s drew to a close.

DSW greatly accelerated its pace of expansion under Value City's control, as Value City itself continued to expand through acquisitions. Value City added another retail chain to its holdings in March 2000, paying $89 million for a bankrupt 19-store chain operating under the name Filene's Basement. DSW by this point had expanded aggressively in the two years since its acquisition by Value City, opening more than ten stores a year. In October 2000, the company opened its 70th store, a grand opening that was significant for two reasons. The store was the largest in the chain, measuring 43,000 square feet, and it was located in Los Angeles, reflecting the more ambitious geographic scope of the company after years of concentrating its expansion in the Midwest and the Northeast. Expanding aggressively and entering new markets, DSW exhibited impressive vitality at the beginning of the 21st century, generating an estimated $300 million in annual revenue, or 18 percent of Value City's annual revenue volume. The same could not be said of Value City, which began to record annual losses as the new century began, suffering from flaws in its merchandise mix and in the layout of its stores. As Value City tried to improve its performance, DSW became involved in the troubles of its parent company, ushering in a period of reorganization within the entire Schottenstein retail empire.

Organizational Changes in the 21st Century

The first attempt to reorganize the businesses controlled by Schottenstein Stores Corp. occurred during the tenth anniversary of the DSW chain. In mid-2001, Schottenstein Stores Corp. announced that it intended to acquire all of Value City's subsidiaries. Schottenstein Stores Corp. submitted a $275 million bid to acquire 19 Filene's Basement stores, five Crown Shoe stores, the 136 shoe departments in other stores leased through Shonac, and 87 DSW Shoe Warehouse outlets. Schottenstein Stores Corp. signed a letter of intent to acquire the subsidiaries, but terminated the agreement in August 2001. Organizational changes resurfaced in 2003, when Value City altered its corporate structure by forming a new holding company named Retail Ventures, Inc. Retail Ventures was formed in October, becoming the corporate umbrella under which Value City, Shonac, DSW, and Filene's Basement operated. The reorganization was effected to allow each retail concept to concentrate exclusively on its own merchandising and store operations, a singular focus Value City desperately needed. The chain continued to post annual losses, however, registering a $20 million loss in 2004, its fifth consecutive year of operating in the red.

While Value City struggled to find a formula for success, DSW performed admirably, becoming the jewel of the Schottenstein retail empire. By mid-2004, the chain consisted of 151 stores, having more than doubled in size during the previous four years. Sales for the year reached $791 million, an increase of nearly 23 percent from the total collected in 2003. Looking ahead, the company's expansion plans reflected the financial vitality of the chain. After opening 22 stores in 2003 and 35 stores in 2004, Retail Ventures executives announced plans to open 30 stores each year through 2009, setting an ultimate target of 500 stores

Key Dates:

1969: Shonac Corporation is formed.
1991: DSW Shoe Warehouse, formed as a subsidiary of Shonac, opens its first discount shoe store in Dublin, Ohio.
1998: Shonac and DSW Shoe Warehouse are acquired by Value City Department Stores, Inc.
2003: Value City forms Retail Ventures as the holding company for assets that include Shonac and DSW Shoe Warehouse.
2005: Shonac changes its name to DSW Inc. and completes its initial public offering of stock.

nationwide. As the company pressed forward with its expansion plans, it used a 30,000-square-foot format, rolling out stores that stocked 40,000 pairs of shoes and offered a range of accessories, including handbags, hosiery, and headwear.

The contrasting fortunes of Value City and DSW led to another organizational change with the Schottensteins' collection of businesses, one that had a profound effect on DSW. Retail Ventures, realizing a need to sharpen its focus on the beleaguered Value City chain and wanting to take advantage of DSW's success, decided to spin off Shonac and the discount shoe chain in an IPO. The offering was expected to raise $185 million, the bulk of which ($165 million) was to be given to Retail Ventures to pay down debt. In February 2005, in anticipation of the IPO, Shonac changed its name to DSW Inc. The following month, as Retail Ventures prepared to file for DSW's IPO with the Securities and Exchange Commission (SEC), a security breach threatened to scuttle plans for the IPO. A computer hacker obtained credit card information from 1.4 million customers who had shopped at more than 100 DSW stores. The U.S. Secret Service launched an investigation into the security breach, casting a pall over DSW's debut as a publicly traded company, but Retail Ventures decided to move forward with its original plan. "We didn't want to allow a computer criminal to hold the process hostage," Retail Ventures' chief financial officer explained in a March 16, 2005 interview with the *Columbus Dispatch.*

DSW made its debut on the New York Stock Exchange in July 2005. Slightly more than 14 million shares were offered for $19 per share, marking the beginning of DSW's new era of independence—although, as ever, the Schottenstein family remained connected to the business it had created. Jay Schottenstein was appointed the company's chairman and chief executive officer. Further, Retail Ventures, which was 60 percent-owned by Schottenstein Stores Corp., owned 60 percent of

DSW's stock and controlled more than 90 percent of the voting rights associated with the company's stock. Positioned within this framework, DSW pushed forward with its ambitious expansion plans, pursuing its goal of becoming a 500-store chain.

Principal Subsidiaries

DSW Shoe Warehouse, Inc.

Principal Competitors

Federated Department Stores, Inc.; Payless ShoeSource, Inc.; Rack Room Shoes Inc.

Further Reading

Belgum, Deborah, "Upscale Shoe Retailer Entering L.A. Market," *Los Angeles Business Journal,* October 23, 2000, p. 3.

Bohman, Jim, "DSW Planning Initial Public Offering," *Dayton Daily News,* March 15, 2005, p. D1.

Crawford, Dan, "Value City Still Mulling Offers for Subsidiaries," *Business First-Columbus,* November 30, 2001, p. A3.

"DSW Hacking Affected 1.4 Million Credit Cards—Far More Than First Reported," *Cardline,* April 22, 2005, p. 1.

"DSW Latest Retailer to Suffer Massive Theft of Credit Card Information," *Atlanta Journal-Constitution,* April 20, 2005, p. B1.

Kraeuter, Chris, "Shoe Retailer Horns in on Union Square," *San Francisco Business Times,* January 28, 2000, p. 5.

Leopold, Jason, "DSW to Merchandise Stein Mart Stores," *Footwear News,* August 19, 2002, p. 2.

Nelson, Bernard, "Columbus, Ohio, Family Makes Bid to Buy Clothing, Shoe Retailers," *Boston Globe,* July 11, 2001, p. B3.

Niemi, Wayne, "Analysts Give DSW IPO Big Thumbs Up," *Footwear News,* March 21, 2005, p. 18.

Roberts, Ricardo, "Schottenstein Bid May Invite Higher Offers," *Mergers & Acquisitions Report,* July 16, 2001.

Scardino, Emily, "DSW Fills Big Footprint for Well-Heeled City Shoppers," *DSN Retailing Today,* November 8, 2004, p. 4.

——, "DSW Promotes Thrill of the Hunt," *DSN Retailing Today,* May 23, 2005, p. 16.

Sheban, Jeffrey, "Columbus, Ohio-Based Retailer Loses $19.4 Million in 2004," *Columbus Dispatch,* March 16, 2005, p. B3.

——, "Columbus, Ohio-Based Retail Company Struggles to Increase Sales," *Columbus Dispatch,* April 16, 2005, p. B2.

——, "Retailer Plans IPO for DSW Shoe Warehouse," *Columbia Dispatch,* March 16, 2005, p. B2.

Thompson, Kelly, "Value City Buyout May Happen Sooner Than Later," *Footwear News,* July 16, 2001, p. 2.

"Value City Terminates Plans to Divest Subsidiaries," *MMR,* February 25, 2002, p. 4.

Zmuda, Natalie, "DSW Plans to Debut 35 New Stores in '04," *Footwear News,* June 14, 2004, p. 4.

——, "DSW to Open First 2 Manhattan Doors," *Footwear News,* October 11, 2004, p. 6.

—Jeffrey L. Covell

E.I. du Pont de Nemours and Company

1007 Market Street
Wilmington, Delaware 19898
U.S.A.
Telephone: (302) 774-1000
Toll Free: (800) 441-7515
Fax: (302) 999-4399
Web site: http://www.dupont.com

Public Company
Incorporated: 1915
Employees: 55,000
Sales: $27.34 billion (2004)
Stock Exchanges: New York
Ticker Symbol: DD
NAIC: 325211 Plastics Material and Resin
  Manufacturing; 313210 Broadwoven Fabric Mills;
  324110 Petroleum Refineries; 325131 Inorganic Dye
  and Pigment Manufacturing; 325188 All Other
  Inorganic Chemical Manufacturing; 325998 All Other
  Miscellaneous Chemical Product Manufacturing

E.I. du Pont de Nemours and Company is undoubtedly better known by consumers under the name DuPont, one of the oldest family names in American business. The company operates in more than 70 countries, selling a wide range of products competing in the agriculture, nutrition, electronics, communications, safety and protection, home and construction, transportation, and apparel markets. After a century of focusing on synthetics derived from oil-based ingredients, DuPont is focused on biological materials as the basis for its products.

Company Founding

Founder Éleuthère Irenée du Pont de Nemours was born to French nobility. He studied with the chemist Antoinne LaVoisier, in charge of manufacturing the French government's gunpowder. The years of turmoil preceding the French Revolution caused him to immigrate to the United States in 1797. He chose to build his production facilities on a site on the Delaware's Brandywine River, which was central to all of the states

at the time and provided sufficient water power to run the mills. Du Pont rapidly established a reputation for superior gunpowder. He died in 1834, leaving his sons Alfred and Henry to buy out French financiers and continue the business. His sons expanded the company's product line into the manufacture of smokeless powder, dynamite, and nitroglycerine.

One century after its founding, the gunpowder and explosives combine faced dissolution when senior partner Eugene du Pont died at the age of 62, after having served 42 years. With no new leadership, the surviving partners decided to sell the company to the highest bidder. Alfred I. du Pont, a distant relative of the founder, purchased the firm with the aid of his cousins. Alfred was intent on saving the family business. Although he had grown up working in gunpowder yards, he lacked the organizational skills needed to run the firm. His cousins Pierre S. du Pont and Thomas Coleman possessed the financial acumen and led the family company to unprecedented success. The purchase price was set at $12 million, but secret investigations by the cousins unveiled company assets conservatively valued at $24 million. The old partnership also held a great deal of undervalued shares in other companies, among them their direct competitors in the gunpowder business, Hazard and Laflin & Rand. Not having the initial capital for the purchase, the young cousins negotiated a leveraged buyout, giving them a 25 percent interest in the new corporation and 4 percent paid on $12 million over the next 30 years. Coleman was president, Pierre treasurer, and Alfred vice-president of E.I. du Pont de Nemours & Company. The only cash involved in the takeover was $8,500 in incorporation fees.

Sound management, luck, and hidden wealth resulted in the acquisition of 54 companies within three years. Pierre set out to dominate the industry through payoffs and by purchasing minority shareholders and vulnerable competitors. When the cousins first incorporated in 1902, the company controlled 36 percent of the U.S. powder market. By 1905 it held a 75 percent share of the market. DuPont alone supplied 56 percent of the national production of explosives, with $60 million in estimated assets; it had become one of the nation's largest corporations.

A new method of operation was required to keep track of the rapidly growing organization. The cousins solicited the aid of Amory Haskell and Hamilton Barksdale, managers who had

Company Perspectives:

Our ability to adapt to change and our foundation of unending scientific inquiry has enabled DuPont to become one of the world's most innovative companies. But, in the face of constant change, innovation and discovery, our core values have remained constant: commitment to safety, health and the environment; high ethical standards; and treating people with respect.

reorganized their dynamite business into an efficient organization. They remodeled the unwieldy company using elaborate family tree charts composed of levels of managers. The new structure revolutionized American business and gave birth to the modern corporation. The system of organization worked so well that Pierre bailed out the then struggling General Motors Corporation, buying 23 percent of the shares and applying the skills DuPont had perfected. (The Department of Justice later ordered DuPont to divest its General Motors holdings in 1951.)

A Gunpowder Monopoly by 1900

DuPont grew to command the entire explosives market. So dominant was the company that by 1907 the U.S. government initiated antitrust proceedings against it. DuPont was deemed a gunpowder monopoly in 1912 and ordered to divest itself of a substantial portion of its business. In addition, early years of incorporation were fraught with tension between Alfred and his more practical cousins. Arguments ensued over the modernization of the Brandywine yards. Coleman and Pierre saw modernization as the only way to fully utilize the plant. The quarrel, along with other incidents, prompted Coleman and Pierre to take away Alfred's responsibilities in 1911. In effect, this left Alfred a vice-president in name only.

Modernization, diversification, good management, and a command of the market characterized DuPont's industrial era phase. The experiments of DuPont chemists with a product known as guncotton, an early form of nitroglycerine, led to the company's involvement in the textile business. The end of World War I proved the peacetime use of artificial fibers to be more profitable than explosives. In the 1920s DuPont acquired French rights for producing cellophane. DuPont made it moistureproof, transforming cellophane from a decorative wrap to a packaging material for food and other products. DuPont also produced the clothing fiber Rayon in the 1920s, and used a stronger version of the fiber for auto tire cord.

Developing Synthetics: Mid-20th Century

DuPont gradually moved away from explosives and into synthetics. Their most important discovery, Nylon, was created in 1935 by a polymer research group headed by Wallace H. Carothers. The synthesis of nylon came from the hypothesis that polymeric substances were practically endless chains held together by ordinary chemical bonds. Long chain molecules could be built one step at a time by carrying out well understood reactions between standard types of organic chemicals. Carothers chose one of nature's simplest reactions—alcohols reacting

with acids to form esters. By reacting compounds with alcohol groups on each end with analogous acids, polyesters were produced. Super polymers were later formed when a molecular still was used to extract the water that was formed in the reaction. The excess water had created a chemical equilibrium that stopped reaction and limited chain growth. Experimentation with diamine-dibasic pairs produced a molten polyamide that could be drawn into filaments, cooled, and stretched to form very strong fibers. DuPont later marketed a 6–6 polymer, which was made from the inexpensive starting compound Benzene. The new fiber proved remarkably successful. It was employed as a material for undergarments, stockings, tire cord, auto parts, and brushes.

A large number of plastics and fibers followed. Products such as Neoprene (synthetic rubber), Lucite (a clear, tough plastic resin), and Teflon (a resin used in nonstick cookware) became commonplace, as did Orlon (a bulky acrylic fiber), Dacron polyester, and Mylar. DuPont quickly became known as the world's most proficient synthesizer. The range of textiles it supplied reoriented the whole synthetic field.

Not every DuPont invention was a success, however. Corfam, a synthetic leather product, proved to be a disaster. Lammont du Pont Copeland, the last du Pont to head the company, invested millions of dollars into promoting Corfam in the 1960s. The product was not successful because, although the material lasted practically forever, it lacked the flexibility and breathability usually found in leather products. Lammont relinquished the chief executive post in 1967 and was succeeded by Charles B. McCoy, son of a DuPont executive. Irving Shapiro took the post in 1974. Shapiro had served DuPont well, acting as the principal lawyer negotiating the antitrust suit brought against DuPont and General Motors Corporation.

Shapiro led DuPont for six years during a period when the fibers industry stagnated from overcapacity. DuPont's stream of synthetic fiber discoveries had led it into a trap, for it left them content to exploit the fiber market without looking elsewhere for new products. The demand for fibers collapsed in the mid-1970s, causing a halt in the company's main business. Climbing raw material costs and declining demand combined to depress the market in 1979. The innovator of a new technology had been the last to recognize that the market it created was losing momentum. The collapse compelled DuPont to concentrate exclusively on repairing its old business, delaying actions to create a new base. DuPont's rebuilding efforts were also hindered by reducing its commitment to research and development. Continued reliance on fibers caused DuPont to be one of the worst hit chemical companies in the 1980 recession.

DuPont's continued attention to the fibers business, however, resulted in an important discovery in 1980. Kevlar was added to the company's assemblage of synthetic textiles. DuPont scientist Stephanie Kwolek discovered the solvent that unclumped the hard chains of molecules comprising an intractable polymer. The resultant revolutionary material proved to be light yet strong, possessing a tensile strength five times that of steel. Fabrics made of Kevlar were heat and puncture resistant. When laminated, Kevlar outstripped fiberglass. DuPont made the largest financial gamble in its history, investing $250 million in a Kevlar plant expansion. Applications for Kevlar ranged from heat resistant

Key Dates:

1802: Éleuthère Irenée du Pont establishes gunpowder production facilities along the Brandywine River in Delaware.
1902: The company is purchased by three distant relatives of the founder, who spearhead DuPont's transformation from an explosives manufacturer into a broader-based chemical company.
1930: DuPont's polymer research group develops the world's first true synthetic fiber, Nylon.
1980: DuPont begins producing Kevlar.
1981: DuPont acquires Conoco, Inc.
1998: Chief Executive Officer Charles Holliday announces the company's emphasis on bioscience.
1999: Conoco is sold and Pioneer Hi-Bred International is acquired.
2001: DuPont sells its pharmaceutical division.
2004: DuPont sells its textile fibers business; Holliday initiates a cost-cutting program aimed at reducing spending by $900 million by 2005.

gloves, fire resistant clothing, and bullet resistant vests to cables and reinforcement belting in tires. Kevlar also proved successful in the fabrics industry: one half of the police force in the United States soon wore Kevlar vests. Kevlar's true success, however, depended on the price of its raw material—oil. Kevlar showed no threat of becoming a steel replacement, since the price of its production was considerably higher.

Diversification in the Early 1980s

DuPont reacted to the depressed market in textiles by arranging mergers and acquisitions of other companies in other industries. DuPont's takeover of Conoco Oil (the United States' number two petroleum firm) was the largest merger in history. Issues of antitrust were prevalent in negotiation for the merger, but in the end DuPont bought Conoco for $7.8 billion. DuPont merged with Conoco to protect itself from the rise in crude oil prices. As oil supplies dwindled, a supply of Conoco oil and coal as raw material for DuPont's chemicals provided a competitive advantage. Conoco's sites in Alberta, Canada, and off the north slope of Alaska provided large amounts of these resources. DuPont's only disadvantage in the Conoco takeover was the introduction of Edgar Bronfman, chairman of the Seagram Company, the world's largest liquor distiller, into a minority position in DuPont-Conoco. Conoco had been a major acquisition target for Seagram. The merger left Seagram with 20 percent of DuPont. Bronfman saw himself as a long-term investor in DuPont and desired an important voice in the company's direction. However, Seagram and DuPont arrived at an agreement whereby Seagram could not purchase more than 25 percent of DuPont stock until 1991.

Growth and greater financial security came to DuPont in 1980 when it bought Remington Arms, a manufacturer of sporting firearms and ammunition. The Remington Arms unit of DuPont made a number of multimillion-dollar contracts with the army to operate government-owned plants. DuPont also

expanded its scope in the early 1980s with other major purchases. New England Nuclear Corporation, a leading manufacturer of radioactive chemicals for medical research and diagnosis, was acquired in April 1981, and Solid State Dielectrics, a supplier of dielectric materials used in the manufacture of multilayer capacitors, was acquired in April 1982.

DuPont management was determined to reduce the company's dependence on petrochemicals. It decided to take some risks in becoming a leader in the life sciences by delving into development and production of biomedical products and agricultural chemicals. In April 1982 DuPont purchased the agrichemicals division of SEPIC. In November the company acquired the production equipment and technology for the manufacture of spiral wound reverse osmosis desalting products. In March 1986 DuPont acquired Elit Circuits Inc., a producer of molded circuit interconnects.

In addition to mergers and acquisitions, DuPont became heavily involved in joint ventures. DuPont had agreements with P.D. Magnetics to develop, manufacture, and sell magnetic tape. It also became involved with PPG Industries to manufacture ethylene glycol. Aided by Olin Corporation, it planned to construct a chlor/alkali production facility. DuPont also forged extensive connections with Japanese industry. The 1980s united them with Sankyo Company (to develop, manufacture, and market pharmaceuticals), Idemitso Petrochemicals (to produce and market butanediol), Mitsubishi Gas Chemical Company, and Mitsubishi Rayon Company. Furthermore, DuPont established connections in Europe, becoming partners with N.V. Phillips (to produce optical discs), EKA AB (to produce and market the Compozil chemical system for papermaking processes), and British Telecom (to develop and manufacture optoelectronic components).

In addition to stock chemicals and petrochemically based synthetic fibers, DuPont looked to the life sciences and other specialty businesses to produce earnings. Edward G. Jefferson, a chemist by training, succeeded Shapiro and directed the company into the biosciences and other specialty lines. DuPont supported these businesses with large amounts of capital investment and research and development expenditures. The company's fields of interest were genetic engineering, drugs and agricultural chemicals, electronics, and fibers and plastics.

DuPont had the kind of multinational marketing capability and resources to become a major influence in the life sciences. The company sought ways to restructure living cells to mass produce specific microorganisms in an attempt to manufacture commercial quantities of interferon, a human protein that was considered potentially useful in fighting viruses and cancer. DuPont claimed to be the first company to have purified fibroblast interferon, one of the three types of human interferon in the mid-1970s. DuPont developed a blood profile system, artificial blood, and a test for acquired immune deficiency syndrome (AIDS). The company created drugs that controlled irregular heartbeats, aid rheumatoid arthritis pain, and were antinarcotic agents. In addition to new drugs, DuPont worked to develop new pesticides and herbicides. DuPont built a $450 million business as a major supplier to the electronics industry, providing sophisticated connectors and the dry film used in making printed circuits. DuPont also developed new high-performance plastics. The company's scientists developed a process called group transfer polymerization for solvent-based polymer acrylics, which was the first major polymerization process developed since the early 1950s.

In the early to mid-1980s DuPont had approximately 90 major businesses selling a wide range of products to different industries, including petroleum, textile, transportation, chemical construction, utility, healthcare, and agricultural industries. Business operations existed in more than 50 nations. DuPont had eight principle business segments: biomedical products; industrial and consumer products; fibers; polymer products; agricultural and industrial chemicals; petroleum exploration and production; petroleum refining, marketing and transportation; and coal. Total expenditure for research and development amounted to more than $1 billion in 1985, and over 6,000 scientists and engineers were engaged in research activities.

Refocusing on Core Businesses in the Late 1980s

However, by this time DuPont was bloated with the numerous businesses it had acquired over the years. Management decided to return to its former policy of focusing on areas of maximum profit. It began moving away from commodity production, instead concentrating on oil, healthcare, electronics, and specialty chemicals.

By 1987 the changes were paying off in some areas, as discretionary cash flow reached $4.5 billion. Biomedical products represented only 4 percent of sales, but the firm was moving into the large markets for cancer and AIDS testing and research. Breaking into its new markets was expensive, however. Earnings soared at rivals Rhone-Poulenc and Dow Chemical, which were less diversified. Meanwhile DuPont's pretax income climbed only 4.5 percent, to 3.8 billion in 1988, although sales climbed by 8 percent. DuPont still had problems with quality control. In 1988 Ford Motor Co. gave DuPont's contract for mirror housings to General Electric because paint kept flaking off DuPont's plastic, according to an April 1989 *Business Week* article.

Edgar Smith Woolard, Jr., became president in 1989, backed by the Bronfman family. As part of his mission to raise the price of DuPont's stock and prevent a takeover, the firm bought back about 8 percent of its outstanding stock. The electronics division had $1.8 billion in annual sales and had won business in films and imaging, though it was losing money in the highly competitive areas of fiber optics and optical disks. In addition, the pharmaceuticals business was still losing money. Investment in research and equipment had reached $1.8 billion since 1982, yet most of the drugs under development were years from the market. One area of clear success was DuPont's textile business. The $5.8 billion division was the firm's most profitable.

Seeking to raise public awareness of its fibers, DuPont started a consumer products catalogue featuring household items made from its products. The catalogue mentioned copyrighted fiber names including Lycra, Zytel, and Supplex as it advertised the clothes, sporting goods, and housewares. DuPont had reason to be interested in maintaining brand-name recognition in fibers. Lucre, a stretch polymer invented in 1959 and originally used for girdles, became a huge hit after being adopted for biking clothes and other exercise outfits during the early 1980s. By the end of the decade, Lucre clothing had become fashionable. Big name designers incorporated it into their wardrobes, and by 1990, Lucre profits topped $200 million a year. DuPont's patent on Lucre, the generic name of which is spandex, had long since expired, but DuPont had continued to improve the fabric and was its only major manufacturer. To make certain things stayed that way, the firm announced in 1990 that it would spend $500 million over three years to build or expand Lucre plants.

Another important area for DuPont was pollution control and cleanup. According to *Forbes* magazine, the firm was one of the country's biggest air polluters and was in the process of spending well over $1 billion on pollution control and cleanup. The firm's chlorofluorocarbon business was being replaced by chemicals less harmful to the ozone layer, at a cost of another $1 billion. DuPont also stood to make money, however, by creating safer herbicides and expanding into the growing recycling market. Partly because of these trends, DuPont's sales of agricultural chemicals tripled between 1985 and 1990, to $1.7 billion.

The Gulf War temporarily drove up oil prices and refinery margins, leading to profits of over $1 billion for Conoco in 1990. But a worldwide recession was hurting most of the rest of the company. Profits for 1991 fell to $1.4 billion on sales of $38.7 billion, down from sales of $40 billion in 1990. The firm's electronics products had garnered little prestige within the industry and had fallen well behind earlier projections. Consequently, DuPont began pulling back, beginning by selling an electronic connectors business with $400 million in annual sales. DuPont also took a step back from pharmaceuticals, putting that division into a joint venture with Merck & Co.

Although the company had been divesting businesses for a few years, it accelerated its efforts at streamlining in the early 1990s. With 133,000 employees and numerous management layers in 1991, DuPont was ready to cut back the bureaucracy. Chairman and CEO Edgar S. Woolard took several classic steps to restructure the company. The number of employees was reduced steadily in the early 1990s, to 97,000 in 1996, and several layers of vice-presidents and managers were eliminated. The remaining employees were given stock options for 600 shares each to encourage a sense of ownership and responsibility for the company. Executives were required to own shares more than equal to their annual salary. "Everyone is now connected to the company," John A. Krol, who became CEO in 1995, told *Forbes* in 1997. "They post the price of DuPont stock on watercoolers and safety signs around the company."

DuPont also continued to sharpen its focus on its core businesses of chemicals and fibers. The firm closed its declining Orlon division and in 1991 it sold half of Consolidation Coal Co. for over $1 billion to Germany's Rheinbraun A.G. In addition, Du Pont sold all of its medical products businesses. In 1993 the company also sold its acrylic business to ICI and in turn bought ICI's nylon business and later its worldwide polyester films, resins, and intermediates businesses. By acquiring the ICI polyester technology, DuPont could make plastic bottles, a growing market, at less cost than any competitor in the world. The company increased its marketing of synthetic fibers. DuPont looked for new uses for its popular spandex fabric

Lycra, its high-performance fiber Tyvek (best-known for its use in Federal Express envelopes), and its synthetic Kevlar.

Record Profits in the Mid-1990s

After several years of declining profits (from $2.5 billion in 1989 to $0.6 billion in 1993), DuPont reaped the rewards from the restructuring years. The company reported a streak of record profits in the mid-1990s, beginning in 1994 with a net income of $2.7 billion and continuing through 1996 with a net income of $3.6 billion. The company's stock price enjoyed a corresponding rise: from a low around $15 a share in 1990 to a high of almost $50 in 1996.

Some of these earnings were used in 1995 to buy back the shares owned by Seagram since 1980. To raise money for a venture into showbusiness, Seagram sold its 24 percent stake in DuPont back to the company for $8.8 billion, a discount of 13 percent from the market value of the stock at the time.

Conoco played an important role in the rejuvenation of DuPont. In 1995 some analysts (and DuPont shareholders) were recommending DuPont sell off the subsidiary, which they felt was not even returning the cost of its capital. After scrutinizing the numbers, the DuPont management team decided to hold on to Conoco but reevaluate its decision in a year. In 1996 Conoco returned $860 million in net earnings and bought the support of DuPont's board. In 1997 Conoco acquired heavy oil reserves in Venezuela and a gas field in Texas, thus increasing its oil reserves by 50 percent.

Joint ventures continued to be an important strategy for DuPont in the mid- to late 1990s. From 12 joint ventures in 1990, DuPont had reached 37 by 1997. Among the most significant were its partnership with the Japanese chemical firm Asahi to market synthetic fibers in Asia, the 50–50 venture with Dow called DuPont Dow Elastomers, and the alliance with Pioneer Hi-Bred International to form Optimum Quality Grains.

DuPont reaffirmed its commitment to the life sciences as a core business in the late 1990s. Bioindustrial, pharmaceutical, and feed and food industries were seen as the new ground for the increasing integration of chemistry and biotechnology. As part of this push, in 1997 DuPont purchased Protein Technologies International, which developed soy-based products, from Ralston Purina for $1.5 billion. The following year the company agreed to buy Merck's 50 percent share in the joint venture DuPont Merck Pharmaceutical Company.

A New Focus for a New Century

In 1998 DuPont announced its intention to sell Conoco, a divestiture that became part of a sweeping restructuring program that had as profound an effect on the organization as its transformation a century earlier from explosives to chemicals manufacturing. The individual who led the company during this period of redefining itself was Charles O. "Chad" Holliday, a career DuPont executive who was named president in 1997, chief executive officer the following year, and chairman in 1999. Holliday's mission centered on using DuPont's legacy in chemistry, begun in 1902 during the company's first great transformation, and using it to usher in a new era of DuPont innova-

tions in bioscience. For years, the company had lacked a breakthrough product to drive its sales and earnings growth. Stainmaster fabric protection, introduced in 1986, was the last of the company's line of synthetics (Nylon, Lycra, Dacron, Mylar, Kevlar, etc.) to become a household name. The company, according to the February 3, 2003 issue of *Forbes*, had suffered from "an overemphasis on 'new-and-improving' its old brands," creating a "mix of mediocrity, malaise, and investor ambivalence." To inject vitality into the company, Holliday demanded that new synthetics be developed, synthetics that would use biological materials rather than the oil-based ingredients that formed the basis of DuPont's pioneering work in the 20th century. The company, for example, directed its resources at developing Sorona—described as a "cousin" to polyester—that used a polymer derived from corn, not petroleum. Fittingly, given the company's new orientation toward bioscience, the 1999 spinoff of Conoco occurred at roughly the same time Holliday spent $7.6 billion to acquire Pioneer Hi-Bred International Inc., the world's largest producer of hybrid corn and soybean seeds. The year also marked the official recognition of the addition of biology to chemistry as DuPont's core science platform. The company's corporate brand identity, which had been expressed in the slogan "Better Things for Better Living," was changed to "The Miracles of Science."

The company's far-reaching restructuring program occupied Holliday's attention in the years before and after DuPont's 200th anniversary. Between 1998 and 2004, the company's divestiture and acquisition transactions totaled $60 billion, a period that saw its annual revenue volume drop from $45 billion to $27 billion and its workforce cut from 98,000 to 55,000. Holliday had decided to exit the drug business, selling the company's pharmaceutical division in 2001 to Bristol-Myers Squibb for $7.8 billion, and he sold the company's textile fibers business in 2004 to Koch Industries for $4.2 billion, which had been responsible for 25 percent of its annual revenue. DuPont was leaner, focused on execution and efficiency, and intent on achieving 6 percent annual sales growth and 10 percent annual earnings growth. To help achieve this goal, Holliday established a target of achieving $900 million in cost savings by 2005, a figure the company was "on track to significantly exceed," according to the September 20, 2004 issue of *Chemical Market Reporter*. An analyst who had attended the company's annual shareholder meeting confirmed the assessment, telling *Chemical Market Reporter*, "We came away with the distinct impression that DuPont had gotten its house in order and both top-line and bottom-line growth are improving." Holliday offered his own assessment in the same article, expressing an optimistic tone as DuPont began its third century of business. "We've been working for six years to put in place the right business mix and the right set of operating processes in this company to deliver our long-term goals. We now have both in place to move us forward. We are clearly in the deliver and execute mode."

Principal Subsidiaries

Agar Cross S.A. (Argentina); Antec International Ltd. (U.K.); Building Media, Inc.; ChemFirst Inc.; Christiana Insurance Limited (Bermuda); Destination Realty, Inc.; DPC (Luxembourg) SARL; DPC S/A Brazil; DPC South America (Brazil); DSRB Ltda (Brazil); DuPont—Kansai Automotive Coatings

Company; DuPont (Australia) Ltd.; DuPont (Korea) Inc.; DuPont (New Zealand) Limited; SuPont (South America), Holdings, LLC; DuPont (Thailand) Co. Ltd.; DuPont (U.K.) Investments; DuPont (U.K.) Limited; DuPont Agricultural Caribe Industries, Ltd. (Bermuda); DuPont Agricultural Chemicals Ltd. (China); DuPont Agro Hellas S.A. (Greece); DuPont Argentina S.A.; DuPont Asia Pacific, Ltd.; AuPont Beteiligungs GmbH (Austria); DuPont de Nemours (Deutschland) GmbH (Germany); Dupont de Nemours (France) S.A.; DuPont de Nemours Italiana S.r.l. (Italy); DuPont Iberica, S.L. (Spain); DuPont Services B.V. (Netherlands); Dupont S.A. de C.V. (Mexico); Griffin, LLC; UNIAX Corporation.

Principal Divisions

Dupont Electronic & Communication Technologies; DuPont Performance Materials; DuPont Coatings & Color Technologies; DuPont Safety & Protection; DuPont Agriculture & Nutrition.

Principal Competitors

BASF Aktiengesellschaft; Bayer AG; The Dow Chemical Company.

Further Reading

Chandler, Alfred D., Jr., and Stephen Salsbury, *Pierre S. du Pont and the Making of the Modern Corporation,* New York: Harper & Row, 1971.

Chang, Joseph, "DuPont Focuses on Execution Following Transformation: Next Big Thing Could Be Biosciences," *Chemical Market Reporter,* September 20, 2004, p. 1.

——, "Major Chemicals Reap Profit Bonanza," *Chemical Market Reporter,* November 1, 2004, p. 1.

Colby, Gerald, *du Pont Dynasty,* Secaucus, N.J.: Lyle Stuart, 1984.

"E.I. du Pont de Nemours and Co.," *Business Record,* August 16, 2004, p. 37.

Lenzer, Robert, and Carrie Shook, "There Will Always Be a DuPont," *Forbes,* October 13, 1997, pp. 60–69.

Lovell, Michael, "Pioneer Finding Place in DuPont Shift to Biotech," *Business Record,* April 21, 2003, p. 1.

Mosley, Leonard, *Blood Relations: The Rise and Fall of the du Ponts of Delaware,* New York: Atheneum, 1980.

Norman, James R., "Turning Up the Heat at DuPont," *Forbes,* August 5, 1991.

Plishner, Emily S., "The Dilemma: Will DuPont's New CEO Spin Off Conoco?," *Financial World,* December 5, 1995, pp. 34–37.

Scherreik, Susan, "Analysts Are Standing by DuPont," *Money,* September 1998, p. 32.

Schoenberger, Chana R., "Greenhouse Effect," *Forbes,* February 3, 2003, p. 54.

——, "A Run in the Stocking," *Forbes,* February 3, 2003, p. 59.

Taylor, Graham D., and Patricia E. Sudnik, *DuPont and the International Chemical Industry,* Boston: Twayne, 1984.

Weber, Joseph, "DuPont's Trailblazer Wants to Get Out of the Woods," *Business Week,* August 31, 1992.

——, "DuPont's Version of a Maverick," *Business Week,* April 3, 1989.

Weiner, Steve, "But Will They Ever Know Zytel from Lycra?," *Forbes,* June 26, 1989.

Westervelt, Robert, "DuPont Confirms Talk on Sale of Textiles Unit," *Chemical Week,* April 23, 2003, p. 8.

Wood, Andrew, "DuPont Expects Lower Growth, but Maintains Earnings Targets," *Chemical Week,* September 22, 2004, p. 7.

—Scott M. Lewis
—updates: Susan Windisch Brown; Jeffrey L. Covell

Elkay Manufacturing Company

2222 Camden Ct.
Oak Brook, Illinois 60523
U.S.A.
Telephone: (630) 574-8484
Fax: (630) 574-5012
Web site: http://www.elkay.com

Private Company
Founded: 1920
Employees: 3,900
Sales: $575 million (2003 est.)
NAIC: 332998 Enameled Iron and Metal Sanitary Ware
   Manufacturing; 332913 Plumbing Fixture Fitting and
   Trim Manufacturing; 337110 Wood Kitchen Cabinet
   and Counter Top Manufacturing

Elkay Manufacturing Company is best known for the residential and commercial sinks it makes under the Celebrity, Lustertone, Gourmet, and Revere labels. In addition, the Oak Brook, Illinois-based private company manufactures faucets, shower systems, associated hardware, and fixtures through Phylrich International; kitchen cabinets through subsidiaries Yorktowne, Medallion, and MasterCraft; and water coolers through Halsey Taylor. Elkay is also involved in a joint venture in Malaysia, Elkay Pacific Rim, which dispenses bottled water and coolers manufactured in Malaysia throughout the Pacific Rim. All told, Elkay is comprised of ten privately held companies employing some 3,900 people, with 14 factories and 24 distribution centers located in the United States, Canada, Mexico, and the Pacific Rim. Elkay's largest customer is Home Depot.

Formation in 1920

Elkay was founded in 1920 by Leopold Katz, his son Louis, and a tinsmith named Ellef Robarth. The company's name was coined by combining the initial sounds of Robarth's first name and Katz's last name. The trio rented 2,100 square feet of space in Chicago and set up shop to produce handmade silver butler pantry sinks, which they sold, delivered by street car, and installed in the homes of Chicago's wealthy. The one-product company quickly built a reputation for quality, so that by the end of the first year in business Elkay increased its workforce from its three founders to seven. Robarth left the company after two years, the reason long forgotten, but Elkay continued to grow without him. By the end of the 1920s Elkay's sinks were best sellers, prompting a move to larger accommodations and the hiring of more employees despite the advent of the Great Depression.

Elkay reached a key moment in its history in 1935 when it offered its first stainless steel sink, the earliest models constructed out of a light gauge of metal, encased in a wooden frame. Within three years, Elkay became the first company to mass produce stainless steel sinks in the United States. As was the case with much of American industry, during World War II Elkay devoted its energies in the first half of the 1940s to aiding the war effort. The company used its expertise to produce sinks for the U.S. Navy as well as scullery and plumbing fixtures. Elkay delivered on average about 10,000 sinks a month to the military during this period.

Following World War II, Elkay shifted its focus from serving upper-class homes to the emerging middle-class. Returning servicemen were getting married and having children at a record rate, leading to the Baby Boom generation, and because of a national housing shortage, suburbs sprouted up across the country. All of these new suburban houses needed sinks and many homeowners were attracted to stainless steel sinks because of the ease of cleanup. Elkay was already well established in the stainless steel sink business, but it further strengthened its hold with a production breakthrough in 1948, when it began to die draw stainless steel bowls. This advance allowed the company to cut in half the cost of producing a stainless steel bowl. As a result, Elkay became the leader in residential sinks.

Third Generation Joining Business in 1950s

In the 1950s a third generation of the Katz family became involved in the company, Louis's son Ron Katz, the company's current chairman and chief executive officer. During the 1950s Elkay began to build a large network of independent sales representatives, and continued to be a leader in innovation in the field. Through continued advances in automation techniques, Elkay was able to lower production costs, so that by the late 1950s it emerged as the largest maker of stainless steel residential sinks in the world and in 1960 began the construction of a new facility in Broadview, Illinois, where the company would also make its headquarters for the next 20 years. In 1979 Elkay moved the corporate offices to its present site in Oak Brook, Illinois.

Elkay began diversifying its business in 1969 by adding water coolers to the mix, then supplemented the line in 1976 with the acquisition of Cordley/Temprite. In the meantime, Elkay maintained its reputation as an industry innovator. In 1970 it introduced a three-compartment stainless steel sink that proved highly popular. Elkay also increased geographic reach and share of the residential sink market through acquisitions in the 1970s. It bought a plant in Lumberton, North Carolina, which became Elkay Southern Corporation, and the Dayton-Ogden Corporation, based in Ogden, Utah.

During the 1980s, Elkay took advantage of its name recognition to move into the retail market, which was especially attractive because of the increasing popularity of such big box retailers as Home Depot and Lowe's catering to the growing do-it-yourself market. To serve these customers, Elkay introduced the Neptune brand of sinks. The company also became interested in other aspects of the kitchen market. Elkay's Gourmet Cuisine Centre, which combined a sink, garbage disposal, drain board, and cutting surface in a single unit, was a step in this direction. In the late 1980s Elkay began eyeing the cabinet industry, offering complementary product lines, since a large percentage of people in the market for a new kitchen sink were also looking for matching kitchen cabinets.

In the early 1990s Elkay hired Jack Edl to investigate the highly fragmented kitchen cabinet marketplace and recommend companies for Elkay to buy. Edl was well suited to the task, having spent five years as the president of Yorktowne Cabinets, and six years working for Elkay as vice-president of marketing. It was not especially surprising that the first cabinet maker Edl recommended that Elkay acquire was Yorktowne. Based in Red Lion, Pennsylvania, Yorktowne had been in business since 1908 making horse-drawn carriages. As automobiles replaced horses, Yorktowne turned its attention in the 1920s to mid-range kitchen cabinets, while also building radio cabinets and later switching to television cabinets. In the mid-1980s Yorktowne changed its emphasis from stock kitchen cabinets to individual kitchens. But a slowing economy hurt Yorktowne in the highly competitive cabinet market, with sales falling from $48 million in 1987 to $38 million in 1991. Ownership changed hands, with a venture capital group buying the business from Wickes Inc., a Santa Monica, California-based furniture retailer. Elkay began negotiating the purchase in early 1992 but did not close on the deal until August 1993.

Just one month after bringing Yorktowne into the fold, Elkay completed a second cabinet acquisition, Medallion

Kitchens of Waconia, Minnesota, a company that had four owners in the previous five years. Like Yorktowne, Medallion had endured recent struggles, experiencing a dropoff in sales from $27 million in 1989 to $21 million in 1991. However, Medallion's business was starting to rebound when Elkay stepped in. Edl was named president of the newly formed Elkay Cabinet Group, which in 1995 recorded combined sales of $75 million. Elkay added further to its cabinet assets in May 1996 with the purchase of MasterCraft Cabinets. As a result, Elkay with $165 million in sales in 1996 became the seventh largest cabinet maker in the United States, as determined by *Wood & Wood Products*. The addition of Salem, Oregon-based Westwood Products in 1998 elevated Elkay to the number four spot. Westwood was renamed Westwood Customers Cabinetry Inc. and folded into the Medallion operation.

Steady Expansion in 1990s

Elkay grew on other fronts as well in the 1990s. Halsey Taylor was acquired in 1991, adding to Elkay's water cooler segment. The company also became international in scope during this period. With Malaysia partner Formosa Prosonic Equipment, it formed a sales and marketing operation, Elkay Pacific Rim Sdn, Bhd., to distribute coolers and bottled water to Pacific Rim countries, shipped out of Port Klang, Malaysia. In 1996 the partnership built a new water cooler manufacturing plant in Malaysia to service the venture. Elkay became involved in the Canadian sink market through the purchase of Ontario-based Wessan Plumbing Manufacturing Ltd., maker of both residential and commercial sinks. The business was renamed Elkay Canada. In addition to the manufacture and marketing of sinks, the division would also distribute water coolers, faucets, and drinking fountains made by the Elkay U.S. operation. The Wessan acquisition also brought with it a subsidiary, Revere Sink Corp. of New Bedford, Massachusetts. A year later, in May 1999, Elkay turned its attention southward, acquiring Mexico's largest sink manufacturer, E.B. Tecnica Mexicana, in business since 1962. The company had started out small, producing just four stainless steel sinks a day, but by 1990 it was in a position to pursue a growth strategy, diversifying into the production of composite sinks and opening warehouses throughout Mexico. When Elkay assumed control, E.B. Tecnica maintained 20 distribution centers in Mexico and a major manufacturing facility in San Luis Potosi.

Although prospering on a number of levels Elkay was not without challenges in the late 1990s. The Wessan acquisition, for one, proved problematic. The inherited facility was filled with antiquated equipment and lacking in contemporary manufacturing and quality systems. Elkay as a whole required some updating: sales were not growing while profit margins were shrinking. Moreover, it was not just the Canadian plant that was behind the times in adopting modern manufacturing methods. To help reorganize the company, to streamline production and grow profit margins, Elkay hired a new vice-president of operations, Cary B. Wood, who brought years of experience in the automotive industry to the job. The company now focused on standardizing operations and making them as efficient as possible. Elkay switched to a just-in-time approach to manufacturing, so that the plants now produced what was actually ordered, not what the company thought it might sell. This required sales,

---

Key Dates:

1920: Company is founded.
1935: Elkay produces first stainless steel sink.
1948: First die draw stainless steel bowls are produced.
1957: Elkay becomes world's largest stainless steel residential sink manufacturer.
1969: Elkay becomes involved in water cooler business.
1979: Oak Brook headquarters opens.
1993: Elkay begins acquiring kitchen cabinet companies.
1999: E.B. Tecnica Mexicana is acquired.
2004: Phylrich International is acquired.

---

manufacturing, and distribution to work closely together, so that on a monthly basis they planned together the production and inventory needs, allowing the company to better anticipate customer demand and smooth out costly production spikes. Although it was not required, Elkay elected to become ISO certified as a way to instill further order and make sure all systems and processes were in optimal shape.

Overall, Elkay adopted five principles of what became known as the "SQDCP" strategy. The first letter of SQDCP stood for "Safety." Elkay made a concerted effort to reduce the amount of employee hours lost to accidents. During the first three years of the program, from 2000 to 2002, the company enjoyed solid success, evinced by an 80 percent decrease in workman's compensation claims. The next principle was the cost of "Quality," or the amount of money the company had to spend reworking products, scrap costs, and appraisal costs. As for the "Delivery" part of SQDCP, Elkay dramatically improved the on-time delivery of products from 75 to 94 percent. Better inventory and production planning also lowered "Costs." Inventory costs were reduced by 30 percent while at the same time productivity improved by 39 percent. The final element was "People." Employees at all levels of the organization were involved in SQDCP, and their participation was essential to the success of the program.

With the start of the new century, Elkay continued to grow its operations. In 2000 it opened a new 100,000-square-foot distribu-

tion center in Bolingbrook, Illinois, which played a major part in Elkay's efforts to improve efficiencies and bolster margins. The company also remained an innovator, becoming in 2001 the first to add sensor-operated faucets to sinks for hospitals, schools, public buildings, and industrial applications. Elkay took steps to become involved in the in-home water delivery and filtration business with the launch of the Elkay Watertech Division. The company also invested in new plants to ensure production efficiencies. The 40,000-square-foot Ogden plant was replaced by a new 106,000-square-foot plant in 2004, while plans were made to replace Yorktowne's Red Lion plant with a larger facility scheduled to open in Virginia in 2006. In addition, Elkay continued to grow by external means. In late 2004 it acquired Phylrich International, maker of decorative plumbing products, a deal that expanded Elkay's faucet collections.

In 2003 67-year-old Chairman and CEO Ron Katz celebrated his 50th anniversary with the company his father and grandfather had founded more than 80 years earlier. Although he received periodic offers for the company, Katz showed no inclination to either sell the business or retire any time soon.

Principal Divisions

Plumbing Products; Cabinetry; Water Dispensing.

Principal Competitors

Fortune Brands, Inc.; Kohler Co.; Masco Corporation.

Further Reading

Adams, Larry, "Elkay Takes Over a Surging Yorktowne Team," *Wood & Wood Products,* October 1994, p. 56.
Christianson, Rich, "Elkay Plunges into Cabinet Market," *Wood & Wood Products,* October 1994, p. 55.
Glowacki, Michael, "Elkay Manufacturing Company: A Tale of Two Sites," *Journal for Quality and Participation,* March/April 2000, p. 59.
McCarthy, Kevin M., "Elkay Manufacturing in No Danger of Going Down Drain," *Manufacturing Today,* September/October 2002.
Spencer, Mark, "A Sparkling Success; Longtime Sink Maker Elkay Seen As Best in Business," *Daily Herald,* February 2, 2000, p. 1.

—Ed Dinger

Encore Acquisition Company

777 Main Street, Suite 1400
Fort Worth, Texas 76102
U.S.A.
Telephone: (817) 877-9955
Fax: (817) 877-1655
Web site: http://www.encoreacq.com

Public Company
Incorporated: 1998
Employees: 164
Sales: $298.53 million (2004)
Stock Exchanges: New York
Ticker Symbol: EAC
NAIC: 211111 Crude Petroleum and Natural Gas
   Extraction

Encore Acquisition Company is an oil and gas company involved in the acquisition, development, and exploitation of North American reserves. Encore's properties are located in the Williston Basin in Montana and North Dakota, the Permian Basin in Texas and New Mexico, the Arkoma and Anadarko Basins in Oklahoma, the North Louisiana Basin, and in the Rocky Mountains. The company's Cedar Creek Anticline property in the Williston Basin represents its most valuable asset, accounting for 66 percent of its total proved reserves. Encore is led by its founder, I. Jon Brumley, an oil industry veteran with a penchant for pursuing growth via acquisitions.

Origins

Encore Acquisition Company was a fitting name for a start-up venture that most likely represented the entrepreneurial swan song of an oil-patch veteran. I. Jon Brumley had achieved success in the energy industry by heading acquisition-driven companies, and Encore was meant to be, in strategic terms, a repeat performance of the successes he enjoyed during his 30-year career. Born in Pampa, Texas, and raised in Austin, Brumley received his master's degree in business from the University of Pennsylvania's Wharton School of Business. After earning his degree, he returned to Texas and settled in Fort Worth, where he accepted a position as an administrative assistant at Southland Royalty. Brumley joined Southland in 1967, when the company operated as an oil exploration firm with a market capitalization (the number of shares held by investors multiplied by the price per share) of $100 million. The company's market worth increased exponentially after it changed its corporate strategy, a significant turning point for the company and a pivotal event in Brumley's professional career.

When Southland completed an acquisition in 1976, the purchase altered the company's strategy for the future, making a lasting impression on Brumley that would be evinced in his actions for decades to come. In a deal with Dallas-based Aztec Oil & Gas, Southland purchased a group of gas properties in the San Juan Basin that possessed roughly a trillion cubic feet of gas reserves. From that point forward, as Brumley earned promotion through the company's executive ranks, Southland shelved its exploration activities and focused on fueling its growth through additional acquisitions. By 1980, four years of aggressively pursuing oil and gas properties had greatly increased the size of the company. Southland entered the decade with a market capitalization of $4 billion, having quickly become one of the country's major players in the oil and gas industry and convincing Brumley of the merits of an acquisition-driven strategy. In 1985, after Brumley had completed his climb up the company's hierarchy to hold the posts of president and chief executive officer, he presided over the sale of the company to Burlington Northern Santa Fe Corp., a transaction that freed him to pursue his next goal: replicate Southland's strategy with another company.

The business model that served as the basis for Encore's strategy already was ingrained in Brumley's mind by the mid-1980s—nearly 15 years before Encore was formed. During the intervening years, the strategy was refined as its practitioner developed into a seasoned oil and gas executive. In 1986, a year after orchestrating the sale of Southland, Brumley cofounded a company named Cross Timbers Oil Co., a Fort Worth-based firm formed to focus on the acquisition and development of established oil and gas properties. Brumley spent a decade running Cross Timbers, overseeing its conversion to a publicly traded company and spearheading the acquisition of more than

Company Perspectives:

Encore Acquisition Company, using the experience of our senior management team, has developed and refined an acquisition program designed to increase our reserves and to complement our core properties. We have over 30 engineering and geoscience professionals who manage our core properties and use their experience and expertise to target attractive acquisition opportunities. Following acquisition, our technical professionals seek to enhance the value of the new assets through a proven development and exploitation program. Since our inception in 1998, Encore has successfully acquired producing oil and natural gas properties totaling over $600 million.

$500 million worth of properties by the time he retired in the summer of 1996. Brumley's retirement only lasted several weeks. Before the summer was over, Fort Worth billionaire Richard Rainwater and T. Boone Pickens, who owned a company named Mesa Inc., asked Brumley and his son, Jon S. (Jonny) Brumley, to help turnaround Pickens's beleaguered company. The elder Brumley, who was appointed chairman, was asked to find a merger partner, which he did a year later, when Mesa merged with Parker & Parsley Petroleum Co., creating a new company, the $546 million-in-sales Pioneer Natural Resources Co. Brumley and his son, who served as the company's manager of commodity risk and corporation development, left Pioneer in 1998, one year after the merger. Brumley chose against a return to retirement, deciding instead to fulfill one more goal in his professional career. He wanted to graft the experience he had gained at Southland and Cross Timbers on a new start-up venture, an enterprise that, in April 1998, became known as Encore Acquisition Company. "For some time," Brumley said in an August 2001 interview with *Oil and Gas Investor*, "Jonny and I wanted to work together in our own company, following the business model that was employed so successfully at Southland and Cross Timbers." Brumley assumed the posts of president, chief executive officer, and chairman, while his son took the title of executive vice-president of business development.

Brumley intended the company to be an acquisition-driven company, an entity that would purchase producing properties from major oil companies and improve their operations while cutting costs. "Reviving Vintage Fields" became the Encore slogan later in its development, as Brumley exercised his skill in churning a profit from properties forsaken by other companies. His timing for launching his venture was regarded by industry onlookers as propitious, occurring at a time when petroleum prices were at a 13-year low and while major energy concerns were directing their efforts offshore and selling their onshore properties for reduced prices. "What's happening," an analyst explained in a December 4, 1998 interview with the *Dallas Business Journal*, "is that a lot of people are thinking they can go and pick up assets that are being sold by larger companies or companies that could become distressed." Brumley, who began with a dozen employees, ten of whom were partners in his venture, intended to focus on onshore properties, ideally selecting those with roughly eight years worth of production remaining.

Given Brumley's achievements in the oil and gas industry, he had no difficulty in raising the capital to get his acquisition-driven company underway. "When I met Jon Brumley in the spring of 1998," the vice-chairman of New York-based E.M. Warburg, Pincus & Co. said in an August 2001 interview with *Oil and Gas Investor*, "the question wasn't whether we were going to invest in him, but whether he was going to take our money. From our viewpoint, he was a proven executive with a proven business model who was approaching a part of the industry then out of favor—oil." Warburg, Pincus & Co. contributed roughly $150 million to Encore, providing start-up capital that was augmented by a $100 million investment from Chase Capital Partners, $30 million from Natural Gas Partners, and $20 million from First Union Capital Partners. Individual investors also contributed to Encore's cause, as well as Brumley himself, who invested several million dollars of his own money, giving his company the cash to begin its acquisition campaign. All totaled, Brumley began with approximately $300 million in equity financing, a sum he first put to use in the summer of 1999.

The First Big Acquisition in 1999

Encore's first acquisition was arguably the most important acquisition completed during the company's first seven years in business. In June 1999, Brumley used $86 million of the company's start-up capital to purchase Shell Oil's Cedar Creek Anticline oil properties for a total purchase price of $172 million (the remainder was borrowed from Bank of America). The Cedar Creek Anticline properties would represent the company's core asset well into the ensuing decade, constituting a substantial percentage of its total reserves. The properties were located in the Williston Basin along a swath of land stretching from southeastern Montana to northwestern North Dakota.

Brumley made further investments in Cedar Creek Anticline acreage and added holdings in other basins during the next two years—the period spanning the company's initial acquisition and its debut as a public company. During this period, the company's annual revenues grew substantially, jumping from $31.4 million in 1999 to $108.9 million in 2000 and to $135.9 million in 2001. By the time of Encore's initial public offering (IPO) of stock in March 2001, Brumley had acquired oil and natural gas properties in the Permian Basin, which contained fields in Texas and New Mexico, the Anadarko Basin of Oklahoma, and the Powder River Basin in Montana. The Cedar Creek Anticline properties, by this point, accounted for 57 percent of Encore's total reserve value. The IPO, which was completed in March 2001, consisted of 7.15 million shares offered at $14 per share, yielding net proceeds of approximately $92 million—capital Brumley intended to use to fund the company's acquisition campaign.

Encore in the 21st Century

Brumley continued to focus on Encore's Cedar Creek Anticline properties as the heart of the company's operations following the IPO. Further investments were made, increasing the company's reliance on acreage in the Williston Basin even as Brumley acquired properties in other regions. By the end of 2004, the Cedar Creek Anticline properties accounted for 66 percent of the company's total proved reserves, up markedly from the 57 percent the properties represented in 2001. "The

CCA (Cedar Creek Anticline) is our most valuable asset today and in the foreseeable future,'' Encore's 2004 annual filing with the Securities and Exchange Commission noted. ''A large portion of our future success revolves around future exploitation of and production from this property through primary, secondary, and tertiary recovery techniques,'' the document stressed. Much emphasis was placed on the aggrandizement of the company's first acquisition, but Brumley did explore and seize opportunities elsewhere, completing several deals during the first years of the 21st century that added meaningfully to the company's portfolio of properties.

The most significant acquisitions completed in the wake of Encore's IPO occurred in 2003 and 2004, representing a substantial portion of the nearly $600 million the company spent on oil and natural gas properties during its first five years. In July 2003, Encore paid $52.5 million for natural gas properties on 1,800 acres located in the Elm Grove Field in Louisiana. In a company press release dated July 31, 2003, Brumley commented on the purchase. ''This acquisition,'' he wrote, ''provides Encore with a new focus area that is expected to show significant growth through drilling and add-on acquisitions.'' Encore's next major acquisition followed in April 2004, when the company acquired Cortez Oil & Gas, Inc., a $127 million purchase that increased its presence in the Cedar Creek Anticline area. Cortez owned Cedar Creek Anticline properties adjacent to properties already owned by Encore, as well as properties in the Permian Basin in Texas and New Mexico, the Arkoma and Anadarko Basins of Oklahoma, and mineral rights for 2,000 acres in the Barnett Shale field near Fort Worth. ''These properties are a nice fit for us because with the exception of the Barnett Shale, we already operate in those areas,'' Jonny Brumley remarked in a March 3, 2004 interview with the *Fort Worth Star-Telegram.* The Cortez acquisition was followed by another purchase that strengthened the company's position in areas where it already operated. In June 2004, the company bought natural gas properties in the Overton Field in Texas that were in the same core area as its properties in the Elm Grove Field acquired one year earlier.

As Encore plotted its future course at the end of 2004, the confidence in Brumley expressed by industry pundits and investors had been substantiated. ''This pint-sized oil and gas driller,'' *Fortune* noted in its August 8, 2005 issue, ''has been a huge success for investors—even relative to most firms in the red-hot energy sector.'' Brumley's tried-and-true approach to growth in the oil and gas industry underpinned Encore's success during its formative years, creating a well-regarded member of the nation's oil and gas community. In the years ahead, with the younger Brumley being groomed to replace his father, the Encore brand of leadership was expected to inspire continued success into the future.

Principal Subsidiaries

EAP Energy, Inc.; EAP Properties, Inc.; EAP Operating, Inc.; EAP Energy Services, L.P.; Encore Operating, L.P.; Encore Operating Louisiana LLC.

Principal Competitors

Anadarko Petroleum Corporation; BP P.L.C.; Exxon Mobil Corporation.

Further Reading

Bounds, Jeff, ''Oil Veteran Starts Energy Firm,'' *Dallas Business Journal,* December 4, 1998, p.1.
Darbonne, Nissa, ''Encore Hunts Oil While Others Pursue Gas,'' *Oil and Gas Investor,* July 2003, p. 17.
''Encore Acquisition Co.,'' *IPO Reporter,* March 5, 2001.
''Encore to Buy More East Texas Assets,'' *America's Intelligence Wire,* May 3, 2004, p. 45.
Holman, Kelly, ''Encore to Pay $123M for Cortez Oil,'' *Daily Deal,* March 3, 2004, p. 31.
Lustgarten, Abrahm, ''Our Picks Pay Off,'' *Fortune,* August 8, 2005, p. 108.
Musero, Frank, ''Curtain Call for Encore?,'' *IPO Reporter,* March 5, 2001.
Pillar, Dan, ''Encore Acquisition Co. to Buy Plano, Texas, Oil, Gas Firm,'' *Fort Worth Star-Telegram,* March 3, 2004, p. B1.
——, ''Encore Acquisition Reveals Conoco As Seller of West Texas Properties,'' *Fort Worth Star-Telegram,* November 13, 2001, p. B3.
——, ''Fort Worth, Texas-Based Encore Acquisition Buys Oil, Gas Properties in Utah,'' *Fort Worth Star-Telegram,* April 20, 2002, p. B1.
——, ''Fort Worth, Texas Energy Company Buys Oil Properties,'' *Fort Worth Star-Telegram,* November 11, 2001, p. B2.
Toal, Brian A., ''One More Time,'' *Oil and Gas Investor,* August 2001, p. 61.

—Jeffrey L. Covell

Enersis S.A.

Avenida Santa Rosa 76, Piso 17
Santiago 833-0099
Chile
Telephone: +56 2 353 4400
Fax: +56 2 378 4768
Web site: http://www.enersis.cl

Public Subsidiary of Endesa SA
Incorporated: 1921 as Compañia Chilectra de
    Electricidad SA (Chilectra); 1981 as Chilectra
    Metropolitana SA; 1988 as Enersis SA
Employees: 11,000
Sales: CLP 271 billion ($4.86 billion) (2004)
Stock Exchanges: Santiago New York
Ticker Symbols: ENE; ENI (ADR)
NAIC: 221122 Electric Power Distribution; 523120
    Securities Brokerage; 551112 Offices of Other
    Holding Companies; 561110 Office Administrative
    Services

Enersis S.A., of Chile, is one of South America's leading electricity utilities, with operations chiefly focused on the power generation and distribution markets. Enersis's generation operations include its control of Endesa Chile, which is not only Chile's leading electricity producer, but also one of the largest in the continent, with 46 power plants in Chile, Argentina, Brazil, Peru, and Colombia. Endesa Chile's total power generation capacity stood at more than 12,000 MW in 2005. Enersis also operates power distribution subsidiaries, including its flagship Chilectra. That subsidiary provides electricity distribution services to nearly 1.4 million customers in the metropolitan Santiago market. Chilectra also serves as the holding company for Enersis's international power distribution operations, including Edesur, the Argentinean market leader; Coelce, serving the state of Ceará, and Ampla, which holds the Rio de Janeiro concession, in Brazil; Edelnor, focused on the region of northern Peru; and Codensa, which serves Bogota and more than 96 other municipalities in Colombia. Altogether, Enersis serves more than ten million customers. Enersis itself is controlled by Spain's Endesa, which acquired a 65 percent stake in the company at the beginning of the 2000s. Enersis is listed on the Santiago and New York stock exchanges. In 2004, the company posted revenues of CLP 271 billion.

Tramway Origins in the 19th Century

Electricity came to Chile, then under British and German dominance, in the early 1880s, not long after the first electricity networks appeared in the United States and England. The first lighting company started up in Santiago in 1882, and by 1883 had installed a power generation plant featuring seven generators, driven by three steam engines.

Santiago's steady growth into the 1890s created a need for a stable and reliable electricity network. By the early 1890s, the city's population had grown to 300,000. In 1896, the city inaugurated a public lighting grid based on incandescent light. Yet the most important factor in the development of a reliable electricity system was the decision in 1893 to build an electric tramway in the city. Until then, the city was served by Ferrocaril Urbano, which operated more than 300 horse-drawn trams on a network of more than 100 kilometers of track.

The contract for the tramway was awarded to the British group Alfred Parish & Co., which in turn founded Chilean Electric Tramway & Light Company (CETLC) in 1898. Registered in London, CETLC was nonetheless more German in nature—its capital, as well as its chairman and most of its board of directors were from Germany. CETLC created a Chilean subsidiary, Compaia de Tranvias I Alumbrado Eléctricos—the tramway operator was nonetheless known by its English name—then acquired Ferrocaril Urbano. CETLC also brought in Berlin-based Allgemeine Elektricitäts Gesellschaft to convert the city's tramway to electric trams.

By the early 1900s, CETLC had largely completed the first phase of its tramway, with 205 motor cars pulling 40 passenger coaches on nearly 100 kilometers of track. The company expanded greatly in the first half of the decade, and by 1905 boasted a fleet of 225 motor cars and 90 primarily double-decker coaches.

Company Perspectives:

Enersis is one of the principal private electric multinationals in Latin America and it has a direct or indirect participation in the business of generating, transmitting and distributing electric power and related activities in five countries: Argentina, Brazil, Colombia, Chile and Peru.

CETLC was acquired by the German consortium Deutsch-Überseeische Elektricitäts Gesellschaft (DUEG, also known as Compañia Alemana Transatlántica de Electricidad in South America), which already controlled the Valparaiso tramway and which had established extensive tramway holdings in Argentina, Uruguay, and elsewhere. Under DUEG, CETLC extended its tramway beyond Santiago for the first time, inaugurating a suburban line in 1906.

DUEG was forced to withdraw from the Latin American market at the end of World War I. CETLC was then taken over by a multinational consortium, including British, Spanish, and Belgian partners. That consortium's control proved shortlived, however. In 1921, a new major shareholder, Whitehall Electric Investment Ltd. of England, led a merger between CETLC and Compañia Nacional de Fuerza Electrica, founded in 1919 in order to produce and distribute electricity for northern Chile. The newly enlarged company adopted the name of Compañia Chilena de Electricidad, or CCE. Whitehall's share of the company stood at 86 percent.

By then, CCE's fleet numbered more than 500 passenger trams, and its network had been extended to 153 kilometers. Yet the fleet and track were in poor repair, and a refurbishment of the line was hampered by the city of Santiago's refusal to allow CCE to raise its fares. CCE was additionally hurt by the appearance of the city's first bus service in 1922. During this period, however, CCE's electricity generation and distribution operations grew strongly, in part due to the decision to convert much of Chile's railroad network to electricity. As a result, CCE was able to carry out an extensive renovation of its Santiago tramway network into the late 1920s. The company also acquired a shuttle service operator, Tranvias Electricos Pedros de Valdivisa in 1925. CCE then formed a new subsidiary for its tramway interests, Compañia de Traccion y Alumbrado de Santiago.

CCE was acquired by a U.S.-based holding company, Electric Bond & Share, in 1929, which expanded the company's fleet again in the early 1930s. Yet the economic crisis of the 1930s brought CCE into financial turmoil. By 1936, the Chilean government pushed through a consolidation of the country's electrical industry. This process began with the formation of South American Power Co. (SAP), which acquired the operations of most of the electrical companies operating in Chile's central region. The companies continued to operate as autonomous units into the middle of the decade.

By the mid-1930s, the state had begun to exert more control over the electricity industry. In 1936, the state engineered a merger of the SAP companies into CCE. The company nonetheless remained a private corporation, still largely under U.S. control. Over the next several decades, CCE acquired most of the electrical companies in operation in its region, establishing a near-monopoly by the early 1960s. Yet CCE gradually lost its own independence, as the Chilean government increased its stake in the business. By 1960, the government's stake had grown to 15 percent.

The massive nationalization of Chile's industries under the Allende government at the beginning of the 1970s removed CCE from the private sphere as well. CCE's nationalization took place in August 1970. Under the Pinochet government, which gained control in 1973, however, the country began a process of re-privatization of many of the formerly private businesses taken over by the state. Nonetheless, the government continued to exert control over a number of industries, including electricity, gas, coal, mining, and others.

Privatizing in the 1980s

The Pinochet government nonetheless began preparations to privatize the electricity industry in the early 1980s. In 1981, the CCE was divided into three parts. The first bundled its power generation operations, which grew into Endesa Chile during the decade; the second became Chilquinta SA, which took over the CCE's power distribution business in Chile's Region V. The third part, which included the CCE's power distribution operations in the Santiago metropolitan region, became Compañia Chilena Metropolitana de Distribucion Electrica SA, or Chilectra.

Chilectra started off as a money loser, riddled by debt and inefficient operations. In 1983, however, Jose Yuraszeck was named as head of Chilectra and charged with restructuring its operations toward its future privatization. Yuraszeck had served in the government's Odeplan, the supervisory body for the free-market reform program instituted by the Pinochet government, before joining Chilectra.

As part of the move toward privatization—and in order to help lower employee resistance—Yuraszeck enacted a program of issuing shares in the company at discounted prices to employees. Another block of shares were sold to a newly created group of private pension fund management companies, while the rest was to be sold in a public offering.

In 1986, Yuraszeck created a new holding company, Enersis SA, which took over Chilectra and its assets. Shares in Enersis were also sold to the company's employees, while another block of shares were sold to the public. Yet Yuraszeck and a number of other company executives structured the sale of Enersis's shares in a way that gave them firm control of the company. As part of the new shareholding structure, the company established five investment groups, called Chispas (''sparks''); yet the Chispas' voting rights were transferred to Yuraszeck and a small number of associates. This setup, at the time, earned Yuraszeck praise as Chile's ''energy czar.''

In 1988, Enersis was floated on the Santiago stock exchange, completing its transfer to the private sector. The following year, the company began buying up shares in Endesa Chile. By 1990, Enersis's more than 12 percent stake in Endesa Chile made it the primary shareholder in the country's largest power generation company. By 1995, Enersis's stake in Endesa Chile had grown to 25.3 percent; the company acquired a controlling share of 60 percent in 1999.

Key Dates:	
1898: Chilean Electric Tramway & Light Company (CETLC) is formed to install electric tramway in Santiago.	sition of stake in Empresa Distribuidora Sur SA (Edesur) of Argentina.
1905: Deutsch-Überseeische Elektricitäts Gesellschaft (DUEG) acquires CETLC.	**1994:** Company acquires 60 percent of Empresa de Distribucion Electrica de Lima Nortes SA (Edelnor) in Peru.
1921: CETLC merges with Compañia Nacional de Fuerza Electrica, becoming Compañia Chilena de Electricidad (CCE).	**1996:** Company enters Brazil with stake in Companhia de Eletricidade do Rio de Janeiro (Cerjm later Ampla).
1936: Chilean government engineers merger of South American Power into CCE, which remains nominally privately controlled.	**1997:** Company acquires stake in Condensa (Colombia); Endesa acquires 32 percent of Enersis.
1970: Allende government nationalizes CCE.	**1998:** Company acquires stake in Companhia Energetic de Ceará (Coelce); Endesa acquires majority control of Enersis.
1981: CCE is broken up into three parts, including Chilectra, as part of privatization process.	**2000:** Enersis launches streamlining and capital expansion in order to streamline debt.
1986: Enersis is formed as a holding company for Chilectra and other electric power interests.	**2002:** Enersis builds new hydroelectric plant at Ralco, in the eight region, and the Fortaleza thermal plant in Ceará, Brazil.
1988: Enersis is privatized and listed on the Santiago exchange.	**2005:** Company begins construction on two new power plants in San Isidro and Palmucho.
1989: Enersis acquires first stake in Endesa Chile.	
1992: Company begins internationalization effort with acqui-	

International Energy Company in the New Century

In the meantime, Enersis had expanded internationally, targeting its neighboring South American markets. This process began in 1992, when the company acquired a stake in Argentina's Empresa Distribuidora Sur SA (Edesur), then in the process of being privatized. By 1995, Enersis had boosted its direct shareholding in Edesur past 39 percent, giving it majority control of that business.

Enersis's attention turned to Peru in 1994, where it purchased 60 percent of Empresa de Distribucion Electrica de Lima Nortes SA (Edelnor). The company then boosted its position to 69 percent of Edelnor. At the same time, Enersis eyed an entry into Brazil, the continent's largest electricity market. That entry came in 1996 when the company joined a consortium, including Spain's Endesa, in the acquisition of Companhia de Eletricidade do Rio de Janeiro (Cerj). Later known as Ampla, the purchase gave Enersis a position as an electricity distributor in the Rio de Janeiro and surrounding market.

In 1997, Enersis traveled to Colombia, once again joining a consortium to acquire Condensa SA, the electricity distributor to the Bogota market, as well as the Cundinamarca department. The following year, Enersis boosted its Brazilian position when, through another consortium, again featuring Endesa, it acquired a controlling stake in Companhia Energetic de Ceará (Coelce). That company's operational sphere included the state of Ceará and elsewhere in northeast Brazil.

Enersis itself became an acquisition target in the late 1990s, as Endesa of Spain began acquiring shares in the company. The Spanish company bought a 32 percent stake in 1997. Then, in 1999, in a deal put together by Yuraszeck, Endesa gained control of another 32 percent, largely represented by the shares held by the five Chispas. Yet the true nature of the deal—which not only gave Endesa control of Enersis but

effective control of all of Enersis's multinational markets by limiting Enersis's ability to make acquisitions outside of Chile. Worse, the deal included a number of hidden clauses—most notably a payment to Yuraszeck and associates worth more than $500 million.

The resulting scandal led to Yuraszeck losing his job, and nearly threatened the Endesa purchase altogether. While Endesa finally succeeded in acquiring a majority stake in Enersis, its position in the Chilean company was weakened by a new agreement guaranteeing Enersis's freedom to conduct its own national and international expansion.

One of Enersis's first moves was to acquire an additional 25 percent in Endesa Chile, making it that company's majority shareholder. The stake in Endesa Chile also placed Enersis among the top electricity companies in South America.

Enersis's expansion had saddled the company with a debt of more than $11 billion, however. In 2000, the company began a streamlining exercise in large part in order to raise funds to reduce its debt. In that year, the company sold off its electricity transmission subsidiary, Transelec, to Quebec, Canada's Hydro Quebec International. The company then sold off several other businesses, as well as a number of real estate properties. The company also launched a capital increase of more than $1.6 billion that year.

Into the mid-2000s, Enersis focused its efforts on building capacity. In 2002, for example, the company built a new hydroelectric plant at Ralco, in the eight region, and the Fortaleza thermal plant in Ceará, Brazil. In 2005, the company launched construction on two more plants in San Isidro and Palmucho, in a combined investment of more than $223 million, which would add some 600 MW to the group's total capacity by 2007. With a customer base of more than ten million, Enersis had grown into South America's electricity giant.

Principal Subsidiaries

Central Costanera S.A. (Argentina); Central Hidroeléctrica de Betania S.A. (Colombia); Chilectra S.A.; Compañía Eléctrica San Isidro S.A.; Compañía Eléctrica Tarapacá S.A.; Compañía Gasoducto Atacama; Edegel S.A. (Peru); Edelnor (Peru); Edesur S.A. (Argentina); Electrogas S.A.; Emgesa S.A. (Colombia); Empresa Eléctrica Pangue S.A.; Empresa Eléctrica Pehuenche S.A.; Endesa Chile; Endesa Fortaleza (Brazil); Hidroeléctrica El Chocón S.A. (Argentina).

Principal Competitors

National Power Corp.; Autoridad de Energia Electrica de Puerto Rico; Centrais Eletricas Brasileiras S.A. Eletrobras; Corporacion Dominicana de Electricidad; Instituto de Recursos Hidraulicos y Electrificacion; EEB S.A.; Electricidad De Caracas C.A.; Corporacion Autonoma Regional del Cauca CVC.

Further Reading

"Endesa Restructures Its Brazilian Shareholdings," *Business Wire*, May 25, 2005.

"Enersis Profits Rise After Restructuring," *Latin American Power Watch*, August 18, 2003, p. 7.

"Enersis Unveils Investment Plan," *Latin American Power Watch*, August 18, 2003, p. 6.

"A Gargantuan Refinancing," *LatinFinance*, February 2004, p. 51.

Kandell, Jonathan, "Fall from Grace," *Institutional Investor*, February 1998, p. 63.

Loft, Kurt, "Endesa Spain Reshapes Enersis-Chile?" *America's Intelligence Wire*, June 30, 2003.

Romans, Christine, and Greg Clarkin, "Enersis to Focus on Distribution Assets from 2004," *America's Intelligence Wire*, November 4, 2003.

"Spain's Endesa Will Invest $140m in Brazil Through Its Chilean Subsidiary, Enersis," *Petroleum Economist*, May 2004, p. 45.

—M.L. Cohen

Eramet

Tour Maine-Montparnasse, 33 av du Maine
Paris F-75755 Cedex 15
France
Telephone: +33 1 45 38 42 42
Fax: +33 1 45 38 74 25
Web site: http://www.eramet.fr

Public Company
Incorporated: 1880 as Société Le Nickel
Employees: 12,806
Sales: EUR 2.52 billion ($3.44 billion) (2004)
Stock Exchanges: Euronext Paris
Ticker Symbol: ERA
NAIC: 331419 Primary Smelting and Refining of
    Nonferrous Metals (Except Copper and Aluminum);
    325131 Inorganic Dye and Pigment Manufacturing;
    331491 Nonferrous Metal (Except Copper and
    Aluminum) Rolling, Drawing, and Extruding; 331492
    Secondary Smelting, Refining, and Alloying of
    Nonferrous Metals (Except Copper and Aluminum)

France's Eramet is a world-leading producer of nickel, manganese, high-performance alloys, and speedsteel. The company has its roots in the nickel mines in New Caledonia, where it continues to operate four mines as well as nickel production facilities. Since the early 1990s, Eramet has successfully diversified, capturing a world-leading share in the high-performance speedsteel market, notably through subsidiaries Erasteel Commentry and Aubert & Duval. The company also has acquired stakes in manganese mining, through its controlling stake in New Caledonia's Comilog, among other businesses. As such, Eramet has become the world's top producer of manganese alloys and chemical derivatives, and the world's number two producer of manganese ore. The company's alloys division is the world's largest producer of nickel alloys and so-called super alloys. Formerly controlled by the French government, which viewed nickel product to be of vital national interest, Eramet has been progressively privatized, with an offering since 1994 on the Paris Stock Exchange. In 1999, the French government further reduced its stake in Eramet. The company posted revenues of EUR 2.5 billion in 2004.

Discovering Nickel in the 1880s

Eramet stemmed from the discovery of nickel deposits in French colonial possession New Caledonia in the late 19th century. French geologist Jules Garnier was the first to discover nickel deposits along the Dumbéa river in the 1860s; for a time, the mineral was even named as "garniérite" by France's Académie des Sciences. By 1873, the first exploitable nickel veins had been discovered by Pierre Coste on his property on the Mont-Dore slopes. Soon after, new deposits of the ore, which contained as much as 14 percent of nickel, were located in Bourail, Canala, Thio, and Houailou. Coste's discovery led to a rush of small-scale miners and mining concessions. Among the larger concessionaires were John Higginson, Jean-Louis Hanckar, and Jules Garnier. Higginson became the first to obtain a contract from the colony's prison administration for the use of prison labor to work his deposits in 1878. This practice became widespread throughout the colony's nickel mines, and spread to other industries as well.

The nickel market proved highly unstable—by 1877, the nickel industry had entered its first crisis, ruining many of the small-scale miners. The situation enabled the larger mining companies, in particular those of Hanckar, Higginson, and Garnier, to buy up the smaller concessions for low prices. In 1880, Hanckar, Higginson, and Garnier decided to pool their concessions into a common company, called Société Le Nickel (SLN). The company received financial backing from the Baron de Rothschild, and SLN remained under control of the Rothschild family until the early 1970s. SLN's operations began with 40 mines under its direct control, and shares in another 20.

SLN remained the dominant nickel producer in New Caledonia. By the outbreak of World War I, however, the company had lost ground amid the entry of a number of competitors, including Canada's International Nickel Company, or INCO, which set up operations in 1902. By 1913, SLN's market share had dropped to 33 percent, compared with INCO's 55 percent.

In the meantime, the local industry also had expanded to include foundries; the first of these had been constructed in 1879, but had gone bankrupt in 1885 amid a new crisis in the nickel market. A more lasting facility was built in 1910 by André Ballande, who founded the Société des Hauts Fourneaux in Nouméa. When the nickel market collapsed again amid the Global Depression of 1929, Ballande's company collapsed and was merged into SLN. Later, during World War II, as France fell under Nazi occupation, SLN turned to INCO for help in refining its nickel production for export to the United States.

The 1960s marked a new boom period for the New Caledonian nickel industry. SLN in particular profited during the period between 1967 and 1971, as nickel prices skyrocketed. The booming Western economies and high demand, as well as the U.S. involvement in the Vietnam War, helped drive up nickel prices. Another important factor in SLN's growth during this period, however, was an extended strike at INCO, which more or less shut down the company's chief rival's production.

SLN grew quickly during the late 1970s, expanding its production facilities and opening new mines. A large part of the population now moved toward the metropolitan region to find employment in the nickel industry. The company's growth was further stimulated by the French government's declaration of nickel as a strategic resource—resulting in the government taking control of research and exploration operations in the former colony. While New Caledonia (now considered a French overseas possession) benefited from the strong nickel market, its reliance on the mineral left it dangerously exposed to vagaries in the market.

Nationalization in the 1970s

Indeed, nickel's boom years proved short-lived. By 1972, the global nickel market had once again collapsed. To make matters worse, the Arab Oil Embargo in 1973 only exacerbated New Caledonia's dependence on its nickel industry. A consequence of the crisis years was the steady increase in ethnic and political tensions, and the growth of a nationalistic movement seeking New Caledonia's independence from France.

SLN's strong growth had led the Rothschilds to restructure its various mining interests, including Pennaroya and Mokta, which were then placed under SLN. Amid the economic crisis of the early 1970s, however, the French government moved to nationalize a number of industries. SLN's nickel interests were reformed into a subsidiary, Société Metallurgique Le Nickel SLN, in 1974. The French government, through Elf Acquitaine, then took a 50 percent stake in the new company. Société Le

Nickel—that is, the company representing the combined Rothschild mining holdings—then changed its name to Imetal, retaining a 50 percent stake in SLN.

As the global nickel market emerged from the extended economic crisis of the 1970s, the French government sought to rebuild SLN's tattered operations. In 1983, the French state-owned oil and gas policy instrument, ERAP, which by then had become majority shareholder in Elf Acquitaine, took over a 70 percent stake in SLN. At that time, both Imetal's and Elf's interests in SLN were reduced to 15 percent. Under ERAP, a new structure was put into place, with the creation of the holding company Eramet-SLN, which in turn took over the operations of Société Metallurgique Le Nickel SLN. ERAP remained the company's principal shareholder into the late 1990s, boosting its stake to 85 percent through the acquisition of Imetal's share in 1990.

SLN enjoyed the benefits of a new boom in the international nickel market. Under ERAP, however, the company not only restructured its operations, it also adopted a new policy of diversification. In this way, SLN sought to reduce its reliance on a single, highly cyclical market.

SLN's first diversification move came in 1989, when the company acquired France-based La Commentryenne, then the world's third largest producer of high-performance speedsteel. This type of steel was used in the production of components requiring high resistance to heat and abrasion, such as the fabrication of tool bits, among many other applications.

In 1991, SLN boosted its new division through a still larger acquisition, that of Sweden's Kloster Speedsteel. The addition of Kloster, then the world's top producer of speedsteel, transformed SLN into the clear global market leader. In that year, as well, SLN formed a cooperation agreement with Japan's Nisshin Steel, one of that country's leading stainless steel producers. Under that agreement, Nisshin agreed to purchase SLN's steels, in exchange for a growing shareholding in SLN. By 1994, Nisshin's stake in SLN had reached its maximum 10 percent.

In 1992, SLN grouped its speedsteel operation under a single holding company, Erasteel. Also that year, SLN made a new diversification move, buying a stake in Eurotunstene Poudres, a producer of cobalt powder and tungsten steel. That shareholding topped 51 percent in 1994. By then, the company had restructured again, with Société Metallurgique Le Nickel SLN renamed as Société Le Nickel, and the Eramet-SLN becoming simply Eramet.

Eramet was then taken public in 1994 in a partial privatization that saw the listing of 30 percent of its shares on the Paris Bourse's Secondary Market. Soon after, Eramet boosted its nickel mining operation, acquiring from the government-run Bureau de Recherches Geologiques et Minieres its subsidiary Cofremmi, which held concessions to a number of mining deposits in New Caledonia.

Diversified Leader in the 2000s

Eramet shifted its listing to the Paris exchange's main Reglement Mensuel in 1995 ahead of its next diversification move. That came that same year when the company acquired a 46 percent stake in Gabon's Comilog. That company was then the

Key Dates:

1864: Jules Garnier discovers the presence of nickel ore in New Caledonia.
1880: Garnier joins with John Higginson and Jean-Louis Hanckar to form Société Le Nickel (SLN) with the financial backing of Baron de Rothschild.
1929: SLN absorbs Société des Hauts Fourneaux in Nouméa.
1969: The French government declares nickel mineral a strategic market, leading to the company's nationalization in 1974.
1983: ERAP takes 70 percent control of SLN.
1985: SLN is renamed as Eramet.
1989: Diversification begins, with the purchase of La Commentryenne, a leading producer of speedsteel.
1991: The acquisition of Sweden's Kloster Speedsteel gives Eramet the lead in the global market.
1994: Eramet is partially privatized, with a listing on the Paris Stock Exchange.
1996: Eramet diversifies into manganese production with the acquisition of control of Comilog of Gabon.
1999: Eramet acquires Elkem's manganese operations; the company acquires control of alloy producer SIMA.
2000: Eramet builds a new industrial complex in Gabon; a capacity increase in nickel production begins in New Caledonia.
2002: Eramet acquires its first production facility in China.
2005: Eramet begins an investment in a one million-ton manganese production increase.

world's second largest producer of manganese, as well as a leading producer of ferromanganese for the steel industry. In 1997, the company acquired an additional 15 percent of Comilog, thereby gaining majority control.

Growing pressure from New Caledonia's nationalist movement led the French government to agree to cede a stake in the company to local control. The French government also agreed to exchange its concession in Koniambo for a lower-yielding concession in Poum in 1998.

Eramet's privatization was completed in 1999, when ERAP ceded a 30 percent stake in Eramet to the locally controlled Société Territoriale Caledonienne de Participation Industrielle. Consequently, the French government's stake in Eramet fell below 50 percent. At that time, as well, the French government announced its intention to exit ERAP's holding in Eramet entirely.

In the meantime, Eramet continued looking for expansion opportunities. In 1999, the company boosted its position in the worldwide manganese market, taking the leadership with the acquisition of the Norwegian Elkem's manganese mining operations. In this way Eramet also emerged as a leader in the production of superalloys and other manganese-based alloys. Eramet confirmed this leadership that same year when it acquired the Société Industrielle de Materiaux Avancés, or SIMA.

The purchase made Eramet the global leader in the production of nickel-based alloys as well.

Eramet opened a new industrial complex in Moanda, in Gabon, in 2000, boosting Comilog's production capacity. The following year, the company also began building up capacity at its nickel operations in New Caledonia, ramping up to a 25 percent increase in production.

Into the mid-2000s, Eramet began seeking to expand its international base as well. In 2000, the company acquired Mexico's Sulfamex, which produced agrochemicals based on manganese. The company then entered China, acquiring the Guilin manganese alloy facility in 2002. The company launched an expansion of its China presence in 2003, investing in a new speedsteel production facility in a joint venture with Tiangong.

After completing its production expansion in New Caledonia, Eramet turned to its manganese operations in Gabon, launching an expansion to boost capacity by 50 percent in 2004. In that year, as well, the company added to its China presence with its announcement of the creation of a new factory producing manganese for use in alkaline batteries.

By 2005, the booming manganese market led Eramet to announce its plans to boost its manganese production again, adding another one million tons by 2006. Eramet had successfully transformed itself into a diversified mining and metals group, capable of resisting downturns in its core nickel market, while claiming leadership in the global manganese, speedsteel, and specialty alloys markets.

Principal Subsidiaries

Aubert & Duval Holding; Bear Metallurgical Corporation (U.S.A.); Brown Europe; Comilog Asia Ltd. (China); Comilog Far East Development Ltd. (China); Comilog International; Comilog US; Erachem Comilog Inc. (USA); Erachem Comilog S.A. (Belgium); Erachem Marietta Inc. (U.S.A.); Eramet Alliages; Eramet Canada Inc. (Canada); Eramet Comilog North America Inc. (U.S.A.); Eramet Holding Manganèse; Eramet Holding Nickel; Eramet Manganèse Alliages; Erasteel Champagnole; Erasteel Commentry; Erasteel GmbH (Germany); Erasteel Inc. (U.S.A.); Erasteel Korea Ltd.; Erasteel Latin America (Brazil); Forges M. Dembiermont; Guangxi Comilog Ferro Alloys Ltd. (China); Stahlschmidt GmbH (Germany).

Principal Competitors

Fushun Aluminium Plant; Mittal Steel Temirtau; Lonmin Platinum Div; Jilin Ferroalloy Works; Kadamzhay Antimony Combine JSC; Norsk Hydro ASA; Degussa AG; Tata Sons Ltd.; Hengyang Xinhua Chemical Metallurgical Company General; Umicore; Solnechniy Mining and Ore-Processing Plant Joint Stock Co.; W.C. Heraeus GmbH; Johnson Matthey PLC.

Further Reading

Carroll, Rory, "Force Majeure at Eramet Fails to Boost Nickel," *American Metal Market,* June 7, 2005, p. 1.
"Eramet Decision Due on SLN Expansion," *American Metal Market,* June 26, 2001, p. 5.

''Eramet Mum on Terms of China Ferroalloy Plant Buy,'' *American Metal Market,* September 27, 2002, p. 6.

''Eramet to Hike Manganese Output,'' *American Metal Market,* May 13, 2005, p. 2.

''Expansion in New Caledonia,'' *Mining Journal,* June 29, 2001, p. 485.

''France's Eramet Acquires Medium-Sized Ferroalloy Plant in Guangxi's Guilin,'' *China Business News,* October 9, 2002.

''Historique du groupe Eramet,'' *Eramet Document de Référence,* 2003.

—M.L. Cohen

FACTSET

FactSet Research Systems Inc.

601 Merritt 7
Norwalk, Connecticut 06851
U.S.A.
Telephone: (203) 810-1000
Fax: (203) 810-1001
Web site: http://www.facset.com

Public Company
Incorporated: 1978 as FactSet Research Corporation
Employees: 1,000
Sales: $251.9 million (2004)
Stock Exchanges: New York
Ticker Symbol: FDS
NAIC: 518111 Internet Service Providers

FactSet Research Systems Inc. is a Norwalk, Connecticut-based company that provides global financial and economic information and analytics, combining more than 200 databases into a single source—covering stock markets, company data, government information, and outside research, as well as proprietary material. The information is delivered online from mainframe computers to the desktop PCs of a select roster of 1,400 institutional subscribers able to afford the pricey service, such as investment managers, wealth managers, investment bankers, law firms, and corporations. FactSet also provides tools and training to allow customers to manipulate the data for analysis and reports. Only a small portion of the business is content, about 10 percent, but in recent years the company has attempted to move beyond its delivery model by acquiring several niche content providers, thus transforming FactSet from a financial data integrator into a solution provider. In addition to its Connecticut headquarters, FactSet maintains operations in New Hampshire, Virginia, Europe, and the Pacific Rim. FactSet is a public company listed on the New York Stock Exchange.

Launching the Company in the Late 1970s

The company was founded in September 1978 as FactSet Research Corporation by Howard E. Wille and Charles J. Snyder, both Wall Street veterans. Wille, the older of the pair, had worked as an analyst and investment manager at a number of firms before becoming the president and chief investment officer at Piedmont Advisory Corporation from 1961 to 1976. He then became a partner and director of research at the New York investment firm of Faulkner, Dawkins & Sullivan, Inc., where he remained until 1977, at which point Shearson Hayden Stone, Inc. acquired the company. Wille stayed on as a manager until deciding to strike out on his own to launch FactSet and become its chief executive officer. Some 14 years younger, Snyder, a self-described "math and science guy," was more technically savvy than Wille. After earning an undergraduate degree from Princeton and a master's degree from New York University, he also worked at Faulkner, Dawkins, from 1964 to 1977, becoming the director of computer research, a position he retained when Shearson took over. "I found the work wasn't much fun anymore," he recalled in an interview he granted to his prep school, Western Reserve Academy, for a fundraising program. He decided to team up with Wille, "took a real deep breath . . . and jumped out the window." He became FactSet's chief technology officer and Wille focused on selling. In a move that hearkened back to another era, the company did not sign contracts with clients, electing instead to do business on a handshake basis, a policy that became entrenched at FactSet.

At the time Wille and Snyder set up shop in Manhattan, computer financial analysis was still very much in the early stages, relegated to the world of bulky mainframe computers, requiring scores of technicians to simply merge different sets of data. Many analysts and fund managers continued just to use paper. FactSet was a forward-looking venture, established to harness the emerging technologies—personal computers, spreadsheets, and user-friendly databases—to bring together data from a number of sources, deliver it to users, and provide them with the tools to slice and dice and, ultimately, make a useful report out of the material. After more than two years of research and development, FactSet had a product ready for its selective market. In 1981 the company released its first client terminal, which connected a subscriber to FactSet's mainframe computers and allowed it to use the Company FactSet report. As Snyder described it to Western Reserve Academy, "We got the data from a wide variety of sources and integrated it so that our clients could get complete portfolio data at the push of a button.'' In essence, FactSet was a pioneering online service, many years before most people had ever heard of the Internet, and well before the invention of the browser and the World Wide Web. To build up a customer base, the company concentrated on service. ''We built service in as part of our product,'' Snyder explained to his prep school, ''and it was a clever strategy. We'd make house calls, give help over the phone, or teach a class. Computers are a great self-teaching tool, but they can also be frustrating. We found that people would use our product when they knew how.''

Continual Upgrades in the 1990s

For the next quarter-century, the bulk of the company's history revolved around the improvements Snyder and his team of computer scientists made to the original product. With the rise of the personal computer in the late 1970s came new spreadsheet applications. However limited in power and capacity, they at least allowed users to store some information and manipulate it. In 1982, in order to better serve customers, Snyder did some reverse engineering on VisiCalc, the first in a generation of spreadsheets, and developed a way that FactSet databases could directly populate the cells of a subscriber's spreadsheet. The product, Data Downloading, was revolutionary in the way it allowed users to blend personal data with FactSet's mainframe databases for more robust analysis and financial modeling. It would remain a key component of the FactSet service 20 years later. In 1983 the company made this feature available to Lotus 1-2-3, which was eclipsing VisiCalc in spreadsheet popularity. Another major improvement in the 1980s was the 1984 addition of screen capabilities, although users were still limited in their range of search items. This deficiency was corrected later in the decade with the introduction of Universal Screen, which permitted users to establish their own screening criteria. Along the way, FactSet increased the speed of delivery, in 1988 adopting the use of 9600 modems, quaint in terms of broadband hundreds of times faster a decade later, but an impressive improvement at the time. Another important development during the 1980s was the 1989 release of the company's Private Database Service. Users could now store proprietary data and integrate it with their own information to perform custom analysis.

FactSet opened the 1990s by relocating its headquarters from New York City to Greenwich, Connecticut, although it continued to maintain a Manhattan computer center. The product also continued to be upgraded. In the early part of the decade real-time earnings estimates databases were included, as was the first non-U.S. data. An application called Alpha Testing was launched, permitting users to compare a number of variables and to project investment returns over time. Other enhancements during this period were the introduction of IB link and Comp Builder for investment bankers, and the release of the

first benchmark. In 1991 FactSet was made available on the increasingly popular Windows platform. The company provided WAN (wide area network) connectivity in 1993, followed later in the decade with WAN connectivity via the Internet. In addition, the company established client bases in new markets, Europe in 1991 and the Pacific Rim in 1992. To support the European business, FactSet opened a London office in 1993 as well as one in San Mateo. A Tokyo office opened in 1995.

By the end of 1995 FactSet had less than 400 customers, but they included 84 of the United States' top investment managers. The company recorded sales of $36.2 million in 1995 and net income of nearly $5 million. The company also changed its name in June 1995, becoming FactSet Research Systems Inc. in preparation for becoming a public company. Although an initial public offering of stock was completed in 1996, there were no new shares issued; thus FactSet received no proceeds. Nevertheless, the company did not lack for funds, holding $12.7 million in cash and short-term investments, and generated more than sufficient cash flow to pay for the major upgrades the company made in 1996 to its two computer centers, located in Greenwich and New York City (each of which ran at 50 percent capacity in order to provide backup capabilities should one experience shutdown). FactSet continued strong growth through the rest of the 1990s. Starting in 1993 sales grew at an annual rate of 20 percent; the same pace was maintained by earnings starting in 1996.

A key to retaining customers and attracting new business was the introduction of new features to the FactSet product. In 1996 the company released Portfolio Management Workstation, empowering global portfolio managers with a host of specialized tools. A year later the Economic Analysis application was unveiled to permit customers to portray big picture information in the form of charts and reports. Also in 1997 FactSet became more user-friendly with the launch of Company Explorer. Now subscribers could access a wide range of company data from a single window. The product became even easier to use in 1998 with the release of the DIRECTIONS interface and the addition of Online Assistant, a web-based help and reference tool. Moreover, the company improved client service with the introduction of 24-hour live telephone support.

Expansion also continued in the second half of the 1990s. Offices in Hong Kong and Sydney, Australia, were opened in 1998. In that same year the New York data center was expanded and a dedicated training center was opened. In 1999 a Boston office and training center also was added.

Management Changes Near End of 1990s

The end of the 1990s and start of a new century also brought a changing of the guard at FactSet. First, Snyder retired as president and chief technology officer in August 1999, staying on as vice-chairman as well as a consultant to help the technical groups make the transition. But after Wille retired as CEO and chairman in May 2000, Snyder stepped in as CEO on an interim basis, serving until September of that year, when Philip A. Hadley was named the new CEO and chairman. The driving force behind the company in recent years, Hadley, an accounting graduate from the University of Iowa, had joined FactSet in 1985 as a consultant after working for Cargill Corporation.

A year later he became vice-president of sales, then in 1989 became senior vice-president and director of sales and marketing, a post he held until ascending to the top of the organization. He took over a company with 764 clients and more than 25,000 users, generating $103.8 million in sales and $18.6 million in earnings in 1999.

FactSet advanced on a number of fronts in the early 2000s, especially in terms of incorporating the Web into its operations. First, the technical infrastructure was upgraded to power client web sites, then necessary products for a web environment were identified and development efforts launched. Of more importance, perhaps, the company decided that the next generation of all applications had to be Web-enabled. The integration of the Internet gave FactSet access to a new source of customers. New products in the early 2000s included a portfolio returns product, SPAR (Style, Performance and Risk), that allowed portfolio managers to analyze the risks and performance of their own funds as well as compare them with peer funds; the Data Central application, which allowed subscribers to create and save their own time-series databases; FactSet Marquee, which combined streaming news and stock quotes with traditional security-level analysis; and Public Information Book Builder, to allow users to quickly assemble reports and news stories into a PDF document.

FactSet also expanded its physical operations during this period, buying a 12,500-square-foot New Hampshire data center from bankrupt Vitts Network Inc. to replace the New York data center. Later, the company purchased a data center in Reston, Virginia, an area that had seen a great deal of buildup in the 1990s before the dot-com bust. FactSet was able to take advantage of available state-of-the-art data center space in Virginia to open a new facility that could house some of the company's Greenwich, Connecticut computer operations. In this way, the company gained geographic diversity, an important factor in a post-9/11 world. The company also would move its headquarters from Greenwich, relocating to larger accommodations in nearby Norwalk in 2004. In addition, FactSet opened an office and training facility in Chicago and new international offices in Frankfurt, Paris, and Milan.

After being in business for more than 20 years, FactSet completed its first acquisition in 2000, paying close to $10 million for Innovative Systems Techniques, Inc., picking up the Vision Technology database management product, thus providing subscribers with advanced data analysis tools. This purchase was the start of a number of niche acquisitions intended to flesh out FactSet's offerings in a bid to shift the company from a financial data integrator to a solution provider. FactSet also began adding content such as the acquisition of LionShares, bought for $2.3 million from Worldly Information Network Inc. LionShares was a share ownership database geared toward the institutional and mutual fund markets, allowing fund holdings to be compared for analysis and business development purposes. Later niche content acquisitions included Mergerstate Holdings L.P., a 40-year-old provider of mergers and acquisitions information; CallStreet, which provided transcripts of quarterly conference calls; and TrueCourse, compiler of corporate takeover defense intelligence. FactSet also expanded its European business by acquiring the JFC Group of companies for $60.4 million in 2004. Based in both London and Paris, JFC provided institutional investors with global broker estimates and other financial and macroeconomic data.

Despite difficult economic conditions, FactSet continued its strong pattern of growth in the first half of the 2000s. Sales topped the $200 million mark for the first time in 2002 and approached $252 million in 2004, when the company also posted net income of $58 million. A sterling reputation, as evidenced by its 96 percent customer retention rate, new state-of-the-art facilities, a strong balance sheet, and recent acquisitions that brought key personnel as well as new product offerings, boded well for the future of FactSet.

Principal Subsidiaries

Factset Data Systems, Inc.; FactSet Mergerstat, LLC; CallStreet, LLC; Innovative Systems Techniques, Inc.

Principal Competitors

Bloomberg L.P.; Reuters Group PLC; The Thomson Corporation.

Further Reading

Alva, Marilyn, "A Little Known Player with Big-Time Result," *Investor's Business Daily,* May 9, 2003, p. A08.
——, "Provider of Investment Research Data Keeps Taking It to the Street," *Investor's Business Daily,* January 31, 2005, p. A05.
Fishman-Lapin, Julie, "FactSet Research Systems Moves Data Center from Connecticut to Virginia," *Stamford Advocate,* February 18, 2004.
Reeves, Amy, "Despite Ailing Market, Data Provider Thrives," *Investor's Business Daily,* April 26, 2002, p. A06.
"Snyder Gift Is Largest in the School's History," *Western Reserve Academy Campaign Update,* Winter 2004.
Tewary, Amrit, "FactSet's Numbers Add Up," *Business Week Online,* January 22, 2003.
Watkins, Steve, "Data Firm Finds Value in Old-School Ways," *Investor's Business Daily,* December 21, 2000, p. A12.

—Ed Dinger

Frito-Lay North America

7701 Legacy Drive
Plano, Texas 75024-4099
U.S.A.
Telephone: (972) 334-7000
Toll Free: (800) 352-4477
Fax: (972) 334-2019
Web site: http://www.fritolay.com

Division of PepsiCo, Inc.
Incorporated: 1961 as Frito-Lay, Inc.
Employees: 44,000
Sales: $10.98 billion (2004)
NAIC: 311919 Other Snack Food Manufacturing; 311340 Nonchocolate Confectionery Manufacturing; 311421 Fruit and Vegetable Canning; 311821 Cookie and Cracker Manufacturing; 311911 Roasted Nuts and Peanut Butter Manufacturing

Frito-Lay North America is the dominant player in the salty snack category in the United States, with a 65 percent share of the market. Led by such blockbuster brands as Lay's, with annual sales of $2.8 billion, and Tostitos, a $1.6 billion brand, Frito-Lay boasts no fewer than 15 brands whose sales each year exceed $100 million. In the United States, Frito-Lay is the leader in several snack categories: potato chips (Lay's, Ruffles), extruded snacks (Cheetos), corn chips (Fritos), tortilla chips (Tostitos, Doritos), multigrain chips (Sun Chips), and pretzels (Rold Gold). Other major brands include Cracker Jack candy-coated popcorn, Grandma's cookies, Quaker Chewy granola bars, and Munchies snack mix. Operating only in the United States and Canada, Frito-Lay North America runs about 50 food manufacturing and processing plants and approximately 1,700 warehouses, distribution centers, and offices. Of PepsiCo, Inc.'s four operating divisions, Frito-Lay North America is the most profitable, generating 39 percent of the parent company's operating profit, and it is also responsible for one-third of PepsiCo's overall revenues.

The original Frito-Lay, Inc. company, whose predecessor firms date back to the 1930s, merged with Pepsi-Cola Company in 1965 to form PepsiCo, Inc., with Frito-Lay becoming a divi-

sion of the new company. The operations of Frito-Lay were later divided into two units, Frito-Lay North America and Frito-Lay International. While the former continues to operate as a division of PepsiCo—and can be considered the successor to the original Frito-Lay company—the latter in 2003 was subsumed within another PepsiCo division, PepsiCo International. This division comprises the parent company's beverages, snacks, and foods businesses outside the United States and Canada. It includes the non-North American manufacturing and distribution of such global brands as Lay's and Doritos as well as regional snack brands, including Walkers in the United Kingdom, Gamesa and Sabritas in Mexico, and Smith's in Australia.

The Frito Company

Frito-Lay traces its origins to the early 1930s. In the midst of the Great Depression, the lack of job prospects spurred a number of young people to turn to entrepreneurship in order to get ahead. Among these were the founders of the two companies that would merge in 1961 to form Frito-Lay. Elmer Doolin's entrance into the snack food industry was one of happenstance. In 1932 the Texas native was running an ice cream business that was struggling because of a price war. Doolin began seeking a new venture and happened to buy a five-cent, plain package of corn chips while eating at a San Antonio café. At the time, corn chips or "fritos" were a common fried cornmeal snack in the Southwest (the word *frito* meaning "fried" in Spanish). Typically, cooks would cut flattened corn dough into ribbons, then season and fry them.

Impressed with his five-cent snack, Doolin discovered that the manufacturer wished to return to Mexico and would sell his business for $100. Doolin borrowed the money from his mother, purchasing the recipe, 19 retail accounts, and production equipment consisting of an old, handheld potato ricer converted for the job. Initially setting up production in his mother's kitchen, Doolin spent his nights cooking Frito brand corn chips and sold them during the day from his Model T Ford. Early production capacity was ten pounds daily, with profits of about $2 on sales ranging from $8 to $10 daily.

Doolin soon expanded to the family garage, and increased production by developing a press that operated more efficiently than the potato ricer. Within a year of his purchase of the business, Doolin moved the headquarters for the Frito Company from San Antonio to Dallas, the latter having distribution advantages. Sales began expanding geographically after Doolin hired a sales force to make regular deliveries to stores. The Frito Company also began selling the products of potato chip manufacturers through license agreements. The company soon had plants operating in Houston, Tulsa, and Dallas.

In early 1941 Doolin expanded to the West Coast by opening a small manufacturing facility in Los Angeles. Only the onset of World War II and rationing slowed Frito's growth. But sales quickly picked up again following the war's end, and by 1947 revenues exceeded $27 million. Doolin moved his company toward national status through licensing agreements. The first came in 1945, when Frito granted H.W. Lay & Company an exclusive franchise to manufacture and distribute Fritos in the Southeast. This marked the beginning of a close relationship between the two companies, and would eventually lead to their 1961 merger. In 1946 another franchise was launched in Bethesda, Maryland, followed by a Hawaii-based franchise in 1947. The following year, Frito introduced Chee-tos brand Cheese Flavored Snacks, which gained immediate popularity. Meantime, the Fritos brand went national in 1949 when Doolin purchased color advertisements in several magazines, including *Ladies' Home Journal, Better Homes and Gardens,* and *Life.*

By 1954, when the firm made its initial offering of public stock, the Frito Company business included 11 plants and 12 franchise operations. In 1953 the Frito Kid made his debut as a company spokesman; the character continued to be used in Fritos advertising until 1967. In 1956 the Frito Kid made an appearance on the *Today* show with host Dave Garroway, marking the Frito Company's first use of television advertising. Fritos gained a new advertising theme in 1958 with the debut of ''Munch a Bunch of Fritos.'' That year, the Frito Company acquired the rights to Ruffles brand potato chips. The following year, Doolin died, having led his company to its status as a

major snack food maker, with revenues exceeding $51 million. The Frito Company continued to operate 11 plants, but its franchise operations had been reduced to six after the company bought out several franchisees. John D. Williamson took over as president of the company. Within two years of Doolin's death, the Frito Company would merge with H.W. Lay.

H.W. Lay & Company

H.W. Lay & Company, Inc. was founded by another entrepreneur, Herman W. Lay. Born in humble circumstances in 1909 in Charlotte, North Carolina, Lay had worked a variety of jobs and run a few small businesses from the age of ten, including an ice cream stand, before taking a position as a route salesman at the Barrett Food Products Company, an Atlanta-based potato chip manufacturer, in 1932. Later that year, Lay borrowed $100 to take over Barrett's small warehouse in Nashville on a distributorship basis. This was coincidentally the same year that Doolin had established the Frito Company.

Lay started out selling Barrett's Gardner brand products from his 1928 Model A Ford, initially pocketing about $23 a month. Growth came rapidly, however. In 1933 Lay hired his first salesman, and by the following year his company had six sales routes. By 1936 Lay employed a workforce of 25 and had moved his company from its original warehouse to another Nashville building. From this location, Lay began manufacturing products himself, including peanut butter cracker sandwiches and french fried popcorn. In 1938 the latter became the first item marketed under the Lay's name, specifically Lay's Tennessee Valley Popcorn. By that year Lay was distributing snack foods throughout central Tennessee and southern Kentucky, and had opened a new warehouse in Chattanooga. The most significant development of 1938, however, came as a result of financial difficulties encountered by Barrett Food Products. After securing $60,000 in financing through business associates and friends, Lay bought Barrett, its plants in Memphis and Atlanta, and the Gardner's brand name. He changed the name of the company to H.W. Lay & Company, Inc., with headquarters in Atlanta.

During the early 1940s H.W. Lay added manufacturing plants in Jacksonville, Florida; Jackson, Mississippi; Louisville, Kentucky; and Greensboro, North Carolina. Lay also built a new plant in Atlanta featuring a continuous potato chip production line, one of the first in the world. In 1944 the company began marketing potato chips under the Lay's name, with the Gardner's brand becoming a historical footnote. That same year, H.W. Lay became one of the first snack food concerns to advertise on television, with a campaign featuring the debut of Oscar, the Happy Potato, the company's first spokesperson. The following year, H.W. Lay gained from the Frito Company an exclusive franchise to manufacture and distribute Fritos corn chips in the Southeast.

After establishing a research laboratory to develop new products in 1949, H.W. Lay expanded its product line during the 1950s to include barbecued potato chips, corn cheese snacks, fried pork skins, and a variety of nuts. The company also expanded outside the Southeast and acquired a number of weaker competitors. In 1956 H.W. Lay went public as a company with a workforce exceeding 1,000, manufacturing facili-

Key Dates:

1932: Elmer Doolin founds the Frito Company in San Antonio, Texas, and begins making Fritos corn chips.

1938: Herman W. Lay buys Atlanta potato chip maker, changes name to H.W. Lay & Company, Inc. the following year.

1944: H.W. Lay begins marketing potato chips under the Lay's name.

1948: Frito Company introduces Chee-tos snacks.

1958: Frito Company acquires the rights to Ruffles brand potato chips.

1961: The Frito Company and H.W. Lay & Company are merged to form Frito-Lay, Inc.

1965: Frito-Lay, Inc. and the Pepsi-Cola Company merge to form PepsiCo, Inc., with Frito-Lay becoming a division of the new company.

1967: Doritos tortilla chips make their national debut.

1970: Frito Bandito advertising campaign is abandoned following complaints from Mexican American organizations.

1981: Company introduces Tostitos tortilla chips.

1991: Sunchips multigrain snacks are introduced.

1997: Company acquires the Cracker Jack brand.

2001: Following PepsiCo's acquisition of the Quaker Oats Company, Frito-Lay gains the Quaker snack business, which includes granola bars and rice cakes.

2003: As part of a restructuring, the international operations of Frito-Lay are subsumed within the PepsiCo International division, while Frito-Lay North America (FLNA) carries on the Frito-Lay legacy in the United States and Canada; FLNA enters the natural and organic snacks category with the launch of the Natural line.

ties in eight cities, and branches or warehouses in 13 cities. Revenues in 1957 stood at $16 million, making Herman Lay's company the largest maker of potato chips and snack foods in the United States. H.W. Lay had also gained fame for carefully developing and utilizing its sales routes. Company salespeople were among the first to go beyond simply delivering their merchandise to store owners, as they also stocked the merchandise for the owners, set up point-of-purchase displays, and helped to assure product quality by pulling stale bags off the shelves and displays before they could be sold. This "store-door" delivery system helped to increase revenues as the salespeople were able to "work" a particular sales territory more intensely. By the spring of 1961, H.W. Lay had operations in 30 states, following the purchase of Rold Gold Foods, makers of Rold Gold Pretzels, from American Cone and Pretzel.

Frito-Lay, Inc.: 1961–65

In September 1961 H.W. Lay and the Frito Company merged to form Frito-Lay, Inc., a snack food giant headquartered in Dallas with revenues exceeding $127 million. The new company began with four main brands—Fritos, Lay's, Ruffles, and Chee-tos—and a national distribution system. Williamson served as the first chairman and CEO of Frito-Lay, with Lay

taking the position of president. In 1962 Lay took over as CEO, with Fladger F. Tannery becoming president; two years later, Lay added the chairmanship to his duties.

In 1963 Frito-Lay began using the slogan "Betcha Can't Eat Just One" in its advertising for Lay's potato chips. Two years later comedian Bert Lahr began appearing in ads in which he attempted—always unsuccessfully—to eat just one Lay's chip. Annual revenues for Frito-Lay exceeded $180 million by 1965, when the company had more than 8,000 employees, 46 manufacturing plants, and more than 150 distribution centers throughout the United States.

June 1965: Frito-Lay + Pepsi-Cola = PepsiCo

In June 1965 Frito-Lay merged with Pepsi-Cola Company to form PepsiCo, Inc., with Frito-Lay becoming an independently operated division of the new company. Pepsi's CEO and president became CEO and president of PepsiCo, while Herman Lay was named chairman, a position he held until 1971. Lay then served as chairman of the executive committee until 1980, when he retired. He died in December 1982.

There were a number of forces that drove the two companies together. The 1960s was an era of consolidation, with a number of food and beverage firms being gobbled up by larger entities. Pepsi-Cola was considered a takeover target not only because it ran a distant second in the soft drink sector to industry giant Coca-Cola Company, but also because little of the company's stock was in the hands of management. Following the creation of PepsiCo, however, the new company's directors held a much larger proportion of shares, with Lay holding a 2.5 percent stake himself. A second force behind the merger was Frito-Lay's desire to more aggressively pursue overseas markets. The company's sales had largely been restricted to the United States and Canada, but it could now take advantage of Pepsi's strong international operations, through which Pepsi products were sold in 108 countries.

A third force was the perceived synergy between salty snacks and soft drinks. As Donald M. Kendall, the head of Pepsi-Cola, succinctly related to *Forbes* in 1968, "Potato chips make you thirsty; Pepsi satisfies thirst." The plan was to jointly market PepsiCo's snacks and soft drinks, thereby giving Pepsi a potential advantage in its ongoing battle with Coke. These plans, however, were eventually scuttled by the resolution of a Federal Trade Commission antitrust suit brought against Frito-Lay in 1963. The FTC ruled in late 1968 that PepsiCo could not create tie-ins between Frito-Lay and Pepsi-Cola products in most of its advertising. PepsiCo was also barred from acquiring any snack or soft drink maker for a period of ten years.

New Products, the Frito Bandito, and Increased Competition: 1965–79

Frito-Lay began its PepsiCo era with the same lineup of brands it had when Frito-Lay was created in 1961: Fritos, Lay's, Ruffles, Chee-tos, and Rold Gold. Shortly after the creation of PepsiCo, Lay's became the first potato chip brand to be sold nationally. Of even greater importance was increased new product development activity. In 1966 Frito-Lay began test-marketing a new triangular tortilla chip under the brand name

Doritos (meaning, when literally translated into Spanish, "little bits of gold"). Compared to regular tortilla chips, Doritos were more flavorful and crunchier. Launched nationally in 1967, Doritos proved successful, but additional market research revealed that many consumers outside the Southwest and West considered the chip to be too bland—not spicy enough for what was perceived as a Mexican snack. Frito-Lay therefore developed taco-flavored Doritos, which were introduced nationally in 1968 and were a tremendous success. Four years later, national distribution began of nacho cheese–flavored Doritos, which were also a hit. Ironically, with increasing popularity, Doritos became less and less identified as a "Mexican snack," a development that echoed the earlier brand history of Fritos. During the 1970s Doritos became Frito-Lay's number two brand in terms of sales, trailing only Lay's. This spectacular growth was fueled by heavy advertising expenditures—as much as half of the company's overall $23 million ad budget in the mid-1970s. The "Crunch" campaign began in the early 1970s, and gained added impetus in 1976 when Avery Schreiber, a bushy-mustached character comedian, began crunching Doritos on national television. Frito-Lay also found lesser success in this period with other new products, including Funyuns onion-flavored rings, which debuted in 1969, and the Munchos potato crisps that were launched in 1971.

In 1968 Frito-Lay began a new Fritos advertising campaign featuring the Frito Bandito, a Mexican bandit complete with a long mustache, sombrero, and six-gun who spoke in a heavy accent. Ads showed the cartoon character robbing and scheming to get his beloved Fritos corn chips. The campaign quickly drew heavy criticism from Mexican American groups who alleged that it showed a prejudice against Mexican Americans and perpetuated a stereotype. Responding to the protests, radio and television stations in California began pulling Frito Bandito spots off the air. Frito-Lay finally ended the campaign in 1970.

During the 1970s Frito-Lay began feeling the effects of increased competition. The Lay's brand was challenged not only by more aggressive regional brands but also by such newfangled chips as Pringles and Chipos. These chips were made from mashed or dehydrated potatoes molded into a uniform shape, which enabled them to be stacked into a can or packaged in a box. In either case, they had several advantages over regular potato chips: they were less fragile, their packaging was less bulky, and they had a longer shelf life. Most importantly, they could be made in one location and shipped nationally, rather than having to be made in a nationwide system of regional plants. Pringles and Chipos were also backed by the national advertising prowess of two consumer product giants—Procter & Gamble Company and General Mills, Inc., respectively. Additional competition in the 1970s came from Nabisco Inc., maker of Mister Salty pretzels and such extruded snacks as Flings and Corkers, and Standard Brands Inc., which was expanding its Planters brand beyond nuts into corn and potato chips, cheese curls, and pretzels. Despite its formidable foes, Frito-Lay remained the clear leader in the U.S. snack industry, with sales by the late 1970s exceeding $1 billion, more than double that of the nearest competitor, Standard Brands. Moreover, Frito-Lay was far from resting on its laurels. It increased its overall production capacity by one-third by 1979 through the opening of a new plant in Charlotte, North Carolina, and the culmination of expansion programs at ten existing plants. Keeping Frito-Lay ahead of the competition during this period

was D. Wayne Calloway, who became president and chief operating officer in early 1976.

New Product Ups and Downs in the 1980s

The 1980s started out promisingly, with Frito-Lay acquiring the Grandma's regional brand of cookies in 1980 for $25 million, in a venture outside of its salty snack stronghold. In 1983 the company made a national launch of the Grandma's brand, and soon was selling five varieties. Among these was a homemade-style cookie that was soft on the inside but crispy on the outside. In 1984 Procter & Gamble sued Frito-Lay and two other cookie makers for infringing on its patent for Duncan Hines crispy-chewy cookies. The parties reached a settlement in 1989, whereby Frito-Lay agreed to pay about $19 million to Procter & Gamble, while the bulk of the $125 million settlement was shared equally by the two other defendants, Nabisco and Keebler Co.

In addition to the acquisition of Grandma's, the early 1980s also saw Frito-Lay introduce Tostitos tortilla chips. Debuting in 1981, Tostitos was the most successful new product introduction yet in Frito-Lay history, garnering sales of $140 million in the first year of national distribution. The development of Tostitos came out of market research on Doritos indicating that some consumers felt the latter chips were too heavy, too thick, and too crunchy; at this time, there was a general trend toward consumer preference for "lighter-tasting" foods, as well as an increased interest in Mexican food. Frito-Lay thus created the thinner, crispier Tostitos, which could be eaten alone, made into nachos, or dipped into increasingly popular salsas. By 1985 Tostitos was Frito-Lay's number five brand, with sales of about $200 million, trailing only Doritos ($500 million), Lay's ($400 million), Fritos ($325 million), and Ruffles ($250 million). Also in 1985 Frito-Lay expanded its tortilla chip line with the introduction of Santitas white and yellow corn round chips.

In 1983 Calloway shifted to the PepsiCo headquarters in Purchase, New York, to become the parent company's CFO (and eventually its chairman and CEO). Taking over as president of Frito-Lay was Michael Jordan, who held the position for two years before also heading to Purchase and eventually becoming PepsiCo president. Willard Korn served as president of Frito-Lay during the mid-1980s, a period coinciding with the company's relocation of its headquarters from Dallas to Plano, Texas, but more importantly with a spate of failed product introductions. In 1986 Frito-Lay rolled out a slew of new products, several in the nonsalty snack sector, including Toppels cheese-topped crackers, Rumbles crispy nuggets, and Stuffers dip-filled shells. The company also attempted to penetrate the growing market for kettle-cooked chips, a variety harder and crunchier than regular potato chips, with a brand called Kincaid. The barrage of new products was too much for Frito-Lay's 10,000-strong sales force to handle; products were lost on store shelves and all of the new brands were quickly killed. Korn resigned from his post in November 1986, with Jordan returning to Texas to head Frito-Lay once again.

Under Jordan's leadership in the late 1980s, Frito-Lay focused on revitalizing its existing brands rather than developing new brands. Among the successful line extensions introduced in this period were Cool Ranch flavor Doritos and a low-fat version of Ruffles. In 1989 Frito-Lay acquired the Smartfood brand of cheddar-cheese popcorn, a regional brand it hoped to roll out nationwide. The company was also finding success in the international market, where profits were increasing 20 percent per year, revenues were exceeding $500 million by the end of the decade, and Frito-Lay products were being sold in 20 countries. Overall sales stood at about $3.5 billion.

Rising Fortunes in the 1990s

Entering the 1990s, Frito-Lay faced continuing challenges from both regional and national players, including the upstart Eagle Snacks brand, owned by beer powerhouse Anheuser-Busch Cos. Eagle Snacks gained market share in the 1980s with premium products that sold for low prices, some of which were 20 percent lower than those of Frito-Lay. In addition to the increased competition, Frito-Lay also suffered in the late 1980s through 1990 from self-inflicted wounds, such as increasing prices faster than inflation, letting the corporate payroll become bloated, and allowing product quality to decline. As a result, profits were on the decline in the early 1990s.

In early 1991, Roger A. Enrico was named to the top spot at Frito-Lay, after most recently serving as president of PepsiCo Worldwide Beverages. Enrico, a former Frito-Lay marketing vice-president, immediately set out to turn around the stumbling but still formidable snack giant. During 1991 the company eliminated 1,800—or about 60 percent—of its administrative and managerial jobs, creating a much more streamlined structure. Four of the company's 40 plants were closed or sold off, and more than 100 package sizes and brand varieties were dropped from what had become an unwieldy product portfolio. These moves resulted in annual savings of approximately $100 million. On the selling side, Frito-Lay created 22 sales/marketing offices to bring decision-making closer to retailers and consumers. The company also slashed its prices. In its first big new product success since Tostitos, Frito-Lay launched SunChips in 1991, garnering $115 million in sales during the first year; the multigrain, low-sodium, no-cholesterol chip/cracker found a ready market among adults seeking a more healthful snack. In moves designed to revitalize its longstanding brands, Frito-Lay redesigned the packaging for several products, including Fritos and Rold Gold pretzels, and reformulated both Lay's and Ruffles potato chips—the first time the Lay's formula had ever been changed. To enhance the flavor of both chips, the company developed a new frying process and switched from soybean oil to cottonseed oil. With consumers preferring less salty snacks, the sodium content of the chips was also reduced. The new Lay's chips were introduced in 1992 through an ad campaign featuring the tag line, ''Too Good to Eat Just One!,'' a variation on the old ''Betcha Can't Eat Just One'' slogan. In 1993 Rold Gold pretzels were the subject of the product's first network television campaign, with ads featuring *Seinfeld* star Jason Alexander as ''Pretzel Boy.'' The following year the formula for Doritos was reformulated to make the chips 20 percent larger, 15 percent thinner, and stronger tasting—changes that were based on careful market research. Frito-Lay also continued to roll out new products, including Wavy Lay's potato chips and Baked Tostitos (1993), Cooler Ranch flavor Doritos (1994), and Baked Lay's (1996).

By the mid-1990s, as the snack food sector entered a slower growth period marked by heavy price competition, it became increasingly clear that Frito-Lay would remain the industry frontrunner by a wide margin. The company increased its share of the salty snack market in the United States from 38 percent in the late 1980s to 55 percent by 1996. Competitive pressure from Frito-Lay led two of its fiercest rivals to wave the white flag. Borden sold most of its snack businesses in the mid-1990s as part of a massive restructuring. In early 1996 Anheuser-Busch shut down its Eagle Snack unit after failing to find a buyer; it sold four of Eagle's plants to Frito-Lay, which converted them to production of its main brands.

In 1996 PepsiCo merged its domestic and international snack food operations into a single entity called Frito-Lay Company, consisting of two main operating units, Frito-Lay North America and Frito-Lay International. That same year, after Enrico had moved up to become CEO of PepsiCo, Steven Reinemund took over as CEO of Frito-Lay. He had been head of the company's North American operations since 1992. Frito-Lay in 1997 bought the Cracker Jack brand from Borden, marking the company's reentrance into the nonsalty snack food sector. Also in 1997 Frito-Lay reentered the sandwich cracker market with the national introduction of seven varieties. Other developments heightened Frito-Lay's importance to its parent company. In 1997 PepsiCo spun off its restaurant operations, and despite PepsiCo's 1998 acquisition of juice maker Tropicana Products, Inc., Frito-Lay generated half of the parent company's revenues and two-thirds of its profits in the late 1990s.

Frito-Lay expanded internationally in 1998 through the acquisition of several salty snack assets in Europe and Smith's Snackfood Company in Australia from United Biscuit Holdings plc for $440 million. In late 1998 Frito-Lay announced that it had formed a broad Latin American joint venture with Savoy Brands International, part of a Venezuelan conglomerate, Empresas Polar SA. Covering Venezuela, Chile, Colombia, Ecuador, Guatemala, Honduras, Panama, Peru, and El Salvador, the joint venture was designed to enable Frito-Lay to better penetrate the $3 billion salty snack sector in Latin America. Also in 1998 Frito-Lay began selling its Wow! line of low-fat and no-fat versions of Doritos, Ruffles, Lay's, and Tostitos. Made with a fake fat called olestra developed by Procter & Gamble (ironically the maker of rival chip Pringles), the Wow! products were controversial because of reports and studies that indicated that the chips could cause gastric distress. All olestra products carried warning labels stating that they ''may cause abdominal cramping and loose stools.'' Despite waves of negative publicity, the Wow! line was the best-selling new consumer product of 1998, garnering a whopping $350 million in sales.

By 1999 Frito-Lay's aggressive new product development, advertising, and marketing efforts had further increased the company's share of the U.S. salty snack market to 60 percent. That year, the company changed its corporate logo for the first time since 1980, and it signed an agreement with Oberto Sausage Company to be the exclusive distributor of Oh Boy! Oberto brand meat snacks, such as beef jerky. Frito-Lay also launched an efficiency drive involving the closure of four of its oldest U.S. plants and the expansion of five others that were among its most efficient. The workforce was reduced by a net 450 people as a result of the restructuring. A second effort also launched in 1999, involving changes to Frito-Lay's much lauded distribution system, aimed at saving as much as $340 million a year by the time of its full implementation. The three-year distribution overhaul was designed to enable its battery of 15,000 salespeople to spend more time merchandising and selling snack products in retail stores as opposed to loading and sorting the products in their trucks. In September 1999 Reinemund moved up to become president and COO of PepsiCo (he would succeed Enrico as chairman and CEO of the parent company in May 2001). Al Bru, a 23-year PepsiCo veteran, took over leadership of Frito-Lay.

Also during the late 1990s, Enrico was placing increased emphasis on building sales of Pepsi in its core supermarket channel. To this end, he launched an initiative called "Power of One" that aimed to take advantage of the synergies between Frito-Lay's salty snacks and Pepsi beverages. This strategy involved persuading grocery retailers to move soft drinks next to snacks, the pitch being that such a placement would increase supermarket sales. In the process, PepsiCo would gain sales of both snacks and beverages while arch-rival Coca-Cola could benefit only in the latter area. Power of One harkened back to one of the original rationales for the merger of Frito-Lay and Pepsi-Cola. At the time, the head of Pepsi, Donald Kendall, had told Herman Lay: "You make them thirsty, and I'll give them something to drink." The promise of this seemingly ideal marriage had never really been achieved, however, until the Power of One campaign, which in 1999 helped increase Frito-Lay's market share by two percentage points and boosted Pepsi's volume by 0.6 percent.

Early 2000s: Adding Quaker Brands, Pushing More Natural and Healthful Products

Late in 2000 PepsiCo reached an agreement to acquire the Quaker Oats Company in a deal valued at $14 billion when completed the following August. Although clearly coveted for its blockbuster Gatorade sports drink, Quaker Oats also brought to PepsiCo brands that meshed well with Frito-Lay. Quaker's snack brands, which included Quaker Chewy granola bars, Quaker Fruit and Oatmeal bars, and Quaker Quakes rice cakes, became part of a new convenience-food unit within Frito-Lay North America. The addition of these brands helped Frito-Lay in its efforts to diversify outside the salty snack sector, and particularly into "on the go" light meals and nutritious snacks. In turn, the Quaker brands were expected to benefit from being placed into Frito-Lay's massive and recently overhauled distribution system.

On the new product front, Frito-Lay attempted to tap into the booming growth in the U.S. Hispanic population by launching a line of products aimed specifically at that market. The line included a mix of new products, such as Doritos Rancheros, several spicy snacks already sold in the United States, and four items that were big sellers for its sister company in Mexico, Sabritas S.A.: Crujitos, Churrumais, El Isleno Plantains, and Abobadas.

Other new product developments during this period centered around Americans' growing concerns about the healthfulness of the foods they were consuming. Sales of the Wow! line had turned disappointing following its stellar launch, perhaps because of the controversies surrounding olestra, but Frito-Lay pushed ahead with non-olestra-based products deemed to be

more healthful, such as Lay's Reduced Fat and Cheetos Reduced Fat snacks, both of which debuted in 2002 with significantly less total fat and saturated fat than the original versions. The nonfried Baked line expanded as well that year with the introduction of Baked Doritos. Frito-Lay announced that it would begin eliminating artery-clogging trans fats from its products. Whereas Lay's, Fritos, and Ruffles had never contained trans fats, Doritos, Tostitos, and Cheetos had, and by 2004 Frito-Lay had eliminated trans fats from all of its products.

Pushing further in this same direction, Frito-Lay in 2003 branched into the natural and organic snacks category for the first time. Under the overall umbrella name "Natural," the company launched a slew of new products made with certified organic ingredients. Among the initial offerings were Natural Reduced Fat Ruffles, Organic Blue Corn Tostitos, Tostitos Organic Salsa, Natural Lay's Potato Chips with Sea Salt, and Natural Cheetos White Cheddar Puffs. Another new product launched in 2003 was Lay's Stax potato crisps, which were packaged in a cardboard can and designed to compete directly with Procter & Gamble's Pringles brand. The fast-growing Baked line, meanwhile, began sporting "Smart Spot" symbols as a further way of alerting consumers to their status as a more healthful choice, and as part of a wider PepsiCo project. To include the symbol, a Frito-Lay product had to contain: 150 calories or less, less than 35 percent of calories from fat, zero grams of trans fats, and 240 milligrams or less of sodium per 1-ounce serving. Sales of these "sensible snacks" totaled more than $1 billion in 2003, out of total Frito-Lay revenues of $9.09 billion.

Another significant development of 2003 was the separation of PepsiCo's two snack businesses, Frito-Lay North America and Frito-Lay International. The former—concentrating solely on the United States and Canada—continued to be one of the main divisions of the parent company, but the latter was subsumed within a newly enlarged international food and beverage division called PepsiCo International. Frito-Lay North America now generated about one-third of the parent company's net revenue—as did PepsiCo International—but Frito-Lay contributed nearly 40 percent of the operating profit, making it the most profitable of PepsiCo's four divisions.

By 2003 the Wow! line was garnering annual sales of just $100 million, despite the U.S. Food and Drug Administration's ruling in August 2003 that the warning label on olestra-laden snacks was "no longer warranted." In September of the following year, Frito-Lay attempted to reposition its olestra line. It was rebranded with a new name, Light, the packaging was revamped, and the marketing began focusing on reduced calories rather than lower fat. In the interim, the American food scene had been roiled by the low-carb craze. Frito-Lay responded quickly with a new line called Edge, which debuted in January 2004 with new versions of Doritos and Tostitos with 60 percent fewer carbohydrates than the originals.

Late in 2003 Frito-Lay North America announced plans to close its Louisville manufacturing plant and shut down older manufacturing lines in two other plants. The restructuring involved 330 employees losing their jobs. In September 2004 Irene Rosenfeld came onboard as chairman and CEO of Frito-Lay, replacing Bru, who became vice-chairman of PepsiCo before retiring in February 2005. Rosenfeld had spent 22 years at Kraft Foods Inc., leaving in July 2003 as president of Kraft's North American businesses, which consisted of five operating units with annual sales of $21 billion. Rosenfeld took over at a time when concerns were mounting that increasingly health-conscious consumers were beginning to buy fewer salty snacks. The new leader responded in February 2005 by announcing that Frito-Lay would begin repositioning itself and its brands to compete within the broader "macrosnacks" category, which included cookies, crackers, yogurt, and candy in addition to Frito-Lay's forte, salty snacks. In this larger category—in which annual U.S. sales totaled about $75 billion—Frito-Lay held the leading share of 15 percent. Initial plans included increasing the advertising budget by 50 percent, bumping up ad and marketing expenditures aimed at minorities, pumping more money into smaller products with high-growth potential such as Sun Chips multigrain snacks, and introducing new products, such as multigrain Tostitos tortilla chips, aimed at meeting consumer demand for more natural and healthful snacks. While North American diet trends seemed to indicate a potentially more troubled future for Frito-Lay, the company had proved adept at changing itself and its products with the times.

Principal Competitors

The Procter & Gamble Company; Kraft Foods Inc.; Kellogg Company; General Mills, Inc.; Campbell Soup Company; Snyder's of Hanover; The Hain Celestial Group, Inc.

Further Reading

Adler, Jerry, "The Soul of a New Snack," *Newsweek,* April 16, 1984, pp. 13, 16.

Bary, Andrew, "Fat Chance," *Barron's,* January 19, 2004, pp. 15–16.

Bayer, Tom, and B.G. Yovovich, "Snacking on Success: New Product Prowess? That's Frito-Lay's Bag," *Advertising Age,* March 15, 1982, p. M10.

Benezra, Karen, "Frito-Lay Dominates, While Others Pick Up Loose Chips," *Brandweek,* February 7, 1994, pp. 31 +.

——, "Frito-Lay's Last Challenge," *Brandweek,* March 18, 1996, pp. 33 +.

Block, Maurine, "Doritos Feel the Crunch—of Success," *Advertising Age,* October 2, 1972, p. 26.

"Boards of Pepsi-Cola and Frito-Lay Approve Merging As PepsiCo," *Wall Street Journal,* February 26, 1965, p. 8.

Bork, Robert H., Jr., "Of Potato Chips and Microchips," *Forbes,* January 30, 1984, pp. 118–19.

Brady, Diane, "A Thousand and One Noshes: How Pepsi Deftly Adapts Products to Changing Consumer Tastes," *Business Week,* June 14, 2004, pp. 54, 56.

Byrne, John A., "PepsiCo's New Formula," *Business Week,* April 10, 2000, pp. 172–76 +.

Calloway, D. Wayne, "Case History of Frito Lay," *Planning Review,* May 1985, p. 13.

Chakravarty, Subrata N., "The King of Snacks," *Forbes,* October 20, 1997, p. 213.

Collins, Glenn, "PepsiCo Pushes a Star Performer," *New York Times,* November 3, 1994, pp. D1, D8.

Deogun, Nikhil, "PepsiCo Forms Big Venture in Latin America," *Wall Street Journal,* November 25, 1998, pp. A12, A13.

——, "PepsiCo's Frito-Lay Unit to Buy Some Assets of United Biscuits," *Wall Street Journal,* November 18, 1997, p. B4.

——, "Sailor Jack and Bingo Join Frito-Lay Team in Cracker Jack Deal: Can Famed Sweet Snack Offer a Prized Change of Pace for Firm's Salty Lineup?," *Wall Street Journal,* October 9, 1997, p. B6.

——, "U.S. Probe into Practices by Frito-Lay Ends Without Charges Being Brought," *Wall Street Journal,* December 22, 1998, p. A4.

Dunkin, Amy, "Frito-Lay's Cooking Again, and Profits Are Starting to Pop," *Business Week,* May 22, 1989, pp. 66, 70.

Feder, Barnaby J., "Frito-Lay's Speedy Data Network," *New York Times,* November 8, 1990, pp. D1, D7.

Feld, Charles S., "Directed Decentralization: The Frito Lay Story," *Financial Executive,* November/December 1990, pp. 22 +.

Fisher, Anne B., "Peering Past PepsiCo's Bad News," *Fortune,* November 14, 1983, pp. 124 +.

Forest, Stephanie Anderson, and Julia Flynn Siler, "Chipping Away at Frito-Lay," *Business Week,* July 22, 1991, p. 26.

Frank, Robert, "Frito-Lay Devours Snack-Food Business," *Wall Street Journal,* October 27, 1995, p. B1.

——, "Frito-Lay Puts Up More Than Chips in Deal for Olestra," *Wall Street Journal,* May 31, 1996, pp. A3, A4.

"Frito-Lay May Find Itself in a Competition Crunch," *Business Week,* July 19, 1982, p. 186.

Gibson, Richard, "Frito-Lay Has Eagle Snacks out on a Limb," *Wall Street Journal,* March 1, 1994, p. B7.

Greenwald, John, "Frito-Lay Under Snack Attack," *Time,* June 10, 1996, pp. 62 +.

Grossman, Laurie M., "Frito-Lay Chief Aims to Cut Unit's Fat and Give Snack Food a Spicier Image," *Wall Street Journal,* July 11, 1991, p. B1.

——, "Price Wars Bring Flavor to Once-Quiet Snack Market," *Wall Street Journal,* May 23, 1991, p. B1.

"Gulp, Munch, and Merge," *Forbes,* July 15, 1968, pp. 20–21.

Hall, Trish, "President Quits at PepsiCo's Largest Unit—Korn Leaves Frito-Lay Job," *Wall Street Journal,* November 25, 1986, p. 2.

"Herman W. Lay of PepsiCo," *Nation's Business,* September 1969, pp. 88–89, 92–95.

"Holders of Pepsi-Cola and Frito-Lay Approve Proposal for Merger," *Wall Street Journal,* June 9, 1965, p. 8.

"Innovators in the Salted-Snacks Market: New Products and New Packaging Challenge Industry Leader Frito-Lay," *Business Week,* October 30, 1978, pp. 73–74.

Johnson, Robert, "In the Chips: At Frito Lay, the Consumer Is an Obsession," *Wall Street Journal,* March 22, 1991, pp. B1 +.

Kaplan, Elisa, "Frito-Lay: Still King of the Snack Food Hill," *Advertising Age,* April 30, 1979, pp. S2, S48–S49.

Lawrence, Jennifer, "Frito Play: New 'Basics' Strategy Takes on Regional Rivals," *Advertising Age,* March 30, 1987, pp. 1, 70, 71.

——, "Taco Bell Calls on Supermarkets: Frito-Lay to Test Mexican Food Line Under Sister PepsiCo Unit's Name," *Advertising Age,* February 8, 1993, pp. 3, 47.

Levine, Art, "Food Fight in Indianapolis: A Test Market for Fat-Free, Olestra-Based Snacks Gets Messy," *U.S. News and World Report,* May 5, 1997, pp. 53 +.

Lisser, Eleena de, "Tortilla Chips Tempt Snackers with Changes," *Wall Street Journal,* May 6, 1993, p. B1.

Lublin, Joann S., and Chad Terhune, "Pepsi Names Ex-Officer of Kraft To Top Posts at Frito-Lay Unit," *Wall Street Journal,* September 2, 2004, p. B2.

McCarthy, Michael J., "Added Fizz: Pepsi Is Going Better with Its Fast Foods and Frito-Lay Snacks," *Wall Street Journal,* June 13, 1991, pp. A1 +.

——, "Frito-Lay Bets Big with Multigrain Chips," *Wall Street Journal,* February 28, 1991, p. B1.

——, "PepsiCo, in a Surprise Reshuffle, Names Roger A. Enrico to Lead Frito-Lay Unit," *Wall Street Journal,* December 12, 1990, p. B6.

McGraw, Dan, "Salting Away the Competition: Frito-Lay Launches a Powerful Snack Attack and Crunches the Competition," *U.S. News and World Report,* September 16, 1996, pp. 71 +.

McKay, Betsy, "Fit to Eat?: PepsiCo Challenges Itself to Concoct Healthier Snacks," *Wall Street Journal,* September 23, 2002, p. A1.

——, ''PepsiCo Reorganizes Some Business Units,'' *Wall Street Journal,* August 9, 2001, p. B4.

——, ''PepsiCo's Frito-Lay Gives Its Baked Chips 'Smart Snack' Label,'' *Wall Street Journal,* August 6, 2003, p. D3.

——, ''Russians Go Nuts for Snacks As Planters, Frito Duke It Out,'' *Advertising Age,* December 13, 1993, pp. I3, I14.

McKay, Betsy, and Jonathan Eig, ''PepsiCo Hopes to Feast on Profits from Quaker Snacks,'' *Wall Street Journal,* December 4, 2000, p. B4.

Morrison, Ann M., ''Cookies Are Frito-Lay's New Bag,'' *Fortune,* August 9, 1982, pp. 64–67.

Neff, Jack, ''When the Chip Are Down,'' *Food Processing,* December 2003, pp. 26–28, 30.

''Our First Fifty Years: The Frito-Lay Story, 1932–1982,'' special issue of *Bandwagon,* Dallas: Frito-Lay, 1982.

Parker-Pope, Tara, and Nikhil Deogun, ''Frito-Lay to Begin Selling Wow! Chips Made with Olestra Later This Month,'' *Wall Street Journal,* February 10, 1998, p. B2.

''Party Gets Rough for Potato Chippers,'' *Business Week,* November 8, 1969, p. 36.

''PepsiCo—More Than Just 'Pepsi,' '' *Financial World,* November 4, 1970, pp. 5, 26.

Pollack, Judann, ''Frito-Lay Revamps Strategy for Struggling Wow!,'' *Advertising Age,* September 14, 1998, p. 1.

——, ''New-Product Feast Readied by Frito-Lay,'' *Advertising Age,* February 12, 1996, pp. 1, 37.

Porter, Eduardo, and Betsy McKay, ''Frito-Lay Adds Spanish Accent to Snacks,'' *Wall Street Journal,* May 22, 2002, p. B4.

Prokesch, Steven E., ''Frito-Lay's Go-It-Alone Policy,'' *New York Times,* December 2, 1985, pp. D1, 4.

Reyes, Sonia, ''Frito-Lay Lays Out Plans for Natural Line,'' *Brandweek,* May 12, 2003, p. 9.

Robinson-Jacobs, Karen, ''Frito-Lay to Rename 'Wow' Chip Light to 'Light,' '' *Dallas Morning News,* June 4, 2004.

——, ''New CEO Thinks Frito-Lay Is Worth Its Salt,'' *Dallas Morning News,* September 3, 2004.

Sellers, Patricia, ''If It Ain't Broke, Fix It Anyway,'' *Fortune,* December 28, 1992, pp. 49+.

''Steady Gains for PepsiCo,'' *Financial World,* March 1, 1972, pp. 7, 19.

Terhune, Chad, ''Frito-Lay to Refocus Marketing,'' *Wall Street Journal,* February 25, 2005, p. B3.

Thomas, Robert McG., Jr., ''Herman W. Lay, 73, Is Dead: Success Tied to Potato Chips,'' *New York Times,* December 7, 1982, p. D30.

Thompson, Stephanie, ''As Fat Fight Rages, Frito Battles Back,'' *Advertising Age,* September 2, 2002, p. 1.

——, ''Frito-Lay Launches Two New Snacks,'' *Advertising Age,* November 25, 2002, p. 6.

Vranica, Suzanne, ''PepsiCo Sets Health-Snack Effort,'' *Wall Street Journal,* September 23, 2003, p. B6.

Warner, Fara, ''Empowered by Enrico,'' *Adweek's Marketing Week,* May 4, 1992, pp. 16+.

Whalen, Jeanne, ''Tostitos Tastes New Life,'' *Advertising Age,* December 11, 1995, p. 42.

''Who Acquired Who?,'' *Forbes,* April 1, 1967, p. 69.

Willman, John, ''Salty Snack Attack on Europe,'' *Financial Times,* February 2, 1998, p. 13.

Yung, Katherine, ''Concerns About Sales Leave Only a Few Making Fat-Free Chips,'' *Dallas Morning News,* January 25, 1999.

Zellner, Wendy, ''Frito-Lay Is Munching on the Competition,'' *Business Week,* August 24, 1992, pp. 52–53.

—David E. Salamie

General Binding Corporation

One GBC Plaza
Northbrook, Illinois 60062
U.S.A.
Telephone: (847) 272-3700
Fax: (847) 272-1389
Web site: http://www.gbc.com

Wholly Owned Subsidiary of ACCO Brands Corporation
Incorporated: 1947
Employees: 3,600
Sales: $712.3 million (2004)
NAIC: 333313 Office Machinery Manufacturing

General Binding Corporation (GBC), in the business of packaging and presenting information for more than a half century, is among the world leaders in binding, laminating, and displaying products. The GBC, Quartet, and Ibico brands are marketed in more than 100 countries. GBC experienced a slump following a 1990s expansion and scaled back product offerings. A merger with Fortune Brands Inc.'s ACCO World Corporation was completed in August 2005.

Bound Together: 1940s–70s

GBC was founded in 1947 by William N. Lane and two business partners when they purchased a small trade bindery in Chicago, Illinois. First year sales totaled $250,000. GBC expanded operations in 1952, opening another domestic manufacturing plant and founding General Binding Corporation Canada, Ltd. In the 1950s GBC laid the groundwork for its international divisions, creating sales and distribution networks in Europe, Mexico, Canada, Venezuela, and Brazil. Sales were slow at first in the European market, where GBC's binding machines were readily available but supplies were not. In response to this situation, GBC established a manufacturing subsidiary in Switzerland in 1954 to produce a full range of plastic binding supplies as well as a limited number of binding machines. Wholly owned subsidiaries were then set up to market GBC machines and supplies throughout England, Germany, Holland, Italy, and France.

In 1958, the European Economic Community established a 30 percent tariff on goods produced in Switzerland and sold throughout Europe. To avoid hefty tariffs, GBC built a second European manufacturing facility in Germany, just across the border from its Swiss concern. One year later, when labor shortages in Switzerland sharply curtailed production at GBC's plant there, the company built a third European manufacturing facility in England.

In 1960, GBC introduced the Combo, its first combination punch/binding system. GBC also continued its international expansion, becoming one of the first foreign companies to set up operations in Japan. Three years later, the company established a fourth European manufacturing plant in Italy. Again, GBC's profits were threatened by high taxes, so the company built an automated plant in a newly created Italian economic development zone that had a lower tax rate. When the Australian government levied high import tariffs on GBC products in 1966, the company established an Australian manufacturing facility and purchased a Sydney-based firm to manufacture binding supplies from raw materials exported from the United States. This persistence in expanding its international sales garnered GBC an "E" Award for excellence in exporting from the U.S. government in 1964.

GBC also established a wholly owned subsidiary in Brazil in 1962. Due to the unstable political situation in the country at that time, however, the company refrained from doing business there until 1971, when it entered into a joint venture with a Brazilian firm to distribute its products.

Sales from 1961 to 1971 rose an average of $2.1 million a year, 30 percent of which came from foreign markets. GBC's domestic sales also expanded greatly, fueled by growth in the office market as well as a surge in the printing and graphics industry. In 1962, GBC ventured into the lamination business with the purchase of Virginia Laminating, a designer and manufacturer of lamination machines. In 1969, GBC purchased Webtron Corp., a maker of specialty presses used for printing tags and labels, and set it up as a wholly owned subsidiary. GBC went public in 1966, listing its securities on the OTC (over the counter) market. Stocks split two-for-one in 1968 and again in 1971. The company declared its first cash dividend in 1975.

Sales in 1973 surpassed $50 million for the first time, and Therm-A-Bind, a revolutionary, heat-activated binding system, was introduced. In 1977 GBC purchased U.S. RingBinder Corporation. GBC founder, Chairman, and CEO William N. Lane passed away in 1978. The Lane family retained control of 57 percent of the company and William N. Lane III was named chairman.

Rebound: 1980s

Sales in 1978 hit the $100 million mark but began to slip around 1981, due to the economic recession in the United States. In an attempt to boost earnings, GBC entered into an agreement with NorthStar Computers to sell its personal computers through GBC's well-established distribution and sales channels. The move proved to be nearly disastrous for GBC. Its sales force devoted the majority of its efforts toward selling new computers under the GBC name. IBM also ventured into the personal computer arena in the early 1980s, however, and within two years cornered the market. In 1983, GBC sold less than 500 computers. Earnings fell to $236,000 on sales of $145.7 million, compared with 1981 earnings of $7.5 million on sales of $149.6 million.

GBC's subsidiary U.S. RingBinder was facing competition from lower priced imports in the metal ringbinder industry. By 1983 U.S. RingBinder had resorted to selling its products at no gross margin in order to stave off its eroding market share. GBC's second subsidiary Webtron also was feeling the squeeze of competition.

In 1984, Rudolph Grua was hired to replace John Preschlack as president and CEO. Under Grua, the company began a back-to-basics marketing effort, dropping its computer line and focusing on its core binding and lamination businesses. Faced with growing threats from European and Japanese imports, Grua earmarked $1.4 million for research and development of new binding and laminating systems and shredders. GBC introduced a number of new products and instituted a combined direct-mail, catalog, and telemarketing drive for its binding and office supplies. U.S. RingBinder became competitive again by establishing a manufacturing plant in Singapore. Sales in 1984 rose 13 percent to $165 million; net earnings soared to $6.4 million.

In 1985, GBC entered into an agreement with VeloBind, Inc., to develop a new binding system that used rigid plastic strips. The company broadened its marketing efforts, introducing an expanded product catalog named Sourcebook and establishing a telemarketing center at corporate headquarters in Northbrook, Illinois. The following year, telemarketing centers were established in England, Australia, and Canada. In 1987, with sales of more than $200 million, GBC stocks split 3-for-2 and dividends increased by 20 percent. In 1988 stocks split 3-for-2 again, earnings jumped 55 percent to $14 million, and sales hit a record $250 million.

Buying Binge: 1990s

GBC continued its expansion into the 1990s, establishing a new Film Products Division in 1989 and also purchasing Loose Leaf Metals Co., Inc., that year. The company also began tapping into the growing desktop publishing and home office market. In 1991, the Film Products Division introduced a high-speed commercial laminating system, which established GBC as a complete marketer of paper finishing products. Also that year, GBC purchased VeloBind, Inc., for approximately $50 million. Research and development spending continued, resulting in the introduction of 14 new products in 1992, including binding machines, improved Therm-A-Bind systems, and shredding machines. The next year, GBC entered the office supply business with the acquisition of Bates Manufacturing Company.

As it moved toward the beginning of the 21st century, GBC planned to focus on improving its international markets, which were hurt by recessions in the overseas operations. In 1993 international sales accounted for 45 percent of unit sales but only 36 percent of dollar sales. With a focus on developing its Mexican and Australian markets, GBC looked for continued growth and profitability.

In 1994, GBC purchased Michigan-based Sickinger Co., a maker of high-volume paper punching machines. Seeking to cut manufacturing costs, the company entered into two joint ventures in China and built a plant in Costa Rica. Concurrently plants in Germany and Mexico City were shut down. Revenue for the year climbed 12 percent to $420.4 million. Earnings were up 5 percent to $15.7 million.

Govi C. Reddy, 18-year GBC veteran and head of the laminating film division, stepped up to the posts of president and CEO in January 1995. Under his leadership the division's annual revenue had grown from $6 million in the late 1980s to $63 million in 1994. Reddy's goal was to boost GBC total revenues to $1 billion by 2000, according to *Crain's Chicago Business*.

As a part of his quest, Reddy ventured into the digital graphics market, with the purchase of Wisconsin-based Pro-Tech in late 1995. He also restructured operations and invested $20 million in the company's information system. The company gained Australian market leadership in office supplies with the acquisition of Fordiograph Inc. The Sydney-based company had sales of $21 million in 1995.

The majority of the company stock remained with the Lane family. Lane Industries Inc. held 62 percent of the common stock with Ariel Capital Management, a mutual fund business, holding 11 percent. Lane Industries controlled all Class B voting stock. The stock had been confined to the $18 to $23 range for a number of years due to the less than stellar results from commodity product ventures such as three-ring binders, computers, and desktop supplies, according to *Crain's*.

GBC purchased Quartet Manufacturing, a visual communication product maker in 1997. U.S. RingBinder was divested in 1998, putting the proceeds toward debt reduction. The company

Key Dates:

1947: The company is founded by William N. Lane and two partners with the purchase of a small trade bindery.

1952: The company begins expanding operations.

1959: The company builds its third European manufacturing plant.

1960: The company becomes one of the first foreign companies to set up operations in Japan.

1962: The company enters the lamination business via an acquisition.

1966: An Australian manufacturing facility is established; GBC goes public.

1978: Sales hit the $100 million mark.

1981: The company enters the PC market through an agreement with a computer maker.

1983: Imports hurt U.S. Ringbinder Corporation, the metal ringbinder business purchased in 1977.

1984: Market pressures send the company back to its core binding and lamination businesses.

1992: R&D spending results in the introduction of 14 new products.

1995: The company enters the digital market.

1997: The company acquires Quartet Manufacturing, maker of bulletin boards, marker boards, and easels.

1998: U.S. Ringbinder is divested.

2001: Dennis J. Martin becomes chairman, president, and CEO.

2005: Fortune Brands Inc. spins off its ACCO World Corporation office products unit, which merges with GBC in August, becoming ACCO Brands Corporation.

was paring itself down to four core business areas of office products, document finishing, films, and emerging markets.

Record sales of $922.4 million, a 20 percent increase over 1997, were achieved in 1998. Net income dropped off due to a downturn in document finishing and digital print finishing businesses; charges related to three new manufacturing plants and the closure of two others; implementation of new distribution and information management systems in Europe; and costs related to the purchase of Ibico AG.

April 1999 announcements of a first quarter earnings decline of 82 percent and a workforce reduction resulted in a 26 percent hit to GBC's stock price. Domestic sales of office supplies were soft and the ongoing integration problems related to the February 1998 buyout of Switzerland-based Ibico AG contributed to the fall-off. The restructuring, which also included a plant closing in Phoenix, the elimination of about 24 field sales offices, and the shuttering of warehouses in Dallas and Atlanta, was expected to save the company about $16 million annually. GBC recorded a net loss of $56.7 million for the year, and its stock fell to the $12 level, a 68 percent drop-off.

GBC returned to profitability in 2000, with $2.4 million in net earnings. In February 2001, Reddy retired. Lane also stepped down as chair in 2001, making room for new leader-

ship. Dennis J. Martin came aboard as chairman, president, and CEO in May 2001. He planned to cut unprofitable products, reduce debt accumulated during the 1990s acquisition spree, and cut overhead. Martin had headed up the $1 billion welding products group for conglomerate Illinois Tool Works Inc.

By the summer of 2003, Martin had reduced product offerings from more than 30,000 to less than 10,000. Instead of producing a slew of models for a piece of equipment such as a paper shredder, GBC began limiting them to the ones favored by high-volume customers. With a decrease in product offerings came a corresponding reduction in sales volume, factories, major distribution centers, and workers. In addition, Martin pushed for the development of technically advanced products.

Martin's plan proceeded in a time of economic recession, taking hold in 2001. Corporate spending and hiring was off from the level that created strong demand for GBC products during the 1990s. GBC responded by outsourcing to low-cost facilities and entering the retail mass market.

Annual sales were around the $700 million mark in 2003 and red ink continued to plague GBC's bottom line despite increased efficiency. ''I don't think the company is losing marketshare to competitors in most of its business lines,'' Walter Liptak, a KeyBank Capital Markets/McDonald Financial Group analyst told *Crain's Chicago Business* in May 2004. ''It's just that corporate spending remains weak. And until demand rises, the company won't be able to raise its prices much, either.''

GBC regained its footing in 2004, producing its most profitable year since 1998. Year-end debt was at its lowest level since 1996.

In March 2005, Fortune Brands Inc. announced plans to spin off its Illinois-based ACCO World Corporation office products unit. ACCO would be merged with GBC, creating the world's largest supplier of branded office products with a combined revenue of nearly $2 billion. ACCO's Swingline brand was the North American leader in stapling and punches and ACCO was the leader in clips and fasteners.

Shareholders of both Fortune Brands and GBC were to receive shares in the newly created company. Fortune shareholders would own 66 percent and GBC shareholders 34 percent. The merger deal drove up GBC shares by 62 percent from mid-March to the beginning of June.

ACCO's profit margins had been under pressure from volume purchasers such as OfficeMax Inc. and Staples Inc. Fortune had attempted to sell ACCO in 2001, but shifted direction when no satisfactory offers were put forth. Cost-cutting and streamlining distribution and production operations produced a turnaround, but contribution to Fortune's overall sales and earnings continued to be limited, according to the *Chicago Tribune*.

The new company, ACCO Brands Corporation, was to be headed by ACCO chief David Campbell. GBC's Martin would not be involved in the combined entity.

Principal Competitors

Fellowes Manufacturing Company; PolyVision.

Further Reading

Allison, Melissa, "Turnaround Expert Sees Success with Northbrook, Ill.-Based Binding Business," *Chicago Tribune,* August 5, 2003.

"Anemic Demand Has Gen'l Binding in a Profit Bind," *Crain's Chicago Business,* May 24, 2004, p. 30.

"Annual Meetings: Lagging Gen'l Bind Paring Jobs, Facilities," *Crain's Chicago Business,* May 31, 1999, p. 14.

Arndorfer, James B., "People: General Binding CEO Trims Product Lines, Pays Off Debt," *Crain's Chicago Business,* July 2, 2001, p. 12.

"Back to Basics," *Barron's,* August 17, 1987, p. 45.

Byrne, Harlan S., "General Binding Corp.," *Barron's,* January 15, 1990, p. 40.

Cecil, Mark, "Fortune Plans to Free Office Products Division," *Mergers & Acquisitions Report,* October 16, 2000.

Defour, Matthew, "CEO Implements Unlikely Recipe for Success," *Daily Herald* (Arlington Heights, Ill.), January 7, 2004, p. 1.

"GBC Cites Overseas Market 'Flexibility,'" *Industrial Marketing,* May 1974, p. 6.

Lashinsky, Adam, "Globetrotter Settles in at General Binding," *Crain's Chicago Business,* September 6, 1993.

"General Binding Looks for Links to Boost Growth," *Crain's Chicago Business,* May 29, 1995, pp. 53+.

McCormick, Jay, "A Farewell to Puberty," *Forbes,* March 11, 1985, p. 108.

Miller, James P., "Northbrook, Ill.-Based Office Supply Firm Needs Complicated Merger," *Chicago Tribune,* June 7, 2005.

Moore, Anne, "New CEO, New Strategy Lifting Office Supplies Maker's Outlook," *Crain's Chicago Business,* August 26, 1996, p. 19.

Tita, Bob, "Office Supplier's Sales in a Bind," *Crain's Chicago Business,* November 29, 2004, p. 4.

Webber, Maura, "General Binding Corp.; Rank: 73," *Crain's Chicago Business,* June 7, 2000, p. 56.

—Maura Troester
—update: Kathleen Peippo

Global Imaging Systems, Inc.

3820 Northdale Boulevard
Suite 200A
Tampa, Florida 33624
U.S.A.
Telephone: (813) 960-5508
Toll Free: (888) 628-7834
Fax: (813) 264-7877
Web site: http://www.global-imaging.com

Public Company
Incorporated: 1994
Employees: 3,200
Sales: $926.5 million (2005)
Stock Exchanges: NASDAQ
Ticker Symbol: GISX
NAIC: 432420 Office Equipment Merchant Wholesalers

Global Imaging Systems, Inc. is the leading provider of many office technology solutions. These include solutions for digital automated office equipment, network integration, and electronic presentation systems. In addition, Global offers a variety of contract services, such as service to machinery, supply, network management, technical support, and training. Global is the most profitable public company among its peers and is committed to consolidating the fragmented office technology solutions industry.

An Idea Coming to Life: 1994–2000

Tom Johnson had a gift for acquiring and turning around underperforming companies. In fact, after his graduation from the University of Florida in 1972, with him in various leadership roles, the revenues of several companies grew. He became widely recognized throughout the office equipment industry for creating the benchmarking model for acquiring and integrating businesses. Finally in 1994, 20 years of experience in acquisitions and integrations, along with smart thinking and the ability to predict market and business trends, had brought him to a milestone. It was time to turn his "ideas into reality." Johnson, through a partnership with a private equity investment firm called Golder, Thoma, Cressey, Rauner Inc. (GTCR), founded Global Imaging Systems, Inc. Johnson, a Harvard Business School graduate, brought to the company not only his benchmark model but ten years of experience examining the office equipment industry through the eyes of his competitors. According to Global's web site, the company was formed "to exploit profitably Tom Johnson's benchmarking model, known throughout the office imaging industry as the premier tool for improving operations and for evaluating potential acquisition candidates."

Johnson created a company with a philosophy of "Think Globally, Act Locally." This meant that Global would be in the business of acquiring core companies that would offer its products and services regionally. In addition, satellite companies would act under the core companies and would be able to offer products and services even more locally, with the core company performing most administrative duties. Acquired companies would keep their original names and management, thereby retaining pre-acquisition customer relationships. While devising this system of companies, Johnson also had the foresight to recognize market trends. According to *Document Imaging Report,* he "realized that, in the future, stand-alone, analog copiers were going to give way to networked digital copiers." He decided to make Global a "one-stop shop," and offer not only a range of digital imaging solutions, but also network integration and management services, along with electronic presentation systems (including online audio/visual presentations). Johnson also recognized a need for office equipment solutions by customers in the middle market and decided that Global would focus on those clients.

In June 1998, Global Imaging Systems held an initial public offering (IPO), with GTCR owning close to 40 percent of the company. The earnings generated by the IPO would be used for general corporate use and to repay debt. By the fall of that same year, Global Imaging Systems had acquired 27 companies and finally turned a profit for the first time. It had ten core companies in different regions of the country, with the goal being that each core would be able to offer all of Global's products and services. Johnson stated that he would like to have 25 core companies covering the entire United States, but admitted that it

---

Company Perspectives:

Global's strategic mission is to be the most efficient, low-cost provider of document and image processing technology and services, including input, storage and output. We are "Passionate about Customer Productivity."

---

could be up to five years before enough companies were acquired and integrated in order to reach this goal.

In March 1999, Global announced that it had acquired Dahill Industries, bringing its total number of acquisitions to 32. With Dahill generating approximately $23 million in annual revenue, Global's acquired revenues rose to $110 million for the fiscal year. Dahill, an Austin, Texas company, was acquired to become a core company for Global's eastern Texas market. In addition, it would oversee satellite companies within the market. This acquisition would become a fairy-tale example of the success of Global's decentralized business model by, three years later, winning the company's award for outstanding performance as measured by revenue growth, operating income growth, and the growth in cash flow, return on assets, and return on investment.

Taking Off: 2001–02

By 2001, Global had acquired 50 companies, but was dealing with the aftermath of four straight quarters of earnings declines. It also was dealing with market value plunges, reportedly because it was simply being lumped together with larger industry leaders in the eyes of investors. While large industry leaders were being stymied by financial problems and internal issues, however, Global was steadily moving forward. Choosing to provide products and services to middle-market companies had been a genius move. Large industry leaders, such as Xerox Corp. and IKON Office Solutions, chose to battle over major business accounts, leaving relatively no competition for Global in the middle market. In 2001, that middle ground made up 45 percent of the entire market. "Global's largest target customer might have $1 billion in sales and a couple thousand employees. But most are far smaller. These companies look for copiers primarily in the $7,000 to $15,000 range," stated *Investor's Business Daily*. Global also offered convenience just by virtue of being a "one-stop shop." Not only did the company offer service contracts on the products it was providing, but it also offered several brands through Global's relationship with multiple vendors. Although the large industry leaders were hitting upon troubled times, Global was experiencing a 90 percent customer retention rate.

Compared with others in the industry, Global's future looked promising. But the company decided to continue operations on a cautious note. Instead of borrowing in order to purchase new businesses, it would use internal cash flow and would be more selective about new acquisitions. Although it seemed to have a strong foothold in the industry, the company was still heavily leveraged, with the debt-to-equity ratio being almost 70 percent, according to a July 2001 *Investor's Business Daily* article.

Global's cautiousness was rewarded in early 2002 when it was able to announce record-high revenues for the third quarter

(ending December 31, 2001). Tom Johnson said, "Our employees came through again and delivered an outstanding quarterly performance, in spite of the ongoing economic uncertainty." Also in 2002, Global announced that it would commence a public offering in an attempt to raise money to repay indebtedness. The offering would yield net proceeds of $39.2 million. Following the public offering, Global was able to make its 53rd acquisition. Johnson commented that the company hoped to return to a more normal pattern of external growth. This pattern would involve possibly acquiring several more businesses within the year, economic conditions permitting. In May 2002, Global was able to announce record-high earnings once again. This time the records were set not only for the quarter, but also for the fiscal year, ending March 31, 2002. After making it through the initial rough patch at its inception, Global seemed to be on the fast track to success.

In the spring of 2002, Tom Johnson brought his managers and top sales and service associates together in order to unveil a new theme. With his company long following the motto "Think Globally, Act Locally," Johnson had decided to add a new idea. The new motto was to be "Passionate about Customer Productivity," and was an initiative that would exemplify Global's commitment to the customer and to their ever-changing needs. According to *PR Newswire*, Johnson said, "Passionate about Customer Productivity says it all. It's who we are, and why we do what we do. This is not just lip service, or a catchy phrase." Johnson explained that being especially conscious of the needs of clients, along with Global's decentralized model of core companies and satellite companies served to truly set the company apart from competitors. It was these unique qualities that would push Global forward to continue to outperform other companies in the industry.

Strong Performances: 2003–05

Defying expectations, Global was able to once again announce record-high fiscal year revenues and net income (for the fiscal year ending March 31, 2003). The success was attributed to the company's steadfast commitment to customers in the middle market and also to Global's decentralized business model. Global also announced that it would be refinancing existing debt at a much lower interest rate. Although the refinancing involved a $5.4 million prepayment penalty, Johnson stated that he expected low interest rates to offset the penalty.

Approximately one month later, Global announced that it had acquired the Dallas, Texas branch of Copy Products, Inc., bringing its total number of acquisitions since 1994 to 60. Copy Products was a leading digital copier dealer in the Dallas area and would expand Global's coverage there. With annual revenues of approximately $3.4 million, Copy Products would become a satellite operation of core company Dahill Industries.

Also in 2003, Johnson, president and chief executive officer of the company, was elected chairman of the board of directors, following the resignation of Carl Thoma. Carl Thoma, who held the position for nine years, was the managing partner of Thoma Cressey Equity Partners, a private equity investment company and a successor to GTCR. Johnson's election was a logical one, following his tenure as president of the company since its founding.

The spring of 2004 brought the acquisition of Imagine Technology Group, Inc., the company's largest acquisition to date. Imagine reported annual revenues of approximately $117 million for 2003 and served the office technology needs of middle-market customers in 22 locations across the western United States. Chairman and CEO Johnson said, ''This transaction puts Global ahead of schedule to meet our three-year acquisition growth target, and we believe the acquisition will be nicely accretive to our earnings.''

Global also reported in 2004 that it had reached an 18 percent increase in revenues, bringing its revenues to a record $212 million for the first quarter. Attaining the record brought the company even closer to Johnson's goal of becoming a $1 billion company. Johnson said, ''We are running ahead of our external-growth goal to acquire, on average, $60 to $100 million in annualized revenues each year for the three-year period ending March 2006.''

Once again, Global was able to announce record-high revenues and net income, this time for the fiscal year ending March 31, 2005. Compared with the previous year, revenues were up 23 percent and operating income was up 24 percent.

Global's 2006 fiscal year started strong with the acquisition of Scottsboro Business Equipment. The business reported annual revenue of approximately $1.7 million and would act as a satellite company within the Alabama and southeast Tennessee markets.

Tom Johnson told the *Business Journal* (Tampa Bay) that one person he would have liked to have met would be Alexander the Great. Johnson said, ''The most impressive thing about him was his ability to win over those whom he conquered.'' As well as appreciating this ability to build a rapport, it appeared as though Johnson had tried to model this trait. As chairman and CEO of the company, he had led Global into its 11th year, forging a relationship with numerous vendors and partners, while continuing to acquire and integrate new companies. In a relatively short amount of time, Global had become a shining example of how to think ''outside of the box.''

Principal Subsidiaries

Dahill Industries.

Principal Competitors

Canon Inc.; CDW Computer Centers, Inc.; Danka; Dell Computer Corporation; Gateway, Inc.; Hewlett-Packard Company; IKON Office Solutions, Inc.; Imagistics; Insight Enterprises, Inc.; Konica Corporation; Minolta Co., Ltd.; PC Connection, Inc.; Xerox Corporation.

Further Reading

Crugal, Robin M., ''Tampa, Florida Office Equipment Firm Doesn't Copy the Rest,'' *Investor's Business Daily,* July 25, 2001, p. A08.
''Integrating Copier Dealers and Imaging Integrators,'' *Document Imaging Report,* October 16, 1998, p. 4.
''Tampa, Fla.-Based Global Imaging Systems Sets $212 Million Revenue Record,'' *Tampa Tribune,* July 23, 2004.

—Sara Poginy

Gol Linhas Aéreas Inteligentes S.A.

Rua Tamoios, 246, Jardim Aeroporto
04630-000 São Paulo
Brazil
Telephone: (55 11) 2125-3200
Fax: (55 11) 5033-4223
Web site: http://www.voegol.com.br

Public Company
Incorporated: 2000
Employees: 3,307
Sales: BRL $2.6 billion ($1.0 billion) (2005 est.)
Stock Exchanges: Bolsa de Valores de São Paulo New
    York
Ticker Symbol: GOL (ADR)
NAIC: 481111 Scheduled Passenger Air Transportation;
    481112 Scheduled Freight Air Transportation

Gol Linhas Aéreas Inteligentes S.A. is a leading Brazilian airline operating a low-cost business model *à la* Southwest Airlines. The name translates to ''Goal Intelligent Airlines.'' Gol flies a uniform fleet of 29 Boeing 737s to about 40 destinations. Aeropar Participacoes S.A. is the major shareholder, with 75.15 percent of total capital. Unlike Southwest, Gol arranges its route network in a hub-and-spoke system, which increases passenger feed and aircraft utilization. According to *Air Transport World,* Gol's employees are trained to think in terms of business objectives and the compensation structure includes various incentives such as profit sharing. Within a few years, revenues have reached the $1 billion mark. This explosive growth has come in spite of global recession, rising fuel prices, high inflation, and one of the airline industry's worst recessions. Gol rivals Ireland's Ryanair Holdings PLC, which also flies the low-cost carrier model, as the world's most profitable airline.

Origins

Gol Linhas Aéreas Inteligentes S.A. was launched in 2000 with backing from the Aurea Group, a bus company entrepreneur Constantino de Oliveira had formed in the 1950s. According to the Associated Press, start-up capital was an estimated $12 million. The Associated Press noted the timing of Gol's formation was helped by a newly relaxed regulatory environment regarding fares and the availability of personnel following massive layoffs at Viaçao Aérea São Paulo S/A (VASP).

Oliveira had reportedly sent his sons across the world to study low-cost carriers such as Southwest, Ryanair, and easyJet. One of the sons, Constantino de Oliveira, Jr., served as the new airline's CEO while his father was chairman. They imported a focus on strict cost control first learned in the bus business. In fact, the airline was priced to compete with intercity buses.

Passenger Flights Beginning in 2001

Gol began passenger operations in January 2001—the middle of the South American summer vacation season. Following the low-fare business model used to great success by Southwest Airlines in the United States, the new airline started with a fleet of three leased medium-range, mid-size Boeing 737 aircraft resplendent in its white and orange livery. By the end of its first year, Gol connected seven destinations in Brazil.

Gol aimed to grow the market by using low fares to attract new segments of the traveling public. When Gol started, its ticket prices were half those of its competitors. According to the Associated Press, Gol kept costs down by relying on ticketless reservations and by cutting out traditional perks such as hot meals and liquor. Gol also had no airport lounges, first or business class seating, frequent flyer program, or in-flight entertainment systems. The no-frills policy extended to its headquarters, a nondescript, four-story building at São Paulo's Guarulhos International Airport that lacked elevators.

Gol had about 1,100 employees in 2001, when it carried two million passengers. After losing $1.5 million on revenues of $95.8 million in 2001, its first year, Gol posted a net profit of $10.0 million (BRL 3.9 million) in 2002 as revenues more than doubled to $191.4 million. Passenger count rose to 4.8 million in 2002. Gol accomplished this in the face of a severe devaluation of the real that hurt all Brazilian airlines, which paid for fuel and aircraft in U.S. dollars.

The fantastic growth continued unabated in spite of a recession. In 2003, net profits were up fivefold to BRL 175.4 million ($60.3 million) as revenues more than doubled for the second consecutive year, reaching BRL 1.4 billion ($481.5 million). Employment was up to 2,453 people, and more than seven million passengers flew the airline.

Gol's fares were said to be an average 25 percent less than those of competitors. The airline began offering discounted night flights in late 2003. These prices compared with those for 20-hour intercity bus journeys.

Going International, Public in 2004

In May 2004, Gol placed a massive aircraft order for 15 Next-Generation Boeing 737s, with an option for up to 28 more. At retail prices, the deal was worth $2.7 billion (BRL 8 billion). By this time, Gol was flying to about 30 destinations.

Gol went public in June 2004, floating 17.6 percent of its total capital on the Bolsa de Valores de São Paulo and the New York Stock Exchange. It was only the second South American airline, after LAN Chile, to list on the New York Stock Exchange, according to *LatinFinance,* which reported that 72 percent of subscribers were international. The shares would peak at double their original price within a year.

The initial public offering (IPO) raised BRL 878 million ($281 million). Some proceeds were earmarked toward the $2.5 billion U.S. Export-Import Bank loan used to finance its large Boeing order. There was a secondary offering in May 2005. The influx of capital helped Gol keep its costs of borrowing down in a country known for exorbitant interest rates. By the time of its IPO, Gol was Brazil's third largest airline (behind VARIG and TAM) with a 22 percent share of the domestic market, according to one estimate.

Gol was chosen as *Exame* magazine's Company of the Year for 2004. *Aviation Week & Space Technology* ranked Gol the world's top publicly traded airline, in terms of competitiveness,

among those with less than $1 billion in sales. Gol also won praise for the transparency of its investor relations.

Revenues were about $622 million (BRL 2 billion) in 2004. Net income was $96.2 million (BLR 256 million). More than three-quarters of sales were from the Internet, making Gol one of Brazil's leading e-commerce companies. However, travel agencies, which charged commissions of up to 15 percent, handled half of these Internet ticket sales.

Gol started a popular service from São Paulo to Buenos Aires, Argentina, in late December 2004. This was its first international route. Dow Jones reported that tickets for this route sold in Brazil cost twice as much as those in Argentina due to government price controls. Gol was adding flights to Bolivia in June 2005 and other countries, such as Uruguay and Paraguay, soon after.

At the same time, the airline was investing in its facilities, building its own BRL 30.5 million ($12.8 million) maintenance center at the Cofins airport in the state of Minas Gerais. Gol was estimating revenues to be BRL 3.0 billion (more than $1 billion) for 2005. The airline leapfrogged debt-laden VARIG to attain the second largest share of the domestic market, 27 percent. (TAM Linhas Aéreas S.A., more oriented to business travelers, was the leading player with a 43 percent market share.)

The Brazilian air travel market was still growing more than 10 percent a year, noted *Institutional Investor International.* Fewer than one-fifth of Brazil's 180 million inhabitants flew once a year or more. Mexico was considered another relatively undeveloped commercial aviation market. A Mexican joint venture with Inversiones y Tecnicas Aeroportuarias S.A. (ITA) was expected to begin operations in 2006.

Gol continued to cut fares in order to keep its growing fleet full. It was placing new emphasis on price-sensitive business travelers. According to *Dow Jones International News,* Gol was second in the domestic market with a 20 percent share. One new regional rival, OceanAir, was also a feeder partner, since its turboprop aircraft operated from short runways in Brazil's interior that Gol's jets could not reach.

The fleet was expected to number 34 planes by the end of 2005 and 69 planes by the end of 2010. Gol enjoyed a relatively untapped market and few strong competitors. Challenges included the rising cost of fuel and instability of the Brazilian economy.

Principal Subsidiaries

Gol Transportes Aéreos S.A.

Principal Competitors

TAM Linhas Aéreas S.A.; Viaçao Aérea Rio-Grandense, S.A.

Further Reading

Adese, Carlos, "Fasten Your Seatbelts: Cutting Costs, TAM Airlines Follows Low-Cost Gol's Model to Cater to Brazil's Growing Airline Business," *Latin Trade,* March 2005, pp. 29+.

"Brazil Gol Eyes 40 Percent Domestic Market Share," *Latin America News Digest,* September 16, 2004.

"Brazil Gol to Boost Passenger Flow by 30 Percent," *Latin America News Digest,* January 13, 2005.

"Brazil Gol to Introduce Flights to Bolivia," *Latin America News Digest,* January 21, 2005.

"Brazil Gol to Invest $12.75 Million in Maintenance Centre," *Latin America News Digest,* June 22, 2005.

"Brazil Gol to Start International Flights Dec. 22, 2004," *Latin America News Digest,* October 22, 2004.

"Brazil Gol Turnover Seen at $1.0 Billion 2005," *Latin America News Digest,* February 18, 2005.

"Brazil's Gol, TAM Grab Airline Market Share from Varig," *Dow Jones International News,* April 12, 2005.

Chozick, Amy, "Discount Airlines Hit Latin America," *Wall Street Journal,* June 8, 2005, pp. D1+.

Clendenning, Alan, "Born from a Bus Company, Brazil's Gol Airline Spreading Wings in South America," *Associated Press,* January 28, 2005.

——, "Brazilian Discount Airline Selling Stock Via IPO Today," *Seattle Times,* June 24, 2004, p. E3.

Cowley, Matthew, "Brazil Airline Gol Thrills Investors, Challenges Abound," *FWN Select,* June 24, 2005.

——, "Brazil's Gol Airline to Add Planes in Latest Market Push," *Dow Jones International News,* March 9, 2005.

——, "Brazil's Gol Airline Well Positioned to Expand—Execs," *Dow Jones International News,* January 27, 2005.

——, "Brazil's Gol Sees 70K Customers a Year from Argentina Route," *FWN Select,* December 23, 2004.

Cowley, Matthew, and Amy Guthrie, "Brazil Gol to Launch Low-Cost Airline in Mexico," *Dow Jones International News,* July 5, 2005.

"Cruising Altitude—Web Exclusive," *LatinFinance,* March 1, 2005.

"Dollar Drives Gol Off Original Route," *Gazeta Mercantil Online* (Brazil), October 28, 2002.

Gille, John, "Big Order for 737s Boosts Boeing," *News Tribune* (Tacoma, Wash.), May 18, 2004.

"Gol Opens New Round in Airline Wars," *Gazeta Mercantil Online* (Brazil), March 11, 2004.

"Gol Reaches 8.3% Market Share and Surpasses Rio Sul," *Gazeta Mercantil Online* (Brazil), February 26, 2002.

"GOL Scores Big with Low Fares and Great Service in Brazil's Travel Market," *Institutional Investor International,* February 2005, p. 69.

Kepp, Michael, "Brazilian Airline Gol Goes Public," *Daily Deal,* June 25, 2004.

Lima, Edvaldo Pereira, "Winning Gol! Brazil's Low-Fare Carrier Soars on Global IPO As It Rewrites the Rules of Competition," *Air Transport World,* October 2004, pp. 22+.

"Low-Cost Leader Gol Airlines Successfully Lists on the NYSE and Bovespa," *LatinFinance,* September 2004, p. 45.

Maslen, Richard, "Brazilian Start-Up Gol Linhas Aereas Confirms 15th January Launch Plan," *Airclaims,* January 5, 2001.

"Pioneering IPOs," *LatinFinance,* February 2005, p. 45.

Samor, Geraldo, "Brazil's Gol Faces Hurdles," *Wall Street Journal,* August 9, 2004, p. C3.

Uphoff, Rainer, "Brazilian Start-Up Gol Eyes Air Force Transport Ops," *Air Transport Intelligence,* September 4, 2000.

—Frederick C. Ingram

Granite Industries of Vermont, Inc.

P.O. Box 537
Barre, Vermont 05641
U.S.A.
Telephone: (802) 479-2202
Toll Free: (800) 451-3236
Fax: (802) 479-7917
Web site: http://www.granitevermont.com

Private Company
Founded: c. 1897 as Valz Granite Company
Employees: 52
Sales: $10 million (2004 est.)
NAIC: 327991 Cut Stone and Stone Product Manufacturing

Based in the small town of Barre, Vermont, privately owned Granite Industries of Vermont, Inc. (GIV) specializes in the manufacture of granite and marble memorials. It is one of a handful of regional companies contracted by the U.S. Department of Veteran Affairs to produce marble headstones for government cemeteries, the memorials provided free to veterans' families. Responsible for the Northeast section of the country, GIV provides all of the headstones for Arlington National Cemetery. Although the bulk of the headstones are for veterans of World War II and Korea, many bear the names of soldiers killed in the war in Iraq, resulting in a great deal of publicity for the tiny company, which employs less than 60 people and does about $10 million in business each year, a third of which comes from veterans' headstones. GIV is also known for its ability to do custom work, and is especially adept at recreating historic monument styles, put to use in the making of replacement headstones, such as the thousands of deteriorating headstones in Confederate graveyards in the South. In addition, the company has won a number of high-profile projects, such as Arlington's Pentagon Victims Memorial dedicated to the people killed in Washington in the September 11, 2001 terrorist attacks, and the black marble wall of the Vietnam Veterans Memorial in Washington. In addition to veterans' headstones and war memorials, GIV also produces public and civic memorials, landscape architecture, and specialized building architecture. Whereas most of the company's raw materials come from local quarries, GIV also imports granite and marble of other colors from countries such as Sweden and South Africa. In addition, the company buys finished product from China, which is able to sell at prices far less than a rough cut GIV could buy at a local quarry. In order to compete against the Chinese, GIV is increasingly turning into a high-quality niche operation.

Emergence of the Vermont Granite Industry in the 1800s

Barre, Vermont, bills itself as the Granite Center of the World, with the industry focused around local quarries that hold an estimated 4,500-year supply of Barre Gray granite, unique to the area, the result of the land being covered and scraped by succeeding tides of ice sheets over the course of many thousands of years. Barre Gray is a favorite material for monuments, markers, and mausoleums because it is almost as hard as sapphire and resists moisture, and so can be exposed to the elements without crumbling or staining. Moreover, it is consistent from piece to piece and the fineness of its crystals is ideal for carving.

The Barre area was settled in the late 1770s, but in the early decades the area's principal industries were dairy, lumber, and farming. But any farmer who tried to clear his land was sure to encounter granite outcroppings, which the practical Yankees used for house foundations and millstones. It was not until the 1810s that the first quarry opened in Barre. Starting in 1833 the stone was hauled by ox teams over nine miles of hills to Montpelier for use in the construction of the State Capitol completed five years later (at a cost of $400). Next, the city of Troy, New York, ordered ten million paving blocks, which inspired other Barre residents to become involved in the business and stone workers to move into the community. But the growth of the industry was hindered for decades because of transportation difficulties. For years Barre Gray had to be hauled ten miles by ox to reach the closest railroad station. The transportation costs for moving raw material to the shops, and finished work to the customer, made Barre granite and products prohibitive in cost and stunted the growth of the industry. The problem was not remedied until 1875 when the Central Vermont railroad built an extension from Barre to Montpelier. Now

Company Perspectives:

For family memorials or individual memorials, trust the people who know, understand and work with granite. Retailers with an eye for the very best memorialization select Granite Industries of Vermont for the most demanding execution of detail.

the industry began to take shape and the community attracted stonecutters and artisans from Europe, especially Italy, many of whom launched their own business.

Predecessor Company's Founding Likely in the Early 1900s

Two of the Italian immigrants who came to Barre were cousins Constantino and Guido Valz, both born in Montesinaro, Italy, and who founded GIV. Constantino came to the United States in his teens and learned stonecutting from his uncle in Fitzwilliam, New Hampshire. Eight years later, after completing his apprenticeship, he moved to Barre and found work. After four years he decided to strike out on his own and formed a partnership with Guido, five years younger. According to GIV, the cousins launched Valz Granite Company in 1897, but this date is contradicted by Arthur W. Brayley's definitive book *History of the Granite Industry of New England,* published in 1913. Brayley lists Constantino's birth date as October 11, 1878, which would make him less than 20 years of age, and his cousin (born on September 23, 1883) would have been 14 or 15 if Valz Granite was indeed founded in 1897. If Brayley's research is accurate, it is more likely that the company was founded a decade later, around 1906 or 1907. Nevertheless, the cousins did become partners, starting out modestly, working out of a shed in a meadow. They did well enough that after two years they were able to build their first plant, located on the same site as GIV's present operation. According to Brayley, they specialized in medium and large monument work.

Valz Granite remained in the Valz family until the 1940s when it was bought by Henry Vanetti, an employee of the company, and his brother Aldo. Henry was born in Italy, and Aldo, ten years his junior, was born in Barre. They elected to keep the Valz Granite name and continued the tradition of concentrating on larger work, especially mausoleums. After Henry's passing in 1963, Aldo continued to run the business. When he died in 1978, his son and daughter inherited Valz Granite. They tried running it for two years, but neither were well versed in the monument business and in 1980 they elected to sell the company.

Partners Silvio Nativi, a Barre native and second-generation Italian-American, and New York City businessman Herman Goldberg bought Valz Granite, changing the name in 1980 to Granite Industries of Vermont. Nativi was already running another company, Nativi Granite Company, founded half a century earlier by his father, specializing in monument work. Nativi and Goldberg decided to devote GIV to the construction industry, to perform ''cladding'' work, putting up sheets of granite or marble on the exterior of buildings. Thus they invested in European equipment such as diamond saws and pol-

ishers and gutted much of the GIV plant to make the transition from monuments to cladding. One of their first major contracts was Manhattan's AT&T Building. Ironically, the company's new cladding capabilities landed it a memorial contract that would become the most famous project in company history: The Vietnam Veterans Memorial in Washington, D.C., ''the wall.'' GIV cut, inscribed, and polished the nearly 150 slabs of black granite imported from Bangalore, India, that made up the two separate walls that comprised the memorial. There were no joints connecting the three-inch-wide panels; they were simply pushed together, connected by stainless steel pins drilled into the sides. GIV warned the architect that the granite would expand and contract with the seasons and likely crack, but the installation was not changed. Several years later the first cracks began to appear in some of the center panels, where outer stress converged. A number of blank panels had been stored at the time the memorial was built, allowed to age at the same pace as the rest of the materials, and would likely be pulled out someday to replace the cracked sections of the wall.

GIV concentrated on cladding during the bulk of the 1980s. Then in 1988 Nativi Granite suffered a major fire and Silvio Nativi decided to get out of the business. He and Goldberg agreed to sell GIV. They found a buyer in Jeff Martell, who formed a partnership with Nativi Granite's office manager, Glenn Atherton, to buy the company.

Martell came to the granite and marble business by chance. He grew up in New Jersey, the son of an airline pilot who flew out of La Guardia. He began his college education at the University of Tampa before transferring to the University of Vermont in Burlington. He graduated in 1977 with a bachelor's of science degree in water quality and environmental science, but his dreams of ridding the world of pollution were soon dashed when he learned that the kind of positions available with the Vermont government paid a pittance. Thus he found a job with a SONY distributor, moved to Maine, and began selling electronics. A year later he returned to Vermont to attend a friend's wedding and met the owner of Cook, Watkins & Patch, a Barre granite company, and was recruited as a salesman. Martell agreed and began selling monuments throughout western Pennsylvania, Ohio, and Illinois. He enjoyed the work and over the next five years he established a solid customer base. When Cook, Watkins began experiencing financial problems, he quit in 1983, shortly before his employer went out of business, and launched Martell Memorials. He represented four different Barre granite manufacturers, selling into his established network of customers in the Midwest. He ran his own brokerage business for the next five years, until the opportunity to buy GIV arose.

Nativi and Goldberg's asking price was in the $1.8 million range. Both Martell and Atherton put up $100,000, but had to approach Vermont National Bank for the balance. Three times the bank rejected their loan application, prompting Nativi and Goldberg to drop their price to $1.6 million. The loan was finally granted—albeit at a steep cost, two points over prime at a time of high interest rates. Moreover, the bank kept a tight rein on the company's capital line and required a monthly look at GIV's profit and loss statement. Martell and Atherton's financial situation was made even more precarious because they soon learned that the plant was in terrible condition and required a

Key Dates:

1897: Valz Granite Company is founded, according to the company.
1940s: The company is sold to the Vanetti brothers.
1980: Valz is sold and is renamed Granite Industries of Vermont (GIV).
1988: Jeff Martell and Glenn Atherton buy GIV.
1994: Atherton dies.
2002: The company regains the marble upright contract with the Veterans Administration.

great number of improvements. The roof was leaking, the heating was shot, and the place was such a fire hazard that the company had to pay a $60,000 premium for fire and liability insurance. The partners would eventually install new ten-inch mains to accommodate a $100,000 sprinkler system, which lowered the insurance premium to just $15,000 a year.

As part of the purchase agreement, Martell and Atherton agreed to complete the construction contracts already on the books, but because Martell and Atherton's backgrounds were in memorials, they wanted to eventually focus on that business. To do so, the company had to incur the expense of leasing space for six months from another area company, Beck & Beck, until it could acquire the specialized equipment it needed to do memorial work in its own plant. With Atherton serving as plant manager and Martell handling sales and the financial responsibilities, GIV and its 26 employees generated about $3 million in revenues in the first year, producing barely enough cash flow to stay afloat.

Mid-1990s Switch to Marble Contract

Nativi Granite had been in the business of producing granite flat markers for the Veterans Administration (VA), but because of its lack of equipment, GIV was unable to pursue the business until 1990 when it won a bid to produce the military markers for the Northeast and Mid-Atlantic states. The company kept the contract for the next four years, but it was a very competitive business, and while GIV's costs continued to rise the VA paid the same price, causing GIV's margins to be compressed to a razor's edge. It was then that the company, which to this point had exclusively worked in granite, began looking at marble, and pursued the VA marble upright contract for military markers. These 42-inch high markers, of which 20 inches were above ground, came in two styles: oval top and "old style," used to replace the markers on the graves of Confederate soldiers from the Civil War. These markers had a peak, making them difficult to sit upon—as well as for Union veterans to desecrate the graves of their erstwhile foes. GIV won the marble upright contract for the Northeast in 1994 and played a major role in the company's improving fortunes in the 1990s, accounting for about 30 percent of revenues. The year 1994 also was marked by misfortune at GIV: Atherton died of a heart attack at the age of 52 while snowmobiling. The company was able to get by until Martell hired a new plant manager, William Perry. Later an office manager was hired, Forrest Rouelle, to whom Martell would eventually sell a 5 percent stake in the company.

As sales grew so did the GIV operations. By the mid-1990s revenues totaled $4 million to $4.5 million, improved to the $6 million to $7 million range in the late 1990s, and settled around $10 million in the 2000s. When Martell and Atherton bought GIV, the plant was about 50,000 square feet in size; over the next 15 years it grew by 50 percent. A shipping room was built in 1992, an addition to handle the veterans' markers came in 1994, an outbuilding dedicated to the preassembly of mausoleums was constructed in 1997, and in 2000 the company added a crating area and a washstand area where markers were not only cleaned but inspected. At this point, the company was told by the state that due to the lack of fire walls the facility could not make any more additions without major renovations.

In the mid-1990s, GIV and others in the granite industry began to feel pressure from imports from India, but later in the 1990s China weighed in and put the entire U.S. memorial industry under severe pricing pressure. GIV had begun taking steps to become more of a high-end niche player, producing personalized monuments and mausoleums and introducing new memorial designs. Around 1993 the company acquired Barre Draft Services, picking up specialized equipment as well as talented draftsmen who proved crucial in the company's efforts to stay ahead of foreign competition. But only a few months after GIV unveiled a new design, a Chinese company would have a copy on the market. Graveyards in the New York City area that were once 95 percent Barre product, according to Martell, were now 70 percent Chinese. The price differential was so great that GIV began to buy blank monuments from the Chinese in the 2000s, since it could not even buy raw materials from a nearby quarry at a lower price. In a 2005 interview, Martell offered an example of a massive buffalo from China, some eight feet in length and six feet high, costing just $600.

GIV lost its upright marble contract with the VA in 2000. Whereas the VA maintained that price was just one factor in awarding bids, along with quality and ability to deliver on time, Martell expressed his belief that the contract was lost on price in 2000. Two years later, the contract was won back, again on the basis of price, according to Martell. It was an important piece of business for GIV, one that would focus on providing the markers for World War II veterans who were dying off at an increasing rate, expected to peak in 2008 at around 675,000. The company also picked up business due to unwanted reasons. It won the contract for the five-sided Pentagon Victims Memorial in Arlington cemetery, dedicated to the people killed at the Pentagon during the September 11, 2001 terrorist attacks. As the war in Iraq dragged on, the company saw an increasing number of orders for markers for soldiers whose birth and death dates were uncomfortably close in time.

Principal Competitors

Rock of Ages, Inc.; Cold Spring Granite Company; Keystone Granite; Wang Li.

Further Reading

Barna, Ed, "Vermont Mining Companies Stay Grounded," *Vermont Business Magazine,* January 1994, p. 36.

Brayley, Arthur Wellington, *History of the Granite Industry of New England,* Boston: National Association of Granite Industries of the United States, 1913.

Buck, Rinker, ''Monument Workers Shape Nation's History,'' *Hartford Courant,* June 7, 2004.

Edelstein, Art, ''Making It in Vermont,'' *Vermont Business Magazine,* January 1, 2003, p. 32.

Green, Peter S., ''A Grave Business,'' *Fortune Small Business,* July 1, 2005, p. 33.

Harris, Francis, ''Iraq Adds to Burden for the Headstone Carvers of Vermont,'' *Daily Telegraph,* April 21, 2005.

Mehren, Elizabeth, ''Headstone Makers Provide Final Mark of Dignity to Fallen Troops,'' *Houston Chronicle,* September 19, 2004, p. 14.

—Ed Dinger

Herschend Family Entertainment Corporation

5445 Triangle Parkway, Suite 200
Norcross, Georgia 30029
U.S.A.
Telephone: (417) 338-2611
Toll Free: (800) 475-9370
Fax: (417) 336-7111
Web site: http://www.hfecorp.com

Private Company
Founded: 1960
Employees: 2,000
Sales: $284 million (2004 est.)
NAIC: 713110 Amusement and Theme Parks

Herschend Family Entertainment Corporation (HFE) is one of the nation's leaders in the themed entertainment business. Since its humble beginnings offering tours of Marvel Cave near Branson, Missouri, in 1950, the family business has grown exponentially. Headquartered in Norcross, Georgia, Herschend Family Entertainment Corporation provides wholesome family-oriented entertainment to people of all ages across the country, and is focused primarily in the Missouri Ozarks, the Tennessee Smoky Mountains, and the Atlanta, Georgia, area.

HFE owns, operates, or partners to operate 24 properties in ten states. The company's hometown properties include Silver Dollar City theme park, Celebration City theme park, White Water water park, Showboat Branson Belle showboat, and The Grand Village shops in Branson. As a partner in the Dollywood Company with country music legend Dolly Parton, HFE operates the Dollywood Theme Park and Dollywood's Splash Country water park in Parton's hometown of Pigeon Forge, Tennessee, and is a shareholder in Parton's Dixie Stampede dinner and show extravaganzas in Pigeon Forge and Branson, as well as Myrtle Beach, South Carolina, and Orlando, Florida. HFE also owns Ride the Ducks International (RTDI), which operates amphibious vehicle tours in five tourist locations: Branson, Baltimore, Atlanta, Philadelphia, and Memphis. Affiliated RTDI locations are in Boston and Seattle. HFE operates an additional theme park in partnership with the state of Georgia:

Stone Mountain Park in Atlanta. Three Hawaiian Falls water parks in Dallas, Garland, and The Colony, Texas, also fall under the HFE umbrella of properties.

1950s: Building on Marvel Cave's Allure

Herschend Family Entertainment Corporation's modest beginnings started with the fascination that so many Americans have for exploring caves. Back in 1894, mining expert William Henry Lynch purchased Missouri's Marvel Cave and opened it to tours. By the 1920s, thanks to Lynch's efforts to establish travel routes through nearby Branson, the cave was an accessible and well established tourist attraction. In 1946, Hugo and Mary Herschend visited and were fascinated by its size, beauty, and mystery. Four years later the Herschends signed a 99-year lease with Lynch's daughters for access to the cave.

Hugo and Mary left their home in Chicago for the Ozarks and began offering tours of Marvel Cave to tourists. They touted the attraction with signs that read "America's Third-Largest Cavern." That first summer they welcomed 8,000 visitors for tours of their amazing cave. Before long they made improvements to enhance the cave's safety and accessibility. After Hugo died in 1955, Mary was committed to preserving the natural beauty of the surrounding area and keeping the cave open to the public with the help of her sons Jack and Peter. Word of mouth helped increase the cave's popularity, and in 1959, 65,000 people visited Marvel Cave. The business's revenues reached $200,000.

In about 1960, Mary and her sons decided it was time to add to the attraction. They created a small tourist village with an 1880s mining town theme to enhance the allure of Marvel Cave. The historic town included a general store, blacksmith shop, ice cream parlor, authentic log buildings, and a church. It provided a fun and effective way to entertain cave visitors while they were waiting to take a tour. The mining village became known as Silver Dollar City because the Herschends gave visitors silver dollars as change. Because of the novelty of silver dollars, this tradition led to increased word of mouth exposure for the park.

With the energy and ideas of her young sons involved in the business, Mary expanded and added more attractions to Silver Dollar City, including 1880s-style native artists creating and

Company Perspectives:

Herschend Family Entertainment is a company dedicated to creating memories worth repeating! We immerse our guests in unique, highly themed environments that bring to life the adventure, entertainment and wonder of another century. We're located in the heart of the Ozark Mountain Country, minutes from the famed Branson, Missouri.

showing traditional Ozarks crafts. The Herschends welcomed 125,000 visitors to Silver Dollar City and the cave in 1960.

1963: Growing into Missouri's Top Tourist Destination

In 1963 the Herschends added to the artistic allure of Silver Dollar City by planning and hosting the first craft festival there. It drew a record 500,000 visitors. Crafters demonstrated woodcarving, shingle splitting, weaving, black-smithing, tie hacking, and soap and candle making. The craft festival event put Silver Dollar City on the map as the state's number one tourist attraction. Not long after, Mary Herschend was named Missouri Small Businessman of the year by the federal Small Business Administration.

Silver Dollar City's popularity grew, drawing more tourists to the Branson area each year. In 1966, 450,000 people visited Silver Dollar City, resulting in revenue of $3 million. The Herschend's business received national exposure in 1969 when the popular television show *Beverly Hillbillies* filmed five episodes at Silver Dollar City. The company could not have paid for better advertising. Soon stagecoach rides and a steam train were added to the park's attractions.

During those early years, the Herschend brothers developed an effective partnership for running their business: Jack handled operations and development, and Peter handled more of the public relations. Mary became a state and community leader for tourist and civic groups. According to HFE's business history, Mary received the Missouri Tourism Award presented at the first Annual Governor's conference on Tourism in 1972. Two years later, the Branson/Lakes Area Chamber of Commerce established its highest honor, the Mary Award, named for Mary Herschend and Mary Trimble, who developed the Shepherd of the Hills Farm and Outdoor Theater. Finally, in 1977, the Missouri Chamber of Commerce honored Mary as the "Leading Lady of Missouri Tourism."

1976: Company Expansion to Pigeon Forge, Tennessee

The Herschends' company undertook its first expansion out of state in 1976, acquiring Gold Rush Junction Park, a run-down theme park in Pigeon Forge, Tennessee. After investing about $1 million in upgrades to the park, the facility reopened as Silver Dollar City, Tennessee. Within three years attendance at the park quadrupled to 500,000. Soon after, the Herschends formally established Silver Dollar City Corporation and set up a four-person board of directors.

The early 1980s was a period of continued expansion for Silver Dollar City Corporation. The company opened White Water water park in Branson in 1980. It also built four other water parks, located in the Oklahoma City and Atlanta areas. Three of the parks were not successful and were later sold by the company. Sadly, Mary Herschend passed away in 1983, but her sons were committed to continuing to evolve and grow the family business that their parents had created.

In 1986, Jack and Peter Herschend entered into their first corporate partnership when they initiated a working relationship with country music star Dolly Parton. They renamed their Tennessee theme park Dollywood, as it was in her hometown, and gave it a Dolly Parton theme throughout.

The Herschends were also committed to keeping the Branson tourism business strong, and worked with other local leaders to extend the tourism calendar in 1988. Silver Dollar City and several other Branson attractions and accommodations stayed open about three weeks into November for the first Ozark Mountain Christmas. Eventually the tourism season was extended through December, a move that would become the single most successful economic development project of the Branson community, according to HFE's business history.

1990s: New Facilities, Special Events, and Festivals

Through the early 1990s Branson tourism saw tremendous growth, catering to families and retirees. The Herschends added to the entertainment allure of the Branson area by erecting a 4,000-seat theater, the area's largest, called the Grand Palace. Many of the biggest names in country and pop music have entertained at the Grand Palace over the years. The following year they opened Grand Village, a themed shopping complex adjacent to the theater. In 1991, Silver Dollar City took in approximately $90 million in revenues from its properties (including Dollywood in Tennessee).

By 1992, the company's revenues were expected to exceed $110 million. That year the corporation began what would be a long-term involvement in special events by partnering with Radio City Entertainment to produce and host the Radio City Christmas Spectacular in the Grand Palace. Adding variety to the mix of tourist attractions and choices in Branson, the Herschends had a 750-seat paddlewheel boat built in 1995, which it launched on nearby Table Rock Lake and christened the *Showboat Branson Belle*. The boat offered lunch and dinner cruises including entertainment. Silver Dollar City attendance reached 1.7 million people in 1995.

The Herschends formed another partnership in 1998. They entered into a long-term lease with the State of Georgia to manage the state's historical theme park, Stone Mountain Park, near Atlanta. The company intended to spend $75 million redeveloping the theme park over a ten-year period to tell the story of the South. With a theme of Southern history, heritage, and spirit, the plan included an indoor roller coaster, theaters, shops, an old-time depot town, large children's play area, a four-dimensional theater, and a main street from reconstruction-era Atlanta.

2000: National Industry Recognition for Excellence

Silver Dollar City added a new water roller coaster called Buzz Saw Falls in 1999. By then the Branson theme park boasted more than two million visitors annually. In 2000 Silver Dollar City gained worldwide recognition when it earned the annual Applause Award. The Applause Award honor was "the theme park industry's top award of excellence based on management, operations, creativity and ingenuity." The next year Silver Dollar City was awarded the Thea Award for excellence and outstanding achievement in themed entertainment from the Themed Entertainment Association.

Company expansion continued in 2001. The Herschends opened another water park, this time in partnership with Dolly Parton; it was Dolly's Splash Country water park in Pigeon Forge, near Dollywood. That year the Herschends began involvement with Ride the Ducks, an established Branson tourist activity that involved taking visitors on exciting and entertaining land and water tours using World War II amphibious vehicles. Silver Dollar City Corporation used its resources to expand the Ride the Ducks concept to Baltimore in 2002, Philadelphia in 2003, and Memphis in 2005.

The company purchased assets and property of an amusement park near Silver Dollar City, called Branson USA, planning to rebuild and reopen the park with a new name in a few years. In the spring of 2003, Celebration City debuted. The renovated complex was now a $40 million theme park which highlighted key periods in the 20th century. It was the largest new theme park development in the country, and featured one section reflecting traditional amusement parks at the turn of the 20th century, and another section reflecting the period from the 1940s through 1960s, "the Route 66 period."

The Herschends intended to market the new theme park as an afternoon and evening venue for entertainment so it would

not compete head-to-head with Silver Dollar City. One of its advertising slogans said, "After a day at Silver Dollar City, Celebration City is the Night Thing to Do." Silver Dollar City closed at 7 p.m., and Celebration City was scheduled to be opened from 3 p.m. until 10 or 11 p.m., with an evening special effects show featuring music, lasers, a huge water screen, and fireworks show at closing time. Attractions included a Victorian style main street, the Ozark WildCat wooden roller coaster, and some 29 additional rides.

2003: Name Change Reflecting Diverse Properties and Family Roots

In 2003, the Herschends officially changed the company name to the Herschend Family Entertainment Corporation (HFE) because this name more accurately reflected the company's diverse holdings, which at the time numbered 19 properties in six states. The name change, however, did not affect the names of any of the Herschends' individual parks. That year the company also helped Dolly Parton open and operate her four Dixie Stampede Dinner Shows in Pigeon Forge, Branson, Myrtle Beach, and Orlando.

The opening of Celebration City appeared to negatively impact attendance at Silver Dollar City. By mid-August, attendance at the 40+ year-old theme park was down 125,000 from the previous year. The overall attendance at the Branson attractions was up slightly, however. To counter revenue problems, HFE did some restructuring in late 2003, including minor job reductions. But according to *Amusement Business* magazine, the reductions were no more than 2 percent at any HFE site.

What also hurt the company at the time was declining attendance at Stone Mountain Park in Atlanta. HFE requested, and was granted, a reduction in rent by the state of Georgia, saving $2.2 million that year. In the previous five years, the Herschends had invested $80 million in Stone Mountain Park improvements.

After a successful three-year partnership with Ride the Ducks International, HFE purchased the company in 2004. At the time RTDI had attractions in Branson, Philadelphia, Baltimore, and Memphis. HFE also purchased Hawaiian Falls water parks in Texas. In November of that year Peter and Jack Herschend were inducted into the International Association of Amusement Parks and Attractions (IAAPA). IAAPA affirmed the brothers for their experience, commitment to family values, sound business development, originality, and strategic vision.

2005 and Beyond

In 2005 the company moved to new headquarters in Georgia, which included expanded creative studios intended to monitor and ensure strict adherence to theming and presentation at all HFE properties. The Herschends' baby, Silver Dollar City, had grown to 50 acres and hosted five festivals each year, including World Fest, American Music Fest, and Children's Fest. Approximately 100 resident crafters regularly demonstrated woodcarving, glassblowing, pottery, basket weaving leather crafts, and candle making. Silver Dollar City attracted more than two million visitors a year and employed 1,500 people. Its offerings included 12 performance stages, 11 rides, 12 restaurants, and 60 shops.

Herschend Family Entertainment was poised for growth and continuing improvements at its many properties. In a 2005 news release, HFE CEO and President Joel Manby stated: "Ever since Herschend Family Entertainment was but one single property almost five decade ago, Silver Dollar City in Branson, leadership has kept a keen eye on bringing to life the colorful history of geographic regions. Our focus remains on our corporate hallmark to capture the imaginations of today's families while immersing them in multi-layered experiences." One colleague in the theme park business commented online (on Thrillnetwork.com) about the Herschend family enterprise: "They are quietly one of the best amusement park chains in existence." Most likely that reputation would carry the company well into a successful and profitable future.

Principal Divisions

Dollywood Corporation; Ride the Ducks International; Silver Dollar City; Hawaiian Falls Water Parks.

Principal Competitors

Busch Entertainment Corporation; Cedar Fair, L.P. (FUN); Hershey Entertainment & Resorts Company.

Further Reading

Chesnut, Mark, "Celebration City Rolls out Good Times in Branson," *Travel Weekly*, May 26, 2003, p. 23.

Gubernick, Lisa, "A curb on the ego," *Forbes*, September 14, 1992, p. 418.

"Herschend Family Entertainment Enters 2005 Season with Expansion Plans," http://www.thrillride.com, April 12, 2005.

"Herschends Join IAAPA Hall of Fame," http://www.mobile .thrillnetwork.com, November 19, 2004.

Medina, Kari, "All-American Celebration: Branson Welcomes the Herschend Family's Second Area Theme Park," *Travel Agent*, April 28, 2003, p. 78.

O'Brien, Tim, "Celebration' Pays Off of Mo.'s White Water," *Amusement Business*, July 21, 2003, p. 5.

——, "$40 M Celebration Brewing in Branson: New Part Set for Spring Debut," *Amusement Business*, January 13, 2003, p. 1.

——, "Herschend President Positions Co. for Future," *Amusement Business*, August 18, 2003, p. 3.

——, "Parent Firm Changes Name," *Amusement Business*, December 16, 2002, p. 8.

——, "Silver Dollar City Expands Holdings in Branson, Mo; Purchases Themer," *Amusement Business*, December 10, 2001, p. 8.

Payton, Crystal, "The Story of Branson's Silver Dollar City," Springfield, Mo.: A Lens & Pen Production, 1997.

Powell, Tim, "Silver Dollar City Flips for Festivals; Park Eyeing Record Attendance," *Amusement Business*, June 17, 1996, p. 31.

Sengupta, Somini, "Georgia Park Is to Hail Southern Spirit," *New York Times*, October 8, 2000, p. 18.

Smith, Ben, "Board Approves Missouri Firm's Proposal to Redevelop Stone Mountain, Ga., Park," *Knight Ridder/Tribune Business News*, September 19, 2000.

—Mary Heer-Forsberg

Hong Kong and China Gas Company Ltd.

23/F 363 Java Road, N Point
Hong Kong
Telephone: +852 2963 3388
Fax: +852 2561 6182
Web site: http://www.towngas.com

Public Company
Incorporated: 1862
Employees: 1,954
Sales: HKD 8.15 billion
Stock Exchanges: Hong Kong OTC
Ticker Symbol: HOKCY (ADR)
NAIC: 221210 Natural Gas Distribution

Hong Kong and China Gas Company Ltd. (also known as Towngas) is the oldest public utility operating in Hong Kong. The company is also the sole supplier of piped gas to the Hong Kong region—the company far outdistances its primary LPG competitors. Towngas company has extended beyond Hong Kong itself, however, to claim a growing presence in mainland China. The company serves more than 1.5 million customers through a pipeline network of some 3,000 kilometers. On the Chinese mainland, the company is active in some 30 city gas pipeline projects—including six new projects added in 2004 alone. Most of the company's mainland operations are carried out through a number of joint ventures, including in Guangzhou, Zhongshan, Fangcun, Panyu, Beijing, Wuhan, Anquing, Maanshan, Shunde, and others. Towngas produces its own gas, mostly from two naphtha-based production plants in Hong Kong. Its entry into the mainland market has been aided by majority shareholder Henderson Investment's strong relationship with the Chinese government. Henderson Chairman Lee Shau Kee is also chairman of Towngas. In 2004, the company posted revenues of HKD 8.15 billion.

Beginnings in the 19th Century

Hong Kong and China Gas Company's origins stretch back to the 1860s, making it Hong Kong's—and China's—oldest public utility. Although incorporated in England in 1862, the company focused from the outset on the Hong Kong market, introducing the town's first piped gas in 1864. The company, which became popularly known as Towngas, built a 24-kilometer pipeline network that provided gas for 500 street lamps, as well as to a number of buildings in the British colony.

The company set up its own gas production facilities, using coal as its feedstock. Hong Kong Island remained the company's sole market until the end of the 19th century and through most of the 20th century as well. In the 1930s, Towngas faced a setback when one of its gasholders was destroyed in an explosion. In 1956, however, the company commissioned a new and larger gasholder at Ma Tau Kok. Four years later, the company listed its shares on the Hong Kong Stock Exchange for the first time.

In the mid-1960s, Towngas began seeking an alternative feedstock source for its gas production. The company switched to fuel oil in 1967. By 1973, however, Towngas begun investigating the use of the more environmentally friendly naphtha for its feedstock. Then in 1977, the company converted most of its gas production to naphtha.

By then, Towngas had begun expanding its range of operations, adding the Chung Hom Kom and Stanley districts of Hong Kong Island in 1975. In that year, also, the company began supplying gas to the nearby Kowloon peninsula for the first time, in a joint venture with the Hong Kong Housing Authority. This new market helped the company boost its total customer base to more than 170,000 by 1980.

After 120 years as a British corporation, Towngas transferred its registration to Hong Kong. Part of the motivation behind this move came from the arrival of Hong Kong property development tycoon Lee Shau Kee, through Henderson Land, as Towngas's majority shareholder. In 1983, Lee took over as Towngas chairman.

Lee Shau Kee, whose father had operated a money-changing business in Guangzhou prior to China's Communist revolution, was sent to Hong Kong in 1948 with half of the family's assets (the other half was sent to Macau with Lee's brother). By 1958, Lee had entered the real estate market, taking advantage of the boom in the Hong Kong property market. In 1972, Lee had

<table>
<tr><td>

Company Perspectives:

Mission: To provide our customers with a safe, reliable supply of gas and the caring, competent and efficient service they expect, while working to preserve, protect and improve our environment.

</td><td>

Key Dates:

1862: Hong Kong and China Gas Company (Towngas) is incorporated in England.
1884: The first gas pipeline is launched in Hong Kong City.
1960: Towngas goes public with a listing on the Hong Kong Stock Exchange.
1975: The company extends its services onto the Kowloon peninsula.
1977: The company switches to naphtha as its primary feedstock.
1982: The company transfers its registration to Hong Kong as Henderson Investment becomes the majority shareholder.
1983: Henderson Chairman Lee Shau Kee becomes Towngas chairman.
1986: A new gas production plant is constructed at Tai Po.
1995: The company's first joint venture is launched on the Chinese mainland, in Panyu, Guangdong province.
2001: The company launches its first joint venture in Jiangsu province.
2005: The company enters Beijing with its first joint venture.

</td></tr>
</table>

decided to focus on property development, founding Henderson Land Development in 1973, and, in 1975, acquiring Wing Tai, which later became Henderson Investment. Through Henderson Land Development, Lee established himself as one of Hong Kong's top businessmen, building a fortune worth billions of dollars.

Powering Growth in the 1980s

Lee, who remained chairman of Henderson, was to play an important role in Towngas's expansion, not least because of his strong relationship with mainland Chinese authorities, as well as his powerful economic position in Hong Kong. Under Lee, Towngas launched a new period of expansion.

Towngas now became interested in widening its reach to include all of the Hong Kong region, including Kowloon and the New Territories. In support of this, the company began building a new high-pressure pipeline to bring gas to the New Territories. Towngas's connection with Henderson provided the company with a solid foundation for growth; Henderson played a leading role in developing the New Territories, outfitting its residential developments so that they could be connected to Towngas's pipeline. At the same time, the Hong Kong government also chose to outfit its own new housing developments for Towngas's gas. Towngas's penetration in the region's new housing developments reached up to 90 percent during the decade.

By 1983, the company boasted more than 300,000 customers. By 1989, the company had more than doubled that figure, topping 617,000 customers by mid-1989. In order to ensure its gas supply for its rapidly growing network, Towngas launched construction of a new gas production plant at Tai Po Plant in the early 1980s. The company commissioned the first phase of that plant in 1986. That facility rapidly ramped up its production, and by the end of the decade, the Tai Po plant supplied some 86 percent of Towngas's supply requirements.

Towngas continued its rapid growth into the new decade, topping 760,000 customers in 1991. The company increased its production capacity, spending some HKD 1 billion (approximately $120 million) to triple capacity at its main Tai Po gasworks in the early 1990s. The company also extended its gas pipeline to new parts of Hong Kong, reaching Yuen Long in 1991, and Tuen Mun and Tin Shui in 1992.

In 1994, Towngas launched construction of a new pipeline to extend its reach to Lantau Island. That area was expected to experience a strong population with the opening of a new airport serving the Hong Kong market. The company also targeted expansion into the fast-growing Discovery Bay area in the mid-1990s. At the same time, Towngas launched a series of initiatives to encourage customers to abandon a number of

electrical appliances in favor of gas-driven appliances. As such, the company teamed up with appliance maker Renal, based in Japan, to develop a gas-powered clothes dryer adapted to the Hong Kong market. The two companies also began designing a new stove incorporating a gas-driven rice cooker. For the restaurant sector, the company helped develop a gas-fired pig roaster capable of roasting from six to ten pigs at a time. These initiatives helped boost the group's customer base past the one million mark by 1994.

Mainland Expansion for the New Century

Yet Towngas began looking forward to new markets by the mid-1990s. Initially, the company investigated expansion opportunities elsewhere in the Southeast Asian region. In 1993, however, the company's interest turned to the underdeveloped Chinese mainland, which led to a first feasibility study that year. This quickly led to a joint venture agreement to establish gas distribution operations in the cities of Panyu and Zhongsan. These projects got underway in 1995. The following year, the company added a new joint venture to enter the city of Zhonshan as well.

Towngas quickly lined up new joint ventures: In 1996, the company signed agreements to enter Guangzhou, Fangcun, Shenzhen, Shantou, Dongguan, and Zhauhai in the Guangdong region. The first of these, Guangzhou and Fangcun, launched operations by the following year. Once again, the company's relationship with Lee Shau Kee helped pave the way for its rapid growth in these new markets.

Towngas's expansion onto the mainland took on greater importance in the early 2000s, as its total customer base topped 1.5 million. While this made the company the largest gas supplier in the Asian region, it also meant that it had reached, for the most part, the limits of its growth in Hong Kong itself, a market that counted only 1.7 million households. Yet the extension of its network onto the mainland was not the company's only effort at future expansion.

In 2000, the company launched a number of diversification efforts, such as the creation of GH-Fusion Ltd., a subsidiary dedicated to the production of polyethylene fittings for the mainland market, launched in 2000. The company also set up ECO Energy Company Ltd., which began constructing LPG filling stations in West Kowloon and Chai Wan. In another direction, Towngas began producing dry ice using the carbon dioxide produced as a byproduct of its gas production process.

Nonetheless, growth on the mainland remained Towngas's primary motor into the 2000s. In 2001, the company formed its first joint venture beyond Guangdong, with a project to begin supplying the Suzhou Industrial Park in Jiangsu province. This was followed shortly after by joint ventures in Yixing, also in Jiangsu, and in Qingdao and Laoshan. By 2002, the company's gas pipeline network topped 3,000 kilometers for the first time.

Towngas's mainland prospects were buoyed with the Chinese government's decision to deregulate the country's piped-gas market. In order to enhance its fast-growing position in the country, Towngas announced its intention to launch investments of more than HKD 1 billion in 2003. The company also stated that it was considering a separate stock market listing for its mainland operations by as early as 2006.

In the meantime, Towngas continued to build out its mainland network, adding six new joint ventures in China in 2004 alone. These included agreements in Anhui province for a gas midstream project, and the creation of a city piped-gas venture in Huzhou. By early 2005, the company had entered the Beijing market as well. Backed by Lee Shau Kee and Henderson Investment, Towngas appeared certain to play a major role in China's gas utility market in the new century.

Principal Subsidiaries

Anquing Hong Kong and China Gas Company Limited (China; 50%); Barnaby Assets Ltd.; Changzhou Hong Kong and China Gas Company Limited (China; 50%); Danetop Services Ltd.; ECO Energy Company Ltd.; Empire Bridge Investments Ltd.; Hong Kong & China Gas (China) Ltd.; Hong Kong & China Gas Investment Ltd.; Maanshan Hong Kong and China Gas Company Limited (China; 50%); Monarch Properties Ltd.; Nanjing Hong Kong and China Gas Company Limited (China; 50%); Pathview Properties Ltd.; Planwise Properties Ltd.; Prominence Properties Ltd.; P-Tech Engineering Company Ltd.; Quality Testing Services Ltd.; Shunde Hong Kong and China Gas Company Limited (China; 50%); Starmax Assets Ltd.; Summit Result Development Ltd.; Superfun Enterprises Ltd.; Suzhou Hong Kong and China Gas Company Limited (China; 50%); Taian Taishan Hong Kong and China Gas Company Limited (China; 50%); Towngas Enterprise Ltd.; Towngas International Company Ltd.; Towngas Investment Company Ltd.; Towngas Technologies Ltd.; Towngas Telecommunications Fixed Network Ltd.; Upwind International Ltd.; U-Tech Engineering Company Ltd.; Uticom Ltd.; Weifang Hong Kong and China Gas Company Limited (China; 50%); Weihai Hong Kong and China Gas Company Limited (China; 50%); Wuhan Natural Gas Company Ltd. (China; 50%); Zibo Hong Kong and China Gas Company Limited (China; 50%).

Principal Competitors

Shenyang Gas Company General; Beijing Coal Gas Co.; XinAo Gas Holdings Ltd.; Hongkong Electric Holdings Limited; Changchun Gas Company Ltd.; Tianjin Tianlian Public Utilities Company Ltd.; Dongguan SHV LPG Company Ltd.; Sinolink Worldwide Holdings Ltd.; Panva Gas Holdings Ltd.; CLP Holdings Limited; CNOOC Limited.

Further Reading

Hayes, David, "Hong Kong and China Gas Seeks New Markets," *Gas World International,* February 1996, p. 10.

"HK & China Gas Approved to Take 30% of Shenzhen Gas," *Business Daily Update,* April 19, 2004.

"Hong Kong and China Gas Plans to Spend HKD 1 Billion in China in Next Year," *Xinhua Financial News—China Focus,* September 2, 2003.

"Hong Kong & China Gas to March into Beijing," *Beijing Modern Business Daily,* June 21, 2005.

—M.L. Cohen

Huttig Building Products, Inc.

555 Maryville University Drive, Suite 240
St. Louis, Missouri 63141
U.S.A.
Telephone: (314) 216-2600
Fax: (314) 216-2601
Web site: http://www.huttig.com

Public Company
Founded: 1885
Employees: 2,427
Sales: $938.4 million (2004)
Stock Exchanges: New York
Ticker Symbol: HBP
NAIC: 423310 Lumber, Plywood, Millwork, and Wood
　　　Panel Merchant Wholesalers

St. Louis-based Huttig Building Products, Inc. is the largest distributor of building products in the United States, selling nearly $1 billion in products each year from about 50 distribution centers. Products are used in new home construction as well as remodeling and repair work. General building products include lumber, panels, roofing, siding, insulation, dry wall, gutters, and nails. Millwork products include interior and exterior doors, storm doors, patio doors, windows, stair parts, frames, columns, and mouldings. The company's primary customers are building material dealers, which in turn serve contractors and professional builders. Huttig is a public company listed on the New York Stock Exchange.

Heritage Dating to the Civil War Era

Huttig was founded by brothers Charles F. and William Huttig, natives of Germany. They immigrated to the United States in the mid-1850s when Charles, the eldest, was just 19, settling in Muscatine, Iowa, because they had friends in the city. Charles worked as a mason and eventually became a masonry contractor. William, meanwhile, became a music teacher. With the outbreak of the Civil War in 1861 he formed a regimental band for the 35th Iowa Volunteer Infantry. When regimental bands were dismissed by order of the war department, William was at loose ends. He

returned to Muscatine, and in 1862 started a grocery store with his brother. In 1868 they turned their attention to lumber, investing $30,000 to establish a sawmill and lumberyard operating under the company name Huttig Brothers Lumber Company, taking advantage of Muscatine's strategic location on the Mississippi River. They brought in a partner in 1869, acquired the mill business of Cadle and Mulford, and began manufacturing doors, blinds, and window sash under the name of Huttig Brothers & Falter. After Falter left six years later, the company changed its name to Huttig Brothers Manufacturing Company. Before then, however, the company was almost put out of business by a flood caused by the destruction of Muscatine's levees in April 1870, which swept away Huttig's stock of lumber. To make matters worse a fire completely destroyed the factory. The brothers wasted no time in replacing the plant with a new, larger facility, located far removed from the river.

In 1880 Huttig Brothers was incorporated, followed a year later by the opening of a new, larger plant in Muscatine. The extra capacity was put to good use during the 1880s, as the growth of the railroads opened up new markets for the company. But it also became apparent that these new markets could be served better by branch offices, thus setting the stage for Huttig's geographic expansion, shepherded by a second generation of the family. In 1883 Charles's eldest son, William, was dispatched to Kansas City, Missouri, to serve as manager of the first branch, Western Sash and Door Company. After this operation proved successful, Charles's second eldest son, Charles H., was sent to St. Louis to establish a second branch, the forefather of today's Huttig Building Products, then known as Huttig Sash & Door Company. With $40,000 in seed money, Charles H. bought an existing business, Gray and Holekamp, in December 1885 and began distributing the door and sash products produced by the Muscatine plant as well as other manufacturers. Less than two years later, the branch added its own manufacturing capabilities by purchasing a small factory. Business was so strong that the company quickly outgrew its facilities, leading to the 1892 acquisition of a building large enough to accommodate both a warehouse and a factory.

The year 1892 was also a turning point because Charles F. Huttig, whose health was beginning to fail, decided to sell the

Muscatine company, Huttig Brothers Manufacturing Company. With that money he then bought stock in the Kansas City and St. Louis branches, which had become separate corporations. Although Huttig Manufacturing Company would continue to do business in Muscatine, it was no longer connected to Huttig Sash and Door Company.

In a relatively short period of time, Charles H. Huttig firmly established himself in the St. Louis business community. Prior to joining the family business he had cut his teeth in banking at Cook, Musser and Company. Now in 1897 he was named president of the Third National Bank of St. Louis. He remained president of Huttig Sash and Door, but increasingly he relied on a chief lieutenant, Alfred J. Siegel, to run the company, serving as secretary and general manager. This arrangement lasted for the next 15 years, during which time the company prospered but also suffered from a June 1911 fire that destroyed the St. Louis complex. A competitor, the William G. Frye Manufacturing Company, was immediately acquired, but it burned to the ground the very next day. Huttig managed to arrange for help from other manufacturers, enough to scrape by. Less than seven months after the fires, the company moved into a new state-of-the-art millwork plant, which opened in January 1912. Around this time, Charles H. Huttig began to experience deteriorating health, leading to an operation in September 1912. He appeared to be on his way to recovery, but he suffered a relapse and returned to the hospital for a second operation in November. He now resigned as Huttig's president, naming Siegel his replacement, and ultimately succumbed in July 1913.

After 26 years in a subordinate role, Siegel took charge of Huttig at a key historical moment, the eve of a world war. Siegel was quick to recognize that despite President Wilson's pledge to keep the country out of the European conflict, the United States would eventually be drawn in, and that Huttig would be called upon to support the war effort. In order to do so effectively, it would need branch offices. The only one established in time was in Memphis, Tennessee, as the Memphis Sash and Door Company. When the United States did declare war in April 1917, Huttig was contracted by the U.S. military to manufacture airplanes, work the company took on in addition to the production of wooden ammunition boxes, ship joinery, and building supplies used to construct 21 army camps, six office training camps, nine air fields, and seven hospitals.

Post-World War I Expansion

When World War I ended in November 1918, pent-up consumer demand led to continued expansion of the Huttig opera-

tion. In July 1919 a subsidiary, the Birmingham Sash & Door Company, was opened in Birmingham, Alabama. A year later Huttig entered into a joint venture with Spokane, Washington-based White Pine Sash Company, to establish a sash factory in Missoula, Montana, which took the name Missoula White Pine Sash Company, with Huttig owning a controlling interest. The pace of Huttig's geographic expansion increased in the 1920s. First, the company looked to the fast-growing Southwest, spurred by the energy industry. In 1920 Dallas Sash & Door Company was established and opened for business in September 1921. Florida also attracted the company's attention, leading to the 1923 creation of a Jacksonville operation. Business quickly overwhelmed the leased warehouse and a new facility was built, opening in February 1925. In that same year a Miami warehouse was built to accommodate the growing Florida business. During the first half of the 1920s Memphis Sash & Door Company became a Huttig subsidiary and constructed a new facility. Birmingham Sash & Door also experienced strong growth during this period, resulting in the construction of a new warehouse as well.

Huttig's growth during the early 1920s occurred despite Siegel's poor health. In 1926 he was heavily involved in putting together a major merger, the creation of United States Door Company by combining the interests of Huttig, White Pine Sash Company, Missoula White Pine Sash Company, and the major Pacific Coast fir door and plywood manufacturers. But Siegel's sudden death in November 1926 scuttled the deal and United States Door Company never came to pass. Moreover, Huttig found itself bereft of seasoned leadership. Siegel's son, Roy R. Siegel, was being groomed as a replacement but was not yet ready to take over. Hence, the board's chairman, E.L. McColm, resigned his post, stepped into the breach and assumed the presidency, with the younger Siegel serving as first vice-president. Turnover at the top did not prevent Huttig from continuing to expand, however. Huttig took over a warehouse operation in Columbus, Ohio, in 1926, and a branch office was established in Charlotte, North Carolina, in 1927 to serve the Carolinas. After 16 months, McColm turned over the presidency to another seasoned executive, George W. Simmons, a vice-president of the Chase National Bank. He was immediately faced with some difficult choices. The Florida land boom collapsed suddenly, forcing the closure of the Jacksonville and Miami branches. In addition, Huttig sold its Charlotte operation in 1929. Simmons's tenure as the Huttig head proved brief, however. He was killed in an accident in May 1930, and this time Roy Siegel was deemed ready to succeed his father as Huttig's president.

The younger Siegel took over under difficult circumstances as the country, a few months after the 1929 stock crash, tumbled into a deep depression. Under his leadership, Huttig instituted a number of belt-tightening measures in order to simply stay in business. In 1931 the Houston operation was sold, but by 1934 the worst was over and Huttig began looking to resume its expansion efforts. Once again the company opened a branch in Charlotte to take advantage of growth in the Carolinas. Also in 1934 Huttig acquired an operation from the Roanoke Glass and Door Company, establishing an operation in Roanoke, Virginia, to serve the Shenandoah Valley and Washington, D.C. markets. Its affairs were in such good shape that in 1936 Huttig was able to complete a major acquisition, the purchase of Louisville,

---

Key Dates:

1868: Huttig Brothers Lumber Company is launched.
1885: Huttig launches the St. Louis operation.
1919: Birmingham Sash & Door Company is established.
1936: W.J. Hughes and Sons Company is acquired.
1957: American Sash & Door Company is acquired.
1968: Crane Co. acquires a controlling interest.
1999: Crane Co. spins off Huttig.
2003: Michael Lupo turns around the company.

Kentucky-based W.J. Hughes and Sons Company, which maintained branches in Paducah, Kentucky, and Knoxville, Tennessee. The Paducah business was shut down but the Louisville and Knoxville operations were brought into the fold and headed by Huttig executives. It was also during the late 1930s that the branch operations began to become less dependent on the St. Louis warehouse, due to the high shipping costs that put the branches at a competitive disadvantage. Huttig now allowed the branches to fill their own orders and limited the St. Louis warehouse to the serving of markets not covered by Huttig branches. Moreover, the company looked to further expand its branch operations to new strategic locations.

With Europe already engulfed in World War II by 1940, the United States began building up its military. For Huttig this meant the increased need for building supplies to construct camps and bases as well as housing for workers in armament plants and other factories supporting the war effort. To meet rising demand Huttig reopened its Miami warehouse in 1940 and a year later opened a large new warehouse in Louisville. After the United States entered the war in December 1941, most of Huttig's business was war-related for the next four years. In addition to building supplies, Huttig produced items for the military such as wood truck body parts and ammunition cases.

After the war ended in 1945 and the country overcame a brief recession, Huttig expanded to keep pace with the postwar building boom, as servicemen returned home, married, and entered the new suburban housing developments where the Baby Boom generation would be raised. The Miami branch moved into a new plant in 1946, followed a year later by a new facility for the Dallas branch, and a new plant in Knoxville in 1948. A new branch was then opened in Nashville, Tennessee, in 1949. Around this time management also began considering what to do with its 40-year-old St. Louis plant, which was outdated, costly to maintain, and no longer conveniently located. In addition, millwork was falling out of favor with the new generation of homeowners, who were in the market for less expensive materials. The company decided to exit this part of the business and the plant was sold in 1951. Huttig began building a new warehouse in the western part of St. Louis, which opened in 1954. Also of note during the 1950s, Huttig opened a branch in Atlanta in 1955 on land purchased a decade earlier when it became apparent that the growing city fell into a crack, unable to be adequately served by Huttig branches in Florida, Alabama, North Carolina, or Tennessee. In addition, in 1955 the Knoxville branch expanded its facility, as did Nashville a year later. The Columbus warehouse was replaced by a

new building in 1957, the same year that Huttig moved into the Kansas City, Missouri market by acquiring American Sash & Door Company. To close the decade, in April 1959 Siegel, after serving the company for 34 years, turned over the presidency to T.R. Armstrong. Siegel stayed on as chairman until November 1963 and died less than a year later in September 1964.

Dissolving the St. Louis Branch in the 1960s and Steady Growth into the 21st Century

During the 1960s Huttig consolidated its operations, merging American Sash & Door Company and Birmingham Sash & Door Company. Missoula White Pine Sash Company merged into the parent company, as did Huttig Sash & Door Company of Texas. The company also grew through acquisitions in the 1960s, purchasing the General Sash & Door Company of Tulsa, Oklahoma, in 1966, followed by the addition of Oklahoma City-based Lumbermens Supply Company in 1967. That year also saw the liquidation of the St. Louis branch due to high wages and other factors. Another significant development in 1967 was the purchase of 20 percent of the company's stock by the Crane Co. A year later Crane acquired more shares, gaining a 51 percent controlling interest, and by March 1971 it owned 87 percent of the business. Crane was founded in 1855 in Chicago to produce copper and brass castings used by the railroad industry. Over the years, Crane expanded beyond metal valves and fittings to manufacture fire hydrants, water pumps, elevators, bathroom fixtures, and basic materials businesses. The addition of Huttig added to Crane's portfolio of building products.

Under the direction of its new parent company, Huttig opened an Orlando, Florida branch in 1968 and added operations in Mobile, Alabama, and New Orleans by acquiring the jobbing division of McPhillips Manufacturing Company. A year later, Huttig acquired nine branches covering four states of the Rock Island Corporation's wholesale division. As it moved into the 1970s, Huttig closed operations in Kansas City and Nashville that were no longer performing up to expectations. At the same time, the company aggressively moved into new growth areas. A Fort Myers, Florida operation was opened in 1973, followed a year later by the acquisition of Lexington, Kentucky-based Combs Company. By now Huttig was operating 27 distribution facilities in 26 states along with its lone millwork manufacturing plant in Oregon, all of which in 1976 combined to generate sales in excess of $100 million for the first time in company history. Huttig continued to expand in the second half of the 1970s, adding facilities in Des Moines, Iowa, and Rockford, Illinois, as well as glazing operations in Charlotte and Louisville. Three more branches were added in 1978: Chicago; Kernersville, North Carolina; and Tri-Cities, Tennessee.

Despite poor economic conditions that resulted in declining housing starts, Huttig managed to grow during the early 1980s. It added Houston and Dallas operations through the acquisition of Lone Star Wholesale Company, and opened yet another Florida distribution center, this one in Clearwater. In 1982 Huttig acquired Palmetto Sash & Door Company and Southern Manufacturing Company of Orangeburg, South Carolina, to expand its presence in the Carolinas. A year later a new distribution center was opened in Dothan, Alabama. The 1985 acquisition of Madison Millwork, Inc. added a branch in Jackson,

Tennessee, strategically located to serve Spring Hill, Tennessee, home to the new General Motors Saturn plant. Also in 1985, Huttig acquired warehouses in Albuquerque, New Mexico, and Green Bay, Wisconsin, to close out its first 100 years in operation.

Over the next 15 years Huttig enjoyed steady growth under Crane ownership, increasing sales in excess of $700 million and expanding the number of distribution centers to 41, but by 1999 it became apparent that both Huttig and Crane would be better off if Huttig were spun off as a separate company to pursue its own business strategy. In this way, Crane could focus on its role as a specialty manufacturer and untie the hands of Huttig's management, which wanted to keep pace with the competition in an industry undergoing consolidation. In conjunction with the spinoff, Huttig achieved much needed scale by acquiring the U.S. building products business of The Rugby Group PLC, which in 1998 posted sales of nearly $600 million from 33 distribution centers located in 35 states. Under the terms of the Huttig spinoff, Crane shareholders received 68 percent of Huttig's common stock and Rugby received the balance.

In addition to the economies of scale it hoped to realize from the addition of the Rugby assets, Huttig also expanded its presence in the Midwest and on the East Coast, thus positioning the company to better adapt to regional downturns. But after posting a profitable year in 2001, Huttig began to struggle despite the start of a major housing construction boom, leading to the resignation of its chief executive officer, Barry Kulpa, in March 2003. He was replaced by 70-year-old Michael Lupo on an interim basis, but after two months he asked to take the job on a permanent basis and the board agreed. A veteran turnaround artist, he quickly sized up the situation at Huttig, which he believed should have held a significant competitive advantage in the marketplace. "Instead," according to a *St. Louis Post Dispatch* profile, "he found chaos, born in part by a multilayered, top-down management structure with almost no accountability for what was happening in the warehouses. When he asked about performance at specific warehouses, he more often than not received shoulder shrugs. . . . Huttig's sales team was in disarray, as well. . . . And despite its national presence, Huttig was not serving several large metropolitan areas."

Lupo cut headcount in management and reallocated the money to beef up sales and field operations. To gain accountability, general managers were hired for each distribution center, responsible for inventory, sales, and marketing. The changes quickly began to pay off, and within the year Huttig was again profitable and looking to expand on its national platform. Lupo was committed to remaining as CEO through 2005; whether he stayed on or not, he already had succeeded in positioning Huttig for long-term growth.

Principal Subsidiaries

Huttig, Inc.; Huttig FSC, Inc.

Principal Competitors

Georgia-Pacific Corporation; Hughes Supply, Inc.; Weyerhaeuser Company.

Further Reading

Garrison, Chad, "Turnaround Specialist Lupo Works His Magic at Huttig," *St. Louis Business Journal,* March 12, 2004, p. 6.

"The Huttig Story," Chesterfield, Mo.: Huttig Sash & Door Company, 1985.

Larson, Scott, "Set Free by Parent, Huttig Buys Rugby," *National Home Center News,* November 8, 1999, p. 1.

Naudi, Jack, "Chief of Missouri-Based Building Products Firm Wants Recognition of Handiwork," *St. Louis Post-Dispatch,* April 22, 2004.

—Ed Dinger

Input/Output, Inc.

12300 Parc Crest Drive
Stafford, Texas 77477
U.S.A.
Telephone: (281) 933-3339
Fax: (281) 879-3626
Web site: http://www.i-o.com

Public Company
Incorporated: 1979
Employees: 743
Sales: $247.29 million (2004)
Stock Exchanges: New York
Ticker Symbol: IO
NAIC: 334519 Other Measuring and Controlling Device
   Manufacturing

Input/Output, Inc. is a leading provider of seismic imaging technology used by the oil and gas companies for the exploration and development of reservoirs both onshore and offshore. The company prides itself on offering its customers full-seismic imaging technology solutions, ranging from the design and planning of seismic surveys to the acquisition and processing of seismic data. Input/Output's products are designed for traditional three-dimensional data collection, as well as time-lapse, or four-dimensional, data collection. The company maintains operations in Europe, China, South America, and the Middle East.

Origins

Input/Output experienced several distinct periods of existence during its business life, operating for years as a small, relatively obscure firm before realizing explosive growth that suddenly disappeared, engendering years of managerial instability and shareholder unrest. The company's roller-coaster ride began in Houston in 1968, when Aubra E. Tilley started a small firm to develop and manufacture seismic equipment for use in the petroleum industry. Initially, the company developed and manufactured products that enhanced and complemented the seismic acquisition systems of other manufacturers, selling components to companies such as Texas Instruments, Sercel, and Geoscience rather than directly to customers involved in oil and gas development and exploration.

Tilley's firm joined an industry whose importance to exploration and drilling efforts would increase as technological advancements improved the capabilities of seismic data gathering. During the early days of seismology, the ability of seismic equipment to identify reservoirs of oil and gas was limited by a number of factors, including the sophistication of computer technology. When Input/Output was formed, massive, expensive mainframe computers possessed less computing power than latter-day desktops, severely reducing the cost-effectiveness, comprehensiveness, and accuracy of seismic studies. The objective of a seismic study was to identify geologic formations that were indicative of nearby oil or gas—a salt dome, for instance, often indicated the presence of an underground lake of oil beneath it. To obtain a picture of formations beneath the earth's surface, seismic engineers triggered a series of dynamite charges, creating sound waves that reverberated off rock layers below. Listening posts, or sensors, that were placed strategically on the surface received the sound waves, which then could be interpreted to yield a crude image of telltale formations. In early seismic studies, receiving sensors were arranged in a line to generate a two-dimensional view along a vertical plane cutting through the earth. As technology advanced and computer processing power became exponentially more powerful, the sensors were arranged in a two-dimensional grid on the surface, processing the reverberations to produce a three-dimensional image. The leap in seismic technology and capability was enormous, evolving into an extremely valuable tool for companies engaged in finding and producing oil and gas. "You drill your dry holes on the computer," an executive of a seismic equipment manufacturer remarked in a June 20, 1994 interview with *Forbes*. Input/Output not only witnessed the significant technological advances that shaped its industry, but also figured as one of the select companies initiating the technological revolution, becoming one of the leading competitors in the seismic equipment manufacturing industry.

For Input/Output, prominence came with time. When Tilley formed the company, his business scope did not pretend to achieve the heights the company later reached—a fundamental change in the company's corporate strategy enabled it assume a greater posture in its industry. Input/Output began its business life by serving the type of company it later became. Initially focused on developing products that improved and complemented the seismic acquisition systems made by others, the company introduced its first product one year after its formation. In 1969, Input/Output introduced the Seismic Source Synchronizer, an instrument that allowed the user to remotely control the timing of explosive seismic energy sources. The company began to assume a greater profile in its industry during the mid-1970s, when it diversified its operations for the first time. In 1975, Input/Output branched out into the development and production of data acquisition systems by introducing the Digital High Resolution Recording System (DHRRS), a system that monitored shallow seismic signals.

A Change of Strategy in the Early 1980s

Input/Output achieved enough recognition during its first decade of business to attract the attention of a much larger competitor in the petroleum industry. In 1980, after work had continued on the DHRRS during the second half of the 1970s in the form of several upgrades, Kidde, Inc. acquired Input/Output and moved the company the following year to new headquarters in Stafford, Texas, 16 miles southwest of Houston. Input/Output's new base of operations, a 35,200-square-foot facility that employed 100 workers, was directed to carry out management's new strategy for the future one year after it was constructed. By 1982, Input/Output senior officials had realized the company's opportunities for growth were limited by its focus on serving primary seismic equipment manufacturers, prompting them to concentrate their future efforts on developing data acquisition systems rather than just on producing components for data acquisition systems. The decision marked a turning point in Input/Output's history, though it would be years before the company would reap the financial rewards produced by its new market focus.

Input/Output engineers began working on developing the company's first primary seismic system in the new Stafford complex, launching research and development efforts that would take most of the decade to complete. During this period, as the small firm geared toward the production of a full system, control over its operations changed hands. In 1985, after Kidde, Inc. decided to divest its petroleum industry assets, Input/

Output was sold, remaining on its own until the end of 1986, when it was acquired by Dallas-based Triton Energy Corp. The acquisition did little to interrupt the work underway in Stafford. Input/Output, though it was a Triton Energy subsidiary, continued to operate as an independent company, enabling it to conclude its research and development work on its primary seismic equipment. After six years of work, the company unveiled its first system, appropriately named the Input/Output System One, in May 1988.

The introduction of System One moved Input/Output into the main sector of the seismic market, where its years of relative anonymity would end. System One, an eight-bit system, was an advanced land seismic acquisition system that made three-dimensional seismic surveys affordable, enabling the petroleum industry to begin the profound transition from two-dimensional to three-dimensional data acquisition. Exploration and production companies, consequently, began to realize a dramatic increase in the success ratios of their efforts. Improvements in the technology followed with the introduction of the System Two in 1991, the same year Input/Output completed its initial public offering (IPO) of stock, debuting on the NASDAQ. System Two, a 24-bit system, dramatically increased the range of recorded seismic signals, which enhanced sub-surface images that helped determine the ideal location for drilling a well. On the strength of System Two, Input/Output began a new chapter in its history, entering a period of explosive financial growth that stood in sharp contrast to the decades of modest growth that had preceded it.

By the beginning of the 1990s, advances in seismic equipment technology had dramatically improved the ability to identify telltale subsurface rock formations. The use of three-dimensional imaging to discover hidden reservoirs of oil and gas could increase the success rate for developmental drilling by as much as 80 percent, helping exploration and production companies avoid losses stemming from drilling dry holes, which could cost roughly $750,000. Input/Output, supported by System Two, was credited with making seismic equipment that was affordable for even small oil and gas companies, enabling the company to secure a substantial share of the market. By 1993, the company was estimated to control slightly more than 50 percent of the market for seismic equipment, maintaining a lead over its chief rival, the French company Sercel Inc., which commanded about 40 percent of the market.

Input/Output's sales grew rapidly during the first half of the decade, ending years of unspectacular growth. Between 1991 and 1995, annual sales swelled from $36 million to $134 million, driven by the demand for the company's affordable seismic equipment. In 1995, Input/Output completed one of the most significant acquisitions in its history, gaining assets that doubled the company's sales and net income. Midway through the year, the company purchased the seismic exploration products assets belonging to Western Atlas Inc. for roughly $120 million, adding offshore capabilities to its established strength in onshore seismic equipment. The assets, which generated $112 million in revenue in 1994, added marine seismic recording systems, vibrator source products, and geophone products to Input/Output's technology portfolio, helping Input/Output generate $278 million in revenue and $38.6 million in net income in 1996. Investors applauded the company's moves, driving its

---

Key Dates:

1968: Input/Output is founded by Aubra E. Tilley.
1975: The company diversifies into the development and production of data acquisition systems.
1980: Kidde, Inc. acquires Input/Output.
1982: Input/Output begins to focus on developing its own data acquisition systems.
1985: Input/Output is sold by Kidde, Inc. and is acquired the following year by Triton Energy Corp.
1988: The Input/Output System One is introduced.
1991: Triton Energy spins off Input/Output in a public offering.
1997: Input/Output begins to struggle financially.
2002: System Four is introduced.
2003: Robert Peebler is appointed president and chief executive officer.
2004: Input/Output acquires Concept Systems Holdings Limited and GX Technology Inc.

---

stock up to roughly $40 per share in mid-1996, a 20-fold increase from the company's share price five years earlier. Input/Output had become the darling of Wall Street. "The company has clearly been the greatest success story in the geophysical subsector for the last five years in terms of both technology and growth," an analyst remarked in an October 10, 1997 interview with the *Houston Business Journal*. But the company quickly faltered. The company's stock plunged to $14 per share by April 1997, 11 months after trading at $40 per share. Net income, which had reached $38.7 million in 1996, fell to $16.6 million the following year.

Problems Surfacing in the Late 1990s

The late 1990s proved to be a troublesome period for Input/Output. The company's chief executive officer, Gary Owens, resigned suddenly in the spring of 1997. The head of marketing resigned weeks later, followed by the company's chief financial officer, Robert Brindley. Shareholders filed a lawsuit against the company, Owens, and Brindley, alleging information about the company's business, products, sales, markets, financial condition, and business prospects had not been disseminated clearly to the public. One source of the company's troubles came from its main rival, the French firm Sercel. By 1996, the seismic technology on the market had matured, which prompted Sercel to cut the price of its products. Input/Output, fearing it would lose market share to Sercel, discounted its prices as well, which substantially reduced its profit margins. "They were too quick to discount products in anticipation of industry conditions," an analyst said in reference to Input/Output in an October 10, 1997 interview with *Houston Business Journal*. "They cut prices when they didn't really need to."

Managerial instability, stagnant sales, and declining stock value hobbled Input/Output's progress for the remainder of the 1990s, as the company fell from the heights it reached earlier in the decade. Owens was replaced by a petroleum engineer named W.J. "Zeke" Zeringue, the former president of Halliburton Energy Services, and Brindley's post was taken by Ron

Harris, but the two new executives left after little more than a year in charge. Zeringue reportedly clashed with Input/Output's board directors as the company's stock value continued to plummet. Commenting on the relationship between Zeringue and the company's board of directors in a June 4, 1999 interview with the *Houston Business Journal*, an analyst said, "It's like a couple that was at each other's throats for two years. Then they finally get divorced, and you ask what caused it? Who knows?" Zeringue and Harris resigned within weeks of each other in the spring of 1999, followed by the resignation of the company's chief technical officer before the end of the year, when Input/Output's stock was trading at a record low of $4.37.

As Input/Output entered the 21st century, the company continued to struggle, recording lackluster financial results and lacking stable leadership. An interim chief executive officer, Sam Smith, guided the company for nine months before Timothy J. Probert, a 27-year veteran at Baker Hughes International, took the helm. Probert resigned in early 2003 to take a job at Halliburton Co., which led to the hiring of a former Halliburton executive, Robert P. Peebler. Peebler, an Input/Output director since 1999, became president and chief executive officer in April 2003, inheriting a company mired in financial mediocrity. After reaching a record high $278 million in revenue in 1996, Input/Output's financial vitality waned. In 2001, the company collected $212 million in sales. In 2002, the total dropped to $118 million. The following year, sales rose to $150 million, but the total was nearly half the revenue volume collected by the company seven years earlier.

During the first years of Peebler's stewardship, encouraging progress was made in restoring Input/Output's financial health and in positioning the company for the future. In 2004, two important acquisitions were completed that helped increase sales nearly 65 percent and strengthen the company's technology portfolio. In February, the company paid $49.8 million for Concept Systems Holdings Limited, a Scotland-based software developer with applications tailored for offshore seismic analysis. The company's software was installed on towed streamer vessels as part of seabed monitoring systems. In June, Input/Output acquired GX Technology Inc., a Houston-based designer of customized imaging solutions for marine environments. The company paid $152.5 million for GX Technology, gaining a company whose services encompassed all elements in the seismic workflow, including survey planning, technology selection, project management, advanced processing, and final image rendering. Thanks in part to the two acquisitions, Input/Output generated $247 million in revenue in 2004. The increase buoyed hopes for the future, but a $3 million loss for the year coupled with the value of the company's stock, which was trading in the $7 range in 2005, showed that more work needed to be done before Input/Output could enjoy the same level of success it enjoyed a decade earlier.

Principal Subsidiaries

Concept Systems Holdings Limited (U.K.); Concept Systems Limited (U.K.); Geophysical Instruments AS (Norway); Global Charter Corporation; Global Charter S.A. (Argentina); GMG/ AXIS, Inc.; GX Technology Canada, Ltd. (Canada); GX Technology Corporation; GX Technology de Venezuela C.A.; GX Technology EAME Limited (U.K.); GX Technology Finance

EURL (France); HGS (India) Ltd.; I/O Cayman Islands, Ltd.; I/O Exploration Products (U.K.), Inc.; I/O Exploration Products (U.S.A.), Inc.; I/O General, LLC; I/O International FSC, Inc. (Barbados); I/O International, Inc. (U.S. Virgin Islands); I/O Luxembourg S.a.r.l.; I/O Marine Systems, Inc.; I/O Nevada, LLC; I/O of Austin, Inc.; I/O Sensors, Inc.; I/O Texas, LP; I/O U.K. Holdings Limited (U.K.); I/O U.K., Ltd. (U.K.); Input/Output Canada, Ltd.; IPOP Management, Inc.; Sensor Nederland B.V. (Netherlands).

Principal Competitors

Dawson Geophysical Company; Compagnie Generale de Geophysique, S.A.; TGS-NOPEC Geophysical Company ASA.

Further Reading

De Rouffignac, Anne, "CEO Zeringue Exits Input/Output As Stock Continues to Languish," *Houston Business Journal,* June 4, 1999, p. 6.

——, "Shareholders Sue After Seismic Shake-Up," *Houston Business Journal,* October 10, 1997, p. 1A.

Gianturco, Michael, "Seeing into the Earth," *Forbes,* June 20, 1994, p. 120.

Perin, Monica, "Another Seismic Shakeup," *Houston Business Journal,* December 31, 1999, p. 1.

"Timothy J. Probert Resigns from Input/Output Board of Directors," *Business Wire,* May 29, 2003, p. 5719.

—Jeffrey L. Covell

Intuit Inc.

2632 Marine Way
Mountain View, California 94043
U.S.A.
Telephone: (650) 944-6000
Toll Free: (800) 446-8848
Fax: (650) 944-3699
Web site: http://www.intuit.com

Public Company
Incorporated: 1984
Employees: 6,700
Sales: $1.87 billion (2004)
Stock Exchanges: NASDAQ
Ticker Symbol: INTU
NAIC: 511210 Software Publishers

Intuit Inc.'s TurboTax software is the number one selling tax software program in the United States. One in four tax returns completed are prepared using an Intuit tax product. Holding the lion's share of the market in its primary business lines, including Quicken personal finance software, Intuit changed strategy in the early years of the 21st century to fuel slowed growth.

Humble Beginnings in the Early 1980s

Intuit was the brainchild of entrepreneur Scott Cook, who cofounded the company with Tom Proulx in 1983. Cook, then only 23 years old, had moved to northern California in 1980 and was working in banking and technology assignments for the consulting firm Bain & Co. One night he and his wife, Signe, were sitting at their kitchen table in San Francisco paying their bills. It occurred to Scott that there must be a better way to manage their household finances and automate the hassle of bill paying. Inspired to start his own software company, he went to Stanford University to place an advertisement for a programmer. When he got to the campus, he stopped a passing student, Tom Proulx, for help in locating a bulletin board. Proulx, it turned out, had done some programming and agreed to write a simple check-balancing program for Cook. In his dorm room he created the first Quicken program, which he and Scott used to launch Intuit.

Cook's idea for a check-balancing program was unique, but he was only one of many people trying to break into the burgeoning personal computer software market at the time. According to several associates, it was his background, intellect, and enthusiasm that separated him from the rest of the pack. Cook earned degrees in both math and economics at the University of Southern California (USC). (He credited summer internships with the federal government with encouraging him to go into business rather than the bureaucratic public sector.) Also at USC, Cook took it upon himself to resurrect the school's ailing ski club. He rented out a cabin at the nearest ski area and charged club members a mere $1 per night to stay. The club became one of the most successful organizations on campus and played an important role in getting him accepted into Harvard's graduate business school. Indeed, Cook was one of only a handful of students to enter Harvard straight out of undergraduate school and was the youngest member of his 800-member class. "When I look back, that ski club success, as much as anything, led me to believe that I could start a successful company," Cook explained in 1992 to the *Business Journal—San Jose.*

Cook was snatched up by the Cincinnati-based marketing giant Procter & Gamble immediately after he graduated from Harvard in 1976 and was placed in charge of the Crisco shortening brand. At Procter & Gamble he met coworker Signe Ostby, his future wife. In 1980 the couple moved to California for its climate, with Cook taking the consulting job with Bain and his wife becoming vice-president of marketing at Software Publishing Corp. During the next few years Cook gained important experience related to banking and technology while his wife learned about marketing software. Meanwhile, Tom Proulx labored in his dorm room creating the first version of Quicken. After polishing up the program the two launched Intuit in 1983.

While Proulx contributed the technical expertise to the original Quicken program, Scott drew on his consumer marketing background to ensure that the program would meet a real need in the marketplace. He conducted numerous telephone interviews and focus groups, for example, in an effort to determine exactly what households needed financially and what features

Company Perspectives:

After 20 years Intuit continues to transform business and financial management for small businesses, accounting professionals and consumers.

were most important to potential customers. Coworkers called his emphasis on customer input fanatical, and Cook's fixation eventually became well known within the software industry. The application resulting from this research allowed people to enter data on screens that looked much like a check and a checkbook. The data was automatically processed, thus eliminating much of the tedium of balancing a checkbook.

Cook and Proulx started Intuit in Proulx's basement with a single product and seven employees. Cook originally planned to sell the software through bank branches, a strategy that soured when he realized that banks were poorly equipped to sell prepackaged software. Moreover, because Intuit was just one of several companies trying to market a personal financial software program, Cook was unable to find a retail distributor that would take his unknown product. By 1985 the company was struggling to stay afloat. Three employees left when Cook and Proulx became unable to pay salaries. The other four, still believing in their product, kept working for six months without any pay.

Cook remained surprisingly upbeat and helped to buoy the Intuit team during their initial struggles. Whenever Proulx's wife would come down into the basement to see how things were going, Cook would tell her that they could not be better. "The truth is that things couldn't be worse," Proulx recalled in 1995 to the *San Francisco Business Times*. "Years later he told me that in 1985, when we were out of money, if someone had agreed to buy the company from him to pay off his loans, he would have done it." In fact, Cook was more than $300,000 in debt and was facing a long 30 years of trying to pay off those obligations if his venture failed. "I never had any doubt that he would eventually succeed," Proulx said. "A large part of my belief was from having been propagandized by Scott."

By 1986 Cook and Proulx were beginning to see some light at the end of the tunnel. Importantly, the Apple version of Quicken was getting positive attention in the trade press, and sales were slowly picking up. Recognizing the power of such trade articles to generate sales, they made a pivotal decision that turned the company around. Instead of selling the programs through banks, they would sell them directly to customers through advertisements. In a risky move that could have quashed the entire venture, Proulx coaxed a reluctant Cook into placing $125,000 worth of advertisements, despite the fact that they had only $95,000 left in the bank. Cook wrote the ads himself, drawing on his marketing experience at Procter & Gamble. He emphasized the benefits of the program as opposed to its features, unlike most software ads of the time. "End financial hassles" was the key benefit touted in Cook's ads.

The advertising campaign was a success, and from that point forward Intuit's fortunes improved. Still, the company lacked a broad retail distribution channel and faced growing competition in the financial software market. In an effort to expand his

advertising efforts and boost Quicken's exposure, Cook approached more than 30 venture capital firms during the mid-1980s. All of them turned him down, including one represented by his former Harvard roommate. Nevertheless, Cook and Proulx persisted. Cook determined that word-of-mouth critiques of his program and customer loyalty would become the most valuable advertising tools at his disposal. For that reason, he decided that customer service and input would take top priority throughout the entire company.

Stories of Cook's obsession with customer service abound. Once, while visiting the office of a software association, Cook walked by a clerk entering data on one of his programs. He immediately stopped to interview her about the application and later incorporated one of her suggestions into a version of the program. When Cook preached customer service to his employees at a meeting in 1988, he told them that he wanted Intuit's service to improve to the point where customers would become "apostles" for Quicken by purchasing other Intuit products and telling their friends about Intuit's offerings.

Rapid Growth in the Late 1980s and Early 1990s

By the late 1980s Intuit was clearly on the fast track to success. In just a few years sales of Quicken exploded, and the program became one of the best-selling personal financial applications. Intuit suddenly had little problem securing more financing. Several well-known venture capital companies, including Sierra, Technology Venture Investors, and Kleiner Perkins Caufield and Byers, were willing to back Intuit's efforts to expand its retail distribution. Thus, during the late 1980s and early 1990s Quicken became one of the top-selling software applications in the world, surpassed only by such industry staples as WordPerfect and Lotus 1-2-3. Sales climbed to $55 million in 1991 from just $20 million three years earlier, and Intuit's workforce more than doubled in 1991 to about 425 employees.

Intuit broadened its scope in 1991 when it introduced Quick-Pay, a software program designed to help small businesses process their payroll. The $60 program, which was designed to work in conjunction with Quicken, was readily accepted by many users of Quicken. Intuit followed that introduction in 1992 with QuickBooks, a full-featured small-business bookkeeping program that provided an easier and less-expensive alternative to traditional accounting software. It was priced at about $140 and was also designed to work in cooperation with both Quicken and QuickPay. By 1992, Quicken (at a retail price of $70) was dominating the personal financial software market with a powerful 70 percent share. Much of that success was attributable to the company's emphasis on customer satisfaction: one 1992 survey showed that 85 percent of all Quicken users had recommended the program to at least one other person.

Having established its dominance in the market for stand-alone personal and small-business financial software, Quicken started looking at the much bigger picture. Indeed, Cook and his associates believed that Intuit's future was in providing a means of electronically linking customers with banks, brokers, and other businesses, and in providing various electronic financial services to the public. To that end, Intuit struck a deal with Visa that allowed Quicken users to download credit card statements directly onto their computers and into Quicken. In 1993 Intuit spent $243 million to purchase ChipSoft, which allowed customers to file tax returns electronically. Intuit scored again later that year when it bought out National Payment Clearinghouse Inc., a processor of electronic transactions, for $7.6 million.

Cook realized in 1993 that Intuit was evolving from an entrepreneurial startup company to an established corporation. The company had even gone public by that time on the OTC market and was rapidly adding employees and facilities in the wake of ongoing acquisitions and surging sales. Early in 1994 Cook selected 53-year-old William V. Campbell to serve in the newly created post of president and chief executive officer. Campbell, a former Apple executive, was skilled in building organizations. In addition to his background in the computer industry, he had also served as the head football coach at his alma mater, Columbia University. Campbell would oversee the day-to-day operations at Intuit while Cook, as chairman of the board, would continue to spearhead the company's strategic plans.

By the mid-1990s Intuit was drawing attention from a much larger suitor, with software giant Microsoft eyeing Intuit as a possible takeover target. To Microsoft, Intuit represented an entry into the only major software category in which it did not have a significant presence. Microsoft was competing successfully with its own personal financial program, Microsoft Money. By 1994, though, that application was serving only 22 percent of the market, compared to Quicken's walloping 70 percent. Furthermore, Intuit owned other programs of interest to Microsoft, such as TurboTax, MacInTax, and ProSeries, all of which were geared for the personal and small-business tax-return-preparation market. Finally, Intuit had valuable experience related to conducting computerized transactions over telephone lines.

Microsoft, with Cook's cooperation, attempted a buyout of Intuit in 1995. Critics and Microsoft competitors balked, claiming that the merger was anticompetitive and would give Microsoft too much power in the software industry. To Cook's dismay, the Justice Department tried to block the deal, which would have been the largest merger in the history of the software industry. Both Microsoft and Intuit fought the Department's efforts, and Microsoft even offered to sell off its Money program. Nevertheless, the $2 billion deal eventually collapsed. With that, Microsoft CEO Bill Gates renewed his efforts to make Microsoft Money a

contender. Microsoft hired away a top Intuit salesman and launched a revamped version of Money to be used with Microsoft's long-awaited new operating system, Windows 95.

Like Microsoft, Intuit turned its attention back to its growing array of products following the failed merger. The company was still trying to digest the flurry of product and company acquisitions completed during the early 1990s. To that end, Intuit was working to consolidate and streamline its information systems and operational and financial controls. Intuit also began its online banking service in 1995 and acquired Japanese software company Milk Way KK. Even though the company's fiscal year was shortened by two months in 1994, revenues surged to about $194 million. In the long term, Intuit was positioning itself to become a leader in the burgeoning electronic banking and financial services industries.

Diversification and Expansion in the Late 1990s

The mid-1990s were a difficult period for Intuit. Not only was the company recovering from the disappointment from the failed Microsoft merger, but Intuit was also facing challenges in the software front. Overall sales of packaged software were declining as an increasing number of computers were sold with software installed, and Intuit's software sales were also affected by a saturated market—many in the target audience for personal finance software already owned Quicken. Another imposing threat to Intuit was the increasing presence of the Internet, which signaled the possibility of the demise of stand-alone software programs. Between November 1995, when Intuit's stock hit a high of $89 per share, and August 1997, the share price fell 72 percent, to $25 per share. The company racked up net losses of $44.3 million and $20.7 million for fiscal 1995 and 1996, respectively. The company was forced to eliminate nearly 10 percent of its workforce in mid-1997. Analyst David Farina of William Blair declared in *Fortune,* "Quicken is over! . . . It's done. It's almost a nonfactor."

Intuit was not about to throw in the towel, however, and it worked to transform itself into a fast-moving Internet company, hoping to leverage its brand equity to attract consumers and gain credibility. "The Net was forcing us to learn fast, change fast, and even fail fast," Cook told *Fast Company.* "The only thing wrong with making mistakes would be not learning from them." Intuit decided to divest itself of non-core operations and sold Intuit Services Corporation, its online banking and electronic transaction processing subsidiary, to Checkfree in 1997. The company also sold its consumer software and direct marketing operations, Parsons, to Broderbund Software, Inc. Meanwhile, Intuit worked to increase its Internet presence. In 1996 Intuit acquired GALT Technologies, Inc., a provider of mutual fund information on the Web, for about $14.6 million. The following year the company invested about $40 million in Excite Inc. Excite, one of the leading Internet search engines, boasted about 2.5 million users daily. Under terms of the agreement, Intuit would be the exclusive provider of financial information on the Excite web page. Early in 1998 Intuit inked a $30 million deal with America Online, Inc. (AOL), and Intuit became the exclusive provider of tax preparation services, life and auto insurance, and mortgage services for AOL members. Intuit launched a revamped version of Quicken.com in 1997 that offered a host of financial services and information, including QuickenMortgage, an online service that allowed customers to search for mortgages from a number of different lenders. Quicken.com quickly became the most popular personal finance site on the Web, and Intuit's stock price began to climb. Intuit's William Harris, who became CEO in 1998, asked in *Fast Company,* "Isn't it amazing . . . how quickly you can become a company of the past—or a company of the future?"

Though Intuit focused its energies on the Internet, it did not neglect its core software operations. The company continued to enhance and improve its personal finance software and worked to bridge the gap between the Internet and packaged software by offering web versions and integrating web links. In fiscal 1999 Intuit introduced its QuickBooks Online Payroll service, which allowed QuickBooks users to connect with banks and tax agencies to facilitate payroll processing. By the end of the fiscal year, more than 6,000 businesses had signed up for the service. The company also offered WebTurboTax, which combined TurboTax features with electronic tax filing capabilities and allowed users to complete their tax returns and file them online. More than 240,000 1998 federal tax returns were completed and filed using WebTurboTax.

Intuit continued to make strategic acquisitions, and in 1997 it purchased Nihon Micom Co. Ltd. through its Japanese subsidiary. Nihon Micom developed accounting software for small businesses. The following year Intuit purchased Lacerte Software Corporation and Lacerte Educational Services Corporation for about $400 million. Lacerte developed professional tax preparation software. In 1999 Intuit bought the customer lists and intellectual property rights of TaxByte, Inc., a professional tax preparation software business, and Compucraft Tax Services, LLC, another professional tax preparation software company. Intuit also acquired Computing Resources, Inc., a payroll services provider, for about $200 million; Boston Light Software Corp., a developer of web products and software geared toward small businesses; SecureTax.com, which developed online tax preparation services; and Hutchison Avenue Software Corporation, a developer of web products and software. Intuit completed its acquisition of mortgage lender Rock Financial Corporation in December 1999.

In September 1999 William Harris stepped down as CEO. Former CEO William Campbell filled in as interim CEO as the search for a permanent replacement commenced. Intuit continued to add features to its Quicken.com web site, including the ability to view and pay bills, as well as view Discover credit card accounts. The company entered another agreement with AOL to be the exclusive provider of bill management services for AOL members, which numbered about 19 million in late 1999. Intuit also formed a number of partnerships with financial organizations, such as Fidelity Investments and Vanguard Group, to provide tax preparation software to online customers of those organizations.

For 1999, Intuit reported total revenues of $847.6 million, up 43 percent from 1998. Net income reached $376.5 million, a significant improvement over a net loss of $12 million in 1998. The leader of personal finance software was banking on becoming the leader of e-finance as well, building upon its legacy as an innovator and provider of personal financial management solutions. With more than 15 million customers, Intuit was in a strong position as it approached a new decade. The company planned to continue dominating the personal finance segment by offering the latest and greatest finance solutions, both online and off.

What Is Old Is New Again: 2000–05

Revenue grew by 16 percent in fiscal 2000, driven by Intuit's well-established products. Only a quarter of the $1.1 billion in sales were web-related, according to *Forbes,* with only three of eight web businesses running in the black. "Quicken Insurance gets clobbered by the likes of InsWeb and traditional advisers. Its flagship online service, Quicken.com, is under siege from major banks and Weblets," wrote Erika Brown.

Former CEOs William Campbell and William Harris had promoted Intuit's entry on the Web, but its customer base was slow to move with them. Stephen Bennett, a former General Electric (GE) who came aboard in January 2000, said, "There is no crisis here, the house isn't burning. But we should be doing a lot better." Quicken customers, by and large, continued to use separate sites for paying bills, checking out mortgage rates, or buying stock, rather than merge all of their financial life onto one Intuit web product.

Bennett, for his part, was eyeing another market segment: businesses with more than 20 and up to 250 employees. Prior to his promotion to GE president, the 23-year veteran of the company led the small business division at GE Capital. Taking a page out of his GE boss Jack Welch's playbook, Bennett began with a revamp of Intuit's organizational structure with more managers reporting directly to him.

Bennett's goal, not surprisingly, was to increase sales and net income. The company's core QuickBooks product already held 85 percent of the retail market for small business accounting software, and Intuit wanted to cross-sell products and services such as inventory management or web design. A potential stumbling block was the speed at which small business owners made computer technology shifts.

Quicken, holding 73 percent of the personal finance software category saw unit sales fall by 27 percent in fiscal 2001, and Intuit registered an $82 million loss for the year. But TurboTax kept humming along powered by the complex U.S. tax laws.

Under Bennett, Intuit moved into the realm of larger small businesses—a segment also in the sights of Oracle, Microsoft, and SAP. QuickBooks Enterprise was introduced to meet those companies' tracking needs. Intuit also began bringing out non-accounting industry specific software. More products were in the offing either to be internally developed or by way of acquisitions.

Intuit rebounded in 2002, in terms of profitability and stock price. Former GE managers were running the company's two major divisions, enforcing tougher internal operating standards, improved quality control, waste reduction, and performance-linked pay incentives. Bennett had spent nearly $500 million on software firm acquisitions. But by comparison Microsoft had spent $2.5 billion over two years doing the same thing.

Intuit's Quicken personal finance, QuickBooks small business finance, and TurboTax income tax filing offerings continued to lead their markets but the growth rate had slowed. The company was looking toward single-digit growth as it approached the mid-2000s.

QuickBooks Enterprise had not taken off as hoped, according to *Business Week Online*, nor had the products produced by the companies Bennett had acquired. The QuickBooks Point-of-Sale system for small retailers on the other hand experienced strong growth. Bennett meanwhile shifted gears, moving toward serving smaller niches with simpler products.

"While some analysts are skeptical about growth prospects, there is a consensus that Bennett's plan makes Intuit a good long-term hold. 'If they grow revenue 10 percent, that's a phenomenal result,' " David Farina, technology analyst at investment bank William Blair & Co. told *Business Week Online*. He added, "In Silicon Valley, you are a failure if you're not growing 30 percent, but Intuit is in a different phase of its life. It's a very good, very dominant business that's well run. It's just in a transition in terms of buyers."

Fiscal 2004 revenue growth fell to 12 percent, down from 26 percent the prior year. But with the return to its roots—following customers home, watching what they do, and then going back and tweaking software—the company had produced positive results and expected better than anticipated numbers for 2005.

Principal Subsidiaries

Blue Ocean Software, Inc.; Greenpoint Software (Canada); Intuit Canada Limited; Intuit Limited (U.K.).

Principal Competitors

H&R Block, Inc.; Microsoft Business Solutions; The Sage Group.

Further Reading

Allen, Mike, "Intuit Staff Looks Forward to Yet Another Taxing Year: From Humble Beginnings As ChipSoft, TurboTax Breaks $400 Million Mark," *San Diego Business Journal*, September 15, 2004, pp. 5+.

Brown, Erika, "Small Is Big," *Forbes*, May 27, 2002, p. 88.

——, "Square Peg, Round Hole," *Forbes*, November 13, 2000, p. 326.

Brown, Eryn, "Is Intuit Headed for a Meltdown?," *Fortune,* August 18, 1997, p. 200.

Buck, Richard, "Intuit Stock Tumbles on Microsoft Ruling," *Seattle Times,* February 16, 1995, p. C1.

Crosariol, Beppi, "US Fights Microsoft's Takeover of Intuit," *Boston Globe,* April 28, 1995, p. 1.

Dillon, Pat, "Conspiracy of Change: How Do You Overthrow a Successful Company?," *Fast Company,* October 1, 1998, p. 182.

Janah, Monua, "Mountain View, Calif.-Based Firm Plans Full-Service Financial Web Site," *San Jose Mercury News,* November 15, 1999.

Krey, Michael, "Scott Cook: Intuit Co-Founder Got up to Speed at USC Ski Club," *Business Journal-San Jose,* July 20, 1992, p. 13.

Lacy, Sarah, "How Intuit Quickened Sales," *Business Week Online*, April 22, 2005.

——, "Intuit Faces a Long Road Back," *Business Week Online*, October 8, 2004.

Levine, Daniel S., "Executive of the Year: After Bringing Bill Gates to His Knees, Scott Cook Plans to Revolutionize the Finance Industries," *San Francisco Business Times,* January 6, 1995, p. 1.

Mullaney, Timothy J., "The Wizard of Intuit," *Business Week*, October 28, 2002, p. 60.

Swisher, Kara, "Intuit CEO Bill Harris Resigns; Bill Campbell to Be Interim Chief," *Wall Street Journal,* September 24, 1999, p. B3.

——, "Intuit to Integrate Web Links into Small-Business Software," *Wall Street Journal,* October 21, 1999, p. B15.

"Welcome Back to the Jungle, Intuit," *Business Week,* June 5, 1995, p. 4.

—Dave Mote
—updates: Mariko Fujinaka, Kathleen Peippo

Jardine Cycle & Carriage Ltd.

239 Alexandra Road
Singapore 159930
Singapore
Telephone: +65 6473 3122
Fax: +65 6475 7088
Web site: http://www.jcclgroup.com

Public Company
Incorporated: 1899 as The Cycle & Carriage Company
Employees: 100,000
Sales: $1.5 billion (2004)
Stock Exchanges: Singapore
Ticker Symbol: JCYC
NAIC: 441110 New Car Dealers; 237210 Land
Subdivision; 441310 Automotive Parts and
Accessories Stores; 551112 Offices of Other Holding
Companies

Jardine Cycle & Carriage Ltd. (JCC) is one of Singapore's 50 largest corporations, in part because of its strategic (49.92 percent as of May 2005) stake in regional automotive powerhouse PT Astra International. In addition to its shareholding in Astra, JCC has built up direct operations in two core areas: motor vehicle distribution and retailing; and property development. The company's motor vehicle arm is one of the largest automobile retailers and distributors in Singapore, and has a strong share of the Malaysian market, through its 59 percent stake in Cycle & Carriage Bintang Bhd. In Singapore, JCC sells Mercedes-Benz, Kia, and Mitsubishi. In Malaysia, the company handles Mercedes-Benz, Peugeot, Ford, and Mazda. The company's operations extend beyond retailing and include, in the case of Mercedes-Benz, the assembly of vehicles for sale in the local market. Since the early 2000s, JCC also has begun a drive to expand its automotive business into the greater regional market, establishing a subsidiary in Thailand. JCC's property development wing is operated through its 66 percent stake in publicly listed subsidiary MCL Land. That company is one of Singapore's largest property developers, with an assets portfolio worth more than SGD 5 billion. Founded in 1899 as Cycle & Carriage, the company has been majority controlled by the Jardine Matheson group since 2002. In 2004, JCC's revenues topped $1.5 billion. The company is listed on the Singapore Stock Exchange and led by Managing Director Adam Keswick.

Late 19th-Century General Store

Jardine Cycle & Carriage was known more simply as Cycle & Carriage for most of its more than 100-year history. The company was originally founded, however, as Federal Stores, by two brothers, named Chua, in Kuala Lumpur in 1899. Federal Stores initially operated as a general store, carrying a variety of items, including spices such as nutmeg. Yet before the end of that year, the Chuas had expanded their trading interests, to include a wide variety of items, such as machine parts, writing paper, soap, and other products. The brothers also became interested in sales of bicycles, then motorcycles and automobiles. For these operations the brothers adopted the name of Cycle & Carriage. In 1918, the company registered as a limited liability company in the Federated Malay States.

By the 1920s, the company's cycle and automotive sales had become its main activity, and Singapore, then a regional center of the British colonial empire, emerged as the company's primary market. This led Cycle & Carriage to move its headquarters to Singapore in 1926. At that time, the company listed its shares on the Singapore Stock Exchange, becoming The Cycle & Carriage Company (1926) Ltd. The company's Malaysian operations in the meantime continued as Cycle & Carriage Bintang Bhd. During this time, Cycle & Carriage built up a network of branches throughout Singapore and Malaysia.

The following decades represented an extended period of turmoil for the company. Cycle & Carriage was buffeted by a global depression, and by World War II. The Malaysian business in particular suffered during the economic chaos of the period, and by 1933 had been forced to shut down all of its Malaysian branches.

The separation of Malaysia and Singapore, and the two countries' independence from colonial rule, launched a new period of growth for Cycle & Carriage. The company's Singapore and Malaysian entities remained closely linked, with the

---

Company Perspectives:

Our objective is to maintain our position as a premier motor vehicle and property group by continually providing customers with the highest-quality products and services. From our humble beginnings more than 100 years ago, we have grown into a regional force comprising close to 200 subsidiaries and associates spanning the region. With a highly-focused business portfolio and dedicated workforce, we are confident of moving ahead and maintaining a strong foothold in the automotive and property markets in the region.

Singapore business serving as Cycle & Carriage Bintang's major shareholder.

The year 1951 marked a major milestone for both companies, when Cycle & Carriage was awarded the franchise for Mercedes-Benz for both countries. The contract led to the reestablishment of Cycle & Carriage Bintang's operations. The popularity of ''import-substitution'' policies in the region, in which governments required companies seeking to import their goods to set up domestic assembly and finishing plants for the final products, led Cycle & Carriage to establish its own assembly plants for its Mercedes-Benz business.

Cycle & Carriage relisted its shares as Cycle & Carriage Limited on the then-joint stock exchanges of Malaysia and Singapore in 1969. When those exchanges split into separate entities, Cycle & Carriage Bintang launched its own public offering on the new Kuala Lumpur stock exchange in 1977. Although Cycle & Carriage remained a major shareholder in the Malaysia company, it nonetheless allowed its shareholding to drop below 50 percent by 1980.

Diversified in the 1990s

By then, Cycle & Carriage had gained another important automobile concession for the Singapore market, that of Mitsubishi. The company launched sales of Mitsubishi vehicles in 1977, establishing a dealer network throughout the territory.

Cycle & Carriage continued seeking new automobile franchise opportunities in the 1980s. By 1989, the company had succeeded in adding two new dealership contracts. The first was the concession for Proton automobiles—the newly developed Malaysian automobile—in Singapore. At the same time, Cycle & Carriage Bintang acquired the Malaysian franchise for Mazda automobiles.

Already one of the largest automotive dealers and distributors in Singapore and Malaysia, Cycle & Carriage launched its first efforts to expand beyond these countries. The Korean automaker Hyundai, then just beginning its own drive to establish itself as an international brand, proved to be the vehicle for Cycle & Carriage's own international expansion. In 1990, the company was awarded the franchise to introduce the Hyundai brand to Australia. At the same time, Cycle & Carriage entered into the joint venture Astra Investments, which acquired the Hyundai franchise in Singapore. The company then leveraged

its existing relationship with Mazda to enter the New Zealand market, establishing Sri Temasek Ltd. for that business.

Yet at the end of the 1980s and into the early 1990s, Cycle & Carriage became interested in diversifying beyond its automotive operations. In 1989, the company entered the food business, acquiring a 43 percent stake in Cold Storage (Malaysia) Berhad. With this purchase, Cycle & Carriage added a food manufacturing business, as well as the distribution of foods and other goods. Cold Storage also led the company into the operations of supermarkets and pharmacies in the Malaysian market.

Real estate became another target market for Cycle & Carriage. In 1990, the company launched its first effort at real estate development, building the Hillview Villas in Singapore. By 1992, the company had expanded its portfolio of properties, forming a new subsidiary, CCL Group Properties, to oversee its properties in Malaysia and Singapore.

The acquisition of Malayan Credit Limited (MCL) that same year, however, launched Cycle & Carriage into the big leagues among the region's real estate groups. As its name indicated, MCL had originally been formed to provide credit services. Established in 1963, MCL went public in 1967, then entered the property development market in 1969. Real estate became the company's core operation, and MCL grew to become one of the region's leading publicly listed developers of hotels and other commercial properties, as well as residential developments. Under Cycle & Carriage, MCL officially changed its name to MCL Land in 1997 as a more accurate reflection of its operations. By the mid-1990s, Cycle & Carriage had extended its shareholding in MCL Land to 60 percent, and then to 66 percent by the mid-2000s.

New Owners for a New Century

Cycle & Carriage continued seeking new automotive franchises in the 1990s. In 1995, for example, Cycle & Carriage acquired the franchise for Kia Motors for both Malaysia and Singapore, although the company dropped the Malaysian franchise in 1999. By then, the company also had gained the franchise for Audi automobiles in Australia.

Throughout this period, Cycle & Carriage had developed a relationship with Hong Kong trading giant Jardine Matheson. That company, founded in Canton, China, by William Jardine and James Matheson in 1832, had been instrumental in the development of Hong Kong into a world financial capital. Jardine Matheson itself grew into one of the largest and most powerful of Hong Kong's ''hongs''—that is, extremely diversified conglomerates, with interests ranging from banking to shipping to property development, as well as interests in retail, food production, and restaurant operations. Jardine Matheson also was involved in motor vehicle dealership operations, the international expansion of which led the company to Cycle & Carriage at the beginning of the 1990s.

In 1992, Jardine Matheson bought a 16 percent stake in Cycle & Carriage, as well as a 15 percent share of Cycle & Carriage Bintang, in order to gain a foothold in the fast-growing Singapore and Malaysian markets. The link-up with Jardine Matheson provided other advantages, notably through the tie between Cold Storage and Jardine Matheson's own retail

Key Dates:

1899: The Chua brothers establish Federal Stores, which become the general merchandiser Cycle & Carriage, in Kuala Lumpur.

1926: The company moves to Singapore and goes public as The Cycle & Carriage Company Ltd.

1951: The company acquires the automotive franchise for Mercedes Benz in Singapore and Malaysia.

1977: The Malaysian operations are listed on the Kuala Lumpur Stock Exchange as Cycle & Carriage Bintang; the Mitsubishi franchise in Singapore is acquired.

1989: Franchises for Proton in Singapore and Mazda in Malaysia are acquired; the company acquires Cold Storage (Malaysia) and enters food production, distribution, and retailing.

1990: The Hyundai franchise in Australia is acquired; the company enters the property development market.

1992: The company acquires Malayan Credit Limited (renamed as MCL Land in 1997); Jardine Matheson acquires a 16 percent stake in the company.

2000: The company acquires 30 percent of Astra International in Indonesia.

2002: Jardine Matheson raises its shareholding to more than 50 percent.

2004: The company changes its name to Jardine Cycle & Carriage.

2005: The company increases its stake in Astra International to 49.92 percent.

food operation in the region, Dairy Farm, which boosted Cold Storage's retail network to more than 40 stores by the end of the decade.

By the mid-1990s, Jardine Matheson had increased its stake in Cycle & Carriage to 23 percent, just shy of the mandatory takeover limit of 25 percent. The two companies continued to strengthen their bonds toward the end of the decade, and in 2000, Jardine Matheson launched an offer to increase its holding in Cycle & Carriage to more than 50 percent. That offer was allowed to lapse; nonetheless, Jardine Matheson continued building its shares in Cycle & Carriage, topping nearly 30 percent of shares. Then, in 2002, Jardine Matheson reached an agreement with Edaran Otomobil National Berhad to acquire its 21.1 percent stake in Cycle & Carriage. The deal placed Cycle & Carriage as a strategic subsidiary in the Jardine Matheson empire. This position was ratified in 2004 when the company adopted a new name, Jardine Cycle & Carriage (JCC). In that year, as well, JCC acquired full control of Cycle & Carriage Bintang.

By then, JCC had itself become a strategic investor, when in 2000 it purchased a 31 percent stake in Indonesia's PT Astra International, the country's leading automotive group and one of Indonesia's largest conglomerates. The Astra holding became the third leg of JCC's three-prong strategy. Into the mid-2000s, JCC continued to acquire shares in Astra, and by 2005 had succeeded in boosting its stake to 49.92 percent.

In the meantime, JCC continued to expand its portfolio of automobile dealerships. In 2002, the group acquired the franchise for Peugeot vehicles in Malaysia and Singapore. The company also transferred its exclusive Mercedes-Benz franchise in Malaysia to a new joint venture with DaimlerChrysler set up in 2003. At the same time, JCC's property arm also maintained its strong growth, with an assets portfolio worth more than SGD 5 billion. At the end of 2004, MCL Land announced a partnership with Sunrise Bhd. to develop the 480-acre Seremban Forest Heights site in Malaysia. After more than 100 years, JCC remained one of Singapore and Malaysia's major corporations.

Principal Subsidiaries

CCL Group Properties Sdn. Bhd. (79%); Cycle & Carriage (Thailand) Ltd.; Cycle & Carriage Automotive Pte Ltd.; Cycle & Carriage Automotive Services Pty. Ltd. (Australia); Cycle & Carriage Bintang Berhad (Malaysia; 59%); Cycle & Carriage Industries Pte Limited; Cycle & Carriage Kia Pte Ltd.; Cycle & Carriage Mitsu (Thailand) Ltd.; MCL Land Limited (66%); PT Astra International Tbk (49.92%); PT Tunas Ridean Tbk (38%).

Principal Competitors

Singapore Technologies Private Ltd.; Borneo Motors Singapore Private Ltd.; Inchcape Motors Private Ltd.; DaimlerChrysler South East Asia Private Ltd.; Champion Motors 1975 Private Ltd.; Tan Chong and Sons Motor Company Singapore Private Ltd.; Malayan Motors; Motor Image Enterprises Private Ltd.; SMRT Road Holdings Ltd.

Further Reading

"Cycle & Carriage Bintang Hopes to Chart Further Growth Ahead," *Bernama*, May 12, 2004.

"Cycle & Carriage Eyes 10–15 Percent Market Share in 2.0cc Segment," *Bernama The Malaysian National News Agency,* September 18, 2004.

Donnan, Shawn, "Astra Rides to 22% Increase in Profits," *Financial Times,* March 22, 2005, p. 26.

"Jardine Sets Cycle & Carriage Deal," *Asian Wall Street Journal,* July 16, 2002.

"JC&C to Acquire Additional 12.3 Percent Stake in CCB for RM 41.59 Million," *Bernama,* May 7, 2004.

Kwok, Ben, "Car Dealer Unit Surges 64pc," *South China Morning Post,* February 25, 2004.

Pilus, Razali, "Sunrise Bhd and MCL Land Ltd to Jointly Develop Seremban Forest Heights," *Bernama,* July 12, 2004.

Shameen, Assif, "Driving into Southeast Asia," *Asiaweek,* June 14, 1996.

—M.L. Cohen

Jostens, Inc.

5501 American Blvd. West
Minneapolis, Minnesota 55437
U.S.A.
Telephone: (952) 830-3300
Fax: (952) 830-3293
Web site: http://www.jostens.com

Private Subsidiary
Incorporated: 1906 as Jostens Manufacturing Company
Employees: 6,300
Sales: $807.2 million (2004)
NAIC: 339911 Jewelry (Including Precious Metal)
   Manufacturing; 511130 Book Publishers

Jostens, Inc. is best known as a manufacturer of high-quality class rings for high school and college students. For more than four decades, the company also has produced specially commissioned rings for contestants in the World Series, the Super Bowl, the NBA Championship, and the NHL Stanley Cup. Despite such high-profile coups and new ventures, the school products segment provided Jostens the lion's share of revenues. A promising educational software venture, for example, ended with disappointment and contributed to the interruption of a three-decade-long streak of earnings and revenue increases. Taken private in 2000, the century old company found itself being traded three times in the span of four years.

From Small-Town Business to Multimillion-Dollar Corporation: Late 1800s–1960s

Begun in 1897 by Otto Josten, Jostens was originally a small jewelry and watch repair business located in Owatonna, Minnesota. In 1900 the founder began manufacturing emblems and awards for nearby schools and in 1906, the year of incorporation, Josten added class rings to his product line, to be sold to schools throughout the Midwest. The company remained small and relatively inconspicuous until Daniel C. Gainey, a former teacher and football coach, was hired in 1922 as the first full-time Jostens ring salesman. The rings at the time carried no gemstones and were all one size. Yet Gainey, with his dynamic and winning personality, secured sales of $18,000 within his first year. The amount was so large that he was forced to return to Owatonna to ensure personally that production demands could be met. By 1923 Gainey had enlisted four more sales representatives—all part-time—and revenues quickly rose to $70,000. Thus class rings became the central concern for the Jostens Manufacturing Company. In 1930 the watchmaking and repair business was sold and the capital was used to construct the company's first ring manufacturing plant. Three years later, with sales approaching the $500,000 mark, Gainey was elected chairman and CEO, positions he held until his retirement in 1968. According to several accounts, Gainey's greatest contribution to the company was his establishment and motivation of a nationwide sales force. Direct sales through independent representatives were the primary source for the company's virtually uninterrupted growth.

During World War II Jostens contributed to the war effort by adapting its plant and equipment to manufacture precision parts and other materials. Major expansion came following the end of the war. In 1946 the company added graduation announcements to its offerings; in 1950 Jostens launched the American Yearbook Company. Both moves further tapped the education market and made the company less dependent on seasonal sales from rings. In 1958 the company made its first acquisition, purchasing the Ohio-based Educational Supply Company, a manufacturer of school diplomas. Jostens went public the following year and a seemingly unending series of acquisitions, which fortified the company's dominance of the high school and college products markets, characterized the next ten years. Sales for 1962 totaled $26 million; three years later the company obtained its listing on the New York Stock Exchange. In 1968 the company expanded into the Canadian photography market with the purchase of Winnipeg-based National School Studios. By this time Jostens was the undisputed domestic leader in both class ring and yearbook sales. Gainey's retirement, however, coupled with Jostens' relocation to Minneapolis in 1969, triggered a tumultuous period that nearly shipwrecked the then nearly $100 million company.

Rocky Start to Leadership Change: 1970s

Star Tribune columnist Dick Youngblood, reflecting back on this period, wrote: "Jostens had been in turmoil since the late

1960s, when company patriarch Daniel C. Gainey, a major stockholder, pretended to retire as CEO. The trouble was, Gainey remained active enough over the ensuing four years to force the resignation of three chairmen and a president, including his own son.'' In 1970, amidst the turmoil, a top-performing Jostens salesman and division manager was appointed executive vice-president and effectively became the company's chief operating officer. His name was H. William (Bill) Lurton. Unbeknownst to senior management, however, including Lurton, Gainey had begun negotiations with acquisition-hungry Bristol-Myers. Once Gainey's plan surfaced, several top Jostens officials tendered their resignations; Lurton was among the few who remained. Although Bristol-Myers halted negotiations after the management fallout, Jostens remained in peril under the leadership of replacement CEO Richard Schall. A former top official at General Mills and Metro-Goldwyn-Mayer, Schall, according to *Corporate Report* editor Terry Fiedler, ''presided over Jostens for about 18 months before the advent of what amounted to a palace coup.'' An outsider with little knowledge of the business, Schall had brought in his own management team and radically disrupted the friendly, teamwork-oriented corporate culture and threatened to move the company too quickly into new, uncharted territory. ''The Lurton-led old guard demanded that Schall leave, threatening to leave themselves if he didn't. The directors sided with the old guard and in February 1972 Lurton became CEO of Jostens.''

Twenty-one years later, Lurton remained in the position, well-liked by his employees and greatly esteemed by his fellow Minnesota CEOs. During his early tenure he moved quickly to reestablish Jostens as a thriving, focused company. Diversification beyond educational products, thought to be the key to the company's future, was renewed only for a short time before being curtailed in large part. In 1974 Lurton divested Jostens of a greeting cards manufacturer and a men's accessories business. Five years later he also rid the company of interests in wedding rings and library supplies. Jostens Travel, first organized in 1972, also was dissolved before the end of the decade. Jostens did keep at least one peripheral acquisition, Artex Enterprises, for the long term. A manufacturer of custom-imprinted athletic and casual wear, the Artex label survived within the Jostens Sportswear division and was marketed primarily through mass merchants.

Changing Demographics: 1980s

Aside from the aftermath of the Gainey debacle, Lurton's greatest challenge as a CEO came in the late 1970s and early 1980s, when demographic studies clearly showed that the last of the baby boom generation had graduated from high school and, therefore, beyond the core products line. According to Jackey

Gold in *Financial World*, ''Lurton's worry was that declining high school enrollments would shake Wall Street's faith in the company's ability to perform. Jostens' board of directors, too, became infected by such concerns and in August 1982 approved Lurton's proposal for a management buyout.'' The decision to go private was, for lack of financing, never realized; neither, however, was the company's forecasted decline.

Instead, Lurton launched a concerted campaign to impress Wall Street and counteract potential downswings in profits by boldly entering the proprietary schools business. Beginning in 1983, he acquired San Gabriel Colleges of California and Metridata Education Systems of Kentucky. Three additional private vocational schools were acquired in 1984. That same year Jostens also entered the audiovisual learning and educational software fields by acquiring the Educational Systems Division of Borg-Warner Corporation, which it later renamed Jostens Learning Systems. The new flurry of purchases carried sales to more than $400 million in 1985, when Jostens was accorded *Fortune* 500 status for the first time. In 1986 the company acquired Illinois-based Prescription Learning Corporation (PLC). A developer of customized computer hardware, software, and support services for the educational market, PLC was merged with Education Systems Corporation three years later to form Jostens Learning Corporation (JLC), a wholly owned subsidiary.

Meanwhile, to the consternation of several analysts, Jostens divested itself of its burgeoning list of proprietary schools, all 36 of them. The company sold the schools to CareerCom Corp. in 1987 for a sizable profit. As then Education Division spokesperson Gary Buckmiller explained, ''We didn't view the sale as getting out of the proprietary school business, but rather as changing the way we're involved in the business.'' The involvement, through JLC, has become one of support and service for, rather than management of, instructors and curriculum. Jostens' one remaining non-educational venture, the Business Products Division, also was sold in 1987, for a gain of $40 million. Now 90 years old, the company had returned to its roots in its service emphasis. By this time Jostens boasted an employee workforce of some 9,000, in addition to an independent sales force numbering approximately 1,400.

Tarnished Hopes: Early 1990s

Jostens' nearly 27 percent average return on investment between the years 1983 and 1989 brought kudos from all corners for the CEO. *Fortune* magazine highlighted Jostens among its 500 in 1989 as one of the ''Companies That Compete Best.'' In 1990 Lurton was accorded the honor of ''Executive of the Year'' by *Corporate Report Minnesota*; further recognition came the same year from *Industry Week,* which celebrated Lurton as one of ''America's Unsung Heroes.'' Until fiscal 1992 the news regarding Jostens and Lurton continued to be highly favorable. The 1990 purchase of Gordon B. Miller & Co. (the oldest recognition products company in North America) and Lenox Awards augured well for the company, as did its multimedia agreement with Western Publishing's Little Golden Books. Even the 1992 performance reports were respectable, considering the lingering effects of a recession: net sales increased 2 percent, while net income showed a 4 percent decline. The announced consolidation of jewelry manufacturing and photo processing operations were expected to contribute to a quick rebound. Jostens hoped that rising school enrollment, a strengthening economy, and a new management team for the Sportswear group would improve the company's performance.

Also fueling hopes for the future was JLC, the leader of the computer-based instructional technology field. Fiscal 1992 revenues for JLC totaled $172 million, or approximately 20 percent of all corporate gross income. JLC, operating in a marketplace that experts estimated as only 15 percent tapped, appeared poised for fast-paced growth, especially considering its August 1992 purchase of chief competitor Wicat Systems and its arrangement with Texas-based Dell Computer to market a Jostens line of 386 and 486 systems. Lurton expected to see an increase of about 25 percent annually. His goal was to return Jostens to "double-digit growth in sales and earnings."

Jostens posted a net loss of $12.1 million in fiscal year 1993. According to an April 1994 Youngblood article, about half of the loss was due to a "poorly managed" consolidation of the

photography operation. Compounding problems, JLC missed some key changes in the market, including tightening school budgets and an accompanying shift in demand toward less expensive products and systems.

Lurton announced his retirement as chairman of the board and CEO in October 1993. Robert P. Jensen, a director since 1980, succeeded him as chairman. The combination of missed earnings projections, losses in the earnings column, and nose-diving stock prices had raised the ire of stockholders and Lurton's long, successful tenure ended on a sour note. Yet, under his leadership, the company had put together an enviable succession of sales and earnings increases even while the student population was shrinking.

Robert C. Buhrmaster, a Corning Inc. senior vice-president who came on board as chief of staff in December 1992 and moved into the president's post in mid-1993, succeeded Lurton as CEO and led a revamping of the company. In rapid order, the sportswear division was sold. Veteran executives were replaced. The photography division and JLC were downsized. The corporate culture itself changed as management layers were cut and divisions reported more closely to headquarters. The design and marketing of traditional products such as rings were also re-examined. But losses continued into a second year; underperformance by JLC contributed to the $16.2 million deficit.

Jostens sold JLC to a group led by Boston-based investment firm Bain Capital, Inc. in June 1995 for $90 million in cash and notes. Wicat Systems, the computer-based aviation training division, was sold separately. The sales marked the end of a two-year restructuring and turned emphasis back on traditional business areas of making and marketing class rings, yearbooks, and other recognition products.

Profits for fiscal 1995 improved in all areas but JLC and net income returned to the plus column with $50.4 million in earnings on $665.1 million in sales. The restructuring and other operational changes resulted in $11 million in cost savings, according to the Jostens annual report. Flush with cash from the JLC sale and the company restructuring, Jostens repurchased seven million shares of stock for $169.3 million in September 1995 through a Modified Dutch Auction tender offer. But the company failed to meet earnings expectations in the latter half of 1996, and Wall Street reacted negatively.

A Second Century of Business; A New Millennium: 1997–99

Buhrmaster continued to fine-tune Jostens in 1997. The company's 100th year in business was celebrated in part with a new logo and identity system. For the first time Jostens consciously worked to extend brand awareness and preference. The effort was part of the larger mission to transform the company from a "ring and yearbook" business to "one that people call upon to help celebrate their most important moments."

The company cut additional costs with the transfer of some ring production to Mexico. In addition, the purchase of the Gold Lance class ring brand from Town & Country Corporation in July 1997 gave Jostens a strong presence in the retail class ring business, which was dominated by companies such as J.C. Penney and Wal-Mart.

Although the retail market accounted for about 33 percent of all U.S. annual class ring sales, Jostens' name-brand appeal helped the company maintain a dominant market share. Scott Carlson wrote in a May 1998 *St. Paul Pioneer Press* article, "Industry observers and Jostens' competitors attribute the company's market strength to making quality products, providing reliable service to students and parents, and hiring enterprising independent sales representatives who build long-term relationships with schools and gain access for in-school marketing." But Jostens' trade practices had drawn fire as well as praise.

Dallas-based Taylor Publishing, one of only two national yearbook companies competing against Jostens (the other was Herff Jones), claimed that the Minnesota company had tried to monopolize the Texas yearbook market. In May 1998 Taylor won a multimillion-settlement, which Jostens planned to appeal. Jostens had been under the scrutiny of the attorney general's office of Minnesota in the mid-1990s in regard to "exclusive supply contracts" with schools. Although the company denied that its sales practices were monopolistic, Jostens agreed to avoid using any techniques that would imply that the schools were locked in long-term exclusive deals. Jostens had been revamping its sales operations as a part of the general company restructuring.

Buhrmaster, who added the company's chairmanship to his roles as president and CEO in the beginning of 1998, had returned the company to profitability. Yet growth continued to be a concern: total sales for 1997 were up only 4.8 percent. Jostens' mature school market had limited growth opportunities, but the company planned to make the most of those through products such as the "Millennium" ring collection, which capitalized on the interest in the new century. The smaller recognition segment of the business, which primarily served U.S. and Canadian corporations and businesses, directed its focus on the fans of professional sports teams for added sales. Additional plant consolidation and infrastructure improvements that continued into 1998 delayed the implementation of any major expansion plans. The success of Buhrmaster's tenure as the head of the century-old business would be measured by his ability to build markets for Jostens brand-name products while embarking on new business ventures.

During 1999, Jostens took a hit from Y2K computer problems. The computer glitches caused lost and missed deliveries and the possible loss of future business, according to *Knight Ridder/Tribune Business News*. These losses were not the company's only concern. Core ring and yearbook sales were falling below expectations.

Taken Private: 2000–05

Investcorp led a leveraged buyout of Jostens, Inc. in 2000. The deal was valued at approximately $950 million, according to *Buyout*. Charles Philippin, a member of Investcorp's management committee, said the investment group's interest in a company such as Jostens was linked to the growth potential for the commemorative school products sector. The number of people in the high school and college age-bracket was on the upswing.

"Investcorp will assist Jostens in a number of Internet initiatives, Philippin said, using technology to further the company's growth. For example, in the future, students will be able to order Jostens' products online, while customizing them to match their individual interests. Philippin said providing these services should increase the company's buy rate by making the products more readily available to its customers," Leslie Green wrote.

During late 2001, Jostens sold off its loss ridden recognition division and tightened its focus on school-based operations. The company also closed a distribution center in Tennessee and a manufacturing plant in Canada. The moves helped Jostens post earnings of $4.1 million versus an $18.7 million loss in 2000.

Investcorp and other equity owners, including MidOcean Partners LP (DB Capital Partners), First Union Leveraged Capital, and Northwestern Mutual Life Insurance Co., sold Jostens in the summer of 2003. DLJ Merchant Banking Partners, a unit of Credit Suisse First Boston (CSFB) acquired the country's largest school yearbook and ring company in a deal valued at about $1.1 billion, according to the *Daily Deal*. During 2002, Jostens' sales were $756 million: 42 percent from yearbooks; 27 percent from jewelry, primarily rings; and 24 percent from diplomas, announcements, caps and gowns.

But the Jostens roller coaster ride was not over. The company lost $25.8 million during the 2003 fiscal year on sales of $788 million. In the summer of 2004 another ownership change was launched. Kolberg Kravis Roberts & Co. (KKR) would come on as a new equity investor, and Jostens was to be combined with educational textbook publisher Von Hoffmann Corp. and sample product maker Arcade Marketing under a new holding company.

The deal prompted the early change in leadership. Jostens President Michael L. Bailey would succeed Buhrmaster as CEO, and Jostens would continue to operate independently under the new structure. Marc Reisch, senior KKR advisor and chair of Canada's Yellow Pages Group, would lead the holding company, 90 percent jointly owned by KKR and DLJ. The remaining 10 percent of the company would be held by Jostens' management and existing investors.

As the complex deal, valued at $2.2 billion, worked toward completion, Jostens began marketing rings to fantasy football leagues via Internet sites. U.S. fantasy sports games participants numbered about 15 million in 2003, according to a *Providence Journal* article. Jostens had produced rings for 25 out of 38 Super Bowl victors and was running with that connection. Each Jostens-made diamond studded ring cost the New England Patriots in excess of $15,000. Fantasy league rings fell in the $99 to $400 range. By comparison, high school students were paying from $270 to $1,155 for their keepsakes.

By September 2004, credit for Jostens Intermediate Holding Corp. (Jostens IH Corp.) and the recapitalization of Jostens, Von Hoffmann, and Arcade by KKR and DLJ was set in place. CSFB was an underwriter along with Bank of America and Deutsche Bank. In early October, the transactions required to create the new specialty printing, marketing, and school-related affinity products and services organization were completed. Jostens IH Corp. produced 2004 fiscal year sales of about $1.5 billion. Jostens sales contributed $807.2 million to the total, a year over year increase of 2.4 percent.

In February 2005, the combined company and holding company took on new names, Visant Corporation and Visant Holding Corp., respectively. In April, Jostens hit the sports news again, when it delivered World Series rings to the Boston Red Sox. At 500, it was Jostens' largest championship ring order ever. Given that the Sox' last victory came in 1918, just 21 years into Jostens' 108 year history, it was no wonder.

Principal Competitors

American Achievement Corporation; Herff Jones Company of Indiana, Inc.; Walsworth Publishing Company, Inc.

Further Reading

Benson, Tracy E., "America's Unsung Heroes," *Industry Week,* December 3, 1990, p.12.

Bjorhus, Jennifer, "Jostens Gets New Owner," *Knight Ridder/Tribune Business News,* July 22, 2004.

Byrne, Harlan S., "Jostens Inc.: Demographics Offer an Earnings Kick," *Barron's,* October 14, 1991, p. 38.

"Business Briefs: Jostens Inc.," *Wall Street Journal,* January 28, 1994, p. B4.

Carlson, Scott, "Running Rings Around Competition," *St. Paul Pioneer Press,* May 17, 1998, pp. 1D, 3D.

Cohen, Amy, "CSFB Shops Mammoth Jostens Recap," *Loan Market Week,* September 13, 2004, pp. 1 + .

Colberg, Sonya, "Del City, Okla.-Based Trophy Maker Buys Division of Yearbook Company Jostens," *Knight Ridder/Tribune Business News,* December 6, 2001.

"Cost of High School Rings Up to $1,100," *UPI NewsTrack,* November 15, 2004.

"Daily Briefing," *Atlanta Journal-Constitution,* July 22, 2004, p. F2.

De Llosa, Patty, "What Business Am I In?" *Fortune,* November 14, 1994, p. 54.

"Digest of Earnings Reports," *Wall Street Journal,* July 30, 1993, p. C14.

"Digest of Earnings Reports," *Wall Street Journal,* August 4, 1995, p. B6.

Ehrlich, David, "DLJ Completes Jostens Buyout," *Daily Deal,* July 30, 2003.

Feyder, Susan, "Jostens Names Buhrmaster President and COO, Filling Positions Left Vacant by Two Retirements." *Star Tribune,* June 24, 1993.

——, "Jostens' New CEO Rings Out Some Old Concepts," *Star Tribune* (Minneapolis), May 23, 1994, p. 1D.

——, "Jostens Taking Charge for Closing Photo Plant," *Star Tribune* (Minneapolis), May 1, 1998, p. 3D.

——, "Jostens to Buy Back 7 Million Shares for $168 Million in "Dutch Auction," *Star Tribune* (Minneapolis), September 2, 1995, p. 1D.

——, "Longtime Jostens CEO Lurton Says He's Retiring," *Star Tribune* (Minneapolis), October 29, 1993, p. 1D.

——, "Rival Wins Suit Against Jostens over the Selling of Yearbooks," *Star Tribune* (Minneapolis), May 15, 1998, p. 3D.

——, "Still Going for the Brass Ring," *Star Tribune* (Minneapolis), April 20, 1998, p. 1D.

Fiedler, Terry, "H. William Lurton: Modesty That Rings True," *Corporate Report Minnesota,* January 1990, pp. 45–51, 92.

Fierman, Jaclyn, and Rayport, Jeffrey, "How to Make Money in Mature Markets," *Fortune,* November 25, 1985, pp. 46–50.

Foster, Jim, "Jostens Plans Consolidation Moves," *Star Tribune* (Minneapolis), January 29, 1992, p. 3D.

Fredrickson, Tom, "Jostens Tries Staff Buyouts to Ring in Costs," *Minneapolis/St. Paul CityBusiness,* April 22–28, 1994, pp. 1, 30.

Freund, Bob, "Class-Ring Giant Jostens Names Rochester, Minn., Native CEO," *Knight Ridder/Tribune Business News,* August 30, 2004.

——, "Rochester, Minn., Native to Preside Over Newly Recapitalized Jostens Inc.," *Knight Ridder/Tribune Business News,* August 30, 2004.

Gold, Jackey, "How to Make a Cash Cow Dance," *Financial World,* June 12, 1990, p. 38.

Green, Leslie, "Live Deals: Investcorp Takes Jostens Private," *Buyouts,* January 10, 2000.

Greenbaum, Jessica, "Lord of the Rings," *Forbes,* May 21, 1984, pp. 108–10.

Grimaldi, Paul, "Jostens Hopes to Score with Fantasy Football Rings," *Providence Journal* (Providence, R.I.), September 9, 2004.

Gross, Steve, "Jostens Learning Expanding PC Line," *Star Tribune* (Minneapolis), April 15, 1992, p. 3D.

"How to Make Money in Mature Markets." *Fortune,* November 25, 1985, pp. 46–50.

Isa, Margaret. "For Jostens, Class Rings Fit the Best," *Wall Street Journal,* August 21, 1995, p. C1.

"Jostens Has Lower Earnings, Sales," *Star Tribune* (Minneapolis), January 19, 1993.

"Jostens Inc.," *Wall Street Journal,* July 7, 1995, p. A2.

"Jostens Moves to Head of the Class," *St. Paul Pioneer Press & Dispatch,* October 14, 1985.

"Jostens Reports Sales and EBITDA Increase for 2001," *Business Wire,* February 14, 2002.

Jostens' Today (special 90th anniversary issue: "90 Years of People, Progress and Pride"), Minneapolis: Jostens, August 1987.

Kosman, Josh, and David Carey, "DLJ Pays $1.1B for Jostens," *Daily Deal,* June 18, 2003.

Marcotty, Josephine, "Boston Investment Group Is Buying Jostens Learning," *Star Tribune* (Minneapolis), May 24, 1995, p. 1D.

McCartney, Jim, "Bloomington, Minn.-Based Jostens Loses Earnings to Year 2000 Bug," *Knight Ridder/Tribune Business News,* July 2, 1999.

Moylan, Martin J., "Jostens Learning Gives Stock an Edge," *St. Paul Pioneer Press & Dispatch,* August 12, 1991.

Peterson, Susan E., "Lower-Than-Expected Earnings Forecast Drops Jostens Stock," *Star Tribune* (Minneapolis), June 15, 1996, p. 1D.

Raley, Marcia A., "Dain Bosworth Research Capsule: Jostens," January 25, 1988.

Reinan, John, "500 in Red Sox Family Get Jostens-Made Series Rings," *Star Tribune,* (Minneapolis), April 12, 2005, p. 1D.

——, "Wall Street Investment Firms Are New Owners of Jostens," *Star Tribune,* (Minneapolis), July 22, 2004, p. 1D.

Saporito, Bill, "Companies That Compete Best," *Fortune,* May 22, 1989, p. 36.

Spiegel, Peter, "Ringing True," *Forbes,* November 6, 1995, p. 12.

"Visant Corporation Announces 2004 Fourth Quarter and Full Year Results," *Business Wire,* March 10, 2005, p. 1.

"Yearbook Specialist OKs Acquisition by Investors," *Graphic Arts Monthly,* July 2003, p. 18.

Youngblood, Dick, "Former CEO of Jostens Explains What Went Wrong After 19 Years of Growth," *Star Tribune* (Minneapolis), April 20, 1994, p. 2D.

——, "In a Shrinking Market, He Gently Led Jostens to New World of Growth," *Star Tribune* (Minneapolis), March 18, 1991.

—Jay P. Pederson
—update: Kathleen Peippo

Keppel Corporation Ltd.

**1 HarbourFront Avenue, Suite 18-01 Keppel Bay
Tower**
Singapore 098632
Singapore
Telephone: + 65 6270 6666
Fax: + 65 6413 6391
Web site: http://www.kepcorp.com

Public Company
Incorporated: 1968 as Keppel Shipyard (Pte) Ltd.
Employees: 22,186
Sales: SGD 3.96 billion ($2.42 billion) (2004)
Stock Exchanges: Singapore
Ticker Symbol: KPP
NAIC: 336611 Ship Building and Repairing; 237210
    Land Subdivision; 334210 Telephone Apparatus
    Manufacturing; 483211 Inland Water Freight
    Transportation; 517110 Wired Telecommunications
    Carriers; 522110 Commercial Banking; 541330
    Engineering Services; 551112 Offices of Other
    Holding Companies

Keppel Corporation Ltd. is one of Singapore's leading and most diversified conglomerates. The publicly listed company, long controlled by the Singapore government, has undergone a thorough restructuring into the mid-2000s, and as a result has refocused on three core areas of operation: Offshore & Marine; Property; and Infrastructure. Offshore & Marine represents the company's largest component, generating some 61 percent of the group's SGD 3.96 billion ($2.4 billion) in 2004 revenues. Offshore & Marine includes subsidiaries Keppel FELS and Keppel Shipyard, and ranks among the world's largest shipbuilders and is the world leader in the construction of jack-up rigs for the offshore oil industry. Keppel Offshore & Marine operates from 16 shipyards located in Singapore, the United States, Norway, The Netherlands, the Philippines, Brazil, Azerbaijan, Kazakhstan, and the United Arab Emirates. Keppel's Property division, represented by Keppel Land Ltd., is a leading property developer primarily active in the Asian region, including in Singapore, China, Thailand, Vietnam, Hong Kong, Indonesia, Malaysia, the Philippines, South Korea, Myanmar, Thailand, and Vietnam, as well as in Australia. The group's total assets portfolio is worth more than SGD 5 billion. The company's Infrastructure division encompasses businesses active in engineering, power generation, and network systems, including the group's Keppel Telecommunications & Transportation Ltd. (Keppel T&T), active in the cellular and microwave communications markets. Before Keppel's restructuring, the largest part of the company's revenues came from its Investments division, which included a 49 percent stake in Singapore Petroleum Company. The divestment of these holdings cut the group's annual revenues by some two-thirds. Keppel is listed on the Singapore Stock Exchange.

Shipbuilding Beginnings in the 1960s

Keppel Corporation derived its name from Singapore's Keppel Bay, the country's primary deepwater harbor. Discovered by Admiral Sir Henry Keppel, the harbour provided a sheltered location for the establishment of the British Empire's colonial outpost in the country. In 1859, the first dock was built in New Harbour. By 1861, the Patent Slip and Dock Company had been established to provide harbor and ship repair services. That company later merged with its chief rival, Tanjong Pagar Dock Company, in 1899, and then changed its name to New Harbour Dock Company. The following year, New Harbour itself was renamed as Keppel Bay.

By 1905, the colonial government had taken the first step toward establishing its control over the harbor. In 1911, government control was solidified with the creation of the Singapore Harbour Board, which took over oversight of the entire Singapore coastline. Following Singapore's independence, the harbor board was placed under the new government's control and became known as the Port of Singapore Authority. Dock operations and services were placed under the Dockyard Department.

In 1968, however, a new company was formed, Singapore Drydock and Engineering Co. (Pte) Ltd., which then took over the Drydock Department. Soon after, the new company changed its name, becoming Keppel Shipyard (Pte) Ltd. The new company was initially operated by the Swan Hunter Group, then a major ship repairer in the region.

Company Perspectives:

Keppel is focused on creating and enhancing value for our shareholders by growing its businesses in Offshore and Marine, Property and Infrastructure to deliver sustainable earnings growth. As the Group pursues opportunities which fit its core competencies to achieve profitable growth, it is also building value on its investments to maximise shareholder wealth. Keppel's objective of maximising shareholder value is translated through its strategic actions of: Growing core competencies; Expanding into key markets worldwide; Investing in proprietary technologies; Leveraging strengths through strategic partnerships; Developing a talented global workforce.

Keppel launched the first wave of its expansion early the following decade. In 1971, the company entered shipbuilding, ship repair, and later, rig-building through the acquisition of a 40 percent stake in Far East Levingston Shipbuilding Ltd. That company had been formed just four years earlier, as Far East Shipbuilding Industries (FELS), then went public in 1969, before adopting the FELS name in 1970.

Controlled by the Singapore government, Keppel was placed under local management in 1972. The company continued to seek expansion opportunities, and in order to fund its growth strategy, the company went public in 1975. Nonetheless, the Singapore government maintained its majority ownership of the company.

Following the public offering, Keppel launched its first foreign expansion, creating Keppel Philippines Shipyard in 1975 and launching operations in that country by 1976. Closer to home, Keppel expanded its shipyard operations through the acquisition of rival Singmarine that same year. Then, in 1977, the company inaugurated its first graving dock, Temasek Dock.

Keppel took full control of FELS in 1980. Two years later, the company added its second graving dock, Raffles Dock. By then, however, Keppel had made its first moves toward becoming one of Singapore's major diversified conglomerates. In 1978, the company took its first step by establishing a finance company, Shing Laong Credit. Then in 1983, the company added a property development wing through the acquisition of Straits Steamship Land.

That company had been founded in 1890 as the Straits Steamship Company Ltd., and focused on shipping operations until the early 1970s. In 1973, however, Straits Steamship launched its own diversification drive, adding property development and warehousing businesses, as well as leisure and distribution businesses. Under Keppel, Straits grew strongly, particularly from the mid-1980s as Straits began buying up a number of major Singapore properties. Into the late 1980s, Straits began expanding into the international property market, quickly establishing itself as a major property group in the Asian region. In 1989, in recognition of the growth of Straits's property portfolio, Keppel spun off the property business into Straits Steamship Land Limited.

At the same time, Keppel restructured the former Straits shipping operation into a new company, Steamers Maritime Holdings, which was then given its own listing on the Singapore Stock Exchange in 1989. Steamers then became Keppel's vehicle for diversification into telecommunications networks and related infrastructure operations, launched in 1990. By 1997, Keppel had exited shipping, and had launched the M1 cellular phone network. In that year, Steamers changed its name, becoming Keppel T&T. At the same time, Keppel renamed its property business as Keppel Land.

Diversified Conglomerate in the 1990s

By then, Keppel itself had changed its name, becoming Keppel Corporation in 1986. The company continued to build its shipbuilding and port operations. In 1987, the company merged Singmarine Shipyard with Singapore Slipway, creating a new company, Singmarine Industries. That company was listed on the Singapore exchange the same year.

Keppel turned to the Philippines the following year, acquiring Cebu Shipyard and Engineering Works. That company was then listed on the Manila and Makati stock exchanges in 1989. The following year, Keppel ventured into the United States for the first time, acquiring a stake in a shipyard in Brownsville, Texas. That company became known as AMFELS in 1992 after Keppel acquired full control. By then, the company also had moved into the Persian Gulf market, acquiring the Arab Heavy Industries shipyard in the United Arab Emirates. The company also entered India at this time, buying a shipyard there.

Other shipyards followed during the decade, including the launch of the Caspian Shipyard Company in Azerbaijan in 1997, initially as a joint venture. The company also established operations in Bulgaria, Vietnam, Thailand, and elsewhere during this time.

Keppel in the meantime continued its diversification. In 1988, the company merged its Shing Laong Credit finance unit with publicly listed Sim Lim Finance, creating Keppel Finance. In that year, also, the company bought a stockbroking business, EG Tan Stockbrokers. Two years later, Keppel moved into banking, acquiring Asia Commercial Bank. The company subsequently renamed the bank Keppel Bank, and listed its shares on the Singapore Stock Exchange in 1993. By then, the company also had created a dedicated engineering business, Keppel Integrated Engineering, composed of the various engineering subsidiaries and businesses operated by its other subsidiaries. That company was later renamed Keppel FELS Energy and Infrastructure during the company's restructuring at the end of the 1990s.

Through the 1990s, Keppel emerged as a major player within the world's shipbuilding industry. Keppel developed leadership in two specialties in particular. The first was the design, engineering, and construction of jack-up rigs for the offshore exploration and production industry. The second was the conversion of ships as Floating Production Storage and Offloading and Floating Storage and Offloading vessels.

Refocused for the New Century

The Asian banking crisis forced Keppel to rein in its highly diversified businesses. The company launched a major restructuring program in 1998. As part of that restructuring, the company agreed to merge Keppel Bank with rival Tatlee Bank in

Key Dates:

1859: The first dock is built in Singapore's New Harbour (later Keppel Bay).

1913: Singapore Harbour Board, which becomes Port of Singapore Authority after the country's independence, is created.

1968: Singapore Drydock and Engineering Co. is established to take over Drydock Department of Port of Singapore Authority; the company adopts the name Keppel Shipyard.

1971: Shipbuilding group FELS is acquired.

1975: Keppel goes public on the Singapore Stock Exchange.

1983: The company acquires Straits Steamship Ltd., which provides an entry into property development, later forming the basis for Keppel Land and infrastructure subsidiary Keppel T&T.

1986: The company changes its name to Keppel Corporation.

1990: Keppel enters the United States with the acquisition of a shipyard in Brownsville, Texas; the company acquires Asia Commercial Bank, which becomes Keppel Bank.

1998: Keppel Bank merges with Tat Lee Bank amid a restructuring of operations.

1999: The company merges Keppel Shipyard with Hitachi Zosen, which becomes Keppel Hitachi Zosen.

2002: The company acquires full control of Keppel Hitachi Zosen, which is integrated into the newly established Keppel Offshore & Marine, as well as Keppel FELS and KFEI.

2003: Keppel enters Kazakhstan with the creation of an offshore engineering and construction subsidiary.

2004: Keppel spins off the Investments division to refocus around a core of Offshore & Marine, Property, and Infrastructure.

1998, marking a first step in the company's exit from the financial industry. Other rationalizations followed. In 1999, the company merged Keppel Shipyard with rival Hitachi Zosen, creating Keppel Hitachi Zosen. In 2002, however, Keppel took full control of that business, and established a new subsidiary, Keppel Offshore & Marine. This new company integrated several of Keppel's businesses, including Keppel FELS, Keppel Shipyard, and Keppel Singmarine, as well as all of the group's international shipyards.

Keppel's international profile expanded again that same year, when the company reached an agreement to acquire Rot-

terdam, The Netherlands-based Verolme Botlek. That shipyard was then renamed Keppel Verolme. Then in 2003, Keppel entered Kazakhstan, setting up an offshore engineering and construction facility there.

Keppel's restructuring continued into the mid-2000s. The company refocused its operations around a three-prong core of Offshore & Marine, Property, and Infrastructure. Into the beginning of 2004, Keppel also operated a fourth division, Investments, which included its 49 percent in Singapore Petroleum Company and a 36 percent stake in k1 Ventures. The Investment division in fact represented the largest part of Keppel's revenues, at some two-thirds of company sales. In 2004, however, Keppel spun off its investment operations. While this reduced the group's sales to slightly less than SGD 4 billion ($2.4 billion) for the year, it represented a major step forward in Keppel's strategy to reinvent itself as a focused Singapore corporate powerhouse for the new century.

Principal Subsidiaries

Alpha Investment Partners Ltd.; Arab Heavy Industries PJSC (UAE); Caspian Shipyard Company Ltd. (Azerbaijan); Dragon Land Ltd. (China); Keppel AmFELS Inc. (U.S.A.); Keppel Bay Pte Ltd.; Keppel Corporation Limited; Keppel Electric Pte Ltd.; Keppel Energy Pte Ltd.; Keppel Engineering Pte Ltd.; Keppel FELS Brasil S.A. (Brazil); Keppel FELS Limited; Keppel FMO Pte Ltd.; Keppel Integrated Engineering Ltd.; Keppel Kazakhstan LLP; Keppel Land International Limited; Keppel Land Limited; Keppel Offshore & Marine Ltd.; Keppel Philippines Marine Inc.; Keppel Philippines Properties Inc.; Keppel Shipyard Limited; Keppel Singmarine Pte Ltd.; Keppel Telecommunications & Transportation Ltd.; Keppel Thai Properties Public Co. Ltd. (Thailand); Keppel Verolme B.V. (The Netherlands); MobileOne Ltd.; Network Engineering; Offshore & Marine A/S (Norway); Offshore Technology Development Pte Ltd.; Seghers Keppel Technology Group N.V. (Belgium); Singapore Petroleum Company Ltd.

Further Reading

"Keppel to Buy 51% of Five Star Property," *Business Day,* January 28, 2000.

Lim, Richard, *Tough Men, Bold Visions: The Story of Keppel,* Singapore: Keppel Corporation, 1993.

Maksoud, Judy, "Newbuild Jackups Keep Keppel Busy," *Offshore,* May 2005, p. 20.

Snyder, Robert E., "Keppel Acquires Dutch Shipyard," *World Oil,* September 2002, p. 29.

Thorpe, Alan, "Ship Repair Majors Talk Merger," *Marine Log,* September 2000, p. 27.

—M.L. Cohen

Klabin S.A.

Rua Formosa 367, 12 andar
São Paulo 01075-900
Brazil
Telephone: 55 (11) 3225-4000
Fax: 55 (11) 3225-4241
Web site: http://www.klabin.com.br

Public Company
Incorporated: 1909 as Companhia Fabricadora del Papel
   S.A.
Employees: 12,800
Sales: BRL 2.73 billion ($931.74 million) (2004)
Stock Exchanges: Bolsa de Valores de São Paulo OTC
Ticker Symbols: KLBN; KLBAY
NAIC: 113110 Timber Tract Operations; 113210 Forest
   Nurseries and Gathering of Forest Products; 113310
   Logging; 322121 Paper (Except Newsprint) Mills;
   322130 Paperboard Mills; 322211 Corrugated and
   Solid Fiber Box Manufacturing; 322212 Folding
   Paperboard Box Manufacturing; 322213 Setup
   Paperboard Box Manufacturing; 322224 Uncoated
   Paper and Multiwall Bag Manufacturing

Klabin S.A. is Brazil's largest manufacturer of pulp and paper products. A vertically organized enterprise, it harvests timber from its own forest tracts and sells lumber to a variety of customers, including the U.S. construction industry. Its timber (and the timber it purchases from others) also is converted in its own factories to cellulose (wood pulp), which is used in the company's plants for the production of packaging paper, paper sacks, and corrugated cardboard boxes. It concentrates on these products because, as a low-cost producer of wood and wood pulp, it specializes in paper grades where the raw material plays a major role in the final cost of the product. Its planted pine trees reach maturity for cutting in only 20 years, compared with 100 years in Europe.

Venerable Papermaking Pioneer: 1911–90

Maurício Klabin was one of the five surviving children of the 11 born to a Lithuanian Jewish couple. He emigrated to Brazil in 1889 and began to make and sell cigarettes in São Paulo. He was soon joined by members of his family who, with the Lafer relatives of his wife, took part in the incorporation of Klabin Irmaos & Cia. in 1899. Initially a firm that imported office stationery supplies, especially paper, it merged with a small factory that made paper from rags. When the Klabins and Lafers decided in 1909 to open a new factory to make paper from imported wood pulp, they organized Companhia Fabricadora de Papel S.A., with the family firm owning 44 percent and 25 shareholders holding the rest. The factory opened in 1911.

Companhia Fabricadora de Papel grew to be among the biggest paper producers in Brazil during the 1920s and attained first place in 1929. But the Klabin-Lafer clan had even bigger plans. The family firm became a holding company that, in the 1930s, developed a ceramics manufacturing company and took in a nitroglcerine enterprise. In addition, in 1933, it purchased a huge tract of land near Monte Alegre in the state of Paraná both for its wood and for a future paper plant. The company founded Indústrias Klabin do Paraná S.A. for this purpose in 1934, with nine shareholders, all family members.

The new company lacked the capital to proceed with its plans until World War II had cut off newsprint imports from Scandinavia and left Brazilian publishers at the mercy of U.S. and Canadian suppliers, who were able to command sharply higher prices. In an era when the only other mass media was radio, this was a matter of serious concern to President Getúlio Vargas, who ruled Brazil as a virtual dictator. He enabled the company to obtain, in 1941, the necessary government credits to purchase imported machinery for the plant and imported electrical equipment to harness the power from a waterfall on a tributary of the Paraná. The plant, which opened in 1947 at Telêmaco Borba, had the capacity to produce 40,000 metric tons of wood pulp a year, half the nation's needs, and 40,000 metric tons of newsprint, 80 percent of the nation's needs. The raw material came from the company's own nearly 1,000 square miles of land. Beginning in 1943, the native trees were interspersed with Araucaria, eucalyptus, and pine plantings.

The death of Wolff Klabin in 1957 left his son Israel, a grandnephew of the founder, as one of four family partners and unofficial president—in charge of the holding company's interests, including what was now Klabin do Paraná de Celulose S.A., South America's biggest paper producer. The family controlled an estimated 80 percent of Brazil's production of newsprint, corrugated and other paper-finishing plants, a rayon and nylon mill, two coffee plantations, a cattle ranch, and the ceramics factory, as well as indirect interests in industrial chemicals, acrylic fibers, land development, and appliances. A $30 million plant expansion, completed in 1963, more than doubled the Paraná plant's newsprint capacity to 135,000 tons. Three years later, the holding company obtained financing from international lending agencies for the construction of a $26 million pulp and paper mill at Lages, in the state of Santa Catarina. Israel Klabin remained president of the group until 1980, shortly after becoming mayor of Rio de Janeiro.

Acquisitions and Divestitures: 1990–2003

The Klabin group purchased other companies during the 1970s and ranked 47th in size among Brazilian enterprises in 1989. In 1990 the holding company had 17 factories, 19,000 employees, revenue of $900 million a year, and it accounted for annual production of one million metric tons of pulp and paper. That year it was renamed Indústrias Klabin de Papel e Celulose S.A. and, although described as a private holding company, was listed on the Borsa de Valores de São Paulo. Klabin Fabricadora de Papel e Celulose S.A. represented about two-thirds of the business. The two other companies were Papel e Celulose Catarinense S.A. (PCC) and Riocell S.A., a pulp and paper producer in Guaíba, Rio Grande do Sul, which was 68 percent owned by Kiv Participaçoes S.A., a holding company in which Klabin held a 52 percent controlling interest. The PCC and Riocell properties included some 217,000 acres of planted forest.

Between 1990 and early 1993 Klabin invested $260 million to expand and modernize its factories. In April 1993 it opened a new PCC unit, in Correia Pinto, Santa Catarina, to increase its production of tissues, toilet paper, and paper towels. A corrugated box plant opened later in the year in Jundiaí, near São Paulo. The group also was planning to invest $300 million to raise production at the Telêmaco Borba plant. In addition, it had purchased at auction in the previous year the Camaçari, Bahia, pulp mill that would become the production facility of Klabin Bacell S.A. and that would require another $200 million to convert to a soluble-pulp plant.

Klabin was producing, in 1993, liquid-packaging board, kraftliner, testliner, and corrugated boxes; newsprint, directory, and wood-containing printing papers; tissue and sanitary products; kraft paper and shipping sacks; and eucalyptus and fluff-market pulps. Of $600 million in annual net sales, exports amounted to 39 percent. Interviewed for *PPI/Pulp & Paper International* by Amanda Marcus, Managing Director Alfredo Claudio Lobl called Klabin "still the lowest-cost producers of

wood in the world." During the late 1990s Brazilian demand for packaging, folding board, and liquid packaging board grew by 15 percent a year. Klabin was the only company in Brazil making both the hardwood and softwood pulp used for these grades, and its biggest problem was to meet demand.

Josmar Verillo, who was president of Klabin from 1998 to 2002, presided over a restructuring of the enterprise that saw the number of its companies reduced from 30 to 17 and the dismissal of more than 2,600 employees. Priority was given to three areas: timber, packaging, and a third to be decided—either bleached cellulose or discarded paper. The existing companies were grouped into five sectors. During 1999–2000 Klabin acquired Laleka, a manufacturer of paper towels and hygienic paper; Bacraft, a producer of absorbent and sanitary papers; and Igaras, primarily a manufacturer of cardboard boxes.

By 2000, when all of its mills were producing at full capacity, Klabin had formed new strategic alliances with at least two companies. A joint venture with Kimberly-Clark Corp., KCK Tissue S.A., controlled much of this market in Brazil. A newsprint joint venture with Norske Skog do Brasil Ltda. was allowing Klabin to leave the newsprint sector of the paper business, which was described as no longer suitable except for the very largest of the world's paper companies. The arrangement involved the Norske Skog joint venture leasing a newsprint machine at Klabin's Monte Alegre for three years, after which Klabin converted the machine to produce more board instead. In 2003 Klabin sold its interest in the joint venture, Klabin Monte Alegre Com. Ind. Ltda., to the Norske Skog unit. Newsprint accounted for only 9 percent of Klabin's net revenues in 2000, compared with a combined 80 percent for pulp, packaging paper, tissue, and corrugated boxes.

Riocell, on the other hand, had been operating at a loss since 1996 because of falling prices for wood pulp, impelling Klabin to seek a buyer or a joint venture partner. The problem was that, although the price of its product had recovered, the facility's capacity needed to at least double in order to be economically viable, which would require significant investment. As preparation for a possible transaction, Klabin purchased the part of Riocell that it did not own in 2000 and renamed the company Klabin Riocell S.A. Then, at the end of 2001, as part of a corporate restructuring, Klabin merged itself into Riocell and renamed the company Klabin S.A. By this time it had raised Riocell's manufacturing capacity by 25 percent. In 2003 Klabin sold Riocell to a rival pulp and paper company, Aracruz Celulose S.A., for $610 million. Another problem subsidiary was Klabin Bacell, the soluble-pulp producer in a joint venture with an Austrian company that began operations in 1995. Klabin increased its share of the enterprise from 62 percent to 82 percent in 2000 and sold it in 2003. Also in 2003, Klabin sold its half-interest in KCK Tissue and Klabin Kimberly S.A.

Of Klabin's acquisitions in this period, the most important was the 2000 purchase of Igaras, Brazil's second largest packaging company, for an arguably too pricey $510 million. This acquisition included a kraftliner mill in Santa Catarina, pine plantations near the mill, two facilities elsewhere that were processing recovered paper, and five box-making plants strategically located throughout Brazil. The latter raised Klabin's share of the Brazilian corrugated-board box market from 18

Key Dates:

1899: Importing family firm Klabin Irmaos & Cia. is incorporated.

1909: A company is incorporated to make paper from imported wood pulp.

1911: This company opens a factory in the São Paulo metropolitan area.

1929: Companhia Fabricadora de Papel S.A. is the largest paper manufacturer in Brazil.

1933: The Klabin holding company buys a huge forested. tract in the state of Paraná.

1947: A papermaking pulp and paper mill opens on this site.

1966: Financing is secured for a second pulp and paper mill, in the state of Santa Catarina.

1990: The Klabin holding company owns 17 factories and has 19,000 employees.

1992: The company purchases the pulp plant that is to be directed by Klabin Bacell S.A.

2000: Klabin purchases Igaras, Brazil's second largest producer of packaging paper.

2002: A four-year restructuring has reduced the number of subsidiary companies from 30 to 17.

2003: Klabin sells newsprint, cellulose, and tissues manufacturing facilities.

to 30 percent. With regard to packaging, it held 40 percent of the domestic market.

Klabin S.A. in 2004

Klabin emerged from these changes somewhat smaller in size but considerably lightened in debt and capable, in the judgment of its chief executive, Miguel Sampol Pou, of investing $1 billion over the next five years. Some $500 million was tentatively earmarked to double annual production of cartonboard at Monte Alegre. Much of this material would be used for packaging liquids such as fruit juices and bulk wine and, along with carrier board and folding boxboard, offered superior profit margins. A company kraftliner mill at Angaratuba, São Paulo, was being converted to cartonboard production. Both these products contained eucalyptus fiber, good for rigidity and also providing a very good surface for printing.

Sampol Pou's plans for Klabin called for annual growth of more than 10 percent through 2009, when its revenues would be 75 percent higher than in 2003. The increase in paper and board production would call for more wood pulp, and hence, timber. Of the company's 353,000 hectares (872,000 acres) of forest, some 230,000 hectares (568,000 acres) adjacent to the Monte Alegre facility continued to be a mosaic of stands of eucalyptus and loboly pine interspersed within large tracts of virgin native forest, a practice that kept pests at bay, in large part by providing haven to their natural predators. As a rule, logs of less

than 20 centimeters (about eight inches) in diameter were going directly to the mill, whereas the larger ones went to sawmills. Small private landowners also were providing the company with timber.

Klabin's production of paper products came to 1.34 million metric tons in 2004, of which exports accounted for 41 percent (excluding wood). Wood sales came to 3.3 million metric tons. Cellulose production of 1.2 million metric tons meant that Klabin was still the second largest pulp producer in Brazil despite its disposal of Riocell. This was now for internal consumption only, however, as the prime raw material for its paper products. The company also was Brazil's largest consumer of recovered fiber. Of Klabin's consolidated net sales of BRL 2.73 billion ($931.74 million), wood sales accounted for 11 percent and exports for 30 percent. The company's net debt (of which 75 percent was long-term) was BRL 498 million ($169.97 million), far below the level of the late 1990s.

Principal Subsidiaries

Antas Serviços Florestais S/C Ltda.; IKAPÉ Emprendimentos Ltda.; Klabin Argentina S.A.; Klabin do Paraná Productos Florestais; Klapart Participaçoes Ltda.

Principal Operating Units

Corrugated Boxes; Forestry; Industrial Sacks; Papers and Cardboards.

Principal Competitors

Aracruz Celulose S.A.; Cia. Suzano de Papel e Celulose; Votorantim Celulose e Papel S.A.

Further Reading

"Brazil to Finance Paper-Pulp Plant," *New York Times,* January 25, 1941, p. 27.

"O céu é o limite para a Klabin," *Exame,* March 21, 1990, pp. 50–52.

Cony, Carlos Heitor, and Sergio Lamarao, *Wolff Klabin,* Rio de Janeiro: Editora FGV, 2001.

"Klabin Continues to Expand in Its Core Areas," *PPI/Pulp & Paper International,* June 2000, p. 48.

Knight, Patrick, "Klabin Pulls Off a Good Deal with Igaras Package," *PPI/Pulp & Paper International,* May 2001, pp. 36–37.

——, "Preparing for a Board Boom," *PPI/Pulp & Paper International,* February 2005, pp. 25–28.

Mano, Cristiane, "Primeiro diminuir, depois crescer," *Exame,* December 8, 2004, pp. 70–71.

Marcus, Amanda, "Klabin Enjoys Lead Role Among Latins," *PPI/ Pulp & Paper International,* November 1993, pp. 39, 41–43.

Raymont, Henry, "New Consortium Plans Latin Aid," *New York Times,* May 18, 1966, p. 60.

Rebouças, Lidia, "A hora da verdade," *Exame,* April 17, 2002, pp. 72–75.

"Rothschilds of the South," *Time,* June 28, 1963, p. 80.

"Who's Who in Foreign Business," *Fortune,* March 1963, p. 64

—Robert Halasz

Lifetime Brands, Inc.

One Merrick Avenue
Westbury, New York 11590-6601
U.S.A.
Telephone: (516) 683-6000
Fax: (516) 683-6116
Web site: http://www.lifetimebrands.com

Public Company
Incorporated: 1945 as Lifetime Cutlery Corporation
Employees: 751
Sales: $189.5 million (2004)
Stock Exchanges: NASDAQ
Ticker Symbol: LCUT
NAIC: 321999 All Other Miscellaneous Wood Product
Manufacturing; 326199 All Other Plastics Product
Manufacturing; 327210 Glass and Glass Product
Manufacturing; 332211 Cutlery and Flatware (Except
Precious) Manufacturing; 332214 Kitchen Utensil,
Pot, and Pan Manufacturing; 442299 All Other Home
Furnishings Stores

Lifetime Brands, Inc., formerly Lifetime Hoan Corporation, designs, develops, markets, and distributes a wide range of household consumer products under both owned and licensed brands. These products include cutlery, kitchenware, cutting boards, bakeware, cookware, pantryware, tabletop products, and bath accessories. Among the trademarks the company owns are Hoffritz, Roshco, Baker's Advantage, Kamenstein, CasaModa, Hoan, Gemco, and USE; licensed brands include Farberware, KitchenAid, Cuisinart, Sabatier, DBK-Daniel Boulud Kitchen, and Joseph Abboud Environments. Each year, Lifetime's 35-person design department creates in excess of 600 new products, ranging from entry-level items through the mid-priced sector and to the upscale. The company farms out production to about 100 contract manufacturers located primarily in the People's Republic of China, where it maintains two showroom/offices. Lifetime sells its products primarily in the United States to about 900 customers, which include national retailers, department store chains, mass merchant retail and discount stores, supermarket chains, warehouse clubs, specialty

stores, off-price retailers, and home centers—more than 33,000 individual retail locations in all. Its largest customer is the Wal-Mart Stores, Inc. chain, which accounts for about 24 percent of net sales. Through its Outlet Retail Stores, Inc. subsidiary, Lifetime Brands also owns and operates about 60 Farberware outlet stores located in 31 states. Most of Lifetime's products are shipped to its customers from the firm's 550,000-square-foot distribution center in Robbinsville, New Jersey.

Cutlery Beginnings

The founder of Lifetime Brands—and the chairman, CEO, and president of the company to the advent of the 21st century—was Milton Cohen, born in 1929, the son of a garment worker. Following high school, Cohen began working as a scissors and shears salesman. He eventually gained a position, at age 26, managing sales on the East Coast for a large cutlery firm.

Wanting to be his own boss, Cohen joined in 1957 with partner Sam Siegel to start a knife factory in Brooklyn under the name Reo Products. In 1960 Reo Products acquired 1945-founded Lifetime Cutlery Corporation, a larger distributor of knives than Reo. Cohen adopted Lifetime's name for his company.

Cohen, in a 1995 interview with the *New York Times,* estimated that there were about 100 cutlery manufacturers in the United States in the late 1950s, but that their numbers dwindled over the decades to three. Most of the companies failed because of increasing imports of cheap goods from Asia. A key to his company's survival, Cohen had concluded, was the 1961 decision to shift manufacturing overseas. That year the company began contracting with manufacturers in Japan for the production of parts. The parts were then shipped to the Brooklyn factory for assembly and packing. Freed from the production of basic parts, Cohen and Siegel could concentrate on design, packaging, and marketing. Over the years, Lifetime Cutlery shifted its production from one east Asian country to the next, progressing to Korea, Taiwan, the Philippines, Malaysia, Indonesia, Thailand, and China.

Between 1965 and 1967 Lifetime sold 50 million steak knives to Shell Oil for ten cents each. Shell gave one of the ivory-plastic-handled knives out to each customer coming in

Company Perspectives:

Lifetime Brands, Inc. continues to grow by utilizing advanced design capabilities to emphasize innovation and quality within its portfolio of premium brands. Lifetime Hoan's in-house design and product development team, composed of 27 professionals, uses advanced training in state-of-the-art design programs to incorporate new materials and technology into our product assortments.

for a fill-up. Cohen told *Business Week* in 1994, "It was a lot of business and just a lot of hard work and no profit."

By staying away from such risky gimmicks and especially through relentless marketing, Cohen, Siegel, and a third partner increased sales by 1980 to $13 million. Within a year, however, both of Cohen's partners died. Needing cash for himself and to provide for his partners' families, Cohen—in collaboration with his former partners' sons, Jeffrey Siegel and Craig Phillips—executed a $16 million leveraged buyout (LBO) of the company in April 1984. Siegel and Phillips became executives at Lifetime, remaining in executive positions and on the board of directors into the early 2000s.

Acquisition of Hoan Products: Mid-1980s

Cohen and his new partners acquired a controlling interest in Hoan Products Ltd. in 1986; they soon owned the company outright, through a total investment of $4 million. Hoan Products was an unprofitable supplier of kitchen tools and gadgets generating annual sales of $14 million (whose name stood for "Housewares of All Nations"). Lifetime Cutlery became Lifetime Hoan Corporation following the takeover.

Still headquartered in low-cost Brooklyn, Lifetime Hoan moved the Hoan operation there, selling its New Jersey headquarters for $5 million. Other changes included redesigning the Hoan line, cutting the costs of manufacturing Hoan products, and selling them through Lifetime's established channels. The last of these maneuvers was particularly strategic as both Lifetime cutlery and Hoan kitchenware were positioned in the entry-level and middle-market sectors, selling well in supermarkets, mass merchandise stores, and specialty shops. By the early 1990s half of the company's sales came from the Hoan line.

In 1987 Lifetime Hoan moved its manufacturing operation to Dayton, New Jersey, maintaining its headquarters in Brooklyn. That same year the company entered into its first licensing agreement. In a deal with The Walt Disney Company, Lifetime obtained the right to develop and market a line of Disney flatware and a line of kitchen gadgets under the Chef Mickey name. After some ups and downs, the two companies settled on profitable lines of children's housewares featuring Mickey and Minnie Mouse on such items as bag clips, party goods, bottle stoppers, and flatware.

Farberware and Pillsbury Licenses Marking Early 1990s

Revenues reached $38.5 million by 1989, while net income stood at $800,000. At this time Lifetime Hoan's cutlery lines,

which included the Tristar and Old Homestead brands, remained on the lower end of the market. The company made its first move up the scale in early 1990 when it entered into a license agreement with Farberware, Inc. to market cutlery, kitchen gadgets, and barbecue accessories under the well-known and respected Farberware name. Founded in 1900, Farberware made its reputation with the stainless steel cookware it introduced soon after the end of World War II and the beginnings of the postwar boom years. In 1966 Farberware was acquired by Walter Kidde & Co., which sold the company to British conglomerate Hanson PLC in 1987. Under Hanson, Farberware began broadening the range of products bearing the famous brand, with the agreement with Lifetime Hoan a notable part of that trend. The Lifetime-created Farberware products were mid-priced and aimed at department stores and specialty shops, a retail sector already well acquainted with the Farberware name. This strategy enhanced both the probability that stores would stock the items and that consumers would buy them.

A similar licensing deal involving the leveraging of a familiar brand was reached in April 1991, this time with the Pillsbury Company for a line of moderately priced bakeware and kitchen accessories. Launched in mid-1992, the line eventually included items such as nonstick cookie sheets and pie pans, spatulas, whisks, and cookie cutters featuring the Pillsbury Doughboy logo, as well as accessories such as peelers, can openers, kitchen hooks, and steamers incorporating the Green Giant character. These products were aimed at the supermarket channel, where the Pillsbury brands were long established.

In June 1991 Lifetime Hoan sold 40 percent of the company to the public in an initial public offering (IPO) that raised $19.4 million. Portions of the proceeds were used to virtually eliminate Lifetime's outstanding debt (some stemming from the 1984 LBO) and to redeem all outstanding preferred stock, leaving about $7.7 million in working capital. The offering not only strengthened the company's balance sheet, it also positioned Lifetime to grow through continued aggressive new product development and through acquisition. In addition, the offering provided some liquidity for Cohen and the second-generation Siegel and Phillips shareholders, a lesson Cohen learned from the surprise deaths of his original partners. As of 1993, Cohen and his family held a 24 percent stake in Lifetime Hoan, while the Siegel and Phillips families held another 27 percent.

The company launched a new brand, Smart Choice, in 1993. This was a line of gadgets, packaged as impulse purchases and geared strictly for supermarkets, drugstore chains, and mass merchandisers. Smart Choice helped fuel a new product blitz whereby Lifetime introduced 500 new items in 1994, compared with 150 the previous year. By 1994 the company offered about 3,000 different products.

Sales reached $77.4 million in 1994, nearly double the figure of 1989. Profits stood at $8.6 million, which translated into a profit margin of 11.1 percent, quite impressive for a maker of mainly low-priced housewares. The Farberware license was responsible for much of the increase in both sales and profits, as the Farberware line accounted for more than a quarter of overall sales and an even larger portion of profits. The decision to sell more higher priced products (a Farberware set of knives might be priced three times higher than a similar set under one of

Key Dates:

1945: Lifetime Cutlery Corporation is founded.

1957: Milton Cohen and partner Sam Siegel start a knife factory in Brooklyn under the name Reo Products.

1960: Reo acquires Lifetime Cutlery and adopts the acquired firm's name.

1961: Company begins contracting with overseas manufacturers.

1984: Cohen, along with Jeffrey Siegel and Craig Phillips, executes a $16 million leveraged buyout of the firm.

1986: The partners acquire a controlling interest in Hoan Products Ltd., maker of kitchen tools and gadgets; after they gain full control of Hoan, Lifetime Cutlery is renamed Lifetime Hoan Corporation.

1987: Lifetime enters into its first licensing agreement, with The Walt Disney Company.

1990: Company agrees to licensing deal with Farberware, Inc.

1991: Company completes an initial public offering (IPO), selling 40 percent of the company to the public.

1995: Upscale Hoffritz brand is acquired.

1996: Lifetime acquires a 200-year, royalty-free, exclusive right to the Farberware name in the cutlery, kitchen gadget, and barbecue accessory categories; as part of the deal, the company also assumes ownership of 50 Farberware outlet stores.

1998: Company acquires Roshco, Inc., maker of betterquality bakeware under the Roshco and Baker's Advantage brands.

2000: Pantryware/woodenware maker M. Kamenstein, Inc. is acquired; Jeffrey Siegel is named CEO.

2001: Under license from Whirlpool Corporation, the KitchenAid line of kitchen gadgets debuts.

2002: In agreement with Conair Corporation, Lifetime gains the right to produce Cuisinart brand cutlery.

2004: The rights to several brands are gained through acquisition of Excel Importing Corp.

2005: Company changes its name to Lifetime Brands, Inc.

Lifetime's other brands) was clearly beginning to pay dividends. The company's shareholders benefited thereby from a 3-for-2 stock split in late 1993.

Lifetime Hoan moved its headquarters to Westbury, New York (on Long Island), in October 1994. The company had outgrown its space in Brooklyn, but also found difficulty in attracting employees there. Of particular importance was hiring new computer-literate designers because the design department was being expanded and computerized during this period. The move to Long Island enabled Lifetime to bring in the highly skilled people it needed and to improve its productivity. The company paid $5 million for a 40,000-square-foot building, used as headquarters and for a showroom for visiting buyers. Previously, because many buyers were reluctant to venture into Brooklyn, Lifetime had had to maintain a showroom in expensive Manhattan, where high rents limited its size. At this new building, the company had a huge showroom, where buyers could tour both it and Lifetime's high-tech design shop at the

same time. Meantime, Lifetime continued to contract out its manufacturing to its Asian partners, with final assembly and packaging handled at its New Jersey factory.

Mid- to Late 1990s Hoffritz, Farberware, and Roshco Deals

The mid- to late 1990s saw an ever more aggressive Lifetime Hoan complete a series of acquisitions and enter into new licensing and partnership deals. Having established itself as a leader in the entry-level and mid-priced segments of the housewares market, Hoan sought to enter the high-end market. To do so, it decided to acquire an instantly recognizable brand, rather than license one. After a two-year search, Lifetime settled upon the upscale 60-year-old Hoffritz brand, acquiring it in September 1995 from Alco Capital Group, Inc., an investment firm that had purchased Hoffritz in late 1992 from the bankrupt C.W. Acquisitions. At one time, there had been 197 Hoffritz stores selling upscale cutlery and kitchenware, but by the time Lifetime acquired the brand there were only six (and these were closed shortly thereafter).

Lifetime launched a new line of Hoffritz products in the spring of 1996, a line that within a few years exceeded 300 items. It featured knives, scissors, and shears; kitchenware, including spatulas, ladles, peelers, ice cream scoops, lemon zesters, serving spoons, graters, thermometers, and colanders; barbecue accessories; cutting boards; pepper grinders; bar accessories; and personal care implements, such as nail files and clippers, tweezers, manicure sets, and pocket knives. Lifetime marketed Hoffritz products in department and specialty stores through a "shop within a store" concept.

In 1995 Hanson spun off Farberware and 33 of its other smaller U.S. subsidiaries, forming U.S. Industries Inc. The new company soon began shopping Farberware around, having designated it a noncore asset. In April 1996 Lifetime Hoan joined with Syratech Corporation, an East Boston-based maker of tabletop and giftware products, to acquire most of the assets of Farberware for a total of about $52 million, $12.7 million of which was paid by Lifetime in cash. Syratech gained Farberware's cookware and small electrical appliances business. Lifetime and Syratech simultaneously entered into a 50–50 joint venture that gained outright ownership of the rights to the Farberware trademarks. Through this joint venture, Lifetime acquired a 200-year, royalty-free, exclusive right to the Farberware name in connection with the cutlery, kitchen gadgets, and barbecue accessories covered by the 1990 licensing agreement; in essence Lifetime thereby owned the trademark for these product categories. The company also acquired 50 Farberware outlet stores. In July 1997 Lifetime struck a deal with Meyer Corporation, the licensed manufacturer of Farberware cookware, in connection with these stores. Lifetime would continue to own and operate the stores, while Meyer and Lifetime would be jointly responsible for merchandising and stocking them, with Meyer handling the cookware and Lifetime the rest of the stock. Meyer would receive all revenue from sale of the cookware and reimburse Lifetime for 62.5 percent of the stores' operating expenses. Through this arrangement, the stores returned to profitability. In the meantime, in October 1997, Lifetime Hoan announced that it had initiated payment of cash dividends on its stock, starting with the third quarter of 1997, a move reflecting a company confident of its long-term prospects.

Not resting on its laurels, Lifetime in August 1998 acquired Roshco, Inc., a Chicago-based, privately held distributor of better-quality bakeware under the Roshco and Baker's Advantage brands. The addition of Roshco, which had revenues of $10 million in 1997, not only extended the company further into the bakeware sector, it also added to the already strong array of higher-end products Lifetime could aim at department and specialty stores. In late 1998 Lifetime achieved similar aims through the signing of a license agreement with Corning Consumer Products Company for the design and marketing of cutlery and cutting boards under the well-known Revere brand. The first products from this line were introduced in early 1999.

Over the course of the 1990s Lifetime Hoan made a dramatic transition from a marketer of lower-end, lesser-known trademarks to that of higher-end, better-known brands. Farberware and Hoffritz quickly became Lifetime's most important brands, with these lines accounting for about 60 percent of overall sales in 1996, 70 percent in 1997, 75 percent in 1998, and 80 percent in 1999. The addition of the Roshco and Revere brands to the company stable were logical extensions of the same strategy. At the very end of the decade, in December 1999, Jeffrey Siegel was named president of Lifetime Hoan, having served as executive vice-president since 1967. Cohen remained chairman and CEO.

Aggressive Expansion in the Early 2000s

Lifetime stepped up its pace of expansion in the early 2000s. In September 2000 the company acquired privately held M. Kamenstein, Inc. Founded in Brooklyn, New York, by Meyer Kamenstein in 1893, M. Kamenstein produced pantryware, teakettles, and home organization accessories crafted of wood, glass, plastic, metal, and combinations thereof. A month later, Lifetime entered into a licensing agreement with Whirlpool Corporation to design, manufacture, and market a line of high-end kitchen utensils under the well-regarded KitchenAid brand. Lifetime's KitchenAid line became the company's top brand within just a couple of years. More than 470 KitchenAid items were introduced in 2001, the debut year, in what management called ''the most successful introduction in the company's history.'' The agreement with Whirlpool was soon expanded to include bakeware, which hit store shelves in the second half of 2002. Also in 2000, after achieving only minimal sales from the Revere products, Lifetime terminated its agreement with Corning Consumer Products for the licensed Revere line. Finally, in December 2000 Siegel assumed the additional title of CEO. He was named chairman as well six months later, taking over for the retiring Cohen.

Following up on the success of the KitchenAid line, Lifetime secured the rights to produce cutlery under another prestigious brand, Cuisinart. This deal, completed in March 2002 with Conair Corporation, led to the introduction late that year of three lines of deluxe fine-edge Cuisinart brand cutlery. Also in late 2002 Lifetime created a new division called CasaModa, whose lines would feature moderately priced barware and serveware.

As the company was implementing this aggressive expansion, which along with organic growth in existing brands translated into fairly steady increases in revenues each year of about 10 percent, a major overhaul of Lifetime's warehouse management system was negatively affecting the bottom line. The systems and software were overhauled in order that the company could shift its warehousing from three separate facilities to a much larger, single, state-of-the-art warehouse in Robbinsville, New Jersey. This new facility, boasting 550,000 square feet, was finally operational in January 2003, by which time Lifetime had suffered through four straight years of depressed earnings ranging from $2.3 million to $4 million. The millions spent on the new warehouse and its critical systems paid off as net income reached $8.4 million in 2003 on record revenues of $160.4 million. Nevertheless, the resulting net profit margin of 5.2 percent, while a large improvement over the immediately preceding years, was a far cry from the 10 to 11 percent figures of the period from 1996 to 1998.

Lifetime Hoan's expansion continued apace in 2003 and 2004. The highly successful KitchenAid line was further broadened with the introductions of ceramic bakeware and serveware as well as premium barbecue tools. Late in the year the company reached an agreement with Whirlpool to expand the line again, to create premium kitchen cutlery, knife storage blocks, knife sharpeners, and wood cutting boards. These KitchenAid products debuted in 2004. One of Lifetime's most successful product introductions of 2003 was the S'mores Maker, a tabletop gadget for making the familiar campfire dessert made from graham crackers, chocolate, and marshmallows. Several different models were offered, sold under three company brands—CasaModa, Hoffritz, and Roshco. In February 2004 Lifetime entered into an agreement with Hershey Foods Corporation to begin producing and marketing S'mores Makers and chocolate fondue sets under the Hershey brand name. Another innovative tabletop item was the CasaModa Smokeless Tabletop Griller, which debuted in 2004.

Three more acquisitions broadened Lifetime's growing array of products still further. In October 2003 the company acquired the USE brand, which had been created in 1995 by noted industrial designer Robert Sonneman. This addition extended Lifetime's reach into the bathroom. USE products included decorative hardware, mirrors, lighting, and window decorations for the bath. One month later, Lifetime bought the assets of the bankrupt Gemco Ware, Inc., based in Hauppauge, New York. Gemco, whose history dated back to the late 1940s, produced a popular line of glassware that included salt and pepper shakers, sugar dispensers, and oil and vinegar cruets. In July 2004 Lifetime Hoan paid about $8.5 million for Excel Importing Corp., based in Westbury, New York. Lifetime thereby gained the license rights to several high-end brands, including Sabatier, DBK-Daniel Boulud Kitchen, and Joseph Abboud Environments, as well as extending its use of the Farberware brand into dinnerware and glassware. The Excel deal was particularly important because it expanded both Lifetime's product line, into flatware, dinnerware, and glassware, and its customer base, to include such high-end retailers as Williams-Sonoma, Crate and Barrel, and Neiman-Marcus.

The diversification drive inspired the company to change its name to Lifetime Brands, Inc. as a reflection of its expanding array of household products. The change took effect in June 2005. Further complementary acquisitions were anticipated as well as the introduction of hundreds of new products as Lifetime's annual revenues were expected to approach a quarter of a billion dollars.

Principal Subsidiaries

Outlet Retail Stores, Inc.; Roshco, Inc.; M. Kamenstein Corp.

Principal Competitors

Newell Rubbermaid Inc.; WKI Holding Company, Inc.; The Pampered Chef, Ltd.; Wilton Industries, Inc.

Further Reading

Bernstein, James, "Lifetime Hoan Pays $41M in Farberware Acquisition," *Newsday,* February 6, 1996, p. A33.

Brammer, Rhonda, "Breaking Out," *Barron's,* February 17, 2003, p. 23.

Byrne, Harlan S., "Cutting Edge," *Barron's,* February 6, 1995, p. 16.

Gault, Ylonda, "Purchase of Hoffritz a Deal of a Lifetime," *Crain's New York Business,* October 2, 1995, p. 27.

Hill, Dawn, "Hoan Adds Hoffritz," *HFD—The Weekly Home Furnishings Newspaper,* September 25, 1995, pp. 47+.

——, "The Next Frontier: Lifetime Hoan Heads for the High End," *HFD—The Weekly Home Furnishings Newspaper,* July 31, 1995, pp. 27+.

Konig, Susan, "Why One Business Planted Its Headquarters in Westbury," *New York Times,* January 8, 1995, Sec. 13, Long Island Weekly, p. 2.

Markus, Stuart, "Lifetime Hoan in KitchenAid Pact," *Long Island (N.Y.) Business News,* October 27, 2000, p. A1.

Meeks, Fleming, "I Work Too Damn Hard to Do It for Nothing," *Forbes,* April 11, 1994, pp. 124–25.

Porter, Thyra, "Lifetime Hoan Division to Offer Gift Sets of Barware, Serveware," *HFN—The Weekly Newspaper for the Home Furnishing Network,* January 13, 2003, p. 170.

——, "Lifetime Hoan Excel Deal Means Bigger Place at Table," *HFN—The Weekly Newspaper for the Home Furnishing Network,* August 2, 2004, p. 1.

——, "Lifetime Hoan's Latest Move: Snagging M. Kamenstein Deal Adds New Categories and Paves Way for Expansion," *HFN—The Weekly Newspaper for the Home Furnishing Network,* October 9, 2000, p. 4.

Reeves, Amy, "Kitchenware Supplier Cooks Up a New Plan," *Investor's Business Daily,* May 12, 2004.

Sinisi, John, "Doughboy's $10M License to Bake," *Brandweek,* September 28, 1992, p. 7.

Solnik, Claude, "Lifetime Hoan Acquires Farberware—Again," *Long Island (N.Y.) Business News,* July 30, 2004, p. 1.

Thau, Barbara, "Lifetime Hoan's New President Outlines Growth Goals," *HFN—The Weekly Newspaper for the Home Furnishing Network,* January 3, 2000, p. 55.

Weiss, Lisa Carey, "Chance of a Lifetime: Lifetime Hoan Corp. Targets New Opportunities in Cutlery, Gadgets in Expansion Plans," *HFD—The Weekly Home Furnishings Newspaper,* December 23, 1991, pp. 43+.

Wolff, Lisa, "Alliance Strengthens Lifetime Hoan's Power," *Gourmet News,* January 2003, pp. 1, 29.

—David E. Salamie

Lonza

Lonza Group Ltd.

Munchensteinerstrasse 38
Basel CH-4002
Switzerland
Telephone: +41 61 316 81 11
Fax: +41 61 316 91 11
Web site: http://www.lonzagroup.com

Public Company
Incorporated: 1897 as Elektrizitätswerk Lonza
Employees: 5,668
Sales: CHF 2.18 billion ($1.87 billion) (2004)
Stock Exchanges: Bourse de Zurich
Ticker Symbol: LON
NAIC: 325188 All Other Inorganic Chemical
    Manufacturing; 325192 Cyclic Crude and Intermediate
    Manufacturing; 541710 Research and Development in
    the Physical Sciences and Engineering Sciences;
    621511 Medical Laboratories

Lonza Group Ltd. is the world's leading manufacturer of custom active ingredients, intermediates, and other pharmaceutical components supporting the global pharmaceuticals and life sciences industries. The company targets the value-added range of complex organic fine chemicals, conducting research and development, and manufacturing for pharmaceuticals and other products, including agro-industrial, dye and pigment, food and feed, adhesives, fragrances, and the like. Lonza's operations are structured into three primary product groups: Exclusive Synthesis and Biopharmaceuticals (31 percent of sales); Organic Fine and Performance Chemicals (39 percent); and Polymer Intermediates (30 percent). Europe, including Switzerland, is the company's major market, accounting for a total of 54 percent of sales; North America adds 31 percent. Key products include phthalic, maleic, trimellitic anhydride, nicotinic and isophthalic acids, as well as biocides, fungicides, oleochemicals, polymer intermediates, polyester resins, and the like. Lonza, formerly part of the Alusuisse group, was spun off in 1999 to facilitate that company's merger with Alcan Aluminum and Pechiney Since then, Lonza has performed a strategic shift in focus,

targeting the life sciences market, and especially the fast-growing biotechnology and custom manufacturing segments. Lonza supports its operations with an international manufacturing presence, including 18 production and research and development subsidiaries in eight countries, including the United States and China. Lonza is listed on the Bourse de Zurich and is led by Chairman Sergio Marchionne and CEO Stefan Borgas.

Electricity Origins in the 19th Century

The original focus of the Lonza Group was on the newly developing electricity industry in Switzerland at the turn of the 20th century. In the late 1800s, the growth of the country's railroad introduced the need for brighter and safer lighting, especially for headlights. Into the 1890s, the various types of lamps available, based on oil, petroleum, or even early filament-based electric lamps, were neither bright enough nor reliable enough for the railroads.

The invention of a new process for producing acetylene gas, based on carbide, provided a new fuel source for locomotive lighting in the early 1890s. Invented by the chemist Henri Moissan, acetylene provided a bright light, and was more reliable—if nonetheless dangerous—to use on the rails.

The production of carbide, however, required enormous amounts of energy. The Lonza River, in the Swiss Alps near Basel, provided a powerful and unlimited energy source, attracting a great deal of companies to the region. In 1897, Aflons Ehinger, a prominent banker, led a group of investors in setting up a new company, called Elektrizitätswerk Lonza. Lonza was able to acquire a downstream concession in Gampel and began building an industrial complex for the production of carbide, and featuring its own power generation station. After a series of setbacks, construction was completed by August 1898.

Lonza began producing carbide using a method devised by the Nuremberg, Germany-based Schukert Co. involving the use of electricity to combine coal and lime. That process proved inefficient, however, resulting in lower yields than initially expected. The search for greater productivity led Lonza to begin improving the process, enabling the company to build up its first expertise in the chemicals industry.

The development of a new generation of electric headlights put an end to the use of carbide—which had been the cause of a large number of accidents throughout Europe. Lonza began seeking new markets, and by the end of the first decade of the 20th century, the company had begun producing fertilizers based on calcium carbide, ammonia, and nitrogen. For this activity, the company moved to larger quarters in Visp, which was to remain its home into the 21st century.

Lonza continued expanding its range of operations through the first half of the century. In 1920, the company began producing nitric acid and ketene derivatives. By the mid-1950s, Lonza had moved into pharmaceuticals, producing intermediates, and foods markets as well. In 1956, for example, the company launched production of niacin, used as a B vitamin supplement.

The 1960s marked a new period for the company, with a move into the petrochemicals market. At that time the company shifted its production base away from carbide, installing its first naphtha cracker in Valais in 1965. This change led to a transformation of the company's product line, which now extended to include agrochemicals, dyes and colorings, adhesives, and the like. Lonza also continued to develop its pharmaceuticals business, widening its range of intermediates and launching production of a variety of additives as well.

Big Pockets in the 1970s

At the end of the 1960s, Lonza also began an international expansion effort, making acquisitions in the United States that led to the creation of its first U.S. subsidiary, Lonza Inc., in 1969. The U.S. extension enabled the company to enter the performance chemical market, notably with the addition of a line of biocides, as well as the production of a range of oleochemicals. Italy became another market for the company, where it acquired expertise in production of dibasic acids and derivatives.

Lonza found a larger partner in 1974, when it was acquired by Alusuisse. The merger into the company enabled Lonza to develop its international operations on a much larger scale. It also led the company to step up its investments, notably in the production of fine chemicals for the pharmaceuticals and agrochemical industries. The expanded company now adopted the name of Alusuisse Lonza.

In 1982, Lonza entered what was to become one of its major areas of operations by the end of the century, that of contract manufacturing for the world's pharmaceutical and agrochemicals companies. This new business area received a boost in 1984, when Lonza launched construction of a new fine chemicals manufacturing complex in Visp. By then, Lonza had taken its first step into the biotechnology market, setting up its first research group to investigate synergies among the company's expertise in the production of organic substances and the developing biotechnology field. Through the 1980s, the company successfully developed a number of chiral compounds and other substances. By 1992, Lonza was ready to launch its first biotechnology complex, acquiring Biotec S.R.O., which operated a fermentation plant in Kourim, in the Czech Republic. By then, the company also had extended its fine chemicals manufacturing capacity in the United States, adding two new facilities in the early 1990s.

New Strategy for a New Century

Lonza's biotechnology investments continued into the mid-1990s. In 1996 the company made an important acquisition to boost this area of its operations when it acquired Celltech Biologics. The Slough, England-based company also provided Lonza with a biotechnology complex in Portsmouth, New Hampshire, in the United States. Lonza also expanded its additives business, particularly its strong maleic anhydride derivatives production with the addition of a new production facility at Ravenna, its base in Italy.

By then, Lonza's sales had topped CHF 1.6 billion ($1.4 billion). The company also eyed further expansion, now in the fast-growing Asian region. In 1996, Lonza entered China for the first time, forming a joint venture to build a facility to produce niacinamide for the local market. Also that year, Lonza established a manufacturing presence in Singapore, setting up a new factory to produce isophthalic acid.

In the late 1990s, however, Alusuisse Lonza began seeking a partner in order to gain scale in the global market. In 1998, the company reached an agreement to merge with Germany's Viag AG, which, among other operations, operated specialty chemicals subsidiaries nearly three times larger than Lonza.

Yet the merger with Viag fell through by 1999. Instead, Alusuisse found two very different partners, when it reached an agreement with Alcan Aluminum Ltd. and Pechiney S.A. to merge their aluminum and packaging operations into a single unit. In this way, Alusuisse hoped to compete against industry leader Alcoa. As part of the merger, however, Alusuisse was forced to spin off Lonza as an independent company that year. Lonza's shares were then listed on the Bourse de Zurich, and former Alusuisse Lonza Chairman and CEO Sergio Marchionne left to join Lonza as its chairman.

The newly independent Lonza now began a strategy shift, placing its future growth more firmly in the life sciences and biotechnology arena. The company supported its change in focus with an ambitious investment program, which saw the company spend some CHF 550 million ($330 million) at the beginning of the decade. Part of this investment went toward expanding its Kourim, Czech Republic facility, completed in 2004. In the United States, Lonza spent $225 million to quadruple capacity at its Portsmouth facility.

Lonza's timing proved unfortunate, however, as the global chemicals and pharmaceuticals markets entered a downturn

Key Dates:

1897: Elektrizitätswerk Lonza is created to build an electrical generation plant to fuel production at a carbide plant.
1898: The carbide plant is completed.
1908: Lonza expands into chemicals production, and opens a larger facility in Visp, Switzerland.
1920: Production of ketene and nitric acid is launched.
1956: The company begins production of niacin (vitamin B) as part of its extension into life sciences.
1965: The company shifts from carbide to naphtha, entering the petrochemicals industry.
1969: The company launches operations in the United States and Italy.
1974: Lonza is acquired by Alusuisse, which becomes Alusuisse Lonza.
1982: The company begins contract manufacturing for the pharmaceuticals and agrochemicals industries.
1983: The company launches a research center for entry into the biotechnology market.
1984: The company builds a new fine chemicals plant at Visp.
1992: A biotechnology unit in the Czech Republic is acquired.
1996: Lonza acquires Celltech Biologics (based in England and the United States); a joint venture for production of niacinamide in China is formed; an isophthalic acid facility in Singapore is added.
1998: Alusuisse announces a merger with Germany's Viag AG but the merger collapses.
1999: Alusuisse merges with Pechiney and Alcan and spins off Lonza as an independent, publicly listed company.
2004: After an investment program worth CHF 550 million, the company expands its biotechnology capacity in the Czech Republic and the United States.

toward mid-decade. Particularly difficult for the company was the slowdown in the contract manufacturing market, brought on in part because of a lower level of new compounds in the pharmaceutical pipeline. The difficult market conditions helped suppress the group's profits, as its revenues receded to just CHF 2.24 billion in 2003, down 11 percent over the previous year,

and again to CHF 2.18 billion in 2004. Despite the difficult market, however, Lonza remained true to its strategy to focus on the life sciences market, including the launch of a new biologics facility in Visp at the end of 2004.

Principal Subsidiaries

LOFO High Tech Film GmbH (Germany); Lonza (China) Investments Co. Ltd.; Lonza America Inc.; Lonza Biologics Inc. (U.S.A.); Lonza Biologics PLC (U.K.); Lonza Biotec S.R.O. Kourim (Czech Republic); Lonza Compounds GmbH & Co. KG (Germany); Lonza Europe B.V. (Netherlands); Lonza Finance Limited (Jersey); Lonza GmbH (Germany); Lonza Group GmbH (Germany); Lonza Group UK Ltd. (U.K.); Lonza Guangzhou Ltd. (China); Lonza Guangzhou Nansha Ltd. (China); Lonza Guangzhou Research and Development Center Ltd. (China); Lonza Inc. (U.S.A.); Lonza Ltd.; Lonza Sales Ltd.; Lonza Singapore Pte Ltd.; Lonza S.p.A. (Italy).

Principal Competitors

Merck and Company Inc.; GlaxoSmithKline PLC; Pfizer Inc.; Bayer AG; Roche Holding AG; Celesio AG; BASF Aktiengesellschaft (BF); Bristol-Myers Squibb Co.; Abbott Laboratories.

Further Reading

Birch, John, "Biotechnology and Contract Manufacturing: Dr. John Birch, Chief Scientific Officer at the Lonza Group, Explains How and Why His Company Has Entered into Biotechnology," *Specialty Chemicals,* April 2003, p. 30.
"Lonza Builds Up Mammalian Cell Capacity," *Chemical Market Reporter,* November 1, 2004, p. 2.
"Lonza Group, the Leading Custom Manufacturer of Chemical and Biotechnological Solutions," *Chemical Week,* January 29, 2003, p. 38.
"Lonza's Results Reflect Struggle in Contract Manufacturing Unit," *Chemical Market Reporter,* July 26, 2004, p. 5.
"Lonza Stuns Investors with Profits Warning, Job Cuts," *Chemical Week,* May 21, 2003, p. 5.
"Lonza's 2003 Profits Plunge, CEO Resigns," *Nutraceuticals International,* February 2004.
Tilton, Helga, "Lonza Supports Its Strategic Shift with More Investments," *Chemical Market Reporter,* September 30, 2002, p. 25.
"Tough Conditions Threaten Lonza's Profits," *Chemical Week,* November 24, 2004, p. 5.

—M.L. Cohen

MANPOWER

Manpower Inc.

<table>
<tr><td>

5301 N. Ironwood Road
Milwaukee, Wisconsin 53217
U.S.A.
Telephone: (414) 961-1000
Fax: (414) 961-7985
Web site: http://www.manpower.com

Public Company
Incorporated: 1948
Employees: 27,000
Sales: $14.9 billion (2004)
Stock Exchanges: New York
Ticker Symbol: MAN
NAIC: 561320 Temporary Help Services

</td></tr>
</table>

Manpower Inc. has come a long way from its humble beginnings as a temp agency; it now provides employment opportunities for a wide range of professionals both in temporary and permanent positions from 4,300 offices in 68 countries worldwide. In addition to staffing needs, Manpower also offers consultations, training, and financial services to some 400,000 domestic and international clients. Its name, however, is a misnomer. Manpower's ranks have often been filled by more women than men in its almost six decades of operations.

Postwar Origins: 1940s–70s

Manpower was founded in 1948 by Elmer L. Winter and Aaron Scheinfeld, two partners in a Milwaukee law firm who saw the labor shortage following World War II as an opportunity to form a temporary agency. A year earlier, Kelly Services, Inc., which would become the second biggest temporary agency, had been formed in Detroit. By 1956 Manpower's reputation was established enough that franchising the company name became profitable. In order to set up a Manpower franchise, an investor paid an initial fee, attended a training course, then set up an office. The franchisee was responsible for recruiting and placement, as well as paying a percentage of his or her gross earnings to Manpower, while the company provided promotion and management guidance.

Under its founders' charge Manpower expanded during the 1960s, establishing franchises all over the world, most prominently in Europe, but also in South America, Africa, and Asia. In 1965 Mitchell S. Fromstein, whose small advertising agency had been handling the Manpower account, joined its board of directors. Fromstein's role in the company's development grew as the company expanded. Its acquisitions in the 1970s included Nationwide Income Tax Service, Detroit; Gilbert Lane Personnel, Inc. of Hartford, Connecticut; and Manpower Southampton Ltd., which had been one of its franchisees. All of these companies were later sold by Manpower.

In 1976 the Parker Pen Company acquired Manpower for $28.2 million. Like Manpower, Parker was a well-known, family-owned business based in Wisconsin. Where Manpower had enjoyed a meteoric rise in the 1950s and 1960s, Parker's sales began faltering in the late 1970s due to its failure to compete with inexpensive writing implements in the marketplace. With Scheinfeld dead and Winter eager to pursue other personal interests, a buyout of all stock was initiated by Fromstein and Parker's president, George S. Parker. Fromstein bought 20 percent of Manpower's stock and moved up to the position of president and chief executive.

When Manpower began, it had initially concentrated its efforts on industrial help. Fromstein made changes in this and many other respects. Practicing a managerial style he credited to Vince Lombardi, the legendary coach of football's Green Bay Packers, for whom he had written speeches, Fromstein was considered responsible for virtually all of the growth and development Manpower underwent during his tenure. His innovative approach to the temporary industry included shifting emphasis from the factory to the office, recognizing that automated equipment was revolutionizing the workplace, and revising the company's Employment Outlook Survey. The survey, initiated in 1962 to measure the hiring intentions of employers and published quarterly, was revised with the assistance of the Survey Research Center of the University of Michigan. Understanding of and sensitivity to its clients needs became hallmarks of Manpower under the guidance of Fromstein.

Above all, it was Fromstein's commitment to take responsibility for training temporary employees, rather than merely finding

---

Company Perspectives:

Manpower Inc. (NYSE: MAN) is a world leader in the employment services industry, offering customers a continuum of services to meet their needs throughout the employment and business cycle. The company specializes in permanent, temporary, and contract recruitment; employee assessment; training; career transition; organizational consulting; and professional financial services. The focus of Manpower's work is on raising productivity through improved quality, efficiency, and cost-reduction, enabling customers to concentrate on their core business activities. In addition to the Manpower brand, the company operates under the brand names of Right Management Consultants, Jefferson Wells, Elan, and Brook Street.

---

places for them to work, which accounted for Manpower's dominance in the industry. In his *Alternative Staffing Strategies* (Bureau of National Affairs, 1988), David Nye wrote, ''Manpower is by no means the only 'temporary' firm involved in training and testing, but its approach is clearly the most extensive.''

In 1978, when the prospect of a computer that would fit inside an office, let alone on top of a desk, seemed preposterous, Fromstein announced that Manpower would invest $15 million in a computer training program called Skillware. An interactive, self-paced program, Skillware enabled Manpower employees to develop competence in a variety of tasks. This approach made temporary employees more valuable to companies because they required less onsite training and made a greater contribution to productivity in a shorter time. Since its inception, Skillware expanded tremendously and became available for 160 software programs in nine languages.

Spurring Growth in the 1980s

The complexion of the job market in the United States and abroad contributed greatly to the ascendancy of the temporary industry in the 1980s. Because the cost of providing benefits rose faster than the cost of providing wages, employers began to view temporary hires as more economical than searching for, hiring, and training permanent workers. It also proved to be an effective way of testing potential permanent workers. Furthermore, the increase in dual-income families bolstered the appeal of temporary work to parents faced with the high cost of daycare. Under Fromstein, Manpower was positioned to capitalize on the situation more effectively than its closest competitors, Kelly and Olsten Corporation. Total sales reached $300 million in 1976 and would mushroom to the billions within little more than a decade.

Manpower's rapid growth meant it was drastically outpacing the pen sales at Parker. For a time, its profits made up for the pen company's losses but by February 1986 the imbalance had become too great, despite Parker's efforts at reducing its workforce and cutting back on the varieties of pens manufactured. The writing instruments division was sold to a group of investors for $100 million, and Manpower became the name of the parent company.

In 1987 Manpower engaged in an important affiliation with International Business Machines Corporation (IBM). Under the agreement, Manpower provided onsite training and support services (such as a hotline for computer questions) to buyers of IBM systems. IBM benefited from having its users more fully acquainted with its systems, and Manpower benefited from the awareness of these users that its temporary workers were computer literate.

In the same year, Manpower was the target of a hostile takeover in what turned out to be a tangled and complex affair. In August, Antony Berry's Blue Arrow Plc, a British employment-services firm with revenues only one-sixth the size of Manpower's, offered to buy Manpower at $75 per share for a total of $1.21 billion. Berry, well known in England from his days as a boxer, had terrific success with Blue Arrow since joining them in 1984, taking them from £410,000 ($725,000) in profits to £30 million ($55 million). Manpower stock had been at $62.38 at the time of the offer, but excitement over the bid drove the price up to $78, beating the $75 offered by Blue Arrow.

In the weeks that followed, Fromstein and Manpower contemplated a return bid on Blue Arrow, considered a joint venture with the Swiss employment firm Adia S.A., then threatened to refuse Blue Arrow unless they increased their bid to $90 per share. Manpower's board also publicly denounced Berry's plans for combining the companies, which included implementing an executive search program—a suggestion that infuriated Fromstein, who told the *Wall Street Journal,* ''We aren't blind or deaf. If we thought it was an opportunity, we could have done it years ago.'' Manpower rejected the bid, prompting a shareholder lawsuit on charges that the directors' decision was financially irresponsible.

Three weeks after the initial offer was made, Manpower finally endorsed the Blue Arrow offer at $82.50 per share for a total of $1.3 billion. Under the terms of the sale, Manpower's operations in the United States would continue under the name ''Manpower.'' Fromstein was allowed to stay on as Manpower president and CEO and one of a five-member Blue Arrow board, though by December 1987 he was fired from this position after a long simmering conflict with Berry became apparent.

Fromstein's separation from Manpower, however, was not long-lasting. In spite of his early successes, Berry proved to be an inept manager. His enthusiasm for sports led Blue Arrow into an expensive and unauthorized investment in a yacht for the America's Cup competition. The stock market crash of October 1987 brought Berry's most substantial impropriety to light. In order to create the funds necessary to purchase Manpower, Berry had secured a loan of $1.3 billion from the National Westminster Bank (NatWest) in England to be repaid from the proceeds of a stock issue.

With the bank as underwriter, 38 percent of the shares were purchased by existing Blue Arrow shareholders, leaving the bank the responsibility of selling the rest. According to an article in *Financial World,* potential buyers might have been scared away had they learned of this situation, so NatWest itself purchased 12 percent in order to boost the amount of sold shares to 50 percent, a more respectable figure. Such a purchase was legal, but the underwriters kept it a secret, and once revealed, this was con-

Key Dates:

1948: Manpower is founded in Milwaukee, Wisconsin.
1954: The first Manpower franchise office is opened.
1956: Manpower's first international office is established in Canada.
1962: The company goes public on the New York Stock Exchange.
1964: Youthpower is launched for the young people seeking jobs.
1976: Manpower is bought by Parker Pen Company.
1985: Manpower bypasses 1,000 offices worldwide.
1987: The company is sold to Blue Arrow Plc.
1998: Manpower sponsors soccer's World Cup in France.
2000: Elan Group, Ltd. is acquired by Manpower.
2001: Jefferson Wells International, Inc. is acquired.
2004: Right Management Consultants, Inc. is acquired.
2005: Manpower partners with the Chinese government to train its labor force.

strued as a deliberate attempt to mislead potential investors. A criminal investigation was launched and by January 1989 top executives at the bank—most notably its chairman, Lord Boardman—were forced to resign and Berry was disgraced by his role in the deal and other financial improprieties.

Backed by Manpower's U.S. franchises, Fromstein mounted a successful campaign to regain control of Blue Arrow. Once back at the helm, his first three decisions were to change the name of Blue Arrow to Manpower, sell all businesses that had belonged to Blue Arrow, and to move the company's headquarters back to Milwaukee.

Swelling Revenues in the 1990s

As promised, Fromstein sold most Blue Arrow businesses in 1990 and 1991 and Manpower became a U.S. corporation again in 1991. As the company began the decade, its major objectives were to stay current with technological advances in the workplace and to further international expansion into previously inaccessible regions like Eastern Europe.

Manpower succeeded in achieving most of its goals from the beginning of the decade: it recorded robust financial growth and exponentially increased its global staffing services. Manpower's revenue growth, which lifted systemwide sales past the $10 billion mark by the decade's conclusion, was propelled by the company's ever increasing expansion rate, particularly overseas—a primary goal when Fromstein led the company.

Most of the company's progress during the decade was achieved without the benefit of any major acquisitions, though its competitors could not make such a claim. The industry was rapidly consolidating, as rivals merged to form global powerhouses, quickly establishing worldwide networks of staffing offices. Nonetheless, by striking an independent pose, Manpower saw its lead over all worldwide rivals disappear. Its relegation to the number two position in the world, caused by the 1997 merger of Adia SA and Ecco SA, was symbolic of the company's progress during the 1990s. Manpower took giant strides forward during the decade, but as it did so the pace of rival firms and the changing dynamics of the temporary staffing industry sometimes passed the company by.

Midway through the decade Manpower's growth began to pick up speed. Coming off $4.3 billion in revenues and a record $83.9 million in net income in 1994, the company began establishing new offices at a frenetic pace, increasing the number of new offices it opened each year from 100 in 1994 to more than 400 by the late 1990s. The spate of new office openings brought Manpower into dozens of new markets, stretching from Milan to Moscow and into Latin America, Asia, and South America. Important alliances were formed as the company fleshed out its global network of offices, highlighted by two partnerships forged in 1996. Manpower signed an exclusive arrangement with Drake Beam Morin Inc., the world's largest executive outplacement company, and formed an alliance with Ameritech to provide call center and help desk agents. Manpower's 50th anniversary marked 50 consecutive years of revenue growth, but during the celebratory year, Adia SA and Ecco SA merged, usurping Manpower as the global leader in its industry.

One year after the merger that created Zurich-based Adecco S.A., Manpower reached an impressive financial milestone. Systemwide sales eclipsed $10 billion in 1998, double the revenues of five years earlier, but the towering growth did not silence all of the company's critics. The emergence of Adecco as the new international leader prompted some industry pundits to cite Adecco's successes as Manpower's failures, specifically Fromstein's belated entry into the fastest-growing segment of the staffing industry, information technology (IT). Adecco derived roughly 20 percent of its revenues from providing IT workers, nearly twice as much as Manpower. Manpower's perceived failure to assume a strong position in a market led *Forbes* magazine's Phyllis Berman and Adrienne Sanders to suggest Fromstein should step aside. Although it was doubtful such criticism materially affected Fromstein's mindset, he was quoted in the January 11, 1999 issue of *Forbes* as saying, "I'm putting pressure on myself to replace myself."

Fromstein retired in 1999 and Jeffrey Joerres was promoted to the posts of CEO and president. A Manpower executive since 1993, Joerres had been credited with spearheading the enormous growth of the company's global accounts, demonstrating a talent that would be instrumental in his efforts to shoulder past Adecco in the 21st century. As Manpower exited the 20th century, the company hoped to have a greater presence in the IT market, after establishing more than 200 offices devoted exclusively to serving technical and IT staffing needs. The company finished 1999 with revenues of just under $9.8 billion and operating profit of $230.6 million.

Manpower in the 2000s

After a decade of little acquisitive growth, Manpower started off the new millennium by acquiring several companies. First was Elan Group, Ltd., a leading IT recruitment and services firm with 52 worldwide offices serving 16 European and Asian countries, for which Manpower paid $146 million in 2000. This was followed by a joint venture with the United Kingdom's SHL Group Plc., a human resources firm, and the formation of the Empower Group.

In 2001 Joerres was named chairman of the board in addition to his duties of president and chief executive. During the year, Manpower segued into the financial services sector with the acquisition of the Wisconsin-based Jefferson Wells International, Inc., an accounting firm, for about $174 million. Revenues for 2001 were a fraction higher than 2000's $10.8 billion, accounting for the new acquisitions and the disruptions caused by the terrorist attacks against the United States of September 11, 2001. The consequences of 9/11 continued to shadow corporate results in 2003, as Manpower brought in revenues of $10.6 billion, but operating profit climbed from the previous year's $234.8 million to $257.9 million.

In 2002 Manpower concentrated on expanding operations in the Middle East and Europe (other than France, its stronghold). The company's four operational divisions (U.S., United Kingdom, Other Europe, and Other Countries) were updated to reflect the company's growth: U.S., France, EMEA (Europe, Middle East, and Africa), and Other Operations. By the end of the year, France led revenues with $3.8 billion, EMEA brought in $3.4 billion, the U.S. topped $1.19 billion, and other miscellaneous operations claimed $1.4 billion.

Manpower went back on the acquisitions trail with the purchase of Right Management Consultants, Inc. (RMC) in January 2004, the world's largest career transition and human resources firm, based in Philadelphia, Pennsylvania, and with 300 offices in nearly three dozen countries. Buying RMC brought Manpower closer to achieving its objective of providing the world's best staffing and to offering its 2.5 million temporary workers the highest quality employment opportunities available. Revenues from services rose to $14.9 billion and operating profit leaped to $395.8 million from the previous year's $257.9 million on revenues of $12.2 billion.

As with the past several years, Manpower's operations in France continued to lead its revenues, bringing in $5.2 billion (up over 12 percent), followed closely by the EMEA segment at just under $5.1 billion. In terms of sheer growth, however, France was not Manpower's top performing segment—it was the EMEA unit with an increase of 29.7 percent in revenues and operating profits shooting from 2003's $51.7 million to $115.1 million. Manpower's U.S. operations had begun to perk up after declining revenues, climbing 4.9 percent for 2004 to revenues of just over $2.0 billion. Another possible rising star was a new joint venture with the government of China, one of the hottest labor markets in the world. Manpower already had over two dozen offices in China, though Joerres planned to open several more to train the burgeoning Chinese workforce.

As Manpower headed into the late 2000s the company was on solid ground—despite remaining the second largest staffing provider in the world. Though Manpower had made great strides in its international goals, rival Adecco continued to dominate the international and domestic employment sector and brought in revenues of $23.4 billion. Adecco's strong presence in the United States remained a thorn in the Milwaukee-based Manpower's side. While the worldwide staffing industry was certainly big enough for Adecco, Manpower, and rising star Vedior N.V. (with revenues of $8.8 billion for 2004), if Manpower hoped to topple the Swiss powerhouse, it needed to pay far greater attention to its North American operations and continue pursuing opportunities in the Chinese labor market.

Principal Subsidiaries

Manpower AB; Manpower A.S.; Manpower France S.A.S.; Manpower GmbH und Company KG; Manpower Israel Ltd.; Manpower Team ETT SAU; Manpower UK Ltd.; Right Management Consultants, Inc.; Jefferson Wells International, Inc., Elan Group, Ltd., Brook Street Bureau Plc.

Principal Competitors

Adecco S.A.; Kelly Services, Inc.; Randstad Holding N.V.; Spherion Corporation; Vedior N.V.

Further Reading

Berman, Phyllis, and Adrienne Sanders, "Time to Go?," *Forbes,* January 1, 1999, p. 82.
Berss, Marcia, "You Can Go Home Again," *Forbes,* October 1990.
"Case Study: Blue Arrow PLC and Manpower Inc.," *Buyouts & Acquisitions,* November/December 1987.
Cronan, Carl, "How to . . . Choose the Right Temp Agency," *Philadelphia Business Journal,* May 11, 2001, p. B11.
Dresang, Joel, "Manpower Launches Joint Venture to Boost China's Job Market," *Milwaukee Journal Sentinel,* May 25, 2005.
Gilbert, Nick, "Manpower Comes Home," *Financial World,* April 30, 1991.
Jensen, Dave, "Temp and Team Spirit," *Management Review,* October 1988.
Kafka, Peter, "Permanent Help," *Forbes,* May 9, 2005, p. 114.
Kapp, Sue, "Titan of Service," *Business Marketing,* November 1991.
"Making a Perfect Match," *Personnel Today,* March 12, 2002, p. 13.
"Manpower," *Information Age,* April 10, 2005.
"Market Outruns Offer by Blue Arrow," *Wall Street Journal,* August 5, 1987.
Mehta, Stephanie N., "The Titans of Temp Reach Out," *FSB,* November 1, 2002, p. 77.
Mullins, Robert, "Manpower's New Man: Fromstein Successor to Update Pioneer Staffing Firm," *Business Journal-Milwaukee,* September 24, 1999, p. 25.
Nye, David, *Alternative Staffing Strategies,* Washington, D.C.: Bureau of National Affairs, 1988. Pei, Jianfeng, "Labor Shortage Restrains Temporary-Staffing Firms," *Purchasing,* May 18, 2000, p. 165.
Sansoni, Silvia, "Move Over, Manpower," *Forbes,* July 7, 1997, p. 64.
Snavely, Brent, "Slowdown Slams Kelly Earnings," *Crain's Detroit Business,* April 30, 2001, p. 3.
Walbert, Laura R., "Menpower Versus Penpower," *Forbes,* December 19, 1983.
"Winter's Tale," *Finance,* September 1969.
"Youthpower Looking for More Employers," *Milwaukee Journal Sentinel,* July 11, 2005.

—Mark Swartz
—updates: Jeffrey L. Covell; Nelson Rhodes

Martha Stewart Living Omnimedia, Inc.

11 West 42nd Street
New York, New York 10036
U.S.A.
Telephone: (212) 827-8000
Fax: (212) 827-8204
Web site: http://www.marthastewart.com

Public Company
Incorporated: 1997
Employees: 480
Sales: $200 million (2005 est.)
Stock Exchanges: New York
Ticker Symbol: MSO
NAIC: 511120 Periodical Publishers; 511130 Book Publishers; 512110 Motion Picture and Video Production

Martha Stewart Living Omnimedia, Inc. (MSLO) encompasses the varied publishing, broadcasting, and merchandising enterprises of its founder, Martha Stewart. With products reflecting the personal tastes and style of Stewart, the company's brands have been compared to the likes of Calvin Klein and Ralph Lauren in terms of name recognition and quality. The company is comprised of four divisions: publishing, television, merchandising, and Internet/direct commerce, though all units took a beating after Stewart was convicted of stock fraud charges and served time from 2004 to 2005. Stewart has long denied any wrongdoing and her attorneys have appealed her conviction. Back in the fold, however, Stewart has been buoyed by public support and has returned to work. A number of television projects were in the works in 2005, including two shows with *Survivor* wunderkind Mark Burnett as well as joint ventures with Kmart, Bernhardt Furniture, Sirius satellite radio, Sherwin-Williams, and others.

In the Beginning, 1970s–80s

Although Martha Stewart bought the company bearing her name from Time Warner and incorporated it in 1997, the beginnings of the business can be traced to Stewart's activities two decades earlier. Stewart's formal education consisted of a bachelor's degree in history and architecture from Barnard College, and, following limited success as a model and a stockbroker, she decided to make a career out of her passion for food preparation and presentation. In 1976 Stewart founded her own business, a catering operation headquartered in the basement of the historic farmhouse she lived in with her husband and daughter in Westport, Connecticut.

By the late 1970s, Stewart was running a successful, upscale catering business on the East Coast and contributing articles to *The New York Times* and *House Beautiful*. She was also hoping to parlay her expertise in party planning into a book on the subject. In 1980 she forged an agreement to write such a book for Crown Publishing, a division of Random House. Stewart reportedly had to fight for the lavish style she envisioned for the book, which included a multitude of color photographs and the large-sized format of a "coffee table book." Published in 1982, Stewart's *Entertaining* helped establish Stewart as an authority on taste; by the mid-1990s the book had sold over half a million copies. The production of her first book also proved to be a blueprint for how Stewart would build her image, and she continued to think big while maintaining a perfectionist's attention to detail.

Stewart authored several more books in the 1980s, including *Martha Stewart's Quick Cook, Martha Stewart's Hors d'Oeuvres, Martha Stewart's Quick Cook Menus,* and *Martha Stewart's Christmas.* The books proved to have an enduring shelf life earning significant income as backlist titles and remained in print well into the next decade. The next step in making Martha Stewart a nationally known brand name came in 1987 when Stewart signed a $5 million five-year consulting contract with Kmart. Stewart was hired to help create home products for the retailer, including a line of Dutch Boy paint colors and bath and bedding products. Stewart's primary role, however, was to lend her name to Kmart's products, to appear in print and television ads, and to make in-store appearances.

Creation of a Magazine, the Early 1990s

Back in the late 1980s Stewart had pitched an idea for a magazine to the publishing house of Condé Nast. The company's chairman, Si Newhouse, was wary of the idea for *Martha Stewart Living,* deeming a product dependent on one person as too risky. Stewart's idea was also turned down by Rupert Murdoch's magazine empire. In 1990, however, Time Inc. approved two test issues of *Martha Stewart Living,* with the first scheduled to come out in November 1990 and the second in March 1991. The public's response was strong enough for Time to commit to six issues a year. Although Stewart had achieved her goal of moving into magazine publishing, the deal with Time was not particularly lucrative, at least not until the maga-zine became profitable—reportedly because other publishers had turned down her concept for *Martha Stewart Living.*

By 1992 Stewart had become dissatisfied with her Kmart consulting and let the contract lapse, though Kmart continued to sell Martha Stewart towels, bedding, and paints. "I thought they wanted me to make real decisions for them," Stewart told *Work-ing Woman* in 1995 about the Kmart deal, "but it turns out I was really hired as a personality, not a consultant . . . they acted on nothing I proposed." While the Kmart venture may have been a disappointment, Stewart's publishing career ramped into high gear. By 1995 there were more than four million copies of her books in print, her magazine was selling over a million copies per issue and had been voted "Magazine of the Year" by *Ad Age,* and she began touring the country. Her book tours soon led to paid lecture appearances, which in turn kept Stewart and her products in the media, popularizing her inimitable style.

The magazine spawned several other new enterprises in the early and mid-1990s. Morning television's *Today* show agreed to fund the production costs of an appearance by Stewart every other week on the program. Stewart appeared at no charge and in return received free publicity for her magazine and books. Time, Inc. also began publishing books that made use of articles from the magazine, grouped according to theme; the first two were titled *Holidays* and *Special Occasions.*

Once again ready to expand into new areas, Stewart con-vinced Time to fund a television show based on the magazine, also to be called *Martha Stewart Living.* The weekly show covered home decorating, entertaining, gardening, cooking, and featured Stewart as the host. By 1993 the show was broadcast in 84 percent of the nation's markets.

MSL Enterprises, 1995 and 1996

New ventures and the continued popularity of her magazine led Stewart to renegotiate her relationship with Time. To help with her negotiations, Stewart gathered a team of lawyers and consultants: Allen Grubman, a prominent entertainment lawyer; Sharon Patrick, strategy consultant; and Charlotte Beers, chair and chief executive of Ogilvy & Mather Worldwide. With these three advisers, Stewart persuaded Time to create a subsidiary of Time Warner called Martha Stewart Living Enterprises and to name Stewart chair and chief executive officer. Time provided all of the funds for the company, and Stewart provided the ideas and her name. The new corporation was jointly owned by Time Inc. Ventures, a division of Time Warner Inc., and Martha Stewart, though neither party revealed the percentage of their ownership. The company encompassed *Martha Stewart Living* magazine, its spinoff books, the new television show, and Stewart's *Today Show* appearances. Outside the company's purview were the books Stewart had written between 1982 and 1995; the royalties from the sales of Kmart bedding, towels, and paints; and Stew-art's lecture fees. In 1995 Stewart continued to expand her reach with Martha by Mail, which had begun as an insert in *Martha Stewart Living* magazine and was expanded into a full direct mail catalogue; a weekly syndicated newspaper column; and even a prime-time Christmas special featuring Hillary Rodham Clinton.

By 1996 Martha Stewart Living Enterprises had a staff of 140 and burgeoning sales. Because Time Warner only an-nounced sales figures for its publishing businesses as a whole, the value of the company was difficult to ascertain. Some industry analysts placed its worth at $70 million and estimated annual revenues at $200 million. Stewart began pushing to renegotiate her relationship with Time again just a year after the formation of Martha Stewart Living Enterprises. She wanted a greater equity stake (40 percent) in the company and the power to expand in new directions as the firm flourished.

A New Name and Rapid Expansion, 1997 and 1998

In 1997 Stewart acquired majority interest in the company and renamed it Martha Stewart Living Omnimedia, L.L.C. With the continued help of Sharon Patrick, Stewart had arranged the pur-chase of at least 80 percent of the company for about $75 million, although figures varied according to different accounts. Time's remaining stake in the company was generally estimated to be between 5 and 10 percent, with the balance of the stock held by Patrick and staff members. The separation from Time was report-edly a friendly one. Don Logan, chair and CEO of Time Inc., agreed to join the new board for Martha Stewart Living Om-nimedia. Stewart initially appointed Patrick president and chief executive officer, but soon took the helm as CEO, while Patrick remained president and COO. The buyout was financed in large part with new contracts from Kmart and Sherwin-Williams.

The Kmart deal added to concern among market analysts that Stewart was clouding her image with too many endorse-ments and target markets. The new Kmart deal, however, was different than the first in that Martha Stewart Living Om-nimedia retained control over the entire production process, from design to advertising, of the newly named Martha Stewart Everyday product line. "Whether it's a hang tag on a dish towel or a label on a paint can, everything has to look as good as the

Key Dates:

1976: Martha Stewart founds a catering company in Connecticut.
1982: Stewart's first book, *Entertaining*, is published.
1987: Kmart signs Stewart to a five-year consulting contract.
1990: The first issue of *Martha Stewart Living* is published by Time Inc.
1993: Stewart begins hosting a weekly television show, *Martha Stewart Living*.
1995: *Martha Stewart Living* is voted "Magazine of the Year" by *Ad Age;* the Martha by Mail catalogue is launched.
1997: Stewart buys the company bearing her name from Time Warner.
1999: Martha Stewart Living Omnimedia, Inc. goes public on the New York Stock Exchange.
2001: Stewart sells shares in ImClone.
2003: Stewart is indicted on securities fraud charges.
2004: Stewart is convicted and asks to begin serving her five-month prison term early.
2005: Stewart is released from prison and welcomed back to her company.

magazine," Production Director Dora Braschi Cardinale explained to the *New York Times.* With such control, the company hoped to maintain a consistent brand image. The contract with Sherwin-Williams was signed in May 1997 for a line of Martha Stewart paints. Originally carried exclusively by Kmart, Sears began offering the paint line in March 1998.

Free to pursue her vision for the company, Stewart led a rapid and varied expansion of Martha Stewart Living Omnimedia in 1997 and early 1998. The *Martha Stewart Living* television show moved from a weekly to a weekday schedule. The show was distributed by CBS and Stewart soon left her biweekly appearance schedule on NBC's *Today Show* to appear weekly on the *CBS This Morning* program. In addition, the company launched a daily 90-second radio feature known as "askMartha" and a web site with a wide range of information about the television show, magazine, and Stewart's books. The site also highlighted items from the Martha by Mail catalogue and allowed users to order over the Internet.

Stewart also had further plans for the lucrative Kmart partnership, hoping to build on her brand's name by introducing new lines of cooking, gardening, and decorating merchandise. Near the end of 1997 the company completed construction on a new $4 million studio in Westport, Connecticut, for taping Stewart's television and radio shows with large kitchens and state-of-the-art equipment. Circulation of *Martha Stewart Living* magazine had grown to 2.3 million for 1997, 30 percent higher than 1996. Total year-end revenues for 1997 came to $132.8 million, with earnings of $13.9 million.

In early 1998 the company's new and established ventures were going strong. The "askMartha" newspaper column was syndicated in 212 papers and the radio program was broadcast on 135 stations. The *Martha Stewart Living* television show had top

ratings and was offered on 197 stations across the nation. Though Stewart had talked about taking the company public since gaining ownership, she became more serious about the issue in 1998. Market analysts debated whether the company had the ability to stand on its own. Linda R. Killian, an analyst and portfolio manager with the Renaissance Capital Corporation, commented to the *New York Times,* "If Martha Stewart got hit by a cab tomorrow, to what extent is there a viable company there?" Others questioned whether profits would be hurt by continued expansion. Stewart, herself, expressed total confidence in the independence of her company to the *New York Times:* "It won't die without me. I think we are now spread very nicely over an area where our information can be trusted." Consumers evidently concurred, helping MSLO bring in revenues of $177.2 million for 1998 with net income climbing to $23.8 million.

Martha Storms Wall Street, 1999 to 2001

Stewart took her road show to Wall Street in October 1999 with an initial public offering of over 8.28 million shares for $18 each. The offering generated funds of more than $132 million and amazed naysayers and fans alike. The new firm, Martha Stewart Living Omnimedia, Inc., under the ticker symbol MSO, became a favorite of Wall Street and consumers alike with stock prices rising as high as $50 a share. It was the perfect time to launch another new venture with the debut of *From Martha's Kitchen,* a half-hour cooking program to air on cable television's Food Network in late 1999. Martha Stewart Living Omnimedia, Inc. finished its maiden year as a public company with revenues topping $229 million.

By 2000 *Martha Stewart Living* magazine's circulation had reached 2.1 million and the homemaking publication went from 10 issues per year to 11, with plans for becoming monthly the following year. Its sibling publication, *Martha Stewart Weddings,* which had debuted in 1994, had gone from an annual publication to biannual then quarterly. Other special interest magazines had also joined the ranks, including *Entertaining* (which had also been the title of Stewart's first book in 1982), *Martha Stewart Baby, Halloween,* and *Clotheskeeping.* A new quarterly magazine for families, called *Kids: Fun Stuff to Do Together* was published in July 2001, filled with recipes, crafts, and games for kids aged three to ten.

Stewart also expanded further into home furnishings through a deal with Bernhardt Furniture Company for a Martha Stewart Signature collection in 2001, the same year MSLO signed with Japan's Seiyu, a retail chain of more than 200 stores. Seiyu was slated to carry a broad range of Stewart branded products, while the two companies were to collaborate on a new magazine called *Martha,* published in Japanese.

An error in judgment with devastating consequences also occurred in 2001. Whether Stewart willingly committed a crime or simply acted irresponsibly, she sold ImClone stock after allegedly receiving a tip from her friend Samuel Waksal, ImClone's chief executive. An adverse FDA report then sent ImClone stock tumbling, and soon Stewart, Waksal, and Stewart's broker Peter Bacanovic were questioned by federal investigators. As the case gained momentum, it became clear Stewart would face charges. While many called the investigation a witch hunt, few believed Stewart would ever face trial. Revenues for 2001 totaled $288.6 million as suspicion of Stewart's actions grew.

Allegations, Court Time, and Prison, 2002–04

By 2002 Stewart was in the middle of a legal maelstrom. Waksal was arrested for insider trading and Bacanovic began cooperating with investigators. Federal prosecutors suspected not only wrongdoing but a coverup as well. With all the publicity affecting MSLO, Stewart cut back her involvement as the company began showing signs of the strain by the middle of the year. Consumer confidence in Stewart teetered despite her protestations of innocence; by the third quarter earnings had fallen and stock value was down by more than half. The end of the year brought revenues of a relatively strong $295 million, but income of only $7.3 million.

By the time Stewart was indicted in July and went on trial in 2003, she had resigned as chief executive and chair of her company, serving as a "creative" officer of the board. Revenues for the troubled year had fallen to $245.8 million and the company suffered its first ever annual loss of $2.7 million. Stewart's five-week trial ended in March 2004 when she was convicted on all charges. She was fined $30,000, sentenced to five months each of prison time and home confinement, and two years probation. She served her time from October 2004 to March 2005, and after her release was allowed to leave her estate for up to 48 hours per week while under house arrest.

While Stewart's legal woes certainly affected MSLO's performance (2004 revenues only reached $187.4 million with a hefty loss of $60 million), there was hope for a brighter future. New deals included broadening the company's branded product line with Bernhardt Furniture Company; extending its licensing agreement with Kmart until 2010; the purchase of *Body & Soul* magazine from New Age Publishing; and collaborating with pet guru Marc Morrone for a new television program called *Petkeeping with Marc Morrone*, which also included newspaper and magazine columns.

A New Era, 2005 and Beyond

In 2005 as Stewart returned to work, she was welcomed back by many of her colleagues and loyal customers. In her absence friend and stockholder Sharon Patrick had taken the helm but stepped down in late 2004, replaced by Susan Lyne, a former television executive, as CEO and president. With Stewart still under a cloud due to a Securities and Exchange Commission lawsuit, she was unable to lead the company in any significant way (her shares had been put in the control of her daughter Alexis while Stewart was in prison). Stewart was, however, front and center in several new television development deals, two of which paired her with *Survivor* and *Apprentice* producer Mark Burnett. Not only would Stewart host an hour-long live program featuring cooking and decorating, but she would also star in a new version of *The Apprentice* made famous by Donald Trump.

Other new ventures included a deal with Sirius satellite radio for a *Martha Stewart Living* radio program, and the cable television Style Network acquiring the rights to run previously-aired episodes of the Emmy-winning *Martha Stewart Living* twice daily along with a few newly produced specials. By the middle of 2005 both Stewart and her company were regaining lost confidence and making strides in all of MSLO's business segments. The television, publishing, merchandising, and Internet/direct commerce divisions were touting new products and partnerships. Though Stewart's legal problems were not over, she was more than ready to move forward and to once again make her empire "a good thing."

Principal Operating Units

Television; Publishing; Merchandising; Internet/Direct Commerce.

Principal Competitors

Advance Publications; Crate & Barrel; Home Depot, Inc.; Pottery Barn; Target Stores, Inc.; Wal-Mart Inc.; Williams Sonoma, Inc.

Further Reading

Brady, Diane, et al., "Sorting Out the Martha Mess," *Business Week,* July 2, 2002, p. 44.

Byrnes, Nanette, "Propping Up the House That Martha Built," *Business Week,* June 16, 2003, p. 38.

Creswell, Julie, "Will Martha Walk?," *Fortune,* November 25, 2002, p. 112.

David, Grainger, "Martha's New TV Boss Makes a Mint," *Fortune,* February 21, 2005, p. 28.

Dugan, I. Jeanne, "Someone's in the Kitchen with Martha," *Business Week,* July 28, 1997, p. 58.

Frank, Jackie, "Martha Stewart May Spin Off Retail Stores," *Reuter Business Report,* November 12, 1996.

Goldsmith, Jill, "Stewart's Stock in a Stew," *Variety,* June 17, 2002, p. 4.

Granastein, Lisa, "MSLO Eyes New Growth Phase," *Brandweek,* November 15, 2004, p. 8.

Hays, Constance L., "Company Says Stewart's Woes Are Taking Toll," *New York Times,* July 25, 2002, p. C1.

——, "Is There Life for Martha Stewart Living Omnimedia Without Martha?," *New York Times,* September 5, 2002, p. C5.

——, "Martha Stewart Indicted by U.S. on Obstruction," *New York Times,* June 5, 2003, p. A1.

——, "Stewart Found Guilty of Lying in Sale of Stock," *New York Times,* March 6, 2004, p. A1.

Kasindorf, Jeanie Russell, "Martha, Inc.," *Working Woman,* June 1995, pp. 26–35.

Kelly, Keith J., "On Her Own, Martha Stewart Eyes IPO," *Advertising Age,* February 10, 1997, p. 1.

"Martha Stewart Thriving," *Business Week,* March 25, 2002, p. 56.

McMurdy, Dierdre, "A Brand Called Martha," *MacLean's,* December 12, 2000, p. 49.

Naughton, Keith, et al., "Martha Breaks Out," *Newsweek,* March 7, 2005, p. 36.

Pogrebin, Robin, "Master of Her Own Destiny," *New York Times,* February 8, 1998, p. 1C.

Pollack, Judann, and Alice Z. Cuneo, "Multitude of Deals Could Hurt Martha," *Advertising Age,* November 18, 1996, p. 26.

Rozhon, Tracie, "Stewart Quits As Director of Big Board," *New York Times,* October 4, 2002, p. C1.

Sellers, Patricia, "Designing Her Defense," *Fortune,* June 23, 2003, p. 27.

Thottam, Jyoti, "Martha's Endgame," *Time,* July 26, 2004, p. 47.

——, "Why They're Picking on Martha," *Time,* June 16, 2003, p. 44.

—Susan Windisch Brown
—update: Nelson Rhodes

MBIA Inc.

113 King Street
Armonk, New York 10504
U.S.A.
Telephone: (914) 273-4545
Fax: (914) 765-3163
Web site: http://www.mbia.com

Public Company
Incorporated: 1986
Employees: 623
Total Assets: $33.02 billion (2004)
Stock Exchanges: New York
Ticker Symbol: MBI
NAIC: 524130 Reinsurance Carriers

MBIA Inc. is a financial guarantee company, primarily insuring municipal bonds, infrastructure finance issues, asset- and mortgage-based securities. In essence the company bestows its own Triple-A rating (issued by Moody's, Standard & Poor's, Fitch and Rating and Investment Information) on the insured issue, making an unconditional and irrevocable guarantee that all financial obligations of the bond will be met. By obtaining insurance the bond issuer is able to negotiate lower interest rates and better market the bonds to buyers who are confident of their investments. MBIA also offers asset management and revenue enhancement services to state and local governments, academic institutions, and other public- and private-sector clients. In addition to its Armonk, New York headquarters, MBIA maintains offices in Denver, San Francisco, Paris, London, Madrid, Milan, Sydney, and Tokyo. MBIA is a public company listed on the New York Stock Exchange.

Introduction of Bond Insurance: Early 1970s

Many cities issue bonds to raise money to build necessary infrastructure. These general obligation bonds (GOs) are backed by an issuing agency, which has the power of taxation to make sure the bonds are paid off. Over the years revenue bonds also became popular. Their financial obligations are met by the revenue generated by the project itself, such as tolls charged to cross a bridge or use a highway. To give investors a sense of the quality of a bond issue, securities are rated, for a fee, by independent rating agencies such as Standard & Poor's and Moody's. The highest rating is Triple-A, the gold standard for bonds, reassuring investors and lenders alike in a project. Because some bond issues receive less than a Triple-A rating, a market developed for insurance, to back the bond with the Triple-A rating of the insurer.

In the early 1970s two bond insurers formed around the same time: American Municipal Bond Assurance Corporation (Ambac), a subsidiary of MGIC Investment Corporation of Milwaukee, and MBIA's predecessor, the Municipal Bond Insurance Association (MBIA), which was managed by Municipal Issuers Service Corporation (MISC). MISC was founded in 1971 after John R. Butler approached William O. Bailey, a senior executive at Aetna Casualty and Surety Company, with the concept of insuring municipal bonds. Bailey then recruited Aetna, St. Paul Fire and Marine Insurance Company, Connecticut General, and United States Fire Insurance Company to form MBIA in 1973. A year later MBIA became the first municipal bond guarantor to receive Standard & Poor's Triple-A rating, giving it a competitive edge over Ambac, which was awarded a Double-A rating. (In 1971 Ambac had become the first company to guarantee a municipal bond, the $650,000 issue for the Greater Juneau (Alaska) Borough Medical Arts Building.) With Bailey serving as its first president while continuing to work at Aetna, MBIA set up shop in White Plains, north of New York City. Initially business was slow, since GO bonds remained the dominant type of municipal bonds and had the power of taxation to back them up. But as taxpayers became increasingly upset about mounting property taxes, local government turned to revenue bonds, which by the end of the 1970s accounted for about two-thirds of all municipal bonds. Revenue bonds were a somewhat riskier investment, and issuers were more inclined to purchase insurance to gain the security of a Triple-A rating. It was not until May 21, 1974, that MBIA guaranteed its first bond, an $8.65 million water and sewer revenue bond issued by Carbondale, Illinois. The company guaranteed 11 more issues by the end of the year, for a total of $82 million worth of par value insured.

When New York City, running a massive deficit, came close to defaulting on its municipal bonds in 1975, the need for bond insurance gained traction, and business picked up for MBIA. Within two years the company had guaranteed 500 new bonds with a par value of $2.3 billion, as rising interest rates prompted many municipalities to insure their bonds in order to lower their interest costs. In 1980 that amount would reach $5 billion, and a year later MBIA insured its 1,000th issue. By 1983 the company held the distinction of having guaranteed bonds in all 50 states. During the early 1980s MBIA insured its first private university bond issue, began insuring healthcare financing bonds as well as bonds issued by housing agencies, and became the first bond insurer to guarantee the municipal bonds contained in unit investment trusts. With its higher rating than Ambac, MBIA dominated the market. Until Ambac was able to earn a Triple-A, it had only insured 115 bond issues, but seeing the profits that MBIA was enjoying, Ambac stepped up efforts in its new issue insurance program. Moreover, new competition arrived in 1983 in the form of Financial Guaranty Insurance Company (FGIC), followed by Bond Investors Guaranty Insurance Co. (BIG) in 1984 and Financial Security Assurance Inc. (FSA) in 1985.

Bond Default in the 1980s Causing Demand

A major factor in the rise of competition, however, was an increasing market for bond insurance, a tide that floated all boats in the industry including MBIA, which continued to grow and prosper during the 1980s. Also contributing to greater demand for insurance was another prominent bond default. In 1983 the Washington Public Power Supply System, known as WHOOPS in a case of unintended irony, defaulted on $2.25 billion worth of bonds after Washington taxpayers balked at backing some of its contracts. Ambac had insured a small portion of the bonds, the holders of which were repaid on time. Investors holding the uninsured bonds, on the other hand, received delayed, reduced payments. The incident proved to be a watershed moment in the bond insurance industry. Later in the 1980s another event took place that further stimulated business. The Tax Reform Act of 1986 eliminated tax-exemptions on private-purpose and non-governmental bonds issued after 1985. As a result, municipalities rushed to issue bonds before the new regulations went into effect, leading to a surge in bond insurance.

In 1985 Ryder System, Inc. acquired MBIA's managing agent, MISC, but Ryder sold the business less than 18 months later. At this point MBIA was reorganized, transforming itself from a consortium of five insurers (now including Travelers Corp.), all of which carried their share of the bond insurance on their own books. While Travelers opted out, the four founding insurers pooled $427 million in an initial investment to create a new entity, MBIA Inc., incorporated in Connecticut in November 1986. A month later it became MBIA's successor. It also acquired MISC from Ryder and reinsured all of the municipal bond insurance portfolios of the shareholding insurance companies.

In 1987 Bailey retired from Aetna and took over as the first chief executive officer and chairman of the new MBIA. Later in the year, in July, the company went public, selling 5.5 million shares priced at $23.50 per share in an initial public offering. The company was subsequently listed on the New York Stock Exchange. A stock market crash in October 1987—the notorious Black Monday—put a severe dent in the price of MBIA shares, but the company soon recovered. It was healthy enough by the end of the 1980s to acquire another municipal bond insurance company, BIG, which in 1990 adopted the name MBIA Insurance Corp. of Illinois. MBIA was also taking steps to begin doing business in Europe. In December 1989 it forged an alliance with Credit Local de France, a major French financial institution, which bought a 5 percent stake in MBIA from Continental Corp. In return, MBIA agreed to provide technical assistance to Credit Local de France, essentially teaching the French financing techniques that might be transferred to Europe, where a market for municipal bonds had not yet emerged. Instead, municipalities relied on banks and other lending institutions to finance projects. MBIA was also hopeful that the alliance with a powerful financial institution would give it a leg up on future business in Europe. In 1991 the company established a French subsidiary to help lay the groundwork for the financial guarantee business in Europe and a year later opened its first international office in Paris.

MBIA entered the 1990s never having paid a claim in its history. The company continued to broaden its services in the early 1990s, launching its Cooperative Liquid Assets Securities System (CLASS) to provide investment management services to school districts and municipalities, and the ASSURETY program that guaranteed a bank's obligations to municipal depositors. In 1993 MBIA established MBIA Investment Management Corp., which served municipal insurers, guaranteeing investment agreements for the proceeds from their municipal bonds. MBIA also experienced a change in leadership. In 1992 David H. Elliott was named CEO, and following Bailey's retirement in 1994 was named chairman as well.

Another seminal moment in the history of the bond insurance industry occurred in 1994 when Orange County, one of the nation's wealthiest areas, possessing a Double-A credit rating, went bankrupt. MBIA was a direct beneficiary, subsequently insuring $900 million worth of recovery bonds issued by Orange County and receiving nearly $30 million in fees. Moreover, as had been the case in 1975 with New York City and 1983 with Washington Public Power Supply defaults, the demand for bond insurance surged, as investors were no longer satisfied with the reputation of a municipality when buying bonds. In short, if Orange County could default, than anyone could. Within a year about 40 percent of newly issued municipal bonds would be insured, and a year later nearly half would be insured.

Mid-1990s Brings Expansion

The company's prominent role in guaranteeing Orange County's recovery bonds also rekindled investor interest in MBIA. In December 1995 the company completed a $75 million public offering, followed a month later by a stock sale that raised $55 million. Flush with cash, MBIA expanded in the second half of the 1990s on a number of fronts, both internally and by way of acquisitions. MBIA Securities Corp. was estab-

Key Dates:

1971: Municipal Issuers Service Corp. (MISC) is formed.
1973: Municipal Bond Insurance Association (MBIA) is formed by four insurance companies, managed by MISC.
1974: MBIA receives Triple-A credit rating.
1986: MBIA is reorganized as a corporation.
1987: MBIA goes public.
1991: Paris office opens.
1998: MBIA merges with CapMac.
2004: MBIA is subpoenaed by state and federal regulators.

lished in 1995 to offer internal fixed-income trading and portfolio management. In that same year, the company launched a joint venture with Ambac, MBIA-Ambac International, to sell financial guarantee insurance around the world. MBIA & Associates Consulting was formed in 1997 to provide management consulting services to state and local governments, colleges and universities, as well as real estate entities and international concerns. Acquisitions included Municipal Tax Bureau, a Philadelphia-based provider of tax discovery, compliance, and administration services that became the backbone of a new subsidiary, MBIA MuniServices. In addition the new unit acquired MuniFinancial, a California company that offered a slate of bond administration services. Also in 1997 MBIA acquired Municipal Resource Consultants, another California company, provider of revenue enhancement audits and other services, and American Money Management Associates, Inc., which offered a variety of investment services to municipalities and other public sector entities.

Expansion continued in the late 1990s. After reaching an agreement in 1997, MBIA and CapMAC Holdings Inc. merged in a stock swap valued at more than $500 million. The addition of CapMAC's expertise in structured financial solutions and credit risk management strengthened MBIA's ability to serve the structured finance marketplace, which was enjoying fast growth worldwide. Also in 1998 MBIA acquired another Philadelphia company, 1838 Investment Advisors, an equity management firm that became a major component in newly formed MBIA Asset Management LLC. But the year would also be marked by the largest claim in the history of MBIA. In 1998 Allegheny Health, Education and Research Foundation, a non-profit hospital chain known as AHERF, filed for bankruptcy, putting $256 million in securities insured by MBIA into default. MBIA subsequently arranged for $170 million of reinsurance from three Triple-A reinsurers, paying a $3.85 million premium. However, these reinsurance agreements would prove troublesome several years later.

In the meantime, Elliott retired as CEO and chairman in 1999, replaced in both posts by Joseph (Jay) W. Brown, Jr. MBIA opened a London office in 2000 and a year later topped the $1 billion mark in adjusted direct premiums. The AHERF episode began to resurface in December 2002 when New York City Hedge fund Gotham Partners issued a white paper that claimed MBIA's reserves were inadequate and that an invest-

ment in the firm was risky. MBIA struck back quickly, accusing Gotham Partners of attempting to drive down the price of MBIA shares in order to profit from Gotham's short position on the company. MBIA's protestations were loud enough, in fact, to prompt an investigation of Gotham by the Securities & Exchange Commission and the New York State Attorney General's office.

In May 2004, Gary Dunton, president of MBIA, was named CEO and Jay Brown became executive chairman. During Jay Brown's tenure at the helm of MBIA, he strengthened MBIA's operations, including pricing, risk management, loss reserving, and human resources.

In November 2004 the company received subpoenas from the Securities and Exchange Commission (SEC) and the New York Attorney General's (NYAG) office requesting information that covered the AHERF reinsurance transactions MBIA had entered into in 1998. In March 2005, MBIA restated its financial results for the previous seven years due to improper accounting related to a 1998 agreement with Converium Re, previously known as Zurich Reinsurance Centre. Later that month, MBIA received a subpoena from the U.S. Attorney's Office for the Southern District of New York seeking information about the reinsurance agreements. Supplemental requests from the NYAG and the SEC sought documents relating to the company's accounting treatment of advisory fees, its methodology for determining loss reserves and case reserves, instances of purchase of credit default protection on itself, and documents relating to Channel Reinsurance Ltd., a reinsurance company of which MBIA was part owner. MBIA began to cooperate fully with these investigations.

The rating agencies supported MBIA throughout this period. Moody's stated, ''The relatively contained nature of the additional request for information, both as to its scope and apparent materiality, suggest a limited impact on MBIA's financial profile. While most questions relate to MBIA specific issues, the accounting for loss and case reserves is a financial guaranty industry issue recently referred by the SEC to the FASB for further guidance.'' S&P stated that, ''they have received no information that would cause them to change the rating or outlook of MBIA Inc. (AA/Stable) and MBIA Insurance Corp. (AAA/Stable).''

Analysts also remained positive throughout, and Rob Ryan of Merrill Lynch reiterated his buy rating on MBIA in April 2005 stating, ''The current perception of regulatory risk for MBIA and the industry is excessive.'' After the March subpoenas, Geoffrey Dunn of Keefe Bruyette & Woods thought the stock presented a positive opportunity. ''We believe that this will prove to be a positive buying opportunity for longer-term investors,'' Dunn said. ''We reiterate our Outperform rating.''

How the investigations and the lawsuits would play out was uncertain. During this time, MBIA stock continued to perform well, and the company maintained a strong market share.

Principal Subsidiaries

MBIA Insurance Corporation; MBIA Asset Managements, LLC; MBIA Municipal Investors Service Corporation; MBIA Investment Management Corp.; MBIA Capital Management

Corp.; MBIA Services Company; MBIA MuniServices Company; CapMac Financial Services, Inc.

Principal Competitors

AMBAC Financial Group, Inc.; Financial Guaranty Insurance Company; Financial Security Assurance Holdings Ltd.

Further Reading

Atlas, Riva D., and Jonathan Fuerbringer, "With MBIA Inc. Under Regulators' Scrutiny, Investors Wonder About the Status of Its Bond Insurer," *New York Times,* April 12, 2005, p. C2.

Bayot, Jennifer, "William Bailey, 78, Dies," *New York Times,* January 29, 2005, p. B7.

Feldman, Amy, "Muni Anxiety," *Forbes,* August 15, 1994, p. 74.

Francis, Theo, "MBIA Is Facing Another Inquiry Over Reinsurance," *Wall Street Journal,* March 10, 2005, p. B2.

Francis, Theo, and Ian McDonald, "MBIA Is Probed for Additional Reinsurer Deal," *Wall Street Journal,* April 6, 2005, p. C1.

Higgins, Carol B., "Keeping Watch Over Cities Is This Insurer's Business," *Across the Board,* September 16, 1988, p. 31.

King, Sharon R., "After Orange County, MBIA's Bond Insurance Is in Demand," *New York Times,* June 18, 1996, p. D10.

McLean, Bethany, "The Mystery of the $890 Billion Insurer," *Fortune,* May 16, 2005, p. 135.

Morgenson, Gretchen, "MBIA Will Restate Results for 7 Years Over Improper Accounting," *New York Times,* March 9, 2005, p. C2.

Richard, Christine, "Outside Audit: Reinsurance Probe Reaches Out to MBIA," *Wall Street Journal,* December 24, 2004, p. C3.

Whitehouse, Mark, and Theo Francis, "Unsettling Claim: Old Deal Bedevils Key Player in World of Municipal Bonds," *Wall Street Journal,* May 2, 2005, p. A1.

—Ed Dinger

Moldflow Corporation

430 Boston Road
Wayland, Massachusetts 01778
U.S.A.
Telephone: (508) 358-5848
Fax: (508) 358-5868
Web site: http://www.moldflow.com

Public Company
Incorporated: 1978 as Moldflow Pty. Ltd.
Employees: 291
Sales: $48.67 million (2004)
Stock Exchanges: NASDAQ
Ticker Symbol: MFLO
NAIC: 511210 Software Publishers; 541511 Customer
  Computer Programming Services

Moldflow Corporation is the leading developer of software solutions that improve the design, analysis, and production of injection-molded plastic parts. Moldflow's products are used by part designers, mold designers, manufacturing engineers, and machine operators, serving as tools used through all phases of the design and production processes for injection-molded plastic parts. Moldflow also is involved in manufacturing the hardware its software helps to perform more effectively, producing equipment-monitoring systems and machine-temperature controls. The company operates globally, maintaining a physical presence in Europe, Asia, and in Australia, where it was originally established.

Origins

Plastic revolutionized manufacturing in the 20th century, becoming the material of choice for innumerable applications. Lightweight, strong, and offering consistent quality, size, shape, and color, plastic afforded many benefits, but producing injection-molded parts could be troublesome, resulting in heavy financial losses if the design of the mold proved flawed. Often, plastic parts were not analyzed before production because of the time and expertise needed to analyze, or simulate, the production of a molded plastic part before it was produced. Consequently, costly re-designs of parts and molds resulted. One manufacturer,

in a June 23, 1997 interview with *Design News,* explained the inherent problem with working with injected-molded plastic parts. "Eighty-five percent of the part designs we receive require design changes to support the manufacturing process. For a $300-million company like ours, verifying part designs up-front would save us about $200,000 per year." The mission of Moldflow was to help manufacturers predict design flaws before the manufacturing process began, offering computer-aided-engineering (CAE) products that reduced the costs and the expertise needed to simulate the intricacies of the flow of plastic into a mold. Moldflow, its name describing its mission, became the leader in its field, increasing the already revolutionary efficacy of plastic in a manufacturing setting.

The company was started in Australia, beginning its corporate life as Moldflow Pty. Ltd. in 1978 when its founder, Colin Austin, turned his attention to resolving the difficulties of working with plastic. The market for simulation software was relatively small, dwarfed by the markets simulation software served. The global market for simulation software did not reach the $100 million mark until 30 years after Austin founded Moldflow, by which time the company had relocated to the United States, establishing its headquarters near Boston. The move occurred in 1996, one year after Ampersand Ventures acquired a substantial stake in the company and before Moldflow significantly expanded its product line, sharpening its assault on the software simulation market.

Moldflow's annual revenue hovered around $10 million when it moved to Boston. The financial total had been built up during the first 20 years of the company's history, a period during which Moldflow relied on a single product line. Known as Moldflow Plastics Insight, the simulation software established the company in its market, but it could only be used by highly specialized engineers conducting in-depth plastics simulation. The expertise required to use Plastics Insight left Moldflow courting only a small customer base in an already small market, holding its financial growth in check. The company did not begin to increase its stature substantially until it developed simulation software that could be navigated by less experienced users, a turning point in Moldflow's history that occurred shortly after it relocated to Boston. The introduction of

Plastics Advisors followed by the introduction of Plastics Xpert enabled Moldflow to develop into the dominant player in the global simulation software market.

New Products in the Late 1990s Igniting Growth

Moldflow's Plastics Advisor Series was introduced in 1997, giving participants in all phases of the design and production process for injection-molded plastic parts a software tool they could use. Plastics Advisor simulated the flow of plastic, offering advice to the part designer on what corrective actions needed to be taken to improve the "manufacturability" of a molded part. The software informed the user whether a part would fill properly, it showed the location of weld lines, and it identified whether and where air traps would appear. "Today," Black & Decker's director of engineering services said in a June 23, 1997 interview with *Design News,* "analysis is done too late, after the part is designed. At that stage, analysis requires 40 to 60 hours of an expert's time, and a fix, which is needed in most cases, is too expensive." Plastics Advisor was a significant product introduction not only because it enabled less experienced users to simulate production but also because it represented the company's attempt to enable what it called "process-wide" plastics simulation. With Plastics Advisor and succeeding products, the company was trying to bridge the gaps between part design, mold design, and part production, offering a comprehensive solution to a number of different disciplines.

Moldflow followed its Plastics Advisor software series with Plastics Xpert, a software package introduced in the fall of 1998. Plastics Xpert attached to injection-molding machines, enabling operators to monitor and to control the manufacturing process. The software tackled problems that typically occurred on the shop floor, giving injection-molding machine operators (individuals generally not trained in plastic part design) the ability to correct design flaws.

The addition of Plastics Advisor and Plastics Xpert to Moldflow's product line ignited financial growth in an expanding

market. Sales in 1998 reached $16.3 million, jumping to nearly $28 million the following year. At the time, the market for simulation software was growing by 20 percent annually, demonstrating a level of vitality that prompted industry participants to consolidate with one another in a bid to capture a greater share of a growing market. In 1998, in a move that foreshadowed a pivotal deal in Moldflow's history, the company's main competitor was busy consolidating with other operators, intensifying the competitive race between the two companies. In June, Moldflow's biggest rival, C-Mold, struck an accord with Matra Datavision to acquire its software simulation operations. In December, C-Mold strengthened its market position further, announcing that it had forged an agreement with one of the smaller simulation software operators, Rapra Technology Ltd. Based in Shawbury, England, Rapra decided to exit the simulation software business, transfer its customers to C-Mold, and become a reseller of C-Mold products. At the time the deal with Rapra was announced, Moldflow estimated that it controlled 65 percent of the global market compared with C-Mold's 22 percent share. Officials at C-Mold disagreed with Moldflow's estimate, claiming that the two companies were equals in the U.S. market and closer rivals on the international front, although the company declined to provide any specific figures.

Acquisitions at the Dawn of the 21st Century

Whatever the size of the gap separating Moldflow and C-Mold, the dispute was rendered moot within months of the Rapra deal. The beginning of the 21st century was a time of decisive action for Moldflow, a period that saw the company make its public debut. In early 2000, Moldflow filed with the Securities and Exchange Commission for an initial public offering (IPO) of stock. Ampersand Ventures, which had taken an equity position in the company five years earlier, was set to own 45 percent of Moldflow after its IPO. The IPO was completed at the end of March, when the company sold three million shares at $13 per share, raising, after expenses, approximately $34 million. The funds raised from the IPO were used to complete a significant acquisition, the purchase of C-Mold, which had necessitated the IPO. Moldflow acquired C-Mold in April 2000, paying $11 million to gain control of its primary competitor.

Moldflow's management charged forward after the acquisition of C-Mold, branching beyond its business base into new facets of the plastics industry. In mid-2000, the company turned its attention to injection-molding machines and to developing its e-commerce business. In June, the company signed an agreement with Milacron Inc., a Batavia, Ohio-based manufacturer of machine control systems. Under the terms of the agreement, Moldflow began loading its Parts Advisor software onto Milacron's machine control systems. On the Internet, the company's web site, www.plasticzone.com, was tailored to deliver Moldflow's software simulation packages to customers online. The web site featured an Internet version of Plastics Advisor, enabling a customer to run an analysis of a computer-aided mold design in less than 30 minutes. Also available was an Internet version of Plastics Xpert, which allowed users to monitor injection press operations from a distant site and perform diagnostic tests.

The beginning of the 21st century witnessed Moldflow's evolution into an integrated company, as it became increas-

Key Dates:

1978: Moldflow is established.
1996: Moldflow moves from Australia to the Boston area.
1997: Plastics Advisor is introduced.
1998: Plastics Xpert is introduced.
2000: Moldflow completes its initial public offering of stock and acquires C-Mold.
2002: A. Roland Thomas is appointed president and chief executive officer.
2003: Moldflow acquires Controle Processus Industriels.
2004: Moldflow acquires American MSI Corp.

ingly involved in aspects of the plastics industry beyond its core simulation software business. As the company carved a new position in the hardware sector, it did so under the guidance of a new leader. A. Roland Thomas was appointed president and chief executive officer in June 2002, a promotion that arrived during his twentieth year of service with Moldflow. Australia-born Thomas served in various management positions related to product development, operations, and general management before being selected as the company's vice-president of research and development, the post he held before becoming its principal executive.

Under Thomas's rule, Moldflow furthered its development into an integrated company. Not long after moving into his new office, Thomas looked overseas to bolster the company's operations. In January 2003, Moldflow acquired a French company named Controle Processus Industriels (CPI) that made production-monitoring systems. Based in Dampart, CPI served roughly 100 customers in French-speaking countries. Commenting on the $800,000 deal in a January 13, 2003 interview with *Plastics News,* Moldflow's executive vice-president for marketing and field services, Ken Welch, explained: "We already are doing a lot of business in Europe. This helps us grow that European base and puts our products in the French market."

Thomas continued to look for other acquisition targets in the wake of the CPI purchase, suggesting, perhaps, that the 25-year-old Moldflow would assume a more aggressive acquisitive stance in its next quarter-century of business. Thomas completed another deal a year after purchasing CPI, acquiring Moorpark, California-based American MSI Corporation, a maker of hot-runner temperature controls. The acquisition represented another move toward building a comprehensive product offering; or, as one analyst put it in a February 2, 2004 interview with *Plastics News:* "I think they're basically getting down, further and further, into the tool." The transaction, a $7.2 million deal, was completed in January 2004, prompting a reorganization of Moldflow into two business units. Tim Triplett, who had been chairman and chief executive officer of American MSI, was appointed executive vice-president and general manager of Moldflow's Manufacturing Solutions segment. Ken Welch was promoted to the posts of executive vice-president and general manager of the company's Design Analysis Solutions unit.

As Moldflow prepared for the future, the company held sway in its market, defining what a well-equipped, comprehensive simulation software firm should look like. Its dominance in software had engendered a move into hardware, making it a total solutions provider to the plastics industry. By acquiring American MSI, a hardware maker, the company could begin to operate all of its products off a single platform, giving its customers a seamless, sophisticated answer to design and production problems. In November 2004, when the absorption of American MSI into the Moldflow fold was still underway, Thomas was awarded the added title of chairman, giving him resolute control over the company. Looking ahead, the company planned to begin hardware manufacturing in Cork, Ireland, by mid-2005. Beyond that date, the company planned to strengthen its already formidable market position, promising to play a prominent role in the plastics manufacturing industry for years to come.

Principal Subsidiaries

Moldflow Scandinavia (Sweden); Moldflow International Pty. Ltd. (Australia); Moldflow Pty. Ltd. (Australia); Moldflow Italia S.R.L. (Italy); Moldflow Korea Limited; Moldflow (Europe) Ltd. (U.K.); Moldflow Vertriebs GmbH (Germany); Moldflow Japan KK; Moldflow Singapore Pte. Ltd.; Moldflow France; Moldflow B.V. (Netherlands); Moldflow Taiwan, Inc.; Moldflow Ireland, Ltd.; Moldflow Iberia s.l. (Spain); Advanced CAE Technology, Inc.; Branden Technologies, Inc.; Moldflow Merger Corporation; Moldflow (Guangzhou) Ltd. (China); Moldflow Mauritius Pty. Ltd.; Moldflow Securities Corporation; American MSI Corporation.

Principal Divisions

Manufacturing Solutions; Design Analysis Solutions.

Principal Competitors

Autodesk, Inc.; Dassault Systemes S.A.; Electronic Data Systems Corporation.

Further Reading

Bregar, Bill, "Moldflow Buys Temperature Control Maker," *Plastic News,* February 2, 2004, p. 9.
——, "Moldflow Launches Plastics Xpert," *Plastics News,* October 12, 1998, p. 42.
——, "Moldflow Takes IPO Plunge," *Plastics News,* April 3, 2000, p. 13.
Colucci, Deana, "Software Promises Perfect Plastic Parts Up Front," *Design News,* June 23, 1997, p. 89.
Grace, Robert, "Moldflow Picks Ireland for Production Site," *Plastics News,* November 29, 2004, p. 9.
Knights, Mikell, "The New Dimension in Mold Simulation," *Plastics Technology,* March 2004, p. 46.
Lauzon, Michael, "Moldflow Plans $46 Million Nasdaq IPO," *Plastics News,* January 31, 2000, p. 4.
"Moldflow," *IPO Reporter,* May 1, 2000.
"Moldflow Buys C-MOLD," *Computer-Aided Engineering,* April 2000, p. 10.
"Moldflow Buys French Controls Developer," *Modern Plastics,* February 2003, p. 25.
"Moldflow Buys French Firm," *Plastics News,* January 13, 2003, p. 19.

Ogando, Joseph, ''Now Get Flow Simulation Without All the Fuss,'' *Plastics Technology,* June 1997, p. 23.

Pryweller, Joseph, ''Moldflow CEO Roland Thomas Talks Automation, Its Future,'' *Plastics News,* February 2, 2004, p. 9.

——, ''Moldflow to Extend Beyond Core Products,'' *Plastics News,* June 19, 2000, p. 30

Toloken, Steve, ''CAE Player Beginning to Flow Together,'' *Plastics News,* December 14, 1998, p. 11.

——, ''Moldflow's Founder Austin Now Has Water-Flow System,'' *Plastics News,* May 26, 2003, p. 19.

—Jeffrey L. Covell

NBGS International, Inc.

3150 IH 35 South
New Braunfels, Texas 78130
U.S.A.
Telephone: (830) 620-5400
Fax: (830) 629-2867
Web site: http://www.nbgsintl.com

Private Company
Founded: 1984 as New Braunfels General Store
Employees: 100
Sales: $20 million (2004 est.)
NAIC: 713110 Amusement and Theme Parks; 713990 All
Other Amusement and Recreation Industries

NBGS International, Inc. is an industry leader in the design, engineering, and fabrication of waterpark rides and attractions, or what the company calls ''Transportainment.'' From original concept to implementation, the award-winning NBGS is a sister company to Waterpark Management Inc., which oversees the Schlitterbahn Waterpark Resort, the nation's most successful waterpark, located in New Braunfels, Texas. In addition to its one-of-a-kind waterpark attractions, NBGS designs and manufactures soft-play areas, playgrounds, and fountains for municipal centers, shopping malls, resorts, campgrounds, and cruise ships.

In the Beginning: 1970s–80s

In modest-sized New Braunfels, Texas, population 36,000, sits a giant: the Schlitterbahn. While fellow Texans had long enjoyed the town for its annual Wurstfest (a ten-day celebration of German pride, represented in tons of wurst [sausage] and beer), it was literally put on the map by the mighty Schlitterbahn Waterpark. The story of NBGS International, Inc. began with the Henry family's desire to create an amazing, one-of-a-kind waterpark near their riverfront hotel, the Landa Resort. Bob and Billye Henry bought the Landa, which was surrounded by the Comal and Guadalupe rivers, in 1966. Landa guests, area residents, and college kids from nearby San Antonio (25 miles south) and Austin (40 miles north) had long enjoyed swimming and sunning themselves on inner tubes, lazily traversing the rivers. The Henrys began thinking a more structured ''waterpark'' would bring vacationers and tourists to the Landa and generate dollars for New Braunfels as well.

Over the next several years Bob Henry created a number of chutes and river rides for the Landa. The resulting waterpark was eventually named the Schlitterbahn, which meant ''slippery road'' in German. The Schlitterbahn was modeled after the Solms Castle in Braunfels, Germany, where the town's original settlers had come from. The waterpark's centerpiece was a 60-foot replica of the German castle's Bergfried Tower, around which Henry designed four water slides. The Schlitterbahn (often referred to as Schlitterbahn West) opened in 1979 and for the next several years the Henrys added additional attractions and water rides to the park. In 1980 came the 50,000-square-foot Lagoon pool (with the first ever swim-up refreshment bar) and the Hillside Tube Chute; in 1983 the Cliffhanger Tube Chute and a recreation facility; and in 1984 the Tunnel Tube Chute, tennis courts, and another pool.

Bob and Billye Henry's son Jeff founded a company called the New Braunfels General Store (later known as NBGS International) in 1984. NBGS provided some maintenance and foam-coated equipment, designed by Jeff, to the Schlitterbahn. The two entities had a working partnership for years, though NBGS would move beyond its role as Schlitterbahn supplier to designing and building recreational complexes around the world. Through the ingenuity of the Henrys, the Schlitterbahn became the most celebrated waterpark in the United States and the standard to which all others aspired.

As the popularity of the Schlitterbahn grew, the Henrys continually sought new ways to keep the waterpark fun, unique, and ahead of the competition. By 1985 the Schlitterbahn's success had spawned a slew of imitators, riding an industry trend as waterparks were built in major tourist attractions across the country. Within a decade there were waterparks throughout most of the nation's popular destinations not only in the South and Southwest, where warm weather permitted attendance most of the year, but in the Midwest and eastern states as well. The trend came to include hotels, beach resorts, campgrounds, park districts, and health clubs—many of which were built using NBGS-designed attractions and equipment. By the close of the decade

Key Dates:

1979: The Schlitterbahn Waterpark opens in New Braunfels, Texas.

1980: The Hillside Tube Chute, first inner tube ride in the United States, is opened at Schlitterbahn.

1984: The New Braunfels General Store is founded by Jeff Henry to supply the Schlitterbahn.

1988: NBGS wins its first World Waterpark Association (WWA) leadership award.

1990: NBGS wins its first WWA safety award.

1997: The Henrys break ground on Schlitterbahn South Padre.

2000: The original Schlitterbahn's German castle gets major renovations.

2001: The South Padre Schlitterbahn opens and wins NBGS several industry awards.

2003: Negotiations begin with city of Galveston to build a Schlitterbahn waterpark.

2004: The New Braunfels Schlitterbahn is named "America's Best Waterpark" by *Amusement Today* for the seventh time.

2005: The first phase of the Galveston, Texas, Schlitterbahn opens.

several new slides, chutes, and concessions had been added to the Schlitterbahn, courtesy of Jeff Henry's designs for NBGS.

Rapid Expansion: 1990s

By 1991 another 25 acres, a few blocks east of the original Schlitterbahn, were added to the megapark and called Schlitterbahn East. The new section included additional concession stands, a gift shop, lockers, and more German-themed water rides including the Boogie Bahn for body surfing. The world's first uphill "water coaster," designed by NBGS and called the Dragon Blaster, wowed guests by the Schlitterbahn's 15th anniversary in 1994. The following year Schlitterbahn became the top seasonal waterpark in the United States, rivaled only by year-round parks.

By 1996 several amazing new rides, designed by NBGS, were added to the Schlitterbahn—rides that solidified its reputation as one of the world's most innovative recreational design companies. The Torrent River rapids ride, the Master Blaster uphill water coaster, the Black Knight dark tube adventure, and the Wolfpack family raft ride not only gave Schlitterbahn's visitors the ride of their lives, but put NBGS on the map.

With the ongoing success of the Schlitterbahn, the Henrys were looking to expand. One area of interest was in southern Texas, at South Padre Island on the Gulf of Mexico. Located less than an hour from the Mexican border and near the city of Harlingen, South Padre was a major hangout for spring breakers, attracting thousands of college students each year. Families and tourists visited too, lured by the beaches and the Gulf's warm waters. The Henrys and several investors broke ground on the 15-acre South Padre Schlitterbahn in 1997. The new water rides and attractions, which Jeff Henry promised would

be cutting edge with surfing areas and large wave pools, came from the increasingly renowned NBGS.

The New Braunfels Schlitterbahn celebrated its 20th anniversary in 1999. With waterpark mania in full swing—both domestically and internationally—Jeff Henry and NBGS had taken advantage of the craze and brought the family's unique recreational designs to the forefront of the amusement industry. Not only would there be two Schlitterbahns gracing U.S. soil, but NBGS had helped design and build six waterparks in Asia: two in China, two in Malaysia, and one each in Guam and Indonesia. Jeff Henry believed the industry would evolve further, especially attractions or waterparks with pervasive themes and those constructed as part of extensive hotel complexes.

The kinds of equipment and rides were changing too. As Henry told *Amusement Business* magazine (October 1999), fiberglass, once practically the only material used in fashioning water rides, could be mixed and matched with other materials. "In the beginning, many parks [used] . . . pre-shaped fiberglass attractions," he said. "But to create a comfortable attractive environment, a park needs to mix in other elements with the fiberglass, such as concrete. A good mix of textures is very important and more and more of the modern parks are realizing [this factor]. It's what we have done at Schlitterbahn, and it works well."

New Century, New Goals: 2000s

The New Braunfels Schlitterbahn experienced record attendance in 2000, with visitors topping the 900,000-mark for the first time. To help the flagship break the million-visitor mark, NBGS renovated the park and added a new two-mile river rapids ride. Schlitterbahn's trademark German castle was given a facelift and its four Castle Slides became part of the river rapids ride. At the same time, NBGS was completing the attractions for the family's new waterpark in South Padre, which included a series of lock-like fun stations and conveyors at differing water levels to eliminate waiting lines. This became the hallmark of NBGS's "Transportainment" system, where any waiting was done in water—on an inner tube—keeping visitors cool and comfortable. The concept was introduced at the opening of the Schlitterbahn Beach Waterpark in South Padre.

The Transportainment concept became the talk of the amusement industry, winning a slew of awards and recognition for NBGS by 2001. The system was so named because it combined the elements of transportation, sport, and entertainment, integrating several of NBGS's most popular rides and chutes to lift, push, and float patrons throughout the park's river system. As Jeff Henry told *Amusement Business,* "It's a continuous loop that will also be used as a transportation system within the park," he said. "When we finish the entire system . . . a person [could] be on it for six hours without standing in a single line. I think this is the wave of the future."

Patrons evidently agreed as the New Braunfels Schlitterbahn was voted the number one waterpark in the nation by *Amusement Today*'s poll for the fourth time in 2001, with the Master Blaster as "Best Waterpark Ride," and its Raging River ride winning second place. To protect its more than 100 products and proprietary designs, NBGS had patented its Master Blaster uphill water coaster and had applied for patents on its innovative Transportainment system and automated control systems.

In early 2002 Abigail Erwin was named president of NBGS and Mike Jaroszewski was appointed to the new position of vice-president of sales. Founder Jeff Henry remained chief executive, and had commented in a company press release that it was "[T]ime to move the company to a new level of industry leadership. With Abby and Mike at the helm we are well positioned to move the company forward." Erwin was new to NBGS, having worked for Wells Fargo, Texas Bancshares, and San Antonio's Resources Connection, a financial and management services company. Jaroszewski had worked at NBGS since 1994 and had worked on the Master Blaster coaster and other products during his tenure.

By 2005 the word "Schlitterbahn" had become part of the lexicon not only for those in the amusement industry but to waterpark enthusiasts in North America and beyond. NBGS and the original Schlitterbahn had been lauded by the press and even on television. The Travel Channel's *America's Best Waterparks* named the 65-acre New Braunfels Schlitterbahn as the country's best, and went on to do an hour-long segment on the park, covering its giant wave and surfing pool, three uphill water coasters, nine chutes, 17 water slides, five swimming pools, five hot tubs, seven children's water playgrounds, five gift shops, and nearly two dozen refreshment centers.

What the Schlitterbahn did for waterparks, NBGS took several steps further: helping recreational centers create unique, high-tech attractions and even schooling clients in the maintenance and repair of these products free of charge. NBGS began offering an annual Tech School session at its New Braunfels headquarters, which included its 300,000-square-foot manufacturing plant. The company also continued to capture more awards and honors, including its ninth World Waterpark Association award (seven had been for Innovation, two for Safety), and its 11th International Association of Amusement Parks & Attractions (IAAPA) award, six of which had been for Innova-

tion, one for "Impact" lauding its Transportainment system, and the remainder for individual rides and attractions.

NBGS continued to expand in the mid-2000s with projects in Delaware, Mississippi, Texas, and Dublin, Ireland. A third Schlitterbahn waterpark was soon to open in Galveston, Texas, south of Houston, while other projects in Florida, Alaska, the East Coast, the Midwest, Spain, and South Korea were underway. With its increasing exposure in Europe, the Middle East, and Asia, NBGS opened an office in the United Kingdom to liaise with its growing roster of international clients.

Principal Competitors

Fun Corporation of America; Six Flags, Inc.; Walt Disney Parks & Resorts; Wet 'n Wild Inc.; Paramount Parks Inc.

Further Reading

Hurtz, Rod, "Company's Innovative Water Rides Extend Beyond New Braunfels Park," *Austin American-Statesman*, July 5, 2002.

O'Brien, Tim, "Henry's New Ideas Put into Action in Texas," *Amusement Business*, December 24, 2001, p. 19.

——, "Pacific Rim Waterparks Seek New Technology," *Amusement Business*, February 10, 1997, p. 26.

——, "Schlitterbahn Gets Funky," *Amusement Business*, October 16, 2000, p. 13.

——, "Schlitterbahn Gives Facelift to Tower with Rapids Ride," *Amusement Business*, May 8, 2000, p. 35.

——, "Schlitterbahn Waterpark Found It Hard to Rise Up After Flood," *Amusement Business*, September 30, 2002, p. 6.

——, "Schlitterbahn Waterpark: South Padre's New Edition," *Amusement Business*, August 14, 1997, p. 22.

——, "Theming, Resorts Seen As Trends," *Amusement Business*, October 4, 1999, p. 28.

Waddell, Ray, "1995 Another Record Year for Texas' Schlitterbahn Park," *Amusement Business*, September 4, 1995, p. 38.

—Nelson Rhodes

Nestlé Waters

20 rue Rouget de Lisle
Issy les Moulineaux
F-92793 Cedex 9
France
Telephone: +33 1 41 23 38 00
Fax: +33 1 41 23 69 00
Web site: http://www.nestle-waters.com

Wholly Owned Subsidiary of Nestlé S.A.
Incorporated: 1992 as Nestlé Source International; 1996
  as Perrier-Vittel S.A.
Employees: 27,600
Sales: CHF 8.0 billion (EUR 5.2 billion) ($6.2 billion)
  (2004)
NAIC: 312111 Soft Drink Manufacturing

Nestlé Waters is the world's leading producer of bottled waters for both the small-format (PET) retail and large-format HOD (Home and Office Delivery) circuits. The company, the Water Division of foods giant Nestlé, has nearly 110 production plants in 33 countries providing sales and distribution to more than 130 countries and, with sales of CHF 8.0 billion ($6.2 billion) in 2005, represents some 10 percent of its parent company's total sales. Whereas HOD contributes approximately one-third of sales, the company's small-format, branded bottles represent its fastest-growing segment, particularly in markets such as South America, Asia, and the United States. Nestlé Waters is also one of Nestlé's fastest-growing divisions, particularly since the launch of its two "multiple-site" water brands, Pure Life and Aquarel. These brands acquire their water from local market sources, rather than from a specific spring, enabling Nestlé to lower its bottling, transportation, and logistics costs. Nestlé Waters also markets five international brands: flagship Perrier; two high-end Italian waters, Acqua Panna and S. Pellegrino; Vittel, the company's first bottled water; and Contrex, which Nestlé Waters markets as a "weight-loss" water (due to its high magnesium and calcium content). Although sales of these brands are significant, the multiple-site and international brands combine to generate just one-third of Nestlé Waters' total sales. The bulk of

the group's revenues comes instead from its impressive portfolio of local brands, which include Valvert (Belgium); Sainte-Alix, Carola, Hepar, Quezac, Opalia (France); Rhenser Mineralburnnen, Rietnauer, Klosterquelle (Germany); Korpi (Greece); Theodora (Hungary); Aqua Claudia, Ulmeta, Lora Recoaro, Levissima (Italy); Buxton, Ashbourne (United Kingdom); and Ice Mountain, Deer Park, Poland Spring, Arrowhead, Calistoga, Zephyrhills (United States), among many others. Altogether, Nestlé Waters' portfolio includes nearly 80 brands, giving the company a 17 percent share of the global market.

Founding a Bottled Water Portfolio in the 1970s

Founded by Henri Nestlé in Switzerland in 1866, Nestlé grew into one of the world's largest and most diversified food groups. Yet the company's interest in bottled beverages came as early as 1843, when Henri Nestlé built a factory in order to produce lemonade. Nestlé also began bottling water around this time. This activity remained marginal in terms of the group's overall operations, however.

Bottled water became a fixture in Europe toward the end of the 19th century, popularized particularly by the continent's many spas. Since water, and various water therapies, were central to the spa business, many began bottling their spring water so that customers could continue their treatments once back at home. Many of the brands in the later Nestlé Waters portfolio appeared during this time, such as Vittel, in the Vosges Mountains, where a spa was constructed in 1855; Perrier, which began spa operations in the 1860s; and Contrexville, discovered in the 18th century, which began bottling its water at the height of the spa fashion in the 1890s.

The popularity of Europe's spas ebbed and flowed through the 20th century, as spa usage gradually fell out of favor. Yet the habit of drinking bottled water persisted, and by the late 1960s had become a fixture among European consumers. The economic boom of the 1960s, and the introduction of new types of packaging, notably the first PVC bottles, helped raise the profile of the bottled water market into a veritable industry.

Never one to be left behind in consumer trends, Nestlé began taking an interest in the bottled water market in the mid-1960s.

Company Perspectives:

Our Mission: Water. Nestlé Waters, world bottled water leader, is the Nestlé Group's Water Division, accounting for approximately 10% of total sales. Established in 130 countries, with a full range of product formats for all distribution channels, Nestlé Waters offers bottled waters and refreshing water-based beverages to meet consumer needs anywhere, anytime.

In a bottled water market where disparities between countries are significant, Nestlé Waters bases its growth on managing a unique portfolio of brands and on a policy of targeted acquisitions around the world.

Since its creation in 1992, Nestlé Waters has continued to strengthen its position, regularly showing faster growth than the bottled water market.

In parallel with growth, Nestlé Waters is committed to scrupulous protection of its springs, drawing only the bare minimum required for its operations. The company also has a policy of continuous optimisation of production processes so as to avoid waste. As a result, despite Nestlé Waters' market leadership, it uses only a tiny share (0.0009%) of the water consumed on the planet.

With this approach, Nestlé Waters ensures the sustainable development of its business model and guarantees its consumers a superior product that stands for quality and purity.

In 1969, the group made its first purchase, taking a 30 percent stake in Société Générale des Eaux Minérales de Vittel (SGEMV). Vittel had been founded by Louis Bouloumié, who acquired the Source Gérémoy in the Vosges in 1854. The Vittel spa opened in 1856, then launched its bottled water in 1882. By the beginning of the 20th century, SGEMV had sold one million bottles, and by 1951, the company's sales had topped 100 million. In the 1960s, Vittel began experimenting with packaging types, and became the first to launch its waters in new PVC bottles in 1968. Although heavier than the later PET bottles, the plastic format made the bottled water lighter to carry and less prone to breakage. These factors helped stimulate a new boom in bottled water consumption.

Nestlé next turned to Germany, where it acquired the Blaue Quellen group in 1974. That purchase gave Nestlé control of a number of mineral water springs, as well as a portfolio of popular German brands, including Klosterquelle and Rietenauer.

The bottled water market had a number of inherent limitations. Most important among these was the difficulty in transporting a brand of spring water far from its source. Shipments were both heavy and fragile, and logistics costs represented a significant share of a bottled water's end price. For these reasons, the bottled water market developed a strong local nature. Although a number of brands succeeded in generating national and even international success, the largest share of the market remained with the many local brands.

Nestlé followed this market by acquiring its own portfolio of local brands, buying up brands throughout most of Europe through the 1980s and 1990s. Nonetheless, the company also

strengthened its hold on Vittel, the third largest selling bottled water brand in France and a growing international brand as well, acquiring the majority control of SGEMV in 1987.

Even though many, if not most, bottled waters on the market represented the continuation of long-popular brands and spa names, Nestlé also began experimenting with the creation of new bottled water brands. The development of a new packaging type—PET bottles, which were lighter than PVC, more flexible and shock-resistant, and also recyclable—encouraged the company to launch a new in-house brand in 1992, called Valvert, based in Belgium. The début of Valvert was also notable in that it marked the first time Nestlé had simultaneously rolled out a brand in five countries.

Bottled Water Leader in the 1990s

Yet a still more important event marked 1992, that of the acquisition of Perrier. Star of the bottled water set, Perrier's origins traced back to a spring in Bouillens, near Nîmes, on a property owned by the Granier family. Alphonse Granier became the first to investigate the spring's naturally carbonated water, and in 1863, after receiving official recognition as a mineral water source, opened a spa on the site. A fire in 1869 destroyed the spa, however; by 1884, Granier was forced to declare bankruptcy and close the spa.

New life came to the site in the form of Doctor Louis Perrier, who leased the spring in 1894, before buying the property outright in 1898. Perrier founded his own company there, called Société des Eaux Minerales, Boissons, et Produits Hygieniques de Vergeze. At the time, water was not a favored beverage among French consumers, but Perrier sought to correct this situation by bottling his naturally carbonated water.

Perrier, however, lacked the capital to launch his bottled water business. Instead, he leased the business to an Englishman, St. John Harmsworth, a paraplegic who had come to France to learn the language. Inspired by the weights he used as part of his physical therapy, Harmsworth developed a new bottle shape for the water. Harmsworth also was credited with creating a new brand name for the water: Perrier.

Targeting the British population, Harmsworth first began selling Perrier to the British army in India, reasoning that the returning soldier would then introduce the product into England itself. Harmsworth's instincts proved correct, and Perrier quickly captivated the British market. By 1908, the company was selling more than five million bottles per year in England; the company then turned to developing the French market, and by 1933, the company's sales of 20 million bottles per year were split almost evenly between France and England. Harmsworth's death that year saw the company fall into a slow decline; during World War II, the German occupying force took over the spring. By 1946, Perrier had more or less ceased operation and its owners put the property up for sale.

In 1947, Gustav Leven, of Paris, bought the property and modernized its production facility, bringing in bottling machinery from the United States. By 1948, Leven had succeeded in raising production to 30 million bottles per year. Yet by 1952, the company's production had soared to 150 million. Coupled with an astute marketing program, Perrier quickly captured the lead of

Key Dates:

1843: Henri Nestlé begins bottling lemonade and water.
1969: Nestlé acquires 30 percent of Vittel, launching its involvement in the bottled water market.
1974: German bottled water producer Blaue Quellen is acquired.
1987: Majority control of Vittel is acquired.
1992: The company acquires Perrier and forms Nestlé Sources International (NSI).
1996: NSI changes its name to Perrier Vittel.
1998: The company launches its first multi-site brand, Pure Life.
2000: The Pure Life brand is expanded into South America; the Aquarel brand is launched.
2002: Perrier Vittel changes its name to Nestlé Waters.
2004: A joint venture is formed with South Korea's Pulmuone Group.

the French bottled water market, before expanding throughout Europe. The company also expanded its drinks portfolio, acquiring the Contrexéville bottled water brand (redeveloped by the company as a ''weight-loss'' water), and then launching its own soft drink, Pschitt, and acquiring the French license to bottle Pepsi Cola. In the 1970s, Perrier turned to the United States, where bottled waters were virtually unknown. The company's distinctive advertising campaigns helped the group become the North American market's dominant bottled water producer. By 1988, Perrier accounted for more than 80 percent of all imported water in the United States and had established itself as a leader in the total U.S. water market.

Yet, in 1990, the discovery of traces of benzene in a bottle of Perrier destined for the United States spelled a near catastrophe for the company. The company was forced to withdraw its products from supermarket shelves and sales of Perrier plummeted worldwide. Amid the scandal, Gustav Leven was forced to resign from the company. Nestlé seized the opportunity, acquiring control of Source Perrier S.A. and the Perrier brand. Backed by Nestlé's marketing clout, Perrier quickly rebuilt its reputation and reasserted itself as the world's leading bottled water brand.

The Perrier acquisition prompted Nestlé to form a dedicated bottled waters division, Nestlé Sources International (NSI). The 1990s saw the bottled water market boom, particularly in the United States, where Nestlé helped successfully reposition bottled water as a status symbol. NSI began buying up North American bottled water brands, including regional leaders such as Ice Mountain, Deer Park, Poland Spring, Arrowhead, Calistoga, and Zephyrhills. In order to reinforce its position as a brand leader, NSI changed its name in 1996, becoming Perrier Vittel.

Into the late 1990s, Nestlé began targeting a wider international market, boosting its presence in South America, Asia, and elsewhere. The company also began expanding into the Home and Office Delivery (HOD) segment. This market, more familiarly recognized for its water coolers, had been in existence since the 19th century and had long been the favored commer-

cialized water source in the North American and South American markets, among others. Despite the growing interest in branded bottled waters in these markets, Nestlé sought to become a major player in the HOD segment as well. In 2000, the company designated the HOD market as a strategic priority.

Global Multi-Site Model for the New Century

If spring water brands had long been associated with specific springs, by the late 1990s, the actual source of a bottled water had become more and more irrelevant. In France, Perrier Vittel faced new competition from a fast-growing new brand, Cristalline. That brand was based on a new multi-site concept, in which the same brand was applied to water bottled at several different sites around France. In this way, Cristalline was able to slash its logistics costs and sell its water at a price far lower than that of premium brands represented by Nestlé and the like. Other similar competitors emerged during the same period, while the large-scale retail distribution began to roll out their own private-label bottled waters.

Nestlé responded by launching its own multi-site brand, Pure Life, in 1998. That brand specifically targeted the nascent markets in developing countries, such as Pakistan, which became the first to test the Pure Life brand. Other markets followed quickly, including China, Thailand, the Philippines, and Vietnam (where the brand became La Vie). The Pure Life rollout continued into South America, including Argentina and Mexico in 2000, then the Middle East, including Lebanon and Jordan in 2001, and Egypt, Uzbekistan, and Turkey in 2002, among others. By 2005, Pure Life had reached Russia, Canada, and the United States. Nestlé expected the brand to become the first truly global bottled water brand, with plans to develop the brand into the world's leading bottled water by 2010.

The success of Pure Life encouraged the company to roll out a multi-site brand specific for the European market. That brand was launched in 2000 as Aquarel. Based on seven production sites around Europe, Aquarel quickly reached Belgium, France, Germany, Hungary, Luxembourg, Poland, Portugal, and Spain, with plans to expand the brand to the entire European market in the second half of the decade.

As Nestlé's brand strategy shifted to the multi-site model, Perrier Vittel changed its name in 2002, becoming Nestlé Waters. The following year, Nestlé Waters made a splash in the European HOD market, buying up the Powwow Group, the European leader in the HOD segment.

Into the mid-2000s, Nestlé Waters continued seeking new expansion opportunities in its quest for global domination of the bottled waters market. In 2004 and 2005, the company joined the trend in flavored waters, rolling out its own lines of flavored waters under a number of its brands, including Perrier, Vittel, Contrexéville, and others. The company also sought new markets, entering South Korea, for example, in a joint venture with Pulmuone Group in 2004. By the beginning of 2005, Nestlé Waters claimed a global market share of 17 percent; the division also had grown to become one of parent company Nestlé's most important, accounting for some 10 percent of its total sales. As the world's thirst for bottled water appeared unquenched, Nestlé Waters looked forward to steadily growing sales in the 2000s.

Principal Competitors

Unilever PLC/Unilever N.V.; Procter & Gamble Co.; PepsiCo Inc.; Embotelladora Metropolitana S.A. de C.V.; Sammons Enterprises Inc.; Coca-Cola Co.; Philip Morris USA; Sara Lee Corporation; Groupe Danone; Cadbury Schweppes PLC.

Further Reading

Castano, Ivan, ''Nestlé Starts Water Plant in Badjoz,'' *just-drinks.com,* May 4, 2005.

''Nestlé Consolidates Leading Position in Bottled Water Market,'' *Europe Agri,* March 10, 2005, p. 504.

''Nestlé Eyes Top Spot for Aquarel,'' *just-drinks.com,* March 11, 2005.

''Nestlé to Launch Flavoured Vittel,'' *just-drinks.com,* April 25, 2005.

Prince, Greg W., ''Spring It On!,'' *Beverage Aisle,,* October 15, 2002, p. 30.

Todd, Stuart, ''NA Growth Keeps Nestlé Waters Stable,'' *just-drinks.com,* March 9, 2005.

Tomlinson, Richard, ''Troubled Waters at Perrier,'' *Fortune,* November 29, 2004, p. 173.

—M.L. Cohen

Nexstar Broadcasting Group, Inc.

909 Lake Carolyn Parkway, Suite 1450
Irving, Texas 75039
U.S.A.
Telephone: (972) 373-8800
Fax: (972) 373-8888
Web site: http://www.nexstar.tv

Public Company
Incorporated: 1996
Employees: 2,072
Sales: $245.7 million (2004)
Stock Exchanges: NASDAQ
Ticker Symbol: NXST
NAIC: 515120 Television Broadcasting

Nexstar Broadcasting Group, Inc. owns, operates, or provides services to 46 television stations in medium-sized markets in 11 U.S. states, which broadcast NBC, CBS, ABC, Fox, and UPN network programming to more than 7 percent of households in the country. The firm owns about two-thirds of the stations itself, and provides services to the rest under "duopoly" agreements in which many services are performed for two stations in the same market by a single Nexstar-owned one. The publicly traded company is run by its founder, broadcast industry veteran Perry Sook.

Beginnings

Nexstar was founded in the summer of 1996 by Perry Sook, to purchase television stations in mid-size markets around the United States. Sook, 38, had worked since high school in both on-air and sales jobs in the broadcasting industry, and in 1991 had founded Superior Communications Group, which acquired television stations in Kentucky and Oklahoma before selling them to Sinclair Broadcast Group for $63 million. Nexstar was backed by ABRY Broadcast Partners II, a Boston-based private equity fund, which would hold a 78 percent stake in the firm. Sook, who took the title of company president, would own most of the remainder.

Deregulation of the U.S. broadcast industry was taking place in the wake of the Communications Act of 1996, which struck down the existing limit of 12 television stations one company could own, and many firms soon began to buy clusters of them. Sook's approach was to target smaller markets where there was less competition for advertisers, audiences, and syndicated programs, and where purchase prices and operating costs were lower.

Shortly after its formation, the company bought WYOU-TV of Scranton, Pennsylvania, for approximately $23 million. Its new parent would be headquartered in the nearby town of Clark's Summit. Over the following year, Nexstar made deals to purchase additional stations in Terre Haute, Indiana; St. Joseph, Missouri; Joplin, Missouri; Wichita Falls, Texas; the Beaumont-Port Arthur, Texas area; Erie, Pennsylvania; and Wilkes-Barre, Pennsylvania. To comply with Federal Communications Commission (FCC) regulations limiting a company's ownership of several stations in a single market, after buying the last-named the company decided to sell its lower-rated Scranton operation.

Formation of First Duopoly: 1997

Nexstar partner ABRY recommended that David Smith, who had once managed a station ABRY owned in Cincinnati, buy the Scranton operation and then let Nexstar run it as a "duopoly," in which many of the functions of the Scranton and Wilkes-Barre stations would be combined. Smith, who had quit the television business several years earlier to become a Lutheran pastor, would serve as nominal figurehead of a new firm called Mission Broadcasting which would own WYOU-TV, while Nexstar would perform the vast majority of duties and keep almost all of the revenues. Though Mission was considered a separate company under FCC rules, its funding came from Nexstar, and all of its stations would be operated by Sook's firm.

Acquisitions continued in early 1999 with the purchase of WROC-TV, a CBS network affiliate serving Rochester, New York, for $46 million, and three CBS affiliates in Peoria, Springfield, and Champaign, Illinois, which were sold by Mid-West Television, Inc. for $110.7 million. Nexstar operated a total of 15 stations, including several which Mission Broadcasting had acquired.

Once a station had been purchased by the company, Sook sought the greatest possible operating efficiencies, typically dismissing unneeded employees, boosting advertising sales staff, and increasing the amount of advertiser-friendly local news programming by an average of five hours per week. In the case of WCIA-TV in Champaign, Illinois, Nexstar replaced the station's general manager with one of its own choosing and let a half-dozen of the station's other 115 employees go. The company also put money into its physical plant, gutting and remodeling offices, building a new set for the local news program, and buying a new remote broadcast truck. Several on-air staffers were also let go, and the station's longtime husband-and-wife news anchors were told to begin working full-time hours instead of part-time, which led them to walk off the job. Nexstar noted that their existing contracts did not specify how many hours they had to work per week, and sued them for breach of contract. They were later fired, and their attempts to win compensation in court proved unsuccessful.

In 2000 the firm purchased KMID of Midland/Odessa, Texas, for $10 million and KTAL of Shreveport, Louisiana, for $35 million. The year also saw Nexstar join the Broadcasters' Digital Cooperative, which was a consortium of 12 station groups that had banded together to find ways to use extra portions of the broadcast spectrum they had been given for digital television. The cooperative hoped to eventually send content including weather and news information to home computers or cellular telephones.

In early 2001 Nexstar received $225 million in additional financing from a group led by Banc of America. The year also saw a duopoly agreement signed between Nexstar's WMBD in Peoria and WXZZ in Bloomington, Illinois. The latter station, owned by Sinclair Broadcast Group, would broadcast news reports created by the Nexstar station, and most of its employees would begin working for Nexstar. For 2001 the firm had revenues of $110.7 million and a loss of $39.5 million. With the U.S. economy having recently hit rough waters, the firm's ad revenues had dropped by 10 percent, at the same time that its interest payments had increased.

In April 2002 Nexstar filed for an initial public offering of stock on the NASDAQ, hoping to raise more than $130 million. By this time the company owned and operated 14 stations, and provided management, sales, or other services to six others. In June the firm announced it would spend $9 million to install new digital transmitters at all of its stations, and replace analog transmitters with a newer generation of equipment.

Early 2003 saw Nexstar, which had recently moved its headquarters to Irving, Texas, acquire stations in Little Rock,

Arkansas, and Dothan, Alabama, from Morris Multimedia, Inc. for $90 million. The firm also set up duopoly arrangements with stations in Abilene and San Angelo, Texas, and Terre Haute, Indiana, that were owned by Mission Broadcasting.

2003: Quorum Acquisition Boosts Holdings to More Than 40 Stations

In the fall the company reached an agreement to acquire Quorum Broadcast Holdings LLC for $230 million in cash, assumption of debt, and shares of stock. Quorum owned 11 stations, one of which was about to be sold for $43 million, and operated or provided services to five others. With two other stations in Arkansas in the pipeline, Nexstar would own or operate 41 stations in nine states when the dust had settled.

In late November the company sold ten million shares of stock on the NASDAQ in an initial public offering (IPO) for $14 each, taking in $140 million. CEO Sook was paid a $4 million ''success fee'' when the IPO was completed, which he used in part to pay back a $3 million loan he had taken out in the company's behalf in 1998.

After the IPO the firm's Nexstar Finance, Inc. subsidiary issued $125 million in senior notes to help pay off the Quorum acquisition, and opened a new $275 million line of credit that refinanced some of its older debt at a more favorable rate. For 2003 the company reported revenues of $214.3 million, and a loss of $87.1 million.

In January 2004 the pending sale of an additional Quorum station fell through, and it was added to the Nexstar acquisition. The year 2004 also saw the firm take on new duopoly agreements for Mission-owned stations in Utica, New York, and Rockford, Illinois, as well as closing deals on new acquisitions in the Ft. Smith/Fayetteville, Arkansas market and in San Angelo, Texas.

In part because of Nexstar's higher profile in the wake of its IPO, the firm's duopoly strategy was drawing scrutiny, and in 2004 the FCC announced that it would begin looking into making new rules for such agreements. The company prepared for a lobbying battle to defend its turf before the FCC, and began drawing up contingency plans if changes were made.

For 2004, Nexstar posted revenues of $245.7 million and a loss of just $20.5 million. The firm's earnings were up due to the presidential election year and its attendant political advertising spending spree, as well as the Olympics, whose coverage on the company's NBC affiliates in August brought a spike in viewership in the otherwise repeat-plagued summer schedule. To boost revenues and ad sales, the firm was now using new promotional tactics including adding online viewers' clubs and informational phone lines, as well as selling sponsorships of news and sports tickers that scrolled on-screen.

Face-Off Over Retransmission in 2005

Despite all these measures, the company was continuing to run in the red, and its management began looking at new ways to increase revenues. One potential source was cable system operators, who retransmitted broadcast television channels to their subscribers along with the signals of cable networks in-

```
┌────────────────────────────────────────────┐
│                 Key Dates:                   │
│                                              │
│ 1996:  Perry Sook forms Nexstar Broadcasting │
│        Group, begins buying TV stations.     │
│ 1998:  Duopoly is formed to run Scranton     │
│        station for new owner Mission         │
│        Broadcasting.                         │
│ 2003:  Company's initial public offering     │
│        (IPO) raises $140 million.            │
│ 2003–04: Acquisition of Quorum Broadcasting  │
│        and other stations doubles firm's     │
│        holdings.                             │
│ 2005:  Nexstar pulls signal from Cox, Cable  │
│        One systems, demands per-subscriber   │
│        fees.                                 │
└────────────────────────────────────────────┘
```

cluding Animal Planet, CNN, and HBO. Though the latter charged fees of as much as several dollars per month per subscriber, over-the-air broadcasters were typically compensated only through ad purchases on their stations. The issue was impacted by a 1992 federal law giving broadcasters the right to require cable systems to carry their signals in a local area, which allowed for negotiations about terms. While cable companies had almost always refused to pay broadcasters cash, they had compensated most of the major networks by offering them a channel on their systems for a new cable network, while local station owners had typically been assuaged with ad buys. Each broadcaster signed a retransmission agreement with cable providers that lasted an average of three years, however, and several of Nexstar's were about to come up for renewal.

On January 1, 2005, Nexstar pulled five of its Texas and Missouri stations off of cable networks owned by Cable One, Inc. and Cox Communications, Inc. when those firms refused the company's demands for a 30-cent per month subscriber fee per station, which would increase to 35 cents in 2006 and 40 cents in 2007. Nexstar noted that the increasingly popular satellite dish networks were all paying for retransmission of broadcast signals, and insisted that it was time wired cable providers did the same.

The move left close to 170,000 cable subscribers without Nexstar channels in Texas, Missouri, and Louisiana, where a station had also been pulled a few weeks later. The affected Nexstar stations, which were affiliated with all three of the major networks, lost as much a third of their viewers, while the cable operators lost some subscribers who changed to satellite networks that carried the channels. Both sides offered different assessments of the impact on their operations, and the cable operators released Nielsen ratings showing significant viewership drops for Nexstar's affected stations that were disputed by the company. Nexstar had recently discontinued most of its use of the Nielsen audience-counting service to determine advertising rates, after chafing at charges which totaled as much as 1 or 2 percent of a station's gross income. The firm, which had turned to alternate ratings sources such as Simmons Research and Media Audit, claimed that its advertising income was only minimally affected by the loss of cable retransmission in those markets.

Nexstar's bold move was considered the first salvo in a battle that was about more than just basic cable. Broadcasters

were beginning to send high-definition digital signals, and the cost of the equipment needed to support such broadcasts totaled $1 million or more per station. Owners were loathe to give away their digital signal for free, and the fight over retransmission was expected to lay the groundwork for agreements in this realm, which was still in an embryonic stage of development. Soon, rumblings were being heard in Washington as the American Cable Association lobbied the FCC to give cable operators more options by rewriting the retransmission rule.

Nexstar had chosen small markets where it felt it had a reasonable chance of winning concessions, but as the year wore on neither side gave an inch, though Nexstar signed a subscriber-fee deal with a separate cable operator in the spring. When the company offered to consider accepting just one cent per subscriber the cable providers still refused to budge, fearing that paying even that small amount would give broadcasters the impetus to seek higher charges down the line. Nexstar was preparing a strategy for future battles, as many of its remaining retransmission deals expired in late 2005 and early 2006. The intransigence of the two sides was evident in such comments as one made by Nexstar's COO Duane Lammers to the *Baltimore Sun:* "If they think we're going to give them our channels for free and then they can charge $10 or $15 a month for digital cable," said Lammers, "then they can drop dead."

In a decade's time Nexstar Broadcasting Group had assembled one of the largest groups of television stations in mid-size markets in the United States. The firm was struggling to turn the corner to profitability, and was seeking to develop a new revenue stream by facing off with cable system operators who had heretofore retransmitted its signal with no direct compensation. With major players on both sides of the fight watching the outcome, the industry was at a turning point that could affect the future fortunes of broadcasters, cable operators, and viewers alike.

Principal Subsidiaries

Nexstar Finance Holdings, Inc.; Nexstar Broadcasting, Inc.

Principal Competitors

Sinclair Broadcast Group, Inc.; Hearst-Argyle Television, Inc.; Emmis Communications Corp.; Cox Television; Gannett Co., Inc.; ACME Communications, Inc.; LIN TV Corp.; Gray Television, Inc.; Raycom Media, Inc.; Media General, Inc.

Further Reading

Deitrich, Matthew, "Effects of New TV Station Ownership Vary," *State Journal-Register* (Springfield, Ill.), February 6, 2000, p. 1.

Dickson, Glen, "Getting Together Over Data," *Broadcasting & Cable,* March 27, 2000, p. 6.

Hennessey, Raymond, "Nexstar IPO Features Unusual Bonus for CEO," *Dow Jones News Service,* November 19, 2003.

McMorris, Frances A., "Nexstar Broadcasting IPO Stumbles," *Daily Deal,* November 25, 2003.

Morrow, Darrell, "Sook Leaves Channel 34 for New Firm," *Journal Record,* June 4, 1996.

Moss, Linda, "Broadcast Television's Hard Bargainers," *Multichannel News,* July 25, 2005.

——, ''Nexstar Claims Ratings Are Up Even with Stations Dropped By Ops,'' *Multichannel News*, May 9, 2005.

——, ''Nexstar Not Hurt By Retrans Fight,'' *Multichannel News*, May 5, 2005.

''Nexstar Builds a Mini Empire in the Midwest,'' *Mediaweek*, July 19, 1999.

Norris, Floyd, ''Making a Mockery of Media Concentration Rules,'' *New York Times*, November 21, 2003, p. 1.

Russell, John, ''Sharon Center, Ohio, Pastor Runs Fast-Growing Broadcasting Company,'' *Akron Beacon Journal*, January 11, 2004.

''TV Broadcaster Nexstar Sets IPO Terms,'' *Reuters News*, May 31, 2002.

Wood, Andrea, ''Erie's WJET-TV Sold for $18 Million,'' *Business Journal of the Five-County Region*, October 1, 1997, p. 21.

—Frank Uhle

Odebrecht S.A.

Avenida Luiz Viana Filho 2841
Salvador, Bahia 41730-900
Brazil
Telephone: 55 (71) 2105-1111
Fax: 55 (71) 3230-0701
Web site: http://www.odebrecht.com.br

Public Company
Incorporated: 1944 as Construtora Norberto Odebrecht
   S.A.
Employees: 24,859
Sales: BRL 21.87 billion ($7.4 billion) (2004)
Stock Exchanges: Bolsa de Valores de São Paulo
Ticker Symbol: ODBE
NAIC: 213111 Drilling Oil and Gas Wells; 213112
   Support Activities for Oil and Gas Field Exploration;
   236210 Industrial Building Construction; 236220
   Commercial and Institutional Building Construction;
   237110 Water and Sewer Line and Related Structures
   Construction; 237120 Oil and Gas Pipeline and
   Related Structures Construction; 237310 Highway,
   Street, and Bridge Construction; 325110 Petrochem-
   ical Manufacturing; 541330 Engineering Services;
   551112 Offices of Nonbank Holding Companies

Odebrecht S.A. is a holding company for Construtora Norberto Odebrecht S.A., the biggest engineering and contracting company in Latin America, and Braskem S.A., the largest petrochemicals producer in Latin America and one of Brazil's five largest private-sector manufacturing companies. The holding company fully controls the former and owns the majority interest in the latter. Odebrecht S.A. is publicly traded but closely held by the founding family and its present and former employees. It stresses reinvestment of profits for long-term results.

Norberto Odebrecht's Empire: 1944–91

Emil Odebrecht arrived in Brazil in 1856 as an immigrant from Germany. Trained as an engineer in Prussia, he was a surveyor and road builder in southern Brazil. Emílio Odebrecht, one of his grandchildren, was a pioneer in the use of reinforced concrete in Brazil. He moved to Recife in 1918 and in the 1920s became a home builder in northeastern Brazil, transferring his company's headquarters to Salvador in 1926. But the business ground to a halt during World War II, when materials imported from Europe became scarce.

Emilio's son Norberto became a construction contractor in 1944, starting without assets except his father's employees, with whom he made a partnership pact. The business, Construtora Norberto Odebrecht S.A., took off in the 1960s, when international loans were plowed into large government infrastructure projects. According to Joel Millman's 1993 article in *Forbes,* "The company excelled in Brazil's rough-and-tumble regional patronage game, making millions on local Bahia state contracts for roads, power plants and refineries." At the end of the decade it began to extend its reach to southern Brazil. In 1969 Odebrecht's revenues came to less than $100 million, but four years later it more than doubled this total with contracts such as the ones it secured to take part in the construction of Rio de Janeiro's international airport and Rio's state university campus.

By 1976 Odebrecht was seeking a role in the huge Itaipú project being built in a part of the country remote from Bahia: the world's largest hydroelectric dam, scheduled to span the Paraná River along the border between Brazil and Paraguay. Odebrecht bought its way into the consortium building this project by paying about $100 million for Companhia Brasileira de Projectos e Obras (CBPO), then among the biggest contractors in the state of São Paulo. According to Millman, CBPO's Itaipú contracts "made Odebrecht a national player overnight." Other important public works in which the company took part in this period included the Angra dos Reis nuclear plant, a bridge in Florianópolis, and a railroad in the Amazon. It also participated in the construction of subways in Brasilia and Recife.

By the end of the 1970s, however, Odebrecht had decided to diversify, foreseeing that an era of lucrative government contracts for big public-works projects was coming to an end because of budgetary problems. Odebrecht paid about $100 million to buy Técnica Nacional de Engenharia S.A. (Tenenge), a major São Paulo-based company engaged in the assembly of

industrial plants. It entered a new field in 1979, when it joined
the state petrochemical holding group Petroquisa in Companhia
Petroquímica de Camaçari (CPC), a producer of polyvinyl chlo-
ride (PVC) in Odebrecht's Bahia. In the same year the company
became a contractor for the government-owned oil company
Petróleos Brasileiros S.A. (Petrobras), prospecting for offshore
oil from platforms in the Atlantic. In collaboration with English
investors, it also searched for gold and vanadium deposits. The
holding company Odebrecht S.A. was established in 1981.

At the same time, Odebrecht started working outside Brazil,
beginning in 1978 with the construction of a hydroelectric plant
in Peru. It became a contractor in Angola—like Brazil, a former
Portuguese colony—in 1984, when it built a hydroelectric
power plant. Later projects in Angola included sanitation and
water-treatment systems, petroleum extraction for shipment to
Brazil, and opening a diamond mine. The company also drilled
for oil off the coasts of Gabon and India, built irrigation dikes in
Ecuador and Peru, power plants in Argentina, Mexico, and
Paraguay, and pulp and paper plants in Chile. It entered Europe
in 1988 by purchasing a Portuguese highway and railroad
builder and secured North Sea oil-drilling contracts by acquiring a British firm, SLP Engineering Ltd., in 1991. Odebrecht
entered the United States that year by winning a contract to
extend Miami's elevated-transit system. By late 1993 the company was active in 18 countries, and in the following year
Brazilian government contracts represented less than 28 percent
of Odebrecht's revenues.

Odebrecht had become a giant, with annual revenue of $2.6
billion and 43,472 employees in 1990. Petrochemicals now
accounted for 30 percent of its assets. Foreign projects brought
in $400 million, equivalent to 22 percent of its operating reve-
nues. The following year Norberto Odebrecht, now 70 years
old, yielded the presidency of the holding company to his eldest
son, Emílio, a workaholic known for putting in 15- and 16-hour
days as president of the construction firm.

Construction and Petrochemicals: 1991–2001

Odebrecht became the largest private investor in the Brazilian petrochemical industry during the early 1990s. The group
bought assets not only from state-owned Petroquisa but also
from numerous private holding companies, investing $350 mil-
lion. It achieved its first controlling interest in a petrochemicals
firm in 1992, when it bought a majority stake in PPH
Companhia Industrial de Polipropileno, a polypropylene pro-

ducer, from Petroquisa and the holding group Petropar. Its
minority direct and indirect holdings included a stake in Unipar
- Uniao de Indústrias Petroquímicas, a holding group participat-
ing in 16 petrochemical downstream companies, and Po-
liolefinas S.A.

Fernando Collor de Mello, president of Brazil, resigned
from office in 1992 after revelations of rampant government
corruption in which major construction companies were said to
have secured contracts by issuing bribes to politicians. A consulting firm founded by an aide to the president in order to
collect money from construction companies accumulated about
$55 million. Odebrecht, as the largest such company, emerged
badly tainted from the scandal. This outcome was a humiliation
for Norberto Odebrecht, who had burnished the family's image
through the Emílio Odebrecht Foundation, an organization established in 1965 that built schools and hospitals and funded
health and education programs. Described by Armin Schmid
and Rob McManamy in *Design-Build* as ''part guru, part phi-
losopher, part prophet,'' he had written five books on what he
called ''entrepreneur technology,'' emphasizing the primacy of
service to the client, decentralization of management, and motivation of employees through profit sharing and participation in
decision making. He stepped down as chairman of the group in
1998 and was succeeded by Emílio.

The scandal gave new impetus to Odebrecht's desire to
diversify its activities. In 1994 it purchased three German construction firms and moved Tenenge's headquarters to London.
The Portuguese transport contractor, Bento Pedroso Construçoes S.A., won the right to construct and operate the Vasco
da Gama bridge over the Tagus River, a contract valued at more
than $1 billion. In 1994 foreign projects accounted for $811
million of Odebrecht's $2.18 billion in consolidated revenues.

Odebrecht Contractors of Florida Inc. earned more than
$400 million in public-works contracts during the 1990s, in-
cluding a prominent part in the expansion and remodeling of
Miami's international airport. Its role in the state was enhanced
by close ties to Church & Tower Inc., a Miami construction firm
run by Cuban exile leader Jorge Mas Canosa and—political
opponents charged—by a $75,000 contribution to a foundation
established by Jeb Bush, a real estate developer who was
elected governor of Florida in 1998. By 2002, it was participat-
ing in the construction of Miami's American Airlines Arena, the
South Terminal of the city's airport, and the city's Performing
Arts Center. Odebrecht had taken part in more than 40 U.S.
projects, including bridges and highways in the Southeast and
the Seven Oaks dam-construction project in California, earning
revenues of about $1.2 billion. The U.S. Army Corps of Engi-
neers voted Odebrecht as its company of the year in 1999 for its
construction of the Seven Oaks earthfill dam.

Odebrecht S.A. tentatively entered a new field, wood-pulp
production, in 1991, when it launched a project to plant fast-
growing eucalyptus trees on a 400-square-mile tract in a coastal
portion of the state of Bahia. This joint venture with a Swedish-
Finnish company seemingly came to an end in 1999.

In the petrochemical field, Odebrecht joined forces with
Petroquímica da Bahia S.A., a member of the Mariani group,
in 2001 to purchase the government-owned holding company

Companhia Nordeste de Participaçoes (Conepar) for BRL 785 million ($320 million). They also, in the same year, acquired control of Petroquímica do Nordeste - Copene Ltda., Brazil's largest petroleum "cracker." The following year they merged several different companies into a new company, Braskem S.A., with majority control by Odebrecht and its head office located in the chemical division's old quarters in Camaçari, Bahia. Braskem immediately became Latin America's largest thermoplastics producer and one of the five largest private-sector manufacturing companies. It integrated the production of feedstocks such as ethylene, propylene, and chlorine with downstream petrochemicals. The raw materials manufactured by Braskem were used to make a number of important final products, including plastics and acrylics for auto panels; synthetic rubber for tires; artificial fibers for upholstery and carpeting; plastic packaging; plastics used to make toys, utensils, and other products; synthetic fibers for the clothing industry; chemical compounds for the pharmaceutical industry; resistant plastic compounds for heavy industry and machinery manufacture; and pipes, tubes, plastic products, and shapes used for finishing by the civil construction industry.

Entering a New Century

Emílio Odebrecht, serving as both president and chairman of Odebrecht S.A., came to feel that he had put the organization at risk by concentrating so much power in his hands and yielded the former position in 2001. The post was assumed by Pedro Novis, an Odebrecht executive who had been working for the company since 1968. Emílio's eldest son, 34-year-old Marcelo, was seen as the future trustee of the family's holdings. Emílio and his four siblings each held equal shares in the family holding company Kieppe Participaçoes, which ultimately controlled Odebrecht S.A., but none of the other four were active in the company.

Odebrecht Holdings had a participation in about 200 companies in 2003 and revenues of $6.1 billion in that year. "Each one of our businesses functions as a small enterprise, led by a kind of owner," Emílio Odebrecht told the Brazilian business magazine *Exame* in 2004. "Basically, we expect two things from such a leader: a return for the client and for the shareholder. He has to confront the challenges and find the solutions. . . . Centralized chiefs don't fit this model, since they retard the development of personnel and of the enterprise itself. Entrepreneurial leaders think long term. Today, for example, we are working on planning for the next 20 years. There are three generations of professionals involved in this . . . to guarantee the perpetuity of the business. . . . This process isn't an abdication. It is a planned delegation."

Principal Subsidiaries

Braskem S.A. (73%); Construtora Norberto Odebrecht S.A.

Principal Competitors

Companhia Petroquímica do Sul; Construçoes e Comércio Camargo Corrêa S.A.; Construtora Andrade Gutierrez S.A.; Construtora Queiroz Galvao S.A.; Petroquímica Triunfo S.A.; Petroquímica Uniao S.A.; Refineria Alberto Pasqualini - Refap S.A.

Further Reading

"Como montar um time venceor," *Exame,* July 21, 2004, pp. 26–27.
"A Family Tradition of Excellence," *Forbes,* October 24, 1994, Brazil supplement.
McManamy, Rob, and Armin Schmid, "Odebrecht's Big Picture," *Design-Build,* August 2001.
——, "Odebrecht: Brazil's Giant Beats Adversity," *ENR/Engineering News Record,* September 20, 1993, pp. 45, 47–48.
Millman, Joel, " 'You Have to Be an Optimist,' " *Forbes,* May 24, 1993, pp. 84–85, 87.
Netz, Clayton, "O vôo livre de tocador de obras," *Exame,* February 7, 1990, pp. 47–53.
"Pimp or Prince?," *Economist,* January 29, 1994, p. 70.
Reveron, Derek, "Friends in High Places," *Latin Trade,* January 2000, pp. 26–27.
Sissell, Kara, "Streamlining Brazil's Chemicals Ownership," *Chemical Week,* October 31, 2001, pp. 21–22.
Turner, Rik, "Brazil Takes the Lead in Latin America's PVC Boom," *Chemical Week,* December 14, 1988, pp. 18–19.
Wood, Andrew, "Brazil's Odebrecht Builds a Major Petrochemical Stake," *Chemical Week,* March 31, 1993, pp. 36, 38.

—Robert Halasz

Old Orchard Brands, LLC

P.O. Box 66
Sparta, Michigan 49345
U.S.A.
Telephone: (616) 887-1745
Toll Free: (800) 330-2173
Fax: (616) 887-8210
Web site: http://www.oldorchardjuice.com

Private Company
Incorporated: 1985
Employees: 67
Sales: $135 million (2003 est.)
NAIC: 311411 Frozen Fruit, Juice, and Vegetable
    Manufacturing; 312111 Soft Drink Manufacturing;
    311421 Fruit and Vegetable Canning

Old Orchard Brands, LLC is the third largest producer of frozen concentrated juice in the United States, and the ninth largest bottled juice maker. Its product lines include 100 percent juice blends, sweetened fruit juice cocktails, reduced-calorie juice drinks, and USDA certified organic juice in nearly 30 frozen configurations and more than 40 bottled versions. The firm is owned and run by founder Mark Saur.

Origins

Old Orchard Brands was founded on the site of an apple orchard in the small town of Sparta, Michigan, in 1985. The company's 23-year-old founder, Mark Saur, purchased the land from his father, Roger, and formed two businesses, Apple Valley International and Old Orchard Brands, to make and sell frozen concentrated apple and orange juice. Over the next several years the small operation began selling its products to growing numbers of retailers in Michigan and in such nearby states as Wisconsin. They were offered in 12- and 16-ounce cans under brand names including Valu Time, Mega, and Old Orchard.

In 1993 Apple Valley International was fined $480,600 by a U.S. District Court judge, and Saur was fined $100,225, for using invert beet sugar in what the firm had labeled frozen unsweetened

orange juice concentrate. While beet sugar was similar to the natural sugars found in orange juice, it was much less expensive to buy, and over the years a number of juice producers had used it to lower production costs and increase profits. FDA investigators had determined that the company sold 475,000 cases of adulterated juice between 1986 and 1988. Saur admitted authorizing the deception, and pled guilty to three misdemeanor counts.

After settling the matter, Saur and the business moved forward, and by 1995 Apple Valley was marketing 12 different varieties of frozen juice and had annual revenues of $35 million, while employing just 23. The juices continued to be distributed primarily in the Midwest, but during the year an agreement was reached with the Orlando Magic basketball team to make the firm its exclusive juice supplier for five years. The team's logo would appear on Apple Valley juices, 11 varieties of which would be marketed in the Orlando area. Orange juice was omitted, as the firm believed it was unlikely to do well in the heart of orange country. The deal had largely come about because the Orlando Magic was owned by Amway Corp. affiliate RDV Corporation, located in nearby Grand Rapids.

Bottled Juice Sales Beginning in 1998

In 1998 the company began to produce bottled ready-to-drink juices in an effort to offset a steady decline in sales of frozen juice. Bottling was initially performed by several outside firms, but in late 1998 the company began the first stage of an expansion that would eventually double its 70,000-square-foot facility in Sparta and add a bottling line. With sales of frozen orange juice dropping especially fast, Old Orchard also reconfigured its frozen juice offerings to focus on apple-based blended flavors. Six new varieties were introduced during the year, including apple kiwi strawberry, apple raspberry, and apple passion mango, with suggested prices of between $1.09 and $1.39 per 12-ounce can of concentrate. Over the next few months, the new frozen juice varieties grew to account for one-quarter of the company's sales. With consumers becoming more aware of the healthy qualities of food, the firm was also increasing the availability of unsweetened 100 percent juice drinks at this time.

The year 1999 saw completion of the firm's $6 million expansion program, which was supported in part by a 12-year,

Company Perspectives:

For twenty-five years, Old Orchard has been making apple interesting. That means we use only the finest ingredients. We carefully craft our juices to make sure they not only beat our expectations, but yours as well!

50 percent tax abatement from Sparta that would save over $21,000 per year in taxes. The company would henceforth be able to bottle its juices onsite in PET plastic containers, rather than relying on outside contractors. Though Old Orchard obtained its juice from Michigan growers where possible, most was imported from such countries as Argentina or China, where the entire apple crop was used for juice production. For 1999, the firm, which was now using Old Orchard Brands LLC as its primary business name, had revenues of $63 million.

The company offered 18 flavors of frozen juice, six bottled juice cocktails that contained 30 percent juice and enhanced vitamin C levels, two lemonades, and Cranberry Raspberry Flavored Iced Tea. In 2000 Old Orchard also begin offering calcium- and vitamin-fortified juices, plus smaller single-serving sizes.

In July 2001 the firm had a small ammonia leak in its plant, and called the local fire department for assistance, which led to a regional Hazardous Materials Team being mobilized. The city later billed the firm $20,000 for this service, and when Old Orchard protested that the response had been excessive, the city sued. The company later settled by agreeing to pay $15,000.

The fall of 2001 saw Old Orchard begin bottling apple cider and fruit punch drinks in new one-gallon plastic jugs. By now the company's distribution area had expanded to include most of the Midwest, the Great Plains states, and the Southwest, and it reached the West Coast over the next few months.

In the fall of 2003 Old Orchard sent five truckloads, containing 45,000 bottles of juice, to Californians affected by wildfires. The company typically donated a truckload of juice per month to food banks and Christian aid organizations. In December the firm also gave 88.5 acres of former orchard land adjacent to its plant to the local school district for construction of a new high school. In addition to its charitable activities, Old Orchard looked after the welfare of its employees, many of whom had been with the firm for years because of good pay, benefits, and a profit sharing program, as well as perks including free lunches one day a week and a weekly case of juice.

The year 2003 also saw the firm's products reach the East Coast, giving Old Orchard coast-to-coast coverage and penetration of about half of the U.S. national market, as well as the Bahamas, Jamaica, and Panama. Riding a wave of 15 to 20 percent growth per year for five years running, the firm racked up sales of more than $135 million for 2003.

New Drinks, Expanded Production in 2004

The year 2004 was a busy one for Old Orchard Brands. In January, a new low-carbohydrate juice cocktail line was introduced, for use by followers of the then popular Atkins and

Key Dates:

1985: Mark Saur founds juice-making business in Sparta, Michigan.
1993: Saur and firm are fined nearly $600,000 for selling adulterated orange juice.
1998: Company adds line of ready-to-drink bottled juices.
1999: A $6 million plant expansion adds in-house bottling capability.
2003: Distribution reaches East Coast, giving firm coast-to-coast coverage.
2004: New low-carb, organic, nectar, and drink mixer lines are introduced.

South Beach diet plans. The diets required that adherents cut down on their intake of carbohydrates, which were abundant in sweet foods, including juice as well as grain-based products such as bread. The new 25 percent juice drinks were sweetened with artificial sweetener Splenda, and contained one-quarter the carbohydrates of pure juice. They were sold in 64-ounce bottles in such flavors as apple, grape, and apple cranberry under the Old Orchard LoCarb brand name.

In the summer the firm started bottling juice at an Anaheim, California plant that was operated as a joint venture with several other companies, and added more new equipment in Sparta. A deal was also signed with retailer Target to put Old Orchard products in its 1,200 stores nationwide, expanding on an existing regional presence with the chain. Other customers included Wal-Mart, Costco, Publix, Kroger, and Food Lion, as well as many smaller retailers. Old Orchard was the third largest frozen juice producer in the United States behind Minute Maid and Welch's, and one of the ten largest bottled juice makers.

Other additions for 2004 included products and services targeted at the growing U.S. Hispanic population, such as the Old Orchard Nectars line in such flavors as Mango and Papaya, and a Spanish-language web site. The firm also added five USDA-certified organic bottled juices and frozen drink mixes in daiquiri, pina colada, and margarita varieties. With the low-carb craze fading rapidly, by year's end the firm had renamed its LoCarb line Old Orchard Healthy Balance, repositioning it as a beverage for consumers on a low calorie diet.

Early 2005 saw the company roll out new ten-ounce plastic bottles of some of its more popular juices including five 100 percent juices and three reduced calorie juice cocktails. In the summer Old Orchard relaunched its 100 percent juice line with new label designs that emphasized their pure juice content. New flavors were also being added, including grape juice with added grape seed extract, and a blend of blueberry and pomegranate, which capitalized on recent reports of the health benefits of their respective ingredients.

The company was now producing some 45 million cans of frozen juice per year and 55 million bottles of ready-to-drink juice. Despite a 50 percent decline in frozen juice sales over the most recent five-year period, the firm was steadfast in its commitment to the category, running radio and television advertisements and adding innovations such as recloseable and micro-waveable plastic cans.

After two decades in business Old Orchard Brands LLC had grown from a small regional frozen juice producer into one of the largest juice makers in the United States. The company offered quality products for a variety of different consumers, and with full national penetration not yet achieved, its future growth appeared certain.

Principal Competitors

The Coca-Cola Company; PepsiCo, Inc.; Cadbury Schweppes Plc; Ocean Spray Cranberries, Inc.; Welch Foods Inc.

Further Reading

Bauer, Julia, "Sparta Juice Maker Sends Some Relief to Californians," *Grand Rapids Press*, November 7, 2003, p. 9A.

Bush, Kathy, "Apple Valley Expands Juice Production Facilities," *Grand Rapids Press*, September 3, 1998, p. 9C.

——, "Juice Company Adds Bottling Operation," *Grand Rapids Press*, October 29, 1999, p. 8A.

"Frozen Juice Concentrate: Orchard Bears Fruit," *Frozen Food Age*, May 2004, p. S25.

Hartnett, Michael, "Squeeze and Freeze," *Frozen Food Age*, September 2000, p. 42.

Hogan, John, "Old Orchard Lands East Coast Deal," *Grand Rapids Press*, September 30, 2004, p. 1C.

——, "Old Orchard's Growth Streak Comes from a Diet of Fresh Juices," *Grand Rapids Press*, April 11, 2004.

Irwin, Tanya, "Juice Maker Seeks Shop for Shot at Consumers," *Adweek* (Midwest Edition), June 24, 2002, p. 2.

"Juice Firm Inks Deal with Orlando Magic," *Grand Rapids Press*, July 26, 1995, p. 10A.

"Juice Processor Pays City," *Grand Rapids Press*, June 16, 2004, p. 2B.

Merli, Richard, "It's Not All Doom and Gloom in Frozen Juice," *Frozen Food Age*, May 1999, p. 15.

Morrison, Gary, "Firm Lauded As Work Begins on New School," *Grand Rapids Press*, June 13, 2005, p. 2B.

"Old Orchard Juices up Concentrate," *Frozen Food Age*, May 2005, p. S22.

Pritchard, James, "Michigan Juice Company a Sweet Success," *Associated Press State & Local Wire*, December 4, 2004.

Rent, Katy, "There's Something New at Old Orchard for 2004," *Grand Rapids Business Journal*, January 5, 2004, p. 6.

Ropp, Kevin L., "Orange Juice Firm Guilty of Adulteration," *FDA Consumer*, October 1993.

Theodore, Sarah, "Rapid Response Is Key for Michigan Juice Company," *Beverage Industry*, May 2000, p. 30.

—Frank Uhle

✔ **Pagnossin** SpA

Pagnossin S.p.A.

Via Noalese 94
Treviso I-31100 TV
Italy
Telephone: +39 0422 2916
Fax: +39 0422 435005
Web site: http://www.pagnossin.com

Public Company
Incorporated: 1919
Employees: 923
Sales: EUR 46.10 million ($55 million) (2004)
Stock Exchanges: Borsa Italiana
Ticker Symbol: PAG
NAIC: 327112 Vitreous China, Fine Earthenware and
   Other Pottery Product Manufacturing; 327123 Other
   Structural Clay Product Manufacturing

Pagnossin S.p.A. is a leading name in the Italian porcelain and ceramics industry, and has established an international reputation for its products. Pagnossin itself specializes in ironstone ceramics-based tableware. The company is also a leading Italian producer of terracotta flowerpots, vases, and other products, primarily through subsidiary Vaserie Trevigiane. Another major part of the Pagnossin S.p.A. stable comes through its controlling share of Richard Ginori 1735, which produces fine china and porcelain tableware, and which represents as much as 50 percent of the group's total sales. Other brands in the Pagnossin brand family include Rio, Smalti, Giuletta & Romeo, Amitis, Elisir, and Giove. Pagnossin has long been an internationally focused company, distributing its products in more than 70 countries, and international sales still account for more than half of company revenues. The wedding gifts market is the company's bread and butter, providing some 70 percent of the group's sales. Pagnossin fell on difficult times into the mid-2000s, with its sales falling to EUR 46 million ($55 million) in 2004, and its losses mounting. The company is listed on the Borsa Italiana and is led by Chairman Carlo Rinaldini.

Brick-Making Foundations in the 1920s

Although Italy had established a reputation worldwide for its quality porcelain and china production, Pagnossin's origins lay in a more mundane area. The company, later to become a major name in Italian tableware, in fact began operations at the turn of the 20th century as a manufacturer of bricks. By 1919, the company had formally incorporated as Pagnossin S.p.A.

Pagnossin's interest in ceramics operations beyond bricks came only in 1950, when the company launched production of ironstone dinnerware. The company's diversification also demonstrated its willingness to adopt and or develop new technology, and for its new line of products the company added kilns capable of heating its ceramics to more than 1,250 degrees Celsius.

The company's ceramics production gradually became its central operation. By the 1960s, Pagnossin decided to specialize in ceramic tableware. The company then abandoned brick making altogether. Over the next decade or more, Pagnossin became a leading name in Italian tableware. As part of that process, the company launched a marketing effort that included the sponsorship of a number of sporting events, notably Formula 1 racing, which had long enjoyed immense popularity among Italians. These efforts played an important role in building Pagnossin's brand name both in Italy and abroad.

Nonetheless, the company's growth stagnated somewhat into the mid-1980s. The company, described as ''sleepy'' by some analysts, had grown inefficient in its production techniques, and its development of new designs and technologies also had slowed. In 1986, however, the company acquired a new major shareholder, financier Carlo Rinaldini, who launched the company on a new period of expansion.

Rinaldini placed Dal Bo' in charge of the company in order to lead a thorough restructuring of its operations. Under Bo', Pagnossin went through a recapitalization, enabling it to invest in developing more modern and efficient production capacity. This restructuring effort continued into the early 1990s, and by 1994 the company boasted near total automation of its production, as well as improvements in its raw materials. Pagnossin also renewed its investment in technology, and by the early 1990s had succeeded in developing an innovative coloring technique that permitted this process, as well, to be automated—a first in the industry.

The new process, based on xeriography, enabled Pagnossin to paint directly onto the surface of its tableware products. The process also allowed the company to paint in up to five colors simultaneously. This compared with the industry standard decalcomania process, which required color to be applied to a separate overlay, only one color at a time. Pagnossin's new and more efficient coloring technique had a number of other advantages. With the color brought on directly to the surface of objects, Pagnossin was able to offer customers a five-year guarantee against fading. Meanwhile, the process also enabled the company to produce shorter and smaller runs of new designs, and more quickly, enabling the company to respond to a growing industry trend toward faster design turnover in the 1990s. Last, the process gave Pagnossin an advantage with department store and other large-scale buyers, permitting the company to prepare prototypes of designs within a matter of hours.

Pagnossin renewed its growth through the 1990s. The international market became particularly receptive to the company's designs, and by the mid-2000s, Pagnossin boasted sales in more than 70 countries. The company's international marketing and distribution network included subsidiaries in Japan, Switzerland, and the United States, among other markets.

Diversifying for a New Century

Pagnossin also sought external growth in the 1990s. In 1992, the company made its first effort to diversify its business when it absorbed the operations of Vaserie Trevigiane. That company was a leading producer of terracotta pots and vases for interior and exterior gardens, noted for its high-quality products. Pagnossin at first leased the Vaserie Trevigiane works, which, due to overspending, had gone into receivership. By 1994, Pagnossin bought the terracotta works outright, paying ITL 3.8 billion.

Following the acquisition, Pagnossin began an investing effort in Vaserie Trevigiane, spending some ITL 2.4 billion on the company's production infrastructure. This effort enabled Vaserie Trevigiane to double its production and its sales by the mid-1990s.

Pagnossin also invested in its own production capacity during this time. In 1996, the company brought a new and innovative gas furnace online. Entirely designed by Pagnossin's own research and development team, the furnace was the first in the world to produce heat levels consistent with electric furnaces. The new oven allowed Pagnossin to boost its production by

some 20 percent. It also allowed the company to produce both cups and plates on the same production line, something that had not been possible with the group's earlier equipment.

Pagnossin continued to target expansion as it approached the dawn of the 21st century. In 1997, Pagnossin made its next major move, when its holding company Retma Holding acquired Richard Ginori 1735 for ITL 65 billion. Richard Ginori 1735 represented one of the oldest and most respected names in Italian bone china and porcelain, tracing its origins back to its founding in 1735 by the Marchese Carlo Ginori.

Until the early 1800s, China had been the major source for porcelain in Europe. The material became highly prized, and even coveted. Yet the Europeans had not yet discovered the formula for producing local versions of porcelain. In the early 1800s, the first successful recipes for producing porcelain based on raw materials found in Europe had been developed, and factories now began to appear across Europe.

Ginori set up his factory in Doccia, in the then-kingdom of Florence. Ginori originally produced porcelain featuring designs by Giovan Battista Foggina. Associated with a number of noted artists and architects of the day, Ginori became known for his large-scale objects. Yet the business proved a money-loser up until Ginori's death in 1757. Son Lorenzo then took over the company's operations, reorienting its production to smaller objects, and transforming the business into a profitable and thriving enterprise.

Through the 18th and 19th centuries, the Ginori works developed its reputation as one of Italy's foremost producers of porcelain and, later, bone china, and the company became a supplier to Italy's royalty. Under management by Carlo Benedetto in the late 1870s, Ginori installed new electric ovens, which greatly increased the company's production capacity.

In 1896, the Ginori family sold the company to Milan's August Richard. The more industrialist-oriented group had been founded in 1873 by Giulio Richard in order to produce ceramics products for the northern Italy market. That business grew quickly, and in the late 1880s had begun to expand elsewhere in Italy, notably with the purchase of Palme, based in Pisa, in 1887, and the establishment of a warehouse in St. Giovanni. Following the purchase of the Ginori company, Richard, or Richard Ginori as it later became known, maintained its production in Milan, as well as in Doccia, and also operated a number of its own shops in Naples, Turin, Rome, and Bologna.

Richard Ginori established its reputation as one of Italy's master porcelain makers, working with a number of noted designers, especially with architect Gio Ponti starting in 1923. Richard Ginori grew again in the 1960s, when it acquired Laveno-based SCI (for the Italian Ceramic Society) in 1965. Richard Ginori itself went through a succession of owners through the 1960s and the 1970s, becoming owned by Italian businessman S. Ligresti, who then sold Richard Ginori to Pagnossin in 1997.

In 1998, Pagnossin listed part of Richard Ginori's shares on the Borsa Italiana. Nonetheless, Pagnossin maintained majority control of its new subsidiary. In that year, as well, Richard Ginori began its association with designer Giovan Battista Vannozzi.

Key Dates:

1735: Carlo Ginori founds a porcelain production plant in Doccia, near Florence.

1896: August Richard acquires Ginori, and the combined company becomes Richard Ginori.

1919: Pagnossin S.p.A., which had begun manufacturing bricks in Treviso at the beginning of the century, is incorporated.

1950: Pagnossin launches production of ceramic tableware, which becomes its sole product in the 1960s.

1986: Carlo Rinaldini acquires Pagnossin and institutes restructuring.

1992: Pagnossin diversifies into terracotta, leasing Vaserie Trevigiane.

1994: Pagnossin acquires Vaserie Trevigiane.

1997: Pagnossin acquires Richard Ginori.

1998: Richard Ginori lists on the Borsa Italiana.

2001: Terracotta producer TTT-Trequanda is acquired.

2005: Pagnossin announces that sales are down by 16 percent and losses amount to EUR 36 million.

That collaboration resulted in the well-received Iubilaeum 2000 Collection, launched for the dawn of the 21st century.

Richard Ginori also became a vehicle for the acquisition of new brands for the Pagnossin stable. In 2001, the company acquired TTT-Trequanda, a producer of terracotta pots. Other brands added to Pagnossin included Laure Japy, based in France.

Pagnossin's fortunes fell into the mid-2000s, however. The company saw its sales slip, while its profits collapsed into losses. By 2004, sales had dropped some 16 percent from the previous year, reaching slightly more than EUR 46 million. Yet the group's losses had grown even larger, reaching some EUR 36 million for the year. With a long history as a top Italian ceramics producer, Pagnossin faced an uncertain future in the early years of the new century.

Principal Subsidiaries

Casa Italiana 3 S.R.L.; Editrice L'Italia a Tavola S.R.L; Gruppo Italiano Tavola S.R.L.; Laure Japy France et RG S.A. (France); Museo Richard-Ginori della Manifattura; Retma Holding B.V. (Netherlands); Richard-Ginori (Svizzera) S.A. (Switzerland); Richard-Ginori 1735 Inc. (U.S.A.); Richard-Ginori 1735 S.p.A.; Richard-Ginori Japan (Japan); Vaserie Trevigiane International S.p.A.

Principal Competitors

Elkem ASA; American Greetings Corporation; Waterford Wedgwood PLC; Villeroy und Boch AG; Noritake Company Ltd.; Mikasa Inc.; Rosenthal AG; Royal Doulton PLC; Lladro S.A. Grupo; Josiah Wedgwood and Sons Ltd.

Further Reading

''KPMG Refuses to Certify Pagnossin Accounts,'' *Europe Intelligence Wire,* June 16, 2005.

''Pagnossin: A fine arzo posizione finanziaria netta,'' *Finanza.com,* May 2, 2005.

''Pagnossin: Perdita 2004 sale a 36.2 mln euro,'' *Borse.it,* June 1, 2005.

''Richard Ginori e Pagnossin a velcita' sostenuta,'' *Finanza.com,* June 15, 2005.

The Richard-Ginori Factory, Milan: A. Mondadori, 1988.

''Un 2003, 'horribilis' per il gruppo Rinaldini,'' *Trend-online.com,* May 27, 2004.

—M.L. Cohen

Paradores de Turismo de Espana S.A.

Requena 3
Madrid E-28013
Spain
Telephone: +34 91 516 67 00
Fax: +34 91 516 66 53
Web site: http://www.parador.es

State-Owned Company
Incorporated: 1928
Employees: 4,086
Sales: $318 million (2004 est.)
NAIC: 721110 Hotels (Except Casino Hotels) and Motels

Paradores de Turismo de Espana S.A. operates one of the world's most unique collections of hotels. Owned by the Spanish government, Paradores oversees more than 90 hotels established almost exclusively in historical locations, such as former castles, monasteries, fortresses, and the like; some of the group's sites date back as far as the ninth century. Paradores was originally formed in 1928 as a means of rescuing and restoring landmark sites in Spain, as well as helping to establish the country's tourism infrastructure, especially in noncoastal areas. Although the company operates a number of hotels on the country's coasts, Spain's primary tourism zones, the bulk of the company's hotels are situated inland. Whereas most of the company's sites are located in landmark buildings, a number of the hotels in its portfolio are modern hotels. These, however, are generally located on sites of historic interest. Paradores functions as a hotel management company; the majority of its locations are owned by Spain's National Heritage Service. The company also takes charge of the renovation and restoration of the sites, which is paid for through the site's hotel operations. Since the early 2000s, Paradores has been in an extensive restructuring and renovation of its hotels, spending more than EUR 150 million per year. The company also has continued adding new properties, including seven slated to open starting in 2005. In 2004, Paradores's revenues were expected to top EUR 350 million. Ana Isabel Marino Ortega serves as the company's chairman of the board.

Historic Tourism Infrastructure in the 1920s

Paradores de Turismo de Espana stemmed from the Spanish government's earliest efforts to create a tourism infrastucture in Spain at the dawn of the 20th century. Indeed, into the early years of the century, the country—especially its rural regions—offered little in the way of accommodations and support for travelers, particularly for those coming from abroad.

In 1910, the government turned over the job of promoting a homegrown tourism industry to the Marquis de la Vega Inclán. The following year, Vega Inclán launched the Royal Tourism Commission. Among Vega Inclán's objectives was the establishment of tourist markets in Spain's remote—and poor—regions, where industrial development was lacking. The Gredos mountains became the commission's first target, and in 1926, construction began on what was to become the first Parador.

The site was developed as a hunting lodge, featuring a relatively modest 30 rooms. Completed in 1928, the first Parador (which means ''inn'' in Spanish) received enthusiastic support from an important source: King Alfonso XIII.

The king's enthusiasm led to the decision to expand the parador concept throughout Spain. Soon after the Gredos site's opening, the government founded the Board of Paradores and Inns of Spain in order to develop and expand the Parador project. The new state-controlled body began refining the concept, recognizing the potential to solve another problem facing the government.

Many of Spain's historical sites had fallen into disrepair by the early 20th century. Maintenance and upkeep of the sites proved too costly for private individuals to afford. Other sites had long been abandoned by their owners. The parador concept was then extended to incorporate the renovation and conversion of the country's sites of historical interest into high-quality hotels. In this way, the revenues generated through the hotel operations would pay off the costs of the sites' renovation. Although the majority of the Paradors were developed from existing buildings, a number of sites also were chosen for their natural beauty. New buildings were then constructed on these sites.

Company Perspectives:

Our Mission. Paradores achieves its success by fulfilling a mission defined by the following objectives: To develop a quality tourism product that is the image of the Spanish hotel industry abroad, and the instrument of the country's policy on tourism. To facilitate the recovery of historical heritage for tourism, permitting the conservation and maintenance of buildings for the learning and enjoyment of present and future generations. To boost tourism in areas with little tourist or economic activity, and support sustainable development, respecting the environment in those areas in which the establishments are located, and to serve to attract private initiatives. To promote traditional regional cuisine by researching and recovering recipes and cooking methods, and boost the consumption of local quality products. To further knowledge of cultural and natural destinations, thus helping to diversify Spanish tourism offerings and to convey a richer image of Spain to visitors. To develop the above activities as profitably as possible, such that they satisfy the State's financial expectations as the sole shareholder, and the expectations of Spanish society as a whole and the company's employees.

Key Dates:

1919: The Marquis de la Vega Inclán is appointed to develop a tourism infrastructure in Spain.
1926: Vega Inclán launches construction on the first Parador hotel in Gredos.
1928: Gredos Parador opens and wins the support of King Alfonso XIII, leading to the creation of the Board of Paradores and Inns of Spain and the development of new Paradors.
1991: Paradores de Turismo de Espana S.A. is incorporated as a state-owned company.
2001: A EUR 165 million refurbishment program is launched.
2005: The Paradores network tops 90 hotels, with seven new hotels slated to open starting in 2005.

The Board of Paradores began selecting sites and launching renovation projects. One of the first of the new Paradors opened in Toledo, in Oropesa, in 1930, followed soon after by the Ubeda site in Jaen. The following year, the parador in Badajoz opened as well.

Extension Under Franco in the 1950s

The Parador project survived the years of the Spanish Civil War and received new interest in the postwar dictatorship established by Francisco Franco. Indeed, under Franco the program was accelerated, and the Paradores network came to be considered as one of the Franco regime's few achievements.

In 1940, Paradores opened its first hotel in the province of Malaga, in Antequera. The Parador San Francisco de Granada opened in 1945, followed by a new hotel in Malaga, in Gibralfaro in 1948. Two years later, Paradores completed the renovation of what some later considered to be the jewel in the Paradores crown: the Hostal de Los Reyes Catolicos in Santiago de Compostela. The 16th-century structure had initially served as a hospice for pilgrims, and the renovated site became one of the most beautiful and unique hotels in Europe.

Franco's interest in the Paradores project enabled the government agency to step up the number of building conversions. The Franco era also represented a period in which Paradores began adding new, modern hotels to its portfolio. Among the company's new openings in the 1950s were the Parador de Pontevedra, opened in 1955 on the site of a 16th-century castle. Opened in 1956, the Pontevedra met with strong success, and led to a rapid expansion of the Paradores network. By the end of that year, the agency had opened the Parador de Almagro. A fourth hotel in Malaga opened that year as well.

Through the 1960s and into the 1970s, Paradores kept up its stream of hotel openings. In 1965, the agency opened its four-star Antiguo Hospital de la Ruta Jacobea, originally built as a hospital providing medical care to pilgrims making their way to Santiago do Compstela. Another opening in 1965, of the Parador de Santo Domingo de la Calzada, included the extensive renovation of the surrounding area as well as the opening of a hotel. The following year Paradores opened a new hotel, the Conde de Gondemar, in Baiona in Galicial. That site had been made famous because it was from there that the *Pinta* was first spotted on its way back from its journey to the New World.

The Paradores program survived another regime change, with the death of Franco in 1975 and the creation of a new democratic government in Spain. One of the oldest of the Paradores hotels opened its doors in 1976, in a fortress at de Cardona that had already been present in the 10th century. Other hotels of this period included the Parador de Chincon, opened in 1982 and built from an Augustinian convent dating back to the 16th century. The renovation of the site, which also had served as a prison and a courthouse over the centuries, took some ten years to complete. A convent served as the setting for another Parador in the 1990s, the Parador de Trujillo, on a site that dated from the 16th century.

Global Reputation in the New Century

The beginning of the 1990s marked a new era for Paradores. In that year, the state-owned agency was converted into a corporation, becoming Paradores de Turismo de Espana S.A. The move signaled the beginning of the end of the group's reputation for bloated payroll and inefficient operations. Paradores now launched a cost-cutting effort, shrinking its payroll in order to bring its average employees per room measurements closer to the industry average. Paradores also launched a refurbishment effort to upgrade a number of its hotels to attract a wealthier clientele.

New hotel openings continued through the 1990s, including the opening of a fifth hotel in Malaga, the Parador de Ronda, which began operations in 1994. Paradores also began looking beyond its own portfolio for revenue sources, and began providing management services to hotels owned by private parties. During the 1990s, Paradores started focusing on its catering and restaurant operations. A number of hotels began opening their restaurants to the outside public, and by the mid-2000s, the group's restaurant operations represented a strategic share of its annual sales.

By 2003, there were 88 Paradores in operation, including the Parador de La Palma, on the Canary Islands, opened in 2000. That hotel was followed by the conversion of the Convent of Santo Domingo, a 15th-century structure, and by the opening of two five-star hotels, the Parador of Lerma in the former Ducal Palace, and the Parador of Monforte, in the former Monastery of San Vincente do Pino, both opened in 2003.

At the same time, Paradores carried out a massive EUR 165 million investment program to refurbish and upgrade parts of its now 90-strong portfolio. The company also began construction on another seven hotels, the first of which was slated for inauguration in 2005. Paradores had by then earned a global reputation as the manager of one of the world's most unique hotel portfolios.

Principal Competitors

Hoteles Turisticos Unidos S.A.; Globalia Corporacion Empresarial S.A.; Bouganville Playa Hoteles S.A.; NH Hoteles S.A; Sol Melia S.A.; Riu Hotels S.A.; Viajes Marsans S.A.; Barcelo Hotels and Resorts; Viajes Iberia S.A.; Grupo Serhs S.A.; Occidental Hoteles Management S.A.; Hosteleria Unida S.A.; Hoteles Hesperia S.A.

Further Reading

Anastasi, Paul, "State-Run Hotels 'Wasted Money,' " *European,* August 8, 1996, p. 21.
Cebrian, Belen, "Paradores amplia sus miras," *El Pais,* March 14, 2004.
Hayley, Julia, "Spain's Historic Inns Try for Up-Market Tourists," *Reuters,* May 29, 1995.
"Historic Conversions Going Strong 75 Years On," *Traveltrade,* October 15, 2003.
"Parador Network Expands," *Travel Agent,* January 31, 2000, p. 101.
"Paradores sale del letargo," *El Pais,* November 4, 2001, p. 5.
"Paradores Will Not Be Privatised," *Expansion,* May 11, 2001, p. 11.
Wilkinson, Isambard, "Paradores Mark 75 Years of B&B with a Flavour of the Real Spain," *Daily Telegraph,* August 30, 2003.

—M.L. Cohen

PFSweb, Inc.

500 North Central Expressway
Plano, Texas 75074
U.S.A.
Telephone: (972) 881-2900
Toll Free: (800) 920-4959
Fax: (972) 633-2615
Web site: http://www.pfsweb.com

Public Company
Incorporated: 1996 as Priority Fulfillment Services, Inc.
Employees: 881
Sales: $321.67 million (2004)
Stock Exchanges: NASDAQ SmallCap
Ticker Symbol: PFSW
NAIC: 423420 Office Equipment Merchant Wholesalers;
 423430 Computer and Computer Peripheral Equip-
 ment and Software Merchant Wholesalers; 488510
 Freight Transportation Arrangement; 493110 General
 Warehousing and Storage; 511210 Software Publishers;
 522320 Financial Transactions Processing, Reserve,
 and Clearinghouse Activities; 541614 Process,
 Physical Distribution, and Logistics Consulting
 Services; 561499 All Other Business Support Services

PFSweb, Inc. is a leading business-to-business and business-to-consumer order fulfillment and call-service provider for such clients as IBM, Raytheon Aircraft Corporation, Hewlett-Packard, Xerox, the Smithsonian Institution, and the U.S. Mint. The company's services include processing and shipping orders; billing; managing inventory; light assembly; and creating and hosting web sites. PFSweb also offers the Entente Suite of software, which can perform a full range of tasks for e-commerce businesses. About four-fifths of the firm's revenue is derived from subsidiary Supplies Distributors, Inc., which performs work for IBM.

Beginnings

PFSweb, Inc. was founded in 1996 as Priority Fulfillment Services, Inc. (PFS) by Texas-based Daisytek International Corporation, a leading wholesale distributor of computer and office automation supplies such as printer ribbons, toner cartridges, and computer disks. The new unit was initially created to perform order-processing, fulfillment, and telemarketing services for other companies, due to a growing demand for outsourcing in this area. Soon after its formation, PFS was chosen to perform telemarketing and distribution services for IBM Printing Systems' Network Printer product line throughout North America.

PFS soon began to take on additional clients, and Daisytek doubled the size of its own "superhub" warehouse/shipping center in Memphis (strategically located near the main shipping hub of Federal Express) in part because of the unit's success. By mid-1997 PFS was distributing close to $200 million worth of goods per year for more than 20 clients.

In the latter half of 1997 the firm opened a new call center in Memphis, which would take incoming calls and perform telemarketing. PFS was also operating call centers in Dallas, Miami, Sydney, Toronto, and Mexico City at Daisytek sites.

In January 1999 the company formed a European division, PFS Europe, which would employ ten at a call- and fulfillment center in Maastricht, Netherlands, and also launched a new division to offer order fulfillment services to Internet-based retailers. It was targeted toward both web-based startups and bricks-and-mortar firms who were adding web ordering capabilities and needed to quickly get systems and staff in place.

PFS was now growing rapidly, and the firm recorded revenues of $101.2 million for the year ended March 31, 1999, double the figure of a year earlier. It had 30 customers, including new web-based firms such as YardMart.com and Bargain Bid.com, as well as established companies including Hewlett-Packard. PFS's primary client continued to be IBM, which accounted for 93 percent of its business.

Initial Public Offering in 1999

At this time many thought the Internet would soon radically change the way Americans did business, and investors were frantically trying to get in on the ground floor of any company that had a connection to "e-commerce." With Daisytek's business model appearing dull in comparison to the "sexier" web-fulfillment services offered by PFS, the parent firm decided to capitalize on the market frenzy for Internet stocks by selling part of it on the NASDAQ.

In early December 1999 one-fifth of the company, now bearing the name PFSweb, Inc. to highlight its e-commerce capabilities, was sold in an initial public offering (IPO). Mark Layton, the 40-year-old CEO of Daisytek, who had recently published a book called *.coms or .bombs ... Strategies for Profit in e-Business,* took the titles of president, CEO, and chairman of PFSweb, while remaining board chairman of the parent firm.

The IPO was an unqualified success, and raised $52.7 million for the firm to help fund growth and pay off $22.3 million worth of assets acquired from Daisytek. PFSweb stock had initially been priced at $17, but closed at $44 on the first day, giving the company a market valuation double that of its parent, and it continued to rise in the following weeks.

Shortly after the successful IPO, the Christmas gift-buying season exposed several cracks in the relatively untested e-commerce model, which caused some firms, including several of PFSweb's clients, to go out of business. The company began looking for more stable firms to work with, and reached an agreement with IBM for the computer maker to promote the company's services to its established e-commerce clients. PFSweb's share price took a beating in the months after Christmas, and by the spring of 2000 had fallen to less than one-third of its opening price.

After PFSweb's IPO Daisytek announced plans to spin off the remaining stock to its own shareholders, and despite the efforts of some to block the move, the deal went forward in the summer, with 14.3 million shares of PFSweb stock distributed. Afterwards, Daisytek would continue to outsource some of its functions to the firm, and several shared assets and board members were gradually disentangled.

In late July 2000 PFSweb introduced the Entente Suite of software, which offered full e-commerce support from web site interface to back-office accounting functions, customizable to meet each customer's needs. In August the firm also formed the Professional Consulting Service Group, which would advise clients about technology and distribution logistics. During the year the company signed new contracts with Adidas, Avaya Communications, Mary Kay Cosmetics, and Pharmacia/Upjohn. For fiscal 2000, the firm reported revenues of $86.6 million.

PFSweb's stock price had never been able to regain its initial spark, and in April 2001 the firm narrowly avoided being delisted by the NASDAQ after it had fallen below $1 per share for an extended period of time. The spring also saw the company sell Daisytek one-third of its 1.2 million-square-foot Memphis superhub facility for $11 million, transferring the employees who had worked there on outsourced Daisytek assignments back to the former parent firm. PFSweb continued to use some 800,000 square feet of the Memphis facility and other sites in Toronto, Canada, and Liege, Belgium, as well as its headquarters in Plano, Texas, to perform services for its clients.

In August PFSweb added managed hosting and web site development services to its offerings. To accomplish the former, the firm established uninterruptible, redundant power supplies and a secure data center. The company also launched a buyback of two million of its 18 million shares of stock in an effort to boost share value, and unveiled a new corporate logo.

Formation of Supplies Distributors: 2001

October 2001 saw the creation of a new affiliate firm, Supplies Distributors, Inc., which would use funds from IBM Global Finance to buy parts from IBM for distribution by PFSweb. The company invested $750,000 and would retain 49 percent ownership. New work was added during the year for several clients, including cosmetics maker Lancome USA, while existing contracts with Hewlett-Packard and Overtoom International were expanded.

In February 2002 PFSweb began offering customized light manufacturing and supplier inventory services to further support its clients. In June, still in danger of NASDAQ delisting, the company's stock was transferred to the exchange's Small-Cap market from the National Market. The same month saw PFSweb sign a five-year, $14 million contract with the Smithsonian Institution's Business Ventures unit to provide fulfillment services for catalog and web orders. The firm had earlier begun assisting the U.S. Mint. The company was now working to cut costs, and in the summer laid off 60, paring its total staff to about 550.

In October, an alliance was formed with eBay that would allow PFSweb's clients to distribute their products via that firm's online auction site. The month also saw acquisition of the remaining 51 percent of Supplies Distributors, Inc.

The second quarter of 2003 was the company's first profitable one since 1999, and the stock price soon crept above $1, saving it from NASDAQ delisting yet again. In September PFSweb added a new package of services to help customers handle product recalls, and November saw a new contract signed with Shell Energy Services Company to support that firm's new web initiative, Shell HomeGenie, which would allow customers to monitor their homes and control some appliances remotely from the Internet. For 2003 PFSweb recorded revenues of $285.8 million and a net loss of $3.7 million.

In the spring of 2004 the firm introduced the Ecometry Commerce Suite, a new direct-marketing software package purchased from an outside vendor, as well as GlobalMerchant CommerceWare 2.0 Software Suite, a simple, low-cost e-commerce program. Spring also saw the company sign service agreements with several new clients including CHiA'SSO, a home design products firm, and Raytheon Aircraft Company,

Key Dates:

1996: Daisytek International Corp. forms Priority Fulfillment Services (PFS).
1996: PFS signs contract with IBM Printing Systems.
1999: Daisytek sells one-fifth of renamed PFSweb, Inc. on the NASDAQ.
2000: Daisytek spins off rest of firm to its stockholders.
2000: Entente Suite of software is introduced.
2001: Firm adds web development and hosting; Supplies Distributors is formed.
2004: PFSweb begins relocating most distribution operations to Southaven, Mississippi.
2004: Company records first profitable year since initial public offering.

for which a new 150,000-square-foot parts distribution facility would be opened in Belgium. Soon afterwards PFSweb was tapped to distribute parts to Raytheon's Western hemisphere customers out of that firm's Grapevine, Texas facility.

Distribution Operations Beginning Shift to Mississippi in 2004

In August 2004 the company signed a lease on a 435,000-square-foot warehouse/shipping center in Southaven, Mississippi, which was located near its Memphis superhub site. The firm had been in a dispute with Memphis officials since 2003, when former parent Daisytek had gone bankrupt and tax breaks for the Memphis site that had been granted to that firm ended, raising PFSweb's costs. When an appeal to the Shelby County Industrial Development Board was denied, the firm had begun seeking a new location outside of Memphis.

The new Mississippi facility was soon put to use providing services for a major corporate retailer that the company was contractually obligated not to reveal. Other new clients included Rene Furterer USA, FLAVIA Beverage Systems, and several other unnamed firms. To help fund its expansion, PFSweb issued $5 million in industrial revenue bonds through the State of Mississippi and boosted its credit facility with Comerica Bank. For 2004 the company's revenues increased to $321.7 million, and it recorded its first profitable year, with net income of $226,000. The firm now had nearly 900 employees, and was shipping approximately $1 billion worth of products per year for its customers.

February 2005 saw PFSweb expand its Southaven capacity by 167,000 square feet to accommodate more work for a consumer electronics firm's spare parts unit, and in April the com-

pany announced it would begin moving most Memphis operations to Southaven, where it had now leased a total of 908,000 square feet in two buildings. Some jobs would remain in Memphis at an expanded call center there.

The history of PFSweb, Inc. encompassed both the highs and lows of the late 1990s/early 2000s dot.com boom and bust, which the firm had survived to become profitable. In just five years of independent operation, the company had grown into a $320 million business, and had built a reputation for solid performance that put it on the road to brighter days ahead.

Principal Subsidiaries

Supplies Distributors, Inc.; Priority Fulfillment Services, Inc.; PFSweb B.V. (Belgium).

Principal Competitors

Ingram Micro, Inc.; Menlo Worldwide, LLC; United Parcel Service Inc.; GENCO Distribution System, Inc.; ClientLogic Corp.; DSC Logistics; Exel Plc; Affiliated Computer Services, Inc.

Further Reading

Cecil, Mark, "Holders Want to Stop Daisytek Spin-Off," *M&A Reporter*, June 19, 2000.

Cruz, Mike, "Daisytek Spin-Off PFSweb Stacks Up," *Computer Reseller News*, October 30, 2000, p. 125.

——, "Putting a Web Face Forward," *Computer Reseller News*, September 3, 2001, p. 55.

Dillich, Sandra, "Daisytek Unloads PFSweb," *Computer Dealer News*, October 22, 1999, p. 10.

"E-Commerce Concern PFSweb Makes Big Debut on NASDAQ," *Dow Jones Business News*, December 2, 1999.

Harrison, Crayton, "Plano, Texas-Based Internet Supply Management Firm Sees Future After Tech Bust," *Dallas Morning News*, January 26, 2003.

——, "Supply Chain Outsourcer PFSweb Says It's Just Shy of Sustained Profit," *Dallas Morning News*, September 17, 2003.

Morton, Kate Miller, "Texas-Based Distribution Firm Decides to Lease Space in DeSoto County, Tenn.," *Commercial Appeal (Memphis)*, August 31, 2004.

Northway, Wally, "PFSweb Has First Profitable Year," *Mississippi Business Journal*, March 21, 2005, p. 10.

Pereira, Pedro, "Daisytek Corners Outsourcing—Priority Fulfillment Unit Boosts Corporate Revenue," *Computer Reseller News*, June 23, 1997, p. 141.

Roberts, Jane, "High-Tech Distributor PFSweb to Move Regional Headquarters to Southaven, Miss.," *Commercial Appeal (Memphis)*, April 6, 2005.

Ward, Leah Beth, "Allen, Texas-Based Web Firm Returns to Top of Its Game," *Dallas Morning News*, July 15, 2001.

—Frank Uhle

Philip Services Corp.

5151 San Felipe Road, Suite 1600
Houston, Texas 77056
U.S.A.
Telephone: (713) 623-8777
Fax: (713) 625-7185
Web site: http://www.contactpsc.com

Private Company
Incorporated: 1990 as Philip Environmental Inc.
Employees: 5,000
Sales: $1.5 billion (2004 est.)
NAIC: 423930 Recyclable Material Merchant
    Wholesalers; 325188 All Other Inorganic Chemical
    Manufacturing; 325998 All Other Miscellaneous
    Chemical Product Manufacturing; 562998 All Other
    Miscellaneous Waste Management

Philip Services Corp. is one of the largest providers of industrial services in North America. The company offers industrial cleaning and maintenance services, environmental and waste services, and oilfield services at more than 120 locations in North America. Philip Services is controlled by investor Carl Icahn.

Origins

Philip Services was formed through a series of transactions at the beginning of the 1990s, but its corporate roots stretch to a Canadian landfill, quarrying, and asphalt business based in Hamilton, Ontario, named Taro Aggregates Inc. that was founded in 1980. Nearly a decade later, in July 1989, Taro sold its landfill and ancillary quarrying assets in an all-stock transaction to a company named Lincoln Capital Corp., which became involved a year later in the transactions that gave birth to Philip Services' predecessor, Philip Environmental. Philip Environmental was formed by brothers Allen and Philip Fracassi, who had begun their business careers when they took over their father's bankrupt Hamilton-based trucking company in 1979. The Fracassis formed Philip Environmental, whose official corporate title initially was Philip Environmental Corporation, in June 1990, the same month Philip Environmental acquired a

Hamilton-based waste management company named Branard Corp., in which each of the Fracassi brothers held an equity stake. Lincoln Capital, at this point, purchased a 50 percent interest in Philip Environmental. In December 1990, Lincoln Capital sold its interests in Taro to Philip Environmental and sold its 50 percent stake back to the company, marking the formal organization of Philip Environmental, which changed its name from Philip Environmental Corporation to Philip Environmental Inc. the following July. In May 1997, the company changed its name to Philip Services Corp.

It would have been difficult for the Fracassi brothers to imagine a more disastrous first decade for the business they cobbled together at the end of 1990. Marked by scandal, a stream of shareholder lawsuits, managerial instability, and profound financial problems, Philip Services lived a brutal existence during the 1990s, one that did not improve by much as the company limped through the first years of the 21st century. The company's pervasive problems, which resulted in one of the biggest annual financial losses in Canadian business history, did not surface until the late 1990s after an ambitious campaign for expansion spectacularly foundered.

Before Philip Services began its precipitous fall, the company moved in the other direction, recording impressive growth during its first years in business. The completion of several acquisitions greatly aided the company's expansion, including the September 1993 purchase of Waxman Resources Inc., a Hamilton-based recycler and processor of copper, aluminum, plastics, and ferrous metals. The purchase was important because its assets represented the future orientation of the company, but for less affirmative reasons the acquisition was significant because it marked the arrival of Robert Waxman at Philip Services' headquarters. (Waxman later became a central figure in the events that led to Philip Services' collapse). Several months after the purchase of Waxman Resources, the company acquired Nortru Inc., a Michigan-based hazardous and nonhazardous recycling business, and Burlington Environmental Inc., a Washington-based chemical waste management and environmental engineering and consulting business. In November 1994, Philip Services purchased Deslan Environmental Group Inc., a decommissioning and remediation services company

---

Company Perspectives:

We will increase the scale and scope of our activities by broadening and deepening our client relationships, and we will differentiate ourselves from our competitors by bundling services for our clients. We will pursue opportunities within and across our two major businesses—Metals and Industrial Services—and build profitable client alliances that complement our size and reflect our capabilities.

---

based in Toronto. The company's acquisitive activities fueled its financial growth, exponentially increasing its revenue volume from CAD 60 million in 1992 to CAD 489 million in 1994. The growth was substantial, but the financial gains became larger after the company looked at the changing dynamics of its marketplace and fashioned a new future for itself as a consolidator in the scrap metals industry. The change in strategic focus made Philip Services a $2 billion-in-sales company (the company began reporting its financial totals in U.S. currency), and it also set the stage for the nightmarish late 1990s.

A Change in Strategy in the Mid-1990s

By 1995, according to Allen Fracassi's letter to shareholders in the company's 1997 annual report, Philip Services ''had reached a crossroad.'' Fracassi, who served as president and chief executive officer while his brother Philip served as executive vice-president and chief operating officer, noted that the company's industrial clients were changing the way they did business. Outsourcing, the great corporate movement of the 1990s, drove companies to seek third-party vendors to take responsibility for functions otherwise performed by the companies themselves. While companies looked to contract out ancillary aspects of their businesses, leaving them more focused on their core pursuits, they also looked to reduce the number of vendors they contracted with, seeking a partner with comprehensive capabilities to meet their outsourcing needs. Such were the changes viewed by Fracassi during the mid-1990s that served as the impetus for his decision, announced in February 1996, to concentrate Philip Services' business on the resource recovery and industrial services market, thereby distancing the company from what Fracassi referred to as ''the traditional environmental sector'' in his letter to shareholders. Philip Services' relationship with its customers in the steel industry exemplified the new ''one-stop-shopping'' approach of the company. The company's early associations with the steel industry involved processing foundry sand for reuse in cement production, but its new approach called for it to not only provide scrap metal to feed its customers' furnaces but also to handle their waste stream, deliver their on-site maintenance and industrial cleaning, and provide final processing and distribution of their products.

Philip Services began fashioning itself into a new type of company first by divesting some of its assets before beginning its ambitious assault on the acquisition front. The company sold its municipal solid waste business in 1996, severing its ties to operations in Quebec, Ontario, and Michigan, and it sold a substantial stake in its utilities management operations. The additions to the company's holdings followed, financed initially

by a $550 million line of credit to fund its acquisition campaign. Allen Fracassi looked at the resource recovery and industrial services sector and saw a wealth of acquisition candidates, aiming his acquisitive sights on a highly fragmented industry populated by a bevy of private companies without the financial and organizational resources required to serve the changing marketplace. The campaign began in earnest in December 1996. Philip Services acquired Houston-based Southwest Limited Partnership, Ohio-based Luntz Corporation, and the Alcan Alloys Plant located in Guelph, Ontario, each of which significantly expanded the geographic scope and service mix of the company's metals recovery group. The drive to consolidate the scrap metals industry took off with abandon the following year, when Fracassi purchased more than 30 companies, spending a staggering $1.3 billion. Among the most significant of the acquisitions were Luria Brothers, a Cleveland-based scrap broker and processor; the Steiner-Liff Group of companies; Allwaste, Inc.; and Allied Metals Limited, a steel scrap and mill services company based in the United Kingdom. Revenue shot upward as a result of the ambitious acquisition campaign, eclipsing $1 billion in 1997, just five years after the company collected CAD 90 million for its annual total. Wall Street— Philip Services' stock was traded on both Canadian and U.S. exchanges—approved of the company's moves to consolidate the industry, fueling an impressive increase in the company's stock and providing easier access to capital. The company's stock was trading for less than $8 per share in June 1996, rising to nearly $20 by September 1997. A $380 million stock offering in November 1997 easily sold out, as investors eagerly seized the opportunity to invest in Fracassi's growth strategy. Within months, the enthusiasm surrounding Philip Services turned to ire, as the company entered the darkest chapter in its history.

Late 1990s Collapse

The debacle of the late 1990s began January 1998. The company intended to spend the first part of the year initiating a program to integrate the numerous acquisitions completed in 1997 into its operations, but the year began with the announcement that there was a discrepancy between the book and physical inventory values in its yard copper business. Roughly 50,000 tonnes of copper had gone missing or had never existed. One month later, the company announced it would restate the financial results posted for the three previous years, further eroding investor confidence and triggering a storm of shareholder lawsuits. Some of the complaints charged that the company had known of its true condition before the November 1997 offering that raised $380 million. In May 1998, Allen Fracassi stepped down as chief executive officer, replaced by an executive touted as a turnaround specialist who was hired to sell assets, lead negotiations with banks, and restructure Philip Service. John G. McGregor occupied the post for five weeks before moving aside for the return of Allen Fracassi. McGregor was given the title of chief restructuring officer, but he left the company entirely before the end of the year.

While Philip Services grappled with leadership issues, the company's problems attracted a renowned executive named Carl Icahn. Described by *Fortune* in its July 10, 2000 issue as one of the ''buccaneers who prowled Wall Street in the 1980s, taking and gutting companies for sport and profit,'' Icahn made his living by preying on companies. Icahn profited handsomely as a corporate raider, accumulating an estimated $5 billion fortune by squaring off against massive companies such as RJR Nabisco, Western Union, and Texaco. When Philip Services began to falter, Icahn sniffed opportunity, believing that the company was undervalued because it was still producing substantial amounts of cash. In May, when Fracassi relinquished his chief executive officer post, Icahn paid CAD 80 million for a 9 percent stake in Philip Services and, along with a Los Angeles investment group, Foothill Partners III LP, acquired most of the company's mounting debt. The following month, Philip Services sued Robert Waxman, who had become president of the company's metals division, and two colleagues, demanding $240 million in damages for the trio's alleged role in the copper trading scandal. The settlement of the case against Waxman, which dragged on for more than five years, could do nothing to help the company in 1998, however. In the fall, the company announced it could not make interest payments on its more than $1 billion of debt, prompting Icahn, who had since increased his stake to more than 14 percent, to demand that Philip Services file for bankruptcy or let him take control of its operations. The company ended the year with a numbing $1.6 billion loss and began 1999 preparing to file for bankruptcy.

After months of negotiations with its lenders, Philip Services filed for bankruptcy in Canada and the United States in June 1999. While the company developed a restructuring plan in preparation for its return, Icahn increased his investment, building up a more than 40 percent stake in Philip Services. Under the company's restructuring program, debt holders became the holders of new secured debt and were given control of 90 percent of a new corporate entity, one whose business was heavily reliant on ferrous scrap sales. Philip Services emerged from bankruptcy protection in April 2000, getting what it hoped to be a fresh start in business. In September, when the company was led by a new president and chief executive officer, Anthony Fernandes, Philip Services moved its headquarters to the United States, where it derived roughly 80 percent of its sales. After operating out of Chicago for a brief period, the company established its headquarters in Houston.

Early 21st Century Offers No Relief

Despite the promise of an improving ferrous scrap market, Philip Services soon began to suffer from severe financial

problems. The company lost $78 million in 2001 and $59 million the following year. In March 2002, as the company headed towards a $59 million loss, Anthony Fernandes resigned as chief executive officer, creating a vacancy that was not filled for more than a year. During the first fiscal quarter of 2003, Philip Services, despite rising prices for ferrous scrap, posted a $12.7 million loss, 45 percent more than it lost during the same period a year earlier. In April 2003, John Correnti, formerly chief executive office of Nucor Corp. and Birmingham Steel Corp., was hired as acting chief executive officer, but the arrival of a new leader did little to bolster Philip Services' cause. In May 2003, the company announced that if it did not reach a new financial agreement with creditors by the beginning of the following month it would be forced to declare bankruptcy again. The deadline passed without the required agreement, forcing Philip Services, for the second time in four years, to seek protection under Chapter 11 of the U.S. Bankruptcy Code.

Another attempt at a restructuring began in June 2003, when the company announced it would try to sell all of its operating units either as a whole or in parts. By September, a winning bidder for the company's assets was announced, Carl Icahn's High River Limited Partnership. Icahn controlled a majority of the outstanding shares of the reorganized company when it emerged from bankruptcy on the last day of 2003. Philip Services pressed ahead with its third attempt at achieving success in the business world, hoping to put its troubled past behind it. "Philip Services is emerging from this restructuring as a financially sound, formidable competitor in the industrial cleaning, environmental, and metals services markets," a company executive remarked in a January 7, 2004 interview with *Canadian Corporate News*.

Principal Subsidiaries

Luntz Corporation; Philip Services (Europe) Limited; Philip Services (Delaware) Inc.; Philip Industrial Services Group, Inc. Philip Metals (USA), Inc.

Principal Competitors

Metal Management, Inc.; Safety-Kleen Systems, Inc.; Waste Management, Inc.

Further Reading

Baxter, Kevin, "New Year, New President Named to Philip Services," *American Metal Market,* January 3, 2000, p. 16.
"Canadian Court Oks Philip's Restructuring," *American Metal Market,* November 10, 1999, p. 9.
Johnson, Greg, "Icahn May Take All of Philip Services," *Daily Deal,* June 5, 2003, p. 32.
Marley, Michael, "Icahn Top Bidder for Philip; Ch. 11 Exit Eyed by Year-End," *American Metal Market,* September 16, 2003, p. 1.
——, "Philip Services Eyes Asset Sale to Pay Off Debts," *American Metal Market,* June 5, 2003, p. 1.
——, "Philip Services Urged to Sell Scrap Business," *American Metal Market,* August 13, 2001, p. 1.
——, "Philip's Red Ink Swells, Mulls Filing Ch. 11," *American Metal Market,* May 22, 2003, p. 8.
McCann, Joseph, "Correnti Acting Top Executive at Scrap Firm," *American Metal Market,* May 21, 2003, p. 1.

Morrison, Scott, "Philip Files for Bankruptcy," *Financial Times,* June 29, 1999, p. 28.

"Philip Services Corporation Emerges from Chapter 11," *Canadian Corporate News,* January 7, 2004, p. 31.

Roggio, Armando, "Philip Services Fends Off Carl Icahn with Equity Capital," *American Metal Market,* November 24, 1998, p. 1.

Weber, Joseph, "Carl Icahn's Toxic Takeover," *Business Week,* December 28, 1998, p. 63.

Worden, Edward, "Philip Looks for Rising Ferrous Scrap Mart to Lift Operations," *American Metal Market,* November 2, 1999, p. 2.

——, "Philip Restructuring Moves Along," *American Metal Market,* March 9, 1999, p. 2.

——, "Philip Sees Light at End of Bankruptcy Tunnel," *American Metal Market,* December 3, 1999, p. 7.

——, "Turnaround Specialist Leaves Philip Services," *American Metal Market,* January 22, 1999, p. 7.

—Jeffrey L. Covell

Pinnacle Airlines Corp.

1689 Nonconnah Boulevard, Suite 111
Memphis, Tennessee 38132
U.S.A.
Telephone: (901) 348-4100
Toll Free: (800) 603-4594
Fax: (901) 348-4130
Web site: http://www.nwairlink.com

Public Company
Incorporated: 1985 as Express Airlines I, Inc.
Employees: 3,400
Sales: $634.45 million (2004)
Stock Exchanges: NASDAQ
Ticker Symbol: PNCL
NAIC: 481111 Scheduled Passenger Air Transportation

Pinnacle Airlines Corp. is the holding company for Pinnacle Airlines, Inc., a regional airline based in Memphis. As Northwest Airlink, Pinnacle operates feeder routes on behalf of Northwest Airlines Corporation. Pinnacle operates a fleet of more than 130 regional jets to more than 100 destinations, with secondary hubs in Detroit and Minneapolis-St.Paul. More than six million people flew the airline in 2004; it has been ranked as the world's fastest-growing airline as well as the eighth largest regional carrier.

Origins

Pinnacle Airlines was incorporated in Georgia in early 1985 as Express Airlines I, Inc. The Roman numeral ''I'' in the company's name indicated plans to build a family of regional feeders under parent company Phoenix Airline Services, Inc. It was led by Atlanta entrepreneur Michael J. Brady, who had formerly been head of Eastern Metro Express, a feeder for Eastern Airlines, and had formed another regional airline, Southeastern Airlines (later part of Atlantic Southeast Airlines). He also helped launch a local fighter aircraft adventure business called Sky Warriors.

Express I soon landed a contract to supply feeder traffic to Republic Airlines and by June 1 was flying as Republic Express. The company's original fleet consisted of three 19-seat British Aerospace Jetstream 3100s, which connected Memphis with three destinations: Columbus and Greenville, Mississippi, and Monroe, Louisiana. By December 1985, it had a dozen turbo-props, including two 33-seat Saab 340s, flying to ten cities. It also started flying out of Minneapolis-St. Paul during the month.

NWAirlink in 1986

The fleet more than doubled to 27 planes by June 1986. Republic Airlines was acquired by Northwest Airlines in October 1986, and Republic Express, also called Express Airlines I, Inc. (Express I for short), began operating as an NWAirlink carrier.

Express I's fleet shifted entirely to the Saab 340s in the 1990s, and grew to 32 aircraft. The route network expanded to include 56 southeastern and midwestern destinations. The airline suffered its first disaster when one of its turboprops crashed on December 1, 1993, killing 18 people.

Like other airlines, Express I was forced to undergo extensive cost-cutting in the early 1990s recession. It was profitable, however, by the mid-1990s. Revenues were about $150 million in 1995, when more than 1.5 million passengers were carried. It was (with Business Express) one of the top two privately owned regional airlines in the United States.

A second company, Express II, was created from the operations at the Minneapolis hub, but it soon was recombined with Express I. Parent company Phoenix Air Services also was providing back-office support to an affiliated company, Chicago Express.

There were a couple of major developments in the Northwest/Express I relationship in 1994. In March of that year, Northwest switched to a very successful new system of connecting flights at Memphis. In October, Express I entered a novel new contract wherein it merely sold all of its seats to NWA for a fixed price, freeing it from fare wars and marketing considerations. NWA handled all booking and scheduling. Express I was leasing all of its aircraft from Northwest.

Acquisition by Northwest: 1997

Northwest bought Express I from founder and CEO Michael J. Brady and CFO Glenn Schabb in April 1997. The price was later reported to be $33 million.

Phil Trenary, founder of Lone Star Airlines, was named its new CEO and president. The Minneapolis-St. Paul operation was transferred to sister Airlink carrier Mesaba Airlines, while the corporate headquarters were relocated from Atlanta to the Memphis base of operations in August 1997.

Trenary was given the task of immediately improving Express I's customer service, operational reliability, and costs. This was accomplished with the help of key executives brought in from Lone Star and Northwest, and an emphasis on staff training and motivation. A new program called ITMAD—Input That Makes a Difference—encouraged employees to contribute ideas.

Express I had about 1,200 employees in 1999 and was flying more than one million passengers a year. Its network connected three dozen destinations in 11 states.

Regional Jets in 2000

Northwest was a little late in transitioning its feeders in the industrywide shift from turboprops to small jets. Express I acquired its first 50-seat Canadair Regional Jet (CRJ) in April 2000; this plane was dubbed "The Spirit of the Memphis Belle" after the storied World War II bomber. A month earlier, the airline had joined FlightSafety International in opening a $23 million Flight Learning Center in Memphis to meet its increased training requirements. (NWA's other Airlink partner, Mesaba, would not get regional jets until 2005.)

Business really took off after the addition of the CRJs, as Northwest increased its flights at Memphis-Shelby County Airport by 25 percent and started a major expansion program of its facilities there. Express I's payroll doubled to 1,300 employees within a year, and it opened a second hub in Detroit as Northwest Airlines reorganized its regional feeders along market-based rather than strictly geographical lines. By this time, Express I was operating 17 CRJs and 26 Saab 340s to 56 destinations. About 650 employees, however, were laid off following the terrorist attacks on the United States on September 11, 2001. The Saabs were divested by November 2001, giving Express I an all-jet fleet.

Renamed Pinnacle Airlines in 2002

Express I was renamed Pinnacle Airlines, Inc. on May 8, 2002. A holding company, Pinnacle Airlines Corp., had been formed in January 2002. According to *Commuter/Regional Airline News*, about 200 advertising agencies around the world were asked to help select the name from a list of 200 sugges-

tions developed by a public relations firm. "We were changing everything—our culture, our fleet, the look of the airline, everything—so we went looking for a new name," explained a company spokesperson. During the year, *Professional Pilot* magazine commended Pinnacle on its management/employee relations.

An initial public offering (IPO) on the NASDAQ followed in November 2003. Northwest retained an 11 percent shareholding and two board seats. Proceeds from the IPO, which raised $271.6 million, went to the Northwest Airlines Pension Plans, which had been transferred the stock earlier.

Pinnacle Airlines Corp., the publicly traded parent company, had revenues of $457.8 million for 2003, with net income of $35.1 million. Its major limitation at the time seemed to be contractual stipulations preventing it from operating larger, 70-seat regional jets, which made up the segment of the market considered by analysts to offer the most potential for growth, according to *Air Transport World*.

Earnings were up 16 percent to $40.7 million on revenues of $635.5 million in 2004. The company ended the year with about 1,100 pilots. It was the fastest-growing of about five dozen regional airlines in the United States.

Pinnacle celebrated the arrival of its 100th regional jet in July 2004, naming it the *Spirit of Beale Street* in honor of a World War II B-24 bomber whose purchase was funded by the Memphis African-American community.

An expansion of Pinnacle's headquarters was underway. To help meet its onboard staffing needs while maintaining flexibility, Pinnacle began hiring large numbers of part-time flight attendants. It also was using more part-timers as ramp workers. Pinnacle was hiring hundreds of pilots, but two new flight crew members were lost when they crashed on a positioning flight on October 14, 2004.

20 in 2005

At the time of the company's 20th anniversary in 2005, Pinnacle was ranked by *Airline Business News* as the world's fastest-growing airline and the eighth largest regional. It had 3,400 employees and was operating 134 jets to about 100 destinations.

Within some limits, Pinnacle was free to pursue business from other carriers. Northwest's guarantee of a minimum operating margin for Pinnacle was set to expire in 2008, and its contract would be up for renewal several years after that.

Principal Subsidiaries

Pinnacle Airlines, Inc.

Principal Competitors

American Eagle Airlines, Inc.; Comair, Inc.; ExpressJet Airlines, Inc.; MAIR Holdings Inc.

Further Reading

"Analyst Urges a Pinnacle Buy After Detailed Study," *Commuter Regional Airline News,* March 15, 2004.

Arnoult, Sandra, "In Memphis, But Not Blue," *Air Transport World,* February 2001, pp. 82+.

——, "Pinnacle of Success: Pinnacle Airlines Has Achieved Remarkable Things Over the Past Few Years, But the Future Brings New Challenges," *Air Transport World,* August 2004, pp. 67+.

Black, Bob, "Pinnacle Airlines: Regional Feeder Soaring to New Heights," *Airline Pilot Careers,* April 2005, pp. 16–20, 23–25.

Dunlap, Stanley, "Memphis-Based Pinnacle Airlines Has Reason to Celebrate," *Commercial Appeal* (Memphis), June 11, 2005.

"Express Airlines I Improves Performance Through New Technology," *Commuter Regional Airline News,* July 23, 2001.

"Express I's Trenary Named Regional Airline Executive of the Year," *Commuter Regional Airline News,* May 8, 2000.

Fedor, Liz, "NWA Jets Promised to Pinnacle, Not Mesabe; Pilot Labor Costs a Question Mark," *Star Tribune* (Minneapolis), September 16, 2003, p. 1D.

——, "Pinnacle IPO Boosts Pension Funds; NWA to Contribute More Cash As Well," *Star Tribune* (Minneapolis), November 26, 2003, p. 2D.

"How They Did It: Express Airlines I Takes on Customer Service, Morale," *Commuter Regional Airline News,* February 16, 1998, p. 4.

Iverson, Doug, "Northwest Airline Operator Averts Pilot Strike," *Knight Ridder/Tribune Business News,* March 5, 1996.

Maki, Amos, "Pinnacle Airlines Overcomes Bad Reputation to Win Over Industry," *Memphis Business Journal,* September 27, 1994.

Moorman, Robert W., "Memphis Belle," *Air Transport World,* August 1999, pp. 46+.

Morton, Kate Miller, "Memphis, Tenn.-Based Pinnacle Airlines to Expand Corporate Headquarters," *Commercial Appeal* (Memphis), June 9, 2004.

Moylan, Martin J., "Pinnacle Airlines' Pilots Pin Hopes on Raise from Northwest Regional Carrier," *Knight Ridder/Tribune Business News,* January 25, 2005.

"One-on-One with Express Airline I's Phil Trenary," *Commuter Regional Airline News,* February 2, 1998, pp. 6+.

"One-on-One with Express I's Michael Brady," *Commuter Regional Airline News,* January 9, 1995, pp. S1+.

Paulk, Michael, "I Have Never Been Bored in the Job. Never," *Memphis Business Journal,* August 25, 2000, p. 13.

"Pinnacle Airlines Seeks Independence from Northwest," *Commuter Regional Airline News,* November 17, 2003.

"Pinnacle Fleet to Grow with Independence; Airline Positions Itself for Successful IPO," *Commuter Regional Airline News,* November 11, 2002.

"Pinnacle's SEC Filing Outlines Potential Risks and Benefits," *Commuter Regional Airline News,* March 4, 2002.

Richfield, Paul, "Red-Tail CRJs Debut in Memphis," *Business & Commercial Aviation,* July 2000, p. 40.

Roberts, Jane, "Memphis, Tenn.-Based Pinnacle Airlines Trains New Flight Attendants," *Knight Ridder/Tribune Business News,* August 5, 2004.

——, "Memphis, Tenn.-Based Regional Airline's Stock Offering Fails to Fly High," *Commercial Appeal* (Memphis), November 26, 2003.

——, "Pinnacle Airlines Celebration in Memphis, Tenn., Features Tuskegee Airman," *Commercial Appeal* (Memphis), July 9, 2004.

——, "Pinnacle Airlines Slashes Hours, Benefits of Some Full-Time Ramp Workers," *Commercial Appeal* (Memphis), August 2, 2003.

——, "Pinnacle Airlines Welcomes Newest Jet to Its Fast-Growing Regional Fleet," *Commercial Appeal* (Memphis), July 8, 2004.

——, "Regional Airline to Cut 140 Jobs at Memphis, Tenn., Airport," *Commercial Appeal* (Memphis), September 26, 2003.

Thurston, Scott, "Northwest in Talks to Buy Atlanta-Based Commuter Affiliate," *Knight Ridder/Tribune Business News,* March 15, 1997.

Wilson, Benet J., and Karen Huffer, "One-on-One with Express Airline's Mike Brady," *Commuter Regional Airline News,* March 10, 1997, pp. 4+.

——, "Out with the Old, In with the New: Trenary Takes Over at Express," *Commuter Regional Airline News,* April 7, 1997, p. 8.

—Frederick C. Ingram

PRG-Schultz International, Inc.

600 Galleria Parkway, Suite 100
Atlanta, Georgia 30339-5986
U.S.A.
Telephone: (770) 779-3900
Toll Free: (800) 752-5894
Fax: (770) 779-3133
Web site: http://www.prgx.com

Public Company
Incorporated: 1996 as Profit Recovery Group
   International, Inc.
Employees: 2,800
Sales: $356.9 million (2004)
Stock Exchanges: NASDAQ
Ticker Symbol: PRGX
NAIC: 541219 Other Accounting Services

Atlanta-based PRG-Schultz International, Inc. specializes in recovery audit services, using proprietary software and well-honed methodology to scour clients' books—invoices, purchase orders, receiving documents, databases, and even correspondence files—to find overpayments, missed discounts, and rebates. The company receives a percentage of the money it recovers, charging companies no other fees for its services. A recovery audit can take as little as three weeks and as long as a full year to complete. Early customers were in retail, such as discounters including Wal-Mart, department stores, and drug and supermarket chains, but today PRG-Schultz works with a broad range of industries, including aerospace, chemicals, consumer electronics, healthcare providers, and pharmaceuticals. The company's clients include nearly 90 percent of the nation's top 25 retailers, almost half of the *Fortune* Global 200, and 54 companies that comprise the *Fortune* 100. The largest company in the world in its field, PRG-Schultz works with clients in more than 40 countries. Efforts launched in the late 1990s to diversify service offerings failed to take hold, leading the company to return to its roots, accounts payable services, although the company continues to provide tax recovery services as well. PRG-Schultz is a public company, listed on the NASDAQ.

1960s Roots

PRG-Schultz was formed in 2002 after Profit Recovery Group International Inc. acquired Howard Schultz & Associates, although the latter was the older of the two firms—and the first company in the United States to provide accounts payable recovery services, founded by Howard Schultz in 1970. Schultz received his inspiration for the business during the late 1960s when he was hired by a large department store as its controller and was charged with the task of clearing up a massive accounting problem. The retailer's payment processing system had become overwhelmed, delaying the payment of bills. In order to meet pending deadlines, the accounts payable department had been forced to ignore its usual verification process in order to cut the necessary checks. Upon taking over, Schultz initiated an audit, which located and recovered about $40,000 in overpayments. He made it a standard practice to conduct audits on his employer's books, recovering money that would have been lost equal to many times his salary. Shrewdly he decided to quit his salaried position and continue to do the audits, but on a contingent basis. Unlike other accountants who performed similar functions on a part-time basis to earn extra money, he recruited the services of other accountants and in 1970 formed Howard Schultz & Associates, Inc. (HS&A) to take on other clients and become the first full-time profit recovery company. In the first month alone, the company recovered more than $250,000.

In the early years the profit recovery business was labor-intensive, requiring auditors to sort through vast amounts of paper records. Nevertheless, the young company was able to unearth a large enough number of overpayments to attract clients and grow the business. In 1975 Howard Schultz took his concept to Canada, and five years later entered the U.K. and Ireland markets. At this stage an increasing number of retailers became more computerized and turned to electronic data interchange (EDI). Although it sped up the bill-paying process, EDI also led to a new breed of errors that went undetected because of an increasing lack of human oversight. "There is a belief out there that if something is listed on a computer printout, then it has to be right," Schultz told the *Dallas Morning News* in a 1992 profile. "I've found that I've been very successful in finding overpayments in that environment . . . because no one is

Company Perspectives:

PRG-Schultz is committed to making our clients worldwide more profitable, improving the potential of our employees, and the value for our shareholders. By creating partnerships with our employees, our business partners, our clients and their suppliers, we meaningfully improve our clients' internal controls and financial performance. Our passion for creativity and innovation, and a disciplined approach creates value for our clients in ways no other firm can.

checking their work.'' In order to audit electronic accounts, HS&A developed the industry's first audit-specific software programs, unveiled in 1987. Clients turned over their computer tapes to HS&A auditors, who then ran the tapes through the program to compare purchases with historical data and other criteria to flag potential errors that required closer examination. Like the company, the auditors were not paid a salary. Rather, they received a percentage of the money they recovered. ''That keeps them from getting bored,'' Schultz told the *Dallas Morning News*. In 1987 the company also topped the $100 million mark in annual recoveries for the first time.

HS&A made further inroads in Europe, in 1988 opening offices in the Benelux region, then in 1993 entering France. Two years later the company moved into the Far East. The company continued to get better at finding overpayments, with recoveries increasing about 13 percent a year during the 1990s. Moreover, waves of mergers and consolidations led to the downsizing of accounts payable departments at many major companies, opening up even greater opportunities for HS&A and other profit recovery companies. In 1996 HS&A was the top company in its field, generating $60 million more than its closest competitor, Atlanta-based Profit Recovery Group International (PRG). Over the next few years, however, that ranking would be reversed.

Longtime company President, CEO, and Chairman John M. Cook first became aware of the potential of a profit recovery company in the late 1980s when he was the chief financial officer at Caldor Stores and hired a small recovery auditing firm, Atlanta-based Roy Greene Associates. But Cook had developed a penchant for the field much earlier in his business career. During the early 1960s he worked his way through Saint Louis University, holding a variety of jobs, including working part-time in the accounting department of a local department store. While working on the accounts of one of the company's parking garages he noticed some discrepancies. Told to ignore them by his supervisor, Cook pored over the books on his own time and was able to document a consistent revenue shortfall that ranged from $700 to $900 a day, the result, it turned out, of a longtime employee raiding the register. The department store offered him a job after he graduated in 1964 and he became an internal auditor. Cook later took a position with May Department Stores and gained experience setting up systems to minimize losses either through fraud or simple clerical errors. Cook left May to become involved in a start-up, but returned for a second stint in 1982, joining May's Kaufmann's Department Store division as vice-president of control. He then became chief financial officer at another May division, Caldor Stores.

Cook was well aware of the large number of accounting errors caused by computer systems. Although impressed by the results of Greene's recovery audit at Caldor, Cook was convinced he could do an even better job if he were in charge, especially if he could develop a recovery audit method that worked in a purely electronic environment. In 1989 he quit Caldor to buy 20 percent of Roy Greene and become president and chief operating officer at Roy Greene. His agreement also allowed him to acquire the rest of the business. To back the $1 million loan he needed for the buy-in, Cook used his home as collateral. In 1991 Cook bought the business outright and he and John M. Toma, a colleague at Caldor who had gone to work for Greene before Cook, cofounded PRG. Two months later he spotted a chance to add customers from different markets and acquired another small audit recovery firm, Bottom Line Associates Inc. In its first full year in business, PRG recorded revenues of $17.7 million. The company also spent heavily to develop the kind of EDI-auditing software Cook had in mind. Like Schultz before him, Cook initially focused on retailers and drummed up business by charging no fees and only making money if the firm recovered money for the client.

Cook was quick to look to foreign markets to fuel growth. As early as 1991 he set up The Profit Recovery Group Mexico and The Profit Recovery Group UK. The company's first international client, a U.K. retailer, was signed in 1993. In that same year, PRG set up operations in Canada, France, and Asia. By the end of 1995 foreign business accounted for one-fifth of all revenues, which totaled more than $56 million for the year. Also in 1995 the company greatly expanded its U.S. business by acquiring competitor Fial & Associates.

To fuel further growth, PRG became the first publicly traded recovery audit company, completing an initial offering of stock in March 1996, raising $50 million. Some of that money, about $3 million, was spent to upgrade the company's computer hardware, and another $5 million funded the work of 50 information technology personnel, including eight computer programmers, working on even more advanced auditing tools. Preparing for the future, PRG also formed new subsidiaries in Australia, Belgium, Germany, The Netherlands, and New Zealand. Being a public company that was transparent about its finances proved useful in signing international clients, who were reassured about the company's financial footing. At the end of 1996, during which the company generated revenues of $77.3 million and recorded net income of $6.7 million, PRG was virtually debt-free and had nearly $17 million in cash on hand.

The long-term plan was to move into new markets and add services to become a one-stop shop for clients. In 1997 PRG targeted the healthcare industry, acquiring a pair of companies heavily involved in the healthcare recovery audit business: Newport Beach, California-based Hale Group, and Houston-based Accounts Payable Recovery Services, which also brought with it energy clients. The acquisition of another California company, Shaps Group, gave PRG a foothold in manufacturing/high-tech auditing. Another 1997 purchase was TradeCheck, LLC, an auditing company that specialized in ocean freight expenses and helped PRG launch its Logistics Management Services unit. PRG also grew internationally in 1997 by acquiring Financier Alma, S.A., a Paris-based tax auditing firm, whose clients were likely prospects for PRG's accounts payable services.

Key Dates:

1970: Howard Schultz forms Howard Schultz & Associates, Inc. (HS&A).
1980: HS&A expands to the United Kingdom.
1990: John M. Cook and John M. Toma cofound Profit Recovery Group International Inc. (PRG).
1991: PRG acquires Roy Green Associates, Inc. and Bottom Line Associates, Inc.
1996: PRG is taken public.
2002: PRG acquires HS&A, becoming PRG-Schultz International, Inc.
2005: Cook announces his retirement.

PRG's aggressive pattern of growth continued in 1998, as revenues nearly doubled 1997's total, increasing from $112.4 million to $202.8 million, while net income topped $18 million. Much of that growth was due to eight acquisitions. The addition of Precision Data Link, The Medallion Group, and Industrial Traffic Consultants bolstered the Logistics Management Services unit, so that it could handle a full range of freight auditing services, whether they be ground, express, or ocean freight. In 1998 PRG also acquired Loder, Drew & Associates, which focused on commercial and industrial firms, and Robert Beck & Associates, focusing on grocers. In Europe, PRG acquired France's Novexel S.A. and Belgium's IP Strategies S.A., both of which specialized in European Union government grant procurement issues. In the Pacific Rim, PRG acquired Australia-based Cost Recovery Professionals, a retail accounts payable auditing form.

PRG closed out the 1990s on a high note, reaching $1 billion in the amount of money it recovered for its clients, resulting in a 44 percent increase in revenues in 1999 to $350 million and net income that doubled to $39 million. PRG was doing especially well with nonretail customers, such as high-tech industries, healthcare, financial services, government agencies, and manufacturing and distribution. During 1999 the company completed a third offering of stock, selling 3.5 million shares at a price of $34 million, money that was put to use in making further strategic acquisitions, such as the purchase of Atlanta-based Integrated Systems Consultants, Inc. and Payment Technologies, Inc. The acquisition of Ireland-based Meridian VAT Corp., a leader in the Value-Added Tax recovery field, provided entry to 13 more countries, including Japan. As a result of its strong performance, PRG received its share of accolades, named as one of *Fortune* magazine's 100 Fastest Growing Companies. Personal honors came as well to Cook, named ''Ernst & Young LLP Entrepreneur of the Year'' in the Financial Services Category.

Acquiring HS&A in 2002

Even as PRG was enjoying a strong 1999, there were questions arising from some quarters about the company's accounting practices and growth potential. A critical report published in a December 1999 hedge-fund subscription newsletter by Off Wall Street Consulting Group in Cambridge, Massachusetts, led to a sell-off in PRG's stock. Management was able to reassure investors and the stock price rebounded, but missed quarterly projections in 2000 led to further decreases in the price of PRG stock. The company took advantage of the situation to buy back a large portion of its stock, but it was becoming apparent that the one-stop shopping plan was not working, the combined business model requiring too much capital and effort from management to be viable. Management hired consultants Bain & Company in the fourth quarter to develop a realignment strategy, which called for the company to divest Meridian and the communications, logistics, and freight divisions in order to focus on the core accounts payable business. It was in the context of this back-to-basics philosophy that in 2002 PRG reached an agreement to acquire HS&A in a deal that closed in early 2002, creating the world's largest recovery audit service provider by a wide margin, some 14 or 15 times larger than its nearest competitor. To pay for the deal, PRG issued nearly $160 million in stock to HS&A and assumed about $37 million in debt. As a result, 72-year-old Howard Schultz and his son Andrew became two of the largest PRG shareholders. They subsequently sold a major portion of those shares to a pair of private equity Firms, Berkshire Partners LLC and Blum Capital Partners LP, which held a combined 27 percent stake in PRG.

PRG now assumed the name PRG-Schultz International, Inc. and had to contend with difficult economic conditions in many of the industries it served. Recovery auditing services had long been considered recession-proof, but that idea was now being put to the test, as PRG-Schultz learned the obvious lesson that when companies do less business there are less mistakes to be found. The company turned in what Cook considered a solid performance, but in 2003 had to contend with continuing poor economic conditions, exacerbated by the Securities and Exchange Commission's inquiries into vendor-supplied promotional allowances that made many clients cautious about pursuing audit claims. As a result, PRG-Schultz saw its revenues slip from $447 million in 2002 to $376 million in 2003. Business continued to fall off in 2004 and PRG-Schultz found itself the recipient of unsolicited offers to buy the company. Management felt that in fairness to its shareholders it should seriously consider the offers, and so in October 2004 it hired CIBC World Markets as a financial advisor to consider strategic alternatives, including the possible sale of the company.

When the results of 2004 were tallied, PRG-Schultz recorded another drop in revenues, to $356.9 million, while losing $71.5 million. Nevertheless, by June 2005 the company concluded that it was still not in the best interests of shareholders to sell the company. Rather, management expressed confidence that PRG-Schultz was on the verge of realizing new growth opportunities in both the United States and internationally. In a separate announcement, Cook declared his retirement, although he agreed to stay on as chairman, president, and CEO until his successor was in place.

Principal Subsidiaries

PRG-Schultz USA, Inc.; PRG-Schultz France, Inc.; PRG-Schultz Canada, Inc.; PRG International, Inc.; PRG-Schultz UK, Ltd.; Howard Schultz & Associates (Asia) Limited.

Principal Competitors

Connolly Consulting, Inc.; Broniec Associates Inc; Hewitt Associates, Inc.; The Corporate Executive Board Associates Inc.

Further Reading

Alva, Marilyn, "Scandals Don't Bring Auditor Down," *Investor's Business Daily,* September 13, 2002, p. A07.

"Blueprint for Success," *Shareholder,* Fall/Winter 2000, p. 5.

Coolidge, Carrie, "Finders, Keepers," *Forbes,* December 25, 2000, p. 74.

Geer, John F., Jr., "Profit Recovery Group: Greener Eyeshades," *Financial World,* August 12, 1996, p. 25.

Pallarito, Karen, "The 'Lost Profit' World: Payment Recovery Firms Target Lucrative Healthcare Industry," *Modern Healthcare,* June 16, 1997, p. 36.

Patrick, Stephanie, "Schultz Recovers Millions in Client Overpayments," *Dallas Business Journal,* November 27, 1998.

Utley, Michael, "Scoring on Errors," *Dallas Morning News,* August 10, 1992.

—Ed Dinger

Quaker Foods North America

Quaker Tower
555 West Monroe, Suite 16-01
Chicago, Illinois 60604-9001
U.S.A.
Telephone: (312) 821-1000
Web site: http://www.quakeroats.com

Division of PepsiCo, Inc.
Incorporated: 1901 as The Quaker Oats Company
Employees: 3,000
Sales: $1.53 billion (2004)
NAIC: 311211 Flour Milling; 311212 Rice Milling;
    311230 Breakfast Cereal Manufacturing; 311423
    Dried and Dehydrated Food Manufacturing; 311822
    Flour Mixes and Dough Manufacturing from
    Purchased Flour; 311823 Dry Pasta Manufacturing;
    311999 All Other Miscellaneous Food Manufacturing

Quaker Foods North America has inherited the mantle of the Quaker Oats Company, which was acquired by PepsiCo, Inc. in August 2001. The product of a rocky union between three 19th-century millers, Quaker Oats originally centered around oats, but it was its Gatorade sports drink brand that was its most coveted asset by the late 20th century. Responsibility for Gatorade, however, was shifted post-merger to PepsiCo's beverage operations, while Quaker Oats' snack business, consisting of granola bars and rice cakes, was transferred to PepsiCo's Frito-Lay snack unit. This left the newly named Quaker Foods North America with a predominantly breakfast-oriented product lineup: the flagship Quaker oatmeal, Quaker grits, Cap'n Crunch and Life cereals, Aunt Jemima syrups and pancake mixes, and the Rice-A-Roni, Pasta Roni, and Near East side dish brands. Several Quaker Foods brands—including both Quaker oatmeal and grits, Aunt Jemima syrup, and Rice-A-Roni—lead their category in the U.S. market, though Quaker's cold cereals rank a distant fourth. Quaker Foods focuses exclusively on the United States and Canada, its former international operations having been transferred to other PepsiCo units following the takeover. Quaker is the smallest of PepsiCo's four divisions, generating about 5 percent of the parent company's revenues and 8 percent of its operating profits.

Oatmeal Battles in the 19th Century

Ferdinand Schumacher undertook an ambitious project in 1856 when he organized his German Mills American Oatmeal Factory in Akron, Ohio. His mission was to introduce steel-cut oats to the American table at a time when oats were considered an inappropriate food for anything but horses. German and Irish immigrants were his initial customers, because they were accustomed to eating oats and unused to the high cost of American meat. Oat milling was a low-cost operation, and competitors quickly appeared as oats gained acceptance as a food.

One competitor with an innovative approach to business was Henry Parsons Crowell of nearby Ravenna, Ohio. Crowell purchased the Quaker Mill in Ravenna, gave his oats the Quaker name, and packed them in a sanitary, two-pound paper package with printed cooking directions. He also advertised in newspapers with German, Scottish, and Irish readers, a practice at the time associated with disreputable showmen. Crowell became the first marketer to register a trademark for cereal, registering his Quaker symbol in 1877. (The Quakers—that is the Society of Friends Christian sect—played no role in the development of the Quaker Oats Company.) Soon Crowell's success impinged on Schumacher's business, with urban customers often specifically requesting Quaker brand oats.

Another competitor, Robert Stuart, emigrated with his father from Embro, Ontario, to establish a mill in Cedar Rapids, Iowa, in 1873. Eventually he helped finance the building of a new oatmeal mill in Chicago and expanded the original mill. Under the same label the two mills established markets throughout the Midwest, especially in Chicago, Milwaukee, and Detroit, carefully avoiding territories dominated by Schumacher or Crowell.

In 1885 Crowell and Stuart joined forces in a price war against Schumacher's larger operation. An attempt to form the Oatmeal Millers Association that year failed when Schumacher refused to join. One year later Schumacher's largest mill burned to the ground; Crowell reacted by immediately raising his prices. Because Schumacher had been uninsured, he finally

Company Perspectives:

You know us by our brands, which have been around for as long as a century. They are symbols of quality, great taste, and nutrition. Holding No. 1 positions in their respective categories are favorites such as Quaker Oats, Quaker Rice Cakes, Chewy Granola Bars and Rice-A-Roni. With its Aunt Jemima brand, Quaker, a unit of PepsiCo Beverages & Foods, is also a leading manufacturer of pancake syrups and mixes. It is among the four largest manufacturers of cold cereals with popular brands like Cap'n Crunch and Life.

agreed to join Stuart and Crowell in their venture. Crowell became president of the Consolidated Oatmeal Company, Stuart was vice-president, and Schumacher, the former oatmeal king, was treasurer.

Consolidated, however, made up only half of the trade, and the other half was determined to destroy it. Competitors built mills they did not want, knowing Consolidated would purchase them simply to keep them out of production. Half of Consolidated's earnings were spent this way, and in 1888, under financial and legal pressure, it collapsed.

A third and finally successful attempt at consolidation came that same year, when seven of the largest American oat millers united as the American Cereal Company. Schumacher ended up with a controlling interest, and he appointed himself president and Crowell vice-president. The company doubled production in two years by consolidating operations into the two major mills at Cedar Rapids and Akron, Ohio. The concentration of facilities gave them the strength to survive the depression of the 1890s.

Crowell promoted Quaker Oats aggressively during the decade. Schumacher, however, insisted that his own brand, F.S. Brand, be sold alongside Quaker, blunting the success of the better-selling Quaker. Then Stuart crossed Schumacher, the company's treasurer, by purchasing two food companies at bargain prices and investing in machinery for the Cedar Rapids mill. Opposed to both actions, Schumacher requested and secured Stuart's resignation in 1897. The following year he also voted Crowell out of the organization.

The ousted Crowell and Stuart, who together owned 24 percent of American Cereal, quietly began to buy available shares. In 1899, after a proxy fight, Schumacher lost control of the company to Stuart and Crowell. Stuart immediately built new facilities and diversified the product line while Crowell increased promotional efforts. Quaker was now producing wheat cereals, farina, hominy, cornmeal, baby food, and animal feed.

Early Years As Quaker Oats

In 1901 American Cereal became the Quaker Oats Company, with sales of $16 million. Twenty years of growth followed, including a wartime peak of $123 million in sales in 1918. With the 1911 acquisition of Mother's Oats, Quaker owned half of all milling operations east of the Rocky Mountains. (The federal government filed a suit against the purchase, but eventually withdrew its last appeal in 1920, when national

interest in trust-busting had faded.) An interest in finding a use for discarded oat hulls led to the establishment of a chemical division in 1921. Although a profitable use for furfural (a chemical produced from oat hulls that has solvent and other properties) did not appear until World War II, postwar sales of the product would exceed oatmeal sales into the 1970s.

Also in 1921 the company weathered a grain-surplus crisis; dealers had been caught with an oversupply and prices fell rapidly, leading that year to the company's first reported loss. Stuart's eldest son John became president of Quaker the following year. John Stuart immediately changed Quaker's retail sales strategy to one of optimum, rather than maximum, sales. The growth of the grocery chains helped to encourage a system of fast turnover rather than bulk purchasing.

Early in the century Crowell and Stuart invested in foreign markets by establishing self-supporting overseas subsidiaries. These subsidiaries operated mills in Europe and sold oats in South America and Asia. Under John Stuart's company reorganization in 1922, foreign operations became a corporate division. Approximately 25 percent of Quaker's sales were derived abroad. During John Stuart's 34 years as CEO, the company increased its toehold on the growing market of ready-to-eat cereals with Puffed Wheat and Puffed Rice. Quaker further diversified its product line by purchasing name brands that were already established, such as Aunt Jemima pancake flour in 1925. Similarly, the company entered the pet food industry through the purchase of Ken-L-Ration in 1942. Internal attempts to develop a cat food failed, and the company eventually purchased Puss 'n Boots brand cat food in 1950.

In 1942 sales reached $90 million. Wartime demand for meat and eggs pumped new life into the sagging animal-feed division as well as boosting sales of the company's grains and prepared mixes. Quaker's furfural became important in the manufacture of synthetic rubber, and during the war Quaker built and ran a bomb-assembly plant for the government.

Postwar Growth and Diversification

In the years that followed World War II, Quaker's sales grew to $277 million generated by 200 different products, a broad product line requiring heavy promotion. John Stuart's younger brother, R. Douglas Stuart, studied under Crowell and assumed control of promotions when John Stuart became CEO. After World War II he adopted the then radical policy of using more than one advertising agency. The Stuart brothers recognized that the grocery industry would continue to expand into pet foods, convenience products, and ready-to-eat cereals, and matched the company's product line and promotions accordingly.

The company's first outside manager, Donald B. Lourie, rose to CEO in 1953. Under Lourie, Quaker retained the atmosphere of a family company with personal leadership. The company needed external support, however, for its increasingly complex marketing decisions. National advertising for the Aunt Jemima brand came at a price of $100,000. The cost of introducing Cap'n Crunch in 1963 was $5 million.

For many food companies, the 1960s were a period of automatic growth as consumer demand for convenience increased and brand recognition grew. For Quaker, however, sales

---

Key Dates:

1856: Ferdinand Schumacher organizes the German Mills American Oatmeal Factory in Akron, Ohio.

1873: Robert Stuart establishes an oatmeal mill in Cedar Rapids, Iowa.

1877: Henry Parsons Crowell, owner of the Quaker Mill in Ravenna, Ohio, becomes the first marketer to register a trademark for cereal: the Quaker symbol.

1886: Schumacher, Stuart, and Crowell join forces as the Consolidated Oatmeal Company.

1888: Seven of the largest American oat millers, including the Consolidated principals, unite as the American Cereal Company.

1899: Schumacher loses control of American Cereal to Stuart and Crowell, who diversify the product line.

1901: American Cereal changes its name to Quaker Oats Company; sales stand at $16 million.

1911: Mother's Oats is acquired, giving Quaker ownership of half of all milling operations east of the Rocky Mountains.

1925: The Aunt Jemima brand is acquired.

1942: Company enters pet food industry through purchase of Ken-L-Ration brand.

1963: The Cap'n Crunch cereal brand is introduced.

1969: Fisher-Price Toy Company is acquired.

1979: William D. Smithburg is named CEO; overall sales reach $2 billion.

1983: Quaker acquires Stokely-Van Camp, maker of Gatorade sports drink.

1986: Quaker acquires Golden Grain Macaroni Company, maker of Rice-A-Roni.

1991: Fisher-Price is spun off.

1993: Company acquires the Near East rice and pasta product brand.

1994: Snapple Beverage Corporation is acquired for $1.7 billion.

1995: U.S. and European pet food operations are divested.

1997: Snapple is sold to Triarc Companies, Inc. for $300 million; Robert S. Morrison replaces Smithburg as CEO.

2001: Quaker Oats is acquired for $14 billion by PepsiCo, Inc. which shifts Gatorade, snacks, and international operations to other units, leaving Quaker Foods North America to focus exclusively on the United States and Canada.

---

rose just 20 percent and profits only 10 percent as long-term development absorbed earnings. Quaker expanded in the industry's fastest-growing areas: pet foods, convenience foods, and ready-to-eat cereals. By the end of the decade growth rates had increased, but not as much as hoped. Robert D. Stuart, Jr., became CEO in 1966. The decade's slow growth and a general corporate trend toward diversification prompted him to make acquisitions outside the food industry for the first time since 1942. Many of these acquisitions were eventually sold, but Fisher-Price Toy Company, purchased in 1969, was held for more than two decades and grew beyond expectations. Within ten years, it made up 25 percent of Quaker's total sales.

Late in 1970 Stuart restructured Quaker's organization around four decentralized businesses: grocery products, which now included cookies and candy; industrial and institutional foods, which contained the newly acquired Magic Pan Restaurants; toys and recreational products; and international. Sales in 1968 had been frustratingly low at $500 million, but with Stuart's acquisitions, the company reported $2 billion in sales by 1979.

Economic recession during the 1970s kept sales down. A second toy company, Louis Marx Toys, was purchased in 1972. During 1974 and 1975, Marx, which was purchased as a "recession-proof" company, drove earnings per share from $2.04 to $1.45. Magic Pan Restaurant's profits fell for four consecutive years. The chemical division reported a net loss of $7 million when a cheaper substitute for furfural came onto the market. This introduction took the company by surprise, as it expected earnings from that division to climb steadily.

Looking to expand its foreign market in grocery and pet foods, Quaker made seven acquisitions of foreign companies during the decade. But while the company focused on diversification, prod-

uct development slipped. Between 1970 and 1978, only one new major product, 100 Percent Natural Cereal, was introduced. Shelf space in major grocery chains did not increase. Stuart had successfully lessened the company's dependence on grocery products, but profits also dropped, to a low of $31 million in 1975.

By the end of the decade, however, a turnaround was in sight. Quaker's least profitable areas were limited to its smallest divisions, and since the entire industrial and restaurant industries had been weakening, the company was already preparing to divest its holdings in that field.

William D. Smithburg replaced Stuart as CEO in late 1979. Smithburg aggressively increased Quaker's sales force and advertising budget, improvements that were badly needed. The company also refocused on its core food business. Quaker had two new successes as the 1980s dawned: Ken-L-Ration's Tender Chunks became the second best-selling dog food in its first year, and Corn Bran had a commendable 1.2 percent share of the ready-to-eat cereal market. In addition, Fisher-Price sales had increased tenfold since 1969, to $300 million. Quaker planned to expand the division by building plants in Europe, raising its target age group, and lowering unit selling prices.

By 1979 Quaker had a return on invested capital of 12.3 percent—higher than the industry average, but well below competitor Kellogg's 19.4 percent. The company still needed to divest its interests in companies that absorbed profits.

Addition of Gatorade and Golden Grain in the 1980s

In the first half of the decade, Quaker sold Burry, a cookie maker; Needlecraft; Magic Pan Restaurants; its Mexican toy operations; and its chemical division. During the same period, the company made several acquisitions. Like many food companies at the time, Quaker entered specialty retailing, with such purchases as Jos. A. Bank Clothiers, the Brookstone mail-order company, and Eyelab, all purchased in 1981; all would be sold in late 1986. By then, Smithburg had decided that the price for retail chains was inflated and that Quaker could get a better return on food. He proved himself right. By 1987 Quaker's return on shareholder equity matched Kellogg's. Quaker confirmed its new path with its 1983 acquisition of Stokely-Van Camp, the maker of Gatorade sports drink and Van Camp's pork and beans. By expanding Gatorade's geographic market, Quaker made the drink its top seller in 1987.

Quaker's revival came about through the strong potential of its low-cost acquisitions. Golden Grain Macaroni Company, the maker of Rice-A-Roni, gave the company a base to expand further into prepared foods. Anderson Clayton & Company, purchased in late 1986, gave Quaker a 15 percent share of the pet-food market with its Gaines brand, effectively challenging Ralston Purina's lead in that market.

With the purchase of Anderson Clayton, financed by the sale of its unwanted divisions, Smithburg managed to strengthen Quaker's position in existing markets and improve its product mix without overloading the company with specialty products. Products with leading market shares made up 75 percent of 1987 sales and over half came from brands that Quaker had not owned six years earlier.

The late 1980s tempered that success, however. Pet food sales were flat throughout the industry, and Quaker took $112 million in charges related to its recently expanded pet division. The corporation was a rumored takeover candidate because of its high volume of shares outstanding and its strong branded products. In response, the company announced in April 1989 that it would repurchase seven million of its nearly 80 million outstanding shares, and that July, Smithburg reassigned some managerial duties. The company also decreased its advertising and marketing expenses.

Refocusing on Food and Beverages in the 1990s

Despite some setbacks, Quaker entered the 1990s with 14 years of unbroken sales growth. The company concentrated on three major divisions: American and Canadian grocery products; international grocery products; and Fisher-Price toys. Still, Quaker continued to streamline its operations into the early 1990s, spinning off Fisher-Price Toys in 1991, a move that made Quaker solely a packaged-foods company for the first time in over 20 years. Sales that year hit a record $5.5 billion, and over 70 percent of the products in Quaker's portfolio held either the first- or second-place position in their segments. Quaker's international sales continued to comprise a significant percentage of the company's total, and in 1991 the company restructured both its European and Latin American operations to focus marketing on a continental, as opposed to a country-by-country, basis.

As it divested itself of its nongrocery products, Quaker continued to expand its packaged foods portfolio. Its concentration was on healthful food brands, such as Near East rice and pasta products, Chico-San rice cakes, and Petrofsky's bagels, all acquired in 1993. The buying spree continued through 1994 and into 1995 with the acquisitions of Proof & Bake frozen bagels,

Maryland Club coffee, Arnie's Bagelicious Bagels, and Nile Spice Foods, a maker of dried soups, pasta, and beans.

Quaker's largest acquisition was its 1994 purchase of Snapple Beverage Corporation, a maker of ready-to-drink juice beverages and teas, for $1.7 billion. Some industry experts considered the price too high for this upstart company with annual sales just below $1 billion, but the purchase boosted Quaker's share of the nonalcoholic beverage market significantly. With combined sales of over $2 billion, Quaker was now the nation's third largest producer of nonalcoholic beverages.

On the international front, Quaker continued its aggressive Gatorade marketing drive, and by 1994 the beverage was available in 25 countries across Latin America, Asia, and Europe. The company also strengthened its foothold in the Latin American food products market with the 1994 acquisition of Adria Produtos Alimenticos, Ltd., Brazil's top pasta manufacturer. Although much of Quaker's expansion was through acquisitions, the company also sought to grow its product portfolio internally, especially in its historically strong rice and grains category. Between 1992 and 1995, volume in that category tripled with the addition of new products such as Quaker chewy granola bars and flavored rice cakes. Companywide sales in 1994 hit $5.95 billion, a record high for the 19th consecutive year.

Despite its record sales figures, Quaker's overall financial outlook was not so bright as it entered 1995. Because of the acquisition of Snapple, Quaker held a high debt to total capitalization ratio and felt it necessary to divest itself of a number of businesses in early 1995. In March, H.J. Heinz Company acquired Quaker's U.S. and Canadian pet foods operations for $725 million. The following month, Quaker's European pet foods division was sold to Dalgety PLC for $700 million. Other 1995 divestitures included a Mexican chocolates business and the Wolf/Van Camp's bean and chili businesses. The selloff continued in 1996 with the sale of the company's U.S. and Canadian frozen food business to Van de Kamp's (eventually part of Pinnacle Foods) for $185.8 million.

While Quaker worked to pay down debt incurred with the Snapple acquisition, it also almost immediately found that it had paid dearly for a faltering brand. In hindsight, it became clear that Quaker had bought Snapple just as the brand reached its peak. Imitators were quick to enter the tea drink market, including Arizona Iced Tea, Mystic, and Nantucket Nectars. Even worse, soft drink giants Coca-Cola Company and PepsiCo, Inc. entered the sector through alliances with Nestea and Lipton, respectively. By the end of 1996 Lipton had claimed 33 percent of the market and Nestea 18 percent, while Snapple was left with only a 15 percent share. In addition to the increased competition, Snapple was also hurt by distribution problems and failed marketing campaigns.

By early 1997 Quaker Oats had suffered Snapple-related losses and charges of more than $100 million. Unable to turn the brand around, and facing pressure from angry shareholders, Quaker sold Snapple to Triarc Companies, Inc., owner of RC Cola and the Arby's restaurant chain, for $300 million. It also took a $1.4 billion pretax charge—essentially the difference between the purchase and selling prices. This led to a net loss for the year of $930.9 million. The Snapple debacle also led to the departure of Smithburg, who was replaced as chairman, president, and CEO by Robert S. Morrison, a former head of Kraft Foods' North American operations, in October 1997.

Almost immediately, Morrison took several decisive measures. Feeling that for a relatively small food company Quaker had an overall complex management structure, Morrison eliminated an entire layer of top management, then elevated ten managers to head the company's main brands, with each reporting directly to the new CEO. He also initiated a number of restructuring moves, including a consolidation of U.S. sales operations, a streamlining of the worldwide supply chain, and the realigning of Quaker's overseas units. These and other moves led to $65 million in savings during 1998. Morrison also took a hard-line approach to the company's brand portfolio, jettisoning those product lines identified as underperforming. Four such brands were sold during 1998 for a total of $192.7 million: Ardmore Farms juice, Continental Coffee, Nile Spice, and Liqui-Dri foodservice biscuits and mixes. The sale of the troubled Adria pasta brand followed in 1999.

Approaching the turn of the millennium, Quaker Oats appeared to be a company on the rebound, with net income increasing from $284.5 million in 1998 to $455 million in 1999. The Gatorade brand was leading the way, generating about 38 percent of overall sales and a like percentage of operating profits. In late 1999 the company announced a 10 percent workforce reduction, equivalent to about 1,400 employees, as part of a cost-saving plan centering around Quaker's slower growing cereal operations. At the same time the company said it would increase production capacity for Gatorade through a $230 million to $245 million expansion program. In addition, as part of revitalized new product development initiatives, Quaker Oats in early 2000 was planning the introductions of a Gatorade-branded bottled water called Propel (which included some of the beneficial nutrients featured in Gatorade but with one-fifth the calories), Gatorade energy bars, and a juice drink dubbed Torq, which was heavier in carbohydrates and calories than Gatorade.

Beginning of the PepsiCo Era in the Early 2000s

As Morrison engineered this turnaround, a number of analysts began predicting that the CEO was getting Quaker Oats in shape for a sale. Quaker was a relatively small player in the U.S. food industry, which was rapidly consolidating, and its powerhouse Gatorade brand made it a particularly attractive target. Sales of Gatorade had reached $1.8 billion in 1999, up from a mere $100 million in 1984 when Quaker bought the brand. It controlled an astounding 86 percent of the sports drink category in the supermarket channel and an equally impressive 83 percent in convenience stores. The desire to gain ownership of Gatorade led three of the largest beverage companies in the world to make bids for Quaker Oats during a rather wild couple of months in late 2000.

In early November PepsiCo offered to pay $14.8 billion in stock for Quaker, but the latter rejected that offer as too low, and PepsiCo walked away. Later that same month the CEO of the Coca-Cola Company, PepsiCo's archrival, engineered a tentative deal to take over Quaker for $15.75 billion in stock, but at the last minute Coca-Cola's board pulled the plug on the deal, mainly concerned that the price was too high. Just days later,

Paris-based Groupe Danone terminated its discussions with Quaker as well. PepsiCo then reentered the picture and finally sealed a deal in early December. The terms were essentially the same as PepsiCo's earlier offer: 2.3 shares of its stock for each share of Quaker. When the deal was completed on August 2, 2001, this translated into a final purchase price of $14 billion.

Once the deal was consummated, there were numerous changes at Quaker. The company was essentially broken apart, with various brands and operations moving to other PepsiCo areas. Responsibility for Gatorade, the biggest prize, was shifted to the parent company's beverage operations. Quaker's snack brands, which included Quaker Chewy granola bars, Quaker Fruit and Oatmeal bars, and Quaker Quakes rice cakes, became part of a new convenience-food unit within Frito-Lay North America, PepsiCo's giant snack food division. Oversight of Quaker's international businesses was transferred to Frito-Lay International and eventually became part of the PepsiCo International division, which was created in 2003 and took over responsibility for all of the parent company's snack, beverage, and food units outside North America. Soon after being acquired by PepsiCo, then, the newly renamed Quaker Foods North America had a much smaller portfolio of brands, and its operations were limited to the United States and Canada. It now had a predominantly breakfast-oriented product lineup consisting primarily of Quaker oatmeal, Quaker grits, Cap'n Crunch and Life cereals, Aunt Jemima syrups and pancake mixes, and the Rice-A-Roni, Pasta Roni, and Near East side dish brands.

The product lineup was trimmed further via two divestments. Late in 2002 Quaker's U.S. bagged cereal business, which had generated 2001 revenues of $100 million, was sold to Malt-O-Meal Company. The deal included a line of 40 bagged cereals marketed under the Quaker brand, including Frosted Flakes, Marshmallow Safari, Apple Zaps, and Cocoa Blasts. The acquirer gained the right to temporarily use the Quaker name under license but converted the products to the Malt-O-Meal brand by early 2004. Early in 2003 Quaker's Golden Grain/Mission pasta brand was sold to American Italian Pasta Company for approximately $43 million plus inventory. Revenues for this divested business totaled $27 million in 2002. These divestments further reduced the revenues generated by Quaker Foods. By far the smallest of PepsiCo's four divisions, Quaker posted sales of just $1.47 billion in 2003, representing 5 percent of the parent company's total. Quaker was nevertheless solidly profitable, and its operating profit of $486 million comprised 8 percent of PepsiCo's overall figure.

Morrison remained in charge of Quaker Foods (and the Gatorade and Tropicana businesses) until February 2003, when he retired. Later in the year Mary Dillon was named president of Quaker Foods, having previously served as vice-president of marketing. In her former position, Dillon had overseen the successful launch earlier in 2003 of Quaker Oatmeal Breakfast Squares, a breakfast bar touted to have a "bowl of instant oatmeal baked into every delicious, moist square." A number of the new products introduced over the next two years were aimed at fulfilling consumers' demands for more healthful food options. Among the products launched in 2004 were Quaker Lower Sugar Instant Oatmeal, which contained half the sugar of regular instant oatmeal, and Cap'n Crunch's Swirled Berries, which included a third less sugar than regular Cap'n Crunch. In early 2005 Quaker

Take Heart Instant Oatmeal debuted, with two features aimed at fighting heart disease: it included 50 percent more soluble fiber from whole-grain oats to help reduce cholesterol, and it supplied higher amounts of potassium to help lower blood pressure.

To at least some observers Quaker Foods was a poor fit for PepsiCo given that the parent company was predominantly a beverage and snack food company. They suggested that PepsiCo would do well to sell off the remaining Quaker brands. But PepsiCo had no immediate plans to do so, one reason being that Quaker enjoyed a reputation as a healthful brand, an important asset in the health-conscious early 21st century. Additionally, PepsiCo adopted a new strategy in 2004 whereby it began seeking ways of gaining growth by marketing the breakfast products of Quaker alongside the quintessential breakfast drinks of Tropicana. To aid in this effort, the juice maker's headquarters were shifted in 2004 from Bradenton, Florida, to Chicago, where Quaker Foods was still based. These developments nevertheless left open the possibility that PepsiCo might divest Quaker's side dish brands, Rice-A-Roni, Near East, and the like, which clearly did not mesh with the new strategy.

Principal Competitors

Kellogg Company; General Mills, Inc.; Kraft Foods, Inc.

Further Reading

Arndorfer, James B., "Quaker Oats Sales Spree in the Cards," *Crain's Chicago Business,* February 17, 2003, p. 4.

Balu, Rekha, "Like Oatmeal, Morrison Proves Good for Quaker," *Wall Street Journal,* October 27, 1998, p. B1.

"A Big Spender—That's What Quaker Oats Has Become, and It Should Pay Off," *Barron's,* January 7, 1985, pp. 45+.

Bruss, Jill, "A Willing Hand: A Gangbuster Year Leaves PepsiCo Holding All the Right Cards," *Beverage Industry,* January 2002, p. 31.

Burns, Greg, "Crunch Time at Quaker Oats," *Business Week,* September 23, 1996, p. 70.

——, "Will Quaker Get the Recipe Right?," *Business Week,* February 5, 1996, p. 140.

Byrnes, Nanette, and Julie Forster, "A Touch of Indigestion: Pepsi's Integration of Quaker Oats Is Not Going As Smoothly As Some Investors Would Like," *Business Week,* March 4, 2002, p. 66.

Campbell, Hannah, "The Story of Quaker Oats," *Country Living,* December 1988, p. 146.

Day, Richard Ellsworth, *Breakfast Table Autocrat: The Life Story of Henry Parsons Crowell,* Chicago: Moody Press, 1946, 317 p.

Deogun, Nikhil, "PepsiCo to Buy Quaker for $13.4 Billion," *Wall Street Journal,* December 4, 2000, p. A3.

Deogun, Nikhil, Betsy McKay, and Jonathan Eig, "PepsiCo Aborts a Play for Quaker Oats," *Wall Street Journal,* November 3, 2000, p. A3.

Dreyfack, Kenneth, "Quaker Is Feeling Its Oats Again," *Business Week,* September 22, 1986, pp. 80+.

Eig, Jonathan, and Thomas Kamm, "Danone SA Drops Bid for Quaker Oats," *Wall Street Journal,* November 24, 2000, p. A3.

Franz, Julie, "Quaker Adapts: Smithburg Puts His Brand on Company," *Advertising Age,* January 19, 1987, pp. 3+.

——, "Quaker Strategy Is to Buy Small, Think Big," *Advertising Age,* June 23, 1986, pp. 6+.

Gibson, Richard, "At Quaker Oats, Snapple Is Leaving a Bad Aftertaste," *Wall Street Journal,* August 7, 1995, p. B4.

——, "Quaker Oats Sets Broad Realignment, Takes Charge of As Much As $130 Million," *Wall Street Journal,* May 17, 1994, p. A2.

——, "Quaker Oats to Spin Off Fisher-Price Unit," *Wall Street Journal,* April 25, 1990, p. A4.

Helliker, Kevin, "Gatorade Set to Stir the (Bottled) Waters with 'Propel,'" *Wall Street Journal,* December 10, 1999, p. B4.

Leonhardt, David, "Stirring Things Up at Quaker Oats," *Business Week,* March 30, 1998, p. 42.

Manring, M.M., *Slave in a Box: The Strange Career of Aunt Jemima,* Charlottesville: University Press of Virginia, 1998, 210 p.

Marquette, Arthur F., *Brands, Trademarks and Good Will: The Story of the Quaker Oats Company,* New York: McGraw-Hill, 1967, 274 p.

McCarthy, Michael J., "Quaker Oats Posts $1.11 Billion Quarterly Loss," *Wall Street Journal,* April 24, 1997, p. A3.

——, "Quaker Oats to Buy Snapple for $1.7 Billion," *Wall Street Journal,* November 3, 1994, p. A3.

McCarthy, Michael J., Richard Gibson, and Nikhil Deogun, "Quaker to Sell Snapple for $300 Million," *Wall Street Journal,* March 28, 1997, p. A3.

McKay, Betsy, "PepsiCo Reorganizes Some Business Units: Quaker Oats CEO Will Play Larger Role," *Wall Street Journal,* August 9, 2001, p. B4.

McKay, Betsy, and Jonathan Eig, "PepsiCo Hopes to Feast on Profits from Quaker Snacks," *Wall Street Journal,* December 4, 2000, p. B4.

McManus, John, "Quaker Matrix Management Models for Turbulent Future," *Brandweek,* May 23, 1993, p. 16.

Moukheiber, Zina, "He Who Laughs Last," *Forbes,* January 1, 1996, p. 42.

Murray, Matt, and Christina Duff, "Heinz Agrees to Acquire Quaker Oats' North American Pet-Food Operations," *Wall Street Journal,* February 7, 1995, p. A3.

Musser, Joe, *The Cereal Tycoon: Henry Parsons Crowell, Founder of the Quaker Oats Co.; A Biography,* Chicago: Moody Press, 1997, 160 p.

Palmeri, Christopher, "Opportunities Lost," *Forbes,* July 20, 1992, pp. 70+.

"PepsiCo Creates New Frito, Quaker Snack Unit," *Snack Food and Wholesale Bakery,* August 2001, p. 10.

Rockford: The Pet Food Story, 1923–1987, Rockford, Ill.: Rockford Pet Foods Division, Quaker Oats Company, 1987, 98 p.

Saporito, Bill, "How Quaker Oats Got Rolled," *Fortune,* October 8, 1990, pp. 129+.

Sorkin, Andrew Ross, "Coke's Retreat Puts Quaker Back in Play," *New York Times,* November 23, 2000, p. C1.

Strahler, Steven R., "Gatorade Extended Quaker's Longevity," *Crain's Chicago Business,* December 11, 2000, p. 4.

Swientek, Bob, "An Unquenchable Thirst for Success," *Prepared Foods,* September 2000, p. 16.

Thackray, John, "The Crunch at Quaker," *Management Today,* October 1983, pp. 82+.

Thornton, Harrison John, *The History of the Quaker Oats Company,* Chicago: University of Chicago Press, 1933, 279 p.

Upbin, Bruce, "Breaking a Sweat: Streaking Past the Snapple Debacle and with a New Guy at the Helm, Quaker Oats Is a Growth Company Again," *Forbes,* December 27, 1999, p. 68.

Vogel, Jason, "How Sweet It Isn't: Snapple Shareholders Made a Killing Selling Out to Quaker. What About Quaker Shareholders?," *Financial World,* July 4, 1995, p. 36.

Whitford, David, "The Gatorade Mystique," *Fortune,* November 23, 1998, pp. 44+.

Wilke, John R., and Chad Terhune, "FTC Lets Pepsi–Quaker Oats Deal Proceed," *Wall Street Journal,* August 2, 2001, p. A3.

—updates: Maura Troester; David E. Salamie

Real Madrid C.F.

Avenida Coucha, Espina Nr. 1
Madrid 28036
Spain
Telephone: +34-91-389-43-32
Fax: +34-91-458-75-78
Web site://www.realmadrid.com

Private Company
Incorporated: 1902 as Madrid Foot Ball Club
Employees: 500
Sales: $115.6 million (2004)
NAIC: 711211 Sports Teams and Clubs

Real Madrid C.F. is the entity governing the Real Madrid football (soccer) team, a Spanish club that ranks as one of the two or three most successful teams in the world. Real Madrid operates as a private, nonprofit club supported financially, in part, by more than 100,000 club members. Real Madrid generates roughly 25 percent of its revenue from ticket sales, 36 percent from television agreements, and 38 percent from merchandise and marketing deals.

Origins

To be a successful business enterprise, a sports team must first excel at its game. In the decades before sports teams became brands, a record of success offered virtually the only way for a sports team to financially survive. Championships and trophies attracted fans, giving the team the gate receipts to sustain itself. In the era after sports teams were regarded as brands, winning lost none of its importance, driving the marketing campaigns that helped pay for players' seven-figure salaries: the price of success in modern sports. Among all sports, there were few teams who could claim to be as successful at its game as Real Madrid, a team whose record of achievement and, at times, dominance in the most popular sport in the world provided the foundation for its success in the business world.

Despite the regal pedigree of the club, Real Madrid began modestly, playing on dirt fields when Spanish football, as an organized, national association, did not exist. On March 6, 1902, a group of students, led by Juan Padrós Rubio, formed the Madrid Foot Ball Club, establishing the small organization in the back room of the Al Capricho store, which was owned by Padrós and his brother. At the meeting, a board of directors was established, with Padrós appointed president of the four-person governing body. The club began with five members. The board decided on the team's uniform during the first meeting, choosing white shirts and shorts, blue socks and caps—the colors worn by the then-famous London Corinthians—and a coat of arms embroidered in purple. The white uniforms later earned the team one of its nicknames, "Los Blancos," but the club's colors were not worn when the team played its first match three days after the first meeting. For its first match, Madrid Foot Ball Club played itself, separating its players on blue and red teams to determine who should play on the club's first team. Each board member played in the scrimmage.

Madrid Foot Ball Club was not the first club formed in Spain—that distinction went to Recreativo de Huelva—but it came into being well before Spanish football was organized into a national association of clubs. In Spain, as elsewhere, football enthusiasts looked to England, the birthplace of the sport, for an organizational model to emulate. England's domestic league was formed in the early 1880s, nearly a half-century before Spain's clubs played against each other in a league format. Not surprisingly, Madrid Foot Ball Club looked to England as a resource for talent and strategies, hiring an Englishman, Arthur Johnson, as its first manager. When Johnson took charge of the club he served not only as the team's chief strategist, but also spearheaded the first efforts to give Spanish football some cohesion.

In later years, a football team's success was measured by its achievements in three areas: its league standing, its progress in domestic tournaments, or cups, and its progress in continental tournaments. When Madrid Football Club was formed, none of the modern benchmarks of success existed in Spanish football. Within weeks of the club's formation, however, the first yardstick of a Spanish club's success was created, a competition that owed its existence to the group of footballers gathered in the back room of the Al Capricho store. Madrid Foot Ball Club's board of directors went to the office of Madrid's mayor in April

Key Dates:

1902: Madrid Foot Ball Club is formed.
1905: The club wins its first major trophy, the Copa del Rey.
1920: King Alfonso XIII grants the title "Real" ("Royal") to the Madrid club.
1932: Real Madrid wins its first league championship.
1955: Real Madrid wins the first of five consecutive European Cups.
2002: Real Madrid wins its ninth European Cup during its centennial season.
2003: The addition of David Beckham improves Real Madrid's marketing exposure in North America, Asia, and Africa.

1902, lobbying for the formation of a football tournament to celebrate the coronation of King Alfonso XIII. The following month, the Copa del Rey (the King's Cup) began, starting with a match between Madrid Foot Ball Club and the team that would be its fiercest rival from that point forward, Barcelona. Madrid Foot Ball Club lost the match to the Catalans and it failed to win the Copa del Rey, but in the years ahead the club would establish an impressive record of success.

Madrid Foot Ball Club's legacy of success was established with the Copa del Rey. The club won its first cup in 1905, the first of four consecutive cups won by the team in white. In 1917, Madrid Foot Ball Club won its fifth Copa del Rey, which, combined with ten regional championships won during the first two decades of the century, drew the praise of the most well-known figure in Spain. In 1920, King Alfonso XIII granted the title "Real," or "Royal," to the club, marking the debut of Real Madrid, a team that spent its first year under its new name on an international tour in Portugal and Italy, its first serious trip abroad. The decade included several more international tours, including trips to England, Denmark, and France in 1925 that saw Real Madrid lose more matches than it won. The club traveled to the United States in 1927, faring better with a record of nine wins, four draws, and four losses, but it would not begin to perform markedly better until a national league was formed. At the end of the decade, in 1928, Spain at last formed a national league, pitting ten teams against each other. Real Madrid placed second during the inaugural season of the Spanish first division, losing the championship (based on points awarded for wins and draws) to Barcelona—the first of 18 times Real Madrid and Barcelona finished in the top two positions during the 20th century. The club won its first championship during the league's fourth season and emerged victorious the following season, beginning to demonstrate the dominance that would see the club win more league championships than any other club during the 20th century.

1943: The Bernabéu Era Begins

In the history of Real Madrid, no figure played a more prominent role in the club's development than Santiago Bernabéu. Bernabéu's affiliation with Real Madrid began in 1912, when he began playing forward for the club, but his greatest contributions came as its president. Bernabéu was appointed president in 1943, beginning a 35-year tenure at the club that represented Real Madrid's definitive era of development. His greatest legacy to the club was one of his first actions undertaken as president: constructing a stadium to befit the royal club from Madrid. Real Madrid spent its first two decades playing on dirt fields before establishing a grass pitch in 1923. The team's home field was destroyed during the Spanish Civil War and rebuilt in 1939, but the new facility, in Bernabéu's estimation, lacked the scale and panache to house what he intended to make the preeminent club in Europe. Bernabéu purchased the land for the club's new stadium in June 1944, broke ground with a symbolic pick in October, and watched his club play its first match in the stadium, originally named La Castellana, in December 1947; Real Madrid won. The stadium, which originally held mostly standing crowds of 75,000, became one of the most famous football grounds in the world, but not as La Castellana. In 1955, when the stadium could accommodate 120,000 fans, La Castellana was renamed Estadio Santiago Bernabéu as a tribute to the individual who was in the process of making Real Madrid the most successful club in Europe.

Real Madrid's claim of superiority was confirmed during the 1950s and reaffirmed during ensuing decades. In 1955, the same year the club's stadium was rechristened as the Bernabéu, a new European tournament was created, one that would represent the ultimate achievement of any club's season. The tournament, known as the European Cup until it was re-branded as the Champions League in the 1990s, ran concurrent with the football season (August to May), pitting the continent's best clubs against one another. Real Madrid won the first tournament and proceeded to win the next four, quickly distinguishing itself as the most successful club in the most prestigious tournament. The club also began asserting itself in its domestic league during the 1950s, winning its first league championship in 21 years during the 1953–54 season. Real Madrid won three more league championships during the 1950s and thoroughly dominated the Spanish first division during the 1960s, securing eight league championships during the decade.

When Bernabéu's presidency ended in 1978, Real Madrid held sway as the champion of champions, boasting a record of success that only one or two clubs in the world came close to emulating. During Bernabéu's 35-year presidency, the club won six European Cups, six Spanish Cups, and 16 league championships: trophies that earned the club an enormous fan base whose presence gave Bernabéu's successors the leverage flourish in the modern era of football. In the decades following Bernabéu's seminal leadership, Real Madrid built on the legacy of its most influential leader, adding four Spanish cup titles by the early 1990s and winning five consecutive league championships during the second half of the 1980s.

Real Madrid Preparing for the 21st Century

As Real Madrid entered the 1990s, the club, along with the ranks of other top-tier clubs, also entered the age of high-stakes football. The financial rewards to be won both on the pitch and on the business front grew enormously during the 1990s, becoming a new benchmark of success for the world's elite football organizations. Transfer fees—the amount paid for one club to purchase another club's player—salaries, and television revenues increased exponentially during the decade, driving the development of the sport into the realm of big business. To reap the financial rewards of the club's success and to pay for the talent to ensure its continued dominance, Real Madrid's management needed to market the Real Madrid name with the same zeal accorded to a consumer product. The club needed to be popular not only in Spain but also throughout the world. "These days football clubs are marketing brands, not just teams," Real Madrid's general director said in a June 22, 2003 interview with the *Washington Times*. "It is no longer just a case of doing well or not on the pitch; that is not the only thing that matters now. It is not just what happens that matters, it's what you say happens. The image is important." Real Madrid, the brand, needed to have appeal in Africa, North America, and Asia, the expansive battleground of the world's leading football clubs as the 21st century neared.

At the turn of the century, Real Madrid's success on the pitch did much to promote the club's success as a brand name. It ranked as the second richest football club in the world, trailing only England-based Manchester United. The club's ownership structure as a private, supporter-based operation helped it defray debt among more than 100,000 Real Madrid club members and freed it from investor scrutiny, facilitating the purchase of the best players in the world. (Manchester United, in contrast, operated as a publicly traded company). "They are the best team and that sells itself. Players go where the money is," a Madrid sportswriter said in the April-May 2003 issue of *Soccer Digest*. "Real Madrid, apart from being a soccer team, is also an economic force." The prestige of the club, coupled with its supporter-owned structure, aided in the purchase of star players nicknamed "Galacticos" by the Spanish media, players such as Brazil's Ronaldo, France's Zinedine Zidane, and Portugal's Luis Figo, each a winner of the Fédération Internationale de Football Association (FIFA) Player of the Year Award. With the skills of such players, Real Madrid celebrated its centennial season by beating Germany's Bayer Leverkusen to win its ninth European Cup, the third European Cup won by the club in the previous six years.

Off the pitch, Real Madrid's greatest challenge during the first years of the 21st century was executing a global marketing strategy. Despite its stellar achievements, the club had a weakness. Its closest rival in terms of fiscal dominance was Manchester United, a club that had spent the late 1990s and the first years of the 21st century expanding its television exposure, completing international tours, and marketing troves of merchandise to ensure that the Manchester United brand name penetrated markets throughout the world. Real Madrid, in contrast, lacked marketing muscle in the United States, Africa, and the Far East, thereby reducing the revenue-producing potential of the club. In mid-2003, in one of a string of high-profile player

acquisitions completed during Florentino Pérez's presidency, Real Madrid strengthened its position overseas, signing Manchester United midfielder David Beckham in a $41 million deal. The acquisition made sense for several reasons, giving Real Madrid a player with an enormous fan base cutting across all demographic, geographic, and socioeconomic lines. Beckham, for instance, made his Real Madrid debut during a tour in Asia, where he was hugely popular, boosting the esteem of the club in an important market. Further, Real Madrid, unlike most clubs, insisted upon retaining 50 percent of the "image rights" for each of its players, which meant that half of every endorsement deal Beckham signed as a Real Madrid player went to the club. Finally, Beckham was a talented player, skilled at free kicks and crosses, giving Real Madrid yet another superstar to ensure its supremacy on the pitch.

As Real Madrid prepared for its future, the club was guided by Florentino Pérez. Elected president in 2000, Pérez was re-elected by an overwhelming margin in 2004, but confidence in his abilities began to wane in 2005 when Real Madrid for the second consecutive season failed to win a major trophy. Not winning a major trophy for two years hardly represented a failure for any club in the world, but at Real Madrid expectations ran exceedingly high. Pérez vowed to stay on, however. "Until 2008," he said in a March 15, 2005 interview with the *America's Intelligence Wire*, "I will continue here because club members are with us."

Principal Subsidiaries

Real Madrid Television.

Principal Competitors

F.C. Barcelona; Manchester United PLC; Milan A.C., S.p.A.

Further Reading

Branom, Mike, "Real Madrid Stars Not for Sale, Club President Says," *America's Intelligence Wire,* March 16, 2005.

Fall, Steve, "The Dream Team," *Soccer Digest,* April-May 2003, p. 52.

Fisher, Eric, "Real Madrid Hits Limelight with Beckham," *Washington Times,* June 22, 2003, p. C3.

Mackey, Stephen, "Embattled Real Madrid President Says He Won't Resign," *America's Intelligence Wire,* March 15, 2005, p. 43.

"Sid Lowe: Reap What You Sow, Real Madrid," *Europe Intelligence Wire,* March 14, 2005, p. 32.

Wahl, Grant, "Eyes on the Prize," *Sports Illustrated,* May 5, 2003, p. 25.

—Jeffrey L. Covell

RedPeg Marketing

727 North Washington Street
Alexandria, Virginia 22314-1924
U.S.A.
Telephone: (703) 519-9000
Fax: (703) 519-9290
Web site: http://www.redpegmarketing.com

Private Company
Founded: 1995
Employees: 65
Gross Billings: $20 million (2004 est.)
NAIC: 541810 Advertising Agencies

RedPeg Marketing, formerly Momentum Marketing Services Corporation, is an award-winning promotional marketing agency specializing in event and experiential marketing. Red-Peg's focus is finding ways to put products in the hands of consumers through special events and promotions, to try to create an "emotional connection" between strategically targeted consumers and a brand or product. Creating engaging "brand experiences" that touch people on a personal level is what RedPeg does best. The full-service agency is headquartered in Alexandria, Virginia, with satellite offices in Westport, Connecticut, and Charlotte, North Carolina. RedPeg's events, however, take place all over the country.

Though the agency is relatively young in the industry, RedPeg's clients have included such large corporations as General Mills, America Online, USAir, Geico, General Electric, Miller Brewing, and the Mexican Bureau of Tourism. The company has achieved national exposure through recognition in *Inc.* and *Fortune Small Business* magazines, as well as numerous performance awards within the promotions industry. The company's ranking in *Promo* magazine's annual top 100 agencies has risen steadily to 23rd place in 2005.

1995: Momentum Marketing Services Born in D.C.

After working for a number of promotional marketing companies, Brad Nierenberg decided he was ready create a business of his own. In 1995 he founded Momentum Marketing Services Corporation in Washington, D.C., along with colleague Brad Beckstrom. Both had experience in promotional marketing. Their first client was Heineken USA.

Early on, Momentum established a reputation for cutting-edge, outside-the-box creative thinking for its clients. Before digital photo technology was well known, the firm used it in a Heineken promotional campaign. In a variety of locations, field representatives took digital photos of potential consumers, then put them in their hands along with information about the product. It got people's attention in part because digital photography was still a novelty to the general public.

Momentum's founders believed that traditional advertising and marketing methodologies were not enough in a market saturated by constant media messages. They set out to create relevant events and experiences, often newsworthy, to capture the attention of specifically targeted consumers. Their campaigns often required hiring and thoroughly training a large number of temporary employees as field representatives. Other corporate clients early on were Dunkin' Donuts, Allied Domecq, United Airlines, and Nestlé Waters. Regardless of who the client was, Momentum Marketing was all about finding the right person to represent the brand that was being promoted. The company was careful to find people with enthusiasm and energy to represent the brand, and then train them more thoroughly than the other shops did.

1996: Using Technology in Promotions and Events

The company also continued to recognize the value of using the latest technology as a part of its promotions. For example, Momentum's field representatives used Palm-based data capture systems, and in response to client feedback designed online portals so people in the field could log on and enter survey information.

Momentum quickly gained a reputation in the industry for hiring and training top notch people, creating mobile marketing tours, being experts at "activation and execution" of a well-designed plan. It arranged for full orchestras to perform in five different business markets on the same day to promote United Airlines' new advertising campaign and encourage consumers to register for United's frequent flier program. Momentum's field staff promoted Perrier and Amstel Light beverages on beaches all over the country, and pushed Dove products in shopping malls. They even put several costumed, muscular Tarzans on the streets of Washington, D.C., handing out T-shirts, coffee, and sweepstakes chances.

Though "products" were often a key part of a promotional plan, Momentum's "experiential" campaigns involved much more than handing out product samples. Nierenberg explained to *Promo* that experiential marketing "gives companies a venue to communicate with customers through a variety of layers. One of the keys to a successful campaign is giving customers a chance to experience a product through the five senses: sight, touch, taste, smell and hearing."

Late 1990s: Collaboration, Creativity, Interaction

Momentum also collaborated with another large agency to implement a highly successful "Towel Amnesty Day" for Holiday Inn Hotels and Resorts. Customers who returned towels that they had previously "borrowed," received as a gift a limited edition Holiday Inn embossed towel and the company made a financial donation to charity on their behalf. The chain not only gave away 60,000 of the towels, but Holiday Inn connected and reconnected with customers in a fun and memorable way, enhancing their corporate image as well as consumer loyalty.

The agency became known for executing creative, interactive, face-to-face marketing for clients. For the Dunkin' Donuts chain, Momentum staff covered large vans with Dunkin' Donuts logos and pictures of products—hot beverages in the fall and winter, and cold beverages in spring and summer. Momentum field staff talked with targeted consumers (parents 35 to 49 years of age) and served them hot lattes during cold months and coolattas and iced lattes in the warm months. The Dunkin' campaign lasted from March through December and included visits to shelters and charity events where specialty beverages and bakery items were distributed.

By the late 1990s, Momentum had attracted the attention of larger agencies with which it was competing for clients. According to the corporate web site, Momentum Marketing's services included "Lifestyle marketing, Event and Tour management, Creative services and production, and Integrated promotional technology."

2001: PRO Award Bringing Recognition

In 2001 Momentum received its first big industry recognition when *Promo* gave the company a top PRO Award for its "Tossed and Found" promotion for GE's financial division. The campaign entailed having trained field representatives drop 10,000 wallets in financial districts of big cities including Los Angeles, San Francisco, and New York, then reacting and following up with consumers who retrieved the wallets. Winners were directed to a web site where two lucky consumers won $100,000 each. The campaign was successful and gained the company media coverage in the process.

The agency's net revenue grew steadily, reaching $2.3 million in 2001. To accommodate company growth, Momentum moved from Washington, D.C., to a larger facility in nearby Alexandria, Virginia's Old Town area. At that time Momentum had 40 employees. The move gave the company 3,000 more square feet and allowed space for future growth in staff.

2002: Rapid Growth Grabbing Headlines

The company's growth got noticed, even outside the advertising and marketing industries. Momentum was cited in the *Inc.* 500 in 2002. *Inc.* magazine profiled 500 of the country's fastest growing private companies. According to Momentum's web site, "Qualifying companies must display 'unbelievable revenue growth' as well as pass an intensive interview process about company structure, policies and overall best practices." Momentum made the prestigious *Inc.* listing two years in a row.

In 2003 Momentum made *Promo* magazine's Top 100 list. For 2002, net revenues were up 6.9 percent to $3.1 million. According to *Promo*, the agency "generated more than 2.6 million web site hits and interacted with over 175,000 consumers around the country with the 6th annual Amstel Light Beach Patrol." At that time Momentum's clients included Heineken USA, Seagram Americas, Ryan Partnership, General Mills, and Nestlé Waters.

The year 2003 was a successful one for the agency, which achieved net revenue of $4.3 million and sales or billings of $10 million. At the end of the year, Nierenberg walked in to the office with a briefcase full of cash and proceeded to give every employee a $1,000 bill as a surprise end of the year bonus. It was a reward for surpassing its sales goal. By 2004 Momentum had grown to 48 permanent employees and hundreds of temporary staff working as field reps.

2004: One of Best Bosses

In October 2004, Momentum founder Brad Nierenberg was selected by *Fortune Small Business* magazine as one of the 15 "Best Bosses" in the country. Nierenberg was lauded for creating and maintaining a strong employee focus and for the company's thorough training programs for permanent and temporary employees. Each permanent employee benefited from regular internal training courses and a $500 allocation for their own education. Even temporary employees were flown in to the home office from all over the country for a weeklong training program.

Rewarding and affirming employees for their work had long been a pattern at the agency. Since the firm opened, Nierenberg and partner Beckstrom had a philosophy of empowering, motivating, and listening to their talented cadre of employees. They also recognized and rewarded employees' contributions to the success of the agency. In addition to the $1,000 bonuses, incentive trips to places such as Cancun or Jamaica were awarded.

Key Dates:

1995: Brad Nierenberg and Brad Beckstrom create Momentum Marketing Services Corporation.
2001: Momentum receives *Promo* magazine's Top PRO Award for Best Overall Campaign.
2002: Momentum is ranked among *Inc.* magazine's list of the fastest growing companies.
2003: Momentum shifts headquarters to Alexandria, Virginia.
2004: Nierenberg is cited by *Fortune Small Business* as one of the 15 ''Best Bosses'' in the country.
2005: Momentum is renamed RedPeg Marketing.

An example of the agency founder's focus on employees was noted in the online publication *Winning Workplaces.* ''When the company decided to move to new office space, [Nierenberg] not only took recommendations for locations, he sat down with a list of his employees' addresses and mapped out where everyone lived to help find a building that was closest to the most people.'' In the new Alexandria office, there were no cubicles. Each employee got to choose the paint and furnishings for his or her office. *Winning Workplaces* described the unusual work environment at Momentum Marketing this way: ''it's the casual culture (including office dogs, a retractable garage door conference room, and a Heineken phone booth) that make it fun to come to work.'' Not surprisingly, the agency's employee turnover was low. Most new hires get their foot in the door through in-house staff referrals.

2005: Renaming and Rebranding

In early 2005, Momentum Marketing Services announced that it was officially changing its name to RedPeg Marketing. Another, larger advertising agency, Momentum Worldwide, had acquired an event company a few years earlier, which had resulted in confusion because both agencies were doing similar kinds of work. Momentum Marketing did not always get credit for work it had done. Those in the field called them Big Mo and Little Mo. In addition, some 20 other agencies had ''Momentum'' somewhere in their names. Nierenberg explained one reason for the new company name to industry publication *Promo Magazine*, ''When you have to go into a pitch and explain that you're not that other agency, it's a bad place to start.''

The name change was not only about renaming, but also rebranding. It was the result of two years of research, evaluation, design, and planning, and sifting through 300 proposed names and 100 logos. The name ''RedPeg'' refers to the red pegs used in the game ''Battleship'' when a player directly hits the opponent's ship. The new logo resembled those red pegs. ''It stands for strategy, precision and impact,'' Nierenberg explained. ''To hit the right consumer in the right place with the right interaction or message? That's a direct hit,'' Nierenberg told *Promo.*

RedPeg received additional industry recognition in early 2005 when *Event Marketer* gave it ''Ex Awards'' for two promotional campaigns. The company received a gold award in the category of Best Activation of an Entertainment Sponsorship for the Rock Boat campaign for Miller Brewing Company.

RedPeg was a silver winner in the category of Best Multi-Venue/Market Event for a Local Market Activation campaign for America Online.

The agency also moved up to number 23 on *Promo*'s list of the top agencies from 2002 to 2004. RedPeg's net revenues increased 151 percent, to $7.7 million, mostly due to work for current clients including AOL, Ryan Partnership, Kobrand, and Bacardi. New clients in 2004 included Miller Brewing Company and Geico.

2005 and Beyond

RedPeg's leaders recognized that its original formula of hand-to-hand promotional experiences created awareness while also being entertaining and fun. Competition in the event marketing arena was increasing as traditional advertising agencies realized that they were missing out on event and promotional planning. RedPeg had been a pioneer in ''Emotional Touch Point Marketing,'' making brands personal and placing companies and their products in the ''hands, heads and hearts'' of targeted consumers.

RedPeg Marketing had been on a steady growth curve since its inception. As of 2005, about 75 percent of the agency's business was event marketing. The company expected growth to continue, and planned to open offices in Los Angeles and Chicago, bringing staff size to 70 or more. In 2004, RedPeg's billings reached $20 million. The company's goal was to see that figure reach $50 million by 2010.

Principal Competitors

GMR Marketing; Pierce Promotions; Einson Freeman, Inc.; Modeme Promotions, Inc.; The Promotions Dept.

Further Reading

''Anatomy of a Promo: The Art of the Drip; Momentum Marketing Really Knows How to Lose a Wallet,'' *Promo Magazine*, http://www.promomagazine.com, February 1, 2002.
De Marco, Donna, ''Name Change Defines RedPeg,'' *Washington Times: Business,* February 14, 2005.
''In Depth: Advertising and Marketing,'' *Washington Business Journal*, May 6, 2005.
Johannes, Amy, ''Live from PROMO EXPO: Lasting Connections Through Experiential Marketing,'' *Promo Magazine*, http://www.promomagazine.com, November 17, 2004.
Lohr, Greg, ''Momentum Motors into Alexandria,'' *Washington Business Journal*, April 4, 2003.
''Momentum Marketing Services Corp.; Empowerment and Shared Success Bolster Business and Employee Satisfaction,'' *Winning Workplaces*, http://www.winningworkplaces.org.
Parry, Tim, ''Road Trip,'' *Promo Magazine*, http://www.promomagazine.com, August 1, 2004.
Spethmann, Betsy, ''Agency Aliases,'' *Promo Magazine,* http://www.promomagazine.com, February 1, 2005.
Spragins, Ellyn, ''The Acting Coach: Brad Nierenberg, Momentum Marketing Services, Alexandria, Va.,'' *Fortune Small Business*, October 1, 2004, p. 40.
''Top 25 Agencies,'' *Promo Magazine*, http://www.promomagazine.com, June 1, 2005.
Watson, Ashley, *Ithaca College Alumni Magazine*, April 26, 2005.

—Mary Heer-Forsberg

Rocky Mountain Chocolate Factory, Inc.

265 Turner Drive
Durango, Colorado 81303
U.S.A.
Telephone: (970) 259-0554
Toll Free: (888) 525-2462
Fax: (970) 259-5895
Web site: http://www.rmcf.com

Public Company
Incorporated: 1982
Employees: 185
Sales: $23.6 million (2004)
Stock Exchanges: NASDAQ
Ticker Symbol: RMCF
NAIC: 311330 Confectionery Manufacturing from
    Purchased Chocolate; 311340 Nonchocolate
    Confectionery Manufacturing

Rocky Mountain Chocolate Factory, Inc. (RMCF) is a leading chain of confectionery stores. The company has about 300 retail locations in the United States (concentrated primarily on the West Coast and in the Sun Belt), Canada, Guam, and the United Arab Emirates, and a 53,000-square-foot factory near Durango, Colorado. The retail stores are typically located in tourist areas or factory outlet malls; all but a handful are franchised. Unable to find a suitable shipper, the company has built its own fleet of brown and bronze refrigerated semis. The factory produces 300 types of candies, and retail stores also produce a number of hand-dipped items using traditional methods. The best-selling items are caramel apples, followed by "Bears" (turtles). One key to the company's success is the experience of many of the confections being whipped up at the stores. Marketing Executive Ed Dudley described it this way in the *Rocky Mountain News:* "Because all of your senses are engaged, it's about giving the customer a five- to 10-minute vacation."

Creating a Sweet Job in Colorado

The Rocky Mountain Chocolate Factory (RMCF) was built around a location and a lifestyle. Franklin E. Crail had owned a thriving company in Newport Beach, California, that produced billing software for the cable TV industry (CNI Data Processing, Inc.). But he and his wife wanted to raise a family in a small town. They settled in Durango, Colorado, where Crail prospected for an entrepreneurial niche. "It came down to either a car wash or a chocolate shop," he says in the company's official history.

Frank Crail later told *Candy Industry* he would have been content to open a See's Candy store, but the California company did not franchise. Instead, he enlisted two partners and opened the first RMCF shop on Durango's Main Street on Memorial Day, 1981. The town was something of a tourist attraction, known for its scenic railroad and outdoor recreation. Many future stores also would be opened in vacation spots in order to be close to a large volume of traffic.

The stores themselves became tourist attractions in their own right, with much of the confection-making process on display. Trademarks included hand-dipped caramel apples and fresh fudge, heated in copper kettles and cooled on a 500-pound marble slab. The selection was staggering, with some stores offering 30 kinds of apples, ranging from basic caramel to a gourmet white chocolate and Oreo masterpiece. Wholesale chocolate was sourced from Burlingame, California's Guittard Chocolate Company and other suppliers.

True to its rugged mountain origins, RMCF became known for its big, chunky portions. One of its peanut butter cups was large enough to be called the "Bucket." The chocolate also won awards for taste.

The venture was successful from the start. Although tourist traffic was strong in the summer, locals shopped for gifts for Christmas and Valentine's Day. Crail's partners opened other stores in Breckenridge and Boulder, Colorado, within a year.

The first franchised stores were opened in 1982 in Colorado Springs and Park City, Utah. Crail later told *ColoradoBiz* that the typical franchisee was a professional who wanted to set out upon a second career in a small, family-oriented town, much as Crail himself had done.

An off-site chocolate factory also was opened in 1982, and Rocky Mountain Chocolate Factory, Inc. was incorporated in November of that year. Crail's two partners left the business in 1983.

Company Perspectives:

Frank Crail had a dream to raise a family in a quiet, small town environment. Not having a plan to support his dream in Durango, Colorado, the quaint Victorian-era town in which they had chosen to settle, he began surveying the town's local residents and merchants. "It came down to either a car wash or a chocolate shop," recalls the father of seven. "I think I made the right choice." Today, a shop still stands on Main Street, with its sights and smells tempting tourists and locals alike to experience a cornucopia of chocolatey treats. . . .

Key Dates:

1981: Rocky Mountain Chocolate Factory (RMCF) is founded by the family of Frank Crail.
1982: The first franchised stores open.
1986: RMCF goes public on the NASDAQ.
1997: RMCF restructures to focus on franchising.
2001: The company logo, packaging, and new store interiors are updated.
2002: The kiosk concept is developed.
2005: The company pays off all outstanding debt.

Public in 1986

Crail took the company public on the NASDAQ in February 1986. Revenues were about $4.1 million for fiscal 1985–86, up more than 10 percent, though the loss tripled to $146,706. The loss increased to $1.8 million in fiscal 1986–87, when revenues were up to $4.5 million. The company then had 55 stores in 13 states.

Revenues rose 14 percent to $5 million in the fiscal year ended February 28, 1991, and net income slipped to $520,006 from $637,385. Ten of about 64 stores had closed, but the company was opening a handful of new ones. RMCF tested a mail-order catalog for Christmas 1991.

The company posted a loss of $34,000 in 1992 but soon recovered. Revenues were up to $13.6 million by 1995, with net income of $1.3 million. *Chain Store Age* pronounced RMCF founder Frank Crail one of its Entrepreneurs of the Year for 1995. A survey in *Money* magazine rated the company's chocolates superior to those from established chocolatiers such as Godiva and Fanny May.

By 1996, RMCF was making about two million pounds of candy a year. Revenues were $18.7 million. It had 350 employees, including 125 at the main factory. There were 162 stores, 45 of which were company-owned, from San Francisco, California, to Hilton Head Island, South Carolina. The company had opened a side venture, FuzziWig's, which sold hard candy (outsourced) for children at five locations.

In the summer of 1996, RMCF created a seven-foot, 430-pound white chocolate alligator for display at the San Francisco Zoo. The replica had more than one million calories and was worth $6,000, reported *Candy Industry*. Miniature versions were available for purchase.

Retooling in the Late 1990s

There were a couple of major refinements to RMCF's formula in the late 1990s. Most of the company-owned retail operations were closed or sold to franchises, allowing RMCF to focus on franchising and manufacturing. Nine stores were closed in 1997; the restructuring led to a full-year loss of $1.2 million. The company also was automating some of its factory operations after years of making almost everything by hand.

Kansas City, Missouri chocolate giant Whitman's Candies Inc., a unit of Russell Stover Candies Inc., made an offer to buy

RMCF for around $16 million in 1999 but was rebuffed by management after RMCF's operating results improved later in the year.

With 125 employees in Durango, Rocky Mountain Chocolate Factory was the town's largest manufacturer, according to *ColoradoBiz*. It still had 34 company-owned stores. RMCF signed a franchisee in the United Arab Emirates in 2000.

New Look in 2001

A new logo and revitalized packaging were introduced in time for the Christmas 2001 season. Sleek new copper gift boxes were designed to reinforce the association with the copper cooking kettles. The stores were modernized as well. The company's logo was meant to represent swirling chocolate. Only 10 percent of sales stemmed from purchases of gifts, and the company was focusing on increasing that, COO Bryan Merryman told the *Rocky Mountain News*.

The product line expanded to include no-sugar-added and sugar-free candies. Factory-made products accounted for half of store sales, according to *Confectioner*; store-made products accounted for another 40 percent, with the remainder coming from other manufacturers. A new factory-made product developed between 2000 and 2002 was a line of licensed chocolates based on the *I Love Lucy* television show.

The retail concept was being modernized and upgraded to a more high-end feel, noted *Confectioner*. By this time, there were 204 stores in the United States, plus 23 in Canada and two in the United Arab Emirates. Of these, only four stores in Colorado were company owned; all the rest were franchised. Distribution had expanded to home shopping channels, FAO Schwartz stores, and Costco warehouse clubs.

In February 2002, the company introduced a 250-square-foot kiosk concept for areas where a traditional 1,000-square-foot shop was not feasible. The compact site did include a cooking area. A 125-square-foot kiosk also was developed. These allowed RMCF to open stores in very expensive malls.

RMCF's annual revenues were $19.4 million in 2002. The company was opening more than two dozen stores a year. Stores cost franchisees an average of $175,000 each to open and were averaging $300,000 to $350,000 in sales per year.

RMCF posted net income of $3.1 million on revenues of $23.6 million in the 2004 calendar year. The company had 285 locations in the United States, Canada, Guam, and the United Arab Emirates. *Fortune* magazine dubbed RMCF one of "America's 100 Fastest-Growing Small Public Companies." RMCF was planning to open between 40 and 50 units per year, an executive told CNBC.

Revenues rose to $24.5 million in the fiscal year ended February 2005, producing net income of $3.3 million. "We were borrowing a little bit here, a little bit there, paying 24, 30 percent in interest rates, whatever it took," Crail told *Candy Industry* of the RMCF's cash-strapped early days. Those days were long gone by June 2005, when the company announced that it had paid off all of its outstanding debt and had another $2 million in the bank.

Principal Competitors

Alpine Confections, Inc.; Godiva Chocolatier Inc.; See's Candies, Inc.

Further Reading

"Alligator Weighs in with 58,000 Grams of Fat, One Million Calories," *Candy Industry,* August 1996, p. 16.

Berta, Dina, "Lucy's Heir Loves Durango Chocolatier; Rocky Mountain Factory to Launch Candy Based on Famous '50s Show," *Rocky Mountain News* (Denver), April 11, 2000, p. 1B.

——, "Rocky Mountain Chocolate Factory Makes Sweet Deal with Lucy's Line," *Rocky Mountain News* (Denver), May 14, 2000, p. 9G.

Brand, Rachel, "Durango Chocolate Chain Upbeat; 20-Year-Old Firm Plans 10 New Concept Stores by the End of This Year," *Rocky Mountain News* (Denver), August 3, 2001, p. 4B.

——, "Selling an Experience; New Trend in Retailing Draws Customers in, Brings Them Back, Proponents Say," *Rocky Mountain News* (Denver), December 10, 2000.

——, "Store Makeovers Draw Customers; Chocolate Retailer Spruces Up Outlets, Enjoys Sweet Sound of Ringing Registers," *Rocky Mountain News* (Denver), November 30, 2001, p. 4B.

"CEO Interview: Bryan Merryman—Rocky Mountain Chocolate Factory Inc. (RMCF)," *Wall Street Transcript Digest,* July 30, 2001.

"CEO Interview: Bryan Merryman—Rocky Mountain Chocolate Factory Inc. (RMCF)," *Wall Street Transcript Digest,* April 29, 2002.

Dudley, Rebecca, "Chocolate Factory Is a Sweet Deal," *Wenatchee Business Journal,* February 2002, p. B6.

Everly, Steve, "Whitman's Withdraws Offer for Durango, Colo.-Based Candy Retailer," *Knight Ridder/Tribune Business News,* November 2, 1999.

"Frank Crail: Chairman of the Board, Rocky Mountain Chocolate Factory," *Chain Store Age,* Retail Entrepreneurs of the Year, December 1995, p. 90.

"Fuzziwig's Creates Candyland," *Chain Store Age,* October 1996, pp. 74 +.

Goldberg, Bruce, and K.C. Keefer, "Candy a Dandy Colorado Business," *Colorado Business Magazine,* September 1996, pp. 56 +.

Govoni, Steve, "Sweet Success," *Financial World,* May 13, 1986, p. 6.

"History of Rocky Mountain Chocolate Factory: One Man's Dream Makes for Smiles and a Sweet Opportunity," Durango, Colo.: Rocky Mountain Chocolate Factory, Inc., 2003.

Kruger, Renée Marisa, "Rocky Mountain Chocolate High: Operating As Manufacturer and Retailer/Franchiser, Rocky Mountain Chocolate Factory Is Taking Its Brand to New Heights of Passion," *Confectioner,* September 2002, pp. 8 +.

Lewis, Pete, "Chocolate Thunder," *ColoradoBiz,* March 2000, pp. 18 +.

Locke, Tom, Christopher Wood, Garrison Wells, and L. Wayne Hicks, "Chocolatier Opening New Stores," *Denver Business Journal,* August 2, 1991, p. 10.

Parker, Penny, "Chocolate-Maker Chains FuzziWig's," *Denver Post,* July 30, 1996.

"Rocky Mountain Shows Loss," *Candy Industry,* May 1997, p. 11.

Sinanoglu, Elif, "We Grade the Top Chocolates (Tough Work, Eh?)," *Money,* February 1995, p. 171.

Tiffany, Susan, "Rocky Mountain Chocolate Factory Celebrates 15 'Beary' Good Years," *Candy Industry,* August 1996, pp. 24 +.

Whitney, Daisy, "Top 100: Rocky Mountain Chocolate Factory; Candy Firm's Sweet Deal; Franchising Lifts Durango Business," *Denver Post,* August 12, 2001, p. D16.

—Frederick C. Ingram

RONA, Inc.

220 Chenin du Tremblay
Boucherville, Quebec J4B 8H7
Canada
Telephone: (514) 599-5100
Fax: (514) 599-5110
Web site: http://www.rona.ca

Public Company
Incorporated: 1939 as Les Marchands en Quincaillerie
   Ltee.
Employees: 16,000
Sales: CAD 4.5 billion (2004)
Stock Exchanges: Toronto
Ticker Symbol: RON
NAIC: 444130 Hardware Stores

RONA, Inc. is Canada's largest retailer of hardware, gardening, and home renovation products. It operates a chain of more than 500 stores across Canada, with its largest concentration in Quebec and Ontario. RONA runs a mix of retail outlets, with some so-called "big box" stores, many more traditionally sized hardware stores, and various specialized stores. As well as the mix of sizes, RONA has a mix of company-owned stores, franchises, and affiliated stores. The chain has grown quickly in the 2000s through a series of acquisitions. RONA was hard pressed to distinguish itself from the other major player in the Canadian hardware market, U.S.-based Home Depot, and the company evolved some unusual retailing concepts borrowed from other successful chains such as The Gap and Starbucks. RONA began as a cooperative, and this governing structure endured until it became a public company in 2002. RONA Inc. is the sole North American member of the European buying group ARENA and is a partner in a U.S.-Canadian buying pool called Alliance International LLC.

Quebec Cooperative in the 1940s–60s

RONA was founded in 1939 as a buying group of 30 Quebec hardware stores. The hardware market still remains highly frag-mented in Canada, with more than half the market share divided between numerous tiny independent retailers. In 1939, one monopoly company had a chokehold on hardware supplies, and Quebec's small retailers needed a way to fight back. The 30 Quebec hardware owners wished to remain independent operators, yet band together to combine their purchasing power. The owners affiliated in a group initially named Les Marchands en Quincaillerie Ltee. The group's first presidents were Rolland Dansereau and Napoleon Piotte. These men remained active directors in the Les Marchands group through the 1960s.

After World War II, the hardware industry in Canada underwent rapid change. Discount department store chains such as Savette, Woolco, and Towers began encroaching on markets long served by small independent stores. Between 1955 and 1965, some 1,000 hardware stores across the country closed down, unable to compete with the new chains. This prompted a new strategy from determined owners. Dansereau and Piotte, who had been with Les Marchands de Quincaillerie since its inception, incorporated a new entity in 1960, a private company called Quincaillerie Ro-Na Inc. The "Ro" and "Na" came from the combined first names Roland Dansereau and Napoleon Piotte. Dansereau took the title of president, with Piotte termed the new company's External Relations Agent. Then in 1962, Piotte and a group of hardware store owners acquired Les Marchands de Quincaillerie. This company was then formally set up as a cooperative, with the shareholders all hardware store owners or dealers. This cooperative structure endured all the way until 2002, when the group became a public company.

Through the 1960s, Les Marchands de Quincaillerie and Quincaillerie Ro-Na were closely linked, governed by the same president. When Napoleon Piotte died in 1968, both companies were presided over by Charles Morency. In 1970, the two companies formally merged under the name Marchands Ro-Na Inc. Meanwhile, other hardware store owners in Canada also were setting up cooperatives. In 1964, a coalition of Ontario hardware store owners founded Home Hardware, a dealer-owned cooperative of 122 area stores. The next year, Ro-Na joined with Home Hardware in Ontario, Winnipeg-based cooperative hardware chain Falcon Hardware, and Link Hardware, a cooperative in Calgary, to form a national hardware buying group. This new affiliation was called United Hardware Warehouse. There were in effect two levels of cooperative hardware groups: regional cooperatives such as Ro-Na, and a national cooperative that allowed the regional groups to combine their buying power. On the local level, stores belonging to the Ro-Na group retained their own names.

Building Slowly in the 1970s and 1980s

In 1970 the two affiliated Quincaillerie groups dissolved into one entity called Marchands Ro-Na Inc. Marchands Ro-Na moved into new quarters in 1970, in Boucherville, Quebec. The cooperative made some technical advances at that time, replacing a paper catalog system with files on microfiche. Ro-Na also expanded its deliveries inside the province of Quebec. Distribution and delivery were standardized and streamlined within the province. Yet Ro-Na did not look beyond Quebec at the time. The group confined its business to its home province as part of an unwritten agreement with the other members of the national cooperative, United Hardware Warehouse, to respect each other's territories.

In the 1980s, Ro-Na made purchases and alliances that expanded the variety of stores in its group. In 1982, Ro-Na purchased a chain of gardening stores called Botanix. The next year, Ro-Na premiered a chain of boutique-style interior decorating stores under the name Ambiance Boutique. Now what had been strictly a hardware chain had branched out into two related areas. In 1988, Ro-Na acquired a building materials cooperative group called Dismat. At this time the company changed its name to Ro-Na Dismat. By the late 1980s, the Ro-Na group contained all of the elements—hardware, gardening, interior decorating, and lumber—that would soon be brought under one roof by the so-called "big box" retailers.

The trend in the 1980s seemed to be toward bigger stores and bigger chains. Ro-Na's sister cooperative Home Hardware also expanded in the 1980s, buying a 55-store chain in the west of the country. Home Hardware and Ro-Na reinforced their ties in 1984, forming a new allied company called Alliance RONA Home Inc. Ro-Na and Home Hardware were still members of the national cooperative, United Hardware Warehouse. By 1990, this national group included some 1,000 Canadian hardware merchants. The Canadian group joined with a Fort Wayne, Indiana-based group of U.S. hardware merchants in 1990, forming a new group called Alliance International.

Bringing on the Big Boxes in the 1990s

The hardware industry in Canada's southern neighbor was put through a major change in the 1980s with the advent of Home

Depot, a company founded in Atlanta, Georgia, in 1978. Home Depot pioneered the big-box format, putting vast, warehouse-like stores down on the edges of suburban areas, and selling a huge array of hardware products, paint, lumber, garden supplies, and nursery plants under one roof. By the late 1980s, Home Depot was a high-flying stock on Wall Street, and the company had plastered its domestic market with stores. Home Depot entered the Canadian market in 1994 by acquiring an Ontario chain called Aikenhead's Home Improvement Warehouse. Because of an agreement with Aikenhead's parent company, Home Depot did not enter the Quebec market until 1998. Thus much of the fiercest competition between Home Depot and Canadian rivals occurred first in Ontario. While Ro-Na's longtime sister company Home Hardware continued with small and medium-sized stores, other Canadian chains, such as Surrey, British Columbia-based Revy Home Centres, Inc., moved into the densely populated suburban Toronto area with football-field sized big-box stores, sometimes building them right across the street from Home Depot. Ro-Na paid close attention to the happenings in Ontario while staying in Quebec. It rolled out its own big-box stores (which the company called "large surface" stores) in Quebec beginning in 1994, under the name RONA L'entrepot. These were warehouse-sized stores, but Ro-Na Dismat hoped to distinguish them from the competition by continuing to offer a high level of customer service.

Canada's economy was doing well in the 1990s, and home improvement was a flourishing business. With the entrance of Home Depot into the country, the several large Canadian chains such as Ro-Na, Home Hardware, Revy, and Montreal-based Reno-Depot Inc. were forced to come up with a strategy that would let them maintain market share. Ro-Na Dismat made a decision to grow larger through acquisition. In 1997, it accepted an investment of $30 million from the French hardware chain ITM Enterprises, to bankroll acquisitions. ITM took partial ownership of Ro-Na, though the company retained its cooperative structure. Ro-Na had total sales of more than $700 million that year. In 1998, the company changed its name to RONA, Inc. It opened some new stores under the names RONA L'express and RONA L'express Materiaux, and made its first foray into the Ontario big-box battlefield with a 145,000-square-foot large-surface store in a suburb of Ottawa. By 1999, RONA had almost 500 stores under various banners in eastern Canada, and sales had risen to $2.1 billion.

Acquisitions in the 2000s

RONA moved quickly in the 2000s, acquiring smaller chains that gave it a coast-to-coast presence. It equaled or surpassed Home Depot in market share, while taking care to make its stores noticeably different from the American competitor. The lesson of the Canadian hardware industry in the 1990s seemed to be adapt or fail. For example, between 1993 and 2001, 34 big-box stores opened in the Toronto area, while 117 traditional-sized stores closed. Industry analysts expected that the largest Canadian chains would have to consolidate in order to combat Home Depot. RONA began buying. In 2000 the company spent $50 million on a chain of 66 Ontario hardware stores called Cashway Building Centres. The following year, the company sold shares to two Quebec pension funds, Caisse de Depot et Placement and SGF, and let the French firm ITM

Key Dates:

1939: Quebec hardware retailers band together as Les Marchands en Quincaillerie Ltee.
1960: Quincaillerie Ro-Na Inc. is founded.
1970: Two firms combine as Marchands Ro-Na Inc.
1982: The company acquires Botanix.
1988: Dismat is acquired.
1994: The company opens the first RONA big-box store in Quebec.
1997: ITM Enterprises buys a partial share in Ro-Na.
1998: The name is changed to RONA, Inc.
2002: The company goes public.
2003: The company buys Reno-Depot.

invest still more, giving RONA another $100 million to spend. With this much cash in hand, RONA bought a chain based in British Columbia called Revy Home Centres. The Revy purchase cost $220 million, and it brought RONA 51 big boxes in Ontario and a chain of stores called Lansing Buildall. For the first time, RONA's territory expanded all the way to the West Coast. The purchase also lifted RONA's total revenue to a level on par with Home Depot Canada.

RONA's stores were consciously different from the blueprint Home Depot brought to the industry. Although many of RONA's new stores used the ''large surface'' format, they were not the stark warehouse design of its competitors. According to a profile of the company in the *Toronto Star* (March 10, 2001), RONA wanted to ''take the warehouse out of the warehouse concept.'' Instead, its stores would offer an enticing shopping experience explained by one RONA spokesman in the *Star* article as ''Disney meets home improvement.'' To advance this concept, RONA used ideas that it found at other successful chains. Its paint departments were modeled in one sense on the coffee shop chain Starbucks. Customers could step into the ''paint café'' and have a clerk pour them a paint sample to take home and test. Sales clerks also wore radio headsets for communication, an idea attributed to the clothing chain The Gap. RONA did not set up its big boxes in long aisles, but broke the interior into several stores within a store. The company also strove foremost to please women consumers, who made the majority of home improvement buying decisions, offering decorating items including mirrors and picture frames. The trend toward so-called ''soft do-it-yourself'' products was particularly strong in Europe, and RONA was a leader in presenting soft do-it-yourself in Canada. However, not all RONA's stores were big boxes, and about half its sales still came from small and medium-sized stores.

In 2002, the company prepared to make a public stock offering. Its market share had grown from 7 percent in 1999 to 11 percent, putting it in third place behind Home Depot, with 14 percent, and the Toronto-based Canadian Tire, at 12 percent. It now had coast-to-coast exposure, though it still ran stores under many names, and the RONA brand had the strongest resonance in Quebec. RONA, Inc. debuted on the Toronto Stock Exchange in October 2002. The company was a public corporation, and it set aside its cooperative structure. In 2003 RONA made another

large acquisition, buying Reno-Depot for $350 million. Reno-Depot was known for its big-box stores in eastern Canada.

After the Reno-Depot purchase, RONA and Home Depot stood alone as the two biggest contenders in the Canadian hardware market. Half the market was still shared by small independent hardware stores, and the Home Hardware cooperative and Canadian Tire also had a good slice of the market. However, RONA had succeeded in the fierce battle set off by Home Depot's entry into Canada in 1994, and it now equaled the American giant in Canadian market share. RONA's task in the 2000s was to build its brand. In 2004, the company announced that it would boost its market share from around 14 percent to 25 percent over the next three years. Its strategy was to have stores in every segment of the market. It would continue to open large-surface stores as well as small neighborhood stores. The company pulled together its image somewhat in the mid-2000s, attaching RONA to the name of all of its stores. There was still a variety of names in use, however, such as RONA Botanix, RONA Lansing, and RONA Home Centres, reflecting the origins of the companies that had combined. In Quebec, where RONA had a market share of more than 40 percent, the company gained more exposure through a television show called *Ma Maison Rona*. The show, which was a number one hit in Quebec, pitted families against each other in a home renovation competition. Not only did RONA show ads at the beginning and ending of each episode, but the show featured much footage of the competitors shopping at RONA stores and conferring with RONA design experts, and viewers could log on to an Internet link with the show to vote for favorites as well as ask questions about hardware and remodeling.

RONA seemed to be reaping the benefits of its acquisitions. It ended 2004 with record sales and profits. It continued to open new stores, but same-store sales, a key measure of sales growth at stores open at least one year, was up by more than 10 percent in 2004. This showed that RONA was doing well even without acquisitions and new stores. The company did continue to acquire, as well. In 2005 it spent $100 million on a chain of building supply stores in Alberta, Totem Building Supplies. Totem ran 14 retail stores and two stores just for contractors. Its annual sales were estimated at $260 million. Totem's location was crucial to RONA, doubling its retail outlets in Alberta, Canada's fastest-growing province.

Principal Competitors

Home Depot Canada, Inc.; Home Hardware Stores Ltd.; Canadian Tire Corporation, Ltd.

Further Reading

Brown, Mark, ''Identity Crisis,'' *Canadian Business,* March 17, 2003, p. 18.
''Building Supply Firm Still a Buyer,'' *Toronto Star,* May 11, 2005, p. E08.
Chilton, David, ''Ma Maison Rona,'' *Marketing Magazine,* December 1, 2003, p. 20.
Flavelle, Dana, ''Home-Improvement Dreams,'' *Toronto Star,* April 7, 2004, p. E01.
——, ''Rona Lumbers Back to Market,'' *Toronto Star,* May 14, 2003, p. E03.

Jenish, D'arcy, "The War for Your Home," *Maclean's,* October 16, 2000, p. 54.

Kucharsky, Danny, "Rona Wants to Build Stronger Image," *Marketing Magazine,* March 24, 2003, p. 3.

"Rona Builds Record Profits on Acquisitions," *Toronto Star,* February 24, 2005, p. D18.

Taylor, Peter Shawn, "Home Fires Burning," *Canadian Business,* October 11, 2004, p. 76.

Theobald, Steven, "Quebec's Rona Cobbles Together National Chain," *Toronto Star,* September 25, 2001, p. BU03.

——, "Rona Jumps into Big-Box Battle," *Toronto Star,* March 10, 2001, p. BU01.

—A. Woodward

Royal Group Technologies Limited

1 Royal Gate Boulevard
Woodbridge, Ontario L4L 8Z7
Canada
Telephone: (905) 264-0701
Fax: (905) 264-0702
Web site: http://www.royalgrouptech.com

Public Company
Incorporated: 1970 as Royal Plastics Group Limited
Employees: 9,000
Sales: $1.52 billion (2004)
Stock Exchanges: New York
Ticker Symbol: RYG
NAIC: 326122 Plastics Pipe and Pipe Fitting
　Manufacturing

Royal Group Technologies Limited is a Canadian manufacturer of polymer-based products primarily used in the home building, home renovation, and construction fields. Although most of its business is conducted in Canada and the United States, Royal is a global company, with additional operations located in South America, Europe, and Asia. Home building and renovation products include siding, roofing, window frames, and patio doors, and construction products include pipe and fittings systems and commercial doors. Royal also offers consumer products such as decking, sheds, shutters, furniture, and some housewares. In addition, the company is involved in component-based home construction through its patented Royal Buildings Systems, which uses hollow polymer panels that are fitted together and filled with concrete to produce a highly durable structure requiring little maintenance. The houses have found a market around the world, especially in developing countries. Royal is vertically integrated, capable of producing most of its raw materials and tools in addition to final products. The company is publicly traded, listed on the New York Stock Exchange.

Founder a 1960s Immigrant

The man behind the birth of Royal was Vic De Zen, a man of Dutch heritage who was born in 1941 in a small town near Venice, Italy. He grew up working on his family's farm, but even as a child, he claimed, he knew that he would make his life across the Atlantic Ocean. As a teenager he learned the tool-and-die craft as an apprentice in Italy, but jobs were scarce in the country and in the late 1950s he had to travel to Switzerland to find work as a tool-and-die maker. Two older brothers moved to Canada, and when he was 20 he decided to join them, borrowing money from an aunt to pay for the airfare for himself and his new bride, Angelina. With just $20 in his pocket, he wasted little time in getting to work. According to a story that has become company lore, De Zen got off the plane in Toronto at five in the evening in November 1962 and within the hour was installing television antennas with his brothers who had set up a business installing storm windows, storm doors, and antennas. Although well trained in the tool-and-die craft, he had trouble finding work in the field because of his inability to speak English. In 1995 De Zen recounted his frustration in a *Canadian Business* profile: "At one point, De Zen took an interpreter into a company with him. 'I said, 'Give me the drawing, give me the steel and the machine. If I cannot make the piece, I'll pay for it,' De Zen shakes his head in recollection. 'He said, 'No. You don't know the language, no job for you.' ''

For five years De Zen supported his family doing manual labor. Finally, in 1967, he was hired by Pillar Plastics Ltd., a small Toronto company. Rather than create plastic shapes from molds, it extruded plastic through a die, the so-called "Black Art" of plastic manufacturing. The *Financial Post* in 1994 described it as "not a pretty business," comparing it with meat going through a grinder: "Extrusion is, however, a highly precise art that demands acute skills and expensive machinery. It involves patience, precision and luck, because every single piece must be an exact clone of its predecessor. So there's a fine line separating a valuable strip of extruded plastic from a useless piece of plastic goop." Building a reputation as an expert tool-and-die craftsman, capable of fashioning virtually any shape out of plastic, De Zen quickly became the key to Pillar's success.

It was during his time at Pillar that De Zen first became involved with plastic houses, for years the goal of many plastic extruders. During the 1950s Monsanto Chemical stoked the dream by displaying a plastic house at a trade show. De Zen did work for a pair of companies creating dies for use in making parts for a plastic house, but both pulled out of the projects, which De Zen considered a mistake. He never forgot the idea, however, and he revisited it 20 years later.

De Zen soon grew disenchanted with Pillar's management: One Christmas his bonus totaled just $2. Management belatedly recognized his valuable contribution and eventually offered him a 10 percent stake in the business only to renege on the promise. Infuriated, De Zen decided to launch his own business, but not before returning to Europe for a year in 1969 to learn the latest developments in the making of dies for vinyl extrusion. Then, in 1970 he joined forces with a pair of fellow immigrants and Pillar employees, Domenic D'Amico and Lorenzo De Meneghi, each of them investing $17,000, although De Zen held a majority stake in the venture. For the name of the new plastic extrusion company, De Zen wanted something to match his ambitions. He considered Imperial Plastics and Monarch Plastics, but because both names were taken he settled on Royal Plastics (the full name becoming Royal Plastics Group Limited).

De Zen acquired Italian-made extruders and cooling devices called vacuum-sizers, worth some CAD 2 million, and set up shop in North York. At the time, European companies dominated the extrusion business, but De Zen's expertise leveled the playing field in terms of quality and Royal's location gave it a pricing edge in the Canadian market. The three-man operation also benefited from the partners' discipline, limiting their own pay to a mere $45 a week. As a result, Royal turned a profit in its first year, posting sales of CAD 273,000 on its first product, PVC weatherstripping. Nevertheless, the partners resisted giving each other a raise. In fact they continued to limit their weekly pay to $45 for another four years.

A major help to Royal's growth was a CAD 250,000 research and development grant from the Canadian government, money the company used to develop technology that essentially reinvented the extrusion process. The Europeans began to turn to Royal to license its cutting-edge technology. Royal also was gaining attention south of the border in the United States, where companies were impressed with both the quality of the product and the price. Royal began importing into the U.S. market in 1973, a watershed moment that marked the beginning of rapid, long-term growth. It was also in 1973 that Royal paid CAD 500,000 to acquire De Zen's former company, Pillar, which had struggled after his departure.

Mid-1970s Expansion

In the mid-1970s Royal began expanding its product offerings in the construction field beyond weatherstripping, becoming the first North American manufacturer to develop PVC window systems. Over the next 15 years a spate of other proprietary products were introduced as well, including garage doors, pipes and gutters, siding, and interior blinds. Aside from his abilities as a master of the Black Art, De Zen also displayed a creative bent for business. According to a 1993 *Forbes* profile, "Royal would grow, then reap some profits; grow, then reap. During the moneymaking phases, De Zen invested some of the profits into commercial and industrial real estate around Toronto, which boomed during the Seventies and Eighties. When it was time to expand Royal again, he would sell property—a selfmade man building a self-financed business the old-fashioned way, out of scrimping, brains and sweat." De Zen also fashioned a structure for the company that enriched his partners while further driving growth. "As his business expanded," as explained by *Forbes,* "he set up plastic extrusion factories throughout Canada, the U.S. and Great Britain and incorporated each one separately, each with different minority partners. In each case, De Zen retained a controlling interest. That puts him at the center of a 'circle' of companies." In this way Royal spawned a collection of small companies. Furthermore, in order to better look after customers, once an account grew large enough Royal would build a dedicated plant and bring in the customer with 50 percent equity. Moreover, De Zen, no doubt remembering his experience at Pillar, made sure to award equity stakes to key employees in the factories they ran. De Zen also proved to be a savvy acquirer of struggling companies. In 1989, for example, Royal tried to buy 35 percent of publicly traded Quebec-based Plastibec Ltd., maker of custom profiles, for $2.20 a share. When that deal fell through, Royal was able six months later to acquire 90 percent of the business for just $1.65 a share. De Zen installed both his corporate structure as well as his patented technology to upgrade the operation, and within two years Plastibec had completed a successful turnaround. Whether home grown or acquired, the Royal collection of companies ran the gamut of the extrusion field, making Royal Group very much a vertically integrated enterprise. About all it needed outside the family was resin and some additives.

During the late 1980s De Zen revisited the dream of developing a commercially viable plastic house. Over the course of the decade both GE Plastics and BF Goodrich had invested millions in the quest, but all they had to show for their efforts were showcase prototypes, not practical products. De Zen proved tenacious in his pursuit of a practical concept, spending $50 million and devoting about five years to the development of a plastic house. Royal's plastic house relied on interlocking panels and connectors. The hollow sections were then filled with concrete to provide stability, while the exterior could be covered with any number of materials, such as brick or stucco. Construction was quick, taking three people using common hand tools just three days to put up a 500-square-foot house, a vast improvement over the months a conventional house required. The marriage of plastic and concrete offered another benefit: the houses tended to stay cool in the summer and warm in the winter. Furthermore, they were virtually maintenance free, impervious to rot, mold, mildew, and insects. The first Royal plastic house was constructed in Germany in 1991 and found ready markets in the Caribbean and Latin America. The structures soon proved their sturdiness, able to ride out hurricane-force winds and major earthquakes while wooden

<table>
<tr><td colspan="2">

Key Dates:
</td></tr>
<tr><td>**1970:**</td><td>Royal Plastics Group Limited is founded by Vic De Zen and two partners.</td></tr>
<tr><td>**1973:**</td><td>The company begins exporting to the United States.</td></tr>
<tr><td>**1991:**</td><td>The first plastic house is constructed.</td></tr>
<tr><td>**1994:**</td><td>The company is taken public.</td></tr>
<tr><td>**1997:**</td><td>The name is changed to Royal Group Technologies Limited.</td></tr>
<tr><td>**2004:**</td><td>Top management is forced out.</td></tr>
</table>

buildings were devastated. Within three years Royal plastic houses, schools, churches, factories, and medical centers were to be found in more than 40 countries, and were especially popular following such natural disasters as hurricanes and earthquakes when speed of construction to replace destroyed buildings was at a premium. As De Zen had always done, Royal spun off separate companies wherever there was strong demand for the housing system. Although there was a limited demand for such structures in Canada and the United States, Royal still found a use for the technology. In January 1995 the company launched a joint venture with Rubbermaid Incorporated, creating Royal Rubbermaid Structures Ltd. to make and market modular consumer storage sheds. Utilizing the same kind of interlocking plastic panels, the sheds could be put up by a lone person without tools in a matter of a few hours. At the end of 1996 Royal bought out Rubbermaid's share of the business.

Strong Growth in the 1990s

De Zen took Royal public in November 1994, keeping most of the voting stock for himself, more than 80 percent of voting shares as opposed to about 17 percent of equity. The fortunes of the company soared over the next several years, with sales improving from 20 to 25 percent each year. In 1997, in light of its increasing emphasis on technology, the company changed its name to Royal Group Technologies Limited. A year later it cracked CAD 1 billion in annual sales and approached CAD 1.3 billion in 1999. Royal continued to make strategic acquisitions that brought with them new product lines including fencing and decking. The company's research and development efforts also led to the introduction of a bevy of new products, such as wood grain finish siding, PVC window blinds that had the feel of fabric, imitation slate roof tile, and roof tiles and door frames that made used of recycled materials.

However business began to sour somewhat with the start of the 2000s. Royal invested a great deal of money to beef up capacity, but was unable to use it efficiently. It also had to contend with the rising cost of raw materials and the high valuation of the Canadian dollar. The company compounded its problems by consistently downgrading its earnings projections. Investors lost faith and the price of Royal shares dropped from more than $32 in June 2002 to just $7 in March 2003. De Zen did not help improve shareholder relations by accepting a $5.6 million bonus for 2002, which led to a contentious annual meeting and a number of shareholders voicing their anger.

No doubt feeling the pressure, De Zen announced his retirement in November 2003, although he retained 80 percent of the voting rights. The situation only turned grimmer for both De Zen and Royal when word leaked out that the Royal Canadian Mounted Police was launching an investigation to address allegations that De Zen and other executives defrauded shareholders by transferring money in 1998 to the St. Kitts Marriott Resort and the Royal Beach Casino, a luxury Caribbean development controlled by De Zen. In an effort at damage control, the Royal board of directors established a special committee of three independent board members to look into the questionable dealings. Although an outside firm hired to do the investigation found no wrongdoing on the part of the company, it uncovered conduct by executives and a lack of controls that the board found troubling. In November 2004 De Zen as well as CEO Douglas Dunsmuir and CFO Ron Groegan were ousted. According to a company press release, in 1998 a De Zen-owned company bought 185 acres of land for $20 million and immediately sold it to Royal for $27 million. The board neither authorized the sale nor was aware of the details of the transactions.

An interim management team was installed and began the task of rebuilding Royal's stock price and reputation. It remained a very valuable property, as demonstrated by the $1.05 billion bid for the company made by New York money manager Cerberus Capital Management LP in the spring of 2005. De Zen and other shareholders entered into an agreement with Cerberus supporting the offer, making it likely that Royal was about to return to being a private company as it entered a new phase in its history, minus its charismatic founder.

Principal Subsidiaries

Plastibec Ltd.; Novo Industries, Inc.; Novo Europe B.V.

Principal Competitors

Certainteed Corporation; Newell Rubbermaid Incorporated; Nortek Holdings, Inc.

Further Reading

Bianchi, Angela, "The Plastic Kingdom," *Financial Post,* May 1, 1994, p. 31.

Gray, John, "Royal Mess," *Canadian Business,* October 25–November 7, 2004, p. 49.

Heinzi, Mark, "Cerberus Plans $1.05 Billion Bid for Royal Group," *Wall Street Journal,* May 17, 2005, p. B2.

Lane, Randall, " 'I Buy from Someone Else, I Got No Edge,' " *Forbes,* December 20, 1993, p. 110.

Onstad, Katrina, "The Midas Touch," *Canadian Business,* December 1995, p. 40.

Raizel, Robin, "A Royal Ruckus," *Canadian Business,* March 17, 2003, p. 9.

Taylor, Sterling, "Firm Molds Big Profits in Vinyl," *Toronto Star,* April 29, 1986, p. D1.

—Ed Dinger

SEGA Corporation

1-2-12 Haneda, Ohta-ku
Tokyo 144-8531
Japan
Telephone: +81-3-5736-7111
Fax: +81-3-5736-7066
Web site: http://www.sega.co.jp

Wholly Owned Subsidiary of Sega Sammy Holdings Inc.
Incorporated: 1960 as SEGA Enterprises Ltd.
Employees: 814
Sales: $1.81 billion (2004)
NAIC: 511210 Software Publishers; 713120 Amusement
    Arcades; 423920 Toy and Hobby Goods and Supplies
    Merchant Wholesalers

SEGA Corporation is a developer of software and games for personal computers, wireless devices, and video-game consoles. SEGA, which once ranked as one of the largest manufacturers of consoles, exited the market in 2001 and began making games for platforms marketed by Sony, Microsoft, and Nintendo. The company merged with Sammy Corporation in 2004, becoming a subsidiary of Sega Sammy Holdings Inc., the largest gaming software company in Japan.

Origins

For SEGA, success came at a price. The company did not begin to endure years of hardship until it evolved beyond its modest beginnings and stood as a global contender in a fiercely competitive industry. In its rise in the business world, the company earned esteem as a technological pioneer and, for brief periods, it held sway as the best in its class, but, ironically, its prize for achievement was to become ensnared in a market that nearly caused its own collapse. At those moments of the greatest despair, SEGA executives could be forgiven for wanting a return to the simpler days of the company's existence, back to the considerably less troublesome era that began when SEGA sprang from a small Hawaiian company founded in 1940.

Although SEGA was not incorporated until 1960, the company's roots stretched to a Honolulu-based company named Standard Games. SEGA's predecessor spent roughly a decade in Honolulu before moving to Tokyo in 1951, when it was renamed Service Games of Japan, the immediate predecessor of SEGA Enterprises. Once in Tokyo, the company began importing U.S.-made pinball machines. The pinball business marked the beginning of SEGA's involvement in operating arcades, an aspect of the company's business into the 21st century, but the core of the company—and the source of its much publicized troubles—was not created until the 1980s, when SEGA entered the video-game console market.

SEGA Entering the Console Market in the 1980s

The console market was in its nascence when SEGA joined the fray, years away from developing into what would become a more than $7 billion market. It would prove to be a difficult market for all competitors. A quarter-century after SEGA introduced its first console, no company dominated the market for consoles for more than one generation of machines. SEGA made its debut with the launch of an eight-bit console called the Master System in 1984, the same year the company's path crossed with an individual who would play an important role in SEGA's development. Isao Ohkawa, an enormously wealthy financier, founded an information-processing firm named CSK Corp. in 1968, a company that first invested in SEGA in 1984, eventually becoming the company's largest shareholder. SEGA became a publicly traded company in 1986, two years after the introduction of the Master System, debuting on the Tokyo Stock Exchange.

SEGA struggled with its first entry in the cartridge-based console market, but it scored its first and greatest success with its second system. The company unveiled its Genesis console in 1988, introducing a product that represented a technological leap beyond competing systems. Genesis was built with a 16-bit computer chip, enabling it to provide more colors, faster action, and better sound than existing systems. At the time of Genesis' introduction, Nintendo dominated the industry, controlling the market in Japan and holding an 80 percent market share in the United States. An overwhelming majority of consumers—typically adolescents—were using the company's eight-bit console to play "Mario Bros.," Nintendo's most popular video game, but with Genesis SEGA had a formidable riposte. The

Key Dates:

1940: Standard Games, the earliest predecessor of SEGA, is formed in Honolulu.
1951: Standard Games' operations are moved to Japan.
1960: SEGA Enterprises is incorporated.
1984: SEGA introduces the Master System, its first gaming console.
1988: A second console, Genesis, is introduced.
1994: SEGA's 32-bit system, Saturn, is introduced.
1998: Dreamcast, a 128-bit system with a built-in modem is released.
2001: SEGA decides to exit the console market and concentrate on developing gaming software.
2004: SEGA merges with Sammy Corporation, creating Sega Sammy Holdings Inc.

company's "Sonic the Hedgehog" video game was hugely popular, tied to a 16-bit console that was superior to Nintendo's eight-bit console because it processed twice as much data at a time. To SEGA's further benefit, Nintendo had the capability to introduce a 16-bit console, but the company chose to wait while it milked whatever it could from the eight-bit market. Nintendo waited until the fall of 1991 to introduce its 16-bit system and SEGA took full advantage of the delay, quickly becoming one of the fastest growing companies in Japan.

Genesis gave SEGA a taste of the rewards a dominant console could deliver, whetting its appetite for similar success with its next generation of technology. By the mid-1990s, gaming had advanced to 32-bit consoles, with the competitive race intensifying as technological capabilities advanced. Both the games and the consoles—the software and hardware—were becoming increasingly expensive to produce, requiring vast sums of money and considerable labor to bring to market. SEGA, as it worked on developing its 32-bit console, faced its familiar foe, Nintendo, which had learned its lesson with the belated launch of its NES system, and a new, towering competitor. The industry was abuzz about the expected entry of Sony Corp. in the console market, a company whose enormous wealth and proven technological expertise gave SEGA and Nintendo little room for error. SEGA introduced its 32-bit system, Saturn, in Japan in 1994 and in the United States in mid-1995, but ineffective marketing coupled with a wait-and-see-what-Sony-introduces attitude by consumers doomed Saturn nearly from the start. After much fanfare leading up to the launch, Sony released its 32-bit PlayStation in September 1995 and quickly crushed all competitors. By December 1995, in the midst of the all-important holiday shopping season, PlayStation was outselling Saturn by a ratio of seven-to-one.

The failure of Saturn to capture the interest of gamers delivered a crippling blow to SEGA. The company began to record devastating financial losses, losing hundreds of millions of dollars in the years immediately following the launch of Saturn. Vital financial support was provided by its chairman, Isao Ohkawa, who kept the company alive with cash infusions. The precarious financial state of SEGA put added pressure on the development of the company's next console, whose success or failure likely would determine whether SEGA would survive or not. "We wanted a return match," a SEGA employee remarked in a March 28, 2001 interview with the *Financial Times.* "We said, 'We'll get them next time.'"

Dreamcast Taking Shape in the Late 1990s

Work was underway on the company's next system one year after the U.S. launch of Saturn, a project begun at a meeting in Tokyo's shopping district, Shibuya, in 1996. The project was known to select SEGA employees under the code-name Katana (an ancient Japanese sword), a project that would produce a console known to the public as Dreamcast. As the project progressed, Dreamcast was developed as a 128-bit system with a built-in modem enabling online play and the ability to download supplements to existing software. Other console designers were shying away from developing systems capable of connecting to the Internet, theorizing that widespread broadband connections would be needed to make online gaming perform suitably, but SEGA executives charged ahead. As it turned out, however, the problem was that SEGA executives were not all charging in the same direction. The enormous pressure on the success of Dreamcast led to an extended decision-making process and to bickering among senior executives, setting the company up for another fall, one that had the potential of being fatal.

Between 1996 and 1998, the debates about Dreamcast's development occupied the attention of SEGA's senior management. Executives argued about the specifications of the graphics chip—the heart of a video game console—which represented 70 percent of the cost of a console. "We wasted three months on the chip debate," a SEGA executive said in a March 28, 2001 interview with the *Financial Times.* As management discussed which type of chip to use, memory prices swelled by 40 percent, greatly increasing manufacturing costs. Executives also mulled over whether to add networking capabilities for months, with some arguing that adding a modem would increase the cost of the console beyond the price consumers would pay. Other debates centered on the launch of Dreamcast, a battle fought between those who wanted to introduce the console in Japan first and those who believed it should be introduced first in the United States, the company's second largest market. By 1998, the bickering was over. The 128-bit, modem-equipped Dreamcast debuted in Japan in November 1998 backed by the exuberance of Shoichiro Irimajiri, SEGA's president and the second leader to oversee the Dreamcast project. "We're not really going to compete with Sony or Nintendo," Irimajiri explained in a December 7, 1998 interview with *Business Week.* "We're going to blow them out of the water."

Despite the protracted debates about various matters related to Dreamcast, critics found little wrong with the console. After the September 1999 launch of the system in the United States, American consumers found little wrong with console as well. Within 24 hours, a quarter-million units were sold. Within five days, 400,000 Dreamcasts were sold, double the company's expectations. Irimajiri's tone, however, contained less enthusiasm than during the console's launch in Japan. "If Dreamcast fails, there is no plan B," he told the *Financial Times* in an October 14, 1999, interview. Perhaps some of Irimajiri's hesitance stemmed from two problems that occurred before the console was launched. Because of the delay in providing chip specifications, the development of software for the console was stunted. Further, a week before the launch in Japan, the manufacturer of the graphics chip informed SEGA that it could supply only 25 percent of the requested amount of chips by the launch date. When Dreamcast entered the Japanese market, there were only 200,000 consoles available instead of the expected 600,000. Instead of 15 games being available at the launch, the delay in providing chip specifications limited new Dreamcast owners to an offering of only four games. In Japan, many gamers opted against purchasing Dreamcast, preferring to wait for the much heralded arrival of Sony's PlayStation 2, which boasted more memory and better graphics than Dreamcast.

Poor management again had tripped up SEGA, delivering a stinging blow to an already injured company. SEGA, largely because of Saturn, lost $412 million in 1999, while sales slipped 12 percent to $2.2 billion. In 2000, the company lost $398 million. Irimajiri stepped down as president in May 2000, replaced by Ohkawa, who was watching his 22 percent investment in Saga plummet in value. The company still ranked as the third largest console maker, but its size offered little solace to senior executives. "SEGA is now facing a difficult live-or-die stage," a video game analyst remarked in a July 1, 2000 interview with *AsiaWeek*. "The next year is crucial."

Before the next year was over, SEGA executives made a decision that marked a profound turning point in the history of their company. With Dreamcast failing to deliver expected results and Microsoft preparing for worldwide launch of its console, X-Box, management announced it would exit the console market. Production of Dreamcast systems ended in March 2001, removing what a SEGA spokesman, in a March 7, 2001, interview with *Investor's Business Daily,* described as a "ball and chain around our ankle." Instead of making consoles, SEGA officials decided to develop games for the other consoles, fashioning itself as a third-party software publisher.

After exiting the console business, SEGA officials expressed relief that the long-fought battle in the hardware market was over. The company's losses did not end immediately, however. The cost of ending Dreamcast production resulted in $689 million in extraordinary losses, contributing to another money-losing year in 2002, when the company's revenue volume was half the total generated a decade earlier. In 2003, thanks largely to growth recorded in its arcade equipment business, the company posted its first annual profit in six years, providing an encouraging sign that a turnaround was underway. As the company celebrated a return to profitability, attention turned to the intriguing announcement that a merger was in the works, an announcement that marked the beginning of another SEGA saga.

Merger Discussions in the 21st Century

In March 2001, just as the production of Dreamcast consoles was winding down, Isao Ohkawa died. The senior executives who replaced the founder of CSK began pressing for a merger, seeking to reduce SEGA's mounting debt by aligning their investment with another corporation. Toward this end, SEGA announced in February 2003 that it had agreed to merge with Sammy Corporation, the largest manufacture of pachinko machines in Japan. The merger was set to be completed in October 2003, when Sammy would gain entry into the game-publishing

business in the United States and SEGA would receive the financial help it needed. Within weeks, SEGA officials began looking for a way out of the deal, reportedly because they felt pressured by CSK, SEGA's largest shareholder, to complete the merger. In April 2003, SEGA executives believed they had received the help they wanted when Namco Ltd., a Japanese developer of gaming software, submitted its own proposal to merge with SEGA. Both deals collapsed, however, with Namco withdrawing its proposal in May 2003 and negotiations with Sammy breaking down over numerous issues, including management control.

SEGA's merger with Sammy was revived in 2004. In January, Sammy acquired the 22.4 percent stake held by CSK, paying $419 million to become SEGA's largest shareholder. In May, a $1.4 billion merger agreement between the two companies was announced, with the completion date for the transaction set for October 2004. The two companies merged in October, creating Sega Sammy Holdings Inc., the largest computer entertainment company in Japan. As SEGA, with Sammy alongside it, prepared for the future, the company faced several years of integrating its operations with those of Sammy. The process was expected to take until 2007 to complete. In the years ahead, the value of the merger would be determined, revealing whether SEGA's role as a software developer represented a business foundation capable of reversing more than a decade of troubles as a console maker.

Principal Subsidiaries

SEGA of America, Inc.; SEGA Enterprises, Inc. (U.S.A.); SEGA Europe Ltd.; SEGA Amusements Europe Ltd.

Principal Competitors

Electronic Arts Inc.; Konami Corporation; Namco Holding Corporation.

Further Reading

Abrahams, Paul, "SEGA Pins Its Hopes on the Dream Machine," *Financial Times,* October 14, 1999, p. 31.

"Business: Competition: Game, Set, and Match?," *AsiaWeek,* July 1, 2000.

Davey, Tom, "Mortal Combat: SEGA Faces Dangerous New Foe," *San Francisco Business Times,* July 7, 1995, p. 3.

Dumaine, Brian, "When Delay Courts Disaster," *Fortune,* December 16, 1991, p. 104.

Ginsberg, Steve, "Sony's Video-Game Player Trounces SEGA's, but Hang on to Your Joystick," *San Francisco Business Times,* December 22, 1995, p. 3.

Harney, Alexandra, "SEGA's Fight Continues As It Plays Again," *Financial Times,* October 6, 2001, p. 18.

——, "How SEGA's Dream Became a Nightmare," *Financial Times,* March 28, 2001, p. 16.

——, "Is This the End of the Dream for Computer Games Pioneer?," *Financial Times,* January 25, 2001, p. 29.

Isaac, David, "Video Games," *Investor's Business Daily,* March 7, 2001, p. A4.

"Japanese Giant Adjusts to Life As a Third Party in Changing Market," *Games Analyst,* July 11, 2003, p. 10.

"Japan's SEGA Ends Game Console Production," *Futures World News,* May 17, 2001.

"Japan's SEGA Enjoys First Profit in Six Years," *Europe Intelligence Wire,* May 19, 2003, p. 12.

Kunii, Irene M., "SEGA: 'We're Going to Blow Them Out of the Water,'" *Business Week,* December 7, 1998, p. 108.

"Late SEGA President Leaves Legacy As Passionate Capitalist," *Asia-Pulse News,* March 19, 2001, p. 143.

Nakamoto, Michiyo, "It's Game over for SEGA in Merger Quest," *Financial Times,* May 9, 2003, p. 15.

"Popcorn Not Included," *Business Week,* June 7, 1999, p. 140E10.

"Sammy Snaps Up Sega Shares As Hostile Takeover Talk Spreads," *AB UK,* January 2004, p. 3.

Sanchanta, Mariko, "Embattled SEGA Looks to Namco to Avoid Merger with Sammy," *Financial Times,* April 21, 2003, p. 16.

"Sega Sammy Holdings Debuts Friday in Tokyo," *America's Intelligence Wire,* October 1, 2004, p. 31.

"SEGA, Sammy Integrate Operations Under Joint Holding Company," *Kyodo News International,'* October 1, 2004, p. 43.

"SEGA's Superhero Vs. the Big Guys," *Business Week,* May 22, 2000, p. 104E2.

Seitz, Patrick, "SEGA Relishes New Role As Maker of Games Software, Not Hardware," *Investor's Business Daily,* June 10, 2002, p. A6.

Shafer, Richard A., "Playing Games," *Forbes,* August 16, 1993, p. 108.

Smith, Charles, "Sammy Snags SEGA in $1.4B Deal," *Daily Deal,* May 19, 2004, p. 32.

——, "SEGA Courted by New Suitor," *Daily Deal,* April 21, 2003, p. 32.

—Jeffrey L. Covell

Seventh Generation, Inc.

212 Battery Street, Suite A
Burlington, Vermont 05401-5281
U.S.A.
Telephone: (802) 658-3773
Toll Free: (800) 456-1191
Fax: (802) 658-1771
Web site: http://www.seventhgeneration.com

Private Company
Incorporated: 1988
Employees: 30
Sales: $30 million (2005 est.)
NAIC: 325610 Soap and Cleaning Compound Manufacturing; 325611 Soap and Other Detergent Manufacturing; 325612 Polish and Other Sanitation Good Manufacturing; 325613 Surface Active Agent Manufacturing; 325620 Toilet Preparation Manufacturing; 446120 Cosmetics, Beauty Supplies, and Perfume Stores

Seventh Generation, Inc. is a leading wholesaler of environmentally conscious household products. Originally a catalog marketer, the company shifted to a focus on wholesale in the early 1990s and within a few years had entered the mass retail market with its nontoxic cleaning products, including dishwasher and laundry detergent and chlorine-free bleach. The company also supplies toilet paper and paper towels with a high recycled fiber content, recycled plastic trash bags, baby wipes and diapers, and other household products. The company develops and markets the products; manufacturing is contracted out to about eight factories. Even though it has won numerous environmental awards, Seventh Generation has begun publishing an annual Corporate Responsibility Report describing how it could do a still better job of minimizing harm to the environment.

Eco-Origins

Seventh Generation, Inc. started as the mail-order catalog of Renew America, a nonprofit in Washington, D.C., that marketed energy- and water-conserving products such as fluorescent light bulbs and low-flow showerheads. In 1988, Renew America handed off the catalog to Alan Newman of Burlington, Vermont.

Newman, a transplant from Oregon, had set out to make the world a better place through enterprise. According to *Inc.* magazine, he learned entrepreneurship through experience, first in 1983 by cofounding Gardener's Supply. This was followed in 1986 with Niche Marketing, a distributor of progressive-oriented products.

The company was dubbed Seventh Generation, Inc. The name, suggested by one of Newman's Native American employees, came from the Great Law of Peace of the Six Nations Iroquois Confederacy: "In our every deliberation we must consider the impact of our decisions on the next seven generations."

First year sales were around $1 million. According to an early profile in *People* magazine, one bestseller was a European-style reusable shopping bag, while another imported idea, reusable sanitary napkins, failed to catch on.

Vermont has quite a tradition of socially and environmentally conscious entrepreneurs (for example, Ben Cohen and Jerry Greenfield of ice cream fame). This prompted Jeffrey A. Hollender, the company's future CEO, to visit the Green Mountain state, where he met Newman while researching a book called *How to Make the World a Better Place*.

Hollender had previously established adult education programs in Toronto and New York City. The latter site eventually developed a library of instructional audiotapes, and was sold to Warner Communications. Hollender then served as president of Warner Audio Publishing.

Hollender came aboard the Seventh Generation team, raising money and becoming president and CEO. Seventh Generation headquarters was relocated to nearby Colchester, Vermont (Hollender maintained an office in Manhattan).

According to *Inc.*, a March 1989 *New York Times* mention of Seventh Generation generated huge publicity, increasing orders several-fold within a year. The 20th anniversary of Earth Day on April 22, 1990, also brought media attention to the green products business. Catalog sales increased from $1 million in 1989 to $7 million in 1990, according to *Inc.* By this time, the company had 120 employees.

The catalog was redeveloped to focus on benefits to the environment beyond energy conservation, such as vegetable-based laundry detergent. The goal was to sell "Products for a Healthy Planet." The product line included a plethora of consumable products intended to be less harmful to the environment, including recycled paper products, cleaning supplies, organic foods, and skin care supplies. There were plenty of items made of alternate, more ecologically sound materials, such as a milkweed floss comforter. Cloth and biodegradable diapers also were offered.

Recession and Retooling in the 1990s

Sales were hit hard during the recession of the early 1990s. About half the workforce of 125 employees was laid off in 1991. The company, however, was still earning environmental kudos. It won the Direct Marketing Association's first ever environmental award, sponsored by Rodale Press, Inc., in 1991.

Newman left Seventh Generation in 1992. He later went on to start a Burlington microbrewery, the "Magic Hat Brewing Co. and Performing Arts Center," with a former Seventh Generation employee. According to *Inc.*, proceeds from the stock sale helped to fund the beer venture.

Around 1992, the company began wholesaling its products to retailers, beginning with natural food stores such as Cambridge Natural Foods, Harvest Co-ops, and Bread & Circus. This became the focus of Seventh Generation's business. Sales reached $6.5 million in 1992 after several years at just $100,000.

Interestingly, the cover of the controversial fall 1992 catalog, mailed to 500,000 homes, featured an attack on President George H.W. Bush, as elections approached. Conservation-minded liberals were generally critical of the GOP's stance on environmental issues. "We have serious questions of whether a business like ours can flourish under President Bush," Hollender told the *Boston Globe*.

Bush lost the election to Clinton and Gore, and Seventh Generation seemed to be ready to flourish, despite losing $3 million in the previous two years. The company went public on November 8, 1993, raising $7 million. It lost another $2.4 million in 1993, however, on sales of $7.2 million. About 500 natural food stores on the East and West Coasts carried Seventh Generation products by the end of 1993. This number would eventually increase to 1,000.

Between 1993 and 1994 the catalog was retooled to appeal to more value-conscious consumers. Half the products were replaced, either for price or performance reasons. The product line expanded to include vegetable-dyed linens and dinnerware manufactured without heavy metals. The revamped catalog was printed on glossy, rather than uncoated paper, a concession to allow the photographs to reproduce (and sell) better.

Employment peaked at 140 people in 1994, when revenues exceeded $8 million. Catalog sales accounted for 80 percent of the total. During the summer, the company had entered the mass retail market with three products: dishwasher detergent, nonchlorine bleach, and liquid laundry detergent.

Boston's Star Market Co. became Seventh Generation's first mainstream supermarket retailer when it agreed to carry the products at its 33 stores. The metro New York area Food Emporium chain soon followed.

In May 1995, the mail-order catalog business was sold to Gaiam, Inc. of Boulder, Colorado, a subsidiary of Transecon. Renamed *Harmony* two years later, the catalog continued to offer Seventh Generation products. Another catalog, *Home Trends,* soon added them as well.

With the catalog in other hands, Seventh Generation had sales of $1.7 million in the 12 months ended March 1995. Sales more than doubled the next year, approaching $4 million.

The next couple of years were difficult ones. The company cut its workforce as its share price crashed. Seventh Generation reported just eight full-time employees at the end of 1998. Sales were nearly $9 million for the year, with a net loss of about $400,000. Seventh Generation was making progress, however, not only with natural food chains such as Wild Oats but also mainstream supermarkets such as Kroger's.

The company was developing new environmentally responsible products suited for supermarket sales. Gaining national supermarket distribution also typically required spending millions of dollars on slotting fees and other expenses, a marketing executive told *Inc.* The company could leverage the uniqueness of its products to the supermarket chains, however, which liked to stock products that warehouse clubs did not carry.

Private Again in 1999

Hollender led a buyout of the company in 1999, making it a private company again. The cost of complying with SEC regulations and analyst indifference for smaller companies were two reasons for the move. Sales were growing rapidly, reaching $11 million in 1999.

A new marketing strategy emphasized the health benefits of using products free of harsh, artificial chemicals: The new tagline was "Healthier for You and the Planet." Seventh Generation invested a fair amount of energy into consumer education, warning of the dangers of toxic chemicals in many cleaning products. The web site was one means for getting information into the hands of customers. Unbleached toilet paper printed with alarming facts about dioxin was another; such rolls were dispensed to distributors and retailers in a 2000 promotion. Company CEO Jeffrey Hollender continued to publish books on environmental issues.

New products included disposable diapers, introduced in April 2003. Seventh Generation, which subcontracted manufacturing to about eight plants, had about 30 employees of its own in 2004. Sales were about $25 million and reportedly growing between 20 and 40 percent a year.

According to *OnEarth,* the natural household product market was worth perhaps $100 million a year, a mere blip compared with the $18 billion in household products mainstream

---

Key Dates:

1988: Seventh Generation, Inc. is launched from the former Renew America catalog business.
1992: The company begins wholesaling to natural food stores.
1993: An initial public offering is made.
1994: The company enters the mass retail market.
1995: The mail-order catalog business is sold to Gaiam, Inc.
1999: The company is taken private.
2004: The company publishes its first Corporate Responsibility Report.

---

supermarkets sold. Supermarkets accounted for 30 percent of Seventh Generation's sales, according to the publication.

Environmental accountability was becoming more mainstream among corporations. Few were as forthcoming as Seventh Generation, however, which began producing an annual Corporate Responsibility Report describing how it could do a better job of minimizing harm to the environment. In 2004, Seventh Generation garnered the U.S. Chamber of Commerce's Corporate Stewardship Award for Small Business.

Principal Competitors

Earth Friendly Products, Inc.; Sun & Earth, Inc.

Further Reading

Bauer, Bob, "Star Market Offering 'Green' Detergent Line," *Supermarket News,* July 25, 1994, pp. 39 + .

Cole, Michelle, "Vermont Maker of Environmental Home Products Struggles with Purity Issues," *Oregonian,* February 28, 2004.

Cronin, Michael P., "Green Marketing Heats Up," *Inc.,* January 1993, p. 27.

Cyr, Diane, "The Nine Lives of Seventh Generation," *Catalog Age,* June 1994, pp. 101 + .

Daley, Yvonne, "Vermont Firm Provides Products That Are Good for the Planet, Pocketbook," *Knight Ridder/Tribune Business News (Boston Globe),* October 25, 1994.

Dowling, Melissa, "A Paler Shade of Green," *Catalog Age,* January 1995, p. 36.

Estabrook, Barry, "Clean 'n' Green: Seventh Generation's Natural Products Are Heading to a Supermarket Chain Near You. Procter & Gamble, Beware," *OnEarth,* Winter 2004, pp. 34 + .

Ferguson, Bob, "Seventh Generation Relaunches," *Catalog Age,* July 1997, p. 28.

Gilje, Shelby, "Direct-Marketing Companies Make Recycling a Priority," *Seattle Times,* October 7, 1990, p. K7.

Hollender, Jeffrey, "Changing the Nature of Commerce," *Sustainable Planet: Roadmaps for the 21st Century,* Boston: Beacon Press, 2002.

——, *How to Make the World a Better Place—116 Ways You Can Make a Difference,* New York: W.W. Norton & Co., 1995.

Hollender, Jeffrey, and Stephen Fenichell, *What Matters Most—How a Small Group of Pioneers Is Teaching Social Responsibility to Big Business, and Why Big Business Is Listening,* New York: Basic Books, 2004.

James, Dana, "Double the Responses, Double the Cash; Seeing Green; Internet Excellent Supplement to P-O-P Tactics," *Marketing News,* November 22, 1999, p. 19.

Janofsky, Michael, "Seventh Generation Takes Its Green Approach to Wall Street," *New York Times,* November 1, 1993, p. D4.

Johnson, Jim, "Seventh Generation Goes Private," *Waste News,* February 14, 2000, p. 4.

Kahlenberg, Rebecca R., "Getting Clean and Green; Earth-Friendly Products Are Going Mainstream, One Shelf at a Time," *Washington Post,* September 18, 2003, p. H1.

Kalish, David E., "Tiny Vermont Eco-Company Wants to Be Green Giant," *Associated Press,* Bus. News, November 25, 1994.

Litvan, Laura M., "Going 'Green' in the '90s," *Nation's Business,* February 1995, p. 30.

London, Simon, "Tough Calls for a Company with a Conscience," *Financial Times* (London), March 2, 2004, p. 12.

McCuan, Jess, "It's Not Easy Being Green," *Inc.,* November 1, 2004, p. 110.

"A National Brand—At What Price?," *Inc.,* February 1995, p. 108.

Neal, Mollie, "Marketers Develop a Green Consciousness," *Direct Marketing,* February 1993, pp. 35 + .

"Playing Politics: Company Takes a Stand on Environment," *Greenwire,* October 8, 1992.

Reed, Susan, "When America Thinks Green, Eco-Preneurs Alan Newman and Jeffrey Hollender Think Greenbacks," *People Weekly,* November 12, 1990, pp. 155 + .

Seventh Generation, Inc., *Frequently Asked Questions About Chlorine,* Burlington, Vt.: Seventh Generation, Inc., 1996.

——, *Frequently Asked Questions About Petroleum and Household Cleaners,* Burlington, Vt.: Seventh Generation, Inc., 1997.

——, *The Seventh Generation Guide to a Toxic Free Home,* Burlington, Vt.: Seventh Generation, Inc., 1998.

Smith, Geoffrey, "Seventh Generation: The 'Green' Mail King," *Business Week,* December 24, 1990, p. 73.

Treadway, Robert, "Double Duty," *Print,* March 2000, p. 8.

Wennen, Ginny, "Toilet Paper Used As Reading Material," *Potentials,* February 2000, p. 14.

—Frederick C. Ingram

The World's Aquarium

Shedd Aquarium Society

1200 South Lake Shore Drive
Chicago, Illinois 60605
U.S.A.
Telephone: (312) 939-2438
Fax: (312) 939-8677
Web site: http://www.sheddaquarium.org

Nonprofit Corporation
Incorporated: 1924 as Shedd Aquarium Society
Employees: 250
Sales: $25 million (2005 est.)
NAIC: 541710 Research and Development in the
    Physical, Engineering, and Life Sciences; 712120
    Historical Sites; 712190 Nature Parks and Other
    Similar Institutions

Shedd Aquarium Society manages the John G. Shedd Aquarium, promoted as "The World's Aquarium." With more than two million visitors a year, Shedd is one of Chicago's top attractions as well as the most-visited aquarium in the United States. Shedd is located on Lake Shore Drive's "Museum Campus" next to the Field Museum and Adler Planetarium. More than 21,000 animals live at Shedd Aquarium. Facilities include a 3,000-square-foot animal hospital. The institution is involved in considerable marine research and conservation activities.

Origins

Chicago business leader John Graves Shedd sponsored the formation of the aquarium with a $2 million gift (later raised to $3 million) in 1924. A native of New Hampshire, he moved to Chicago in 1872 and worked his way up the ranks at Marshall Field & Company. He succeeded the retailer's founder as company president in 1906 and was named chairman of the board in 1923. Shedd intended to give Chicago one thing it lacked among the world's great cities; nothing less than the best would do.

The Shedd Aquarium Society was formed in 1924 and soon secured a location on a vacant lot on 12th Street (later called Roosevelt Road). The architects Graham, Anderson, Probst &

White were hired to design the aquarium. Europe's top aquariums were benchmarked. For example, new water filtration systems and ample viewing and working areas were included.

Construction began on November 2, 1927. The aquarium cost $3.25 million to build and was housed in a 300-foot-diameter octagonal building made of white Georgian marble. A swamp exhibit was housed inside its 70-foot-tall rotunda.

John G. Shedd passed away before the aquarium that bears his name was finished. The public was allowed in beginning in December 1929—a welcome distraction from the first bitter winter of the Great Depression. There were no fish in the tanks yet. It took another few months to ship one million gallons of seawater by rail from Key West, Florida.

Shedd Aquarium was the world's largest aquarium when it officially opened on May 30, 1930. It was unique for an inland aquarium in having permanent exhibits of both saltwater and freshwater fish. In 1931, the aquarium had 4.7 million visitors, which would be an enduring record.

From the beginning, Shedd claimed the world's largest single collection of sea life. This included a sawfish, the only one on exhibit at the time. In 1933, the facility received two rare lungfish from Australia. One of them, "Granddad," would still be living there at the time of Shedd's 75th anniversary in 2005, making him the oldest known animal in a public display institution.

Other unique species displayed in the early years included the spotted wobbegong shark, Atlantic tarpon, and neon tetra. The tetra, the first of its kind on public display, arrived from Germany via the *Hindenburg* and was nicknamed "Lindy" after the famous aviator of the day. President Teddy Roosevelt sent the aquarium some triggerfish he caught in the Caribbean in 1933.

Many of the fish were brought to Shedd aboard the *Nautilus,* a custom Pullman car that cost $40,000 to build and equip. It was in service until 1957. Its successor lasted until 1975, when it was given to the Monticello Railway Museum in Champaign, Illinois.

A notable addition to the collection in 1965 was Chico, a freshwater dolphin from the Amazon. He lived until 1982, set-

Key Dates:

1930: Shedd Aquarium opens.
1931: A record 4.7 million people visit the aquarium.
1936: First public display of the neon tetra draws thousands.
1971: Coral Reef/Caribbean Reef Exhibit opens.
1991: New Oceanarium nearly doubles Shedd's size.
1998: Popular "Seahorse Symphony" begins two-year run.
2000: Amazon Rising exhibit opens.
2003: Wild Reef exhibit is opened.
2005: Shedd celebrates 75th anniversary.

ting a record for his species. The aquarium eventually established a 3,000-square-foot animal hospital and was an innovator in the treatment and rehabilitation of sea life.

Caribbean Reef Opening: 1971

Shedd began producing its own synthetic seawater in 1970. The next year, Shedd opened its $1.2 million, 90,000-gallon Caribbean Reef. This replaced the original swamp exhibit in the rotunda and included about 1,000 fish in one of the earlier multispecies exhibits. There were about 200 smaller tanks apart from the central, 90,000-gallon tank. The Caribbean Reef would be revamped in 1999.

By the early 1980s, Shedd had 5,000 specimens of more than 500 different species, according to the *New York Times*. Exotic creatures were not only obtained from distant seas. The paddlefish, with an exceedingly long nose, came from rivers in the Midwest. Shedd added sea otters to the collection in 1989, a first among the continent's inland aquariums.

Oceanarium Opening: 1991

In April 1991, after years of planning and fundraising, Shedd opened its Oceanarium, a representation of the Northwest Pacific coast. Covering 170,000 square feet, it was the largest indoor marine mammal habitat in the world, and housed Pacific white-sided dolphins and beluga whales in a two million gallon indoor pool, the world's deepest. Six other pools added another one million gallons and contained sea otters and penguins. A 300-speaker sound system played nature recordings taken from the Pacific Northwest. The Oceanarium hosted several daily demonstrations of dolphin and whale behaviors. The Oceanarium was the aquarium's first expansion and cost $47 million to build, including about $5 million on a landfill extending into Lake Michigan. The opening was delayed by the need to reapply an epoxy coating to the tanks.

The man credited as the driving force behind the creation of the Oceanarium, William Braker, retired at the end of 1993. He had been only the second director in more than 60 years. Braker

had started at Shedd in 1950 and replaced Walter Chute, the original director, in 1964.

After Braker retired, Shedd hired Ted A. Beattie, formerly director of zoos in Knoxville and Fort Worth, to head the institution. Beattie was experienced in public relations, and Shedd had to maintain its image in the face of vocal animal rights activists opposed to keeping mammals in captivity. Aquariums had a role in promoting respect for wildlife as well as in conservation of endangered species, said Beattie.

Shedd's annual budget was about $20 million in the early 1990s and the aquarium employed 220 people. Research and education were important parts of the mission. Shedd offered the public classes in taking care of tropical fish and aquatic plants.

Shedd was a pioneer in seahorse husbandry (its popular Seahorse Symphony exhibit in the late 1990s featured a number of different seahorses and related creatures). Cetaceans (toothed whales) were another focus of research. Shedd was also researching the reproduction of lungfish, which were notoriously difficult to breed.

More Ambitious Exhibits in 2000 and Beyond

Amazon Rising: Seasons of the River was a unique exhibit that opened in 2000. It represented the wildlife of the world's largest river over the course of a year. The wide range of species included bullet ants, pygmy marmosets, and a green anaconda. The role of indigenous people was also included. In addition, this was Shedd's first exhibit to incorporate live plants. Seasons of the River cost $17 million to build.

The Wild Reef exhibit opened in April 2003. Based on a Philippine coral reef, considered the most diverse of marine ecosystems, Wild Reef was comprised of 26 interconnected habitats. It featured the Midwest's largest public collection of live corals. The 27,000-square-foot, $45 million exhibit also housed more than two-dozen sharks.

Wild Reef also became home to Bubba the Grouper, believed to be the first fish to receive chemotherapy treatment for cancer. This Queensland grouper was literally left on Shedd's doorstep in 1987 while less than a foot long. Bubba had since quadrupled in size and changed sex from female to male, following the development of most groupers. In 2003 he developed systems of connective tissue cancer.

The aquarium's wildlife conservation activities focused on the critically endangered blue iguana. Shedd was displaying two of the species in 2005 in an exhibit meant to encourage breeding.

Shedd's roofs were upgraded by the addition of a new soybean polymer system installed in 2004. White in color, it was energy efficient as well as environmentally sound in its production, installation, and recycling phases.

75th Anniversary in 2005

Shedd was home to more than 21,000 animals. It was drawing more than two million visitors a year at the time of its 75th anniversary in 2005. A temporary exhibit of more than 30 different species of crabs helped celebrate the milestone.

According to the *Chicago Sun Times,* admissions, concessions, and gift sales funded nearly two-thirds of Shedd's annual budget of about $38 million. The aquarium was staffed by 600 volunteers in addition to its 250 employees.

Principal Competitors

Monterey Bay Aquarium; National Aquarium.

Further Reading

"Beautiful Creatures Star in 'Seahorse Symphony'," *Chicago Tribune,* Friday Sec., May 8, 1998, p. 66.

Bertagnoli, Lisa, "Shedding Light on the Amazon," *Crain's Chicago Business,* July 17, 2000, p. 34.

Bianchi, Laura, "Tanks for the Memories; As Chicago's Shedd Aquarium Turns 75, Take a Look at What You Might Have Been Missing," *Daily Herald* (Arlington Heights, Ill.), May 20, 2005, p. 32.

Bodamer, Ralph, and Mary C. Wagner, "Taking Care of Tropical Fish Is Like Taking Care of Children: Tales of the Deep from a Senior Aquarist at Shedd Aquarium," *Chicago Tribune,* August 4, 1985, p. 46.

"Chicago Plans to Keep Octopi Alive in $3,000,000 Aquarium to Be Built There," *The New York Times,* April 11, 1927, p. 2.

Dale, Steve, "Dreams Stay Afloat; Tides of Turmoil Didn't Sink Oceanarium," *Chicago Tribune,* Friday Sec., April 26, 1991, p. 5.

Davenport, Misha, "Shedd's History As Colorful As Its Inhabitants, Founder," *Chicago Sun Times,* May 27, 2005.

Fortin, Cassandra, "Who's Afraid of the Water?," *Chicago Tribune,* Tempo Northwest Sec., February 28, 1999, p. 6.

Grable, Grant, "Soy Restores the Shedd: Environmental ELMS Replaces Aquarium Roof in Chicago," *Environmental Design & Construction,* January/February 2005, pp. 14 + .

Herrmann, Andrew, "Shedd Aquarium at 75," *Chicago Sun Times,* May 27, 2005.

John G. Shedd Aquarium, "Chicago's Shedd Aquarium Celebrates 75! History Spans 75 Years—Cultural Icon of Chicago Looks Back," Chicago: John G. Shedd Aquarium, 2004.

——, "Fast Facts," Chicago: John G. Shedd Aquarium, 2004.

——, "History Makers: Shedd Aquarium's 75 Years of Firsts," Chicago: John G. Shedd Aquarium, 2004.

——, "Shedd Aquarium: 75 Years of Firsts and Favorites," Chicago: John G. Shedd Aquarium, 2004.

——, *Tarpons, Tetras and Terra Cotta Turtles: Shedd Aquarium's First 75 Years,* Chicago: John G. Shedd Aquarium, in press.

Johnson, Steve, "Peeling Tanks Have Aquarium Painted into a Corner," *Chicago Tribune,* Tempo Sec., September 3, 1990, p. 1.

"Making a Difference at the Aquarium," *Chicago Tribune,* March 19, 1993, Editorial Sec., p. 18.

McCormick, Douglas, "The Age of Aquariums," *Sea Frontiers,* March/April 1993, pp. 23 + .

Mullen, William, "After Being Raised by Humans, Beluga Learns to Be a Whale," *Chicago Tribune,* January 4, 2005.

——, "Bit of Chicago History Written in Canada: Shedd Gets Its Whales," *Chicago Tribune,* News Sec., July 30, 1989, p. 1.

——, "Bubba the Grouper Believed to Be First Fish to Undergo Chemotherapy," *Chicago Tribune,* October 15, 2003.

——, "Shedd Sails Into Different Waters for New Chief," *Chicago Tribune,* November 17, 1993.

——, "Sound Advice May Help Aquarium Get Lungfish in the Mood," *Chicago Tribune,* News Sec., September 6, 1995, p. 1.

"New Aquarium in Chicago Gets Water from the Sea," *New York Times,* May 25, 1930, p. 54.

Olmstead, Rob, "My Blue Heaven: Iguanas at Shedd," *Daily Herald* (Arlington Heights, Ill.), February 11, 2005, p. 1.

"Roosevelt Fish Reach Chicago," *New York Times,* April 6, 1933, p. 19.

Schultz, Beth, "Aquarium Net Does Just Swimmingly; Attention to Security Keeps Users—Eels, Sharks and Whales—Off the Rocks," *Network World,* December 20, 2004, p. 1.

Sheppard, Nathaniel, Jr., "Chicago's Glassed-In Sea," *New York Times,* January 17, 1982, pp. XX12.

Washburn, Gary, "Aquarium to Get Multimillion-Dollar Face Lift; Highlights Include Reef, Shark Exhibits," *Chicago Tribune,* News Sec., October 11, 1997, p. 1.

Wright, Gordon, "Aquatic Addition Melds Diverse Environments," *Building Design & Construction,* November 1991, pp. 30 + .

—Frederick C. Ingram

Siliconware Precision Industries Ltd.

123 Chung Shan Road, Section 3, Tantzu Hsiang
Taichung 427
Taiwan
Telephone: +886 4 2534 1525
Fax: +886 4 2534 6278
Web site: http://www.spil.com.tw

Public Company
Incorporated: 1984
Employees: 10,613
Sales: TWD 35.25 billion ($1.11 billion) (2004)
Stock Exchanges: Taiwan NASDAQ
Ticker Symbol: SPIL
NAIC: 334412 Printed Circuit Board Manufacturing

Siliconware Precision Industries Ltd. (SPIL) is the number two integrated circuit (IC) packager in Taiwan (behind Advanced Semiconductor Engineering) and the number three worldwide (behind Amkor Technology). Based in Taipei, SPIL offers turnkey IC packaging and testing services to many of the world's largest semiconductor manufacturers—including Intel, for which SPIL is a Preferred Quality Supplier. SPIL services include packaging consultation, design, and simulation; wafering, sorting, and assembly; and final testing and burn-in, as well as direct shipment. The company also offers testing services separately from its packaging operations. Packaging represents the largest part of the company's business, however, at more than 95 percent of revenues of $1.1 billion in 2004. SPIL operates three production facilities in Taiwan. SPIL's substrate and lead frame packaging capabilities cover the wide range of IC product applications, including PCs, cameras, modems, cellular phones, PDAs, and LCD and plasma screens. SPIL was established in 1984 by a group led by Bough Lin, and is listed on both the Taiwan Stock Exchange and the NASDAQ. Bough Lin serves as executive vice-president and chairman, while Chi Wen Tsai acts as CEO.

IC Packager in the 1980s

Siliconware Precision Industries Ltd. had its roots in another prominent Taiwanese IC company, Lingsen Precision, which had been launched in the 1950s to provide IC assembly services to the local electronics industry. IC assemblers served as a midstep between the semiconductor manufacturers and electronic appliance developers, receiving unfinished semiconductors, testing them, and then packaging them for specific applications.

In 1984, Bough Lin, Chung Li Lin, and C.W. Tsai led a group of former engineers from Lingsen in the formation of a new company specialized in IC assembly packaging in Taichung. That company became Siliconware Precision Industries Ltd., or SPIL. From the start, SPIL focused primarily on servicing the packaging requirements of fellow Taiwanese United Microelectronics Corporation. That company was to remain SPIL's largest client until well into the 1990s.

SPIL set up a factory at Taichung and began packaging production by the end of 1984. The company initially specialized in the simpler Plastic Dual In-Line Packages (PDIP) format. The company continued to develop its technologies, however, in order to enter higher value-added packaging segments. As part of this effort, the company opened its second production facility, at Tan Fu, in 1987. The completion of that plant in 1988 enabled the company to extend its operations into new packaging areas, such as Small Outline Plastics (SOP). By 1990, SPIL had expanded its engineering technologies, and in that year launched production of Quad Flat Packages (QFP). Other higher-end packaging sectors added by the company included Plastic Lead Chip Carrier Packages (PLCC) and, beginning in 1992, Enhanced QFP. In that year, as well, SPIL received ISO 9002 certification.

SPIL's technology extension was matched to an ambitious expansion strategy that was to lift the company to the rank of the number two IC packaging company in Taiwan by the mid-1990s. Vertical integration, as well as expansion of the company's production capacity and technology, formed the major features of the company's growth plans. In 1992, SPIL made a first step, when it acquired a stake in High-Tech, a manufacturer of lead frames, a raw material in the packaging process. In that year, as well, the company bought a shareholding in Vate Technology, which provided testing services.

SPIL stepped up its expansion in 1993, backed by an initial public offering (IPO) on the Taiwan Stock Exchange that year. The company's IPO was highly successful, and SPIL became one of the most favored technology stocks on the Taiwan Stock Exchange through the 1990s. Concurrent with its IPO, the company extended its operations to the United States for the first time, opening Siliconware USA in San Jose, California.

The company's IPO backed a brief but important acquisition drive. In 1993, the company acquired three fellow IC assemblers, Talent Electronics, Taicera, and More Power Electronics, boosting the company's range of technologies and its production capacity. Also that year, SPIL enhanced its in-house testing component, acquiring Silicon Ware Corporation, which specialized in IC testing.

These acquisitions enabled SPIL to begin offering turnkey IC packaging and testing services by 1994. The company extended its packaging technologies to include new quad flat packaging applications, including LQFP in 1994 and TQFP by 1996. By then, the company had completed construction of its second production facility, Da Fong. Construction on the plant was launched in October 1994, and quadrupled the company's capacity, including space enough to add more than 600 wire bonders. The Da Fong site also became the company's headquarters in 1995.

IC Packaging Leader in the New Century

SPIL by then had claimed the number two IC packaging spot in Taiwan, behind leader Advanced Semiconductor Engineering (ASE). Unlike ASE, which targeted the global IC market, SPIL for the most part focused on the local Taiwanese market through the 1990s. The rapid growth of Taiwan's technology sector, which by then had become one of the world's most important centers for IT and semiconductor development, gave SPIL a strong basis for continued growth.

SPIL continued to enhance its technologies as well, adding next-generation packaging capacity for technologies such as Ball Grid Arrays (BGA), starting with PBGA in 1996. In 1998, the company extended its range of assemblies to include the full spectrum of BGA assemblies. In that year, as well, the company launched production of new Multi Chip Modules (MCM). Also in that year, SPIL gained QS 9000 and ISO 9001 certification. By then, the company's total wire bonder capacity neared 850, placing it among the world's top five IC assembly subcontractors.

Of importance, SPIL continued to invest in adding new technologies by acquiring stakes in a number of assembly and testing companies, including two major IC substrate specialists,

Unimicron Technology and Phoenix Precision Technology; ChipMOS, which specialized in LCD driver and memory assemblies; testing specialist Kyec, and others, including Artest, Caesar Technology, and Sigurd. In 1997, the company launched a partnership with Abpac, which operated an advanced IC packaging facility in Phoenix, Arizona. Also in 1997, the company's U.S. subsidiary added a technology center there in 1997. In this way, the company kept pace with new industry developments.

Entering the 2000s, SPIL inaugurated a new production facility at Chung Shan. The addition of the new capacity helped boost the group's total wire bonding capacity to 3,000 by 2005. The new facility enabled the company to add new technologies as well. In 2001, for example, the company licensed Kulicke & Soffa Industries' Flip Chip Technologies wafer bumping and redistribution processes. By then, the company had completed a secondary public offering, listing its shares on the NASDAQ.

SPIL boosted its production capacity again in 2002, when it broke ground on a new plant in Suzhou, the fast-growing "high-tech" city in mainland China's Jiangsu Province. The new capacity allowed SPIL to extend its technology expertise into new-generation, high-end packaging sectors, such as TCP (tape carrier package), TAB (tape automated bonding), and the small form-factor CSP (chip scale packaging) technologies.

SPIL's growth continued into the mid-2000s. An important feature of the company's growth was its shifting focus from a reliance on the Taiwan market to an increasing position in international markets. A primary example of this extension was the launch of the company's involvement with Intel Corporation. By 2005, the company had become a Preferred Quality Supplier, winning an award from Intel that year. With sales of TWD 35 billion ($1.1 billion), SPIL appeared certain to remain among the world's leading IC packaging and testing companies.

Principal Subsidiaries

Siliconware Investment Company Ltd.; Siliconware Technology (Suzhou) Ltd. (China); Siliconware USA Inc. (U.S.A.); SPIL (BVI) Holding Ltd. (British Virgin Islands); SPIL (Cayman) Holding Ltd. (Cayman Islands).

Principal Competitors

Advanced Semiconductor Engineering Inc.; Amkor Technology Inc.; Kyec Electronics Co. Ltd.; Micro-Star International Company Ltd.; Agere Systems Singapore Private Ltd.; Sichuan Changhong Electric Company Ltd.; Intel Microelectronics Phils Inc.; Mosel Vitelic Corporation; MiTAC Technology Corporation; Silicon Integrated Systems Corporation; Behaviour Tech Computer Corporation.

Further Reading

Levine, Bernard, "Siliconware USA, Inc.," *Electronic News,* June 8, 1998, p. 55.
"Siliconware Precision Expanding IC Packaging Capacity," *Taiwan Economic News,* April 16, 2002.
"Siliconware Precision Sees Revenue Continue Growing," *Taiwan Economic News,* March 15, 2002.
"Top Two Taiwanese Chip Assemblers Hit New High Revenues in Nov.," *Taiwan Economic News,* December 12, 2003.

—M.L. Cohen

Sistema JSFC

Leontevskiy Per. 10
Moscow 125009
Russia
Telephone: +7 95 229 36 83
Fax: +7 95 232 33 91
Web site: http://www.sistema.ru

Public Company
Incorporated: 1993
Employees: 30,000
Sales: $5.7 billion (2004)
Stock Exchanges: Moscow London
Ticker Symbol: SSA
NAIC: 334210 Telephone Apparatus Manufacturing;
236116 New Multi-Family Housing Construction
(Except Operative Builders); 236220 Commercial and
Institutional Building Construction; 334419 Other
Electronic Component Manufacturing; 453998 All
Other Miscellaneous Store Retailers (Except Tobacco
Stores); 515112 Radio Stations; 515120 Television
Broadcasting; 524128 Other Direct Insurance Carriers
(Except Life, Health, and Medical); 551112 Offices of
Other Holding Companies; 561510 Travel Agencies;
561520 Tour Operators

Sistema JSFC is one of Russia's largest and most diversified private sector consumer-oriented services companies in Russia and the Commonwealth of Independent States (CIS). Whereas other Russian business empires have been built on a foundation of the country's natural resources, Sistema has gathered a portfolio of leading companies in the telecommunications, banking, insurance, press and media, and retail industries, among others. The company's primary asset is its 50.6 percent control of Mobile TeleSystems (MTS), the number one provider of mobile telephone services in Russia and the CIS, with more than 34 million subscribers at the end of 2004. MTS alone accounts for more than 90 percent of Sistema's net profits. MTS is grouped under subsidiary Sistema Telecom, which also controls the Sky-

Link satellite telephone service, Moscow's leading fixed line telephone operator MGTS, and, since the end of 2004, a nearly 30 percent stake in MTT, a nationally operating telecommunications and network interconnection services provider. Altogether, Sistema Telecom oversees more than 50 subsidiaries in Russia and the CIS. Sistema's Insurance division focuses on its control of Rosno, a leading provider of a full range of insurance products in Russia. Germany's Allianz is a strategic partner in Rosno, with a 47 percent stake. Sistema Hals is one of Russia's most profitable and successful real estate development groups, with a variety of high-profile projects under its belt, including properties for DaimlerChrysler, Raiffeisenbank, Samsung, and Banque Nationale de Paris. Sistema also controls the Moscow Bank for Reconstruction & Development (MBRD), providing both corporate and retail banking products and services. The company also controls the Detsky Mir Group, which operates Russia's leading children's clothing retail chain. Under its Media division, Sistema is active in pay-TV, through a 50 percent stake in Kosmos TV, and has interests in radio broadcasting and print media and news distribution, including the Moscow newspaper *Metro,* the national newspaper *Rossiya,* and the daily *Smena,* as well as the Rosbalt news agency. Other company investments include pharmaceuticals, helicopters, biotechnology, and the Intourist travel and tourism agency network. In 2004, Sistema reported revenues of $5.7 billion, up from $3.8 billion in 2003. The company is listed on the Moscow Stock Exchange, and, since early 2005, on the London Stock Exchange. Founder Vladimir Yevtushenkov retains control of 75 percent of Sistema's stock.

New Markets in the 1990s

The collapse of the Soviet regime and the institution of a free market system in Russia and the CIS opened a range of new business opportunities at the beginning of the 1990s. A small number of entrepreneurs managed to seize these opportunities, and by the end of the decade, the country boasted a handful of billionaires, at least on paper. Nearly all of the country's new business leaders built their fortunes based on what appeared as more or less a ''land grab'' for the country's natural resources. In almost each case, these resources were acquired at a nominal price. By the early 2000s, many of the initial generation of

303

entrepreneurs had fallen—and a number, such as Yukos's head Mikhail Khodorkovsky, found themselves facing arrest.

Amid the somewhat chaotic early period of Russia's transition to a free market economy, Vladimir Yevtushenkov proved to be one of the few to build a business empire based on consumer-oriented products and services. Yevtushenkov (also spelled as Evtushenkov) was born in 1948, and had attended the D. Mendelev Moscow Chemical Engineering Institute, before earning a doctorate in economics from Moscow State University. Under the Soviet regime, Yevtushenkov started his career at the Karacharovo Plastic Works, rising to the rank of deputy director and chief engineer by 1982. He then transferred to the Polymerbyt Scientific and Production Association, serving as chief engineer and then deputy general director. In 1987, however, Yevtushenkov came to Moscow, becoming the chief of the city's Technical Administration and the chief of the Central Administration on Science and Engineering of the Moscow City Executive Committee. By 1990, Yevtushenkov had become chairman of the city's Committee on Science and Engineering.

As Moscow emerged from Soviet dominance, Yevtushenkov found a powerful ally at the head of Moscow's government: his brother-in-law and close friend, Yuri Luzhkov, who became mayor of the city. Luzhkov's government itself proved highly entrepreneurial. Over the course of the next decade, the city bought stakes in some 400 countries, in industries ranging from fast food to oil refineries.

The climate appeared right for Yevtushenkov to go into business for himself. In 1993, Yevtushenkov led a group of investors in the creation of Sistema JFSC. Yevtushenkov nonetheless retained majority control of the company, with nearly 80 percent of its shares.

From the outset, Sistema was organized as a holding company seeking to acquire former state-run businesses as they came up for privatization. Sistema's strategy was to acquire companies, which as often as not were unprofitable, and play an active and direct role in their management. As such the company launched a series of takeovers starting in 1993, acquiring operations in a variety of industries, ranging from telecommunications, to tourism, to electronics, to oil and petroleum products. The company also launched its own real estate development and construction businesses. By 1995, Sistema controlled nearly 40 companies.

Sistema had not ventured into business alone—the city of Moscow often held significant stakes in companies acquired by Sistema. The company also received a large number of high-profile construction and development contracts from the city. Of importance, Sistema also was awarded an early license to set up a mobile telephone service in Moscow. For this, Sistema backed the founding of pioneering cellular phone provider Vimpelcom in 1993. That company launched its first pilot network, based on the U.S.-standard AMPS protocol, in Moscow that year. The service began with an initial subscriber base of just 400. By June 1994, Vimpelcom had launched full-scale operations, and its subscriber base soared past 5,000. By 1995, Vimpelcom claimed the leadership of the nascent Russian cellular phone market, leading to the company's listing on the New York Stock Exchange—the first Russian company to do so since 1903.

Sistema's other operations were growing strongly as well. In 1994, the company set up Sistema Hals, grouping its real estate and construction operations, which had grown with a number of acquisitions of other companies established in Moscow since the liberalization of 1990. The company also acquired control of the children's clothing chain Detsky Mir (Children's World). Under Sistema, Detsky Mir quickly grew into Russia's second largest retail group, and one of the country's best-known retail names. Helping to fuel the group's acquisition strategy was its own bank, the Moscow Bank for Reconstruction & Development (MBRD), established in 1993. Although MBRD offered both commercial and retail banking services, it remained relatively small in terms of assets. Nonetheless, the bank played a central role in financing Sistema's acquisition strategy.

The oil industry also became an early target for the company, in part in partnership with the city of Moscow. The company formed Sistema-Invest in order to oversee its investments in this area, which included the development of oil fields in Komi Republic, and the creation of a network of Kedr-M service stations in the Moscow area.

Leading Consumer-Driven Private Sector Corporation in the New Century

The public listing of Vimpelcom in 1996 enabled Sistema to exit its shareholding in that company in favor of the acquisition of a new mobile telephone company, Mobile TeleSystems (MTS), that year. Unlike Vimpelcom, MTS launched operations using the more advanced GSM mobile standard that had been adopted on a European-wide scale. Sistema quickly brought in the expertise of Deutsche Telekom to help it develop MTS's network in Moscow and then on a national level. In exchange, Deutsche Telekom acquired a minority stake in MTS.

With the investment in MTS, telecommunications took on a major role in Sistema's balance sheet and future development. MTS grew quickly, and by the mid-2000s had become the leading mobile telephone service provider in Russia and the CIS. MTS also formed the most profitable area of Sistema's holdings, accounting for more than 90 percent of the group's total profits.

Sistema continued to invest in the telecommunications sector, acquiring Moscow's leading fixed line telephone operator MGTS, and a 50 percent stake in the satellite telecommunications service Skylink. In 1998, Sistema established a new subsidiary for its telecommunications holdings, Sistema Telecom. That subsidiary then brought MTS public, with a listing on the New York Stock Exchange, in 2000.

In the meantime, Sistema had targeted a new area for expansion, acquiring one of Russia's leading insurance groups, Rosno, in 1998. Once again, Sistema sought a more experienced

Key Dates:

1993: Vladimir Yevtushenkov leads in the creation of Sistema as a holding company for diversified investments; the company establishes its own bank, MBRD, and begins acquisition of former state-owned businesses in tourism, retail, oil, construction, and other industries; the company joins in the creation of Vimpelcom, a pioneering mobile telecommunications group in Russia.

1995: Sistema now holds stakes in more than 100 companies.

1996: Vimpelcom is listed on the New York Stock Exchange, allowing Sistema to exit that company's shareholding and launch a new mobile telephone service MTS, based on the GSM standard, in partnership with Deutsche Telekom.

1998: Sistema acquires Rosno insurance group, one of the leading insurance companies in Russia.

2000: MTS is listed on the New York Stock Exchange.

2001: Allianz AG becomes a strategic partner in Rosno.

2002: Sistema begins restructuring to focus on consumer-oriented businesses, with a core of telecommunications and high technology.

2004: The company completes the sale of its oil industry interests; Sistema launches stock on the Moscow Stock Exchange.

2005: Sistema launches an IPO on the London Stock Exchange, selling 16.5 percent of its shares in the largest Russian IPO to date.

partner for its new business. In 2001, the company signed a strategic partnership agreement with Germany's Allianz AG. Under the guidance of Allianz, Rosno solidified its status in the Russian insurance market.

Sistema's business interests also continued to expand, encompassing diverse areas such as pharmaceuticals, electronics, trucks—in a partnership with Volvo Truck Corp. signed in 2000—and other manufacturing areas. The company also began building a portfolio of media holdings, including newspaper titles such as the Moscow-oriented *Metro,* the national daily *Rossiya,* and the daily *Smena,* as well as the Rosbalt news agency.

In 2002, Sistema launched a restructuring as it began to refocus its holdings in an effort to become a pure-play consumer-oriented products and services company. As part of that restructuring, Sistema began selling its oil industry holdings, including its Kedr-M service station network. That process was completed, in large part, in 2004.

Instead, the company began focusing more closely on its telecommunications and electronics businesses. The company made a number of acquisitions to boost these operations, including the purchase of OAO Science Center Corporation, a 50 percent stake in Comstar Company, 50 percent of ZAO Cosmos-TV, and 100 percent of the Czech Republic's Strom Telecom S.R.O. The company also boosted its stake in MTS, buying another 10 percent in 2003. At the same time, Sistema

moved to bring a number of its other businesses under tighter company control. As such the company boosted its shareholding in its travel and tourism business Intourist to 91 percent in 2002, and its shares of two banks, MBRR Commercial Bank and East-West United Bank, to 52 percent and 30 percent, respectively.

These changes led the company to the next phase of its development in 2004, when it listed its shares on the Moscow Stock Exchange. This step, given the relatively limited size of the Moscow market, was seen as only a preliminary to the group's full market listing, however. At the beginning of 2005, Sistema turned to the London Stock Exchange, launching what became Russia's largest-ever initial public offering (IPO). In the IPO, Sistema sold more than 16 percent of its shares, a block valued at $1.56 billion. Vladimir Yevtushenkov nonetheless retained control of the company, holding 65 percent of Sistema's stock. In little more than a decade, Sistema had grown into Russia's leading consumer-oriented private sector company.

Principal Subsidiaries

Bs Telecom; Detsky Mir Group; East-West United Bank; Fram Resource (Sweden); Intourist Hotel Group; Intourist Japan (Japan); Intourist Warsaw (Poland); Intours Corporation (Canada); Iskratel; Kamov Holding; Kosmos TV; Literaturnaya Gazeta; Maxima Communications Group; Mediatel; Medical Technologies Holding Company; Metro Newspaper; Metroreklama Group; Moscow Bank for Reconstruction & Development (MBRD); Nasha Pressa Group; Niidar Research & Production Complex; Niime and Mikron; Radio Centre Concern; Radio Tesla Sistema; Rosbalt News Agency; Rosno; Rossiya Public Newspaper; Rti-Sistemy Concern; Sistema Hals; Sistema Multimedia; Sistema Telecom; Strom Telecom Group of Companies; Ten Viaggi (Italy); Tesla Tech (Prague); Vzpp-Mikron Industrial & Consumer Electronics.

Principal Competitors

Interros Holding Co.; Sovtransavto; Moskhleb Joint Stock Co.; Perm Timber Producers Joint Stock Co.; Evraz Holding Group; Urals Mining and Metals Co.; Pipe Metallurgical Co; Avtoselkhozmash-Holding Joint Stock Co.; Metalloinvest Holding Co.; RBC Information Systems Joint Stock Co.; Transmash Holding.

Further Reading

"Forgive and Forget?," *Economist (US),* February 12, 2005, p. 74US.
"Investors Eat out of Sistema's Hand As IPO Show Gets Going," *Euroweek,* January 28, 2005, p. 27.
"Sistema Continuing to Diversify," *Euromoney,* January 2002, p. 81.
"Sistema Floats for $1.4bn As Top Funds Flock to Russia," *Euroweek,* February 11, 2005, p. 1.
"Sistema (Launches Public Offering)," *Corporate Finance,* March 2005, p. 10.
"Sistema $1.6bn IPO on Track Say Bankers, Despite Analyst Doubt Over Price Range," *Euroweek,* February 4, 2005, p. 32.
Yevtushenkov, Vladimir, "Sistema JSFC: A Holding Company with Interests That Span 12 Key Business Areas," *Worldlink,* January-February 2002, p. 158.

—M.L. Cohen

Smith & Wesson Corp.

2100 Roosevelt Avenue
Springfield, Massachusetts 01104-1606
U.S.A.
Telephone: (413) 781-8300
Toll Free: (800) 331-0852
Fax: (413) 747-3677
Web site: http://www.smith-wesson.com

Wholly Owned Subsidiary of Smith & Wesson Holding Corporation
Incorporated: 1856 as Smith & Wesson, Inc.
Employees: 682
Sales: $119.5 million (2004)
NAIC: 332994 Small Arms Manufacturing; 332999 All Other Miscellaneous Fabricated Metal Products Manufacturing

Smith & Wesson Corp. is the leading manufacturer of handguns in the United States. Among the company's best known products over the years have been the .22 rimfire revolver (Model 1), which became a worldwide success in the mid-1800s; the .38 special revolver (Model 10), a 20th-century model used extensively by police forces; the .44 Magnum revolver made famous by Clint Eastwood in his *Dirty Harry* movies; and the line of .357 Magnums, which, according to the company, became the most popular line of revolvers of all time. Smith & Wesson also sells pistols, handcuffs, and bicycles designed for law enforcement use, as well as licensed products, including apparel, knives, coffee mugs, and watches, affixed with the company logo. Smith & Wesson Corp. is the main operating subsidiary of the publicly traded Smith & Wesson Holding Corporation.

Mid-19th-Century Origins

The history of Smith & Wesson begins in the 1850s with a partnership between Horace Smith and Daniel B. Wesson. Smith was born in 1808 in Cheshire, Massachusetts. His father, a carpenter, moved the family to Springfield, Massachusetts, four years later, taking a job in the U.S. Armory. After finishing his public school education at age 16, Smith joined his father at the Armory as a gunsmith's apprentice. He gained expertise in the manufacture of guns through the 18 years he spent at the Armory. In the 1840s Smith worked for a number of gun manufacturers and spent three years running his own gun-making concern. In 1851 he patented an improvement on the breech-loading rifle. He next took a position at Allen, Brown & Luther, a rifle barrel manufacturer based in Worcester, Massachusetts. It was there that he met Wesson.

Born in 1825 in Worcester, Wesson worked on the family farm and attended school until the age of 18. He then apprenticed himself to his eldest brother, a gunsmith. After completing his apprenticeship in 1846, Wesson worked as a journeyman gunsmith before taking over his brother's business after his death in 1850. Soon thereafter, he joined Allen, Brown & Luther.

This was still the era of the muzzle loaders, firearms that had to be reloaded with loose powder, ball, and primer. Through their partnership, Smith and Wesson played a key role in the ending of the muzzle-loading era. They formed their first partnership, the Smith & Wesson Arms Company, in 1852, working to perfect a lever-action pistol with a metallic cartridge and a new repeating action, for which the partners received a patent in February 1854. According to Smith & Wesson historian Roy G. Jinks, ''The fire power of this lever action pistol was so impressive, that in 1854 when the gun was reviewed by *Scientific American,* it was nicknamed the Volcanic since its rapid fire sequence had the force of an erupting volcano.''

The repeating action of the pistol was not entirely successful and when the Norwich, Connecticut-based company encountered financial problems, Oliver Winchester stepped in as a new investor. The factory was moved to New Haven, Connecticut, and the company name was changed to Volcanic Arms Company. In 1855 Smith retired while Wesson accepted a position as superintendent of the company. Wesson soon departed as well. The company later adapted the 1854 patent to rifles, creating the Winchester repeating rifle, which became world famous. In 1866 this firm changed its name again, to the Winchester Repeating Arms Company.

Meanwhile, in 1856 Smith and Wesson joined in a new partnership and began manufacturing the first Smith & Wesson revolver ("Model 1") in Springfield, Massachusetts. This revolver was based on a patent the partners had received in August 1854 for a central-fire metallic cartridge, which contained not only powder but also a lubricant located within the case between the powder and the ball. The revolver included what was called a "rimfire" cartridge (later known as the .22 rimfire), featured repeating action and an open cylinder, and was manufactured with interchangeable parts. Its unique design helped make it an enormous success, including its adoption by U.S. military authorities. When demand exceeded the capacity of the firm's small, 25-person workshop, Smith & Wesson built a new factory in central Springfield on Stockbridge Street near the Armory, and expanded its workforce to 600. Improving on the original model, the company soon introduced the Model 2, which featured a .32-caliber cartridge.

Late 19th-Century Growth

During the Civil War, demand for Smith & Wesson revolvers increased further and helped establish the company as one of the top gunmakers in the United States. Following the war, however, sales fell to just a few guns per month as the ensuing depression hit Smith & Wesson hard. To drum up new sales, the partners established sales agencies in England, France, and Germany. They also exhibited their wares at the international exhibition in Paris in 1867, resulting in large contracts with several European and South American countries, as well as Japan and China. The Russian government alone placed an order for 200,000 revolvers. With a larger international market secured, the company proceeded to introduce its first large caliber gun, a .44-caliber revolver, the Model 3. This gun proved popular around the world and in the American West.

In addition to making improved models based on their own inventions, Smith and Wesson also purchased patents from other inventors. One of the most important of these was a design by William C. Dodge that automatically emptied shells from a gun—a patent Smith & Wesson bought in 1869. In July 1873 Smith sold his interest in the company to Wesson and retired. He died 20 years later, leaving no direct descendants. Wesson carried on as the sole principal for ten years before bringing his two sons on board as partners in 1883. Four years later, Wesson patented a safety revolver designed to prevent accidental firing. Smith & Wesson in 1899 introduced its most famous revolver, the .38 Military & Police, also known as the Model 10—a gun

popular with law enforcement officials for nearly the entire 20th century. After Wesson died in 1906, the company he cofounded continued to be owned and managed by members of the Wesson family well into the 20th century.

New Models and War Contributions in the First Half of the 20th Century

The early decades of the 20th century were marked by the introduction of the N frame line of revolvers. This line featured a new larger frame, and first appeared in 1908 with a .44-caliber S&W Special cartridge. The N frame revolver received international notice during World War I, when Smith & Wesson supplied 75,000 N frame revolvers to the British government. For one year during the war, the U.S. government took over Smith & Wesson, operating it as part of the Springfield Armory.

The 1930s saw the debut of the K-22 Outdoorsman, a model designed for the competitive shooter, and the .357 Magnum, a more powerful handgun designed for law enforcement officers. The .357, introduced in 1935, marked the debut of the Magnum line, which became famous later in the century. Like most companies, Smith & Wesson was hit hard by the Great Depression. At one point, its workforce was reduced to just 24 employees, and the firm pursued diversification, making other products such as a toilet flush valve. In the end, it was Smith & Wesson's growing popularity with law enforcement officials—particularly after the introduction of the .357 Magnum—coupled with rising crime rates, that saved the company.

During World War II, Smith & Wesson supplied arms to the United States and its allies; by 1941 the company was entirely dedicated to war production. By war's end, the company had supplied more than 1.1 million .38 Military & Police revolvers.

In 1946 C.R. Hellstrom was named president of Smith & Wesson, becoming the first person outside the Wesson family to run the company. Three years later Smith & Wesson completed construction of a new and much larger factory in Springfield. Among the first new models to roll off the assembly lines were Model 39, the first U.S.-made 9mm double-action pistol, and Model 29, the legendary .44 Magnum, which debuted in 1955.

Bangor Punta/Lear Siegler Era, 1965–87

By the mid-1960s Smith & Wesson reigned as a leading maker of handguns, with an emphasis on revolvers used in law enforcement, and had also begun to sell handcuffs. It was still largely in the hands of the Wesson family, with some stock selling over the counter. For the year ending in June 1965, the company posted earnings of $1.5 million on sales of $10.4 million. During 1965 Smith & Wesson introduced Model 60, the first all stainless steel revolver. Late that year, the firm's era of independence came to an end with its acquisition by Bangor Punta Alegre Sugar Corp., a conglomerate based in Bangor, Maine, with operations in railroads, textiles, foundry equipment, sewage disposal systems, yacht manufacturing, commercial finance, grain elevators, and other areas. Bangor Punta paid about $22.6 million to gain control of Smith & Wesson.

Under Bangor Punta ownership, Smith & Wesson expanded its product line into areas related to handguns and handcuffs in the 1970s. For the law enforcement market, Smith & Wesson began selling riot control equipment, night vision apparatus, breath-testing instruments, police car lights, and sirens. Another new law enforcement product was the Identi-Kit software program, which helped investigations create facial composite drawings of suspects. In the sporting market, Smith & Wesson began offering its dealers a full line of products, including ammunition, holsters, and long guns. By the late 1970s about 25 percent of the company's sales were for nongun products.

The 1970s was a period of slow or no growth for the U.S. firearms industry, which faced a host of problems, concisely summarized in a 1978 *Business Week* article: "skyrocketing product liability costs, highly restricted export markets, burgeoning labor and materials costs, an aging plant and skilled labor force, foreign gunrunning scandals, the recurring threat of federal gun controls, diminishing hunting grounds and shorter hunting seasons, stiff competition from imports, and, recently, competition from foreign companies manufacturing firearms in the U.S." While Smith & Wesson was not immune to these problems, it was, according to *Business Week,* "the envy of the industry" because of its grip on the law enforcement market and its efficient, modern plants. The company was also highly profitable, posting operating profits of $18.4 million on sales of $84 million for the year ending in September 1977.

In the early 1980s Smith & Wesson began making 9mm semiautomatic pistols for the U.S. military and for law enforcement agencies seeking more powerful weapons to do battle with heavily armed criminals. In January 1984 Santa Monica, California-based Lear Siegler Corporation acquired Bangor Punta, giving Smith & Wesson a new parent. Under the direction of Lear Siegler, whose primary holdings were in the manufacture of aerospace and automotive parts and systems, Smith & Wesson divested numerous noncore areas in order to concentrate on its main areas of strength: making and selling handguns, handcuffs, and police Identi-Kits.

In spite of the divestments, Smith & Wesson was a company on the decline in the early to mid-1980s. Its entry into the semiautomatic handgun market was the move of a follower, not a market leader. The U.S. units of two foreign gunmakers, Austria's Glock GmbH and Italy's Beretta S.p.A., had led the introduction of semiautomatic weapons into the U.S. market. With overall sales of guns remaining flat, the new competition not only ate away at Smith & Wesson's market share, they also cut into its sales. It was also becoming clear, as summarized by Charles E. Petty writing in *American Rifleman,* that the quality of Smith & Wesson guns was on the decline. Although sales had surpassed the $100 million mark by the early 1980s, growth slowed by the mid-1980s and profits were down. For the fiscal year ending in June 1986, the gunmaker reported operating profits of $14.1 million on sales of $116.1 million. The profits figure represented a decline of 41 percent from the level in 1982.

The Tomkins Era of the Late 1980s and 1990s

It was in this troubled state that Smith & Wesson would once again see its ownership change hands. In December 1986 leveraged buyout (LBO) specialist Forstmann Little & Co. led a group that took Lear Siegler private in a $2.1 billion LBO, with a new holding company created called Lear Siegler Holdings Corporation. As was typical of 1980s LBOs, the new holding company quickly sought to sell off noncore assets to pay down the debt incurred in the buyout. Smith & Wesson was one of the companies identified as noncore, as Lear Siegler Holdings intended to concentrate on its aerospace and automotive operations. Among the firms bidding to acquire Smith & Wesson was fellow firearms maker Sturm, Ruger & Company, Inc. Prevailing in the end, however, was U.K. conglomerate F.H. Tomkins PLC (later simply Tomkins PLC), which paid $112.5 million in June 1997 to purchase Smith & Wesson, marking its first foray into the United States.

Tomkins saw in Smith & Wesson "a company with a good name and market position with a strong potential for growth through management achievement," according to Robert Muddimer, as quoted in *American Rifleman.* Muddimer, who was installed as interim president of the gunmaker, said that Tomkins' initial goal was "to enhance quality, and to service the market in terms of quality and accuracy with a blend of new technology and traditional gunsmithing arts." In recognition of the company's problems with the quality of its products, Tomkins set out to make improvements by modernizing the design and manufacturing process through the addition of computer-aided design equipment and a host of high-tech manufacturing apparatus. Tomkins also instituted a much more rigorous testing process. Already by mid-1989 the new equipment and programs had helped significantly lower the rate at which guns were being returned for warranty repair. For automatic pistols, the return rate had fallen from 6.3 percent to a record low of 1.2 percent, while only 2 percent of Smith & Wesson revolvers were being returned for service, halving the previous rate of 4 percent.

Although Tomkins was clearly aware of the declining quality of Smith & Wesson guns prior to its purchase of the company, the British firm came to believe that Forstmann Little had misled it about a jamming problem in a line of L-frame .357 Magnum revolvers. In 1994 Tomkins sued Forstmann Little for damages and indemnification.

Meanwhile, the Tomkins-led Smith & Wesson was showing a renewed vigor in the area of product development. In 1988 the company launched an improved, third-generation line of semiautomatic pistols. With interest in gun ownership increasing among women, Smith & Wesson introduced the LadySmith line of handguns in 1989. Under the leadership of Ed Shultz, who became president in 1992, Smith & Wesson introduced the Sigma Series of pistols. Debuting in March 1994, the Sigma Series was the company's first line to feature plastic frames. Glock sued Smith & Wesson over the design of the Sigma, alleging patent infringement and other charges, leading to a 1997 settlement whereby Smith & Wesson agreed to make a multimillion-dollar payment to Glock and to slightly modify the Sigma pistols. Another light-weight line, the AirLite Ti titanium revolvers, was introduced in 1999.

In January 1998 Smith & Wesson began selling bicycles designed specifically for police work. During the late 1990s the company also opened up eight retail stores around the United States, selling apparel and a variety of other nongun products affixed with the company logo. This latest diversification away from guns came at a time when gun sales remained stagnant. Americans already owned approximately 230 million guns, which last for a long time, dampening demand. Other reasons given for the sales stagnation included a decreasing interest in hunting and falling crime rates, the latter of which might have been resulting in decreased demand for self-protection weapons. At the same time, the gun industry was under an increasing legal assault, with more and more municipalities suing gun manufacturers alleging negligence in the manufacturing, marketing, and distribution of guns. These suits were somewhat similar to the largely successful suits brought against the tobacco industry in the late 1990s. The potential for large liability judgments, along with increasing calls for stiffer federal gun control measures, gave added impetus to Smith & Wesson's and other gunmakers' moves to diversify. For its part, Smith & Wesson aimed to increase its sales of nongun products to 50 percent of overall sales, which would be a substantial increase over the 18 percent level of the late 1990s.

Early 2000s: Beset by Troubles, Returning to American Ownership

By early 2000 more than two dozen cities and counties had filed lawsuits against gun manufacturers. Early legal decisions represented a mixed bag, although there were several clear victories for the gunmakers. Nevertheless, Smith & Wesson, still led by Shultz, broke ranks with others in the gun industry by entering into an agreement with the Clinton administration in March 2000. Among other provisions, the firm agreed to demand background checks on buyers at gun shows, install safety locks on all its guns, and work on a high-tech gun that could be fired only by its owner. In return, many local governments dropped Smith & Wesson from their lawsuits, and the Clinton administration agreed not to name the company in any future suit it might file against the industry.

Hailed as a landmark deal at the time, the agreement was the precipitating factor in a crisis that soon engulfed the firm. Other gun manufacturers quickly denounced the company for making the deal, and many gun enthusiasts—feeling that the lawsuits were part of a larger attempt to limit gun rights—began boycotting the company, some vowing never to buy a Smith & Wesson gun again. Sales plunged. Adding to the turmoil at the company was Tomkins' announcement in July 2000 that it intended to sell Smith & Wesson as part of a streamlining aimed at shedding noncore units. This same divestiture plan led to Shultz's departure in October. He had been serving simultaneously as president of another Tomkins' unit, Murray Inc., maker of lawn mowers, go-carts, and bicycles. When Tomkins sold Murray, Shultz resigned from Smith & Wesson in order to remain president of Murray. George Colclough, vice-president of administration, succeeded Shultz. Meanwhile, the steep sales decline mainly attributable to the consumer boycott led Smith & Wesson to announce, also in October, the layoff of 15 percent of its workforce—125 employees.

In a seeming case of a minnow swallowing a whale, Tomkins ended up selling Smith & Wesson to Saf-T-Hammer Corporation in May 2001. The purchase price, apparently reflecting the firm's troubled nature, was only $15 million, although Saf-T-Hammer also agreed to assume $53 million in debt. Based in Scottsdale, Arizona, Saf-T-Hammer was a manufacturer of gun locks that had been founded in 1998 and had begun selling its products in late 2000. The company's president, Robert Scott, had spent ten years as a Smith & Wesson vice-president before joining Saf-T-Hammer in 1999. He was named the new president of Smith & Wesson Corp., now American-owned again and still headquartered in Springfield, Massachusetts.

The precipitous decline in sales not only cost Smith & Wesson its place as the leading U.S. maker of handguns to Sturm, Ruger, it also led to a $14 million loss for the fiscal year ending in April 2001. Scott moved quickly to turn the company's fortunes around, particularly by mending fences within the gun industry. Buyers slowly began returning, and sales grew from $70.7 million in the fiscal year ending in April 2001 to $79.3 million the following, before jumping to $98.5 million the year after that. After suffering a net loss of $10.8 million in the fiscal year ending in April 2002, Smith & Wesson returned to profitability one year later, $15.7 million in the black. Aiding this turnaround were a number of other Scott initiatives, including improving the production process and turning out new gun products, although the firm's efforts to aggressively license the company's name for myriad items—such as fine art prints, watches, body armor, safes, footwear, and golf clubs—yielded little in the way of profits. During this same period, the legal threat that had been hanging over the gun industry more or less evaporated. A growing number of the lawsuits were dismissed, and the newly installed, pro-gun Bush administration backed away from the "landmark" deal between the government and Smith & Wesson.

In early 2002, meanwhile, Saf-T-Hammer renamed itself Smith & Wesson Holding Corporation. In January of the following year, Scott was named chairman and CEO of Smith & Wesson Corp. (the operating subsidiary). Taking over as president was Roy C. Cuny, a former president of Peerless Manufacturing Co., a maker of air filtering equipment. Cuny had joined Smith & Wesson in November 2002 as vice-president for operations. As president, he oversaw the launch of nine new handguns in early 2003. These guns garnered strong interest at national and international trade shows held in February and March. Among them was the Model 500, a .50-caliber revolver weighing 4.5 pounds, which was the largest, most powerful handgun ever made, and the .45-caliber Model 1911 pistol, which was a modernized replica of the military sidearm that the U.S. Army used for most of the first half of the 20th century.

Although Smith & Wesson was seemingly on the road to recovery, it was soon engulfed in a new round of controversy, mainly revolving around machinations at the parent holding company. In December 2003 Smith & Wesson Holding filed its annual report five months after the deadline because it needed to restate its results for 2002 owing to a series of mistakes in the way it had accounted for its acquisition of the gunmaker. That same month, Chairman and CEO Mitchell A. Saltz and President Colton R. Melby of the parent company stepped down from their posts while retaining spots on the board of directors. Saltz and Melby were the firm's two largest shareholders. Cuny was named chairman, president, and CEO of Smith & Wesson Holding, but just one month later a new chairman was appointed, James J. Minder, a management consultant and member of the board of directors since 2001. Also in January 2004 the holding company announced that it would close its Scottsdale headquarters and move its functions to the subsidiary's Springfield offices. Then in February 2004 came more embarrassment when Minder resigned the chairman's post while maintaining a seat on the board after it was revealed that he was a felon who in the 1950s and 1960s had served 15 years in Michigan prisons for dozens of armed robberies, including a bank heist, and an attempted escape from jail. Taking over as chairman was another member of the board, G. Dennis Bingham.

Smith & Wesson Corp. attempted to put all these distractions behind it by refocusing on its core gun line during 2004. The firm shut down a nascent and ill-conceived venture into home decor cataloging and divested other businesses as well, including its Identi-Kit software program. Millions were spent to improve and expand production at the Springfield plant. During the year, Smith & Wesson regained its position as the top maker of handguns in the United States. This positive note, however, was followed by the announcement in November

2004 that Cuny had left the company with no indication of the reason for the sudden departure. Bingham resigned as well around this same time and was replaced as chairman by Barry M. Monheit, a management consultant and independent board member. In December 2004 Michael F. Golden was brought onboard as the company's fifth leader in as many years. The new president and CEO had previously held management positions with three leading U.S. manufacturing firms: Kohler Company, Black & Decker Corporation, and Stanley Works.

Several other changes in the top management were made around this same time as Smith & Wesson attempted to assemble a more marketing-savvy leadership team. Early in 2005 the parent company completed a refinancing that reduced its total debt by $21.3 million and offered $1.5 million in savings on interest expense for the fiscal year ending in April 2006. The Golden-led team also began working on a plan to broaden the firm's focus to include "safety, security, protection, and sport." After more than 150 years in the handgun market, Smith & Wesson was considering moving into the production of shotguns or rifles and was also looking into licensing its name for such products as ammunition, nonlethal weapons, and home security systems. The company was also stepping up efforts to bolster sales to law enforcement agencies and the military, both areas in which Smith & Wesson once dominated but had been lagging for some time. Perhaps most important was Golden's intention to bolster marketing and to turn what he called "a quiet company" into a much more visible one.

Principal Competitors

Sturm, Ruger & Company, Inc.; Taurus International Manufacturing, Inc.; Glock GmbH; SIGARMS, Inc.; Fabbrica D'Armi Pietro Beretta S.p.A.; Peerless Handcuff Company.

Further Reading

"Bangor Punta Plans Bid to Buy Stock of Smith & Wesson," *Wall Street Journal,* October 7, 1965, p. 19.

Barrett, Paul M., "Attacks on Firearms Echo Earlier Assaults on Tobacco Industry," *Wall Street Journal,* March 12, 1999, pp. A1, A6.

——, "Gun Industry Seeks to Shut a Trade Group," *Wall Street Journal,* June 7, 1999, pp. A3, A6.

——, "Smith & Wesson CEO Is Gun Industry's Maverick," *Wall Street Journal,* January 17, 2000, p. B1.

——, "Uneasy Gun Makers Add Gentler Product Lines," *Wall Street Journal,* March 25, 1999, pp. B1, B10.

Bravin, Jess, and Sara Calian, "Smith & Wesson to Be Acquired by Arizona Firm," *Wall Street Journal,* May 15, 2001, p. B10.

Butterfield, Fox, and Raymond Hernandez, "Gun Maker's Accord on Curbs Brings Pressure from Industry," *New York Times,* March 30, 2000, p. A1.

Carr, Robert E., "Women's Market Is Not Gun-Shy: S&W," *Sporting Goods Business,* March 1989, p. 29.

Dao, James, "Under Legal Siege, Gun Maker Agrees to Accept Curbs," *New York Times,* March 18, 2000, p. A1.

Fields, Gary, "White House Retreats from Smith & Wesson Deal," *Wall Street Journal,* August 1, 2001, p. A4.

Freebairn, William, "Corporate Misfires Take Toll on Image," *Springfield (Mass.) Republican,* February 29, 2004, p. D1.

——, "New CEO: Gunmaker an 'Absolute Gem,'" *Springfield (Mass.) Republican,* November 28, 2004, p. D1.

——, "New Smith & Wesson Chief Eager to Grow Gunmaker," *Springfield (Mass.) Union-News,* January 12, 2003, p. E1.

——, "Shakeup at Top of Firearms Company," *Springfield (Mass.) Republican,* December 6, 2003, p. A1.

——, "Smith & Wesson at 150: Springfield Gunmaker Defined by Controversy, Innovation," *Springfield (Mass.) Union-News,* August 4, 2002, p. E1.

——, "Smith & Wesson CEO Sees Broader, Loud Future," *Springfield (Mass.) Republican,* June 5, 2005, p. D1.

——, "Smith & Wesson Returning Home," *Springfield (Mass.) Republican,* January 22, 2004, p. A1.

——, "Smith & Wesson to Restate Results," *Springfield (Mass.) Republican,* August 15, 2003, p. C7.

Fried, Joseph P., "Gun Marketing Is Issue in Trial Against Makers," *The New York Times,* January 6, 1999, pp. A1, B7.

Fuhrman, Peter, "A Conglomerate of His Own," *Forbes,* February 27, 1995, pp. 106 +.

Furchgott, Roy, "Packing Heat—and a Big Wheel, Too," *Business Week,* March 9, 1998, p. 6.

Hull, Jennifer Bingham, "Lear Siegler Inc. Agrees to Buy Bangor Punta," *Wall Street Journal,* December 13, 1983, p. 2.

Humphreys, Noel D., "Dangerous Deal: How a Fast Sell-Off Haunts an LBO Firm," *Mergers & Acquisitions,* November/December 1994, pp. 39 +.

Jinks, Roy G., *History of Smith & Wesson: No Thing of Importance Will Come Without Effort,* North Hollywood, Calif.: Beinfeld Publishing, 1977, 290 p.

Lambert, Wade, and Richard B. Schmitt, "Tomkins to Sell Smith & Wesson in Plan to Shed Its Noncore Units," *Wall Street Journal,* July 24, 2000, p. A6.

"Lear Siegler Holdings Says It Will Sell Units, Posts Loss for Quarter," *Wall Street Journal,* February 19, 1987.

Maines, John, "Can Females Be Friends with Firearms?," *American Demographics,* June 1992, pp. 22 +.

Maremont, Mark, "A Raider's New World," *Business Week,* June 15, 1987, pp. 49–50.

O'Connell, Vanessa, "Smith & Wesson Chairman Quits As Past Armed Robberies Surface," *Wall Street Journal,* February 27, 2004, p. A1.

——, "Under the Gun: How Troubled Past Finally Caught Up with James Minder," *Wall Street Journal,* March 8, 2004, p. A1.

O'Connell, Vanessa, and Paul M. Barrett, "Firearms Firms, Amid Rising Litigation, Take Steps to Reduce Criminal Gun Use," *Wall Street Journal,* July 22, 1999, p. B10.

——, "Line of Fire: As Lawsuits Falter, a Big Gun Maker Retools Its Image," *Wall Street Journal,* October 16, 2002, p. A1.

Petty, Charles E., "Inside Smith & Wesson," *American Rifleman,* August 1989, pp. 46–49, 85–86, 94.

Rasmusson, Erika, "A Company Under Siege," *Sales and Marketing Management,* April 2000, pp. 90–96.

Stevenson, Richard W., "Smith & Wesson Is Sold to Britons," *New York Times,* May 23, 1987, pp. 33, 35.

Taylor, Roger, "Too Big for Its Own Good?," *Financial Times,* January 17, 1998, p. FTM5.

Thurman, Russ, "S&W and Glock Settle Suit," *Shooting Industry,* June 1997, p. 62.

——, "Smith & Wesson Is Back!," *Shooting Industry,* May 2003, pp. 24–26.

Wagner, Eileen Brill, "Under the Gun: How Saf-T-Hammer Snared Smith & Wesson," *Phoenix Business Journal,* June 22, 2001, pp. 1, 44–45.

"Why the Firearms Business Has Tired Blood," *Business Week,* November 27, 1978, pp. 107, 110, 112.

Widem, Allen M., "Smith & Wesson Aims Its Mace at the Public," *Advertising Age,* May 31, 1984, pp. 3, 53.

—David E. Salamie

Société BIC S.A.

14 rue Jeanne d'Asnieres
Clichy F-92611
France
Telephone: +33 1 45195200
Fax: +33 1 45195299
Web site: http://www.bicworld.com

Public Company
Incorporated: 1945
Employees: 8,706
Sales: EUR 1.37 billion ($1.9 billion) (2004)
Stock Exchanges: Euronext Paris
Ticker Symbol: BB
NAIC: 339941 Pen and Mechanical Pencil Manufacturing;
    325620 Toilet Preparation Manufacturing; 332211
    Cutlery and Flatware (Except Precious) Manufacturing;
    339942 Lead Pencil and Art Good Manufacturing

Société BIC S.A. (Bic) is the world's leading manufacturer of ball-point pens, selling some 22 million pens and other stationery items every day. The company's ball-point pens—which revolutionized the writing world upon their introduction in the late 1940s—remain its core product, and sales of pens and stationery items, including the Wite-Out and Tipp-Ex brands of correction products, represented 52 percent of the group's sales of EUR 1.37 billion ($1.9 billion) in 2004. One of the world's best-known brands, Bic is almost equally recognized for its disposable lighters, launched in the mid-1970s, which continue to sell more than four million each day. Lighters account for 25 percent of group sales. Bic also is a top contender in the global disposable shaver market, selling 11 million razors daily, which contributes an additional 19 percent to sales. Bic also has acquired a strong stable of brands, including luxury pen maker Sheaffer, Conte pencils, Stypen and Tipp-Ex, both acquired in 2004, and Wite Out, as well as the new Bic Kids brand, launched in 2004. Beyond its core consumer products, Bic produces windsurf boards, kayaks, and similar sports equipment under its Bic Sports subsidiary. The company also operates Bic Graphic, which provides promotional products to the corporate market. Bic has been an international operation almost from its beginning; in 2005, the company included 23 factories worldwide, with sales and distribution to 160 countries. The North American and Oceania markets accounted for 46 percent of sales. Western Europe represented 33 percent of sales. Eastern Europe, the Middle East, Africa, and Asia added 8 percent to sales, and Latin America generated 13 percent of the group's sales. Listed on the Euronext Paris Stock Exchange, Bic is led by Bruno Bich, son of the company's founder.

Writing Revolution in the 1950s

The first ''practical'' writing pens, such as developed by Lewis Waterman in 1884, began to appear in the late 19th century. Yet these pens remained of the fountain pen variety, and retained many of their disadvantages, such as the need to refill frequently, and a tendency to leak. The first patents for a new type of ''ball-point'' pen were filed toward the end of the century. One of the earliest of these was filed by John Loud, a New York tanner, in 1888. Loud's pen featured a ball point, and was designed to write on leather. Yet Loud never launched production of his ball-point pen.

The next step forward in the development of the ball-point pen came in the 1930s, when Hungary's Ladislao (or Laszlo) Biro took up the cause. Biro had a gift for invention—at a young age, he had invented a manual washing machine that brought him some success. During the 1930s, while working as an editor for a cultural magazine, Biro became frustrated with his fountain pen, the sharp tip of which often tore at the paper. Yet on a visit to the printer, Biro recognized the potential for developing a pen capable of using a thicker ink such as used in a printing press. Biro and brother George, a chemist, began working on a prototype for a new type of ball-point pen, coming up with their first design by 1938.

In that year, however, the Biros fled Hungary for Paris. While on a vacation in Yugoslavia, the brothers had a chance meeting with the president of Argentina. Impressed by the Biros' ball-point pen design, the president invited them to immigrate to Argentina. Once set up in Buenos Aires, the Biros continued working on their ball-point pen. By 1943, the Biros had developed a workable design, filed for a patent, and set up a company to begin manufacturing the pens. The new type of pen proved a quick success in Argentina, and was then introduced in the United Kingdom, where it also became a quick seller. At the same time, Milton Reynolds launched a copy of the pen (which had not been patented in the United States) and was soon joined by others.

Yet the success of the early generation of ball-point pens was short-lived. By the late 1940s, as Biro's and other designs revealed their own flaws, including a propensity for leaking, sales of ball-point pens dropped off dramatically. New designs arrived to take their place, such as the Parker company's Jotter and the Frawley company's Papermate, both of which became popular sellers in the 1950s.

The true ball-point revolution, however, arrived from France in the 1950s. Baron Marcel Bich, whose family originated from Italy and had received their title from King Charles Albert of Savoy in 1848, had started his career as a door-to-door salesman in France. Bich later went to work as a production manager for an ink manufacturer, before gaining a background in working with plastics and using molding technology. When the first ball-point pens began to arrive in France in the mid-1940s, Bich was alarmed at their poor quality, and recognized the potential for developing an improved ball-point design.

In 1945, Bich and partner Edouard Buffard bought a pen factory in Clichy, near Paris, launching production of fountain pens and mechanical pencils. But Bich was determined to launch a new ball-point pen design, and in 1950 acquired the patent rights from the Biro brothers. Bich began studying the different ball-point pens then available, even using a microscope to examine their construction. By 1952, Bich had succeeded in creating his own design—a streamlined pen made of clear plastic that was far less prone to leaking than existing designs, was able to write upside down, and could reportedly draw a line more than two kilometers long. Of importance, Bich's design could be sold very inexpensively, with an initial price set at just 50 centimes, or about one cent.

Bich also recognized the need for a catchy name for his product and dropped the "h" from his name to create what was to become one of the world's best-known brands: BIC. The product was instantly successful; by 1954, the company had sold 21 million pens. Bic was an international success almost from the start, as the ball-point pen became a strong seller throughout Europe. By 1953, the company's sales topped more than 40 million pens per year.

Bic expanded beyond Europe in the mid-1950s, opening a subsidiary in Brazil in 1956, before expanding into nearly every South American market. That year, the company also launched a successful follow-up to the original Bic, a retractable ball-point called the M10 Clic, and later known as the Bic Clic. The company's international expansion continued, with an entry into the Middle East and Africa. In the meantime, Bic sought an entry into the vast U.S. market.

That entry came in 1958, when Bic paid $1 million to acquire a 60 percent stake in the Waterman Pen Company, based in Connecticut. Once the world's largest manufacturer of fountain pens, Waterman had fallen on hard times with the skyrocketing sales of ball-point pens in the 1950s. Following the acquisition, Bic discovered the full extent of Waterman's financial problems—and added the remaining 40 percent as part of the original purchase price. The U.S. operation then took on the name of Waterman-Bic Pen Corporation. The company's entry into the United States, where the Bic was launched as the Bic Stick, was backed by a highly successful advertising campaign based on the slogan, "writes first time, every time."

Consumables Innovator in the 1970s

Bic expanded again in the late 1950s, buying Sweden's Ballograf in 1959. The company entered the Japanese market in the mid-1960s. By the end of that decade, Bic had begun its first efforts to diversify beyond its ball-point pens. In 1969, Bic launched a division producing promotional items for corporations, which formed the basis for later subsidiary Bic Graphic.

Yet low-cost, consumable goods remained the company's bread and butter. After going public with a listing on the Paris Stock Exchange in 1972, Bic launched a new international success: a disposable cigarette lighter. The butane-filled Bic Lighter represented a new success in a market long dominated by refillable—and often leaky and unreliable—lighters. Yet again, Bic had not been the first to produce a disposable lighter—that distinction went to French luxury cigarette lighter company S.T. Dupont, which had developed its own disposable lighter, called Cricket. Dupont was acquired by Gillette, which launched the lighter in the United States a full year ahead of Bic. Once again, however, savvy advertising played a strong role in the Bic brand's success, as advertising campaigns exhorted consumers to "flick my Bic." By 1978, Bic had established itself as the market leader, and by 1983, Gillette sold off the Cricket brand.

The 1970s held one more product success in store for the company. In 1975, Bic became the first to introduce a one-piece disposable razor. The product helped spark a whole new razor market, bringing Bic into competition with market leaders Schick and Gillette; the latter even responded by launching its own disposable razor in the United States, called the Good

---

Key Dates:

1945: Marcel Bich buys a factory in Clichy, France, producing fountain pens and mechanical pencils.
1950: The company acquires the patent rights for the Biro ballpoint pen and begins developing its own ballpoint pen.
1952: The launch of BIC pens is an immediate success.
1956: The company begins sales outside of Europe, launching a subsidiary in Brazil.
1958: The company acquires the Waterman pen company in the United States, which later becomes BIC Corp.
1972: BIC goes public on the Paris Stock Exchange.
1973: The BIC disposable lighter is launched.
1975: The BIC disposable razor is launched.
1979: The company acquires Conte, of France.
1981: The company creates BIC Sport and begins production of sailboards.
1989: Parfum BIC is launched (but discontinued in 1991).
1992: BIC Corp. acquires Wite-Out.
1994: Bruno Bich takes over the company.
1995: The company acquires full control of U.S. subsidiary BIC Corp.
1997: Tipp-Ex and Sheaffer are acquired.
2004: Stypen in France and Kosaido in Japan are acquired.

News. Although Bic never captured a leading share in the overall razor market, it captured the lead in the disposable segment, and its razor sales nonetheless became an important part of its revenues, with sales of more than 11 million razors daily into the mid-2000s.

The company's U.S. subsidiary, which adopted the simplified name Bic Corporation in the early 1980s, later launched its own public offering, becoming nominally separate from its French parent. Bic Corp. quickly emerged as the group's most dynamic operation. This came in large part because of the buoyancy and intense competitiveness of the U.S. market. Joining the company in the early 1970s was Bich's son Bruno, who began his career as a salesman for the company. By 1982, however, the younger Bich had taken over as the U.S. subsidiary's CEO.

Bic expanded its writing materials operations in 1979 with the acquisition of fellow French company Conte, which specialized in pencils of all varieties. Conte had its origins in the late 18th century, when Nicolas Jacques Conte invented modern pencil lead with a mixture of graphite and clay. Conte received a patent—number 32 in France—and launched production of pencils in 1795.

The 1980s marked Marcel Bich's attempt to steer the company into new product categories. Bich, a yachting enthusiast who led France's entry in the America's Cup, set up Bic Sport in 1981. That subsidiary took up Bich's interests in water sports, launching production of windsurf equipment and sailboards. Although that operation achieved some success, other attempts by Bich to diversify the company did not. Among these was the group's attempt to enter the pantyhose market, with the launch of the "Fannyhose" in the late 1970s. That product failed to inspire consumers.

Instead, the company attempted to buy into the hosiery market, acquiring French market leader Dim in the mid-1980s. Bic continued to expand into the clothing market, acquiring Rosy, a lingerie maker, and the fashion house Guy La Roche. In the late 1980s, the company attempted to do for the perfume market what it had done for pens, launching a line of inexpensive "spritzers" under the Parfum Bic brand in 1989. Sales of the company's perfume were so dismal that the company pulled the product by the end of 1991.

In the meantime, the company found itself embattled by a growing number of lawsuits involving the safety of its disposable lighters. Although the company successfully defended itself against many of the claims, citing user negligence, a number of losses led the company to discontinue certain lighter models and to introduce new child-resistant lighters in the early 1990s.

New Acquisitions in the New Century

Marcel Bich died in 1994, and Bruno Bich took his place as company chairman. Under the younger Bich, Bic regrouped around its core product categories of writing materials, lighters, and razors, selling off its clothing and fashion holdings; that process was completed in 2001 with the sale of the Guy La Roche brand. Bic also moved to take firmer control of its flagship U.S. subsidiary, increasing its stake to nearly 90 percent in 1995, and removing its stock market listing.

Meanwhile, Bic had launched a new strategy designed to expand the Bic name beyond its writing business into a more extensive line of stationery. The company had taken a step in that direction when Bic Corp. acquired the Wite-Out brand of correction products in 1992. This acquisition led the company to launch a Wite-Out branded correction pen in 1996.

The following year, Bic made two more significant acquisitions, buying up Germany's Tipp-Ex, which produced its own line of correction and stationery products, and, in an extension into the luxury writing tools segment, Sheaffer.

Into the 2000s, Bic focused on rolling out new products within its core categories, such as the twin blade Softwin in 1999, the Megalighter in 2001, and the Exact Liner, branded under both the Tipp-Ex and Wite-Out names. In 2002, the company launched a new sporting goods product as well, the Bic Kayak.

In 2004, Bic relaunched part of Conte's range of children-oriented pens and stationery products as the Bic Kids brand. The company expected to convert the full range of Conte's coloring products to the Bic Kids brand through the middle of the decade.

In the meantime, Bic completed two more acquisitions, acquiring France's Stypens, which produced a range of pens under its own brand name, but also produced a wide range of licensed pens for brands including Kenzo, Harley Davidson, Harry Potter, and the like. Also in 2004, Bic signaled its intention to boost its presence in the Asian market with the purchase of its Japanese distributor. Bic by then had become one of the world's most recognized brand names.

Principal Subsidiaries

Ballograf BIC (Austria); BIC (NZ) Ltd.; BIC (South Africa) Pty. Ltd.; BIC Argentina S.A.; BIC Australia Pty. Ltd.; BIC

Belgium SPRL; BIC Botswana Pty. Ltd.; BIC Brasil S.A. (Brazil); BIC Chile S.A.; BIC CIS; BIC Colombia S.A.; BIC Corporation (U.S.A.); BIC de Guatemala S.A.; BIC de Venezuela; BIC Ecuador S.A.; BIC GBA Sdn. Bhd. (Malaysia); BIC Graphic Europe S.A.; BIC Holdings Southern Africa Pty. Ltd.; BIC Iberia S.A. (Spain); BIC Inc. (Canada); BIC India Pvt. Ltd.; BIC International Co. (U.S.A.); BIC Italia S.p.A. (Italy); BIC Kosaido KK (Japan); BIC Malawi Pty. Ltd.; BIC Mozambique; BIC Netherlands B.V.; BIC Polska Sp. z.o.o. (Poland); BIC Portugal S.A.; BIC Product (Asia) Pte. Ltd. (Singapore); BIC Product (Korea) Ltd.; BIC Product (Singapore) Pte. Ltd.; BIC Product Thailand Ltd.; BIC Stationery (Shanghai) Co. Ltd. (China); BIC UK Ltd.; BIC Ukraine; BIC Uruguay S.A.; BIC Violex S.A. (Greece); BIC Zambia Ltd.; No Sabe Fallat S.A. de C.V. (Mexico); PT Buana Inti Cakrawala (Indonesia); Société BIC (Suisse) S.A. (Switzerland).

Principal Competitors

Schick Wilkinson Sword; Esselte Sverige AB; Gillette Group Italy S.p.A.; Mitsubishi Pencil Company Ltd.; Herlitz AG; Faber-Castell AG; Staedtler Mars GmbH und Company; Schreib- und Zeichengerate-Fabriken; KOH-I-NOOR HARDTMUTH A.S; China First Pencil Company Ltd.; Productos Pelikan S.A. de C.V.

Further Reading

Bannister, Nicholas, "Fine Line Between Biro and Fame: Brand Values: Bic," *Guardian,* June 26, 1999, p. 28.

"Bic Acquires As Chief's Confidence Burgeons," *Office Products International,* July 2004, p. 17.

"Company Focus: Bic," *Office Products International,* January 2003, p. 36.

Higgins, Steve, "Parisian Parent of Pen-Maker Bic in Milford, Conn Sees Increase in Revenue," *Knight Ridder/Tribune Business,* October 15, 2004.

Rhyle, Sarah, "Stroke of Luxury As Ballpoint Pen-Maker Bic Picks Up Sheaffer for £30m," *Guardian,* August 1, 1997, p. 19.

Rigby, Rhymer, "Inventor Whose Fame Is Writ Large," *Management Today,* March 1998, p. 104.

Saget, Estelle, "Bruno Bich ou le mondialisation à visage humain," *L'Expansion,* May 28, 1998.

Troise, Damian J., "Restructuring Hits Société Bic's Profits," *New Haven Register,* March 4, 2005.

—M.L. Cohen

South Beach Beverage Company, Inc.

40 Richards Avenue
Norwalk, Connecticut 06854-2327
U.S.A.
Telephone: (203) 899-7111
Toll Free: (800) 588-0548
Fax: (203) 899-7177
Web site: http://www.sobebev.com

Wholly Owned Subsidiary of PepsiCo, Inc.
Incorporated: 1995
Employees: 100
Sales: $300 million (2005 est.)
NAIC: 312111 Soft Drink Manufacturing

South Beach Beverage Company, Inc. is a leading marketer of noncarbonated juice and tea-based drinks. The firm's offerings include herb- and vitamin-enhanced beverages with such names as Tsunami, Love Bus Brew, and Orange-Carrot Elixir; energy drinks including Adrenaline Rush and No Fear Super Energy Supplement; and related products including SoBe Gum, SoBe Chocolate bars, SoBe Ice frozen fruit juices, and SoBe clothing. The firm has been a unit of PepsiCo, Inc. since 2001.

Beginnings

The South Beach Beverage Company traces its origins to January 1995, and a lunch meeting in Norwalk, Connecticut, between John Bello and Tom Schwalm. Bello, who had earned his M.B.A. from Dartmouth, had worked for the National Football League's marketing arm for 15 years, including five as its president, and also briefly at Pepsi-Cola and AriZona Beverages. Schwalm had worked for The Stroh Brewery Co., Dribeck Importers, and Barton Beers, and had headed consulting firm Greenwich Beverage Group. Inspired by the success of recent start-up AriZona, which had reached $300 million in sales in less than three years, they decided to form a new beverage company to produce noncarbonated "new age" drinks.

Feeling that a regional identity would help distinguish their brand, they chose the health- and fashion-conscious South Beach area of Miami Beach, Florida, for the company's name, and appropriated a lizard design from the Art Deco façade of the Abbey Hotel in Miami Beach for its logo. The pair assembled a small group of investors to back the venture with $5 million in capital, and signed on the Stroh Brewery Co. to bottle the products at its Winston-Salem, North Carolina plant.

In December 1995 the first South Beach drinks hit stores in Connecticut and Florida. Packaged in 20-ounce bottles with the firm's lizard mascot embossed on the glass, they sported slogans like "Shake well," "Drain the Lizard," and "Grab a Lizard" on their caps. Flavors included Boca Berry-Grape and Palm Peach-Mango, several iced teas, nonalcoholic cocktails such as Pina-Colada Nite Cap, and a blend of orange and carrot juice called Orange Elixir. To promote the launch, the firm's executives began making the rounds of beverage industry conventions and outdoor festivals to give out samples. After a few months the brand name evolved into SoBe, which was Florida shorthand for South Beach.

During its first full year in operation the company shipped 200,000 cases of beverages to stores and took in revenues of $2.1 million, but also recorded $2 million in losses. The firm's products, while good, were not different enough from competitors' to stand out, and distributors were unenthusiastic about the brand. One bright spot was South Beach's healthful orange/carrot juice blend, which had generated a fair amount of positive consumer feedback. Having recently noticed media reports about the health benefits of herbs, Bello decided that adding more health-promoting ingredients to his drinks might reverse the company's fortunes. When Billy Bishop, Jr., the 26-year-old son of Executive Vice-President Bill Bishop, Sr., suggested a new product that blended tea with Oriental medicinal herbs, SoBe 3G Black Tea was born.

The 3G name was a reference to ginseng, gingko, and guarana, herbal derivatives that purportedly improved concentration, endurance, and energy, respectively. Although such benefits were not scientifically proven, and the amounts contained in the drinks were relatively small, the inclusion of herbs in a drink marketed to mainstream consumers struck a chord, and upon its introduction in December 1996 the tea began to fly off shelves.

The firm quickly decided to roll out new Green Tea, Red Tea, and Oolong Tea drinks, which contained such exotic ingredients as echinacea, selenium, and bee pollen. With funds running perilously low, Bello put his house up as collateral on a $1 million loan, and persuaded the company's other shareholders to help raise a total of $4.5 million to finance this new direction. The company also negotiated extended credit agreements with its glassmaker, flavor supplier, and packagers.

Functional Drinks Bringing Success in 1997

By the spring of 1997 the firm's product line had been revamped to feature eight tea and fruit-flavored "wellness" or "functional" drinks that bore designations such as 3G, 3C, and SoBe Energy, each of which contained various combinations of exotic herbs, vitamins, and minerals. South Beach had by now junked all but two of its original flavors, Orange Elixir and Cranberry-Grapefruit Elixir, and the single lizard logo on labels had become a pair of lizards entwined in "yin-yang" complementarity, courtesy of Bello's design student daughter. The flavors had been developed by the firm's in-house nutritionist in consultation with formulation experts Wild Flavors of Erlanger, Kentucky.

Unlike the first round of South Beach products, which had gotten minimal shelf space in stores already crowded with similar Snapple and Mistic drinks, distributors were now enthusiastic about pushing the reformulated line. The company had been helped by distribution changes at rival AriZona, which had left some territories open to new brands, as well as the increasing media attention being given to the firm's products. Whereas other companies had marketed beverages with one or two herb or vitamin additives, South Beach was taking the concept to a higher level, which meshed with the American public's new-found interest in the benefits of herbs.

In September 1997 the company appointed Michael B. Schott, former Snapple president and AriZona Beverages CEO, to the posts of president and chief operating officer, and gave him a stake in the firm. By this time, South Beach products were being distributed in 30 states and Bermuda, and were being manufactured at six locations.

Early 1998 brought more new drinks, including Zen Blend, Wisdom, and Orange-Tomato 3C Elixir, and by summer the firm was selling a total of 12 juice-based drinks and teas, including the most recent addition, Eros, which used the tagline, "Who Needs Viagra?" The beverages were priced at between 99 cents and $1.49. Because the company contracted its manufacturing, it had only 92 employees.

In the fall South Beach introduced dairy-based Lizzard Blizzard, as well as a three-product tea- and fruit-based line called SoBe Essentials, which contained higher "supplement levels" of herbal extracts. They were marketed in 14-ounce bottles. Sales for the year jumped from $13 million to $67 million, with 5.4 million cases of drinks sold. Threatened by the firm's success, Snapple owner Triarc attempted to buy South Beach during the year but was rebuffed, and soon afterward Snapple Elements, a thinly-veiled knockoff of the successful SoBe Essentials line, was introduced.

The spring of 1999 saw a number of new products added. In April, three flavors of SoBe Lean Metabolic Enhancer were introduced, which contained an appetite suppressant and were sweetened with a blend of aspartame and Ace-K, and in May Lizard Fuel, a dairy-based strawberry-banana drink, hit stores. During the summer the firm added Lemon Tea, and began offering many of its products in 11.5-ounce cans for use on beaches and other glass-free places, priced at between 99 cents and $1.29. Other new drinks included Passion, Drive, and Soy Essentials, which contained soy protein, which was touted for its health benefits. Another dairy-based drink, Lizard Lightning, also appeared, containing herbs that were thought to boost the immune system. Distribution continued to expand during the year, with a deal reached to produce SoBe drinks in Canada.

Adding Sports Sponsorships in 1999

South Beach was now working to build visibility in "extreme sports" activities like mountain biking and snowboarding, using multi-sport athlete Bode Miller as an endorser and linking with bike maker Cannondale Corp. to sponsor its HeadShok Racing Team. The firm also launched its first ad campaign, buying $2 million worth of radio spots on the East and West Coasts that touted the purported health and energy-enhancing qualities of its drinks.

Other elements of the firm's $5 million marketing campaign included sending two vintage school buses ("SoBe Love Buses") to festivals, fairs, sports events, and concerts on the East and West Coasts, a web site, a toll-free "Lizard Line," and a catalog of hats, shirts, and other "Lizard Gear." Billy Bishop, Jr., had been named vice-president of marketing to coordinate these activities, which were aimed at young, active individualists. The firm now had 300 distributors selling SoBe drinks to stores in all 50 states.

By the end of 1999 the company had sold 14.8 million cases of drinks and taken in $166.4 million. South Beach had recently surpassed rival AriZona in sales and was second only to Snapple in the new age drink category. Less than pleased, rival AriZona slapped the company with a lawsuit claiming that SoBe had copied its bottle design.

In February 2000 the U.S. Food and Drug Administration (FDA) warned the firm that its product labels contained exaggerated claims of health benefits, asking that it delete copy such as that on Lizzard Blizzard that stated it was "loaded with nature's most powerful cold and flu fighters." The firm subsequently changed its packaging to adhere to the FDA's guidelines.

Early 2000 saw the introduction of Tsunami, a dairy/fruit drink, which featured a surfing lizard on the label. Laird Hamilton, one of the world's top surfers, was engaged to help promote it. South Beach was now budgeting $9 million per year for radio ads and $3 million for sampling vehicles, athletic sponsorships including the Major League Lacrosse circuit, and other events including the Warped music tour. The firm's ads used the tagline, "SoBe Yourself," and sought to position the brand as one for individuals who wanted to stand out. In June the company announced plans to introduce ten of its best-selling products in the United Kingdom through distributor Food Brands Group Ltd.

Sale to PepsiCo in 2001

In the summer of 1999 South Beach had begun looking for an outside investor to fund growth, improve distribution, and allow its investors to cash out, and the following spring the company announced that it would sell a 70 percent ownership stake to Boston-based investment firm J.W. Childs Associates LP, for a reported $260 million. By fall the Coca-Cola Company had opted in for 20 percent, but negotiations bogged down, and an exclusivity window lapsed at the end of September. With little advance warning, PepsiCo, Inc. swooped in with an offer of close to $370 million for a 90 percent stake in South Beach, and within two weeks a deal had been struck.

Sales of carbonated soft drinks including Pepsi had been stagnant for some time, but the alternative juice drink and tea category was growing by 12 percent a year. Pepsi already made Aquafina water, Lipton tea, Frappuccino coffee, Tropicana juices, and Fruit-Works fruit drinks, and the purchase of the hot new SoBe brand was expected to help it increase its hold on this growing market.

After the purchase SoBe would be operated as an independent unit of the firm, with CEO Bello remaining in place, although Pepsi installed new sales and marketing executives. The deal had come shortly after Snapple and Mistic's acquisition by Cadbury Schweppes PLC, and just before PepsiCo acquired Quaker Oats, makers of Gatorade, for $13.8 billion.

The latter half of 2000 saw the launch of a line of plastic-bottled sports drinks called the SoBe Sports System, as well as

Adrenaline Rush, which was designed to compete with energy drinks such as Red Bull. It was priced at $1.99 per 8.2-ounce can, though it was later repackaged in a 6.5-ounce amber bottle. Also introduced were 11-ounce aseptic containers called Lizard Packs, and frozen fountain drinks for sale in convenience stores and restaurants under the name SoBe Ice. For 2000, the firm sold 19 million cases of drinks for revenues of $203.2 million.

In early 2001 the Pepsi deal was finalized, and soon afterward the firm's Canadian distribution was taken over by SoBe's new parent, as was distribution to much of the United States. Integration of the formerly independent SoBe was not going entirely smoothly, however. The firm's new sports drinks had been overshadowed by a similar Pepsi line, and when the highly successful Adrenaline Rush was encroached upon by Pepsi's new Amp energy drink, Bello wrote a defensive memo to the firm's remaining non-Pepsi distributors warning them to be on guard.

Late 2001 saw the introduction of more new drinks including chocolate-flavored Love Bus Brew, Nirvana, Lizard Lava, Dragon, and MacLizard's Lemonade. In November, the firm agreed to modify claims in advertisements that promoted SoBe Lean as a drink that would help users lose weight.

Adding Carbonated Drinks, Chocolate, and Gum in 2002

New offerings for 2002 included Bodacious Brew, named in honor of spokesperson and Olympic medalist Bode Miller, and the company's first carbonated product, Mr. Green, which contained herbal extracts and had a flavor likened to Dr. Pepper. In the summer a SoBe Chocolate Bar was introduced, as was SoBe Gum, which had been created in partnership with retailer 7-Eleven. The gum contained liquid centers that were based on several of the firm's most popular beverages.

In December 2002 South Beach recalled several thousand cases of SoBe Green Tea and Energy drinks, because they had accidentally been bottled with dextromethorphan, an ingredient in cough medicine. That same month the firm agreed to pay nearly $1.8 million to settle sexual harassment claims brought by five female employees.

At the end of 2002 founder and CEO John Bello left the company. He later formed an investment firm, Quest Capital, and then Firefighter Brand Products, which produced chili, chips, and soda. Tom Bene took over leadership of the unit after his departure.

New products for 2003 included Long John Lizard's Grape Grog, which contained grapeseed extracts; SoBe No Fear Super Energy Supplement, which was co-branded with an edgy apparel maker; and SoBe Fuerte, a mango-passionfruit blend that was targeted at Hispanics. The firm also relaunched its SoBe Lean line with supermodel Molly Sims as spokesperson, and created SoBe Synergy, a five-flavor line of 50 percent juice drinks packaged in cans for vending machines such as those found in schools.

Early 2004 saw a marketing partnership formed with Buy Music.com, Inc., an online music store. A promotion was soon launched that gave one in 12 buyers of SoBe drinks prizes such as free downloads, Rio MP3 players, and more. In March 2004

Scott Moffitt was named to head the firm. He was an 11-year veteran of PepsiCo who had run SoBe's marketing efforts for more than a year. Products introduced during the year included sugar-free versions of No Fear and Adrenaline Rush, as well as carbonated SoBe Rush, introduced in Mexico. The year also saw a $219,000 fine levied by the state of Connecticut stemming from former claims of cold- and flu-fighting qualities on some of the firm's bottles.

In early 2005 PepsiCo announced a new $20 million advertising push for SoBe and its other alternative beverage lines. Upscale, urban-themed TV ads began running in April for Adrenaline Rush on channels including Comedy Central, Fuse, and MTV, while No Fear, the firm's biggest recent success, was promoted with billboards and print ads featuring professional surfers and a female motocross team. The year 2005 also saw the Lean line expanded and the logo of the South Beach Diet added.

In little more than a decade, South Beach Beverage Company Inc.'s SoBe had become one of the top brands in the U.S. noncarbonated beverage market through its functional drinks that contained herbs, vitamins, and minerals. The deep pockets and marketing muscle of new owner Pepsi gave the firm a strong foundation for continued success.

Principal Subsidiaries

SoBe Operating Corp., Inc.

Principal Competitors

The Coca-Cola Company; Cadbury Schweppes PLC; Ferolito, Vultaggio & Sons; Red Bull GmbH.

Further Reading

Dzikowski, Don, "Leapin' Lizards!," *Fairfield County Business Journal,* March 31, 1997, p. 1.

Hein, Kenneth, "Necessity and Invention," *Brandweek,* February 19, 2001, p. 22.

Holleran, Joan, "A So Big Deal," *Beverage Industry,* December 1, 2000, p. 24.

——, "SoBe It," *Beverage Industry,* July 1, 1998, p. 17.

Kelley, Kristine Portnoy, "Lizard Wizards Try to Put Drinks in Your Gizzard," *Beverage Industry,* February 1, 1996, p. 16.

Khasru, B.Z., "SoBe Sets Sights on Surpassing Snapple," *Fairfield County Business Journal,* January 24, 2000, p. 1.

Lenderman, Max, "South Beach Washed Out? Bello Declares, 'SoBe It,' " *Beverage World Periscope Edition,* September 30, 1997, p. 1.

Martorana, Jamie, "Apocalizard Flies into LI to Take on Snapple, AriZona Iced Tea," *Newsday,* May 3, 1999, p. 5.

McKay, Betsy, and Nikhil Deogun, "Pepsi Edges Coke in Deal to Buy New Age SoBe," *Wall Street Journal,* October 30, 2000, p. B1.

Prezioso, Jeanine, "Lizard King's Story," *Fairfield County Business Journal,* December 10, 2001, p. 1.

Ross, Julie Ritzer, "Leapin' Lizards!," *Food & Beverage Marketing,* June 1, 1999, p. 8.

Sierpina, Diane, "Pushing a Product with Herbal Punch," *New York Times,* May 18, 1997, Sec. 13CN, p. 12.

"SoBe Succeeds by Selling Lifestyle," *Food Processing,* September 1, 1999, p. 28.

Todd, Heather, "Sink or Swim: Can a Small Fish Stay True to Its Identity When Thrown into a Large Corporate Pond?," *Beverage World,* October 15, 2004, p. 40.

Wallace, Phil, "Beverage Company Agrees to Change Weight-Loss Ads," *Food Chemical News,* November 19, 2001, p. 24.

Winter, Greg, "Pepsico Buys a 90% Stake in South Beach Beverage," *New York Times,* October 31, 2000, p. 2C.

—Frank Uhle

Spear & Jackson, Inc.

6001 Park of Commerce Blvd., Suite 2
Boca Raton, Florida 33487
U.S.A.
Telephone: (561) 999-9011
Fax: (561) 999-9076
Web site: http://www.spear-and-jackson.com

Public Company
Incorporated: 1760 as Spear & Love
Employees: 755
Sales: $101.18 million (2004)
Stock Exchanges: OTC
Ticker Symbol: SJCK
NAIC: 332212 Hand and Edge Tool Manufacturing;
   332213 Saw Blade and Handsaw Manufacturing;
   333991 Power-Driven Handtool Manufacturing;
   334513 Instruments and Related Products Manufactur-
   ing for Measuring, Displaying, and Controlling
   Industrial Process Variables; 332999 All Other
   Miscellaneous Fabricated Metal Product Manufacturing

Spear & Jackson, Inc. is one of the world's oldest manufacturers of hand and garden tools, and also makes magnetic
equipment and measuring tools. The firm's brands include
Spear & Jackson garden tools, Neill hand tools, Elliot Lucas
pincers and pliers, Robert Sorby wood turning tools, Moore &
Wright precision tools, Eclipse magnetic equipment, and
Bowers measuring tools and bore gauges. Headquartered in
Florida, Spear & Jackson's operations are primarily located in
the United Kingdom.

Beginnings

The roots of Spear & Jackson date to 1760, when drapery
maker John Love decided to found a steelmaking company in
Sheffield, England, where that country's production of steel,
cutlery, and tools were becoming centered due to an abundance
of raw materials. He was joined in the business by Alexander
Spear, a wealthy merchant from the nearby town of Wakefield,
and the new firm took the name Spear & Love.

Over the following decades the company came to focus on
producing saws, and business grew. In 1814, with the firm now
run by Alexander Spear's nephew John Spear, an apprentice
named Sam Jackson was added. Jackson proved a capable assistant, and in 1830 the company was renamed Spear & Jackson.

The firm continued to produce saws and other tools throughout the 19th and into the 20th century. In 1962 the company
acquired Brades Nash & Tyzack Industries Ltd., and in 1971
bought Spearwell Tools. In 1974 two firms, John Bedford and
AMV, were also acquired. The year 1985 saw Spear & Jackson
purchased by the James Neill Group following a heated takeover battle.

Neill had been founded in 1889 by accountant James Neill,
who like John Love had decided to change careers and become
a steelmaker. He spent the better part of a decade developing a
patented process for making ''composite steel,'' which combined the best qualities of steel and iron. In 1909 he registered
the trademark Eclipse (after a famous British racehorse of the
1760s), and in 1911 began making the world's first composite
hacksaw blade. Neill continued to make improvements in his
designs, and in 1924 the firm introduced a hacksaw frame
design, the 20T, which was later adopted as the standard shape
for this type of tool.

In 1914 Neill had been approached by the British government
to produce magnets for use in engines, as the country was then at
war with Germany, their primary producer. After the cessation of
hostilities the company continued to make magnets under the
Eclipse name, and in 1934 its engineers developed a new me-
chanically switchable magnetic chuck. This patented invention
proved a great advancement in the manufacture of grinding machinery, and was soon being sold around the world, bringing the
firm significant revenues. Eclipse later branched out into production of other types of magnetic tools and magnet products.

Over the years Neill made a number of acquisitions, includ-
ing William Smith Tool & Steel Co., Ltd. in 1948, Standard
Hacksaw Ltd. and the John Shaw Group (which included Moore
& Wright and Britool Ltd.) in 1970, and Elliot Lucas, Ltd. in
1971. In 1989, four years after it acquired Spear & Jackson, the
Neill Group purchased the French firm Forges de Lavieu and

the German company Wilhelm Abt. That same year the descendants of James Neill sold their business holdings to Apax Partners for £78 million. At this time the combined firms employed 2,000, mainly in Sheffield.

The early 1990s saw tool and magnet sales decline due to an economic recession, and in 1992 Jeffrey Wilkinson was put in charge of the James Neill Group to revive its sagging fortunes. Over the next several years he was able to boost the firm's results from £3 million in annual losses to a profit of £6 million by selling off money-losing operations like Britool and by investing £5 million in improvements to the firm's manufacturing processes.

In 1995 the Neill Group was renamed Spear & Jackson, Ltd. By this time, the company's annual sales had grown to £74.6 million, and profit stood at £2.45 million. The firm's various units offered nearly 2,000 different products that were manufactured at four sites in the United Kingdom and France, and distributed to 120 countries internationally. Employment had fallen to 1,200, with 750 workers remaining in Sheffield.

U.S. Industries Buys Firm in 1997

In December 1997 Spear & Jackson was purchased by U.S. Industries, Inc. (USI) for cash and stock worth £63.75 million ($107 million). USI, formed in 1995 from some 30 former units of the British conglomerate Hanson Plc, had $2.3 billion in annual revenues from such companies as Lighting Corporation of America, bath fixture maker Jacuzzi, and Ames Lawn & Garden Tools, the U.S. market leader. Spear & Jackson soon began distributing Ames tools in the United Kingdom and to about 120 other countries where it had a strong presence including France, Australia, and New Zealand.

In early 1998 Spear & Jackson's Sheffield factory and headquarters moved into a new £8 million facility, which boasted £1 million worth of new equipment. The year saw export sales boosted by the introduction of the first dedicated sharpening machine for tools used in the steel industry. The machines, which cost £50,000, could sharpen blades as long as eight meters in diameter.

The year 1998 also saw the company's Eclipse Magnetics unit launch Supermill, a high-powered heavy-duty chuck line that helped double or triple production output for some customers. The product was recognized with the 1998 Manufacturing Industry Achievement Award for Mechanical Engineering Innovation. The following year, Eclipse Magnetics acquired Magnacut, Ltd., a magnet processing firm.

In September 2000, with debt-laden USI's stock falling, that firm announced it would spin off several units to shareholders, including Spear & Jackson. The move was delayed for over a year, however, while larger companies such as Ames Lawn & Garden were sold. After the firm's commercial saws division

was sold in March 2001, in August 2002 Spear & Jackson was sold to a Florida-based company called MegaPro Tools, Inc. for a 29.5 percent stake in the latter, which was valued at less than $8 million.

For 2002 Spear & Jackson recorded revenues of $87.9 million, down from the $95.5 million of a year earlier. The reported loss of $3.5 million was a sizable improvement over the $13.5 million lost in 2001.

Not long after making the acquisition, MegaPro Tools changed its name to Spear & Jackson, Inc., whose stock would now trade on the U.S. over-the-counter market. Florida resident Dennis Crowley, the owner of MegaPro who had engineered the reverse takeover, took the titles of CEO, board chairman, secretary, and treasurer of the 240-year-old British firm.

Over the following months a stream of press releases was issued announcing new products, including The World's Strongest Shovel and a new line of power tools, as well as sizable orders from chains including Super Cheap Auto in Australia, Bauhaus in Turkey, Tesco in the United Kingdom, and OBI in France. The firm had, however, also lost its largest U.K. customer, wholesaler Toolbank.

The apparent growth of Spear & Jackson as reported in its press releases helped send the stock price soaring, and it increased by more than 200 percent over a year's time, eventually hitting nearly $16 per share. In July 2003 stock watchdog web site Stocklemon.com released a report alleging improprieties in the firm's accounting practices and in its disclosure of certain facts to shareholders. CEO Dennis Crowley, who owned approximately two-thirds of the firm's stock, had been banned for life from the securities industry in 1991 for giving faulty advice to investors, but had not revealed this information when he took control of the company. Stocklemon.com also criticized Crowley's relationship with International Media Solutions (IMS), which was promoting Spear & Jackson stock, noting that IMS principals Yolanda Velazquez and Kermit Silva had received stock as part of their compensation.

SEC Forcing CEO to Step Down in 2004

Shortly after the Stocklemon.com report was published, the U.S. Securities and Exchange Commission (SEC) launched a formal investigation into Spear & Jackson's activities. In April 2004 the SEC filed a restraining order barring Crowley from serving as an officer or director of a public company, and put in place a court-appointed monitor. Crowley, Velazquez, and Silva's assets were also frozen, and their passports seized.

The agency alleged that Crowley had sold $3 million worth of improperly obtained company stock through accounts in the British Virgin Islands, and that IMS had sold $1.6 million in stock it received from Crowley. The price had allegedly been hyped upward by a combination of false statements about financial progress made by Crowley and by the efforts of IMS sales agents, who had convinced investors they were impartially recommending the stock when they were actually receiving a commission of up to 10 percent for sales of its shares. Spear & Jackson was cited by the SEC for its failure to report the full extent of Crowley's ownership of the firm.

```
┌─────────────────────────────────────────────────┐
│                  Key Dates:                      │
│                                                  │
│  1760:  John Love and Alexander Spear form steel │
│         company in Sheffield, England.           │
│  1830:  Firm is renamed Spear & Jackson in honor │
│         of new partner Sam Jackson.              │
│  1889:  James Neill founds steelmaking business  │
│         in Sheffield.                            │
│  1911:  Neill introduces Eclipse composite steel │
│         hacksaw blades.                          │
│  1934:  New Eclipse switchable magnetic chuck    │
│         boosts Neill's revenues.                 │
│  1970:  Neill acquires John Shaw Group including │
│         Britool and Moore & Wright.              │
│  1985:  James Neill Group purchases Spear &      │
│         Jackson.                                 │
│  1989:  Apax Partners acquires Neill Group.      │
│  1995:  Neill Group is renamed Spear & Jackson   │
│         Plc.                                     │
│  1997:  U.S. Industries purchases firm.          │
│  1998:  Sheffield operations move into new       │
│         facility.                                │
│  2002:  U.S. Industries sells firm to Dennis     │
│         Crowley's MagnaPro Tools.                │
│  2005:  Crowley pays $6.1 million Securities and │
│         Exchange Commission (SEC) fine, sells    │
│         majority ownership back to firm.         │
└─────────────────────────────────────────────────┘
```

The company's stock price was soon in freefall, and by year's end it had dropped to less than a quarter of its earlier peak value. A number of class-action lawsuits were also being filed against the firm by unhappy shareholders. After denying ownership of the offshore accounts or a relationship with IMS, in February 2005 Crowley agreed to settle with the SEC, admitting no guilt but paying the $4.1 million he had received from the company plus a $2 million civil penalty. He also agreed to sell the six million shares he owned in Spear & Jackson back to the company for $100, and was permanently banned from holding a position as a director or officer of a public company. IMS and Velazquez agreed to settle with the SEC as well, paying a total of $2.4 million. The money would be placed in a fund to reimburse defrauded investors. Spear & Jackson itself was not forced to pay any fines, but was admonished to strictly adhere to SEC rules in the future.

Following Crowley's removal, the firm's board put its Florida office and a small warehouse facility there up for sale. The return of Crowley's shares, which constituted 51 percent of the total, effectively boosted the stake owned by the remnants of USI, now known as Jacuzzi Brands, Inc., to 61.2 percent. Jacuzzi Brands immediately announced plans to sell its stake in Spear & Jackson within a year's time. Some months earlier, management of two of the firm's largest subsidiaries had offered $26 million to buy those units back from the parent company, and this remained a possible option.

For the fiscal year ending in September 2004, the firm had reported revenues of $101.2 million and net earnings of $436,000, an improvement over previous years that was largely attributed to currency fluctuation between markets. Garden, digging, and cutting tools made up the largest share of revenues, at 31 percent, while industrial cutting tools accounted for 20

percent, metrology tools and products 15 percent, and electrical tools about 12 percent. The Neill Tools unit took in $44.4 million in 2004, Bowers Metrology $15.4 million, Eclipse Magnetics $9.4 million, Robert Sorby $5.1 million, Spear & Jackson Australia and Spear & Jackson New Zealand a combined $17.4 million, and Spear & Jackson France $9.6 million.

With nearly 250 years of history behind it, Spear & Jackson, Inc. was looking to right its ship and move forward after several changes of ownership and a devastating stock promotion scandal. Ownership was likely to revert to management, and the possibilities for a return to stability looked positive.

Principal Subsidiaries

Spear & Jackson Plc (U.K.); Bowers Group Plc (U.K.); S and J Acquisition Corp.; Bowers Metrology Ltd. (U.K.); Bowers Metrology UK Ltd. (U.K.); Coventry Gauge Ltd. (U.K.); CV Instruments Ltd. (U.K.); Eclipse Magnetics Ltd. (U.K.); Spear & Jackson (New Zealand) Ltd.; James Neill Canada, Inc.; James Neill Holdings Ltd. (U.K.); James Neill U.S.A., Inc.; Spear & Jackson (Australia) Pty Ltd.; Magnacut Ltd. (U.K.); Neill Tools Ltd. (U.K.); Spear & Jackson Garden Products Ltd. (U.K.); Spear & Jackson Holdings Ltd. (U.K.); Spear & Jackson France S.A.; Societe Neill France S.A.; C.V. Instruments Europe BV (Netherlands).

Principal Competitors

The Stanley Works; Fiskars Corp.; Ames True Temper Inc.; Mitutoyo America Corp.; Pfeil; Henry Taylor Tools, Ltd.

Further Reading

Burns, Judith, ''SEC Files Action Vs. Spear & Jackson Inc., Removes CEO,'' *Dow Jones News Service*, April 16, 2004.

Burns, Judith, and Carol S. Remond, ''Spear & Jackson's CEO Is Barred from Firm amid Stock Probe,'' *Wall Street Journal*, April 19, 2004, p. B4.

''Eclipse Magnetics History,'' *http://www.eclipse-magnetics.co.uk/History/*, July 28, 2005.

Enrich, David, ''Jacuzzi Brands May Get Boost from Spear & Jackson Stake,'' *Dow Jones Corporate Filings Alert*, February 24, 2005.

''Former CEO of Spear & Jackson, Inc. Pays Over $6.1 Million to Settle SEC Fraud Charges,'' *SEC News Digest*, February 11, 2005.

Griffin, Rob, ''Exports Surge for Sawblade Firm at the Cutting Edge,'' *Yorkshire Post*, December 8, 1998, p. 12.

Higgins, David, and Geoffrey Tweedale, ''Asset or Liability? Trade Marks in the Sheffield Cutlery and Tool Trades,'' *Business History*, July 1, 1995, p. 1.

Jackson, Ted, ''Boca Tool Maker's Stock Plunges As Web Site Questions Accounting,'' *Palm Beach Post*, July 12, 2003, p. 10B.

''Jacuzzi Brands to Sell Spear & Jackson Stake,'' *Reuters News*, April 26, 2005.

Pickard, Wilfrid, ''Spear & Jackson Is Sold for Nearly #64M,'' *Yorkshire Post*, December 5, 1997, p. 12.

Poirer, John, ''Spear & Jackson Ex-CEO to Pay $6.1 Mln in SEC Case,'' *Reuters News*, February 10, 2005.

Rae, Bob, ''Spear & Jackson Put Up for Sale,'' *Sheffield Star*, February 26, 2002.

Remond, Carol S., ''Digging Through Spear & Jackson's Books,'' *Dow Jones News Service*, July 11, 2003.

——, ''SEC Launches Formal Probe into Spear & Jackson,'' *Dow Jones News Service*, February 17, 2004.

——, "Spear & Jackson Case Spotlights Promoters," *Dow Jones News Service*, April 16, 2004.

"Spear & Jackson Includes US Ames Lines in 1999 UK Launches," *DIY Week*, March 5, 1999, p. 17.

"U.S. Indus. to Delay Light, Tool Unit Spinoff," *Dow Jones News Service*, February 20, 2001.

"U.S. Industries Buys European Manufacturer," *Reuters News*, December 3, 1997.

"U.S. Industries Says It Will Spin Off Two Businesses," *New York Times*, September 15, 2000, p. 3C.

Willets, Susan, "MegaPro Tools Buys Spear & Jackson from US Industries," *Dow Jones News Service*, August 26, 2002.

—Frank Uhle

Strattec Security Corporation

3333 W. Good Hope Road
Milwaukee, Wisconsin 53209
U.S.A.
Telephone: (414) 247-3333
Fax: (414) 247-3329
Web site: http://www.strattec.com

Public Company
Incorporated: 1994
Employees: 2,000
Sales: $195.6 million (2004)
Stock Exchanges: NASDAQ
Ticker Symbol: STRT
NAIC: 336399 All Other Motor Vehicle Parts
  Manufacturing

Milwaukee, Wisconsin-based Strattec Security Corporation is a spinoff of Briggs & Stratton Corporation's automotive lock division. Since gaining its independence in 1995, Strattec has become the largest maker of automotive locks and keys in the world. The company also serves the heavy truck, recreational vehicle, marine, and industrial markets. Product offerings include mechanical and electromechanical locks as well as security/access control products and latches. In addition to automakers, Strattec supports automotive aftermarket customers. More than 80 percent of the company's revenues come from four customers, automakers Ford, General Motors (GM), and Daimler-Chrysler, and auto parts manufacturer Delphi Corporation. Through a series of joint ventures in Germany, Brazil, and China, Strattec has gained a global presence. Strattec is a public company listed on the NASDAQ.

Lineage Dating to the Early 1900s

Although Briggs & Stratton is best known today for its lawnmower and other outdoor power equipment engines, when the company was founded it was very much focused on the automobile, eventually establishing a lucrative automotive key business. The men behind the Briggs & Stratton name were Stephen Foster Briggs, an electrical engineer and inventor, and Harold M. Strat-

ton, who had launched a successful business career at his uncle's grain trading partnership. The two young men became partners in 1908, interested in manufacturing the six-cylinder, two-cycle automobile engine Briggs had designed while a student at South Dakota State College, from which he had recently graduated. Unfortunately the engine was not suited to mass production and the partners tried to become involved in automaking, creating a model called the Superior assembled from third-party parts. When this effort failed as well, all but forcing the company into bankruptcy, Briggs & Stratton looked to the specialty parts market. Briggs invented a new starter that gave the young company a foothold in the electrical specialties sector. By the start of the 1920s Briggs & Stratton was the United States' largest maker of ignitions, starting switches, regulators, and specialty lights. The company was casting about for other profitable niches as well, trying any number of products that it soon abandoned, such as oil filters and air cleaners. It also looked outside the automotive industry, trying its hand at producing radios, refrigerators, candy display stands, soap containers, and calendar banks. In 1924 Briggs & Stratton became involved in the automotive key business, a niche that proved profitable and became a mainstay.

Briggs & Stratton developed a new zinc die-cast lock cylinder that was far superior to the standard brass models. During this period, automobiles relied on a bevy of locks and keys, not just for the doors and ignition system but also the transmission, spare tire, and radio. Briggs & Stratton took advantage of this arrangement by creating a system of locks that could be opened by a single master key, which the company sold for 75 cents to many a frustrated driver. In 1929 Briggs & Stratton shipped more than 11 million automotive locks, more than 75 percent of the market, making it the largest maker of automotive locks in the world. The company added ancillary products, such as key cutting machines, key depth deciders, key code books, coding tools, and specialized tools used to service the locks. Automotive locks and accessories became Briggs & Stratton's main business, accounting for 70 percent of all sales, but the company also was pursuing a new product line that would eventually surpass locks in importance: small engines.

In 1919 Briggs & Stratton acquired the A.O. Smith Motor Wheel, which used a small gasoline engine that could propel a bicycle. The company reengineered the engine and found various applications for its different models, including lawnmowers and garden tractors, and compressors, generators, and pumps. But the most popular use of a Briggs & Stratton small engine was in washing machines, which became the main market in the 1930s. By the early 1940s Briggs & Stratton's business was almost equally divided between automotive locks and small engines.

With automobile production severely limited during World War II Briggs & Stratton's automotive key unit shifted its focus to war-related items such as ignition switches for airplanes and aircraft guns, and detonating fuses for bombs and artillery shells. The company's small engines found a multitude of applications in all branches of the military, used in generators, mobile kitchens, repair shops, emergency hospitals, water purification systems, pumps, compressors, and ventilating fans. Demand was so strong for the engines that sales, less $800,000 in 1938, grew to $6 million in 1944, the last full year of the war.

World War II: A Watershed Moment

World War II proved to be a watershed moment for Briggs & Stratton, as the automotive key business was surpassed in importance by the company's small engines. During the post-war housing boom, as servicemen returned home and began raising the Baby Boom generation of children in the country's new suburbs, Briggs & Stratton's small gasoline engines found an increasing market in lawn and garden equipment, so much so that Briggs & Stratton in the mind of many consumers became synonymous with the lawnmower. The lock business was now part of Briggs & Stratton's Automotive Division and, although overshadowed by the company's small engines, remained a leader in its field, due in large part to the contributions of Edward Jacobi, who during his 53 years with Briggs & Stratton was responsible for more than 225 patents relating to locks. During the 1940s, for example, Jacobi invented the unit shutter, the ubiquitous flap that slides over an exterior car lock to prevent the interior from being contaminated by the elements. Another important Jacobi contribution during this time was the pick-resistant side-bar lock.

Locks and the Automotive Division in general lessened in importance to Briggs & Stratton over the succeeding decades. By 1980 the company was in a dominant position in the world's small engine market, but new competition in the form of Japanese companies including Honda, Kawasaki, Suzuki, and Mitsubishi soon began to have an impact. Not only did the company have to deal with a shifting marketplace in small engines, as well as labor problems, it had to contend with a lock and key division that now accounted for just 7 percent of Briggs and Stratton's revenues. It too was struggling during the mid-1980s. Failing to win wage concessions from labor, and unable to gain further advantages through automation, the automotive divi-

sion, renamed the Technologies Division in 1987, built a plant in Mexico, resulting in the loss of 200 jobs in Milwaukee.

For the first time in half a century Briggs & Stratton posted a major loss in 1989, some $20 million. The company began to rebound in the 1990s, regaining market share from its Japanese rivals. But to remain competitive in its core business, Briggs & Stratton needed to focus its resources and, to accomplish this task, management decided in May 1994 to spin off the automotive lock business, which would likely benefit as well from the separation, because an independent public company would be able to sell stock and secure loans to gain the funding it needed to pursue its own business strategies.

In September 1994 Briggs & Stratton formed a subsidiary to house the automotive key assets, naming it Strattec Security Corporation. A plan was then announced to distribute one share of Strattec as a special dividend to Briggs & Stratton shareholders for every five shares of the parent company they owned. At the same time, a shareholders rights plan, a poison pill, would be implemented, set to be triggered if any entity accumulated as much as 20 percent of Strattec's common stock. The distribution took place on February 27, 1995.

Life After Briggs & Stratton in the Late 1990s

Strattec, headed by President and CEO Harry Stratton, began its independent existence on an uptick. Revenues had improved more than 18 percent from the fiscal year ending June 30, 1993, to fiscal 1994, when sales totaled $97.1 million and net income amounted to $7.8 million. Through the first half of 1995, sales were up another 17 percent. Moreover, the company had little debt and recently landed new business from Ford, contracted to make locks for the Ford F150 pickup truck and the Ford Taurus, North America's number one selling pickup and auto. But now that it was on its own and a pure-play automotive parts company, Strattec had to contend with Wall Street's misgivings about auto industry stocks. It also faced rising competition from European and Japanese companies, which were beginning to enter the North American market.

Ironically, to curry favor with Ford, Strattec had to support one of its foreign rivals, German corporation Hulsbeck and Furst GmbH and its effort to break into the market through subsidiary Huf-North America. When Ford opted to drop Tennessee-based Hurd Corp. as its lockset supplier because, unlike Strattec, it failed to keep up with new developments in the field, the automaker divided its business between Strattec and Huf. Ford did not want to be dependent on a single supplier, and as a result be left vulnerable in pricing as well as to labor problems the supplier might encounter. Thus Ford strongly urged Strattec to help Huf get up to speed in establishing its North American manufacturing operation. Although the level of cooperation between the two companies was confidential, it was likely that Strattec was helping Huf in designing lock systems for automakers, a role the company had assumed over the years. The relationship between the two firms was cooperative, but remained competitive as well. Huf planned to gain market share in the United States, and that necessarily meant it would go after some of Strattec's business. On the other hand, Strattec was looking overseas, with a long-term plan to do business in Europe and compete with Huf in its home market.

Key Dates:

1908: Briggs & Stratton is founded to produce automobile engines.
1924: Briggs & Stratton becomes involved in the automotive key business.
1994: Strattec is formed as a Briggs & Stratton automotive key subsidiary.
1995: Strattec is spun off as a separate company.
2000: A joint venture with German company E. Witte Verwaltungsgesellschaft GmbH is established, forming Witte-Strattec LLC; Witte-Strattec enters into a joint venture with IFER Estamparia e Ferramentaria Ltda., forming Witte-Strattec do Brasil.
2002: The Witte-Strattec China joint venture is formed.
2004: Witte-Strattec Great Shanghai Co. is formed.

According to the *Milwaukee Journal Sentinel* in a June 1995 article, the newly independent Strattec displayed an entrepreneurial spirit and enthusiasm usually found in a young company, rather than one that had been exploiting its niche for 70 years. The article also quoted analyst David Leiker who believed that Strattec was "well-positioned to benefit from the evolution to electro-mechanical and, eventually, electronic lock systems. 'The real sizzle here and the real growth is on the ignition switch,' Leiker said. 'Thieves can break windows to bypass door locks, but steering wheel systems like the Strattec-developed GM Pass-Key are more difficult to penetrate.'" Moreover, these newer products offered a higher margin, and as the company continued in efforts to reduce costs, it improved its profitability, which in turn allowed it "to pick up additional business from this lower cost base," according to Leiker.

The price of Strattec shares grew over the ensuing months, but the company was unable to control all the variables inherent in its business. The production side fell short, turning out far too many parts that failed to meet requirements. Manufacturing was unable to keep up with sales, resulting in shipping delays, and greater than expected shipping costs because the late parts would have to go air freight. This led to lower profits, missed financial projections, and dissatisfied investors who in turn bid down the price of Strattec stock.

Not only did the company have to sort out its production problems, it had to gear up to be more of a global player to simply keep pace with its customers, automakers who were planning operations around the world and needed suppliers to follow suit. Strattec planned to expand internationally either through joint ventures or acquisitions. It first looked to Europe, where the automotive key business was highly fragmented and where there were ample opportunities for Strattec to ally itself with a small or mid-sized company. The first step in this direction was a 1996 alliance with British lock manufacturer C.E. Marshall Ltd. to produce locksets for Ford's Jaguar subsidiary.

As the U.S. economy soared during the second half of the 1990s, U.S. automakers prospered as well, as did Strattec. Sales grew from $139.8 million in fiscal 1996 to $202.6 million in fiscal 1999, while net income during this period increased from

$7.7 million to $17 million. A 1998 GM strike caused some layoffs but did little to hinder Strattec's strong growth in the late 1990s. Throughout this time the company invested heavily in research and development to keep pace with the increasing influence of electronics in vehicle security. It also pursued globalization efforts, and in 1999 began talks with German company E. Witte Verwaltungsgesellschaft GmbH, which culminated in the November 2000 signing of an alliance agreement that allowed Strattec to sell Witte products in North America and Witte to sell Strattec products in Europe. The two companies also established a joint venture, Witte-Strattec LLC, to sell both companies' products outside of North America and Europe. Witte-Strattec then entered into a joint venture with IFER Estamparia e Ferramentaria Ltda., forming Witte-Strattec do Brasil to sell the parent companies' products in South America.

After completing a stellar year in 2000, when sales reached $224.8 million and net income totaled $18.5 million, Strattec experienced a challenging 2001. As the U.S. economy slumped, auto sales slipped, resulting in reduced automotive production and less demand for lockset and security systems. Strattec was further hurt by labor problems. Company and union negotiators reached a new three-year contract in June 2001 only to have the union's rank and file reject the deal. A 16-day strike ensued, not ending until the two sides hammered out a four-year agreement, which the union members finally ratified. In 2001, sales dipped to $203 million and net income dropped to $13 million.

Globalization efforts continued in the 2000s, as Witte-Strattec China was formed in 2002 and Witte-Strattec Great Shanghai Co. was formed in 2004. Strattec also had to contend with other changes in the automotive industry. Because of new remote keyless locking systems, automakers were eliminating trunk and passenger side lock cylinders. As a result, Strattec was providing fewer parts per car, leading to lower sales, which now hovered below the $200 million mark. Management took steps to restructure the company to make it less dependent on traditional product lines and the big three automakers. New products included ignition lock housings and integrated key systems. Moreover, a beefed-up sales team began to push Strattec's door latches and access control-related products. Strattec remained profitable, netting $17.3 million on sales of $195.6 million in 2004, but the company's future was both promising and uncertain.

Principal Subsidiaries

STRATTEC de Mexico S.A. de C.V.; STRATTEC Componentes Automotrices S.A. de C.V.

Principal Competitors

Chubb PLC; Directed Electronics, Inc.; The Eastern Company.

Further Reading

Content, Thomas, "Glendale, Wis.-Based Car Lock, Key Maker Ventures into International Territory," *Milwaukee Journal Sentinel,* April 12, 2002.
——, "Strike Called at Strattec Plant," *Milwaukee Journal Sentinel,* June 2, 2001, p. 1.
Fauber, John, "Strattec Will Enter Market at a Crossroads," *Milwaukee Journal Sentinel,* February 16, 1995, p. C8.

Gallagher, Kathleen, "Former Briggs Unit Strattec Overlooked, But Has Potential," *Milwaukee Journal Sentinel,* June 19, 1995, p. D10.

Kirchen, Rich, "A 'Fairly Unusual' Lock Combination," *Business Journal Milwaukee,* June 3, 1995, p. A3.

——, "As Spinoff Date Nears, Briggs' Lock Division Seeks Own Identity," *Business Journal Milwaukee,* February 11, 1995, p. 8.

Rovito, Rich, "Strattec Locks into Cost Cuts," *Business Journal Milwaukee,* May 16, 2003, p. A3.

Savage, Mark, "Strattec Seeks Expansion into European Market," *Milwaukee Journal Sentinel,* October 20, 1999, p. 3D.

—Ed Dinger

SYNNEX Corporation

44201 Nobel Drive
Fremont, California 94538
U.S.A.
Telephone: (510) 656-3333
Fax: (510) 668-3777
Web site: http://www.synnex.com

Public Company
Incorporated: 1980 as COMPAC Microelectronics, Inc.
Employees: 2,676
Sales: $5.31 billion (2004)
Stock Exchanges: New York
Ticker Symbol: SNX
NAIC: 541512 Computer Systems Design Services

SYNNEX Corporation is a Fremont, California-based information technology company involved in two core business segments. It offers supply chain services to original equipment manufacturers (OEMs) and value-added resellers (VARs). The company distributes personal computers, notebooks, servers, central processing units, memory, communications products, networking products, and software manufactured by 3Com, Computer Associates, Hewlett-Packard, IBM, Intel, Microsoft, Seagate, and others. In addition, Synnex provides OEMs with contract assembly services, manufacturing such products as PCs, printed circuit boards, and networking equipment. Synnex maintains sales offices and distribution centers throughout North America, as well as in China and Japan. Contract assembly is conducted in plants located in California, Tennessee, and the United Kingdom. Synnex is a public company listed on the New York Stock Exchange, but is 70 percent owned by Taiwan-based MiTAC International.

Company Formation: 1980

Synnex was founded by its longtime chief executive officer, Robert Huang. He was born in Taiwan in 1945, the son of a Japanese-educated father who launched a paper trading company, Nichidai Trading, which he relocated to Osaka, Japan, in 1955 to be closer to Western markets, which at the time were beginning to import a great deal of Chinese noodles and relied on the paper boxes Nichidai Trading manufactured. Huang attended high school in Japan and stayed in the country to earn an Electrical Engineering degree from Kyushyu University. Then in 1968 he moved to the United States for his postgraduate studies, earning a master's degree in electrical engineering from the University of Rochester, followed by a master's in management science from the Massachusetts Institute of Technology's Sloan School of Management. Huang returned to Japan to take a job with chipmaker Advanced Micro Devices, eventually becoming an international sales manager. There he learned a great deal about Japanese management styles, attention to detail, and frugality. He applied these lessons when he returned to California and struck out on his own in 1980 to launch Compac Microelectronics, Inc., later to take the Synnex name.

Compac started out exporting computer parts into Asian markets, but soon Huang became fearful of instability in the region and around 1983 focused the company on domestic markets, particularly the West Coast. Overall, the company fared well but after several years, when annual sales reached around $40 million, it hit a ceiling. Huang told *Silicon Valley/ San Jose Business Journal* in a 2004 profile, "I felt we were stretching cash." As a result he sold control of the company and stayed on to run it. Compac enjoyed solid growth over the next few years, expanding from its West Coast base, where it maintained distribution centers in Fremont and Anaheim, California, and Redmond, Washington, to include operations in Addison, Illinois; West Caldwell, New Jersey; and Norcross, Georgia. When Compac's owner began to have financial problems, Huang was able to find a new backer in the form of Taiwan-based MiTAC International, which acquired majority control of the company in 1992.

Adoption of Synnex Name: 1994

MiTAC now provided Compac with computer cases, power supplies, and motherboards, and used its purchasing power to allow Compac to buy other components, like hard drives, at cheaper prices. The MiTAC connection was important in transitioning Compac from a mere "high volume, box-pushing distributor of mass-storage products," in the words of *Computer*

Reseller News, to a value-added business orientation. "They actually brought us manufacturing," Huang told *Silicon Valley/ San Jose Business Journal.* "Combined with our logistic expertise, we went to AT&T and got our manufacturing contract. The model worked so well, we were able to sell to Compaq. Before long we were manufacturing 10,000 (PCs) a day." The ability to now manufacture PCs also brought the company into conflict with one of its suppliers, Compaq Computer Corporation. In 1993 Compac announced a plan to manufacture a line of Compac-branded PCs, leading Houston-based Compaq to sue over trademark infringement. Compac filed a counterclaim, maintaining that it had prior rights to the name. The two parties soon reached a settlement, since it was in the best interest of both to prevent customer confusion. Thus, in early 1994 Compac Microelectronics took the name Synnex Information Technologies Inc. Pronounced "sin-nuks," the name was the fusion of "synergy" and "nexus," which Huang viewed as core components of the company's success. According to *Silicon Valley/ San Jose Business Journal,* "Outsiders familiar with the company note it's one of the prospering survivors in one of the lowest-margin parts of high-tech, with profits akin to supermarkets. The key to success, they say, is to keep products moving and not sitting in inventory, watching all expenses and building a close-knit team." Another important factor in the company's success was its ability to limit the number of vendors it carried to around 40.

With MiTAC's backing, Synnex was able to grow internally as well as through strategic acquisitions during the 1990s. In 1993 it acquired some assets, including eight Novell-authorized training centers, from Microware Distributor Inc. that made it a top Novell-authorized distributor and spurred its growing VAR business. The company also added Microware's contract to distribute very important networking lines of Intel Corporation and Standard Microsystems Corp. Synnex was further strengthened when its parent company added its U.S. operation to the mix, so that the company now began assembling Mitak's PCs and Mitak-branded mass storage products. In early 1994 the company, which was already strong on the East and West Coasts, opened a seventh distribution center, located near Houston, Texas, which helped to fill in coverage in the middle of the country. Later in the year Synnex bolstered its mass-storage line by signing distribution agreements with a number of important manufacturers, including Western Digital Corp., which had many loyal customers; Exabyte Corp., to serve the high-end LAN and Unix markets; and Fujitsu Computer Products of America, an aspiring player in the high capacity market. Also in 1994, Compac launched a Technical Products division to take advantage of its Novell alliance and further position itself as a distributor of higher-end networking products. As a result of these moves, Compac went from an obscure, regional distributor to one of the top ten in the country and revenues began to increase at a rapid clip. Sales totaled $140 million in 1993 and

improved to about $250 million in 1994. Synnex landed its first manufacturing contract with a major tier-one computer company in 1995 and revenues ballooned to $730 million.

To help drive the company to the $1 billion annual sales level in 1996, Synnex reached distribution agreements on a number of product lines, including U.S. Robotics Mobile Communications Corp.'s Megahrtz line of mobile modems complementing the Sportster line, already top sellers for Synnex; Motorola's full line of SURFR modems; Intel networking products; multimedia solutions by Creative Labs; and Iomega Corporation's removable storage drives. According to *Computer Reseller News,* $1 billion was a magic number because distributors believed that "vendors' perception of them changes for the better. Big-name manufacturers, such as Compaq or Hewlett-Packard Co., may not even look at smaller wholesalers as potential partners, but distributors believe that reaching the $1 billion level proves to vendors that they can handle large volumes for a wide customer base." It was an even more important milestone for a company like Synnex, more of a specialized distributor, focused on mass storage and networking products.

Synnex grew by external means in 1997 with the acquisition of Merisel FAB Inc., a subsidiary of Merisel, Inc. that included the ComputerLand chain of nearly 200 franchised operations providing computer products and services to business clients, and the Datago aggregation business comprised of 500 affiliated resellers. In one stroke, Synnex jumped over the $2 billion sales mark and set the stage for ongoing growth, as the Merisel FAB acquisition paved the way for the company to begin distributing top-tier PC lines from IBM and Hewlett-Packard on a channel assembly basis. A channel assembly program allowed a distributor to make PCs bearing the logo and warranty of the manufacturer to fill orders on a more timely, thus cost-effective, basis. In 1998 Synnex launched certified channel assembly programs for both IBM and Hewlett-Packard to assemble PCs. In 1999 Synnex was ranked as Hewlett-Packard's top channel partner.

Synnex expanded into a new area in 1999 with the formation of a computer-telephony division to offer call center, unified messaging, and IP-based solutions. A year later Synnex created a subsidiary, ecLand.com, to help smaller resellers create customized web sites where customers could buy from them online and have access to more than 100,000 products and services available in a virtual warehouse. A companion business, eManage.com, was created to run the customer's web site. Also in 2000 Synnex opened a sales office in Beijing, China, and acquired MiTAC U.K. to gain a contract assembly plant in the United Kingdom. Synnex was flying high, on its way to recording more than $3.8 billion in sales in 2000 and taking steps to make an initial public offering (IPO) of stock. But then the Internet bubble burst and the high-tech market collapsed, forcing the postponement of the IPO.

Synnex's discipline and ability to survive on razor-thin margins helped the company to weather the downturn in the economy. Sales dipped to $3.2 billion in 2001 and net income dropped by a third, but Synnex remained profitable, posting $25.8 million in net income for the year. Unlike some competitors, Synnex was healthy enough to take advantage of conditions to make strategic acquisitions. In 2001 it acquired Merisel Canada Inc. for $20 million. In that same year the company also added five new distribution centers in the United States, and was named IBM's number one domestic distributor, as well as Hewlett-Packard's number one growth distributor of the year.

In 2002 Synnex completed additional purchases. It acquired distribution and sales assets from Novitech S.A. de C.V. and launched a Mexico operation. It also added to its web business with the $3.3 million acquisition of License Online, Inc., which provided web-based software licensing technology. Synnex added software to the business mix through the $44.5 million acquisition of Gates/Arrow Distributing from Arrow Electronics, Inc. Software allowed Synnex to tap into a different customer base. It was already distributing software in Canada, but the Gates acquisition opened up the Quebec marketplace for the Canadian operation. During 2002 Synnex was active in signing distribution agreements with other major vendors, such as Abit, Creative Labs, Intel, Seagate, and Storcase. In addition, the Hewlett-Packard and Compaq merger opened up the way for Synnex to expand its channel assembly program to include Compaq's Access Business Group line of desktops, notebooks, and handheld devices. Previously Synnex was relegated to distributing Compaq products on an indirect basis. Sales rebounded in 2002, totaling nearly $3.8 billion and net income improved to $28 million, but another attempt to take the company public was scrapped in 2002.

Taken Public in 2003

Synnex had now emerged as the number three broadline distributor, albeit a distant third, trailing Ingram Micro Inc. with $22.5 billion in sales and Tech Data Corporation with $15.7 billion. In 2003 Synnex was finally able to complete its IPO. In preparation the company was reincorporated in Delaware in October 2003 and changed its name to Synnex Corporation. The offering was conducted in November 2003, with the company netting almost $49 million in what was considered a lukewarm reception from investors. Nevertheless, Synnex continue to post strong results, recording nearly $4.2 billion in sales in 2003, the surge continuing in 2004, when the company completed a pair of acquisitions. Greenville, South Carolina-based BSA Sales was acquired for $4.5 million, adding outsourced sales and marketing services to manufacturers and solution providers. Both Ingram Micro and Tech Data offered such services, but rather than start an operation from scratch, Synnex concluded that it was better to buy into the field. Also in 2004, Synnex

acquired a Canadian niche distributor, EMJ Data Systems, which had competed with Synnex Canada in some product lines. The addition of EMJ not only eliminated some competition in Canada, it also provided the U.S. operation with EMJ's expertise in bar code, point-of-sale, and autoID Technology. To some observers, the deal was a harbinger of things to come: broadbase distributors such as Synnex gaining value-adding capabilities by picking up niche distributors, with both hopefully able to play off each other's strengths. One of those new markets Synnex was interested in entering was enterprise storage products. The first step was taken in January 2005 when Hewlett-Packard authorized Synnex to sell its enterprise storage products.

With more than $5.3 billion in sales in 2004, Synnex was well positioned to continue enjoying long-term growth, especially in light of a resurgence in high-tech spending by U.S. companies after a prolonged slump. Huang, now 60 years old, was also grooming a successor, hiring John Paget, a former General Electric Commercial Finance executive, to take over as president and chief operating officer. Paget took advantage of his ties to GE to arrange a program to work with resellers to offer financing to end users. Synnex could be expected to add other types of services to broaden its core distribution business in the years to come.

Principal Subsidiaries

SYNNEX Canada Limited; SYNNEX de Mexico; Computer-Land Corporation; SIT Funding Corporation; MiTAC Industrial Corporation; ECLand.com.

Principal Competitors

Ingram Micro Inc.; Tech Data Corporation.

Further Reading

Caldwell, Douglas E., "Small Fish Grew into a Whale," *Silicon Valley/ San Jose Business Journal,* December 10, 2004, p. 39.

Campbell, Scott, "A Detail-Oriented Risk Taker, Huang Sets Brisk Pace for SYNNEX," *CRN,* December 13, 2004.

Del Nibletto, Paolo, "Gates/Arrow Deal Boosts Synnex in Quebec," *Computer Dealer News,* May 31, 2002, p. 9.

Kerstetter, Jim, "Don't Be Fooled by This Low Profile," *Business Week,* June 19, 2000, p. 136.

Lai, Eric, "Entrepreneur Robert Huang: Low Profit Margins, High Ambition," *East Bay Business Times,* December 14, 2004, p. 19.

Longwell, John, "Bob Huang: Chairman and Ceo, Synnex," *CRN,* November 17, 2003, p. 100.

——, "Synnex Enters Value-Added Market, Broadens Line Card," *Computer Reseller News,* January 31, 1994, p. 97.

Pereira, Pedro, "Distributors Roll Dice, Hope to Land $1B Goal," *Computer Reseller News,* November 18, 1996, p. 255.

——, "Synnex Becoming a Quiet Giant, Slowly," *Computer Reseller News,* May 20, 1996, p. 157.

Zarley, Craig, and Scott Campbell, "Price Champion," *CRN,* November 24, 2003, p. 16.

—Ed Dinger

Techtronic Industries Company Ltd.

Unit B-F 24/F CDW Building, 388 Castle Peak Road, Tsuen Wan
New Territories
Hong Kong
Telephone: +852 2402 6888
Fax: +852 2413 5971
Web site: http://www.tti.com.hk

Public Company
Incorporated: 1985
Employees: 21,000
Sales: $2.10 billion (2004)
Stock Exchanges: Hong Kong
Ticker Symbol: TTNDY
NAIC: 333991 Power-Driven Hand Tool Manufacturing; 334413 Semiconductor and Related Device Manufacturing; 334515 Instrument Manufacturing for Measuring and Testing Electricity and Electrical Signals; 335129 Other Lighting Equipment Manufacturing; 335211 Electric Houseware and Fan Manufacturing

Techtronic Industries Company Ltd. is one of the world's leading manufacturers of corded and cordless power hand tools as well as a leading manufacturer of vacuum cleaners and other floor care products. Based in Hong Kong, and initially an original equipment manufacturer (OEM) behind such brands as Craftsman, RIDGID (for Home Depot), Bissell, and Dirt Devil, Techtronic has made a drive into the branded arena at the beginning of the 21st century. Since the late 1990s, Techtronic has acquired a number of major brand names, including Ryobi (excluding Japan); Vax, the U.K. and Australian vacuum cleaner leader; Homelite, in the United States, a maker of lawn and garden tools and equipment; and Royal Appliances Mfg. Co., also in the United States, a leading maker of vacuum cleaners and floor care products. In January 2005, Techtronic completed its acquisition of Atlas Copco's tool division, adding the Milwaukee Electric Tool Corporation, in the United States, and Germany's AEG Power Tools, as well as the DreBo brand of carbide drill bits. These acquisitions have not only given the company a global brand portfolio, they also have enabled the company to establish a manufacturing presence worldwide. Techtronic Industries is listed on the Hong Kong Stock Exchange and is led by founder and Chairman Horst Pudwill. In 2004, the company's sales topped $2.1 billion.

Cordless Niche in the 1980s

Techtronic Industries was founded in Hong Kong in 1985 by German native Horst Pudwiller in order to produce rechargeable battery packs for use in hand tools and other appliances. Pudwiller, who previously had been an executive with Volkswagen, teamed up with Hong Kong businessman Roy Chung, and began producing for the OEM market from a factory in Hong Kong. Pudwiller served as company chairman and CEO, and Chung became Techtronic's managing director.

Although cordless hand tools had by then become popular among professionals, they remained out of reach for the ordinary consumer. Techtronic recognized the potential for entering this niche, and designed a line of cordless tools specifically for the consumer market. By 1986, the company had secured its first major client, Sears, which commissioned the company to begin production of a new line of Craftsman-branded cordless power tools. That same year, Techtronic entered the vacuum cleaner market as well, supplying cordless vacuum and handheld vacuum cleaners for the Bissell brand. Sales of these products were launched by 1987.

Techtronic's timing was right—that year witnessed the start of a large-scale Do-It-Yourself (DIY) boom in the United States. The company initially planned for production of only 200,000 tools; by the end of 1987, sales had soared past one million. This success, and promises of continuing growth in the DIY market, encouraged Techtronic to expand its production capacity. For this, the company turned to mainland China, becoming one of the first from outside China to establish manufacturing facilities on the mainland. In 1988, Techtronic's new facility opened in Dongguan. Over the next decade, Techtronic added two more manufacturing plants in China.

To prepare for stronger growth in the 1990s, Techtronic went public in 1990, listing on the Hong Kong Stock Exchange. The offering allowed Techtronic to begin an effort at diversification.

Company Perspectives:

Operating philosophy

People with passion. We care passionately about everything we do, our products, our service, our customer relationships.

Solutions through innovation. Innovation can solve the most challenging problems. Customers and partners regard TTI as the industry leader for technical innovation.

A culture that worships quality. For TTI, compromise is unacceptable. We invest heavily in cutting edge technology and the most capable employees.

Highly responsive. Rapidly translating market data into strategic intelligence gives us a competitive edge. Consistently we are first to market with innovative products.

Adding value. TTI is dedicated to building value and growth for our shareholders and customers. We do this by continuously improving our core competencies and increasing the scale of our operations.

The company chose the field of healthcare appliances, and in 1991 paid $36 million for 51 percent of Gimelli Productions AG. Based in Switzerland, Gimelli specialized in the OEM production of dental and healthcare appliances for a range of clients, including Bausch & Lomb, Philips, and AEG. At the time of its acquisition, Gimelli was operating at a loss. Following the purchase, however, Techtronic shifted a large part of Gimelli's production to its Hong Kong and China facilities, helping to reduce manufacturing costs. By 1992, Gimelli had become profitable.

In that year, Techtronic spotted its next diversification opportunity, paying $67 million to acquire a 76 percent stake in Solar Wide. This company specialized in the OEM production of solar-powered appliances, such as lighting and alarm systems and measurement and monitoring devices, as well as consumer electronics products. The addition of Solar Wide, together with Gimelli, helped Techtronic reduce its reliance on the U.S. market to some extent.

In another attempt at diversification, Techtronic bought the manufacturing and distribution rights for the Jetstream oven from American Harvest. Terms of the agreement gave Techtronic worldwide rights, excluding the U.S. and South Korean markets. Yet this business, as well as the company's healthcare and solar power operations, remained small in comparison with Techtronic's core power tools and vacuum cleaner operations. By 1994, Techtronic's sales had topped HKD 1 billion. Power tools accounted for some 63 percent of this total, and floor care added another 17 percent to sales.

Floor care took on still greater weight with the company following the launch of the Superbroom in 1996. This product, a handheld, broom-shaped vacuum cleaner, became a huge success. By the end of 1997, the Superbroom had helped propel the group's sales past HKD 2.36 billion.

Branded Strategy for the 2000s

The growing success of the company's power tools and floor care appliances led Techtronic to refocus around these opera-

tions in 1998. By then, as well, the company had shifted nearly all of its production to its three mainland China plants. In 1998, the company expanded its production capacity again, opening a new production facility in Indonesia. Also in 1998, the company launched a new type of cutter, featuring a revolving blade magazine. To support sales of this new tool in its core U.S. market, the company acquired a 20 percent stake in distributor Nack that year.

The late 1990s witnessed a sea-change in the global manufacturing market, as more and more manufacturers shut down their local production facilities and turned to predominantly Asian-based third-party contract manufacturers. Yet, as the new century neared, Techtronic took the opposite approach. In 1999, the company introduced an ambitious new strategy—that of re-creating itself as a brand-name producer.

Techtronic's first brand acquisition came that year, when it acquired Vax, a leading producer of vacuum cleaners and floor care products for the U.K., Australian, New Zealand, and Indian markets. Vax had been founded in 1977 in Worcestershire, England, and launched its first product, a machine that combined wet and dry vacuuming with a carpet washing function. At first, the Vax machine was sold door-to-door, but by the early 1980s, the company had begun distributing through the United Kingdom's retail network as well. By 1988, Vax had launched distribution in the Australia and New Zealand markets; in 1998, Vax formed a joint venture with Videocon International, launching its floor care products in India as well. Paying $8 million for Vax, Techtronic then began introducing the brand into new markets.

The acquisition that put Techtronic on the global power tools brand map came in 2000, when the company acquired Ryobi US and exclusive manufacturing and distribution rights for the Ryobi brand in the North American markets. Ryobi had been founded in 1943 in Japan as Ryobi Seisakusho, and began as a manufacturer of metal die-cast products. In the 1950s, Ryobi had added plastic die-cast production, and then began diversifying its production through the 1960s, entering areas such as the production of offset printing presses. In 1972, Ryobi created its power tool division, which grew into a Japanese market leader, before becoming a major global power tool brand.

Techtronic paid Ryobi's Japanese parent $95 million for its U.S. subsidiary. In 2001, Techtronic returned to Ryobi, buying up its European operations for $6.8 million. The following year, the company paid Ryobi another $3 million to take over its business in Australia and New Zealand. By mid-decade, Techtronic had succeeded in acquiring global control of the Ryobi brand, excluding the Japanese market. The acquisition of Ryobi helped Techtronic gain another major client, when in 2002 it signed an exclusive distribution deal with Home Depot for the Ryobi brand. That agreement placed Home Depot as the company's leading client, ahead of Sears.

By then, Techtronic had gained two new brands for its growing stable. In November 2001, the company acquired John Deere's Homelite brand of garden and lawn care tools and equipment, paying $24 million. Homelite had been founded in Port Chester, New York, in 1921 as the Home Electric Lighting Company, originally to develop gas-powered electric genera-

Key Dates:

1985: Horst Pudwill and Roy Chung found Techtronic in Hong Kong in order to produce cordless appliances based on rechargeable batteries.

1986: The company receives a major original equipment manufacturer (OEM) contract for the Craftsman line from Sears Roebuck and begins supplying vacuum cleaners for the Bissell brand.

1990: The company goes public on the Hong Kong Stock Exchange.

1991: Gimelli, an OEM producer of dental and healthcare appliances, is applied.

1992: Solar Wide, producer of solar-powered appliances, is acquired.

1999: The company adopts a branded strategy, acquiring Vax floor care products.

2000: The company acquires the Ryobi US power tools business, and then adds Ryobi operations in Europe and Australia.

2001: Homelite lawn and garden equipment is acquired from John Deere.

2002: Home Depot becomes the exclusive North American distributor for the Ryobi brand.

2003: The company acquires Royal Appliances; the RIDGID professional power tools joint venture is formed.

2004: The company acquires the Ryobi outdoor equipment business in North America.

2005: The company acquires the Atlas Copco Power Tools division, including the Milwaukee and AEG brands.

tors. Homelite began producing gardening tools, including powered pumps and blowers in the 1920s, then added its first chain saw in 1946. Over the next decade, the company introduced a variety of other products, including hedge trimmers, string trimmers, and other handheld powered gardening and lawn care products.

Global Leadership in the New Century

Techtronic next expanded its floor care business, when it reached an agreement at the end of 2002 to acquire the Royal Appliances Mfg. Co. for $105.5 million. The Royal brand had been introduced in 1905 by Cleveland, Ohio-based P.A. Geier Company. Royal's major innovation came in 1937, when it introduced the Royal Prince, the world's first handheld vacuum cleaner. The company's spirit of innovation continued into the 1980s, especially with the highly successful launch of its Dirt Devil Hand Vac in 1984. That product quickly became the company's flagship. The Royal acquisition was completed in April 2003.

Soon after, Techtronic solidified its position in the North American power tools market with the creation of a joint venture with Emerson Professional Tools to launch the RIDGID brand of professional grade power tools. The joint venture, which launched production in October 2003, also helped

strengthen Techtronic's relationship with Home Depot, which became the major retail distributor of the RIDGID line.

Techtronic continued building on its brand success as it approached mid-decade. In 2004, the company added to its Ryobi branded range when it acquired the North American rights to Ryobi's outdoor power equipment products line.

At the beginning of 2005, Techtronic's latest acquisition placed it among the world leaders in the power tools segment. In January of that year, Techtronic agreed to pay $626 million to acquire the Power Tools division of Sweden's Atlas Copco. That purchase gave Techtronic control of two major brands, Milwaukee, based in the United States and founded in 1924, and AEG, based in Germany and one of Europe's leading power tool brands. The purchase also gave the company control of DeBro, a manufacturer of carbide drill bits. Techtronic had succeeded in reinventing itself as one of the world's leading branded power tools manufacturers for the new century.

Principal Subsidiaries

A & M Electric Tools GmbH (Germany); DreBo GmbH (Germany); Gimelli Laboratories Co. Ltd.; Homelite Asia (Dongguan) Co. Ltd. (China); Homelite Consumer Products, Inc. (U.S.A.); Homelite Far East Co. Ltd.; Milwaukee Electric Tool Corporation (U.S.A.); OWT Industries, Inc. (U.S.A.); Royal Appliance International GmBH (Germany); Royal Appliance Mfg. Co. (U.S.A.); Ryobi Technologies (New Zealand) Ltd.; Ryobi Technologies (UK) Ltd.; Ryobi Technologies Australia Pty Ltd.; Ryobi Technologies Canada, Inc.; Ryobi Technologies France S.A.S.; Ryobi Technologies GmbH (Germany); Solar Wide Industrial Ltd.; Techtronic Appliances (Hong Kong) Ltd.; Techtronic Appliances Assembly Factory 1 (China); Techtronic Appliances Assembly Factory 2 (China); Techtronic Industries (Taiwan) Co. Ltd.; Techtronic Industries Assembly Factory (China); Techtronic Industries Co. Ltd.; Techtronic Industries North America, Inc. (U.S.A.); Vax Appliances (Australia) Pty Ltd.; Vax Ltd. (U.K.).

Principal Competitors

Wurth Group; Danaher Corporation; Black and Decker Corporation; Cooper Industries Ltd.; Beijing Tiantan Furniture Co.; Stanley Works; Husqvarna AB; Electrolux Construction Products Inc. Target Div.; Snap-On Inc.; Pentair Inc.; Scintilla AG; Makita Corporation; Alba PLC.

Further Reading

"Atlas Copco Completes Sale," *Australasian Business Intelligence,* March 15, 2005.

Beatty, Gerry, "Royal Agrees to Be Acquired in Order to Focus on Floor Care," *HFN The Weekly Newspaper for the Home Furnishing Network,* December 23, 2002, p. 3.

"HJ Techtronic to Buy Swedish Power Tools Company," *Australasian Business Intelligence,* October 12, 2004.

"Horst J. Pudwill, Chairman, Techtronic Industries, Hong Kong," *Business Week,* June 9, 2003, p. 44.

Leahy, Joe, "Techtronic Branding Breaks New Ground for HK," *Financial Times,* November 26, 2001, p. 18.

"Power Play," *Australasian Business Intelligence,* July 24, 2002.

''Ryobi's Parent Company Buying Milwaukee Electric,'' *Do-It-Yourself Retailing,* October 2004, p. 19.

''Ryobi Technologies Expands South Carolina Facility Operation,'' *Outdoor Power Equipment,* March 2002, p. 12.

''Techtronic Gears Up on Ryobi,'' *South China Morning Post,* June 2, 2000.

''Techtronic in Demand,'' *South China Morning Post,* April 10, 2001.

Tomasulo, Kay, ''TTI Buys Atlas Copco Brands Acquisition Includes Milwaukee, AEG, and Drebo,'' *Tools of the Trade,* November-December 2004, p. 17.

—M.L. Cohen

TEPPCO Partners, L.P.

2929 Allen Parkway
Houston, Texas 77252
U.S.A.
Telephone: (713) 759-3636
Toll Free: (800) 877-3636
Fax: (713) 759-3957
Web site: http://www.teppco.com

Public Company
Incorporated: 1990
Employees: 1,104
Sales: $5.95 billion (2004)
Stock Exchanges: New York
Ticker Symbol: TPP
NAIC: 424710 Petroleum Bulk Stations and Terminals;
486910 Pipeline Transportation of Refined Petroleum
Products; 551112 Offices of Other Holding Companies

TEPPCO Partners, L.P. is a major pipeline company, operating nearly 12,000 miles of pipeline as well as storage and related facilities that serve the downstream, midstream, and upstream segments of its industry. TEPPCO's downstream assets are located in 14 states, highlighted by a 5,500-mile pipeline that carries refined petroleum products from Texas to New England and the Mid-Atlantic. The company's midstream activities involve transporting roughly 2.5 billion cubic feet of natural gas per day through a 1,900-mile network of pipeline in Colorado, New Mexico, and Texas. On the upstream side, TEPPCO transports crude oil to destinations in Oklahoma and Texas through 3,500 miles of pipeline.

Origins

Although TEPPCO was founded in 1990, its assets enjoyed a lengthier history, constituting the core of the company's operations as it expanded during its inaugural decade. The foundation of the company was created during World War II, when the prosecution of the war effort was hampered by the attacks of German U-boats on oil tankers trying to reach the United States' eastern coast. Ships transporting oil vital to the war effort were being sunk, prompting U.S. officials to search for a safer means of transporting crude oil from fields in Texas to refineries on the East Coast. As a solution, the federal government constructed two pipelines, the two-foot diameter Big Inch Pipeline and its slightly smaller sister pipeline, the 20-inch diameter Little Big Inch, through which crude oil was delivered from Texas to destinations eastward. At the end of the war, the War Assets Administration put the Big Inch and Little Big Inch up for sale, an offering that attracted the Texas Eastern Transmission Company, the predecessor to TEPPCO. Texas Eastern paid $143 million for the two pipelines and chose to use them for a different purpose than the federal government had used them, deciding the Big Inch and the Little Big Inch would be best used as pipelines to deliver natural gas.

Senior officials at Texas Eastern soon changed their minds about how the Little Big Inch should best be used, adopting a strategy that would be employed by TEPPCO during its first years in business. In 1955, after a decade of using the 20-inch pipeline to deliver natural gas, Texas Eastern converted much of the Little Big Inch into a pipeline geared for transporting refined petroleum products, the aspect of TEPPCO's business that would form its downstream segment. In 1958, the company completed its first test shipment of refined products from Texas to the Midwest, inaugurating regular shipments of liquefied petroleum gases (LPGs) by the end of the year. Texas Eastern's shipments of LPGs was a groundbreaking event in the pipeline industry, with the first test shipments representing the longest single shipments of LPGs ever made and the first time LPGs had ever traveled through a pipeline as large as the Little Big Inch.

With its pipeline business as its core, Texas Eastern developed into a formidable competitor during the 1960s, 1970s, and 1980s. The company diversified into other areas of the energy industry and strengthened its base of operations, emerging as a pipeline company with $3.5 billion in annual sales by the end of the 1980s. Much of the expansion and diversification completed during the decades would have little bearing on TEPPCO, but the expansion of Texas Eastern's pipeline system, which occurred gradually from the 1960s through the 1980s, was relevant, giving TEPPCO, at its birth, a pipeline system significantly more robust than the one created in the wake of World War II. TEPPCO's inheritance from Texas Eastern's sprawling operations became clear at the end of the 1980s, when Texas Eastern was under siege, its assets the object of another company's fancy.

A company named The Coastal Corporation launched a hostile takeover against Texas Eastern at the end of the 1990s, but the company was saved by what the business community referred to as a "white knight." The white knight was Panhandle Eastern Corporation, which acquired Texas Eastern in the spring of 1989 to thwart the unsolicited advances of The Coastal Corporation. Not long after acquiring Texas Eastern, Panhandle began selling all of Texas Eastern's non-pipeline assets and all of its pipeline assets not related to natural gas. Panhandle only wanted Texas Eastern's more than 10,000-mile network of natural gas pipelines. Panhandle sold La Gloria Oil and Gas Co., a crude oil refinery, Petrolane Inc., a marketer of LPGs, and oil and gas reserves in the North Sea that were valued at $1.4 billion. At the end of 1989, the company announced another divestiture, stating that it planned to sell Texas Eastern's petroleum products pipeline by forming a master limited partnership (MLP) named TEPPCO Partners L.P. and spinning off the MLP in a $215 million public offering. "It's not a financial decision," an analyst explained in a December 11, 1989 interview with the *Houston Business Journal*, referring to the spinoff that created TEPPCO. "It's part of Panhandle's ongoing program to sell its non-strategic assets. They're selling because the history of pipeline diversification is that 90 percent have not turned out well."

Transporting Refined Petroleum in 1990

TEPPCO was formed on March 7, 1990, as an MLP, a corporate structure designed by the U.S. House of Representatives to provide tax incentives that were expected to stimulate investment. Panhandle spun off the company in a public offering so it could retain a 10 percent interest in the company, which left TEPPCO with 90 percent ownership of a 4,100-mile petroleum products pipeline system that extended from southeastern Texas to the Northeast. At its outset, TEPPCO's assets represented roughly 10 percent of what had constituted Texas Eastern's business before its piecemeal breakup by Panhandle.

Compared to its stature at the beginning of the 21st century, TEPPCO was a small company during the early 1990s. Although the company was distinguished by its ownership of one of the largest common carrier pipelines of refined petroleum products in the nation, it generated only a fraction of the revenue it collected after its first decade of business. The difference in size between 1990 and 2000 stemmed from the scope of

the company's business, which was confined to the downstream sector of the petroleum industry during much of the 1990s. As a company operating exclusively in the downstream segment, TEPPCO acted as a transporter of refined products to the Midwest and of propane to the Midwest and Northeast, a role that limited its opportunities for growth. TEPPCO collected $166 million in sales in 1992, a total that eclipsed $200 million by 1995 and reached $429 million by 1998—the first year the company entered the upstream segment of the petroleum sector, a segment that included crude oil transportation, storage, gathering, and marketing activities.

TEPPCO, pressed by the need to diversify and to broaden its business scope, had acquired two crude oil fractionation (chemical separation) facilities in Colorado from Duke Energy Field Services, Inc., giving it a presence in the crude (upstream) market to complement its presence in the refined (downstream) market. The move into the upstream segment enabled TEPPCO to nearly double its sales total in 1998, a move that was buttressed by the November 1998 acquisition of Duke Energy Transport & Trading Co., which stored, transported, and marketed crude oil primarily in Texas and Oklahoma. When the financial totals for 1999 were released, the addition of upstream-related business greatly increased the company's financial stature. Sales for the year reached $1.93 billion, with $1.69 billion of the total derived from crude oil and petroleum products.

On the heels of its aggressive move into the upstream segment, TEPPCO launched a major expansion campaign, increasing its size and scope at a rapid rate. The first major acquisition of the campaign occurred in March 2000, when TEPPCO paid $318 million for assets belonging to Arco. The assets included crude oil terminal facilities in Cushing, Oklahoma, and Midland, Texas, a crude oil pipeline stretching from western Texas to Houston, and a 50 percent interest in the Seaway crude and refined products system. The Seaway assets included a crude oil pipeline connecting Freeport, Texas, and Cushing, a refined products pipeline from Pasadena, Texas, to Cushing, and a crude oil terminal in Texas City, Texas.

Entering the Natural Gas Business in 2001

After strengthening both its upstream and downstream businesses, TEPPCO completed its diversification by entering the midstream segment, making the company a comprehensive player in the nation's pipeline industry. In September 2001, TEPPCO paid $360 million for Alberta Energy Co.'s subsidiary, Jonah Gas Gathering Co., which owned a system of pipeline that collected natural gas from Wyoming's Green River Basin, considered to be one of the country's most active gas basins. The acquisition included 300 miles of pipeline, five compressor stations, and 50 miles of additional pipeline under construction at the time of the transaction. When the construction was completed, the Jonah system was capable of collecting and carrying more than 700 million cubic feet of gas per day. Roughly a year after the Jonah acquisition, TEPPCO completed another significant natural gas purchase, part of nearly $1.6 billion the company spent at the dawn of the new century to bolster it market presence. The company paid $444 million to Burlington Resources Gathering Inc. to acquire the company's Val Verde Gathering System in New Mexico's San Juan Basin. The purchase included 360 miles of pipeline, 14 compressor stations, and a large amine treating station for the removal of carbon dioxide.

By the end of 2002, TEPPCO's annual revenue volume had swelled to $3.24 billion, more than 20 times the total collected a decade earlier. During this period, the company had been led by William L. Thacker, a former president of Unocal Pipeline Company. Thacker retired as chairman and chief executive officer in May 2002, making room for the promotion of Barry R. Pearl from the posts of president and chief operating officer. Under Pearl's stewardship, TEPPCO lost none of the momentum built up during Thacker's last years in charge as it pressed forward with the objective of completing between $300 million and $400 million per year in acquisitions. In 2003, the company and Louis Dreyfus Energy Services formed Mont Belvieu Storage Partners L.P. to serve Mont Belvieu, Texas, a major LPG and natural gas liquid (NGL) storage and fractionation hub for the United States, and acquired crude oil supply and transportation assets located along the upper Texas Gulf Coast, shoring up its supply and transportation capabilities.

As TEPPCO plotted its course for its second decade of business, the company held sway as a formidable competitor in the pipeline industry, having achieved much of its growth after entering the upstream and midstream market segments. The company's revenue total marched upward during the first years of Pearl's command, reaching $4.25 billion in 2003 before making a massive leap to $5.95 billion in 2004. The company's progress during the first half of 2005 provided every indication that continued expansion remained one of Pearl's priorities. In February 2005, the company announced a $122 million expansion project of the Jonah system that was expected to increase capacity to 1.5 billion cubic feet per day. The project was slated for completion by December 2005. In April 2005, the company acquired crude oil storage assets in Cushing and a 158-mile crude oil pipeline connecting Mexia, Texas, to Houston. In July 2005, TEPPCO acquired a 90-mile pipeline and storage assets capable of handling 5.8 million barrels from Texas Genco LLC. TEPPCO paid $62 million for the assets, which were intended to strengthen the company's refined products capabilities in the Houston and Texas City areas.

Principal Subsidiaries

TE Products Pipeline Company, Limited Partnership; TCTM, L.P.; TEPPCO Midstream Companies, L.P.; TEPPCO Crude Oil, L.P.

Principal Competitors

El Paso Corporation; Kinder Morgan, Inc.; The Williams Companies, Inc.

Further Reading

"EPCO Inc. Acquires Texas Eastern Products Pipeline Co.," *Pipeline & Gas Journal,* March 2005, p. 38.

McNamara, Victoria, "Panhandle Spinning off TEPPCO in $215 Million Public Offering," *Houston Business Journal,* December 11, 1989, p. 6.

"TEPPCO Buys Certain Texas Genco Assets in Expansion," *America's Intelligence Wire,* July 15, 2005, p. 21.

"TEPPCO Moves into Natural Gas; Buys Wyoming Pipe System," *Energy Daily,* September 13, 2001, p. 4.

"TEPPCO Partners, L.P. General Partner Acquired by EPCO, Inc.," *America's Intelligence Wire,* February 24, 2005, p. 32.

—Jeffrey L. Covell

3i Group PLC

91 Waterloo Road
London SE1 8XP
United Kingdom
Telephone: + 44 20 7928 3131
Fax: + 44 20 7928 0058
Web site: http://www.3i.com

Public Company
Incorporated: 1945 as Industrial and Commercial
    Finance Corporation Limited
Employees: 833
Sales: $480.20 million (2004)
Stock Exchanges: London
Ticker Symbol: III
NAIC: 523999 Miscellaneous Financial Investment
    Activities

3i Group PLC is one of the leading venture capital groups in Europe and one of only a handful of publicly listed private equity and investment groups in the United Kingdom. Founded in 1945 as a government-inspired initiative to provide investment funding for the United Kingdom's SME (small and medium enterprise) market, 3i has distinguished itself by establishing operations across all major funding areas, ranging from early-stage venture capital to growth capital investment, and including buyouts. Into the mid-2000s, the company's investments average EUR 1.3 billion ($1.6 billion) across 200 or more deals per year. Unlike many of its competitors, which operate small firms of ten people or less, 3i boasts a team of more than 250 investment professionals, backed by a support staff of more than 600 worldwide. The company operates offices in 13 countries. The United Kingdom represents its core market; in the 2000s, however, 3i's European investments topped its U.K. investments for the first time. The United States is also a strategic market, and the company has established a target of boosting its Asian investment portfolio to 5 percent of its overall investments by 2006. As part of this effort, the company began building an investment team in India in 2005, while also beginning preparations to open its first office in China, in Shanghai. 3i Group is listed on the London Stock Exchange and is led by

CEO Philip Yea and non-Executive Chairman Baroness Sarah Hogg, who also serves as chairperson of the BBC.

Filling the Capital Gap in the 1940s

Prior to the 1940s, there existed no true venture capital market. As early as the 1930s, in Britain, this situation led to the recognition of a gap in corporate financing among British businesses struggling to cope with the effects of the global depression. While larger companies were able to turn to the country's banks or to the public market for investment capital, the country's smaller and midsized companies faced the banks' reluctance, or even unwillingness, to provide capital. At the same time, these businesses, especially the many small family-owned companies, were too small and unprepared to turn to the public market for funding.

The British government launched a commission, known as the Macmillan committee after its chairman, to investigate the situation. The lack in access to capital funding became known as the Macmillan gap. In the 1940s, the government began working on a proposal to fill the gap, with the Board of Trade and the Treasury coordinating the effort with the Bank of England and the country's clearing banks. If the Board of Trade favored a government-sponsored institution, the Treasury, in conjunction with the Bank of England, insisted on the formation of a body that raised its capital in the private sector. The Bank of England went further, suggesting the new institution be created by the country's five clearing banks, and thus entirely removed from the government. As for the clearing banks, they remained hostile to the idea altogether.

Nonetheless, the discussion led to the creation of two new corporate financing companies in 1945. The first was the Finance Corporation for Industry (FCI), which was set up to provide long-term financing for large-scale businesses. The second, called the Industrial and Commercial Finance Corporation (ICFC), was more directly aimed at filling the MacMillan gap. The ICFC in particular was marked by the disagreements among the various founding members, resulting in the new corporation's independence from the government as well as from the Bank of England and the clearing banks.

The ICFC's mission was to provide funding to small and midsized businesses on a national scale. Despite the corporation's independence, it was nonetheless subjected to funding limits, set at a range between £5,000 and £200,000. The ICFC's independence, however, placed it in a competing situation with the clearing banks, which, with the Bank of England, were also the company's shareholders. Although the clearing banks were expected to support the ICFC's development by providing operational support and by passing on investment opportunities that fell outside of their own sphere of operations, in practice the banks did little to help the ICFC. Indeed, the banks attempted to hamper the company's growth, sending it only hopeless investment cases, and even wooing potential ICFC clients with their own funding offers. The clearing banks also attempted to restrict the ICFC's access to capital and, when loaning to the ICFC, attempted to do so at high interest rates.

The result of the hostility of its own shareholders was that the ICFC gained a strong sense of self-reliance. The need to maintain its own commercial viability obliged the company to build its own risk assessment and evaluation methods, with expertise in evaluating all levels of a potential investment. The ICFC was also adept at attracting business. Two important factors played a role in many customers' decisions. The first was that the ICFC, unlike the banks, did not usually take an active role in its investee companies, including not placing its staff on their boards of directors. The second factor was ICFC's ability to play off small firms' reluctance to turn over an equity stake in their business in exchange for capital funding from a bank. Instead, these firms preferred to turn over equity to the ICFC. In this way, as well, the ICFC was able to share in the successful growth of the companies it supported, which helped to minimize the losses from less successful investments.

Through the 1950s and into the 1960s, the ICFC expanded on a national scale, launching a network of branch offices that eventually reached 14 in number. This network gave the group greater access to local and regional markets. The company's expansion became especially strong after 1959, when it received permission from its bank shareholders to begin raising capital externally. At the same time, the company began adding subsidiary operations, such as the Estate Duties Investment Trust (EDITH), which placed institutional investors in companies faced with the loss of major shareholders.

In 1962, the company, acting on government fears of a growing "technology gap," joined in the creation of Technical Develop Capital (TDC), which targeted technology-based investments. In this way, the ICFC took on the characteristics more commonly associated with the American version of venture capital (which coupled technology investments with hands-on investment management) then providing financial foundation for the first boom in the U.S. technology market.

Broadening Scope in the 1980s

Yet the vast majority of the ICFC's business lay in less glamorous investments with the nation's small business sector. Many of these relationships were extremely long-term, and the ICFC was credited with laying the foundation for the growth of a strong percentage of the United Kingdom's industry. Yet, as *Business Week* described the firm, the ICFC "grew into a sprawling bureaucracy with 14 offices responsible for lending in their regions. These regional groups gained a reputation for small, cookie-cutter deals, relying on legions of relatively junior managers to make decisions according to strict guidelines."

The ICFC began broadening its scope in the 1970s. An important moment came when the company acquired its sister corporation, FCI. Unlike ICFC, which had made thousands of deals by the early 1970s, the FCI's long-term, large-scale lending operations had rarely been used. The merged company, now called Finance for Industry (FFI), combined not only the ICFC's focus on the SME market, but also extended its brief to include investment in large corporations as well.

The arrival to power of the Conservative government led by Margaret Thatcher sparked a new era for FFI. The British economy began to grow again in the early 1980s after nearly a decade of economic recession. The resurgent economy, combined with the Thatcher government's support of entrepreneurism, stimulated a boom in the investment market. In response, FFI restructured its operations, adopting a division structure, and changed its name to Investors in Industry (or 3i) in 1983.

By then, 3i had expanded its range of operations to include an important and fast-growing segment of venture capitalism—the buyout market. The company also launched itself onto the increasingly international buyout market by adding its own international operations. In 1982, for example, the company opened an office in Boston. The following year, 3i moved into France, with the opening of its Paris office. By 1986, 3i had added an office in Frankfurt, Germany. The company's international growth culminated in its entry into Italy (Milan) and Spain (Madrid) in 1990.

3i also prepared to launch its own public offering—a rare move among venture capitalists—at the start of the 1990s. As the global economy slipped into recession, however, the company was forced to put off its listing. At the same time, 3i also launched a streamlining of its operations in order to maintain its profitability in the difficult market climate. This led the company to close its U.S. offices.

Global Ambitions in the 2000s

3i at last came to market in 1994, with a listing on the London Stock Exchange. Just two months after its initial public offering, the company joined the prestigious FTSE 100 index. By then, the company had adopted an increasingly international strategy. In 1994, for example, the company launched its first

Key Dates:

1945: The Industrial and Commercial Finance Corporation (ICFC) and the Finance Corporation for Industry (FCI) are established.
1959: ICFC gains the right to raise capital externally, sparking national growth.
1962: ICFC enters the technology ventures market with a stake in Technical Develop Capital.
1975: ICFC and FCI merge and form Finance for Industry.
1982: The company opens an office in the United States.
1983: The company changes its name to Investing in Industry (3i) and broadens its scope to include buyouts.
1985: The company name is formally changed to 3i.
1986: The company opens an office in Germany.
1990: The company opens offices in Italy and Spain.
1991: The U.S. operations are closed.
1994: A public offering is made on the London Stock Exchange.
1999: Offices are opened in Japan and Hong Kong and the company re-enters the U.S. market.
2001: The company completes an acquisition spree, adding four companies in Germany, Austria, Finland, and Sweden
2003: The company closes the Japanese office.
2005: The company announces plans to open offices in India and in Shanghai, China.

foray into external fund management, launching a £225 million fund in partnership with a number of British, Swiss, U.S., and Pacific Rim investors, targeting the continental European growth businesses market.

By the late 1990s, 3i's interest in continental Europe had become a key part of its aim to transform itself into a leading globally active venture capital group. Part of the company's strategy came through the lack of growth prospects in the United Kingdom. Indeed, in 1999, 3i had attempted to acquire new scale at home when it launched a takeover bid for its chief rival, Electra Investment Trust. That bid was rejected, however, after 3i's CEO publicly acknowledged that its interest in Electra was for its assets, and not its people.

Instead, 3i turned to the overseas market. The company stepped up its investment activities in continental Europe. It also returned to the United States in 1999, establishing new offices on the East and West Coasts. By 2000, the company's portfolio in the United States topped $300 million. The company also made its first entry into the Asian market, opening offices in Hong Kong and Japan.

3i next went on something of a spending spree in order to establish a solid presence on the European continent. In late 2000 and into 2001, the company completed four strategic acquisitions. In Germany, the company acquired Technologieholding, that country's leading specialist in early-stage technology ventures. In Sweden, 3i bought Atle, one of the Scandinavian market's oldest and largest private equity specialists. The company added venture capital and fund management operations in Austria, through the purchase of Bank Austrai TFV High Tech Unternehmens Beteiligung. Then the company returned to Scandinavia, picking up Finland's SFK Finance, which specialized in telecommunications, IT, and environmental technology investments.

Having secured a dominant position in the European venture capital market, 3i turned to the next phase in its global strategy, that of boosting its operations in the Asian region. 3i's strategy called for its Asian investments to top 5 percent of its total portfolio by 2006. The company's Hong Kong office, overseeing the Korean and fast-growing Chinese markets, soon became the focal point for the company's regional growth. In 2003, the company closed its less active Japanese office.

By 2005, 3i began preparation for the next phase in its Asian region expansion, initiating recruiting for personnel to back the launch of an office in India. At the same time, the company announced its intention to open its first office on the Chinese mainland, in Shanghai, at mid-decade. After 60 years in business, 3i remained one of the world's largest venture capital groups.

Principal Subsidiaries

3i Asia Pacific PLC; 3i Corporation (U.S.A.); 3i Deutschland Gesellschaft für Industriebeteiligungen GmbH; 3i Europe PLC; 3i Gestion S.A. (France); 3i Holdings PLC; 3i International Holdings; 3i Investments PLC; 3i Nordic PLC; 3i PLC; Gardens Pension Trustees Limited; Ship Mortgage Finance Company.

Principal Competitors

Candover Investments PLC; CVC Capital Partners Limited; Investcorp S.A.; Electra Investment Trust.

Further Reading

Bradley, Sandrine, "Private Equity Growth Capital, a New Path for Mid-Caps?," *Acquisitions Monthly,* July 2003, p. 50.
Campbell, Katharine, "3i Looking for European Buy," *Financial Times,* May 28, 1999, p. 19.
Coopey, Richard, and Donald Clarke, *3i: Fifty Years of Investing in Industry,* Oxford, n.p., 1995.
"More Exits for 3i," *Acquisitions Monthly,* August 2003, p. 55.
Paisner, Guy, "Compromise," *Red Herring,* September 15, 2001, p. 50.
Sheahan, Mathew, "3i Says Sayonara to Tokyo Office," *Private Equity Week,* February 24, 2003, p. 10.
Smart, Victor, "Retooling 3i," *Institutional Investor International Edition,* October 2002, p. 43.
"This Risk-Taker Is Ready to Roll the Dice," *Business Week,* July 1, 2002, p. 50.

—M.L. Cohen

Timber Lodge Steakhouse, Inc.

1801 E. 79th St., Suite 27
Bloomington, Minnesota 55425
U.S.A.
Telephone: (952) 920-9353
Fax: (952) 929-5658
Web site: http://www.timberlodgesteakhouse.com

Private Company
Incorporated: 1991 as Q-Steaks Incorporated
Employees: 1,300
Sales: $42.9 million (2004)
NAIC: 722110 Full Service Restaurants; 722410 Drinking
    Places (Alcoholic Beverages)

Timber Lodge Steakhouse, Inc. is a chain of steakhouse restaurants known for its northwoods lodge-like décor and its moderately priced menu. The company operates 24 Timber Lodge restaurants covering seven different markets in Minnesota, Wisconsin, Illinois, South Dakota, Nebraska, North Dakota, and New York. Food choices include steak, chicken, pork, seafood, and a variety of accompaniments. The restaurants also feature wine and spirits and a lengthy list of appetizers.

The company was once publicly traded on the NASDAQ but in successive buyouts Timber Lodge went private when a group of former management signed a deal to buy the company. CEO and President Peter Bedzyk owns the majority of stock, holding 45 percent in 2005.

Minnesota Steakhouse

In 1991, when two St. Louis Park, Minnesota, partners formed Q-Steaks Incorporated, the restaurant business in the Midwest was characterized by small town supper clubs and meat and potato fare. Unlike many other parts of the country where national and regional chain restaurants were taking root all over the place, the Midwest market was just opening up to chain restaurants. Several non-fast food thematic establishments had only just successfully entered the local landscape.

Minnesota restaurateurs Doren Jensen and Dermot F. Rowland took note of the regional carnivorous diet and began a chain of steakhouses, naming the establishments The Minnesota Steakhouse. The two settled on a cabin-like northwoods theme for The Minnesota Steakhouse. The restaurant atmosphere guaranteed the relaxation of an up-North cabin with its roaring fire and log timbers, an atmosphere many Midwesterners longed for. The company was to change its name, ownership, and management over its lifetime but the one constant would be its emphasis on meat, particularly red meat and its generous Midwestern portion size.

When the chain opened two Buffalo, New York, restaurants in 1994, Q-Steaks decided to drop the Minnesota reference and name those operations after Minnesota legend Paul Bunyan. The company introduced P. Bunyan's Steakhouse to the Niagara Falls area, an important tourist destination and an expanding restaurant market.

In 1993 Q-Steak went public and company shares were listed on the NASDAQ. The company needed investment for expansion, and thus had turned to an initial public offering (IPO) to secure that funding. In 1995 the company sought to rename its six restaurant establishments Timber Lodge Steakhouse. Shareholders of the company's stock granted permission for the name change in the early summer of 1995. The company issued a statement to the press explaining the reason for the name change saying, ''This is intended to raise consumer awareness of [the restaurant chain's] distinctive style and to increase name recognition throughout the company's current and potential market area.'' Timber Lodge opened in Sioux Falls, South Dakota, at this time and the company closed its restaurant in Williamsville, New York. Timber Lodge management cited problems with the strip mall location in Williamsville as its reason for the closure.

By August 1996 Timber Lodge opened its 12th restaurant, and had rebounded from some losses it had incurred as a result of its name change and the confusion it created with its customers. Timber Lodge won the Minnesota Beef Council Beef Backer Award that same year, a prize it was awarded for selling approximately $17 million in steaks during its calendar year.

In the early weeks of 1997, Timber Lodge benefited from a surge of investor interest in the company. Analysts had marked Timber Lodge stock as a good buy and it had jumped in a three-

Company Perspectives:

Timber Lodge Steakhouse, Inc. develops, owns and operates Timber Lodge Steakhouses. These are full-service, casual restaurants serving dinners of generous portions at moderate prices and featuring a ''northwoods'' atmosphere. The menu features steaks, prime rib, barbequed ribs, fresh seafood, chicken, pasta and specialty regional entrees and appetizers.

week period from $3.50 to $5.12 per share. In May 1997 Timber Lodge opened its 14th steakhouse. The company chose St. Cloud, Minnesota, for its 240-seat dining facility.

The 1990s Buyout and Expansion

In December 1997 G.B. Foods Corporation (GBFC) announced that it intended to acquire all the outstanding shares of capital stock, taking over the company. GBFC, based in California, owned and operated or franchised 185 Green Burrito quick-service Mexican restaurants. Its chairman, William Foley II, also was chairman of CKE Restaurants, which owned the Hardee's and Carl's Jr. fast-food chains. GBFC planned to take Timber Lodge west to Arizona, Utah, Idaho, and New Mexico. The $32.4 million acquisition allowed for an influx of capital needed to expand the restaurant into new markets.

Timber Lodge reported strong fourth quarter earnings in 1997, up 33 percent over the same period the prior year. While net income had increased, expenditures at the company had also increased. Timber Lodge reported costs up 5.2 percent in 1997. The company blamed the higher expenses on increased advertising, leases, and short-term borrowing.

The acquisition was finalized in January 1998, with Timber Lodge shareholders receiving 0.8 shares of GBFC common stock for each Timber Lodge share. GBFC made public its plan to convert 16 JB's Restaurants into Timber Lodges over the next several years. JB's Restaurants was a wholly owned subsidiary of CKE Restaurants Inc.

In February 1998 CKE announced its plan to sell GBFC JB's Restaurants for one million shares of GBFC common stock. At the close of the deal GBFC became Santa Barbara Restaurant Group (SBRG)

By July 1998, Timber Lodge had added its 18th location. The restaurant was the first Timber Lodge Steakhouse to open in Rochester, Minnesota. Timber Lodge parent company GBFC signed a letter of intent in August 1998 with Franchise Finance Corporation of America for financing properties the company hoped to buy. The strategic alliance allowed GBFC to expand its new concept restaurants without raising capital for the projects.

Timber Lodge Steakhouse began airing a new advertising campaign in October 1998. The company hired Cevette and Company of Minneapolis to produce the spot, which featured an ambulance rushing a hungry patient to one of its restaurants. The concept was hailed as unusual because the advertisement

did not feature any food items, only the suggestion to head to Timber Lodge when one was really hungry.

The company opened its ninth Twin Cities location in November 1999, a Timber Lodge Steakhouse in the Southtown Shopping center in Bloomington, Minnesota. The company continued its rapid growth with the addition of two more Twin Cities steakhouses the following year, one in Maple Grove and another in Stillwater, Minnesota. Timber Lodge ventured into North Dakota by opening a restaurant in Fargo towards the end of 2000.

The company opened several converted JB's Restaurants to Timber Lodges in the Salt Lake City area and Phoenix and Tucson, Arizona, which brought its number of steakhouses to 23 by June 2000.

In March 2000, Santa Barbara Restaurant Group, Inc., agreed to sell the remainder of its JB's Family Restaurants to the chief operating officer of the restaurant chain. The deal included 52 company operated establishments and 29 franchised facilities. SBRG also agreed to sell its six Galaxy Diners. A number of JB's Family Restaurants had already been converted to Timber Lodge Steakhouses in Arizona and Utah and those six restaurants were not included in the sale.

Sales declined for the company in the first and second quarters of 2001. Revenue was down by 1.1 percent in the first quarter compared to an increase of 8 percent the previous year, and second quarter results showed even further decline, with a loss of 5.8 percent, compared to an increase of 2.8 percent the same quarter in 2000.

SBRG President and CEO Andrew Puzder spoke regarding the disappointing trend when the company announced its earnings report through *PR Newswire:* ''Regarding Timber Lodge Steakhouse, I am certainly disappointed with the negative sales trends, and we are working very hard to reverse them. Fortunately, in spite of the soft sales, we have been able to improve operating margins at Timber Lodge, which positions us very well to capitalize on any future sales improvement.''

News of a buyout of SBRG by closely related CKE Restaurant Group surfaced in November 2001. CKE announced its intent to purchase SBRG despite its own struggles with debt mostly incurred by its holding of Hardee's. Hardee's was purchased by CKE in 1998 for more than $750 million, but the chain was poorly managed and in need of a turnaround.

The sluggish American economy took its toll on restaurants throughout the years 2001 and 2002. Still, according to a *Minneapolis Star Tribune* article, consumers seeking the convenience of ready-made meals were still buying food on the go. In 2000, according to the *Star Tribune,* ''the restaurant industry took in 45 percent of all dollars spent on food.''

The web site Beef.org reported that 3.8 percent of American households visited a steakhouse in an average two-week period, and steakhouses continued to be one of the fastest-growing areas in foodservice. The site claimed that from 1993 to 2000 consumer expenditures at casual steakhouses increased 150 percent.

Timber Lodge parent company CKE signed a beverage deal with Coca-Cola Fountain in January 2003. Coca-Cola

<table>
<tr><td colspan="2">Key Dates:</td></tr>
<tr><td>1991:</td><td>Q-Steaks Incorporated is started.</td></tr>
<tr><td>1993:</td><td>Q-Steaks goes public.</td></tr>
<tr><td>1994:</td><td>New York P. Bunyan's restaurants open.</td></tr>
<tr><td>1995:</td><td>Company adopts the name Timber Lodge Steakhouse.</td></tr>
<tr><td>1998:</td><td>G.B. Foods buys Timber Lodge.</td></tr>
<tr><td>2001:</td><td>CKE buys Santa Barbara Restaurant Group.</td></tr>
<tr><td>2004:</td><td>CKE sells Timber Lodge to T. Lodge Acquisition.</td></tr>
</table>

provided all Timber Lodge Steakhouses with soft drinks and bottled water.

Low carbohydrate diets became the craze of the new decade and the push for protein was only countered by the fear that shocked the nation when a possible positive report of bovine, spongiform encephalopathy was reported in an adult Holstein cow in Washington state. The report was the first confirmed case of mad cow disease in the United States. CKE issued statements in December 2003 that none of its suppliers purchased meat from the implicated Washington beef packer.

2000 and Beyond: Back in Private Hands

In September 2004 CKE Restaurants sold its Timber Lodge holdings to T. Lodge Acquisition, a privately held group of former management and other investors. The deal was for approximately $8.8 million, with $7 million in cash and $1.8 million in secured notes.

The menu at Timber Lodge was recreated in February 2004. Although the standard entrees remained, Executive Chef Tim Ristow received some assistance from Corporate Chef Scott Foster to tweak the offerings and raise the bar a notch. The company included extra features listed as Timber Toppers that were added to traditional entrees for a minimal extra charge. The toppers allowed patrons to custom order a meat or fish entree with specialty crusting or additional sauces and rubs.

The company hired Medvec-Eppers Advertising in the spring of 2004 to produce radio spots promoting the restaurant.

The campaign featured local Twin Cities talent, including Mick Sterling and the Stud Brothers and Jack Knife and the Sharps. Another campaign, featuring Minnesota Vikings Head Coach Mike Tice, was aired throughout the Twin Cities radio market and brought a great deal of publicity to the company.

The American diet, despite the diversity of its culture, was a diet committed to the consumption of meat products. The Midwest restaurant market catered to the demand for quality affordable steaks and Timber Lodge Steakhouse was poised to meet the growing needs of a public eager for prepared foods, creating a warm, homey retreat atmosphere and affordable prices.

Principal Competitors

American Restaurant Group, Inc.; Landry's Restaurants, Inc.; Outback Steakhouse, Inc.

Further Reading

Blahnik, Mike, "Beef Prices Dropping; Analysts Expect Several Days of Declines," *Minneapolis Star Tribune,* December 25, 2003, p. 1D.

——, "Lessons Learned; Steak with More Sizzle; The Situation: A Steakhouse Chain Faces Increasing Competition," *Minneapolis Star Tribune,* February 2, 2004, p. 4 D.

Keenan, John, "A Feast Fit for a Hunting Party; The Timber Lodge Offers Mountains of Food and Friendly Service in Rustic Surroundings, *Omaha World Herald,* March 14, 2003, p. 1E.

Kennedy, Tony, "Minnesota Steakhouse Gets New Name," *Minneapolis Star Tribune,* April 21, 1995, p. 3D.

Levy, Melissa, "Timber Lodge Steakhouse Agrees to Be Acquired for About $32.4 Million," *Minneapolis Star Tribune,* December 13, 1997, p. 4D.

Merrill, Ann, "Details of Timber Lodge Steakhouse Deal Revealed," *Minneapolis Star Tribune,* January 21, 1998, p. 3D.

Montgomery, Tiffany, "California-Based CKE Restaurant Group to Buy Santa Barbara Restaurant Group," *Orange County Register,* November 20, 2001.

Phelps, David, "Timber Lodge Steakhouse Finally Doing Better with Name Change," *Minneapolis Star Tribune,* August 19, 1996, p. 1D.

Wallenfang, Maureen, "Steakhouses Flourish in Appleton, Wis., Area," *Post-Crescent,* October 16, 2002.

Zate, Maria, " Santa Barbara, Calif., Restaurant Group Sells Stake in Steakhouse Chain," *Santa Barbara News-Press,* September 9, 2004.

—Susan B. Culligan

Tropicana

Tropicana Products, Inc.

555 West Monroe Street
Chicago, Illinois 60661
U.S.A.
Telephone: (312) 821-1000
Web site: http://www.tropicana.com

Division of PepsiCo, Inc.
Incorporated: 1947 as Manatee River Packing Company
Employees: 4,000
Sales: $3 billion (2004 est.)
NAIC: 311421 Fruit and Vegetable Canning; 311411
    Frozen Fruit, Juice, and Vegetable Processing

A division of PepsiCo, Inc. since August 1998, Tropicana Products, Inc. is the leading producer of orange juice in the United States, outselling archrival Minute Maid (fittingly owned by PepsiCo's archrival The Coca-Cola Company). In the $2.63 billion U.S. chilled juice sector, Tropicana holds a commanding 44 percent share. The company was a pioneer in the not-from-concentrate, chilled orange juice sector, and it accounts for as much as two-thirds of U.S. not-from-concentrate sales. Operating only in the United States and Canada, Tropicana's main brands include the flagship Tropicana Pure Premium (the number three food brand in the U.S. supermarket sector), Tropicana Season's Best, Dole juices, Tropicana Twister, and Tropicana Smoothies. The firm's former international operations are now the responsibility of a separate PepsiCo division, PepsiCo International. Tropicana Products was headquartered in Bradenton, Florida, from 1949 (two years after the firm's founding) to 2004, when PepsiCo management shifted the head office to Chicago, the home of the PepsiCo Beverages & Foods North America division. The company's products continue to be made at and distributed from its Bradenton plant.

Midcentury Founding by Sicilian Immigrant

The founder of Tropicana was Anthony T. Rossi, who was born in Messina, Sicily, in 1900, and had immigrated to the United States in 1921. Sailing from Naples, Italy, he landed in New York City with $30 in his pocket. He and four other friends came to the big city to make enough money to finance an adventure in Africa, where they planned to make a film. But Rossi found that he liked the United States and its money-making opportunities too much to leave, and the African expedition was quickly forgotten. After working in a machine shop, and as a cabdriver and chauffeur, in the late 1920s he purchased the first self-service grocery store in the country, the Aurora Farms market on Long Island, which he ran for 13 years.

In the early 1940s, longing to live in a climate similar to his native Sicily, Rossi—after first relocating in Virginia where he was a farmer—moved to Florida, settling in Bradenton, a small gulf coast town in Manatee County south of Tampa. He grew tomatoes on a 50-acre rented farm there, and also bought a cafeteria in downtown Bradenton, where his freshly prepared food proved popular. Dreaming of owning a chain of restaurants, he bought the Terrace restaurant in Miami Beach in 1944. Wartime gasoline rationing, however, crippled the Florida tourism industry, leading Rossi to exit the restaurant business.

The same week he sold his restaurant, Rossi embarked on a new venture, that of selling gift boxes of Florida citrus fruit to such department stores as Macy's and Gimbel's in New York City. Finding surprising success in this business, he moved in 1947 to Palmetto, a town just north of Bradenton, where he purchased the Overstreet Packing Company, renaming it the Manatee River Packing Company. Rossi was now able to buy his citrus directly from nearby growers rather than from retail supermarkets in Miami, cutting his costs and improving his product's freshness.

Rossi's gift boxes grew even more popular, and were soon being distributed across the country. He next expanded into selling jars of chilled fruit sections. But since only the largest fruit was selected for the boxes and the sections, Rossi needed to find a way to use the smaller fruit that was going to waste. He decided to squeeze the smaller oranges into juice, and ship it to the Northeast along with jars of fresh fruit sections, using specially modified refrigerated trucks. In 1949 the company moved to Bradenton and changed its name to Fruit Industries, Inc. That same year Rossi also entered the burgeoning market for frozen orange juice concentrate, purchasing an evaporator to extract the water from the juice. In addition, he registered

"Tropicana" as a trademark and began using it on his fruit section and juice products, which proved so successful that he abandoned the marketing of the fruit gift boxes.

Personified brands, such as Speedy Alka Seltzer, were popular in the early television days of the 1950s, and Rossi joined the trend in 1951 when he commissioned the creation of "Tropic-Ana," a grass skirt- and lei-wearing, pigtailed girl balancing a large bowl of oranges on her head. The character provided an instantly recognizable symbol for the still-young company and helped establish it in the consumer market as Tropicana products began appearing in supermarket cases, mainly in the Northeast and Southeast. In 1953 the company moved to larger quarters, the former Florida Grapefruit Canning Plant in Bradenton, which served as the firm's headquarters until its relocation to Chicago in 2004.

Pioneer of Chilled Juice, Mid-1950s

The key event in the early years of the company came in 1954. That year Rossi, not wanting to be just one of a number of frozen juice concentrate producers, pioneered a flash pasteurization method that raised the temperature of freshly squeezed orange juice for a very short time, extending the juice's shelf life to three months while maintaining its flavor. This method—combined with American Can Company-commissioned packaging consisting of waxed paper cartons in half-pint, pint, and quart sizes—made possible the mass marketing of fresh chilled, not-from-concentrate juice into supermarkets and through home delivery services. Although Tropicana Pure Premium chilled orange juice quickly gained a following in much of the country, sales to New York City were particularly large, accounting for as much as 40 percent of overall sales in the 1960s and early 1970s.

Rossi now had a product that clearly distinguished his company from its competitors; he soon stopped offering Tropicana in frozen concentrate form. In 1957 he changed the name of the company to Tropicana Products, Inc. to reflect the increasing popularity of the brand. That same year Tropicana—not able to expand its truck fleet—began shipping orange juice from Florida to New York via an 8,000-ton ship the company had purchased, which it christened the SS *Tropicana*. Carrying at its peak use 1.5 million gallons of juice each week, the ship would land at Whitestone, Queens, where Tropicana had built a plant for receiving, packaging, and distribution. The *Tropicana* made its final orange juice voyage in 1961, and the company began relying exclusively on truck and rail transport.

In 1958 Tropicana Coffee made its debut. Marketed as a concentrated liquid in a push-button aerosol can, the product failed in part because it had a faulty valve that made it difficult to accurately shoot the liquid into a cup. In 1962 the citrus industry was rocked by one of its periodic freezes. More than one-third of the Florida orange crop was destroyed by a December freeze. Desperately in need of fruit, Tropicana boldly put processing equipment on a ship, which it anchored off the coast of Mexico, a nation with a large and cheap orange crop. After some initial and profitable success in getting Mexican orange juice to the U.S. market, the Mexican government raised the price of oranges, scuttling the venture. Tropicana sold the ship and the equipment onboard, losing $2 million in the process.

Public Company, 1969–78

Tropicana in the early 1960s began shipping more of its orange juice in glass bottles, aided by the company's development of a high-speed vacuum-packing method. With its base in sand-rich Florida, Tropicana took the next logical step of building its own glass plant, for the manufacture of the increasing amounts of glass bottles that were needed. The glass plant opened in 1964. Five years later the company became the first citrus industry company to operate its own plastic container manufacturing plant. Meantime, Tropicana in 1966 began selling its not-from-concentrate Florida orange juice overseas for the first time, shipping 14,000 cases of juice in glass bottles to France. The 1960s ended on another high note, when Tropicana Products, Inc. went public in 1969. Initially sold over the counter, the stock soon gained a listing on the New York Stock Exchange under the symbol TOJ. Revenues increased from $31.2 million in 1964 to $68.4 million by the end of the decade.

The infusion of capital from the stock offering set the stage for even more rapid growth at Tropicana. By 1973, in fact, revenues had reached $121.2 million, while net income grew nearly sixfold, to $10 million. Among the developments of the early 1970s was the launch of a company-owned train (the "Great White Train," later painted orange), which shipped bottles of juice from Bradenton to a distribution center in New Jersey. Continuing its moves to lessen its dependence on outside suppliers, Tropicana opened a box plant in 1972 and began making its own corrugated boxes. The following year Tropicana opened a new processing facility in Fort Pierce, Florida, a town on the Atlantic side of the state.

Although the so-called orange juice wars would not begin in earnest until the 1980s, a few skirmishes between Tropicana and Coca-Cola's Minute Maid took place in the 1970s. Coca-Cola in 1973 took direct aim at Tropicana's stranglehold on both the New York metropolitan area market and the chilled juice sector with the introduction into that area of Minute Maid chilled juice that had been reconstituted from frozen concentrate. This was the beginning of a long-running debate between the companies over which had the superior product. Tropicana contended that not-from-concentrate chilled juice was obviously superior because it was bottled (after being pasteurized) right out of the orange. Minute Maid argued that the concentrating process gave it the opportunity to blend the juice of oranges picked at different times of the year, thereby overcoming seasonal variations in orange taste and quality and giving the resultant juice a more consistent flavor and better overall quality. In any event, Minute Maid, backed by Coke's deep pockets, gained one edge—it quickly became the first nationally available chilled orange juice. The Tropicana-Minute Maid rivalry heated up further in 1975 when the former reentered the market for frozen concentrate.

Key Dates:

1947: Sicilian immigrant Anthony T. Rossi founds Manatee River Packing Company in Palmetto, Florida, originally to ship gift boxes of Florida citrus fruit to the Northeast but soon shifting to orange juice.

1949: Rossi moves the company to nearby Bradenton, changes its name to Fruit Industries, Inc., enters the market for frozen orange juice concentrate, and begins using the Tropicana brand.

1951: First use of the "Tropic-Ana" character.

1954: After pioneering a flash pasteurization method, company begins selling fresh chilled, not-from-concentrate juice.

1957: Company changes its name to Tropicana Products, Inc.

1969: Tropicana is taken public.

1978: Beatrice Company purchases Tropicana for $490 million.

1986: Kohlberg Kravis Roberts & Co. takes Beatrice private through LBO and begins stripping it of assets to pay down debt.

1988: Tropicana is sold to The Seagram Company Ltd.

for $1.2 billion; company introduces Tropicana Twisters.

1995: After acquiring the global juice business of Dole Food Company, Tropicana is rechristened Tropicana Dole Beverages.

1998: Seagram sells Tropicana to PepsiCo, Inc. for $3.3 billion; now a division of PepsiCo, it once again adopts the name Tropicana Products, Inc.

2001: PepsiCo's acquisition of Quaker Oats Company (and the Gatorade brand) leads to numerous changes at Tropicana, to the latter's detriment; responsibility for Tropicana's international operations is shifted to PepsiCo Beverages International, meaning that Tropicana Products is now focused exclusively on the United States and Canada.

2002: Tropicana becomes part of the PepsiCo Beverages & Foods North America division.

2004: The headquarters of Tropicana is shifted to Chicago, home of PepsiCo Beverages & Foods North America, in order to market Tropicana and Quaker Foods breakfast products together.

By the mid-1970s, Tropicana had expanded its market range within the United States (though it still was not a national brand) and had gained a presence in the Bahamas, Bermuda, the West Indies, and several countries in Europe. Despite the Minute Maid entry into the chilled juice sector, Tropicana was the main beneficiary of the faster growth of chilled juice versus frozen concentrate. Whereas in the late 1960s chilled juice accounted for only 20 percent of the overall orange juice market, by the late 1970s it accounted for 31 percent. Tropicana was growing rapidly, with sales increasing 19 percent each year on average, reaching $244.6 million in 1977. Earnings were increasing 21 percent a year, standing at $22.5 million in 1977.

The health of Tropicana was reflected in an endless stream of suitors that attempted to woo the company in the 1970s. Among these were Philip Morris, PepsiCo (in an ironic twist), and Kellogg. On three separate occasions—in April 1974, June 1976, and July 1977—Tropicana and Kellogg, the cereal giant which sought to extend its breakfast offerings to include orange juice, agreed in principal to merge only to have Rossi walk away from the deal before it became final. Following the third failed Kellogg takeover, articles in the press focused on Rossi's inability to "let go." The company founder still controlled 20 percent of Tropicana stock, dominated a more or less rubber-stamp board of directors, and held onto the positions of chairman, CEO, and president at the age of 77. Observers also worried about the company's lack of a succession plan. In October 1977 Rossi finally gave up the presidency, appointing to that post Kenneth A. Barnebey, an executive vice-president and director who had joined the company in 1955 as sales supervisor.

Era As Beatrice Subsidiary, 1978–86

In August 1978 Tropicana was finally sold to Beatrice Company for $490 million in cash and stock. The acquisition immediately ran into regulatory difficulties, and in 1980 a Federal Trade Commission (FTC) administrative law judge ruled that the purchase violated antitrust law because Beatrice could have expanded its own chilled juice brand, which had a market share of 1 percent, instead of buying Tropicana. The judge ordered Beatrice to divest Tropicana and pay to the government any Tropicana-derived profits. Following Beatrice's appeal, the FTC overturned the judge's ruling in 1983, finding that the acquisition was not illegal.

Barnebey headed up Tropicana Products following the acquisition, but by 1982 Richard Walrack, a 30-year Beatrice veteran, had taken over as president of the Beatrice subsidiary (Rossi died in 1993 at the age of 92). Two important events in 1983 shook the orange juice industry and intensified the "orange juice wars." The Procter & Gamble Company (P&G) launched the Citrus Hill brand, offering both frozen concentrate and from-concentrate chilled juice. By 1984 the marketing power of P&G had quickly made Citrus Hill into a fairly strong third player. That year the declining frozen concentrate sector was led by Minute Maid's 25 percent share, with Citrus Hill holding 7 percent and Tropicana 4 percent. Tropicana still held the top spot in the rapidly growing chilled juice sector with a 28 percent share, with Minute Maid claiming 18 percent and Citrus Hill 9 percent. The second key event of 1983 was an orange freeze that forced Tropicana to raise the price of its not-from-concentrate chilled juice three times in quick succession. Amazingly, the company saw no drop-off in purchasing, as customers were clearly willing to pay a premium for what they perceived to be a superior product—the not-from-concentrate juice. Funds from the higher prices were used to begin expanding the Tropicana brand outside of its strongholds in the Northeast and Southeast. Around this time, Tropicana, with the help of Beatrice, became more sophisticated in its marketing and product positioning. It rebranded its not-from-concentrate chilled juice Tropicana Pure

Premium, while the from-concentrate version, which it had sold for a number of years, was first called Gold 'n Pure and then Tropicana Season's Best. Under Beatrice, Tropicana was also more aggressive about introducing new products, such as the 1985-debuted Tropicana Pure Premium HomeStyle orange juice, which featured added pulp.

Meanwhile the door to the Tropicana president's office became a revolving one, as Walrack resigned in June 1984 for "personal reasons," and his replacement—Wesley M. Thompson, who had been hired away from a Coca-Cola executive marketing position—did the same only nine months later. Stephen J. Volk, who had previously worked at PepsiCo, was named president in March 1985. Sales in the United States of chilled orange juice outpaced concentrate for the first time in 1986, as consumers continued to buy increasing amounts of convenience foods. Tropicana was well-positioned to take advantage of this trend.

KKR/Seagram Era, 1988–98

In April 1986 Beatrice was taken private through a $6.2 billion, highly leveraged buyout led by Kohlberg Kravis Roberts & Co. (KKR). Over the next two years, Beatrice was stripped of much of its assets to pay down debt. Tropicana was part of this asset sale; it was sold to The Seagram Company Ltd., the Canadian alcoholic beverage maker, for $1.2 billion in March 1988. By that time, Tropicana was a company with annual sales of $740 million and pretax profits of $100 million.

Under Seagram, Tropicana continued to expand within the United States, becoming a truly national brand for the first time. Also in an aggressive expansion mode, Minute Maid aimed squarely at Tropicana with the 1988 introduction of its own not-from-concentrate chilled juice brand, Minute Maid Premium Choice. Tropicana subsequently sued Coca-Cola over its advertising and packaging slogan for Premium Choice, which included the phrase "straight from the orange." Coca-Cola dropped the slogan rather than fight the suit. Despite the lawsuit, by 1990 Minute Maid had 11.7 percent of the not-from-concentrate, ready-to-serve orange juice market. That year, however, Tropicana edged past Minute Maid in the overall U.S. orange juice market, with 22.3 percent to its rival's 22.2 percent. The orange juice wars soon claimed their first victim when the top two orange juice brands proved to be too formidable even for P&G, which discontinued the Citrus Hill brand in September 1992. Tropicana and Minute Maid were soon battling anew to gain share in the aftermath of Citrus Hill's withdrawal. Tropicana gained the initial upper hand, and by 1993 had extended its lead in the overall orange juice market to a somewhat comfortable 30.1 percent to 25.9 percent.

Even while it was ascending to the top spot, Tropicana continued to be beset by management turnover. Robert L. Soran, who had headed the company at the time of its acquisition by Seagram and continued as president afterward, was forced to resign in September 1991 following his failure to report to Seagram $20 million in cost overruns on construction projects in Florida, New Jersey, and California, according to Alix M. Freedman of the *Wall Street Journal*. In February 1992 William Pietersen, president of the Seagram Beverage Group, was named president of Tropicana as well. He resigned in

January 1993 for "family considerations," with Myron A. Roeder taking over.

From the late 1980s through the mid-1990s, Tropicana expanded aggressively, both outside of its core orange juice products and outside of the United States. In 1988 the company introduced the Twister line of bottled and frozen juice blends. The "flavors Mother Nature never intended" were eventually to include apple-berry-pear, orange-peach, cranberry-raspberry-strawberry, and orange-strawberry-guava. Three years later, a low-calorie Twister Light line made its debut. By 1991 annual sales of the Twister lines reached $170 million. That year Tropicana Pure Premium was launched in Canada, the United Kingdom, Ireland, and France; Germany, Argentina, and Panama were added to Pure Premium's market area in 1994. Also in 1991 a joint venture between Tropicana and Kirin Brewery Company, Limited of Japan began importing and marketing orange juice in that country. In 1993 Tropicana introduced Grovestand orange juice, a ready-to-serve product that was touted to have the consistency and taste of fresh-squeezed juice. The company acquired Hitchcock, the number one premium fruit juice brand in Germany, from Deinhard & Company in 1994. By that time, about 12 percent of Tropicana's overall sales (which were about $1.3 billion in fiscal 1994) were generated from overseas markets, compared to just 5 percent in 1992. The company gained further overseas power through the May 1995 $276 million purchase of the global juice business of Dole Food Company, which had a strong presence in western Europe. Brands gained thereby were Dole juices in North America and Dole, Fruvita, Looza, and Juice Bowl juices and nectars in Europe. Tropicana then became known as Tropicana Dole Beverages, with Ellen Marram heading up the unit and Gary M. Rodkin serving as president of Tropicana Dole Beverages North America.

As the 1990s continued, Tropicana expanded further internationally, entering several more Latin American countries as well as Hong Kong and China. The company also scored a promotional coup in 1996 when it signed a 30-year naming-rights deal—for $46 million—to have the new stadium for the Tampa Bay Devil Rays major league baseball team named Tropicana Field (which opened in March 1998). In 1997, in addition to celebrating its 50th anniversary, Tropicana began construction of a $17 million research and development center in Bradenton; opened its Midwest Distribution Center in Cincinnati, Ohio; launched Tropicana Pure Premium juice products into Portugal; acquired Copella Fruit Juices Ltd., the leading producer and marketer of chilled apple juice in the United Kingdom; introduced Tropicana Fruitwise Smoothies and Tropicana Fruitwise Healthy Fruit Shakes; and also launched a calcium-fortified version of Tropicana Pure Premium.

The PepsiCo Era, 1998 and Beyond

While Tropicana was expanding rapidly into a company with 1997 worldwide sales of $1.93 billion, Seagram was increasing its involvement in the entertainment industry. In May 1998 Seagram announced it would acquire PolyGram N.V., the world's largest music company, for $10.4 billion. To help fund the purchase, Seagram said it would divest Tropicana. Originally, Seagram planned to sell the unit to the public through an initial public offering. However, the IPO market was not as attractive as it had been earlier in the decade, and Seagram struck a deal with

PepsiCo, Inc., consummated in August 1998, whereby the juice business was sold to the beverage giant for $3.3 billion in cash. Tropicana became a division of PepsiCo, once again adopting the name Tropicana Products, Inc. Marram elected to pursue opportunities elsewhere, so Rodkin was named president and CEO of the company. One sign that Tropicana was poised for a bright future was an August 1998 Tropicana press release announcing that for the first time in U.S. history, sales of not-from-concentrate chilled orange juice had surpassed those of from-concentrate juice. In November 1998 the company announced that it had agreed to license the Tropicana brand name to Greene River Marketing, Inc. of Vero Beach, Florida, for use on ruby red fresh grapefruit. This marked the first time that the Tropicana name would appear in the produce section of supermarkets.

At the time of the PepsiCo takeover, Tropicana was enjoying surging sales. This trend continued over the next two years, with revenues jumping 10 percent to $2.25 billion in 1999 and 6 percent to $2.4 billion the following year. Between 1998 and 2000, profits doubled from $110 million to $220 million thanks to Rodkin's belt-tightening initiatives. International expansion occurred during these years, including the introduction of the Tropicana brand into India for the first time and the company's entry into the Spanish market through the acquisition of Alimentos de Valle S.A., a leading producer of chilled, not-from-concentrate orange juice in Spain that sold juice in France, Portugal, and Belgium as well. In the United States, Tropicana continued to pump out new products, introducing calcium-fortified formulations of Tropicana Pure Premium Grovestand and Tropicana Pure Premium Ruby Red Grapefruit. In September 1999 Rodkin was promoted to CEO of Pepsi-Cola North America. Succeeding him as president and CEO of Tropicana Products was Brock Leach, a seasoned marketer who had spent 17 years at Frito-Lay, the snack food division of PepsiCo, most recently heading up Frito-Lay's product development, innovation initiatives, and technology. In early 2000 Tropicana announced that it would increase its fleet of refrigerated railcars to more than 400, and that their orange color would gradually be phased out in favor of a return to the original white for the sake of cooling efficiency. That year, Tropicana Pure Premium passed Campbell's Soup to become the third largest brand in U.S. grocery stores behind only Coca-Cola Classic and Pepsi-Cola.

Tropicana reached another milestone in 2001 when it squeezed its 300 billionth orange into juice. On the new product front that year, the company introduced a low acid version of Tropicana Pure Premium, targeting another health-related niche of the juice sector. The firm also launched a $60 million expansion of its juice storage facilities in Bradenton, to bolster capacity by 32 percent, to nearly 100 million gallons, and provide enough room to store juice between citrus harvests. Late in the year Tropicana announced that it would shut down its glass manufacturing plant in Bradenton, ending its use of glass containers and making its shift to cartons and plastic containers complete. The glass plant, dating back to 1964, had been operated since 1993 as a joint venture with Saint-Gobain Containers Inc., a Muncie, Indiana-based glassmaker. The shutdown was completed in 2003 and entailed the elimination of about 220 jobs.

The big event in 2001 at the PepsiCo parent, and one destined to have a major impact on Tropicana, was the acquisition of Quaker Oats Company for $14 billion. Quaker was coveted mainly for its powerhouse Gatorade sports-drink brand. Following the acquisition, PepsiCo implemented a reorganization in which Tropicana was placed within the same PepsiCo division as Gatorade. Furthermore, the independent brokers who had been selling Tropicana products were fired, and sales and marketing was turned over to members of Gatorade's in-house sales force. Tropicana sales suffered, however, because the new salespeople were not as adept at selling chilled orange juice. Around this same time, responsibility for manufacturing and marketing Tropicana Twister and Season's Best products was likewise shifted to the Gatorade team. The rationale was that these products, which did not require refrigeration, were manufactured the same way as Gatorade. Sales again suffered. In yet another organizational change from 2001, oversight of Tropicana's international operations were merged with those of Pepsi-Cola and Gatorade, creating PepsiCo Beverages International. Tropicana Products, Inc. was now focused exclusively on the United States and Canada. (Two years later, PepsiCo created a new division called PepsiCo International, which took over responsibility for all of the parent company's snack, beverage, and food units outside North America.)

Tropicana tried to stem its sagging sales through new product launches. Rolled out nationally in March 2002 were Tropicana Smoothies, touted as delicious and nutritious combinations of juice and yogurt, packaged in convenient single-serving resealable plastic bottles. Simultaneously, four kinds of Tropicana Pure Premium products also debuted in single-serving bottles, which were in part aimed at the convenience store consumer. Later in the year the Tropicana Pure Premium Healthy Kids line was launched, which was designed to provide children with calcium and vitamins A, C, and E.

In mid-2002, as Tropicana's travails continued, Leach was replaced as president by Jim Dwyer, a former senior executive at the company who had more recently served a stint overseeing the merger of PepsiCo and Quaker Oats. Tropicana's operations were affected by yet another PepsiCo reorganization that same year. All of PepsiCo's North American beverage operations, including Pepsi-Cola, Tropicana, and Gatorade, were united within one division, PepsiCo Beverages & Foods North America.

Starting in 2003 in particular, overall orange juice sales were down as it appeared that people on low-carb diets, such as the Atkins and South Beach plans, were shunning the product because of its high carbohydrate content. Tropicana seemed slow to react to the trend, only releasing its Light 'n Healthy product in early 2004. The new product was lower in sugar and calories and had a third less carbohydrates than Tropicana Pure Premium. In December 2003, just prior to this launch, PepsiCo shocked the community of Bradenton with the announcement that the headquarters of Tropicana Products would be shifted to Chicago, the base for PepsiCo Beverages & Foods North America. The move was completed in 2004. It affected 300 Tropicana staffers in Bradenton but left the 1,900-person manufacturing and distribution operation intact. The change in headquarters location was precipitated by another shift in strategy, again related to Quaker. In this case, however, it was the Quaker Foods operation that was involved. PepsiCo officials now wanted to market Tropicana products alongside those of Quaker Foods, because the two lines were comprised predominantly of breakfast products. The Quaker brands included Quaker Oats oatmeal, Aunt Jemima syrup, and Life and Cap'n Crunch cereals. In addition to gaining such synergies, the change in Tropicana's headquarters was also aimed at cutting costs.

Following the relocation, Dwyer left the company. Appointed as new president was Greg Shearson, who previously headed beverage operations for PepsiCo in Canada. Tropicana's struggles continued in 2004 as a price war in the orange juice industry prevented the company from increasing prices despite rising fruit costs stemming from a summer of hurricanes that devastated Florida's citrus crop. Needing to trim costs, Tropicana late in the year announced a plan to cut as many as 200 jobs from its Bradenton operations, aiming to do so by offering retirement incentives to its staff.

Principal Competitors

Coca-Cola North America; Florida's Natural Growers.

Further Reading

"Beatrice Foods: Adding Tropicana for a Broader Nationwide Network," *Business Week,* May 15, 1978, pp. 114–16.

Braga, Michael, "Does Tropicana's Move Make Sense? PepsiCo Doesn't Have a Record of Sound Decisions with the Juice Giant," *Sarasota (Fla.) Herald-Tribune,* December 6, 2003, p. A1.

——, "Squeezing the Competition: Competitors Say Tropicana Uses Lawsuits to Gain Market Dominance," *Sarasota (Fla.) Herald-Tribune,* November 3, 2002, p. D1.

——, "Tropicana Products Has New President," *Sarasota (Fla.) Herald-Tribune,* June 8, 2002, p. D1.

Braga, Michael, and Rich Shopes, "Tropicana Move to Affect 300," *Sarasota (Fla.) Herald-Tribune,* December 23, 2003, p. A1.

Brennan, Peter, "Tropicana Tries Squeezing into Latin Markets," *Journal of Commerce,* December 27, 1995, pp. A1, 5B.

Buss, Dale D., "Fresh Markets for Tropicana," *Food Processing,* November 1996, pp. 53+.

Chen, Kathy, "Tea and Tropicana? Seagram Wants Juice to Be Chinese Staple," *Wall Street Journal,* January 2, 1998, pp. 1, 4.

"Coca-Cola Invades Tropicana's Market," *Business Week,* December 1, 1973, pp. 26, 28.

Cox, Meg, "Beatrice's Great Expectations for Tropicana Tempered by Host of Unforeseen Problems," *Wall Street Journal,* December 15, 1980, p. 27.

Dawson, Havis, "The Chill Leader," *Beverage World,* July 1997, pp. 46–47, 50, 52.

Dyslin, John, "New Beverage President Charts New Seas for Seagram," *Prepared Foods,* September 1993, pp. 13+.

"Fifty Years of Growth," Bradenton, Fla.: Tropicana Products, Inc., 1997, 27 p.

Freedman, Alix M., "Tropicana Officials Fired by Seagram Kept Quiet About $20 Million Overrun," *Wall Street Journal,* September 24, 1991, p. A4.

Freedman, Alix M., and Ed Bean, "Seagram to Buy Beatrice Unit for $1.2 Billion," *Wall Street Journal,* March 11, 1988, pp. 2, 12.

Gazel, Neil R., *Beatrice: From Buildup to Breakup,* Urbana: University of Illinois Press, 1990, 235 p.

Giges, Nancy, "Tropicana Puts Ad Squeeze on Foes," *Advertising Age,* June 14, 1984, pp. 1, 43.

Halleron, Chris, "Tough Break: Tropicana Kisses Glass Goodbye," *Beverage World,* January 15, 2002, p. 14.

Hwang, Suein L., "Seagram Is Set to Buy Dole's Juice Business," *Wall Street Journal,* January 5, 1995, pp. A3, A6.

——, "Seagram Ousts President at Tropicana, Seeks New Course As Juice Unit Sours," *Wall Street Journal,* October 5, 1992, p. B1.

Ingram, Frederick C., "Tropicana," *Encyclopedia of Consumer Brands,* volume 1, edited by Janice Jorgensen, Detroit: St. James Press, 1994, pp. 598–601.

Jacobs, Cherie, and Alison North Jones, "Tropicana Relocates Managers to Chicago," *Tampa Tribune,* December 3, 2003.

Keefe, Robert, "Seagram's Tropicana Unit a Marketing and Fruit-Juice Powerhouse," *Knight-Ridder/Tribune Business News,* October 29, 1996.

King, Wayne, "Tropicana's Boss Finds His 'Crazy' Ways Work," *New York Times,* June 16, 1974.

Lawrence, Jennifer, "Coca-Cola to Shake Tropicana Juice," *Advertising Age,* May 23, 1988, pp. 3, 89.

Louis, Arthur M., "Tony Rossi Can't Let Go," *Fortune,* January 16, 1978, pp. 120–21, 124.

Marsteller, Duane, "Tropicana Products to Expand Its Line of Lighter Juices," *Bradenton (Fla.) Herald,* May 14, 2004.

McCarthy, Michael J., "Squeezing More Life into Orange Juice: Premium Juice Is Focal Point of Fierce Battle," *Wall Street Journal,* May 4, 1989, p. B1.

McKay, Betsy, "Juiced Up: Pepsi Edges Past Coke, and It Has Nothing to Do with Cola," *Wall Street Journal,* November 6, 2000, p. A1.

——, "PepsiCo Makes Moves to Fill Marineau's Void," *Wall Street Journal,* September 8, 1999, p. B4.

——, "PepsiCo Reorganizes Some Business Units," *Wall Street Journal,* August 9, 2001, p. B4.

——, "Tropicana Is Planning to Sell Orange Juice As a Heart Protection," *Wall Street Journal,* October 31, 2000, p. A3.

Murphy, Joan, "FTC Bars Tropicana from Using Specific Health Benefit Claims," *Food Chemical News,* June 13, 2005, p. 20.

O'Connell, Vanessa, "Seagram May Be About to Seek a Buyer for Tropicana," *Wall Street Journal,* May 18, 1998, p. B10.

Ono, Yumiko, "Tropicana Is Trying to Cultivate a Global Taste for Orange Juice," *Wall Street Journal,* March 28, 1994, p. B10.

Orwall, Bruce, and Eben Shapiro, "Seagram to Sell Tropicana Unit to Public," *Wall Street Journal,* May 22, 1998, pp. A3, A12.

"Pepsi's Sitting on Trop of the World After Making Juicy Deal with Seagram," *Beverage World,* August 15, 1998, p. 14.

Prince, Greg W., "Shoot for the Moon," *Beverage World,* December 1995, pp. 30, 32.

Recio, Irene, and Zachary Schiller, "They're All Juice Up at Tropicana," *Business Week,* May 13, 1991, p. 48.

Rossi, Sanna Barlow, *Anthony T. Rossi, Christian and Entrepreneur: The Story of the Founder of Tropicana,* Downers Grove, Ill.: InterVarsity Press, 1986.

Sauer, Matthew, "Frito-Lay Exec to Lead Tropicana," *Sarasota (Fla.) Herald-Tribune,* September 15, 1999, p. 1A.

——, "Tropicana CEO Rodkin Takes New Job," *Sarasota (Fla.) Herald-Tribune,* September 8, 1999, p. 1A.

Schiller, Zachary, and Gail DeGeorge, "What's for Breakfast? Juice Wars," *Business Week,* October 5, 1987, pp. 110, 115.

Shapiro, Eben, "Tropicana Squeezes Out Minute Maid to Get Bigger Slice of Citrus Hill Fans," *Wall Street Journal,* pp. B1, B10.

Steinriede, Kent, "Pepsi Buys Tropicana," *Beverage Industry,* September 1998, pp. 27–28, 30.

Terhune, Chad, "OJ Brands Fight Carbs, Each Other," *Wall Street Journal,* May 14, 2004, p. B3.

Todd, Heather, "OJ Gets a Boost," *Beverage World,* March 2004, p. 14.

"Tropicana Goes It Alone," *Financial World,* May 22, 1974, p. 24.

"Tropicana Settles with Feds over Juice Health Claims," *Sarasota (Fla.) Herald-Tribune,* June 3, 2005, p. D1.

"What Makes Rossi Run?," *Forbes,* November 15, 1971, pp. 50–51.

White, Dale, "Juice King Revolutionized Industry," *Sarasota (Fla.) Herald-Tribune,* February 22, 1999, p. 1B.

—David E. Salamie

&⃝ UNIBANCO

Unibanco Holdings S.A.

Avenida Eusebio Matoso 891
São Paulo 05423-901
Brazil
Telephone: 55 (11) 3097-1980
Fax: 55 (11) 3813-6182
Web site: http://www.unibanco.com.br

Public Company
Incorporated: 1967
Employees: 27,408
Total Assets: $29.32 billion (2004)
Stock Exchanges: São Paulo New York
Ticker Symbols: UBBR; UBB (ADR)
NAIC: 522110 Commercial Banking; 522210 Credit Card
    Issuing; 522291 Consumer Lending; 522293
    International Trade Financing; 522310 Mortgage and
    Other Loan Brokers; 523110 Investment Banking and
    Securities Dealing; 523120 Securities Brokerage;
    523920 Portfolio Management; 523930 Investment
    Advice; 523991 Trust, Fiduciary and Custody
    Activities; 524210 Insurance Agencies and
    Brokerages; 525110 Pension Funds

Unibanco Holdings S.A. is the holding company for Unibanco - Uniao de Bancos Brasileiros S.A., one of Brazil's leading financial institutions and among the five largest banks in the country. A full-service institution, it provides a wide range of financial products and services to a diverse individual and corporate customer base throughout Brazil, including deposit banking, consumer and mortgage loans for individuals, corporate loans and other financial services, brokerage and underwriting, investment banking, leasing, factoring, trade finance, foreign exchange trading, private banking, asset management, and credit cards.

The Making of a Major Financial Institution: 1924–95

Unibanco's roots go back to 1909, when Joao Moreira Salles opened a general store in a small village in the state of Minas Gerais. He also acted as a correspondent for banks in distant cities.

In 1924 he founded Seçao Bancária da Moreira Salles e Cia. in Poços de Caldas. This became Casa Bancária Moreira Salles in 1931, a wholesale bank financing government agencies and grand hotels. Two years later Joao and his son Walter became the only shareholders, Walter succeeding Joao Afonso Jonqueira. This bank, now under Walter's operating control, began an expansion program in 1940 by merging its $1.6 million in assets with two others under the name Banco Moreira Salles. It established branches in Rio de Janeiro and São Paulo in 1941 and 1942 and had 34 offices in 1945.

During the next decade Walter Moreira Salles developed a personal empire that included the world's largest coffee plantation and 1.1 million acres of cattle-ranching land, and he was Brazil's ambassador to the United States for two years. Professionals managed the bank on a day-to-day basis, allowing him to serve a later term as ambassador to Washington and to hold the position of finance minister twice. Banco Moreira Salles grew to 167 branches and $130 million in assets by 1959. In 1964 it opened a 33-story office building in São Paulo. An investment bank was added in 1966.

Banco Moreira Salles merged with Banco Agrícola Mercantil do Rio Grande do Sul in 1967 to form Uniao de Bancos Brasileiros S.A. (Union of Brazilian Banks). UBB, as it was popularly termed, was the result of a series of recent mergers of smaller institutions and became Brazil's fourth largest private-sector bank, with over a million depositors and more than 26,000 shareholders. Its offerings included such services as credit cards, mutual funds, and insurance. It became publicly traded on the São Paulo exchange in 1968. By 1972, with the establishment of branches in Brazil's north and northeast, UBB was truly a national bank. There were 15 companies in the Grupo Uniao de Bancos in 1975, when Unibanco was added to the corporate name. Walter Moreira Salles yielded the presidency in 1976 and became chairman of the board.

The 20 Unibanco subsidiaries in 1980 included a brokerage; insurance, real estate, credit card, and import-export agencies; custody and asset management units; a publishing, printing, and

Company Perspectives:

Our Mission (Why we exist): To contribute actively, as a financial institution, for the economic development of the country, attending, in balanced form, to the expectations, necessities, and interests of customers, functionaries, and shareholders.

advertising subsidiary; and three tourist agencies, two of them associated with Club Mediterranée. Unibanco opened a New York office in 1980 and initiated a campaign to attract wealthy clients and to serve businesses with annual revenues of over $100 million a year. In 1981 it acquired majority control of Banco Mineiro and opened new quarters in Rio de Janeiro. Round-the-clock automated teller machines (ATMs) were introduced in 1983.

The Brazilian government, in 1986, put into effect a program to wean the nation from its traditional dependence on high inflation. Up to that time the banks had greatly benefited from the overnight ''float'' between the time they received deposits to the time they paid out money. Unibanco, like its great rivals, Banco Bradesco and Banco Itaú, realized Brazilian banking would never be the same. Over the next few years it cut more than half of its staff, turned away many customers, and devoted itself to what proved to be the lucrative area of trade financing.

By the end of 1991 Unibanco had $4.5 billion in assets and three important foreign shareholders: the Bank of America, Japan's Kangyo Bank Ltd., and Germany's Commerzbank A.G. It was also the local advisor and administrator of a Morgan Stanley & Co. Inc. Brazilian investment fund and provided management, advisory, and brokerage services to a number of other major international institutional investors. Unibanco accounted for over 20 percent of the Brazilian market in debt and equity issues in 1991.

Unibanco, in 1993, reversed course and began seeking ordinary depositors as part of a new policy of expansion through economy of scale. An incentive program encouraged the executives of its 438 branches to compete aggressively for business, targeting consumers with minimum income of $1,000 a month. By mid-1994 the bank had more than doubled its assets since the end of 1991, to $9.6 billion. The Moreira Salles family formed a new holding company—Unibanco Holdings S.A.—that was structured in a way to allow the family to raise more equity capital for Unibanco's continued growth without losing control of the enterprise.

Staying in the Game: 1995–2004

Unibanco's next big move was to purchase Banco Nacional S.A. in 1995. This bank, only slightly smaller than Unibanco, offered the same products and services and placed the same emphasis on automated banking, but Nacional had many depositors below Unibanco's level of interest, earning as little as $500 a month, and it was teetering on the edge of bankruptcy. Nevertheless, Unibanco felt it had to grow larger to compete with Banco Brandesco and Banco Itaú. The transaction closed on a weekend, and staffers worked around the clock to meld Nacional's computer operations into Unibanco's by the next Monday morning. The acquisition (valued at about $1 billion) increased Unibanco's scope to 2.1 million customers, 764 branches, and BRL 23.8 billion ($21.9 billion) in assets. *Latin-Finance* named it the bank of the year in 1996.

In making the Nacional purchase, Unibanco entered negotiations not with the bank owners but with Brazil's central bank, which held it in receivership. ''Now to do the acquisition and get the liabilities,'' Israel Vainbolm, chief executive officer of Unibanco Holdings told *LatinFinance* in 1998, ''since in this structure we didn't get the bad loans, we got cash to back up these liabilities—we needed the capital base to be able to face those liabilities. So we said to the central bank, 'The only way that we can do this is if we choose assets that we want to buy out of this group.' We never bought Banco Nacional itself, we bought assets and liabilities, branches and selected assets. We said, 'For those assets, we will issue stock, and you keep the stock.' ''

At least 90 percent of Nacional's customers retained their accounts with Unibanco, which further solidified its courtship of the lower middle class by purchasing a half-interest in Fininvest, Brazil's largest consumer-finance company, in 1996. This acquisition offered Unibanco the opportunity to increase its share of the nation's still small but growing credit card market. The bank also responded adroitly to a government directive requiring 85 percent of deposits to be in low-interest government bonds; it reclassified accounts as money-market funds rather than demand deposits, not only to deal with the new rule but also to charge added fees. Moreover, the acquisition of Nacional's large insurance operation put Unibanco in fourth place in this sector. Also in 1996, the bank purchased Interbanco, one of the largest banks in Paraguay, and took a stake in Surinvest, a Uruguayan bank.

Unibanco had paid for the Nacional acquisition by issuing to the central bank one-third of the shares of both the holding company and bank. This stake was converted to cash in 1997, after the holding company raised $1.23 billion by offering stock worldwide in Latin America's fourth largest equity sale. The offering also made Unibanco the first Brazilian banking company to trade on the New York Stock Exchange by selling American depositary receipts. Also in 1997, Unibanco established a partnership with American Insurance Group, Inc. (AIG), acquiring about half of the equity of AIG Brasil Companhia de Seguros, while AIG acquired almost half of Unibanco's insurance subsidiary. During the next two years Unibanco, like Brazil's other banks, struggled to overcome the effects of a financial crisis that resulted in the devaluation of the national currency, the real.

Unibanco resumed its expansion in 2000 by purchasing three smaller banks, Banco Creditbanco S.A., Banco Bandeirantes S.A., and Portugal's Caixa Geral de Depósitos. It now had 1,623 points of sale and four million account holders. The bank's wholesale operations, especially its corporate credit business, was considered among the best in Brazil, but analysts judged its retail customer base (five million account holders in late 2001) too small to compete with Bradasco (11.8 million account holders) or Itaú (11.4 million). In order to increase its customer base, it initiated a program to enroll 1.8 million retail clients over three years by spending BRL 190 million

Key Dates:

1924: Joáo Moreira Salles founds a banking institution in the state of Minais Gerais.

1941–42: Banco Moreira Salles establishes branches in Rio de Janeiro and São Paulo.

1967: The bank merges with another to form Uniao de Banco Brasileiros S.A. (UBB).

1975: UBB, Brazil's fourth largest bank, adds Unibanco to its corporate name.

1980: Unibanco's 20 subsidiaries include a brokerage and an insurance firm.

1991: Unibanco has $4.5 billion in assets.

1995: Purchase of Banco Nacional S.A. increases Unibanco's number of branches to 764.

1996: Unibanco takes a half-share in Finivest, Brazil's largest consumer finance company.

1997: The bank raises $1.23 billion in its first worldwide equity offering.

2000: Unibanco resumes its expansion by purchasing three smaller banks.

2003: Unibanco acquires the leading credit card in Brazil's northeast; bank raises $1.42 billion from a variety of sources.

($68.5 million) on advertising, direct marketing, and hiring additional staff.

One way Unibanco was enhancing its customer base was by relaxing its monthly earnings standard for an account providing that a prospective client deposited a guaranteed minimum of BRL 100 each month. Another method was to increase the number of minibranches in supermarkets and other heavily frequented outlets. A third was to exploit Fininvest's base of 3.3 million active customers, typically buying just one or two products, whereas Unibanco's account holders bought, on average, five products each—generally including checking and savings accounts, a credit card, and insurance. New depositors could also be lured from the ranks of rival banks by a larger credit line and an extra credit or debit card, especially since it was quite common to bank at more than one institution. The danger, as a Unibanco official told Jonathan Wheatley for an article published by the *Banker,* was that ''We have a population of 170 million, most of them in the low-income sector. That means they have a limited capacity to generate income and an unlimited capacity to generate costs, depending on how you proceed.''

Unibanco unified its credit card operations under the Unicard label in 2003 and acquired HiperCard, principal credit card of Brazil's northeast, the following year. It raised $218 million in a 2003 equity offering, part of a series of bond, equity, asset-backed, and subordinated-debt issues that raised $1.42 billion in that year. In some cases, broker/dealers expressed a reluctance to proceed, whereupon the company successfully followed through itself. For these reasons *Latin-Finance* named Unibanco its Bank Issuer of the Year. In 2004 Unibanco enhanced its position by purchasing Banco BNL de Brasil S.A. and formed a credit partnership with the Sonae supermarket group. It also acquired Creditec-Credito Finan-

ciamento e Investimento S.A., a company with a significant presence in personal loans and consumer finance.

Walter Moreira Salles retired in 1991 and died in 2001. Pedro Moreira Salles, the third of his four sons, became chairman of the board of Unibanco Holdings in 1997, despite suffering from muscular dystrophy, which increasingly confined him to a wheelchair. He became chief executive officer of the bank in 2004. Although many observers wondered how long Unibanco could resist a takeover from a bigger financial group—probably a foreign one—management was not under pressure since the Moreira Salles family had firm control of the holding company's voting stock. Unibanco Holdings owned 96.6 percent of Unibanco's outstanding common stock at the end of 2004. The Moreira Salles family had 78.6 percent of the holding company's shares.

Unibanco in 2004

At the end of 2004 Unibanco had 895 full-service branches. There were also 253 Fininvest stores. Counting Fininvest's more than 11,000 points of sale, Unibanco had over 15,000 points of distribution throughout Brazil. A separate network of 380 branches located on the premises of corporate customers offered retail banking services both to corporate customers and their employees. Unibanco was operating about 7,500 ATMs for the use of its customers. A variety of retail banking services were also being offered on the Internet, with 1.7 million registered users. Unibanco had 4.8 million credit cards issued, while Fininvest had 7.6 million private-label accounts.

Unibanco's wholesale business included corporate lending, trade finance, capital markets and investment banking services, investment and brokerage services, project finance, and mergers and acquisitions advice to approximately 400 institutional investors and 2,028 economic groups. The wholesale network had five regional offices and 11 regional branches within Brazil, plus branches in Nassau, The Bahamas, and the Cayman Islands. Unibanco had banking subsidiaries in Luxembourg and the Cayman Islands and representative offices and a brokerage firm in New York.

Principal Subsidiaries

Unibanco - Uniao de Bancos Brasileiros S.A.; Banco Fininvest S.A.; Interbanco S.A.; Unibanco Asset Management - Banco de Investimiento S.A.; Unibanco Corretora de Valores Mobilarios S.A.; Unibanco Leasing S.A. - Arrendamiento Mercantil; Unibanco Representaçao e Participaçoes Ltda.; Unicard Banco Multiplo S.A.; Unipart Participaçoes Internacionais Ltda.

Principal Operating Units

Retail; Insurance and Pension Plans; Wealth Management; Wholesale.

Principal Competitors

Banco Bradasco S.A.; Banco do Brasil S.A.; Banco Itaú S.A.

Further Reading

Fucs, José, ''E Agora?,'' *Exame,* February 6, 1995, pp. 19–23.

Griffith, Victoria, "Positive Aggression," *LatinFinance,* October 1996, pp. 20–22, 24.

"Israel Vainboim, Unibanco Holdings," *LatinFinance,* July 1998, pp. 192–93.

Karp, Jonathan, "Dollars and Conscience," *Wall Street Journal,* February 22, 2001, p. A18.

O'Brien, Maria, "Aiming for a Local Following," *LatinFinance,* November 2003, p. 64.

Tangeman, Michael, "Bonanza for a Brazilian Bank," *Institutional Investor* (National Edition), January 1998, p. 85.

"Unibanco," *Institutional Investor* (International Edition), February 1994, Brazil supplement, pp. 12–13.

"Walter Moreira Salles," *Fortune,* May 1959, p. 80.

Wheatley, Jonathan, "Unibanco Turns Takeover Tables," *Banker,* November 2001, pp. 61–63.

Zappa, Sergio, "Co-Piloting Capital Raising," *LatinFinance,* February 2004, p. 56.

—Robert Halasz

United Press International, Inc.

1510 H Street, Northwest
Washington, D.C. 20005
U.S.A.
Telephone: (202) 898-8000
Fax: (202) 898-8057
Web site: http://www.upi.com

Wholly Owned Subsidiary of News World Communications
Incorporated: 1907 as United Press
Employees: 100
NAIC: 519110 News Syndicates; 519190 All Other
Information Services

United Press International, Inc. (UPI), like its rival The Associated Press (AP), is a name recognized around the world for news and photography. Though UPI has downsized and narrowed its scope, the renowned company still brings up-to-the-minute news, sports, and in-depth reports to its clients, primarily over the Internet. With a century of experience behind its dispatches, UPI has continued to forge alliances and remain at the cutting edge of information collection and delivery.

In the Beginning: 1907–57

Newspaper publisher Edward "E.W." Scripps founded United Press (UP) on June 21, 1907, to make national and international news coverage available to all existing newspapers and newspaper startups. In a dig at the older and larger Associated Press wire service, Scripps reportedly said, "I do not believe it would be good for journalism in this country if there should be one big news trust." United Press was created by a merger of Publisher's Press with Scripps-McRae Press Association and Scripps News Associations. There were several organizations then using the name "United Press," and it took Scripps two years of legal wrangling to gain ownership of the name.

On its first day of business the news service used leased telegraph lines to send 12,000 words of Morse code to 369 afternoon newspapers, including those belonging to the Scripps chain. Early "Unipressers," as the correspondents were called, were the first wire service reporters to conduct interviews and to put bylines on stories. They were also the first to send feature stories over the wire and to include laborers' views in coverage of industrial disputes.

In 1935 UP expanded its services and became the first wire service to tailor news for radio broadcasters. Radio announcer Ronald Reagan at WHO in Des Moines, Iowa, used the newly launched UP radio wire in 1936. In contrast to the well known AP, Unipressers generally worked solo and were encouraged to keep their expenses down, and to be both speedy and brief. Opinions were not welcome, just the facts. To beat their competitors, UP reporters resorted to both creative and common sense methods. A Unipresser in Madrid in 1936 tricked the censors to get the first story out announcing the beginning of the Spanish Civil War. His message to London was a mishmash of words, with the first letter of each word spelling out "foreign legion revolted martial law declared." Decades later, during President Nixon's first visit to China in 1972, UPI White House reporter Helen Thomas filed her story from the tunnels of the ancient, underground Ming tombs simply by asking a Chinese attendant if there was a telephone anywhere around. He led her to one nearby. In 1981 the "mystery man" sought by police for running from the scene of the assassination attempt on President Reagan turned out to be a UPI reporter trying to get to a telephone to call in the story.

In the early 1950s the E.W. Scripps Company (then known as Scripps Howard) sold its Acme Newspictures photo agency to United Press, beginning a relationship that would result in a number of Pulitzer Prizes for news photography.

Mergers, Acquisitions, and Losses: 1958–85

In May 1958 United Press merged with International News Service (INS), owned by William Randolph Hearst, and was renamed United Press International. Early discussions between UP and INS had focused on merging their newsphoto services. But in 1955 the negotiations began examining consolidation of the two parent organizations. After three years of secret talks, the two companies reached an agreement. United Press Associations absorbed International News Service, buying the Hearst assets and assuming responsibility for fulfilling all INS news and picture contracts. Frank Bartholomew, president of UP,

Company Perspectives:

Since 1907, United Press International (UPI) has been a leading provider of critical information to media outlets, businesses, governments and researchers worldwide. UPI is a global operation headquartered in Washington, D.C. with offices in Beirut, Hong Kong, London, Santiago, Seoul, and Tokyo. UPI licenses content directly to print outlets, online media, and institutions of all types. In addition, UPI's distribution partners provide our content to thousands of businesses, policy groups and academic institutions worldwide. Our audience consists of millions of decision-makers who depend on UPI's insightful and analytical stories to make better business or policy decisions.

remembered that the eight sets of the final agreement weighed 17 pounds, as measured on a bathroom scale.

UP and INS jointly announced UPI's birth at noon on May 24, 1958. The announcement read: "This is the first dispatch of the news service which will embrace the largest number of newspaper and radio clients ever served simultaneously by an independently operated news and picture agency." At the time of its founding, UPI had 6,000 employees and served 5,000 newspapers and broadcast clients. Later that year UPI introduced the first wire service radio network, with correspondents reading their reports from around the globe. Among the voices with which radio listeners became familiar were those of Eric Sevareid, David Brinkley, and Walter Cronkite.

Reporting news internationally, as well as domestically, turned out to be an expensive business. UPI operated at a loss for years, with its parent company carrying it. Those losses increased as afternoon newspapers, the service's primary market, began to close. In 1978 E.W. Scripps Company proposed an arrangement for its clients to invest in the news service, becoming co-owners. When the effort failed, the company began looking for a buyer.

E.W. Scripps Company celebrated UPI's diamond anniversary in 1982 by selling the news service to Media News Corporation, a new company formed by four investors who owned U.S. newspaper, cable, and television stations. Scripps received $1 from the new owners and agreed to spend a further $5 million to support the service during the transition. At the time of its sale UPI was serving more than 7,500 newspapers, as well as radio, television, and cable systems in more than 100 countries. Its 2,000 full-time employees in 224 news and picture bureaus sent some 13 million words of news and other information out each day. More than 550 cable systems subscribed to UPI Cable Newswire, making UPI the largest provider of written news for cable television screens.

Revenues for UPI reached $110 million in 1982, but it was operating with a $4 million loss. Much of this was caused by huge telephone bills: $14 million a year in the United States and $30 million worldwide. Media News determined it could save as much as $7 million by using satellites rather than telephone lines to send its articles and pictures. The new owners announced they would spend $20 million to improve communica-

tions and to beef up state and regional news coverage. They also planned to study the pricing of the news service. Unfortunately, their efforts failed. In April 1985 UPI declared bankruptcy and filed for Chapter 11 protection from its creditors. Employee layoffs began as the company reported $40.2 million in debt and about $24 million in assets.

Rebirth and More Losses: 1986–92

In June 1986 a company called New UPI Inc., owned by Mexican businessman Mario Vazquez-Rana and Texas real estate investor Joe Russo, bought the financially troubled UPI. New UPI Inc. paid $41 million for UPI, beating out Financial News Network (FNN) in the bidding. Employees took a 25 percent pay cut to keep UPI going, as Vazquez-Rana, who owned 90 percent of the company, pledged to keep it as a general news service. After two years—during which UPI lost between $1 million and $2 million a month—Vazquez-Rana sold the company to Infotech Inc., which held 46 percent of cable business channel FNN. The agreement transferred operational control but not ownership to Infotech, with Vazquez-Rana setting up lines of credit to cover costs.

Infotech planned to make UPI "the cornerstone of a high-tech information network," according to Elizabeth Tucker in a 1988 *Washington Post* article. UPI Chairman Earl Brian envisioned UPI reporters feeding information to FNN and its 30 million viewers, while financial information from FNN correspondents would be available for UPI's print business products. As part of this strategy, Infotech broke up UPI's generalized wire service into specific segments—national sports, business news, photographs, and international news—and concentrated more heavily on covering local and regional news.

By late 1990 with Infotech heavily in debt and unable to meet its daily operating expenses, the company put UPI and FNN up for sale. The following August, with $65.2 million in liabilities and $22.7 million in assets, UPI sought once again to reorganize under Chapter 11. The news service was down to 586 employees and its future was uncertain. By the middle of 1992 it appeared religious broadcaster Pat Robertson would buy UPI, but he withdrew his bid, offering instead to buy just the name, UPI's photo archive, and its overseas news photo distribution business. In June the bankruptcy judge selected Middle East Broadcasting Centre, Ltd. (MBC) of London over Robertson and a Dutch foundation. Middle East Broadcasting paid $3.95 million in cash for UPI.

The principal owner of MBC was Sheik Walid Al-Ibrahim, brother-in-law of King Fahd of Saudi Arabia, and the company broadcasted news and entertainment from Arabia to Europe, Africa, and the Middle East. MBC was UPI's fifth owner in a decade, a period that also included two bankruptcies, a court-ordered liquidation, management upheaval, and labor disputes. For the second time in its 85-year history, UPI was foreign-owned.

UPI Recovering, Somewhat: 1993–97

In 1993 and 1994 the new owners reorganized UPI into six regional bureaus, made significant investments to upgrade the company's communications system, and started expanding into new areas. The management team who took over in early 1994 symbolized MBC's new strategic direction for UPI. Chief Executive L. Brewster Jackson and his management team came from high-tech media companies and international businesses. In a 1994 interview, Jean AbiNader, vice-president of operations, told the *Canada NewsWire,* ''Our worldwide technology investment alone should tell the world that we aren't resting on our laurels. Our new global satellite system, delivering an array of news and information services to desktop computers anywhere in an instant says a lot about our future direction.''

The company began selling electronic news services to a wider array of subscribers and created 35 worldwide sales positions to market UPI's products to corporate and government markets as well as media customers. It also upgraded its photos and other images, so they could be delivered by satellite. By 1995 UPI had completed a satellite transmission system and no longer needed to send news over telephone lines.

One of UPI's first new services was ''World View,'' a global satellite network to provide information important to corporate clients. Using UPI's network program, clients could access text, audio, photographs, and live video information. UPI's management came to believe the company's future lay in broadcasting, not in wire service writing. By the end of 1996 the company was concentrating its efforts on expanding its broadcast and online computer services and in early 1997 nearly all of UPI's news bureaus in Europe (except London) and the United States were closed, leaving the company to depend on freelance ''stringers'' for coverage. To strengthen its radio broadcast activities, the broadcast and news desks were merged.

Focusing on broadcasting made sense; UPI Radio Network, with 120 affiliates, accounted for half of the company's income. The network's clients included Salem Broadcasting, Skylight, and People's Radio Network, three religious broadcasters, as well as the Armed Forces Radio Network and Bloomberg News Radio. Employment at UPI was down to 300 staff members and 800 stringers with about 1,000 broadcast clients and 1,000 newspaper and Internet clients.

Still far from profitable, UPI was developing what the *New York Times,* in a March 1997 article, described as ''a kind of niche journalism, selling fragments of news to customers ranging from a San Francisco paging service that puts headlines on pager screens to a Kentucky enterprise that wants to flash headlines in small streaming lights installed in bars, to religious broadcasters who have been adding news broadcasts as a way of keeping their listeners tuned in.'' The headline service, which UPI called ''Short Service,'' provided two-sentence news summaries. For its news articles, UPI adopted a new writing style limited to 350 words. ''We provide details to reporters and editors to use in their own reports,'' a UPI executive explained in the *Times* article.

In mid-1997 James Adams, who had been the Washington bureau chief for London's *Sunday Times* after serving as its defense correspondence and managing editor, was named chief executive. Adams greatly accelerated the company's move to becoming an electronic information source, aimed at developing ways individual consumers could access specific ''knowledge'' at any time. One new service was UPI MEMO, an online joint venture with Meridian Emerging Markets Ltd. of Virginia. For $10,000 a year, a client received comprehensive coverage on 16,000 companies in emerging markets and the necessary software to screen and analyze the data. Reports addressed the political and cultural issues influencing the economic outlook in a market as well as pricing and dividend information, earnings estimates, and historical fundamental financial data on individual companies.

New Facets: 1998 to the 2000s

In 1998 Adams announced UPI was getting into the production business, with the formation of UPI Productions to create documentary and news programs for television, video, and the Internet. He also moved to develop new markets and customers for UPI's extensive archives. To this end, he developed a joint venture with Microsoft Corporation, called UPI-Microsoft Knowledge Center, to convert and distribute text, photos, audio, and video/film over the Internet. He also discussed the launch of a new entity to sell its library of films and videos as well as make UPI material available through Media Exchange International's web site on a per-use basis to general users. In May, Adams announced an agreement with Geoworks Corporation to deliver headlines and news summaries to wireless devices. With Geoworks' software, customers could search for news by topics, names, or keywords.

Adams continued to have high expectations for UPI, predicting the company would be profitable by 1999 and might even go public. His words rang hollow, however, as the company fell deeper into debt. Adams resigned in late 1998 and took several top staffers with him to create a new information services firm. UPI's Saudi owners brought in Arnaud de Borchgrave, a longtime UPI bureau chief, as their new chief executive. Next came the all-too-familiar: UPI was sold again, this time to Reverend Sun Myung Moon's News World Communications (NWC). Moon and the NWC owned the venerable *Washington Post* newspaper, as well as other papers including the *World Peace Herald, Middle East Times,* and Latin America's *Tiempos del Mundo.*

UPI staffers were told the controversial Moon's ownership would have little impact on them; such sentiments failed to convince veteran White House correspondent Helen Thomas,

UPI's only jewel in the crown, who resigned as soon as the sale to Moon and NWC became final. Chief Executive de Borchgrave nevertheless tried to put a positive spin on UPI's latest ownership change and was quoted in *U.S. News & World Report* (December 4, 2000) as saying, ''UPI, which also stands for Unlimited Possibilities and Ideas, will consign the humdrum to oblivion, think out-of-the-box, and look over-the-horizon.''

Over the next few years UPI quietly went about its business, trying to stay abreast of technological advances and holding on to the few loyal clients it had. For the most part it succeeded, by extending coverage and bringing new providers into the fold. In 2004 UPI expanded its decades-old partnership with information services firm LexisNexis, as well as Thomson Gale (a subsidiary of Toronto-based Thomson Corporation) and EBSCO Publishing. Thomson Gale and EBSCO Publishing, both providers of educational and information services, began offering UPI's English, Spanish, and some Arabic content in their extensive online databases. In addition, UPI formalized an agreement with the Sports Network to provide scores and sports information to media, interactive, and corporate clients nationwide.

In early 2005 UPI partnered with Country Briefings, Ltd. to add the latter's content to its news and informational offerings. Country Briefings, which published current political, economic, and business reports on 32 major world markets, also possessed an archive with more than a decade's worth of international news.

Although the UPI that existed in the late 2000s was a fraction of its competitors' sizes, it had weathered a century of ups and downs and transitioned from a telegraph and phone news agency to an established information services provider. Its numerous owners and financial woes did not keep UPI from carving itself a niche within the information collection industry to provide media outlets, companies, governments, schools, and researchers with news and information in English, Spanish, and Arabic. The company's partnerships with ABC-CLIO Schools, LexisNexis, EBSCO Publishing, Thomson Gale, NewsCom, Omnivex Corporation, and the Copyright Clearance Center brought its products to the broadest possible range of clients from the boardroom and the classroom to individual homes. In the electronic and digital age of the 21st century, competition was all about delivery and speed and UPI continued to make strides in both of these areas.

Principal Competitors

Agence France-Presse; The Associated Press; Bell & Howell Company; Bloomberg L.P.; Dow Jones & Company, Inc.; Gannett Company, Inc.; Knight Ridder-Tribune News Service; New York Times Company; Reuters Group PLC.

Further Reading

Barringer, Felicity, ''A New Boss Vows to Take Beleaguered UPI Upscale,'' *International Herald Tribune*, December 30, 1998, p. 3.

Bartholomew, Frank H., ''Putting the 'I' into U.P.I.,'' *Editor & Publisher*, September 25, 1982, p. 25.

Bedard, Paul, et al., ''UPI, Part X,'' *U.S. News & World Report*, December 4, 2000, p. 16.

——, ''UPI's Final Bell?,'' *U.S. News & World Report*, May 8, 2000, p. 6.

Berry, John F., ''New Hope at Distressed Wire Service; Youthful Owners Set Out to Make UPI Profitable,'' *Washington Post*, October 3, 1982, p. M1.

Day, Kathleen, ''Financial News Network, UPI Are Put Up for Sale,'' *Washington Post*, November 8, 1990, p. B15.

Farhai, Paul, ''UPI's Fate Goes Down to Wire,'' *Washington Post*, November 16, 1990, p. C11.

Friendly, Jonathan, ''UPI to Spend $20 Million to Improve and Expand Operation,'' *New York Times*, October 3, 1982, p. 40.

''From Threatened to Just Threadbare, U.P.I. Adjusts to Buyout,'' *New York Times*, July 20, 1992, p. D6.

Jayne, Micah, ''UPI Hopes New Information Service Will Do Big Business with Big Business,'' *Washington Times*, July 27, 1994, p. B7.

Jones, Alex S., ''Mideast Broadcaster Acquires UPI in Bankruptcy Court,'' *New York Times*, June 24, 1992, p. D2.

Lattin, Don, ''Robertson Gives Mixed Signals About Religion's Role in UPI,'' *San Francisco Chronicle*, May 15, 1992, p. A9.

Lilling, Adam, ''UPI's Latest Survival Strategy,'' *American Journalism Review*, September 1997, p. 15.

Lord, Lewis, ''Thank You, Ms. Thomas,'' *U.S. News & World Report*, May 29, 2000, p. 8.

Manning, Robert, ''When UP Had No I,'' *New York Times*, June 12, 1982, p. 31.

''Pat Robertson Backs Out of UPI Deal,'' *Star Tribune* (Minneapolis), June 11, 1992, p. 3D.

Peterson, Iver, ''In News Business, UPI Plans to Thrive in 350 Words or Less,'' *New York Times*, March 31, 1997, p. D1.

Quigg, H.D., ''UPI's Diamond Anniversary: From Morse Code to Satellites,'' *U.P.I.*, June 19, 1982.

Schuch, Beverly, ''UPI CEO Interview,'' *CNNfn Business Unusual*, April 21, 1998.

Spiegal, Peter, ''Old Dog, New Tricks,'' *Forbes*, June 1, 1998, p. 47.

''Suddenly UPI Is in Demand As 3 Groups Wrestle for Control,'' *Chicago Tribune*, June 19, 1992, p. 2.

Sugawara, Sandra, ''UPI Proves Too Much for Vazquez-Rana: Owner Hands Over Operating Control of Troubled Wire Service to Former Rival,'' *Washington Post*, February 21, 1988, p. A4.

Tharp, Paul, ''UPI Upgrades Wires Service to the 'Net,'' *New York Post*, March 20, 1998, p. 034.

Tucker, Elizabeth, ''Brian's Aggressive Plans for Troubled UPI,'' *Washington Post*, November 28, 1988, p. F37.

''UPI Eyes TV, Video Internet,'' *AP Online*, March 19, 1998.

Wolper, Allan, ''Down to One Suitor at UPI,'' *Editor & Publisher*, February 14, 2000, p. 4.

——, ''UPI Looks for Way Out of Massive Debt,'' *Editor & Publisher*, April 24, 1999, p. 8.

——, ''UPI Will Still Fly Under Own Flag,'' *Editor & Publisher*, May 22, 2000, p. 13.

—Ellen D. Wernick
—update: Nelson Rhodes

Value Line, Inc.

220 East 42nd Street
New York, New York 10017
U.S.A.
Telephone: (212) 907-1500
Toll Free: (800) 634-3583
Fax: (212) 818-9748
Web site: http://www.valueline.com

Public Company
Incorporated: 1931 as Arnold Bernhard & Company
Employees: 249
Sales: $84.7 million (2004)
Stock Exchanges: NASDAQ
Ticker Symbol: VALU
NAIC: 523920 Portfolio Management; 511110
   Newspaper Publishers; 511120 Periodical Publishers;
   511140 Database and Directory Publishers; 511210
   Software Publishers; 541810 Advertising Agencies

Value Line, Inc. is best known for publishing the *Value Line Investment Survey,* the most widely used independent investment service in the world. The company publishes more than a dozen print and electronic products, read by more than half a million people. The company's flagship weekly periodical, which provides comprehensive information on approximately 1,700 stocks, more than 90 industries, the stock market, and the economy, earned the moniker the bible of Wall Street. Long known for its strong and consistent record, the seven-decade-old information service was widely regarded by many as the world's best-performing financial newsletter. The *Investment Survey* had been perennially ranked number one by the *Hulbert Financial Digest.* Other publications bearing the venerable company name include the *Value Line Mutual Fund Survey,* which ranks and evaluates mutual funds. The company's Value Line Family of Mutual Funds, consisting of 15 investment companies, which manages investments for private and institutional clients, has generally failed to match the success of its information segment.

Early History

Value Line was founded in 1931 by legendary financier Arnold Bernhard. Following a brief stint as a reporter and playwright, the would be "Dean of Wall Street" made his entry into the business world as a trainee in the Railroad Department of Moody's Investment Service during the late 1920s. The neophyte investor, like the rest of the Wall Street community, was ill prepared for the disastrous events to come. The Great Crash of 1929 and the ensuing collapse in the early 1930s, however, proved to be the catalyst for his entrepreneurial drive.

Having realized that not even Moody's, one of the most respected sources of financial opinion in the world, had been able to predict the impending collapse of stock values to come, Bernhard concluded that what his investors needed was a standard of normal value that would signal when stocks were overvalued and when they were undervalued. Instead of accepting the conventional wisdom of the time, that the value of a stock is revealed completely in its market price, he began examining the correlation between the monthly price of stocks and such factors as annual earnings and book values over 20-year periods.

Bernhard's new ideas, along with the continued decline in the market in the early 1930s, did not sit well with one of his clients who suffered heavy losses during the period and eventually brought suit against Moody's for allowing Bernhard to manage his account. In 1931, the young investment counselor was fired. The apparent catastrophe, though, proved to be a blessing: not only did many of his clients retain his services, but he now had the freedom and the time to work on his Ratings of Normal Value.

By 1935, Bernhard had worked out equations for 120 individual stocks, assigning each a rating based on the charting of prices and earnings over time. He bought a multilith press and printed 1,000 copies of the book, which he called the *Value Line Ratings of Normal Value,* setting the price at $200 each. "It was hard for me to realize how little the world would be interested," Bernhard said 50 years later in a speech before the Newsletter Association of America. His numerous calls to banks and other financial institutions resulted mostly in polite stares and only one sale, to a skeptical portfolio manager.

With an embarrassingly large inventory of 999 books in his office and much of his time and energy diverted from his investment counsel accounts, Bernhard was paid a visit by Major L.L.B. Angas, the publisher of an enormously influential financial newsletter. Although Angas refused to purchase a copy of the book, he agreed to review it in the forthcoming edition of his bulletin. A few days later, Angas made good on his promise, advising his readers that they "should own" a copy of the "young fellow's" book; however, the price had been lowered to $55. Not only was the value of Bernhard's inventory reduced by nearly 75 percent overnight, but he received a bill for $800 from the Major to cover the cost of printing the bulletin in which the endorsement appeared. The recommendation, though, proved to be a worthy investment: 600 checks for $55 appeared on Bernhard's desk shortly after the publication of the newsletter.

The lesson Bernhard had learned from the crafty publisher would guide his future marketing strategy. Instead of relying merely on personal representation, Bernhard channeled his resources into print advertisements to build the circulation of his fledgling newsletter. He invested $70 in a two-week advertisement in *Barron's* for $5 samples of the *Value Line Ratings of Normal Value*. Although the two ads brought in only nine leads and a $45 initial return, follow-up letters that included more information about the ratings resulted in the sale of three books at $55 each. Once again, what appeared to be a setback turned out to be a blessing.

Postwar Growth and Innovation

For the first decade, Bernhard's formula for rating stocks consisted of simply tracking a security's past price and earnings history and projecting that into the future by multiplying a percentage of the company's book value by a conservative multiple of anticipated earnings per share. This relatively simple equation underwent a significant revision with the hiring of Samuel Eisenstadt, who brought his extensive knowledge of statistics theory to the company upon his arrival in 1946. Among the more sophisticated measuring instruments he helped to introduce was "multiple regression analysis"—the simultaneous comparison of a number of variables. The added complexity to Bernhard's basic formula did not, however, significantly improve the accuracy of the ratings. As Eisenstadt recalled in the *Wall Street Journal,* Value Line's predictive performance during this period was "ho-hum—just a little better than average."

The availability of computer technology in the 1960s enabled Bernhard and his chief statistician to add the missing variable to their formula. Using the computer's power to measure each stock's price and earnings characteristics against the comparable characteristics of all other Value Line stocks, they developed what became known as a "cross-sectional" method of analysis. In April 1965, they introduced what would become the hallmark of the Value Line rating system: the "timeliness" ranking, whereby all stocks in the survey receive a ranking of 1 to 5 based on the computer-aided analysis of several variables of financial strength and a prediction of investment suitability over the next 12 months. Despite widespread skepticism among mainline sources of financial opinion, the new methodology proved successful almost from the start. Value Line's team of statisticians noticed immediately that on average the top 100 stocks—those that received a Group 1 rating—performed better than their counterparts in other categories, rising more in strong markets and declining less in weak ones.

Challenges of the 1970s

During the late 1960s and early 1970s, the stock market experienced a period of strong growth. Value Line fund managers, according to Tim Metz's profile in the *Wall Street Journal,* however, maintained a conservative outlook and were slow to react to the bullish market. When the company finally did take a more aggressive course, the market declined, causing some investors to lose money and confidence in the Value Line system.

A number of wide-ranging investigations by the Securities and Exchange Commission (SEC) provided other obstacles for the company during this period. In the late 1960s, the SEC accused Bernhard and another company official of taking fees in connection with two company funds without informing investors in the fund prospectus or remitting the funds. The agency also charged some company analysts with withholding information from Value Line subscribers and shareholders regarding their agreements to serve as financing or acquisition finders for companies they were following. Without admitting or denying the SEC charges, the defendants consented to a 1971 federal court injunction against future securities law violations.

In 1974, new scandals emerged that threatened to further tarnish the esteemed Value Line reputation. A former editor was accused of accepting a $15,000 bribe from two brokers in 1972 in exchange for writing bullish recommendations on two selected stocks. The 1971 injunction and the charges against the editor generated a host of civil lawsuits. While Bernhard denied the charges, they remained a hindrance throughout the decade, costing the company more than $500,000 in out of court settlements.

Recovery and Growth in the 1980s

Consistent with its proven ability to turn adversity into growth, Value Line did not fail to learn from its mistakes. By tightening investment standards and improving the methodology behind its stock rankings, the company succeeded in doubling subscriptions to the then $365-a-year *Value Line Investment Survey* between 1978 and 1983, while boosting annual revenues to approximately $40 million. Meanwhile, profits increased more than 80 percent, to $6.7 million, between 1980 and 1983. First, in an attempt to make its forecasts more objective by further removing the "human element," the company ended a three-year "experiment" that allowed the ana-

---

Key Dates:

1931: Value Line is founded by Arnold Bernhard.
1935: Company publishes the *Value Line Ratings of Normal Value.*
1946: Statistical theory expert Samuel Eisenstadt joins company.
1965: Forerunner of the "timeliness" ranking is introduced.
1971: Investigations by SEC lead to federal court injunction.
1974: Value Line reputation again under threat with new allegations.
1983: Bernhard offers 19 percent of Value Line to public.
1992: Profits hit all-time high of $26 million.
1995: First online service is offered.
2003: Wall Street firms agree to begin offering independent research to clients.

---

lysts' judgment factor to account for 20 percent of the weight in its stock rankings. The company also stopped its earlier practice of purchasing unregistered "letter stock" for which there was not yet a public market. In addition to boosting subscriptions, such policies contributed to the strong performance of the flagship Value Line Fund, which demonstrated average annual returns of nearly 33 percent between 1974 and 1981.

By 1983, the 375-employee firm had expanded its survey to include ratings on 1,700 stocks, while controlling $1.2 billion in assets through its six mutual funds. The success of the "timeliness" rankings, well publicized in such popular magazines as *Time* and *Newsweek,* contributed to the excitement surrounding Bernhard's decision to make a public offering of 19 percent of his company in April 1983. Widespread interest in new issues and stock investments in general at the time brought the selling price to $17 a share and helped the price to climb to a record high of $40 by the summer of 1984.

The company, aided by the more than $30 million brought in by the public offering, grew steadily during the latter part of the decade, boosting revenue to nearly $70 million by 1987, largely on the strength of the *Investment Survey*'s 30 percent to 35 percent operating margins. Although cautious with his approach to new ventures, Bernhard worked to expand the company by diversifying profitably into the money-management business, adding several new publications, and entering the investment software market.

In the midst of this period of expansion, though, the company also had to overcome a new challenge: a transition in leadership brought on by the death of its founder and leader, Arnold Bernhard. Although Bernhard's son, Van, who had worked for the firm for several years, seemed the probable successor, he declined the job, and his sister, Jean Buttner, who joined the company in 1982, was appointed CEO and given the task of leading the company through the challenges of a recessionary economy and a new era in technology. While the company enjoyed record total revenue and profits during the first year of Buttner's tenure, it suffered from a general malaise in the investment market following the stock market crash of 1987

and the ensuing recession of the late 1980s. Value Line, like many other businesses in the field, saw its pattern of vibrant growth come to a halt at the close of the decade.

Strong Start to the 1990s

With the new decade came the start of market recovery and a concomitant increase in the *Investment Survey*'s circulation. In 1992, Value Line's revenue returned to near record levels and profits climbed to an all-time high of $26 million. Despite the strong balance sheets, Buttner drew criticism for what *Business Week*'s Anthony Bianco described as an "autocratic" style of leadership that lowered employee morale. The company, long known for its ability to hold down costs and a forerunner of the downsizing trend, reduced its workforce from approximately 425 to 325 during this period, largely through resignations and firings that some believed threatened the stability of the company.

Despite drawing heavy criticism from disgruntled former employees and the media for her management techniques, Buttner, who received recognition as one of the top 50 businesswomen by *Working Mother* magazine, led the company to three straight years of record earnings, building on the growth that led *Forbes* magazine to name Value Line the best small company in the United States, based on return on equity. She was also moved to update the company to the demands of the Information Age, initiating and expanding the "Value/Screen" electronic database/software service, which covered 1,600 stocks, and DataFile, the institutional equity database covering 5,200 U.S. and foreign companies.

A number of new publications and features were also added to the *Value Line* fold during Buttner's tenure. The company more than doubled its coverage of the market by providing investors with the *Value Line Investment Survey—Expanded Edition,* which reported on 1,800 stocks not included in the flagship publication. Moreover, it added a separate 16-page newsletter called "Selection & Opinion," which highlighted individual stocks, reported general market and interest rate conditions, and offered three different model portfolios of 20 stocks to suit different types of investors. In 1993, the firm added mutual funds to its survey through the introduction of the *Value Line Mutual Fund Survey,* a biweekly publication that covered more than 2,000 funds. In 1995, the company also offered its first online service, negotiating a deal with CompuServe through which subscribers could access both the *Value Line Investment Survey* and the *Value Line Mutual Fund Survey* and could view individual company and industry reports.

Fading in the Late 1990s

While Value Line's stock picking ability had made its reputation, the company's own mutual fund family, drawn from the survey list, underperformed. The disparity, according to *Forbes,* arose from transaction costs tied to Value Line real world funds coupled with stock price spikes as Value Line readers and its own funds purchased top picks.

Moreover, Value Line's own stock lagged behind its publishing and money management peer group, according to *Crain's New York Business.* Value Line had been slow to sign on when the mutual fund market heated up; Morningstar would become the brand name in the mutual fund rating business.

While the company had added electronic versions of its print products, subscribers switching from one format to another offered no net gain in market share. Competition had also heated up, coming from the vast stores of financial information of the Internet and from Morningstar, which had entered into the stock ranking business in 1997. Finally, mergers in the financial world created competitors with deeper pockets.

''Despite the stock's less-than-stellar returns the past few years, Ms. Buttner was paid about $1.4 million in fiscal 1997 and $1.2 million in fiscal 1996. About the same time, she won a nasty public fight with her twin, Arnold Van Hoven Bernhard, for control of the company,'' wrote Anna Robaton for *Crain's.*

A bull market did little to help Value Line revenues, according to *Crain's,* up only 2 percent for fiscal 1998, to $93.6 million. Net income suffered a drop of nearly 23 percent, to $35.2 million, due to a special dividend paid as part of the ownership settlement.

New Century, New Game

By 2000, Value Line's top picks had fallen below market returns for five straight years. The system depending on historical data and offering only weekly updates could not keep pace with the overheated market and light speed technology of the day. Most of the hottest dotcom stocks, lacking two-year price and earnings data, did not make the rankings. Some observers were writing off the service as out of step with the times; others pointed to the ongoing need for a reliable independent source of information, according to *Money* magazine.

Value Line, for its part, upgraded its technology during 1999 and 2000. Drawing in the new breed of investors, who did not even recognize the name, was another story. A hopeful sign was the reversal of the half-decade slippage by the end of 1999. Stock picks such as Qualcomm and JDS Uniphase pushed Value Line past the market once again, Lisa Reilly Cullen reported for *Money.* Value Line beat the S&P 500 by 20 points in 2000. Although top picks dropped 7 percent in 2001, Value Line stayed five points ahead of its large cap weighted rival, according to *Kiplinger's Personal Finance Magazine.*

Value Line's own large stock mutual funds continued to be ''pedestrian performers,'' observed Steven T. Goldberg for *Kiplinger's.* In addition, stellar small stock funds lacked promotion. The Value Line's 15 mutual funds managed only about $4 billion in assets.

The financial world faced turmoil on many levels in the new century, ranging from the 9/11 attacks to internal misdeeds. In the midst of if all, the name Value Line was again on people's lips, as a possible remedy to what ailed Wall Street. Regulators were pushing to force investment bankers to provide clients with independent research in addition to their own. In 2003, ten major Wall Street firms settled with New York Attorney General Eliot Spitzer over conflict of interest claims and Value Line was among those companies likely to benefit from the new requirements.

Despite the ups and downs of its recent history, Value Line's predictive acumen had staying power. In 2005, the *Hulbert Financial Digest* ranked the *Value Line Investment Survey* second among rating investment newsletters for risk-adjusted performance over the past 25 years, according to the *America's Intelligence Wire.*

Principal Subsidiaries

Value Line Securities, Inc.; Vanderbilt Advertising, Inc.; Value Line Distribution Center; Value Line Publishing, Inc.

Principal Competitors

McGraw-Hill Companies, Inc.; Morningstar Inc.; Thomson Corporation.

Further Reading

Baldwin, William, ''Paying the Piper,'' *Forbes,* October 19, 1987, p. 208.

Bianco, Anthony, ''Value Line: Too Lean, Too Mean?,'' *Business Week,* March 16, 1992, pp. 104–06.

Choe, Sang-Hung, ''Value Line Had Another Bad Year—and Still Beat Market,'' *America's Intelligence Wire,''* February 11, 2005.

''Coming Out: A Top Stock Picker Goes Public,'' *Time,* April 25, 1993, p. 98.

Cullen, Lisa Reilly, ''What Happened to Value Line?,'' *Money,* September 1, 2000, pp. 96 + .

Curran, John J., ''Value Line's Winning Way,'' *Fortune,* April 18, 1983, pp. 131–32.

Gandel, Stephen, ''Stock Watch: Value Line Stands to Gain from Wall Street's Rehab,'' *Crain's New York Business,* October 28, 2002, p. 43.

Fredrickson, Tom, ''Stock Watch: Value Line Proves to Be the Gift That Keeps Giving,'' *Crain's New York Business,* May 31, 2004, p. 47.

Goldberg, Steven T., ''Civil Warriors: Value Line's Oldest Employee Spars with the Founder's Daughter,'' *Kiplinger's Personal Finance Magazine,* August 2002, pp. 36 + .

Gorham, John, ''The Momentum Formula,'' *Forbes,* January 25, 1999, p. 114.

Hopkins, Brent, ''Value Line in First Place for Performance Since 1980,'' *America's Intelligence Wire,''* July 11, 2003.

Hulbert, Mark, ''Tweaking the Numbers,'' *Forbes,* February 13, 1995, p. 214.

''In Memoriam: Arnold Bernhard,'' New York: Value Line, Inc., 1988.

Kahn, Virginia Munger, ''Nice Try,'' *Financial World,* March 14, 1995, pp. 77–80.

Metz, Tim, ''Better Days,'' *Wall Street Journal,* January 14, 1981, pp. 1, 19.

——, ''Value Line Plans to Sell 19% of Concern to Public for As Much As $34.2 Million,'' *Wall Street Journal,* April 8, 1983, p. 13.

Miller, Annetta, and Ellyn E. Spragins, ''Family Values,'' *Newsweek,* October 10, 1994, pp. 48–50.

Opdyke, Jeff, and Jane Kim, ''Stock Picker's Fund Lags,'' *Grand Rapids Press,* September 19, 2004, p. 16.

Robaton, Anna, ''Investors See Less Value in Bible of Stocks: Buttner's Value Line Struggling with New Ventures, More Competition,'' *Crain's New York Business,* October 5, 1998, p. 18.

Solomon, Robert S., ''Value Line's Self-Defeating Success,'' *Forbes,* June 15, 1998, p. 294.

Vartan, Vartanig G., ''The Downturn at Value Line,'' *New York Times,* August 28, 1995, p. D6.

Weiss, Gary, ''Arnold Bernhard Is a Tough Act to Follow,'' *Business Week,* January 25, 1988, pp. 93–94.

—Jason Gallman
—update: Kathleen Peippo

Variety Wholesalers, Inc.

3401 Gresham Lake Road
Raleigh, North Carolina 27615
U.S.A.
Telephone: (919) 876-6000
Fax: (919) 790-5349
Web site: http://www.vwstores.com

Private Company
Founded: 1932
Employees: 7,500
Sales: $502 million (2003 est.)
NAIC: 452111 Department Stores (Except Discount Department Stores)

Privately held Variety Wholesalers, Inc. is a Raleigh, North Carolina-based operator of several discount retail chains, offering a wide variety of clothing and accessories, housewares, health and beauty aids, sporting goods, toys, snack foods, and furniture. All told, the company owns about 550 stores located in southeastern and Mid-Atlantic states, including Delaware, Maryland, Virginia, West Virginia, North Carolina, Kentucky, Tennessee, South Carolina, Georgia, Florida, Alabama, Mississippi, Arkansas, and Louisiana. The units are divided among three primary divisions. More than 200 stores in the 5,000- to 10,000-square-foot range make up the Super 10 Division. In addition to the Super 10 name, these stores operate as ''Pope's,'' ''Eagle,'' and ''Super Dollar'' stores. Slightly larger stores, 10,000 to 30,000 square feet, form the 150-plus Maxway Division, operating under the Maxway banner. Finally, the stores in the Rose's Division range in size from 30,000 to 70,000 square feet, all operating under the Rose's name. In addition, some Variety stores operate under the Bargain Town, Treasure Mart, and Value Mart Super Center names. The company is headed by the patriarch of the Pope family, John W. Pope, Sr., known as a keen retailer, able to buy struggling retail chains and turn them around, and a man not afraid to close failing stores. *Business, North Carolina* in a 1999 profile, described Pope as frugal: ''Some might say downright cheap. His stores can go 15 or 20 years without a makeover.'' He shies away from larger markets, avoiding going head-to-head with Wal-Mart, for example, preferring instead areas that have minimum populations of 2,500 within one mile of a site, at least a 25 percent African-American population within five miles, and a median household income of less than $40,000. He also likes second- or third-generation shopping centers, especially ones anchored by a supermarket.

History Dating to the 1930s

Variety traces its history to 1932 when John Pope's father, James Pope, himself the son of a dry-goods store owner, opened a five-and-dime store in Angier, North Carolina. John Pope learned the business as a child and was known to sleep under the counter on Saturday nights when his father kept the store open until midnight to attract the business of farming families who came in town for the movies and might stay to shop after the show was over. Pope also picked up some shrewdness from his father, who was quick to realize that as war approached in the early 1940s there were shortages to come, so he stockpiled goods in anticipation. As a result, he was able to open additional stores in North Carolina. When the United States entered the war, John Pope, despite being 17, was in his second year at the University of North Carolina, where he majored in Commerce. His father called him home in 1942 to take the place of a manager who had entered the military, but the younger Pope wanted to enlist in the service. He was not of age and his father refused to sign the permission form, and so in an act of defiance, John Pope convinced a woman at the store to forge his mother's name and he left home to join the Army Air Force. Although trained as a navigator he never saw action, was discharged in 1945, returned to college, and graduated in 1947.

With his savings and backing from his father, who apparently forgave his insubordination, John Pope launched his own business career, which in the beginning was a string of failures that included a jewelry store and a wet-mop factory. In the meantime, his father died, leaving the five-and-dime stores he owned to his brothers. They had no interest in running them, however, and sold out to John Pope and his two brothers in 1949. John Pope then bought out his siblings two years later and began to grow the business, relying purely on cash flow for the next 20 years. In 1953 he opened his first self-service dime

store, and then in July 1957 incorporated his business in North
Carolina as Variety Wholesalers, Inc. Pope proved nimble in
adapting to a changing marketplace, quick to make the transition from the full-price dime stores his father founded to the
variety store format of the 1950s and early 1960s. Veteran
retailers including Woolworth failed to follow suit and eventually fell by the wayside, while others, such as Sam Walton, who
started his retailing career by owning a Ben Franklin franchise
switched from variety stores to the discount store format. Pope
carved out his own niche, concentrating on small southern and
Mid-Atlantic towns and pursuing the downmarket business of
the "dollar store" in the 1970s, and later turned to a mix of
formats in the 1980s and 1990s.

Pace of Expansion Picking Up in the 1970s

After reaching the 50-store mark and generating about $8
million in annual sales, Variety began to accelerate its growth in
the 1970s, as many of the small family-run dime store and
variety store chains were now in the hands of second-generation
owners, many of whom were Pope's friends and whose children
were not interested in taking over the business. Pope would buy
the chains and convert them to his lean way of doing things. In
1971, for the first time taking on debt to make a deal, he
acquired the North Carolina chain of 52 Eagle Stores, which
produced about $10 million in annual revenues, a move that
effectively doubled Variety's size. Next, Pope bought 54
McCrory/United Stores in 1978, followed two years later by the
acquisition of 188 Value Mart Stores, mostly located in Alabama, Louisiana, and Mississippi. In 1981 Variety added the
145 Super Dollar Stores, which relied on advertised sales to
bring in customers. Many of Pope's other stores pursued a
similar strategy, but again the retail landscape was changing,
forcing Pope to adjust once more.

The legal requirement that retailers abide by the "manufacturer's suggested retail price" had started to be discarded in
many states during the 1970s. As a result, the large chains could
use their economies of scale and purchasing power to buy and
sell merchandise at a discount, putting the squeeze on smaller
players. After acquiring 55 P.H. Rose's variety stores in 1984,
Variety was operating close to 400 stores under the Pope's,
Value Mart, Super Dollar, and P.H. Rose's names. But the
company was under pressure from discounters such as
Wal-Mart which were sweeping across the South. The old
formula of heavily advertising loss leader items at or below cost
in the hope that customers would also buy profitable items as
well was no longer working, forcing Pope to close stores in the
wake of decreasing sales. Pope read in a trade journal about a

California merchant who was taking a different approach, giving up on sales and instead offering all items at or below an
everyday threshold price. After 1985 brought a 10 percent drop
in sales for Variety, he decided to try out the new formula on 15
failing stores that he would have to close if they did not turn
around soon. Now called Super 10, the stores priced everything
at $10 or less. The experiment worked and over the next few
years Pope applied the concept to other stores. To gain an edge
he ceased advertising altogether, relying on the consistent pricing approach to bring back customers.

Using different formats, and by a willingness to close stores
that could not be saved, Variety was able to rebound from the
lean years of the mid-1980s and continue to expand through
acquisitions, picking up the pieces of retailers who proved less
adept at changing gears. In 1989 Variety acquired 106 stores
from Allied Department Stores/Savannah Wholesale Co. from
Michigan General Corp., a company that had recently emerged
from Chapter 11 bankruptcy protection. A year later Variety
added 33 Maxway stores, acquired from another company in
Chapter 11. The units, mostly located in North Carolina, Georgia, and South Carolina, were then converted to an everyday
low-price format. In 1992 Variety acquired 60 Bargain Town
stores, almost all of which were located in Alabama, Georgia,
and Mississippi.

By 1995 Variety owned about 550 stores, although that
number fluctuated as Pope continued to show no hesitancy in
shutting down struggling units. Pope employed a number of
relatives, including son John Pope, Jr., and Art Pope. The
former retired from the business in 1995 to concentrate on "his
personal finances and his golf game," according to the father.
John, Jr., a Duke law school graduate, had other interests aside
from retailing and golf. He also was devoted to Republican
politics, serving as a state representative from 1989 to 1992
before losing his bid to become North Carolina's lieutenant
governor. He also chaired the conservative John Locke Foundation, a Raleigh organization he helped to found, and which the
Pope family helped to fund. It was somewhat ironic that a
couple of years later he would meet a drug saleswoman at a
Christmas party who was an active Democrat and marry her, a
situation that would prove nettlesome down the road. His younger brother Art was also a lawyer, serving as Variety's legal
counsel and chief negotiator. He harbored no illusions that he
possessed the retail instincts of his father, who despite his
mounting years remained very much in charge of the company.

Acquiring Rose's in the Late 1990s

In 1997 Variety acquired Rose's Stores Inc. to go with the 55
P.H. Rose's variety stores it bought 20 years earlier—another
example of Pope picking the bones of a less flexible retailer.
Rose's had an even longer history than Variety, its origins
dating to 1915 when Paul Rose opened a general store in North
Carolina's Henderson County. Rose built up a chain of dime
stores and in 1960 began opening large discount stores, on
which it eventually elected to focus, selling the smaller formats
to Variety in the 1980s. By 1990 the chain totaled 260 stores,
but more than half were in markets occupied by giant competitors Kmart and Wal-Mart. Moreover, management had lost its
edge and failed to keep pace with current business practices,
was slow to computerize the accounts, and even failed to adopt

Key Dates:

1932: James Pope opens a general store.
1949: Pope's three sons acquire the family's five-store operation.
1951: John Pope, Sr., buys out his brothers.
1957: Pope forms Variety Wholesalers, Inc.
1971: Eagle Stores is acquired.
1981: Super Dollar Stores is acquired.
1986: The Super 10 format is launched.
1997: Rose's Stores is acquired.

other standard industry money-saving techniques. After the last of the Rose family left in 1991, a new management team, headed by a former Target executive, was unable to turn around the chain and compete against Wal-Mart large-format stores by concentrating on cheap clothing and beauty and health supplies. The company was forced to enter Chapter 11 bankruptcy protection in 1993, and when it emerged in 1995 the chain had been cut in half to 106 units. Pope made a bid for the assets in 1996, offering a $20 million loan for a 65 percent stake, a move that would have given Variety a chance to acquire the chain if it returned to bankruptcy. That and a second offer were rejected, and it appeared that Rose's faced liquidation. Then Art Pope persuaded his father to make one more attempt. This time the two sides were able to reach a $19.2 million cash deal that closed in December 1997.

Variety quickly imposed its own operating strategy on Rose's, applying the everyday pricing strategy and dramatically cutting back on the advertising budget. Instead of producing a circular every week, the chain now offered a monthly advertising piece. Previous management had been ready to make some of the same changes, but the chain carried too much debt and its poor reputation made suppliers wary to ship merchandise to the stores. No such fears existed with Variety, which was not hindered by the fear of creditors as it worked to turn around Rose's. Although sales fell off, Variety was able to squeeze a profit from Rose's in the first year.

John Pope continued to run his collection of retail stores well into his 70s, converting some to new smaller express formats while continuing to show no reluctance about closing stores. Since the 1980s it was estimated that he had closed about 500 stores, or about the same number as Variety operated in 2004. His announced goal was to reach $2 billion in sales by 2007, at which point he would be 83 years old. Because Variety was guarded about its business, it was uncertain if Pope's dream was on pace.

Pope would, however, outlive his eldest son, John, Jr., who died of a heart attack at the age of 53 in March 2004. According to court records Art Pope and sister Amanda Pope then moved about $100 million in company stock from their brother's personal trust fund into a family foundation, which they said was in keeping with the individual trusts the siblings had established in 1986. According to the Associated Press, Art and Amanda Pope maintained that the trusts were designed "to bypass spouses and go to the family's foundation when they died, unless they had a birth child; John Pope, Jr., had only a stepdaughter." As a result of the transfer of stock, the stepdaughter and John, Jr.'s, wife, Jane, were prevented from receiving about $50 million, or half of the trust fund. They received about $4.2 million from a separate estate. Jane Pope filed suit to stake a claim to the money, with the situation complicated by her willingness to donate money to Democratic candidates, which was not well received by her Republican-leaning in-laws. The Pope family also was facing criticism at John Pope, Sr.'s, alma mater, The University of North Carolina. The Pope Foundation proposed funding a new Western cultures program at the school, leading to protests from students fearful that the program would simply become another way for the Popes to espouse their conservative views. For their part, the Popes dismissed the students as "radicals." No matter what their politics or how they chose to divide their fortune, the Pope family remained master retailers, able to find profit where others failed.

Principal Divisions

Super 10; Maxway; Rose's.

Principal Competitors

Dollar General Corporation; Family Dollar Stores, Inc.; Fred's, Inc.

Further Reading

Busillo, Teresa, "Rose's Is Bought by Discount Chain," *Home Textiles Today,* November 3, 1997, p. 2.
Degross, Renee, "Changes Help Put Roses Back in Black," *News & Observer* (Raleigh, N.C.), March 9, 1999, p. D1.
"Heirs of N.C. Retail Chain Fortune Split by $50 Million, Politics," *Associated Press,* November 14, 2004.
"John Pope," *Triangle Business Journal,* June 25, 1999, p. 8A.
Traugot, Catherine Liden, "Variety Is the Spice," *Business, North Carolina,* September 1, 1999, p. 22.
"Variety Wholesalers Inc. Plans to Make Rose's Blossom," *Chain Store Age,* January 1998, p. 52.
Wilensky, Dawn, "Variety Takes Over Rose's," *Discount Store News,* November 17, 1997, p. 1.

—Ed Dinger

VAUXHALL

Vauxhall Motors Limited

Griffin House
Osborne Road
Luton
Bedfordshire LU1 3YT
United Kingdom
Telephone: (01582) 721122
Fax: (01582) 426926
Web site: http://www.vauxhall.co.uk

Wholly Owned Subsidiary of General Motors Corporation
Incorporated: 1907
Employees: 5,150
Sales: £3.57 billion ($6.37 billion) (2003)
NAIC: 336111 Automobile Manufacturing

Vauxhall Motors Limited, a subsidiary of General Motors Corporation (GM), is the number two seller of automobiles in the United Kingdom, just behind market leader Ford Motor Company. During 2004, Vauxhall sold 373,540 cars at home, capturing 13.9 percent of the market. Among the firm's leading models are the Astra, which comes in coupe, hatchback, and convertible versions; the Corsa three-door hatchback; the Vectra, available as a hatchback, sedan, or wagon; the Zafira minivan; the Meriva compact minivan; the Signum premium wagon; the Monaro performance coupe; the Tigra convertible coupe; and the VX220 sports car. Vauxhall also sells a line of light commercial vehicles. Vauxhall is based in Luton, Bedfordshire, just north of London, where it operated a plant for nearly 100 years before it was closed down in March 2002. The company now operates only one plant, in Ellesmere Port, Cheshire, in northwestern England, southeast of Liverpool. There, about 200,000 cars roll off the assembly line each year. Other vehicles sold by Vauxhall are produced at other GM-affiliated plants in the United Kingdom and elsewhere.

Early History: From Marine Engines to Vauxhall Motors

Although the first Vauxhall automobile was produced in 1903, the origins of the company date well back into the previ-

ous century. In 1857 a Scottish engineer named Alexander Wilson established a manufacturing firm near the fashionable Vauxhall Gardens and the Vauxhall Bridge in London. Originally called Alexander Wilson and Co., but known locally as the Vauxhall Works, the firm initially focused on large steam-powered marine engines but soon diversified into other machinery, such as donkey engines (an American invention of the 1880s) for boiler water feeders. Wilson left the company he founded to become an engineering consultant in 1894, around the same time that the firm began experimenting with internal combustion engines. The company soon ran into financial difficulties, and in 1896 the company was reorganized as the Vauxhall Iron Works Company Limited, with a workforce of 150.

At this time, motor cars were beginning to appear on London streets, particularly with the raising of the speed limit from 4 to 12 miles per hour in November 1896. At Vauxhall Iron Works, the experiments with internal combustion engines, now under the engineering guidance of Frank William Hodges, resulted in the development in 1897 of a single-cylinder gasoline engine that successfully powered a small river launch named *Jabberwock*. It is believed that this engine provided the inspiration for the 5-horsepower, single-cylinder engine that was placed into a light car chassis to create the first Vauxhall production car, launched in mid-1903. This "horseless carriage" featured only two forward speeds and no reverse, was controlled by a hand throttle, was steered by a tiller arm, and came in two- and four-seat models, the four-seater putting the two extra passengers over the engine compartment in front of the driver. Approximately 40 of these were sold at prices starting at £136. Early in 1904 a new model debuted with a more powerful 6-horsepower engine and a reverse gear. In September of that year the company changed over from tiller arm steering to the more popular steering wheel. Forty-four of this model were sold before Vauxhall introduced a 12/14-horsepower model in late 1904 selling for £375.

Vauxhall's successful move into motor cars prompted a need for expanded factory space. The solution came via a 1905 merger with West Hydraulic Company, forming the Vauxhall and West Hydraulic Company Limited. This enabled the company to set up a car factory in Luton, in Bedfordshire just north

Company Perspectives:

Our cars and vans embody our strategy for being the best automotive manufacturer in the UK by 2005—bar none. This involves a mixture of design, style, driving excitement and ultimately, bringing the best of GM to the UK.

of London, on land West Hydraulic had owned. Soon thereafter, the management concluded that the widely diversified manufacturing activities of Vauxhall and West Hydraulic were holding back the development of its automobile business. In 1907 the latter was spun off into a newly incorporated, entirely independent firm called Vauxhall Motors Limited. (Vauxhall and West limped along through World War I, but was eventually wound down in 1918.) Serving as chairman and joint managing director was Leslie Walton, who had a background in finance and was a major company shareholder. The other managing director was Percy Kidner, an engineer who had joined Vauxhall Iron Works in 1903.

1908–19: Pomeroy-Engineered, Competition-Based Success

The earliest Vauxhall models, when Hodges was the chief engineer, were of a fairly pedestrian design. The shift to the production of cars with more distinction came via Hodges's successor, Laurence Henry Pomeroy, who, like many early automobile engineers, had apprenticed as a locomotive engineer. In a twist of fate, Pomeroy was given the chance to design a more powerful engine when Vauxhall's directors decided to build a special car to compete in the newly formed Royal Automobile Club's 2,000-mile Trial of 1908. At the time of the decision, Hodges was on vacation in Egypt, so the task fell to the 25-year-old Pomeroy. He designed a more powerful and technically advanced 20-horsepower engine, which powered a model eventually called the A-type. This car went on to win the trial for its class, beating out the Rolls-Royce ''Silver Ghost.'' The A-type also later set several speed and distance records, all of which fueled public interest. Nearly 200 of this model left the factory in 1909, and production reached 246 the next year. The next model, the B-type, set four world speed records and performed superbly at the 1911 Russian reliability trials. Engine power was at this time a preeminent factor in selling cars, and the B-type was soon fitted with Vauxhall's first six-cylinder engine; the power of its engine increased from 27 to 35 horsepower between 1910 and 1913.

Pomeroy solidified the reputation of Vauxhall through the design of two more well-received models, the C-type, also known as the Prince Henry, and the 30/98. A doorless four-seater selling for about £580, the Prince Henry is generally considered to be the first true sports car. Between 1911 and 1914, 190 Prince Henrys were produced in Luton, and the car achieved a great deal of success in various races and contests in which it competed. The 30/98 was first produced in 1913 to compete in the Shelsley Walsh hill-climb, a competition it won handily, setting a course record that stood for 15 years. Only a few of these cars had been sold to sporting enthusiasts by 1914

(at a price of £900), but after World War I production increased; 600 were produced before the model was discontinued in 1926, and the 30/98 proved to be a strong rival to Bentley products.

Overall production reached 387 by 1913, when Vauxhall employed 575 workers. Production was slowly increasing, but Vauxhall was not yet a mass production operation, and it lacked the capital to become one. Its focus during this period was on medium luxury cars—not the cheaper and smaller models of the mass producers—and it was steadily making money doing so. In 1913, for instance, pretax profits of £30,868 were posted on sales of £220,690. Nevertheless, the Pomeroy-designed models were in great demand, and the Vauxhall board recapitalized the company in the spring of 1914 in order to provide funds to boost production. The outbreak of World War I in August, however, thwarted these plans.

Vauxhall's entire production went toward the war effort for the duration of the conflict. The U.K. War Office chose a less glamorous Vauxhall model, the 25-horsepower D-type, as an army staff car, and the company supplied 2,000 of them during the war. Vauxhall also was awarded large contracts for the manufacture of fuses, and it built and equipped a new factory adjacent to the car plant to meet these demands.

Financial Travails and GM Takeover in the 1920s

The Pomeroy era ended abruptly in 1919 when the chief engineer resigned in order to embark for the United States to escape an unhappy marriage. His immediate successors, while fine engineers, lacked the knack for innovation that was characteristic of Pomeroy. A larger problem for Vauxhall Motors, however, came in the form of management blunders in the post–World War I era. Anticipating a postwar boom based on pent-up demand for automobiles, Vauxhall and other British carmakers stepped up production. Output at Vauxhall reached 689 by 1920, but the company was still using handcraft methods rather than mass production, which limited capacity, and its focus remained on higher-priced medium luxury vehicles, which limited its potential market. When the postwar boom collapsed in 1920 and 1921, demand for cars fell 50 percent, and Vauxhall and other higher-end producers suffered disproportionately. Vauxhall was forced to slash both prices and production, leading to a huge loss of more than £221,000 for 1921, as revenues fell from £812,600 to £519,200. The firm suffered another loss of £76,710 the following year.

Vauxhall's board responded to this predicament by turning to the production of a smaller, less expensive vehicle, while still making the larger ones as well. The 14-horsepower M-type, introduced in 1922, sold for £650. This was considerably more than the under-£300 models being mass-produced elsewhere but well below Vauxhall's £1,000-plus D-type sold from 1919 to 1922. The M-type was followed by the slightly modified LM-type, also 14-horsepower, which debuted in 1924 and sold for as little as £495. As Vauxhall was attempting this shift in focus, there occurred a not-coincidental shift in the wider market as commercial success for automakers would no longer come from achievements in races and competitors but from producing cheaper cars aimed at middle-class families. Vauxhall, therefore, withdrew from competitive racing in 1923.

Although production at the company grew to 1,366 vehicles by 1924, Vauxhall still lacked the capital to increase output to a level high enough to compete with its rivals. With the firm saddled by debt, its future in doubt, the board agreed in late 1925 to sell Vauxhall to General Motors Corporation (GM) for $2,575,291. Vauxhall gained much needed capital to shore up its finances and fund production increases, while GM secured its first production base in Europe—though a tiny one by GM standards, with Vauxhall then producing about 1,500 vehicles per year versus the American giant's 836,000.

Not much actually changed in the immediate aftermath of the GM takeover, although production did reach as high as 2,589 in 1928. Vauxhall, however, began suffering heavy losses again in 1927, leading GM to push for changes at its British subsidiary. By 1928 most of the holdovers on the management team from the pre-GM days had left, and the following year Charles Bartlett was named managing director. Trained in business practices and accounting, Bartlett was a GM man, having worked since 1920 for the GM subsidiary in England that imported GM cars from the United States. But he also was an Englishman through and through, which fit with GM's plan to keep Vauxhall 100 percent British—in management, staff, and product. Bartlett would lead Vauxhall into the ranks of the "Big Six" British automakers by the late 1930s.

Into the Big Six in the 1930s

The move of Vauxhall Motors into the top ranks of the U.K. auto market stemmed from GM's firm backing and guidance. Perhaps most important was the reorganization of production along mass assembly lines, but the Bartlett-led firm also benefited from GM's tutelage in intensive marketing practices and the transference of some American engineering and design principles to the British company. The first visible result of the "new" Vauxhall was the Cadet, introduced in 1930. Although this was not a small car, offered in 17- and 26-horsepower, six-cylinder versions, the Cadet propelled Vauxhall into the lower end of the market as the smaller version sold for less than £300. Sales of the Cadet, however, proved disappointing, in large part because the U.K. market had shifted solidly toward smaller cars—those of 14 horsepower and below. The Cadet was nevertheless noteworthy for two other reasons. It was the first British car to feature the synchromesh gearbox, which made shifting easier and smoother, and its design was actually based in large part on that of the Opel Kadett. This marked the first connection between Vauxhall Motors and the German firm Adam Opel AG, which GM had acquired in 1929.

Production at Luton neared 4,000 in 1931, but it was the introductions of the Light Six in 1933 and the Big Six two years later that propelled Vauxhall into mass production. These proved to be big sellers thanks in no small part to their low prices. The Light Six was available in 12- and 14-horsepower versions for £195 and £215, respectively, while similar versions of the Big Six went for £205 and £225, respectively. Production topped 26,000 vehicles by 1935, by which time revenues had surpassed the £7 million mark. A good portion of this turnover now came from the sale of light trucks. In April 1931 Vauxhall introduced the rugged and reliable Bedford truck, initially offered in a two-ton version and later in a more popular 3,000-pound model. The Bedford was an immediate success, quickly capturing one-quarter of the British output of commercial vehicles as production grew from more than 11,000 in 1931 to more than 31,000 in 1937.

Rounding out the 1930s was the introduction of the Vauxhall Ten in 1938. With this model, Vauxhall became the first British manufacturer to produce a car with an integrated body and chassis. The company sold 55,000 of these £168 cars by 1940. The success of the Ten propelled Vauxhall car production to more than 35,000 vehicles in 1938. That year the company captured 10.4 percent of the U.K. car market, a remarkable advance from 1929, when its share amounted to less than 1 percent. It trailed only Morris, Austin, and Ford in market share, while ranking just ahead of the other two members of the Big Six, Rootes, and Standard.

Production of cars virtually ceased with the outbreak of World War II in 1939, but Vauxhall continued churning out Bedford trucks, producing a quarter of a million of them for the British army by war's end. The company also was commissioned to design and build a new tank. Within one year, the first of 5,640 Churchill tanks exited the production line at Luton.

Vauxhall produced a variety of other war materials as well, including more than five million fuel cans, four million rocket engine components, and three-quarters of a million helmets. The Luton plant became a target for German bombers, and in August 1940 several dozen bombs were dropped on the plant, killing 39 employees and injuring 40 more. Remarkably, production resumed less than a week later.

Postwar Period of Prosperity

Immediately following the war, Vauxhall resumed production of its prewar models. The company soon ended 10-horsepower engine production, however, when the British government shifted from horsepower-related car taxation to a flat-rate system in mid-1947. After the Vauxhall Twelve and Fourteen, the next big shift in car styling came with the 1951 introduction of the E-type, available in several versions, including the Wyvern, the Velox, and the luxury Cresta. Among the typical accessories of this period, the Wyvern featured a sun visor above the windshield and antiglare "eyebrows" on the headlamps. Some 342,000 of the E-type vehicles were produced before their run ended in 1957. By this time, it should also be noted, Vauxhall was exporting its models to more than 130 countries. Around this time, Vauxhall, under pressure from its parent GM, adopted the practice of updating its models every year, as American carmakers did.

Meanwhile, in 1953, 50 years after production of the first Vauxhall car, annual production reached 100,000 and the millionth car rolled off the assembly line. The company posted after-tax profits of £3.4 million on sales of £58.6 million. That same year Bartlett stepped aside as managing director to briefly become chairman, ending 24 years at the helm. Increased demand for cars led the company in 1954 to begin a series of investments in production facilities totaling £36 million. In July 1955 production of Bedford trucks was shifted from Luton to a new plant in nearby Dunstable, thus enabling the Luton plant to put all of its energies into car production. On the new model side, the F-type Victor, debuted in 1957, and the 1958 Victor Estate model became the first Vauxhall-produced station wagon.

In the early 1960s Vauxhall managers decided to add a smaller car to its lineup to sell alongside the larger Victor and to build it in a new factory. The Merseyside town of Ellesmere Port was selected as the site for the new plant in part based on incentives offered by the British government to companies locating in economically depressed areas. In designing the car, for the first time a "shared platform" was developed by sister GM companies Vauxhall and Opel. The first HA Viva rolled off the new production line in 1963 (the same year Opel began making its version of the same car, the Kadett A). The Viva became immensely popular. By the time production ended in early 1966, more than 307,000 had been built. Its successor, the HB Viva, sold from 1966 to 1970, did even better as production totaled more than 556,000. Revenues at Vauxhall reached a record £216.4 million in 1968, when after-tax profits totaled £5.3 million.

Struggles in the 1970s and 1980s

Despite the success of the Viva, which continued throughout the 1970s when more than 640,000 HC Vivas were sold, Vauxhall fell into a prolonged slump. From 1969 through 1986, the company made money during only one year, 1978. Its share of the British car market fell to as low as 7.3 percent (1973) before recovering in the early 1980s, hitting 16.2 percent in 1984. The reasons for this poor performance were multifold. Vauxhall's larger models, the Victor and Ventora, did not sell well in part because of quality problems stemming from the Luton plant. Operations there were affected by production cutbacks and two major strikes in 1977 and 1979. More generally, the U.K. car market was hit hard by the oil crisis, economic recession, and increased competition, particularly from Japanese and European imports. Ironically, during this same period Vauxhall's Bedford truck and van operation was highly profitable, but GM elected to separate it from Vauxhall in 1983, creating the Bedford Commercial Vehicle Division.

In the meantime, a key shift occurred in 1978 when GM officials further pulled the reins back on Vauxhall's autonomy by assigning Opel engineers in Rüsselsheim, Germany, the task of designing new cars for both Opel and Vauxhall. This brought an end to British-designed Vauxhalls, with the FE Victor, produced from 1972 to 1976, representing the last of that breed. This decision, though painful to British pride, helped to bring about Vauxhall's recovery by the mid-1980s. The Chevette, sporting the hatchback that became common on later Vauxhall models, was successfully introduced in 1978 as the replacement for the Viva. Vauxhall also began selling the Cavalier, an Opel-designed model filling the gap between the Chevette and Victor ranges. Starting in the early 1980s, the Cavalier became immensely popular with buyers of "fleet" or company cars, a sector that comprised as much as half of the U.K. market. Sales of the Cavalier passed the one million mark by July 1988, and Vauxhall continued producing the model in Luton through 1995. During this period, the Cavalier represented as much as one-third of Vauxhall's overall production. Also Opel-designed was the Astra, introduced in 1980 as Vauxhall's first front-wheel-drive car. The Cavalier and the Astra were consistently among the top ten—and sometimes the top five—best-selling cars in Britain. Rounding out the 1980s model lineup were the high-end Carlton, introduced in 1979, and the Nova subcompact, which debuted in 1983 as a two-door sedan.

1990s and Beyond

Vauxhall remained profitable throughout the 1990s, though the amount of profits fluctuated substantially. Its share of the U.K. car market reached as high as 17.2 percent (1993). In July 1993 Vauxhall gained the leading share of the U.K. market for the first time in its 90-year history, garnering 23.2 percent of sales versus 20.3 percent for Ford, the longstanding market leader—just a one-month achievement, but an achievement nonetheless. A number of new vehicles saw their way into the Vauxhall lineup, including the Frontera four-wheel-drive recreational vehicle (1991); the Corsa hatchback (1993), which replaced the Nova; the Tigra sports coupe (1993); the Omega (1994), successor on the luxury end to the Carlton; the Vectra sedan and wagon (1995), which replaced the Cavalier; and the Sintra minivan (1996), which was quickly replaced by the better-received Zafira (1999), a seven-person, flexible-seat minivan based on the Astra platform. In addition the Astra was completely redesigned in 1998. The Vectra did not sell as well as the Cavalier and was panned in the press, but the Astra remained a bestseller in its class.

GM backed up Vauxhall with several large capital investments during the decade. In late 1992 production began at a new £193 million engine facility at the Ellesmere Port plant. The V6 engines produced there were slated for use in higher-end models of not only Vauxhalls but Opels and Saabs as well (GM having purchased a 50 percent interest in Saab Automobile AB in 1989). In 1996 Vauxhall announced a £300 million modernization program at Ellesmere Port to raise capacity from 135,000 cars and vans per year to 200,000 and to prepare for the 1998 introduction of the next-generation Astra.

Then came the stunning news from GM in December 2000 that production would cease at the Luton plant, leading to the elimination of 2,000 jobs. This was part of a larger GM restructuring aiming in part to address the overcapacity that was plaguing carmakers worldwide. The Luton plant in particular was selected for closure in part because it was an older and less efficient facility. It did not help that it was the struggling Vectra model that was being produced there. Part of the Vectra production was slated to be shifted to GM plants in Spain and Germany, but in 2001 the Ellesmere Port factory received a £200 million capital injection in order to transform it into a so-called flex plant, capable of producing both a new version of the Vectra, which debuted in mid-2002, and the Astra at the same time. On March 21, 2002, the 7,415,045th—and last—car rolled off the assembly line at Luton, bringing to a close 97 years of auto production in that facility. Vauxhall Motors remained headquartered in Luton.

Along with the entire GM European operation, Vauxhall posted losses throughout the early 2000s. Its models were criticized for being unimaginative, and it was hurt by an image of being a maker of fleet cars. The car market was stagnant during this period, and the competition fierce. GM turned to centralization as a way of turning things around in Europe. Late in 2003 the company announced that it would integrate the sales, marketing, and after-sales operations of its European brands, including Vauxhall, Opel, and Saab. Then in June 2005 a major overhaul of GM's European operations was launched that further reduced the autonomy of Vauxhall, Opel, and Saab, shifting responsibility for engineering and manufacturing to the regional headquarters in Zurich. This was part of a larger effort to centralize global product development, cutting overlapping engineering projects and reducing costs worldwide. Whether this would reduce the Vauxhall company itself to merely a marketing and sales organization was not initially clear. One certainty was that the Vauxhall lineup would be thoroughly overhauled, because GM planned to replace 90 percent of its models by 2008. Vauxhall had found great success with the new fifth-generation version of the Astra, which debuted in May 2004. Stellar sales of the Astra pushed Vauxhall ahead of Ford in U.K. market share for two of the first four months of 2005, prompting hopes in Luton that Vauxhall might beat out its arch-rival for the full year and finally end Ford's quarter-century-long dominance of the British car market. Meanwhile,

an all-new version of the Zafira minivan hit the market in July 2005. GM also was considering assembling some Vauxhall (and Opel) vehicles in North America and then shipping them to Europe.

Principal Competitors

Ford Motor Company; Volkswagen AG; DaimlerChrysler AG; Toyota Motor Corporation.

Further Reading

Brady, Rosemary, "Battle for Britain," *Forbes,* July 2, 1984, pp. 164–65.

Broatch, Stuart Fergus, *Vauxhall,* Stroud, U.K.: Sutton Publishing, 1997.

Burgess-Wise, David, *Vauxhall: A Century in Motion, 1903–2003,* Oxford: CW Publishing, published on behalf of Vauxhall Motors Limited, 2003.

Burt, Tim, "Spotlight Turns Towards Vauxhall's Cost Drive," *Financial Times,* October 18, 1999, p. 3.

——, "Vauxhall Chief Making Progress," *Financial Times,* September 16, 1999, p. 7.

Burt, Tim, and Jim Pickard, "Vauxhall Puts £200m into Merseyside Vectra Plant," *Financial Times,* February 6, 2001.

Burt, Tim, and John Griffiths, "Vauxhall Chief Blames Price Cuts for Closure," *Financial Times,* December 16, 2000.

Champion, Marc, "U.K. Hit Hard in Europe's Auto Cutbacks," *Wall Street Journal,* December 15, 2000, p. A15.

Church, Roy, *The Rise and Decline of the British Motor Industry,* Basingstoke, U.K.: Macmillan, 1994.

Copelin, P.W., "Development and Organisation of Vauxhall Motors Limited," in *Studies in Business Organisation,* edited by Ronald S. Edwards and Harry Townsend, London: Macmillan, 1961.

Holden, Len, *Vauxhall Motors and the Luton Economy, 1900–2002,* Woodbridge, Suffolk, U.K.: Boydell Press, 2003.

Johnson, Richard, "NUMMI Payoff: Hendry Brings New Approach to Rebuild Vauxhall Operation," *Automotive News,* June 20, 1988, pp. 1, 50.

Kimberly, William, "Vauxhall Ups Its Flexibility in Ellesmere Port," *Automotive Design and Production,* September 2002, p. 28.

Kurylko, Diana L., "GM Struggles to Regain Status in Europe," *Automotive News,* August 3, 1998, p. 47.

"Less of the Cavalier Attitude," *Marketing Week,* March 28, 2002, p. 23.

Power, Stephen, "GM Europe to Get a Major Tune-Up," *Wall Street Journal,* May 17, 2004, p. A6.

——, "GM Plans Major Overhaul of Business in Europe," *Wall Street Journal,* June 17, 2004, p. A3.

Simison, Robert L., "GM's Europe Unit Unveils Astra Line of Compact Cars," *Wall Street Journal,* July 12, 1991.

"Vauxhall's Lukewarm Drive for a Cool Image," *Marketing News,* May 13, 2004, p. 23.

The Vauxhall Story, Luton, Bedfordshire: Vauxhall Motors Limited, Education Service, 2001.

Wendt, Ed, "Tune-Up Helps Vauxhall Gain on Ford," *Automotive News,* April 27, 1992, p. 9.

—David E. Salamie

Verint Systems Inc.

330 S. Service Road
Melville, New York 11747
U.S.A.
Telephone: (631) 962-9600
Fax: (631) (62-9300
Web site: http://www.verint.com

Public Company
Incorporated: 1994 as Interactive Information Systems
    Corporation
Employees: 1,200
Sales: $249.8 million (2005)
Stock Exchanges: NASDAQ
Ticker Symbol: VRNT
NAIC: 541512 Computer Systems Design Services

Melville, New York-based Verint Systems Inc. portrays itself as a provider of analytic software-based solutions for both law enforcement and the business community. In essence the company sells software that helps customers to collect, store, and sift through voice, video, fax, e-mail, Internet, and data transmissions for security purposes—to turn raw data into ''actionable intelligence.'' Verint's Star-Gate product line is aimed at communications service providers such as wired and cellular telephone companies and Internet service providers, and is used to set up a communications intercept for law enforcement organizations and other government agencies as authorized. The Reliant and Vantage products are sold to law enforcement and government agencies, used to collect, store, and analyze intercepted communications. Verint's Network Video Solutions business segment is represented by the Nextiva platform and suite of software applications, which identifies unusual activity and then sends notification to security personnel for review. Finally Verint offers contact center business intelligence solutions through the Ultra product line, used by call centers to record and analyze customer interactions with call center employees, whether they be by phone, e-mail, online chat, or co-browsing sessions on the Internet. Verint maintains operations across the United States and Canada, as well as in Europe,

Africa, the Middle East, Asia, and the Pacific Rim. Verint is a public company, listed on the NASDAQ.

Chairman Launching Business Career: 1980s

Verint grew out of Comverse Technology, a company founded by Verint's chairman, Kobi Alexander, in 1984. Born in Israel, he graduated with honors from the Hebrew University of Jerusalem, receiving a degree in economics. After serving in the Israeli military and intelligence services, he moved to New York to continue his education, earning an M.B.A. at night while working as a full-time investment banker at Shearson Lehman during the day. An aspiring entrepreneur, Alexander was quick to seize a chance to strike out on his own. In 1982 he met Israeli engineer Boaz Misholi, who had had an idea for a voice and fax messaging system that was far more advanced than anything available at the time. Alexander quit his job and moved back to Israel to take advantage of government subsidies for high-tech start-ups, and together with Misholi founded Efrat Future Technology Ltd. to develop the messaging system, aided in large measure by Alexander's brother-in-law, Yechiam Yemini, who became Efrat's chief scientist. When the product was just about ready for the market, the three men returned to New York in 1984 to set up a U.S. company, based in Woodbury, New York, called Comverse, which was coined to play off the words ''communication'' and ''versatility.''

Comverse became Efrat's parent and went public in 1986 with Misholi initially acting as chief executive. After he left in 1988, Alexander stepped in to lead the company. There was no doubt that Comverse offered an innovative product, perhaps the first to integrate voice, fax, and call processing into a single unit, but it also had to contend with such giant competitors as AT&T. As a result, Alexander focused on international markets, especially Europe, and enjoyed great success with the Trilogue product, which allowed cell phone callers who failed to reach a party to leave a message in a mailbox. Trilogue could also serve as virtual telephone service for individuals without phone service—especially people in undeveloped countries where the telecommunications infrastructure was rudimentary—they could rent an electronic mailbox and use a public telephone to retrieve messages.

Company Perspectives:

Today, over 1000 organizations in more than 50 countries deploy Verint's actionable intelligence solutions as an integral part of their security and business intelligence initiatives.

Alexander was also eager to develop new niche products, encouraging employees to pursue ideas, which if they showed promise formed the basis of a new business unit. In the late 1980s Comverse began working on a product that would one day lead to the creation of Verint. It was called AudioDisk, a digital surveillance product intended to be used by police and intelligence agencies in the recording and storing of wiretap material. AudioDisk offered vast improvements over the old reel-to-reel tape recording systems. Not only could the product monitor hundreds of telephone and fax machine lines simultaneously, the information could be stored in "jukeboxes" and was available immediately. Moreover, instant search functions replaced the tedious chore of winding and rewinding tape to locate a key passage of an intercepted communication. Aside from law enforcement and intelligence agencies, AudioDisk also found customers in the private sector, as companies used the Ultra product, launched in April 1996, for internal uses, such as monitoring incoming calls and the activities of call center representatives.

AudioDisk: Early 1990s

Comverse began marketing AudioDisk in the early 1990s. Sales were strong and accounted for half of Comverse's revenues in 1993. Because of the discreet nature of the product, AudioDisk was not as well known as Trilogue, and in February 1994 that entire surveillance business was broken off and housed in a new subsidiary called Interactive Information Systems Corporation. Two years later, the company changed its name to Comverse Information Systems Corporation. In 1999 Comverse Technology reorganized its operations, which were now split into two divisions. Comverse Information Systems merged with Comverse InfoMedia Systems to create Comverse Infosys. In addition, some Efrat assets were also included in the new division.

Because Comverse Infosys did business with the U.S. Department of Defense, which used the intercept products in a classified manner, the unit had to be insulated from foreign ownership. As a result, control of the unit—other than the right to sell or liquidate the business—was placed in the hands of three U.S. citizens possessing the required security clearances, as specified in a proxy agreement sign with the Department of Defense in January 1999, superseded by another such agreement in 2001. Acting as the government's security committee, these three individuals oversaw Verint's efforts to prevent unauthorized disclosure or export of controlled information, and provided an annual report to the Department of Defense, which also conducted periodic inspections to make sure Verint was in compliance with the proxy agreement.

While Comverse Information Systems quietly sold its AudioDisk systems under the new Reliant (launched in August 1999) and Star-Gate (launched in May 2000) names, Comverse

Technology's other division, Comverse Network Systems Inc., was thriving with its wireless voice messaging systems, spurred by the tremendous popularity of cell phones in the late 1990s. But with nearly three-quarters of its $1.2 billion in revenues coming from the sale of Mobile mailboxes, and the cell phone market reaching saturation, Comverse Technology was in danger of having too many eggs in one basket, voice mail. As a result, management began to aggressively pursue acquisitions in order to add promising technologies in the hopes of developing new products and achieving some diversity. In the process it also added assets to Comverse Infosys. Acquired in July 2000 was Loronix Information Systems, Inc., a company that developed software-based digital video recording, networking, and live Internet video streaming technology. From Loronix came a digital video monitoring system that was used by government agencies, such as the U.S. Department of the Treasury, as well as commercial customers including Mohegan Sun Casino and FedEx.

Comverse Technology completed several other acquisitions, prompting management in 2001 to reorganize the company again, this time splitting it into five divisions, one of which remained Comverse Infosys. In many respects Comverse Infosys did not fit in with the rest of the company, given that it sold to an entirely different market than the telecommunications companies that bought Comverse's voice and data messaging services. It was not surprising, therefore, that management would begin looking for a way to split off the security unit.

Demand in Wake of 9/11 Attacks

An opportunity arose following the terrorist attacks against the United States on September 11, 2001, when the need for all manner of security products increased dramatically. Although the demand for initial public offerings was weak due to a struggling economy and depressed stock market, Alexander felt the time was right to sell shares of Comverse Infosys in a "carveout" arrangement that would leave Comverse Technology with a majority stake in the company while unlocking shareholder value. Thus, in February 2002, Comverse Infosys was renamed Verint Systems, Inc. and prepared to be taken public. Media assets housed under Comverse Media Holding Inc. were sold back to the parent company, while at the same time Verint, through Lorinix, beefed up its video surveillance business with the acquisition of the digital video recording business of Lanex, LLC. Alexander assumed the chairmanship of Verint, while Dan Bodner served as president and CEO, positions he had held since Comverse Technology established Interactive Information Systems in 1994. An electrical engineer with degrees from the Technion, Israel Institute of Technology and Tel Aviv University, he joined Comverse in 1987.

One drawback to the offering, however, was Verint's lack of profitability. Like many high-tech companies it spent a great deal of money on research and development and needed time for sales to catch up with investments. Although the unit was narrowing its losses, it still lost $4.6 million on $131.2 million in revenues in 2002, which ended on January 31 of that year. When the stock offering, led by Lehman Brothers Holdings Inc., was finally made in May 2002, investors focused on the financials rather than Verint's prospects, and as a result the company was only able to price its shares at the low end of the $16 to $18 a share range touted by the underwriters and

Key Dates:

1984: Comverse Technology is founded.
1990: Comverse begins selling AudioDisk wiretapping product.
1994: Subsidiary Interactive Information Systems is created for AudioDisk product.
1996: Interactive Information Systems is renamed Comverse Information Systems Corporation.
1999: Comverse Information Systems is renamed Comverse Infosys, Inc.
2002: Comverse Infosys is taken public as Verint Systems, Inc.

the company. In addition, the shares quickly lost $1.51 on the first day of trading on the NASDAQ, making it the second-worst launch of a stock in 2002. After a week the stock lost about a third of its value.

Before the year was out, however, Verint changed some minds on Wall Street, as the increased demand for surveillance products in the fight against terrorism finally began to factor in Verint's favor. The company's stock regained lost ground and began creeping upward. Then, an industry newsletter in late December 2002 predicted higher demand for Verint's data-analysis programs, leading to a bump of about 20 percent to well over $21. The company used some of its higher-price stock in a $10 million deal to purchase Montreal-based SmartSight Networks Inc. in May 2003, in keeping with a strategy to acquire companies possessing complementary technologies that would broaden Verint's product offerings. SmartSight produced Internet Protocol-based systems for wireless video transmission, the addition of which permitted the Verint digital video system to cover remote locations of large complexes, such as airports, oil refineries, ports, or military bases, as well as borders and critical infrastructure including power systems and pipelines. The Verint video surveillance system software would then track motion and identify unusual activity, prompting security personnel with an on-screen message or audible alarm.

When Verint made a secondary stock offering in June 2003, it was met with a far more enthusiastic response from investors. The company priced five million shares at $23 per share, raising more than $100 million for Verint and about $3.5 million for insiders whose 150,000 shares were part of the offering. After recording sales of $157.8 million and net income of $10.1 million in 2003, Verint saw revenues improve to $192.8 million and net income to $18 million in 2004. More strategic acquisitions followed in 2004. Verint bought the government surveillance business of ECtel Ltd., a subsidiary of Israeli company ECI Telecom. Like Verint, ECtel was involved in the monitoring of telephone calls, e-mail, and Internet usage. The addition of ECtel was helpful in moving Verint into new markets, expanding on its North American and European base of customers, which accounted for 85 percent of all sales, to gain a presence in the Middle East and South America. Later in 2004 Verint added to its technology by acquiring RPO Sicherheitssysteme GmbH, a German company that developed mobile video security products used in mass-transit systems, which were likely to receive greater attention given terrorist mass transit bombings in Spain and London.

Sales continued to build, approaching $250 million in 2005, while net income improved to $19 million. Given the state of the world and the need for advanced security systems, there was every reason to believe that Verint was well positioned to enjoy sustained growth for the foreseeable future.

Principal Subsidiaries

Verint Technology Inc.; Lorinx Information Systems, Inc.

Principal Competitors

ADC Telecommunications, Inc.; ECtel Ltd.; NICE Systems Inc.

Further Reading

Duffy, Maureen Nevin, "Voice Recording Technology Takes Off," *Wall Street & Technology,* November 1995, p. 14.
"Entrepreneur of the Year Finalists: Kobi Alexander," *Long Island Business News,* June 15, 2001, p. C6.
Hennessey, Raymond, and Kara Scannell, "Wiretapping, Apparel Firms Brave an IPO," *Wall Street Journal,* May 16, 2002, p. C4.
Howell, Donna, "Surveillance Software Maker Finds Focus," *Investor's Business Daily,* March 12, 2003, p. A08.
Labate, John, "Companies to Watch: Comverse Technology," *Fortune,* May 17, 1993, p. 102.
Schachter, Ken, "Comverse Tech Eyes IPO of Spyware Unit," *Long Island Business News,* March 29, 2002, p. A5.

—Ed Dinger

Vestas Wind Systems A/S

Smed Sorensens Vej 5
Ringkobing DK-6950
Denmark
Telephone: +45 96 75 25 75
Fax: +45 96 75 24 36
Web site: http://www.vestas.com

Public Company
Incorporated: 1928 as Dansk Staalvindue Industri
Employees: 9,504
Sales: EUR 2.54 billion ($2.9 billion) (2004)
Stock Exchanges: Copenhagen
Ticker Symbol: VVS
NAIC: 333611 Turbine and Turbine Generator Set Unit
   Manufacturing

Vestas Wind Systems A/S is the world leader in the design, engineering, and manufacturing of aeolian power generation systems—in other words, windmills. The company develops and manufactures its own proprietary wind turbine technologies, selling a range of products from the bare turbine components to complete turnkey systems, and even entire wind farms. Vestas has been riding the winds of change since the end of the 20th century, as the reduction of global pollution has taken on a greater urgency, and as more and more governments have begun mandating the installation of clean and renewable energy sources. Vestas is also a global manufacturer, with headquarters in Ringkobing, Denmark, and production facilities in the United States, Australia, Germany, Sweden, India, and elsewhere. In 2005, the company began construction on a production facility in Tianjin, China, marking its entry into that market. The company is the world leader, with a 40 percent market share. More than 70 percent of revenues, which topped EUR 2.5 billion in 2004, are generated in Europe, and the United States accounts for most of the rest. Vestas is one of the wind turbine industry's primary innovators, with projects including the development of turnkey offshore wind platforms. In 2003, the company handed over its first major offshore platform, at Horns Reef, in the North Sea off the Danish coast. Although Vestas stems from a blacksmith business founded at the beginning of the 20th century, its entry into wind turbines came in

the late 1970s, and only became its core operation in the mid-1980s. Vestas is listed on the Copenhagen Stock Exchange.

Forging Origins at the Beginning of the 20th Century

Vestas started out as a small blacksmith shop in Lem, Denmark, when H.S. Hansen set up for business there in 1898. Hansen was said to have inspired the creation of the blacksmith industry in Lem, which became a center of the Danish smithy market in the early part of the century. By 1928, Hansen, joined by son Peder, had entered industrial production, producing window frames for factories and other industrial buildings, founding Dansk Staalvindue Industri.

Following World War II, Peder Hansen led a team of nine fellow employees from Dansk Staalvindue in setting up a new business to produce household appliances. Founded in 1945, that company was called Vestjysk Stalteknik, and then became known as Vestas. Before long, however, Vestas added the production of farm trailers, which became the company's chief product by 1950. Almost from the start, Vestas produced for the export market.

Vestas's introduction into engineering came in 1956, when it agreed to design and manufacture an intercooler for the ship engines built by the Danish B&W shipyard, where Hansen's brother Soren served as deputy chief executive. Intercoolers became the group's core product line in 1959 when Hansen bought out his partners, and then sold off its noncore operations to another of the original founders.

Vestas showed its willingness to transform itself yet again in the late 1960s, when it launched production of truck-mounted hydraulic cranes in 1969. That product line was a success, especially on the import market. Yet the oil crisis of the early 1970s and the resulting slump in the international transport industry placed sales of the company's hydraulic cranes under pressure. Vestas once again began looking for a new product line.

By the end of the decade, Vestas had hit on the product that would bring it into the next century. As a new oil crisis plunged Denmark and much of Europe into a new recession, Vestas became convinced that a future lay in the development of renewable energy sources, especially in harnessing the power of wind. The company's background in engineering enabled it to begin developing its first wind turbine, initially focused on the Darrieus turbine. By 1979, however, Vestas had designed its own three-blade turbine, which it introduced in 1979. The three-blade turbine quickly became an industry standard and helped stimulate the creation of the early wind turbine market.

Vestas launched full-scale production of its turbine in 1980 as the wind farm market entered its first boom phase. Demand for the company's turbines grew strongly on the basis of government policies, which included subsidies and other incentives, both in Denmark and in the United States. With large-scale orders arriving, in particular from the United States, Vestas began to vertically integrate its production, launching the manufacture of fiberglass components in 1981. By 1983, the company's capacity had expanded enough for the company to begin producing its own turbine blades. In that year as well, the company established its first overseas subsidiary, in the United States. By then, the United States had become the company's major customer. The company also quickly added new employees, boosting its payroll to 800 by the middle of the decade.

New Life in the 1980s

A breakthrough came in 1985, when the company developed turbines with pitch regulation, which adjusted the angle of the turbine blades to the direction of the wind, optimizing their efficiency. The innovation helped boost the company's sales, and by the end of that year, the company's total turbine sales to the United States alone had topped 2,500. Wind turbines also had become Vestas's primary source of growth, despite its continued production of its legacy products.

Yet the wind turbine industry remained at the mercy of government policy. In 1986, the company slipped into financial crisis when the United States failed to renew the legislation that had provided special tax benefits for the wind turbine market. The company's heavy exposure to the U.S. market plunged the company into financial disarray. By the end of that year, Vestas was forced to declare bankruptcy.

Nonetheless, Vestas's problems were recognized as legislative; the company's turbine technology remained an industry leader. In particular, Vestas had begun experimenting with the concept of developing large-scale wind "farms." The new concept was immediately promising, pointing to the company's technological viability. The promise held by Vestas's wind turbine business led to the company's reorganization in 1987. A new management led by Johannes Poulson now took over operations of the company, and refocused Vestas as a wind

turbine specialist. The company's payroll by then had been reduced to just 60 employees.

Vestas immediately turned toward the international market. In 1987, Vestas set up a subsidiary in India; by 1988, the company had won a bid to build six wind farm projects for Danida in India. Back at home, Vestas, encouraged by the Danish government, began to grow externally. As H.S. Hansen had inspired the creation of a blacksmith market in Lem at the beginning of the century, Vestas had helped stimulate a buoyant market for wind turbine production in Denmark in the 1980s. By the end of the decade, however, the Danish government had begun to promote a consolidation of the industry's many small players in order to create a smaller number of internationally competitive wind turbine leaders. As part of that process, Vestas took over rival Danish Wind Technology in 1989, boosting its production capacity, as well as its sales and marketing reach.

Vestas also sought to expand its international network. In 1989, the company created a German subsidiary, followed by the establishment of new production subsidiaries in Sweden and the United States in 1992. Other buoyant new markets at the beginning of the 1990s included the United Kingdom, Australia, and New Zealand. New government legislation, particularly in Germany, helped boost the company's fortunes into the early 1990s. By 1993, the company's German subsidiary had nearly tripled its production. The company also carried out an expansion of its Danish production facilities.

Vestas continued to develop new models and innovative new features, helping it to resist the tide of a steadily increasing array of new competitors. The company added to its production capacity through the acquisition of Volund Stalteknik, based in Varde, Denmark, in 1994. In that year, as well, Vestas entered Spain, forming a joint venture with that country's Gamesa, with Vestas's stake at just 40 percent. The partnership started strongly, and by the end of the decade, Spain had become one of Vestas's fastest-growing markets.

Global Wind Turbine Leader in the New Century

Vestas went public in 1998, listing its stock on the Copenhagen Stock Exchange. The highly successful initial public offering signaled the beginning of a new era for Vestas as its growth went into overdrive into the new century. By the end of that year, Vestas had opened a new production facility in Italy in a joint venture partnership with that country's Wind Energy System Taranto S.p.A. By the end of its first year, the Italian venture had produced more than EUR 35 million in revenues. The company also expanded its production capacity in Denmark, building a new blade factory in Nakskov in 1999. The following year, Vestas boosted its international presence with a distribution partnership agreement with Japan's Vestech, owned by Toyota, Kawasaki, and other major Japanese companies.

During this time, Vestas had begun developing new turbine technologies for a new and highly promising market—that of offshore wind farms. In 2001, the company was chosen to supply the turbines for the world's first major offshore wind farm being constructed on Horns Reef in the North Sea off the Danish coast. The company delivered the completed platform in 2003.

Johannes Poulson resigned as company CEO in 2002, replaced by longtime CFO Svend Sigaard. In the meantime, the

Key Dates:

1898: H.S. Hansen sets up a blacksmith shop in Lem, Denmark.

1928: Hansen and son Peder establish Dansk Staalvindue Industri in order to produce window frames.

1945: Peder Hansen and others launch Vestjysk Stalteknik at first to produce appliances, later producing farm trailers, intercoolers for ship engines, and hydraulic cranes.

1977: Vestas begins developing wind turbines in response to the oil crisis and growing environmental concerns.

1978: Vestas introduces the first three-blade turbine.

1986: After a change in legislation in the United States, Vestas collapses into bankruptcy.

1987: Vestas is reorganized as Vestas Wind Systems A/S, specialized in wind turbines.

1989: The company acquires Danish Wind Technology and establishes a subsidiary in Germany.

1992: The company forms a joint venture with Gamesa in Spain.

1998: Vestas goes public with a listing on the Copenhagen Stock Exchange.

2001: The company is chosen to supply turbines for the world's first major offshore wind farm at Horns Reef in the North Sea.

2003: Vestas delivers the Horns Reef platform.

2004: Vestas acquires Danish rival NEG Micon.

2005: Vestas receives its first large contract in China and announces plans to build a factory in Tianjin.

company had pulled out of its joint venture with Gamesa in Spain, after that company began to position itself as a major competitor in the wind turbine industry. Vestas faced another new rival in the United States, when General Electric Corporation bought up the wind farm operations of failed energy giant Enron in 2002.

Despite a downturn in the global wind turbine market, amid a generalized economic slowdown, Vestas's longstanding expertise and market-leading position enabled it to solidify its international standing. The group's work on the Horns Reef project helped it attract a significant number of new orders for offshore wind farm platforms, such as an order to supply the turbines for the first major British offshore wind farm in 2002. In support of its growth, Vestas opened two new factories that year, in Cambeltown, Scotland, and in Lauchhammer, Germany.

A major milestone in Vestas's growth came at the end of 2003, when the company announced its acquisition of rival Danish wind power producer NEG Micon. The merger, completed at the end of 2004, established Vestas as the clear global leader, with a market share of some 40 percent. The completion of the merger process also signaled the departure of Svend Sigaard, who turned over the CEO position to former Hempel A/S executive Ditlev Engel.

Into the mid-2000s, Europe remained Vestas's dominant market, representing more than 70 percent of its sales at the end of 2004. Most of the remainder of the group's revenues was generated by the North American market. However Vestas launched a new strategy to step up its presence in the Asian markets, where the renewable energy market was expected to grow strongly through the end of the decade. After setting up a sales and marketing office in Beijing, Vestas scored its first major order on the mainland in February 2005, with an order for 50 turbines for the Rudong Wind Power Concession project. By July of that year, Vestas announced its intention to build a new factory in Tianjin to supply the blades for that project, and to support the company's further growth in China and elsewhere. Vestas appeared to be soaring toward a strong future as the world's wind turbine leader.

Principal Subsidiaries

Eissengiesserei Magdeburg GmbH (Germany); Global Renewable Energy Partners A/S (GREP); NEG Micon A/S; Vestas – American Wind Technology, Inc.; Vestas – Australian Wind Technology Pty. Ltd.; Vestas – Canadian Wind Technology, Inc.; Vestas – Celtic Wind Technology Ltd.; Vestas – Danish Wind Technology A/S; Vestas – Italian Wind Technology S.R.L.; Vestas – Nederland Windtechnologie B.V.; Vestas – Scandinavian Wind Technology A/S; Vestas Americas A/S; Vestas Argentina S.A.; Vestas Asia Pacific A/S; Vestas Assembly A/S; Vestas Blades A/S; Vestas Blades Australia Pty. Ltd.; Vestas Blades Deutschland GmbH; Vestas Blades Italia S.R.L.; Vestas Blades UK Ltd.; Vestas Brasil Ltda.; Vestas Central Europe A/S; Vestas China Ltd.; Vestas Control Systems A/S; Vestas Deutschland GmbH; Vestas Eólica SAU; Vestas France S.A.S.; Vestas Hellas S.A.; Vestas Japan KK; Vestas Machining A/S; Vestas Mediterranean East A/S; Vestas Mediterranean West A/S; Vestas Mexico S.A.; Vestas Nacelles A/S; Vestas Nacelles Australia Pty. Ltd.; Vestas Nacelles Italia S.R.L.; Vestas Nacelles Spain S.A.; Vestas New Zealand Wind Technology Ltd.; Vestas Northern Europe A/S; Vestas Poland Sp. z.o.o.; Vestas RRB India Ltd.; Vestas Svenska AB; Vestas Technology UK Limited; Vestas Towers A/S; VestasPor – Servicos de Technologia Eólica Ltda.; Wind Power Invest A/S; Windcast Group A/S.

Principal Competitors

General Electric Corporation; Abengoa S.A.; Azure Dynamics Inc.; Domnick Hunter Group PLC; Gamesa Corporacion Tecnologica S.A.; Solarworld GmbH.

Further Reading

"Danish Wind Turbine Maker Vestas to Build Factory in Tianjin," *AsiaPulse News,* July 8, 2005.

Dolan, Kerry A., "Clean and Green," *Forbes,* July 25, 2005, p. 111.

"European Wind Power Giant Expands in US," *Natural Life,* May-June 2002, p. 21.

"Giant Windmill Manufacturers Combine," *Modern Power Systems,* January 2004, p. 3.

Passariello, Christina, "Where the Blackout Was Happy News," *Business Week,* September 15, 2003, p. 32.

"Vestas CEO Resigns," *Modern Power Systems,* December 2004, p. 3.

Wustenhagen, Rolf, "Sustainability and Competitiveness in the Renewable Energy Sector: The Case of Vestas Winds Systems," *Greener Management International,* Winter 2003, p. 105.

—M.L. Cohen

Viad Corp.

Viad Tower, 1850 N. Central Avenue
Phoenix, Arizona 85004-4545
U.S.A.
Telephone: (602) 207-4000
Fax: (602) 207-5900
Web site: http://www.viad.com

Public Company
Incorporated: 1926 as Motor Transit Corp.
Employees: 3,025
Sales: $785.7 million (2004)
Stock Exchanges: New York
Ticker Symbol: VVI
NAIC: 561920 Convention and Trade Show Organizers

Viad Corp. is a Phoenix, Arizona-based descendant of the Greyhound Bus line. The publicly traded company is primarily engaged in providing services for trade shows, conventions, and special events. Subsidiary GES Exposition Services, Inc. offers trade show layout and design, logistics planning, and show execution services for approximately 2,000 events each year. The Exhibitgroup/Giltspur subsidiary works with major companies to design, build, and dismantle trade show exhibitions, and provides exhibitor show program management services. To a lesser degree, Viad is also involved in the travel and recreation field. Brewsters Tours, Inc. offers travel services to attractions in the Canadian Rocky Mountains, such as The Columbia Icefield and Banff Gondola. A fourth Viad subsidiary, Glacier Park, Inc., is the principal concessionaire in Montana's Glacier Park, operating four lodges and three motor inns in the area.

1920s Roots

Viad's Greyhound corporate lineage dates to 1926 when Motor Transit Corp. was formed to provide bus service and become a consolidator in the young industry. In 1930 the company changed its name to Greyhound Corp., then survived the Great Depression of the 1930s and emerged as the country's premiere bus line. But as business began to tail off in the 1960s, the company, under the leadership of Gerald H. Trautman, began to diversify into a wide range of businesses and refashioned itself as a conglomerate. In 1962 Greyhound became involved in equipment leasing through the acquisition of Boothe Leasing Corp. Two years later it turned to food services, picking up Prophet Co., renamed Greyhound Food Management Inc. In 1965 Greyhound added financial services to the mix, acquiring Travelers Express Co., Inc., which processed money orders. Greyhound acquired Carey Transportation, Inc. and 80 percent of Nassau Air Dispatch in 1969 to provide ground support to airlines serving the Bahamas. This business was then supplemented by the addition of Freeport Flight Services.

The most significant move Greyhound made to diversify was the 1970 $400 million acquisition of Chicago-based Armour & Company, the famous meatpacker founded in the 1860s. However, 100 years later the company faced a hostile takeover bid by General Host Corp. and convinced the Greyhound board to act as a white knight. After some legal wrangling, General Host sold its Armour stock to Greyhound, which acquired the rest of the company as well. Greyhound then unloaded much of Armour's assets, retaining the meatpacking business, renamed Armour Foods and the consumer productions division, Armour-Dial. Dial soap had been part of the Armour company since 1948 when its researchers used the packing operation's tallow byproduct to develop a new germicidal deodorant soap. In the 1950s Dial adopted the advertising slogan, "Aren't you glad you use Dial? Don't you wish everybody did?," which proved instrumental in Dial emerging as the leading deodorant soap in the country. So enduring was the slogan that Dial employed it for the next 40 years.

On some levels Trautman had assembled a successful conglomerate, but the company was not embraced by Wall Street, which derisively referred to Greyhound as "the dog." Its earnings were erratic, up one year and down the next, and instead of viewing Greyhound as diversified, analysts criticized it for lacking focus. In 1982, a new chairman and chief executive officer, John W. Teets, was brought in to overhaul Greyhound. When his work was completed 14 years later, he would emerge as the chairman and CEO of Viad Corp.

Teets grew up in Chicago in a blue collar home, the son of a crane operator who later started his own construction company.

An indifferent student, Teets was uninterested in becoming a civil engineer as his father desired, instead finding himself drawn to the restaurant business. In his early 20s, with backing from his father, Teets bought an interest in the Winter Garden, a Chicago complex that included a shopping center, restaurant, and ice skating rink. The venture proved highly successful and Teets may have likely remained involved in this field and never worked for Greyhound had it not been for a string of tragedies that struck his life in 1963. First his wife died in her sleep from unknown causes, followed a few weeks later by the death of a brother from a gas leak on the job. Finally, in November of that year the Winter Garden was completely destroyed by fire. Teets was in total despair and it was only at the insistence of a close friend that he applied for a food management job that Greyhound was advertising. He was hired to run the Greyhound restaurants at the 1964 New York World's Fair and performed so well at the task that Greyhound made him president of Posts Houses, a bus terminal restaurant operator. After a few years Teets left Greyhound for stints with other restaurant operations, including Canteen Corp., where he worked for a taskmaster and conglomerate wizard Harold Geneen, who taught him the importance of being detail-oriented and how to squeeze the utmost from managers. In 1976 a much more seasoned Teets returned to Greyhound, lured back by Trautman to take over the struggling Food Service Group. With Geneen as his model, Teets whipped the subsidiary into shape and became heir to Trautman's top post.

Teets told *Fortune* in 1985 that "Trautman wasn't much of a tire kicker," and that "Greyhound was run with benign neglect." All that changed when Teets took charge in 1982. Insisting that all subsidiaries had to return at least 15 percent on equity, he was especially hard on the bus lines and meatpacking units which fell far short of that mark. He moved aggressively to take on the unions, demanding wage cuts from workers at Armour Foods, and when they refused he shuttered the company's 29 plants and sold the business to Conagra Inc., which in days reopened with thousands of non-union workers. Teets then turned his attention to his unionized bus drivers, which Greyhound paid at a much higher rate than the competition. His demand for a 17 percent wage and benefit cut resulted in a 47-day strike marred by violence. In the end he achieved a 15 percent giveback, but Greyhound had been severely hurt and despite a number of cost-cutting measures never fully recovered. In 1987 Teets sold the Greyhound bus company to Dallas investors for $350 million, although the company retained the Greyhound Corp. name.

While casting off major assets, Teets added to existing businesses. In 1986 the consumer products division acquired Ellio's Pizza and Purex Corp., maker of soap, bleach, and other household products that filled in gaps in Greyhound's product lines. A year later Greyhound acquired Carson Pirie Scott & Co.'s in-flight catering and airport terminal concession business. The 20 Mule Team division of United States Borax & Chemical Corp. and its household products were brought into the fold in 1988. The addition of Republic Money Orders, Inc. added to the financial services area. In 1990 Greyhound acquired the Breck hair care products business. In that same year, the company changed its name to Greyhound-Dial in the hopes of creating some distance from its erstwhile bus line while still providing a connection to the ten subsidiaries, such as Greyhound Exhibit group, that continued to carry the Greyhound name. The distinction was lost on the public, however, as people continued to call the corporate switchboard with bus route and fare questions. Less than a year later, in February 1991, the company adopted a less confusing name: The Dial Corp.

Teets undertook a further restructuring of Dial in 1992, creating a spinoff company—GFC Financial Corp. later taking the name of Finova Capital Corp.—composed of Greyhound Financial Corp., Greyhound European Financial Group, and Verex Corp. The result was that a lot of hidden value was unlocked in these assets and Finova enjoyed strong growth, prompting investors to clamor for even more streamlining in Dial, convinced there was additional unrealized wealth in the remaining assets, split between consumer products and service companies. Unlike Finova, Dial was only able to achieve growth through further acquisitions.

Teets resisted the idea of further divestiture until 1996 when Michael Price of Heine Securities began accumulating a significant stake in Dial, which for years had been trading in the $20 range but had an estimated breakup value around $40. In a proactive move Teets announced that Dial would be split into two publicly held companies, with consumer products and the service assets going their separate ways. The consumer products side kept the Dial name, while the service companies inherited the corporate entity that was once Greyhound Corp. and took a new name, Viad Corp. It also retained Teets as chairman and CEO, if only for a brief period. He announced plans to retire at the start of 1997 while at the same time naming his handpicked successor, Robert H. Bohannon, the 51-year-old head of the Travelers Express subsidiary. Bohannon also brought 17 years of experience at General Electric's financial unit.

After the split-up was completed in 1996, Viad consisted of companies involved in airline catering through Dobbs International Service; airplane fueling and ground-handling through Aircraft Service International; convention and exhibit services through GES Exposition Services and Exhibitgroup/Giltspur; contract foodservices through Restaura, Inc.; airport and cruise ship duty-free concessions through Greyhound Leisure Services; travel services through Brewster Transport, Jetsave, and Crystal Holidays; and payment services through Travelers Express. The best of the group were Travelers Express, GES Exposition, and Exhibitgroup/Giltspur, all of which were major players in their fields and enjoying strong growth.

Upon taking over for Teets, Bohannon began to refine Viad's business mix, shedding some assets while adding others. In 1998 Viad cast off Aircraft Services International Group and the duty-free business, then a year later sold Restaura and Dobbs

Key Dates:

1926: Motor Transit Corp. is formed.
1930: Name is changed to Greyhound Corp.
1970: Armour & Company is acquired.
1991: Name is changed to The Dial Corp.
1992: Financial services unit is spun off.
1996: Viad splits from Dial.
1998: MoneyGram Payment Systems is acquired.
2004: Payment services segment is spun off.

International Services. During this period, the company bolstered Travelers Express with the $50 million acquisition of Game Financial Corporation, providing patrons of casinos and other gaming establishments with cash through credit card advance and check cashing services, and automated teller machines. In June 1998 Travelers Express paid $287 million to acquire MoneyGram Payment Systems Inc., a nonbank provider of consumer wire-transfer services, which complemented Travelers Express's money order business.

Exhibitgroup/Giltspur also grew externally, acquiring Dimension Works in November 1998, just one in a series of acquisitions that commenced before the creation of Viad Corp. and resulted in the largest exhibition company in the world. Headed by Charles Corsentino, the Dial subsidiary Exhibitgroup began its growth spurt in 1995 with the acquisition of its top competitor, Giltspur, with both companies generating about $130 million in annual sales. In addition, in 1995, the company added All West Display and Displaymasters & Deaton. The acquisition of Color & Design Exhibits followed in July 1996, then in 1998 T.L. Horton, Germany's Volbo Innenausbau, and Dimension Works were brought into the fold of the world's largest full-service exhibition company, maintaining offices in 17 cities in the United States as well as Toronto, Canada, and Dusseldorf, Germany.

By the new century Viad was involved in two primary areas: payment services and convention and event services. Revenues totaled more than $1.57 billion in 1999, yielding net income of $347.5 million. Both business segments enjoyed solid growth in 2000, a 16 percent increase for payment services and 11 percent for convention and event services. However, events outside the company's control intervened in 2001 and adversely affected Viad's fortunes. While payment services added nearly $100 million in sales for the year, convention and event services experienced a 14.3 percent drop in revenues due to a sagging economy, which caused some convention customers to forgo building new exhibits, and the terrorist attacks of September 11, leading to travel concerns and the cancellation of some trade shows and exhibit orders.

Difficult conditions continued in 2002, as Viad's total revenues decreased 2.1 percent to $1.62 billion and net income slipped to $57.9 million. Again, payment services held steady, increasing revenues by 9.5 percent, but the convention and event services' sales declined by another 11.1 percent. In 2003 payment services was adversely impacted by lower interest rates and widespread mortgage refinancing that resulted in the segment growing at a modest 3.6 percent clip. Convention and event services lost another 8.8 percent in sales, although it was able to produce profitable results in spite of a shrinking marketplace for trade shows and conventions.

It had become clear to investors and management alike that Viad's two principal business segments were hardly capable of achieving synergy. As had been true during the Greyhound and Dial days, the assets were building up unrealized value that could hopefully be unlocked by splitting the two segments into separate companies. In 2003 Viad began the process of engineering a reverse tax-free spinoff of the payment services unit. Thus, a new subsidiary was formed, MoneyGram International, Inc., which early in 2004 received the payment services business and its stock was distributed to Viad stockholders. Viad then conducted a one-for-four reverse stock split to increase the price of Viad shares. For the year, continuing operations generated $785.7 million in revenues. The company that had once been involved in buses, meat, soap, and money orders was now focused almost entirely on the trade show and convention business. Given its size and breadth there was every reason to expect that with a rebounding economy, Viad was well positioned to enjoy success in its chosen field.

Principal Subsidiaries

EXG, Inc.; GES Exposition Services, Inc.; Brewster Tours Inc.; Glacier Park, Inc. (80%).

Principal Competitors

Audio Visual Services Corporation; The Freeman Companies; George P. Johnson Company.

Further Reading

Galarza, Pablo, "Dialing Up the Next Spin-Off," *Financial World,* September 16, 1996, p. 42.

Lipin, Steven, "Viad of Phoenix Agrees to Acquire Colorado Company," *Wall Street Journal,* April 6, 1998, p. 1.

Mattera, Philip, "A Bodybuilding Lifts Greyhound," *Fortune,* October 28, 1985, p. 124.

McCall, Margo, "Subsidiaries May Benefit from Viad Spin-Off," *Tradeshow Week,* November 24, 2003, p. 9.

Rose, Frederick, "Viad Names Bohannon Chairman, CEO to Succeed Longtime Chief John Teets," *Wall Street Journal,* November 22, 1996, p. B2.

—Ed Dinger

Weight Watchers International Inc.

175 Crossways Park West
Woodbury, New York 11797
U.S.A.
Telephone: (516) 390-1400
Toll Free: (800) 651-6000
Fax: (516) 390-1334
Web site: http://www.weightwatchers.com

Public Company
Incorporated: 1963
Employees: 46,000
Sales: $1.02 billion (2004)
Stock Exchanges: New York
Ticker Symbol: WTW
NAIC: 812990 All Other Personal Services

Weight Watchers International Inc., the world's leading weight loss service provider, grew from the dream of one woman into a global franchise with annual sales exceeding $1 billion. Sarah Ferguson, the Duchess of York, has replaced the founder as the personality most associated with the enterprise. More than a million and a half people attend the company's weight loss classes in about 30 countries around the world. In 1999 parent firm H.J. Heinz sold the company's diet center enterprise to the European investment firm Artal Luxembourg SA. Weight Watchers, a public company since 2001, faced a downturn in enrollment during the early years of the 21st century as dieters turned to quick result weight loss solutions.

The Early Years

In 1961 Jean Nidetch was an overweight, 40-year-old homemaker living in Queens, New York. At 214 pounds and wearing a size 44 dress, Nidetch was always on a diet but never lost any weight. Thoroughly discouraged by dieting fads that did not help her, she attended a diet seminar offered by the City Board of Health in New York City. Although she lost 20 pounds following the advice provided, she soon discovered her motivation diminishing. Determined to stay on her diet and lose weight, she phoned a few overweight friends and asked them to come to her apartment. When her friends arrived, Nidetch confessed that she had an obsession with eating cookies. Her friends not only sympathized but also began to share their own obsessions about food. Soon Nidetch was arranging weekly meetings for her friends in her home. The women shared stories about food and offered each other support. Most important, they all began to lose weight.

Within a short time, Nidetch was arranging meetings for more than 40 people in her small apartment. Not long afterward, she began to arrange support group meetings at other people's homes. As more and more people attended the meetings, Nidetch realized that losing weight was not merely adhering to a diet, but encouraging people to support each other and change their eating habits. One couple, Felice and Al Lippert, invited Nidetch to speak to a group of overweight friends at their house in Baldwin Harbor. After meeting every week for four months, Al lost 40 pounds and Felice lost nearly 50. Al Lippert, a merchandise manager for a women's apparel chain, began to give Nidetch advice on how to organize and expand her activities, and soon a four-person partnership was formed among Nidetch and her husband, Marty, and Al and Felice Lippert. In May 1963, Weight Watchers was incorporated and opened for business in Queens, New York.

The company's first public meeting was held in a space located over a movie theater. Although the meeting was not advertised, more than 400 people waited in line to hear Nidetch speak. Nidetch divided the crowd into groups of 50 and spent the entire day addressing the overwhelming guilt and hopelessness that many people felt about being overweight, as well as providing advice about shedding pounds effectively. Nidetch began to hold meetings three times a day, seven days a week. When she started to show signs of fatigue, Al Lippert suggested that she pick key people who had lost weight themselves and had strong communication skills to help her expand the program. The first 100 people chosen to run meetings throughout New York City shared their personal stories and helped people gain control over their eating habits. Nidetch's extraordinary speaking skills and Al Lippert's genius for organization helped raise Weight Watchers to the level of an evangelical movement.

Company Perspectives:

Weight Watchers has always believed that dieting is just one part of long-term weight management. A healthy body results from a healthy lifestyle—which means mental, emotional and physical health. Weight Watchers does not tell you what you can or can't eat. We provide information, knowledge, tools and motivation to help you make the decisions that are right for you about nutrition and exercise. We help you to make healthy eating decisions, and we encourage you to enjoy yourself by becoming more active. To provide motivation, mutual support, encouragement and instruction from our leaders, Weight Watchers organizes group Meetings around the world. Meeting members often become Meeting leaders and receptionists, sharing the story of their personal success with others.

Dynamic Growth in the Middle to Late 1960s

From 1963 to 1967, Lippert organized training programs, expanded the number of company locations throughout the United States, and implemented a franchising system. By 1968, Weight Watchers had 102 franchises in the United States, Canada, Great Britain, Israel, and Puerto Rico. It was relatively easy for a person to get a franchise for Weight Watchers programs. Lippert sold the territory for a minimal fee, then charged the franchisee a royalty rate of 10 percent on the gross income. The most important requirement was that the franchisee had graduated from the company's programs and kept off the weight that he or she had lost. Most of the franchisees were women from New York City who were willing to travel to establish a Weight Watchers franchise. This group was emotionally involved in the program and had a great deal of faith in its principles; as a result, their commitment to the franchise sometimes bordered on religious fervor.

The middle and late 1960s saw a boom for the company. In 1965 Lippert contracted various food companies in the United States to produce Weight Watchers food lines for supermarkets and grocery stores, including low-calorie frozen entrees and dry and dairy low-calorie foods. Lippert was also creative in other ways. He designed a billfold that held small packets of sugar substitutes, skim milk, and bouillon that enabled adherents of the Weight Watchers program to more easily control their diet when away from home. Lippert began to sell items for use in the Weight Watchers classroom; established a joint venture with *National Lampoon* to publish *Weight Watchers Magazine*; and opened a summer camp for children with weight problems.

One of the company's most successful ideas, created under the direction of Felice Lippert, was the publication of a Weight Watchers cookbook. Since the inception of the company, Felice Lippert had been in charge of new recipe development, nutrition, and food research. Her first Weight Watchers cookbook catapulted to the top of the bestseller lists and sold more than 1.5 million copies. In 1968 the company made its first stock offering to the public. Although some financial analysts on Wall Street were skeptical of the offering, the general public was overwhelmingly enthusiastic. The first day of trading saw Weight Watchers stock shoot up from an initial price of $11 to $30.

Changes in the 1970s

In 1973 Weight Watchers held its tenth anniversary celebration in Madison Square Garden in New York City. Host of past Republican and Democratic party presidential conventions, legendary boxing matches, and other historic national events, the Garden was filled to the rafters with admirers of the Weight Watchers program. It was a far cry from the celebration just five years earlier, held in a high school auditorium. Although celebrities in attendance included Bob Hope and Pearl Bailey, people had really come to see and hear Jean Nidetch. She spoke until 1:30 a.m., with the crowd captivated by her inspiring stories.

With the company's rapid growth, in 1973 Nidetch decided to resign from her position as president of Weight Watchers to devote herself entirely to public relations. She traveled the world granting an endless number of radio, newspaper, and magazine interviews and speaking to huge audiences about the success of Weight Watchers programs. Al Lippert continued to organize the operation, hiring Dr. Richard Stuart, an expert in behavioral psychology, to help the company create a training department and design the first guides and manuals for the Weight Watchers program. Lippert also hired Carol Morton, a Weight Watchers graduate and German teacher, to begin operations in Europe. From 1974 to 1976, Lippert, along with a growing list of professional staff members in the areas of marketing, advertising, licensing, and nutrition, began to formalize a strategy for continued growth. Weight Watchers was not only an inspirational program that helped people lose weight, but a highly successful business venture. Lippert and his staff focused on the best way to attract people to Weight Watchers meetings and to sell them food, cookbooks, magazines, camps, spas, and various other weight loss products.

By the late 1970s, however, Al Lippert had experienced two heart attacks and recognized that the phenomenal growth of Weight Watchers was much too rapid for his small management group to handle. Annual revenues had grown to approximately $50 million, and it was at this point that Lippert started searching for a larger corporate partner to help Weight Watchers achieve the next level of organization and success. H.J. Heinz Company approached Lippert about purchasing Foodways National, one of Weight Watchers' frozen food licensees. Heinz initially sought to merge Foodways with Ore-Ida, its own frozen food and controlled-portion entree producer. Heinz management, however, soon realized that it was the Weight Watchers International brand name that was valuable, not its licensee. As a result, Heinz acquired Weight Watchers and Foodways National in 1978 for approximately $100 million. Lippert remained chief executive officer and chairman of the board at Weight Watchers.

Between 1978 and 1981, management at Heinz assimilated Weight Watchers into its corporate organization. Heinz divided the company into three parts: Foodways National's frozen food business was subsumed under Ore-Ida; Camargo Foods, a condiments, dry snacks, and dairy producer, and a licensee of Weight Watchers that was also purchased by Heinz, was merged with Heinz U.S.A.; and Weight Watchers' meeting service business remained Weight Watchers International. Heinz's strategy was to incorporate the food business of Weight Watchers into its own food operations, while allowing the meeting service business to continue functioning separately.

Key Dates:

1963: Weight Watchers is founded.
1965: Weight Watchers food line debuts.
1978: H.J. Heinz Company buys Weight Watchers and divides company into three divisions, including Weight Watchers International.
1997: ''1,2,3 Success'' program is introduced.
1999: Heinz sells Weight Watchers International to Artal Luxembourg.
2001: Weight Watchers goes public once again.
2004: The Core Plan is introduced in response to competition of popular carbohydrate-restrictive diets.
2005: Company acquires stake in WeightWatchers.com from Artal Luxembourg.

Expansion and Diversification in the 1980s

Chuck Berger, the new president of Weight Watchers International, initiated an aggressive strategy that included an innovative program for weight loss, an improved meeting service, and a plan to buy back the company's franchise territories. In 1983 Berger became CEO of Weight Watchers International and, along with Andrew Barrett and Dr. Les Parducci, laid the foundation for a brand new weight loss diet. Dubbed ''Quick Start,'' the diet aimed to quicken the rate of weight loss during the first two weeks. Launched with a well-conceived media blitz, the new program helped to double the company's revenues within two years. Barrett, as executive vice-president, improved marketing, added new food product lines, and concentrated on the lifestyle needs of people with weight control problems. One of his most successful ideas was the ''At Work Program,'' which organized meetings for professional women at their place of work.

Between 1982 and 1989, Weight Watchers International experienced unprecedented growth in product sales. In 1982 the Weight Watchers brand name food items switched from aluminum-tray to fiberboard packaging and introduced one of the world's first lines of microwaveable frozen food entrees. Foodways National also introduced low-calorie dessert products, and by 1988 the company's desserts had a larger market share than Sara Lee and Lean Cuisine. In 1982 *Weight Watchers Magazine* had a circulation of approximately 700,000 readers; by 1986, circulation had increased to more than one million. The magazine had changed its focus and was marketed to women committed to ''self-improvement.'' Collaborating with Time-Life's books division, Weight Watchers International developed a series of highly successful fitness tapes for the video market and started additional projects for books, audiotapes, and videos in the areas of exercise, weight loss, and health awareness.

By 1988, each of the three separate business units of Weight Watchers was recording skyrocketing revenues. When combined, sales for the Weight Watchers businesses amounted to more than $1.2 billion. Even as these figures were released, however, the weight control business was changing dramatically. In 1989 and 1990, numerous competitors including Jenny Craig, Slim-Fast, Healthy Choice, and Nutri/System began to challenge Weight Watchers for a share of the market. During 1990 and 1991, after nearly seven years of increasing market share, the company suddenly stopped growing. Sales of Weight Watchers brand food products declined precipitously, and even the renowned support group meetings began to fall in attendance.

In 1991 Brian Ruder, a vice-president in marketing at Heinz, was hired as the president of a newly reconstituted Weight Watchers Food Company. Ruder immediately embarked on a comprehensive reorganization strategy, implementing new sales, marketing, finance, manufacturing, and research and development procedures. Within 15 months of the new company's formation, Ruder had redesigned almost half of its products. New product development time amounted to a mere 14 weeks, down from the 22-month cycle previously adhered to. One product line, low-fat, low-calorie entrees called ''Smart Ones,'' was an immediate success. During the same time, Dr. Les Parducci was appointed by Heinz management as the head of Weight Watchers International. Parducci revamped the company's strategy for meeting services by simplifying the contents of programs, relocating meetings to more attractive surroundings, introducing more fun and interesting materials for members, and developing an entire new line of convenience food products.

Trouble in the Mid-1990s

Although these changes helped Weight Watchers stem defections to its rivals and revive its food sale business, the entire weight loss industry suffered a downturn in the mid-1990s. Many consumers had tired of feeling a perpetual need to count calories and of the perceived regimentation of diet classes. Spurred on by fitness gurus such as Susan Powter, whose rallying cry ''Stop the Insanity'' summed up many people's frustrations with the diet business, consumers began to look to health clubs and nutritional guides as a path to losing unwanted pounds. As an industry analyst explained to *Business Week,* ''The whole industry has been under pressure. There has been a shift from dieting to general health concerns such as fat intake and general lifestyle.'' Moreover, a new generation of diet drugs was coming on the market, offering the hope that weight loss would become as simple as popping a pill. Weight Watchers also received some adverse publicity in 1993, when the Federal Trade Commission filed suit against it, alleging that it had engaged in misleading advertising. (The suit was eventually settled with no admission of wrongdoing in 1997.) As a result of these events, attendance at Weight Watchers classes dropped 20 percent in 1994 alone.

The company responded quickly to these events. In 1995 Weight Watchers International began to craft what *Business Week* described as a ''health-first, vanity-second message.'' This approach stressed the health values of losing weight through Weight Watchers classes over the cosmetic effects of ''looking better.'' To buttress this message, Weight Watchers negotiated agreements with insurance companies to give premium rebates on life insurance policies to Weight Watcher members. The company also made a more concerted effort to reach out to men, who had long been neglected by the diet industry (understandably so, however, as 95 percent of customers were female), holding male-only classes in some of its centers.

In an effort to streamline the company's operations further, Heinz sold *Weight Watchers Magazine* (whose circulation had dropped significantly from its mid-1980s peak of more than a million readers) to Southern Progress Corp., a subsidiary of Time Inc., in 1996. Although these changes were unable to return Weight Watchers to its former, robust growth levels, they did allow the company to remain profitable throughout the middle of the decade.

By 1997, the diet industry's fortunes were improving. The new class of diet drugs had not only failed to become the panacea for which many consumers had hoped, but were in fact linked to significant health problems. In addition, consumers had found that losing weight through exercise or fad diets had proved no simpler or more successful than the formula offered by Weight Watchers and its competitors. However, Weight Watchers had changed with the times as well. Recognizing that consumers still wanted to have more flexibility in the food they ate, the company unveiled its "1,2,3 Success" program. This innovative plan assigned point values to all foods, allowing dieters to eat whatever they chose, so long as they did not exceed the prescribed number of points. The company also hired the former Duchess of York, Sarah Ferguson, to be its spokesperson for the campaign. "1,2,3 Success" proved a tremendous boon to the company, driving up attendance at its classes worldwide by nearly 50 percent and boosting profits substantially.

Despite this revitalization, Heinz—in the course of a sweeping corporate reorganization—sold Weight Watchers International to the European investment firm Artal Luxembourg for $735 million in July 1999. Artal was a private investment group, which had as its sole investment advisor The Invus Group, Ltd. of New York. In an odd sort of synergy, Artal had also invested heavily in Keebler cookies and Sunshine biscuits. Discussing the sale in a press release, Heinz CEO William R. Johnson remarked, "Weight Watchers is the gold standard in the global weight control business, but its services orientation does not fit with Heinz's long-term food growth strategy, and this sale enables us to focus on Weight Watchers foods and our other global food businesses." Heinz retained the rights to the Weight Watchers name for use on its food and beverage products through 2004.

Dieting Trends Trimming Weight Watchers: 2000–05

In January 2001, Weight Watchers purchased its largest franchisee, Weighco. (Additional franchisee purchases continued into 2003.) The company went public in November 2001, at $24 per share. The stock added 23 percent in value on its first trading day and continued to post a strong performance through early 2002. Artal Luxembourg remained majority shareholder with almost 80 percent of the stock.

Weight Watchers' good fortune was dependent on dieters showing up for their meetings. Dues brought in about 70 percent of revenue. The sale of books, scales, and nutrition bars to meeting attendees brought in additional income. The U.S. operations generated 51 percent of the total and nearly 23 percent came from Britain, according to *The New York Times.* The rest was generated by company-owned operations elsewhere in Europe and in Australia and New Zealand. The company also received royalty fees from franchisees.

Weight Watchers moved to lure more to their meetings with a redesigned magazine, introduced with the January/February 2003 issue and coinciding with the onslaught of post-holiday weight loss resolutions. The company had reacquired the license to publish the magazine from Time Inc. in 2000. Since that time, circulation had nearly tripled to one million. Ad circulation, despite the tough economy, rose 42 percent in 2002. The magazine had performed poorly under Time.

"Weight Watchers has an amazing story," Dan Capell, publisher of *Capell's Circulation Report*, told *Crain's New York Business* in January 2003. "Newsstand sales have gone through the roof, and subscriptions are strong, too." But new diet trends had already begun to show signs of eating away at Weight Watchers' main source of revenue during 2002.

Competition generated by the Atkins and South Beach diets prompted Weight Watchers' first major change in its diet plan since 1997. The Core Plan, introduced in August 2004, eliminated point counting and portion size restrictions. The traditional plan continued to be an option for Weight Watchers members.

Weight Watchers stock lagged behind the overall U.S. market during 2004, even as other companies' stock rose with the economic recovery. But Standard & Poor's Equity Research Services' Hoard Choe, writing in *Business Week Online*, saw positive signs for the company's future, including the growing problem of obesity among Americans and increased disenchantment with low-carb diets.

To expand its line of branded food products, Weight Watchers entered into agreements with a number of food manufacturers in early 2005, including George Weston Bakeries, Organic Milling, Whitman's, and Well's Dairy. In mid-2005, the company acquired a 53 percent stake in WeightWatchers.com from Artal Luxembourg. WeightWatchers.com, founded in September 1999, offered a free site with information on weight loss, healthy lifestyle, and meeting locations. Subscription options targeted people unable to attend meetings and people interested in various tools as a supplement to the meeting.

Weight Watchers two-year North American enrollment erosion was brought to a halt. The new plan and a push for office place meetings—tapping into employer concerns about skyrocketing healthcare costs—had helped reinvigorate the brand. The Internet site was also gaining in popularity.

As of mid-August 2005, the company's stock had increased by 27 percent, and competitors were struggling. "The waning of the low-carb phenomenon was punctuated this month when privately held Atkins Nutritionals Inc., founded in 1989 by Dr. Robert C. Atkins, filed for Chapter 11 bankruptcy protection," Leon Lazaroff reported for the *Chicago Tribune* in August 2005.

Principal Subsidiaries

Weight Watchers Direct, Inc.; Weight Watchers (Accessories & Publications) Ltd.; Weight Watchers (Exercise) Ltd.; Weight Watchers (Food Products) Ltd.; Weight Watchers Funding Inc.; Weight Watchers Camps, Inc.

Principal Competitors

eDiets.com; Jenny Craig, Inc.; NutriSystem, Inc.

Further Reading

Alexander, Keith L., ''A Health Kick at Weight Watchers,'' *Business Week,* January 16, 1995.

Block, Valerie, ''Weighty Issues,'' *Crain's New York Business,*'' January 6, 2003, p. 3.

Choe, Howard, ''Weight Watchers' Attractive Figures,'' *Business Week Online*, November 30, 2004.

Dienstag, Eleanor Foa, ''The Weight Watchers Story,'' in *Good Company: 125 Years at the Heinz Table,* New York: Warner Books, 1994.

Fannin, Rebecca A., ''Corporate Close Up: Slimmer Pickings in U.S. Prompt Weight Watchers to Look Abroad,'' *Advertising Age International,* February 17, 1997.

Freeman, Sholnn, ''European Firm Buys Division of H.J. Heinz Co.,'' *New Orleans Times-Picayune,* July 23, 1999.

Fridman, Sherman, ''Weight Watchers to Shed Y2K Fat or Maybe Not,'' *Newsbytes,* November 22, 1999.

''H.J. Heinz Co. Sells Weight Watchers Weight Control Business to Artal,'' *Market News Publishing,* July 22, 1999.

The History of Weight Watchers, Jericho, N.Y.: Weight Watchers International Inc., 1995.

Lazaroff, Leon, ''Fad-Diet Failures Add Heft to Value of Weight Watchers,'' *Chicago Tribune*, August 14, 2005, p. 5.

Leder, Michelle, ''Real Belt-Tightening As Part of a Portfolio,'' *The New York Times*, January 20, 2002, p. BU9.

Pollack, Judann, ''Fed Up with Promoting Diets, Weight-Loss Rivals Branch Out,'' *Advertising Age,* March 29, 1999.

Sabatini, Patricia, ''Slimming Down Heinz Plans to Shut 20 Plants, Sell Weight Watchers Classes,'' *Pittsburgh Post-Gazette,* February 18, 1999.

Schroeder, Michael, ''The Diet Business Is Getting a Lot Skinnier,'' *Business Week,* June 24, 1991.

Spangler, Todd, ''Heinz to Slim Down: Its Weight Watchers Classrooms Are Being Sold,'' *York Daily Record,* July 23, 1999.

''Weight Watchers: A Little Debt-Heavy?,'' *Business Week*, December 10, 2001, p. 100.

—Thomas Derdak
—updates: Rebecca Stanfel; Kathleen Peippo

Xcel Energy Inc.

414 Nicollet Mall
Minneapolis, Minnesota 55401-1993
U.S.A.
Telephone: (612) 330-5500
Toll Free: (800) 328-8226
Fax: (612) 330-2900
Web site: http://www.xcelenergy.com

Public Company
Incorporated: 1909 as Washington County Light &
  Power Company
Employees: 10,650
Sales: $8.35 billion (2004)
Stock Exchanges: New York
Ticker Symbol: XEL
NAIC: 221122 Electric Power Distribution; 551112
  Offices of Other Holding Companies

Xcel Energy Inc., one of the largest combination electric and gas companies in the nation, serves Colorado, Kansas, Michigan, Minnesota, New Mexico, North Dakota, Oklahoma, South Dakota, Texas, and Wisconsin. In 2004 Xcel Energy had 3.3 million electricity customers and 1.8 million natural gas customers. The company was formed in 2000 upon the merger of Minneapolis-based Northern States Power Company (NSP) with Denver-based New Century Energies.

Early Development of Electric Utilities

Predecessor NSP's roots go back to 1881 when Henry Marison Byllesby, NSP's founder—then a 22-year-old dropout from engineering school—joined Thomas Edison as a draftsman to build a power plant in New York City. Byllesby went on to design plants for Edison in Chile and Montreal. In 1885 Edison's rival George Westinghouse offered Byllesby $10,000 a year to become vice-president and general manager of Westinghouse Electric, and Byllesby accepted.

In his four years with Westinghouse, Byllesby invented and designed more than 40 electric lighting devices. In 1891 he received a job offer from another competitor, Charles A. Coffin,

president of Thomson-Houston Electric Company. Coffin sent Byllesby to St. Paul, Minnesota, to run a subsidiary there. In St. Paul, Byllesby noted that most Midwestern electric companies had inadequate finances and resources to meet customer demand. The weakest companies quickly went bankrupt or were swallowed by their competitors. Byllesby spent four years in St. Paul, until Thomson-Houston merged with Edison's General Electric Company. Unwilling to work for Edison again, Byllesby went to Oregon and became vice-president of the Portland General Electric Company, where he designed, financed, and built four hydroelectric developments in four years.

In 1902 he put his years in St. Paul to use and organized his own engineering and operating firm in Chicago, with Samuel Insull and other backers, to buy and upgrade struggling midwestern utilities. Insull was a leading financier and acquirer of utilities. Financially troubled electric companies would approach Insull, and Insull would bail them out in exchange for stock in the company and an executive position. Byllesby bought companies in Illinois, Ohio, and Oklahoma, then in 1909 returned to Minnesota, where he organized the Washington County Light & Power Company in June 1909. In December 1909, the company's name was changed to Consumers Power Company. Byllesby and Insull also organized two utility holding companies: Northern States Power Company of Delaware in 1909 and Standard Gas and Electric in 1910.

Byllesby, like Insull, ended up acquiring many of the companies he helped. The companies for which Byllesby built steam and hydroelectric plants became insolvent. Byllesby's company would take over these troubled companies and provide engineering, management, and financial assistance. In 1912 Byllesby made his most important acquisition when he bought Minneapolis General Electric of Minnesota. That company was destined to become NSP's flagship company. Also in 1912 Byllesby and Insull parted ways.

World War I to the Depression: Expansion and Interconnection

On February 5, 1916, Byllesby changed his company's name to Northern States Power Company. The United States' entry into World War I in 1917 put a great strain on NSP's generating

Company Perspectives:

Our name reflects our core value—excellence in energy products and services. We are dedicated to providing you the best in service, value and information to enhance your professional and personal life. We are committed to customer satisfaction by continuously improving our operations to be a low-cost, reliable, environmentally sound energy provider. We have been successfully providing this to our customers for the past 130 years and will work hard to continue with this commitment in the future.

capabilities as wartime production and industrial customers' demands grew. After the war, the country experienced a brief depression followed by a business boom that saw increased demand for electricity and encouragement of merger activity.

In the company's first 20 years, NSP bought 25 more Upper Midwest utility companies. It acquired the Northwest Light & Power Company in 1917 and the Brainerd Gas & Electric Company, St. Cloud Water Power Company, Hutchinson Light & Manufacturing Company, and Ottumwa Railway & Light Company in 1920. Ottumwa's electric and steam-heating business was reorganized in 1923 as the Northern States Power Company (New Jersey), while its railway business became the Ottumwa Traction Company. All of the old Ottumwa properties were sold in 1925, except transmission lines in northern Iowa. NSP acquired the Wisconsin-Minnesota Light and Power Company in 1923; the Minnesota Valley Electric Company, Renville County Electric Company, and St. Cloud Public Service Company in 1924; Glenwood Electric Light, Heat & Power Company, Farmers Light & Power Company, and the St. Cloud Electric Power Company in 1926; and the St. Paul Gas Light Company, Sauk Rapids Water Power Company, South St. Paul Gas & Electric Company, St. Croix Power Company, and the Minnesota Power Company in 1927.

As NSP expanded its network of operating companies, it interconnected them. Interconnection allowed massive power production and brought customers lower rates and more reliable service. NSP also replaced old plants with newer, more efficient ones, constructing major hydroelectric units at Rapidan, Cannon Falls, and Coon Rapids, Minnesota, in addition to many smaller installations all over the Midwest. The company put a great deal of effort into improving its steam-generating plants, focusing attention on the Riverside plant in Minneapolis. Riverside was huge by the standards of the day, and its expansion illustrated Byllesby's belief that it was less expensive to generate power at a favorable site and transmit it than to generate power at the site where it is used. Byllesby died in 1924, but numerous associates carried on his work, especially Robert F. Pack, general manager and later president of NSP.

1930s: Federal Action Bringing Changes

Between 1921 and 1929, 3,744 U.S. public utility companies were absorbed in mergers and acquisitions. This meant that 84 percent of all U.S. utility assets were in the hands of slightly more than 1 percent of all utility corporations. During the Great

Depression, large holding companies such as NSP became the subjects of much scrutiny.

The scrutiny resulted in the Public Utility Holding Company Act of 1935, under which utilities had to simplify their structures. As a result of this law, NSP had to dissolve Standard Gas and Electric, and NSP's Chicago-based financial backers had to sell their stock back to the company.

During this period, NSP experienced major financial problems. The Securities and Exchange Commission (SEC) forced the company to reevaluate assets it had overvalued for stock issuing purposes in 1924, and NSP lost $75 million through this readjustment. The SEC also ordered NSP to eliminate its Class B voting stock, which had been created by Byllesby to guarantee him control of NSP, since the company could no longer pay dividends.

Another part of U.S. President Franklin D. Roosevelt's New Deal that affected NSP was the agency he developed to help finance electrical lines for impoverished farmers, the Rural Electrification Administration (REA). The REA encouraged farmers to form electric cooperatives in order to borrow federal funds for line extensions. These cooperatives competed directly with private utilities.

The third blow the New Deal dealt power companies was government sponsorship of municipal power company ownership. The government agreed to pay 45 percent of the cost for any community willing to build, generate, and distribute its own power. After an extensive battle and many town hall debates, most communities ended up choosing NSP's service anyway, for NSP had made voluntary rate reductions consistently since it started operating.

Roosevelt's final implementation that affected NSP was his National Recovery Act, which guaranteed employees the right to organize, bargain collectively, and strike. This act, and the safer working conditions encouraged by a union, was welcomed by NSP linemen, who had lost nearly half their workers to electrical accidents. On February 23, 1937, NSP suffered its first labor strike. By the eighth day of the strike, Robert Pack decided to cut his losses and agreed to recognize the workers' union International Brotherhood of Electrical Workers. NSP was one of the first utility companies in the United States to become unionized.

1940s: War Years and Postwar Demand

In 1939 the company continued to expand in Wisconsin. On August 29, 1941, NSP merged the wholly owned subsidiaries Minneapolis General Electric Company, St. Croix Falls Minnesota Improvement Company, and Minnesota Brush Electric Company into NSP. On December 27 NSP dissolved Northern States Power Company (New Jersey) after selling certain assets to South Dakota Public Service Company and transferring the remainder to itself.

After the United States entered World War II in 1941, demand for electricity rose rapidly, as industry contributed to the war effort. NSP responded by adding a 50,000-kilowatt steam turbine to its St. Paul High Bridge plant. NSP employees were fingerprinted, as a precaution against sabotage and theft.

Key Dates:

1909: Washington County Light & Power Company is formed.
1916: Name is changed to Northern States Power Company (NSP).
1924: Founder Henry Marison Byllesby dies.
1935: Public Utility Holding Company Act forces NSP to simplify structure.
1937: NSP is hit by first major labor strike.
1945: Company reaches $53 million in sales.
1955: Company is ranked among top 10 U.S. utilities.
1967: NSP substitutes gas-fired steam boiler for the nuclear reactor in its first atomic power plant.
1973: Prairie Island nuclear plant begins operation, joining one already underway in Monticello.
1979: Three Mile Island accident scuttles NSP plans to build third nuclear plant.
1990: Company increases dividends for 16th consecutive year.
2000: NSP merges with New Century Energies, creating Xcel Energy Inc.
2002: NRG Energy, a subsidiary operating in unregulated arena, declares bankruptcy.

Most of NSP's advertising during the war focused on conservation and salvage programs. The electric-utility industry's cartoon-character spokesperson, Reddy Kilowatt, regularly promoted victory gardens. More than 600 NSP employees served in the war. In 1942 NSP's president, Robert Pack, retired, turning over his office to his assistant, Ted Crocker.

While many utility companies saw demand slow after the war, NSP reported a record load on December 17, 1945, almost 10 percent higher than in 1944. Sales for 1945 were a record $53 million. NSP became heavily involved in a postwar planning program that helped businesses expand and convert their wartime production to peacetime needs. While NSP helped these businesses, the businesses' growth often helped NSP enlarge its customer base.

NSP's customer base grew so rapidly that when President Ted Crocker died unexpectedly on June 29, 1947, and B.F. Braheney took over, he was faced with a power shortage. Braheney quickly developed a demand-control system and called on customers to conserve. NSP also built new plants, many of them diesel-powered. During the 1950s the company launched its largest ever construction program, investing nearly $400 million. After 1947 NSP's daily kilowatt-hour output surpassed that of the entire year 1916. Operating revenues doubled from 1941 to 1951.

1950s: Consolidation and Entry into the Nuclear Age

In 1950 NSP sold the utility properties of its Illinois-based subsidiary, Interstate Light & Power Company, and dissolved it. In 1955 NSP ranked among the top ten utilities in the United States. In 1956 NSP consolidated three of its subsidiaries—St. Croix Falls Wisconsin Improvement Company, St. Croix Power Company, and Interstate Light & Power Company—into its already existing principal subsidiary, Northern States Power Company (Wisconsin) (NSP-Wisconsin). In October 1956 NSP sold its gas property in Brainerd, Minnesota, to Minnesota Valley Natural Gas Company and bought electrical distribution properties that served 13 Minnesota communities and surrounding rural areas, from Interstate Power Company.

In March 1957 NSP continued to consolidate, acquiring hydroelectric developments at St. Anthony Falls on the Mississippi River in Minneapolis from its wholly owned subsidiaries, St. Anthony Falls Water Power Company and the Minneapolis Mill Company. In August of that year NSP acquired an electrical distribution system in Farmington, Minnesota, from Central Electric & Gas Company. The following month NSP added more electrical distribution facilities in Delhi and North Redwood, Minnesota, from the city of Redwood Falls. In October 1957, NSP-Wisconsin acquired properties from Wisconsin Hydro Electric Company.

NSP had been interested in nuclear energy since 1945, and in the early 1950s it became one of the first utilities to receive access to information from the Atomic Energy Commission. In 1957 the company announced plans for its first full-scale atomic power plant, the Pathfinder, and chose a site on the Big Sioux River. Pathfinder began operating in 1964, but operating and safety costs were so high that in 1967 NSP substituted a gas-fired steam boiler for the nuclear reactor.

1960s: Environmental Concerns

In January 1960 NSP acquired NSP-Wisconsin's Minnesota properties, as well as the Wisconsin properties of Mississippi Valley Public Service Company. Later that year, NSP acquired NSP-Wisconsin's Minnesota gas properties, which were in the Winona and Red Wing areas. In May 1961 NSP acquired Western Power and Gas Company's eastern business, which served the southeastern portion of South Dakota. In 1962 NSP sold its Tracy, Minnesota, water utility to the city of Tracy.

In March 1964 NSP acquired the properties and assets of Deichen Power, Inc. that had supplied southern Minnesota. In 1964 NSP began construction of the Allen S. King steam electric plant in Wisconsin on the St. Croix River and stirred up an environmental confrontation. The public outcry raised by the construction of this plant, which was perceived as a threat to the area's wildlife, was NSP's next real experience with public opposition and foreshadowed the controversy NSP's nuclear plant would raise. Despite an injunction—later lifted—brought by the Wisconsin attorney general, the company went ahead with the plant, which began production in 1968.

Around that time Allen King, NSP president until 1965, and his successor, Earl Ewald, created Mid-Continent Area Power Planners (MAPP), which brought 22 Upper Midwest power suppliers together to coordinate the planning, construction, and operation of new electrical plants throughout the region, in hopes of maximizing efficiency and minimizing duplication and waste. Through interconnection and coordination these companies were able to help each other supply the area.

All went smoothly for NSP through 1965. In June 1965 NSP acquired distribution facilities in Grand Forks, North Dakota, from the Nodak Rural Electric Cooperative. The tide turned in 1966, however, when NSP announced its plans for the Monticello nuclear plant. Demonstrators rose in opposition. Although ground for the plant was broken in 1966, it took five years and $20 million in losses before the plant became operational. The controversy led NSP to create an environmental affairs department in 1969.

NSP continued expanding; in 1967 it acquired distribution facilities from Wright-Hennepin Cooperative Electric Association, as well as the electric distribution facilities of the village of Bayport, Minnesota. In 1968 NSP acquired the electric generating, transmission, and distribution facilities of the village of Mazeppa, Minnesota, and sold the electric distribution system of the village of Fischer, Minnesota, to the Otter Tail Power Company. In December 1969 NSP acquired several electric distribution facilities from Interstate Power Company.

1970s and 1980s: Rates and Resources

In 1971 NSP donated land skirting the Upper St. Croix River to the states of Minnesota and Wisconsin and to the National Park Service to be managed cooperatively. In 1973 as the OPEC oil embargo drove home the importance of conservation, NSP began researching solar energy, wind power, burning garbage as fuel, and even enormous underwater sea turbines. However, 94 percent of NSP's power still came from nuclear and coal-fired plants in 1978. It had added a second nuclear plant, Prairie Island, in 1973.

The 1970s were tough for NSP. As taxes and interest rates went up, NSP's earnings dropped, although revenues reached record highs. NSP, which had cut rates in earlier years, sought rate increases, but not all were approved by regulators. Near the end of the 1970s, NSP began to explore the possibilities of another nuclear power plant to produce low-cost energy. The company planned to participate in a plant called Tyrone, located in western Wisconsin. In early 1979, however, in the middle of NSP's battle with the Wisconsin Public Service Commission, came the nuclear accident at Three Mile Island, Pennsylvania. Soon after, NSP and other Tyrone owners voted to cancel the project.

NSP spent nearly $1 billion on pollution control from 1977 to 1987. The company also continued consolidating its principal subsidiaries. In 1987 NSP merged its subsidiary, Lake Superior District Power Company, into NSP-Wisconsin.

From 1980 to 1990, both NSP's sales and profits nearly doubled. It increased dividends for the 16th consecutive year in 1990. The company, however, contended that many of its costs, such as property taxes, were beyond its control and in 1989 had sought a $120 million electric rate increase from the Minnesota Public Utilities Commission. The commission rejected the request in 1990, and the Minnesota Court of Appeals upheld the commission's decision. In December 1991 the commission granted a smaller increase, $53.5 million. Also in 1991, NSP won rate increases in South Dakota and Wisconsin, although these, too, were smaller than initially requested. In North Dakota, a court case over a rate increase was pending. NSP also reported that its pollution control efforts of the 1970s and 1980s meant the company would not face great setbacks as a result of the restrictions of the Clean Air Act amendments passed in 1990.

Anticipating a Deregulated World: 1990s

In 1992 the Minnesota Public Utilities Commission approved the storage of spent fuel rods in 17 above-ground casks outside the Prairie Island nuclear power plant. The Mdewakanton Sioux Indian tribe, whose reservation was adjacent to the site, and environmentalists were among those protesting the action. NSP said the 1,060 megawatt plant, which produced 20 percent of its total generating capacity, would have to be shut down by 1995 if additional storage space was not created. A planned permanent federal nuclear waste depository had yet to be established. Ruling that the above ground casks amounted to permanent storage, the Court of Appeals sent the issue to the Minnesota state legislature which gave final approval in 1994.

In 1995 NSP and Milwaukee-based Wisconsin Energy Corporation (WEC) announced a $6 billion merger plan which would create a new holding company, Primergy Corporation, based in Minneapolis and serving five states. The companies expected $2 billion in savings to come through consolidation over a ten-year period. Although market analysts and stockholders supported the merger, electric coops, industry groups, environmentalists, consumer organizations, and government regulators had reservations.

The merger plan was part of NSP's preparation for a future in which electric utilities would operate in a more competitive marketplace. In 1992, the federal government moved to allow the Federal Energy Regulatory Commission (FERC) to order electric companies to provide transmission service to other utilities and electric wholesalers, an action which supported the concept of increased competition among electric utilities. NSP Chairman and CEO James J. Howard, an executive in the telephone industry during deregulation, anticipated a time when the company would have to compete for business and pushed for streamlined operations. The company began to cut its workforce, including corporate positions, and revamp inefficient operations.

By late 1996 the NSP-WEC merger was in limbo. Tom Meersman and Susan E. Peterson wrote in a November 19, 1996, *Star Tribune* article, "Much of the debate in Minnesota as well as in previous hearings in Wisconsin and Washington, D.C., focuses on four issues: rates, control, market domination and the environment." NSP stock, which had risen at the time of the announcement of the merger, fluctuated during the prolonged approval process.

In spite of difficulties related to the merger, NSP stayed on track. NSP Gas added 14,000 customers in 1996: the business was growing at twice the national average. A new subsidiary, Seren Innovations, Inc., was created to provide services such as energy management, security control, and business information services by way of two-way communication networks.

Other nonregulated NSP subsidiaries included NRG Energy, Inc., the seventh fastest growing independent power producer in the world. The company built, managed, and operated power plants and was involved in projects using everything from coal to landfill gas. NRG Energy was expected to bring in 20 percent of NSP's earnings by the year 2000. Cenerprise, Inc., a gas and electric products and services company, operated nationwide, while Eloigne Company, which invested in affordable housing, operated primarily within NSP's service area.

In April 1997, Viking Gas Transmission Company, acquired by NSP in 1993, announced plans for an 800-mile pipeline to be built with TransCanada PipeLines Limited, one of North America's leading transporters of natural gas. The $1 billion gas transportation line was to begin in Emerson, Manitoba, and extend to Joliet, Illinois. NICOR Inc., a Naperville, Illinois-based holding company, also joined the partnership.

In May, NSP and WEC terminated their merger agreement. Approval had been granted by the state regulatory commissions in Michigan and North Dakota, but not in Minnesota or Wisconsin or by the FERC. Howard said in a press release, "What we encountered were regulatory agencies that were changing their merger policies as they were considering our filing." The two companies determined that changes in federal regulation would significantly reduce the benefits of the proposed merger.

NSP, of the late 1990s, was one of the most efficiently run utilities in the country and provided some of the cheapest energy to its customers. The company's two nuclear plants, in particular, were considered some of the best-run in the nation. But growth in the electric utility industry was slow under the system of regulation. Expansion of the company's nonregulated businesses, especially NRG Energy, appeared crucial to future growth. Although NSP's success in gaining natural gas customers—the gas business was regulated but not divided into designated territories—seemed to be of no less concern as NSP headed toward a less regulated future.

As the 20th century moved toward a close, the problem of nuclear waste storage heated up for power producers. The Department of Energy was required by Congress to have a permanent storage facility set to operate by January 31, 1998. It did not. NSP was looking at the potential of an early shut down of its Prairie Island plant because of the problem. The company responded by pushing for federal approval of the lawsuit-stalled storage site in Yucca Mountain, Nevada; suing the federal government for storage costs it had incurred; and planning for private storage options along with other utilities.

NSP was not alone in its desire to be rid of its radioactive waste; the Prairie Island Tribe also shared this goal. "The tribe contends its members have suffered from unexplained health problems including an unusually high number of cancer deaths," Julie Forster wrote in a July 1999 *Corporate Report-Minnesota* article.

On-site storage cost the company in other ways. While the Minnesota legislature allowed NSP to store its waste in above ground casks, it required the company to establish a renewable-energy fund to which it had to contribute $500,000 per year for each cask. The first payment of $3.5 million for seven casks came due in January 1999. The company was also required to generate 425 megawatts of electricity, or about 8 percent of total sales, from wind energy by 2002, according to the *National Journal*. Additionally, 2 percent of its gross operating revenue had to be earmarked for energy conservation programs.

Meanwhile, NSP had another plan in the works: a merger with Denver-based New Century Energies (NCE). Anticipating changes related to industry deregulation, the nation's mid-sized electric utilities were in a merger and acquisition mode, creating, they hoped, greater chances for survival in a more competitive climate. The merger between the two required regulatory approval from each state served and the Federal Energy Regulatory Commission. Combined, the company would rank among the nation's ten largest with nearly five million customers in 12 states.

While NCE had been growing its basic utility business at a faster rate than NSP, the Minnesota-based utility had excelled in the area of deregulated services. Mark Reilly reported in *CityBusiness* that NRG not only had become an important earnings generator for NSP but had risen in the ranks of independent power producers worldwide. Its core markets were in the U.S. Southwest and Northeast, Australia, and the Czech Republic. NRG had snapped up plants sold off by large utility companies shifting their concentration from power generation to transmission and distribution of power. Once in hand, NRG implemented cost cutting measures and made management changes at the plants.

While NRG flourished in 1999, NSP's energy sagged. The utilities industry as a whole lost value as investors moved into high growth technology stocks. Moreover, investors saw little immediate gain from the planned merger. The year's mild winter kept customers' gas and electric meters from spinning too fast, and the Minnesota Public Utilities Commission did not grant NSP's request for $35 million in conservation incentives.

Hoping to Excel in the 21st Century

The days looked brighter in 2000 for NSP. The spring spinoff NRG Energy ranked as the largest initial public offering in Minnesota history. Although NSP did not receive any of the nearly $600 million in proceeds, it held 82 percent of NRG's stock. Concurrently, a downturn on NASDAQ sent investors back into the utility sector.

In the summer, NSP merged with NCE, creating Xcel Energy Inc. with a service area stretching from the Canadian to the Mexican borders. In 2001, Xcel received the go ahead to build a power line linking Colorado to the eastern power grid.

However, the lights dimmed in 2002 when Xcel Energy needed to buy back NRG from the public. Wholesale power prices had fallen 90 percent since 1999, putting NRG on the ropes. Banks wanted more collateral to secure its $9 billion in debt. As majority shareholder, Xcel Energy already faced the potential of creditor lawsuits. According to Eric Wieffering of the *Star Tribune* (Minneapolis), a bankrupt NRG would cost the utility some $2.5 billion, the amount shareholders had invested in the unregulated power generating business.

Conversely from 1999 to 2001, Xcel Energy's combined gas and electricity revenue had grown by 40 percent and net income per share was up by 35 percent despite the rate freeze agreements made at the time of the merger. New factories and office towers and larger homes had increased usage. But demand dropped off in 2002, and profits Xcel Energy planned to use to bolster NRG dwindled. NRG Energy Inc. filed for bankruptcy in 2003.

During 2004, five electric utilities, Xcel Energy among them, faced a lawsuit brought by the attorneys general for eight states asking the companies to reduce carbon dioxide emissions which were contributing to global warming. Also during the year, the company began the process of seeking a 20-year extension of the license on its Monticello nuclear power plant. Xcel Energy said keeping the nuclear plant operating would be less costly to ratepayers than building a replacement plant. As the year wound down, Xcel Energy reached agreement with Colorado environmental and conservation groups paving the way for an expansion of its Comanche coal-burning plant near Pueblo. The fourth largest combination electric and natural gas company in the United States brought in total earnings of $356 million in 2004, down from $622 million in 2003.

Without admitting any wrongdoing, in early 2005 Xcel Energy agreed to pay $88 million to settle three lawsuits related to NRG Energy. Participating shareholders claimed Xcel Energy had hidden the extent of the impact its subsidiary's insolvency would have on the company's value.

The Xcel Energy of 2005 had gone back to basics, focusing on electric and natural gas service. The company was not alone. The Enron collapse of 2001 and California energy crisis of 2002 had helped drive utilities back to their more conservative roots. Out with the new and in with the old, Xcel Energy was building new plants and lobbying for rate increases.

Principal Subsidiaries

Northern States Power Company (Minnesota); Northern States Power Company (Wisconsin); Public Service Company of Colorado; Southwestern Public Service Company; Eloigne Company; Seren Innovations, Inc.; Quixx Corporation; Xcel Energy Services, Inc.

Principal Competitors

AEP Industries, Inc.; Aquila, Inc.; CenterPoint Energy.

Further Reading

Aven, Paula, "New Century on Brink of Merger," *Denver Business Journal*, February 18, 2000, p. 14B.

Dukart, James R., "Middleman No More," *CityBusiness* (Minneapolis), March 3, 2000, p. S50.

Forster, Julie, "Power Play," *Corporate Report—Minnesota*, July 1999, pp. 16+.

Geiselman, Bruce, "Eyes on the Five; States File Lawsuit Against 5 Utilities," *Waste News*, August 2, 2004.

Hanners, David, "Xcel Power Production Subsidiary Files for Bankruptcy Protection," *Knight-Ridder Tribune Business News*, May 15, 2003.

Huber, Tim, "Xcel Energy Gets Back to Basics with New Projects," *Saint Paul Pioneer Press*, April 24, 2005.

——, "Xcel Energy Seeks 20-Year Extension for Minnesota Nuclear Power Plant," *Knight-Ridder Tribune Business News*, October 17, 2004.

Kriz, Margaret, "Mountain of Trouble," *National Journal*, September 11, 1999.

McCartney, Jim, "Xcel Energy Will Pay $88 Million to Settle Securities Suits," *Saint Paul Pioneer Press* (St. Paul, Minnesota), January 15, 2005.

Meersman, Tom, "Radioactive Waste," *Star Tribune* (Minneapolis), December 16, 1995, p. 3B.

Meersman, Tom, and Susan E. Peterson, "The NSP Merger," *Star Tribune* (Minneapolis), November 19, 1996, p. 1A.

Niemela, Jennifer, "Mild Weather Was Least of NSP's Blows," *CityBusiness* (Minneapolis), July 7, 2000, p. S41.

Peterson, Susan E., "NSP Shareholders Overwhelmingly Approve Merger of Equals with Wisconsin Energy," *Star Tribune* (Minneapolis), September 14, 1995, p. 1D.

——, "NSP: Wired for Change," *Star Tribune* (Minneapolis), June 23, 1997, p. 1D.

——, "Two Executive Vice Presidents Are Leaving NSP As Part of a Reorganization of Top-Level Positions," *Star Tribune* (Minneapolis), December 2, 1992, p. 1D.

Pine, Carol, *NSP, Northern States People: The Past 70 Years,* Minneapolis: North Central Publishing, 1979.

Proctor, Cathy, "New Century Phasing Out Public Service," *Denver Business Journal*, July 28, 2000, p. 1A.

Raabe, Steve, "Colorado Clears Xcel Energy to Link State Power Grid to East Coast Supply," *Denver Post*, July 19, 2001.

——, "Industry Experts Say Xcel's Pueblo, Colo., Power Plant Deal Unprecedented," *Knight-Ridder Business News*, December 7, 2004.

Rebuffoni, Dean, "NSP Can Store Nuclear Waste," *Star Tribune* (Minneapolis), June 27, 1992, p. 1A.

Reilly, Mark, "A Power Surge," *CityBusiness* (Minneapolis), March 10, 2000, p. 1.

Rohloff, Greg, "Xcel Energy Mega-Merger Clears Final Hurdle," *Knight Ridder/Tribune Business News*, September 26, 2000.

Schafer, Lee, "Power Play," *Corporate Report Minnesota,* April 1996, pp. 36–41.

Wieffering, Eric, "Revenue Brownout; NRG Isn't Xcel Energy's Only Problem," *Star Tribune* (Minneapolis, MN), September 25, 2002, p. 1D.

——, "Xcel, NSP, NRG: What's It All Mean?," *Star Tribune* (Minneapolis), September 8, 2002, p. 1D.

—Maya Sahafi
—update: Kathleen Peippo

Xstrata PLC

Bahnhofstrasse 2, Postfach 102
Zug CH-6301
Switzerland
Telephone: +41 41 726 60 70
Fax: +41 41 726 60 89

4th Floor, Panton House, 25 Haymarket
London
SW1Y 4EN
United Kingdom
Telephone: +44 20 7968 2800
Fax: +44 20 7968 2810
Web site: http://www.xstrata.com

Public Company
Incorporated: 1926 as Suedelektra Holding AG; 1999 as
   Xstrata AG
Employees: 17,062
Sales: $6.09 billion (2004)
Stock Exchanges: London Zurich
Ticker Symbol: XTA
NAIC: 212234 Copper Ore and Nickel Ore Mining;
   212111 Bituminous Coal and Lignite Surface Mining;
   212112 Bituminous Coal Underground Mining;
   212291 Uranium-Radium-Vanadium Ore Mining;
   212299 Other Metal Ore Mining; 331511 Iron
   Foundries; 331522 Nonferrous (Except Aluminum)
   Die-Castings

Xstrata PLC has risen rapidly in the early 2000s to become one of the world's major mining groups. The company is active in commodity mining markets: coal; copper; zinc; and alloys. Xstrata is the world's leading producer of export thermal coal, with mines in South Africa and in New South Wales and Queensland in Australia, and is also a major producer of coking coal from its site in Queensland. The company owns or has interests in more than 30 coal mines, and produces more than 70 million tons per year, more than two-thirds of which are in Australia. Some 90 percent of the group's coal production is destined for the export market. Coal represents approximately 35 percent of the group's total revenues, which topped $6 billion in 2004. Xstrata's Copper production takes place in mines in Queensland, Australia, and in Argentina and Peru, including the group's 50 percent share of Argentina's Alumbrera open-pit gold and copper mine. Copper accounts for nearly half of the group's revenues. Zinc (including lead) production is based on the former Asturiana de Zinc, acquired in 2001, with zinc and lead smelters in Spain, Germany, Australia, and the United Kingdom. Xstrata's Alloys division is the world's largest producer of ferroalloys, including chrome and vanadium, with operations centered on South Africa and Australia. Xstrata's transformation into a major mining firm was achieved through an ambitious acquisition program costing more than $3 billion. This process has been led by former Billiton executive, and one of the architects of the BHP Billiton merger, Mick Davis. Xstrata continues to seek large-scale acquisitions into the mid-2000s. Its takeover bid for Australia's WMC Resources in 2005 failed, however. Xstrata is listed on the London Stock Exchange but is headquartered in Zug, Switzerland.

Financial Investments in the 1920s

Xstrata originated as a financial investment vehicle founded in 1926 as Suedra Holding AG in Zug, Switzerland. Suedelektra's founders included a number of privately owned banks, as well as a group of industrialists. The company's initial targets were the newly developing South American energy and infrastructure markets. Among the group's earliest investments were stakes in Lima Light & Power in Peru, and Argentina's Empresas Electricas de Bahia Blanca and Americana de Luz y Traccion.

The Depression era, however, quickly wiped out much of Suedelektra's investments, and the company lay relatively dormant until the end of World War II. Activity at Suedelektra picked up again following the war, and the company developed a strong assets portfolio throughout the Latin American region. Political upheavals in the region during the 1960s and 1970s once again dragged down the value of the group's investments; by the end of the 1970s, many of Suedelektra's assets had been nationalized. Although the company was to receive compensation for part of its holdings in the late 1980s, Suedelektra abandoned its active infrastructure investments, converting to

Company Perspectives:

We will grow and manage a diversified portfolio of metals and mining businesses with the single aim of delivering industry-leading returns for our shareholders. We can achieve this only through genuine partnerships with employees, customers, shareholders, local communities and other stakeholders, which are based on integrity, co-operation, transparency and mutual value-creation.

the less volatile securities market. Suedelektra also had gone public, with a listing on the Zurich Stock Exchange. By the end of the 1980s, however, a majority of Suedelektra's stock was held by the Union Bank of Switzerland.

In 1990, Union Bank decided to sell its majority stake to the Swiss trading group Glencore International. Formed in 1974, Glencore had risen to become a major, diversified corporation, with a particular interest in the trading of natural resources as well as a number of industrial holdings. Glencore achieved a degree of notoriety, however, after its founder, Marc Rich, was accused of racketeering by the United States. (Rich later received a controversial pardon from personal friend and departing President Bill Clinton.)

Under Glencore, Suedelektra embarked on its second life. Nonetheless, the company clung to its roots as a venture capitalist, now with a focus more directed at the natural resources market. In 1991, Suedelektra entered the oil and gas industry with the purchase of a stake in Argentina's newly privatized Santa Cruz 1 oil fields. By 1992, however, Suedelektra had acquired control of Santa Cruz, marking the company's transition from venture capitalist to an investment group with direct control of its holdings.

Second Life in the 1990s

Suedelektra's interests became increasingly industrial. In 1994, for example, the company acquired Chromecorp Holdings, a major ferrochrome producer based in South Africa. In that year, as well, the company acquired Chile's Forestal del Sur, a producer of wood chips for the paper industry. In 1995, the company turned to Australia, entering the coal industry with the purchase of a 70 percent stake in Abelshore Limited. That purchase boosted Suedelektra's revenues by more than one-third. Fueling the group's expansion was the successful listing of Chromecorp on the Johannesburg Stock Exchange that year.

Yet Suedelektra remained something of an oddity within the overall Glencore group, which by then was more focused on its metals and mining commodities trading activities. Suedelektra's traditional structure, as a hands-off investment vehicle, also appeared out of place in fast-growing Glencore International. In 1996, therefore, Glencore put a new management team in place at Suedelektra, led by Daniel Sauter and Jean-Pierre Conrad. Sauter and Conrad then launched Suedelektra on a corporate makeover, with a focus on the steel metals market.

Suedelektra made its first purchase in that direction, paying $90 million to acquire a 23 percent share of Mount Holly, an

aluminum smelter operation based in South Carolina in the United States. In 1997, Suedelektra stepped up its metals business with an entry into the ferrochrome alloys market, acquiring South Africa's Rhoex, a major vanadium producer, for $61 million. By the end of that year, Suedelektra had completed the purchase of a second vanadium producer, Vantech, also in South Africa, paying $82 million.

In order to fuel its transformation, Suedelektra began selling off its now noncore assets in 1997. That effort helped to raise more than $220 million by the beginning of the 2000s, compared with expenditures nearing $700 million since 1992. Part of that spending went toward the purchase of full control of Chromecorp and Rhoex, for $35 million and $14 million, respectively, in 1998. That year saw the group's largest acquisition to date, of South Africa's ferrochrome producer CMI, for $215 million. In 1999, to reflect the change in the nature of its operations, Suedelektra took on the new name of Xstrata AG.

Xstrata's transformation was completed, in large part, by 2001, when the company expanded into the zinc and lead market with the acquisition of Spain's Asturiana de Zinc S.A. The purchase placed Xstrata among the world's leaders in the zinc and lead market, paving the way for Xstrata's developing zinc operations not only in Spain, but in Germany, the United Kingdom, and Australia. The Asturiana acquisition, however, saddled Xstrata with a heavy debt, and the company was forced to consider raising equity to bring down its gearing ratio, which stood at a dangerous 80 percent. In 2001, however, Sauter and Conrad abruptly resigned from the company.

Mining Major for the 2000s

Glencore, which was busy preparing the launch of a new publicly listed company, called Enex, for its own South African and Australian mining interests, went looking for a replacement for Sauter and Conrad. Glencore's choice fell to South African native Mick Davis, who, as finance director with Billiton, had played a pivotal role in orchestrating its massive $40 billion merger with BHP. The merger had created BHP Billiton, the world's second largest mining group, with a listing in London but headquarters in Melbourne. Davis, however, was unwilling to uproot his family to move to Melbourne. As a result, following the merger Davis was offered the somewhat secondary position as development director at the company's London office.

Davis let his discontent be known and was quickly approached by Glencore to become Xstrata's CEO. Davis agreed, a decision that initially raised eyebrows in the mining industry. In Davis's own words, Xstrata was ''going nowhere.'' Yet Davis, who had long played second fiddle in the finance director position, saw an opportunity to take on a leadership role and transform Xstrata into a world player in the mining industry.

That transformation came more quickly than Davis expected. Glencore had reached the final stage of Enex's initial public offering (IPO), and by September 2001 had entered the final days of an international road show in order to drum up interest in the investment community. Yet the terrorist attacks of September 11 pulled the rug out from under the Enex IPO.

The collapse of the Enex offering signaled an opportunity for Davis and Xstrata. At the end of September 2001, Davis

Key Dates:

1926: Suedelektra Holding is founded by a group of Swiss banks and industrialists in order to acquire investments in South American energy and infrastructure industries.

1990: Suedelektra, by now a securities management group, is acquired by Glencore International.

1992: Suedelektra acquires a stake in Santa Cruz oil and gas fields in Argentina.

1994: The company acquires Chromecorp in South Africa and Forestal, a wood chips producer, in Chile.

1995: Abelshore, an Australian coal miner, is acquired.

1996: A new management team shifts strategy to focus on metals, acquiring a stake in Mount Holly in the United States.

1997: The company acquires Rhoex and Vantech in South Africa and begins selling off noncore assets.

1998: The company acquires CMI in South Africa and completes control of Chromecorp and Rhoex.

1999: The company changes its name to Xstrata AG.

2000: Asturiana de Zinc in Spain is acquired.

2001: Mick Davis becomes company CEO and leads the acquisition of Glencore's coal mining interests in Australia and South Africa.

2003: The company acquires MIM Holdings in Australia and its coal and metals mining operations.

2004: The company launches a hostile takeover bid for WMC Resources in Australia.

2005: The company loses its bid for WMC; plans to seek new acquisitions are announced.

approached Glencore with the proposal that Xstrata buy up Glencore's Australian and South African coal interests. The companies reached an agreement by March 2002. As part of the deal, Xstrata relaunched itself as Xstrata PLC, with a highly successful IPO on the London Stock Exchange. Xstrata then paid Glencore more than $2.5 billion for the acquisition of the Enex operations.

Through 2002, Xstrata continued making a series of bolt-on acquisitions, spending some $230 million to buy up additional coal mines in Australia, as well as a new zinc smelter in Nordenham from Metaleurope. In the meantime, Davis continued looking for the next transformational deal.

That deal came in 2003, as the industry cycle bottomed out, leaving Australia's MIM Holdings, the country's largest remaining independent mining group, in financial difficulties. Davis approached MIM with a takeover offer worth $1.7 billion which was considered as too low by many, including MIM's own managing director. Nonetheless, the offer was accepted by a majority of MIM's shareholders and the deal went through.

The addition of MIM's vast mining holdings in Australia, which included coal as well as copper, lead, and zinc, boosted Xstrata into the ranks of world mining leaders, with sales of more than $6 billion by the end of 2004. The timing of the acquisition was considered by some as a "masterstroke"—

soon after the acquisition, commodities prices began a steady upswing.

Buoyed by the success of the MIM acquisition, Davis began seeking out a new major acquisition. In November 2004, Xstrata launched a bid worth AUD 7.4 billion ($5.8 billion) for Australian mining giant WMC Resources. Yet that offer quickly became a hostile one, and in early 2005 a new suitor for WMC appeared—Davis's former employer, BHP Billiton, which topped Xstrata with an offer for more than $8 billion in March 2005.

The WMC deal might have boosted Xstrata into the ranks of global giants such as BHP Billiton and Anglo American. Undaunted, Davis announced his intention to continue to pursue large-scale acquisitions in his effort to transform Xstrata into a global mining major for the 2000s.

Principal Subsidiaries

Abelshore Pty. Limited (Australia); Alloys; Asturiana de Zinc S.A. (Spain); AZSA Holdings Pty. Limited (Australia); Britannia Refined Metals Limited; Char Technology (Pty.) Ltd. (South Africa); Cook Resources Mining Pty. Limited (Australia; 95%); Cumnock Coal Limited (Australia; 84%); Enex Foydell Limited (Australia); Enex Liddell Pty. Limited (Australia); Enex Oakbridge Pty. Limited (Australia); Ernest Henry Mining Pty. Ltd. (Australia); Hunter Valley Coal Corporation Pty. Limited (Australia); Jonsha Pty. Limited (Australia); Maloma Colliery Ltd. (South Africa; 75%); Minera Alumbrera Limited Antigua (50%); Mount Isa Mines Limited (Australia); Oakbridge Pty. Limited (Australia; 78%); Oceanic Coal (Australia) Limited (Australia); Ravensworth Operations Pty. Limited (Australia); Saxonvale Coal Pty. Limited (Australia); Tavistock Collieries (Pty.) Ltd. (South Africa); The Wallerawang Collieries Limited (Australia; 74.1%); Ulan Coal Mines Limited (Australia; 90%); Xstrata (South Africa) (Pty.) Ltd. (South Africa); Xstrata Coal Investments Limited (Australia); Xstrata Coal Marketing AG (Switzerland); Xstrata Coal Pty. Limited (Australia); Xstrata Coal Queensland Pty. Limited (Australia); Xstrata Technology Pty. Ltd. (Australia); Xstrata Windimurra Pty. Ltd. (Australia); Xstrata Zinc GmbH (Germany).

Principal Competitors

Anglo American PLC; BHP Billiton PLC; Societe Nationale Industrielle et Miniere; Samancor Ltd.; Highveld Steel and Vanadium Corporation Limited; Corporacion Nacional Del Cobre De Chile; Gordo y Cia; Umicore; WMC Resources Ltd.; Elkem ASA.

Further Reading

Cooper, Mike, "Xstrata Combines Global Copper Businesses," *American Metal Market,* January 15, 2004, p. 5.

Cope, Nigel, "Mick Davis: Big Hitter Prepares Xstrata for Joining the Market's Elite," *Independent,* March 11, 2002, p. 15.

"Deep Down Under," *Economist,* April 12, 2003.

Gooding, Ken, "Xstrata on the Acquisition Trail," *Africa News Service,* February 12, 2003.

Hall, William, and Matthew Jones, "Mining Group Moves to Scale Up Its Operations," *Financial Times,* February 22, 2002, p. 30.

Klinger, Peter, ''Xstrata on the Acquisition Trail,'' *Times* (London), March 12, 2005, p. 63.

Laurance, Ben, ''The Mining Boss Who Struck Gold with a Deal That He Mapped Out on a Matchbox,'' *Mail on Sunday,* August 17, 2003.

Lynch, Martin, ''One–Trick Pony,'' *Australasian Business Intelligence,* January 6, 2005.

Wisenthal, Stephen, ''Xstrata Goes Universal,'' *Australasian Business Intelligence,* March 14, 2005.

''Xstrata (XTA),'' *Investors Chronicle,* November 26, 2004.

—M.L. Cohen

Zappos.com, Inc.

500 E. Warm Springs Rd., Suite 100
Las Vegas, Nevada 89119
U.S.A.
Telephone: (702) 943-7777
Fax: (702) 943.7778
Web site: http://www.zappos.com

Private Company
Founded: 1999 as Shoesite.com
Employees: 400
Sales: $300 million (2005 est.)
NAIC: 448210 Shoe Stores

While its name only hints at its raison d'être, Zappos.com, Inc. is the Internet's premier shoe source, with styles and sizes to fit every foot and desire. In addition to 500 well known brands of shoes, sandals, boots, and athletic footwear, Zappos.com sells a growing range of accessories including designer handbags, belts, wallets, socks, and even diaper bags. What sets Zappos.com apart from other shoe sites is its fast, free shipping and ironclad return policy; any item may be returned within one year of purchase with no shipping or restocking fees. For fiscal 2005, Zappos.com had estimated revenues of $300 million.

In the Beginning, 1999

Zappos.com was born of one man's frustration to find his favorite pair of boots. He looked high and low for the size and color he wanted and came up empty-handed. It should not be so hard to find a pair of shoes, right? So thought Nick Swinmurn, an Internet entrepreneur who decided to put his money where his mouth was and start his own shoe store. The catch was that this would be no ordinary shoe store, but an online megastore stocking all colors, styles, and sizes—and shipping orders anywhere in the world. Swinmurn reasoned that plenty of people shopped for clothing and shoes from catalogues, so why not an online footwear showcase, complete with photos and sizing charts?

Swinmurn was born and raised in California. He attended the University of California at Santa Barbara and earned a degree in film studies in 1996. After graduation, Swinmurn worked for the San Diego Padres before joining Internet pioneer Autoweb.com as marketing manager. His success there led to a position as webmaster for Silicon Graphics, then to his own startup in 1999. After managing to raise about $150,000 in initial capital, Swinmurn christened his Internet shoe store Shoesite.com and launched it in June 1999.

By the end of July, however, Swinmurn changed his mind and revamped the cyber shoe source, calling it Zappos.com. The name played off the Spanish word for shoes, *zapatos*, and the new site had more selection (over 100 brands for men, women, and children) and offered accounts and passwords for returning customers. In addition, Swinmurn made deals with shoe manufacturers to ship orders, partnered with AOL and several shopping sites to be a featured link, and in a stroke of marketing genius sponsored the Golden State Warriors NBA basketball team for the 1999–2000 season.

After the name change and relaunch, Swinmurn and a handful of employees tried to give Zappos.com the feel of a specialized brick-and-mortar retailer. There were separate pages for major shoe brands, sizing charts (complete with a printable form to measure feet), and a toll free number to speak to a live customer service representative. The timing seemed right too, since Forrester Research, Inc., an Internet trend watcher, released data finding that online shopping would top $1.6 billion in 1999 and footwear purchasing alone would account for some $120 million for the year.

If the Shoe Fits (or Even If It Does Not): 2000–03

Within months of its founding Zappos gained a boost with the hiring of a former footwear buyer from Nordstrom, Fred Mossler, who came on board as senior vice-president. Another important addition came from within its office space. Located in the well known Marquee building in the Bay Area was another firm called Venture Frog Incubators. Tony Hsieh, a Harvard graduate, had vast experience in the dot.com industry after working for Oracle and founding LinkExchange, which he sold to Microsoft in 1998. Hsieh founded Venture Frog to invest in Internet startups, and one such success was web browser AskJeeves.

In 2000 Venture Frog and Zappos came together when Hsieh invested $1.1 million in the e-tailer and came on board as co-chief executive with Swinmurn. By this time Zappos was luring buyers to its site through a number of innovations including more famous brands, contests and giveaways, and an agreement with the West Coast's Shoe Pavilion to run its e-commerce site (shoepavilion.com) and showcase its footwear. *Footwear News* (May 15, 2000) called the partnership "another marriage of bricks and clicks," which seemed to benefit both traditional retailers and their online counterparts. Zappos had grown to 30 employees, offered customers more than 150 different brands of shoes, and reached sales of $1.6 million for 2000.

Zappos quickly gained a foothold in the online retail industry, becoming the world's largest shoe store by early 2001 despite the onset of a recession. Zappos was succeeding because it had more selection than any shoe retailer, on or off the Internet, and shoppers took notice. While retail analysts still considered shoes a difficult sell over the Internet—photos were not always accurate, it was impossible to try them on, and so forth—Zappos no-fuss money-back guarantee won glowing reviews from shoppers, and more importantly, loyalty. This allegiance helped propel the firm's revenues to $8.6 million for 2001, despite the crash and burn of hundreds of dotcoms. Two key elements set Zappos apart from its rivals, according to Swinmurn: "The best strategy is selection and service," he told *Footwear News* (February 26, 2001). "If customers can find what they're looking for and have a great experience doing so, they'll be back."

An important facet of service, Swinmurn and Hsieh had learned, was to no longer outsource shipping. Order fulfillment could only be controlled and quality maintained if Zappos had its own warehouse and merchandise. Accordingly, warehouse space of over 100,000 square feet was secured in Kentucky and Zappos took over all aspects of order fulfillment.

The firm's return policy also continued to evolve, becoming a primary attraction for shoppers. Not only did Zappos provide free shipping on orders, often overnight, but free shipping on returns (within 60 days) and no restocking fees as well. With fast service, no-hassle returns, and an ever-increasing selection of footwear, Zappos was not your average shoe retailer. By 2002 the cyberstore had again surpassed expectations, with sales more than tripling from the previous year to $32 million. Swinmurn and Hsieh believed Zappos would more than double its revenues the next year, despite the instability of the economy as a whole.

As Zappos became the darling of the online retail shoe industry, Swinmurn and Hsieh fine-tuned the firm. For marketing, the executives believed word-of-mouth testimonials were more important than traditional media spending—though Zappos did spend about 15 percent of its revenues on advertising, usually for ads with online browsers and portals. Customer referrals, however, proved far more effective as more and more shoppers visited the Zappos site and literally walked away happy. Zappos also made itself available to comparison shopping sites, attracting buyers through reasonable prices and its lack of shipping charges. By making returns as easy as ordering (upping the return policy from 60 days to 365 from date of purchase), Zappos continued to set itself apart from the other online retailers flooding the Web.

Not only were new Internet-created retailers popping up, but popular brick-and-mortar retailers had begun offering their products to online shoppers. From higher-end merchandisers (such as Nordstrom, Nike, and Coach) to bargain stores (such as Kmart, Wal-mart, and Target), every retailer worth its salt had realized the value of the Internet as a business tool. Zappos, however, remained ahead of the curve. By 2003 sales had soared to $70 million and the online retailer had opened two brick-and-mortar stores as well as a warehouse in Kentucky to expedite shipping. Zappos had also begun to sell accessories including purses and handbags that matched some of its designer shoe lines, with apparel a possibility for the future.

Onward and Upward, 2004 and Beyond

In 2004 Swinmurn, as chairman, and Hsieh, as chief executive, made several critical decisions regarding Zappos.com's future, including a move from its offices in Silicon Valley to Las Vegas, Nevada, and securing funding for the cyber retailer's expansion. The former helped cut costs across the board; the latter came from two sources: $20 million from Sequoia Capital Partners and an increase of its line of credit with Wells Fargo to $40 million. By this time the Zappos site was as much about style and content as sales. The online e-tailer's production staff had grown to ten employees whose mission was to provide each major shoe brand its own "boutique" or page, with merchandise shot from multiple angles for viewing from the top, side, and even 360 degrees. Zappos offered its shoppers over 200 brands of shoes for men, women, and children, including Adidas, Airwalks, Birkenstock, Dr. Martens, Nike, Skechers, Timberland, Vans, and designer labels including Steven Madden, Charles David, Kenneth Cole, Isaac Mizrahi, Michael Kors, and Calvin Klein.

From 2003 to 2004 Zappos had more than doubled its inventory from over $5 million to $13 million according to *Footwear News* (April 12, 2004) and had plans to double its warehouse space as well. By the end of 2004 Zappos outperformed both analysts' and its management's projections, finishing the year with sales exceeding $180 million.

By 2005 designers and customers alike flocked to Zappos, which had proven itself as the Internet's leading shoe source as brick-and-mortar retailers suffered flat sales. To stay ahead of its growing competition Zappos continued to add to its lineup—which now topped 500 brands, nearly 60,000 styles, and more than a million pairs of shoes—including luxe offerings from

---

Key Dates:

1999: Zappos.com is founded by Nick Swinmurn.
2000: Zappos.com gets $1.1 million in funding and a new CEO from Venture Frog.
2001: Sales climb to $8.6 million as Zappos gains momentum.
2002: Sales for Zappos.com top $170 million and the firm relocates to Las Vegas.
2003: Two brick-and-mortar Zappos stores are opened.
2004: Zappos relocates to Las Vegas and secures venture capital.
2005: The Zappos site offers nearly 60,000 styles of footwear for men, women, and children.

Donna Karan, Pucci, Marc Jacobs, and even celebrity designs from Carlos Santana and Jennifer Lopez. Additionally, Zappos had expanded its accessories line to include socks, wallets, belts, and diaper bags, while Zappos Couture debuted with its own web address (couture.zappos.com). For those against the use of leather, Zappos even had "vegetarian" footwear. To support its rapid expansion the e-tailer's workforce had grown to more than 400 employees. Sales for the year were projected to reach as high as $300 million, and even higher for 2006.

Zappos.com's success was due in large part to its loyal customers and a return rate the company reported as high as 40 percent. By providing a simple, easy to use site and an unending inventory of shoes in virtually every style, size, and color, Zappos gave prospective buyers what brick-and-mortar retailers could not—a virtually stress-free shopping experience with no down side—no shipping charges, no-hassle returns, no problems.

Principal Competitors

Bluefly.com; FogDog.com; Gear.com; Onlineshoes.com; Shoebuy.com; Shoedini.com; Shoemallusa.com; Shoes.com; shoesonthenet.com.

Further Reading

Abel, Katie, "Sole Searching," *Footwear News,* August 2, 2004, p. 46.

Bernard, Sharyn, "Webbed Feet," *Footwear News,* February 4, 2000, p. 34.

Carr, Debra, "Zappos.com Out to Mirror 'Store' Service," *Footwear News,* November 1, 1999, p. 7.

Case, John, "Great Timing," *Inc.,* October 15, 2004.

DeMazza, Mike, "The Digital Players," *Footwear News,* April 12, 2004, p. 19.

"Footwear Briefs," *Footwear News,* August 23, 1999, p. 23.

"Footwear Briefs," *Footwear News,* May 15, 2000, p. 6.

Kooser, Amanda, et al, "Beyond Their Years [Profiles]," *Entrepreneur,* November 2003, pp. 74+.

Lambert, Phineas, "Zappos Taps Sequoia," *Daily Deal,* November 1, 2004.

Lenetz, Dana," In an Uncertain Cyber Retail World, Zappos Shows Promise," *Footwear News,* May 21, 2001, p. 6.

LoRusso, Maryann, "Shoe Bytes," *Footwear News,* March 6, 2000, p. 12S.

Materna, Jessica, "Seeking a Glass Slipper," *San Francisco Business Times,* June 23, 2000, p. 18.

Muir, Lucie, "Footwear Dotcoms Stride Ahead," *International Herald Tribune,* February 25, 2005, p. 14.

Mullins, David P., "Click Backs," *Footwear News,* February 19, 2001, p. 39.

Selinsky, Debbie, "If the Shoe Fits," *Success,* April 2001, p. 18.

Waters, Richard, "Trial and Error Show the Path to Success: Online Footwear," *Financial Times,* March 9, 2005, p. 9.

Zmuda, Natalie, "Retailers Sharpen Growing Online Strategies," *Footwear News,* December 1, 2003, p. 10.

—Nelson Rhodes

Ziff Davis Media Inc.

28 East 28th Street
New York, New York 10016-7930
U.S.A.
Telephone: (212) 503-3500
Fax: (212) 503-5696
Web site: http://www.ziffdavis.com

Wholly Owned Subsidiary of Ziff Davis Holdings Inc.
Founded: 1927 as Popular Aviation Company
Employees: 525
Sales: $204.5 million (2004)
NAIC: 511120 Periodical Publishers; 516110 Internet
  Publishing and Broadcasting

Ziff Davis Media Inc. is one of the largest publishers of technology and video game magazines in the United States. Among the company's key publications are the consumer-oriented *PC Magazine, Sync,* and *ExtremeTech;* the business-focused *eWEEK, CIO Insight,* and *Baseline;* and in the gaming world, *Electronic Gaming Monthly, Computer Gaming World,* and *Official U.S. PlayStation Magazine.* These titles garner a collective 20 percent of the advertising pages in the U.S. technology magazine industry. Their combined circulation is 2.5 million, led by the flagship *PC Magazine,* which boasts a paid circulation of 700,000, and the titles are estimated to reach more than 22 million people per month. The company also licenses its content and brands to licensees who produce titles in some 40 international markets, in 20 languages, and Ziff Davis Media also manages a number of Internet web sites, both magazine companion sites and independent sites for technology and video game enthusiasts. About 64 percent of Ziff Davis's revenue is derived from advertising, while subscription and newsstand sales accounts for about 17 percent. The remaining 19 percent comes from other revenue sources, including mailing list rentals, custom conferences and events, and eNewsletters.

The history of Ziff Davis Media is unusually complex, highlighted by three major events—a huge asset sale (1985) and two breakups of the company into several separate pieces (1994 and 2000). The company also evolved significantly over the years. It started out publishing specialty consumer magazines and then branched out into business niche publications, before refocusing on the computer magazine niche following the 1985 divestments. It then branched out again, into such related areas as trade shows and exhibitions, database and CD-ROM publishing, and online publishing. Following the 1994 breakup, it focused on its technology publications and the ZDNet online content site. The company soon regained a presence in the trade show field and launched a cable television channel, ZDTV (later TechTV). But then in 2000, the company was broken apart yet again, with the technology publications gaining independence within Ziff Davis Media Inc., and the other Ziff units going their separate ways. Since 2000 Ziff Davis Media has been wholly owned by Ziff Davis Holdings Inc., a publicly traded holding company majority owned and controlled by Willis Stein & Partners, L.P., a private equity investment firm.

Niche Magazine Pioneer

The ultimate predecessor of the company was effectively formed in 1927—initially as Popular Aviation Company, becoming Ziff-Davis Publishing Company shortly thereafter. Founded by majority partner William B. Ziff, World War I flyer, author, and lecturer, and minority partner Bernard Davis, the company launched a line of hobby and leisure magazines with *Popular Aviation* (still published today as *Aviation*). During the early years, the company grew at a tremendous rate (expanding to 32 times its initial size in its first ten years), publishing a combination of reference, trade, and juvenile books; "pulp" magazines such as *Amazing Stories, Air Adventures, Mammoth Detective, Mammoth Mystery,* and *Mammoth Western;* and specialty consumer magazines such as *Modern Bride, Popular Aviation, Popular Electronics,* and *Radio News.* Although the company was successful with most of its various publishing ventures, William Ziff never devoted his full attention to the business, preferring to focus on his writing, flying, and other interests, so Davis effectively handled day-to-day operations. By the early 1950s, the company was losing money.

When Ziff died of a heart attack in 1953, his share in the company passed to his son, William B. Ziff, Jr., then 24 and a student of philosophy. He surprised his family by deciding to

---

Company Perspectives:

We distinguish ourselves as the premier technology authority at work, home and play *through comprehensive labs-based evaluations, trusted buying advice, recognized industry experts, and thought-provoking news, reviews, opinions and insights. Reaching more than 22 million passionate readers and event attendees, Ziff Davis Media provides total market coverage, from corporate technology buyers and users to consumer enthusiasts and gamers, through our portfolio of award-winning brands.*

We provide our readers, who are well-educated, influential buyers of technology and other products and decision-makers in their professional fields and households, with the information they need to make important purchasing decisions.

To our advertising and marketing customers, we deliver access to the content environment and community necessary to reach their most important audience, and, most importantly, help them drive sales growth for their companies.

This passion, focus and commitment have made us a leader within our industry.

---

give up his promising academic career to run Ziff-Davis. Unlike his father, he immediately immersed himself in the business, buying out Davis in 1956. He concentrated on expanding the company's specialty consumer line by aggressively acquiring additional niche magazines. His timing was perfect in that the arrival of television as *the* medium for mass communication spelled the downturn for general-interest magazines such as *Life* and the *Saturday Evening Post.* Ziff's response to television was to focus on publications that were tightly focused on narrow topics, giving readers specialized information they could obtain nowhere else and providing advertisers an audience tailored for their products. Over the next 30 years, Ziff-Davis acquired such titles as *Car & Driver, Popular Mechanics, Psychology Today,* and *Stereo Review,* identifying each as the market leader in its particular field or one that Ziff-Davis could move into that position.

Meanwhile Ziff recognized another lucrative area for growth through the acquisition of what *Newsweek* called "obscure but highly profitable trade publications." Similar to Ziff's consumer titles, these business journals were each targeted at a narrow audience, primarily people in the travel and aviation industries for whom the titles became "must" reading. The titles included *Business & Commercial Aviation, Hotel & Travel Index, Travel Weekly, World Aviation Directory,* and the flagship of the group, *Meetings & Conventions,* which by 1983 generated $12 million in annual revenues.

In 1969 Ziff Communications Company was formed and Ziff-Davis became one of its divisions. At this time, Ziff, Jr., transferred ownership through trust funds to his three sons, who held a 90 percent interest, and three nephews, who held the remaining 10 percent. Ziff himself remained in firm control of the company throughout this period as chairman, with a hands-on management style criticized by some as autocratic but difficult to question given the company's continued profitability.

Besides innovation in developing special interest magazines, Ziff Communications also pioneered in its approaches to market research and advertising. Through heavy expenditures on market research, the company gathered detailed profiles of who was reading each magazine, the content they sought, and the advertising to which they might respond. This data helped each editor tailor his or her magazine to the readership and enabled the advertising salespeople to precisely target potential clients. The market research data was also shared with the advertisers themselves to design campaigns in what was known as "consultative selling." Another advertising innovation was offering clients discounts for placing the same ad in a group of related magazines. By 1984, these strategies had fueled the company's continuing growth, with the group of Ziff consumer magazines alone posting estimated annual revenues of $140 million.

Early 1980s: Expanding into Computer Magazines and Databases

According to many observers, Ziff had become bored with the business and with his success when in the early 1980s he began to take Ziff Communications into new territory. In 1979 he spent $89 million to purchase Rust Craft Greeting Cards Incorporated for its six television stations, but within a few years he sold them for $100 million, saying that television was not the "turn-on" he had hoped for. A longer-lasting and eventually more successful foray was into a new area of specialty publishing: computer magazines. The initial titles in this line, such as *PCjr,* were developed in-house beginning in 1981, but Ziff Communications soon returned to its acquisition strategy, most notably through the purchase of *PC Magazine* in 1982. The beginning years for these magazines were difficult, however, as the boom in the computer industry spawned a boom in the publication of specialty computer magazines. Although most of these titles were losing money in the early 1980s, the losses eventually represented an investment that was recouped many times over. Similarly, another new Ziff venture at this time was the 1980 acquisition of Information Access Company (IAC), a pioneer in electronic publishing and one of the first companies to produce databases on CD-ROM, including *Magazine Index, National Newspaper Index,* and *Trade and Industry Index.* IAC designed its InfoTrac workstations that accessed these databases to be user-friendly and offered full text on some of them, providing a competitive advantage over other indexes that offered only article abstracts.

Meanwhile, Ziff's consumer and business publications were reaching their peak of success. By 1984, many of these magazines were the circulation and/or revenue leaders in their respective markets. *Car & Driver* outpaced *Road & Track, Popular Photography* was the top choice for photographers, and *Cycle* led *Cycle World* for motorcyclists. Annual revenue for the most part was increasing. For example, *Car & Driver* posted $33 million in revenue in 1983, a gain of 18.6 percent over the previous year. The business publications were in similarly strong positions as market leaders—with $12 million in 1983 revenue for *Meetings & Conventions,* an increase of 20.5 percent—and enjoyed particularly high margins. Many in the industry were surprised, then, by the October 1984 announcement that Ziff was placing 24 magazines up for sale, 12 in its consumer group and 12 in its business group. Rumors soon began to circulate that William Ziff, Jr., was becoming progres-

Key Dates:

1927: William B. Ziff and Bernard Davis found Popular Aviation Company, publisher of *Popular Aviation* magazine; the company is soon renamed Ziff-Davis Publishing Company.

1953: Ziff dies and is succeeded by his son, William B. Ziff, Jr.

1956: Ziff, Jr., buys out Davis.

1969: Ziff Communications Company is formed, with Ziff-Davis becoming one of its divisions.

1980: Database publisher Information Access Company (IAC) is acquired.

1981: Ziff completes its first foray into computer magazines, with launch of *PCjr*.

1982: Company acquires *PC Magazine*.

1984: Company sells consumer and business magazines to focus on computer magazines and IAC.

1993: Ziff, Jr., retires; Eric Hippeau takes over as chairman.

1994: First consumer computing magazines debut; Ziff-Davis Publishing is sold to Forstmann Little & Co.; IAC is sold to The Thomson Corporation; and Ziff-Davis Exhibitors is sold to Softbank Corporation; Ziff-Davis Publishing launches online news service ZDNet.

1996: Ziff-Davis Publishing is sold to Softbank.

1998: Softbank takes company public as Ziff-Davis Inc.

2000: Ziff-Davis sells its publishing arm to private investors, who rename the unit Ziff Davis Media Inc.

2002: Buffeted by the tech ad recession and verging on bankruptcy, company completes a sweeping financial reorganization.

sively more ill with prostate cancer and wished to simplify his estate and protect his family's future. His three sons were 14, 18, and 20.

Mid-1980s Through Early 1990s: Focusing on Computer Magazines, Expanding into Trade Shows, Internet

After much speculation about possible purchasers, receipt of a variety of bids (for the whole lot, for one group or the other, and for individual magazines), and estimates that Ziff would receive between $300 million and $750 million for all 24 titles, CBS Inc. announced on November 20, 1984, that it had reached an agreement with Ziff to purchase the complete consumer group for $362.5 million, thought to be a record at the time for the sale of a group of magazines. The very next day, Rupert Murdoch announced that he had bought the entire business group for $350 million. Following these sales, Ziff Communications was essentially reduced to its computer magazines and IAC—none of which were offered in the auction, in part because their financial situations were less robust.

William Ziff, Jr., reduced his role in the operation of Ziff Communications for the next few years as he successfully battled against cancer. How closely the fortunes of the company were tied to his involvement is evident from the company's struggles during these years: 1985 saw the company post a loss of $10 million on $100 million in revenue. With his cancer in remission, he returned to full-time leadership of the company in 1987 and oversaw a second application of the Ziff formula for special interest publishing, this time fueling a growth spurt through the computer magazines left out of the 1984 sale. Like the business niche publications so recently sold, the computing publications developed and acquired by Ziff targeted a specific audience needing help with their purchase decisions—buyers of personal computers in the business world. Such magazines as *PC Magazine* and *MacUser* thus focused tightly on product specifications, evaluations, and recommendations from the editors. Using similar market research and advertising techniques honed through the company's decades of innovative magazine publishing, Ziff's line of computer magazines soon began to dominate the industry. By 1991, *PC Magazine* boasted a circulation of more than 800,000, more than $160 million in advertising revenue, and a ranking as the tenth-largest U.S. magazine.

There were some failures along the way as well. Contributing to them was the development of significant competitors in the computer magazine industry, notably International Data Group, Inc. (IDG), publisher of *InfoWorld* and *PC World,* and CMP Publications, publisher of *VAR Business* and *Windows Magazine.* Ziff had acquired *Government Computer News* in 1986 and invested heavily in it, but finally surrendered to IDG and its competitive title when it sold the magazine to Cahners Publishing. Among Ziff's start-ups that failed were *PCjr*—one of the first Ziff computer magazines—and *Corporate Computing*. The latter was launched with great fanfare early in 1992 and positioned as the one magazine for executives needing to make computer purchases. To meet its objective, it had to cover all bases from personal computers to networks to mainframes. At the time, however, the business market was shifting toward personal computers and thus right back to the strength of Ziff's other magazines. Feeling that *Corporate Computing* was beginning to compete with the flagship *PC Magazine,* as well as *PC Week,* the company folded the title just over one year after launch, having invested $10 million in it.

With increasing competition leading to slowing growth in advertising revenue, Ziff Communications reacted with three strategies. First, to lessen reliance on the U.S. market, Ziff launched an ambitious line of European computer magazines early in 1991. The second response was to move beyond the corporate computing world, said by some observers to be maturing, into home computing, which was viewed as the next big growth area. In another combination of organic and acquired growth, the company purchased *Computer Gaming World* and launched two new titles in 1994—*Computer Life* and *FamilyPC,* the latter in a joint venture with Walt Disney Company. The third area was a recommitment to electronic publishing through IAC and the development of online systems.

From the mid-1980s IAC had continued to expand, and by 1992 the company was the leader in full text with more than two million articles culled from more than 1,000 sources. The sheer amount of information offered through the products spun out of its databases began about this time to run up against the limits of CD-ROM technology. One option—almost a stopgap measure—offered to large libraries having large enough mainframes was to mount the database directly on it for patrons to access via the same terminals used for searching the library's catalog. The longer-term solution that IAC began to implement in 1993 was dubbed InfoTrac Central 2000 and allowed libraries to have their patrons access the IAC databases directly via the Internet.

IAC, whose strength had traditionally rested in the library market, now sought ways to achieve a longstanding goal of lessening the company's dependence on its main market. It formed a new consumer/educational division to target the home market, and it increased its presence in the corporate market through acquisitions. In 1991 it acquired Predicasts Inc., whose databases included *PROMT,* a competitor of IAC's *Trade and Industry Index.* In 1994 IAC acquired Sandpoint, which had developed a software application called Hoover designed to run on Lotus Notes, a groupware application that was becoming increasing popular with corporations. Hoover was an interface similar to InfoTrac, but a much more powerful one because it allowed a user to access information from many different types of platforms, from CD-ROMs to online systems to broadcast news sources (the name was derived from its being like a vacuum cleaner for information). Users of Hoover would also find a system more flexible in the different ways it allowed users to access information. By 1994, there were 16,000 users of Hoover at 70 companies.

Further electronic publishing initiatives in the early 1990s were highlighted by the development of the Interchange Online Network. The company had successfully tested the online services market over several years with Ziffnet, which was an online extension of its computer magazines offered through such services as CompuServe and Prodigy. Interchange was designed as an online service of its own and promised to be the first one to fully implement a graphical-user interface (GUI). True to Ziff tradition, it was designed to be a special interest service as opposed to the existing general-interest services. The first interest area to be developed was, predictably, computers, but plans were made to develop other areas including sports, health, and personal finance. Interchange would offer more than simply electronic text of magazines, adding such features as discussion groups, product information, and reference sources. As the Internet and the "information superhighway" became household names in the early 1990s, Interchange represented Ziff's claim to its piece of the multibillion-dollar digital information market.

1994: Breakup of Ziff Communications

Late in 1993, as revenue for Ziff Communications approached $1 billion, William Ziff, Jr., announced that he was retiring as chairman of the company and would have only an advisory role in the future as chairman emeritus. Eric Hippeau, who had already been in charge of all operations except corporate finance as chairman and CEO of Ziff-Davis Publishing, now assumed full control of Ziff Communications as chairman. That an outsider was placed in charge of what had always been a family-run business was telling to some observers who predicted that the company would either be sold or go public, but such rumors were denied for several months, with Ziff pointing out that two of his sons and one nephew were vice-presidents at the company. Nevertheless, in June 1994, the company an-

nounced that it had hired Lazard Freres & Company to handle the sale of the company, seeking $2 billion or more. The decision to sell stemmed from William Ziff's sons' wishes not to make running the company their career. The two brothers who had been vice-presidents at the company, Dirk and Robert, wished to invest the proceeds from the sale in their investment company, Ziff Brothers Investments. The third brother, Daniel, was a college student at this time (he later joined Ziff Brothers Investments).

At the time of the sale, the company was the unquestioned leader in computer magazine publishing and a leading electronic information provider through IAC. In 1994 the company expected a profit of $160 million on $950 million in revenue. Still, some observers thought that William Ziff was again selling out at a time when the company's most prized possessions—the computer publications—were past their peak. Others, however, pointed to numbers showing that the business magazine group (all the U.S. computer magazines except those aimed at consumers) alone was expecting revenues of $505 million and operating income of $146 million in 1994. The figures did show that Ziff's other units were either marginally profitable or losing money, in many cases from heavy investing in new ventures, such as the new consumer magazines and the Interchange system. In the end, these variances in the divisions, perhaps coupled with the enormity of the company, forced the sellers to accept a piecemeal sale rather than a sale of the whole company as they had hoped for. In October 1994 the New York investment firm of Forstmann Little & Co. purchased Ziff-Davis Publishing Co.—the business and consumer computer magazines, the international magazine group, a market research division, and the Ziffnet online service—for $1.4 billion. Ziff-Davis Exhibitors, a unit that managed computer trade shows, was bought by Softbank Corporation of Japan for $202 million, and The Thomson Corporation, a huge Canadian publisher, purchased Information Access Company for $465 million. Finally, in December 1994 AT&T purchased the Interchange Online Network, at the time still undergoing final testing, for $50 million. All told, the sales exceeded $2.1 billion.

1994–96: The Forstmann Little Interregnum

Ziff-Davis Publishing remained largely intact following its purchase by Forstmann Little, with Hippeau continuing as chairman and the editorial contact remaining unaltered. Revenues for 1994 were an estimated $852 million. Ziff-Davis continued to thrive under its new ownership, with the company producing three of the top four publications in high-tech ad dollars in the first nine months of 1995: *PC Magazine, PC Week,* and *Computer Shopper.* Operating earnings increased to $190 million in 1995 from the $140 million figure of the previous year. Seeking to benefit from the burgeoning Internet, Ziff-Davis in late 1994 launched ZDNet, a web site featuring online versions of a number of Ziff-Davis publications. ZDNet almost immediately faced stiff competition from a competing online news service, CNET. ZDNet, however, was one of the first web sites to make its content free to all users and rely on advertising as its primary revenue stream; it also was a pioneer in e-commerce through its 1996 launch of a web site spinoff of *Computer Shopper* magazine, computershopper.com. In 1995 Ziff-Davis entered into a joint venture with Internet portal Yahoo! Inc. to launch the consumer-oriented *Yahoo! Internet Life,* envisioned as the "TV Guide of the Internet." This title faced formidable competition as numerous Internet magazines were hitting the newsstands at this time, but by 1996 its advertising rate base had risen to 200,000.

The Forstmann Little era proved short-lived. Softbank, which had purchased Ziff-Davis Exhibitors after having lost out to Forstmann Little in the bidding for Ziff-Davis Publishing, came forward in late 1995 with an offer that was too rich for Forstmann Little to pass up. The purchase price was $2.1 billion, with the deal, completed in February 1996, providing Forstmann Little with a hefty profit on a less than 18-month investment. Softbank was the leading distributor of computer software in Japan and had augmented its computer trade show unit with the purchase earlier in 1995 of Comdex, the industry's largest trade show. It now also owned the number one U.S. publisher of computer and high-tech magazines.

1996–99: Ownership by Softbank

Under Softbank's ownership, as well as the continued leadership of Hippeau, Ziff-Davis rapidly expanded its publication line, particularly with new overseas titles in Europe and China. By 1998 the company was publishing 26 titles worldwide by itself or through joint ventures. Ziff-Davis also licensed its name or the name of a publication to other companies for more than 50 additional titles. On the domestic front, the video game title *Official U.S. PlayStation Magazine* debuted in 1997. In April of the following year, Softbank took the company public under the name Ziff-Davis Inc., selling 26 percent of the common stock through an initial public offering (IPO) that raised nearly $400 million. At the same time, Ziff-Davis restructured its debt, resulting in a reduction in its debt load from $2.5 billion to $1.6 billion. Interest payments had led the company to post net losses during both 1996 and 1997.

A public company for the first time in its long and convoluted history, Ziff-Davis Inc. began with three main operations: magazine publishing; tradeshows and conferences, including the former Ziff-Davis Exhibitors and Comdex, which were combined into ZD Events Inc.; and the Internet activities of ZDNet. A fourth segment was added in May 1998, a 24-hour cable television channel called ZDTV, which was launched despite the failures of previous ventures by the company into cable, two computer TV shows. Although Ziff-Davis helped launch ZDTV, it was initially owned by another subsidiary of Softbank. Ziff-Davis then purchased ZDTV in February 1999.

During 1998 Ziff-Davis's magazine operations suffered from a combination of factors that cut into ad revenues: fewer new computer product introductions, computer industry consolidation, and the Asian economic crisis, which dampened computer sales in that region. Late in the year the company announced that it would cut its workforce by 10 percent, or about 350 employees, and shutter three niche technology publications. A $46 million charge was taken in connection with these moves, leading to another net loss for the year.

While revenue was declining in the publishing sector, ZDNet's sales were on the rise, increasing from $32.2 million in 1997 to $56.1 million in 1998. Like most early Internet ventures, ZDNet was in the red, but its net loss narrowed in 1998 to $7.8 million, compared to $21.2 million the previous year. In April 1999 Ziff-Davis created a tracking stock for ZDNet and sold 16 percent of the unit to the public through an initial public offering (IPO). In the topsy-turvy world of the late 1990s Internet stock bubble, ZDNet by mid-1999 had a market capitalization greater than that of Ziff-Davis, despite Ziff-Davis's 84 percent stake in ZDNet. Also by this time, Softbank had invested heavily in Internet companies, including such stalwarts as Yahoo! and E*Trade, gaining billions in the process. With Softbank wishing to shift its focus completely to the Internet, Ziff-Davis announced in July 1999 that it was exploring strategic options, including a possible sale of the company.

Turn of the Millennium: Breakup of Ziff-Davis, with Ziff Davis Media Emerging

Eventually, Softbank settled on a plan to retain only ZDNet, and began selling off the other parts of Ziff-Davis piecemeal. In January 2000 ZDTV was sold to Vulcan Ventures, Inc. (and soon renamed TechTV). In April 2000 the magazine unit was sold for $780 million to Willis Stein & Partners, L.P. and James D. Dunning, Jr., a U.S. magazine industry veteran. The ZD Events unit was to be spun off to shareholders as a new company called Key3Media Group, Inc. Then, in the original plan, ZDNet was slated to emerge as a standalone publicly traded company, in which Softbank would hold about a 45 percent stake. But in July 2000 Ziff-Davis, which in essence at that point consisted only of ZDNet, agreed to be purchased by ZDNet's arch-rival, CNET Networks Inc., for $1.6 billion in stock.

As a result of this maze of transactions it was the publishing unit that emerged as the most direct successor to the publishing company founded more than 70 years earlier by a Ziff and a Davis. Fittingly, the unit's new owners, who were granted the exclusive use of the Ziff-Davis name, created a holding company called Ziff Davis Media Inc., with its main subsidiary called Ziff Davis Publishing Inc. Ziff Davis Media in turn was wholly owned by a publicly traded holding company called Ziff Davis Holdings Inc., which was controlled by the Willis Stein-led partners. Dunning was named chairman, president, and CEO of both Ziff Davis Media and Ziff Davis Publishing. The sale of the publishing unit, which did not include *Computer Shopper,* retained by ZDNet because of its related e-commerce web site, included a licensing agreement with ZDNet, whereby Ziff Davis Media would not be allowed to use the content of its existing magazines on the Internet for a three-year period and would then have to share the content with ZDNet for another two years. In return, Ziff Davis Media would receive a royalty of up to 5 percent of ZDNet's revenues during the first three years.

Under Dunning's leadership, a more aggressive and savvier strategy quickly became evident at Ziff Davis Media. Titles were revamped and renamed to reflect the increasing importance of the Internet and the so-called New Economy—*PC Computing* became *Ziff Davis SMART BUSINESS for the New Economy* and *PC Week* was redubbed *eWeek*—as well as to deemphasize the somewhat passé term "PC." In September 2000 the company began publication of *The Net Economy* magazine, which was aimed at business and technical managers, Internet service providers, telecommunications firms, cable and wireless service providers, and other companies that provided network-based services. Ziff Davis also began developing new titles in areas outside of technology but with a focus on what was assumed to be the Internet-centered economy of the 21st century. With e-commerce revolutionizing shopping, the company launched *eShopper*. Similarly, Ziff Davis saw the need for a new travel magazine that would inform consumers about how to use the Internet to enhance their travel planning and experiences. The company joined with Expedia, Inc., operator of a leading online travel service, to launch *Expedia Travels* in the fall of 2000, with an initial circulation of 200,000. This title in some ways brought the company full circle, returning it to its travel magazine roots. Meantime, in August 2000 Ziff Davis Media sold its publishing subsidiaries in the United Kingdom, France, and Germany, along with the ten titles they produced, to VNU N.V., a Dutch publishing group. The move meant that Ziff Davis Media would directly own only U.S. publications. All international titles, with the exception of those in China, would be produced through licensing arrangements with third parties. The company continued to publish four magazines in China through joint ventures.

Early 2000s: Surviving the Severe Post-Bubble Downturn

Despite the bursting of the technology stock bubble in early 2000 and the resulting precipitous decline in tech advertising spending that began late that year, Ziff Davis Media plowed ahead with new magazine launches in 2001. These included another video game title, *Xbox Nation,* as well as two business-oriented titles that, like *eWeek,* were of the controlled-circulation variety (that is, distributed directly to qualified professionals at no charge, with revenue mainly generated through the sale of advertising). Both were aimed at senior-level information technology decision makers, but *CIO Insight,* with a controlled circulation of 50,000, included more general coverage of strategies, management techniques, and technology perspectives related to information technology, whereas the 125,000-circulation *Baseline* was more of a guide to selecting and managing the implementation of leading-edge information systems. Ziff also reached an important agreement with CNET in 2001, whereby the content licensing agreement between the two companies was trimmed from five years to two, giving Ziff the sole rights to the web addresses and content of its magazines by March 1, 2002.

The deep downturn, which affected both ad spending and circulation figures, claimed its first Ziff Davis victim in July 2001 when *Family PC* was shut down. The second victim was a more surprising one—Dunning himself, who was ousted in August 2001. The falling out between Dunning and Willis Stein & Partners resulted in much acrimony coupled with suits and countersuits. For Ziff Davis, Dunning's ouster brought an end to the executive's plan to sell *Expedia Travels, Yahoo! Internet Life,* and four gaming titles to American Media, Inc. for between $100 million and $150 million. His replacement, Robert F. Callahan, a former president of Walt Disney Company's ABC Broadcasting Group who came onboard as chairman and CEO in October 2001, took a different approach. He shut down the short-lived *Expedia Travels* and *Sm@rt Partner* (the latter having been launched in 1999 as *Sm@rt Reseller*) and merged *Interactive Week* into *eWeek*. Needing to severely cut costs,

more than 500 staff members lost their jobs, salaries for senior employees were frozen, facilities were consolidated, and capital spending was cut. Restructuring and asset-impairment charges of $277.4 million, mainly related to the magazine closures, contributed to a net loss of $415.4 million on revenues of $215.9 million for the nine-month transition period ending in December 2001.

As the ad recession continued in 2002, so too did Callahan's restructuring. Between May and July, three of the company's remaining 11 magazine titles ceased publication: *Ziff Davis Smart Business,* the *Net Economy,* and *Yahoo! Internet Life,* all of which resided in the troubled new economy category. Overall, from September 2001 to July 2002, the Ziff workforce was reduced from 1,150 to 450. Callahan's moves were insufficient to turn the company's fortunes around, however, because of the heavy load of debt Ziff had been saddled with since the Willis Stein buyout. By July 2002 the firm verged on the edge of bankruptcy. What saved Ziff Davis was a sweeping financial reorganization implemented in August following approval by all of the company's bank lenders and nearly all of its bondholders. The restructuring reduced its bond debt from $250 million to $102.6 million, resulting in a reduction in annual debt service from about $50 million to $15 million.

Over the next couple of years, Ziff Davis improved its financial performance considerably, while nonetheless remaining in the red. On firmer ground, the company moved cautiously forward with expansion plans. Late in 2003 Ziff reentered the conference business through the acquisition of TM Media, which formed the basis for the newly created Ziff Davis Event Marketing Group. The following October, this unit held its first DigitalLife consumer electronics ''event'' at the Jacob K. Javits Conference Center in New York City. This was followed in 2005 by the debut of *DigitalLife* magazine, a newsstand-only title published twice a year, for the summer and holiday seasons. In June 2004 the company launched its first new non-gaming consumer magazine since 2000. *Sync,* which started with an advertising rate base of 200,000, was positioned as a ''consumer lifestyle'' magazine aimed at men aged 25 to 44. Filled with humor, it focused on the latest digital gadgets—camera phones, high-definition TVs, iPods, and the like. Also launched in 2004 was *ExtremeTech,* a newsstand-only magazine aimed at the hardcore technology do-it-yourselfer. Finally, in October 2004, Ziff Davis Media acquired Connexus Media Inc. (CMI), a business-to-business online publishing company based in Topsfield, Massachusetts. Among CMI's holdings were 25 business-to-business, vertical, and technology specific web sites; ten weekly e-newsletters; and 25 list rental databases and ancillary paid content programs. Further launches and acquisitions were likely as Ziff Davis Media continued to recover from its near-death experience.

Principal Subsidiaries

Ziff Davis Development Inc.; Ziff Davis Internet Inc.; Ziff Davis Publishing Inc.

Principal Competitors

International Data Group, Inc.; CMP Media LLC.

Further Reading

Auerbach, Jon G., and Joseph Pereira, "With PC Ads on Hold, Ziff-Davis Takes a Hit," *Wall Street Journal,* October 9, 1998, p. B1.

Block, Valerie, "Investors Hope to Reboot Ziff-Davis," *Crain's New York Business,* December 13, 1999, p. 3.

Bulkeley, William M., "Ziff-Davis to Explore Its Options, Including a Sale," *Wall Street Journal,* July 15, 1999, p. B4.

Callahan, Sean, "Ziff-Davis Faces Uncertain Future," *Advertising Age's Business Marketing,* August 1999, pp. 2, 50.

Carmody, Deirdre, "Forstmann to Acquire Ziff-Davis," *New York Times,* October 28, 1994, pp. D1–D2.

Carr, David, "Ziff Davis, Its Fortunes Tied to Technology Magazines, Is Said to Plan a Bankruptcy," *New York Times,* July 29, 2002, p. C8.

Churbuck, David C., "Motivated Seller," *Forbes 400,* October 17, 1994, pp. 350–54.

Doan, Amy, "Geek TV," *Forbes,* July 5, 1999, pp. 150–51.

Dugan, I. Jeanne, "I Live, Breathe, Sleep Computer," *Business Week,* December 1, 1997, p. 126.

Fabrikant, Geraldine, "For a Ziff Sale, Spit and Polish and Good Timing," *New York Times,* September 9, 1994, pp. D1–D2.

——, "For Ziffs, Sale Is a Family Affair," *New York Times,* June 10, 1994, pp. 37, 46.

Fine, Jon, "Charges Fly over Ailing Ziff Davis," *Advertising Age,* November 12, 2001, p. 14.

——, "Ziff Davis in Scuffle with CNET," *Advertising Age,* November 6, 2000, p. 1.

——, "Ziff Davis Shuts *Family PC* Title," *Advertising Age,* July 30, 2001, p. 4.

Fine, Jon, and Mercedes M. Cardona, "Ziff Davis Coming Unzipped," *Advertising Age,* August 20, 2001, p. 4.

Furman, Phyllis, "Ziff's Favorite Son," *Crain's New York Business,* August 5, 1996, p. 3.

Garigliano, Jeff, "Ziff-Davis' Intriguing IPO," *Folio,* April 1, 1998, p. 13.

Granatstein, Lisa, "Rocky Road: After Months of Bloodletting, Ziff's Callahan Says the Company Is Now on the Right Course," *Mediaweek,* July 15, 2002, pp. 38–39.

——, "Ziff Syncs Up," *Mediaweek,* June 14, 2004, pp. 32, 34.

Harvey, Mary, "Is 'PC' Passé?: Defining the New Ziff Davis," *Folio,* May 2000, pp. 15+.

Johnson, Bradley, "Wm. Ziff Retires, but His Company Stays in Family," *Advertising Age,* November 23, 1993, p. 22.

——, "ZDTV Marries Computers, Cable, but Who Will See It?," *Advertising Age,* April 13, 1998, p. S20.

——, "Ziff-Davis Goes Public," *Advertising Age's Business Marketing,* May 1998, pp. 3, 48.

Kleinfield, N.R., "The Big Magazine Auction," *New York Times,* November 16, 1994, pp. D1, D3.

——, "CBS to Buy 12 of Ziff's Magazines," *New York Times,* November 21, 1984, pp. D1, D3.

Landler, Mark, "Auctioning Off an Empire," *Business Week,* June 27, 1994, p. 27.

Levison, Andrew, "Ziff-Davis: For Sale," *Online,* September/October 1994, pp. 31–38.

Lindsay, Greg, "After the Tech Wreck," *Folio,* April 2002, pp. 28–33.

Lipin, Steven, "Persistence Pays Off in Second Sale of Ziff-Davis," *Wall Street Journal,* December 29, 1995, p. C1.

——, "Ziff-Davis Unit of Forstmann Set to Be Sold," *Wall Street Journal,* November 9, 1995, p. A3.

Mangalindan, Mylene, and Jennifer L. Rewick, "CNET's $1.48 Billion Deal for Ziff-Davis Unites Rivals in Internet Publishing," *Wall Street Journal,* July 20, 2000, p. B14.

Manly, Lorne, "Ziff Re-Boots," *Folio,* April 15, 1995, pp. 36–38, 57.

Palmeri, Christopher, "The Idea That Print Is Dead Is Preposterous," *Forbes,* June 10, 1991, pp. 42–44.

Prior, Teri Lammers, "CMP, IDG, and Ziff-Davis: Can They Still Fly High?," *Upside,* October 1996, pp. 100–02+.

Rose, Matthew, "Ziff Davis Media Ousts Dunning As Chairman, President, and CEO," *Wall Street Journal,* August 14, 2001, p. B2.

——, "Ziff Davis Media Restructures, Avoiding a Bankruptcy Filing," *Wall Street Journal,* August 12, 2002, p. B4.

——, "Ziff-Davis to Sell Its Magazine Unit for $780 Million," *Wall Street Journal,* December 7, 1999, p. B15.

——, "Ziff-Davis to Spin Off Events Business, Merge What Is Left of Firm into ZDNet," *Wall Street Journal,* March 7, 2000, p. B8.

Schwartz, Matthew, "Back from Financial Brink, Ziff Davis Logs Solid Results," *B to B,* March 10, 2003, p. 4.

——, "New Ziff Davis CEO Acts Fast to Stem Losses," *B to B,* November 26, 2001, p. 3.

——, "Ziff Davis Media Forges Ahead," *B to B,* March 19, 2001, p. 14.

Wayne, Leslie, "Murdoch Buys 12 Ziff Publications," *New York Times,* November 22, 1984, pp. D1, D13.

Weber, Jonathan, "Mogul for a New Age: Bill Ziff's Media Empire Is Built on High Tech—and High Standards," *Los Angeles Times,* October 10, 1993, p. D1.

Weinberg, Neil, and Amy Feldman, "Bubble, Bubble . . . ," *Forbes,* March 11, 1996, p. 42.

—update: David E. Salamie

INDEX TO COMPANIES

Index to Companies

Listings in this index are arranged in alphabetical order under the company name. Company names beginning with a letter or proper name such as Eli Lilly & Co. will be found under the first letter of the company name. Definite articles (The, Le, La) are ignored for alphabetical purposes as are forms of incorporation that precede the company name (AB, NV). Company names printed in bold type have full, historical essays on the page numbers appearing in bold. Updates to entries that appeared in earlier volumes are signified by the notation **(upd.)**. Company names in light type are references within an essay to that company, not full historical essays. This index is cumulative with volume numbers printed in bold type.

Avimo, **47** 7–8

Avion Coach Corporation, **11** 363

Avionics Specialties Inc. *See* Aerosonic Corporation.

Avions Marcel Dassault-Breguet Aviation, I 44–46; **7** 11; **7** 205; **8** 314. *See also* Groupe Dassault Aviation SA.

Avis Rent A Car, Inc., 6 356–58; **8** 33; **9** 284; **10** 419; **16** 379–80; **22** 54–57 **(upd.)**, 524; **25** 93, 143, 420–22

Avista Corporation, 69 48–50 **(upd.)**

Avisun Corp., **IV** 371

Aviva PLC, 50 65–68 **(upd.)**

Avnet Electronics Supply Co., **19** 311, 313

Avnet Inc., 9 55–57; **10** 112–13; **13** 47; **50** 41

Avocent Corporation, 65 56–58

Avon Products, Inc., III 15–16; **19** 26–29 **(upd.)**; **46** 43–46 **(upd.)**

Avon Rubber plc, **23** 146

Avondale Industries, Inc., 7 39–41; **41** 40–43 **(upd.)**

Avondale Mills, Inc., **8** 558–60; **9** 466

Avonmore Foods Plc, **59** 205

Avril Alimentaire SNC, **51** 54

Avro. *See* A.V. Roe & Company.

Avstar, **38** 72

Avtech Corp., **36** 159

AVTOVAZ Joint Stock Company, 65 59–62

AVX Corporation, 21 329, 331; **67** 21–22; **41–43**

AW Bruna Uitgevers BV, **53** 273

AW North Carolina Inc., **48** 5

AWA. *See* America West Holdings Corporation.

AWA Defence Industries (AWADI). *See* British Aerospace Defence Industries.

AwardTrack, Inc., **49** 423

AWB Ltd., 56 25–27

Awesome Transportation, Inc., **22** 549

Awrey Bakeries, Inc., 56 28–30

AXA Colonia Konzern AG, III 210–12; **15** 30; **21** 147; **27** 52–55; **49** 41–45 **(upd.)**

AXA Financial, Inc., **63** 26–27

AXA Private Equity. *See* Camaïeu S.A.

AXA UK plc, **64** 173

Axe-Houghton Associates Inc., **41** 208

Axel Johnson Group, I 553–55

Axel Springer Verlag AG, IV 589–91; **20** 50–53 **(upd.)**; **23** 86; **35** 452; **54** 295

Axon Systems Inc., **7** 336

Ayala Corporation, **70** 182

Ayala Plans, Inc., **58** 20

Aydin Corp., 19 30–32

Aynsley China Ltd. *See* Belleek Pottery Ltd.

Ayr-Way Stores, **27** 452

Ayres, Lewis, Norris & May, Inc., **54** 184

AYS. *See* Alternative Youth Services, Inc.

AZA Immobilien AG, **51** 196

Azcon Corporation, 23 34–36

Azerty, **25** 13

Azienda Generale Italiana Petroli. *See* ENI S.p.A.

AZL Resources, **7** 538

Aznar International, **14** 225

Azon Limited, **22** 282

AZP Group Inc., **6** 546

Aztar Corporation, 13 66–68; **71** 41–45 **(upd.)**

Azteca, **18** 211, 213

B&D. *See* Barker & Dobson.

B&G Foods, Inc., 40 51–54

B&J Music Ltd. *See* Kaman Music Corporation.

B & K Steel Fabrications, Inc., **26** 432

B & L Insurance, Ltd., **51** 38

B&M Baked Beans, **40** 53

B & O. *See* Baltimore and Ohio Railroad.

B&Q plc. *See* Kingfisher plc.

B&S. *See* Binney & Smith Inc.

B.A.T. Industries PLC, 14 77; **16** 242; **22** 70–73 **(upd.)**; **25** 154–56; **29** 196; **63** 260–61. *See also* Brown & Williamson Tobacco Corporation.

B. B. & R. Knight Brothers, **8** 200; **25** 164

B.B. Foods, **13** 244

B-Bar-B Corp., **16** 340

B.C. Rail Telecommunications, **6** 311

B.C. Sugar, **II** 664

B.C. Ziegler and Co. *See* The Ziegler Companies, Inc.

B. Dalton Bookseller Inc., 10 136; **13** 545; **16** 160; **18** 136; **25** 29–31; **30** 68

B-E Holdings, **17** 60

B/E Aerospace, Inc., 30 72–74

B.F. Goodrich Co. *See* The BFGoodrich Company.

B.F. Walker, Inc., **11** 354

B.I.C. America, **17** 15, 17

B.J.'s Wholesale, **12** 335

B.J. Alan Co., Inc., 67 44–46

The B. Manischewitz Company, LLC, 31 43–46

B. Perini & Sons, Inc., **8** 418

B Ticino, **21** 350

B.V. Tabak Export & Import Compagnie, **12** 109

BA. *See* British Airways.

BAA plc, 10 121–23; **29** 509, 511; **33** 57–61 **(upd.)**; **37** 8

Bålforsens Kraft AB, **28** 444

Baan Company, 25 32–34; **26** 496, 498

Babbage's, Inc., 10 124–25. *See also* GameStop Corp.

Babcock International Group PLC, 37 242–45; **57** 142; **69** 51–54

BABE. *See* British Aerospace plc.

Baby Dairy Products, **48** 438

Baby Lock USA. *See* Tacony Corporation.

Baby Phat. *See* Phat Fashions LLC.

Baby Superstore, Inc., 15 32–34; **57** 372

Babybird Co., Ltd. *See* Nagasakiya Co., Ltd.

BabyCenter.com, **37** 130

Babyliss, S.A. *See* Conair Corporation.

BAC. *See* Barclays American Corp.; Beverage Associates Corp.; British Aircraft Corporation.

Bacardi Limited, 18 39–42; **63** 264, 266

Baccarat, 23 241; **24** 61–63; **27** 421, 423

Bache & Company, **III** 340; **8** 349

Bachman Foods, **15** 139

Bachman Holdings, Inc., **14** 165; **34** 144–45

Bachman's Inc., 22 58–60; **24** 513

Bachoco. *See* Industrias Bacholo, S.A. de C.V.

Back Bay Investments Ltd., **64** 217

Back Bay Restaurant Group, Inc., 20 54–56

Back Yard Burgers, Inc., 45 33–36

Backer & Spielvogel, **12** 168; **14** 48–49; **22** 296

Backer Spielvogel Bates Worldwide. *See* Bates Worldwide, Inc.

Bacon's Information, Inc., **55** 289

Bacova Guild, Ltd., **17** 76

Bad Boy Worldwide Entertainment Group, 31 269; **58** 14–17

Badak LNG Transport Inc., **56** 181

Baddour, Inc. *See* Fred's, Inc.

Badger Illuminating Company, **6** 601

Badger Meter, Inc., 22 61–65

Badger Paper Mills, Inc., 15 35–37

Badin-Defforey, **27** 93

BAe. *See* British Aerospace plc.

BAE-Newplan Group Ltd. *See* SNC-Lavalin Group Inc.

BAE Systems Ship Repair, 73 46–48

BAFS. *See* Bangkok Aviation Fuel Services Ltd.

Bahamas Air Holdings Ltd., 66 24–26

Bahlsen GmbH & Co. KG, 44 38–41

Bailey, Banks & Biddle, **16** 559

Bailey Nurseries, Inc., 57 59–61

Bailey Street Trading Company, **71** 60

Bailey's Pub and Grille. *See* Total Entertainment Restaurant Corporation.

Bain & Company, 9 343; **21** 143; **55** 41–43

Bain Capital, Inc., **14** 244–45; **16** 466; **20** 18; **24** 456, 482; **25** 254; **26** 184; **38** 107–09; **63** 133, 137–38

Baird, **7** 235, 237

Bairnco Corporation, 28 42–45

Bajaj Auto Limited, 39 36–38

BÅKAB. *See* Bålforsens Kraft AB.

Bakelite Corp., **13** 231

Baker. *See* Michael Baker Corporation.

Baker and Botts, L.L.P., 28 46–49

Baker & Hostetler LLP, 40 55–58

Baker & McKenzie, 10 126–28; **42** 17–20 **(upd.)**

Baker & Taylor Corporation, 16 45–47; **43** 59–62 **(upd.)**

Baker Cummins Pharmaceuticals Inc., **11** 208

Baker Extract Co., **27** 299

Baker Hughes Incorporated, III 428–29; **11** 513; **22** 66–69 **(upd.)**; **25** 74; **57** 62–66 **(upd.)**; **59** 366; **63** 306

Baker Industries, Inc., **8** 476; **13** 124

Baker Oil Tools. *See* Baker Hughes Incorporated.

Baker-Raulang Co., **13** 385

Bakers Best Snack Food Corporation, **24** 241

Bakers Square. *See* VICORP Restaurants, Inc.

Bakersfield Savings and Loan, **10** 339

Bakery Feeds Inc. *See* Griffin Industries, Inc.

Bal-Sam India Holdings Ltd., **64** 95

Balance Bar Company, 32 70–72

Balatongáz Kft. (Ltd.), **70** 195

Balchem Corporation, 42 21–23

Balco, Inc., **7** 479–80; **27** 415

Balcor, Inc., **10** 62

Bald Eagle Corporation, **45** 126

Baldor Electric Company, 21 42–44

Baldwin & Lyons, Inc., 51 37–39

Baldwin-Ehret-Hill Inc., **28** 42

Baldwin Filters, Inc., **17** 104

Baldwin Hardware Manufacturing Co. *See* Masco Corporation.

Baldwin-Montrose Chemical Co., Inc., **31** 110

INDEX TO INDUSTRIES

Index to Industries

ACCOUNTING

ADVERTISING & OTHER BUSINESS SERVICES

CONSTRUCTION

ENTERTAINMENT & LEISURE

FOOD PRODUCTS

FOOD PRODUCTS (continued)

FOOD SERVICES & RETAILERS

HEALTH & PERSONAL CARE PRODUCTS

MINING & METALS

REAL ESTATE

TEXTILES & APPAREL

UTILITIES

WASTE SERVICES

GEOGRAPHIC INDEX

Geographic Index

Germany

Ghana

Greece

Hong Kong

United States

NOTES ON CONTRIBUTORS

Notes on Contributors

COHEN, M. L. Novelist and researcher living in Paris.

COVELL, Jeffrey L. Seattle-based writer.

CULLIGAN, Susan B. Minnesota-based writer.

DINGER, Ed. Writer and editor based in Bronx, New York.

HALASZ, Robert. Former editor in chief of *World Progress* and *Funk & Wagnalls New Encyclopedia Yearbook*; author, *The U.S. Marines* (Millbrook Press, 1993).

HEER-FORSBERG, Mary. Minneapolis-based researcher and writer.

INGRAM, Frederick C. Utah-based business writer who has contributed to *GSA Business, Appalachian Trailway News,* the *Encyclopedia of Business,* the *Encyclopedia of Global Industries,* the *Encyclopedia of Consumer Brands,* and other regional and trade publications.

PEIPPO, Kathleen. Minneapolis-based writer.

POGINY, Sara. Ohio-based writer.

RHODES, Nelson. Editor, writer, and consultant in the Chicago area.

ROTHBURD, Carrie. Writer and editor specializing in corporate profiles, academic texts, and academic journal articles.

SALAMIE, David E. Part-owner of InfoWorks Development Group, a reference publication development and editorial services company.

UHLE, Frank. Ann Arbor-based writer; movie projectionist, disc jockey, and staff member of *Psychotronic Video* magazine.

WOODWARD, A. Wisconsin-based writer.